D1134815

CHRISTIAN HERITAGE COLLEGE
BY HIM ALL THINGS CONSIST
SAN DIEGO, CALIFORNIA 1970

MEANING AND KNOWLEDGE

Systematic Readings in Epistemology

Meaning and Knowledge

SYSTEMATIC READINGS IN EPISTEMOLOGY

Ernest Nagel
COLUMBIA UNIVERSITY

Richard B. Brandt
THE UNIVERSITY OF MICHIGAN

HARCOURT, BRACE & WORLD, INC.
NEW YORK / CHICAGO / SAN FRANCISCO / ATLANTA

Library of Congress Catalog Card Number: 65-19847

Printed in the United States of America

PREFACE

We have long felt a need, which we suspect is shared by many other teachers of philosophy, for a collection of readings containing representative statements of all the important views on the major problems in the theory of knowledge. The present book is an attempt to fill this need. Deciding what to include has been difficult, and we have been obliged to omit many important contributions to the subject that we initially planned to use, but for which in the end we could find no room—indeed, we have had to omit some contributions for which we ourselves will continue to send students to the library. In making our selections, we have placed a high premium on relatively short, self-contained, lucidly written, and carefully reasoned statements of the views we wished to have represented. We believe that most of the essays in the volume are eminently readable and that many of them are suitable for introducing the problems they discuss to beginning students. However, in order to provide material that can serve as a basis for discussing a number of fundamental issues, we have not hesitated to include some essays that assume considerable philosophical maturity and make large demands on the reader's ability to follow a complex philosophical argument.

We have grouped the selections into chapters, each centered on some major epistemological problem. In some instances, however, a chapter contains essays that deal not only with the question to which the chapter is chiefly addressed, but with others as well. In arranging the chapters sequentially, we have been guided by both logical and pedagogic considerations. However, the order we have adopted is not the only sound one, either logically or pedagogically, and the material can be taught in an order quite different from the one in the present volume. In any case, the chapters contain more essays than can be covered in a one-semester course or seminar in the theory of knowledge; thus teachers may select according to their own tastes and the level of preparation of their students.

Each of us had primary responsibility for writing the introductions to certain chapters, and for selecting and editing the essays in those chapters: Ernest Nagel for the first five chapters, and Richard Brandt for the last five. Final decisions about the content and organization of the volume were made in consultation, and both of us are responsible for the entire book. The general Introduction to the volume is in a special sense a joint product and represents the efforts both of us made to improve several earlier drafts.

ERNEST NAGEL
RICHARD B. BRANDT

CONTENTS

INTRODUCTION

Like most labels in general use, the term "theory of knowledge" (or "epistemology," with which it is often used interchangeably) has a wide range of meanings. At one extreme, it designates a severely limited group of problems, or answers to problems, focused exclusively on how the data directly apprehended in sense perception are related to the objects of common sense and science. At the other extreme, it is a name for a miscellaneous assortment of questions about the nature and relations of various types of mental state, such as knowing, believing, assuming, imagining, dreaming, and the like. The conception of the task of epistemology that underlies the choice of materials for this book coincides with neither extreme. It may be useful to the reader if we briefly indicate how we conceive this task, especially since none of the essays we have included discusses the aims of epistemological inquiry, and some of the authors represented take a view of its scope different from ours.

As we read the history of theories of knowledge in Western philosophy, most of them were developed as generalized critiques of currently held notions of what constitutes knowledge, and can be interpreted as so many proposals of policies for obtaining reliable if not completely certain beliefs. Such critiques were undertaken in some cases to locate and eliminate specific sources of error in perceptual and other judgments, in some cases to supply a comprehensive foundation for adjusting traditional beliefs to scientific and social innovations, and in many cases simply to satisfy theoretical curiosity concerning the power of human reason. But whatever the specific purposes of historic theories of knowledge may have been, we share the conception to which their authors in the main subscribed: the central task of epistemology is to provide a generalized critique of the grounds on which claims to knowledge are supported, by constructing a systematic account of the principles by which the truth of statements may be properly assessed, as well as of the rationale of these principles. A theory of knowledge so understood is indistinguishable from a theory of logic that is general enough to deal not only with the formal validity of arguments, but with the basis on which cognitive claims of any sort can be judged to be warranted, either as cases of knowledge or as instances of probable or reasonable belief.

Accordingly, epistemology is a normative discipline, in the sense that it provides standards for measuring the worth of cognitive claims, along with a systematic defense of the reasonableness of those standards. But it is in part also a descriptive discipline. For the standards it proposes can be neither stated nor defended without factual assumptions about man's intellectual capacities (for example, that men are equipped with memory, though with a fallible one) and about modes of reasoning or other procedures by which human beings have achieved ostensibly reliable beliefs (for example, by performing so-called controlled experiments). Thus it is not just a coincidence that fundamental discoveries (or "revolutions" of thought) in various branches of science—in biology and psychology, as well as in mathematics, physics, and astronomy—have frequently been followed by important shifts in epistemological doctrine. Partly because of its dual normative-descriptive nature, the questions ultimately raised by a theory of knowledge are manifold and diversified, so much so that the selections in this book necessarily fail to touch on all of them.

The major themes that a fully adequate epistemology, as we conceive the subject, must discuss may be classified as follows. The themes fall into two main divisions, which we shall designate as "Theory of knowledge proper" and "Metaepistemology."

Theory of knowledge proper. Let us call a statement an "epistemological statement" if it can be contradicted by a statement (or by the denial of a statement) having the following form: "The person *S* has greater warrant for believing *h* than *i*." Moreover, the phrase "having greater warrant," and other words or phrases definable with its help, will be called "epistemological terms." More generally, epistemological terms are those whose occurrence in statements distinguishes those statements from nonepistemological statements. Although just what is to be understood by "having greater warrant" (or even by "warrant") is highly controversial, we cannot canvass the issues in the controversy; we will simply assume that the meaning of the phrase (or one of its relevant meanings) is sufficiently familiar to the reader for the purposes of this survey.

We can now define the content of the theory of knowledge proper as the presentation, in some systematic order, of *general* epistemological statements and the reasoned defense or criticism of those that have been proposed. Such statements (or epistemic principles) are sometimes said to be of two kinds; although the tenability of this claim is very much disputed, the distinction can nevertheless be stated without prejudice to the issues at stake. The first kind may be called "rules of inference": on the assumption that some statements of given types are already known or are believed with warrant, these epistemic principles formulate what *further* statements of indicated types we can claim to know or to believe with warrant. The following is a quite uncontroversial example of such a rule: "If *S* knows *h*, and also knows that *h* logically implies *i*, then *S* is warranted in accepting *i*." The second kind of epistemic principle may be called "generalizations about independently credible statements": they specify which classes of statements we may claim to know, or to believe with warrant, *independently* of their logical relations to other statements that we either know or have reason to believe. One example of such generalizations that is accepted by some philosophers—among them C. I. Lewis and A. J. Ayer—is the following: "If at time *t* a person *S* believes the statement *h* he makes about his experiences at time *t*, then *S* knows *h*."

Questions belonging to the theory of knowledge proper are treated in a large number of the essays in this book. Epistemic rules of inference are discussed (though not under this label) especially, but not exclusively, in Chapter 5; and generalizations about independently credible statements receive much attention (but again not under this title or exclusively) in Chapters 7, 8, and 9.

Metaepistemology. There is a manifest difference between presenting arguments for or against some proposed epistemic principle and presenting or defending some thesis about *how* epistemic principles may be validated. As has just been explained, the former task belongs to the theory of knowledge proper; the latter task falls into the province of metaepistemology, the second main division of the theory of knowledge.

But metaepistemology itself can be conveniently divided into two parts. The first part is a conceptual inquiry. It tries to make clear the meanings of epistemological terms and statements and of other expressions that are indispensable for an understanding of epistemological terms and statements. It thereby prepares the way for an effective treatment of problems in the theory of knowledge proper as well as in the validation of epistemic principles. Thus, the notion of warrant obviously requires clarification; and the same must be said of other concepts which, so it turns out, enter decisively but at first sight not so obviously into epistemological discussions—such as the concepts of meaning, reference, truth, analyticity, and necessity, though not all of them are epistemological terms. The essays in the first four chapters are devoted largely to this task.

The second part of metaepistemology is an investigation of how, in view of the meanings of epistemic terms, and in view of anything else that may be relevant, we can reasonably support epistemic principles. Some aspects of this question are discussed in Chapters 4 and 5, but with the exception of the selection from Chisholm in Chapter 10, none of the other essays deals with it explicitly. The reader may therefore find it useful if we state the three main positions philosophers have taken on the nature and validation of epistemic principles. Each of these positions has a close parallel in ethical theory, and our designations for them are borrowed from the current literature on ethics.

The first view may be called "nonnaturalism" in epistemology. It is distinguished by two theses: (1) Epistemological terms are meaningful, and epistemological statements are either true or false. (2) However, epistemological terms do not name observable (or "naturalistic") qualities such as shapes, colors, or sounds, and epistemic principles cannot in consequence be confirmed by any conceivable observation. Accordingly, epistemological terms cannot be defined or explained except by way of other epistemological terms, and knowledge of epistemic principles that are not analytically true (for example, the principle that "it is reasonable to believe what one distinctly remembers") must be synthetic a priori knowledge.

The second view can be called "naturalism" in epistemology. It agrees with the first thesis of nonnaturalism, but denies its second thesis. It therefore maintains that epistemological terms can be explained by way of empirical and logical concepts exclusively, without using other epistemological terms in the process. It also claims that epistemic principles have the same cognitive status as statements in the empirical sciences, and that like the latter they must be judged in the light of relevant data obtained by sensory observation.

The third view may be designated "noncognitivism" in epistemology. It rejects the thesis, common to the other two positions, that epistemic principles are either true or false (analytically true principles are of course excepted), although it agrees with nonnaturalism (and disagrees with naturalism) in holding that epistemological terms cannot be defined on the basis of empirical concepts. Nevertheless, epistemological statements are said to have a function—

for example, a statement of the form "It is reasonable to believe *h*" may be uttered to lend the speaker's authority to belief in *h,* to express his confidence in *h,* to recommend that *h* be believed, and the like.

Is it necessary to come to a decision about these metaepistemological views before one can begin to discuss profitably the subject matter of the theory of knowledge proper? We do not think it is; but irrespective of the merits of our answer—we lack the space to give reasons for it—familiarity with that subject matter is useful if not indispensable for handling both this large question and the more limited issues raised in each of these metaepistemological positions. For, after all, while the distinction between the theory of knowledge proper and metaepistemology seems to us clarifying, to take a reasoned stand on these positions is to be engaged in a discussion belonging to the theory of knowledge proper at a "higher" level.

In any event, although we have found the distinction convenient for mapping the large territory occupied by the theory of knowledge, the selections in the book have not been arranged according to the various divisions appearing on the map. One reason they have not is that the distinction is firmly entrenched neither in the recent nor in the older literature of epistemology; another is that even a single piece of writing in the theory of knowledge often deals with problems that fall into more than one division. The ten chapters into which the selections are fitted correspond to the traditional classification of epistemological questions. However, this organization of the essays also fails to yield sharply delimited classes of problems; indeed the introductions to several of the chapters indicate that a problem to which a given chapter is chiefly devoted may nevertheless have aspects that are discussed in another one.

As was suggested at the outset of this Introduction, many philosophers who have interested themselves in the theory of knowledge have viewed the subject as a means to an end—as a road to some practical, or metaphysical, or theological goal. Although when it is so viewed it is surely debatable how much nourishing bread epistemology has succeeded in baking during its long history, we think there is considerable evidence to show that the study of the subject has often contributed to more enlightened appraisals of cognitive claims than would have been made otherwise. Moreover, such a study can provide as a minimum a broad perspective on the powers of the human mind; and there is also reason to believe that the theory of knowledge can place in clearer light similarities and differences among the requirements for warranted beliefs in various branches of inquiry—especially in mathematics, the natural sciences, and the many disciplines that are directly concerned with human values. Philosophy as well as science is better off when such things are made clear.

MEANING AND KNOWLEDGE

Systematic Readings in Epistemology

1

PROBLEMS OF MEANING

Language in the sense of a culturally transmitted system of signs or symbols is a distinctive human achievement, without close parallels elsewhere in nature, and it performs a variety of important functions in the human economy. Perhaps the most remarkable of them is its role as an instrument in the acquisition, organization, and communication of knowledge. Indeed, until the second half of the eighteenth century, students of language were occupied almost exclusively with questions related to this function. It is with certain broad problems connected with language as such an instrument that the essays in this chapter are mainly concerned.

Adult members of a linguistic community are generally successful in communicating their ideas to one another, at any rate in carrying on the customary affairs of life, so that their use of language in such contexts appears to most of them as unproblematic. However, failures in communication do occur, in activities controlled by narrowly practical aims as well as in others. In particular, the pursuit of knowledge is often hampered by misleading interpretations of linguistic constructions—interpretations that are sometimes based on mistaken though not always explicit assumptions about how language is related to thought, or on other nonlinguistic facts. In short, habitual ways of using language may for the most part create no difficulties when language is employed in familiar situations; but the adequacy of those habits is limited, and their uncritical extension to novel contexts may be the source of serious confusion and error.

The hope of preventing such error has been a continuing stimulus to philosophical reflection on language since Greek antiquity. But identifying linguistic sources of error and constructing rules for avoiding or eliminating them have not been the sole aims of such reflection. As happens in other domains of inquiry, even though the critical study of language is frequently initiated by practical objectives, it may eventually be directed toward purely theoretical ends. And indeed, much philosophical discussion of language has at best only a remote bearing on the removal of linguistic sources of error. Much of it seeks to distinguish and analyze various aspects of language, with the intent to make explicit their detailed characteristics and interrelations and to contribute thereby to the clarification of the nature of knowledge.

The essays in this chapter deal mainly with two questions central to the philosophical critique of language, though each question involves a number of subsidiary issues. The first, based on the supposition that linguistic constructions may have the form of grammatically correct sentences but may for various reasons nevertheless appear to be devoid of any meaningful content, raises the problem of whether rules or criteria can be stated for distinguishing between meaningful and meaningless sentences, and if so, what they are. The second question, based on the assumption that the linguistic expressions being discussed are in some sense meaningful and successfully perform their function as instruments of communication, asks what is to be understood by the "meanings" that are conventionally associated with these expressions, what is the nature of that which is communicated with their help. We will briefly survey the major positions philosophers have taken on each of these questions.

A. CRITERIA OF MEANING

Most of the difficulties encountered in unraveling the meanings of linguistic utterances have their source in familiar linguistic faults—for example, in faults stemming from violations of conventional rules of grammar, or from the use of ambiguous or excessively vague locutions. But while such faults may make the meanings of sentences problematic, they can be handled normally by well-known techniques; and the obscurities they produce have rarely been the impetus to a search for criteria of meaningful discourse. Such a search has usually been undertaken—characteristically during periods of vigorous growth in some major branch of systematic inquiry—when advances in knowledge create doubts whether certain classes of sentences previously accepted as formulations of intelligible assumptions or beliefs are cognitively meaningful (that is, whether truth or falsity can be intelligibly predicated of them), even though the sentences do not seem to differ structurally from others that continue to be regarded as significant. In particular, criteria of meaning have been frequently sought in disciplines in which customary manipulations of language are found to generate antinomies—such as the logical paradoxes discovered by Russell in set theory and the foundations of mathematics; and in experimental sciences in which crucial theoretical assumptions come to be suspected of lacking definite empirical content—such as the assumptions of classical physics involving the notions of absolute time and simultaneity. They have also been sought in many other domains in which the language used lends itself to the formulation of ostensibly important questions that have long been subjects of inquiry, but which come to be regarded by many students as incapable of resolution, not because of lack of skill or knowledge on the part of those who have pursued them, but because of the very nature of the questions—as in various sectors of natural science as well as in moral philosophy, metaphysics, and theology.

The criteria of cognitive meaning that have exerted most influence on contemporary thought were designed primarily for that class of sentences whose truth or falsity is said to be contingent rather than necessary. Moreover, those criteria are usually based on the general though obviously vague assumption that a meaningful sentence must refer in some fashion to what is observable, so that on these criteria a sentence is meaningless if no conceivable observation can serve as evidence for its truth or falsity. Proposed rules for distinguishing between meaningful and meaningless sentences that are based on this assumption are commonly called "verifiability" criteria. However, such rules may differ considerably among themselves in the limitations placed upon what is covered by the term "observable," as well as in the prescriptions laid down for the relations that must hold between sentences and what is observable if the sentences are to count as meaningful.

Three distinguishable though overlapping types of historically influential verifiability criteria are discussed in Section A of this chapter. The first type (illustrated by Hume's proposal) reduces the question of whether a sentence is meaningful to whether the terms contained in it are analyzable into ultimate components, each of which represents something directly observable. The second type reduces the question to whether the sentence as a whole represents some determinate mode of observable human action (exemplified by Peirce), or alternatively to whether it states something that can be verified by observation as true or false, whether conclusively or only with probability (advanced in certain writings of Schlick and Carnap). The third type (adopted by Hempel and Marhenke) reduces the question to whether the sentence can be translated into the formulations of some specified language, whose legitimate sentences are assumed to be meaningful. But there are also other ways of classifying criteria of meaning—for example, according to whether a sentence is held to be meaningful by reason of its supposed "origins" in experience (as in Hume's criterion), or by reason of the supposed "consequences" that result from its acceptance (as in Peirce's proposal). Criteria for which questions of origins are central are often based on alleged but dubious facts of empirical psychology. According to Hume, for example, the ultimate terms of meaningful discourse must represent elementary "impressions" or "perceptions of the mind," from which all other ideas are said to be "derived"; and his criterion is sometimes rejected on the ground that the "atomistic" psychology upon which it rests is untenable. It is nevertheless possible to restate criteria such as Hume's, and to retain what is logically essential to them, without commitment to any particular psychological theory.

But however this may be, no criterion of cognitive meaning yet proposed has won universal acceptance, and philosophers continue to disagree on the adequacy of those that have been advanced, on the conditions a satisfactory criterion should fulfill, and even on whether the construction of a reasonably adequate one is logically possible. Some of the proposals upon which much attention has been focused during the present century are critically surveyed in the essays of Hempel, Marhenke, and Waismann; and a number of difficulties that face attempts to devise satisfactory criteria are examined, especially by Hempel and Waismann. The consequences of applying to various areas of inquiry some of the proposed criteria are briefly indicated in several selections in this chapter; and a fuller account of their import for theology is contained in the essays by Ayer and Flew in Section A.

B. MEANING AND REFERENCE

When two linguistic expressions are assumed to have the same meaning, whether or not both belong to the same language, they are often said to have something in common that is distinct from any physical characteristic possessed by either expression. For example, the Greek sentence Euclid used to state the Pythagorean theorem and the physically quite different English sentence that translates it in, say, Heath's rendition of *The Elements* are equivalent in meaning, but whatever may be common to them that is germane to this equivalence cannot be identified with any property intrinsic to the two sentences as spatiotemporal objects or configurations of events. Just what such expressions do have in common is the central problem raised by the second of the two questions listed earlier in this Introduction.

A quick answer to the question is that one thing such expressions surely do have in common is their meaning. But while this answer is formally correct, it would be satisfactory only if the notion of meaning were either unproblematic or so ultimate that its explication in terms of clearer notions is inherently impossible—and neither alternative is prima facie plausible. In any event, less summary attempts to deal with the question have been made. They can be classified as falling into three types, although each has many variant forms (only some of which can be mentioned in this survey).

The first approach has a complicated history going back to Plato. It assumes that linguistic expressions are by and large like proper names representing particular objects, and it equates the meaning of an expression with that which it supposedly names, and with that to which it supposedly refers. On this approach, for example, just as the meaning of the proper name "Dido" is the Carthaginian queen who is named by it, so the meaning of the common noun "queen" is identified with that to which this term refers and which it allegedly names.

However, as this example helps to disclose, the so-called "referential" view of linguistic meaning as frequently presented and just stated is ambiguous. For it does not make clear, among other things, just what an expression is supposed to name (or refer to), and to clarify this point it is useful to recall the familiar logical distinction between what a term *denotes* and what it *connotes*. A term is said to denote the things to which it is correctly applicable—for example, the term "man" denotes all those individuals (Plato, Euclid, Mozart, and so on) who possess the characteristics stipulated to be necessary and sufficient for truly predicating the term; on the other hand, a term connotes the characteristics whose presence in a thing constitute the necessary and sufficient conditions for predicating the term of that thing—for example, the term "man" connotes, among other properties, that of being a rational animal. Philosophers are not in agreement on whether every linguistic expression both denotes and connotes, or on just what kind of "reality" the connotations of expressions possess. However, those who maintain that the meaning of an expression is what the expression names sometimes equate the meaning with its denotation (John Stuart Mill did this for certain terms, though not for all); in some cases with its connotation (this was Frege's view); and in some cases with both its denotation and connotation (sometimes without awareness of the distinction, in other instances with careful indications of the sense of "meaning" intended in a given context).

Moreover, proponents of a referential view of meaning may be divided on further issues. They may disagree on whether the primary reference of linguistic signs is to the ideas (that is, to psychic events such as mental images) allegedly associated with the signs by their users, or, in the case of most signs, to nonpsychic things. Thus, Locke adopted the first alternative, and Mill the second; however, Locke also believed that language usually "stands for" nonmental realities, even if only indirectly and by way of ideas as intermediaries. Some of the difficulties in views such as Locke's are canvassed by Ayer in Section B of this chapter. A paramount problem with such views is to explain how it is possible for linguistic meanings to be relatively stable and to be communicable from person to person, since according to these views expressions denote particular psychic occurrences that are impermanent and differ with the individuals employing them. One proposed solution to this problem involves some shift of ground and consists essentially in equating meanings, not with transitory ideas in the minds of individual users of linguistic signs, but with relatively stable *dispositions* to manifest various kinds of ideas under specified conditions. An explication of linguistic meaning in terms of certain dispositional traits is attempted by both Ayer and Stevenson in Section B of this chapter, but it should be noted that neither is an exponent of a referential theory of meaning.

Proponents of referential theories may also differ in how they conceive the meaning of complex linguistic expressions (especially sentences) to be related to the meanings of their component parts (such as phrases or individual words). For example, Mill assumed that the meaning of a sentence is the resultant of the meanings of its constituent words. However, Mill made no serious attempt to establish this thesis by examining in detail how the meanings of various types of sentences are connected to different expressions contained in them; this task is undertaken in Frege's essay, since he subscribed in essentials to Mill's thesis. On the other hand, many philosophers have either rejected the thesis entirely or accepted it only in a considerably modified form, largely because of certain difficulties that arise in attempts to interpret various sentential forms in a manner consonant with Mill's assumption. For example, it is argued in Russell's essay "On Denoting" that although sentences containing so-called "denoting" words or phrases are meaningful when taken as a whole, those words and phrases do not "in themselves" have any meaning. Russell therefore maintained that the meaning of a sentence is not in general determined by the meanings of its constituent expressions. A more radical form of this latter contention is advanced in Strawson's essay "On Referring"; however, his discussion of this issue, as well as his criticism of Russell, are based on a rejection of referential theories of meaning.

A second but very different approach to the nature of meaning attempts to develop what is commonly called a "behavioral theory" of meaning. Those who adopt it identify the meanings of linguistic signs with various circumstances connected with the overt behavior of the individuals who employ them. Some exponents of this approach locate the meaning of an expression in the relevant causal conditions that lead to its use; others, like Russell at one period in his intellectual history, equate it with the responses individuals make to the expression because of conditioning processes that the individuals have undergone; and still others locate it in a disposition for manifesting such responses under specified conditions, where the disposition itself may be ascribed either to the individuals making the responses (as is done by Ayer) or to the linguistic sign (as is done by Stevenson). Certain special aspects of a behavioral theory are also discussed in Carnap's paper in Chapter 3. A criticism directed against all behavioral and causal accounts of linguistic meaning is contained in Chisholm's essay in this chapter. Chisholm's argument is based on the allegedly distinctive and irreducible character of the mental phenomena that he believes are essentially involved when language is employed.

A third approach to linguistic meaning is less easy to describe briefly than the other two and is perhaps best characterized as a combination of two contentions, one negative and the other positive. The first is a vigorous rejection of all views which assume that an expression has a determinate meaning irrespective of context or which identify the meaning of a linguistic sign with some "entity"—whether the entity is the denotation or the connotation of the sign, a mental or overtly behavioral process associated with its use, or a disposition. The positive contention is the claim that there is in general a great multiplicity of different uses to which a linguistic expression may be put in various contexts. To the extent that exponents of this approach believe it is possible to state in a nutshell what meanings are, they define their conception by saying that the meaning of an expression is "a function of what its users do with it," or even more briefly that its meaning is "its use." Those who subscribe to this view therefore believe it is a capital mistake to conclude that because an expression has an application in each of several contexts, the contexts have some unique property in common that constitutes *the* meaning of the expression. For, according to them, the rules governing the use of an expression (whether they be tacit or explicit) may vary continuously with context, even if there are strong "family resemblances" among them. In consequence, even if it were possible to specify with unlimited precision the various uses (or "functions") of an expression or the resemblances between them (this possibility is generally denied), it would be misleading as well as arbitrary to designate as *the* meaning of the expression either one particular function or the features in which its different functions resemble each other—for in neither case would the proposed identification exhaust the expression's meaning.

This third approach to the study of linguistic meaning—sometimes called the "functional theory"—has been cultivated in variant forms by many thinkers in the past as well as by recent ones (for example, by Aristotle in some of his writings, by Ernst Mach and P. W. Bridgman in their critiques of the language of physics, and by Peirce and Dewey in their analyses of numerous logical, psychological, moral, and legal concepts), and is illustrated by Peirce's essay in this chapter. However, much of its current impetus comes from the ideas of the late Ludwig Wittgenstein, whose style of composition was too aphoristic and disconnected to permit the inclusion of a reasonably brief statement by him of his approach to linguistic meaning, but whose general point of view is reflected in the selections in Section B of this chapter by Ayer, Strawson, and Waismann.

A. CRITERIA OF MEANING

David Hume

Of the Origin of Ideas

Everyone will readily allow that there is a considerable difference between the perceptions of the mind when a man feels the pain of excessive heat or the pleasure of moderate warmth, and when he afterwards recalls to his memory this sensation or anticipates it by his imagination. These faculties may mimic or copy the perceptions of the senses, but they never can entirely reach the force and vivacity of the original sentiment. The utmost we say of them, even when they operate with greatest vigor, is that they represent their object in so lively a manner that we could *almost* say we feel or see it. But, except the mind be disordered by disease or madness, they never can arrive at such a pitch of vivacity as to render these perceptions altogether undistinguishable. All the colors of poetry, however splendid, can never paint natural objects in such a manner as to make the description be taken for a real landscape. The most lively thought is still inferior to the dullest sensation.

We may observe a like distinction to run through all the other perceptions of the mind. A man in a fit of anger is actuated in a very different manner from one who only thinks of that emotion. If you tell me that any person is in love, I easily understand your meaning and form a just conception of his situation, but never can mistake that conception for the real disorders and agitations of the passion. When we reflect on our past sentiments and affections, our thought is a faithful mirror and copies its objects truly, but the colors which it employs are faint and dull in comparison of those in which our original perceptions were clothed. It requires no nice discernment or metaphysical head to mark the distinction between them.

Here, therefore, we may divide all the perceptions of the mind into two classes or species, which are distinguished by their different degrees of force and vivacity. The less forcible and lively are commonly denominated "thoughts" or "ideas." The other species want a name in our language, and in most others; I suppose, because it was not requisite for any but philosophical purposes to rank them under a general term or appellation. Let us, therefore, use a little freedom and call them "impressions," employing that word in a

---

From David Hume, *An Inquiry Concerning Human Understanding,* Section II, first published in 1748.

Born in Scotland, David Hume (1711–76) never held an academic post and acquired a literary reputation during his lifetime by his writings on economic and historical, as well as philosophical, subjects.

sense somewhat different from the usual. By the term "impression," then, I mean all our more lively perceptions, when we hear, or see, or feel, or love, or hate, or desire, or will. And impressions are distinguished from ideas, which are the less lively perceptions of which we are conscious when we reflect on any of those sensations or movements above mentioned.

Nothing, at first view, may seem more unbounded than the thought of man, which not only escapes all human power and authority, but is not even restrained within the limits of nature and reality. To form monsters and join incongruous shapes and appearances costs the imagination no more trouble than to conceive the most natural and familiar objects. And while the body is confined to one planet, along which it creeps with pain and difficulty, the thought can in an instant transport us into the most distant regions of the universe, or even beyond the universe into the unbounded chaos where nature is supposed to lie in total confusion. What never was seen or heard of, may yet be conceived, nor is anything beyond the power of thought except what implies an absolute contradiction.

But though our thought seems to possess this unbounded liberty, we shall find upon a nearer examination that it is really confined within very narrow limits, and that all this creative power of the mind amounts to no more than the faculty of compounding, transposing, augmenting, or diminishing the materials afforded us by the senses and experience. When we think of a golden mountain, we only join two consistent ideas, "gold" and "mountain," with which we were formerly acquainted. A virtuous horse we can conceive, because, from our own feeling, we can conceive virtue; and this we may unite to the figure and shape of a horse, which is an animal familiar to us. In short, all the materials of thinking are derived either from our outward or inward sentiment; the mixture and composition of these belongs alone to the mind and will, or, to express myself in philosophical language, all our ideas or more feeble perceptions are copies of our impressions or more lively ones.

To prove this, the two following arguments will, I hope, be sufficient. *First,* when we analyze our thoughts or ideas, however compounded or sublime, we always find that they resolve themselves into such simple ideas as were copied from a precedent feeling or sentiment. Even those ideas which at first view seem the most wide of this origin are found, upon a nearer scrutiny, to be derived from it. The idea of God, as meaning an infinitely intelligent, wise, and good Being, arises from reflecting on the operations of our own mind and augmenting, without limit, those qualities of goodness and wisdom. We may prosecute this inquiry to what length we please; where we shall always find that every idea which we examine is copied from a similar impression. Those who would assert that this position is not universally true, nor without exception, have only one, and that an easy, method of refuting it by producing that idea which, in their opinion, is not derived from this source. It will then be incumbent on us, if we would maintain our doctrine, to produce the impression or lively perception which corresponds to it.

Secondly, if it happen, from a defect of the organ, that a man is not susceptible of any species of sensation, we always find that he is as little susceptible of the correspondent idea. A blind man can form no notion of colors, a deaf man of sounds. Restore either of them that sense in which he is deficient by opening this new inlet for his sensations, you also open an inlet for the ideas, and he finds no difficulty in conceiving these objects. The case is the same if the object proper for exciting any sensation has never been applied to the organ. A Laplander or Negro has no notion of the relish of wine. And though there are few or no instances of a like deficiency in the mind where a person has never felt or is wholly incapable of a sentiment or passion that belongs to his species, yet we find the same observation to take place in a less degree. A man of mild manners can form no idea of inveterate revenge or cruelty, nor can a selfish heart easily conceive the heights of friendship and generosity. It is readily allowed that other beings may possess many senses of which we can have no conception, because the ideas of them have never been introduced to us in the only manner by which an idea can have access to the mind, to wit, by the actual feeling and sensation.

There is, however, one contradictory phenomenon which may prove that it is not absolutely impossible for ideas to arise independent of their correspondent impressions. I believe it will readily be allowed that the several distinct ideas of color, which enter by the eye, or those of sound, which are conveyed by the ear, are really different from each other, though at the same time resembling. Now, if this be true of different colors, it must be no less so of the different shades of the same color; and each shade produces a distinct idea, independent of the rest. For if this should be denied, it is possible, by the continual gradation of shades, to run a color insensibly into what is most remote from it; and if you will not allow any of the means to be different, you cannot, without absurdity, deny the extremes to be the same. Suppose, therefore, a person to have enjoyed his sight for thirty years and to have become perfectly acquainted with colors of all kinds, except one particular shade of blue, for instance, which it never has been his fortune to meet with; let all the different shades of that color, except that single one, be placed before him, descending gradually from the deepest to the lightest, it is plain that he will perceive a blank where that shade is wanting, and will be sensible that there is a greater distance in that place between the contiguous colors than in any other. Now I ask whether it be possible for him, from his own imagination, to supply this deficiency and raise up to himself the idea of that particular shade, though it had never been conveyed to him by his senses? I believe there are few but will be of opinion that he can; and this may serve as a proof that the simple ideas are not always, in every instance, derived from the correspondent impressions, though this instance is so singular that it is scarcely worth our observing, and does not merit that for it alone we should alter our general maxim.

Here, therefore, is a proposition which not only seems in itself simple and intelligible, but, if a proper use were made of it, might render every dispute equally intelligible, and banish all that jargon which has so long taken possession of metaphysical reasonings and drawn disgrace upon them. All ideas, especially abstract ones, are naturally faint and obscure. The mind has but a slender hold of them. They are apt to be confounded with other resembling ideas; and when we have often employed any term, though without a distinct meaning, we are apt to imagine it has a determinate idea annexed to it. On the contrary, all impressions, that is, all sensations either outward or inward, are strong and vivid. The limits between them are more exactly determined, nor is it easy to fall into any error or mistake with regard to them. When we entertain, therefore, any suspicion that a philosophical term is employed without any meaning or idea (as is but too frequent), we need but inquire, *from what impression is that supposed idea derived?* And if it be impossible to assign any, this will serve to confirm our suspicion. By bringing ideas in so clear a light, we may reasonably hope to remove all dispute which may arise concerning their nature and reality.

Charles Sanders Peirce

How to Make Our Ideas Clear

The very first lesson that we have a right to demand that logic shall teach us is, how to make our ideas clear; and a most important one it is, depreciated only by minds who stand in need of it. To know what we think, to be masters of our own meaning, will make a solid foundation for great and weighty thought. It is most easily learned by those whose ideas are meagre and restricted; and far happier they than such as wallow helplessly in a rich mud of conceptions. A nation, it is true, may, in the course of generations, overcome the disadvantage of an excessive wealth of language and its natural concomitant, a vast, unfathomable deep of ideas. We may see it in history, slowly perfecting its literary forms, sloughing at length its metaphysics, and, by virtue of the untirable patience which is often a compensation, attaining great excellence in every branch of mental acquirement. The page of history is not yet unrolled that is to tell us whether such a people will or will not in the long run prevail over one whose ideas (like the words of their language) are few, but which possesses a wonderful mastery over those which it has. For an individual, however, there can be no question that a few clear ideas are worth more than many confused ones. . . .

The principles set forth in the first [of these papers ("The Fixation of Belief")] lead, at once, to a method of reaching a clearness of thought of higher grade than the "distinctness" of the logicians. It was there noticed that the action of thought is excited by the irritation of doubt, and ceases when belief is attained; so that the production of belief is the sole function of thought. All these words, however, are too strong for my purpose. It is as if I had described

From C. S. Peirce, "How to Make Our Ideas Clear," *Popular Science Monthly,* Vol. 12 (1878). It is the second of the six papers Peirce published in that periodical during 1877 to 1878 under the general title "Illustrations of the Logic of Science." The paper has been reprinted many times and is included in the definitive, eight-volume edition of Peirce's writings, *Collected Papers of Charles Sanders Peirce,* 1931–58.

Charles Peirce (1839–1914) was born in Cambridge, Massachusetts. For many years he was associated with the U. S. Coastal and Geodesic Survey, but except for a brief period (1879–84) as an Instructor in Logic at the Johns Hopkins University he had no academic post.

the phenomena as they appear under a mental microscope. Doubt and Belief, as the words are commonly employed, relate to religious or other grave discussions. But here I use them to designate the starting of any question, no matter how small or how great, and the resolution of it. If, for instance, in a horse-car, I pull out my purse and find a five-cent nickel and five coppers, I decide, while my hand is going to the purse, in which way I will pay my fare. To call such a question Doubt, and my decision Belief, is certainly to use words very disproportionate to the occasion. To speak of such a doubt as causing an irritation which needs to be appeased, suggests a temper which is uncomfortable to the verge of insanity. Yet, looking at the matter minutely, it must be admitted that, if there is the least hesitation as to whether I shall pay the five coppers or the nickel (as there will be sure to be, unless I act from some previously contracted habit in the matter), though irritation is too strong a word, yet I am excited to such small mental activity as may be necessary to deciding how I shall act. Most frequently doubts arise from some indecision, however momentary, in our action. Sometimes it is not so. I have, for example, to wait in a railway-station, and to pass the time I read the advertisements on the walls. I compare the advantages of different trains and different routes which I never expect to take, merely fancying myself to be in a state of hesitancy, because I am bored with having nothing to trouble me. Feigned hesitancy, whether feigned for mere amusement or with a lofty purpose, plays a great part in the production of scientific inquiry. However the doubt may originate, it stimulates the mind to an activity which may be slight or energetic, calm or turbulent. Images pass rapidly through consciousness, one incessantly melting into another, until at last, when all is over—it may be in a fraction of a second, in an hour, or after long years—we find ourselves decided as to how we should act under such circumstances as those which occasioned our hesitation. In other words, we have attained belief.

In this process we observe two sorts of elements of consciousness, the distinction between which may best be made clear by means of an illustration. In a piece of music there are the separate notes, and there is the air. A single tone may be prolonged for an hour or a day, and it exists as perfectly in each second of that time as in the whole taken together, so that, as long as it is sounding, it might be present to a sense from which everything in the past was as completely absent as the future itself. But it is different with the air, the performance of which occupies a certain time, during the portions of which only portions of it are played. It consists in an orderliness in the succession of sounds which strike the ear at different times; and to perceive it there must be some continuity of consciousness which makes the events of a lapse of time present to us. We certainly only perceive the air by hearing the separate notes; yet we cannot be said to directly hear it, for we hear only what is present at the instant, and an orderliness of succession cannot exist in an instant. These two sorts of objects, what we are *immediately* conscious of and what we are *mediately* conscious of, are found in all consciousness. Some elements (the sensations) are completely present at every instant so long as they last, while others (like thought) are actions having beginning, middle, and end, and consist in a congruence in the succession of sensations which flow through the mind. They cannot be immediately present to us, but must cover some portion of the past or future. Thought is a thread of melody running through the succession of our sensations.

We may add that just as a piece of music may be written in parts, each part having its own air, so various systems of relationship of succession subsist together between the same sensations. These different systems are distinguished by having different motives, ideas, or functions. Thought is only one such system, for its sole motive, idea, and function is to produce belief, and whatever does not concern that purpose belongs to some other system of relations. The action of thinking may incidentally have other results; it may serve to amuse us, for example, and among *dilettanti* it is not rare to find those who have so perverted thought to the purposes of pleasure that it seems to vex them to think that the questions upon which they delight to exercise it may ever get finally settled; and a positive discovery which takes a favourite subject out of the arena of literary debate is met with ill-concealed dislike. This disposition is the very debauchery of thought. But the soul and meaning of thought, abstracted from the other elements which accompany it, though it may be voluntarily thwarted, can never be made to direct itself toward anything but the production of belief. Thought in action has for its only possible motive the attainment of thought at rest; and whatever does not refer to belief is no part of the thought itself.

And what, then, is belief? It is the demi-cadence which closes a musical phrase in the symphony of our intellectual life. We have seen that it has just three properties: First, it is something that we are aware of; second, it appeases the irritation of doubt; and, third, it involves the establishment in our nature of a rule of action, or, say for short, a *habit*. As it appeases the irritation of doubt, which is the motive for thinking, thought relaxes, and comes to rest for a moment when belief is reached. But, since belief is a rule for action, the application of which involves further doubt and further thought, at the same time that it is a stopping-place, it is also a new starting-place for thought. That is why I have permitted myself to call it thought at rest, although thought is essentially an action. The *final* upshot of thinking is the exercise of volition, and of this thought no longer forms a part; but belief is only a stadium of mental action, an effect upon our nature due to thought, which will influence future thinking.

The essence of belief is the establishment of a habit; and different beliefs are distinguished by the different modes of action to which they give rise. If beliefs do not differ in this respect, if they appease the same doubt by producing the same rule of action, then no mere differences in the manner of consciousness of them can make them different beliefs, any more than playing a tune in different keys is playing different tunes. Imaginary distinctions are often drawn between beliefs which differ only in their mode of expression;—the wrangling which ensues is real enough, however. To believe that any objects are arranged among themselves as in Fig. 1, and to believe that they are arranged [as] in Fig. 2, are one and the same belief; yet it is conceivable that a man should assert one proposition and deny the other. Such false distinctions do as much harm as the confusion of beliefs really different, and are among the pitfalls of which we ought constantly to beware, especially when we are upon metaphysical ground. One singular deception of this sort, which often occurs, is to mistake the sensation produced by our own unclearness of thought for a character of the object we are thinking. Instead of perceiving that the obscurity is purely subjective, we fancy that we contemplate a quality of the object which is essentially mysterious; and if our conception be afterward presented to us in a clear form we do not recognize it as the same, owing to the absence of the feeling of unintelligibility. So long as this deception lasts, it obviously puts an impassable barrier in the way of perspicuous thinking; so that it equally interests the opponents of rational thought to perpetuate it, and its adherents to guard against it.

Another such deception is to mistake a mere difference in the grammatical construction of two words for a distinction between the ideas they express. In this pedantic age, when the general mob of writers attend so much more to words than to things, this error is common enough. When I just said that

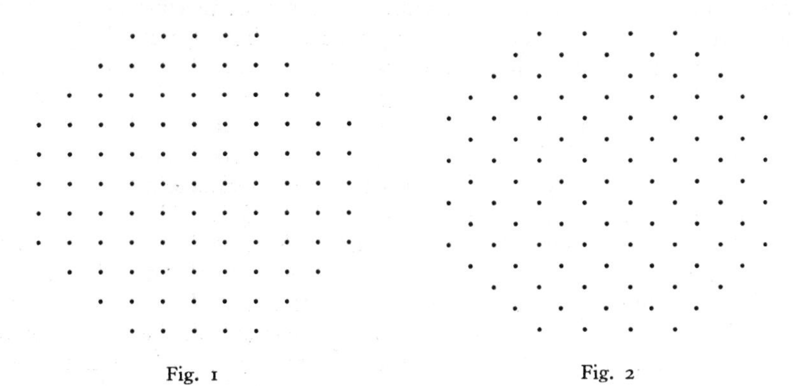

Fig. 1 Fig. 2

thought is an *action,* and that it consists in a *relation,* although a person performs an action but not a relation, which can only be the result of an action, yet there was no inconsistency in what I said, but only a grammatical vagueness.

From all these sophisms we shall be perfectly safe so long as we reflect that the whole function of thought is to produce habits of action; and that whatever there is connected with a thought, but irrelevant to its purpose, is an accretion to it, but no part of it. If there be a unity among our sensations which has no reference to how we shall act on a given occasion, as when we listen to a piece of music, why we do not call that thinking. To develop its meaning, we have, therefore, simply to determine what habits it produces, for what a thing means is simply what habits it involves. Now, the identity of a habit depends on how it might lead us to act, not merely under such circumstances as are likely to arise, but under such as might possibly occur, no matter how improbable they may be. What the habit is depends on *when* and *how* it causes us to act. As for the *when,* every stimulus to action is derived from perception; as for the *how,* every purpose of action is to produce some sensible result. Thus, we come down to what is tangible and conceivably practical, as the root of every real distinction of thought, no matter how subtile it may be; and there is no distinction of meaning so fine as to consist in anything but a possible difference of practice.

To see what this principle leads to, consider in the light of it such a doctrine as that of transubstantiation. The Protestant churches generally hold that the elements of the sacrament are flesh and blood only in a tropical sense; they nourish our souls as meat and the juice of it would our bodies. But the Catholics maintain that they are literally just meat and blood; although they possesss all the sensible qualities of wafer-cakes and diluted wine. But we can have no conception of wine except what may enter into a belief, either—

1. That this, that, or the other, is wine; or,
2. That wine possesses certain properties.

Such beliefs are nothing but self-notifications that we should, upon occasion, act in regard to such things as we believe to be wine according to the qualities which we believe wine to possess. The occasion of such action would be some sensible perception, the motive of it to produce some sensible result. Thus our action has exclusive reference to what affects the senses, our habit has the same bearing as our action, our belief the same as our habit, our conception the same as our belief; and we can consequently mean nothing by wine but what has certain effects, direct or indirect, upon our senses; and to talk of something as having all the sensible characters of wine, yet being in reality blood, is senseless jargon. Now, it is not my object to pursue the theological question; and having used it as a logical example I drop it, without caring to anticipate the theologian's reply. I only desire to point out how impossible it is that we should have an idea in our minds which relates to anything but conceived sensible effects of things. Our idea of anything *is* our idea of its sensible effects; and if we fancy that we have any other we deceive ourselves, and mistake a mere sensation accompanying the thought for a part of the thought itself. It is absurd to say that thought has any meaning unrelated to its only function. It is foolish for Catholics and Protestants to fancy themselves in disagreement about the elements of the sacrament, if they agree in regard to all their sensible effects, here and hereafter.

It appears, then, that the rule for attaining the third grade of clearness of apprehension is as follows: Consider what effects, that might conceivably have practical bearings, we conceive the object of our conception to have. Then, our conception of these effects is the whole of our conception of the object.

Let us illustrate this rule by some examples; and, to begin with the simplest one possible, let us ask what we mean by calling a thing hard. Evidently that it will not be scratched by many other substances. The whole conception of this quality, as of every other, lies in its conceived effects. There is absolutely no difference between a hard thing and a soft thing so long as they are not brought to the test. Suppose, then, that a diamond could be crystallized in the midst of a cushion of soft cotton, and should remain there until it was finally burned up. Would it be false to say that that diamond was soft? This seems a foolish question, and would be so, in fact, except in the realm of logic. There such questions are often of the greatest utility as serving to bring logical principles into sharper relief than real discussions ever could. In studying logic we must not put them aside with hasty answers, but must consider them with attentive care, in order to make out the principles involved. We may, in the present case, modify our question, and ask what prevents us from saying that all hard bodies remain perfectly soft until they are touched, when their hardness increases with the pressure until they are scratched. Reflection will show that the reply is this: there would be no *falsity* in such modes of speech. They would involve a modification of our present usage of speech with regard to the words hard and soft, but not of their meanings. For they represent no fact to be different from what it is; only they involve arrangements of facts which would be exceedingly maladroit. This leads us to remark that the question of what would occur under circumstances which do not actually arise is not a question of fact, but only of the most perspicuous arrangement of them. For example, the question of free-will and fate in its simplest form, stripped of verbiage, is something like this: I have done something of which I am ashamed; could I, by an effort of the will, have resisted the temptation, and done otherwise? The philosophical reply is, that this is not a question of fact, but only of the arrangement of facts. Arranging them so as to exhibit what is particularly pertinent to my question—namely, that I ought to blame myself for having done wrong—it is perfectly true to say that, if I had willed to do otherwise than I did, I should have done otherwise. On the other hand, arranging the facts so as to exhibit another important consideration, it is equally true that, when a temptation has once been allowed to work, it will, if it has a certain force, produce its effect, let me struggle how I may. There is no objection to a contradiction in what would result from a false supposition. The *reductio ad absurdum* consists in showing that contradictory results would follow from a hypothesis which is consequently judged to be false. Many questions are involved in the free-will discussion, and I am far from desiring to say that both sides are equally right. On the contrary, I am of opinion that one side denies important facts, and that the other does not. But what I do say is, that the above single question was the origin of the whole doubt; that, had it not been for this question, the controversy would never have arisen; and that this question is perfectly solved in the manner which I have indicated.

Let us next seek a clear idea of Weight. This is another very easy case. To say that a body is heavy means simply that, in the absence of opposing force, it will fall. This (neglecting certain specifications of how it will fall, etc., which exist in the mind of the physicist who uses the word) is evidently the whole conception of weight. It is a fair question whether some particular facts may not *account* for gravity; but what we mean by the force itself is completely involved in its effects.

This leads us to undertake an account of the idea of Force in general. This is the great conception which, developed in the early part of the seventeenth century from the rude idea of a cause, and constantly improved upon since, has shown us how to explain all the changes of motion which bodies experience, and how to think about all physical phenomena; which has given birth to modern science, and changed the face of the globe; and which, aside from its more special uses, has played a principal part in directing the course of modern thought, and in furthering modern social development. It is, therefore, worth some pains to comprehend it. According to our rule, we must begin by asking what is the immediate use of thinking about force; and the answer is, that we thus account for changes of motion. If bodies were left to themselves, without the intervention of forces, every motion would continue unchanged both in velocity and in direction. Furthermore, change of motion never takes place abruptly; if its direction is changed, it is always through a curve without angles; if its velocity alters, it is by degrees. The gradual changes which are constantly taking place are conceived by geometers to be compounded together according to the rules of the parallelogram of forces. . . . If the actual changes of motion which the different particles of bodies experience are each resolved in its appropriate way, each component acceleration is precisely such as is prescribed by a certain law of Nature, according to which bodies, in the relative positions which the bodies in question actually have at the moment, always receive certain accelerations, which, being compounded by geometrical addition, give the acceleration which the body actually experiences.

This is the only fact which the idea of force represents, and whoever will take the trouble clearly to apprehend what this fact is, perfectly comprehends what force is. Whether we ought to say that a force *is* an acceleration, or that it *causes* an acceleration, is a mere question of propriety of language, which has no more to do with our real meaning than the difference between the French idiom *"Il fait froid"* and its English equivalent *"It is cold."* Yet it is surprising to see how this simple affair has muddled men's minds. In how many profound treatises is not force spoken of as a "mysterious entity," which seems to be only a way of confessing that the author despairs of ever getting a clear notion of what the word means! In a recent admired work on *Analytic Mechanics* it is stated that we understand precisely the effect of force, but what force itself is we do not understand! This is simply a self-contradiction. The idea which the word force excites in our minds has no other function than to affect our actions, and these actions can have no reference to force otherwise than through its effects. Consequently, if we know what the effects of force are, we are acquainted with every fact which is implied in saying that a force exists, and there is nothing more to know. The truth is, there is some vague notion afloat that a question may mean something which the mind cannot conceive; and when some hair-splitting philosophers have been confronted with the absurdity of such a view, they have invented an empty distinction between positive and negative conceptions, in the attempt to give their non-idea a form not obviously nonsensical. The nullity of it is sufficiently plain from the considerations given a few pages back; and, apart from those considerations, the quibbling character of the distinction must have struck every mind accustomed to real thinking.

Carl Gustav Hempel

Problems and Changes in the Empiricist Criterion of Meaning

1. INTRODUCTION

The fundamental tenet of modern empiricism is the view that all non-analytic knowledge is based on experience. Let us call this thesis the principle of empiricism. Contemporary logical empiricism has added to it the maxim that a sentence makes a cognitively meaningful assertion, and thus can be said to be either true or false, only if it is either (1) analytic or self-contradictory or (2) capable, at least in principle, of experiential test. According to this so-called *empiricist criterion of cognitive meaning, or of cognitive significance,* many of the formulations of traditional metaphysics and large parts of epistemology are devoid of cognitive significance—however rich some of them may be in non-cognitive import by virtue of their emotive appeal or the moral inspiration they offer. Similarly certain doctrines which have been, at one time or another, formulated within empirical science or its border disciplines are so contrived as to be incapable of test by any conceivable evidence; they are therefore qualified as pseudo-hypotheses, which assert nothing, and which therefore have no explanatory or predictive force whatever. This verdict applies, for example, to the neo-vitalist speculations about entelechies or vital forces, and to the "telefinalist hypothesis" propounded by Lecomte du Noüy.

The preceding formulations of the principle of empiricism and of the empiricist meaning criterion provide no more, however, than a general and rather vague characterization of a basic point of view, and they need therefore to be elucidated and amplified. And while in the earlier phases of its development, logical empiricism was to a large extent preoccupied with a critique of philosophic and scientific formulations by means of those fundamental principles, there has been in recent years an increasing concern with the positive tasks of analyzing in detail the logic and methodology of empirical science and of clarifying and restating the basic ideas of empiricism in the light of the insights thus obtained. In the present article, I propose to discuss some of the problems this search has raised and some of the results it seems to have established.

From "Problems and Changes in the Empiricist Criterion of Meaning" (without the footnotes in the original), *Revue Internationale de Philosophie,* Vol. 4 (1950). Reprinted by permission of the author and of *Revue Internationale de Philosophie.* The paper appears without omission of the footnotes in Leonard Linsky (ed.), *Semantics and the Philosophy of Language,* 1952.

C. G. Hempel (1905–) is currently Stuart Professor of Philosophy at Princeton University.

2. CHANGES IN THE TESTABILITY CRITERION OF EMPIRICAL MEANING

As our formulation shows, the empiricist meaning criterion lays down the requirement of experiential testability for those among the cognitively meaningful sentences which are neither analytic nor contradictory; let us call them sentences with empirical meaning, or empirical significance. The concept of testability, which is to render precise the vague notion of being based—or rather baseable—on experience, has undergone several modifications which reflect an increasingly refined analysis of the structure of empirical knowledge. In the present section, let us examine the major stages of this development.

For convenience of exposition, we first introduce three auxiliary concepts, namely those of observable characteristic, of observation predicate, and of observation sentence. A property or a relation of physical objects will be called an *observable characteristic* if, under suitable circumstances, its presence or absence in a given instance can be ascertained through direct observation. Thus, the terms "green", "soft", "liquid", "longer than", designate observable characteristics, while "bivalent", "radioactive", "better electric conductor", and "introvert" do not. Terms which designate observable characteristics will be called *observation predicates.* Finally, by an *observation sentence* we shall understand any sentence which—correctly or incorrectly—asserts of one or more specifically named objects that they have, or that they lack, some specified observable characteristic. The following sentences, for example, meet this condition: "The Eiffel Tower is taller than the buildings in its vicinity", "The pointer of this instrument does not cover the point marked '3' on the scale", and even, "The largest dinosaur on exhibit in New York's Museum of Natural History had a blue tongue"; for this last sentence assigns to a specified object a characteristic—having a blue tongue—which is of such a kind that under suitable circumstances (e.g., in the case of my Chow dog) its presence or absence can be ascertained by direct observation. Our concept of observation sentence is intended to provide a precise interpretation of the vague idea of a sentence asserting something that is "in principle" ascertainable by direct observation, even though it may happen to be actually incapable of being observed by myself, perhaps also by my contemporaries, and possibly even by any human being who ever lived or will live. Any evidence that might be adduced in the test of an empirical hypothesis may now be thought of as being expressed in observation sentences of this kind.

We now turn to the changes in the conception of testability, and thus of empirical meaning. In the early days of the Vienna Circle, a sentence was said to have empirical meaning if it was capable, at least in principle, of complete verification by observational evidence; i.e., if observational evidence could be described which, if actually obtained, would conclusively establish the truth of the sentence. With the help of the concept of observation sentence, we can restate this requirement as follows: A sentence S has empirical meaning if and only if it is possible to indicate a finite set of observation sentences, $O_1, O_2, \ldots, O_n$, such that if these are true, then S is necessarily true, too. As stated, however, this condition is satisfied also if S is an analytic sentence or if the given observation sentences are logically incompatible with each other. By the following formulation, we rule these cases out and at the same time express the intended criterion more precisely:

(2.1) *Requirement of complete verifiability in principle:* A sentence has empirical meaning if and only if it is not analytic and follows logically from some finite and logically consistent class of observation sentence.

This criterion, however, has several serious defects. The first of those here to be mentioned has been pointed out by various writers:

(*a*) The verifiability requirement rules out all sentences of universal form and thus all statements purporting to express general laws; for these cannot be conclusively verified by any finite set of observational data. And since sentences of this type constitute an integral part of scientific theories, the verifiability requirement must be regarded as overly restrictive in this respect. Similarly, the criterion disqualifies all sentences such as "For any substance there exists some solvent", which contain both universal and existential quantifiers (i.e., occurrences of the terms "all" and "some" or their equivalents); for no sentences of this kind can be logically deduced from any finite set of observation sentences.

Two further defects of the verifiability requirement do not seem to have been widely noticed:

(*b*) Suppose that S is a sentence which satisfies the proposed criterion, whereas N is a sentence such as "The absolute is perfect", to which the criterion attributes no empirical meaning. Then the alternation SvN (i.e., the expression obtained by connecting the two sentences by the word "or"), likewise satisfies the criterion; for if S is a consequence of some finite class of observation sentences, then trivially SvN is a consequence of the same class. But clearly, the empiricist criterion of meaning is not intended to countenance sentences of this sort. In this respect, therefore, the requirement of complete verifiability is too inclusive.

(*c*) Let "P" be an observation predicate. Then the purely existential sentence "$(Ex)P(x)$" ("There exists at least one thing that has the property P") is completely verifiable, for it follows from any observation sentence asserting of some particular object that it has the property P. But its denial, being equivalent to the universal sentence "$(x) \backsim P(x)$" ("Nothing has the property P") is clearly not completely verifiable, as follows from comment (*a*) above. Hence, under the criterion (2.1), the denials of certain empirically—and thus cognitively—significant sentences are empirically meaningless; and as they are neither analytic nor contradictory, they are cognitively meaningless. But however we may delimit the domain of significant discourse, we shall have to insist that if a sentence falls within that domain, then so must its denial. To put the matter more explicitly: The sentences to be qualified as cognitively meaningful are precisely those which can be significantly said to be either true or false. But then, adherence to (2.1) would engender a serious dilemma, as is shown by the consequence just mentioned: We would either have to give up the fundamental logical principle that if a sentence is true or false, then its denial is false or true, respectively (and thus cognitively significant); or else, we must deny, in a manner reminiscent of the intuitionistic conception of logic and mathematics, that "$(x) \backsim P(x)$" is logically equivalent to the negation of "(Ex) $P(x)$". Clearly, the criterion (2.1), which has disqualified itself on several other counts, does not warrant such drastic measures for its preservation; hence, it has to be abandoned.

Strictly analogous considerations apply to an alternative criterion, which makes complete falsifiability in principle the defining characteristic of empirical significance. Let us formulate this criterion as follows: A sentence has empirical meaning if and only if it is capable, in principle, of complete refutation by a finite number of observational data; or, more precisely:

(2.2) *Requirement of complete falsifiability in principle:* A sentence has empirical meaning if and only if its denial is not analytic and follows logically from some finite logically consistent class of observation sentences.

This criterion qualifies a sentence as empirically meaningful if its denial satisfies the requirement of complete verifiability; as is to be expected, it is therefore inadequate on similar grounds as the latter:

(*a*) It rules out purely existential hypotheses, such as "There exists at least one unicorn", and all sentences whose formulation calls for mixed—i.e., universal and existential—quantification; for none of these can possibly be conclusively falsified by a finite number of observation sentences.

(*b*) If a sentence S is completely falsifiable whereas N is a sentence which is not, then their conjunction, S.N (i.e., the expression obtained by connecting the two sentences by the word "and") is completely falsifiable; for if the denial of S is entailed by some class of observation sentences, then the denial of S.N is, *a fortiori,* entailed by the same class. Thus, the criterion allows empirical significance to many sentences which an adequate empiricist criterion should rule out, such as, say "All swans are white and the absolute is perfect."

(*c*) If "P" is an observation predicate, then the assertion that all things have the property P is qualified as significant, but its denial, being equivalent to a purely existential hypothesis, is disqualified (cf. (*a*)). Hence, criterion (2.2) gives rise to the same dilemma as (2.1).

In sum, then, interpretations of the testability criterion in terms of complete verifiability or of complete falsifiability are inadequate because they are overly restrictive in one direction and overly inclusive in another, and because both of them require incisive changes in the fundamental principles of logic.

Several attempts have been made to avoid these difficulties by construing the testability criterion as demanding merely a partial and possibly indirect confirmability of empirical hypotheses by observational evidence.

(2.3) A formulation suggested by Ayer is characteristic of these attempts to set up a clear and sufficiently comprehensive criterion of confirmability. It states, in effect, that a sentence S has empirical import if from S in conjunction with suitable subsidiary hypotheses it is possible to derive observation sentences which are not derivable from the subsidiary hypotheses alone.

This condition is suggested by a closer consideration of the logical structure of scientific testing; but it is much too liberal as it stands. Indeed, as Ayer himself has pointed out in the second edition of his book, *Language, Truth, and Logic,* his criterion allows empirical import to any sentence whatever. Thus, e.g., if S is the sentence "The absolute is perfect", it suffices to choose as a subsidiary hypothesis the sentence "If the absolute is perfect then this apple is red" in order to make possible the deduction of the observation sentence "This apple is red," which clearly does not follow from the subsidiary hypothesis alone.

(2.4) To meet this objection, Ayer has recently proposed a modified version of his testability criterion. The modification restricts, in effect, the subsidiary hypotheses mentioned in (2.3) to sentences which are either analytic or can independently be shown to be testable in the sense of the modified criterion.

But it can readily be shown that this new criterion, like the requirement of complete falsifiability, allows empirical significance to any conjunction S.N where S satisfies Ayer's criterion while N is a sentence such as "The absolute is perfect," which is to be disqualified by that criterion. Indeed: whatever consequences can be deduced from S with the help of permissible subsidiary hypotheses can also be deduced from S.N by means of the same subsidiary hypotheses, and as Ayer's new criterion is formulated essentially in terms of the deducibility of a certain type of consequence from the given sentence, it countenances S.N together with S. Another difficulty has been pointed out by Professor A. Church, who has shown that if there are any three observation sentences none of which alone entails any of the others, then it follows for any sentence S whatsoever that either it or its denial has empirical import according to Ayer's revised criterion.

3. TRANSLATABILITY INTO AN EMPIRICIST LANGUAGE AS A NEW CRITERION OF COGNITIVE MEANING

I think it is useless to continue the search for an adequate criterion of testability in terms of deductive relationships to observation sentences. The past development of this search—of which we have considered the major stages—seems to warrant the expectation that as long as we try to set up a criterion of testability for individual sentences in a natural language in terms of logical relationship to observation sentences, the result will be either too restrictive or too inclusive, or both. In particular it appears likely that such criteria would allow empirical import, in the manner of (2.1) (*b*) or of (2.2) (*b*), either to any alternation or to any conjunction of two sentences of which at least one is qualified as empirically meaningful; and this peculiarity has undesirable consequences becauses the liberal grammatical rules of English as of any other natural language countenance as sentences certain expressions ("The absolute is perfect" was our illustration) which even by the most liberal empiricist standards make no assertion whatever; and these would then have to be permitted as components of empirically significant statements.

The predicament would not arise, of course, in an artificial language whose vocabulary and grammar were so chosen as to preclude altogether the possibility of forming sentences of any kind which the empiricist meaning criterion is intended to rule out. Let us call any such language an *empiricist language.* This reflection suggests an entirely different approach to our problem: Give a general characterization of the kind of language that would qualify as empiricist, and then lay down the following:

(3.1) *Translatability criterion of cognitive meaning:* A sentence has cognitive meaning if and only if it is translatable into an empiricist language.

This conception of cognitive import, while perhaps not explicitly stated, seems to underlie much of the more recent work done by empiricist writers; as far as I can see it has its origin in Carnap's essay *Testability and Meaning* (especially part IV).

As any language, so also any empiricist language can be characterized by indicating its vocabulary and the rules determining its logic; the latter include the syntactical rules according to which sentences may be formed by means of the given vocabulary. In effect, therefore, the translatability criterion proposes to characterize the cognitively meaningful sentences by the vocabulary out of which they may be constructed and by the syntactical principles governing their construction. What sentences are singled out as cognitively significant will depend, accordingly, on the choice of the vocabulary and of the construction rules. Let us consider a specific possibility:

(3.2) We might qualify a language L as empiricist if it satisfies the following conditions:

(a) *The vocabulary of L* contains:
(1) The customary locutions of logic which are used in the formulation of sentences; including in particular the expressions "not", "and", "or", "if . . . then . . .", "all", "some", "the class of all things such that . . .", ". . . is an element of class . . .";
(2) Certain *observation predicates.* These will be said to constitute the basic empirical vocabulary of L;
(3) Any expression definable by means of those referred to under (1) and (2).

(b) *The rules of sentence formation for L* are those laid down in some contemporary logical system such as *Principia Mathematica.*

Since all defined terms can be eliminated in favor of primitives, these rules stipulate in effect that a language L is empiricist if all its sentences are expressible, with the help of the usual logical locutions, in terms of observable characteristics of physical objects. Let us call any language of this sort a thing-language in the narrower sense. Alternatively, the basic empirical vocabulary of an empiricist language might be construed as consisting of phenomenalistic terms, each of them referring to some aspect of the phenomena of perception or sensation. The construction of adequate phenomenalistic languages, however, presents considerable difficulties, and in recent empiricism, attention has been focussed primarily on the potentialities of languages whose basic empirical vocabulary consists of observation predicates; for the latter lend themselves more directly to the description of that type of intersubjective evidence which is invoked in the test of scientific hypotheses.

If we construe empiricist languages in the sense of (3.2), then the translatability criterion (3.1) avoids all of the shortcomings pointed out in our discussion of earlier forms of the testability criterion:

(*a*) Our characterization of empiricist languages makes explicit provision for universal and existential quantification, i.e., for the use of the terms "all" and "some"; hence, no type of quantified statement is generally excluded from the realm of cognitively significant discourse;

(*b*) Sentences such as "The absolute is perfect" cannot be formulated in an empiricist language (cf. (*d*) below); hence there is no danger that a conjunction or alternation containing a sentence of that kind as a component might be qualified as cognitively significant;

(*c*) In a language L with syntactical rules conforming to *Principia Mathe-*

matica, the denial of a sentence is always again a sentence of L. Hence, the translatability criterion does not lead to the consequence, which is entailed by both (2.1) and (2.2), that the denials of certain significant sentences are non-significant;

(*d*) Despite its comprehensiveness, the new criterion does not attribute cognitive meaning to *all* sentences; thus, e.g., the sentences "The absolute is perfect" and "Nothingness nothings" cannot be translated into an empiricist language because their key terms are not definable by means of purely logical expressions and observation terms.

4. THE PROBLEM OF DISPOSITION TERMS AND OF THEORETICAL CONSTRUCTS

Yet, the new criterion is still too restrictive—as are, incidentally, also its predecessors—in an important respect which now calls for consideration. If empiricist languages are defined in accordance with (3.2), then, as was noted above, the translatability criterion (3.1) allows cognitive import to a sentence only if its constitutive empirical terms are explicitly definable by means of observation predicates. But as we shall argue presently, many terms even of the physical sciences are not so definable; hence the criterion would oblige us to reject, as devoid of cognitive import, all scientific hypotheses containing such terms—an altogether intolerable consequence.

The concept of temperature is a case in point. At first glance, it seems as though the phrase "Object x has a temperature of c degrees centigrade", or briefly "$T(x) = c$" could be defined by the following sentence, (D): $T(x) = c$ if and only if the following condition is satisfied: If a thermometer is in contact with x, then it registers c degrees on its scale.

Disregarding niceties, it may be granted that the definiens given here is formulated entirely in reference to observables. However, it has one highly questionable aspect: In *Principia Mathematica* and similar systems, the phrase "if p then q" is construed as being synonymous with "not p or q"; and under this so-called material interpretation of the conditional, a statement of the form "if p then q" is obviously true if (though not only if) the sentence standing in the place of "p" is false. If, therefore, the meaning of "if . . . then . . ." in the definiens of (D) is understood in the material sense, then that definiens is true if (though not only if) x is an object not in contact with a thermometer—no matter what numerical value we may give to c. And since the definiendum would be true under the same circumstances, the definition (D) would qualify as true the assignment of any temperature value whatsoever to any object not in contact with a thermometer! Analogous considerations apply to such terms as "electrically charged", "magnetic", "intelligent", "electric resistance", etc., in short to all disposition terms, i.e., terms which express the disposition of one or more objects to react in a determinate way under specified circumstances: A definition of such terms by means of observation predicates cannot be effected in the manner of (D), however natural and obvious a mode of definition this may at first seem to be.

There are two main directions in which a resolution of the difficulty might be sought. On the one hand, it could be argued that the definition of disposition terms in the manner of (D) is perfectly adequate provided that the phrase "if . . . then . . ." in the definiens is construed in the sense it is obviously intended to have, namely as implying, in the case of (D), that even if x is not actually in contact with a thermometer, still if it *were* in such contact, then the thermometer *would* register c degrees. In sentences such as this, the phrase "if . . . then . . ." is said to be used counterfactually; and it is in this "strong" sense, which implies a counterfactual conditional, that the definiens of (D) would have to be construed. This suggestion would provide an answer to the problem of defining disposition terms if it were not for the fact that no entirely satisfactory account of the exact meaning of counterfactual conditionals seems to be available at present. Thus, the first way out of the difficulty has the status of a program rather than that of a solution. The lack of an adequate theory of counterfactual conditionals is all the more deplorable as such a theory is needed also for the analysis of the concept of general law in empirical science and of certain related ideas. A clarification of this cluster of problems constitutes at present one of the urgent desiderata in the logic and methodology of science.

An alternative way of dealing with the definitional problems raised by disposition terms was suggested, and developed in detail, by Carnap. It consists in permitting the introduction of new terms, within an empiricist language, by means of so-called reduction sentences, which have the character of partial or conditional definitions. Thus, e.g., the concept of temperature in our last illustration might be introduced by means of the following reduction sentence, (R): If a thermometer is in contact with an object x, then $T(x) = c$ if and only if the thermometer registers c degrees.

This rule, in which the conditional may be construed in the material sense, specifies the meaning of "temperature," i.e., of statements of the form "$T(x) = c$", only partially, namely in regard to those objects which are in contact with a thermometer; for all other objects, it simply leaves the meaning of "$T(x) = c$" undetermined. The specification of the meaning of "temperature" may then be gradually extended to cases not covered in (R) by laying down further reduction sentences, which reflect the measurement of temperature by devices other than thermometers.

Reduction sentences thus provide a means for the precise formulation of what is commonly referred to as operational definitions. At the same time, they show that the latter are not definitions in the strict sense of the word, but rather partial specifications of meaning.

The preceding considerations suggest that in our characterization (3.2) of empiricist languages we broaden the provision *a* (3) by permitting in the vocabulary of L all those terms whose meaning can be specified in terms of the basic empirical vocabulary by means of definitions or reduction sentences. Languages satisfying this more inclusive criterion will be referred to as thing-languages in the wider sense.

If the concept of empiricist language is broadened in this manner, then the translatability criterion (3.1) covers—as it should—also all those statements whose constituent empirical terms include "empirical constructs," i.e., terms which do not designate observables, but which can be introduced by reduction sentences on the basis of observation predicates.

Even in this generalized version, however, our criterion of cognitive meaning may not do justice to advanced scientific theories, which are formulated in terms of "theoretical constructs", such as the terms "absolute temperature", "gravitational potential", "electric field", "ψ function", etc. There are reasons to think that neither definitions nor reduction sentences are adequate to introduce these terms on the basis of observation predicates. Thus, e.g., if a system of reduction sentences for the concept of electric field were available, then—to oversimplify the point a little—it would be possible to describe, in terms of observable characteristics, some necessary and some sufficient conditions for the presence, in a given region, of an electric field of any mathematical description, however complex. Actually, however, such criteria can at best be given only for some sufficiently simple kinds of fields.

Now theories of the advanced type here referred to may be considered as hypothetico-deductive systems in which all statements are logical consequences of a set of fundamental assumptions. Fundamental as well as derived statements in such a system are formulated either in terms of certain theoretical constructs which are not defined within the system and thus play the rôle of primitives, or in terms of expressions defined by means of the latter. Thus, in their logical structure such systems equal the axiomatized uninterpreted systems studied in mathematics and logic. They acquire applicability to empirical subject matter, and thus the status of theories of empirical science, by virtue of an empirical interpretation. The latter is effected by a translation of some of the sentences of the theory—often derived rather than fundamental ones—into an empiricist language, which may contain both observation predicates and empirical constructs. And since the sentences which are thus given empirical meaning are logical consequences of the fundamental hypotheses of the theory, that translation effects, indirectly, a partial interpretation of the latter and of the constructs in terms of which they are formulated.

In order to make translatability into an empiricist language an adequate criterion of cognitive import, we broaden therefore the concept of empiricist language so as to include thing-languages in the narrower and in the wider sense as well as all interpreted theoretical systems of the kind just referred to. With this understanding, (3.1) may finally serve as a general criterion of cognitive meaning.

5. ON "THE MEANING" OF AN EMPIRICAL STATEMENT

In effect, the criterion thus arrived at qualifies a sentence as cognitively meaningful if its non-logical constituents refer, directly or in certain specified indirect ways, to observables. But it does not make any pronouncement on what "the meaning" of a cognitively significant sentence is, and in particular it neither says nor implies that that meaning can be exhaustively characterized by what the totality of possible tests would reveal in terms of observable phenomena. Indeed, *the content of a statement with empirical import cannot, in general, be exhaustively expressed by means of any class of observation sentences.*

For consider first, among the statements permitted by our criterion, any purely existential hypothesis or any statement involving mixed quantification. As was pointed out earlier, under (2.2) (*a*), statements of these kinds entail no observation sentences whatever; hence their content cannot be expressed by means of a class of observation sentences.

And secondly, even most statements of purely universal form (such as "All flamingoes are pink") entail observation sentences (such as "That thing is pink") only when combined with suitable other observation sentences (such as "That thing is a flamingo").

This last remark can be generalized: The use of empirical hypotheses for the prediction of observable phenomena requires, in practically all cases, the use of subsidiary empirical hypotheses. Thus, e.g., the hypothesis that the agent of tuberculosis is rod-shaped does not by itself entail the consequence that upon looking at a tubercular sputum specimen through a microscope, rod-like shapes will be observed: a large number of subsidiary hypotheses, including the theory of the microscope, have to be used as additional premises in deducing that prediction.

Hence, what is sweepingly referred to as "the (cognitive) meaning" of a given scientific hypothesis cannot be adequately characterized in terms of potential observational evidence alone, nor can it be specified for the hypothesis taken in isolation: In order to understand "the meaning" of a hypothesis within an empiricist language, we have to know not merely what observation sentences it entails alone or in conjunction with subsidiary hypotheses, but also what other, non-observational, empirical sentences are entailed by it, what sentences in the given language would confirm or disconfirm it, and for what other hypotheses the given one would be confirmatory or disconfirmatory. In other words, the cognitive meaning of a statement in an empiricist language is reflected in the totality of its logical relationships to all other statements in that language and not to the observation sentences alone. In this sense, the statements of empirical science have a surplus meaning over and above what can be expressed in terms of relevant observation sentences.

6. THE LOGICAL STATUS OF THE EMPIRICIST CRITERION OF MEANING

What kind of a sentence, it has often been asked, is the empiricist meaning criterion itself? Plainly it is not an empirical hypothesis; but it is not analytic or self-contradictory either; hence, when judged by its own standard, is it not devoid of cognitive meaning? In that case, what claim of soundness or validity could possibly be made for it?

One might think of construing the criterion as a definition which indicates what empiricists propose to understand by a cognitively significant sentence; thus understood, it would not have the character of an assertion and would be neither true nor false. But this conception would attribute to the criterion a measure of arbitrariness which cannot be reconciled with the heated controversies it has engendered and even less with the fact, repeatedly illustrated in the present article, that the changes in its specific content have always been determined by the objective of making the criterion a more adequate index of cognitive import. And this very objective illuminates the character of the empiricist criterion of meaning: It is intended to provide a clarification and *explication* of the idea of a sentence which makes an intelligible assertion. This idea is admittedly vague, and it is the task of philosophic explication to replace it by a more precise concept. In view of this difference of precision we cannot demand, of course, that the "new" concept, the explicatum, be strictly synonymous with the old one, the explicandum. How, then, are we to judge the adequacy of a proposed explication, as expressed in some specific criterion of cognitive meaning?

First of all, there exists a large class of sentences which are rather generally recognized as making intelligible assertions, and another large class of which this is more or less generally denied. We shall have to demand of an adequate explication that it take into account these spheres of common usage; hence an explication which, let us say, denies cognitive import to descriptions of past events or to generalizations expressed in terms of observables has to be rejected as inadequate. As we have seen, this first requirement of adequacy has played an important rôle in the development of the empiricist meaning criterion.

But an adequate explication of the concept of cognitively significant statement must satisfy yet another, even more important, requirement: Together with the explication of certain other concepts, such as those of confirmation and of probability, it has to provide the framework for a general theoretical account of the structure and the foundations of scientific knowledge. Explication, as here understood, is not a mere description of the accepted usages of the terms under consideration: it has to go beyond the limitations, ambiguities, and inconsistencies of common usage and has to show how we had better construe the meanings of those terms if we wish to arrive at a consistent and comprehensive theory of knowledge. This type of consideration, which has been largely influenced by a study of the structure of scientific theories, has prompted the more recent extensions of the empiricist meaning criterion. These extensions are designed to include in the realm of cognitive significance various types of sentences which might occur in advanced scientific theories, or which have to be admitted simply for the sake of systematic simplicity and uniformity, but on whose cognitive significance or non-significance a study of what the term "intelligible assertion" means in everyday discourse could hardly shed any light at all.

As a consequence, the empiricist criterion of meaning, like the result of any other explication, represents a linguistic proposal which itself is neither true nor false, but for which adequacy is claimed in two respects: First in the sense that the explication provides a reasonably close *analysis* of the commonly accepted meaning of the explicandum—and this claim implies an empirical assertion; and secondly in the sense that the explication achieves a *"rational reconstruction"* of the explicandum, i.e., that it provides, together perhaps with other explications, a general conceptual framework which permits a consistent and precise restatement and theoretical systematization of the contexts in which the explicandum is used—and this claim implies at least an assertion of a logical character.

Though a proposal in form, the empiricist criterion of meaning is therefore far from being an arbitrary definition; it is subject to revision if a violation of the requirements of adequacy, or even a way of satisfying those requirements more fully, should be discovered. Indeed, it is to be hoped that before long some of the open problems encountered in the analysis of cognitive significance will be clarified and that then our last version of the empiricist meaning criterion will be replaced by another, more adequate one.

Paul Marhenke

The Criterion of Significance

A criterion of significance is a statement to the effect that a sentence is significant if it satisfies such and such conditions, and that it is meaningless if it does not satisfy the specified conditions. When one examines the various formulations of this criterion, it is not always clear whether the criterion is intended as a definition of the term 'significant sentence,' or whether it is intended as a generalization about significant sentences. If the criterion is intended as a definition the conditions referred to are the defining properties of a significant sentence. Thus, a sentence is often said to be significant if and only if it expresses a proposition. This formulation of the criterion is perhaps intended as a definition of the term "significant sentence," rather than as a generalization about significant sentences. If the criterion is intended as a generalization, it specifies some property that belongs to all significant sentences and only to such sentences. When the criterion of significance is formulated as the thesis that a sentence is significant if and only if it is verifiable, this thesis is perhaps intended as a generalization about significant sentences rather than as a definition.

The formulation of a criterion of significance in the sense of a generalization about significant sentences can get under way only if we already know how to distinguish between significant and meaningless sentences. Assuming that we know how to divide any given group of sentences into significant and meaningless sentences, the initial step in the formulation of this generalization is the ascertainment of the common properties of the sentences in the two groups. And assuming that these have been found, we may next find it possible to select a subset of the common properties of the significant sentences which is not also a subset of the common properties of the meaningless sentences. This subset can then be used in the formulation of a criterion of significance, and any sentence that was not used in the formulation of the criterion can be subjected to the test provided by the criterion. The sentence is significant if it has all the properties belonging to the subset, otherwise meaningless.

. . .

From Paul Marhenke, "The Criterion of Significance" (a Presidential address to the Pacific Division of the American Philosophical Association, delivered in 1949), *Proceedings and Addresses of the American Philosophical Association,* Vol. 23 (1950). Reprinted by permission of the *American Philosophical Association.* The address can also be found in its entirety in Leonard Linsky (ed.), *Semantics and the Philosophy of Language,* 1952.

Paul Marhenke (1899–1952) was Professor of Philosophy at the University of California, Berkeley.

It would be very desirable if we had a criterion of significance either in the sense of a definition or in the sense of a true generalization about all significant sentences. But such a definition or generalization has not yet been found. It will be maintained in this paper that the criteria of significance that have been proposed suffer from two defects. (1) If they are intended as definitions of significance they are either inadequate or else reducible to the criterion for which significance is a primitive notion. (2) If they are intended as generalizations about the class of significant sentences, they are false. It will be maintained instead that the criterion of significance in its presesnt form amounts, roughly speaking, to the statement that a sentence is significant if and only if it is transformable into a significant sentence. This is the criterion which is in fact always used when we seek to determine whether or not a sentence is significant.

In order to see how we arrive at the decision that a sentence is significant or meaningless, let us review first some of the necessary conditions that do not presuppose the notion of significance. For this purpose we need to consider only declarative sentences. . . . If a sentence is significant, it must be constructed in accordance with the grammatical rules or else it must be transformable into a sentence that satisfies these rules. A string of words may also fail to be a sentence under the foregoing characterization if there is a violation of the rules of orthography. If a string of this nature can not be transformed into a sentence, grammatical or ungrammatical, by restoring the offending words to orthographic perfection, it is meaningless. In other words, if a sentence is significant, the words of the sentence satisfy the rules of orthography or else it is transformable into a sentence whose component words do satisfy these rules.

The two conditions mentioned are, I think, sufficiently trivial to be acceptable as necessary conditions of significance without further argument. These conditions assure us only that a string of words that resists grammatical and orthographic correction is nonsensical. If a sentence is significant, the grammatical and orthographic defects can always be removed, provided we know what the intended meaning is. We shall therefore use the term 'sentence' henceforth as a synonym for the term 'grammatically correct sentence.' Since a sentence may be grammatically and orthographically correct without being significant, a significant sentence has to satisfy further conditions that are stronger than these two. The necessary condition of significance I propose to examine next is as trivial as these two, but, I think, will not be found acceptable without argument.

The condition I have in mind is one that is imposed whenever we encounter a sentence whose significance we question. If a sentence is significant, we require that it be translatable into the ordinary idiom. The ordinary idiom may be characterized, somewhat vaguely it must be admitted, as the idiom we use in communicating with one another. It is the idiom in which most conversations are conducted and in which almost all books are written. Translatability into this idiom is a necessary condition of significance, because we have but one recourse when we are asked to clarify the meaning of a sentence that is not in this idiom. It would not be to the purpose to answer the question by translating the sentence into another sentence of the same idiom, for its meaning, if it has one, would not thereby become any clearer. The problem can be met only, if at all, by translating the sentence into the ordinary idiom. But since translatability into this idiom is only a necessary condition of significance, there is no guarantee that the result of the translation is a significant sentence. Russell's nonsense sentence "Quadruplicity drinks procrastination" is a sentence in the ordinary idiom. The sentence happens to be formulated in English, but it is a simple matter to produce its translation in the ordinary idiom of French or German. Moreover, this sentence can easily be transformed into another sentence in the ordinary idiom of English by replacing "Quadruplicity" and "Procrastination" by their defined equivalents. These translations are of course in every instance as nonsensical as the original sentence.

. . .

That translatability is at least a necessary condition of significance is shown by the fact that we answer a question of the form "What does the sentence S mean?" by producing some sentence we believe to be synonymous with S. If you do not know what a given sentence means you ask someone who does know, and he answers you by translating the sentence into one that has the same meaning. This question is answered in exactly the same way in which a dictionary answers the question "What does the word W mean?" The dictionary specifies the meaning of a given word by means of other words. Hence, if you are ignorant of the meanings of all words, the dictionary is of no help, and similarly, if you are ignorant of the meanings of all sentences, the meaning of a given sentence can not be explained to you. The procedure we use in explaining the meaning of a sentence suggests that a necessary and sufficient condition of significance is obtained by simply strengthening the requirement of translatability: a sentence is significant if and only if it is translatable into a significant sentence. In one sense of the term "criterion" this condition is of course not a criterion of significance. For if a criterion is formulated with the intention of providing us with a method by which we can determine whether or not a given sentence is significant, then the notion of significance can not itself be used in the formulation of such a criterion. A criterion must enable us to make this determination without the prior knowledge that any sentence is significant or meaningless. We shall now turn to the examination of two formulations of the criterion that appear to answer to this description. One of these specifies the necessary and sufficient condition of significance by means of the concept of a proposition: a sentence is significant if and only if it expresses a proposition. The other specifies it by means of the concept of verifiability: a sentence is significant if and only if it is verifiable.

The first of these formulations is based on the view that a significant sentence is related to an entity which is the significance or meaning of the sentence. This entity is the proposition expressed by the sentence. The existence of the entity demanded by this view can of course be guaranteed by defining the phrase "the proposition expressed by S" by means of the phrase "the class of sentences that are synomymous with S." However, the proponents of the view under consideration do not reckon with the possibility of defining the former phrase by means of terms that refer to linguistic entities; they assume, rather, that this phrase designates an extra-linguistic entity. Some philosophers believe that the propositions expressed by sentences are psychical or psycho-physical occurrences, others that they are of the nature of Platonic universals and thus non-physical and non-psychical. Now if there are propositions and if sentences express them, and if we can identify the proposition a sentence expresses whenever such a sentence is significant, then we can decide whether or not a given sentence is significant without the prior knowledge that it is significant or meaningless. But if we are forced to make this decision independently of the fact, if it is a fact, that the sentence does or does not express a proposition, it is useless to tell us that all significant sentences and only such sentences express propositions. For this characteristic of significant sentences can not be used to distinguish sense from nonsense, if we do not know how to determine whether a sentence possesses it.

The most recent version of the view that propositions are psycho-physical entities is due to Russell. Propositions, according to Russell, are to be defined as "psychological and physiological occurrences of certain sorts—complex images, expectations, etc. Such occurrences are expressed by sentences." But nonsense can also cause the occurrence of complex images and expectations, and it therefore becomes necessary to differentiate the kinds of images and expectations that are expressed by significant from the images and expectations that are expressed by meaningless sentences. Russell dismisses this problem with the declaration that "the exact psychological definition of propositions is irrelevant to logic and theory of knowledge." [1] Russell finds it necessary to look for an extra-linguistic entity as the significance of a sentence in the first instance, because he thinks that the syntactical rules of significance are arbitrary unless we can find a reason for them. Apparently he thinks that this reason is to be found in the psychological and physiological occurrences that are expressed by sentences. Now perhaps there is a difference between the psychological and physiological effects that are expressed by significant and by meaningless sentences, but if there is one Russell has certainly not found it. The problem whose solution is to lead him to the discovery of the proposition is formulated by Russell in two ways. (1) "What do we believe when we believe something?" (2) "When a number of people all believe that there is going to be an explosion, what have they in common?" There is only one conceivable kind of answer that can be given to the first question, and that is the kind of answer that is customarily given. Depending on what we take to be the import of the question "What do you believe when you believe there is going to be an explosion?", we give one or the other of the following answers: (1) There is going to be an explosion; (2) I believe there is going to be an explosion; (3) When I believe there is going to be an explosion, I believe there is going to be an explosion. In each case the answer is given by formulating a sentence. To the second question "What is common to a number of people who believe that there is going to be an explosion?", Russell proposes the following answer: "A certain state of tension, which will be discharged when the explosion occurs, but, if their belief was false, will continue for some time, and then give place to surprise." [2] But this answer can not be quite correct. We can not rest satisfied with it because the psychological and physiological states of people who hear about an impending explosion are not the same. Even when the con-

[1] Russell, *An Inquiry into Meaning and Truth,* p. 237.
[2] *Loc. cit.,* p. 223.

ditions are otherwise the same, people react in different ways to such information. And when the conditions are not the same, the state of tension aroused in a man who knows he is within one hundred yards of the impending explosion is quite different from the state of tension of a man who knows that the site of the explosion is one hundred miles away. Russell is quite well aware of such differences, but he thinks that they are probably only differences of degree.[3] As a matter of fact, the degree of the state of tension may be so low that the state is undetectable, again by his own admissison: "When I believe something less exciting—that tomorrow's 'Times' will contain a weather forecast, or that Caesar crossed the Rubicon—I cannot observe any such occurrences in myself." [4] But if the state of tension may be of such low degree as to be undetectable, this state of tension, i.e., the proposition expressed by a sentence, can not be used for differentiating between sense and nonsense. Every significant sentence may express a proposition, as Russell claims, but this fact does not help us to distinguish significant from nonsensical sentences. The majority of sentences that come before us are too uninteresting and too unexciting; if any of them do express propositions these are too feeble to be observable. Russell's justification of the rules of syntax must hence be considered as a failure. In view of Russell's demand for a justification of these rules, he might have been expected to show that a given sentence is significant by showing that it expresses a proposition. But he never actually uses this procedure. Instead he shows that a sentence is significant by showing that it can be transformed into a significant sentence, i.e., into a sentence that is constructed in accordance with the syntactical rules.

The view that propositions are non-physical and non-psychic entities is the orthodox form of the proposition theory. The chief defect of this theory is that it forces us to hold that propositions belong to a realm of being that is inaccessible to inspection. A sentence does not come before us with the proposition it expresses, if the sentence is significant. Hence how are we going to determine, in the instance of a given sentence, whether or not it expresses a proposition, and, if we decide that it does, how are we going to determine the proposition it expresses? When we are in doubt whether a given sentence is significant, the doubt can not be removed by finding out whether or not it expresses a proposition. The criterion of significance of the proposition theory is formally similar to the criterion we use in determining whether or not a man is married. In the instance of a man, we can remove any doubt regarding his marital status by producing his wife. When we are in doubt whether a sentence is significant, the doubt can not be similarly resolved by producing the proposition it expresses. In order to resolve the doubt concerning a sentence, we are limited to an examination of the sentence and its logical relations to other sentences.

. . .

If propositions were given with the sentences that express them, the criterion of significance of the proposition theory would be an adequate test of significance. But since only one member of this relation is ever given, this criterion must be rejected as inadequate. If the criterion is taken as a defini-

[3] Cf. *Inquiry*, p. 225.
[4] *Inquiry*, p. 224.

tion, it is inadequate, because the defining property can not be used in the identification of sentences as significant or meaningless. And if it is taken as a generalization, it is at best an untestable hypothesis. On the proposition theory the decision that a sentence is significant should be based on the antecedent ground that the sentence expresses a proposition. Instead, the doctrine of the proposition theory that certain sentences express propositions is based on the antecedent ground that these sentences are significant.

We come now to the much debated verifiability criterion of logical positivism. This criterion has appeared in innumerable formulations in the last twenty-five years, but we shall limit this examination to the more or less official versions of Schlick and of Carnap. An early formulation of the criterion is given by Schlick in the following terms: "It is impossible to specify the meaning of an assertion otherwise than by describing the state of affairs that must obtain if the assertion is to be true." [5] From this formulation it appears that a sentence is significant if it is translatable into a significant sentence. To take only one example, let us apply Schlick's test to the sentence "Caesar crossed the Rubicon." In the instance of this sentence we can all doubtlessly describe the state of affairs that must have obtained if the sentence is true. Presumably what is here wanted as a description of the state of affairs is not the sentence "Caesar crossed the Rubicon," though this sentence describes the state of affairs in question quite adequately, but rather some other sentence which uses a different set of words but describes the same state of affairs. We may offer the sentence "Caesar went from one bank of the Rubicon to the other" as a description of the state of affairs that must have obtained if and only if Caesar crossed the Rubicon. According to Schlick's own statement, then, the criterion of significance amounts to the assertion that a sentence is significant if it is possible to formulate another sentence which is synonymous with the given sentence. Schlick himself does not say that the second sentence must be significant, but this is of course included in the demand that this sentence be the description of a state of affairs.

Schlick appears to think that the criterion he has formulated is equivalent to the following: A sentence is significant if and only if it is possible to specify for every descriptive word that occurs in it a definitional chain (or a set of such chains) whose last link is an ostensive definition. For he says: "In order to find the meaning of a sentence we have to transform it by the introduction of successive definitions until finally it contains only words that are not further defined, but whose meanings can be given only by direct ostension." [6] We have observed previously that the condition that is here formulated is only a necessary condition of significance, unless we add the further proviso that the transformed sentence be significant. That the criterion as it stands is only a necessary condition of significance becomes obvious when we consider that Russell's nonsense sentence "Quadruplicity drinks procrastination" can easily be transformed into a sentence that contains only ostensively defined terms. But this sentence is not thereby transformed into a significant sentence.

Schlick's second formulation of the criterion may be rendered as follows: A sentence is significant if and only if it is possisble to specify the circumstances under which the sentence is true. This formulation is evidently equivalent to

[5] *Erkenntnis*, v. 3. p. 6.
[6] *Loc. cit.*, p. 7.

the first. For the specification of the circumstances under which a sentence is true is effected by means of sentences. The only circumstance that is at all relevant to the truth of the sentence "Caesar crossed the Rubicon" is the circumstance that Caesar did cross the Rubicon, and the only method known to man of specifying this circumstance is the formulation of a sentence such as the sentence "Caesar crossed the Rubicon" or of some other sentence synonymous with this sentence. There is another version of the foregoing formulation of the criterion in which the notion of verifiability is used. A sentence is significant if and only if it is verifiable, and it is verifiable if it is possible to give a description of the conditions under which it is true as well as of those under which it is false.[7] The property of verifiability that is mentioned in this formulation has nothing to do with verification. To say that a sentence is verifiable is simply a shorthand way of saying that it is possible to give a description of the conditions under which the sentence is true and false respectively.

Schlick's third formulation of the criterion also makes use of the notion of verifiability. But here we get a different account of what is meant by "verifiability." A sentence is significant if and only if it is verifiable, and to say that it is verifiable is to say that it is logically possible to verify it. Schlick says that "a fact or a process is logically possible if it can be *described,* i.e., if the sentence which is supposed to describe it obeys the rules of grammar we have stipulated in our language."[8] If Schlick were now called upon to show that a given sentence is verifiable, we would expect him to show that the procedure of verifying the sentence is logically possible, i.e., that the procedure of verifying the sentence can be described. But this he fails to do. He considers the sentence "Rivers flow uphill," but instead of demonstrating the logical possibility of verifying this sentence, he demonstrates the logical possibility of rivers flowing uphill. It is logically possible that rivers flow uphill, because the sentence is not self-contradictory. Schlick does not say how he determines that a sentence is not self-contradictory. He apparently holds that this determination is made by examining its logical form. However, a sentence that is not self-contradictory in form may nevertheless be nonsensical. Neither the sentence S nor the sentences that describe the procedure of verifying S may have the logical form of a contradiction. But this is no guarantee that these sentences are not nonsense. Schlick's test therefore comes to nothing, because in order to apply it we must know in advance that the sentence S is significant.

. . .

The criterion of significance has so far been formulated by Schlick simply as a test of significance. We must now consider a formulation of the criterion which does not merely specify the conditions a significant sentence must satisfy, but beyond this tells us what the meaning of the sentence is. The formulation reads as follows: "Stating the meaning of a sentence amounts to stating the rules according to which the sentence is to be used, and this is the same as stating the way in which it can be verified. The meaning of a proposition is the method of its verification."[9] One wonders whether Schlick, and with

[7] Schlick, *Gesammelte Aufsaetze,* p. 340.
[8] *Loc. cit.,* p. 348.
[9] *Loc. cit.,* p. 340.

him many other logical positivists who have repeated the slogan that the meaning of a sentence is the method of its verification, was quite clear in his own mind as to the meaning of the term 'method' when the meaning of a sentence is identified with the method of its verification. A method of verification is a procedure one selects for the purpose of verifying a sentence. Thus I verify the sentence "This is vinegar" by smelling the bottle or by reading the label. But the sentence obviously does not mean smelling the bottle or reading the label. It might be objected that this interpretation of the slogan is a gross misinterpretation. That this objection is without force becomes quite plain when Schlick takes occasion to refute an opponent who maintains that statements about the future are meaningless under the verifiability criterion on the ground that such statements are not verifiable. In this refutation Schlick is fully conscious of the meaning of the term "method of verification." He repels the attack and wins an easy victory by telling the opponent that statements about the future are verified by waiting for the event to happen and that waiting is a legitimate method of verification. Schlick apparently never noticed that all statements about future events must be synonymous, if we should choose to verify them by waiting, and if the meaning of a statement is identical with the method of its verification.

In so far as Schlick has established a connection between the meaning of a sentence and its verifiability, he uses the term "verifiable" simply as a synonym for "transformable into a significant sentence." If, however, the term "verifiability" is understood in the ordinary sense as the possibility of describing a method by which the truth-value of a sentence may be ascertained, then verifiability is not a test of significance. For a method of testing, i.e., the test sentences, can be formulated only if we know the meaning of the sentence we are going to test. In other words, the decision that the sentence is significant must be made in advance of the testing.

. . .

We have seen that the logical positivists use the term "verifiable" in both an improper and a proper sense. In the improper sense, a sentence is said to be verifiable when it is possible to transform the sentence into a significant sentence. In the proper sense it is said to be verifiable when it is possible to formulate the observation sentences that would verify the sentence if the sentence were true. But the possibility of formulating these observation sentences presupposes that the decision that the sentence is significant has already been made. You can not devise an observation test until you know the meaning of the sentence you are going to test.

That the question whether a sentence is verifiable can be raised only after the decision that the sentence is significant has already been made becomes especially clear when one examines Ayer's definition of the term "verifiable": the sentence S is verifiable if and only if there is some sentence R and an observation sentence O such that O is deducible from S and R, but is not deducible from S alone nor from R alone. This definition presupposes that the sentences S, R, and O are all significant, for the rules of deduction apply to significant sentences only. If, however, the rules of deduction apply to nonsense also, then every sentence is verifiable and hence significant under the definition Ayer proposes. Ayer has sought to remedy this defect by revising the definition. But the revised form suffers from the same defect as the original: either the sentence that is tested by means of the criterion is known to be significant independently of the criterion or else every sentence is significant.[10]

If a sentence can not be shown to be significant otherwise than by showing that it is convertible into a significant sentence, we may expect this criterion to be used as the test of significance even by those philosophers whose official criterion would indicate a different procedure. This expectation is fully confirmed by an examination of the text. Russell never demonstrates that an apparently nonsensical sentence is significant by finding the proposition the sentence expresses. He always makes this demonstration by showing that the sentence is transformable into a significant sentence. Thus he decides that the sentence "The sound of a trombone is blue" is significant, because this sentence asserts the identity of two objects that have different names. The sentence is thus merely false, but not nonsensical. Again he shows that the paradox to which the sentence "I am lying" gives rise, on the hypothesis that it is significant, can be avoided, if this sentence is regarded as an infinite conjunction of the sentences "I am asserting a false sentence of the first order," "I am asserting a false sentence of the second order," etc. The resulting translation is again merely false.[11] In one of his examples Russell considers the result of translating the sentence "Quadruplicity drinks procrastination" when the word "Quadruplicity" is replaced by its defined equivalent "That property of a propositional function which consists in being true for exactly four values of the variable," and he wonders how we know that the resulting translation is nonsense.[12] On his own theory it should not be too difficult to remove any doubt on this subject: you investigate the body and find out whether the resulting sentence expresses a proposition. If you fail to detect the complex images and expectations which are the components of propositions, you may be sure that the sentence is nonsense. Russell never avails himself of this procedure. The procedure would indeed be quite useless, even if it were feasible to investigate the body, since nonsense is as prolific in the production of complex images and expectations as the soundest sense.

Carnap holds that a sentence is significant when it is possible to formulate an observation sentence by which the sentence in question can be tested. But he never uses this test when he determines whether or not a sentence is significant. Like Russell he uses the test of translatability. Carnap shows how this test operates in his paper on the repudiation of metaphysics. In this paper he is concerned with showing that a great many of the sentences that occur in Heidegger's *Was ist Metaphysik?* are pseudo-sentences. These sentences are shown to be pseudo-sentences, not by applying the criterion of verifiability, or, as Carnap now prefers, of confirmability, but by showing that these sentences can not be transformed into significant sentences of the ordinary idiom.

In order to see on what grounds the metaphysical sentences of Heidegger are repudiated, it is necessary to translate some of these sentences into English.

[10] Ayer, *Language, Truth and Logic,* p. 11 sq.
[11] *Inquiry,* p. 218.
[12] *Inquiry,* p. 222.

If we have to do violence to the English language in making these translations, this is unavoidable, since Heidegger had to do violence to the German language when he constructed the originals. Heidegger begins by defining the domain of metaphysics. Science, he says, is concerned with the exploration of the real and aside from that with nothing. He then immediately asks the question which is the theme of his paper "How about this nothing?". Since science has preëmpted the realm of the real, there is nothing left for metaphysics but the exploration of the nothing. The question is then followed by sentences of which the following are typical:

> Why are we concerned about this nothing? The nothing is rejected by science and sacrificed as the unreal. Science wants to have nothing to do with the nothing. What is the nothing? Does the nothing exist only because the not, i.e., negation, exists? Or do negation and the not exist only because the nothing exists? We maintain: The nothing is more primitive than the not and negation. We know the nothing. The nothing is the simple negation of the totality of being. Anxiety reveals the nothing. The nothing itself nots.

Carnap shows that none of these sentences can be transformed into significant sentences of the natural language. For in this idiom the word "nothing" is not used as a name. When it appears to be used as a name in a sentence, as for instance in the sentence "Outside there is nothing," the sentence is always transformable into the negation of an existential statement. Every one of Heidegger's sentences in which "the nothing" is used as a designative expression is accordingly nonsensical, since these sentences are not transformable into sentences of this kind. Furthermore, even if it were assumed that the phrase "the nothing" is used as a descriptive phrase in Heidegger's sentence "The nothing exists," the contextual definition of this phrase would have to be so formulated as to yield the sentence "The nothing does not exist" as a logical consequence. Finally, Carnap points out that Heidegger introduces the meaningless verb "to not." This neologism—the original is likewise a neologism—appears in Heidegger's sentences without having been previously defined and can therefore not be eliminated from the sentences in which it occurs. The sentence "The nothing nots" is therefore nonsensical for a two-fold reason. Carnap concludes that Heidegger's sentences can not be constructed in a logically correct language.

A sentence is thus condemned as nonsensical by Carnap not because it is not verifiable, but because it can not be transformed into a significant sentence of the natural language or of a logically correct language which takes the place of the latter. The criterion Carnap actually uses may thus be formulated as follows: A sentence is significant if and only if it is transformable into a significant sentence of standard logical form. A sentence is of standard logical form when it is either a simple sentence or else constructible from sentences of that kind by truth-functional composition and quantification, and it is moreover significant if and only if the simple components from which the sentence is constructed are themselves significant. The conditions a sentence in standard logical form must satisfy in order to be significant are thus specified in such a way that one can decide in a finite number of steps whether or not the sentence is significant. In other words, when we examine a sentence in standard logical form with the view of determining whether it satisfies the conditions of a significant sentence, we are finally led back to the simple sentences from which the given sentence was constructed. And unless these are significant, the original sentence is not significant.

In the absence of a criterion of significance, either in the sense of a definition or a generalization, we are forced, at the present time, to take significance, with respect to simple sentences, e.g., atomic sentences, as a primitive notion. The decision whether or not a sentence not of this form is significant is made by a recursion procedure. For the simple sentences to which we are led by this procedure we have no test of significance. The criterion of significance for sentences of this form has yet to be discovered.

Friedrich Waismann

Verifiability

When we reflect on such a sentence as 'The meaning of a statement is the method of its verification', we should, first of all, be quite clear as to what we mean by the term 'method of verification'. From a logical point of view we are not interested in the various activities that are involved in verifying a statement. What, then, is it we have in mind when we talk of such things? Take an example. Suppose there is a metal ball in front of me, and I have the task of finding out whether the ball is charged with electricity. To do that I connect the ball with an electroscope and watch whether the gold leaves diverge. The statement 'The gold leaves of the instrument diverge' (s) describes the verification of the statement 'The ball is charged' (p). Now what exactly am I doing when I describe the verification of the statement p? I establish a connection between two statements by declaring that the one (s) is to follow from the other (p). In other words, I lay down a *rule of inference* which allows me to pass from the statement 'The ball is charged with electricity' to another that describes an observable situation. By doing this I connect the statement with another one, I make it part of a system of operations, I incorporate it into language, in short, *I determine the way it is to be used*. In this sense giving the verification of a statement is an important part of giving its use, or, to put it differently, explaining its verification is a contribution to its grammar.

In everyday life we understand sentences without bothering much as to the way they are verified. We understand them because we understand the single words which occur in them and grasp the grammatical structure of the sentence as a whole. The question of the verification arises only when we come

---

From Friedrich Waismann, "Verifiability," *Proceedings of the Aristotelian Society,* Supplementary Vol. 19 (1945). Reprinted by permission of the secretary and editor of the Aristotelian Society. The selection is reprinted in A. G. N. Flew (ed.), *Logic and Language,* first series, 1951.

Friedrich Waismann (1896–1959) was born in Vienna. From 1939 until his death he was Reader in the Philosophy of Mathematics at Oxford University.

across a new sort of combination of words. If, for instance, someone were to tell us that he owned a dog that was able to think, we should at first not quite understand what he was talking about and would ask him some further questions. Suppose he described to us in detail the dog's behaviour in certain circumstances, then we should say 'Ah, now we understand you, that's what you call thinking'. There is no need to inquire into the verification of such sentences as 'The dog barks', 'He runs', 'He is playful', and so on, as the words are then used as we may say in their *normal* way. But when we say 'The dog thinks', we create a new context, we step outside the boundaries of common speech, and then the question arises as to what is meant by such a word series. In such cases explaining the verification is explaining the meaning, and changing the verification is changing the meaning. Obviously meaning and verification *are* connected—so why say they are not?

But when I say that the statement p is connected with the statements s_1, $s_2 \ldots s_n$ which describe evidences for it, I do *not* say that p is *identical* with s_1, $s_2 \ldots s_n$ or their conjunction. To say this would only be true if s_1, $s_2 \ldots s_n$ or their conjunction entailed p. Now is that so? There *may* be statements which are nothing more than abbreviations for all that which is unfolded in their verification. There are, however, other sorts of statements of which this is certainly not true. Recent discussions on phenomenalism, for example, tend to show that no conjunction or disjunction of sense-datum statements, however complex, entails the existence or the non-existence of a certain material object. If that is so, a material object statement, though it *is* connected with sense-datum statements, is not just an abbreviation for them; rather has it a logical status of its own, and is not equivalent to any truth-function of the latter ones. I think that the result of these discussions is essentially right, and I ask for permission, to make my point quite clear, to add one word more.

The failure of the phenomenalist to translate a material object statement into terms of sense-data is not, as has been suggested, due to the poverty of our language which lacks the vocabulary for describing all the minute details of sense experience, nor is it due to the difficulties inherent in producing an *infinite* combination of sense-datum statements though all these things may contribute to it. In the main it is due to a factor which, though it is very important and really quite obvious, has to my knowledge never been noticed—to the 'open texture' of most of our empirical concepts. What I mean is this: Suppose I have to verify a statement such as 'There is a cat next door'; suppose I go over to the next room, open the door, look into it and actually see a cat. Is this enough to prove my statement? Or must I, in addition to it, touch the cat, pat him and induce him to purr? And supposing that I had done all these things, can I then be absolutely certain that my statement was true? Instantly we come up against the well-known battery of sceptical arguments mustered since ancient times. What, for instance, should I say when that creature later on grew to a gigantic size. Or if it showed some queer behaviour usually not to be found with cats, say, if, under certain conditions, it could be revived from death whereas normal cats could not? Shall I, in such a case, say that a new species has come into being? Or that it was a cat with extraordinary properties? Again, suppose I say 'There is my friend over there'. What if on drawing closer in order to shake hands with him he suddenly disappeared?

'Therefore it was not my friend but some delusion or other.' But suppose a few seconds later I saw him again, could grasp his hand, etc. What then? 'Therefore my friend was nevertheless there and his disappearance was some delusion or other.' But imagine after a while he disappeared again, or seemed to disappear—what shall I say now? Have we rules ready for all imaginable possibilities?

An example of the first sort tends to show that we can think of situations in which we couldn't be certain whether something was a cat or some other animal (or a *jinni*). An example of the second sort tends to show that we can consider circumstances in which we couldn't be certain whether something was real or a delusion. The fact that in many cases there is no such thing as a conclusive verification is connected with the fact that most of our empirical concepts are not delimited in all possible directions. Suppose I come across a being that looks like a man, speaks like a man, behaves like a man, and is only one span tall—shall I say it *is* a man? Or what about the case of a person who is so old as to remember King Darius? Would you say he is an immortal? Is there anything like an exhaustive definition that finally and once for all sets our mind at rest? 'But are there not exact definitions at least in science?' Let's see. The notion of gold seems to be defined with absolute precision, say by the spectrum of gold with its characteristic lines. Now what would you say if a substance was discovered that looked like gold, satisfied all the chemical tests for gold, whilst it emitted a new sort of radiation? 'But such things do not happen.' Quite so; but they *might* happen, and that is enough to show that we can never exclude altogether the possibility of some unforeseen situation arising in which we shall have to modify our definition. Try as we may, no concept is limited in such a way that there is no room for any doubt. We introduce a concept and limit it in *some* directions; for instance, we define gold in contrast to some other metals such as alloys. This suffices for our present needs, and we do not probe any farther. We tend to *overlook* the fact that there are always other directions in which the concept has not been defined. And if we did, we could easily imagine conditions which would necessitate new limitations. In short, it is not possible to define a concept like gold with absolute precision, i.e. in such a way that every nook and cranny is blocked against entry of doubt. That is what is meant by the open texture of a concept.

Vagueness should be distinguished from *open texture*. A word which is actually used in a fluctuating way (such as 'heap' or 'pink') is said to be vague; a term like 'gold', though its actual use may not be vague, is non-exhaustive or of an open texture in that we can never fill up all the possible gaps through which a doubt may seep in. Open texture, then, is something like *possibility of vagueness*. Vagueness can be remedied by giving more accurate rules, open texture cannot. An alternative way of stating this would be to say that definitions of open terms are *always* corrigible or emendable.

Open texture is a very fundamental characteristic of most, though not of all, empirical concepts, and it is this texture which prevents us from verifying conclusively most of our empirical statements. Take any material object statement. The terms which occur in it are non-exhaustive; that means that we cannot foresee completely all possible conditions in which they are to be used; there will always remain a possibility, however faint, that we have not taken into account something or other that may be relevant to their usage; and that means that we cannot foresee completely all the possible circumstances in which the statement is true or in which it is false. There will always remain a margin of uncertainty. Thus the absence of a conclusive verification is directly due to the open texture of the terms concerned.

This has an important consequence. Phenomenalists have tried to translate what we mean by a material object statement into terms of sense experience. Now such a translation would be possible only if the terms of a material object statement were completely definable. For only then could we describe completely all the possible evidences which would make the statement true or false. As this condition is not fulfilled, the programme of phenomenalism falls flat, and in consequence the attempts at analysing chairs and tables into patterns of sense-data—which has become something of a national sport in this country—are doomed to fail. Similar remarks apply to certain psychological statements such as 'He is an intelligent person'; here again it is due to the open texture of a term like 'intelligent' that the statement cannot be reduced to a conjunction or disjunction of statements which specify the way a man would behave in such-and-such circumstances.

It may have been a dim awareness of this fact that induced Locke to insist on corporeal, and Berkeley on mental substance. Doing away with their metaphysical fog, we may restate what seems to be the grain of truth in their views by saying that a material object statement, or a psychological statement has a logic of its own, and for this reason cannot be reduced to the level of other statements.

But there is a deeper reason for all that, and this consists in what I venture to call the *essential incompleteness* of an empirical description. To explain more fully: If I had to describe the right hand of mine which I am now holding up, I may say different things of it: I may state its size, its shape, its colour, its tissue, the chemical compound of its bones, its cells, and perhaps add some more particulars; but however far I go, I shall never reach a point where my description will be completed: logically speaking, it is always possible to extend the description by adding some detail or other. Every description stretches, as it were, into a horizon of open possibilities: however far I go, I shall always carry this horizon with me. Contrast this case with others in which completeness is attainable. If, in geometry, I describe a triangle, e.g. by giving its three sides, the description is *complete*: nothing can be added to it that is not included in, or at variance with, the data. Again, there is a sense in which it may be said that a melody is described completely in the musical notation (disregarding, for the moment, the question of its interpretation); a figure on a carpet, viewed as an ornament, may be described in some geometrical notation; and in this case, too, there is a sense in which the description may be called complete. (I do not mean the *physical* carpet, but its pattern.) The same applies to a game of chess: it can be described, move by move, from the beginning to the end. Such cases serve merely to set off the nature of an empirical description by the contrast: there is no such thing as completeness in the case in which I describe my right hand, or the character of a person; I can never exhaust all the details nor foresee all possible circumstances which would make me modify or retract my statement. (This was already seen by Leibniz when he said that anything actual is always inexhaustible in its properties and a true image of the Infinite Mind.)

The situation described has a direct bearing on the open texture of concepts. A term is defined when the sort of situation is described in which it is to be used. Suppose for a moment that we were able to describe situations completely without omitting anything (as in chess), then we could produce an exhaustive list of all the circumstances in which the term is to be used so that nothing is left to doubt; in other words, we could construct a *complete definition,* i.e. a thought model which anticipates and settles once for all every possible question of usage. As, in fact, we can never eliminate the possibility of some unforeseen factor emerging, we can never be quite sure that we have included in our definition everything that should be included, and thus the process of defining and refining an idea will go on without ever reaching a final stage. In other words, every definition stretches into an open horizon. Try as we may, the situation will always remain the same: no definition of an empirical term will cover all possibilities. Thus the result is that the incompleteness of our verification is rooted in the incompleteness of the definition of the terms involved, and the incompleteness of the definition is rooted in the incompleteness of empirical description; that is one of the grounds why a material object statement p can *not* be verified conclusively, nor be resolved into statements s_1, s_2 . . . s_n which describe evidences for it. (In mathematics such a reduction is often possible: thus a statement about rational numbers *can,* without loss of meaning, be translated into statements about integers; but here you have complete description, complete definition and conclusive proof and refutation.)

One word more. Why is it that, as a rule, an experiential statement is not verifiable in a conclusive way? Is it because I can never exhaust the description of a material object or of a situation, since I may always add something to it—something that, in principle, can be foreseen? Or is it because something quite new and unforeseen may occur? In the first case, though I know all the tests, I may still be unable to perform them, say, for lack of time. In the second case I cannot even be sure that I know all the tests that may be required; in other words, the difficulty is to state completely what a verification would be in this case. (Can you foresee all circumstances which would turn a putative fact into a delusion?) Now the answer to the question is that *both factors combine* to prevent a verification from being conclusive. *But they play a very different part.* It is due to the first factor that, in verifying a statement, we can never finish the job. But it is the second that is responsible for the open texture of our terms which is so characteristic of all factual knowledge. To see this more clearly, compare the situation in mathematics: here a theorem, say Goldbach's hypothesis, which says that every even number can be represented as the sum of two primes, may be undecidable as we cannot go through all the integers in order to try it out. But this in no way detracts from the *closed* texture of the mathematical concepts. If there was no such thing as the (always present) possibility of the emergence of something new, there could be nothing like the open texture of concepts; and if there was no such thing as the open texture of concepts, verification would be incomplete only in the sense that it could never be finished (just as in the case of Goldbach).

To sum up: An experiential statement is, as a rule, not conclusively verifiable for two different reasons;

(1) because of the existence of an unlimited number of tests;
(2) because of the open texture of the terms involved.

These two reasons correspond to two different senses of 'incompleteness'. The first is related to the fact that I can never conclude the description of a material object, or of a situation. I may, for instance, look at my table from ever new points in space without ever exhausting all the possibilities. The second (and more exciting one) is due to the fact that our factual knowledge is incomplete in another dimension: there is always a chance that something unforeseen may occur. That again may mean two different things:

(*a*) that I should get acquainted with some totally new experience such as at present I cannot even imagine;
(*b*) that some new discovery was made which would affect our whole interpretation of certain facts.

An illustration of the first sort would be supplied by a man born blind who later obtained the experience of seeing. An illustration of the second sort would be the change brought about by the discovery of a new agent of nature, such as electricity. In this case we perceive that the data of observation are connected in a new and unforeseen way, that, as it were, new lines can now be traced through the field of experience. So we can say more exactly that the open texture of concepts is rooted in that particular incompleteness of our factual knowledge which I have just adumbrated.

What I have said modifies to a more or less extent the account I have given of verification. I said that in giving the method of verification we lay down a rule (or rules) of inference. We should, however, feel grave doubts whether that is so. If a material object statement were to entail a sense datum statement, to entail it in a strictly *logical* sense, then the premiss would be cancelled together with the conclusion: or, to put it differently, a single negative instance would suffice to refute the premiss. Suppose someone told me, 'Look, there is your friend, he is just crossing the street'. Now if I looked in the direction indicated, but failed to perceive the person who is my friend, would I say that the statement was refuted beyond the shadow of a doubt? There may be cases in which I may say that. But there are others in which I would certainly not think that the statement was refuted on the strength of such a single glance (for instance, when I was led to expect my friend at this hour, or received a letter from him saying that he will arrive at that time, and the like). A discrepancy between a material object statement and a single sense experience may always be explained away by some accessory assumption: I haven't looked thoroughly, my friend happened in this very second to be behind someone else, he just stepped into a doorway, and so on, not to mention more fanciful theories. I can never exclude the possibility that, though the evidence was against it, the statement may be true.

Whoever considers these facts with unbiassed eyes will, I trust, assent to the conclusion that a single sense experience, strictly speaking, never excludes a material object statement in the sense in which the negation of p excludes p. That means that no sense-datum statement s can ever come into *sharp logical conflict* with a material object statement p; in other words: $p . \backsim s$

never represents a *contradiction* in the sense that $p. \backsim p$ does. In the light of this we can no longer adhere to the view that p entails s. How, then, should we formulate the 'method of verification'—that is, the connection between a proposition p and the statements $s_1, s_2 \ldots s_n$ which are evidences for it? I propose to say that the evidences $s_1, s_2 \ldots s_n$, *speak for* or *against* the proposition p, that they *strengthen* or *weaken* it, which does not mean that they prove or disprove it strictly.

There is a striking analogy to that in the relation that holds between a law of nature L and certain observational statements $s_1, s_2 \ldots s_n$, an analogy which may help to clarify the situation. It is often said that the statements of observation *follow* from the law (the latter being regarded as a sort of universal premiss). Since an unlimited number of consequences can be derived from a law, the ideal of complete verification is, of course, unattainable; whereas, on the other hand, a single counter observation seems to suffice to overthrow the law. From this it would follow that, while a law cannot be strictly verified, it can be strictly confuted; or that it can be decided only one way.[1] That is unrealistic. What astronomer would abandon Kepler's laws on the strength of a single observation? If, in fact, some anomaly in a planet's behaviour were detected, the most varied attempts at explaining the phenomenon would first be made (such as the presence of unknown heavy masses, friction with rarefied gases, etc.). Only if the edifice of hypotheses thus erected has too little support in experience, if it becomes too complex and artificial, if it no longer satisfies our demand for simplicity, or again if a better hypothesis presents itself to us, such as Einstein's theory, would we resolve to drop those laws. And even then the refutation would not be valid finally and once for all: it may still turn out that some circumstance had escaped our notice which, when taken into consideration, would cast a different light upon the whole. Indeed, the history of science exhibits cases (Olaf Römer, Leverrier) in which the apparent defeat of a theory later turned into complete victory. Who can say that such a situation will not repeat itself?

Here again the view suggests itself strongly that the relationship between a statement and what serves to verify it was too crudely represented in the past; that it was a mistake to describe it in logical terms such as 'entailment'; that a law is not a sort of universal statement from which particular statements follow; that its logic is still unexplored, and that it may possibly take the form of rules according to which the law's truth-weight—if I am allowed to use such a term—is increased or lessened by the data of observation. Be that as it may, the mere fact that a single counter observation $\backsim s$ can always be reconciled with a general law L by some accessory assumption shows that the true relation between a law and the experiential evidence for it is much more complicated and only superficially in accord with the customary account.

. . .

All this tends to suggest that the relation between a law of nature and the evidences for it, or between a material object statement and a sense-datum statement, or again between a psychological statement and the evidence concerning a person's behaviour is a looser one than had been hitherto imagined.

[1] See Karl Popper, *Logik der Forschung*.

If that is correct, the application of logic seems to be limited in an important sense. We may say that the known relations of logic can only hold between statements which belong to a *homogeneous* domain; or that the deductive nexus never extends beyond the limits of such a domain.

Accordingly we may set ourselves the task of arranging the statements of our language in distinct strata, grouping in the same stratum all those statements linked by clearly apprehended logical relations. It is in this way, for instance, that the theorems of mechanics are organized in a system the elements of which stand in known logical relations with one another and where it is always possible to decide of two theorems in what logical relation they stand—whether one is a consequence of the other, whether they are equivalent, or independent of, or in contradiction with each other. In like manner the statements of a physicist in describing certain data of observation (such as the position of a pointer on his gauges) stand in exactly defined relations to one another. Thus a pointer on a scale cannot possibly be opposite 3 and 5 at the same time: here you have a relation of strict exclusion. On the other hand, no statement of mechanics can ever come into sharp logical conflict with a statement of observation, and this implies that between these two kinds of statements there exist no relations of the sort supplied to us by classical logic. So long as we move only among the statements of a single stratum, all the relations provided by logic remain valid. The real problem arises where two such strata make contact, so to speak; it is the problem of these planes of contact which to-day should claim the attention of the logician. We may, in this context, speak of the looseness of the chains of inference which lead from statements of one stratum to those of another; the connection is no longer coercive—owing to the incompleteness of all our data.

You will find that it is this fact to which the rise of philosophical troubles often can be traced. (Think of how confusing it is to assert or to dispute the statement, 'The floor is not solid', as it belongs to two quite distinct strata.) The fracture lines of the strata of language are marked by philosophical problems: the problem of perception, of verification, of induction, the problem of the relation between mind and body, and so on.

You will have noticed that I have used the term 'incompleteness' in very different senses. In one sense we may say of a description of a material object that it is incomplete; in another sense we may say that of our knowledge of the boundary conditions in a field of force. There is a sense in which we say that a list of laws of nature is always incomplete, and another sense in which even our knowledge of the agents of nature is so; and you may easily find more senses. They all combine, to a varying degree, to create what I have called the open texture of concepts and the looseness of inferences.

Incompleteness, in the senses referred to, is the mark of empirical knowledge as opposed to *a priori* knowledge such as mathematics. In fact, it is the criterion by which we can distinguish perfectly *formalized* languages constructed by logicians from *natural* languages as used in describing reality. In a formalized system the use of each symbol is governed by a definite number of rules, and further, all the rules of inference and procedure can be stated completely. In view of the incompleteness which permeates empirical knowledge such a demand cannot be fulfilled by any language we may use to express it.

That there is a very close relation between content and verification is an important insight which has been brought to light by empiricists. Only one has to be very careful how to formulate it. Far from identifying the meaning of a statement with the evidences we have for it, the view I tried to sketch leads to a sort of many-level-theory of language in which 'every sort of statement has its own sort of logic'.

Alfred Jules Ayer

Critique of Theology

It is now generally admitted, at any rate by philosophers, that the existence of a being having the attributes which define the god of any non-animistic religion cannot be demonstratively proved. To see that this is so, we have only to ask ourselves what are the premises from which the existence of such a god could be deduced. If the conclusion that a god exists is to be demonstratively certain, then these premises must be certain; for, as the conclusion of a deductive argument is already contained in the premises, any uncertainty there may be about the truth of the premises is necessarily shared by it. But we know that no empirical proposition can ever be anything more than probable. It is only *a priori* propositions that are logically certain. But we cannot deduce the existence of a god from an *a priori* proposition. For we know that the reason why *a priori* propositions are certain is that they are tautologies. And from a set of tautologies nothing but a further tautology can be validly deduced. It follows that there is no possibility of demonstrating the existence of a god.

What is not so generally recognised is that there can be no way of proving that the existence of a god, such as the God of Christianity, is even probable. Yet this also is easily shown. For if the existence of such a god were probable, then the proposition that he existed would be an empirical hypothesis. And in that case it would be possible to deduce from it, and other empirical hypotheses, certain experiential propositions which were not deducible from those other hypotheses alone. But in fact this is not possible. It is sometimes claimed, indeed, that the existence of a certain sort of regularity in nature constitutes sufficient evidence for the existence of a god. But if the sentence "God exists" entails no more than that certain types of phenomena occur in certain sequences, then to assert the existence of a god will be simply equiva-

---

From *Language, Truth and Logic,* Chapter 6, by Alfred Jules Ayer, 2nd edition, 1946. Published by Dover Publications, Inc., New York 14, N. Y., and reprinted through permission of the publisher. Also published by Victor Gollancz, Ltd., London, 1936, and reprinted with their permission.

A. J. Ayer (1910–) was Grote Professor of the Philosophy of Mind and Logic at the University of London from 1946 to 1959, and since then he has been Wykeham Professor of Logic at the University of Oxford.

lent to asserting that there is the requisite regularity in nature; and no religious man would admit that this was all he intended to assert in asserting the existence of a god. He would say that in talking about God, he was talking about a transcendent being who might be known through certain empirical manifestations, but certainly could not be defined in terms of those manifestations. But in that case the term "god" is a metaphysical term. And if "god" is a metaphysical term, then it cannot be even probable that a god exists. For to say that "God exists" is to make a metaphysical utterance which cannot be either true or false. And by the same criterion, no sentence which purports to describe the nature of a transcendent god can possess any literal significance.

It is important not to confuse this view of religious assertions with the view that is adopted by atheists, or agnostics. For it is characteristic of an agnostic to hold that the existence of a god is a possibility in which there is no good reason either to believe or disbelieve; and it is characteristic of an atheist to hold that it is at least probable that no god exists. And our view that all utterances about the nature of God are nonsensical, so far from being identical with, or even lending any support to, either of these familiar contentions, is actually incompatible with them. For if the assertion that there is a god is nonsensical, then the atheist's assertion that there is no god is equally nonsensical, since it is only a significant proposition that can be significantly contradicted. As for the agnostic, although he refrains from saying either that there is or that there is not a god, he does not deny that the question whether a transcendent god exists is a genuine question. He does not deny that the two sentences "There is a transcendent god" and "There is no transcendent god" express propositions one of which is actually true and the other false. All he says is that we have no means of telling which of them is true, and therefore ought not to commit ourselves to either. But we have seen that the sentences in question do not express propositions at all. And this means that agnosticism also is ruled out.

Thus we offer the theist the same comfort as we gave to the moralist. His assertions cannot possibly be valid, but they cannot be invalid either. As he says nothing at all about the world, he cannot justly be accused of saying anything false, or anything for which he has insufficient grounds. It is only when the theist claims that in asserting the existence of a transcendent god he is expressing a genuine proposition that we are entitled to disagree with him.

It is to be remarked that in cases where deities are identified with natural objects, assertions concerning them may be allowed to be significant. If, for example, a man tells me that the occurrence of thunder is alone both necessary and sufficient to establish the truth of the proposition that Jehovah is angry, I may conclude that, in his usage of words, the sentence "Jehovah is angry" is equivalent to "It is thundering." But in sophisticated religions, though they may be to some extent based on men's awe of natural process which they cannot sufficiently understand, the "person" who is supposed to control the empirical world is not himself located in it; he is held to be superior to the empirical world, and so outside it; and he is endowed with super-empirical attributes. But the notion of a person whose essential attributes are non-empirical is not an intelligible notion at all. We may have a word which is used as if it named this "person," but, unless the sentences in which it occurs express propositions which are empirically verifiable, it cannot be said to symbolize anything. And this is the case with regard to the word "god," in the usage in which it is intended to refer to a transcendent object. The mere existence of the noun is enough to foster the illusion that there is a real, or at any rate a possible entity corresponding to it. It is only when we enquire what God's attributes are that we discover that "God," in this usage, is not a genuine name.

It is common to find belief in a transcendent god conjoined with belief in an after-life. But, in the form which it usually takes, the content of this belief is not a genuine hypothesis. To say that men do not ever die, or that the state of death is merely a state of prolonged insensibility, is indeed to express a significant proposition, though all the available evidence goes to show that it is false. But to say that there is something imperceptible inside a man, which is his soul or his real self, and that it goes on living after he is dead, is to make a metaphysical assertion which has no more factual content than the assertion that there is a transcendent god.

It is worth mentioning that, according to the account which we have given of religious assertions, there is no logical ground for antagonism between religion and natural science. As far as the question of truth or falsehood is concerned, there is no opposition between the natural scientist and the theist who believes in a transcendent god. For since the religious utterances of the theist are not genuine propositions at all, they cannot stand in any logical relation to the propositions of science. Such antagonism as there is between religion and science appears to consist in the fact that science takes away one of the motives which make men religious. For it is acknowledged that one of the ultimate sources of religious feeling lies in the inability of men to determine their own destiny; and science tends to destroy the feeling of awe with which men regard an alien world, by making them believe that they can understand and anticipate the course of natural phenomena, and even to some extent control it. The fact that it has recently become fashionable for physicists themselves to be sympathetic towards religion is a point in favour of this hypothesis. For this sympathy towards religion marks the physicists' own lack of confidence in the validity of their hypotheses, which is a reaction on their part from the anti-religious dogmatism of nineteenth-century scientists, and a natural outcome of the crisis through which physics has just passed.

It is not within the scope of this enquiry to enter more deeply into the causes of religious feeling, or to discuss the probability of the continuance of religious belief. We are concerned only to answer those questions which arise out of our discussion of the possibility of religious knowledge. The point which we wish to establish is that there cannot be any transcendent truths of religion. For the sentences which the theist uses to express such "truths" are not literally significant.

An interesting feature of this conclusion is that it accords with what many theists are accustomed to say themselves. For we are often told that the nature of God is a mystery which transcends the human understanding. But to say that something transcends the human understanding is to say that it is unintelligible. And what is unintelligible cannot significantly be described. Again, we are told that God is not an object of reason but an object of faith. This may be nothing more than an admission that the existence of God must be taken on trust, since it cannot be proved. But it may also be an assertion that God is the object of a purely mystical intuition, and cannot therefore be defined in terms which are intelligible to the reason. And I think there are many theists who would assert this. But if one allows that it is impossible to define God in intelligible terms, then one is allowing that it is impossible for a sentence both to be significant and to be about God. If a mystic admits that the object of his vision is something which cannot be described, then he must also admit that he is bound to talk nonsense when he describes it.

For his part, the mystic may protest that his intuition does reveal truths to him, even though he cannot explain to others what these truths are; and that we who do not possess this faculty of intuition can have no ground for denying that it is a cognitive faculty. For we can hardly maintain *a priori* that there are no ways of discovering true propositions except those which we ourselves employ. The answer is that we set no limit to the number of ways in which one may come to formulate a true proposition. We do not in any way deny that a synthetic truth may be discovered by purely intuitive methods as well as by the rational method of induction. But we do say that every synthetic proposition, however it may have been arrived at, must be subject to the test of actual experience. We do not deny *a priori* that the mystic is able to discover truths by his own special methods. We wait to hear what are the propositions which embody his discoveries, in order to see whether they are verified or confuted by our empirical observations. But the mystic, so far from producing propositions which are empirically verified, is unable to produce any intelligible propositions at all. And therefore we say that his intuition has not revealed to him any facts. It is no use his saying that he has apprehended facts but is unable to express them. For we know that if he really had acquired any information, he would be able to express it. He would be able to indicate in some way or other how the genuineness of his discovery might be empirically determined. The fact that he cannot reveal what he "knows," or even himself devise an empirical test to validate his "knowledge," shows that his state of mystical intuition is not a genuinely cognitive state. So that in describing his vision the mystic does not give us any information about the external world; he merely gives us indirect information about the condition of his own mind.

These considerations dispose of the argument from religious experience, which many philosophers still regard as a valid argument in favour of the existence of a god. They say that it is logically possible for men to be immediately acquainted with God, as they are immediately acquainted with a sense-content, and that there is no reason why one should be prepared to believe a man when he says that he is seeing a yellow patch, and refuse to believe him when he says that he is seeing God. The answer to this is that if the man who asserts that he is seeing God is merely asserting that he is experiencing a peculiar kind of sense-content, then we do not for a moment deny that his assertion may be true. But, ordinarily, the man who says that he is seeing God is saying not merely that he is experiencing a religious emotion, but also that there exists a transcendent being who is the object of this emotion; just as the man who says that he sees a yellow patch is ordinarily saying not merely that his visual sense-field contains a yellow sense-content, but also that there exists a yellow object to which the sense-content belongs. And it is not irrational to be prepared to believe a man when he asserts the existence of a yellow object, and to refuse to believe him when he asserts the existence of a transcendent god. For whereas the sentence "There exists here a yellow-coloured material thing" expresses a genuine synthetic proposition which could be empirically verified, the sentence "There exists a transcendent god" has, as we have seen, no literal significance.

We conclude, therefore, that the argument from religious experience is altogether fallacious. The fact that people have religious experiences is interesting from the psychological point of view, but it does not in any way imply that there is such a thing as religious knowledge, any more than our having moral experiences implies that there is such a thing as moral knowledge. The theist, like the moralist, may believe that his experiences are cognitive experiences, but, unless he can formulate his "knowledge" in propositions that are empirically verifiable, we may be sure that he is deceiving himself. It follows that those philosophers who fill their books with assertions that they intuitively "know" this or that moral or religious "truth" are merely providing material for the psycho-analyst. For no act of intuition can be said to reveal a truth about any matter of fact unless it issues in verifiable propositions. And all such propositions are to be incorporated in the system of empirical propositions which constitutes science.

A. G. N. Flew

Theology and Falsification

Let us begin with a parable. It is a parable developed from a tale told by John Wisdom in his haunting and revelatory article 'Gods'. Once upon a time two explorers came upon a clearing in the jungle. In the clearing were growing many flowers and many weeds. One explorer says, 'Some gardener must tend this plot'. The other disagrees, 'There is no gardener'. So they pitch their tents and set a watch. No gardener is ever seen. 'But perhaps he is an invisible gardener.' So they set up a barbed-wire fence. They electrify it. They patrol with bloodhounds. (For they remember how H. G. Wells's *The Invisible Man* could be both smelt and touched though he could not be seen.) But no shrieks ever suggest that some intruder has received a shock. No movements of the wire ever betray an invisible climber. The bloodhounds never give cry. Yet

From A. G. N. Flew, R. M. Hare, and Basil Mitchell, "Theology and Falsification" (symposium), in A. G. N. Flew and A. Macintyre (eds.), *New Essays in Philosophical Theology*, published by Student Christian Movement Press Limited, London, 1955, and reprinted with their permission. The entire symposium, of which the selection above is only the first part, was first published in *University*, 1950–51.

A. G. N. Flew (1923–   ) is Professor of Philosophy at University College of North Staffordshire, England.

still the Believer is not convinced. 'But there is a gardener, invisible, intangible, insensible to electric shocks, a gardener who has no scent and makes no sound, a gardener who comes secretly to look after the garden which he loves.' At last the Sceptic despairs, 'But what remains of your original assertion? Just how does what you call an invisible, intangible, eternally elusive gardener differ from an imaginary gardener or even from no gardener at all?'

In this parable we can see how what starts as an assertion, that something exists or that there is some analogy between certain complexes of phenomena, may be reduced step by step to an altogether different status, to an expression perhaps of a 'picture preference'. The Sceptic says there is no gardener. The Believer says there is a gardener (but invisible, etc.). One man talks about sexual behaviour. Another man prefers to talk of Aphrodite (but knows that there is not really a superhuman person additional to, and somehow responsible for, all sexual phenomena). The process of qualification may be checked at any point before the original assertion is completely withdrawn and something of that first assertion will remain (Tautology). Mr. Wells's invisible man could not, admittedly, be seen, but in all other respects he was a man like the rest of us. But though the process of qualification may be, and of course usually is, checked in time, it is not always judiciously so halted. Someone may dissipate his assertion completely without noticing that he has done so. A fine brash hypothesis may thus be killed by inches, the death by a thousand qualifications.

And in this, it seems to me, lies the peculiar danger, the endemic evil, of theological utterance. Take such utterances as 'God has a plan', 'God created the world', 'God loves us as a father loves his children'. They look at first sight very much like assertions, vast cosmological assertions. Of course, this is no sure sign that they either are, or are intended to be, assertions. But let us confine ourselves to the cases where those who utter such sentences intend them to express assertions. (Merely remarking parenthetically that those who intend or interpret such utterances as crypto-commands, expressions of wishes, disguised ejaculations, concealed ethics, or as anything else but assertions, are unlikely to succeed in making them either properly orthodox or practically effective.)

Now to assert that such and such is the case is necessarily equivalent to denying that such and such is not the case. Suppose then that we are in doubt as to what someone who gives vent to an utterance is asserting, or suppose that, more radically, we are sceptical as to whether he is really asserting anything at all, one way of trying to understand (or perhaps it will be to expose) his utterance is to attempt to find what he would regard as counting against, or as being incompatible with, its truth. For if the utterance is indeed an assertion, it will necessarily be equivalent to a denial of the negation of that assertion. And anything which would count against the assertion, or which would induce the speaker to withdraw it and to admit that it had been mistaken, must be part of (or the whole of) the meaning of the negation of that assertion. And to know the meaning of the negation of an assertion, is as near as makes no matter, to know the meaning of that assertion. And if there is nothing which a putative assertion denies then there is nothing which it asserts either: and so it is not really an assertion. When the Sceptic in the parable asked the Believer, 'Just how does what you call an invisible, intangible, eternally elusive gardener differ from an imaginary gardener or even from no gardener at all?' he was suggesting that the Believer's earlier statement had been so eroded by qualification that it was no longer an assertion at all.

Now it often seems to people who are not religious as if there was no conceivable event or series of events the occurrence of which would be admitted by sophisticated religious people to be a sufficient reason for conceding 'There wasn't a God after all' or 'God does not really love us then'. Someone tells us that God loves us as a father loves his children. We are reassured. But then we see a child dying of inoperable cancer of the throat. His earthly father is driven frantic in his efforts to help, but his Heavenly Father reveals no obvious sign of concern. Some qualification is made—God's love is 'not a merely human love' or it is 'an inscrutable love,' perhaps—and we realize that such sufferings are quite compatible with the truth of the assertion that 'God loves us as a father (but, of course, . . .).' We are reassured again. But then perhaps we ask: what is this assurance of God's (appropriately qualified) love worth, what is this apparent guarantee really a guarantee against? Just what would have to happen not merely (morally and wrongly) to tempt but also (logically and rightly) to entitle us to say 'God does not love us' or even 'God does not exist'? I therefore put to the succeeding symposiasts the simple central questions, 'What would have to occur or to have occurred to constitute for you a disproof of the love of, or of the existence of, God?'

B. MEANING AND REFERENCE

John Locke

The Signification of Words

OF WORDS OR LANGUAGE IN GENERAL

1. God, having designed man for a sociable creature, made him not only with an inclination, and under a necessity to have fellowship with those of his own kind, but furnished him also with language, which was to be the great instrument and common tie of society. Man, therefore, had by nature his organs so fashioned, as to be fit to frame articulate sounds, which we call words. But this was not enough to produce language; for parrots, and several other birds, will be taught to make articulate sounds distinct enough, which yet by no means are capable of language.

2. Besides articulate sounds, therefore, it was further necessary that he should be able to use these sounds as signs of internal conceptions; and to make them stand as marks for the ideas within his own mind, whereby they might be made known to others, and the thoughts of men's minds be conveyed from one to another.

3. But neither was this sufficient to make words so useful as they ought to be. It is not enough for the perfection of language, that sounds can be made signs of ideas, unless those signs can be so made use of as to comprehend several particular things: for the multiplication of words would have perplexed their use, had every particular thing need of a distinct name to be signified by. To remedy this inconvenience, language had yet a further improvement in the use of *general terms,* whereby one word was made to mark a multitude of particular existences: which advantageous use of sounds was obtained only by the difference of the ideas they were made signs of: those names becoming general, which are made to stand for *general ideas,* and those remaining particular, where the *ideas* they are used for are *particular.*

4. Besides these names which stand for ideas, there be other words which men make use of, not to signify any idea, but the want or absence of some ideas, simple or complex, or all ideas together; such as are *nihil* in Latin, and in English, *ignorance* and *barrenness.* All which negative or privative words cannot be said properly to belong to, or signify no ideas: for then they would

---

From John Locke, *An Essay Concerning Human Understanding,* Book III, Chaps. 1–3, first published in 1690.

John Locke (1632–1704) was a physician by profession and never held an academic teaching post.

be perfectly insignificant sounds; but they relate to positive ideas, and signify their absence.

5. It may also lead us a little towards the original of all our notions and knowledge, if we remark how great a dependence our words have on common sensible ideas; and how those which are made use of to stand for actions and notions quite removed from sense, have their rise from thence, and from obvious sensible ideas are transferred to more abstruse significations, and made to stand for ideas that come not under the cognizance of our senses; v.g. to *imagine, apprehend, comprehend, adhere, conceive, instil, disgust, disturbance, tranquillity,* &c., are all words taken from the operations of sensible things, and applied to certain modes of thinking. *Spirit,* in its primary signification, is breath; *angel,* a messenger: and I doubt not but, if we could trace them to their sources, we should find, in all languages, the names which stand for things that fall not under our senses to have had their first rise from sensible ideas. By which we may give some kind of guess what kind of notions they were, and whence derived, which filled their minds who were the first beginners of languages, and how nature, even in the naming of things, unawares suggested to men the originals and principles of all their knowledge: whilst, to give names that might make known to others any operations they felt in themselves, or any other ideas that came not under their senses, they were fain to borrow words from ordinary known ideas of sensation, by that means to make others the more easily to conceive those operations they experimented in themselves, which made no outward sensible appearances; and then, when they had got known and agreed names to signify those internal operations of their own minds, they were sufficiently furnished to make known by words all their other ideas; since they could consist of nothing but either of outward sensible perceptions, or of the inward operations of their minds about them; we having, as has been proved, no ideas at all, but what originally come either from sensible objects without, or what we feel within ourselves, from the inward workings of our own spirits, of which we are conscious to ourselves within.

6. But to understand better the use and force of Language, as subservient to instruction and knowledge, it will be convenient to consider:

First, *To what it is that names, in the use of language, are immediately applied.*

Secondly, Since all (except proper) names are general, and so stand not particularly for this or that single thing, but for sorts and ranks of things, it will be necessary to consider, in the next place, what the sorts and kinds, or, if you rather like the Latin names, *what the Species and Genera of things are, wherein they consist, and how they come to be made.* These being (as they ought) well looked into, we shall the better come to find the right use of words; the natural advantages and defects of language; and the remedies that ought to be used, to avoid the inconveniences of obscurity or uncertainty in the signification of words: without which it is impossible to discourse with any clearness or order concerning knowledge: which, being conversant about propositions, and those most commonly universal ones, has greater connexion with words than perhaps is suspected.

These considerations, therefore, shall be the matter of the following chapters.

OF THE SIGNIFICATION OF WORDS

1. Man, though he have great variety of thoughts, and such from which others as well as himself might receive profit and delight; yet they are all within his own breast, invisible and hidden from others, nor can of themselves be made to appear. The comfort and advantage of society not being to be had without communication of thoughts, it was necessary that man should find out some external sensible signs, whereof those invisible ideas, which his thoughts are made up of, might be made known to others. For this purpose nothing was so fit, either for plenty or quickness, as those articulate sounds, which with so much ease and variety he found himself able to make. Thus we may conceive how *words,* which were by nature so well adapted to that purpose, came to be made use of by men as the signs of their ideas; not by any natural connexion that there is between particular articulate sounds and certain ideas, for then there would be but one language amongst all men; but by a voluntary imposition, whereby such a word is made arbitrarily the mark of such an idea. The use, then, of words, is to be sensible marks of ideas; and the ideas they stand for are their proper and immediate signification.

2. The use men have of these marks being either to record their own thoughts, for the assistance of their own memory; or, as it were, to bring out their ideas, and lay them before the view of others: words, in their primary or immediate signification, stand for nothing but *the ideas in the mind of him that uses them,* how imperfectly soever or carelessly those ideas are collected from the things which they are supposed to represent. When a man speaks to another, it is that he may be understood: and the end of speech is, that those sounds, as marks, may make known his ideas to the hearer. That then which words are the marks of are the ideas of the speaker: nor can any one apply them as marks, immediately, to anything else but the ideas that he himself hath: for this would be to make them signs of his own conceptions, and yet apply them to other ideas; which would be to make them signs and not signs of his ideas at the same time; and so in effect to have no signification at all. Words being voluntary signs, they cannot be voluntary signs imposed by him on things he knows not. That would be to make them signs of nothing, sounds without signification. A man cannot make his words the signs either of qualities in things, or of conceptions in the mind of another, whereof he has none in his own. Till he has some ideas of his own, he cannot suppose them to correspond with the conceptions of another man; nor can he use any signs for them: for thus they would be the signs of he knows not what, which is in truth to be the signs of nothing. But when he represents to himself other men's ideas by some of his own, if he consent to give them the same names that other men do, it is still to his own ideas; to ideas that he has, and not to ideas that he has not.

3. This is so necessary in the use of language, that in this respect the knowing and the ignorant, the learned and the unlearned, use the words they speak (with any meaning) all alike. They, in every man's mouth, stand for the ideas he has, and which he would express by them. A child having taken notice of nothing in the metal he hears called *gold,* but the bright shining yellow colour, he applies the word gold only to his own idea of that colour, and nothing else; and therefore calls the same colour in a peacock's tail gold.

Another that hath better observed, adds to shining yellow great weight: and then the sound gold, when he uses it, stands for a complex idea of a shining yellow and a very weighty substance. Another adds to those qualities fusibility: and then the word gold signifies to him a body, bright, yellow, fusible, and very heavy. Another adds malleability. Each of these uses equally the word gold, when they have occasion to express the idea which they have applied it to: but it is evident that each can apply it only to his own idea; nor can he make it stand as a sign of such a complex idea as he has not.

4. But though words, as they are used by men, can properly and immediately signify nothing but the ideas that are in the mind of the speaker; yet they in their thoughts give them a secret reference to two other things.

First, *They suppose their words to be marks of the ideas in the minds also of other men, with whom they communicate*; for else they should talk in vain, and could not be understood, if the sounds they applied to one idea were such as by the hearer were applied to another, which is to speak two languages. But in this men stand not usually to examine, whether the idea they, and those they discourse with have in their minds be the same: but think it enough that they use the word, as they imagine, in the common acceptation of that language; in which they suppose that the idea they make it a sign of is precisely the same to which the understanding men of that country apply that name.

5. Secondly, Because men would not be thought to talk barely of their own imagination, but of things as really they are; therefore they often suppose the *words to stand also for the reality of things*. But this relating more particularly to substances and their names, as perhaps the former does to simple ideas and modes, we shall speak of these two different ways of applying words more at large, when we come to treat of the names of mixed modes and substances in particular: though give me leave here to say, that it is a perverting the use of words, and brings unavoidable obscurity and confusion into their signification, whenever we make them stand for anything but those ideas we have in our own minds.

6. Concerning words, also, it is further to be considered:

First, that they being immediately the signs of men's ideas, and by that means the instruments whereby men communicate their conceptions, and express to one another those thoughts and imaginations they have within their own breasts; there comes, by constant use, to be such a connexion between certain sounds and the ideas they stand for, that the names heard, almost as readily excite certain ideas as if the objects themselves, which are apt to produce them, did actually affect the senses. Which is manifestly so in all obvious sensible qualities, and in all substances that frequently and familiarly occur to us.

7. Secondly, That though the proper and immediate signification of words are ideas in the mind of the speaker, yet, because by familiar use from our cradles, we come to learn certain articulate sounds very perfectly, and have them readily on our tongues, and always at hand in our memories, but yet are not always careful to examine or settle their significations perfectly; it often happens that men, even when they would apply themselves to an attentive consideration, do set their thoughts more on words than things. Nay, because words are many of them learned before the ideas are known for which they

stand: therefore some, not only children but men, speak several words no otherwise than parrots do, only because they have learned them, and have been accustomed to those sounds. But so far as words are of use and signification, so far is there a constant connexion between the sound and the idea, and a designation that the one stands for the other; without which application of them, they are nothing but so much insignificant noise.

. . .

OF GENERAL TERMS

1. All things that exist being particulars, it may perhaps be thought reasonable that words, which ought to be conformed to things, should be so too,—I mean in their signification: but yet we find quite the contrary. The far greatest part of words that make all languages are general terms: which has not been the effect of neglect or chance, but of reason and necessity.

2. First, It is impossible that every particular thing should have a distinct peculiar name. For, the signification and use of words depending on that connexion which the mind makes between its ideas and the sounds it uses as signs of them, it is necessary, in the application of names to things, that the mind should have distinct ideas of the things, and retain also the particular name that belongs to every one, with its peculiar appropriation to that idea. But it is beyond the power of human capacity to frame and retain distinct ideas of all the particular things we meet with: every bird and beast men saw; every tree and plant that affected the senses, could not find a place in the most capacious understanding. . . .

3. Secondly, If it were possible, it would yet be useless; because it would not serve to the chief end of language. Men would in vain heap up names of particular things, that would not serve them to communicate their thoughts. Men learn names, and use them in talk with others, only that they may be understood: which is then only done when, by use or consent, the sound I make by the organs of speech, excites in another man's mind who hears it, the idea I apply it to in mine, when I speak it. This cannot be done by names applied to particular things; whereof I alone having the ideas in my mind, the names of them could not be significant or intelligible to another, who was not acquainted with all those very particular things which had fallen under my notice.

4. Thirdly, But yet, granting this also feasible, (which I think is not,) yet a distinct name for every particular thing would not be of any great use for the improvement of knowledge: which, though founded in particular things, enlarges itself by general views; to which things reduced into sorts, under general names, are properly subservient. These, with the names belonging to them, come within some compass, and do not multiply every moment, beyond what either the mind can contain, or use requires. And therefore, in these, men have for the most part stopped: but yet not so as to hinder themselves from distinguishing particular things by appropriated names, where convenience demands it. And therefore in their own species, which they have most to do with, and wherein they have often occasion to mention particular persons, they make use of proper names; and there distinct individuals have distinct denominations.

5. Besides persons, countries also, cities, rivers, mountains, and other the like distinctions of place have usually found peculiar names, and that for the same reason; they being such as men have often an occasion to mark particularly, and, as it were, set before others in their discourses with them. And I doubt not but, if we had reason to mention particular horses as often as we have to mention particular men, we should have proper names for the one, as familiar as for the other, and Bucephalus would be a word as much in use as Alexander. And therefore we see that, amongst jockeys, horses have their proper names to be known and distinguished by, as commonly as their servants: because, amongst them, there is often occasion to mention this or that particular horse when he is out of sight.

6. The next thing to be considered is,—How general words come to be made. For, since all things that exist are only particulars, how come we by general terms; or where find we those general natures they are supposed to stand for? Words become general by being made the signs of general ideas: and ideas become general, by separating from them the circumstances of time and place, and any other ideas that may determine them to this or that particular existence. By this way of abstraction they are made capable of representing more individuals than one; each of which having in it a conformity to that abstract idea, is (as we call it) of that sort.

7. But, to deduce this a little more distinctly, it will not perhaps be amiss to trace our notions and names from their beginning, and observe by what degrees we proceed, and by what steps we enlarge our ideas from our first infancy. There is nothing more evident, than that the ideas of the persons children converse with (to instance in them alone) are, like the persons themselves, only particular. The ideas of the nurse and the mother are well framed in their minds; and, like pictures of them there, represent only those individuals. The names they first gave to them are confined to these individuals; and the names of *nurse* and *mamma,* the child uses, determine themselves to those persons. Afterwards, when time and a larger acquaintance have made them observe that there are a great many other things in the world, that in some common agreements of shape, and several other qualities, resemble their father and mother, and those persons they have been used to, they frame an idea, which they find those many particulars do partake in; and to that they give, with others, the name *man,* for example. And thus they come to have a general name, and a general idea. Wherein they make nothing new; but only leave out of the complex idea they had of Peter and James, Mary and Jane, that which is peculiar to each, and retain only what is common to them all.

8. By the same way that they come by the general name and idea of *man,* they easily advance to more general names and notions. For, observing that several things that differ from their idea of man, and cannot therefore be comprehended under that name, have yet certain qualities wherein they agree with man, by retaining only those qualities, and uniting them into one idea, they have again another and more general idea; to which having given a name they make a term of a more comprehensive extension: which new idea is made, not by any new addition, but only as before, by leaving out the shape, and some other properties signified by the name man, and retaining only a body, with life, sense, and spontaneous motion, comprehended under the name animal.

9. That this is the way whereby men first formed general ideas, and general

names to them, I think is so evident, that there needs no other proof of it but the considering of a man's self, or others, and the ordinary proceedings of their minds in knowledge. And he that thinks *general natures* or *notions* are anything else but such abstract and partial ideas of more complex ones, taken at first from particular existences, will, I fear, be at a loss where to find them. For let any one effect, and then tell me, wherein does his idea of *man* differ from that of *Peter* and *Paul,* or his idea of *horse* from that of *Bucephalus,* but in the leaving out something that is peculiar to each individual, and retaining so much of those particular complex ideas of several particular existences as they are found to agree in? Of the complex ideas signified by the names *man* and *horse,* leaving out but those particulars wherein they differ, and retaining only those wherein they agree, and of those making a new distinct complex idea, and giving the name *animal* to it, one has a more general term, that comprehends with man several other creatures. Leave out of the idea of *animal,* sense and spontaneous motion, and the remaining complex idea, made up of the remaining simple ones of body, life, and nourishment, becomes a more general one, under the more comprehensive term, *vivens.* And, not to dwell longer upon this particular, so evident in itself; by the same way the mind proceeds to *body, substance,* and at last to *being, thing,* and such universal terms, which stand for any of our ideas whatsoever. To conclude: this whole mystery of genera and species, which make such a noise in the schools, and are with justice so little regarded out of them, is nothing else but *abstract ideas,* more or less comprehensive, with names annexed to them. In all which this is constant and unvariable, That every more general term stands for such an idea, and is but a part of any of those contained under it.

. . .

11. To return to general words: it is plain, by what has been said, that *general* and *universal* belong not to the real existence of things; but are the inventions and creatures of the understanding, made by it for its own use, and concern only signs, whether words or ideas. Words are general, as has been said, when used for signs of general ideas, and so are applicable indifferently to many particular things; and ideas are general when they are set up as the representatives of many particular things: but universality belongs not to things themselves, which are all of them particular in their existence, even those words and ideas which in their signification are general. When therefore we quit particulars, the generals that rest are only creatures of our own making; their general nature being nothing but the capacity they are put into, by the understanding, of signifying or representing many particulars. For the signification they have is nothing but a relation that, by the mind of man, is added to them.

12. The next thing therefore to be considered is, What kind of signification it is that general words have. For, as it is evident that they do not signify barely one particular thing; for then they would not be general terms, but proper names, so, on the other side, it is as evident they do not signify a plurality; for *man* and *men* would then signify the same; and the distinction of numbers (as the grammarians call them) would be superfluous and useless. That then which general words signify is a *sort* of things; and each of them does that, by being a sign of an abstract idea in the mind; to which idea, as things exist-

ing are found to agree, so they come to be ranked under that name, or, which is all one, be of that sort. Whereby it is evident that the *essences* of the sorts, or, if the Latin word pleases better, *species* of things, are nothing else but these abstract ideas. For the having the essence of any species, being that which makes anything to be of that species; and the conformity to the idea to which the name is annexed being that which gives a right to that name; the having the essence, and the having that conformity, must needs be the same thing: since to be of any species, and to have a right to the name of that species, is all one. As, for example, to be a *man,* or of the *species* man, and to have right to the *name* man, is the same thing. Again, to be a man, or of the species man, and have the *essence* of a man, is the same thing. Now, since nothing can be a man, or have a right to the name man, but what has a conformity to the abstract idea the name man stands for, nor anything be a man, or have a right to the species man, but what has the essence of that species; it follows, that the abstract idea for which the name stands, and the essence of the species, is one and the same. From whence it is easy to observe, that the essences of the sorts of things, and, consequently, the sorting of things, is the workmanship of the understanding that abstracts and makes those general ideas.

John Stuart Mill

Of Names

OF THE NECESSITY OF COMMENCING WITH AN ANALYSIS OF LANGUAGE

. . .

FIRST STEP IN THE ANALYSIS OF PROPOSITIONS

The answer to every question which it is possible to frame, must be contained in a Proposition, or Assertion. Whatever can be an object of belief, or even of disbelief, must, when put into words, assume the form of a proposition. All truth and all error lie in propositions. What, by a convenient misapplication of an abstract term, we call a Truth, means simply a True Proposition; and errors are false propositions. To know the import of all possible propositions, would be to know all questions which can be raised, all matters which are susceptible of being either believed or disbelieved. How many kinds of inquiries can be propounded; how many kinds of judgments can be made;

From John Stuart Mill, *A System of Logic,* 10th ed. (first published in 1843), Book I, Chaps. 1 and 2, Longmans, Green & Co., London, 1879.

John Stuart Mill (1806–73) was for many years an administrator in the London office of the British East India Company and a member of Parliament from 1865 to 1868. He never held an academic teaching post.

and how many kinds of propositions it is possible to frame with a meaning; are but different forms of one and the same question. Since, then, the objects of all Belief and of all Inquiry express themselves in propositions; a sufficient scrutiny of Propositions and of their varieties will apprize us what questions mankind have actually asked of themselves, and what, in the nature of answers to those questions, they have actually thought they had grounds to believe.

Now the first glance at a proposition shows that it is formed by putting together two names. A proposition, according to the common simple definition, which is sufficient for our purpose, is, *discourse, in which something is affirmed or denied of something.* Thus, in the proposition, Gold is yellow, the quality *yellow* is affirmed of the substance *gold.* In the proposition, Franklin was not born in England, the fact expressed by the words *born in England* is denied of the man Franklin.

. . .

NAMES MUST BE STUDIED BEFORE THINGS

This first step in the analysis of the object of belief, which, though so obvious, will be found to be not unimportant, is the only one which we shall find it practicable to make without a preliminary survey of language. If we attempt to proceed further in the same path, that is, to analyse any further the import of Propositions; we find forced upon us, as a subject of previous consideration, the import of Names. For every proposition consists of two names; and every proposition affirms or denies one of these names, of the other. Now what we do, what passes in our mind, when we affirm or deny two names of one another, must depend on what they are names of; since it is with reference to that, and not to the mere names themselves, that we make the affirmation or denial. Here, therefore, we find a new reason why the signification of names, and the relation generally between names and the things signified by them, must occupy the preliminary stage of the inquiry we are engaged in.

. . .

OF NAMES

NAMES ARE NAMES OF THINGS, NOT OF OUR IDEAS

"A name," says Hobbes, "is a word taken at pleasure to serve for a mark which may raise in our mind a thought like to some thought we had before, and which being pronounced to others, may be to them a sign of what thought the speaker had before in his mind." This simple definition of a name, as a word (or set of words) serving the double purpose of a mark to recall to ourselves the likeness of a former thought, and a sign to make it known to others, appears unexceptionable. Names, indeed, do much more than this; but whatever else they do, grows out of, and is the result of this: as will appear in its proper place.

Are names more properly said to be the names of things, or of our ideas of things? The first is the expression in common use; the last is that of some metaphysicians, who conceived that in adopting it they were introducing a highly important distinction. The eminent thinker, just quoted, seems to countenance the latter opinion. "But seeing," he continues, "names ordered in speech (as is defined) are signs of our conceptions, it is manifest they are not signs of the things themselves; for that the sound of this word *stone* should be the sign of a stone, cannot be understood in any sense but this, that he that hears it collects that he that pronounces it thinks of a stone."

If it be merely meant that the conception alone, and not the thing itself, is recalled by the name, or imparted to the hearer, this of course cannot be denied. Nevertheless, there seems good reason for adhering to the common usage, and calling (as indeed Hobbes himself does in other places) the word *sun* the name of the sun, and not the name of our idea of the sun. For names are not intended only to make the hearer conceive what we conceive, but also to inform him what we believe. Now, when I use a name for the purpose of expressing a belief, it is a belief concerning the thing itself, not concerning my idea of it. When I say, "the sun is the cause of day," I do not mean that my idea of the sun causes or excites in me the idea of day; or in other words, that thinking of the sun makes me think of day. I mean, that a certain physical fact, which is called the sun's presence (and which, in the ultimate analysis, resolves itself into sensations, not ideas) causes another physical fact, which is called day. It seems proper to consider a word as the *name* of that which we intend to be understood by it when we use it; of that which any fact that we assert of it is to be understood of; that, in short, concerning which, when we employ the word, we intend to give information. Names, therefore, shall always be spoken of in this work as the names of things themselves, and not merely of our ideas of things.

But the question now arises, of what things? and to answer this it is necessary to take into consideration the different kinds of names.

. . .

GENERAL AND SINGULAR NAMES

All names are names of something, real or imaginary; but all things have not names appropriated to them individually. For some individual objects we require, and consequently have, separate distinguishing names; there is a name for every person, and for every remarkable place. Other objects, of which we have not occasion to speak so frequently, we do not designate by a name of their own; but when the necessity arises for naming them, we do so by putting together several words, each of which, by itself, might be and is used for an indefinite number of other objects; as when I say, *this stone:* "this" and "stone" being, each of them, names that may be used of many other objects besides the particular one meant, though the only object of which they can both be used at the given moment, consistently with their signification, may be the one of which I wish to speak.

Were this the sole purpose for which names, that are common to more things than one, could be employed; if they only served, by mutually limiting each other, to afford a designation for such individual objects as have no names of their own: they could only be ranked among contrivances for economizing the use of language. But it is evident that this is not their sole function. It is by their means that we are enabled to assert *general* propositions; to affirm or deny any predicate of an indefinite number of things at once. The distinction, therefore, between *general* names, and *individual* or *singular* names, is fundamental; and may be considered as the first grand division of names.

A general name is familiarly defined, a name which is capable of being truly affirmed, in the same sense, of each of an indefinite number of things. An individual or singular name is a name which is only capable of being truly affirmed, in the same sense, of one thing.

Thus, *man* is capable of being truly affirmed of John, George, Mary, and other persons without assignable limit; and it is affirmed of all of them in the same sense; for the word man expresses certain qualities, and when we predicate it of those persons, we assert that they all possess those qualities. But *John* is only capable of being truly affirmed of one single person, at least in the same sense. For, though there are many persons who bear that name, it is not conferred upon them to indicate any qualities, or anything which belongs to them in common; and cannot be said to be affirmed of them in any *sense* at all, consequently not in the same sense. "The king who succeeded William the Conqueror," is also an individual name. For, that there cannot be more than one person of whom it can be truly affirmed, is implied in the meaning of the words. Even "*the* king," when the occasion or the context defines the individual of whom it is to be understood, may justly be regarded as an individual name.

It is not unusual, by way of explaining what is meant by a general name, to say that it is the name of a *class*. But this, though a convenient mode of expression for some purposes, is objectionable as a definition, since it explains the clearer of two things by the more obscure. It would be more logical to reverse the proposition, and turn it into a definition of the word *class:* "A class is the indefinite multitude of individuals denoted by a general name."

. . .

CONCRETE AND ABSTRACT

The second general division of names is into *concrete* and *abstract.* A concrete name is a name which stands for a thing; an abstract name is a name which stands for an attribute of a thing. Thus *John, the sea, this table,* are names of things. *White,* also, is a name of a thing, or rather of things. Whiteness, again, is the name of a quality or attribute of those things. Man is a name of many things; humanity is a name of an attribute of those things. *Old* is a name of things; *old age* is a name of one of their attributes.

I have used the words concrete and abstract in the sense annexed to them by the schoolmen, who, notwithstanding the imperfections of their philosophy, were unrivalled in the construction of technical language, and whose definitions, in logic at least, though they never went more than a little way into the subject, have seldom, I think, been altered but to be spoiled. A practice, however, has grown up in more modern times, which, if not introduced by Locke, has gained currency chiefly from his example, of applying the expression "abstract name" to all names which are the result of abstraction or generalization, and consequently to all general names, instead of confining it to the names of attributes. The metaphysicians of the Condillac school,—whose admiration of Locke, passing over the profoundest speculations of that truly original genius, usually fastens with peculiar eagerness upon his weakest points,—have gone on imitating him in this abuse of language, until there is now some difficulty in restoring the word to its original signification. A more wanton alteration in the meaning of a word is rarely to be met with; for the expression *general name,* the exact equivalent of which exists in all languages I am acquainted with, was already available for the purpose to which *abstract* has been misappropriated, while the misappropriation leaves that important class of words, the names of attributes, without any compact distinctive appellation. The old acceptation, however, has not gone so completely out of use, as to deprive those who still adhere to it of all chance of being understood. By *abstract,* then, I shall always, in Logic proper, mean the opposite of *concrete;* by an abstract name, the name of an attribute; by a concrete name, the name of an object.

Do abstract names belong to the class of general, or to that of singular names? Some of them are certainly general. I mean those which are names not of one single and definite attribute, but of a class of attributes. Such is the word *colour,* which is a name common to whiteness, redness, &c. Such is even the word whiteness, in respect of the different shades of whiteness to which it is applied in common: the word magnitude, in respect of the various degrees of magnitude and the various dimensions of space; the word weight, in respect of the various degrees of weight. Such also is the word *attribute* itself, the common name of all particular attributes. But when only one attribute, neither variable in degree nor in kind, is designated by the name; as visibleness; tangibleness; equality; squareness; milkwhiteness; then the name can hardly be considered general; for though it denotes an attribute of many different objects, the attribute itself is always conceived as one, not many. To avoid needless logomachies, the best course would probably be to consider these names as neither general nor individual, and to place them in a class apart.

It may be objected to our definition of an abstract name, that not only the names which we have called abstract, but adjectives, which we have placed in the concrete class, are names of attributes; that *white,* for example, is as much the name of the colour as *whiteness* is. But (as before remarked) a word ought to be considered as the name of that which we intend to be understood by it when we put it to its principal use, that is, when we employ it in predication. When we say snow is white, milk is white, linen is white, we do not mean it to be understood that snow, or linen, or milk, is a colour. We mean that they are things having the colour. The reverse is the case with the word whiteness; what we affirm to *be* whiteness is not snow, but the colour of snow. Whiteness, therefore, is the name of the colour exclusively: white is a name of all things whatever having the colour; a name, not of the quality whiteness, but of every white object. It is true, this name was given to all those various objects on account of the quality; and we may therefore say, without impropriety, that the quality forms part of its signification; but a name can only be said to stand for, or to be a name of, the things of which it can be predicated. We shall presently see that all names which can be said to have any signification, all names by applying which to an individual we give any information respecting that individual, may be said to *imply* an attribute of some sort; but they are not names of the attribute; it has its own proper abstract name.

CONNOTATIVE AND NON-CONNOTATIVE

This leads to the consideration of a third great division of names, into *connotative* and *non-connotative,* the latter sometimes, but improperly, called *absolute.* This is one of the most important distinctions which we shall have occasion to point out, and one of those which go deepest into the nature of language.

A non-connotative term is one which signifies a subject only, or an attribute only. A connotative term is one which denotes a subject, and implies an attribute. By a subject is here meant anything which possesses attributes. Thus John, or London, or England, are names which signify a subject only. Whiteness, length, virtue, signify an attribute only. None of these names, therefore, are connotative. But *white, long, virtuous,* are connotative. The word white, denotes all white things, as snow, paper, the foam of the sea, &c., and implies, or in the language of the schoolmen, *connotes,* the attribute *whiteness.* The word white is not predicated of the attribute, but of the subjects, snow, &c.; but when we predicate it of them, we convey the meaning that the attribute whiteness belongs to them. The same may be said of the other words above cited. Virtuous, for example, is the name of a class, which includes Socrates, Howard, the Man of Ross, and an undefinable number of other individuals, past, present, and to come. These individuals, collectively and severally, can alone be said with propriety to be denoted by the word: of them alone can it properly be said to be a name. But it is a name applied to all of them in consequence of an attribute which they are supposed to possess in common, the attribute which has received the name of virtue. It is applied to all beings that are considered to possess this attribute; and to none which are not so considered.

All concrete general names are connotative. The word *man,* for example, denotes Peter, Jane, John, and an indefinite number of other individuals, of whom, taken as a class, it is the name. But it is applied to them, because they possess, and to signify that they possess, certain attributes. These seem to be, corporeity, animal life, rationality, and a certain external form, which for distinction we call the human. Every existing thing, which possessed all these attributes, would be called a man; and anything which possessed none of them, or only one, or two, or even three of them without the fourth, would not be so called. For example, if in the interior of Africa there were to be discovered a race of animals possessing reason equal to that of human beings, but with the form of an elephant, they would not be called men. Swift's Houyhnhnms would not be so called. Or if such newly-discovered beings possessed the form of man without any vestige of reason, it is probable that some other name than that of man would be found for them. How it happens that there can be any doubt about the matter, will appear hereafter. The word *man,* therefore, signifies all these attributes, and all subjects which possess these attributes. But it can be predicated only of the subjects. What we call men, are the subjects, the individual Stiles and Nokes; not the qualities by which their humanity is constituted. The name, therefore, is said to signify the subjects *directly,* the attributes *indirectly;* it *denotes* the subjects, and implies, or involves, or indicates, or as we shall say henceforth *connotes,* the attributes. It is a connotative name.

It has been seen that all concrete general names are connotative. Even abstract names, though the names only of attributes, may in some instances be justly considered as connotative; for attributes themselves may have attributes ascribed to them; and a word which denotes attributes may connote an attribute of those attributes. Of this description, for example, is such a word as *fault;* equivalent to *bad* or *hurtful quality*. This word is a name common to many attributes, and connotes hurtfulness, an attribute of those various attributes. When, for example, we say that slowness, in a horse, is a fault, we do not mean that the slow movement, the actual change of place of the slow horse, is a bad thing, but that the property or peculiarity of the horse, from which it derives that name, the quality of being a slow mover, is an undesirable peculiarity.

In regard to those concrete names which are not general but individual, a distinction must be made.

Proper names are not connotative: they denote the individuals who are called by them; but they do not indicate or imply any attributes as belonging to those individuals. When we name a child by the name Paul, or a dog by the name Caesar, these names are simply marks used to enable those individuals to be made subjects of discourse. It may be said, indeed, that we must have had some reason for giving them those names rather than any others; and this is true; but the name, once given, is independent of the reason. A man may have been named John, because that was the name of his father; a town may have been named Dartmouth, because it is situated at the mouth of the Dart. But it is no part of the signification of the word John, that the father of the person so called bore the same name; nor even of the word Dartmouth, to be situated at the mouth of the Dart. If sand should choke up the mouth of the river, or an earthquake change its course, and remove it to a distance from the town, the name of the town would not necessarily be changed. That fact, therefore, can form no part of the signification of the word; for otherwise, when the fact confessedly ceased to be true, no one would any longer think of applying the name. Proper names are attached to the objects themselves, and are not dependent on the continuance of any attribute of the object.

But there is another kind of names, which, although they are individual names, that is, predicable only of one object, are really connotative. For, though we may give to an individual a name utterly unmeaning, which we call a proper name—a word which answers the purpose of showing what thing it is we are talking about, but not of telling anything about it; yet a name peculiar to an individual is not necessarily of this description. It may be significant of some attribute, or some union of attributes, which, being possessed by no object but one, determines the name exclusively to that individual. "The sun" is a name of this description; "God," when used by a monotheist, is another. These, however, are scarcely examples of what we are now attempting to illustrate, being, in strictness of language, general, not individual names: for, however they may be *in fact* predicable only of one object, there is nothing in the meaning of the words themselves which implies this: and, accordingly, when we are imagining and not affirming, we may speak of many suns; and the majority of mankind have believed, and still believe, that there are many gods. But it is easy to produce words which are real instances of connotative individual names. It may be part of the meaning of the connotative name itself, that there can exist but one individual possessing the attribute which it connotes: as, for instance, "the *only* son of John Stiles;" "the *first* emperor of Rome." Or the attribute connoted may be a connexion with some determinate event, and the connexion may be of such a kind as only one individual could have; or may at least be such as only one individual actually had; and this may be implied in the form of the expression. "The father of Socrates" is an example of the one kind (since Socrates could not have had two fathers); "the author of the Iliad," "the murderer of Henri Quatre," of the second. For, though it is conceivable that more persons than one might have participated in the authorship of the Iliad, or in the murder of Henri Quatre, the employment of the article *the* implies that, in fact, this was not the case. What is here done by the word *the,* is done in other cases by the context: thus, "Caesar's army" is an individual name, if it appears from the context that the army meant is that which Caesar commanded in a particular battle.

. . .

From the preceding observations it will easily be collected, that whenever the names given to objects convey any information, that is, whenever they have properly any meaning, the meaning resides not in what they *denote,* but in what they *connote.* The only names of objects which connote nothing are *proper* names; and these have, strictly speaking, no signification.

If, like the robber in the Arabian Nights, we make a mark with chalk on a house to enable us to know it again, the mark has a purpose, but it has not properly any meaning. The chalk does not declare anything about the house; it does not mean, This is such a person's house, or This is a house which contains booty. The object of making the mark is merely distinction. I say to myself, All these houses are so nearly alike that if I lose sight of them I shall not again be able to distinguish that which I am now looking at, from any of the others; I must therefore contrive to make the appearance of this one house unlike that of the others, that I may hereafter know when I see the mark—not indeed any attribute of the house—but simply that it is the same house which I am now looking at. Morgiana chalked all the other houses in a similar manner, and defeated the scheme: how? simply by obliterating the difference of appearance between that house and the others. The chalk was still there, but it no longer served the purpose of a distinctive mark.

When we impose a proper name, we perform an operation in some degree analogous to what the robber intended in chalking the house. We put a mark, not indeed upon the object itself, but, so to speak, upon the idea of the object. A proper name is but an unmeaning mark which we connect in our minds with the idea of the object, in order that whenever the mark meets our eyes or occurs to our thoughts, we may think of that individual object. Not being attached to the thing itself, it does not, like the chalk, enable us to distinguish the object when we see it; but it enables us to distinguish it when it is spoken of, either in the records of our own experience, or in the discourse of others; to know that what we find asserted in any proposition of which it is the subject, is asserted of the individual thing with which we were previously acquainted.

When we predicate of anything its proper name; when we say, pointing to a man, this is Brown or Smith, or pointing to a city, that it is York, we do not, merely by so doing, convey to the reader any information about them, except that those are their names. By enabling him to identify the individuals, we may connect them with information previously possessed by him; by saying, This is York, we may tell him that it contains the Minster. But this is in virtue of what he has previously heard concerning York; not by anything implied in the name. It is otherwise when objects are spoken of by connotative names. When we say, The town is built of marble, we give the hearer what may be entirely new information, and this merely by the signification of the many-worded connotative name, "built of marble." Such names are not signs of the mere objects, invented because we have occasion to think and speak of those objects individually; but signs which accompany an attribute: a kind of livery in which the attribute clothes all objects which are recognised as possessing it. They are not mere marks, but more, that is to say, significant marks; and the connotation is what constitutes their significance.

As a proper name is said to be the name of the one individual which it is predicated of, so (as well from the importance of adhering to analogy, as for the other reasons formerly assigned) a connotative name ought to be considered a name of all the various individuals which it is predicable of, or in other words *denotes,* and not of what it connotes. But by learning what things it is a name of, we do not learn the meaning of the name: for to the same thing we may, with equal propriety, apply many names, not equivalent in meaning. Thus, I call a certain man by the name Sophroniscus: I call him by another name, The father of Socrates. Both these are names of the same individual, but their meaning is altogether different; they are applied to that individual for two different purposes: the one, merely to distinguish him from other persons who are spoken of; the other to indicate a fact relating to him, the fact that Socrates was his son. I further apply to him these other expressions: a man, a Greek, an Athenian, a sculptor, an old man, an honest man, a brave man. All these are, or may be, names of Sophroniscus, not indeed of him alone, but of him and each of an indefinite number of other human beings. Each of these names is applied to Sophroniscus for a different reason, and by each whoever understands its meaning is apprised of a distinct fact or number of facts concerning him; but those who knew nothing about the names except that they were applicable to Sophroniscus, would be altogether ignorant of their meaning. It is even possible that I might know every single individual of whom a given name could be with truth affirmed, and yet could not be said to know the meaning of the name. A child knows who are its brothers and sisters, long before it has any definite conception of the nature of the facts which are involved in the signification of those words.

In some cases it is not easy to decide precisely how much a particular word does or does not connote; that is, we do not exactly know (the case not having arisen) what degree of difference in the object would occasion a difference in the name. Thus, it is clear that the word man, besides animal life and rationality, connotes also a certain external form; but it would be impossible to say precisely what form; that is, to decide how great a deviation from the form ordinarily found in the beings whom we are accustomed to call men, would suffice in a newly-discovered race to make us refuse them the name of man. Rationality, also, being a quality which admits of degrees, it has never been settled what is the lowest degree of that quality which would entitle any creature to be considered a human being. In all such cases, the meaning of the general name is so far unsettled and vague; mankind have not come to any positive agreement about the matter. When we come to treat of Classification, we shall have occasion to show under what conditions this vagueness may exist without practical inconvenience; and cases will appear in which the ends of language are better promoted by it than by complete precision; in order that, in natural history for instance, individuals or species of no very marked character may be ranged with those more strongly characterized individuals or species to which, in all their properties taken together, they bear the nearest resemblance.

Gottlob Frege

On Sense and Nominatum

Now it is plausible to connect with a sign (name, word combination, expression) not only the designated object, which may be called the nominatum of the sign, but also the sense (connotation, meaning) of the sign in which is contained the manner and context of presentation. Accordingly, in our examples the *nominata* of the expressions 'the point of intersection of a and b' and 'the point of intersection of b and c' would be the same;—not their senses. The nominata of 'evening star' and 'morning star' are the same but not their senses.

From what has been said it is clear that I here understand by 'sign' or 'name' any expression which functions as a proper name, whose nominatum accordingly is a definite object (in the widest sense of this word). But no concept or relation is under consideration here. These matters are to be dealt with in another essay. The designation of a single object may consist of several words or various signs. For brevity's sake, any such designation will be considered as a proper name.

The sense of a proper name is grasped by everyone who knows the language or the totality of designations of which the proper name is a part;[1] this,

[1] In the case of genuinely proper names like 'Aristotle' opinions as regards their sense may diverge. As such may, e. g., be suggested: Plato's disciple and the teacher of Alexander the Great. Whoever accepts this sense will interpret the meaning of the statement "Aristotle was born in Stagira" differently from one who interpreted the sense of 'Aristotle' as the Stagirite teacher of Alexander the Great. As long as the nominatum remains the same, these fluctuations in sense are tolerable. But they should be avoided in the system of a demonstrative science and should not appear in a perfect language.

From "On Sense and Nominatum," by Gottlob Frege, translated by Herbert Feigl, in *Readings in Philosophical Analysis,* edited by Herbert Feigl and Wilfrid Sellars. Copyright, 1949, Appleton-Century-Crofts, Inc. Reprinted by permission of Appleton-Century-Crofts. The article was originally published as "Ueber Sinn und Bedeutung," *Zeitschr. f. Philos. u. Philos. Kritik,* Vol. 100 (1892).

Gottlob Frege (1848–1925) was Professor of Mathematics at the University of Jena, Germany.

however, illuminates the nominatum, if there is any, in a very one-sided fashion. A complete knowledge of the nominatum would require that we could tell immediately in the case of any given sense whether it belongs to the nominatum. This we shall never be able to do.

The regular connection between a sign, its sense and its nominatum is such that there corresponds a definite sense to the sign and to this sense there corresponds again a definite nominatum; whereas not one sign only belongs to one nominatum (object). In different languages, and even in one language, the same sense is represented by different expressions. It is true, there are exceptions to this rule. Certainly there should be a definite sense to each expression in a complete configuration of signs, but the natural languages in many ways fall short of this requirement. We must be satisfied if the same word, at least in the same context, has the same sense. It can perhaps be granted that an expression has a sense if it is formed in a grammatically correct manner and stands for a proper name. But as to whether there is a denotation corresponding to the connotation is hereby not decided. The words 'the heavenly body which has the greatest distance from the earth' have a sense; but it is very doubtful as to whether they have a nominatum. The expression 'the series with the least convergence' has a sense; but it can be proved that it has no nominatum, since for any given convergent series, one can find another one that is less convergent. Therefore the grasping of a sense does not with certainty warrant a corresponding nominatum.

When words are used in the customary manner then what is talked about are their nominata. But it may happen that one wishes to speak about the words themselves or about their senses. The first case occurs when one quotes someone else's words in direct (ordinary) discourse. In this case one's own words immediately name (denote) the words of the other person and only the latter words have the usual nominata. We thus have signs of signs. In writing we make use of quotes enclosing the word-icons. A word-icon in quotes must therefore not be taken in the customary manner.

If we wish to speak of the sense of an expression 'A' we can do this simply through the locution 'the sense of the expression 'A''. In indirect (oblique) discourse we speak of the sense, e.g., of the words of someone else. From this it becomes clear that also in indirect discourse words do not have their customary nominata; they here name what customarily would be their sense. In order to formulate this succinctly we shall say: words in indirect discourse are used *indirectly,* or have *indirect* nominata. Thus we distinguish the *customary* from the *indirect* nominatum of a word; and similarly, its *customary* sense from its *indirect* sense. The indirect nominatum of a word is therefore its customary sense. Such exceptions must be kept in mind if one wishes correctly to comprehend the manner of connection between signs, senses and nominata in any given case.

Both the nominatum and the sense of a sign must be distinguished from the associated image. If the nominatum of a sign is an object of sense perception, my image of the latter is an inner picture [2] arisen from memories of sense im-

[2] With the images we can align also the percepts in which the sense impressions and activities themselves take the place of those traces left in the mind. For our purposes the difference is unimportant, especially since besides sensations and activities recollections of such help in completing the intuitive presentation. 'Percept' may also be understood as the object, inasmuch as it is spatial or capable of sensory apprehension.

pressions and activities of mine, internal or external. Frequently this image is suffused with feelings; the definiteness of its various parts may vary and fluctuate. Even with the same person the same sense is not always accompanied by the same image. The image is subjective; the image of one person is not that of another. Hence, the various differences between the images connected with one and the same sense. A painter, a rider, a zoölogist probably connect very different images with the name 'Bucephalus'. The image thereby differs essentially from the connotation of a sign, which latter may well be common property of many and is therefore not a part or mode of the single person's mind; for it cannot well be denied that mankind possesses a common treasure of thoughts which is transmitted from generation to generation.[3]

While, accordingly, there is no objection to speak without qualification of the sense in regard to images, we must, to be precise, add *whose* images they are and at what time they occur. One might say: just as words are connected with different images in two different persons, the same holds of the senses also. Yet this difference would consist merely in the manner of association. It does not prevent both from apprehending the same sense, but they cannot have the same image. *Si duo idem faciunt, non est idem.* When two persons imagine the same thing, each still has his own image. It is true, occasionally we can detect differences in the images or even in the sensations of different persons. But an accurate comparison is impossible because these images cannot be had together in one consciousness.

. . .

We can now recognize three levels of differences of words, expressions and complete sentences. The difference may concern at most the imagery, or else the sense but not the nominatum, or finally also the nominatum. In regard to the first level, we must note that, owing to the uncertain correlation of images with words, a difference may exist for one person that another does not discover. The difference of a translation from the original should properly not go beyond the first level. Among the differences possible in this connection we mention the shadings and colorings which poetry seeks to impart to the senses. These shadings and colorings are not objective. Every listener or reader has to add them in accordance with the hints of the poet or speaker. Surely, art would be impossible without some kinship among human imageries; but just how far the intentions of the poet are realized can never be exactly ascertained.

We shall henceforth no longer refer to the images and picturizations; they were discussed only lest the image evoked by a word be confused with its sense or its nominatum.

In order to facilitate brief and precise expression we may lay down the following formulations:

A proper name (word, sign, sign-compound, expression) expresses its sense, and designates or signifies its nominatum. We let a *sign express* its sense and *designate* its nominatum.

. . .

[3] It is therefore inexpedient to designate fundamentally different things by the one word 'image' (or 'idea').

Thus far we have considered sense and nominatum only of such expressions, words and signs which we called proper names. We are now going to inquire into the sense and the nominatum of a whole declarative sentence. Such a sentence contains a proposition.[4] Is this thought to be regarded as the sense or the nominatum of the sentence? Let us for the moment assume that the sentence has a nominatum! If we then substitute a word in it by another word with the same nominatum but with a different sense, then this substitution cannot affect the nominatum of the sentence. But we realize that in such cases the proposition is changed; e. g., the proposition of the sentence "the morning star is a body illuminated by the sun" is different from that of "the evening star is a body illuminated by the sun". Someone who did not know that the evening star is the same as the morning star could consider the one proposition true and the other false. The proposition can therefore not be the nominatum of the sentence; it will instead have to be regarded as its sense. But what about the nominatum? Can we even ask this question? A sentence as a whole has perhaps only sense and no nominatum? It may in any case be expected that there are such sentences, just as there are constituents of sentences which do have sense but no nominatum. Certainly, sentences containing proper names without nominata must be of this type. The sentence "Odysseus deeply asleep was disembarked at Ithaca" obviously has a sense. But since it is doubtful as to whether the name 'Odysseus' occurring in this sentence has a nominatum, so it is also doubtful that the whole sentence has one. However, it is certain that whoever seriously regards the sentence either as true or as false also attributes to the name 'Odysseus' a nominatum, not only a sense; for it is obviously the nominatum of this name to which the predicate is either ascribed or denied. He who does not acknowledge the nominatum cannot ascribe or deny a predicate to it. It might be urged that the consideration of the nominatum of the name is going farther than is necessary; one could be satisfied with the sense, if one stayed with the proposition. If all that mattered were only the sense of the sentence (i. e., the proposition) then it would be unnecessary to be concerned with the nominata of the sentence-components, for only the sense of the components can be relevant for the sense of the sentence. The proposition remains the same, no matter whether or not the name 'Odysseus' has a nominatum. The fact that we are at all concerned about the nominatum of a sentence-component indicates that we generally acknowledge or postulate a nominatum for the sentence itself. The proposition loses in interest as soon as we recognize that one of its parts is lacking a nominatum. We may therefore be justified to ask for a nominatum of a sentence, in addition to its sense. But why do we wish that every proper name have not only a sense but also a nominatum? Why is the proposition alone not sufficient? We answer: because what matters to us is the truth-value. This, however, is not always the case. In listening to an epic, for example, we are fascinated by the euphony of the language and also by the sense of the sentences and by the images and emotions evoked. In turning to the question of truth we disregard the artistic appreciation and pursue scientific considerations. Whether the name 'Odysseus' has a nominatum is therefore immaterial to us as long as we accept

[4] By 'proposition' I do not refer to the subjective activity of thinking but rather to its objective content which is capable of being the common property of many.

the poem as a work of art.[5] Thus, it is the striving for truth which urges us to penetrate beyond the sense to the nominatum.

We have realized that we are to look for the nominatum of a sentence whenever the nominata of the sentence-components are the thing that matters; and that is the case whenever and only when we ask for the truth value.

Thus we find ourselves persuaded to accept the *truth-value* of a sentence as its nominatum. By the truth-value of a sentence I mean the circumstance of its being true or false. There are no other truth-values. For brevity's sake I shall call the one the True and the other the False. Every declarative sentence, in which what matters are the nominata of the words, is therefore to be considered as a proper name; and its nominatum, if there is any, is either the True or the False. These two objects are recognized, even if only tacitly, by everyone who at all makes judgments, holds anything as true, thus even by the skeptic. To designate truth-values as objects may thus far appear as a capricious idea or as a mere play on words, from which no important conclusion should be drawn. What I call an object can be discussed only in connection with the nature of concepts and relations. That I will reserve for another essay. But this might be clear even here: in every judgment [6]—no matter how obvious—a step is made from the level of propositions to the level of the nominata (the objective facts).

. . .

If our conjecture (that the nominatum of a sentence is its truth value) is correct, then the truth-value must remain unchanged if a sentence-component is replaced by an expression with the same nominatum but with a different sense. Indeed, Leibnitz declares: *"Eadem sunt, quae sibi mutuo substitui possunt, salva veritate"*. What else, except the truth-value, could be found, which quite generally belongs to every sentence and regarding which the nominata of the components are relevant and which would remain invariant for substitutions of the type indicated?

Now if the truth-value of a sentence is its nominatum, then all true sentences have the same nominatum, and likewise all false ones. This implies that all detail has been blurred in the nominatum of a sentence. What interests us can therefore never be merely the nominatum; but the proposition alone does not give knowledge; only the proposition together with its nominatum, i. e., its truth-value, does. Judging may be viewed as a movement from a proposition to its nominatum, i. e., its truth-value. Of course this is not intended as a definition. Judging is indeed something peculiar and unique. One might say that judging consists in the discerning of parts within the truth-value. This discernment occurs through recourse to the proposition. Every sense that belongs to a truth-value would correspond in its own manner to the analysis. I have, however, used the word 'part' in a particular manner here: I have transferred the relation of whole and part from the sentence to its nominatum. This I did by viewing the nominatum of a word as part of the nominatum of a

[5] It would be desirable to have an expression for signs which have sense only. If we call them 'icons' then the words of an actor on the stage would be icons; even the actor himself would be an icon.

[6] A judgment is not merely the apprehension of a thought or proposition but the acknowledgment of its truth.

sentence, when the word itself is part of the sentence. True enough, this way of putting things is objectionable since as regards the nominatum the whole and one part of it does not determine the other part; and also because the word 'part' in reference to bodies has a different customary usage. A special expression should be coined for what has been suggested above.

We shall now further examine the conjecture that the truth-value of a sentence is its nominatum. We have found that the truth-value of a sentence remains unaltered if an expression within the sentence is replaced by a synonymous one. But we have as yet not considered the case in which the expression-to-be-replaced is itself a sentence. If our view is correct, then the truth-value of a sentence, which contains another sentence as a part, must remain unaltered when we substitute for the part another of the same truth-value. Exceptions are to be expected if the whole or the part are either in direct or indirect discourse; for as we have seen, in that case the nominata of the words are not the usual ones. A sentence in direct discourse nominates again a sentence but in indirect discourse it nominates a proposition.

Our attention is thus directed to subordinate sentences (i. e., dependent clauses). These present themselves of course as parts of a sentence-structure which from a logical point of view appears also as a sentence, and indeed as if it were a main clause. But here we face the question whether in the case of dependent clauses it also holds that their nominata are truth-values. We know already that this is not the case with sentences in indirect discourse. The grammarians view clauses as representatives of sentence-parts and divide them accordingly into subjective, relative, and adverbial clauses. This might suggest that the nominatum of a clause is not a truth-value but rather that it is of similar nature as that of a noun or of an adjective or of an adverb; in short, of a sentence-part whose sense is not a proposition but only part thereof. Only a thorough investigation can provide clarity in this matter. We shall herein not follow strictly along grammatical lines, but rather group together what is logically of comparable type. Let us first seek out such instances in which, as we just surmised, the sense of a clause is not a self-sufficient proposition.

Among the abstract clauses beginning with 'that' there is also the indirect discourse, of which we have seen that in it the words have their indirect (oblique) nominata which coincide with what are ordinarily their senses. In this case then the clause has as its nominatum a proposition, not a truth-value; its sense is not a proposition but it is the sense of the words 'the proposition that . . . ', which is only a part of the proposition corresponding to the total sentence-structure. This occurs in connection with 'to say', 'to hear', 'to opine', 'to be convinced', 'to infer' and similar words.[7] The situation is different, and rather complicated in connection with such words as 'to recognize', 'to know', 'to believe', a matter to be considered later.

One can see that in these cases the nominatum of the clause indeed consists in the proposition, because whether that proposition is true or false is immaterial for the truth of the whole sentence. Compare, e. g., the following two sentences: "Copernicus believed that the planetary orbits are circles" and "Copernicus believed that the appearance of the sun's motion is produced by the real motion of the earth". Here the one clause can be substituted for the

[7] In "*A* lied, that he had seen *B*" the clause denotes a proposition of which it is said, firstly, that *A* asserted it as true, and, secondly, that *A* was convinced of its falsity.

other without affecting the truth. The sense of the principal sentence together with the clause is the single proposition; and the truth of the whole implies neither the truth nor the falsity of the clause. In cases of this type it is not permissible to replace in the clause one expression by another of the same nominatum. Such replacement may be made only by expressions of the same indirect nominatum, i. e., of the same customary sense. If one were to infer: the nominatum of a sentence is not its truth-value ("because then a sentence could always be replaced by another with the same truth-value"), he would prove too much; one could just as well maintain that the nominatum of the word 'morning star' is not Venus, for one cannot always substitute 'Venus' for 'morning star'. The only correct conclusion is that the nominatum of a sentence is *not always* its truth-value, and that 'morning star' does not always nominate the planet Venus; for this is indeed not the case when the word is used with its indirect nominatum. Such an exceptional case is before us in the clauses just considered, whose nominatum is a proposition.

When we say "it seems that . . ." then we mean to say "it seems to me that . . ." or "I opine that . . .". This is the same case over again. Similarly with expressions such as: 'to be glad', 'to regret', 'to approve', 'to disapprove', 'to hope', 'to fear'. When Wellington, toward the end of the battle of Belle-Alliance was glad that the Prussians were coming, the ground of his rejoicing was a conviction. Had he actually been deceived, he would not have been less glad, as long as his belief persisted; and before he arrived at the conviction that the Prussians were coming he could not have been glad about it, even if in fact they were already approaching.

Just as a conviction or a belief may be the ground of a sentiment, so it can also be the ground of another conviction such as in inference. In the sentence "Columbus inferred from the roundness of the earth that he could, traveling westward, reach India" we have, as nominata of its parts two propositions: that the earth is round, and that Columbus traveling westward could reach India. What matters here is only that Columbus was convinced of the one as well as of the other and that the one conviction furnishes the ground for the other. It is irrelevant for the truth of our sentence whether the earth is really round and whether Columbus could have reached India in the manner he fancied. But it is not irrelevant whether for 'the earth' we substitute 'the planet accompanied by one satellite whose diameter is larger than one-fourth of its own diameter'. Here also we deal with the indirect nominata of the words.

Adverbial clauses of purpose with 'so that', likewise belong here; obviously the purpose is a proposition; therefore: indirect nominata of the words, expressed in subjunctive form.

The clause with 'that' after 'to command', 'to request', 'to forbid' would appear in imperative form in direct discourse. Imperatives have no nominata; they have only sense. It is true, commands or requests are not propositions, but they are of the same type as propositions. Therefore the words in the dependent clauses after 'to command', 'to request', etc. have indirect nominata. The nominatum of such a sentence is thus not a truth-value but a command, a request, and the like.

We meet a similar situation in the case of dependent questions in phrases like 'to doubt if', 'not to know what'. It is easy to see that the words, here too, have to be interpreted in terms of their indirect nominata. The dependent interrogatory clauses containing 'who', 'what', 'where', 'when', 'how', 'whereby', etc. often apparently approximate closely adverbial clauses in which the words have their ordinary nominata. These cases are linguistically distinguished through the mode of the verb. In the subjunctive we have a dependent question and the indirect nominata of the words, so that a proper name cannot generally be replaced by another of the same object.

In the instances thus far considered the words in the clause had indirect nominata; this made it intelligible that the nominatum of the clause itself is indirect, i. e., not a truth-value, but a proposition, a command, a request, a question. The clause could be taken as a noun; one might even say, as a proper name of that proposition, command, etc., in whose rôle it functions in the context of the sentence-structure.

We are now going to consider clauses of another type, in which the words do have their customary nominata although there does not appear a proposition as the sense or a truth-value as the nominatum. How this is possible will best be elucidated by examples.

"He who discovered the elliptical shape of the planetary orbits, died in misery".

If, in this example, the sense of the clause were a proposition, it would have to be expressible also in a principal sentence. But this cannot be done because the grammatical subject 'he who' has no independent sense. It merely mediates the relations to the second part of the sentence: 'died in misery'. Therefore the sense of the clause is not a complete proposition and its nominatum is not a truth-value, but Kepler. It might be objected that the sense of the whole does include a proposition as its part; namely, that there was someone who first recognized the elliptical shape of the planetary orbits; for if we accept the whole as true we cannot deny this part. Indubitably so; but only because otherwise the clause "he who discovered the elliptical shape, etc." would have no nominatum. Whenever something is asserted then the presupposition taken for granted is that the employed proper names, simple or compound, have nominata. Thus, if we assert "Kepler died in misery" it is presupposed that the name 'Kepler' designates something. However, the proposition that the name 'Kepler' designates something is, the foregoing notwithstanding, not contained in the sense of the sentence "Kepler died in misery". If that were the case the denial would not read "Kepler did not die in misery" but "Kepler did not die in misery, or the name 'Kepler' is without nominatum". That the name 'Kepler' designates something is rather the presupposition of the assertion "Kepler died in misery" as well as of its denial. Now, it is a defect of languages that expressions are possible within them, which, in their grammatical form, seemingly determined to designate an object, nevertheless do not fulfill this condition in special cases; because this depends on the truth of the sentence. Thus it depends upon the truth of the sentence "there was someone who discovered the ellipticity of the orbits" whether the clause 'he who discovered the ellipticity of the orbits' really designates an object, or else merely evokes the appearance thereof, while indeed being without nominatum. Thus it may seem as if our clause, as part of its sense, contained the proposition that there existed someone who discovered the ellipticity of the orbits. If this were so, then the denial would have to read "he who first recognized the ellipticity of the orbits did not die in misery, or there was no one who discovered the ellipticity of the orbits." This, it is obvious, hinges upon an imperfection of language of which, by the way, even the symbolic language of analysis is not entirely free; there, also, sign compounds may occur which appear as if they designated something, but which at least hitherto are without nominatum, e. g., divergent infinite series. This can be avoided, e. g., through the special convention that the nominatum of divergent infinite series be the number 0. It is to be demanded that in a logically perfect language (logical symbolism) every expression constructed as a proper name in a grammatically correct manner out of already introduced symbols, in fact designate an object; and that no symbol be introduced as a proper name without assurance that it have a nominatum. It is customary in logic texts to warn against the ambiguity of expressions as a source of fallacies. I deem it at least as appropriate to issue a warning against apparent proper names that have no nominata. The history of mathematics has many a tale to tell of errors which originated from this source. The demagogic misuse is close (perhaps closer) at hand as in the case of ambiguous expressions. 'The will of the people' may serve as an example in this regard; for it is easily established that there is no generally accepted nominatum of that expression. Thus it is obviously not without importance to obstruct once for all the source of these errors, at least as regards their occurrence in science. Then such objections as the one discussed above will become impossible, for then it will be seen that whether a proper name has a nominatum can never depend upon the truth of a proposition.

Our considerations may be extended from these subjective clauses to the logically related relative and adverbial clauses.

. . .

We may hope we have considered the simple types of sentences. Let us now review what we have found out!

The sense of a subordinate clause is usually not a proposition but only part of one. Its nominatum is therefore not a truth-value. The reason for this is *either:* that the words in the subordinate clause have only indirect nominata, so that the nominatum, not the sense, of the clause is a proposition, *or,* that the clause, because of a contained indeterminately indicating constituent, is incomplete, such that only together with the principal clause does it express a proposition. However, there are also instances in which the sense of the dependent clause is a complete proposition, and in this case it can be replaced by another clause of the same truth-value without altering the truth-value of the whole; that is, inasmuch as there are no grammatical obstacles in the way.

. . .

It is difficult to exhaust all possibilities that present themselves in language; but I hope, in essence at least, to have disclosed the reasons why, in view of the invariance of the truth of a whole sentence, a clause cannot always be replaced by another of the same truth-value. These reasons are:

1. that the clause does not denote a truth-value in that it expresses only a part of a proposition;

2. that the clause, while it does denote a truth-value, is not restricted to this function in that its sense comprises, beside one proposition, also a part of another.

The first case holds

a. with the indirect nominata of the words;
b. if a part of the sentence indicates only indirectly without being a proper name.

In the second case the clause is to be interpreted in a twofold manner; namely, once with its usual nominatum; the other time with its indirect nominatum; or else, the sense of a part of the clause may simultaneously be a constituent of another proposition which, together with the sense expressed in the dependent clause, amounts to the total sense of the main and the dependent clause.

This makes it sufficiently plausible that instances in which a clause is not replaceable by another of the same truth-value do not disprove our view that the nominatum of a sentence is its truth-value and its sense a proposition.

Bertrand Russell

On Denoting

By a "denoting phrase" I mean a phrase such as any one of the following: a man, some man, any man, every man, all men, the present King of England, the present King of France, the centre of mass of the Solar System at the first instant of the twentieth century, the revolution of the earth round the sun, the revolution of the sun round the earth. Thus a phrase is denoting solely in virtue of its *form*. We may distinguish three cases: (1) A phrase may be denoting, and yet not denote anything; e.g., "the present King of France". (2) A phrase may denote one definite object; e.g., "the present King of England" denotes a certain man. (3) A phrase may denote ambiguously; e.g., "a man" denotes not many men, but an ambiguous man. The interpretation of such phrases is a matter of considerable difficulty; indeed, it is very hard to frame any theory not susceptible of formal refutation. All the difficulties with which I am acquainted are met, so far as I can discover, by the theory which I am about to explain.

The subject of denoting is of very great importance not only in logic and

From Bertrand Russell, *Logic and Knowledge,* published by George Allen & Unwin Ltd., London, 1956, and reprinted with their permission. This selection originally appeared as "On Denoting," *Mind,* Vol. 14 (1905).

Bertrand Russell (1872–) was for many years Fellow of Trinity College, Cambridge, and Lecturer in Philosophy at the University.

mathematics, but also in theory of knowledge. For example, we know that the centre of mass of the Solar System at a definite instant is some definite point, and we can affirm a number of propositions about it; but we have no immediate *acquaintance* with this point, which is only known to us by description. The distinction between *acquaintance* and *knowledge about* is the distinction between the things we have presentations of, and the things we only reach by means of denoting phrases. It often happens that we know that a certain phrase denotes unambiguously, although we have no acquaintance with what it denotes; this occurs in the above case of the centre of mass. In perception we have acquaintance with the objects of perception, and in thought we have acquaintance with objects of a more abstract logical character but we do not necessarily have acquaintance with the objects denoted by phrases composed of words with whose meanings we are acquainted. To take a very important instance: There seems no reason to believe that we are ever acquainted with other people's minds, seeing that these are not directly perceived; hence what we know about them is obtained through denoting. All thinking has to start from acquaintance; but it succeeds in thinking *about* many things with which we have no acquaintance.

The course of my argument will be as follows. I shall begin by stating the theory I intend to advocate; [1] I shall then discuss the theories of Frege and Meinong, showing why neither of them satisfies me; then I shall give the grounds in favour of my theory; and finally I shall briefly indicate the philosophical consequences of my theory.

My theory, briefly, is as follows. I take the notion of the *variable* as fundamental; I use "C (x)" to mean a proposition [2] in which x is a constituent, where x, the variable, is essentially and wholly undetermined. Then we can consider the two notions "C (x) is always true" and "C (x) is sometimes true".[3] Then *everything* and *nothing* and *something* (which are the most primitive of denoting phrases) are to be interpreted as follows:

C (everything) means "C (x) is always true";
C (nothing) means " 'C (x) is false' is always true";
C (something) means "It is false that 'C (x) is false' is always true".[4]

Here the notion "C (x) is always true" is taken as ultimate and indefinable, and the others are defined by means of it. *Everything, nothing,* and *something,* are not assumed to have any meaning in isolation, but a meaning is assigned to *every* proposition in which they occur. This is the principle of the theory of denoting I wish to advocate: that denoting phrases never have any meaning in themselves, but that every proposition in whose verbal expression they occur has a meaning. The difficulties concerning denoting are, I believe, all the result of a wrong analysis of propositions whose verbal expressions contain denoting phrases. The proper analysis, if I am not mistaken, may be further set forth as follows.

[1] I have discussed this subject in *Principles of Mathematics,* ch. v, and § 476. The theory there advocated is very nearly the same as Frege's, and is quite different from the theory to be advocated in what follows.
[2] More exactly, a propositional function.
[3] The second of these can be defined by means of the first, if we take it to mean, "It is not true that 'C (x) is false' is always true".
[4] I shall sometimes use, instead of this complicated phrase, the phrase "C (x) is not always false," or "C (x) is sometimes true," supposed *defined* to mean the same as the complicated phrase.

Suppose now we wish to interpret the proposition, "I met a man". If this is true, I met some definite man; but that is not what I affirm. What I affirm is, according to the theory I advocate:

"'I met *x*, and *x* is human' is not always false".

Generally, defining the class of men as the class of objects having the predicate *human,* we say that:

"C (a man)" means "'C (*x*) and *x* is human' is not always false".

This leaves "a man," by itself, wholly destitute of meaning, but gives a meaning to every proposition in whose verbal expression "a man" occurs.

. . .

It remains to interpret phrases containing *the.* These are by far the most interesting and difficult of denoting phrases. Take as an instance "the father of Charles II was executed". This asserts that there was an *x* who was the father of Charles II and was executed. Now *the,* when it is strictly used, involves uniqueness; we do, it is true, speak of *"the* son of So-and-so" even when So-and-so has several sons, but it would be more correct to say *"a* son of So-and-so". Thus for our purposes we take *the* as involving uniqueness. Thus when we say "*x* was *the* father of Charles II" we not only assert that *x* had a certain relation to Charles II, but also that nothing else had this relation. The relation in question, without the assumption of uniqueness, and without any denoting phrases, is expressed by *"x begat Charles II"*. To get an equivalent of "*x* was the father of Charles II," we must add, "If *y* is other than *x*, *y* did not beget Charles II," or, what is equivalent, "If *y* begat Charles II, *y* is identical with *x*". Hence "*x* is the father of Charles II" becomes "*x* begat Charles II; and 'if *y* begat Charles II, *y* is identical with *x*' is always true of *y*".

Thus "the father of Charles II was executed" becomes:

"It is not always false of *x* that *x* begat Charles II and that *x* was executed and that 'if *y* begat Charles II, *y* is identical with *x*' is always true of *y*".

This may seem a somewhat incredible interpretation; but I am not at present giving reasons, I am merely *stating* the theory.

To interpret "C (the father of Charles II)," where C stands for any statement about him, we have only to substitute C (*x*) for "*x* was executed" in the above. Observe that, according to the above interpretation, whatever statement C may be, "C (the father of Charles II)" implies:

"It is not always false of *x* that 'if *y* begat Charles II, *y* is identical with *x*' is always true of *y*,"

which is what is expressed in common language by "Charles II had one father and no more". Consequently if this condition fails, *every* proposition of the form "C (the father of Charles II)" is false. Thus, e.g., every proposition of the form "C (the present King of France)" is false. This is a great advantage in the present theory. I shall show later that it is not contrary to the law of contradiction, as might be at first supposed.

The above gives a reduction of all propositions in which denoting phrases occur to forms in which no such phrases occur. Why it is imperative to effect such a reduction, the subsequent discussion will endeavour to show.

The evidence for the above theory is derived from the difficulties which seem unavoidable if we regard denoting phrases as standing for genuine constituents of the propositions in whose verbal expressions they occur. Of the possible theories which admit such constituents the simplest is that of Meinong.[5] This theory regards any grammatically correct denoting phrase as standing for an *object*. Thus "the present King of France," "the round square," etc., are supposed to be genuine objects. It is admitted that such objects do not *subsist,* but nevertheless they are supposed to be objects. This is in itself a difficult view; but the chief objection is that such objects, admittedly, are apt to infringe the law of contradiction. It is contended, for example, that the existent present King of France exists, and also does not exist; that the round square is round, and also not round; etc. But this is intolerable; and if any theory can be found to avoid this result, it is surely to be preferred.

The above breach of the law of contradiction is avoided by Frege's theory. He distinguishes, in a denoting phrase, two elements, which we may call the *meaning* and the *denotation.*[6] Thus "the centre of mass of the Solar System at the beginning of the twentieth century" is highly complex in *meaning,* but its *denotation* is a certain point, which is simple. The Solar System, the twentieth century, etc., are constituents of the *meaning;* but the *denotation* has no constituents at all.[7] One advantage of this distinction is that it shows why it is often worth while to assert identity. If we say "Scott is the author of *Waverley,*" we assert an identity of denotation with a difference of meaning. I shall, however, not repeat the grounds in favour of this theory, as I have urged its claims elsewhere (*loc. cit.*), and am now concerned to dispute those claims.

One of the first difficulties that confront us, when we adopt the view that denoting phrases *express* a meaning and *denote* a denotation,[8] concerns the cases in which the denotation appears to be absent. If we say "the King of England is bald," that is, it would seem, not a statement about the complex *meaning* "the King of England," but about the actual man denoted by the meaning. But now consider "the King of France is bald". By parity of form, this also ought to be about the denotation of the phrase "the King of France". But this phrase, though it has a *meaning* provided "the King of England" has a meaning, has certainly no denotation, at least in any obvious sense. Hence one would suppose that "the King of France is bald" ought to be nonsense; but it is not nonsense, since it is plainly false. Or again consider such a proposition as the following: "If u is a class which has only one member, then that one member is a member of u," or, as we may state it, "If u is a unit class, *the* u

[5] See *Untersuchungen zur Gegenstandstheorie und Psychologie,* Leipzig, 1904, the first three articles (by Meinong, Ameseder and Mally respectively).

[6] See his "On Sense and Nominatum," in this volume.

[7] Frege distinguishes the two elements of meaning and denotation everywhere, and not only in complex denoting phrases. Thus it is the *meanings* of the constituents of a denoting complex that enter into its *meaning,* not their *denotation.* In the proposition "Mont Blanc is over 1,000 metres high," it is, according to him, the *meaning* of "Mont Blanc," not the actual mountain, that is a constituent of the *meaning* of the proposition.

[8] In this theory, we shall say that the denoting phrase *expresses* a meaning; and we shall say both of the phrase and of the meaning that they *denote* a denotation. In the other theory, which I advocate, there is no *meaning,* and only sometimes a *denotation.*

is a *u*". This proposition ought to be *always* true, since the conclusion is true whenever the hypothesis is true. But "the *u*" is a denoting phrase, and it is the denotation, not the meaning, that is said to be a *u*. Now if *u* is *not* a unit class, "the *u*" seems to denote nothing; hence our proposition would seem to become nonsense as soon as *u* is not a unit class.

Now it is plain that such propositions do *not* become nonsense merely because their hypotheses are false. The King in "The Tempest" might say, "If Ferdinand is not drowned, Ferdinand is my only son". Now "my only son" is a denoting phrase, which, on the face of it, has a denotation when, and only when, I have exactly one son. But the above statement would nevertheless have remained true if Ferdinand had been in fact drowned. Thus we must either provide a denotation in cases in which it is at first sight absent, or we must abandon the view that the denotation is what is concerned in propositions which contain denoting phrases. The latter is the course that I advocate. The former course may be taken, as by Meinong, by admitting objects which do not subsist, and denying that they obey the law of contradiction; this, however, is to be avoided if possible. Another way of taking the same course (so far as our present alternative is concerned) is adopted by Frege, who provides by definition some purely conventional denotation for the cases in which otherwise there would be none. Thus "the King of France," is to denote the null-class; "the only son of Mr. So-and-so" (who has a fine family of ten), is to denote the class of all his sons; and so on. But this procedure, though it may not lead to actual logical error, is plainly artificial, and does not give an exact analysis of the matter. Thus if we allow that denoting phrases, in general, have the two sides of meaning and denotation, the cases where there seems to be no denotation cause difficulties both on the assumption that there really is a denotation and on the assumption that there really is none.

. . .

The relation of the meaning to the denotation involves certain rather curious difficulties, which seem in themselves sufficient to prove that the theory which leads to such difficulties must be wrong.

When we wish to speak about the *meaning* of a denoting phrase, as opposed to its *denotation,* the natural mode of doing so is by inverted commas. Thus we say:

> The centre of mass of the Solar System is a point, not a denoting complex;
>
> "The centre of mass of the Solar System" is a denoting complex, not a point.

Or again,

> The first line of Gray's *Elegy* states a proposition.
>
> "The first line of Gray's *Elegy"* does not state a proposition.

Thus taking any denoting phrase, say C, we wish to consider the relation between C and "C", where the difference of the two is of the kind exemplified in the above two instances.

We say, to begin with, that when C occurs it is the *denotation* that we are speaking about; but when "C" occurs, it is the *meaning*. Now the relation of meaning and denotation is not merely linguistic through the phrase: there must be a logical relation involved, which we express by saying that the meaning denotes the denotation. But the difficulty which confronts us is that we cannot succeed in *both* preserving the connexion of meaning and denotation *and* preventing them from being one and the same; also that the meaning cannot be got at except by means of denoting phrases. This happens as follows.

The one phrase C was to have both meaning and denotation. But if we speak of "the meaning of C", that gives us the meaning (if any) of the denotation. "The meaning of the first line of Gray's *Elegy*" is the same as "The meaning of 'The curfew tolls the knell of parting day'," and is not the same as "The meaning of 'the first line of Gray's *Elegy*' ". Thus in order to get the meaning we want, we must speak not of "the meaning of C", but of "the meaning of 'C'," which is the same as "C" by itself. Similarly "the denotation of C" does not mean the denotation we want, but means something which, if it denotes at all, denotes what is denoted by the denotation we want. For example, let "C" be "the denoting complex occurring in the second of the above instances". Then C = "the first line of Gray's *Elegy*", and the denotation of C = The curfew tolls the knell of parting day. But what we *meant* to have as the denotation was "the first line of Gray's *Elegy*". Thus we have failed to get what we wanted.

The difficulty in speaking of the meaning of a denoting complex may be stated thus: The moment we put the complex in a proposition, the proposition is about the denotation; and if we make a proposition in which the subject is "the meaning of C", then the subject is the meaning (if any) of the denotation, which was not intended. This leads us to say that, when we distinguish meaning and denotation, we must be dealing with the meaning: the meaning has denotation and is a complex, and there is not something other than the meaning, which can be called the complex, and be said to *have* both meaning and denotation. The right phrase, on the view in question, is that some meanings have denotations.

But this only makes our difficulty in speaking of meanings more evident. For suppose C is our complex; then we are to say that C *is* the meaning of the complex. Nevertheless, whenever C occurs without inverted commas, what is said is not true of the meaning, but only of the denotation, as when we say: The centre of mass of the Solar System is a point. Thus to speak of C itself, i.e., to make a proposition about the meaning, our subject must not be C, but something which denotes C. Thus "C", which is what we use when we want to speak of the meaning, must be not the meaning, but something which denotes the meaning. And C must not be a constituent of this complex (as it is of "the meaning of C"); for if C occurs in the complex, it will be its denotation, not its meaning, that will occur, and there is no backward road from denotations to meanings, because every object can be denoted by an infinite number of different denoting phrases.

Thus it would seem that "C" and C are different entities, such that "C" denotes C; but this cannot be an explanation, because the relation of "C" to C remains wholly mysterious; and where are we to find the denoting complex "C" which is to denote C? Moreover, when C occurs in a proposition, it is not *only* the denotation that occurs (as we shall see in the next paragraph); yet, on the view in question, C is only the denotation, the meaning being wholly relegated to "C". This is an inextricable tangle, and seems to prove that the whole distinction of meaning and denotation has been wrongly conceived.

That the meaning is relevant when a denoting phrase occurs in a proposition is formally proved by the puzzle about the author of *Waverley*. The proposition "Scott was the author of *Waverley*" has a property not possessed by "Scott was Scott," namely the property that George IV wished to know whether it was true. Thus the two are not identical propositions; hence the meaning of "the author of *Waverley*" must be relevant as well as the denotation, if we adhere to the point of view to which this distinction belongs. Yet, as we have just seen, so long as we adhere to this point of view, we are compelled to hold that only the denotation can be relevant. Thus the point of view in question must be abandoned.

It remains to show how all the puzzles we have been considering are solved by the theory explained at the beginning of this article.

According to the view which I advocate, a denoting phrase is essentially *part* of a sentence, and does not, like most single words, have any significance on its own account. If I say "Scott was a man," that is a statement of the form "x was a man," and it has "Scott" for its subject. But if I say "the author of *Waverley* was a man," that is not a statement of the form "x was a man," and does not have "the author of *Waverley*" for its subject. Abbreviating the statement made at the beginning of this article, we may put, in place of "the author of *Waverley* was a man," the following: "One and only one entity wrote *Waverley,* and that one was a man". (This is not so strictly what is meant as what was said earlier; but it is easier to follow.) And speaking generally, suppose we wish to say that the author of *Waverley* had the property ϕ, what we wish to say is equivalent to "One and only one entity wrote *Waverley,* and that one had the property ϕ".

The explanation of *denotation* is now as follows. Every proposition in which "the author of *Waverley*" occurs being explained as above, the proposition "Scott was the author of *Waverley*" (i.e., "Scott was identical with the author of *Waverley*") becomes "One and only one entity wrote *Waverley,* and Scott was identical with that one"; or, reverting to the wholly explicit form: "It is not always false of x that x wrote *Waverley,* that it is always true of y that if y wrote *Waverley* y is identical with x, and that Scott is identical with x". Thus if "C" is a denoting phrase, it may happen that there is one entity x (there cannot be more than one) for which the proposition "x is identical with C" is true, this proposition being interpreted as above. We may then say that the entity x is the denotation of the phrase "C". Thus Scott is the denotation of "the author of *Waverley*". The "C" in inverted commas will be merely the *phrase,* not anything that can be called the *meaning*. The phrase *per se* has no meaning, because in any proposition in which it occurs the proposition, fully expressed, does not contain the phrase, which has been broken up.

The puzzle about George IV's curiosity is now seen to have a very simple solution. The proposition "Scott was the author of *Waverley*," which was written out in its unabbreviated form in the preceding paragraph, does not contain any constituent "the author of *Waverley*" for which we could substitute "Scott". This does not interfere with the truth of inferences resulting from making what is *verbally* the substitution of "Scott" for "the author of *Waverley*," so long as "the author of *Waverley*" has what I call a *primary* occurrence in the proposition considered. The difference of primary and secondary occurrences of denoting phrases is as follows:

When we say: "George IV wished to know whether so-and-so," or when we say "So-and-so is surprising" or "So-and-so is true," etc., the "so-and-so" must be a proposition. Suppose now that "so-and-so" contains a denoting phrase. We may either eliminate this denoting phrase from the subordinate proposition "so-and-so," or from the whole proposition in which "so-and-so" is a mere constituent. Different propositions result according to which we do. I have heard of a touchy owner of a yacht to whom a guest, on first seeing it, remarked, "I thought your yacht was larger than it is"; and the owner replied, "No, my yacht is not larger than it is". What the guest meant was, "The size that I thought your yacht was is greater than the size your yacht is"; the meaning attributed to him is, "I thought the size of your yacht was greater than the size of your yacht". To return to George IV and *Waverley,* when we say, "George IV wished to know whether Scott was the author of *Waverley*," we normally mean "George IV wished to know whether one and only one man wrote *Waverley* and Scott was that man"; but we *may* also mean: "One and only one man wrote *Waverley,* and George IV wished to know whether Scott was that man". In the latter, "the author of *Waverley*" has a *primary* occurrence; in the former, a *secondary.* The latter might be expressed by "George IV wished to know, concerning the man who in fact wrote *Waverley,* whether he was Scott". This would be true, for example, if George IV had seen Scott at a distance, and had asked "Is that Scott?" A *secondary* occurrence of a denoting phrase may be defined as one in which the phrase occurs in a proposition p which is a mere constituent of the proposition we are considering, and the substitution for the denoting phrase is to be effected in p, not in the whole proposition concerned. The ambiguity as between primary and secondary occurrences is hard to avoid in language; but it does no harm if we are on our guard against it. In symbolic logic it is of course easily avoided.

. . .

The whole realm of non-entities, such as "the round square," "the even prime other than 2," "Apollo," "Hamlet," etc., can now be satisfactorily dealt with. All these are denoting phrases which do not denote anything. A proposition about Apollo means what we get by substituting what the classical dictionary tells us is meant by Apollo, say "the sun-god". All propositions in which Apollo occurs are to be interpreted by the above rules for denoting phrases. If "Apollo" has a primary occurrence, the proposition containing the occurrence is false; if the occurrence is secondary, the proposition may be true. So again "the round square is round" means "there is one and only one entity x which is round and square, and that entity is round," which is a false proposition, not, as Meinong maintains, a true one. "The most perfect Being has all perfections; existence is a perfection; therefore the most perfect Being exists" becomes:

"There is one and only one entity x which is most perfect; that one has all perfections; existence is a perfection; therefore that one exists". As a proof, this fails for want of a proof of the premiss "there is one and only one entity x which is most perfect".[9]

. . .

It is important to observe the effect of our theory on the interpretation of definitions which proceed by means of denoting phrases. Most mathematical definitions are of this sort: for example, "$m - n$ means the number which, added to n, gives m". Thus $m - n$ is defined as meaning the same as a certain denoting phrase; but we agreed that denoting phrases have no meaning in isolation. Thus what the definition really ought to be is: "Any proposition containing $m - n$ is to mean the proposition which results from substituting for '$m - n$' 'the number which, added to n, gives m' ". The resulting proposition is interpreted according to the rules already given for interpreting propositions whose verbal expression contains a denoting phrase. In the case where m and n are such that there is one and only one number x which, added to n, gives m, there is a number x which can be substituted for $m - n$ in any proposition containing $m - n$ without altering the truth or falsehood of the proposition. But in other cases, all propositions in which "$m - n$" has a primary occurrence are false.

The usefulness of *identity* is explained by the above theory. No one outside a logic-book ever wishes to say "x is x," and yet assertions of identity are often made in such forms as "Scott was the author of *Waverley*" or "thou art the man". The meaning of such propositions cannot be stated without the notion of identity, although they are not simply statements that Scott is identical with another term, the author of *Waverley,* or that thou art identical with another term, the man. The shortest statement of "Scott is the author of *Waverley*" seems to be: "Scott wrote *Waverley*; and it is always true of y that if y wrote *Waverley*, y is identical with Scott". It is in this way that identity enters into "Scott is the author of *Waverley*"; and it is owing to such uses that identity is worth affirming.

One interesting result of the above theory of denoting is this: when there is anything with which we do not have immediate acquaintance, but only definition by denoting phrases, then the propositions in which this thing is introduced by means of a denoting phrase do not really contain this thing as a constitutent, but contain instead the constituents expressed by the several words of the denoting phrase. Thus in every proposition that we can apprehend (i.e., not only in those whose truth or falsehood we can judge of, but in all that we can think about), all the constituents are really entities with which we have immediate acquaintance. Now such things as matter (in the sense in which matter occurs in physics) and the minds of other people are known to us only by denoting phrases, i.e., we are not *acquainted* with them, but we know them as what has such and such properties. Hence, although we can form propositional functions C (x) which must hold of such and such a material particle, or of So-and-so's mind, yet we are not acquainted with the

[9] The argument can be made to prove validly that all members of the class of most perfect Beings exist; it can also be proved formally that this class cannot have *more* than one member; but, taking the definition of perfection as possession of all positive predicates, it can be proved almost equally formally that the class does not have even one member.

propositions which affirm these things that we know must be true, because we cannot apprehend the actual entities concerned. What we know is "So-and-so has a mind which has such and such properties" but we do not know "A has such and such properties," where A *is* the mind in question. In such a case, we know the properties of a thing without having acquaintance with the thing itself, and without, consequently, knowing any single proposition of which the thing itself is a constituent.

Of the many other consequences of the view I have been advocating, I will say nothing. I will only beg the reader not to make up his mind against the view—as he might be tempted to do, on account of its apparently excessive complication—until he has attempted to construct a theory of his own on the subject of denotation. This attempt, I believe, will convince him that, whatever the true theory may be, it cannot have such a simplicity as one might have expected beforehand.

Bertrand Russell

Language

The subject of language is one which has not been studied with sufficient care in traditional philosophy. It was taken for granted that words exist to express "thoughts," and generally also that "thoughts" have "objects" which are what the words "mean". It was thought that, by means of language, we could deal directly with what it "means", and that we need not analyse with any care either of the two supposed properties of words, namely that of "expressing" thoughts and that of "meaning" things. Often when philosophers intended to be considering the objects meant by words they were in fact considering only the words, and when they were considering words they made the mistake of supposing, more or less unconsciously, that a word is a single entity, not, as it really is, a set of more or less similar events. The failure to consider language explicitly has been a cause of much that was bad in traditional philosophy. I think myself that "meaning" can only be understood if we treat language as a bodily habit, which is learnt just as we learn football or bicycling. The only satisfactory way to treat language, to my mind, is to treat it in this way, as Dr. Watson does. Indeed, I should regard the theory of language as one of the strongest points in favour of behaviourism.

. . .

There are three matters to be considered in beginning the study of language. First: what words are, regarded as physical occurrences; secondly, what are

From Bertrand Russell, *Philosophy,* Chap. 4, W. W. Norton & Co., New York, 1927. Also published by George Allen & Unwin, Ltd., London, and reprinted with their permission.

the circumstances that lead us to use a given word; thirdly, what are the effects of our hearing or seeing a given word. But as regards the second and third of these questions, we shall find ourselves led on from words to sentences and thus confronted with fresh problems perhaps demanding rather the methods of *Gestaltpsychologie*.

Ordinary words are of four kinds: spoken, heard, written, and read. It is of course largely a matter of convention that we do not use words of other kinds.

. . .

So much for the physical side of language, which is often unduly neglected. I come now to the psychological side, which is what really concerns us in this chapter.

The two questions we have to answer, apart from the problems raised by sentences as opposed to words, are: First, what sort of behaviour is stimulated by hearing a word? And secondly, what sort of occasion stimulates us to the behaviour that consists in pronouncing a word? I put the questions in this order because children learn to react to the words of others before they learn to use words themselves. It might be objected that, in the history of the race, the first spoken word must have preceded the first heard word, at least by a fraction of a second. But this is not very relevant, nor is it certainly true. A noise may have meaning to the hearer, but not to the utterer; in that case it is a heard word but not a spoken word. (I shall explain what I mean by "meaning" shortly.) Friday's footprint had "meaning" for Robinson Crusoe but not for Friday. However that may be, we shall do better to avoid the very hypothetical parts of anthropology that would be involved, and take up the learning of language as it can be observed in the human infant of the present day. And in the human infant as we know him, definite reactions to the words of others come much earlier than the power of uttering words himself.

A child learns to understand words exactly as he learns any other process of bodily association. If you always say "bottle" when you give a child his bottle, he presently reacts to the word "bottle", within limits, as he formerly reacted to the bottle. This is merely an example of the law of association which we considered in the preceding chapter. When the association has been established, parents say that the child "understands" the word "bottle", or knows what the word "means". Of course the word does not have *all* the effects that the actual bottle has. It does not exert gravitation, it does not nourish, it cannot bump onto the child's head. The effects which are shared by the word and the thing are those which depend upon the law of association or "conditional reflexes" or "learned reactions". These may be called "associative" effects or "mnemic" effects—the latter name being derived from Semon's book *Mneme,* in which he traces all phenomena analogous to memory to a law which is, in effect, not very different from the law of association or "conditioned reflexes".

It is possible to be a little more precise as to the class of effects concerned. A physical object is a centre from which a variety of causal chains emanate. If the object is visible to John Smith, one of the causal chains emanating from it consists first of light-waves (or light-quanta) which travel from the object to John Smith's eye, then of events in his eye and optic nerve, then of events in his brain, and then (perhaps) of a reaction on his part. Now mnemic effects belong only to events in living tissue; therefore only those effects of the bottle which happen either inside John Smith's body, or as a result of his reaction to the bottle, can become associated with his hearing the word "bottle". And even then only certain events can be associated: nourishment happens in the body, yet the word "bottle" cannot nourish. The law of conditioned reflexes is subject to ascertainable limitations, but within its limits it supplies what is wanted to explain the understanding of words. The child becomes excited when he sees the bottle; this is already a conditioned reflex, due to experience that this sight precedes a meal. One further stage in conditioning makes the child grow excited when he hears the word "bottle". He is then said to "understand" the word.

We may say, then, that a person understands a word which he hears if, so far as the law of conditioned reflexes is applicable, the effects of the word are the same as those of what it is said to "mean". This of course only applies to words like "bottle", which denote some concrete object or some class of concrete objects. To understand a word such as "reciprocity" or "republicanism" is a more complicated matter, and cannot be considered until we have dealt with sentences. But before considering sentences we have to examine the circumstances which make us use a word, as opposed to the consequences of hearing it used.

Saying a word is more difficult than using it, except in the case of a few simple sounds which infants make before they know that they are words, such as "ma-ma" and "da-da." These two are among the many random sounds that all babies make. When a child says "ma-ma" in the presence of his mother by chance she thinks he knows what this noise means, and she shows pleasure in ways that are agreeable to the infant. Gradually, in accordance with Thorndike's law of effect, he acquires the habit of making this noise in the presence of his mother, because in these circumstances the consequences are pleasant. But it is only a very small number of words that are acquired in this way. The great majority of words are acquired by imitation, combined with the association between thing and word which the parents deliberately establish in the early stages (after the very first stage). It is obvious that using words oneself involves something over and above the association between the *sound* of the word and its meaning. Dogs understand many words, and infants understand far more than they can say. The infant has to discover that it is possible and profitable to make noises like those which he hears. (This statement must not be taken quite literally, or it would be too intellectualistic.) He would never discover this if he did not make noises at random, without the intention of talking. He then gradually finds that he can make noises like those which he hears, and in general the consequences of doing so are pleasant. Parents are pleased, desired objects can be obtained, and—perhaps most important of all—there is a sense of power in making intended instead of accidental noises. But in this whole process there is nothing essentially different from the learning of mazes by rats. It resembles this form of learning, rather than that of Köhler apes, because no amount of intelligence could enable the child to find out the names of things—as in the case of the mazes, experience is the only possible guide.

When a person knows how to speak, the conditioning proceeds in the opposite direction to that which operates in understanding what others say. The reaction of a person who knows how to speak, when he notices a cat, is naturally to utter the word "cat"; he may not actually do so, but he will have a reaction leading towards this act, even if for some reason the overt act does not take place. It is true that he may utter the word "cat" because he is "thinking" about a cat, not actually seeing one. This, however, as we shall see in a moment, is merely one further stage in the process of conditioning. The use of single words, as opposed to sentences, is wholly explicable, so far as I can see, by the principles which apply to animals in mazes.

Certain philosophers who have a prejudice against analysis contend that the sentence comes first and the single word later. In this connection they always allude to the language of the Patagonians, which their opponents, of course, do not know. We are given to understand that a Patagonian can understand you if you say "I am going to fish in the lake behind the western hill", but that he cannot understand the word "fish" by itself. (This instance is imaginary, but it represents the sort of thing that is asserted.) Now it may be that Patagonians are peculiar—indeed they must be, or they would not choose to live in Patagonia. But certainly infants in civilized countries do not behave in this way, with the exception of Thomas Carlyle and Lord Macaulay. The former never spoke before the age of three, when, hearing his younger brother cry, he said, "What ails wee Jock?" Lord Macaulay "learned in suffering what he taught in song", for, having spilt a cup of hot tea over himself at a party, he began his career as a talker by saying to his hostess, after a time, "Thank you, Madam, the agony is abated". These, however, are facts about biographers, not about the beginnings of speech in infancy. In all children that have been carefully observed, sentences come much later than single words.

Children, at first, are limited as to their power of producing sounds, and also by the paucity of their learned associations. I am sure the reason why "ma-ma" and "da-da" have the meaning they have is that they are sounds which infants make spontaneously at an early age, and are therefore convenient as sounds to which the elders can attach meaning. In the very beginning of speech there is not imitation of grownups, but the discovery that sounds made spontaneously have agreeable results. Imitation comes later, after the child has discovered that sounds can have this quality of "meaning". The type of skill involved is throughout exactly similar to that involved in learning to play a game or ride a bicycle.

We may sum up this theory of meaning in a simple formula. When through the law of conditioned reflexes, A has come to be a cause of C, we will call A an "associative" cause of C, and C an "associative" effect of A. We shall say that, to a given person, the word A, when he hears it, "means" C, if the associative effects of A are closely similar to those of C; and we shall say that the word A, when he utters it, "means" C, if the utterance of A is an associative effect of C, or of something previously associated with C. To put the matter more concretely, the word "Peter" means a certain person if the associated effects of hearing the word "Peter" are closely similar to those of seeing Peter, and the associative causes of uttering the word "Peter" are occurrences previously associated with Peter. Of course as our experience increases in complexity this simple schema becomes obscured and overlaid, but I think it remains fundamentally true.

. . .

On behaviourist lines, there is no important difference between proper names and what are called "abstract" or "generic" words. A child learns to use the word "cat", which is general, just as he learns to use the word "Peter", which is a proper name. But in actual fact "Peter" really covers a number of different occurrences, and is in a sense general. Peter may be near or far, walking or standing or sitting, laughing or frowning. All these produce different stimuli, but the stimuli have enough in common to produce the reaction consisting of the word "Peter". Thus there is no essential difference, from a behaviourist point of view, between "Peter" and "man". There are more resemblances between the various stimuli to the word "Peter" than between those to the word "man", but this is only a difference of degree. We have not names for the fleeting particular occurrences which make up the several appearances of Peter, because they are not of much practical importance; their importance, in fact, is purely theoretic and philosophical. As such, we shall have a good deal to say about them at a later stage. For the present, we notice that there are many occurrences of Peter, and many occurrences of the word "Peter"; each, to the man who sees Peter, is a set of events having certain similarities. More exactly, the occurrences of Peter are *causally* connected, whereas the occurrences of the word "Peter" are connected by similarity. But this is a distinction which need not concern us yet.

General words such as "man" or "cat" or "triangle" are said to denote "universals", concerning which, from the time of Plato to the present day, philosophers have never ceased to debate. Whether there are universals, and, if so, in what sense, is a metaphysical question, which need not be raised in connection with the use of language. The only point about universals that needs to be raised at this point is that the correct use of general words is no evidence that a man can think about universals. It has often been supposed that, because we can use a word like "man" correctly, we must be capable of a corresponding "abstract" idea of man, but this is quite a mistake. Some reactions are appropriate to one man, some to another, but all have certain elements in common. If the word "man" produces in us the reactions which are common but no others, we may be said to understand the word "man". In learning geometry, one acquires the habit of avoiding special interpretations of such a word as "triangle". We know that, when we have a proposition about triangles in general, we must not think specially of a right-angled triangle or any one kind of triangle. This is essentially the process of learning to associate with the word what is associated with *all* triangles; when we have learnt this, we understand the word "triangle". Consequently there is no need to suppose that we ever apprehend universals, although we use general words correctly.

Hitherto we have spoken of single words, and among these we have considered only those that can naturally be employed singly. A child uses single words of a certain kind before constructing sentences; but some words presuppose sentences. No one would use the word "paternity" until after using such sentences as "John is the father of James"; no one would use the word "causality" until after using such sentences as "the fire makes me warm". Sentences introduce new considerations, and are not quite so easily explained on behaviourist lines. Philosophy, however, imperatively demands an understanding of sentences, and we must therefore consider them.

As we found earlier, all infants outside Patagonia begin with single words, and only achieve sentences later. But they differ enormously in the speed with which they advance from the one to the other. . . . And no doubt the first sentences used by children are always repetitions, unchanged, of sentences they have heard used by others. Such cases raise no new principle not involved in the learning of words. What does raise a new principle is the power of putting together known words into a sentence which has never been heard, but which expresses correctly what the infant wishes to convey. This involves the power to manipulate form and structure. It does not of course involve the apprehension of form or structure in the abstract, any more than the use of the word "man" involves apprehension of a universal. But it does involve a causal connection between the form of the stimulus and the form of the reaction. An infant very soon learns to be differently affected by the statement "cats eat mice" from the way he would be affected by the statement "mice eat cats"; and not much later he learns to make one of these statements rather than the other. In such a case, the cause (in hearing) or the effect (in speaking) is a whole sentence. It may be that one part of the environment is sufficient to cause one word, while another is sufficient to cause another, but it is only the two parts in their relation that can cause the whole sentence. Thus wherever sentences come in we have a causal relation between two complex facts, namely the fact asserted and the sentence asserting it; the facts as wholes enter into the cause-and-effect relation, which cannot be explained wholly as compounded of relations between their parts. Moreover, as soon as the child has learned to use correctly relational words, such as "eat", he has become capable of being causally affected by a relational feature of the environment, which involves a new degree of complexity not required for the use of ordinary nouns.

Thus the correct use of relational words, *i.e.* of sentences, involves what may be correctly termed "perception of form", *i.e.* it involves a definite reaction to a stimulus which is a form. Suppose, for example, that a child has learnt to say that one thing is "above" another when this is in fact the case. The stimulus to the use of the word "above" is a relational feature of the environment, and we may say that this feature is "perceived" since it produces a definite reaction. It may be said that the relation *above* is not very like the word "above". That is true; but the same is true of ordinary physical objects. A stone, according to the physicists, is not at all like what we see when we look at it, and yet we may be correctly said to "perceive" it. This, however, is to anticipate. The definite point which has emerged is that, when a person can use sentences correctly, that is a proof of sensitiveness to formal or relational stimuli.

The structure of a sentence asserting some relational fact, such as "this is above that", or "Brutus killed Caesar", differs in an important respect from the structure of the fact which it asserts. *Above* is a relation which holds between the two terms "this" and "that"; but the *word* "above" is not a relation. In the sentence the relation is the temporal order of the words (or the spatial order, if they are written), but the word for the relation is itself as substantial as the other words. In inflected languages, such as Latin, the order of the words is not necessary to show the "sense" of the relation; but in uninflected languages this is the only way of distinguishing between "Brutus killed Caesar" and "Caesar killed Brutus". Words are physical phenomena, having spatial and temporal relations; we make use of these relations in our verbal symbolisation of other relations, chiefly to show the "sense" of the relation, *i.e.* whether it goes from A to B or from B to A.

A great deal of the confusion about relations which has prevailed in practically all philosophies comes from the fact, which we noticed just now, that relations are indicated, not by other relations, but by words which, in themselves, are just like other words. Consequently, in thinking about relations, we constantly hover between the unsubstantiality of the relation itself and the substantiality of the word. Take, say, the fact that lightning precedes thunder. If we were to express this by a language closely reproducing the structure of the fact, we should have to say simply: "lightning, thunder", where the fact that the first word precedes the second means that what the first word means precedes what the second word means. But even if we adopted this method for temporal order, we should still need words for all other relations, because we could not without intolerable ambiguity symbolise them also by the order of our words.

. . .

In the present chapter I have confined myself to a behaviouristic explanation of the effects of words heard as stimuli, and the causes of words spoken when the words apply to something sensibly present. I think we shall find that other uses of words, such as the narrative and imaginative, involve only new applications of the law of association. But we cannot develop this theme until we have discussed several further psychological questions.

Charles Leslie Stevenson

Pragmatic Aspects of Meaning

. . . Our first task will be to single out the generic sense of "meaning" that is required.

There is one sense (among many others) which, though conventional enough, will be unsuitable for our purpose. In this sense the "meaning" of a sign is that *to which* people *refer* when they use the sign. (E.g.: "The meaning of 'cake' is edible"; "The meaning of 'hardness' is a characteristic of flint.") It will be convenient to replace "meaning," so used, by the term "referent," following Ogden and Richards. The sense cannot be the generic one required, for we shall want to say that some words (such as "alas") have no referent, but do have a kind of meaning—namely, emotive meaning.

Another sense of "meaning" promises to be more serviceable. In this sense, the "meaning" of a sign must be defined in terms of the psychological reac-

From C. L. Stevenson, *Ethics and Language,* Chap. 3, published by Yale University Press, New Haven, Conn., 1944, and reprinted with their permission.

C. L. Stevenson (1908–) is Professor of Philosophy at the University of Michigan.

tions of those who use the sign. It may be called "meaning in the psychological sense," or in Morris' terminology, "meaning in the pragmatic sense." (E.g.: "The meaning of 'cake' cannot conceivably be eaten, even though cake is edible." "The meaning of 'hardness' is not a characteristic of flint, even though hardness itself is.") If this sense of "meaning" were sufficiently clear, it could readily be taken as designating the required genus, of which emotive and descriptive meanings would be species; for the species could be distinguished by the kind of psychological processes that were involved.

But this generic, psychological sense of "meaning" is unfortunately not clear. Indeed, a proper definition of it has long been one of the most troublesome aspects of linguistic theory. The reason for this can readily be seen:

One of the requirements for any definition of "meaning," so long as that term is to remain suitable for talking about language, is that meaning *must not vary* in a bewildering way. Some variation must of course be allowed, else we shall end with a fictitious entity, serene and thoroughly useless amid the complexities of actual practice; but "meaning" is a term wanted for marking off something relatively constant amid these complexities, not merely for paying them deference. A sense is needed where a sign may "mean" less than it "suggests"—a sense in which meanings are helpful to the understanding of *many* contexts, not some vagrant sense in which a word has a wholly different "meaning" every time it is used.

If the meaning of a sign must be relatively constant, how can "meaning" possibly be defined in terms of the psychological reactions that attend the sign? These reactions are by no means constant, but vary markedly from situation to situation. At a football game "hurrah" may express vigorous emotion, but elsewhere it may be attended by only the faintest echo of emotion. For one who assorts mail, "Connecticut" may cause only a toss of the hand, but for an old resident it may bring a train of reminiscences. How can a constant "meaning" be found amid this psychological flux?

As the latter example shows, the problem of defining a psychological sense of "meaning" is by no means confined to emotive situations; it is equally perplexing for situations which involve a referent. Between sign and referent (e.g., between the word "Connecticut" and the state of Connecticut) a rather constant relation must hold. This relation is preserved by *meaning* in the psychological sense in question; for if "Connecticut" is divorced from the psychological habits of those who use the word, it becomes devoid of any referent, no more interesting than any other complex noise. And yet the psychological responses that attend the word are observed to vary. How can a constant relation be maintained by such inconstant means? How is it possible (so one may confusedly picture the situation) to suspend a weight at a fixed distance from a frame, when the only string that can suspend it is continually varying in length?

. . .

A clue is readily given by the word "power." This term, so familiar in Locke, and a descendant of Aristotle's "potentiality," is in many cases very misleading, since it tempts one to hypostatization and anthropomorphism; but in several modern studies the important aspects of its use have been subject to a very promising analysis. In these studies the term "power" usually gives place to the term "dispositional property," and from now on the latter term will be used here. Before employing the term for present purposes, however, let us become clearer about its usage. Space will permit only a cursory study, in which accuracy will often have to be sacrificed to simplicity; but such a treatment will even so be helpful. It will lead us to a better understanding of "meaning," and so in the direction of a definition of "emotive meaning."

The word "disposition" (or "power," or "potentiality," or "latent ability," or "causal characteristic," or "tendency," etc.) is useful in dealing with complicated *causal* situations, where some specified sort of event is a function of many variables. To illustrate: . . . Although coffee often "causes" stimulation, it is never the *only* cause. The degree of stimulation will depend as well on many other factors—the initial state of a man's fatigue, the absorptive state of his stomach, the constitution of his nervous system, and so on. The situation may accordingly be schematized in this way:

$$\text{Variations in} \left\{ \begin{array}{l} \text{C (amount of coffee drunk)} \\ \text{A} \\ \text{B} \end{array} \right\} \left\{ \begin{array}{l} \text{determine} \\ \text{variations} \\ \text{in} \end{array} \right\} \text{S} \left\{ \begin{array}{l} \text{(actual} \\ \text{stimulation).} \end{array} \right.$$

Here A stands for a *set* of conditions which are subject to change from time to time—the "attendant circumstances" under which the coffee is drunk. B stands for other conditions, less markedly subject to change, such as the chemical components of the coffee. The B factors have an important place in any discussion of dispositional properties; but for the next few pages let us be content to ignore them, to simplify exposition.

There will, of course, be no constant correlation between C and S taken alone; for the correlation will vary with variations in A. And yet the relation of C to S may be very important. With *each* constant condition of A, S may vary with C in *some* way; and with certain conditions of A, variations in C may cause S to vary greatly. To designate this relation, it is convenient to say that coffee (to which C makes conspicuous reference) has a "disposition" to produce S—which is of course only another way of saying that coffee "is a stimulant."

. . .

We must now consider in what sense an object may have an "unchanging" disposition to produce some effect, even though no fixed degree of that effect constantly attends it. This, of course, is simply our problem of explaining how the stimulating power of coffee may remain unchanged, even though the degree of stimulation that attends drinking it does not; and we shall soon see that much the same explanation must be given for *meaning*. With reference to the symbols previously used, the explanation is briefly this:

If for each constant state of A, there is some or another *fixed* way in which C is correlated with S, then the disposition of coffee to stimulate (and so, *mutatis mutandis,* for parallel examples) is said to remain unchanged.

More specifically: Let A retain some constant state, say A_1, and suppose that on each day of a given week it is found that the number of units of C is always double the number of units of S. Again, let A retain some other constant state, say A_2, and suppose that on each day of the same week it is found that the number of units of C is always triple the number of units of S. By a continuation of such experiments it would be possible to conclude, inductively, that for *each* constant condition of A, there is *some* correlation between C and S that remains fixed over the week; or in other words, that the disposition of coffee to stimulate has remained unchanged during that interval. (Note that this correlation need not be the same for all states of A; all that is required is that for each state of A there should be one or another fixed correlation.)

On the other hand, let A retain some constant state, say A_1; and suppose that on *one day* the number of units of C is double the number of units of S, but that on a *later day* it is triple. Here the correlation between C and S has not remained fixed, *even though A has.* The disposition of coffee to stimulate has *changed* during the interval.

Thus the disposition *need* not be said to change just because the effects do; though a change in the effects may *sometimes* indicate a change in the disposition. The unchanging disposition does not require an unchanging S, but rather a correlation between C and S that changes *only* if A changes.

It will be obvious that our imagined experimental tests have been artificially simple. The references to the "number of units" of stimulation, for instance, are more definite than practice may permit, and "more-or-less" comparisons must often take the place of numerical ones. Again, it may be practically impossible to hold the A factors constant; hence their variation must be "allowed for," or be made to cancel out, roughly, by statistical methods. But these and other points, however important they would be to a full study, are more detailed than our simplified treatment can include, and will be granted no further attention.

Let us now give somewhat closer attention to the several factors that any dispositional property involves, and provide a terminology for discussing them:

(a) There will be some relatively simple factor, like C above, which conspicuously affects the object that *has* the disposition. Let us call this a "stimulus." For dispositions assigned to living organisms, this term will have the sense that is current in psychology. For other dispositions it must be taken in an extended sense. Thus the stimulus for the disposition of water to freeze is a temperature of 32° F. or less.

In a similarly extended sense we may use "response" to designate whatever it is that an object has a disposition to do.

. . .

(b) There will be a more complicated set of factors, like A above, which are the "attendant circumstances" under which the disposition may be realized. A variation in these factors may alter the precise form that the response assumes, but as we have seen the disposition is not said to alter *merely* because these factors do. It is sometimes convenient to say that the disposition continues to exist when certain of these factors are totally absent, even though the response may then fail to occur with the stimulus; but unless they are usually present in some form, the disposition will be realized so infrequently that it probably will not be worth mentioning.

(c) There will be other factors, like B [above], that have hitherto been relatively neglected, and must now receive more attention. They are likely to be more permanent than the attendant circumstances, and differ conspicuously in that a variation in them *does* lead us to say that the disposition has varied. Whether or not a given factor is to be classified as belonging to this group, rather than to the attendant circumstances, will largely be determined by the usage of the specific names for dispositions, such as "solubility," "resiliency," "stimulating power," and so on. When a person decides that a variation in a certain factor is to be a criterion for saying that a dispositional property, so named, has itself varied (as distinct from saying that the manner of its realization has varied), he thereby decides that this factor is a B factor, relative to the specific name in question. . . . Some of the B factors will be remote and others immediate. Thus in the example of the "stimulating powers" of coffee, a remote factor would be the way the coffee was grown, and an immediate one would be the amount of caffeine present. The most immediate set of factors, varying when and only when the disposition is said to vary, will be called the "basis" of the disposition.

. . .

It is tempting to hypostatize a disposition, taking it as a special "object" that exists over and above its more "tangible" components. In point of fact, one who gives the stimulus, response, attendant circumstances, and basis of a disposition, and who states in detail their correlation, has said all about the disposition that there is to say. The correlation between the several factors is of primary importance, but a correlation is not, to be sure, an extra object. In the same quest for "tangibility," it is tempting to identify a disposition with its basis; but this again will not do. One may know a great deal about certain factors that in fact constitute the basis of a disposition, but unless he knows how these factors are correlated with the stimulus, response, and attendant circumstances, he cannot be said to know a great deal about the disposition.

. . .

Broad has called attention to "orders" of dispositions, in a way that is best clarified by example. If magnetism is taken as a disposition of the first order, then the disposition of a metal to *acquire* magnetism (which iron has, but copper has not) will be a disposition of the second order. In general, a first-order disposition may be the response of a second-order disposition, which may conceivably be the response, in turn, of a third-order one, and so on. Once we have seen, as above, that a *disposition* may be the *effect,* in an intelligible sense, of something else, we can readily see that it may itself be a response—i.e., that kind of effect whose causes are constituted by some stimulus, basis, and attendant circumstances. The possibility of orders of dispositions is thus manifest.

Having now explained (very roughly, but perhaps serviceably) the nature of dispositional properties, and the sense in which a disposition may be "unchanging," we may return to our problem about meaning. Let us at first consider meaning-situations entirely from the point of view of a hearer, neglecting any reader, speaker, or writer. So simplified, the view to be defended is essentially this:

The meaning of a sign, in the psychological sense required, is not some specific psychological process that attends the sign at any one time. It is rather a dispositional property of the sign, where the response, varying with varying attendant circumstances, consists of psychological processes in a hearer, and where the stimulus is his hearing the sign.

This implies that the relation between the hearing of a sign and the reaction to the sign is an elaborate causal one; for dispositional properties always involve a causal milieu. Although causal theories of meaning are often criticized, it is difficult to see how, for the sense of "meaning" in question, any other view can be plausible. The sign produces certain effects in the ear or eye, and in the nerves; and any further processes must be effects of a more remote sort. Moreover, the hearing of the sign (stimulus) is not the only cause of the psychological processes that ensue (response); and for the remaining causal factors, it is possible to indicate attendant circumstances, and infer to the presence of a basis, in the way that any dispositional property requires.

Such a view all but eliminates the difficulty that was mentioned [earlier]—the need, and seeming impossibility of obtaining, a sense in which the "meaning" of a sign can remain constant even though its psychological effects vary. We shall find that the difficulty reappears for certain of the more controversial aspects of the analysis; but on the whole it vanishes when the problem is freed from artificial simplification and hypostatization. Variations in the response do not imply, necessarily, variations in the disposition. We have seen, for the analogous case of coffee, that whenever a variation in the response can be accounted for by a variation in the attendant circumstances, the disposition can be said to remain unchanged. This holds no less obviously for the particular sort of disposition which is called the meaning of a sign. The psychological processes that attend the sign may vary, but the meaning of the sign need not be said to vary to the same extent; for the meaning is a disposition, whereas the psychological processes are simply the response. Thus a sign's meaning, for the dispositional sense of "meaning" in question, will be more constant than the sign's psychological effects. . . . It cannot be pretended, of course, that these remarks stipulate any precise test for determining when the meaning of a given sign has changed. Any such precision would require a sharp demarcation between the factors that are to be considered among the attendant circumstances of a meaning and those that are not, whereas the present account will provide the demarcation only by means of occasional examples. Hence the phrase "change in meaning" will itself be vague; there will be border-line cases in which it becomes arbitrary whether one says, "The meaning of this sign has changed," or, "Although the meaning of this sign has not changed, the attendant circumstances have come to be such that people's usual reaction to it has changed." The vagueness can *partially* be eliminated for the phrase "change in descriptive meaning," as we shall later see; but it cannot, within the compass of the present work, be eliminated for the phrase "change in emotive meaning"—nor is it likely that any more exhaustive account would be able, in practice, to attain full precision. It can reasonably be hoped, however, that the vagueness will not be fatal to our present purposes. The phrase "change in meaning" is roughly serviceable in common usage, and becomes confusing only when, amid the artificialities of insensitive theory, it is pressed into some hypostatic sense, where unique "entities" take the place of analysis. . . . Passing attention must now be given to a point that might otherwise be misunderstood. Meaning has been taken as a dispositional property of a *sign,* not of the *persons* who *use* the sign. The latter alternative, however, would not have been impossible. In general, whenever a dispositional property has factors that involve several objects (as distinct from events) it makes little difference which object is said to *have* the disposition. Thus one may say either that sugar has a disposition to dissolve in water or that water has a disposition to dissolve sugar, and one may say either that coffee has a disposition to stimulate people or that people have a disposition to be stimulated by coffee. In the same way, one may say either that a sign has a disposition to produce responses in people or that people have a disposition to respond to the sign. The former way of speaking, though not mandatory, will here be adopted. We usually ascribe meaning to a sign, not a person; so if "meaning" is to designate a disposition, the disposition too had better be ascribed to the sign.

. . .

In adopting the idiom, "This sign has a meaning," we must remember that the phrase is elliptical, and must often be expanded to the form "This sign has a meaning for people of sort K." This is parallel to saying that "X is a stimulant" is elliptical, and must often be expanded to the form "X is a stimulant for people of sort K." Just as an X may be a stimulant for certain people and not for others, so a sign may have a meaning for certain people and not for others.

Let us now proceed, still seeking no more than a rough analysis, to limit the *kind* of disposition that is to be called a "meaning." To all words, even nonsense syllables, may be ascribed *some* disposition to affect a hearer; and we shall not want to say that all of them are meaningful. The restriction can partially be obtained by specifying the causes of the disposition, as follows:

A sign's disposition to affect a hearer is to be called a "meaning" (for the not unconventional sense in question) only if it has been caused by, and would not have developed without, an elaborate process of conditioning which has attended the sign's use in communication.

This proviso, though it will be subject to implicit qualification as we proceed, does much to limit "meaning" to a sense that is suitable for linguistic theory. It excludes nonsense syllables, and the ordinary "nonlinguistic" signs. A cough may, in a sense, "mean" that a person has a cold, but will not have a meaning in the present sense; for the elaborate conditioning, developed for purposes of communication, will be lacking.

Let us next drop the artificial restriction of considering only the hearer, and include the reader, speaker, and writer as well. The reader is easily included. We need only recognize that meaning is a disposition whose stimulus must be specified disjunctively, as *either* reading *or* hearing the sign. This is often done in the case of other dispositional properties. E.g., the stimulus for the disposition of powder to explode may be *either* a shock *or* a spark.

The speaker and writer introduce greater complexity into the analysis. They call attention to the need of recognizing a "passive" disposition of a sign—that is to say, a disposition *to be* used. If there is a correlation between some range of a person's psychological processes and his use of a sign, we may say, granted that the other factors can be classified as attendant circumstances and basis, that the sign has a disposition *to be* used. This disposition will be a part of the "meaning" of the sign, granted the proviso introduced just above. The psychological processes, which from the hearer's point of view were the response, become from the speaker's point of view the stimulus.

Meaning thereby becomes a conjunction of dispositions, one passive and one not. But it will be convenient to speak of it as "one" disposition, in spite of this. The criterion of unity for a disposition is rarely precise in ordinary parlance, and often need not be. Thus we may say that magnetism is "one" disposition; or we may say that it is "two," namely, a disposition of an object to draw certain others to it *and* a disposition to induce electric currents in a coil of wire. The criterion of unity is often conveniently allowed to vary with one's purposes.

Having seen that the psychological correlates of a sign may be both a stimulus and a response, we must note that their relationship with signs is often reciprocal. When a man is trying to "clear up his ideas," for instance, he may "talk things over with himself," or "write them down" with many revisions. Certain crude psychological processes lead to certain words, which in turn lead to less crude processes, which in turn lead to other words, which in turn lead to still less crude processes, and so on. As Sapir has remarked, "The product grows with the instrument, and thought may be no more conceivable, in its genesis and daily practice, without speech than is mathematical reasoning practicable without the lever of an appropriate symbolism." In addition to clarifying one's ideas in this way, one may give form to one's moods by use of poetic language. The causal relation between the physical and psychological aspects of language is thus not confined to one simple interplay. It is as if, to press an analogy now grown painfully forced, a man who was stimulated by coffee used his increased energy to make and drink more coffee.

It is this complicated interplay between signs and their psychological correlates which may have led certain theorists to view causal theories of meaning with suspicion. Language has so elaborate a function that any causal explanation seems too clumsy. But one need only imagine the causal situation more sensitively, with a full appreciation of its complexities. The present emphasis on dispositions, with parallels to nonpsychological examples, only hints at the complexity; it is half analysis, half analogy. But so far as it is analogy, it must be taken not as a permanent substitute for a more involved scheme, but only as a device for pointing to it, and for suggesting the further work that must be done. Advances in biology have come not from postulating vital forces, but from a sensitivity to multiple causes; and those who have come to realize, with Wittgenstein, that "colloquial language is a part of the human organism and is not less complicated than it," will expect linguistic theory to take the same course.

Roderick Milton Chisholm

Intentionality and the Theory of Signs

Franz Brentano wrote, in a well-known passage, that *intentionality* is peculiar to psychical phenomena. No *physical* phenomenon, he said, shows anything like it; hence intentionality affords us a criterion of the mental or psychical. Let us refer to this view as "Brentano's thesis." Among the phenomena which he would have called "intentional" is the interpretation of *signs*. One may ask, is it possible to provide an adequate theory of signs which will show Brentano's thesis to be mistaken? In the present paper I shall make certain general points which, I believe, must be considered in any attempt to answer this question. I shall first attempt to state Brentano's thesis somewhat more exactly; then I shall turn to the analysis of the concept *sign*.

I

Psychical phenomena, according to Brentano's thesis, are those "which intentionally contain an object in themselves." Part, at least, of what Brentano had in mind is quite clear, I think. The psychical phenomena which most clearly illustrate his thesis are what are sometimes called *psychological attitudes,* e.g., believing, desiring, hoping, wishing, and the like. When he said that they are characterized by "intentional inexistence," he was referring to the fact that these attitudes can truly be said to have objects even though the objects which they can be said to have do not exist. Even if there weren't any honest men, for example, it would be quite possible for Diogenes to *look for* one. Diogenes' quest has an object, namely an honest man, but, on our supposition, there *aren't* any honest men. The horse can *expect* to receive his oats in ten minutes, even though the event which he expects does not in fact occur. William James would be able to *believe* that there are tigers in India, even if there weren't any tigers in India. Even if there aren't any disembodied spirits, it is quite possible for someone to *take something to be* one. But mere physical phenomena, on the other hand, cannot thus "intentionally contain an object in themselves." In order for Diogenes to sit in his tub, for example, there must be a tub for him to sit in. In order for the horse to eat his oats, there must be oats for him to eat. In order for William James to shoot a tiger in India, there must be a tiger there for him to shoot. And so on.

The statements in which we have described our examples seem to have the

---

From R. M. Chisholm, "Intentionality and the Theory of Signs," *Philosophical Studies,* Vol. 3 (1952). Reprinted by permission of the author, *Philosophical Studies,* and the University of Minnesota Press.

R. M. Chisholm (1916–) is Professor of Philosophy at Brown University.

form of relational statements: "Diogenes *looks for* an honest man"; "Diogenes *sits in* his tub." But the relations described in the psychological statements, if they can be called "relations," are of a peculiar sort, for they can hold even though one of their terms, if it can be called a "term," does not exist. For, it would seem, one can be intentionally related to a such-and-such, even though there aren't any such-and-suches.

These points can be put somewhat more precisely by referring to the *language* we have used. Thus we could say that in the language we have been using, the expressions "looks for," "expects," and "believes" are *intentional,* or are used *intentionally,* whereas "sits in," "eats," and "shoots" are not. We can formulate a working criterion by means of which we can distinguish expressions which are intentional or are used intentionally in a certain language from expressions which are not. It is easy to see, I think, what this criterion would be like, if stated for ordinary English.

A simple categorical statement (for example, "Parsifal sought the Holy Grail") is intentional if it uses a substantival expression (in this instance, "the Holy Grail") without implying either that there is or that there isn't anything to which the expression truly applies. We may also say that the verb of such a statement is intentional or is used intentionally. And we could say that a compound statement (for example, "If Parsifal sought the Holy Grail, he was a Christian") is intentional if any of its components would be intentional when asserted categorically. We should interpret the term "substantival expression" in such a way that it will apply to the grammatical objects in such sentences as "Parsifal believed that he could find the Holy Grail" and "Parsifal believed himself capable of finding the Holy Grail." (Possibly, instead of speaking of such clauses as "applying" or "not applying" to something, we should use a more elaborate terminology; but for the present purposes, I think, our briefer statement will not be misleading.)

It seems clear that, according to our criterion, the verbs "believe," "desire," "look for," "expect," and many others are used intentionally in ordinary English, and that "eats," "shoots," "kills," and many others are not. And there are still other terms which are ambiguous in that they are sometimes used intentionally and sometimes not; possible examples are such psychological terms as "need," "adjust to," "adapt to."

It would be an easy matter, of course, to invent a new terminology which would not be intentional by our criterion. Russell once suggested, for example, that, instead of saying "I perceive a cat," we say "I am cat-perceptive." Instead of saying "The dog expects food," a psychologist may say, "The dog has a food-expectancy," or "The dog has an F-expectancy." And by similar techniques he could re-express in nonintentional terms such statements as "James believes that there are tigers in India."

In all probability, however, the psychologist has only one means of conveying what such expressions as "F-expectancy" or even "food expectancy" might mean; namely, he can tell us that an animal may be said to have a food-expectancy if and only if the animal expects food. Hence we might say that an English expression in a certain use is intentional if in that use it conforms to our original criterion or is defined, or its meaning explained, in terms of other expressions which conform to our original criterion. It must be admitted that, with the introduction of such a qualification, our criterion becomes even less precise. But it is still precise enough, I think, to yield some interesting results.

In addition to statements describing psychological attitudes, there is another important class of statements which are intentional according to our criterion, viz., statements describing *relations of comparison.* For example: "This lizard is smaller than a dragon," "This goblet is other than the Holy Grail," etc. But all the other intentional statements of ordinary English, if I am not mistaken, are readily transformed into statements containing only familiar terms which are not intentional. Thus many statements describing dispositions, tendencies, and potentialities may be intentional: "The roof is vulnerable to future hurricanes," "The storm is now tending to go out to sea," "An atomic bomb, suitably placed, is capable of causing the devastation of Boston." But these could be re-expressed in some such way as the following: "If there should be future hurricanes, the roof would be damaged," "If the storm should continue as it is now, it would go out to sea," "If an atomic bomb were suitably placed, Boston would be devastated."

What may seem to be still other types of intentional statements may be seen, upon closer inspection, to be statements describing psychological attitudes. Examples are statements about language: "The English expression 'the Holy Grail' refers to such-and-such a goblet." It will be generally agreed, I think, that such statements are elliptical and, when properly expanded, can be seen to fall within our first category; for example, "English-speaking people refer to such-and-such a goblet by means of the expression 'the Holy Grail'."

Statements about teleological phenomena, for example, "The purpose of this acorn is that it grow into an oak," may be intentional, but these can be paraphrased so that they may be seen either to concern the purpose of some agent or else to concern dispositions and tendencies.

Certain modal statements are intentional according to our criterion: "It is possible that it will rain," "It is probable that . . ." "It appears that . . ."; also certain ethical statements: "Virtue ought to be rewarded in Heaven." There are various plausible analyses which would relegate these to our other categories; but whether these analyses are adequate need not now concern us.

Brentano's thesis may be construed as saying, then, that the intentional statements which describe psychological attitudes, unlike those describing dispositions, tendencies, and potentialities, *cannot* be re-expressed in familiar terms which are not intentional. The question to which we shall now turn is whether this thesis, in its application to *sign* situations, is mistaken. We shall ask, in short, whether intentional terms (other than those designating relations of comparison) are needed for describing in English the interpretation of signs.

II

We cannot be satisfied with the traditional analyses of sign situations since these, almost invariably, define such terms as "sign" by means of other intentional concepts. That is, we cannot say merely that an object is a sign if it causes someone to *believe,* or *expect,* or *think of* something, since "believe," "expect," and "think of" are clearly intentional terms. Nor can we say merely that an object is a sign if it causes someone to be *set for,* or to be *ready for,* or to *behave appropriately* to something, for these terms, despite their behavioristic overtones, are also intentional. Moreover, if we are to *show* that Brentano is mistaken, then we must not introduce any new technical terms into our analysis of sign behavior unless we can show that these terms apply also to nonpsychological situations. If we take our cue from previous investigations, we will find that two rather different nonintentional conceptions of *sign* are at hand. According to the one, a sign is essentially a *substitute* stimulus; according to the other, it is a *preparatory* stimulus. The second of these conceptions, I believe, is somewhat more promising than the first.

If we use the term "referent" as short for "what is signified," we may say that, according to the first view, the sign is a substitute for the referent. It is a substitute in the sense that, as a stimulus, it causes effects upon the organism similar to those which the referent would have caused. According to this conception, something S may be said to be a sign of something E for an organism O, if and only if S affects O in a manner similar to that in which E would have affected O. Hence the bell may be said to be a sign of food to the dog, since it affects the dog's responses, or dispositions to respond, in a manner similar to that in which the food would have affected them.

This type of definition involves many difficulties of detail, but we shall concern ourselves with only one, viz., that of specifying the respect or degree of similarity which must obtain between the effects caused by the sign and the effects which the referent would have caused. Shall we say that S is a sign of E provided merely that S has *some* of the effects which E would have had? This would have the unacceptable consequence that all stimuli signify each other, since any two stimuli have at least some effects in common. Every stimulus causes neural activity, for example; hence, to that extent at least, any two stimuli will have similar effects. Shall we say that S is a sign of E provided that S has *all* the effects which E would have had? If the bell is to have all the effects which the food would have had, then, as Morris notes, the dog must try to eat the bell. Shall we say that S is a sign of E provided that S has the effects which *only* E would have had? If the sign has effects which only the referent can have, then the sign *is* the referent and only food can be a sign of food. The other methods of specifying the degree or respect of similarity required by the substitute stimulus theory, so far as I can see, have equally unacceptable consequences. Let us turn, therefore, to the preparatory-stimulus theory.

According to the preparatory-stimulus theory, the sign is to be viewed as affecting the organism's responses, or dispositions to respond, to the referent. As a result of being stimulated by the sign, the organism will respond differently, if subsequently stimulated by the referent, than it otherwise would have done. In order to formulate a paradigm for this type of definition, let us borrow Husserl's terms "fulfill" and "disrupt" (or "disappoint"). We may say, then: S is a sign of E for O, if and only if S occasions in O a disposition which would be *fulfilled* if E were to occur, or which would be *disrupted* if E were not to occur. Our problem now becomes that of finding appropriate meanings for the terms "fulfill" and "disrupt."

Russell's terms, "yes feeling" (or "quite-so feeling") and "surprise," may be suggestive in this context. Thus we might say that, as a result of being stimulated by the bell, the dog would have a yes-feeling if food were provided and would be surprised if it were not. Let us assume that we can provide causal nonintentional accounts of *yes-feelings* and *surprises*; possibly they can be defined by means of such terms as "reinforcement," "disequilibration," and "shock."

It may well be that, with these concepts, we can provide an account of the dog and the bell which will show that this elementary sign situation is *not* intentional. It is possible that the dog, in virtue of the sound of the bell, is put into a bodily state such that he will be shocked or surprised if he does not receive food within the moment. And it may be that this bodily state which would lead to the shock or surprise can be specified in physiological terms, independently of the stimulus and of the shock. Whether this is so, of course, is a psychological question. But if it is so, then we must conclude that some sign situations are not intentional. Nevertheless, difficulties in principle seem to be involved when we attempt to extend the preparatory-stimulus theory to human behavior.

These difficulties concern the specification of the occasions upon which the appropriate fulfillments or disruptions must occur. According to our paradigm, these must be caused by the occurrence, or nonoccurrence, of the referent. But it is easy to think of elementary human sign situations where the appropriate events do not occur in the manner required. And to accommodate our definition to such cases, we seem required to make qualifications which reintroduce the intentional concepts we are trying to eliminate.

An example will clarify this point. Jones, let us suppose, interprets certain words or noises as a sign that his aunt is waiting at the railroad station. Our definition, in application to this situation, gives us: "As a result of being stimulated by the words, Jones would experience a yes-feeling if his aunt were at the station or would experience surprise if she were not." If Jones avoids the station, however, the requisite fulfillment or disruption may not occur. Shall we add, then, the qualification ". . . provided Jones visits the station"?

If his visit to the station is brief and if he is not concerned about his aunt, the requisite experiences may still fail to occur. Shall we add: ". . . provided he *looks for* his aunt"? But now we have an intentional term again. And even if we allow him to look for her, the experiences may not occur if some diversion happens to interrupt his search.

Moreover, even after we have made the necessary qualifications, we must still add something about what Jones would *perceive*; for example, ". . . if Jones were to perceive that his aunt is there (or isn't there)." We cannot, at this point, interpret the term "perceive" nonintentionally, construing it merely in terms of light waves, sensible stimulation, etc. For if Jones were to meet his aunt and if she were to serve as visual stimulus object, etc., he might yet *take her to be* someone else; or he might meet and be visually stimulated by someone else and yet *take her to be* his aunt. In such cases, the surprises and yes-feeling would not occur in the manner required by our definition.

Moreover, even if we allow ourselves the intentional terms "look for" and "perceive," our definition will still be inadequate. If Jones visits the bus terminal, *believing* it to be the railroad station, or if he visits the railroad station, *believing* it to be the bus terminal, the conditions prescribed by the definition may well fail to occur. Hence we must add to our other intentional qualifications further qualifications about what Jones must *believe,* or *not* believe. And so on.

The difficulties which we have encountered in connection with this example are of the following sorts: We have found it necessary to add that the organism, rather than be merely stimulated by the referent, must *perceive* it, or *recognize* it, or have it *manifested* to him, or take *something to be* it, or else we must add that these intentional events do *not* occur. We have seen that it may be necessary to add that the organism must *look for* the referent. And we have seen that it is necessary to add that the organism must have certain *beliefs* concerning the nature of the conditions under which he perceives, or fails to perceive, the referent. Similar difficulties can readily be seen to apply to any example which may come to mind.

The analysis of signs, then, seems to lead us back to the intentional concepts with which we began. We noted, however, that there may be simple sign situations, involving the behavior of animals, which can be described nonintentionally. Possibly infants are involved in such situations. And possibly as Ogden and Richards intimated ordinary sign situations may be shown somehow to be "theoretically analysable" into such simple situations. But to show how this might be done is a program or project for the science of semiotics; it is certainly not yet one of its accomplishments. And until this is shown, we can say, I think, that the presumption lies with the thesis of Brentano.

Alfred Jules Ayer

Thinking and Meaning

V

I have been arguing first that the various modes of thinking are not, in any straightforward sense, mental acts; and secondly that the only sense in which they are directed towards an object is that they involve the use of symbols which are meaningful. But at this point the objection may be raised that the use of symbols which are meaningful is itself just such a mental occurrence as I am trying to eliminate. Thus, it will be said that using a symbol is not just making certain noises, or having certain images, or making certain marks on paper; neither is understanding a symbol, which is used by someone else, merely hearing certain sounds or seeing certain shapes. It is necessary in either case that the signs in question should be taken to refer to something. And must not these objects of reference be apprehended by the mind? For otherwise how could the signs be either intelligently used or understood?

This is not an easy objection to answer. For certainly there is a difference between talking intelligently and merely babbling; and certainly there is a

---

From A. J. Ayer, *Thinking and Meaning,* published by H. K. Lewis & Co., London, 1947, and reprinted with their permission. This was Ayer's inaugural lecture as Grote Professor of the Philosophy of Mind and Logic at University College, London.

difference between understanding what another person says and merely hearing the noises that he makes; and it is difficult to give a precise account of what these differences are. All the same, I am sure that they do not consist in the presence or absence of anything that could be reasonably described as a cognitive act. Indeed it is very far from clear to me what such a cognitive act could be supposed to be. It might be suggested that it involved some process of imagination; so that to understand a symbol, as opposed to merely perceiving a sign, would be to have an image of what it stood for. But, in the first place, it is empirically false that one's understanding of symbols is always characterized by the presence of such images. In my experience at least, it is the exception rather than the rule. And secondly, the assumption that understanding consists in having images leads to a vicious infinite regress. For these images must themselves be symbols if they are to do the work that is required of them; and in that case further images will have to be supplied for their interpretation, and so *ad infinitum*. What is true is that if I am to understand a symbol, I must, in some sense, know what it stands for. But my knowing what it stands for does not imply that I am actually imagining anything, or indeed that anything is going on "in my mind." It is, if you like, a matter of my being familiar with the symbols in question; but this familiarity is purely dispositional. In the case of an empirical statement it is a matter of my being able to describe, and ultimately to recognize, the situations that would make it true. And this ability to describe or recognize is not something that I actually have, like a cold in my head, or a shilling in my pocket. I have it only in the sense that I should behave in the appropriate way if the appropriate occasions arose.

Again, my talking intelligently, whether to another person or to myself, consists partly at least in my "knowing what I am saying"; and this is one way in which it may be distinguished from the mere utterance of noises. But, once more, my knowing what I am saying is not a process which goes on independently of the saying; and if it were, the same problem would arise in connection with it. For to be a cognitive process it must itself involve the intelligent use of symbols. Accordingly, the assumption that every intelligent use of symbols comprises not only the formulation of certain signs but also a separate process of "knowing what is being said" leads to another infinite regress. For the knowing what is being said will then itself be a saying which requires a further process of knowing what is being said, and so *ad infinitum*. This does not mean that I do not know what I am saying when I am talking intelligently. But my knowing what I am saying is something for which the criteria are to be sought in my behaviour. It consists in the way in which I formulate the signs, or in the tone in which I express myself, or in my being able subsequently to recall what I have said, or in the way in which I make my discourse hang together; and it also involves the criteria by which it is established that the signs which I am using are such as I am able myself to understand. Thus, if enough of these conditions are satisfied—and although it is not possible to determine *a priori* exactly how many are required, it is easy enough to tell in a particular case—their being satisfied *is* the knowing what is being said; and it is neither necessary nor justifiable to regard this as a separate mental process. Similarly, in the case where one person is conversing intelligently with another it may be said that his conversation is further to be distinguished from mere babbling, or from "talking without thinking," by the fact that he *intends* to make the statements that he does, or to ask the questions, or whatever it may be. But, here again, this intention is not something that has a separate existence in his mind. It may indeed happen that he stops to plan what he is going to say; but then the making of such a plan is itself a case of the intelligent use of symbols; and what makes it intelligent cannot in this case be the presence of an intention, if the presence of an intention is to consist in having a plan. For this would give rise to another infinite regress of plans to make plans to make plans to make plans. Besides it is perfectly possible to converse intelligently without making any plan at all. Thus, if we are going to take the presence of an intention as a criterion for the intelligent use of symbols, this intention must not be conceived as a distinct mental process. The conditions of its existence must again be sought in the subject's behaviour, and its existence will just consist in their being satisfied.

But now it may be argued that even if we can account for the use and understanding of symbols without invoking any cognitive *acts,* we cannot equally dispense with the notion of persisting cognitive *states*. Thus, Professor Price maintains [1] that what he calls "thinking in absence," that is to say, the thought of objects that are not actually present to the senses, would not be possible unless we were aware of classes; and this "awareness of classes" he construes as a "permanent familiarity with universals". He concludes, therefore, that there must be universals, not necessarily subsisting in a Platonic heaven, but at least existing objectively *in rebus*: for otherwise how could we be familiar with them?

I do not think that this argument is sound. It is true that we cannot describe anything without using general terms, that is to say, class-symbols of various sorts; and since these class-symbols have a meaning, we can introduce the word "universal" as a way of referring indefinitely to what they mean. Then the members of the class in question may be said to be instances of the universal which is designated by the class-symbol; and the existence of the universal will simply consist in the fact that the class is not empty. Thus the word "yellow" designates a universal, and since it is a fact that some things are yellow, we can say, if we like, that this universal exists. But we do not in any way explain the fact that some things are yellow by saying that they are instances of the universal "yellow," or by saying that this universal exists. We merely re-state it in a more mystifying way. Nor do we explain the fact that we use and understand class-symbols by saying, as Price does, that we are familiar with universals: here again we do no more than re-state it. It is not *because* I am familiar with the universal "manhood" that I am able to think, or to talk intelligently, about men. My familiarity with this universal just consists in the fact that I am able to use the word "man" correctly. And what is meant by my using the word correctly is, first, that I adhere to the conventions which determine the possibilities of its combination with other words, and secondly, that I apply it to the appropriate situations. Now it is this second condition that raises the difficulty. For in order to apply a word to its appropriate object, say the word "man" to men, it seems necessary that I should both know the connotation of the word, in this case what it is to be a

[1] H. H. Price, *Thinking and Representation*. Lecture to British Academy, 1946.

man, and be able to see that the particular object before me comes under that heading: and it is assumed that these are two intellectual operations of which the first must take place on every occasion on which a word is correctly used, and the second must also take place on every occasion that an object is actually identified. But this is a mistake. My knowing what it is to be a man is not my performing an intellectual operation of apprehending a universal. In so far as it is not merely a matter of my being able to give a nominal definition, it consists in my being able to recognize a man when I see one. And for this it is not at all necessary, as the believers in universals seem to be suggesting, that I should carry a little picture of a man around with me in my head. For, apart from the fact that this assumption is not borne out by the empirical evidence, it does not even furnish the desired explanation: for even if I were to recognize objects by means of such little pictures, the pictures themselves would have to be recognized. And if it is to be held that recognizing an object always involves comparing it with something else, which was the only reason for postulating the little pictures in the first place, we are landed with yet another infinite regress. But, in fact, it is no more necessary that I should have an intellectual idea of something in order to be able to recognize it than it is necessary that a ticket-machine should have an intellectual idea of a shilling in order to give me the correct amount of change. The criteria for my recognizing an object lie wholly in my behaviour; and an important part of this behaviour is just my disposition to use the appropriate signs.

Peter Frederick Strawson

On Referring

I

We very commonly use expressions of certain kinds to mention or refer to some individual person or single object or particular event or place or process, in the course of doing what we should normally describe as making a statement about that person, object, place, event, or process. I shall call this way of using expressions the "uniquely referring use". The classes of expressions which are most commonly used in this way are: singular demonstrative pronouns ("this" and "that"); proper names (*e.g.* "Venice", "Napoleon", "John"); singular personal and impersonal pronouns ("he", "she", "I", "you", "it"); and phrases beginning with the definite article followed by a noun, qualified or unqualified, in the singular (*e.g.* "the table", "the old man", "the king of

---

From P. F. Strawson, "On Referring," *Mind*, Vol. 59 (1950). Reprinted by permission of the author and of the editor of *Mind*.

P. F. Strawson (1919–) is Fellow of University College, Oxford.

France"). Any expression of any of these classes can occur as the subject of what would traditionally be regarded as a singular subject-predicate sentence; and would, so occurring, exemplify the use I wish to discuss.

I do not want to say that expressions belonging to these classes never have any other use than the one I want to discuss. On the contrary, it is obvious that they do. . . .

I think it is true to say that Russell's Theory of Descriptions, which is concerned with the last of the four classes of expressions I mentioned above (*i.e.* with expressions of the form "the so-and-so") is still widely accepted among logicians as giving a correct account of the use of such expressions in ordinary language. I want to show, in the first place, that this theory, so regarded, embodies some fundamental mistakes.

What question or questions about phrases of the form "the so-and-so" was the Theory of Descriptions designed to answer? I think that at least one of the questions may be illustrated as follows. Suppose some one were now to utter the sentence, "The king of France is wise". No one would say that the sentence which had been uttered was meaningless. Everyone would agree that it was significant. But everyone knows that there is not at present a king of France. One of the questions the Theory of Descriptions was designed to answer was the question: how can such a sentence as "The king of France is wise" be significant even when there is nothing which answers to the description it contains, *i.e.,* in this case, nothing which answers to the description "The king of France"? And one of the reasons why Russell thought it important to give a correct answer to this question was that he thought it important to show that another answer which might be given was wrong. The answer that he thought was wrong, and to which he was anxious to supply an alternative, might be exhibited as the conclusion of either of the following two fallacious arguments. Let us call the sentence "The king of France is wise" the sentence S. Then the first argument is as follows:

(1) The phrase, "the king of France", is the subject of the sentence S.

Therefore (2) if S is a significant sentence, S is a sentence *about* the king of France.

But (3) if there in no sense exists a king of France, the sentence is not about anything, and hence not about the king of France.

Therefore (4) since S is significant, there must in some sense (in some world) exist (or subsist) the king of France.

And the second argument is as follows:

(1) If S is significant, it is either true or false.

(2) S is true if the king of France is wise and false if the king of France is not wise.

(3) But the statement that the king of France is wise and the statement that the king of France is not wise are alike true only if there is (in some sense, in some world) something which is the king of France.

Hence (4) since S is significant, there follows the same conclusion as before.

These are fairly obviously bad arguments, and, as we should expect, Russell rejects them. The postulation of a world of strange entities, to which the king of France belongs, offends, he says, against "that feeling for reality which ought to be preserved even in the most abstract studies". The fact that Russell rejects these arguments is, however, less interesting than the extent to which, in rejecting their conclusion, he concedes the more important of their principles. Let me refer to the phrase, "the king of France", as the phrase D. Then I think Russell's reasons for rejecting these two arguments can be summarised as follows. The mistake arises, he says, from thinking that D, which is certainly the *grammatical* subject of S, is also the *logical* subject of S. But D is not the logical subject of S. In fact S, although grammatically it has a singular subject and a predicate, is not logically a subject-predicate sentence at all. The proposition it expresses is a complex kind of *existential* proposition, part of which might be described as a "uniquely existential" proposition. To exhibit the logical form of the proposition, we should re-write the sentence in a logically appropriate grammatical form; in such a way that the deceptive similarity of S to a sentence expressing a subject-predicate proposition would disappear, and we should be safeguarded against arguments such as the bad ones I outlined above. Before recalling the details of Russell's analysis of S, let us notice what his answer, as I have so far given it, seems to imply. His answer seems to imply that in the case of a sentence which is similar to S in that (1) it is grammatically of the subject-predicate form and (2) its grammatical subject does not refer to anything, then the only alternative to its being meaningless is that it should not really (*i.e.* logically) be of the subject-predicate form at all, but of some quite different form. And this in its turn seems to imply that if there are any sentences which are genuinely of the subject-predicate form, then the very fact of their being significant, having a meaning, guarantees that there *is* something referred to by the logical (and grammatical) subject. Moreover, Russell's answer seems to imply that there are such sentences. For if it is true that one may be misled by the grammatical similarity of S to other sentences into thinking that it is logically of the subject-predicate form, then surely there must be other sentences grammatically similar to S, which *are* of the subject-predicate form. To show not only that Russell's answer seems to imply these conclusions, but that he accepted at least the first two of them, it is enough to consider what he says about a class of expressions which he calls "logically proper names" and contrasts with expressions, like D, which he calls "definite descriptions". Of logically proper names Russell says or implies the following things:

(1) That they and they alone can occur as subjects of sentences which are genuinely of the subject-predicate form;
(2) that an expression intended to be a logically proper name is *meaningless* unless there is some single object for which it stands: for the *meaning* of such an expression just is the individual object which the expression designates. To be a name at all, therefore, it *must* designate something.

It is easy to see that if anyone believes these two propositions, then the only way for him to save the significance of the sentence S is to deny that it is a logically subject-predicate sentence. Generally, we may say that Russell recognises only two ways in which sentences which seem, from their grammatical structure, to be about some particular person or individual object or event, can be significant:

(1) The first is that their grammatical form should be misleading as to their logical form, and that they should be analysable, like S, as a special kind of existential sentence;
(2) The second is that their grammatical subject should be a logically proper name, of which the meaning is the individual thing it designates.

I think that Russell is unquestionably wrong in this, and that sentences which are significant, and which begin with an expression used in the uniquely referring way fall into neither of these two classes. Expressions used in the uniquely referring way are never either logically proper names or descriptions, if what is meant by calling them "descriptions" is that they are to be analysed in accordance with the model provided by Russell's Theory of Descriptions.

There are no logically proper names and there are no descriptions (in this sense).

Let us now consider the details of Russell's analysis. According to Russell, anyone who asserted S would be asserting that:

(1) There is a king of France.
(2) There is not more than one king of France.
(3) There is nothing which is king of France and is not wise.

It is easy to see both how Russell arrived at this analysis, and how it enables him to answer the question with which we began, *viz.* the question: How can the sentence S be significant when there is no king of France? The way in which he arrived at the analysis was clearly by asking himself what would be the circumstances in which we would say that anyone who uttered the sentence S had made a true assertion. And it does seem pretty clear, and I have no wish to dispute, that the sentences (1)-(3) above do describe circumstances which are at least *necessary* conditions of anyone making a true assertion by uttering the sentence S. But, as I hope to show, to say this is not at all the same thing as to say that Russell has given a correct account of the use of the sentence S or even that he has given an account which, though incomplete, is correct as far as it goes; and is certainly not at all the same thing as to say that the model translation provided is a correct model for all (or for any) singular sentences beginning with a phrase of the form "the so-and-so".

It is also easy to see how this analysis enables Russell to answer the question of how the sentence S can be significant, even when there is no king of France. For, if this analysis is correct, anyone who utters the sentence S to-day would be jointly asserting three propositions, one of which (*viz.* that there is a king of France) would be false; and since the conjunction of three propositions, of which one is false, is itself false, the assertion as a whole would be significant, but false. So neither of the bad arguments for subsistent entities would apply to such an assertion.

II

As a step towards showing that Russell's solution of his problem is mistaken, and towards providing the correct solution, I want now to draw certain distinctions. For this purpose I shall, for the remainder of this section, refer to an expression which has a uniquely referring use as "an expression" for short; and to a sentence beginning with such an expression as "a sentence" for short. The distinctions I shall draw are rather rough and ready, and, no doubt, difficult cases could be produced which would call for their refinement. But I think they will serve my purpose. The distinctions are between:

(A1) a sentence,
(A2) a use of a sentence,
(A3) an utterance of a sentence,

and, correspondingly, between:

(B1) an expression,
(B2) a use of an expression,
(B3) an utterance of an expression.

Consider again the sentence, "The king of France is wise". It is easy to imagine that this sentence was uttered at various times from, say, the beginning of the seventeenth century onwards, during the reigns of each successive French monarch; and easy to imagine that it was also uttered during the subsequent periods in which France was not a monarchy. Notice that it was natural for me to speak of "the sentence" or "this sentence" being uttered at various times during this period; or, in other words, that it would be natural and correct to speak of *one and the same* sentence being uttered on all these various occasions. It is in the sense in which it would be correct to speak of one and the same sentence being uttered on all these various occasions that I want to use the expression (A1) "a sentence". There are, however, obvious differences between different *occasions of the use* of this sentence. For instance, if one man uttered it in the reign of Louis XIV and another man uttered it in the reign of Louis XV, it would be natural to say (to assume) that they were respectively talking about different people; and it might be held that the first man, in using the sentence, made a true assertion, while the second man, in using the same sentence, made a false assertion. If on the other hand two different men simultaneously uttered the sentence (*e.g.* if one wrote it and the other spoke it) during the reign of Louis XIV, it would be natural to say (assume) that they were both talking about the same person, and, in that case, in using the sentence, they *must* either both have made a true assertion or both have made a false assertion. And this illustrates what I mean by a use of a sentence. The two men who uttered the sentence, one in the reign of Louis XV and one in the reign of Louis XIV, each made a different use of the same sentence; whereas the two men who uttered the sentence simultaneously in the reign of Louis XIV, made the same use [1] of the same sentence. Obviously in the case of this sentence, and equally obviously in the case of many others, we cannot talk of *the sentence* being true or false, but only of its being used to make a true or false assertion, or (if this is preferred) to express

[1] This usage of 'use' is, of course, different from (*a*) the current usage in which 'use' (of a particular word, phrase, sentence) = (roughly) 'rules for using' = (roughly) 'meaning'; and from (*b*) my own usage in the phrase "uniquely referring use of expressions" in which 'use' = (roughly) 'way of using'.

a true or a false proposition. And equally obviously we cannot talk of *the sentence* being *about* a particular person, for the same sentence may be used at different times to talk about quite different particular persons, but only of *a use* of the sentence to talk about a particular person. Finally it will make sufficiently clear what I mean by an utterance of a sentence if I say that the two men who simultaneously uttered the sentence in the reign of Louis XIV made two different utterances of the same sentence, though they made the same *use* of the sentence.

If we now consider not the whole sentence, "The king of France is wise", but that part of it which is the expression, "the king of France", it is obvious that we can make analogous, though not identical distinctions between (1) the expression, (2) a use of the expression and (3) an utterance of the expression. The distinctions will not be identical; we obviously cannot correctly talk of the expression "the king of France" being used to express a true or false proposition, since in general only sentences can be used truly or falsely; and similarly it is only by using a sentence and not by using an expression alone, that you can talk about a particular person. Instead, we shall say in this case that you *use* the expression to *mention* or *refer to* a particular person in the course of using the sentence to talk about him. But obviously in this case, and a great many others, the *expression* (B1) cannot be said to mention, or refer to, anything, any more than the *sentence* can be said to be true or false. The same expression can have different mentioning-uses, as the same sentence can be used to make statements with different truth-values. "Mentioning", or "referring", is not something an expression does; it is something that some one can use an expression to do. Mentioning, or referring to, something is a characteristic of *a use* of an expression, just as "being about" something, and truth-or-falsity, are characteristics of *a use* of a sentence.

A very different example may help to make these distinctions clearer. Consider another case of an expression which has a uniquely referring use, *viz.* the expression "I"; and consider the sentence, "I am hot". Countless people may use this same sentence; but it is logically impossible for two different people to make *the same use* of this sentence: or, if this is preferred, to use it to express the same proposition. The expression "I" may correctly be used by (and only by) any one of innumerable people to refer to himself. To say this is to say something about the expression "I": it is, in a sense, to give its meaning. This is the sort of thing that can be said about *expressions*. But it makes no sense to say of the *expression* "I" that it refers to a particular person. This is the sort of thing that can be said only of a particular use of the expression.

Let me use "type" as an abbreviation for "sentence or expression". Then I am not saying that there are sentences and expression (types), *and* uses of them, *and* utterances of them, as there are ships *and* shoes *and* sealing-wax. I am saying that we cannot say *the same things* about types, uses of types, and utterances of types. And the fact is that we do talk about types; and that confusion is apt to result from the failure to notice the differences between what we can say about these and what we can say only about the *uses* of types. We are apt to fancy we are talking about sentences and expressions when we are talking about the uses of sentences and expressions.

This is what Russell does. Generally, as against Russell, I shall say this. Meaning (in at least one important sense) is a function of the sentence or expression; mentioning and referring and truth or falsity, are functions of the use of the sentence or expression. To give the meaning of an expression (in the sense in which I am using the word) is to give *general directions* for its use to refer to or mention particular objects or persons; to give the meaning of a sentence is to give *general directions* for its use in making true or false assertions. It is not to talk about any particular occasion of the use of the sentence or expression. The meaning of an expression cannot be identified with the object it is used, on a particular occasion, to refer to. The meaning of a sentence cannot be identified with the assertion it is used, on a particular occasion, to make. For to talk about the meaning of an expression or sentence is not to talk about its use on a particular occasion, but about the rules, habits, conventions governing its correct use, on all occasions, to refer or to assert. So the question of whether a sentence or expression *is significant or not* has nothing whatever to do with the question of whether the sentence, *uttered on a particular occasion,* is, on that occasion, being used to make a true-or-false assertion or not, or of whether the expression is, on that occasion, being used to refer to, or mention, anything at all.

The source of Russell's mistake was that he thought that referring or mentioning, if it occurred at all, must be meaning. He did not distinguish B1 from B2; he confused expressions with their use in a particular context; and so confused meaning with mentioning, with referring. If I talk about my handkerchief, I can, perhaps, produce the object I am referring to out of my pocket. I can't produce the meaning of the expression, "my handkerchief", out of my pocket. Because Russell confused meaning with mentioning, he thought that if there were any expressions having a uniquely referring use, which were what they seemed (*i.e.* logical subjects) and not something else in disguise, their meaning must *be* the particular object which they were used to refer to. Hence the troublesome mythology of the logically proper name. But if some one asks me the meaning of the expression "this"—once Russell's favourite candidate for this status—I do not hand him the object I have just used the expression to refer to, adding at the same time that the meaning of the word changes every time it is used. Nor do I hand him all the objects it ever has been, or might be, used to refer to. I explain and illustrate the conventions governing the use of the expression. This *is* giving the meaning of the expression. It is quite different from giving (in any sense of giving) the object to which it refers; for the expression itself does not refer to anything; though it can be used, on different occasions, to refer to innumerable things. Now as a matter of fact there is, in English, a sense of the word "mean" in which this word does approximate to "indicate, mention or refer to"; *e.g.* when somebody (unpleasantly) says, "I mean you"; or when I point and say, "That's the one I mean". But *the one I meant* is quite different from *the meaning of the expression* I used to talk of it. In this special sense of "mean", it is people who mean, not expressions. People use expressions to refer to particular things. But the meaning of an expression is not the set of things or the single thing it may correctly be used to refer to: the meaning is the set of rules, habits, conventions for its use in referring.

It is the same with sentences: even more obviously so. Every one knows that the sentence, "The table is covered with books", is significant, and every one knows what it means. But if I ask, "What object is that sentence about?" I am asking an absurd question—a question which cannot be asked about the sentence, but only about some use of the sentence: and in this case the sentence hasn't been used, it has only been taken as an example. In knowing what it means, you are knowing how it could correctly be used to talk about things: so knowing the meaning hasn't anything to do with knowing about any particular use of the sentence to talk about anything. Similarly, if I ask: "Is the sentence true or false?" I am asking an absurd question, which becomes no less absurd if I add, "It must be one or the other since it's significant". The question is absurd, because the *sentence* is neither true nor false any more than it's *about* some object. Of course the fact that it's significant is the same as the fact that it *can* correctly be used to talk about something and that, in so using it, some one will be making a true or false assertion. And I will add that it will be used to make a true or false assertion *only* if the person using it *is* talking about something. If, when he utters it, he is not talking about anything, then his use is not a genuine one, but a spurious or pseudo-use: he is not making either a true or a false assertion, though he may think he is. And this points the way to the correct answer to the puzzle to which the Theory of Descriptions gives a fatally incorrect answer. The important point is that the question of whether the sentence is significant or not is quite independent of the question that can be raised about a particular use of it, *viz.* the question whether it is a genuine or a spurious use, whether it is being used to talk about something, or in make-believe, or as an example in philosophy. The question whether the sentence is significant or not is the question whether there exist such language habits, conventions or rules that the sentence logically could be used to talk about something; and is hence quite independent of the question whether it is being so used on a particular occasion.

III

Consider again the sentence, "The king of France is wise", and the true and false things Russell says about it.

There are at least two true things which Russell would say about the sentence:

(1) The first is that it is significant; that if anyone were now to utter it, he would be uttering a significant sentence.
(2) The second is that anyone now uttering the sentence would be making a true assertion only if there in fact at present existed one and only one king of France, and if he were wise.

What are the false things which Russell would say about the sentence? They are:

(1) That anyone now uttering it would be making a true assertion or a false assertion;
(2) That part of what he would be asserting would be that there at present existed one and only one king of France.

I have already given some reasons for thinking that these two statements are incorrect. Now suppose some one were in fact to say to you with a perfectly serious air: "The king of France is wise". Would you say, "That's untrue"? I think it's quite certain that you wouldn't. But suppose he went on to *ask* you whether you thought that what he had just said was true, or was false; whether you agreed or disagreed with what he had just said. I think you would be inclined, with some hesitation, to say that you didn't do either; that the question of whether his statement was true or false simply *didn't arise,* because there was no such person as the king of France.[2] You might, if he were obviously serious (had a dazed astray-in-the-centuries look), say something like: "I'm afraid you must be under a misapprehension. France is not a monarchy. There is no king of France." And this brings out the point that if a man seriously uttered the sentence, his uttering it would in some sense be *evidence* that he *believed* that there was a king of France. It would not be evidence for his believing this simply in the way in which a man's reaching for his raincoat is evidence for his believing that it is raining. But nor would it be evidence for his believing this in the way in which a man's saying, "It's raining" is evidence for his believing that it is raining. We might put it as follows. To say, "The king of France is wise" is, in some sense of "imply", to *imply* that there is a king of France. But this is a very special and odd sense of "imply". "Implies" in this sense is certainly not equivalent to "entails" (or "logically implies"). And this comes out from the fact that when, in response to his statement, we say (as we should) "There is no king of France", we should certainly *not* say we were *contradicting* the statement that the king of France is wise. We are certainly not saying that it's false. We are, rather, giving a reason for saying that the question of whether it's true or false simply doesn't arise.

And this is where the distinction I drew earlier can help us. The sentence, "The king of France is wise", is certainly significant; but this does not mean that any particular use of it is true or false. We use it truly or falsely when we use it to talk about some one; when, in using the expression, "The king of France", we are in fact mentioning some one. The fact that the sentence and the expression, respectively, are significant just is the fact that the sentence *could* be used, in certain circumstances, to say something true or false, that the expression *could* be used, in certain circumstances to mention a particular person; and to know their meaning is to know what sort of circumstances these are. So when we utter the sentence without in fact mentioning anybody by the use of the phrase, "The king of France", the sentence doesn't cease to be significant: we simply *fail* to say anything true or false because we simply fail to mention anybody by this particular use of that perfectly significant phrase. It is, if you like, a spurious use of the sentence, and a spurious use of the expression; though we may (or may not) mistakenly think it a genuine use.

. . .

Overtly fictional uses apart, however, I said just now that to use such an expression as "The king of France" at the beginning of a sentence was, in

[2] Since this article was written, there has appeared a clear statement of this point by Mr Geach in *Analysis* Vol. 10, No. 4, March, 1950.

some sense of "imply", to imply that there was a king of France. When a man uses such an expression, he does not *assert,* nor does what he says *entail,* a uniquely existential proposition. But one of the conventional functions of the definite article is to act as a *signal* that a unique reference is being made—a signal, not a disguised assertion. When we begin a sentence with "the such-and-such" the use of "the" shows, but does not state, that we are, or intend to be, referring to one particular individual of the species "such-and-such". *Which* particular individual is a matter to be determined from context, time, place and any other features of the situation of utterance. Now, whenever a man uses any expression, the presumption is that he thinks he is using it correctly: so when he uses the expression, "the such-and-such", in a uniquely referring way, the presumption is that he thinks both that there is *some* individual of that species, and that the context of use will sufficiently determine which one he has in mind. To use the word "the" in this way is then to imply (in the relevant sense of "imply") that the existential conditions described by Russell are fulfilled. But to use "the" in this way is not to *state* that those conditions are fulfilled. If I begin a sentence with an expression of the form, "the so-and-so", and then am prevented from saying more, I have made no statement of any kind; but I may have succeeded in mentioning some one or something.

. . .

The general moral of all this is that communication is much less a matter of explicit or disguised assertion than logicians used to suppose. The particular application of this general moral in which I am interested is its application to the case of making a unique reference. It is a part of the significance of expressions of the kind I am discussing that they can be used, in an immense variety of contexts, to make unique references. It is no part of their significance to assert that they are being so used or that the conditions of their being so used are fulfilled. So the wholly important distinction we are required to draw is between:

(1) using an expression to make a unique reference; and
(2) asserting that there is one and only one individual which has certain characteristics (*e.g.* is of a certain kind, or stands in a certain relation to the speaker, or both).

This is, in other words, the distinction between

(1) sentences containing an expression used to indicate or mention or refer to a particular person or thing; and
(2) uniquely existential sentences.

What Russell does is progressively to assimilate more and more sentences of class (1) to sentences of class (2), and consequently to involve himself in insuperable difficulties about logical subjects, and about values for individual variables generally. . . .

This shows the need for distinguishing two kinds (among many others) of linguistic conventions or rules: rules for referring, and rules for attributing and ascribing; and for an investigation of the former. If we recognise this distinction of use for what it is, we are on the way to solving a number of ancient logical and metaphysical puzzles.

For Further Reading

A. CRITERIA OF MEANING

Alston, William P., *Philosophy of Language,* 1964, Chap. 4.
Ayer, A. J., *Language, Truth, and Logic,* 2nd ed., 1950, Introd. and Chap. 1.
Berlin, Isaiah, "Verifiability in Principle," *Proceedings of the Aristotelian Society,* Vol. 39 (1938–39).
Bridgman, P. W., *The Logic of Modern Physics,* 1927, Chap. 1.
Carnap, Rudolf, "The Elimination of Metaphysics Through Logical Analysis of Language," in Ayer, A. J. (ed.), *Logical Positivism,* 1959, Chap. 3.
———, "Testability and Meaning," *Philosophy of Science,* Vol. 3 (1936) and Vol. 4 (1937); reprinted with omissions in Feigl, H., and Brodbeck, M. (eds.), *Readings in the Philosophy of Science,* 1953.
Cohen, L. Jonathan, *The Diversity of Meaning,* 1962, Chap. 6.
Ewing, A. C., "Meaninglessness," *Mind,* Vol. 46 (1937).
Lewis, C. I., "Experience and Meaning," in Feigl, H., and Sellars, W. (eds.), *Readings in Philosophical Analysis,* 1949.
Mehlberg, Henry, *The Reach of Science,* 1958, Part III.

B. MEANING AND REFERENCE

Austin, J. L., *Philosophical Papers,* 1961, Chaps. 2 and 10.
Black, Max, "The Limitations of a Behavioristic Semiotic," *Philosophical Review,* Vol. 56 (1947); reprinted with the title "The Semiotic of Charles Morris" in Black, M., *Language and Philosophy,* 1949.
Brentano, Franz, "Genuine and Fictitious Objects," in Chisholm, R. M. (ed.), *Realism and the Background of Phenomenology,* 1960, Chap. 3.
Brown, Roger, *Words and Things,* 1958, Chap. 3.
Carnap, Rudolf, *Meaning and Necessity,* 2nd ed., 1955, Chap. 1 and Supplement.
Farrell, B. A., "Intentionality and the Theory of Signs," *Philosophy and Phenomenological Research,* Vol. 14 (1954–55).
Frankena, William, "Some Aspects of Language," in Henle, P. (ed.), *Language, Thought, and Culture,* 1958, Chap. 5.
Frege, Gottlob, "The Thought: A Logical Inquiry," *Mind,* Vol. 65 (1956).
Grice, H. P., "Meaning," *Philosophical Review,* Vol. 66 (1957).
James, William, "The Tigers in India," *The Meaning of Truth,* 1909, Chap. 2.
Leonard, Henry, *Principles of Right Reason,* 1957, Unit 14.
Meinong, Alexius von, "The Theory of Objects," in Chisholm, *Realism and the Background of Phenomenology,* Chap. 4.
Morris, Charles, *Signs, Language, and Behavior,* 1946, Chap. 1.
Mowrer, O. H., "A Psychologist Looks at Language," *American Psychologist,* Vol. 9 (1954).

Quine, W. V. O., *Word and Object,* 1960, Chap. 6.
Ryle, Gilbert, "The Theory of Meaning," in Mace, C. E. (ed.), *British Philosophy in the Mid-Century,* 1957.
Waismann, Friedrich, "Language Strata," in Flew, A. G. N. (ed.), *Logic and Language,* 2nd Series, 1953, Chap. 1.
Wittgenstein, Ludwig, *Philosophical Investigations,* 1953, Part I, Parags. 1 through 137.
———, *The Blue and Brown Books,* 1958, pp. 1–44.

2

CONCEPTIONS AND CRITERIA OF TRUTH

Although the pursuit of knowledge is often said to be a "search for truth," those engaged in it are rarely concerned with the nature of the alleged objective of their search. Certainly few investigators in the natural or social sciences have devoted much thought to defining what truth is; and there is no evidence to show that failure to do so has been a handicap in the conduct of scientific inquiry. Except for philosophy, perhaps the only branch of systematic study in which technical problems of the discipline call for explicit considerations of the nature of truth is formal or mathematical logic (including investigations into the foundations of mathematics). On the other hand, men who contribute to the advancement of knowledge in any field usually pay some attention to problems related to the attainment of truth. For the pursuit of knowledge is notoriously subject to error; and to minimize the risk of falling into it, those engaged in the pursuit must acquire some familiarity with possible sources of mistakes in judgment and some skill in evaluating evidence for cognitive claims.

Two quite different questions concerning truth have in fact often been confounded and must be distinguished—but with the explicit understanding that the word "truth" as used in both of them is a colloquial abbreviation for such phrases as "true belief" or "true statement." One question, often stated in the form "What is the nature of truth?" asks for an *analysis* (or some type of definition) of the notion of truth in terms of presumably clearer or simpler ideas. A relevant answer to the question must in effect provide an account of what it *means* for a belief or statement to be true rather than false, whether or not its truth or falsity happens to be known to anyone. The second question asks whether there are any rules or criteria for *recognizing* truth and, if so, what they are and what their scope is. Accordingly, this question requires an examination of the grounds that presumably warrant claims to knowledge, and it thus merges with the much debated problem of how genuine knowledge is to be distinguished from mere belief. However, although the two questions are formally distinct, many thinkers have maintained that they cannot be discussed separately—indeed, some of them have based their accounts of the nature of truth on their conception of what constitutes warranted knowledge. But most such accounts explicitly deny that their analyses have any bearing on how truth may be discovered or cognitive claims established.

Many of the issues encountered in analyzing the grounds of knowledge are discussed elsewhere in this book, and the essays in the present chapter deal mainly with problems related to the first of the above two questions. All currently influential accounts of the nature of truth agree that the meanings of "true" and "false" have an objective import, so that adequate definitions of them must include a reference to something independent of personal whim and individual acts of thought. But within this broad area of general consensus there is considerable disagreement on a number of issues, even if some of them are of relatively minor importance. Since one of these less important disagreements is reflected in the terminology employed in proposed definitions of truth, we will describe it briefly. Philosophers sometimes differ over the sorts of "things" or "entities" they believe can be properly characterized as either true or false—among the candidates for such characterization are propositions, statements, sentences, utterances, judgments, beliefs, and ideas. Although differences on this issue are sometimes associated with differences in views held on other philosophical questions, they appear to be unrelated to how truth is defined. Indeed, philosophers who disagree on what entities can be said to be true or false, and who therefore formulate their theories of truth with the help of correspondingly different locutions, often subscribe to essentially similar definitions of truth. Accordingly, we shall in this introduction ignore the distinctions marked by terms such as "statement" and "belief," and will use them interchangeably.

Undoubtedly the major difference among theories of truth lies in their conceptions of how a statement, if true, must be related to whatever objectively determines its truth. In respect to this difference, three types of theories are commonly distinguished, and they are labeled as "correspondence," "coherence," and "pragmatic" (or "instrumentalist") theories of truth. The distinctions among them are explained in Ewing's essay, which also contains a critique of definitions of truth illustrative of the types, and a variant of each type is defended in the articles by Russell, Blanshard, and Dewey, respectively. It does not seem entirely gratuitous to note explicitly that Dewey dissociates himself from the view, widely assumed to be the substance of the pragmatic theory (in part because of careless statements of it by some pragmatists), that the meaning of "true" is rendered by "useful to believe."

Although this tripartite classification can serve as a rough map of the territory it surveys, some theories of truth cannot be readily accommodated to any single division set up by it, and it makes no provision for distinguishing among theories that may fall into the same division but which nevertheless differ in significant ways. For example, Dewey's account of truth is usually counted (and we have so counted it) as an example of a pragmatic theory, but this classification is misleading if it suggests that his account is incompatible with definitions of truth in terms of correspondence. On the other hand, though both Dewey and Russell can be classified as exponents of the correspondence notion of truth, in view of the quite different accounts they give of "correspondence" the classification contributes very little to an understanding of their theories. An analogous comment is in order concerning what has been called Austin's "purified version" of the correspondence theory. For according to him, the relation of correspondence in terms of which he explicates the notion of truth is "a purely conventional correlation" between statements and states of affairs. He therefore denies that for the relation to hold there must be any structural similarities between language and things in the world, and he rejects correspondence theories like Russell's for which such similarities are essential, on the ground that these theories commit the error of "reading back into the world the features of language."

But however this may be, discussions of theories of truth have in point of fact been chiefly concerned with ascertaining the sense in which a true statement allegedly either "corresponds to" some segment of reality (as correspondence theories maintain) or "coheres with" the totality of experience (as coherence theories assert). Proponents as well as critics of these theories have made it plain that to interpret these key expressions in certain ways would be fatal to the theories—for example, "corresponds to" cannot have the same meaning as "is an image (or copy) of," and "coheres with" cannot be equated with "is consistent with." Nevertheless, none of the traditional explications for them is without difficulties—at any rate, none has been generally accepted as either sufficiently clear or free from circularity. Dissatisfaction with those analyses has been a goad to the development, on the one hand, of the instrumentalist interpretation of "corresponds to" as equivalent to "is a solution to a given problem," and, on the other hand, of what is currently known as the "performatory" account of truth.

The theories mentioned thus far are based on the assumption that "true" is a predicate of statements or beliefs and is employed to signify whether or not they stand in a certain relation to the subject matter mentioned by them. This assumption has been recently challenged, by Strawson, among others, on the ground that it ignores what is claimed to be an important if not the sole function of the word—namely, to signalize assent, endorsement, concession, and the like. His essay in this chapter criticizes the assumption, especially in connection with the role it plays in the so-called semantic conception of truth that contemporary mathematical logicians have defined in developing a formal theory of semantics for languages conforming to precise rules of construction, and he presents the substance of the performatory theory.

As has already been noted, criteria of truth are not the main burden of this chapter. They are discussed explicitly only in the articles by Blanshard and Ewing, and at a level of generality considerably removed from the specific problems that arise in actual inquiries when statements are required to be tested for their truth. The selection from Blanshard lists a number of proposed criteria, argues against the possibility of using correspondence to fact as even a partial test of a statement's validity, and defends coherence both as a criterion and as a definition of truth. On the other hand, Ewing's essay denies that the notion of truth can be explicated in terms of coherence, but maintains nevertheless that while neither coherence nor correspondence can be taken as the sole criterion of truth, neither of them is dispensable. The discussion in these articles suggests that commitment to some theory as to the nature of truth may be associated with, but does not necessarily imply, acceptance of some particular view concerning criteria of truth.

Alfred Cyril Ewing

Truth

DEFINITIONS OF TRUTH

Philosophers have been—like Pontius Pilate, though out of more respectable motives—much concerned with the question what truth is, and it is obviously of great importance for our whole philosophical outlook what we take as the criterion or criteria of truth. Considering first the question of definition, we find three main theories in the field.

THE CORRESPONDENCE THEORY[1]

This maintains that truth consists in or depends on a relation between a belief or piece of knowledge and a fact in the real world. This is the common-sense theory in so far as common sense can be said to have a theory at all. We ordinarily think that, when we hold a belief, say, about the physical world, the belief is made true or false not by other beliefs but by something in the physical world to which it refers. My belief that this room contains a table is true because it corresponds to the facts about the room; the belief that there is an elephant in the room is false because it does not correspond to the facts about the room. I have taken examples from the physical world, but the same thing applies to beliefs about minds or experiences. My belief that I had toothache yesterday is only made true by the fact that I had toothache.

This theory seems only too obviously true, but there are three perversions of it against which we must be on our guard.

(*a*) I have used the terms, 'belief' or 'judgement' for what is true or false. Now this may be understood as referring either to our mental state of believing or to what is believed. But our state of believing is plainly not true; a psychological state cannot be sensibly called true or false. The theory therefore applies, if at all, only to 'belief' or 'judgement' in the sense of what is believed or 'judged'. ('Judgement' is used by philosophers as a term to cover both knowledge and belief.) The technical term in philosophy for what we judge or believe is 'proposition', and, strictly speaking, it is only propositions which can be true. We speak indeed of 'statements' as true, but they are not true in their own right but only because they stand for propositions which are true. Now, since in a discussion of this sort it is easy and indeed necessary to hypostatize propositions, we are apt to slip into thinking of them as entities which have a being of their own quite independent of being thought by any-

[1] Sometimes called 'accordance'.

Reprinted with permission of The Macmillan Co. from *The Fundamental Questions of Philosophy* by A. C. Ewing. First published in 1951 by Routledge & Kegan Paul Limited.
A. C. Ewing (1899–) is Reader in Philosophy at Cambridge.

body, and some philosophers have taken this view literally. But propositions, taken thus, would be such a queer kind of entities that it is better to avoid the view if we can possibly do so, and I do not see that it is necessary to regard them as anything more than elements in the states of mind of people who do what is called 'think of' or 'contemplate' the propositions. At any rate the correspondence theory is not necessarily committed to taking them as anything more than this. In that case there would still be *facts* if there were no minds, but nothing would then be *true* except in the hypothetical sense in which to say that S is P is true means that, if a mind were to judge S is P, that mind would be judging truly. But, granted that there are minds who do judge, the truth of their judgements may still be dependent on something which is not a mind, though there would not be judgements without a mind. There would be no answers to examination questions if there were no candidates, but it does not follow from this that whether a given answer is right or not depends on the candidate.

(*b*) The word correspondence suggests that, when we make a true judgement, we have a sort of picture of the real in our mind and that our judgement is true because this picture is like the reality it represents. But our judgements are not *like* the physical things to which they refer. The images we use in judging may indeed in certain respects copy or resemble physical things, but we can make a judgement without using any imagery except words, and words are not in the least similar to the things which they represent. We must not understand 'correspondence' as meaning copying or even resemblance.

(*c*) The theory must not be worded in such a way as to imply that we are never aware of the real but only of our judgements or propositions. If that were the case, we could never know that they did correspond. You cannot tell by inspecting a photograph whether it is a good likeness of [illegible] you have never seen.

The correspondence theory as stated often seemed to fall under one or more of these perverted forms, and this aroused in philosophers the desire to find another theory which would avoid the notion of correspondence altogether.

THE COHERENCE THEORY

Thus the coherence theory was developed in the nineteenth century under the influence of Hegel and the associated school of idealists. According to this theory truth is not constituted by the relation between a judgement and something else, a fact or reality, but by the relations between judgements themselves. This avoided the difficulty as to how we could know that judgements corresponded to something which was not itself a judgement. It was held that to say a judgement was true meant that it fitted into a coherent system with other judgements. Since coherence admits of degrees, it follows from this theory that a judgement can be more or less true. No judgement is absolutely true because we never attain a completely coherent system, but some judgements are truer than others because they approach nearer to this ideal.

The above is an objection to the coherence theory, because it is hard to believe such a conclusion. It would seem that a judgement is, strictly speaking, always either true or false and cannot be more or less true, and it is surely obvious that '2 + 2 = 4' and 'Washington is the capital of the United States' are absolutely true. It might be replied that the advocates of the coherence theory were not using 'truth' in the ordinary sense of the term, but we are looking for a definition of the word in the ordinary sense, not in some exotic sense. 'Truth' in the ordinary sense is such a fundamental notion that it is a prime task of the philosopher to search for a definition of it in that sense, if one is indeed available. Further, I do not know how coherence itself could be defined without already presupposing truth. To say A coheres with B is either to say that A is consistent with B or that A necessarily follows from B, or something more complex definable in terms of consistency or of 'necessarily following from'. But these notions themselves already presuppose the notion of truth. To say A is consistent with B is to say that A and B may both be true; to say that A follows necessarily from B is to say that, if B is true, A must be true. So it seems that anyone who defines truth in terms of coherence is defining truth in terms of itself, thus committing a vicious circle. Finally, it is surely obvious that judgements are true not because of their relation to other judgements, but because of their relation to something objective which is not itself a judgement. This brings us back to the correspondence theory of truth.

THE PRAGMATIST THEORY

Truth has been defined by 'pragmatists' as standing for beliefs which 'work'. Certainly true beliefs in general work better than false, but it does not follow that this is what is meant by truth. The pragmatist defends such a view on the ground that we cannot attain absolute truth and therefore must be content with what works. He points out that the object throughout evolution and in at least vastly the greatest part of human life has been not theoretical truth but practical success, and he insists that theory ought to be subordinated to what really counts. No doubt he will agree with everybody else that true beliefs must be consistent with each other and with experience, but he will say that this is only because, if they are not so consistent, they will not work.

The pragmatist definition of truth is open to the following objections. (*a*) It is quite conceivable that a belief might work well and yet not be true or work badly and yet be true. There are very many drunkards who would be greatly benefited if they believed that next time they took alcohol it would kill them, but this does not make the belief true. (*b*) While true beliefs *usually* work, this is usually only because they are first true. It pays to believe that there is a motor car coming when this is true because if I do not believe it I may be run over, but it only pays because there really is a motor car, i.e. because the belief is first true. (*c*) What works for one man may not work for another, and what works for him at one time may not work for him at another. Does it follow that it has ceased to be true when it ceases to work, or that it is true for one man and not for another? The view that reality is a system in which everything is completely determined has worked for some men and the view that there was undetermined individual freedom for others, but both views cannot be true. God cannot both exist and not exist even if some men are helped by belief in his existence and others hindered. And he cannot have all the characteristics which have worked for all believers in all religions, for these are not all compatible. If a proposition is true at all, it surely must be true for everybody, and not just true for some men for whom it works and false for others for whom it does not work? Some pragmatists have welcomed such a subjective view of truth as is here suggested, but it is surely one that we cannot really accept. To take only one instance, if men evolved from animals at all, it will always be true that they did so, and will not become false in a particular generation when the effects of believing it happen to be bad and true again in another. (*d*) The pragmatist definition of truth is open to an objection already brought against the definition in terms of coherence, namely, that the truth of a belief depends on its relation to something objective not just on its functioning as a belief.

RETURN TO THE CORRESPONDENCE THEORY THE VIEW THAT TRUTH IS INDEFINABLE

But the correspondence theory while, I think, true of at any rate most truths, does not give us much information unless we can succeed in defining correspondence, and unfortunately nobody has been able yet to give a satisfactory definition. This does not indeed destroy the theory, for it may well be that correspondence is indefinable. But, if this view is taken we shall have to admit that the theory has very little to tell us, for it will then have done little more than substitute an undefined technical term 'correspond' for the ordinary term 'is true'. Its only service seems to be that it has called attention to something which is obviously a fact but has been overlooked by certain theories, namely, the dependence of truth on a relation to something not itself a judgement at all. It would surely have been better frankly to admit that truth was indefinable and then say what could further be said about it, namely, that it was a relation between propositions and facts, without claiming to have given a definition and veiled the difficulty by the use of a technical term. Further, it may be objected that the correspondence theory only applies to certain kinds of true propositions and not to other kinds. It is hard to apply it to propositions about the future, because there is nothing for these propositions to correspond to, as the future does not yet exist. It is also hard to see how it can be applied to those hypothetical propositions where neither the protasis nor the apodosis expresses a fact, e.g. if Germany had won the war Britain would have been ruined, or if I had six wives I should have $4 + 2$ wives. There is no fact in the existent world to which such propositions correspond, and yet they are true propositions. The examples I have given may sound unimportant, but many such hypothetical propositions are of the greatest practical importance, since our motive for refraining from doing most things that we deliberately refrain from doing is the belief that, if we did them, such and such consequences would ensue. This is a belief in a hypothetical proposition such that, since we are not going to do them, neither the protasis nor (we hope) the apodosis is or ever will be true.

To say that truth is indefinable is not to say that we cannot know anything about it. It is only to say that we cannot analyse it in terms of anything else, and this is by no means an unplausible statement. It seems that we must admit some indefinables if there are to be definitions at all, since we cannot define A in terms of B and C, B and C in terms of D and E, and so on *ad infinitum*. But, if there are indefinables, truth seems as likely to be one as is any concept. It is such a fundamental notion that it is not in the least surprising if it turns out that there is nothing more fundamental in terms of which to analyse it. Only it must be emphasized that, if we are to attach any meaning to an indefinable, as opposed to an undefined term, we must be able to point to an experience in which the characteristic can be seen immediately to be present. To take an example of an indefinable that has commonly been used by philosophers, the colour yellow, we cannot analyse yellow in terms of anything else, otherwise we could explain sufficiently what it was like to a person who had never seen it; [2] but if we are not colour-blind, we can know perfectly well what yellow is like by seeing it, and this is the only way of knowing it. Can we point to an experience that tells us what truth is like in an analogous way so that, though we cannot define it, we can understand what is meant by the term? Surely we can. For we sometimes know something with immediate certainty to be true, if only of our present experience. And in doing that we surely see what truth is. If we did not, we certainly could not see any particular proposition to be true any more than we could see the colour of a yellow thing without seeing its yellowness. Having acquired the notion of truth in such experiences, we can apply it to propositions the truth of which is very much in doubt or is a matter of probable inference. But even if truth is indefinable, philosophers may still dispute about its relations, its criteria and exactly what it qualifies.

CRITERIA OF TRUTH

We shall now turn to the question of the criterion or criteria of truth. This question has not always been carefully separated from the question of the definition of truth, but I think it ought to be. The question, what truth is, is in itself different from the question how we are to find out whether a proposition is true. If we know that truth is to be defined as *A,* it may be thought that this at once gives us also the criterion of truth, because we could then always look for the characteristic *A* in order to decide whether a proposition was true. But it might well be the case that *A* was something which we could not thus directly discover but must determine by indirect means. For instance, only at the best in a minority of cases could we claim to see by direct inspection whether a proposition corresponded to the real, since to do so we should have to have an immediate awareness of the latter, whereas most of the propositions which we believe are established by inference and not thus immediately seen to be true. Yet this admission would not necessarily contradict the view that correspondence constituted the definition of truth. So we had better handle separately the question of the criterion and the question of the definition of truth. The only way of determining the criterion or criteria is to investigate the different kinds of well-authenticated knowledge and belief we have and see what the criteria are that convince us of their truth. There is no means of proving *a priori* what the criteria should be apart from such an investigation of what we find we must actually believe in ordinary cases.

We might well speak of 'correspondence' as the criterion of truth in cases

[2] The scientific 'definition' of yellow in terms of wave-lengths is not an analysis of what the colour is, but of certain physical phenomena which accompany it. People knew what yellow was long before they knew anything about the wave theory of light.

of straightforward sense-experience or introspection. We can then observe the fact in question immediately and see whether our judgement corresponds. But, as we shall discover later, it is difficult to hold that we ever directly sense external physical objects, and in any case most of our judgements about them certainly go beyond anything we experience immediately.

What is to be the criterion of these? It may be contended that the best single word to describe it is 'coherence'. Certainly something that we may describe as a coherence test is needed to decide between rival scientific theories or even to distinguish illusion from genuine perception. Many of our sense-perceptions are unhesitatingly rejected just because they do not fit into a coherent system. That is the case with dreams. Why do we not believe our dreams when awake? Because they do not cohere with the perceptions of waking life. A dreamt that he was hanged last night, but that does not agree (cohere) with the fact that he is still alive. I sometimes dream that I am in a place hundreds or thousands of miles away from where I am when I wake, though no known means of locomotion can have transported me from there. The lack of coherence with waking life would be still more obvious if somebody else were in the room at the time I dreamt and could observe my presence. Again, if we always believed in the sense-perceptions even of waking life, we should have to suppose that the same physical thing had all manner of different shapes, since the shape varies with the position of the observer, and rather than do this we reject very many of our perceptions as illusory. In water an oar appears bent, but to assume that it is really bent would not agree (cohere) well with the fact that we can use it to row effectively. All this can be cited to show the very important part which coherence plays in our actual thinking as a test of truth. It may be said to be the sole criterion by which we distinguish illusions and correct perceptions.

A great deal of stress has rightly been laid on the supreme importance for science of observation, but it may be doubted whether there is a single accepted proposition of science which could be established by observation alone, and I do not think this is altered when we add to observation deductive logic and mathematics. An obstinate person could always adopt the course of the opponents of Galileo when the latter claimed to have discovered the satellites of Jupiter. When they denied the existence of these bodies, Galileo challenged them to look through the newly invented telescope and see them for themselves. They replied that they knew already there were no such satellites and would not look through the telescope because, if they did, the devil might make them see them although they were not there. This is ridiculous enough, but it must be admitted both that the view is logically possible and that a similar course is adopted by all of us in regard to the objects of dreams and other appearances condemned as illusory (except that we do not attribute the deception to the devil but to our sense-organs). These objects do not conform to our intellectual standards of coherence, and so we just say they were not really there, though we have seen them perfectly well. (Of course we do not mean they are not real at all. We give them reality as a sort of mental images, but not as physical things.) Even without resorting to such heroic expedients as Galileo's opponents, most physical theories that have been held at any time could avoid outright refutation if a sufficient number of arbitrary *ad hoc* assumptions were made. Take the Ptolemaic theory, for instance. If we relied on observation primarily, the right reply to Copernicus's suggestion would be that put by Bernard Shaw in the mouth of a medieval soldier: 'The utter fool! Why could not he use his eyes?' It may be retorted that the Ptolemaic theory, although in accordance with experiences such as that of seeing the sun rise, was logically incompatible with observations of a more recondite order, so that these latter refuted it. But this is not the case: it would be possible to maintain the Ptolemaic system compatibly with the evidence of the senses provided we made sufficient arbitrary *ad hoc* assumptions unconnected by any principle. This was what was done in face of the first criticisms of Copernicans, but eventually as the number of such assumptions became greater the Ptolemaic theory became less and less plausible until it was quite dead, although never strictly refuted, and this is what happens with most discarded theories of science.

Advocates of the coherence theory are well aware that complete coherence must be regarded as an unattainable ideal, but views may still be judged according to their greater or less distance from it. The nearest approach to it is to be found in mathematics. Here the different propositions are so connected that each follows necessarily from others and that you could not deny any one without contradicting a vast number of others. If we assumed that $2 + 2$ was equal to 5 we could, I think, without making any further mistake draw conclusions which contradicted every arithmetical truth there is about any number. Other sciences cannot attain to this degree of coherence, but in any science we assume that of two theories, equally compatible with observed facts, the one which brings us nearer to this ideal is the more likely to be true. To be successful a theory must not be inconsistent with empirical facts, but coherence must not be interpreted in terms of mere consistency. Two truths might be quite compatible and yet quite independent and logically unconnected, e.g. that Washington is the capital of the United States and that I have a pain in my big toe. A successful theory must not just enumerate logically compatible facts without connecting them or causally explaining them. It must, if possible, bring them under laws, and the only evidence for the laws may be said to be their coherence with experience. We bring together into a coherent system what previously appeared unconnected by deducing different facts from the same set of laws, e.g. the fall of apples in an orchard and the movements of the stars. We may have no insight into the causal laws governing nature, but nevertheless in deciding what these laws are we can be swayed only by two considerations. Either we must see the laws accepted to be those which can easiest be reconciled with our experience, i.e. cohere best with it. Or we must see that they increase the coherence of our experience by bringing different elements of it together under the same law, instead of two separate unconnected laws. It is difficult to see what other criteria there could be for a scientific law, and these certainly can be brought under the heading of the principle of coherence. In our psychological interpretation of people's actions and testimony we similarly apply the coherence test, accepting the explanation which we say 'makes the best sense' of their actions. We presuppose it even in a detective story, for the correct theory as to the origin of the crime will be the one which accounts for the facts and fits them into a coherent system. The fundamental principles of logic themselves can be justified by this criterion on the ground that there could be no coherent system at all without these principles. But the argument does not in any way support the view that coherence by itself is the sole criterion, but rather *coherence with experience*. This would probably be admitted by most advocates of the coherence theory, but it may then be urged that 'coherence with experience' really means 'coherence with propositions based on experience', so that we have now admitted a second set of propositions not themselves based on coherence but on the mere fact that we can see them to correspond to our experience. The coherence criterion cannot without being thus supplemented by the correspondence criterion ever do justice to the empirical element in our knowledge. Only we must not think of the empirical data as known completely quite apart from the use of the coherence test and thus serving as an altogether independent starting-point already there in its entirety. In order really to know the empirical data, we must have already fitted them into some rough kind of system. We cannot know them, still less communicate our knowledge, without classifying them and bringing them under universal concepts, and this already presupposes a conceptual system in the light of which we make all our judgements and which is tested by its ability to give a coherent interpretation of our empirical data. We must remember that with the exception of proper names almost every word we use stands for a universal concept of one sort or other, and this means that it is part of a conceptual system which men have gradually built up in order to describe their experiences to each other and interpret them to themselves.

There are other gaps in a purely coherence theory of truth besides its inability to deal with empirical data. It is true that the coherence theory cannot get on without admitting immediate empirical cognitions not just based on coherence. But it is true also that it cannot get on without immediate cognitions of a different sort. The advocates of the coherence theory reject the view that any propositions are self-evident in their own right. They would say that the fundamental logical propositions, like the law of contradiction, which seem self-evident, are validated not by their self-evidence, but by the fact that they are presupposed if there is to be any knowledge or any coherent system at all. Of subordinate principles they would say that they must be accepted as true because, although these are not themselves necessary presuppositions of knowledge, they follow from general principles which are. But I find it hard to believe that we only know the law of contradiction because we see that without it we could have no knowledge or that we only know that numbers can be summed because we see that otherwise we could have no arithmetic or no consistent arithmetic. But, however that may be, there is in any case a definite proof that the coherence theory cannot dispense altogether with the notion of self-evidence or intuition. Suppose a belief is accepted or a proposition known because it coheres with the system. But how do we see that it coheres with the system? We might see it as the result of a process of mediate inference, but that could not go on *ad infinitum*. Sooner or later we should have to come to a proposition of which we could only say that it is evident that it coheres with the others or that we just see immediately that it coheres. We may thus apply to the coherence test the general argument which I used earlier to show that all inference must presuppose intuition.

Again, I do not see how, if we were never immediately aware of the presence of goodness or badness, rightness or wrongness in any particular instance, we could ever establish any ethical proposition by the coherence test. Ethical propositions cannot be proved by argument from non-ethical, so some ethical propositions must be known immediately if we are to know any at all. Finally, I do not see how the coherence theory can give a satisfactory account of memory judgements. These are clearly not inferences, they are not established, though they may be confirmed, by coherence; they are as much given as the data of sense-perception. They represent still another kind, and a very important and all-pervasive kind of immediate cognitions.

It seems to me therefore that 'coherence with experience' is not a formula adequate to cover the whole of knowledge and justified belief. There are other immediate cognitions besides those of objects of our present introspection and sense-experience. But a parallel formula might be found to cover all cases. We might say that the criterion is 'coherence with direct cognitions in general'. By an 'immediate cognition' or 'direct awareness' I mean a 'cognition otherwise than by inference', thus covering alike sense-perception, introspection, memory, intuition of the logically self-evident and of immediately apprehended ethical propositions. To say that correspondence was the sole criterion would be to try to bring all criteria under the heading of this direct awareness, but the correspondence theory has to admit that we are able to make inferences beyond our immediate experience or memory. Similarly, the coherence theory has to admit that coherence by itself is not the sole criterion, but at least coherence with experience, and, I should say, 'coherence with immediate cognitions in general'. When this has been admitted, either theory has left a place for the other, and the difference between them has become one of relative emphasis.

It is clear in any case that we cannot do with just one criterion of truth. Neither sense-experience nor coherence can fulfil this role for all truths, if only because there are both *a priori* and empirical propositions. Intuition we have to introduce as a third criterion, if only because all inference presupposes intuitions by which we see that a stage in the inference follows from the preceding one. Since intuitions are usually concerned with facts of a kind that could not be confirmed or refuted by sense-experience or memory, coherence provides a specially valuable test for them; but coherence is also absolutely essential for building up our ordinary conception of the physical world and of human minds. Nor can we dispense with memory as a fourth means of attaining knowledge and justified belief. Memory is not sense-perception or present introspection, nor is it inference, and it can rightly claim to be its own adequate guarantee in a vast multitude of cases. Memory, introspection and perception of the immediate object of sense may perhaps be all appropriately brought under the correspondence formula as cases where we just see immediately that the propositions believed or known correspond to the facts, but it seems less appropriate to apply this formula to knowledge by inference.

The discussion has brought out the fact that there are two elements in knowledge and true belief to both of which it is essential to give an adequate place in our philosophy, (1) active construction and systematizing by the mind, (2) an objectively given basis independent of the first element and the foundation of its work. Extreme empiricism neglects the former element, most forms of the coherence and pragmatist theories the latter.

Are we to add to the other criteria the pragmatic test of which so much is said nowadays? Now no doubt a belief in a true proposition will usually (though not always) work well and a belief in a false proposition badly, and therefore practical success may commonly serve as a criterion which will at least make it likely that the proposition in question is true. But I cannot regard this criterion as an ultimate one. How are we to know that a belief works badly? Because the consequences which should follow if the belief were true do not in fact occur? But this is a direct theoretical refutation which every theory recognizes. The point which shows the belief false is not its practical bearing, i.e. that it injures somebody, but the fact that it conflicts with experience. A false belief might be refuted by a conflict with experience of a kind which was highly agreeable to the believer, as when he has a pleasant surprise. And it may be urged that we know by perception and inference a great many propositions without seeing how they work at all. To this it may be retorted that, since we do not assume all our perceptions to be correct and do not see the canons of at least inductive arguments to be logically self-evident, we must in judging what we perceive and making inductive inferences at any rate presuppose certain general principles which can only be justified by their working. The question is not whether a particular proposition works, but whether it is a consistent deduction from the application of principles of inference which have worked in dealing with experience and are justified by their working. But we may reply that this is a vicious circle. What the pragmatist is trying to justify is the belief in induction, i.e. the argument from what we have observed to the unobserved, and the argument offered to justify it is that the belief has worked in the past. But this is no argument that it will work in the future unless he already assumes the principles of induction which he is trying to justify. And, since he has not yet shown that they will work, these principles must be assumed independently of any test by their working. We may of course interpret 'working' as 'systematizing empirical facts', but then we shall be falling back on the coherence test. The question is: Can the mere fact that some belief produces good consequences, apart from any further argument which shows that the belief in question would not be likely to produce good consequences if it were not true, itself supply a criterion of truth? I am not clear why it should. If we were perfectly adjusted to the real, true beliefs would perhaps always work better than false, but then nobody can claim that we are perfectly adjusted.

Bertrand Russell

Truth and Falsehood

Our knowledge of truths, unlike our knowledge of things, has an opposite, namely *error*. So far as things are concerned, we may know them or not know them, but there is no positive state of mind which can be described as erroneous knowledge of things, so long, at any rate, as we confine ourselves to knowledge by acquaintance. Whatever we are acquainted with must be something: we may draw wrong inferences from our acquaintance, but the acquaintance itself cannot be deceptive. Thus there is no dualism as regards acquaintance. But as regards knowledge of truths, there is a dualism. We may believe what is false as well as what is true. We know that on very many subjects different people hold different and incompatible opinions: hence some beliefs must be erroneous. Since erroneous beliefs are often held just as strongly as true beliefs, it becomes a difficult question how they are to be distinguished from true beliefs. How are we to know, in a given case, that our belief is not erroneous? This is a question of the very greatest difficulty, to which no completely satisfactory answer is possible. There is, however, a preliminary question which is rather less difficult, and that is: What do we *mean* by truth and falsehood? It is this preliminary question which is to be considered in this chapter.

In this chapter we are not asking how we can know whether a belief is true or false: we are asking what is meant by the question whether a belief is true or false. It is to be hoped that a clear answer to this question may help us to obtain an answer to the question what beliefs are true, but for the present we ask only "What is truth?" and "What is falsehood?" not "What beliefs are true?" and "What beliefs are false?" It is very important to keep these different questions entirely separate, since any confusion between them is sure to produce an answer which is not really applicable to either.

There are three points to observe in the attempt to discover the nature of truth, three requisites which any theory must fulfil.

(1) Our theory of truth must be such as to admit of its opposite, falsehood. A good many philosophers have failed adequately to satisfy this condition: they have constructed theories according to which all our thinking ought to have been true, and have then had the greatest difficulty in finding a place for falsehood. In this respect our theory of belief must differ from our theory of acquaintance, since in the case of acquaintance it was not necessary to take account of any opposite.

(2) It seems fairly evident that if there were no beliefs there could be no

---

From Bertrand Russell, *The Problems of Philosophy,* published by Oxford University Press, London, and reprinted with their permission. The book first appeared in 1912.

falsehood, and no truth either, in the sense in which truth is correlative to falsehood. If we imagine a world of mere matter, there would be no room for falsehood in such a world, and although it would contain what may be called "facts," it would not contain any truths, in the sense in which truths are things of the same kind as falsehoods. In fact, truth and falsehood are properties of beliefs and statements: hence a world of mere matter, since it would contain no beliefs or statements, would also contain no truth or falsehood.

(3) But, as against what we have just said, it is to be observed that the truth or falsehood of a belief always depends upon something which lies outside the belief itself. If I believe that Charles I died on the scaffold, I believe truly, not because of any intrinsic quality of my belief, which could be discovered by merely examining the belief, but because of an historical event which happened two and a half centuries ago. If I believe that Charles I died in his bed, I believe falsely: no degree of vividness in my belief, or of care in arriving at it, prevents it from being false, again because of what happened long ago, and not because of any intrinsic property of my belief. Hence, although truth and falsehood are properties of beliefs, they are properties dependent upon the relations of the beliefs to other things, not upon any internal quality of the beliefs.

The third of the above requisites leads us to adopt the view—which has on the whole been commonest among philosophers—that truth consists in some form of correspondence between belief and fact. It is, however, by no means an easy matter to discover a form of correspondence to which there are no irrefutable objections. By this partly—and partly by the feeling that, if truth consists in a correspondence of thought with something outside thought, thought can never know when truth has been attained—many philosophers have been led to try to find some definition of truth which shall not consist in relation to something wholly outside belief. The most important attempt at a definition of this sort is the theory that truth consists in *coherence*. It is said that the mark of falsehood is failure to cohere in the body of our beliefs, and that it is the essence of a truth to form part of the completely rounded system which is The Truth.

There is, however, a great difficulty in this view, or rather two great difficulties. The first is that there is no reason to suppose that only *one* coherent body of beliefs is possible. It may be that, with sufficient imagination, a novelist might invent a past for the world that would perfectly fit on to what we know, and yet be quite different from the real past. In more scientific matters, it is certain that there are often two or more hypotheses which account for all the known facts on some subject, and although, in such cases, men of science endeavour to find facts which will rule out all the hypotheses except one, there is no reason why they should always succeed.

In philosophy, again, it seems not uncommon for two rival hypotheses to be both able to account for all the facts. Thus, for example, it is possible that life is one long dream, and that the outer world has only that degree of reality that the objects of dreams have; but although such a view does not seem inconsistent with known facts, there is no reason to prefer it to the common-sense view, according to which other people and things do really exist. Thus coherence as the definition of truth fails because there is no proof that there can be only one coherent system.

The other objection to this definition of truth is that it assumes the meaning of "coherence" known, whereas, in fact, "coherence" presupposes the truth of the laws of logic. Two propositions are coherent when both may be true, and are incoherent when one at least must be false. Now in order to know whether two propositions can both be true, we must know such truths as the law of contradiction. For example, the two propositions "this tree is a beech" and "this tree is not a beech," are not coherent, because of the law of contradiction. But if the law of contradiction itself were subjected to the test of coherence, we should find that, if we choose to suppose it false, nothing will any longer be incoherent with anything else. Thus the laws of logic supply the skeleton or framework within which the test of coherence applies, and they themselves cannot be established by this test.

For the above two reasons, coherence cannot be accepted as giving the *meaning* of truth, though it is often a most important *test* of truth after a certain amount of truth has become known.

Hence we are driven back to *correspondence with fact* as constituting the nature of truth. It remains to define precisely what we mean by "fact," and what is the nature of the correspondence which must subsist between belief and fact, in order that belief may be true.

In accordance with our three requisites, we have to seek a theory of truth which (1) allows truth to have an opposite, namely falsehood, (2) makes truth a property of beliefs, but (3) makes it a property wholly dependent upon the relation of the beliefs to outside things.

The necessity of allowing for falsehood makes it impossible to regard belief as a relation of the mind to a single object, which could be said to be what is believed. If belief were so regarded, we should find that, like acquaintance, it would not admit of the opposition of truth and falsehood, but would have to be always true. This may be made clear by examples. Othello believes falsely that Desdemona loves Cassio. We cannot say that this belief consists in a relation to a single object, "Desdemona's love for Cassio," for if there were such an object, the belief would be true. There is in fact no such object, and therefore Othello cannot have any relation to such an object. Hence his belief cannot possibly consist in a relation to this object.

It might be said that his belief is a relation to a different object, namely "that Desdemona loves Cassio"; but it is almost as difficult to suppose that there is such an object as this, when Desdemona does not love Cassio, as it was to suppose that there is "Desdemona's love for Cassio." Hence it will be better to seek for a theory of belief which does not make it consist in a relation of the mind to a single object.

It is common to think of relations as though they always held between *two* terms, but in fact this is not always the case. Some relations demand three terms, some four, and so on. Take, for instance, the relation "between." So long as only two terms come in, the relation "between" is impossible: three terms are the smallest number that render it possible. York is between London and Edinburgh; but if London and Edinburgh were the only places in the world, there could be nothing which was between one place and another. Similarly *jealousy* requires three people: there can be no such relation that does not involve three at least. Such a proposition as "A wishes B to promote C's marriage with D" involves a relation of four terms; that is to say,

A and B and C and D all come in, and the relation involved cannot be expressed otherwise than in a form involving all four. Instances might be multiplied indefinitely, but enough has been said to show that there are relations which require more than two terms before they can occur.

The relation involved in *judging* or *believing* must, if falsehood is to be duly allowed for, be taken to be a relation between several terms, not between two. When Othello believes that Desdemona loves Cassio, he must not have before his mind a single object, "Desdemona's love for Cassio," or "that Desdemona loves Cassio," for that would require that there should be objective falsehoods, which subsist independently of any minds; and this, though not logically refutable, is a theory to be avoided if possible. Thus it is easier to account for falsehood if we take judgment to be a relation in which the mind and the various objects concerned all occur severally; that is to say, Desdemona and loving and Cassio must all be terms in the relation which subsists when Othello believes that Desdemona loves Cassio. This relation, therefore, is a relation of four terms, since Othello also is one of the terms of the relation. When we say that it is a relation of four terms, we do not mean that Othello has a certain relation to Desdemona, and has the same relation to loving and also to Cassio. This may be true of some other relation than believing; but believing, plainly, is not a relation which Othello has to *each* of the three terms concerned, but to *all* of them together: there is only one example of the relation of believing involved, but this one example knits together four terms. Thus the actual occurrence, at the moment when Othello is entertaining his belief, is that the relation called "believing" is knitting together into one complex whole the four terms Othello, Desdemona, loving, and Cassio. What is called belief or judgment is nothing but this relation of believing or judging, which relates a mind to several things other than itself. An *act* of belief or of judgment is the occurrence between certain terms at some particular time, of the relation of believing or judging.

We are now in a position to understand what it is that distinguishes a true judgment from a false one. For this purpose we will adopt certain definitions. In every act of judgment there is a mind which judges, and there are terms concerning which it judges. We will call the mind the *subject* in the judgment, and the remaining terms the *objects*. Thus, when Othello judges that Desdemona loves Cassio, Othello is the subject, while the objects are Desdemona and loving and Cassio. The subject and the objects together are called the *constituents* of the judgment. It will be observed that the relation of judging has what is called a "sense" or "direction." We may say, metaphorically, that it puts its objects in a certain *order,* which we may indicate by means of the order of the words in the sentence. (In an inflected language, the same thing will be indicated by inflections, *e.g.* by the difference between nominative and accusative.) Othello's judgment that Cassio loves Desdemona differs from his judgment that Desdemona loves Cassio, in spite of the fact that it consists of the same constituents, because the relation of judging places the constituents in a different order in the two cases. Similarly, if Cassio judges that Desdemona loves Othello, the constituents of the judgment are still the same, but their order is different. This property of having a "sense" or "direction" is one which the relation of judging shares with all other relations. The "sense" of relations is the ultimate source of order and series and a host of mathematical concepts; but we need not concern ourselves further with this aspect.

We spoke of the relation called "judging" or "believing" as knitting together into one complex whole the subject and the objects. In this respect, judging is exactly like every other relation. Whenever a relation holds between two or more terms, it unites the terms into a complex whole. If Othello loves Desdemona, there is such a complex whole as "Othello's love for Desdemona." The terms united by the relation may be themselves complex, or may be simple, but the whole which results from their being united must be complex. Wherever there is a relation which relates certain terms, there is a complex object formed of the union of those terms; and conversely, wherever there is a complex object, there is a relation which relates its constituents. When an act of believing occurs, there is a complex, in which "believing" is the uniting relation, and subject and objects are arranged in a certain order by the "sense" of the relation of believing. Among the objects, as we saw in considering "Othello believes that Desdemona loves Cassio," one must be a relation—in this instance, the relation "loving." But this relation, as it occurs in the act of believing, is not the relation which creates the unity of the complex whole consisting of the subject and the objects. The relation "loving," as it occurs in the act of believing, is one of the objects—it is a brick in the structure, not the cement. The cement is the relation "believing." When the belief is *true,* there is another complex unity, in which the relation which was one of the objects of the belief relates the other objects. Thus, *e.g.,* if Othello believes *truly* that Desdemona loves Cassio, then there is a complex unity, "Desdemona's love for Cassio," which is composed exclusively of the *objects* of the belief, in the same order as they had in the belief, with the relation which was one of the objects occurring now as the cement that binds together the other objects of the belief. On the other hand, when a belief is *false,* there is no such complex unity composed only of the objects of the belief. If Othello believes *falsely* that Desdemona loves Cassio, then there is no such complex unity as "Desdemona's love for Cassio."

Thus a belief is *true* when it *corresponds* to a certain associated complex, and *false* when it does not. Assuming, for the sake of definiteness, that the objects of the belief are two terms and a relation, the terms being put in a certain order by the "sense" of the believing, then if the two terms in that order are united by the relation into a complex, the belief is true; if not, it is false. This constitutes the definition of truth and falsehood that we were in search of. Judging or believing is a certain complex unity of which a mind is a constituent; if the remaining constituents, taken in the order which they have in the belief, form a complex unity, then the belief is true; if not, it is false.

Thus although truth and falsehood are properties of beliefs, yet they are in a sense extrinsic properties, for the condition of the truth of a belief is something not involving beliefs, or (in general) any mind at all, but only the *objects* of the belief. A mind, which believes, believes truly when there is a *corresponding* complex not involving the mind, but only its objects. This correspondence ensures truth, and its absence entails falsehood. Hence we account simultaneously for the two facts that beliefs (*a*) depend on minds for their *existence,* (*b*) do not depend on minds for their *truth.*

We may restate our theory as follows: If we take such a belief as "Othello believes that Desdemona loves Cassio," we will call Desdemona and Cassio the *object-terms,* and loving the *object-relation.* If there is a complex unity "Desdemona's love for Cassio," consisting of the object-terms related by the object-relation in the same order as they have in the belief, then this complex unity is called the *fact corresponding to the belief.* Thus a belief is true when there is a corresponding fact, and is false when there is no corresponding fact.

It will be seen that minds do not *create* truth or falsehood. They create beliefs, but when once the beliefs are created, the mind cannot make them true or false, except in the special case where they concern future things which are within the power of the person believing, such as catching trains. What makes a belief true is a *fact,* and this fact does not (except in exceptional cases) in any way involve the mind of the person who has the belief.

Brand Blanshard

Coherence as the Test and Nature of Truth

THE TESTS OF TRUTH

. . .

5. . . . There are six distinct tests of truth that are today accepted in various quarters as providing a court of last appeal. Indeed there are no doubt more; but at any rate these are the most widely accepted. They are: (1) correspondence with fact, (2) self-evidence, (3) coherence, (4) 'working' as defined by the pragmatist, (5) the peculiar warrant that attaches to mystical intuition, and (6) the voice of authority. The pragmatic test has been dealt with. Correspondence, self-evidence and coherence are all so important that the reader will be invited shortly to listen to a debate between them.

. . .

15. . . . When we are thinking about historical facts, or events reported in the newspapers, or things actually seen and heard, it seems to the plain man obvious that our thought could be tested only by correspondence with fact. But if we were to take this same man by the hand, lead him off to another room in the gallery of knowledge, and set him down before a law of logic

From Brand Blanshard, *The Nature of Thought,* Vol. 2, Chaps. 25 and 26, published by George Allen & Unwin, Ltd., London, 1940, and reprinted with their permission.

Brand Blanshard (1892–) is Sterling Professor Emeritus of Philosophy at Yale University.

or a mathematical proof, he would probably desert his former standard without misgiving. These insights do not need comparison with fact; they are self-evident as they stand. If he had met these first, instead of judgements about things and events, he would probably have laid it down with confidence that the test was a certain clearness and convincingness apparent at once to anyone who could grasp the truth at all. But then disillusionment would again have overtaken him when he began to move from one region to another. For just as correspondence deserts us when we move from facts to abstractions, so self-evidence deserts us when we move back again from abstractions to facts. Where is the self-evidence in the judgement that it rained yesterday in Guatemala?

On the face of it common sense is without any consistent standard. It keeps swinging back and forth between two different standards, correspondence for matters of fact and self-evidence for the abstract and formal. But we hold that this oscillation and inconsistency are superficial only. We hold that these two standards are not so far apart as they seem and that both resolve themselves on analysis into a single standard, coherence. The way to establish this is to show that even in matters of fact it is coherence rather than correspondence that we actually use, and that even in regions of the abstractest formality it is once more coherence rather than self-evidence that is in the end our court of appeal. We shall not argue that these types of judgement cover between them the whole of knowledge, though many philosophers would say they do. It is enough to point out that they are the kinds traditionally placed at the poles of knowledge. If types so far apart can be shown to depend on a single criterion, it is unlikely that any third type will come forward to challenge its universality. We shall open the case for coherence, then, by considering the two types of judgement that seem to demand most obviously another standard.

16. Take first the judgement of fact. 'Burr killed Hamilton in a duel.' 'That is a cardinal on the branch yonder.' To the plain man it seems obvious that the test of such judgements is whether they correspond with fact. But as regards the first of them, there is a simple distinction which, if perceived, would shake his confidence. When he reflects on the judgement, 'Burr killed Hamilton in a duel', he sees, or thinks he sees, that its truth *means* correspondence; and it is natural to say that if truth means this, then it must also be tested by this. But the two questions are distinct, and in saying that the test here is correspondence, he is pretty clearly confusing the test of truth with its meaning. For the slightest consideration will show that the use of correspondence as a test is here out of the question; one of the terms that are to correspond is irrecoverably gone. There is no person living who could have witnessed the famous duel; and even if there were, he could not, through correspondence merely, validate his memories. Our test in such cases must clearly be found elsewhere. And the more we reflect, the plainer it becomes that this test is the way our judgement is implicated with a host of further judgements that we are compelled to make when we investigate. If this belief about Hamilton is true, then a thousand references in newspapers, magazines, and books, and almost endless facts about the fortunes of Hamilton's family, about the later life of Burr, and about American constitutional history, fall into place in a consistent picture. If it is false, then the most credible journalists, historians

and statesmen, generation after generation, may be so deluded about events that happen before the eyes of a nation that no single historical fact is any longer above suspicion. If evidence of this weight is to be rejected, then in consistency we must go on to reject almost every hint that takes us beyond immediate perception. And intellectually speaking, that would pull our house about our heads. What really tests the judgement is the extent of our accepted world that is implicated with it and would be carried down with it if it fell. And that is the test of coherence.

17. 'But in any such judgement', it may be replied, 'the value of correspondence is seen in a false light. *Of course* it cannot be used in those special cases where one of the terms has vanished. But that does not disqualify it where it *is* applicable, nor does it show that any other test can really supplant it where it is not. Indeed, in an instance like this, where correspondence cannot be applied, we see that our judgement is incapable of proof altogether, by coherence or anything else; every judgement of historical fact must retain to the end a touch of uncertainty. It must do so for the reason that it is beyond reach of the one thing that could establish it, namely, that perception of the event itself which would make appeal to correspondence possible. On the other hand, when we turn to the judgements where appeal to correspondence *is* possible, we find that it is always resorted to, and that in such cases uncertainty is banished. Take the judgement, "That bird is a cardinal". If you heard someone make that remark, how would you test it? You would look and see. If there was a correspondence between what was asserted and what you saw, you would call the judgement true; if not, false. This is the way we actually assure ourselves of the truth of all such judgements, and it is correspondence that assures us.'

18. Now, plausible as this argument is, it goes to pieces on inspection. It assumes that, corresponding to our judgement, there is some solid chunk of fact, directly presented to sense and beyond all question, to which thought must adjust itself. And this 'solid fact' is a fiction. What the theory takes as fact and actually uses as such is another judgement or set of judgements, and what provides the verification is the coherence between the initial judgement and these.

Consider the cardinal. This is supposed to be fact, unadulterated brute fact, given directly to our senses and providing a solid reality to which our thought is to correspond. But no bird is a mere sense datum, or even a collection of sense data. Suppose that standing in our place were an animal with all our senses, each developed to the highest acuteness, but unable to attach meanings to sense data as we do, or note likenesses, implications, and differences. Would such a creature perceive what we perceive? Plainly not. To recognize a cardinal is a considerable intellectual achievement, for to do it one must grasp, implicitly but none the less really, the *concept* of cardinal, and this can only be done by a leap far out of the given into ideal classification. The most ignorant person among us who achieves such recognition could unpack from it a surprising wealth of contents. The idea of living organisms, the thought of the bird kingdom and its outstanding characteristics, the notions of flight and a peculiar song and a determinate colour—these and many other notions are so bound up with the identification that our thought would lose its character with the removal of any one of them. Not that they are logical implicates which later analysis might find to be entailed by our identification; they are parts or components of it, as truly as 'plane' is part of 'plane triangle'; they are part of what we mean when we use the word 'cardinal'. And these essential elements, at least at the time and for the most part, are not given in sense at all. They are elements in a theory, and a theory of no little complexity, which is based on sense data if you will, but could not possibly consist of them.

Indeed, that the brute-fact view of perception is untrue is proved by this alone, that perception may be mistaken; I may take the cardinal for a robin. If the object were mere given fact, such a mistake would be impossible. A fact is what it is, and cannot possibly be something else. If it appears to be something else, the seeming must be in our thought, and the perception that involves such seemings has advanced beyond the given into the region of judgement. What makes the error possible is a theory of ours.

It may be said that if perception is itself theory, that only means that we must look a little further for the verifying fact. Somewhere the bow of theory must come to earth; it cannot float loose in the clouds; a theory that rests on nothing but theory is a mere intellectual caprice. Very well; let us go on in our search for fact. By way of testing our perception, we stealthily approach the bird, observe it from new angles, and note fresh characteristics. Does *this* bring us our ultimate fact unmixed with theory? Obviously not. Suppose we proceed with this method to its farthest possible limit; suppose we shoot the bird, seize it, carry it off to a biological laboratory, and subject it to minute and exhaustive dissection; would *that* give us our solid facts? No again. For every notation of a new trait, or even remarking of an old one, would as truly go beyond brute fact and as truly involve an element of theory as would the original judgement. And so long as it contains this element of theory, it must of course be checked by further perceptions; but then these further perceptions once again are judgements; in no case are they brute facts. Thus the facts with which our judgements were to tally seem forever to elude us, and we find ourselves in a region where, on every side, there are only judgements and still more judgements.

. . .

20. To all this it may be replied that we are begging some important questions. It is true enough that in the judgement there are elements not to be found among sense data. But in the first place, why assume that given facts must be confined to sense data? Surely 'two and two make four' and 'pleasure is better than pain' are as much given facts as pleasure and pain themselves. And if so, this attempt to show that given fact is too meagre to verify anything proceeds on a false assumption. In the second place, it begs the question of the structure of judgement. Granting that in the judgement there are elements not present in the answering fact, still there does remain in the judgement the reference to that fact, and it is absurd to say that because the correspondence is incomplete, there is no correspondence at all. When I think of this toothache I may also have to think of irrelevancies, but the fact remains that I do think of this toothache, and that my thought does in part correspond to it.

To the first point we answer as follows: It is true that fact may be, and often has been, identified with something other than what is given in sense. It is generally so taken by the Cambridge philosophers, for whom a fact is a *fact that,* such as that I now have a toothache, or that this table is black; nor is there anything in such usage to object to. But to adopt it here would not help us in the least. Let us suppose that such facts exist, and ask how we can know them. We plainly do not sense them; to say we sense *that* A is B is mere confusion. We apprehend the Bness of A through the judgement, A is B. But judgements, as we have seen, are in principle capable of error; this judgement, therefore, stands in need of verification. But if we attempt to verify it by correspondence, what is the fact that it corresponds to? The Bness of A? But we have seen that we can get at that fact only by the judgement, A is B. To take this as infallible is groundless and arbitrary; to take it as self-evident is to resort to another criterion of truth; to appeal to its coherence with the rest of our knowledge is to join us in this criticism; to say that at any rate what one means by truth is correspondence with such fact is to shift the issue. Indeed, that correspondence is the test seems more difficult to defend on this definition of fact than on the other.

21. Returning then to that other, we are told, secondly, that the correspondence between judgement and fact may be at least partial. Whatever extras judgement introduces, it does contain the assertion that a particular pain exists. Now are we to say that the content of this special assertion cannot correspond just because certain extras that come along with it do not correspond? Surely not, it is said. We can analyse this out from its context and consider its correspondence in isolation. But this itself makes two assumptions, neither of which, I think, can be justified. First, it assumes that the nature of the component it is to isolate is unaffected by the others. There is a fact b^1 and there is a judgement *abc*, and between the b^1 which stands outside the context and the *b* that stands within it there is to be precise correspondence. And the element *b* would still correspond with b^1, no matter how varied or complicated became its context within the judgement. It is thus assumed that the nature of *b* is unaffected by its context. This is not only an assumption but, we believe, a false assumption. Unfortunately since to discuss it would involve us at once in the tortured question of internal relations, we must defer its consideration. But the notion of partial correspondence contains another assumption, which is perhaps the main assumption of the theory generally. It assumes that sensory fact is accessible in its purity, and usable in this form as a test. We have looked into this matter critically in our study of thought in perception, where we were forced to conclude that it is without grounds. This is not to deny, for example, that there are approximations, greater and less, to pure sensory pain. But more particularly in an adult mind, with its innumerable and subtle influences from past experience, its fears and premonitions, its knowledge of causes and results, its flights of classification in which everything received through sense is given its place in a hierarchy of species and genera and related to extensive ranges of remote experience—to suppose that in such experience pain has the sort of purity that it may be presumed to have in the lower orders of life is certainly false to fact.

. . .

24. To those who wish the other kind of evidence it is easy to show that in the actual work of science correspondence is not considered enough. In 1874 Sir William Crookes published an account of an extended series of observa-

tions made in his own laboratory to test the claims of a spiritualist medium that while in a state of trance she was able to produce fully-formed materializations of disembodied spirits. Crookes arranged the conditions in a way that, to his own satisfaction, completely precluded both deception and the co-operation of other persons with the medium; and under these circumstances he reported the following: There appeared a fully materialized figure of a woman some four and one half inches taller than the medium, whose features were larger and complexion lighter, whose pulse-rate by count was 75 while the medium's was 90, who was seen simultaneously with the medium, 'by myself and eight other persons, in my own house, illuminated by the full blaze of the electric light', and who was photographed by a battery of assorted cameras. Now Crookes was a careful and exact observer, of unimpeachable honesty and great scientific distinction. Did science accept his observations? It did not. Though he published in technical journals precise accounts of what he had seen and heard, and described in detail his elaborate precautions, and though a quarter-century later, in his presidential address of 1898 to the British Association he took occasion to say that in all this he had nothing to retract, still in the scientific world his statements met with an incredulity that was steadfast and all but universal. They still do. Nor is this really untypical of the attitude of science toward the claims of perceived facts. If these facts may be read as cohering with the body of established science, in the way of supporting it or extending it, well and good; if they conflict with it, then 'observation and experience are not treated as guides to be meekly followed, but as witnesses to be broken down in cross-examination. Their plain message is disbelieved. . . .' This does not mean, of course, that no observation at variance with received beliefs can get accepted; science would be bound hand and foot if this were true. What it does mean is that observation of this kind is never taken by *itself* as conclusive, as it ought to be if correspondence with perceived fact is to be our test. In case of conflict it is accepted only if the consequences of rejecting generally the sort of evidence here presented would be intellectually more disastrous than those of accepting it. And this is the appeal to coherence.

COHERENCE AS THE NATURE OF TRUTH

1. It has been contended [earlier] that coherence is in the end our sole criterion of truth. We have now to face the question whether it also gives us the nature of truth. We should be clear at the beginning that these are different questions, and that one may reject coherence as the definition of truth while accepting it as the test. . . .

2. The view that truth *is* coherence rests on a theory of the relation of thought to reality, and since this is the central problem of the theory of knowledge, to begin one's discussion by assuming the answer to it or by trying to make one out of whole cloth would be somewhat ridiculous. But as this was our main problem in the long discussions [earlier], we may be pardoned here for brevity. First we shall state in *résumé* the relation of thought to reality that we were there driven to accept, and sketch the theory of truth implicit in it. We shall then take up one by one the objections to this theory and ask if they can pass muster.

To think is to seek understanding. And to seek understanding is an activity of mind that is marked off from all other activities by a highly distinctive aim. This aim, as we saw in our chapter on the general nature of understanding, is to achieve systematic vision, so to apprehend what is now unknown to us as to relate it, and relate it necessarily, to what we know already. We think to solve problems; and our method of solving problems is to build a bridge of intelligible relation from the continent of our knowledge to the island we wish to include in it. Sometimes this bridge is causal, as when we try to explain a disease; sometimes teleological, as when we try to fathom the move of an opponent over the chess board; sometimes geometrical, as in Euclid. But it is always systematic; thought in its very nature is the attempt to bring something unknown or imperfectly known into a sub-system of knowledge, and thus also into that larger system that forms the world of accepted beliefs. That is what explanation is. *Why* is it that thought desires this ordered vision? Why should such a vision give satisfaction when it comes? To these questions there is no answer, and if there were, it would be an answer only because it had succeeded in supplying the characteristic satisfaction to this unique desire.

But may it not be that what satisfies thought fails to conform to the real world? Where is the guarantee that when I have brought my ideas into the form my ideal requires, they should be *true*? Here we come round again to the tortured problem of Book II. In our long struggle with the relation of thought to reality we saw that if thought and things are conceived as related only externally, then knowledge is luck; there is no necessity whatever that what satisfies intelligence should coincide with what really is. It may do so, or it may not; on the principle that there are many misses to one bull's-eye, it more probably does not. But if we get rid of the misleading analogies through which this relation has been conceived, of copy and original, stimulus and organism, lantern and screen, and go to thought itself with the question what reference to an object means, we get a different and more hopeful answer. To think of a thing is to get that thing itself in some degree within the mind. To think of a colour or an emotion is to have that within us which if it *were developed and completed,* would identify itself with the object. In short, if we accept its own report, thought is related to reality as the partial to the perfect fulfilment of a purpose. The more adequate its grasp the more nearly does it approximate, the more fully does it realize in itself, the nature and relations of its objects.

. . .

4\. . . . We may look at the growth of knowledge, individual or social, either as an attempt by our own minds to return to union with things as they are in their ordered wholeness, or the affirmation through our minds of the ordered whole itself. And if we take this view, our notion of truth is marked out for us. Truth is the approximation of thought to reality. It is thought on its way home. Its measure is the distance thought has travelled, under guidance of its inner compass, toward that intelligible system which unites its ultimate object with its ultimate end. Hence at any given time the degree of truth in our experience as a whole is the degree of system it has achieved. The degree of truth of a particular proposition is to be judged in the first instance by its coherence with experience as a whole, ultimately by its coherence with that further whole, all-comprehensive and fully articulated, in which thought can come to rest.

5. But it is time we defined more explicitly what coherence means. To be sure, no fully satisfactory definition can be given; and as Dr. Ewing says, 'it is wrong to tie down the advocates of the coherence theory to a precise definition. What they are doing is to describe an ideal that has never yet been completely clarified but is none the less immanent in all our thinking.' Certainly this ideal goes far beyond mere consistency. Fully coherent knowledge would be knowledge in which every judgement entailed, and was entailed by, the rest of the system. Probably we never find in fact a system where there is so much of interdependence. What it means may be clearer if we take a number of familiar systems and arrange them in a series tending to such coherence as a limit. At the bottom would be a junk-heap, where we could know every item but one and still be without any clue as to what that remaining item was. Above this would come a stone-pile, for here you could at least infer that what you would find next would be a stone. A machine would be higher again, since from the remaining parts one could deduce not only the general character of a missing part, but also its special form and function. This is a high degree of coherence, but it is very far short of the highest. You could remove the engine from a motor-car while leaving the other parts intact, and replace it with any one of thousands of other engines, but the thought of such an interchange among human heads or hearts shows at once that the interdependence in a machine is far below that of the body. Do we find then in organic bodies the highest conceivable coherence? Clearly not. Though a human hand, as Aristotle said, would hardly be a hand when detached from the body, still it would be something definite enough; and we can conceive systems in which even this something would be gone. Abstract a number from the number series and it would be a mere unrecognizable x; similarly, the very thought of a straight line involves the thought of the Euclidean space in which it falls. It is perhaps in such systems as Euclidean geometry that we get the most perfect examples of coherence that have been constructed. If any proposition were lacking, it could be supplied from the rest; if any were altered, the repercussions would be felt through the length and breadth of the system. Yet even such a system as this falls short of ideal system. Its postulates are unproved; they are independent of each other, in the sense that none of them could be derived from any other or even from all the others together; its clear necessity is bought by an abstractness so extreme as to have left out nearly everything that belongs to the character of actual things. A completely satisfactory system would have none of these defects. No proposition would be arbitrary, every proposition would be entailed by the others jointly and even singly,[1] no proposition would stand outside the system. The integration would be so complete that no part could be seen for what it was without seeing its relation to the whole, and

[1] Coherence can be defined without this point, which, as Dr. Ewing remarks (*Idealism*, 231), makes the case harder to establish. In no mathematical system, for example, would anyone dream of trying to deduce all the other propositions from any proposition taken singly. But when we are describing an ideal, such a fact is not decisive, and I follow Joachim in holding that in a perfectly coherent system every proposition would entail all others, if only for the reason that its meaning could never be fully understood without apprehension of the system in its entirety.

the whole itself could be understood only through the contribution of every part.

. . .

8. Does acceptance of coherence as a test commit us not only to a view about the structure of reality but also to a view about the nature of truth? This is a more difficult question. As we saw at the beginning of the chapter, there have been some highly reputable philosophers who have held that the answer to 'What is the test of truth'? is 'Coherence', while the answer to 'What is the nature or meaning of truth?' is 'Correspondence'. These questions are plainly distinct. Nor does there seem to be any direct path from the acceptance of coherence as the test of truth to its acceptance as the nature of truth. Nevertheless there is an indirect path. If we accept coherence as our test, we must use it everywhere. We must therefore use it to test the suggestion that truth *is* other than coherence. But if we do, we shall find that we must reject the suggestion as leading to *in*coherence. Coherence is a pertinacious concept and, like the well-known camel, if one lets it get its nose under the edge of the tent, it will shortly walk off with the whole.

Suppose that, accepting coherence as the test, one rejects it as the nature of truth in favour of some alternative; and let us assume, for example, that this alternative is correspondence. This, we have said, is incoherent; why? Because if one holds that truth is correspondence, one cannot intelligibly hold either that it is tested by coherence or that there is any dependable test at all. Consider the first point. Suppose that we construe experience into the most coherent picture possible, remembering that among the elements included will be such secondary qualities as colours, odours, and sounds. Would the mere fact that such elements as these are coherently arranged prove that anything precisely corresponding to them exists 'out there'? I cannot see that it would, even if we knew that the two arrangements had closely corresponding patterns. If on one side you have a series of elements a, b, c . . . , and on the other a series of elements α, β, γ . . . , arranged in patterns that correspond, you have no proof as yet that the *natures* of these elements correspond. It is therefore impossible to argue from a high degree of coherence within experience to its correspondence in the same degree with anything outside. And this difficulty is typical. If you place the nature of truth in one sort of character and its test in something quite different, you are pretty certain, sooner or later, to find the two falling apart. In the end, the only test of truth that is not misleading is the special nature or character that is itself constitutive of truth.

Feeling that this is so, the adherents of correspondence sometimes insist that correspondence shall be its own test. But then the second difficulty arises. If truth does consist in correspondence, no test can be sufficient. For in order to know that experience corresponds to fact, we must be able to get at that fact, unadulterated with idea, and compare the two sides with each other. And we have seen in the last chapter that such fact is not accessible. When we try to lay hold of it, what we find in our hands is a judgement which is obviously not itself the indubitable fact we are seeking, and which must be checked by some fact beyond it. To this process there is no end. And even if we did get at the fact directly, rather than through the veil of our ideas, that would be no less fatal to correspondence. This direct seizure of fact presumably gives us truth, but since that truth no longer consists in correspondence of idea with fact, the main theory has been abandoned. In short, if we can know fact only through the medium of our own ideas, the original forever eludes us; if we can get at the facts directly, we have knowledge whose truth is not correspondence. The theory is forced to choose between scepticism and self-contradiction.

Thus the attempt to combine coherence as the test of truth with correspondence as the nature of truth will not pass muster by its own test. The result is *in*coherence. We believe that an application of the test to other theories of truth would lead to a like result. The argument is: assume coherence as the test, and you will be driven by the incoherence of your alternatives to the conclusion that it is also the nature of truth.

The theory that truth *consists* in coherence must now be developed more specifically. The theory has been widely attacked, and the average reader will not improbably come to it with numerous and dark suspicions. In presenting the theory we shall therefore follow a somewhat unusual procedure. We shall [deal with some] of these suspicions and objections . . . seeking in our answers to bring the nature and implications of the theory gradually to light.

. . .

13. (5) We come now to an objection more frequently made than any we have been considering. Granting that propositions, to be true, must be coherent with each other, may they not be coherent without being true? Are there not many systems of high unity and inclusiveness, which nevertheless are false? We have seen, for example, that there are various systems of geometry each of which seems to be as coherent internally as the others. Since they are mutually inconsistent, not more than one of them can be true, and there are many mathematicians who would say that *none* of them are true; yet if truth lies merely in coherence, are we not compelled to take all of them as true? Again, a novel, or a succession of novels such as Galsworthy's *Forsyte Saga,* may create a special world of characters and events which is at once extremely complex and internally consistent; does that make it the less fictitious? To say that it does would imply that if we could only dream constantly enough and consistently enough our dreams would literally come true.

(i) This objection, like so many other annihilating criticisms, would have more point if anyone had ever held the theory it demolishes. But if intended to represent the coherence theory as responsibly advocated, it is a gross misunderstanding. That theory does not hold that any and every system is true, no matter how abstract and limited; it holds that one system only is true, namely the system in which everything real and possible is coherently included. How one can find in this the notion that a system would still give truth if, like some arbitrary geometry, it disregarded experience completely, it is not easy to see.

14. (ii) The objection gains point, however, when it goes on to inquire whether all that is actual might not be embraced in more than one system. When a murder is committed, there may be two theories of the crime which do complete and equal justice to all the known facts and yet are inconsistent

with each other. Is it not conceivable similarly that there should be two perfect but conflicting systems in which all known and knowable facts should fall into place? If so, our standard would require us to say that both were true; yet since they conflict, this would be absurd. Now we might reply that such a contingency, though possible, is highly improbable. In the case of the murder, every new bit of evidence narrows the range of available hypotheses, and it does not even occur to us that if we knew *all* the relevant facts we might find ourselves at the end with conflicting theories. If such an issue is improbable where the facts are so few, is it not far more improbable where the facts are infinitely many?

Still, this answer seems inadequate, since a theory that leaves it even possible that in the ultimate nature of truth there should be inconsistency ought to be met, we feel, with some decisive disproof. Can it be shown that such an issue is not only improbable, but impossible? I think it can. There are to be two systems, each including all facts known or knowable, but differing in internal structure. Now if the first system is constructed according to plan A, and the second according to plan B, then the possession by the first of plan A is not a fact that is included in the second, and the possession of plan B by the second is not a fact included in the first. The two systems are thus *not,* as they are supposed to be, each inclusive of all the known facts. To put it otherwise, if the systems differ neither in facts nor in structure, they are not two systems but one. If, with the same facts, they are to differ at all, they must differ in structure, but then there will be at least one fact that each of them must omit, namely, the fact that the other possesses the particular structure it does. Thus that all actual and possible facts should be embraced in conflicting systems is unthinkable.

On the other hand, if the objector lowers his claim and says only that the facts *as so far known* may be ordered in different systems, he is saying nothing against our theory. For this certainly does not show that if all the facts were known these rivals would still stand as rivals; it shows only that with the facts now available we should not on our view be justified in making a choice. And this really confirms our view, through bringing it into line with science. Such suspension of judgement is precisely what is enjoined by scientific practice, which holds that so long as two rival hypotheses equally cover the facts, neither is to be preferred to the other, but that as soon as there appears an *instantia crucis* which one hypothesis can assimilate and the other not, we are justified in adopting the first.[2]

15. (iii) Suppose, however, that no crucial instance ever did arise. Suppose (to put an extreme but conceivable case) that we spent from twelve midnight to twelve noon of every day in dreaming, that our dreams were as vivid and orderly as our waking life, and that when we resumed them every night we did so at exactly the point at which we left off the day before. Would

[2] It may be said that the truth is not established until *all* rivals have been eliminated. But this is not the view on which the natural sciences actually proceed. Of course in formal logic an argument from the affirmation of the consequent is fallacious, and when this is carried over into science it is often said to provide verification without proof; the proof is attained only when it is shown that from no other antecedent could these consequences have sprung. But it will be evident that in the ordinary work of science proof of this kind is seldom if ever practicable; one cannot be sure that *all possible* alternatives have been excluded. 'The character of relativity and non-finality, which attaches to mere verification and causes it to be called the fallacy of the consequent, is really inevitable in the pursuit of truth,'—Bosanquet, *Implication and Lin. Inf.*, 102.

there then be any difference between sleep and waking? Would there be any sense in saying that one world was real and the other unreal, that in the one our perceptions and beliefs were true and in the other delusions merely? I think not. And our inability to make any choice in such a conjuncture confirms our theory. The argument runs: if truth did lie in coherence, then, confronted with two worlds equally coherent, we should be unable to select one as truer than the other; on reflection we can see that such inability is just what we should find; hence the equation of truth with coherence is so far verified.

16. (iv) It is further verified by our way of choosing between systems which in the above sense are *not* equal. There are various cases. Consider how we recognize dreams or delusions for what they are. When we are suddenly roused from a vivid dream, we may be momentarily dazed, not knowing the dream from the actuality. How do we establish which is which? Mere vividness does not decide the matter; the dream may be of nightmare intensity while the perception of our familiar surroundings may be comparatively dim. The deciding factor in the battle is what may be called the mass and integration of the household troops. The bureau and windows of our familiar bedroom and the sound of a familiar voice throw out innumerable lines of connection that bring our everyday world around us again in irresistible volume. Against the great bulk of this world, and without any lodgement in it, the figures of our dream appear unsubstantial and fugitive, quickly dissolving for want of support; and it is just the recognition that what we have been experiencing will not fit into our common-sense world that we mean when we say we wake from dream. The power to measure such fancies and phantasms against the ordered mass of experience is the logical meaning of sanity; its disappearance is insanity. There may be organic differences between the man who thinks himself Napoleon, the man who is sure he has committed the unpardonable sin, and the man who is persuaded that there is a universal conspiracy to keep him down; but intellectually they are alike; there are certain beliefs which resist appraisal by the mass of their general experience, and stand in the midst of it like solid capsules impervious to outer influences. In these cases that is what insanity means.

. . .

19. (6) It may be said that such a view is a 'rationalization' of conservatism. 'We are to accept whatever agrees with the body of received belief, and reject whatever disagrees. But the great advances in human knowledge have been precisely those in which the mind broke loose from the received system, set up claims that ran counter to it, and in spite of opposition and derision made them good. Scientific progress, like political, has sometimes come through revolutions. But how can revolutions occur, how can there be any but the most trivial sort of progress, if it is acknowledged in advance that nothing can be true which does not accord with what is already established?'

A little reflection will show that this begs the question. It is assumed that according to the coherence theory what is established, in the sense of merely holding the ground, is to be taken as established logically, whereas the theory expressly denies this. It says on the contrary that no system can be taken as final except that system, all-inclusive and perfectly integrated, in which the ideal of thought is realized. Indeed the two charges of dogmatism and scepticism, the charge that the theory accepts received truth as final and the opposite charge that it admits no truth at all, might well be left to cancel each other out, except that, rightly interpreted, they reveal complementary values in the theory.

An objector who concedes this may feel a genuine difficulty, however, about the way in which the dogmatism of a particular period is, on the theory, to be broken down. Granting our right to say in the abstract that the system of beliefs of any particular time is defective, how is the system in practice to be corrected if there is no measure of its correctness but itself? Judged by the system of Ptolemy, the system of Newton was false; judged by the system of Newton, the system of Einstein is false. In each of these cases the older system has in fact given way; but if the only measure of its truth was coherence with what was already received, then it ought *not* to have given way. And to say that seems ridiculous. We commonly believe that in each case the newer system won a justified victory, but how could it ever have done so if the coherence view had been followed?

But the critic is here limiting in arbitrary fashion the body of beliefs from which we start. He is assuming that the only beliefs it contains are beliefs of the first order. By 'beliefs of the first order' are meant beliefs about any objects of direct experience such as tables and chairs; by 'beliefs of the second order' are meant beliefs about these beliefs. Now, of course, scientific observation runs counter very frequently to established beliefs of the first order, and if these alone were decisive, the new result would have to go. Take, as a recent example, one of the observations by which the general theory of relativity was verified. It was implied in this theory that as light rays passed the sun on their journey from distant stars they would be bent by the sun's attraction, and hence that stars seen under such conditions would appear to be slightly displaced from their normal positions. Accordingly observers waited impatiently for a moment when an eclipse of the sun would render such stars visible. When it came, they found the stars displaced as Einstein had predicted. The positions actually seen conflicted with those required by Newtonian astronomy; and it may be said that if truth is to be measured by its accord with existing belief, the new observations would have had to be rejected. But at this point beliefs of the second order enter the scene. We not only hold beliefs about tables and chairs, the sun and the stars; we also hold *beliefs about the technique of acquiring beliefs*. We believe that perceptual judgements made under conditions exclusive of bias, ambiguity and vagueness are more to be relied upon than judgements made only casually. Now let us suppose that such careful observations as the one described are rejected because of their conflict with accepted 'fact'. Consistency would require us to hold that *all* observations made with similar care and accuracy must be set down as giving uncertainty and perhaps falsehood, and that would conflict with the very important second-order belief just mentioned. We are thus left in a position where acceptance of the observed result would conflict with our first-order beliefs, while rejection of it would conflict with an important second-order belief; and it may be thought that the first-order beliefs would win by their sheer volume. This is a mistake. For if the second-order belief goes, an enormous mass of first-order beliefs will obviously go with it. If every judgement made under conditions as stringent as those described must be called in question, is there any perceptual judgement that can be any longer relied on? A policy that would reject such judgements consistently would involve science in general ruin. To be sure, if they are accepted, certain old first-order beliefs must be revised, but this is as nothing to the chaos that would follow from a loss of faith in the observations of science. Thus stability itself demands that the new results be given admission.

The charge of conservatism is thus a mistake. It assumes that the system we must take as base is a system of first-order beliefs. But we have seen that when beliefs of the second order are included, as they have every right to be, we have a system that provides for its own correction.

John Dewey

Propositions, Warranted Assertibility, and Truth

I propose in what follows to restate some features of the theories I have previously advanced on the topics mentioned above. I shall shape this restatement on the basis of ascriptions and criticisms of my views found in Mr. Russell's *An Inquiry into Truth and Meaning.* . . .

I

Mr. Russell refers to my theory as one which "substitutes 'warranted assertibility' for truth."[1] Under certain conditions, I should have no cause to object to this reference. But the conditions are absent; and it is possible that this view of "substitution" as distinct from and even opposed to *definition,* plays an important rôle in generating what I take to be misconceptions of my theory in some important specific matters. Hence, I begin by saying that my analysis of "warranted assertibility" is offered as a *definition* of the nature of knowledge in the honorific sense according to which only *true* beliefs are knowledge. The place at which there is pertinency in the idea of "substitution" has to do with *words.* As I wrote in my *Logic: The Theory of Inquiry,* "What has been said helps explain why the term "warranted assertibility" is preferred to the terms *belief* and *knowledge.* It is free from the ambiguity of the latter

[1] *An Inquiry into Truth and Meaning,* p. 362. This interpretation is repeated on p. 401, using the words "should take the place of" instead of "substitutes."

From John Dewey, "Propositions, Warranted Assertibility, and Truth," *The Journal of Philosophy,* Vol. 38 (1941). Reproduced by permission of Mrs. John Dewey and of *The Journal of Philosophy.* The article is a rejoinder to criticisms of Dewey's views by Bertrand Russell, and it also appears in John Dewey, *Problems of Men,* 1946.

John Dewey (1859–1952) was Professor of Philosophy at Columbia University from 1905 until his retirement in 1929.

terms."[2] But there is involved the extended analysis, given later, of the nature of assertion and of warrant.

. . .

The position which I take, namely, that all knowledge, or warranted assertion, depends upon inquiry and that inquiry is, truistically, connected with what is questionable (and questioned) involves a sceptical element, or what Peirce called "fallibilism." But it also provides for *probability,* and for determination of degrees of probability in rejecting all intrinsically dogmatic statements, where "dogmatic" applies to *any* statement asserted to possess inherent self-evident truth. That the only alternative to ascribing to some propositions self-sufficient, self-possessed, and self-evident truth is a theory which finds the test and mark of truth in *consequences* of some sort is, I hope, an acceptable view. At all events, it is a position to be kept in mind in assessing my views.

II

In an earlier passage Mr. Russell ascribes certain views to "instrumentalists" and points out certain errors which undoubtedly (and rather obviously) exist in those views—as *he* conceives and states them. My name and especial view are not mentioned in this earlier passage. But, aside from the fact that I have called my view of propositions "instrumental" (in the particular technical sense in which I define propositions), comment on the passage may assist in clarifying what my views genuinely are. The passage reads:

> There are some schools of philosophy—notably the Hegelians and the instrumentalists—which deny the distinction between data and inference altogether. They maintain that in all our knowledge there is an inferential element, that knowledge is an organic whole, and that the test of truth is coherence rather than conformity with "fact." I do not deny an element of truth in this view, but I think that, if taken as a whole truth, it renders the part played by perception in knowledge inexplicable. It is surely obvious that every perceptive experience, if I choose to notice it, affords me either new knowledge which I could not previously have inferred, or, at least, as in the case of eclipses, greater certainty than I could have previously obtained by means of inference. To this the instrumentalist replies that any statement of the new knowledge obtained from perception is always an interpretation based upon accepted theories, and may need subsequent correction if these theories turn out to be unsuitable.[3]

I begin with the ascription to instrumentalists of the idea that "in all our knowledge, there is an inferential element." This statement is, from the stand-

[2] *Logic,* p. 9. Perhaps in the interest of clearness, the word "term" should have been italicized. The ambiguities in question are discussed in previous pages. In the case of *belief,* the main ambiguity is between it as a state of mind and as *what* is believed—subject-matter. In the case of *knowledge,* it concerns the difference between knowledge as an outcome of "competent and controlled inquiry" and knowledge supposed to "have a meaning of its own apart from connection with, and reference to, inquiry."

[3] *Logic,* p. 154. To clear the ground for discussion of the views advanced in the passage quoted in the text, and as a means of shortening my comments, I append a few categorical statements, which can be substantiated by many references to "instrumentalist" writings. Instrumentalists do *not* believe that "knowledge is an organic whole"; in fact, the idea is meaningless upon their view. They do *not* believe the test of truth is coherence; in the operational sense, stated later in this paper, they hold a correspondence view.

point of my view, ambiguous; in one of its meanings, it is incorrect. It is necessary, then, to make a distinction. If it means (as it is apparently intended to mean) that an element due to inference appears in *propria persona,* so to speak, it is incorrect. For according to my view (if I may take it as a sample of the instrumentalists' view), while to infer something is necessary if a warranted assertion is to be arrived at, this inferred somewhat never appears *as such* in the latter; that is, in knowledge. The inferred material has to be checked and tested. The means of testing, required to give an inferential element any claim whatsoever to be *knowledge* instead of conjecture, are the data provided by observation—and *only* by observation. Moreover, as is stated frequently in my *Logic: The Theory of Inquiry,* it is necessary that data (provided by observation) be *new,* or different from those which first suggested the inferential element, if they are to have any value with respect to attaining knowledge. It is important that they be had under as many different conditions as possible so that data due to *differential* origins may supplement one another. The necessity of both the distinction and the coöperation of inferential and observational subject-matters is, on my theory, the product of an analysis of scientific inquiry; this necessity is, as will be shown in more detail later, the heart of my whole theory that knowledge is warranted assertion.

It should now be clear that the instrumentalist would not dream of making the kind of "reply" attributed to him. Instead of holding that "*accepted* theories" are always the basis for interpretation of what is newly obtained in perceptual experience, he has not been behind others in pointing out that such a mode of interpretation is a common and serious source of wrong conclusions; of dogmatism and of consequent arrest of advance in knowledge. In my *Logic,* I have explicitly pointed out that one chief reason why the introduction of experimental methods meant such a great, such a revolutionary, change in natural science, is that they provide data which are new not only in detail but in *kind*. Hence their introduction compelled new kinds of inference to new kinds of subject-matters, and the formation of new types of theories—in addition to providing more exact means of testing old theories. Upon the basis of the view ascribed to instrumentalists, I should suppose it would have been simpler and more effective to point out the contradiction involved in holding, on one side, that the instrumentalist has no way of discovering "need for further correction" in accepted theories, while holding, on the other side, that all accepted theories are, or may be, "unsuitable." Is there not flat contradiction between the idea that "any statement of new knowledge obtained by perception is always an interpretation based upon accepted theories," and the view that it may need subsequent correction if these theories prove "unsuitable"? How in the world, upon the ground of the first part of the supposed "reply" of the instrumentalist, could any theory once "accepted" ever be shown to be unsuitable?

I am obliged, unfortunately, to form a certain hypothesis as to how and why, in view of the numerous and oft-repeated statements in my *Logic* of the *necessity* for distinguishing between inferential elements and observational data (necessary since otherwise there is no approach to warranted assertibility), it could occur to anyone that I denied the distinction. The best guess I can make is that my statements about the necessity of hard data, due to experimental observation and freed from all inferential constituents, were not taken seriously because it was supposed that upon my theory these data themselves represent, or present, *cases of knowledge,* so that there must be on my theory an inferential element also in them. Whether or not this is the source of the alleged denial thought up by Mr. Russell, it may be used to indicate a highly significant difference between our two views. For Mr. Russell holds, if I understand him, that propositions about these data are in some cases instances of knowledge, and indeed that such cases provide, as basic propositions, the models upon which a theory of truth should be formed. In my view, they are not cases of *knowledge,* although propositional formulation of them is a *necessary* (but not sufficient) condition of knowledge.

I can understand that my actual view may seem even more objectionable to a critic than the one that has been wrongly ascribed to me. None the less, in the interest of understanding and as a ground of pertinent criticism, it is indispensable that this position, and what it involves, be recognized as fundamental in my theory. It brings me to what is meant, in my theory, by the instrumental character of a proposition. I shall, then, postpone consideration of the ascription to me of the view that propositions are true if they are instruments or tools of successful action till I have stated just what, on my theory, a proposition is. The view imputed to me is that "Inquiry uses 'assertions' as its tools, and assertions are 'warranted' insofar as they produce the desired result."[4] I put in contrast with this conception the following statement of my view:

> Judgment may be identified as the settled outcome of inquiry. It is concerned with the concluding objects that emerge from inquiry in their status of being *conclusive.* Judgment in this sense is distinguished from *propositions.* The content of the latter is intermediate and representative and is carried by symbols; while judgment, as finally made, has *direct* existential import. The terms *affirmation* and *assertion* are employed in current speech interchangeably. But there is a difference, which should have linguistic recognition, between the logical status of intermediate subject-matters that are taken for use in connection *with what they lead to as means,* and subject-matter which has been prepared to be final. I shall use *assertion* to designate the latter logical status and *affirmation* to name the former. . . . However, the important matter is not the words, but the logical properties characteristic of different subject-matters.[5]

Propositions, then, on this view, are what are affirmed but not asserted. They are means, instrumentalities, since they are the operational agencies by which *beliefs* that have adequate grounds for acceptance, are reached as *end* of inquiry. As I have intimated, this view may seem even more objectionable than is the one attributed to me, i.e., the one which is not mine. But in any case the difference between the instrumentality of a *proposition* as means of attaining a grounded *belief* and the instrumentality of a *belief* as means of reaching certain "desired results," should be fairly obvious, independently of acceptance or rejection of my view.

Unless a critic is willing to entertain, in however hypothetical a fashion, the view (i) that *knowledge* (in its honorific sense) is in every case connected

[4] *Inquiry,* pp. 401–402.

[5] *Logic,* p. 120 (not all italics in original). The word "logical," as it occurs in this passage, is, of course, to be understood in the sense given that term in previous chapters of the volume; a signification that is determined by connection with operations of inquiry which are undertaken because of the existence of a problem, and which are controlled by the conditions of that problem—since the "goal" is to resolve the problem which evokes inquiry.

with inquiry; (ii) that the conclusion or end of inquiry has to be demarcated from the intermediate means by which inquiry goes forward to a warranted or justified conclusion; that (iii) the intermediate means are formulated in discourse, i.e., as propositions, and that as means they have the properties appropriate to means (viz., relevancy and efficacy—including economy), I know of no way to make my view intelligible. If the view is entertained, even in the most speculative conjectural fashion, it will, I think, be clear that according to it, truth and falsity are properties only of that subject-matter which is the *end,* the close, of the inquiry by means of which it is reached. The distinction between true and false conclusions is determined by the character of the operational procedures through which propositions about data and propositions about inferential elements (meanings, ideas, hypotheses) are instituted. At all events, I can not imagine that one who says that such things as hammers, looms, chemical processes like dyeing, reduction of ores, when used as means, are marked by properties of fitness and efficacy (and the opposite) rather than by the properties of truth-falsity, will be thought to be saying anything that is not commonplace.

IV

. . .

Coming to the main point at issue, I hold that the first propositions we make as means of resolving a problem of any marked degree of difficulty are indeed likely to be too vague and coarse to be effective, just as in the story of invention of other instrumentalities, the first forms are relatively clumsy, uneconomical, and ineffective. They have then, as means, to be replaced by others which are more effective. Propositions are vague when, for example, they do not delimit the problem sufficiently to indicate what kind of a solution is relevant. It is hardly necessary to say that when we don't know the conditions constituting a problem we are trying to solve, our efforts at solution at best will be fumbling and are likely to be wild. Data serve as tests of any idea or hypothesis that suggests itself, and in this capacity also their definiteness is required. But, upon my view, the degree and the quality of definiteness and of simplicity, or elementariness, required, are determined by the problem that evokes and controls inquiry. However the case may stand in epistemology (as a problem based upon a prior assumption that knowledge is and must be a relation between a knowing subject and an object), upon the basis of a view that takes knowing (inquiry) as it finds it, the idea that simplicity and elementariness are *inherent* properties of propositions (apart from their place and function in inquiry), has no meaning. If I understand Mr. Russell's view, his test for the simple and definite nature of a proposition applies indifferently to all propositions and hence has no indicative or probative force with respect to any proposition in particular.

Accepting, then, Mr. Russell's statement that his "problem has been, throughout, the relation between events and propositions," . . . I would point out what seems to be a certain indeterminateness in his view of the relation between events and propositions, and the consequent need of introducing a distinction: *viz.,* the distinction between the problem of the relation of events and propositions *in general,* and the problem of the relation of a *particular* proposition to the *particular* event to which it purports to refer. I can understand that Mr. Russell holds that certain propositions, of a specified kind, are such direct effects of certain events, and of nothing else, that they "must be true." But this view does not, as I see the matter, answer the question of how we know that *in a given case* this direct relationship actually exists. It does not seem to me that his theory gets beyond specifying the kind of case *in general* in which the relation between an event, as causal antecedent, and a proposition, as effect, is such as to confer upon instances of the latter the property of being true. But I can not see that we get anywhere until we have means of telling *which* propositions in particular *are* instances of the kind in question.

. . . These comments are intended to indicate both that I hold a "correspondence" theory of truth, and the sense in which I hold it;—a sense which seems to me free from a fundamental difficulty that Mr. Russell's view of truth can not get over or around. The event *to be* known is that which operates, on his view, as cause of the proposition while it is also its verifier; although the proposition is the sole means of knowing the event! Such a view, like any strictly epistemological view, seems to me to assume a mysterious and unverifiable doctrine of pre-established harmony. How an event can be (i) what-is-to-be-known, and hence by description is unknown, and (ii) what is capable of being *known* only through the medium of a proposition, which, in turn (iii) in order to be a case of knowledge or be true, must correspond to the to-be-known, is to me *the* epistemological miracle. For the doctrine states that a proposition is true when it conforms to that which is not known save through itself.

In contrast with this view, my own view takes correspondence in the operational sense it bears in all cases except the unique epistemological case of an alleged relation between a "subject" and an "object"; the meaning, namely, of *answering*, as a key answers to conditions imposed by a lock, or as two correspondents "answer" each other; or, in general, as a reply is an adequate answer to a question or a criticism—; as, in short, a *solution* answers the requirements of a *problem*. On this view, both partners in "correspondence" are open and above board, instead of one of them being forever out of experience and the other in it by way of a "percept" or whatever. Wondering at how something in experience could be asserted to correspond to something by definition outside experience, which it is, upon the basis of epistemological doctrine, the sole means of "knowing," is what originally made me suspicious of the whole epistemological industry.[6]

[6] In noting that my view of truth involves dependence upon consequences (as his depends upon antecedents, not, however, themselves in experience), and in noting that a causal law is involved, Mr. Russell concludes: "These causal laws, if they are to serve their purpose, must be 'true' in the very sense that Dr. Dewey would abolish" (*Inquiry,* p. 408). It hardly seems unreasonable on my part to expect that my general theory of truth be applied to particular cases, that of the truth of causal laws included. If it was unreasonable to *expect* that it would be so understood, I am glad to take this opportunity to say that such is the case. I do not hold in this case a view I have elsewhere "abolished." I *apply* the general view I advance elsewhere. There are few matters with respect to which there has been as much experience and as much testing as in the matter of the connection of means and consequences, since that connection is involved in all the details of every occupation, art, and undertaking. That warranted assertibility is a matter of probability in the case of causal connections is a trait it shares with other instances of warranted assertibility; while, apparently, Mr. Russell would deny the name of knowledge, in its fullest sense, to anything that is not certain to the point of infallibility, or which does not ultimately rest upon some absolute certainty.

In the sense of correspondence as operational and behavioral (the meaning which has definite parallels in ordinary experience), I hold that my *type* of theory is the only one entitled to be called a correspondence theory of truth.

V

I should be happy to believe that what has been said is sufficiently definite and clear as to the nature and function of "consequences," so that it is not necessary to say anything more on the subject. But there are criticisms of Mr. Russell's that I might seem to be evading were I to say nothing specifically about them. He asserts that he has several times asked me what the goal of inquiry is upon my theory, and has seen no answer to the question.[7] There seems to be some reason for inferring that this matter is connected with the belief that I am engaged in *substituting* something else for "truth," so that truth, as he interprets my position, not being the goal, I am bound to provide some other goal. A person turning to the Index of my *Logic: The Theory of Inquiry* will find the following heading: "Assertibility, warranted, as end of inquiry." Some fourteen passages of the text are referred to. Unless there is difference which escapes me between "end" and "goal," the following passage would seem to give the answer which Mr. Russell has missed:

> Moreover, inference, even in its connection with test, is not logically final and complete. The heart of the entire theory developed in this work is that the resolution of an indeterminate situation is the end, in the sense in which "end" means *end-in-view* and in the sense in which it means *close*.[8]

The implication of the passage, if not in its isolation then in its context, is that inquiry begins in an *indeterminate* situation, and not only begins in it but is controlled by its specific qualitative nature.[9] Inquiry, as the set of operations by which the situation is resolved (settled, or rendered determinate) has to discover and formulate the conditions that describe the problem in hand. For *they* are the conditions to be "satisfied" and the determinants of "success." Since these conditions are existential, they can be determined only by observational operations; the operational character of observation being clearly exhibited in the experimental character of all scientific determination of data. (Upon a non-scientific level of inquiry, it is exhibited in the fact that we *look* and see; *listen* and hear; or, in general terms, that a motor-muscular, as well as sensory, factor is involved in any perceptual experience.) The conditions discovered, accordingly, in and by operational observation, constitute the *conditions of the problem* with which further inquiry is engaged; for data, on this view, are always data of some specific problem and hence are not given ready-made to an inquiry but are determined in and by it. (The point previously stated, that propositions about data are not cases of knowledge but means of attaining it, is so obviously an integral part of this view that I say nothing further about it in this connection.) As the problem progressively assumes definite shape by means of repeated acts of observation,

[7] *Inquiry*, p. 404.
[8] *Logic*, pp. 157–158.
[9] *Logic*, p. 105. "It is a unique doubtfulness" that not only evokes the particular inquiry, but as explicitly stated "exercises control" over it. To avoid needless misunderstanding, I quote also the following passage: "No situation which is *completely* indeterminate can possibly be converted into a problem having definite constituents" (*Logic*, p. 108).

possible solutions suggest themselves. These possible solutions are, truistically (in terms of the theory), *possible* meanings of the data determined in observation. The process of reasoning is an elaboration of them. When they are checked by reference to observed materials, they constitute the subject-matter of *inferential* propositions. The latter are means of attaining the goal of knowledge as warranted assertion, not instances or examples of knowledge. They are also operational in nature since they institute new experimental observations whose subject-matter provides both tests for old hypotheses and starting-points for new ones or at least for modifying solutions previously entertained. And so on until a determinate situation is instituted.

If this condensed statement is taken in its own terms and not by first interpreting its meaning in terms of some theory it doesn't logically permit, I think it will render unnecessary further comment on the notion Mr. Russell has ascribed to me: the notion, namely, that "a belief is warranted, if as a tool, it is useful in some activity, i.e., if it is a cause of satisfaction of desire," and that "the only essential result of successful inquiry is successful action." [10]

In the interest of mutual understanding, I shall now make some comments on a passage which, if I interpret it aright, sets forth the nature of Mr. Russell's wrong idea of my view, and which also, by implication, suggests the nature of the genuine difference between our views:

> If there are such occurrences as "believings," which seems undeniable, the question is: Can they be divided into two classes, the "true" and the "false"? Or, if not, can they be so analyzed that their constituents can be divided into these two classes? If either of these questions is answered in the affirmative, is the distinction between "true" and "false" to be found in the success or failure of the effects of believings, or is it to be found in some other relation which they may have to relevant occurrences? [11]

On the basis of other passages, such as have been quoted, I am warranted in supposing that there is ascribed to me the view that "the distinction between 'true' and 'false' is to be found in the success or failure of the effects of believings." After what I have already said, I hope it suffices to point out that the question of truth-falsity is *not,* on my view, a matter of the effects of *believing,* for my whole theory is determined by the attempt to state what conditions and operations of inquiry *warrant* a "believing," or justify its assertion as true; that propositions, as such, are so far from being cases of believings that they are means of attaining a warranted believing, their worth as means being determined by their pertinency and efficacy in "satisfying" conditions that are rigorously set by the problem they are employed to resolve.

At this stage of the present discussion, I am, however, more interested in the passage quoted as an indication of the difference between us than as a manifestation of the nature of Mr. Russell's wrong understanding of my view.[12] I believe most decidedly that the distinction between "true" and "false" is to be

[10] *Inquiry,* pp. 404, 405.
[11] *Inquiry,* p. 405.
[12] I venture to remark that the words "wrong" and "right" as they appear in the text are used intentionally instead of the words "false" and "true"; for, according to my view, understanding and misunderstanding, conception and misconception, taking and mis-taking, are matters of propositions, which are not final or complete in themselves but are used as means to an end—the resolution of a problem; while it is to this resolution, as *conclusion* of inquiry, that the adjectives "true" and "false" apply.

found in the relation which *propositions,* as means of inquiry, "have to relevant occurrences." The difference between us concerns, as I see the matter in the light of Mr. Russell's explanation, the question of *what* occurrences *are* the relevant ones. And I hope it is unnecessary to repeat by this time that the relevant occurrences on my theory are those existential consequences which, in virtue of operations existentially performed, satisfy (meet, fulfill) conditions set by occurrences that constitute a problem. . . .

Peter Frederick Strawson

Truth

In the following discussion, I confine myself to the question of the truth of empirical statements. My positive thesis is an elaboration of what was said, a long time ago, by F. P. Ramsey.[1] My negative purpose is the criticism of a current misconception—the Semantic or Meta-linguistic Theory of Truth—which seems to me to repeat, in a new way, some old mistakes. In so far as this theory is simply a contribution to the construction of artificial languages, and is not intended to be regarded as relevant to the use of actual languages, I am not concerned with it. But I think the theory has been claimed by some, and it has certainly been thought by many, to throw light on the actual use of the word 'true'; or (which I take to be the same claim) on the philosophical problem of truth. I think it *does* throw some light; but I think it is also seriously misleading. Nothing that follows, however, is to be taken as implying that the word 'true' is *never* used in the way described by the semantic theory. It is certainly so used for some technical purposes, and may sometimes be so used for non-technical purposes as well; though I know of no such non-technical purposes.

I

In recent discussions of truth, one or both of two theses are commonly maintained. These are:

First, any sentence beginning 'It is true that . . .' does not change its assertive meaning when the phrase 'It is true that' is omitted. More generally, to say that an assertion is true is not to make any further assertion at all; it is to make the same assertion. This I shall call Thesis I.

Second, to say that a statement is true is to make a statement about a sentence of a given language, viz., the language in which the first statement was made. It is (in other and more technical terms) to make a statement in a meta-language ascribing the semantic property of truth (or the semantic predicate

[1] Ramsey, *Foundations of Mathematics,* pp. 142–143.

From P. F. Strawson, "Truth," *Analysis,* Vol. 9 (1949). Reprinted by permission of the author and of the editor of *Analysis.*

'true') to a sentence in an object-language. The object-sentence concerned should strictly be written in inverted commas to make it clear that we are talking *about the sentence*; and the phrase 'is true' should strictly be followed by some such phrase as 'in L', where 'L' designates the object-language concerned. This I shall call Thesis 2.

Of these two theses, the first is true, but inadequate; the second is false, but important. The first thesis is right in what it asserts, and wrong in what it suggests. The second thesis is wrong in what it asserts, but right in what it implies. The first thesis is right in asserting that to say that a statement is true is not to make a further statement; but wrong in suggesting that to say that a statement is true is not to do something different from, or additional to, just making the statement. The second thesis is right in implying that to say that a statement is true is to do something different from just making the statement; but wrong in asserting that this 'something different' consists in making a further statement, viz. a statement about a sentence.

Although both theses are sometimes maintained by the same philosopher, it is easy to see that they cannot both be correct. For if it is true that to say (1) "Moths fly by night" is to make the same assertion as to say (2) "It is true that moths fly by night", then it is false that to say (2) is to say anything about the English sentence "Moths fly by night"; i.e. false that (2) ought strictly to be written "'Moths fly by night' is true in English". If to say (2) is to make the same assertion as to say (1), then to say (2) cannot be to say anything about an English sentence; for to say (1) is not to say anything about an English sentence, but is to say something about moths.

Independently of this, one sees how misleading it is to say that the phrase '. . . is true' is used to talk *about sentences,* by comparing it with other phrases which certainly are used to talk about sentences (or words, or phrases). For example, someone says, in French, "Il pleuve"; and someone else corrects him, saying: "'Il pleuve' is *incorrect* French. 'Il pleut' is the right way of saying it". Or, criticising the style of a passage, someone says: "The sentence '. . . .' is *badly expressed.*" Similarly, one may ask what a sentence *means,* or say that a sentence is *ungrammatical, misspelt, a poor translation*. In all these cases, it is natural to say that one is talking *about a sentence.* If any statement of this kind were correctly translated into any language at all, the sentence which was being discussed would re-appear, quoted and untranslated, in the translation of the statement as a whole. Otherwise the translation would be incorrect. But it is perfectly obvious that a correct translation of any statement containing the phrase 'is true' (used as it is ordinarily used) never contains a quoted and untranslated sentence to which the phrase 'is true' was *applied* in the original sentence. The phrase 'is true' is not *applied to* sentences; for it is not *applied to* anything.

Truth is not a property of symbols; for it is not a property.

II

. . .

We may express, then, the main contention of the semantic theory as follows: to say that a statement is true is not to say something further *about the subject-matter* of the statement, but is to say the same thing about the subject-matter of the statement, *by means of a further statement, namely a statement about a sentence.* Now I said that Thesis 1 is true. A fortiori, a modification of Thesis 1 is true, which I shall call Thesis 1A, and which runs as follows:

To say that a statement is true is not to say something further about the subject-matter of the statement, but, in so far as it is to say anything about that subject-matter, is to say the same thing about it.

Now Thesis 1A, but not Thesis 1, is compatible with Thesis 2. The semantic theory consists in the joint assertion of 1A and 2. I suggest that the semantic theory borrows a lot of its plausibility from the truth of 1A. We swallow 2 for the sake of 1A. I now wish to show that the unmodified thesis 1 is true, and that we therefore can and must assert 1A while rejecting 2 and, therefore, rejecting the semantic theory.

. . .

III

The best way of showing that Thesis 1 is true is to correct its inadequacy. The best way of correcting its inadequacy is to discover the further reasons which have led to Thesis 2. To bring out those features of the situation which lead to the mistake of saying that the word 'true' is used meta-linguistically (to talk about sentences), I want first to compare the use of 'true' with that of 'Yes'. If you and I have been sitting together in silence for some time, and I suddenly say 'Yes', you would, perhaps, look at me with surprise and answer "I didn't say anything". Of course, a man may say 'Yes' to himself; and this will be a sign that he has resolved a doubt in his own mind, or come to a decision. But the normal use of 'Yes' is to answer: and where no question is asked, no answer can be given. Suppose you now ask: "Was Jones there?" and I say 'Yes'; there seems no temptation whatever to say that, in so answering, I am *talking about* the English sentence "Was Jones there?" So, in the case of 'Yes', we have a word of which the normal use requires some linguistic occasion (a question), without there being any temptation at all to say that it is used to *talk about* the sentence of which the utterance is the occasion for its use. There is indeed a temptation to go further in the opposite direction and say that in answering 'Yes' I am not talking *about* anything, not making any assertion, at all; but simply answering. In a way, this is correct; but in a way, it's wrong. For it would be perfectly correct for you, reporting our dialogue, to say of me: "He said Jones was there". So of the ordinary use of 'Yes', we may say: first, that it demands a linguistic occasion, namely the asking of a question; second, that it is not used meta-linguistically, to talk about the question, but to answer it; third, that in so far as we are making an assertion at all in using it, the content of the assertion is the same as the content of the question. Now imagine a possible, and perhaps vulgarly current, use of the expression 'Ditto'. You make an assertion, and I say 'Ditto'. In so far as I assert anything, talk about anything, I talk about and assert what you talk about and assert. Of course—and this points to the inadequacy of Thesis 1 and the reason for the meta-linguistic error—to say 'Ditto' is not *the same as* to make the statement in question; for, whereas I might have made the statement before anyone else had spoken, it would be meaningless for me to say 'Ditto' before anyone else had spoken. 'Ditto', like 'Yes', requires a linguistic occasion. But again, and largely, I think, because the expression 'Ditto' does not consist of a grammatical subject and a grammatical predicate, there is absolutely no temptation to say that in thus using 'Ditto', I should be talking *about the sentence* you used, and the utterance of which was the linguistic occasion for my use of this expression. I am not talking about what you said (the noise you made, or the sentence you spoke, or the proposition you expressed). I am agreeing with, endorsing, underwriting what you said; and, unless you had said something, I couldn't perform *these* activities, though I could *make the assertion* you made. Now the expression 'That's true' sometimes functions in just the way in which I have suggested the expression 'Ditto' might function. A says "Jones was there" and B says 'That's true'; and C, reporting the conversation, can correctly say: "Both A and B said that Jones was there". But the point is that B couldn't have said that Jones was there in the way he *did* say it, (i.e. by the use of the expression 'That's true'), unless A had previously uttered the *sentence* "Jones was there", or some equivalent sentence. It is, perhaps, *this* fact about the use (*this* use) of the word 'true', together with the old prejudice that any indicative sentence must describe (be 'about') something, which encourages those who have become chary of saying that truth is a property of propositions to say instead that in using the word 'true', we are talking about sentences. (What I have said about the use of 'That's true' applies, of course, with suitable alterations, to the use of 'That's false').

Now those who assert that 'true' is a predicate of sentences have not, in general, considered these simple cases of the use of 'true' (and 'false'), but the more puzzling cases which lead, or seem to lead, to paradoxes: such as the case where someone utters the isolated sentence "What I am saying now is false", or writes on an otherwise clean blackboard the sentence "Every statement on this blackboard is false". The solution on meta-linguistic lines is to treat these sentences as making statements of the second order to the effect:

(1) that there is some statement of the first order written on the blackboard (or said by me now); and (2) that any first-order statement written on the blackboard (or said by me now) is false.

By means of this distinction of orders, the distinction between meta and object-language, the puzzling sentences are said no longer to engender contradictions: either they are simply false, since the existential part of what they assert is false; or, alternatively, leaving out the existential part of the analysis, and treating them solely as hypotheticals, they are seen to be vacuously true, since no first-order statements occur. This solution is formally successful in avoiding the apparent contradictions. But it seems to me to achieve this success only by repeating the fundamental mistake from which the contradictions themselves arise, and also, and consequently, involving the difficulties mentioned at the beginning of this paper. That is, first, it involves the view that to say that a statement is true (or false) is to make a further, second-order, statement (thus contradicting Thesis 1); and, second, it (usually) involves the unplausibility of saying that this second-order statement is *about* a sentence or sentences. Now the point of the previous discussion of the actual use of 'Yes', the possible use of 'Ditto' and the actual use of 'That's true' is to show that these expedients are unnecessary. When no-one has spoken, and I say 'Ditto', I am not making a false statement to the effect that something true has been said, nor a true statement to the effect that nothing false has been said. I am not making a statement at all; but producing a pointless utterance. When somebody has made an assertion previously, my saying 'Ditto' acquires a point, has an occasion: and, if you like, you may say that I am now making a statement, repeating, in a manner, what the speaker said. But I am not making an additional statement, a meta-statement. It would perhaps be better to say that my utterance is not a statement at all, but a linguistic performance for which in the first case there was not, and in the second case there was, an occasion: so that in the first case it was a spurious, and in the second case a genuine, performance. Similarly, the words 'true' and 'false' normally require, as an occasion for their significant use, that somebody should have made, be making or be about to make (utter or write), some statement. (The making of the statement need not precede the use of 'true': it may follow it as in the case of the expression "It is true that . . ."—a form of words I shall discuss later). But in all cases the indicative clause of which the grammatical predicate is the phrase 'is true' does not in itself make any kind of statement at all (not even a meta-statement), and *a fortiori* cannot make the statement, the making of which is required as the occasion for the significant use of the words 'true' or 'false'. This is not, as it stands, quite accurate. For an indicative sentence of which the grammatical predicate is the phrase 'is true' may sometimes, as I shall shortly show, be used to make an implicit meta-statement. But when this is so, the phrase 'is true' plays no part in the making of this meta-statement. The phrase 'is true' *never* has a statement-making role. And when this is seen, the paradoxes vanish without the need for the meta-linguistic machinery; or at least without the need for regarding the words 'true' and 'false' as part of that machinery. The paradoxes arise on the assumption that the words 'true' and 'false' can be used to make first-order assertions. They are formally solved by the declaration that these words can be used only to make second-order assertions. Both paradoxes and solution disappear on the more radical assumption that they are not used to make assertions of any order, are not used to make assertions at all.

I said, however, that indicative sentences of which the grammatical predicate is the phrase 'is true' or the phrase 'is false' may be used to make an implicit meta-statement, in the making of which these phrases themselves play no part. To elucidate this, consider the following sentences:

(1) What I am saying now is false
(2) All statements made in English are false
(3) What the policeman said is true.

It is certainly not incorrect to regard each of these sentences as implicitly making an *existential* meta-statement, which does not involve the words 'true' or 'false'. The implicit meta-statements in these cases might be written as follows:

(1a) I have just made (am about to make) a statement
(2a) Some statements are made in English
(3a) The policeman made a statement.

These are all second-order assertive sentences to the effect that there are some first-order assertive sentences, uttered (*a*) by me, (*b*) in English, (*c*) by the policeman.

These second-order assertive sentences we can regard as part of the analysis of the sentences (1), (2) and (3). Obviously they are not the whole of their analysis. The sentence "The policeman made a statement" clearly has not the same use as the sentence "What the policeman said is true". To utter the second is to do something more than to assert the first. What is this additional performance? Consider the circumstances in which we might use the expression "What the policeman said is true". Instead of using this expression, I might have *repeated* the policeman's story. In this case, I shall be said to have *confirmed* what the policeman said. I might, however, have made exactly the same set of statements as I made in repeating his story, but have made them *before* the policeman spoke. In this case, though the assertions I have made are no different, I have not done what I did in the other case, namely 'confirmed his story'. So to confirm his story is not to say anything further, *about* his story, or the sentences he used in telling it, though it is to do something that cannot be done unless he has told his story. Now, unlike the confirming narrative which I might have told, the sentence "What the policeman said is true" has no use *except* to confirm the policeman's story [2]; but like the confirming narrative, the sentence does not say anything further *about* the policeman's story or the sentences he used in telling it. It is a device for confirming the story without telling it again. So, in general, in using such expressions, we are confirming, underwriting, admitting, agreeing with, what somebody has said; but (except where we are implicitly making an existential meta-statement, in making which the phrase 'is true' plays no part), we are not making any assertion additional to theirs; and are *never* using 'is true' to talk *about* something which is *what they said*, or the sentences they used in saying it. To complete the analysis, then, of the entire sentence (3) "What the policeman said is true", we have to add, to the existential meta-assertion, a phrase which is not assertive, but (if I may borrow Mr. Austin's word) performatory. We might, e.g., offer, as a complete analysis of one case, the expression: "The policeman made a statement. I confirm it"; where, in uttering the words "I confirm it", I am not describing something I do, but *doing* something. There is, then, a difference between the more complicated cases in which the phrase 'is true' is preceded by a descriptive phrase, and the simpler sentences (e.g. 'That's true') in which the phrase 'is true' is preceded by a demonstrative. The former may be regarded as involving an implicit meta-statement, while the latter are purely confirmatory (or purely 'admittive'). But in neither sort of case has the phrase 'is true' any assertive (or meta-assertive) function.

. . .

Of course, the formula that I have adopted in the discussion of one use of 'true' is not immune from another variant of that argument from grammar which leads to treating 'true' as a descriptive word. Someone might say: in order for you to *confirm* anything, there must be some *object* of this activity; a sentence or a proposition: and to perform this activity upon this object is nothing other than to assert that the object has the property, stands in the relation, referred to by the word 'true'. Anyone who says this is misled partly

[2] This needs qualification. Uttered by a witness, the sentence is a *confirmation*; wrung from the culprit, it is an *admission*. No doubt there are other cases.

by the fact that the verb 'confirm' takes a grammatical object; and partly by the fact that the linguistic performance (of 'confirming') requires, not an object, but an *occasion*—a fact which I declared to be the misunderstood element of truth in the semantic theory. Even this assertion—that there must be, or be thought to be, some kind of sign-occasion for the significant, or genuine, use of the word 'true'—is not quite correct, if it means that some spoken or written utterance must occur, or be thought to occur. For it would not be incorrect, though it would be unusual, to say: "What you are thinking is true"; when nothing has been said. (But, then, a conversation *can* be carried on by glances and nods).

John Langshaw Austin

Truth

§ 1

"What is truth?" said jesting Pilate, and would not stay for an answer. Pilate was in advance of his time. For "truth" itself is an abstract noun, a camel, that is, of a logical construction, which cannot get past the eye even of a grammarian. We approach it cap and categories in hand: we ask ourselves whether Truth is a substance (the Truth, the Body of Knowledge), or a quality (something like the colour red, inhering in truths), or a relation ("correspondence").[1] But philosophers should take something more nearly their own size to strain at. What needs discussing rather is the use, or certain uses, of the word "true." *In vino,* possibly, "*veritas,*" but in a sober symposium "*verum.*"

§ 2

What is it that we say is true or is false? Or, how does the phrase "is true" occur in English sentences? The answers appear at first multifarious. We say (or are said to say) that beliefs are true, that descriptions or accounts are true, that propositions or assertions or statements are true, and that words or sentences are true: and this is to mention only a selection of the more obvious candidates. Again, we say (or are said to say) "It is true that the cat is on the

[1] It is sufficiently obvious that "truth" is a substantive, "true" an adjective and "of" in "true of" a preposition.

From J. L. Austin, "Truth," *Proceedings of the Aristotelian Society,* Supplementary Vol. 24 (1950). Reprinted by permission of the author and of the secretary and editor of the Aristotelian Society. This selection is the first essay in a symposium entitled "Truth"; P. F. Strawson and D. R. Cousin were the two other contributors. Austin's paper is reprinted in his *Philosophical Papers,* 1961.

Until his death, J. L. Austin (1911–60) was White's Professor of Moral Philosophy at Oxford University.

mat," or "It is true to say that the cat is on the mat," or " 'The cat is on the mat' is true." We also remark on occasion, when someone else has said something, "Very true" or "That's true" or "True enough."

Most (though not all) of these expressions, and others besides, certainly do occur naturally enough. But it seems reasonable to ask whether there is not some use of "is true" that is primary, or some generic name for that which at bottom we are always saying "is true." Which, if any, of these expressions is to be taken *au pied de la lettre?* To answer this will not take us long, nor, perhaps, far: but in philosophy the foot of the letter is the foot of the ladder.

I suggest that the following are the primary forms of expression:—

> It is true (to say) that the cat is on the mat.
> That statement (of his, etc.) is true.
> The statement that the cat is on the mat is true.

But first for the rival candidates.

(*a*) Some say that "truth is primarily a property of beliefs." But it may be doubted whether the expression "a true belief" is at all common outside philosophy and theology: and it seems clear that a man is said to hold a true belief when and in the sense that he believes (in) *something which* is true, or believes that *something which* is true is true. Moreover if, as some also say, a belief is "of the nature of a picture," then it is of the nature of what cannot be true, though it may be, for example, faithful.[2]

(*b*) True descriptions and true accounts are simply varieties of true statements or of collections of true statements, as are true answers and the like. The same applies to propositions too, in so far as they are genuinely said to be true (and not, as more commonly, sound, tenable and so on).[3] A proposition in law or in geometry is something portentous, usually a generalisation, that we are invited to accept and that has to be recommended by argument: it cannot be a direct report on current observation—if you look and inform me that the cat is on the mat, that is not a proposition though it is a statement. In philosophy, indeed, "proposition" is sometimes used in a special way for "the meaning or sense of a sentence or family of sentences": but whether we think a lot or little of this usage, a proposition in this sense cannot, at any rate, be what we say is true or false. For we never say "The meaning (or sense) of this sentence (or of these words) is true": what we do say is what the judge or jury says, namely that "*The words* taken in this sense, or if we assign to them such and such a meaning, or so interpreted or understood, *are true*."

(*c*) Words and sentences are indeed said to be true, the former often, the latter rarely. But only in certain senses. Words as discussed by philologists, or by lexicographers, grammarians, linguists, phoneticians, printers, critics (stylistic or textual) and so on, are not true or false: they are wrongly formed, or ambiguous or defective or untranslatable or unpronouncable or misspelled or archaistic or corrupt or what not.[4] Sentences in similar contexts are elliptic or

[2] A likeness is true *to* life, but not true *of* it. A *word* picture can be true, just because it is *not* a picture.

[3] Predicates applicable also to "arguments," which we likewise do not say are true, but, for example, valid.

[4] Peirce made a beginning by pointing out that there are two (or three) different senses of the word

involved or alliterative or ungrammatical. We may, however, genuinely say "His closing words were very true" or "The third sentence on page 5 of his speech is quite false": but here "words" and "sentence" refer, as is shown by the demonstratives (possessive pronouns, temporal verbs, definite descriptions, etc.), which in this usage consistently accompany them, to the words or sentence *as used by a certain person on a certain occasion.* That is, they refer (as does "Many a true word spoken in jest") to *statements.*

A statement is made and its making is a historic event, the utterance by a certain speaker or writer of certain words (a sentence) to an audience with reference to a historic situation, event or what not.[5]

A sentence is made *up of* words, a statement is made *in* words. A sentence is not English or not good English, a statement is not in English or not in good English. Statements are made, words or sentences are used. We talk of *my* statement, but of *the English* sentence (if a sentence is mine, I coined it, but I don't coin statements). The *same* sentence is used in making *different* statements (I say "It is mine," you say "It is mine"): it may also be used on two occasions or by two persons in making the *same* statement, but for this the utterance must be made with reference to the same situation or event.[6] We speak of "the statement that S," but of "the sentence 'S' ", not of "the sentence that S." [7]

When I say that a statement is what is true, I have no wish to become wedded to one word. "Assertion," for example, will in most contexts do just as well, though perhaps it is slightly wider. Both words share the weakness of being rather solemn (much more so than the more general "what you said" or "your words"),—though perhaps we are generally being a little solemn when we discuss the truth of anything. Both have the merit of clearly referring to the historic use of a sentence by an utterer, and of being therefore precisely not equivalent to "sentence." For it is a fashionable mistake to take as primary "(The sentence) 'S' is true (in the English language)." Here the addition of the words "in the English language" serves to emphasize that "sentence" is not being used as equivalent to "statement," so that it precisely is not what can be true or false (and moreover, "true in the English language" is a solecism, mismodelled presumably, and with deplorable effect, on expressions like "true in geometry").

"word," and adumbrated a technique ("counting" words) for deciding what is a "different sense." But his two senses are not well defined, and there are many more,—the "vocable" sense, the philologist's sense in which "grammar" is the same word as "glamour," the textual critic's sense in which the "the" in 1.254 has been written twice, and so on. With all his 66 divisions of signs, Peirce does not, I believe, distinguish between a sentence and a statement.

[5] "Historic" does not, of course, mean that we cannot speak of future or possible statements. A "certain" speaker need not be any definite speaker. "Utterance" need not be public utterance,—the audience may be the speaker himself.

[6] "The same" does not always mean the same. In fact it has no meaning in the way that an "ordinary" word like "red" or "horse" has a meaning: it is a (the typical) device for establishing and distinguishing the meanings of ordinary words. Like "real," it is part of our apparatus *in* words for fixing and adjusting the semantics *of* words.

[7] Inverted commas show that the words, though uttered (in writing), are not to be taken as a statement by the utterer. This covers two possible cases, (i) where what is to be discussed is the sentence (ii) where what is to be discussed is a statement made elsewhen in the words "quoted." Only in case (i) is it correct to say simply that the token is doing duty for the type (and even here it is quite incorrect to say that "The cat is on the mat" is the *name* of an English sentence, —though possibly *The Cat is on the Mat* might be the title of a novel, or a bull might be known as *Catta est in matta*). Only in case (ii) is there something true or false, *viz.* (not the quotation but) the statement made in the words quoted

§ 3

When is a statement true? The temptation is to answer (at least if we confine ourselves to "straightforward" statements): "When it corresponds to the facts." And as a piece of standard English this can hardly be wrong. Indeed, I must confess I do not really think it is wrong at all: the theory of truth is a series of truisms. Still, it can at least be misleading.

If there is to be communication of the sort that we achieve by language at all, there must be a stock of symbols of some kind which a communicator ("the speaker") can produce "at will" and which a communicatee ("the audience") can observe: these may be called the "words," though, of course, they need not be anything very like what we should normally call words—they might be signal flags, etc. There must also be something other than the words, which the words are to be used to communicate about: this may be called the "world." There is no reason why the world should not include the words, in every sense except the sense of the actual statement itself which on any particular occasion is being made about the world. Further, the world must exhibit (we must observe) similarities and dissimilarities (there could not be the one without the other): if everything were either absolutely indistinguishable from anything else or completely unlike anything else, there would be nothing to say. And finally (for present purposes—of course there are other conditions to be satisfied too) there must be two sets of conventions:—

Descriptive conventions correlating the words (= sentences) with the *types* of situation, thing, event, etc., to be found in the world.

Demonstrative conventions correlating the words (= statements) with the *historic* situations, etc., to be found in the world.[8]

A statement is said to be true when the historic state of affairs to which it is correlated by the demonstrative conventions (the one to which it "refers") is of a type [9] with which the sentence used in making it is correlated by the descriptive conventions.[10]

3*a*. Troubles arise from the use of the word "facts" for the historic situations, events, etc., and in general, for the world. For "fact" is regularly used in con-

[8] Both sets of conventions may be included together under "semantics." But they differ greatly.

[9] "Is of a type with which" means "is sufficiently like those standard states of affairs with which." Thus, for a statement to be true one state of affairs must be *like* certain others, which is a natural relation, but also *sufficiently* like to merit the same "description," which is no longer a purely natural relation. To say "This is red" is not the same as to say "This is like those", nor even as to say "This is like those which were called red". That things are *similar,* or even "exactly" similar, I may literally see, but that they are the *same* I cannot literally see—in calling them the same colour a convention is involved additional to the conventional choice of the name to be given to the colour which they are said to be.

[10] The trouble is that sentences contain words or verbal devices to serve both descriptive and demonstrative purposes (not to mention other purposes), often both at once. In philosophy we mistake the descriptive for the demonstrative (theory of universals) or the demonstrative for the descriptive (theory of monads). A sentence as normally distinguished from a mere word or phrase is characterised by its containing a minimum of verbal demonstrative devices (Aristotle's "reference to time"); but many demonstrative conventions are non-verbal (pointing, etc.), and using these we can make a statement in a single word which is not a "sentence". Thus, "languages" like that of (traffic, etc.) *signs* use quite distinct media for their descriptive and demonstrative elements (the sign on the post, the site of the post). And however many verbal demonstrative devices we use as auxiliaries, there must *always* be a non-verbal *origin* for these coordinates, which is the point of utterance of the statement.

junction with "that" in the sentences "The fact is that S" or "It is a fact that S" and in the expression "the fact that S," all of which imply that it would be true to say that S.[11]

This may lead us to suppose that

(i) "fact" is only an alternative expression for "true statement." We note that when a detective says "Let's look at the facts" he doesn't crawl round the carpet, but proceeds to utter a string of statements: we even talk of "stating the facts";

(ii) for every true statement there exists "one" and its own precisely corresponding fact—for every cap the head it fits.

It is (i) which leads to some of the mistakes in "coherence" or formalist theories; (ii) to some of those in "correspondence" theories. Either we suppose that there is nothing there but the true statement itself, nothing to which it corresponds, or else we populate the world with linguistic *Doppelgänger* (and grossly overpopulate it—every nugget of "positive" fact overlaid by a massive concentration of "negative" facts, every tiny detailed fact larded with generous general facts, and so on).

When a statement is true, there is, *of course,* a state of affairs which makes it true and which is *toto mundo* distinct from the true statement about it: but equally of course, we can only *describe* that state of affairs *in words* (either the same or, with luck, others). I can only describe the situation in which it is true to say that I am feeling sick by saying that it is one in which I am feeling sick (or experiencing sensations of nausea)[12]: yet between stating, however, truly that I am feeling sick and feeling sick there is a great gulf fixed.[13]

"Fact that" is a phrase designed for use in situations where the distinction between a true statement and the state of affairs about which it is a truth is neglected; as it often is with advantage in ordinary life, though seldom in philosophy—above all in discussing truth, where it is precisely our business to prise the words off the world and keep them off it. To ask "Is the fact that S the true statement that S or that which it is true of?" may beget absurd answers. To take an analogy: although we may sensibly ask "Do we *ride* the word 'elephant' or the animal?" and equally sensibly "Do we *write* the word or the animal?" it is nonsense to ask "Do we *define* the word or the animal?" For defining an elephant (supposing we ever do this) is a compendious description of an operation involving both word and animal (do we focus the image or the

[11] I use the following *abbreviations*:—

S *for* the cat is on the mat.
ST *for* it is true that the cat is on the mat.
tst *for* the statement that.

I take tstS as my example throughout and not, say, tst Julius Caesar was bald or tst all mules are sterile, because these latter are apt in their different ways to make us overlook the distinction between sentence and statement: we have, apparently, in the one case a sentence capable of being used to refer to only one historic situation, in the other a statement without reference to at least (or to any particular) one.

If space permitted other types of statement (existential, general, hypothetical, etc.) should be dealt with: these raise problems rather of meaning than of truth, though I feel uneasiness about hypotheticals.

[12] If this is what was meant by " 'It is raining' is true if and only if it is raining," so far so good.

[13] It takes two to make a truth. Hence (obviously) there can be no criterion of truth in the sense of some feature detectable in the statement itself which will reveal whether it is true or false. Hence, too, a statement cannot without absurdity refer to itself.

battleship?); and so speaking about "the fact that" is a compendious way of speaking about a situation involving both words and world.[14]

3*b*. "Corresponds" also gives trouble, because it is commonly given too restricted or too colourful a meaning, or one which in this context it cannot bear. The only essential point is this: that the correlation between the words (= sentences) and the type of situation, event, etc., which is to be such that when a statement in those words is made with reference to a historic situation of that type the statement is then true, is *absolutely and purely* conventional. We are absolutely free to appoint *any* symbol to describe *any* type of situation, so far as merely being true goes. In a small one-spade language tst nuts might be true in exactly the same circumstances as the statement in English that the National Liberals are the people's choice.[15] There is no need whatsoever for the words used in making a true statement to "mirror" in any way, however indirect, any feature whatsoever of the situation or event; a statement no more needs, in order to be true, to reproduce the "multiplicity," say, or the "structure" or "form" of the reality, than a word needs to be echoic or writing pictographic. To suppose that it does, is to fall once again into the error of reading back into the world the features of language.

The more rudimentary a language, the more, very often, it will tend to have a "single" word for a highly "complex" type of situation: this has such disadvantages as that the language becomes elaborate to learn and is incapable of dealing with situations which are non-standard, unforeseen, for which there may just be no word. When we go abroad equipped only with a phrase-book, we may spend long hours learning by heart—

A^{i}-moest-fa^{i}nd-^{e}tschâ^{r}woum^{e}n,
Ma^{i}-hwîl-iz-wau^{r}pt (bènt),

and so on and so on, yet faced with the situation where we have the pen of our aunt, find ourselves quite unable to say so. The characteristics of a more developed language (articulation, morphology, syntax, abstractions, etc.), do not make statements in it any more capable of being true or capable of being any more true, they make it more adaptable, more learnable, more comprehensive, more precise and so on; and *these* aims may no doubt be furthered by making the language (allowance made for the nature of the medium) "mirror" in conventional ways features descried in the world.

Yet even when a language does "mirror" such features very closely (and does it ever?) the truth of statements remains still a matter, as it was with the most rudimentary languages, of the words used being the ones *conventionally appointed* for situations of the type to which that referred to belongs. A picture, a copy, a replica, a photograph—these are *never* true in so far as they are reproductions, produced by natural or mechanical means: a reproduction can be accurate or lifelike (true *to* the original), as a gramophone recording or a transcription may be, but not true (*of*) as a record of proceedings can

[14] "It is true that S" and "It is a fact that S" are applicable in the same circumstances; the cap fits when there is a head it fits. Other words can fill the same role as "fact"; we say, *e.g.*, "The situation is that S."

[15] We could use "nuts" even now as a code-word: but a code, as a transformation of a language, is distinguished from a language, and a code-word despatched is not (called) "true."

be. In the same way a (natural) sign *of* something can be infallible or unreliable but only an (artificial) sign *for* something can be right or wrong.[16]

There are many intermediate cases between a true account and a faithful picture, as here somewhat forcibly contrasted, and it is from the study of these (a lengthy matter) that we can get the clearest insight into the contrast. For example, maps: these may be called pictures, yet they are highly conventionalised pictures. If a map can be clear or accurate or misleading, like a statement, why can it not be true or exaggerated? How do the "symbols" used in map-making differ from those used in statement-making? On the other hand, if an air-mosaic is not a map, why is it not? And when does a map become a diagram? These are the really illuminating questions.

§ 4

Some have said that—

> To say that an assertion is true is not to make any further assertion at all.
>
> In all sentences of the form "*p* is true" the phrase "is true" is logically superfluous.
>
> To say that a proposition is true is just to assert it, and to say that it is false is just to assert its contradictory.

But wrongly. TstS (except in paradoxical cases of forced and dubious manufacture) refers to the world or any part of it exclusive of tstS, *i.e.,* of itself.[17] TstST refers to the world or any part of it *inclusive* of tstS, though once again exclusive of itself, *i.e.,* of tstST. That is, tstST refers to something to which tstS cannot refer. TstST does not, certainly, include any statement referring to the world exclusive of tstS which is not included already in tstS—more, it seems doubtful whether it does include that statement about the world exclusive of tstS which is made when we state that S. (If I state that tstS is true, should we really agree that I have stated that S? Only "by implication." [18]) But all this does not go any way to show that tstST is not a statement different from tstS. If Mr. Q writes on a notice-board "Mr. W is a burglar," then a trial is held to decide whether Mr. Q's published statement that Mr. W is a burglar is a libel: finding "Mr. Q's statement was true (in substance and in fact)." Thereupon a second trial is held, to decide whether Mr. W is a burglar, in which Mr. Q's statement is no longer under consideration: verdict "Mr. W is a burglar." It is an arduous business to hold a second trial: why is it done if the verdict is the same as the previous finding? [19]

What is felt is that the evidence considered in arriving at the one verdict is the same as that considered in arriving at the other. This is not strictly correct.

[16] Berkeley confuses these two. There will not be books in the running brooks until the dawn of hydro-semantics.

[17] A statement may refer to "itself" in the sense, *e.g.,* of the sentence used or the utterance uttered in making it ("statement" is not exempt from all ambiguity). But paradox does result if a statement purports to refer to itself in a more full-blooded sense, purports, that is, to state that it itself is true, or to state what it itself refers to ("This statement is about Cato").

[18] And "by implication" tstST asserts something about the making of a statement which tstS certainly does not assert.

[19] This is not quite fair: there are many legal and personal reasons for holding two trials,—which, however, do not affect the point that the issue being tried is not the same.

It is more nearly correct that whenever tstS is true then tstST is also true and conversely, and that whenever tstS is false tstST is also false and conversely.[20] And it is argued that the words "is true" are logically superfluous because it is believed that generally if any two statements are always true together and always false together then they must mean the same. Now whether this is in general a sound view may be doubted: but even if it is, why should it not break down in the case of so obviously "peculiar" a phrase as "is true"? Mistakes in philosophy notoriously arise through thinking that what holds of "ordinary" words like "red" or "growls" must also hold of extraordinary words like "real" or "exists." But that "true" is just such another extraordinary word is obvious.[21]

There is something peculiar about the "fact" which is described by tstST, something which may make us hesitate to call it a "fact" at all; namely, that the relation between tstS and the world which tstST asserts to obtain is a *purely conventional* relation (one which "thinking makes so"). For we are aware that this relation is one which we could alter at will, whereas we like to restrict the word "fact" to *hard* facts, facts which are natural and unalterable, or anyhow not alterable at will. Thus, to take an analogous case, we may not like calling it a fact that the word elephant means what it does, though we can be induced to call it a (soft) fact—and though, of course, we have no hesitation in calling it a fact that contemporary English speakers use the word as they do.

An important point about this view is that it confuses falsity with negation: for according to it, it is the same thing to say "He is not at home" as to say "It is false that he is at home." (But what if no one has said that he *is* at home? What if he is lying upstairs dead?) Too many philosophers maintain, when anxious to explain away negation, that a negation is just a second order affirmation (to the effect that a certain first order affirmation is false), yet, when anxious to explain away falsity, maintain that to assert that a statement is false is just to assert its negation (contradictory). It is impossible to deal with so fundamental a matter here.[22] Let me assert the following merely. Affirmation and negation are exactly on a level, in this sense, that no language

[20] Not *quite* correct, because tstST is only in place at all when tstS is envisaged as made and has been verified.

[21] *Unum, verum, bonum,*—the old favourites deserve their celebrity. There *is* something odd about each of them. Theoretical theology is a form of onomatolatry.

[22] The following two sets of logical axioms are, as Aristotle (though not his successors) makes them, quite distinct:—

(*a*) No statement can be both true and false.
No statement can be neither true nor false.

(*b*) Of two contradictory statements—
Both cannot be true.
Both cannot be false.

The second set demands a definition of contradictories, and is usually joined with an unconscious postulate that for every statement there is one and only one other statement such that the pair are contradictories. It is doubtful how far any language does or must contain contradictories, however defined, such as to satisfy both this postulate and the set of axioms (*b*).

Those of the so-called "logical paradoxes" (hardly a genuine class) which concern "true" and "false" are *not* to be reduced to cases of self-contradiction, any more than "S but I do not believe it" is. A statement to the effect that it is itself true is every bit as absurd as one to the effect that it is itself false. There are *other* types of sentence which offend against the fundamental conditions of all communication in ways *distinct from* the way in which "This is red and is not red" offends,—*e.g.*, "This does (I do) not exist," or equally absurd "This exists (I exist)." There are more deadly sins than one; nor does the way to salvation lie through any hierarchy.

can exist which does not contain conventions for both and that both refer to the world equally directly, not to statements about the world: whereas a language can quite well exist without any device to do the work of "true" and "false." Any satisfactory theory of truth must be able to cope equally with falsity [23]: but "is false" can only be maintained to be logically superfluous by making this fundamental confusion.

§5

There is another way of coming to see that the phrase "is true" is not logically superfluous, and to appreciate what sort of a statement it is to say that a certain statement is true. There are numerous other adjectives which are in the same class as "true" and "false," which are concerned, that is, with the relations between the words (as uttered with reference to a historic situation) and the world, and which nevertheless no one would dismiss as logically superfluous. We say, for example, that a certain statement is exaggerated or vague or bald, a description somewhat rough or misleading or not very good, an account rather general or too concise. In cases like these it is pointless to insist on deciding in simple terms whether the statement is "true or false." Is it true or false that Belfast is north of London? That the galaxy is the shape of a fried egg? That Beethoven was a drunkard? That Wellington won the battle of Waterloo? There are various *degrees and dimensions* of success in making statements: the statements fit the facts always more or less loosely, in different ways on different occasions for different intents and purposes. What may score full marks in a general knowledge test may in other circumstances get a gamma. And even the most adroit of languages may fail to "work" in an abnormal situation or to cope, or cope reasonably simply, with novel discoveries: is it true or false that the dog goes round the cow? [24] What, moreover, of the large class of cases where a statement is not so much false (or true) as out of place, *inept* ("All the signs of bread" said when the bread is before us)?

We become obsessed with "truth" when discussing statements, just as we become obsessed with "freedom" when discussing conduct. So long as we think that what has always and alone to be decided is whether a certain action was done freely or was not, we get nowhere: but so soon as we turn instead to the numerous other adverbs used in the same connexion ("accidentally," "unwillingly," "inadvertently," etc.), things become easier, and we come to see that no concluding inference of the form "Ergo, it was done freely (or not freely)" is required. Like freedom, truth is a bare minimum or an illusory ideal

[23] To be false is (not, of course, to correspond to a non-fact, but) to mis-correspond with a fact. Some have not seen how, then, since the statement which is false does not describe the fact with which it mis-corresponds (but misdescribes it), we know which fact to compare it with: this was because they thought of all linguistic conventions as descriptive,—but it is the demonstrative conventions which fix which situation it is to which the statement refers. No statement can state what it itself refers to.

[24] Here there is much sense in "coherence" (and pragmatist) theories of truth, despite their failure to appreciate the trite but central point that truth is a matter of the relation between words and world, and despite their wrong-headed *Gleichschaltung* of all varieties of statemental failure under the one head of "partly true" (thereafter wrongly equated with "part of the truth"). "Correspondence" theorists too often talk as one would who held that every map is either accurate or inaccurate; that accuracy is a single and the sole virtue of a map; that every country can have but one accurate map; that a map on a larger scale or showing different features must be a map of a different country; and so on.

(the truth, the whole truth and nothing but the truth about, say, the battle of Waterloo or the *Primavera*).

§ 6

Not merely is it jejune to suppose that all a statement aims to be is "true," but it may further be questioned whether every "statement" does aim to be true at all. The principle of Logic, that "Every proposition must be true or false," has too long operated as the simplest, most persuasive and most pervasive form of the descriptive fallacy. Philosophers under its influence have forcibly interpreted all "propositions" on the model of the statement that a certain thing is red, as made when the thing concerned is currently under observation.

Recently, it has come to be realized that many utterances which have been taken to be statements (merely because they are not, on grounds of grammatical form, to be classed as commands, questions, etc.) are not in fact descriptive, nor susceptible of being true or false. When is a statement not a statement? When it is a formula in a calculus: when it is a performatory utterance: when it is a value-judgment: when it is a definition: when it is part of a work of fiction—there are many such suggested answers. It is simply not the business of such utterances to "correspond to the facts" (and even genuine statements have other businesses besides that of so corresponding).

It is a matter for decision how far we should continue to call such masqueraders "statements" at all, and how widely we should be prepared to extend the uses of "true" and "false" in "different senses." My own feeling is that it is better, when once a masquerader has been unmasked, *not* to call it a statement and *not* to say it is true or false. In ordinary life we should not call most of them statements at all, though philosophers and grammarians may have come to do so (or rather, have lumped them all together under the term of art "proposition"). We make a difference between "You said you promised" and "You stated that you promised": the former can mean that you said "I promise," whereas the latter must mean that you said "I promised": the latter, which we say you "stated," is something which is true or false, whereas for the former, which is not true or false, we use the wider verb to "say." Similarly, there is a difference between "You say this is (call this) a good picture" and "You state that this is a good picture." Moreover, it was only so long as the real nature of arithmetical formulae, say, or of geometrical axioms remained unrecognised, and they were thought to record information about the world, that it was reasonable to call them "true" (and perhaps even "statements,"—though were they ever so called?): but once their nature has been recognized, we no longer feel tempted to call them "true" or to dispute about their truth or falsity.

In the cases so far considered the model "This is red" breaks down because the "statements" assimilated to it are not of a nature to correspond to facts at all,—the words are not descriptive words, and so on. But there is also another type of case where the words *are* descriptive words and the "proposition" does in a way have to correspond to facts, but precisely not in the way that "This is red" and similar statements setting up to be true have to do.

In the human predicament, for use in which our language is designed, we may wish to speak about states of affairs which have not been observed or are not currently under observation (the future, for example). And although we *can* state anything "as a fact" (which statement will then be true or false [25]) we need not do so: we need only say "The cat *may be* on the mat." This utterance is quite different from tstS,—it is not a statement at all (it is not true or false; it is compatible with "The cat may *not* be on the mat"). In the same way, the situation in which we discuss whether and state that tstS is *true* is different from the situation in which we discuss whether it is *probable* that S. Tst it is probable that S is out of place, inept, in the situation where we can make tstST, and, I think, conversely. It is not our business here to discuss probability: but is worth observing that the phrases "It is true that" and "It is probable that" are in the same line of business,[26] and in so far incompatibles.

§ 7

In a recent article in *Analysis* Mr. Strawson has propounded a view of truth which it will be clear I do not accept. He rejects the "semantic" account of truth on the perfectly correct ground that the phrase "is true" is not used in talking about *sentences*, supporting this with an ingenious hypothesis as to how meaning may have come to be confused with truth: but this will not suffice to show what he wants,—that "is true" is not used in talking about (or that "truth is not a property of") *anything*. For it *is* used in talking about *statements* (which in his article he does not distinguish clearly from sentences). Further, he supports the "logical superfluity" view to this extent, that he agrees that to say that ST is not to make any further assertion at all, beyond the assertion that S: but he disagrees with it in so far as he thinks that to say that ST *is* to *do* something more than just to assert that S,—it is namely to *confirm* or to *grant* (or something of that kind) the assertion, made or taken as made already, that S. It will be clear that and why I do not accept the first part of this: but what of the second part? I agree that to say that ST "is" very often, and according to the all-important linguistic occasion, to confirm tstS or to grant it or what not; but this cannot show that to say that ST is not also and at the same time to make an assertion about tstS. To say that I believe you "is" on occasion to accept your statement; but it is also to make an assertion, which is not made by the strictly performatory utterance "I accept your statement." It is common for quite ordinary statements to have a performatory "aspect": to say that you are a cuckold may be to insult you, but it is also and at the same time to make a statement which is true or false. Mr. Strawson, moreover, seems to confine himself to the case where I *say* "Your statement is true" or something similar,—but what of the case where you state that S and I *say* nothing but "*look and see*" that your statement is true? I do not see how this critical case, to which nothing analogous occurs with strictly performatory utterances, could be made to respond to Mr. Strawson's treatment.

One final point: if it is admitted (*if*) that the rather boring yet satisfactory relation between words and world which has here been discussed does genuinely occur, why should the phrase "is true" not be our way of describing it? And if it is not, what else is?

[25] Though it is not yet in place to call it either. For the same reason, one cannot lie or tell the truth about the future.

[26] Compare the odd behaviours of "was" and "will be" when attached to "true" and to "probable."

For Further Reading

Ayer, A. J., *The Concept of a Person,* 1963, Chap. 6.
Black, Max, "The Semantic Definition of Truth," *Language and Philosophy,* 1949, Chap. 4.
Bradley, F. H., *Essays on Truth and Reality,* 1914, Chaps. 5, 7, and 8.
Brentano, Franz, "On the Concept of Truth," in Canfield, J. V., and Donnell, D. H. (eds.), *Readings in the Theory of Knowledge,* 1964, Chap. 15.
Coffey, Peter, *Epistemology,* 1917, Vol. 2, Chap. 23.
Dummet, Michael, "Truth," *Proceedings of the Aristotelian Society,* Vol. 59 (1958–59).
Ezorsky, Gertrude, "Truth in Context," *Journal of Philosophy,* Vol. 60 (1963).
Hobhouse, L. T., *The Theory of Knowledge,* 3rd ed., 1921, Part III, Chaps. 1, 2, and 8.
James, William, "A Word More About Truth," *The Meaning of Truth,* 1909.
Kaufmann, Felix, "Three Meanings of 'Truth,'" *Journal of Philosophy,* Vol. 45 (1948).
Royce, Josiah, "The Nature of Truth," in Ewing, A. C. (ed.), *The Idealist Tradition,* 1957.
Russell, Bertrand, *Human Knowledge,* 1948, Part II, Chap. 11.
Strawson, P. F., "Truth," *Proceedings of the Aristotelian Society,* Supplementary Vol. 24 (1950).
Tarski, Alfred, "The Semantic Conception of Truth," *Philosophy and Phenomenological Research,* Vol. 4 (1944); also in Feigl, H., and Sellars, W. (eds.), *Readings in Philosophical Analysis,* 1949.
Warnock, G. J., "Truth and Correspondence," in Rollins, C. D. (ed.), *Knowledge and Experience,* 1963.
Wilson, John, *Language and the Pursuit of Truth,* 1956, Chap. 3.
Wood, Ledger, *The Analysis of Knowledge,* 1941, Chap. 11.
Woozley, A. D., *Theory of Knowledge,* 1949, Chaps. 6 and 7.

3

NECESSARY TRUTH AND A PRIORI KNOWLEDGE

Even beginners in mathematics are made quickly aware that mathematical theorems, unlike the laws of natural science, are established apparently by reasoning alone, without appealing to observations on the course of events. Moreover, the truths of mathematics seem to be valid in all "possible worlds" since they deal with matters that cannot be consistently conceived to be different from what the theorems assert, and in this respect also they are unlike the truths of the empirical sciences, which are about features of the actual world that might conceivably have been organized differently. For example, that the sum of two odd numbers is always even can be shown to be true without any empirical study of nature, and the statement would be true even if the physico-chemical composition of the world were different from what it is in fact. On the other hand, Galileo's law for bodies falling freely near the earth's surface (that is, that the distance traversed by such a body is proportional to the square of the time of its fall) requires support from empirical evidence, and it would not be even approximately true were the world differently constituted (for example, if bodies did not exert gravitational forces on each other in the manner that they now do).

Statements such as the arithmetical one in the example are therefore said to be knowable "a priori" (because their truth or falsity can be established without recourse to sensory observation), and also to be "necessary" (because they supposedly assert or deny what must be the case by the very "nature" of the things mentioned in them, so that their truth or falsity is not contingent on features of the world that might change). Correspondingly, statements like Galileo's law are said to be knowable "a posteriori," and to be "contingent." This pair of distinctions has been recognized in Western thought under various labels at least since the development of demonstrative geometry in ancient Greece. During many centuries geometry was taken to embody the ideal of absolutely certain knowledge and was regarded as the model to which every branch of inquiry aspiring to be a "genuine" science must finally conform. For an endless series of geometric theorems is logically derivable from a handful of axioms, and since the latter were believed to be necessary truths capable of being known a priori, the entire edifice of geometrical knowledge seemed to rest on unshakable foundations. A similar axiomatic formulation was eventually achieved for arithmetic and other parts of mathematics, though not until comparatively recent times. The notion that other branches of science, such as physics, can be organized deductively, with axioms or "first principles" that are necessary and knowable a priori, was taken for granted by outstanding scientists and philosophers down through the ages—for example, by Aristotle and Archimedes in antiquity, by Descartes and Kant, and in some respects even by Maxwell and Eddington, in modern times.

Two points should be noted in connection with these distinctions. In the first place, the term "necessary" is used to characterize either certain *statements* or what the statements are about, while the term "a priori" is employed in the first instance as a characterization of *knowledge* (although the term is commonly used elliptically to label statements that are knowable a priori). Accordingly, to say of a statement that it is necessary means something *prima facie* different from what is meant by saying that it is known a priori. It is therefore not logically impossible that there might be a posteriori knowledge of necessary truth. In point of fact, however, most thinkers who have expressed themselves on the subject have maintained that sensory experience (and more generally so-called inductive procedures, involving the generalization of observed connections among sensory data) cannot establish the necessity of any statement. In consequence, the class of necessary statements has usually been held to be coextensive with the class of statements knowable a priori, and this assumption is implicit in all the selections in this chapter.

Secondly, although a priori knowledge is by definition not grounded in sensory experience, such experience may *suggest* statements that are eventually claimed to be knowable a priori, and it is usually admitted to be indispensable for *acquiring* the concepts that enter into such statements. It may well be the case, for example, that if men had never observed and compared collections of discrete objects they would not have arrived at the notion of number, or the notion of numbers being odd or even. It is also possible that without repeated manipulation of such collections it would not have occurred to anyone that when two collections, neither of which can be divided into two equinumerous aggregates, are combined to form a larger aggregate, the latter can always be divided in the manner indicated. It is nonetheless an a priori truth that the sum of two odd numbers is always even. Accordingly, the question whether a statement has its *origins* in experience must be distinguished from the question whether it is *validated* by experience.

It is however a matter of historical record that many statements believed at one time to be necessary have subsequently been found to be at best only contingently true. Similarly, many claims to a priori knowledge have had to be revised, and traditional conceptions about its scope whittled down. In the hope of preventing the recurrence of such errors, thinkers have throughout the centuries given serious attention to two related questions that continue to be actively discussed today. (1) Are any statements (including those of mathematics) indisputably necessary and, if so, what class of statements can be so characterized and on what grounds? (2) Is any knowledge indisputably a priori and, if so, how is such knowledge possible—why can some truths but not others be known in this way?

No thinker of note has denied that there are some statements which are necessary, though there has been much disagreement on which statements can properly be so judged as well as on the content of such statements. For example, with some exceptions (such as John Stuart Mill, whose views are stated in the selection from his writings included in this chapter) philosophers since Aristotle have claimed necessity for the laws of logic and, in particular, for the law of contradiction. However, while Aristotle and many of his successors maintained that these laws formulate the fundamental structure of everything that is, and that they are the most certain principles of all things, other philosophers (for example, C. I. Lewis in his article in the present chapter) have argued that logical laws are necessary simply as the result of explicit or tacit stipulations for the use of the terms contained in them, and that they assert nothing about reality.

The contrast in doctrines just noted is pervasive in discussions of other allegedly necessary statements, and the views that have been advanced on the nature of necessary truth may be conveniently classified into two main types, on the basis of a distinction that was canonized by Kant. According to this distinction, statements fall into two exclusive classes, those which are *analytic* and those which are *synthetic*. A statement is said by many writers (including Hume and Kant) to be *analytic* if its denial is logically self-contradictory (so that on this definition, only true statements can be analytic); other writers with essentially the same distinction in mind consider a statement to be analytic if it is true or false solely in virtue of the meanings of its terms (so that on this explanation, false as well as true statements can be analytic). On the other hand, a statement is usually said to be *synthetic* if it is not analytic—that is, if neither the statement nor its formal contradictory is logically impossible, so that each represents a logically possible state of affairs.

This distinction has played an important role in the theory of knowledge since Kant. Nevertheless, its soundness has been frequently disputed on various grounds. For example, the sharp antithesis between analytic and synthetic assumed in customary definitions of the distinction has been denied by writers influenced by Hegelian ideas, for reasons similar to those presented in Bosanquet's article in this chapter. More recently, the general validity of the distinction has been challenged by a number of philosophers from the perspective of behavioral and functional theories of meaning—among others by Quine, whose essay raises what seem to him grave difficulties in defining the term "analytic" precisely. Carnap's and Grice and Strawson's articles are attempts to meet this challenge, though in different ways. Carnap adopts for this purpose the technique of axiomatization familiar from foundational studies in mathematics, while Grice and Strawson deny the cogency of the grounds on which the distinction has been criticized by appealing to standards of intelligibility governing the ordinary use of language.

However, if such doubts about the distinction are put aside and it is assumed to be tenable, the two types of views on the nature of necessary truth can be quickly described. According to views of the first type, a statement is necessary if and only if it is analytic; and, since the truth or falsity of an analytic statement can by hypothesis be established by purely logical means, necessary statements are knowable a priori. In consonance with this position, mathematical statements count as necessary only if they are analytic. Thus, many contemporary philosophers take arithmetical truths to be necessary, because the axioms of arithmetic (and therefore the theorems logically implied by them) are assumed to be transcriptions of the laws of formal logic (in accordance with the thesis developed in minute detail by Frege and Russell), and hence to be analytic. On the other hand, the theorems of, say, Euclidean geometry, understood as bona fide statements about so-called "physical space," are commonly held to be contingent in much current thought because the axioms of the system as well as the theorems are not analytic—even though conditional statements (that is, those having the form "If *A* then *B*") whose antecedents are the axioms of the system and whose consequents consist of some theorem logically derivable from the axioms are admittedly necessary truths. Moreover, philosophers who hold views of this type frequently (though not invariably) subscribe to the further thesis that since analytic truths are compatible with anything that might actually obtain in nature, necessary truths have no descriptive content (that is, they assert nothing about the order of nature or the character of experience). In consequence, although philosophers who accept this thesis usually count arithmetical truths as necessary, they deny that these truths have any ontological significance.

According to views of the second type, the class of necessary statements includes not only all analytic ones, but a large variety of synthetic statements as well. Indeed, according to some extreme versions of this type (for example, that of Leibniz) *all* synthetic truths are necessary, even though men are incapable of recognizing most of them to be such because of the weakness of the human intellect. Views of the second type can be further divided: some maintain that necessary synthetic statements formulate structures inherent in the objective nature of things independently of our apprehension of them, and others construe such statements to be about modes of experience and cognition determined by the constitution of the human mind. This first subtype is illustrated by the selection in this chapter from Blanshard, the second by the selection from Kant. Kant's claim that the truths of arithmetic as well as of geometry are synthetic runs counter to what is perhaps the dominant view of the subject which Frege and Russell helped to establish in the early years of the present century, but his view continues to be influential, and versions of it underlie the outlook of important current schools of thought in the foundations of logic and mathematics.

As in the case of necessary statements, no prominent thinker appears to have denied outright the possibility of a priori knowledge. Even Mill, who maintained that the truths of arithmetic and geometry as well as the laws of logic are inductions from experience rather than a priori truths, did not question that what he called "verbal propositions" (for example, that a man's grandfather is the father of one of his parents) are knowable a priori. But, as the example shows, philosophers differ in their conceptions of the nature and scope of the a priori.

The various conceptions that have been advanced often reflect the current state of mathematics or some branch of empirical science, and the supporting arguments for them can frequently be evaluated only on the basis of technical developments in some specialized area of inquiry. But, in any case, conceptions of the a priori can be classified in a number of ways, three of which will be mentioned here. One way is based on the analytic-synthetic distinction, and therefore assumes that the distinction is sound. It divides theories of the a priori into those which maintain that only analytic truths can be known a priori and those for which synthetic as well as analytic a priori truths are possible. Theories of the first kind (exemplified by Carnap and Lewis) therefore hold that the laws of logic and statements about relations between the intensions of linguistic expressions are the sole instances of a priori knowledge. Theories of the second kind (exemplified by Kant) maintain that there are other sorts of a priori truths, but that these can be established only by methods that depend on considerations that are not purely logical.

A second basis for classifying theories of the a priori is the alleged "source" of a priori knowledge. On one view, for example, many statements (synthetic as well as analytic) require no support from inductive evidence because their necessary truth can be recognized as "self-evident" in virtue of a "natural light of reason" inborn in men—a view held, among other thinkers, by Leibniz and in essentials also by Blanshard. On another view, a priori truths are those "presupposed" in all intelligible discourse and purposeful action, so that their denial (even if not self-contradictory) leads to their reaffirmation—a type of argument employed by Aristotle in his defense of the law of contradiction against sceptics. And, on a still different view, a priori truths can be "deduced" from the nature of the human intellect and the character of scientific knowledge—a view advocated by Kant and his followers.

A third way of distinguishing among conceptions of the a priori is in terms of whether or not a priori truths state any fixed "limits" for human knowledge. According to Kant, for example, the content of possible experience is determined by certain forms prescribed by the constitution of human sensibility, and the findings of all empirical inquiry must conform to various principles (such as the axioms of geometry or the principle of causality) that are allegedly derivable a priori from the unalterable nature of the human understanding. According to Lewis, on the other hand, although there are a priori components in all knowledge, they in no way limit the content of experience, nor is the mind inherently compelled to use any particular set of a priori principles—for such principles are freely chosen rules for classifying and interpreting experience and can be abandoned in favor of other principles if our purposes would be better served by the latter. For example, some non-Euclidean system of geometry can be adopted as the framework for classifying figures and making physical measurements, if this geometry provides a more convenient way than does the traditional Euclidean system to achieve a comprehensive ordering of physical knowledge.

It is of course obvious that these three ways of classifying conceptions of a priori knowledge do not yield exclusive types of theories, and some of the articles that follow illustrate more than one of them.

Aristotle

The Principle of Contradiction

He who knows best about each genus must be able to state the most certain principles of his subject, so that he whose subject is being *qua* being must be able to state the most certain principles of all things. This is the philosopher, and the most certain principle of all is that regarding which it is impossible to be mistaken; for such a principle must be both the best known (for all men may be mistaken about things which they do not know), and non-hypothetical. For a principle which every one must have who knows anything about being, is not a hypothesis; and that which every one must know who knows anything, he must already have when he comes to a special study. Evidently then such a principle is the most certain of all; which principle this is, we proceed to say. It is, that the same attribute cannot at the same time belong and not belong to the same subject in the same respect; we must presuppose, in face of dialetical objections, any further qualifications which might be added. This, then, is the most certain of all principles, since it answers to the definition given above. For it is impossible for any one to believe the same thing to be and not to be, as some think Heraclitus says; for what a man says he does not necessarily believe. If it is impossible that contrary attributes should belong at the same time to the same subject (the usual qualifications must be presupposed in this premise too), and if an opinion which contradicts another is contrary to it, obviously it is impossible for the same man at the same time to believe the same thing to be and not to be; for if a man were mistaken in this point he would have contrary opinions at the same time. It is for this reason that all who are carrying out a demonstration reduce it to this as an ultimate belief; for this is naturally the starting-point even for all the other axioms.

There are some who, as we have said, both themselves assert that it is possible for the same thing to be and not to be, and say that people can judge this to be the case. And among others many writers about nature use this language. But we have now posited that it is impossible for anything at the same time to be and not to be, and by this means have shown that this is the most indisputable of all principles.—Some indeed demand that even this shall be demonstrated, but this they do through want of education, for not to know of what things one may demand demonstration, and of what one may not, argues simply want of education. For it is impossible that there should be demon-

---

From Aristotle, *Metaphysica*, Book IV, trans. by W. D. Ross, published by The Clarendon Press, Oxford, 1908, and reprinted with their permission.

Born in Stagira, a city in northeastern Greece, Aristotle (384–322 B.C.) was for twenty years a member of Plato's Academy. He eventually established his own school at the Lyceum in Athens, where he directed as well as carried on researches in various branches of scientific and philosophical inquiry.

stration of absolutely everything; there would be an infinite regress, so that there would still be no demonstration. But if there are things of which one should not demand demonstration, these persons cannot say what principle they regard as more indemonstrable than the present one.

We can, however, demonstrate negatively even that this view is impossible, if our opponent will only say something; and if he says nothing, it is absurd to attempt to reason with one who will not reason about anything, in so far as he refuses to reason. For such a man, as such, is seen already to be no better than a mere plant. Now negative demonstration I distinguish from demonstration proper, because in a demonstration one might be thought to be begging the question, but if another person is responsible for the assumption we shall have negative proof, not demonstration. The starting-point for all such arguments is not the demand that our opponent shall say that something either is or is not (for this one might perhaps take to be a begging of the question), but that he shall say something which is significant both for himself and for another; for this is necessary, if he really is to say anything. For, if he means nothing, such a man will not be capable of reasoning, either with himself or with another. But if any one grants this, demonstration will be possible; for we shall already have something definite. The person responsible for the proof, however, is not he who demonstrates but he who listens; for while disowning reason he listens to reason. . . .

First then this at least is obviously true, that the word 'be' or 'not be' has a definite meaning, so that not everything will be 'so and not so'.—Again, if 'man' has one meaning, let this be 'two-footed animal'; by having one meaning I understand this:—if 'man' means '*X*', then if *A* is a man '*X*' will be what 'being a man' means for him. And it makes no difference even if one were to say a word has several meanings, if only they are limited in number; for to each formula there might be assigned a different word. For instance, we might say that 'man' has not one meaning but several, one of which would be defined as 'two-footed animal', while there might be also several other formulae if only they were limited in number; for a peculiar name might be assigned to each of the formulae. If, however, they were not limited but one were to say that the word has an infinite number of meanings, obviously reasoning would be impossible; for not to have one meaning is to have no meaning, and if words have no meaning reasoning with other people, and indeed with oneself, has been annihilated; for it is impossible to think of anything if we do not think of one thing; but if this *is* possible, one name might be assigned to this thing. Let it be assumed then, as was said at the beginning, that the name has a meaning and has one meaning; it is impossible, then, that 'being a man' should mean precisely 'not being a man', if 'man' is not only predicable of one subject but also has one meaning (for we do not identify 'having one meaning' with 'being predicable of one subject', since on that assumption even 'musical' and 'white' and 'man' would have had one meaning, so that all things would have been one; for they would all have had the same meaning).

And it will not be possible for the same thing to be and not to be, except in virtue of an ambiguity, just as one whom we call 'man', others might call 'not-man'; but the point in question is not this, whether the same thing can at the same time be and not be a man in name, but whether it can in fact. Now if 'man' and 'not-man' mean nothing different, obviously 'not being a man' will mean nothing different from 'being a man'; so that 'being a man' will be 'not being a man'; for they will be one. For being one means this—what we find in the case of 'raiment' and 'dress'—viz. that the definitory formula is one. And if 'being a man' and 'not being a man' are to be one, they must mean one thing. But it was shown earlier that they mean different things. Therefore, if it is true to say of anything that it is a man, it must be a two-footed animal; for this was what 'man' meant; and if this is necessary, it is impossible that the same thing should not be a two-footed animal; for this is what 'being necessary' means—that it is impossible for the thing not to be. It is, then, impossible that it should be at the same time true to say the same thing is a man and is not a man.

. . .

Again, if all contradictory statements are true of the same subject at the same time, evidently all things will be one. For the same thing will be a trireme, a wall, and a man, if it is equally possible to affirm and to deny anything of anything,—and this premise must be accepted by those who share the views of Protagoras. For if any one thinks that the man is not a trireme, evidently he is not a trireme; so that he also is a trireme, if, as they say, contradictory statements are both true.

. . .

Again, is he in error who judges either that the thing is so or that it is not so, and is he right who judges both? If he is not right, what can they mean by saying that the nature of existing things is of this kind? And if he is not right, but more right than he who judges in the other way, being will already be of a definite nature, and this will be true, and not at the same time also not true. But if all are alike both right and wrong, one who believes this can neither speak nor say anything intelligible; for he says at the same time both 'yes' and 'no'. And if he makes no judgement but 'thinks' and 'does not think', indifferently, what difference will there be between him and the plants?—Thus, then, it is in the highest degree evident that neither any one of those who maintain this view nor any one else is really in this position. For why does a man walk to Megara and not stay at home thinking he is walking? Why does he not walk early some morning into a well or over a precipice, if one happens to be in his way? Why do we observe him guarding against this, evidently not thinking that falling in is alike good and not good? Evidently he judges one thing to be better and another worse. And if this is so, he must judge one thing to be a man and another to be not-man, one thing to be sweet and another to be not-sweet. For he does not aim at and judge all things alike, when, thinking it desirable to drink water or to see a man, he proceeds to aim at these things; yet he ought, if the same thing were alike man and not-man. But, as was said, there is no one who does not obviously avoid some things and not others. Therefore, it seems, all men make unqualified judgements, if not about all things, still about what is better and worse. . . .

Immanuel Kant

A Priori Knowledge: How Is Pure Mathematics Possible?

PREAMBLE ON THE PECULIARITIES OF ALL METAPHYSICAL KNOWLEDGE

§ 2

CONCERNING THE KIND OF KNOWLEDGE WHICH CAN ALONE BE CALLED METAPHYSICAL

a. On the Distinction between Analytical and Synthetical Judgments in General. The peculiarity of its sources demands that metaphysical knowledge must consist of nothing but *a priori* judgments. But whatever be their origin or their logical form, there is a distinction in judgments, as to their content, according to which they are either merely *explicative*, adding nothing to the content of knowledge, or *expansive*, increasing the given knowledge. The former may be called *analytical*, the latter *synthetical*, judgments.

Analytical judgments express nothing in the predicate but what has been already actually thought in the concept of the subject, though not so distinctly or with the same (full) consciousness. When I say: "All bodies are extended," I have not amplified in the least my concept of body, but have only analyzed it, as extension was really thought to belong to that concept before the judgment was made, though it was not expressed. This judgment is therefore analytical. On the contrary, this judgment, "All bodies have weight," contains in its predicate something not actually thought in the universal concept of body; it amplifies my knowledge by adding something to my concept, and must therefore be called synthetical.

b. The Common Principle of All Analytical Judgments Is the Law of Contradiction. All analytical judgments depend wholly on the law of contradiction, and are in their nature *a priori* cognitions, whether the concepts that supply them with matter be empirical or not. For the predicate of an affirmative analytical judgment is already contained in the concept of the subject, of which it cannot be denied without contradiction. In the same way its

---

Immanuel Kant (1724–1804) was born in Königsberg, East Prussia, and from 1755 until his retirement in 1797 taught in various capacities and lectured on a large variety of subjects (including mathematics, physics, anthropology, as well as philosophy) at the University of Königsberg.

opposite is necessarily denied of the subject in an analytical, but negative, judgment, by the same law of contradiction. Such is the nature of the judgments: "All bodies are extended," and "No bodies are unextended (that is, simple)."

For this very reason all analytical judgments are *a priori* even when the concepts are empirical, as, for example, "Gold is a yellow metal"; for to know this I require no experience beyond my concept of gold as a yellow metal. It is, in fact, the very concept, and I need only analyze it without looking beyond it.

c. Synthetical Judgments Require a Different Principle from the Law of Contradiction. There are synthetical *a posteriori* judgments of empirical origin; but there are also others which are certain *a priori,* and which spring from pure understanding and reason. Yet they both agree in this, that they cannot possibly spring from the principle of analysis, namely, the law of contradiction, alone. They require a quite different principle from which they may be deduced, subject, of course, always to the law of contradiction, which must never be violated, even though everything cannot be deduced from it. I shall first classify synthetical judgments.

1. *Judgments of Experience* are always synthetical. For it would be absurd to base an analytical judgment on experience, as our concept suffices for the purpose without requiring any testimony from experience. That body is extended is a judgment established *a priori,* and not an empirical judgment. For before appealing to experience, we already have all the conditions of the judgment in the concept, from which we have but to elicit the predicate according to the law of contradiction, and thereby to become conscious of the necessity of the judgment, which experience could not in the least teach us.

2. *Mathematical Judgments* are all synthetical. This fact seems hitherto to have altogether escaped the observation of those who have analyzed human reason; it even seems directly opposed to all their conjectures, though it is incontestably certain and most important in its consequences. For as it was found that the conclusions of mathematicians all proceed according to the law of contradiction (as is demanded by all apodictic certainty), men persuaded themselves that the fundamental principles were known from the same law. This was a great mistake, for a synthetical proposition can indeed be established by the law of contradiction, but only by presupposing another synthetical proposition from which it follows, but never by that law alone.

First of all, we must observe that all strictly mathematical judgments are *a priori,* and not empirical, because they carry with them necessity, which cannot be obtained from experience. But if this be not conceded to me, very good; I shall confine my assertion to *pure mathematics,* the very notion of which implies that it contains pure *a priori* and not empirical knowledge.

It must at first be thought that the proposition $7 + 5 = 12$ is a mere analytical judgment, following from the concept of the sum of seven and five, according to the law of contradiction. But on closer examination it appears that the concept of the sum of $7 + 5$ contains merely their union in a single number, without its being at all thought what the particular number is that unites them. The concept of twelve is by no means thought by merely thinking of the combination of seven and five; and, analyze this possible sum as we may, we shall not discover twelve in the concept. We must go beyond these concepts, by calling to our aid some intuition which corresponds to one of the concepts—that is, either our five fingers or five points (as Segner has it in his *Arithmetic*)—and we must add successively the units of the five given in the intuition to the concept of seven. Hence our concept is really amplified by the proposition $7 + 5 = 12$, and we add to the first concept a second concept not thought in it. Arithmetical judgments are therefore synthetical, and the more plainly according as we take larger numbers; for in such cases it is clear that, however closely we analyze our concepts without calling intuition to our aid, we can never find the sum by such mere dissection.

Just as little is any principle of geometry analytical. That a straight line is the shortest path between two points is a synthetical proposition. For my concept of straight contains nothing of quantity, but only a quality. The concept "shortest" is therefore altogether additional and cannot be obtained by any analysis of the concept "straight line." Here, too, intuition must come to aid us. It alone makes the synthesis possible. What usually makes us believe that the predicate of such apodictic judgments is already contained in our concept, and that the judgment is therefore analytical, is the duplicity of the expression. We must think a certain predicate as attached to a given concept, and necessity indeed belongs to the concepts. But the question is not what we must join in thought *to* the given concept, but what we actually think together with and in it, though obscurely; and so it appears that the predicate belongs to this concept necessarily indeed, yet not directly but indirectly by means of an intuition which must be present.

Some other principles, assumed by geometers, are indeed actually analytical, and depend on the law of contradiction; but they only serve, as identical propositions, as a method of concatenation, and not as principles—for example $a = a$, the whole is equal to itself, or $a + b > a$, the whole is greater than its part. And yet even these, though they are recognized as valid from mere concepts, are admitted in mathematics only because they can be represented in some intuition.

The essential and distinguishing feature of pure mathematical knowledge among all other *a priori* knowledge is that it cannot at all proceed from concepts, but only by means of the construction of concepts.[1] As therefore in its propositions it must proceed beyond the concept to that which its corresponding intuition contains, these propositions neither can, nor ought to, arise analytically, by dissection of the concept, but are all synthetical.

I cannot refrain from pointing out the disadvantage resulting to philosophy from the neglect of this easy and apparently insignificant observation. Hume being prompted to cast his eye over the whole field of *a priori* cognitions in which human understanding claims such mighty possessions (a calling he felt worthy of a philosopher) heedlessly severed from it a whole, and indeed its most valuable, province, namely, pure mathematics; for he imagined its nature or, so to speak, the state constitution of this empire depended on totally different principles, namely, on the law of contradiction alone; and although he did not divide judgments in this manner formally and universally as I have done here, what he said was equivalent to this: that mathematics contains only analytical, but metaphysics synthetical, *a priori* propositions. In this, however, he was greatly mistaken, and the mistake had a decidedly injuri-

[1] *Critique of Pure Reason,* "Methodology," Ch. I, Sec. 1.

ous effect upon his whole conception. But for this, he would have extended his question concerning the origin of our synthetical judgments far beyond the metaphysical concept of causality and included in it the possibility of mathematics *a priori* also, for this latter he must have assumed to be equally synthetical. And then he could not have based his metaphysical propositions on mere experience without subjecting the axioms of mathematics equally to experience, a thing which he was far too acute to do. The good company into which metaphysics would thus have been brought would have saved it from the danger of a contemptuous ill-treatment, for the thrust intended for it must have reached mathematics, which was not and could not have been Hume's intention. Thus that acute man would have been led into considerations which must needs be similar to those that now occupy us, but which would have gained inestimably by his inimitably elegant style.

. . .

§5

THE GENERAL PROBLEM: HOW IS KNOWLEDGE FROM PURE REASON POSSIBLE?

We have already learned the significant distinction between analytical and synthetical judgments. The possibility of analytical propositions was easily comprehended, being entirely founded on the law of contradiction. The possibility of synthetical *a posteriori* judgments, of those which are gathered from experience, also requires no particular explanations, for experience is nothing but a continued synthesis of perceptions. There remain therefore only synthetical propositions *a priori,* of which the possibility must be sought or investigated, because they must depend upon other principles than the law of contradiction.

But here we need not first establish the possibility of such propositions so as to ask whether they are possible. For there are enough of them which indeed are of undoubted certainty; and, as our present method is analytical, we shall start from the fact that such synthetical but purely rational knowledge actually exists; but we must now inquire into the ground of this possibility and ask *how* such knowledge is possible, in order that we may, from the principles of its possibility, be enabled to determine the conditions of its use, its sphere and its limits. The real problem upon which all depends, when expressed with scholastic precision, is therefore: "How are synthetic propositions *a priori* possible?"

For the sake of popular understanding I have above expressed this problem somewhat differently, as an inquiry into purely rational knowledge, which I could do for once without detriment to the desired insight, because, as we have only to do here with metaphysics and its sources, the reader will, I hope, after the foregoing reminders, keep in mind that when we speak of knowing by pure reason we do not mean analytical but synthetical knowledge.[2]

[2] It is unavoidable that, as knowledge advances, certain expressions which have become classical after having been used since the infancy of science will be found inadequate and unsuitable, and a newer and more appropriate application of the terms will give rise to confusion. [This is the case with the

Metaphysics stands or falls with the solution of this problem; its very existence depends upon it. Let anyone make metaphysical assertions with ever so much plausibility, let him overwhelm us with conclusions; but if he has not previously proved able to answer this question satisfactorily, I have a right to say: This is all vain, baseless philosophy and false wisdom. You speak through pure reason and claim, as it were, to create cognitions *a priori* not only by dissecting given concepts, but also by asserting connections which do not rest upon the law of contradiction, and which you claim to conceive quite independently of all experience; how do you arrive at this, and how will you justify such pretensions? An appeal to the consent of the common sense of mankind cannot be allowed, for that is a witness whose authority depends merely upon rumor. Says Horace:

"Quodcunque ostendis mihi sic, incredulus odi." [3]

The answer to this question is as indispensable as it is difficult; and although the principal reason that it was not sought long ago is that the possibility of the question never occurred to anybody, there is yet another reason, namely, that a satisfactory answer to this one question requires a much more persistent, profound, and painstaking reflection than the most diffuse work on metaphysics, which on its first appearance promised immortal fame to its author. And every intelligent reader, when he carefully reflects what this problem requires, must at first be struck with its difficulty, and would regard it as insoluble and even impossible did there not actually exist pure synthetical cognitions *a priori*. This actually happened to David Hume, though he did not conceive the question in its entire universality as is done here and as must be done if the answer is to be decisive for all metaphysics. For how is it possible, says that acute man, that when a concept is given me I can go beyond it and connect with it another which is not contained in it, in such a manner as if the latter *necessarily* belonged to the former? Nothing but experience can furnish us with such connections (thus he concluded from the difficulty which he took to be impossibility), and all that vaunted necessity or, what is the same thing, knowledge assumed to be *a priori* is nothing but a long habit of accepting something as true, and hence of mistaking subjective necessity for objective.

Should my reader complain of the difficulty and the trouble which I shall occasion him in the solution of this problem, he is at liberty to solve it himself in an easier way. Perhaps he will then feel under obligation to the person who has undertaken for him a labor of so profound research and will rather feel some surprise at the facility with which, considering the nature of the subject, the solution has been attained. Yet it has cost years of work to solve the problem in its whole universality (using the term in the mathematical

term "analytical."] The analytical method, so far as it is opposed to the synthetical, is very different from one that consists of analytical propositions; it signifies only that we start from what is sought, as if it were given, and ascend to the only conditions under which it is possible. In this method we often use nothing but synthetical propositions, as in mathematical analysis, and it were better to term it the *regressive* method, in contradistinction to the *synthetic* or *progressive*. A principal part of logic too is distinguished by the name of analytic, which here signifies the logic of truth in contrast to dialectic, without considering whether the cognitions belonging to it are analytical or synthetical.

[3] ["To all that which thou provest me thus, I refuse to give credence, and hate"—*Epistle* II, 3, 188.]

sense, namely, for that which is sufficient for all cases), and finally to exhibit it in the analytical form, as the reader will find it here.

All metaphysicians are therefore solemnly and legally suspended from their occupations till they shall have adequately answered the question, "How are synthetic cognitions *a priori* possible?" For the answer contains the only credentials which they must show when they have anything to offer us in the name of pure reason. But if they do not possess these credentials, they can expect nothing else of reasonable people, who have been deceived so often, than to be dismissed without further inquiry.

. . .

FIRST PART OF THE MAIN TRANSCENDENTAL PROBLEM

HOW IS PURE MATHEMATICS POSSIBLE?

§ 6

Here is a great and established branch of knowledge, encompassing even now a wonderfully large domain and promising an unlimited extension in the future, yet carrying with it thoroughly apodictic certainty, that is, absolute necessity, and therefore resting upon no empirical grounds. Consequently it is a pure product of reason; and, moreover, it is thoroughly synthetical. [Hence the question arises:] "How then is it possible for human reason to produce such knowledge entirely *a priori?"*

Does not this faculty [which produces mathematics], as it neither is nor can be based upon experience, presuppose some ground of knowledge *a priori,* which lies deeply hidden but which might reveal itself by these its effects if their first beginnings were but diligently ferreted out?

§ 7

But we find that all mathematical cognition has this peculiarity: it must first exhibit its concept in intuition and indeed *a priori;* therefore in an intuition which is not empirical but pure. Without this mathematics cannot take a single step; hence its judgments are always *intuitive;* whereas philosophy must be satisfied with *discursive* judgments from mere concepts, and though it may illustrate its doctrines through an intuition, can never derive them from it. This observation on the nature of mathematics gives us a clue to the first and highest condition of its possibility, which is that some pure intuition must form its basis, in which all its concepts can be exhibited or constructed, *in concreto* and yet *a priori.* If we can uncover this pure intuition and its possibility, we may thence easily explain how synthetical propositions *a priori* are possible in pure mathematics, and consequently how this science itself is possible. For just as empirical intuition [namely, sense-perception] enables us without difficulty to enlarge the concept which we frame of an object of intuition by new predicates which intuition itself presents synthetically in experience, so also pure intuition does likewise, only with this difference, that in the latter case the synthetical judgment is *a priori* certain and apodictic, in the former only *a posteriori* and empirically certain; because this latter contains only that which occurs in contingent empirical intuition, but the former that which must necessarily be discovered in pure intuition. Here intuition, being an intuition *a priori,* is inseparably joined with the concept *prior to all experience* or particular perception.

§ 8

But with this step our perplexity seems rather to increase than to lessen. For the question now is, "How is it possible to intuit anything *a priori?*" An intuition is such a representation as would immediately depend upon the presence of the object. Hence it seems impossible to intuit spontaneously *a priori,* because intuition would in that event have to take place without either a former or a present object to refer to, and in consequence could not be intuition. Concepts indeed are such that we can easily form some of them *a priori,* namely, such as contain nothing but the thought of an object in general; and we need not find ourselves in an immediate relation to the object. Take, for instance, the concepts of quantity, of cause, etc. But even these require, in order to be meaningful and significant, a certain concrete use—that is, an application to some intuition by which an object of them is given us. But how can the intuition of the object precede the object itself?

§ 9

If our intuition were of such a nature as to represent things as they are in themselves, there would not be any intuition *a priori,* but intuition would be always empirical. For I can only know what is contained in the object in itself if it is present and given to me. It is indeed even then incomprehensible how the intuition of a present thing should make me know this thing as it is in itself, as its properties cannot migrate into my faculty of representation. But even granting this possibility, an intuition of that sort would not take place *a priori,* that is, before the object were presented to me; for without this latter fact no ground of a relation between my representation and the object can be imagined, unless it depend upon a direct implantation.

Therefore in one way only can my intuition anticipate the actuality of the object, and be a cognition *a priori,* namely: *if my intuition contains nothing but the form of sensibility, antedating in my mind all the actual impressions through which I am affected by objects.*

For that objects of sense can only be intuited according to this form of sensibility I can know *a priori.* Hence it follows that propositions which concern this form of sensuous intuition only are possible and valid for objects of the senses; as also, conversely, that intuitions which are possible *a priori* can never concern any other things than objects of our senses.

§ 10

Accordingly, it is only the form of sensuous intuition by which we can intuit things *a priori,* but by which we can know objects only as they *appear* to us (to our senses), not as they are in themselves; and this assumption is absolutely necessary if synthetical propositions *a priori* be granted as possible or if, in case they actually occur, their possibility is to be comprehended and determined beforehand.

Now, the intuitions which pure mathematics lays at the foundation of all its cognitions and judgments which appear at once apodictic and necessary are space and time. For mathematics must first present all its concepts in intuition, and pure mathematics in pure intuition; that is, it must construct them,

If it proceeded in any other way, it would be impossible to take a single step; for mathematics proceeds, not analytically by dissection of concepts, but synthetically, and if pure intuition be wanting there is nothing in which the matter for synthetical judgments *a priori* can be given. Geometry is based upon the pure intuition of space. Arithmetic achieves its concept of number by the successive addition of units in time, and pure mechanics cannot attain its concepts of motion without employing the representation of time. Both representations, however, are only intuitions; for if we omit from the empirical intuitions of bodies and their alterations (motion) everything empirical, that is, belonging to sensation, space and time still remain, which are therefore pure intuitions that lie *a priori* at the basis of the empirical. Hence they can never be omitted; but at the same time, by their being pure intuitions *a priori,* they prove that they are mere forms of our sensibility, which must precede all empirical intuition, that is, perception of actual objects, and conformably to which objects can be known *a priori,* but only as they appear to us.

§ 11

The problem of the present section is therefore solved. Pure mathematics, as synthetical cognition *a priori,* is possible only by referring to no other objects than those of the senses. At the basis of their empirical intuition lies a pure intuition (of space and of time) which is *a priori,* because the latter intuition is nothing but the mere form of sensibility, which precedes the actual appearance of the objects, since in fact it makes them possible. Yet this faculty of intuiting *a priori* affects not the matter of the phenomenon (that is, the sensation in it, for this constitutes that which is empirical), but its form, namely, space and time. Should any man venture to doubt that these are determinations adhering not to things in themselves, but to their relation to our sensibility, I should be glad to know how he can find it possible to know *a priori* how their intuition will be characterized before we have any acquaintance with them and before they are presented to us. Such, however, is the case with space and time. But this is quite comprehensible as soon as both count for nothing more than formal conditions of our sensibility, while the objects count merely as phenomena; for then the form of the phenomenon, that is, pure intuition, can by all means be represented as proceeding from ourselves, that is, *a priori.*

§ 12

In order to add something by way of illustration and confirmation, we need only watch the ordinary and unavoidable procedure of geometers. All proofs of the complete congruence of two given figures (where the one can in every respect be substituted for the other) come ultimately to this, that they may be made to coincide, which is evidently nothing else than a synthetical proposition resting upon immediate intuition; and this intuition must be pure or given *a priori,* otherwise the proposition could not rank as apodictically certain, but would have empirical certainty only. In that case, it could only be said that it is always found to be so and holds good only as far as our perception reaches. That everywhere space (which [in its entirety] is itself no longer the boundary of another space) has three dimensions and that space cannot in any way have more is based on the proposition that not more than three lines can intersect at right angles in one point; but this proposition cannot by any means be shown from concepts, but rests immediately on intuition, and indeed on pure and *a priori* intuition because it is apodictically certain. That we can require a line to be drawn to infinity (*in indefinitum*) or that a series of changes (for example, spaces traversed by motion) shall be infinitely continued presupposes a representation of space and time, which can only attach to intuition—namely, so far as it in itself is bounded by nothing—for from concepts it could never be inferred. Consequently, the basis of mathematics actually is pure intuitions, which make its synthetical and apodictically valid propositions possible. Hence our transcendental deduction of the notions of space and of time explains at the same time the possibility of pure mathematics. Without such a deduction and the assumption "that everything which can be given to our senses (to the external senses in space, to the internal one in time) is intuited by us as it appears to us, not as it is in itself," the truth of pure mathematics may be granted, but its existence could by no means be understood.

§ 13

Those who cannot yet rid themselves of the notion that space and time are actual qualities inherent in things in themselves may exercise their acumen on the following paradox. When they have in vain attempted its solution and are free from prejudices at least for a few moments, they will suspect that the degradation of space and time to mere forms of our sensuous intuition may perhaps be well founded.

If two things are quite equal in all respects as much as can be ascertained by all means possible, quantitatively and qualitatively, it must follow that the one can in all cases and under all circumstances replace the other, and this substitution would not occasion the least perceptible difference. This in fact is true of plane figures in geometry; but some spherical figures exhibit, notwithstanding a complete internal agreement, such a difference in their external relation that the one figure cannot possibly be put in the place of the other. For instance, two spherical triangles on opposite hemispheres, which have an arc of the equator as their common base, may be quite equal, both as regards sides and angles, so that nothing is to be found in either, if it be described for itself alone and completed, that would not equally be applicable to both; and yet the one cannot be put in the place of the other (that is, upon the opposite hemisphere). Here, then, is an internal difference between the two triangles, which difference our understanding cannot describe as internal and which only manifests itself by external relations in space. But I shall adduce examples, taken from common life, that are more obvious still.

What can be more similar in every respect and in every part more alike to my hand and to my ear than their images in a mirror? And yet I cannot put such a hand as is seen in the glass in the place of its original; for if this is a right hand, that in the glass is a left one, and the image or reflection of the right ear is a left one, which never can take the place of the other. There are in this case no internal differences which our understanding could determine by thinking alone. Yet the differences are internal as the senses teach, for, notwithstanding their complete equality and similarity, the left hand cannot be enclosed in the same bounds as the right one (they are not congruent); the glove of one hand cannot be used for the other. What is the solution? These objects are not representations of things as they are in themselves and as some mere understanding would know them, but sensuous intuitions, that is, appearances whose possibility rests upon the relation of certain things unknown in themselves to something else, namely, to our sensibility. Space is the form of the external intuition of this sensibility, and the internal determination of every space is possible only by the determination of its external relation to the whole of space, of which it is a part (in other words, by its relation to the outer sense). That is to say, the part is possible only through the whole, which is never the case with things in themselves, as objects of the mere understanding, but which may well be the case with mere appearances. Hence the difference between similar and equal things which are not congruent (for instance, two symmetric helices) cannot be made intelligible by any concept, but only by the relation to the right and the left hands which immediately refers to intuition.

REMARK I

Pure mathematics, and especially pure geometry, can have objective reality only on condition that they refer merely to objects of sense. But in regard to the latter the principle holds good that our sense representation is not a representation of things in themselves, but of the way in which they appear to us. Hence it follows that the propositions of geometry are not the results of a mere creation of our poetic imagination, and that therefore they cannot be referred with assurance to actual objects; but rather that they are necessarily valid of space, and consequently of all that may be found in space, because space is nothing else than the form of all external appearances, and it is this form alone in which objects of sense can be given to us. Sensibility, the form of which is the basis of geometry, is that upon which the possibility of external appearance depends. Therefore these appearances can never contain anything but what geometry prescribes to them.

It would be quite otherwise if the senses were so constituted as to represent objects as they are in themselves. For then it would not by any means follow from the representation of space, which, with all its properties, serves to the geometer as an *a priori* foundation, that this foundation and everything which is thence inferred must be so in nature. The space of the geometer would be considered a mere fiction, and it would not be credited with objective validity because we cannot see how things must of necessity agree with an image of them which we make spontaneously and previous to our acquaintance with them. But if this image, or rather this formal intuition, is the essential property of our sensibility by means of which alone objects are given to us, and if this sensibility represents not things in themselves but their appearances, then we shall easily comprehend, and at the same time indisputably prove, that all external objects of our world of sense must necessarily coincide in the most rigorous way with the propositions of geometry; because sensibility, by means of its form of external intuition, namely, by space, with which the geometer is occupied, makes those objects possible as mere appearances.

. . .

REMARK II

Whatever is given us as object must be given us in intuition. All our intuition, however, takes place by means of the senses only; the understanding intuits nothing but only reflects. And as we have just shown that the senses never and in no manner enable us to know things in themselves, but only their appearances, which are mere representations of the sensibility, we conclude that "all bodies, together with the space in which they are, must be considered nothing but mere representations in us, and exist nowhere but in our thoughts." Is not this manifest idealism?

Idealism consists in the assertion that there are none but thinking beings, all other things which we think are perceived in intuition, being nothing but representations in the thinking beings, to which no object external to them in fact corresponds. I, on the contrary, say that things as objects of our senses existing outside us are given, but we know nothing of what they may be in themselves, knowing only their appearances, that is, the representations which they cause in us by affecting our senses. Consequently I grant by all means that there are bodies without us, that is, things which, though quite unknown to us as to what they are in themselves, we yet know by the representations which their influence on our sensibility procures us. These representations we call "bodies," a term signifying merely the appearance of the thing which is unknown to us, but not therefore less actual. Can this be termed idealism? It is the very contrary.

Long before Locke's time, but assuredly since him, it has been generally assumed and granted without detriment to the actual existence of external things that many of their predicates may be said to belong, not to the things in themselves, but to their appearances, and to have no proper existence outside our representation. Heat, color, and taste, for instance, are of this kind. Now, if I go farther and, for weighty reasons, rank as mere appearances the remaining qualities of bodies also, which are called primary—such as extension, place, and, in general, space, with all that which belongs to it (impenetrability or materiality, shape, etc.)—no one in the least can adduce the reason of its being inadmissible. As little as the man who admits colors not to be properties of the object in itself, but only as modifications of the sense of sight, should on that account be called an idealist, so little can my thesis be named idealistic merely because I find that more, nay, *all the properties which constitute the intuition of a body belong merely to its appearance.*

The existence of the thing that appears is thereby not destroyed, as in genuine idealism, but it is only shown that we cannot possibly know it by the senses as it is in itself.

I should be glad to know what my assertions must be in order to avoid all idealism. Undoubtedly, I should say that the representation of space is not only perfectly conformable to the relation which our sensibility has to objects —that I have said—but that it is quite similar to the object—an assertion in which I can find as little meaning as if I said that the sensation of red has a similarity to the property of cinnabar which excites this sensation in me.

REMARK III

Hence we may at once dismiss an easily foreseen but futile objection, "that by admitting the ideality of space and of time the whole sensible world would be turned into mere sham." After all philosophical insight into the nature of sensuous cognition was spoiled by making the sensibility merely a confused mode of representation, according to which we still know things as they are, but without being able to reduce everything in this our representation to a clear consciousness, I proved that sensibility consists, not in this logical distinction of clearness and obscurity, but in the genetic one of the origin of knowledge itself. For sensuous perception represents things not at all as they are, but only the mode in which they affect our senses; and consequently by sensuous perception appearances only, and not things themselves, are given to the understanding for reflection. After this necessary correction, an objection rises from an unpardonable and almost intentional misconception, as if my doctrine turned all the things of the world of sense into mere illusion.

When an appearance is given us, we are still quite free as to how we should judge the matter. The appearance depends upon the senses, but the judgment upon the understanding; and the only question is whether in the determination of the object there is truth or not. But the difference between truth and dreaming is not ascertained by the nature of the representations which are referred to objects (for they are the same in both cases), but by their connection according to those rules which determine the coherence of the representations in the concept of an object, and by ascertaining whether they can subsist together in experience or not. And it is not the fault of the appearances if our cognition takes illusion for truth, that is, if the intuition, by which an object is given us, is considered a concept of the thing or even of its existence which the understanding can only think. The senses represent to us the course of the planets as now progressive, now retrogressive; and herein is neither falsehood nor truth, because as long as we hold this to be nothing but appearance we do not judge of the objective character of their motion. But as a false judgment may easily arise when the understanding is not on its guard against this subjective mode of representation being considered objective, we say they appear to move backward; it is not the senses however which must be charged with the illusion, but the understanding, whose province alone it is to make an objective judgment from appearances.

. . .

But if I venture to go beyond all possible experience with my concepts of space and time, which I cannot refrain from doing if I proclaim them characters inherent in things in themselves (for what should prevent me from letting them hold good of the same things, even though my senses might be different, and unsuited to them?), then a grave error may arise owing to an illusion, in which I proclaim to be universally valid what is merely a subjective condition of the intuition of things and certain only for all objects of senses—namely, for all possible experience; I would refer this condition to things in themselves, and not limit it to conditions of experience.

My doctrine of the ideality of space and of time, therefore, far from reducing the whole sensible world to mere illusion, is the only means of securing the application of one of the most important kinds of knowledge (that which mathematics propounds *a priori*) to actual objects and of preventing its being regarded as mere illusion. For without this observation it would be quite impossible to make out whether the intuitions of space and time, which we borrow from no experience and which yet lie in our representation *a priori*, are not mere phantasms of our brain to which objects do not correspond, at least not adequately; and, consequently, whether we have been able to show its unquestionable validity with regard to all the objects of the sensible world just because they are mere appearances.

Bernard Bosanquet

Analytic and Synthetic

Every judgment is both analytic and synthetic. This would not by itself be a sufficient ground for refusing to employ these terms as heads of classification, for it is more or less the case through the whole of Logic that terms must be employed to mark predominant aspects rather than exclusive characters. Nor do I find a sufficient ground of objection in the psychological comment that the judgment which adds a fresh predicate to a subject to-day must become tautologous or analytic if repeated to-morrow, and that therefore it merely depends on individual knowledge and memory whether a given judgment is synthetic or analytic. Any conception of dominant quality, function, or essence, is enough to make this comment futile, and without such a conception it would seem that science is impossible. It is a superstition to suppose that the progress of theoretical explanation in terms of general law threatens the doctrine of essence, form, or function. However clearly an individual thing may be explained as a section of evolution or a meeting-point of forces, there will always be a definite continued identity conferred by characteristic form or function. No explanation can destroy the actual relations of whole and parts which form the essence of everything that is real. Knowledge has quite enough fixity to give meaning to the contrast of analytic and synthetic judgments wholly apart from the progress of individual minds.

The reason why I no longer care to lay emphasis on the antithesis in question is not that it is purely 'subjective'—for this is not the case—nor even that it is only a distinction of degree—for that is the character of most distinctions in Logic; but simply that it is not a sufficiently specific antithesis to be of practical value in classification. I suppose that if the terms were to be employed, we should call those judgments analytic which attain to an adequate explanation or appreciation of a complex whole. The best instances might be the definition or the disjunction, the equation, and judgments passed upon moral and aesthetic value. In all these cases we have the whole completely given in its parts, the identity in its differences, and therefore we are entitled to con-

---

From Bernard Bosanquet, *Logic,* 2nd ed., Vol. 1, Chap. 1, published by The Clarendon Press, Oxford, 1911, and reprinted with their permission.

Bernard Bosanquet (1848–1923) had private means and held no academic post during most of his life. He was Fellow and Lecturer at University College, Oxford, from 1871 to 1881 and Professor of Moral Philosophy at St. Andrews from 1903 to 1908.

sider not so much the nature of the whole reconstructed, as the exhaustiveness of the reconstruction. But, as the above instances show, adequacy or exhaustiveness exhibits itself in contents whose nature is wide apart, and therefore it has no convenient place as a general character in a classification.

On the other hand, as terms belonging to the general theory of judgment, analytic and synthetic are of profound significance. I said at the beginning of this section that every judgment is both analytic and synthetic. This assertion demands no explanation, if we remember our account of judgment as always involving identity in difference. But I will attempt to illustrate its meaning more fully.

If I say 'Caesar crossed the Rubicon', I start with an individual Caesar, whose continued identity extended through a certain space of time and revealed itself in a variety of acts, and I exhibit his identity in one of the acts and moments —its differences—through which it persisted. What I mean by the affirmation is that he, *the* Caesar who had before conquered Gaul, and who was afterwards murdered on the Ides of March, displayed his character and enacted part of his history by crossing the Rubicon. This is a clear case of exhibiting an identity in difference. But the process has inevitably two aspects. On the one hand, I analyse the individual whole that is called Caesar by specifying one of the differences that may be considered as a part within it; on the other hand, I construct or make synthesis of the individual whole in question, by exhibiting it as a whole that pervades, and absorbs in itself, each or all of its differences. It is only an *individual* whole that is obviously present in *each* as well as in *all* of its differences, as the individual Caesar in the act of crossing the Rubicon. A totality whose unity is incomplete, such as 'all men', is only *implied* in *each* of its differences, and is not *given as* a whole in anything short of *all*. But this does not alter the fundamental nature of assertion. Every judgment exhibits a whole in its parts, and parts as contributory to a whole.

Much has lately been said of Kant's celebrated instance, the equation $7 + 5 = 12$. We have here a total, twelve, which can be compounded in an immense variety of ways, and we display this total as identical, whether expressed by its place in the series of numbers (which implies one and the simplest mode of its formation) or treated as the sum of two other totals, each of which is expressed in the same simple way. It is obvious that if analytic and synthetic were reciprocally exclusive characters, the question 'Is this equation an analytic or a synthetic judgment?' would be wholly unanswerable. If 12 were not the same number as $7 + 5$, the judgment would not be true; if $7 + 5$ gained nothing by being defined as 12, the judgment would cease to be a judgment at all. $7 + 5$ is one of the differences which constitute the nature of the total 12, and by *constructing* 12 in this way we ipso facto *analyse* it.

The relation of these two processes, or rather two aspects of the same process, is so fundamental in all knowledge, being in fact *the* relation which especially characterises knowledge as such, that I may be pardoned for continuing to insist on it by help of another set of considerations. The notion of a plain difference between taking to pieces and putting together arises from actual operation on material things. This origin of the metaphor involved in 'analysis' and 'synthesis' has reacted and still reacts injuriously on our conceptions of intellectual processes. In mechanical operations we cannot pull to pieces and put together the same thing by the same act, and which of the two we can do is determined by the material handed to us. If a thing is complete already, we cannot put it together any further; the only alternative then open to us, as between these two processes, is to pull it to pieces; and so *vice versa.* But this feature of material operation cannot be transferred to thought, and for this reason, that the essence of thought is to show the process in the result, and exhibit each as necessary to the other. Therefore, if we construct in thought, the materials out of which we construct have not lost their separateness when the fabric is finished; the fabric as it is still issues from them as they were; if not, we have dropped a link, and our construction is unwarranted. The synthesis, one might say, is based on the analysis; but this would ascribe a false priority, because the fragments supplied to us only *become* an analysis as the synthesis, which relates them to a whole, progresses. Apart from the synthesis they are mere fragments, and therefore are not an analysis of anything. The workman who puts together the parts of a watch has first the handful of wheels and springs, and then the completed watch; he cannot have both at once, and in as far as he has one he has not the other. Moreover, when he has made the watch the wheels and springs are together and are not separate, nor are they separable consistently with the existence of the watch. Synthesis in this sphere is incompatible with analysis, and *vice versa.* But a man who wishes in thought or calculation to construct any instrument out of parts has a very different task. Every element of the handful of parts must have its place and functions clearly retained in the intelligence which constructs the whole; for the whole, as a whole of intellectual synthesis, exists no longer than its parts are clearly apprehended in their relations. 'Yes,' it may be said, 'but the distinction must remain that even in thought you may *either* begin by considering detached wheels, &c., and finding out how they must act in the watch, *or* by looking at a watch and detecting, within its completed system, the separate parts and their relations. The former process is synthesis, the latter analysis.'

This is true so far as judgment or inference is an activity in time, and includes within itself a transition in time. In so far as it has this character, the process of thought can simulate or share the characteristics of material operation. But this does not affect the internal nature of judgment, as I have pointed out in discussing its temporal character. The question is not whether you begin with the whole or with the parts, but merely what sort of whole and what sort of parts you begin with. Given an escapement wheel, I may chance even to be ignorant that it belongs to a watch at all; but none the less I judge of it as a part in a whole, which whole I can at first only think of, perhaps, as 'some piece of mechanism that depends on a catch playing into a delicately toothed wheel'. The further intellectual construction of this mechanism and the ultimate definition of it as a watch, is, according to the views of the passage just referred to, not a transition from S to P, but a transition from the judgment s–p to the judgment S–P. We therefore find analysis no less than synthesis to be the internal essence of every minutest section of the judgment or inference in question. In the same way, if a watch is put into my hand with instructions to find out what makes it go as it does, I have primarily a thing in space as the given whole, and indefinite wheels, springs, &c. (which as yet I cannot distinguish by position or characteristic shape) as given parts. No doubt in space all the parts which I shall need to learn are given in position within the whole, and so we tend to describe the problem as one of analysis, in contrast to the other (in which I had to find out or imagine the position of the parts in the whole) as synthesis; and these titles serve well enough as superficial descriptions of certain cases to which judgment and inference are applied—not of *any* judgment or inference as such. But the whole is not, in the latter case any more than in the former, given as an intelligible machine, nor are the parts given within the whole of knowledge because they are within the whole of space. In other words, to see the escapement wheel lying inside the watch does *not* 'give' me this wheel as a part of a mechanical arrangement; to know it as a part of *such* a whole I must understand it; and in understanding it, i.e. in my analysis, perform the synthesis of the watch as a definite mechanical contrivance.

Therefore not only is every judgment both analytic and synthetic, but it is analytic only as far as it is synthetic. It can only be called analytic or synthetic *par excellence* if, by the same confusion that causes the judgment to be regarded as a transition from S to P, we consider the joint analysis and synthesis of one whole as the analysis or synthesis of another; because in that case we seem to have a fixed and given whole, and to predicate of it nothing but parts, or *vice versa*. In this confusion there is an element of truth. Though s must become S when p becomes P, yet s has continued identity with S and p with P, and therefore the transition in time from s–p to S–P does all that could be done by the unreal transition from s to P. Present me with a pattern s which is a tissue of intersecting curves p, and when I have analysed it into the thistle design P, the pattern s is transformed to my eye into a distinct and beautiful design S; but S is the same that was s, and in that sense we have connected s with P, and we may represent P as the analysis of s, only not forgetting that it is the synthesis of S which is the same as s, and that therefore in predicating P of s we *ipso facto* transform s into S. And thus the complete understanding of a watch as a mechanical system, expressed in the joint analysis and synthesis S–P, may be accepted as happening to involve, *par excellence, either* the intellectual analysis of the watch as a given whole in space s, *or* the intellectual synthesis of the watch out of given separate parts in space s_1, s_2, s_3, &c. The given whole, or given parts, can be thus allowed to pass as merely whole, or merely parts, because they are not respectively whole and parts in the sense contemplated by the judgment S–P, and therefore it does not press home their relation to one another. The watch seems to be from the first a ready-made whole, a round thing s in space, which can only be analysed, and not constructed, by the judgment S–P. But it *is* further constructed, not as a round thing in space, but as a mechanical system, by means of that judgment.

John Stuart Mill

Of Demonstration and Necessary Truths

THE THEOREMS OF GEOMETRY ARE NECESSARY TRUTHS ONLY IN THE SENSE OF NECESSARILY FOLLOWING FROM HYPOTHESES

If, as laid down in the two preceding chapters, the foundation of all sciences, even deductive or demonstrative sciences, is induction, if every step in the ratiocinations even of geometry is an act of induction, and if a train of reasoning is but bringing many inductions to bear upon the same subject of inquiry and drawing a case within one induction by means of another, wherein lies the peculiar certainty always ascribed to the sciences which are entirely, or almost entirely, deductive? Why are they called the exact sciences? Why are mathematical certainty and the evidence of demonstration common phrases to express the very highest degree of assurance attainable by reason? Why are mathematics by almost all philosophers, and (by some) even those branches of natural philosophy which, through the medium of mathematics, have been converted into deductive sciences, considered to be independent of the evidence of experience and observation and characterized as systems of necessary truth?

The answer I conceive to be that this character of necessity ascribed to the truths of mathematics and (even with some reservations to be hereafter made) the peculiar certainty attributed to them is an illusion, in order to sustain which, it is necessary to suppose that those truths relate to, and express the properties of, purely imaginary objects. It is acknowledged that the conclusions of geometry are deduced, partly at least, from the so-called definitions, and that those definitions are assumed to be correct representations, as far as they go, of the objects with which geometry is conversant. Now we have pointed out that from a definition as such no proposition, unless it be one concerning the meaning of a word, can ever follow, and that what apparently follows from a definition follows in reality from an implied assumption that there exists a real thing conformable thereto. This assumption, in the case of the definitions of geometry, is not strictly true; there exist no real things exactly conformable to the definitions. There exist no points without magnitude; no lines without breadth, nor perfectly straight; no circles with all their radii exactly equal, nor squares with all their angles perfectly right. It will perhaps be said that the assumption does not extend to the actual, but only to the possible, existence of such things. I answer that, according to any test we have of possibility, they are not even possible. Their existence, so far as we can form any judgment, would seem to be inconsistent with the physical

---

From John Stuart Mill, *System of Logic,* 10th ed., Book II, Chaps. 5, 6, and 7, Longmans, Green & Co., 1879.

constitution of our planet at least, if not of the universe. To get rid of this difficulty and at the same time to save the credit of the supposed system of necessary truth, it is customary to say that the points, lines, circles, and squares which are the subject of geometry exist in our conceptions merely and are part of our minds, which minds, by working on their own materials, construct an *a priori* science, the evidence of which is purely mental and has nothing whatever to do with outward experience. By howsoever high authorities this doctrine may have been sanctioned, it appears to me psychologically incorrect. The points, lines, circles, and squares which anyone has in his mind are (I apprehend) simply copies of the points, lines, circles, and squares which he has known in his experience. Our idea of a point I apprehend to be simply our idea of the *minimum visibile,* the smallest portion of surface which we can see. A line, as defined by geometers, is wholly inconceivable. We can reason about a line as if it had no breadth, because we have a power, which is the foundation of all the control we can exercise over the operations of our minds, the power, when a perception is present to our senses or a conception to our intellects, of *attending* to a part only of that perception or conception instead of the whole. But we cannot *conceive* a line without breadth; we can form no mental picture of such a line; all the lines which we have in our minds are lines possessing breadth. If anyone doubts this, we may refer him to his own experience. I much question if anyone who fancies that he can conceive what is called a mathematical line thinks so from the evidence of his consciousness; I suspect it is rather because he supposes that, unless such a conception were possible, mathematics could not exist as a science, a supposition which there will be no difficulty in showing to be entirely groundless.

Since, then, neither in nature nor in the human mind do there exist any objects exactly corresponding to the definitions of geometry, while yet that science cannot be supposed to be conversant about nonentities, nothing remains but to consider geometry as conversant with such lines, angles, and figures as really exist, and the definitions, as they are called, must be regarded as some of our first and most obvious generalizations concerning those natural objects. The correctness of those generalizations, *as* generalizations, is without a flaw; the equality of all the radii of a circle is true of all circles, so far as it is true of any one, but it is not exactly true of any circle; it is only nearly true, so nearly that no error of any importance in practice will be incurred by feigning it to be exactly true. When we have occasion to extend these inductions or their consequences to cases in which the error would be appreciable—to lines of perceptible breadth or thickness, parallels which deviate sensibly from equidistance, and the like—we correct our conclusions by combining with them a fresh set of propositions relating to the aberration, just as we also take in propositions relating to the physical or chemical properties of the material if those properties happen to introduce any modification into the result, which they easily may, even with respect to figure and magnitude, as in the case, for instance, of expansion by heat. So long, however, as there exists no practical necessity for attending to any of the properties of the object except its geometrical properties or to any of the natural irregularities in those, it is convenient to neglect the consideration of the other properties and of the irregularities and to reason as if these did not exist; accordingly, we formally announce in the definitions that we intend to proceed on this plan. But it is an error to suppose, because we resolve to confine our attention to a certain number of the properties of an object, that we therefore conceive, or have an idea of, the object denuded of its other properties. We are thinking, all the time, of precisely such objects as we have seen and touched and with all the properties which naturally belong to them, but, for scientific convenience, we feign them to be divested of all properties except those which are material to our purpose and in regard to which we design to consider them.

The peculiar accuracy supposed to be characteristic of the first principles of geometry thus appears to be fictitious. The assertions on which the reasonings of the science are founded do not, any more than in other sciences, exactly correspond with the fact, but we suppose that they do so, for the sake of tracing the consequences which follow from the supposition. The opinion of Dugald Stewart respecting the foundations of geometry is, I conceive, substantially correct: that it is built on hypotheses; that it owes to this alone the peculiar certainty supposed to distinguish it; and that in any science whatever, by reasoning from a set of hypotheses, we may obtain a body of conclusions as certain as those of geometry, that is, as strictly in accordance with the hypotheses and as irresistibly compelling assent, *on condition* that those hypotheses are true.[1]

When, therefore, it is affirmed that the conclusions of geometry are necessary truths, the necessity consists in reality only in this, that they correctly follow from the suppositions from which they are deduced. Those suppositions are so far from being necessary that they are not even true; they purposely depart, more or less widely, from the truth. The only sense in which necessity can be ascribed to the conclusions of any scientific investigation is that of legitimately following from some assumption which, by the conditions of the inquiry, is not to be questioned. In this relation, of course, the derivative truths of every deductive science must stand to the inductions or assumptions on which the science is founded, and which, whether true or untrue, certain or doubtful in themselves, are always supposed certain for the purposes of the particular science.

. . .

SOME OF THE FIRST PRINCIPLES OF GEOMETRY ARE AXIOMS,
AND THESE ARE NOT HYPOTHETICAL BUT ARE EXPERIMENTAL TRUTHS

It remains to inquire what is the ground of our belief in axioms—what is the evidence on which they rest? I answer, they are experimental truths, generalizations from observation. The proposition, "Two straight lines cannot

[1] It is justly remarked by Professor Bain (*Logic,* II, 134) that the word Hypothesis is here used in a somewhat peculiar sense. An hypothesis, in science, usually means a supposition not proved to be true, but surmised to be so, because if true it would account for certain known facts, and the final result of the speculation may be to prove its truth. The hypotheses spoken of in the text are of a different character; they are known not to be literally true, while as much of them as is true is not hypothetical, but certain. The two cases, however, resemble in the circumstance that in both we reason, not from a truth, but from an assumption, and the truth, therefore, of the conclusions is conditional, not categorical. This suffices to justify, in point of logical propriety, Stewart's use of the term. It is, of course, needful to bear in mind that the hypothetical element in the definitions of geometry is the assumption that what is very nearly true is exactly so. This unreal exactitude might be called a fiction as properly as an hypothesis, but that appellation, still more than the other, would fail to point out the close relation which exists between the fictitious point or line and the points and lines of which we have experience.

inclose a space"—or, in other words, "Two straight lines which have once met, do not meet again, but continue to diverge"—is an induction from the evidence of our senses.

. . .

It is not necessary to show that the truths which we call axioms are originally *suggested* by observation and that we should never have known that two straight lines cannot inclose a space if we had never seen a straight line, thus much being admitted by Dr. Whewell and by all, in recent times, who have taken his view of the subject. But they contend that it is not experience which *proves* the axiom, but that its truth is perceived *a priori*, by the constitution of the mind itself, from the first moment when the meaning of the proposition is apprehended, and without any necessity for verifying it by repeated trials, as is requisite in the case of truths really ascertained by observation.

They cannot, however, but allow that the truth of the axiom, "Two straight lines cannot inclose a space," even if evident independently of experience, is also evident from experience. Whether the axiom needs confirmation or not, it receives confirmation in almost every instant of our lives, since we cannot look at any two straight lines which intersect one another without seeing that from that point they continue to diverge more and more. Experimental proof crowds in upon us in such endless profusion, and without one instance in which there can be even a suspicion of an exception to the rule, that we should soon have stronger ground for believing the axiom, even as an experimental truth, than we have for almost any of the general truths which we confessedly learn from the evidence of our senses. Independently of *a priori* evidence, we should certainly believe it with an intensity of conviction far greater than we accord to any ordinary physical truth, and this, too, at a time of life much earlier than that from which we date almost any part of our acquired knowledge, and much too early to admit of our retaining any recollection of the history of our intellectual operations at that period. Where, then, is the necessity for assuming that our recognition of these truths has a different origin from the rest of our knowledge when its existence is perfectly accounted for by supposing its origin to be the same? when the causes which produce belief in all other instances exist in this instance, and in a degree of strength as much superior to what exists in other cases as the intensity of the belief itself is superior? The burden of proof lies on the advocates of the contrary opinion; it is for them to point out some fact inconsistent with the supposition that this part of our knowledge of nature is derived from the same sources as every other part.[2]

[2] Some persons find themselves prevented from believing that the axiom, "Two straight lines cannot inclose a space," could ever become known to us through experience, by a difficulty which may be stated as follows: If the straight lines spoken of are those contemplated in the definition—lines absolutely without breadth and absolutely straight—that such are incapable of inclosing a space is not proved by experience, for lines such as these do not present themselves in our experience. If, on the other hand, the lines meant are such straight lines as we do meet with in experience, lines straight enough for practical purposes, but in reality slightly zigzag, and with some, however trifling, breadth; as applied to these lines the axiom is not true, for two of them may, and sometimes do, inclose a small portion of space. In neither case, therefore, does experience prove the axiom.

Those who employ this argument to show that geometrical axioms cannot be proved by induction show themselves unfamiliar with a common and perfectly valid mode of inductive proof: proof by approximation. Though experience furnishes us with no lines so unimpeachably straight that two of them are incapable of inclosing the smallest space, it presents us with gradations of lines possessing

This, for instance, they would be able to do, if they could prove chronologically that we had the conviction (at least practically) so early in infancy as to be anterior to those impressions on the senses upon which, on the other theory, the conviction is founded. This, however, cannot be proved, the point being too far back to be within the reach of memory and too obscure for external observation.

. . .

ALL DEDUCTIVE SCIENCES ARE INDUCTIVE

. . .

What we have now asserted, however, cannot be received as universally true of deductive or demonstrative sciences until verified by being applied to the most remarkable of all those sciences, that of Numbers, the theory of the Calculus, Arithmetic and Algebra. It is harder to believe of the doctrines of this science than of any other, either that they are not truths *a priori* but experimental truths, or that their peculiar certainty is owing to their being not absolute but only conditional truths. This, therefore, is a case which merits examination apart, and the more so because on this subject we have a double set of doctrines to contend with: that of the *a priori* philosophers on one side; and, on the other, a theory the most opposite to theirs which was at one time very generally received and is still far from being altogether exploded among metaphysicians.

THE PROPOSITIONS OF THE SCIENCE OF NUMBER ARE NOT VERBAL, BUT GENERALIZATIONS FROM EXPERIENCE

This theory attempts to solve the difficulty apparently inherent in the case by representing the propositions of the science of numbers as merely verbal and its processes as simple transformations of language, substitutions of one expression for another. The proposition, "Two and one is equal to three," according to these writers, is not a truth, is not the assertion of a really existing fact, but a definition of the word three, a statement that mankind have agreed to use the name three as a sign exactly equivalent to two and one, to call by the former name whatever is called by the other more clumsy phrase. According to this doctrine, the longest process in algebra is but a succession of changes in terminology by which equivalent expressions are substituted one for another, a series of translations of the same fact from one into another language; though how, after such a series of translations, the fact itself comes out changed (as when we demonstrate a new geometrical theorem by algebra) they have not explained, and it is a difficulty which is fatal to their theory.

It must be acknowledged that there are peculiarities in the processes of arithmetic and algebra which render the theory in question very plausible, and have not unnaturally made those sciences the stronghold of Nominalism.

less and less either of breadth or of flexure, of which series the straight line of the definition is the ideal limit. And observation shows that just as much and as nearly as the straight lines of experience approximate to having no breadth or flexure, so much and so nearly does the space-inclosing power of any two of them approach to zero. The inference that if they had no breadth or flexure at all they would inclose no space at all, is a correct inductive inference from these facts, conformable to one of the four Inductive Methods hereinafter characterized, the Method of Concomitant Variations, of which the mathematical Doctrine of Limits presents the extreme case.

The doctrine that we can discover facts, detect the hidden processes of nature, by an artful manipulation of language is so contrary to common sense that a person must have made some advances in philosophy to believe it: men fly to so paradoxical a belief to avoid, as they think, some even greater difficulty which the vulgar do not see. What has led many to believe that reasoning is a mere verbal process is that no other theory seemed reconcilable with the nature of the science of numbers. For we do not carry any ideas along with us when we use the symbols of arithmetic or of algebra. In a geometrical demonstration we have a mental diagram, if not one on paper; AB, AC, are present to our imagination as lines, intersecting other lines, forming an angle with one another, and the like; but not so *a* and *b*. These may represent lines or any other magnitudes, but those magnitudes are never thought of; nothing is realized in our imagination but *a* and *b*. The ideas which, on the particular occasion, they happen to represent are banished from the mind during every intermediate part of the process between the beginning, when the premises are translated from things into signs, and the end, when the conclusion is translated back from signs into things. Nothing, then, being in the reasoner's mind but the symbols, what can seem more inadmissible than to contend that the reasoning process has to do with anything more? We seem to have come to one of Bacon's prerogative instances, an *experimentum crucis* on the nature of reasoning itself.

Nevertheless, it will appear on consideration that this apparently so decisive instance is no instance at all; that there is in every step of an arithmetical or algebraical calculation a real induction, a real inference of facts from facts; and that what disguises the induction is simply its comprehensive nature and the consequent extreme generality of the language. All numbers must be numbers of something; there are no such things as numbers in the abstract. *Ten* must mean ten bodies, or ten sounds, or ten beatings of the pulse. But though numbers must be numbers of something, they may be numbers of anything. Propositions, therefore, concerning numbers have the remarkable peculiarity that they are propositions concerning all things whatever, all objects, all existences of every kind known to our experience. All things possess quantity, consist of parts which can be numbered, and in that character possess all the properties which are called properties of numbers. That half of four is two must be true whatever the word four represents, whether four hours, four miles, or four pounds weight. We need only conceive a thing divided into four equal parts (and all things may be conceived as so divided) to be able to predicate of it every property of the number four, that is, every arithmetical proposition in which the number four stands on one side of the equation. Algebra extends the generalization still farther; every number represents that particular number of all things without distinction, but every algebraical symbol does more; it represents all numbers without distinction. . . .

There is another circumstance which, still more than that which we have now mentioned, gives plausibility to the notion that the propositions of arithmetic and algebra are merely verbal. That is that when considered as propositions respecting things, they all have the appearance of being identical propositions. The assertion, "two and one is equal to three," considered as an assertion respecting objects, as for instance, "two pebbles and one pebble are equal to three pebbles," does not affirm equality between two collections of pebbles, but absolute identity. It affirms that if we put one pebble to two pebbles, those very pebbles are three. The objects, therefore, being the very same, and the mere assertion that "objects are themselves" being insignificant, it seems but natural to consider the proposition, "two and one is equal to three," as asserting mere identity of signification between the two names.

This, however, though it looks so plausible, will not bear examination. The expression "two pebbles and one pebble" and the expression "three pebbles" stand, indeed, for the same aggregation of objects, but they by no means stand for the same physical fact. They are names of the same objects, but of those objects in two different states; though they *de*note the same things, their *con*notation is different. Three pebbles in two separate parcels, and three pebbles in one parcel, do not make the same impression on our senses; and the assertion that the very same pebbles may by an alteration of place and arrangement be made to produce either the one set of sensations or the other, though a very familiar proposition, is not an identical one. It is a truth known to us by early and constant experience, an inductive truth, and such truths are the foundation of the science of number. The fundamental truths of that science all rest on the evidence of sense; they are proved by showing to our eyes and our fingers that any given number of objects—ten balls, for example —may by separation and rearrangement exhibit to our senses all the different sets of numbers the sum of which is equal to ten. All the improved methods of teaching arithmetic to children proceed on a knowledge of this fact. All who wish to carry the child's *mind* along with them in learning arithmetic, all who wish to teach numbers, and not mere ciphers—now teach it through the evidence of the senses, in the manner we have described.

We may, if we please, call the proposition, "Three is two and one," a definition of the number three and assert that arithmetic, as it has been asserted that geometry, is a science founded on definitions. But they are definitions in the geometrical sense, not the logical; asserting not the meaning of a term only, but along with it an observed matter of fact. The proposition, "A circle is a figure bounded by a line which has all its points equally distant from a point within it," is called the definition of a circle; but the proposition from which so many consequences follow and which is really a first principle in geometry is that figures answering to this description exist. And thus we may call "three is two and one" a definition of three; but the calculations which depend on that proposition do not follow from the definition itself, but from an arithmetical theorem presupposed in it, namely, that collections of objects exist which, while they impress the senses thus, °o°, may be separated into two parts, thus, oo o. This proposition being granted, we term all such parcels threes, after which the enunciation of the above-mentioned physical fact will serve also for a definition of the word *three*.

The science of number is thus no exception to the conclusion we previously arrived at that the processes even of deductive sciences are altogether inductive and that their first principles are generalizations from experience.

. . .

EXAMINATION OF SOME OPINIONS OPPOSED TO THE PRECEDING DOCTRINES

SIR W. HAMILTON'S OPINION ON THE PRINCIPLES OF CONTRADICTION AND EXCLUDED MIDDLE

. . .

As I have hitherto said nothing of the two axioms in question, those of Contradiction and of Excluded Middle, it is not unseasonable to consider them here. The former asserts that an affirmative proposition and the corresponding negative proposition cannot both be true; which has generally been held to be intuitively evident. Sir William Hamilton and the Germans consider it to be the statement in words of a form or law of our thinking faculty. Other philosophers, not less deserving of consideration, deem it to be an identical proposition; an assertion involved in the meaning of terms; a mode of defining Negation, and the word Not.

I am able to go one step with these last. An affirmative assertion and its negative are not two independent assertions, connected with each other only as mutually incompatible. That if the negative be true, the affirmative must be false, really is a mere identical proposition; for the negative proposition asserts nothing but the falsity of the affirmative, and has no other sense or meaning whatever. The Principium Contradictionis should therefore put off the ambitious phraseology which gives it the air of a fundamental antithesis pervading nature, and should be enunciated in the simpler form, that the same proposition cannot at the same time be false and true. But I can go no farther with the Nominalists; for I cannot look upon this last as a merely verbal proposition. I consider it to be, like other axioms, one of our first and most familiar generalizations from experience. The original foundation of it I take to be, that Belief and Disbelief are two different mental states, excluding one another. This we know by the simplest observation of our own minds. And if we carry our observation outwards, we also find that light and darkness, sound and silence, motion and quiescence, equality and inequality, preceding and following, succession and simultaneousness, any positive phenomenon whatever and its negative, are distinct phenomena, pointedly contrasted, and the one always absent where the other is present. I consider the maxim in question to be a generalization from all these facts.

In like manner as the Principle of Contradiction (that one of two contradictories must be false) means that an assertion cannot be *both* true and false, so the Principle of Excluded Middle, or that one of two contradictories must be true, means that an assertion must be *either* true or false: either the affirmative is true, or otherwise the negative is true, which means that the affirmative is false. I cannot help thinking this principle a surprising specimen of a so-called necessity of Thought, since it is not even true, unless with a large qualification. A proposition must be either true or false, *provided* that the predicate be one which can in any intelligible sense be attributed to the subject; (and as this is always assumed to be the case in treatises on logic, the axiom is always laid down there as of absolute truth). "Abracadabra is a second intention" is neither true nor false. Between the true and the false there is a third possibility, the Unmeaning: and this alternative is fatal to Sir William Hamilton's extension of the maxim to Noumena. That Matter must either have a minimum of divisibility or be infinitely divisible, is more than we can ever know. For in the first place, Matter, in any other than the phenomenal sense of the term, may not exist: and it will scarcely be said that a non-entity must be either infinitely or finitely divisible. In the second place, though matter, considered as the occult cause of our sensations, does really exist, yet what we call divisibility may be an attribute only of our sensations of sight and touch, and not of their uncognizable cause. Divisibility may not be predicable at all, in any intelligible sense, of Things in themselves, nor therefore of Matter in itself; and the assumed necessity of being either infinitely or finitely divisible, may be an inapplicable alternative.

Brand Blanshard

Necessities in Nature

1. We have held that the prime office of reason was the discovery of necessary connections. The tendency of recent thought has been to restrict this office by confining necessity within increasingly narrow limits. It is insisted, first, in the spirit of Hume, that necessity never links existents, but only our own meanings. It is then added that not all meanings admit of such linkage, but only those that can stand as terms in propositions, simple or compound. Next propositions themselves are scrutinized, and many that were thought to be necessary are excluded; only analytic propositions are admitted to the inner fold. Finally, many even of these are questioned, on the ground that they contain empirical elements. 'All bachelors are unmarried' is analytic, of course, but the content of its terms is drawn from experience, and, strictly speaking, empirical contents are never linked by necessity. So we are left in the end with such luminous assertions as '*a* is *a*', or '*a* is not non-*a*', or $p \supset \cdot p \vee q$ as the most characteristic achievements of reason.

In the minds of many philosophers there is a rising revolt against all this. They feel that the retreat of reason has gone too far, that it is time to call a halt and to start reclaiming territory needlessly surrendered. This retreat seems to them to evince a strange failure of nerve. Philosophy has suffered from a creeping palsy of suspicion that reason, its chief weapon, is not much more than a toy, of use only in playing 'language games' or arranging symbols in arbitrary patterns.

It is possible, to be sure, that the philosophers from Plato downwards who have relied upon reason to provide knowledge of the nature and structure of the world were uniformly mistaken. A sceptical inquiry into their procedure

From Brand Blanshard, *Reason and Analysis,* Chap. 10, published by George Allen & Unwin, Ltd., London, 1962, and reprinted with their permission.

must at all times be welcomed, and indeed the findings of recent years have shown that with regard to both the terms and the connections of our so-called rational knowledge, earlier philosophies were unduly complacent. They floated a paper currency of terms only part of which could be redeemed in coin, and they often indulged lavishly in a priori argumentation without any clear view of its true nature and limits. It is therefore conceivable that their whole speculative enterprise was an uncritical dream. Contemporary analytic philosophers have alleged that it was, and have brought particularly severe charges against the traditional employment of reason. Necessary knowledge, they insist, is not knowledge in the strict sense at all. The connections it reveals, if not always purely formal, are at any rate conventional, and provide us merely with the rules of our linguistic practice. Of nature it tells us nothing. And even if it did, what it said would be tautologous, containing only what a clear enough eye could see in that which was already before us.

We have examined these contentions in our discussion of a priori knowledge, finding in them some truth, but not a little also that was superficial and confused. We found no good ground whatever for regarding necessity as arbitrary or conventional or linguistic, nor again as analytic merely. And if these charges fail, there is no good ground, either, for saying that necessary judgments can tell us nothing of nature.

Let us suppose now that reason is acquitted of these charges. How much light on nature may be hoped for from its exercise? Have we any intimations that nature is governed by necessity, either as a whole or in any considerable part? Even if necessity does hold among existent characters and things, it may hold in so small an area that the fullest success we could hope for would bring little illumination. Our best course would seem to be to make an inventory of such necessities as we have already in possession, and then to raise the further question how far we may legitimately hope that such knowledge may be extended. Our first question, then, must be, How large a capital of necessary knowledge do we now have?

2. (1) First, we have logical law. . . .

Professor Popper has pointed out that there are 'three main views on the nature of logic'.[1] It is worth seeing that on all of these views logical laws must be interpreted as asserting about the world. The three are (A) that such laws are laws of thought which either (*a*) describe how we actually think, or (*b*) tell us how we ought to think; (B) that they report about the constitution of all actual and possible objects; (C) that they are rules for the use of words and sentences.

3. When theory (A*a*) says that these laws describe how we actually think, it is pointing out that in a sense we always think logically, that we cannot violate a law of logic if we try. We can say both that Caesar did, and that he did not ride a three-toed horse, but in a sense we cannot *think* both. But in *what* sense? Is it in the sense that we cannot *believe* both, or that we cannot *see* or *understand* how both could be true, or that we can see that both *cannot*

[1] In a symposium on 'Why are the Calculuses of Logic and Arithmetic Applicable to Reality?', *Proc. of the Arist. Soc.*, Sup. Vol. 20 (1946), 48.

be true? Not the first, certainly, because we often do in fact accept contradictory beliefs. The second sense, that we cannot in fact see both sides to be true, is undoubtedly correct, but it does not content us as a final answer, for we are at once moved to ask the further question, *Why* can we not see both sides to be true? Is it because of the limitations of our own thought or because we can see of the real that it *could not* be self-contradictory? The view that logic gives us laws of thought only would take the first line. It would presumably say that though we cannot conceive how Caesar could both ride and not ride a three-toed horse, he might in fact have done so. But if this latter statement has any meaning for us, then we *are* conceiving of his both doing and not doing it, which is precisely what was declared inconceivable, and we have contradicted ourselves. The statement that the laws of logic are laws of thought only, and not of things, cannot be coherently stated.

The second form of the first theory (A*b*), to the effect that these laws are normative and tell us how we ought to think, seems more promising. In saying that we ought to think in accordance with them, it assumes that we can also break them. And in a sense we plainly can; most of us have surprising gifts for believing contradictory things. But granting that we can do this, why should we seek to avoid it? The answer seems clear enough. It is because if we do not think in accordance with logical law, we shall not think in accordance with fact. The 'ought' is a hypothetical imperative; it tells us that we must avoid thinking illogically if we want to think truly. And this implies that the reality of which our thought is true is itself governed by logic. If contradictory assertions cannot both be true, it is because the reality of which they are asserted does not admit contradictory characteristics.

4. Leaping next to the third view (C), that logical laws are linguistic rules, we may content ourselves with adding a consideration or two to the many that have been mentioned earlier.

If a logical law is a rule of usage, we may always legitimately ask why this rule has been adopted rather than some alternative. Suppose, for example, we adopt *ponendo ponens* as a rule, that is, we decide so to regulate our thought and speech that when we have asserted sentence S^1 and the further sentence 'S^1 implies S^2', we should go on to assert S^2. How should we justify this procedure? Those who take the linguistic line do not generally hold this rule to be purely arbitrary, and to do so would certainly not be plausible. They ordinarily fall back on a statement of the calculus of propositions, namely $(p.(p \supset q)) \supset q$, and show by the truth-table method that this is necessary because a tautology. But to say that it is a tautology means that the *truth* of q is among the assertions already made by $(p.(p \supset q))$. The rule of language is adopted because of a set of relations holding among the *truth*-values of propositions expressed by that language. It may be said that a relation among truth-values, for example that p and $\sim p$ are not both true, is itself a rule of language. But (1) the linguistic logicians never so interpret it. They would think it absurd to accept $(p.\sim p)$ as a rule of procedure, though if $\sim(p.\sim p)$ is only such a rule, we should be at liberty to do so. (2) If it is only such a rule, we may again legitimately ask how to justify it. Why should we shrink from saying that p and its contradictory, that this crow is black and that it is not black, are both true? To which the simple and sufficient answer is: Because the crow itself cannot have incompatible attributes, and we see that it cannot.

. . .

5. We are left with position (B), namely that logical law tells us something about the actual structure of things. This has been the view of all the rationalist philosophers, and it has been defended in recent times by Bertrand Russell in Britain, by Morris Cohen in America, and by Ferdinand Gonseth in Europe. The view has been brushed aside in a sentence by Wittgenstein on the ground that while 'it is raining' gives us information about fact, 'it is either raining or not raining' gives us none. And obviously enough it gives us none if the only things counting as information are ruled beforehand to be items verifiable in sense. But we have found no ground for this dogma. And the fact that a logical law applies necessarily and to everything does not show that it says nothing. Nor does the fact of its being empirically irrefutable. To say this would commit one to saying also that nothing a logician or mathematician said was true, for how could it be true without saying anything? And we have found no plausible alternative to the position that such laws are true. That the desk I am writing on is either a desk or not may be admitted to be a most unhelpful truth and one in which nobody but a philosopher would take the slightest interest. Does it say something true, however? Try to deny it and see. Does it say something about this particular desk? Yes, and this is not controverted by pointing out that what it says holds equally of all desks, clouds, and lamp-posts. We must repeat that a statement does not say nothing simply because it applies to everything.

6. (2) In apprehending logical law, then, we know something about the nature of things. Do we have other rational insights of the kind? In descending order of abstractness the next step is to arithmetic. The multiplication table has generally been taken as offering prime examples of propositions which are at once necessary and true, and there is no good reason to deny this. Their applicability to nature, however, is a curiously treacherous matter and has often been misunderstood. Mill thought that it was guaranteed by our having found them to hold with unbroken regularity among experienced things. If this is true, they are not really necessities apprehended by reason, but connections that have so impressed themselves on our minds as to have induced fixed habits of expectation. Laws thus empirically arrived at should be capable of empirical confirmation or disproof. But the evident truth is that we never seriously resort to either. Would it occur to us that a bank teller, because he counts money all day long, knows with more certainty than the rest of us that 5 and 5 = 10? And can we think of an instance in which any sort of perceptual experience would make us doubt the truth of this proposition? Someone may, indeed, put 5 drops and 5 more drops of water into a dry pitcher and challenge us to get 10 out; he may put 5 rabbits and 5 more in a hutch and find 20 when he comes back; and he may then say triumphantly that in the first case 5 and 5 make less than 10, and in the second case more. Should we be ready, in the light of such cases, to say that, after all, 5 and 5 sometimes fail to make 10? Obviously not. We are far more certain that they do than we are of the validity

of any alleged exceptions. We can usually see by a moment's reflection that these are not exceptions at all. The multiplication table says nothing about what will *causally* ensue if we put drops in a pitcher or rabbits in a hutch; it leaves out everything that characterizes any of its units as opposed to any other, and interests itself only in units as units, that is as entities regarded simply as distinguishable. It says: Take any set of 5 units, of which, for the present purpose, we know nothing except that they are distinct, add to them in thought 5 other such units, and you *must* have 10. If one sees this *must*, one will not be shaken by suggestions that in this or that queer instance an exception has turned up. One will merely start hunting for the fallacy that led anyone to suppose he had found such an exception.

7. Now does this fact that in arithmetic the appeal to empirical confirmation is needless show that arithmetic is not true of the empirical order? I do not see that it does. The assertion seems to rest on two confusions. (*a*) The first is the now familiar confusion of supposing that because a statement says nothing about this rather than that, it says nothing at all. What arithmetic says is that so far as things are regarded merely as classes of units, certain necessary relations will be found among these classes. Now things *can* be so regarded. One may abstract in a set of ten clothespins from everything about them—everything that they have in common and everything that differentiates them—except that here are ten somethings distinguishable from each other. We know that to this group of ten *X*'s all the properties applying to the number ten will also apply. We know, further, that all actual and possible groups, because their members are distinguishable somethings, will have arithmetical properties, and that every thing and quality will be a member of many such groups. Thus our knowledge of the multiplication table supplies us, so far as it goes, with knowledge of the world. As Whitehead says, 'the first noticeable fact about arithmetic is that it applies to everything, to tastes and sounds, to apples and angels, to the ideas of the mind and to the bones of the body'.[2]

(*b*) A second source of the error that arithmetic tells us nothing of the real is a confusion about form and content. It is supposed that form would still be significant if there were nothing it could apply to, and that when we talk logic or mathematics, we are saying something not only without reference to this or that thing, but without reference to any possible content. This is not true. In a world that lacked distinguishable things, numbers would be meaningless, like 'up' with no 'down', or 'out' with no 'in'. Number means number *of* something. Where there is nothing numerable, there is no number. Not that the numerable things need be of any specified type; numerical statements do not have to wait for what is called 'interpretation' in order to become meaningful. They are of the highly abstract but important kind that says something about all that is.

. . .

10. (3) We have seen that logic and arithmetic supply us with their own highly abstract truth about things and classes. Can we say the same of geometry? There are three different questions here, corresponding to the three levels

[2] *An Introduction to Mathematics*, 2.

of abstractness on which geometry may be pursued. Pure geometry starts from primitive terms and propositions so abstract that the ordinary connotations of 'point', 'straight line', and 'surface' are not involved, and there may be nothing to indicate that one is dealing with spatial relations at all. Such geometry does not advance beyond the kind of knowledge we have been discussing. Secondly, Euclidean and non-Euclidean geometries do go beyond this and deal with space, but each with its own kind of space, defined by its special postulates, and with no assumption that its space is that of the actual world. Euclid's space, for example, is that in which, if one starts with a straight line, one can draw through a point outside that line only one parallel line; Lobatschevsky's space is one in which a variety of such parallels can be drawn; and Riemann's is one in which none can be drawn. Each system is valid, and each tells us, therefore, what would be true in a space constructed according to its postulates. But none of them, as developed by modern geometers, offers itself as an account of relations in physical space. Thirdly, at a lower level of abstraction than either of these types, stands physical geometry. It is this that particularly interests the philosopher, since what it seeks is a geometrical knowledge of nature. Is there really any such thing? Does it make sense to speak of a *rational* knowledge of actual spatial relations?

That we do possess such knowledge was for many centuries taken for granted; Euclid had supplied it and Newton's physics assumed that he had. But a very simple reflection is enough to call the assumption in question. The points, lines, and planes of which Euclid was speaking were not empirical things at all. A geometrical point, for example, was supposed to be without parts and without magnitude, and it is obvious that what has no size would be invisible; we can see nothing smaller than a dot. Further, a line is supposed to be a continuous series of points; but if a point is really without size, you cannot produce something that does have size by putting a great many points side by side; indeed they have no sides. Thus the lines of the geometer are as far removed from chalk lines on a blackboard as his points are from dots. Again geometrical surfaces are made up of an infinite number of lines drawn side by side, and geometrical solids of an infinite series of stratified surfaces; but neither sort of entity has ever been felt or seen. If it is such remote and fictional things as these that geometry deals with, what reason have we to say that it tells us anything about nature at all? The logical positivist would say quite simply that it tells us nothing, and that our knowledge of actual space is purely empirical. But in view of the confident and successful use of geometrical theorems in the building of bridges, the construction of tennis courts, and the guidance of rockets, this is a paradox. 'It is surely not insignificant to ask whether there may be constructed with ruler and compass a circle equal in area to a given square.'[3] Does the geometrical demonstration that this is impossible tell us nothing about what we may expect in actual experience?

11. At least two suggestions have been made in recent years that help us to bridge the gap between the ideal figures of geometry and the actual ones of experience. One comes from C. D. Broad.[4] Broad points out that empirical

[3] M. R. Cohen, *Preface to Logic*, 54.

[4] *Examination of McTaggart's Philosophy*, I, 42–45.

series may be of different kinds: we can see of some of them a priori that they have no limits, and of others that they have. If we take a series of increasing hotnesses, for example, we can see that there is nothing in the series to require a halt at any point; when we had reached the hotness of boiling water, we could go on to that of a furnace, and from there to the heat of the sun, and so on apparently without limit. On the other hand, suppose we take first a very jagged line, like that of the edge of a cross-cut saw, and then a less jagged one like the edge of a carpenter's saw, and proceed to decrease the jaggedness at each step; is this series without limit? No; we can see a priori that there is a limit to it; when we have reached zero jaggedness, we have a straight line, beyond which the continuation of the series is logically impossible. Now if this suggestion is correct, we have a priori knowledge about empirical fact, in the sense that of some empirical series we can see a priori that they have a certain kind of limit. Even if no line that we ever see is perfectly straight, we can still say of a given line that it belongs to an imaginable series whose limit would be a line of a certain kind, and we can talk of that line with the aid of any member of the series. Similarly of the arc of the moon or a rocket or a rainbow in relation to the perfect geometrical circle. Actual figures may always fall short of geometrical ones, and still be related to them necessarily. Such a theory, instead of having Platonic figures 'laid up in heaven', builds an intelligible bridge to them from the figures of actual space.

12. Another pregnant suggestion was made by Whitehead in his 'principle of extensive abstraction'. He proposed to regard a point, or a line, or a surface, not as the limit of a series, but as the series itself. This is a welcome suggestion to those who are averse to Euclidean points and Platonic figures. Suppose one holds, for example, that the Euclidean point, something with position but no parts or magnitude, is unreal and inconceivable; is geometry therefore to be bereft of meaning? Not at all, says Whitehead. For even if there is no such thing as this shadowy point, we can still conceive the series of volumes that would ordinarily be said to converge upon it. We can conceive of a series of Chinese boxes one inside the other, or a series of concentric spheres growing smaller and smaller. Whitehead's discovery was that for geometrical purposes, the series of these concentric volumes had all the properties traditionally assigned to points while at the same time requiring us to deal only with finite and verifiable magnitudes, and that lines, surfaces, and other mathematical entities could be dealt with in the same way.

It might be objected that volumes are different in kind from points, and that one is not solving the problem of their relation by substituting the one for the other. There are two answers. First, in mathematics a thing is defined by its properties, and if, for all purposes of the science, the properties of the converging series of volumes are the same as those of the original points, the two concepts are interchangeable. Secondly, even if one sticks to points, the new notion can be made to approximate to the old within any desired degree. One of the functions of a pair of points, for example, is to determine the connection between them which we call a straight line. If we substitute basketballs for these points, the line that connects them, being an imaginary cable as thick as the balls themselves, will hardly be accepted as a line at all. But substitute billiard balls for the basketballs, marbles for the billiard balls, and birdshot for the marbles, and the terms will come closer and closer to defining your notion of a line; and the series provides for making the line as gossamer as you please. The older geometry would have it that the line talked about is the line of zero thickness forming the limit of this series. Whitehead held that for all purposes of the physical geometer this line could be dismissed as an airy nothing in favour of the series of converging volumes, and geometry would retain all its validity. We can conceive of any actual dot or ball as enclosed in such a series, and base on the latter our geometrical deductions. We shall thus have a genuinely geometrical knowledge of the physical world.[5]

. . .

14. (4) Further chains of necessary connections in which all existing things are bound are those of *serial order*. Some types of order, such as those of ordinal numbers and of points on a line, may be fairly thought to belong among the arithmetical and geometrical relations already considered, but the orders of degree, of temporal succession, and of the series that lead to the infinitely large and infinitely small may well have separate mention.

When an order is called 'serial', it is usually assumed to have a direction, so that A is not related to B as B is to A. But where these relations are the same—in technical usage 'symmetrical'—the type of order remains unchanged, however the terms are re-disposed. The order of equality is an example. Necessity enters into this order in the sense that things equal to the same thing are necessarily all equal to each other. Of course the equality must be in the same respect. A is equal to B in height or weight or speed, and B to C in the same respect; hence in that respect A and C are equal. Are such insights purely formal, or can we see them to hold of actual things? Where the respect in which things are declared equal is numerical, we can often reason thus with a certainty that it would be merely captious to question. If the graces equal the muses in number, and the muses equal the team that the New York Yankees now have on the field, then it must be conceded, however surprising, that in one respect the Yankees equal the graces. Where the respect in which equality is ascribed is height, weight, or speed, the principle of the inference is still certain, but whether the conclusion is true will depend on the material truth of the premises, and this in turn on the exactitude of our measurements. Exact equality in any respect would be identity in that respect, as we have argued earlier, and there is no reason to deny that such identities occur in nature. But even where they do, the best we can assert in fact will as a rule be similarity.

The term 'order', however, is usually reserved for series in which one cannot move indifferently forward or backward. Such series are asymmetrical; if A precedes B, B cannot also precede A; they are often transitive also, in the sense, for example, that if A precedes B, and B, C, then A precedes C. Now the beads of our particular experiences are strung on a large number of such serial threads, each of them constituting lines of necessary relation. As Kant pointed out, every quality we ever sense is on the same scale of intensity with every other of the same kind; everything that is hot or hard, sweet or sour,

[5] Whitehead's explanation of extensive abstraction is given in *The Concept of Nature,* Ch. IV, and *The Principles of Natural Knowledge,* Pt. III. There is a brief and clear account of it also in Broad's *Scientific Thought,* 38–52.

bright or loud, sharp or heavy, rough or large, is related, and necessarily related, to all other things possessing a quality falling under the same 'determinable'. 'When one term does, by virtue of one and the same point in it, stand in a relation of degree with two or more other terms, then these others are also related in degree.' Of anything that is visible we may say a priori not merely that it is identical with or similar to everything else that is visible in respect to having brightness, but also that if it differs in brightness from B in the same way as B differs from C, then it differs itself in the same way from C. Such a priori knowledge of serial order does not apply to intensities only. It applies to length of lines and acuteness of angles, to sizes, masses, and velocities; and it is the basis of every variety of *a fortiori* argument. Perhaps its most obvious application is to times, for we are arguing constantly that if A comes before B, it will also precede anything contemporary with or subsequent to B. Sometimes we intertwine several strands of serial reasoning together. If General Wolfe died in 1759, Macaulay in 1859, and G. E. Moore in 1959, if Moore was a better philosopher than Macaulay and Macaulay than Wolfe, and if Wolfe was a better soldier than Macaulay and Macaulay than Moore, then there died, two centuries after another, a man who was a worse soldier but a better philosopher.

. . .

16. (5) Differing attributes and even categories may be so connected that we can see that whatever has one must also have another. Shape and size are different attributes, but if a thing has shape it must have size also. Colour is not the same attribute as extension, but if we know that something is coloured, we need not wait till we inspect it to assure ourselves that it covers some extent in space. If we know that a sound has some pitch, is it a matter of probability only that it will also have some degree of loudness? Clearly not. We can see that, different as they are, the first character could not occur without the other. Once more, according to Aristotle and others who have drawn up lists of categories, qualities are ultimately different from relations. But could qualities exist without relations? Obviously qualities in the plural could not, since they would be connected at least by the relation of difference. Could a *single* quality exist in a world where there were no relations at all? It could not exist in time, for if it did, an earlier phase of it would be related to a later phase. Nor could it exist in space, since if it occupied space, its parts would be spatially related, and if it existed somehow at a point, the point would have to be somewhere, and this 'somewhere' again implies relations. Even in a world in which space and time were done away—if such a world can be conceived—a single scent, for example, could be what it was only by being different from other possible qualities; in short, to be at all is to be this rather than that, and the rather-than-that is an inseparable adjunct of being this.

. . .

17. (6) There are similar relations of necessity that link, both positively and negatively, the determinates of the same determinable. Consider the interrelation of colours. There have been many attempts in recent years to show that statements of colour relation are merely empirical. No doubt the statements

that this patch of grass is green and that patch of sky is blue are, so far as present insight goes, empirical purely. Is this also true of the statement that in the table of colour affinities, orange is between red and yellow, or the statement that it is nearer to yellow than to blue? Is it true of the statement that purple is more closely related to blue and red than it is to green? No answers I have seen have effectively challenged what seems to be the position of common sense on these points. If one asked the ordinary man, who had just remarked that a given orange shade fell between given shades of red and yellow whether it would also fall between them in other instances where the shades were the same, he would think the question a silly one; of course they would, for if the relation is really between the colours, it must hold wherever the colours are the same. As Isaiah Berlin puts it, 'invited to conceive of a world in which the shades we call pink, red, black, occurred in some order other than that presented in ours, we must say that we cannot do so: not because of a failure of imagination, but because it is inconceivable: the invitation is itself nonsensical'.[6]

Thus determinates of the same determinable may be necessarily linked with each other. There is also a negative linkage: they exclude each other necessarily when asserted of the same subject. A surface that is pure red cannot, at the same time and to the same observer, be pure green. It has been alleged that this is an analytic statement, that it says only that the two colours are different, which is already involved in their being two. But the statement clearly goes beyond this. A colour and a shape are different, but they can belong at once to the same surface; what our statement tells us is not merely that the colours are different, but that in the same subject they are exclusive of each other. Again, being exclusive of green, though it is entailed by being red, is hardly part of what we *mean* by being red, nor not-being-red part of what we mean by being green. Nor is there any *formal* contradiction in saying that what is red is also green, any more than in saying that what is red is also square. The *must* arises from the content; it is in virtue of the special character of being red, in distinction for example from being square, that the red excludes the green. What we have is a particular kind of incompatibility, based not on the form of the propositions but on the nature of the predicates.

[6] *Proc. of the Arist. Soc.*, Supplementary Vol. 16 (1937), 77.

Clarence Irving Lewis

A Pragmatic Conception of the A Priori

The conception of the *a priori* points two problems which are perennial in philosophy; the part played in knowledge by the mind itself, and the possibility of "necessary truth" or of knowledge "independent of experience." But traditional conceptions of the *a priori* have proved untenable. That the mind approaches the flux of immediacy with some godlike foreknowledge of principles which are legislative for experience, that there is any natural light or any innate ideas, it is no longer possible to believe.

Nor shall we find the clue to the *a priori* in any compulsion of the mind to incontrovertible truth or any peculiar kind of demonstration which establishes first principles. All truth lays upon the rational mind the same compulsion to belief; as Mr. Bosanquet has pointed out, this character belongs to all propositions or judgments once their truth is established.

The difficulties of the conception are due, I believe, to two mistakes: whatever is *a priori* is necessary, but we have misconstrued the relation of necessary truth to mind. And the *a priori* is independent of experience, but in so taking it, we have misunderstood its relation to empirical fact. What is *a priori* is necessary truth not because it compels the mind's acceptance, but precisely because it does not. It is given experience, brute fact, the *a posteriori* element in knowledge which the mind must accept willy-nilly. The *a priori* represents an attitude in some sense freely taken, a stipulation of the mind itself, and a stipulation which might be made in some other way if it suited our bent or need. Such truth is necessary as opposed to contingent, not as opposed to voluntary. And the *a priori* is independent of experience not because it prescribes a form which the data of sense must fit, or anticipates some preëstablished harmony of experience with the mind, but precisely because it prescribes nothing to experience. That is *a priori* which is true, *no matter what.* What it anticipates is not the given, but our attitude toward it: it concerns the uncompelled initiative of mind or, as Josiah Royce would say, our categorical ways of acting.

The traditional example of the *a priori par excellence* is the laws of logic. These can not be derived from experience since they must first be taken for granted in order to prove them. They make explicit our general modes of classification. And they impose upon experience no real limitation. Sometimes we are asked to tremble before the spectre of the "alogical," in order

From C. I. Lewis, "A Pragmatic Conception of the *A Priori*," *The Journal of Philosophy,* Vol. 20 (1923). Reprinted by permission of the author and of the editor of *The Journal of Philosophy.*

C. I. Lewis (1883–1964) was Professor of Philosophy at Harvard University until his retirement in 1953.

that we may thereafter rejoice that we are saved from this by the dependence of reality upon mind. But the "alogical" is pure bogey, a word without a meaning. What kind of experience could defy the principle that everything must either be or not be, that nothing can both be and not be, or that if *x* is *y* and *y* is *z*, then *x* is *z*? If anything imaginable or unimaginable could violate such laws, then the ever-present fact of change would do it every day. The laws of logic are purely formal; they forbid nothing but what concerns the use of terms and the corresponding modes of classification and analysis. The law of contradiction tells us that nothing can be both white and not-white, but it does not and can not tell us whether black is not-white, or soft or square is not-white. To discover *what contradicts what* we must always consult the character of experience. Similarly the law of the excluded middle formulates our decision that whatever is not designated by a certain term shall be designated by its negative. It declares our purpose to make, for every term, a complete dichotomy of experience, instead—as we might choose—of classifying on the basis of a tripartite division into opposites (as black and white) and the middle ground between the two. Our rejection of such tripartite division represents only our penchant for simplicity.

Further laws of logic are of similar significance. They are principles of procedure, the parliamentary rules of intelligent thought and speech. Such laws are independent of experience because they impose no limitations whatever upon it. They are legislative because they are addressed to ourselves—because definition, classification, and inference represent no operations of the objective world, but only our own categorical attitudes of mind.

And further, the ultimate criteria of the laws of logic are pragmatic. Those who suppose that there is, for example, *a* logic which everyone would agree to if he understood it and understood himself, are more optimistic than those versed in the history of logical discussion have a right to be. The fact is that there are several logics, markedly different, each self-consistent in its own terms and such that whoever, using it, avoids false premises, will never reach a false conclusion. Mr. Russell, for example, bases *his* logic on an implication relation such that if twenty sentences be cut from a newspaper and put in a hat, and then two of these be drawn at random, one of them will certainly imply the other, and it is an even bet that the implication will be mutual. Yet upon a foundation so remote from ordinary modes of inference the whole structure of *Principia Mathematica* is built. This logic—and there are others even more strange—is utterly consistent and the results of it entirely valid. Over and above all questions of consistency, there are issues of logic which can not be determined—nay, can not even be argued—except on pragmatic grounds of conformity to human bent and intellectual convenience. That we have been blind to this fact, itself reflects traditional errors in the conception of the *a priori*.

We may note in passing one less important illustration of the *a priori*—the proposition "true by definition." Definitions and their immediate consequences, analytic propositions generally, are necessarily true, true under all possible circumstances. Definition is legislative because it is in some sense arbitrary. Not only is the meaning assigned to words more or less a matter of choice—that consideration is relatively trivial—but the manner in which the precise classifications which definition embodies shall be effected, is something not dictated by experience. If experience were other than it is, the definition and its corresponding classification might be inconvenient, fantastic, or useless, but it could not be false. Mind makes classifications and determines meanings; in so doing it creates the *a priori* truth of analytic judgments. But that the manner of this creation responds to pragmatic considerations, is so obvious that it hardly needs pointing out.

If the illustrations so far given seem trivial or verbal, that impression may be corrected by turning to the place which the *a priori* has in mathematics and in natural science. Arithmetic, for example, depends *en toto* upon the operation of counting or correlating, a procedure which can be carried out at will in any world containing identifiable things—even identifiable ideas—regardless of the further characters of experience. Mill challenged this *a priori* character of arithmetic. He asked us to suppose a demon sufficiently powerful and maleficent so that every time two things were brought together with two other things, this demon should always introduce a fifth. The implication which he supposed to follow is that under such circumstances $2 + 2 = 5$ would be a universal law of arithmetic. But Mill was quite mistaken. In such a world we should be obliged to become a little clearer than is usual about the distinction between arithmetic and physics, that is all. If two black marbles were put in the same urn with two white ones, the demon could take his choice of colors, but it would be evident that there were more black marbles or more white ones than were put in. The same would be true of all objects in any wise identifiable. We should simply find ourselves in the presence of an extraordinary physical law, which we should recognize as universal in our world, that whenever two things were brought into proximity with two others, an additional and similar thing was always created by the process. Mill's world would be physically most extraordinary. The world's work would be enormously facilitated if hats or locomotives or tons of coal could be thus multiplied by anyone possessed originally of two pairs. But the laws of mathematics would remain unaltered. It is because this is true that arithmetic is *a priori*. Its laws prevent *nothing;* they are compatible with anything which happens or could conceivably happen in nature. They would be true in any possible world. Mathematical addition is not a physical transformation. Physical changes which result in an increase or decrease of the countable things involved are matters of everyday occurrence. Such physical processes present us with phenomena in which the purely mathematical has to be separated out by abstraction. Those laws and those laws only have necessary truth which we are prepared to maintain, no matter what. It is because we shall always separate out that part of the phenomenon not in conformity with arithmetic and designate it by some other category—physical change, chemical reaction, optical illusion—that arithmetic is *a priori*.

The *a priori* element in science and in natural law is greater than might be supposed. In the first place, all science is based upon definitive concepts. The formulation of these concepts is, indeed, a matter determined by the commerce between our intellectual or our pragmatic interests and the nature of experience. Definition is classification. The scientific search is for such classification as will make it possible to correlate appearance and behavior, to discover law, to penetrate to the "essential nature" of things in order that behavior may become predictable. In other words, if definition is unsuccessful, as early scientific definitions mostly have been, it is because the classification thus set up corresponds with no natural cleavage and does not correlate with any important uniformity of behavior. A name itself must represent *some* uniformity in experience or it names nothing. What does not repeat itself or recur in intelligible fashion is not a thing. Where the definitive uniformity is a clue to other uniformities, we have successful scientific definition. Other definitions can not be said to be false; they are merely useless. In scientific classification the search is, thus, for *things worth naming*. But the naming, classifying, defining activity is essentially prior to investigation. We can not interrogate experience in general. Until our meaning is definite and our classification correspondingly exact, experience can not conceivably answer our questions.

In the second place, the fundamental laws of any science—or those treated as fundamental—are *a priori* because they formulate just such definitive concepts or categorical tests by which alone investigation becomes possible. If the lightning strikes the railroad track at two places, *A* and *B*, how shall we tell whether these events are simultaneous? "We . . . require a definition of simultaneity such that this definition supplies us with the method by means of which . . . we can decide whether or not both the lightning strokes occurred simultaneously. As long as this requirement is not satisfied, I allow myself to be deceived as a physicist (and of course the same applies if I am not a physicist), when I imagine that I am able to attach a meaning to the statement of simultaneity. . . .

"After thinking the matter over for some time you then offer the following suggestion with which to test simultaneity. By measuring along the rails, the connecting line *AB* should be measured up and an observer placed at the mid-point *M* of the distance *AB*. This observer should be supplied with an arrangement (e.g., two mirrors inclined at 90°) which allows him visually to observe both places *A* and *B* at the same time. If the observer perceives the two flashes at the same time, then they are simultaneous.

"I am very pleased with this suggestion, but for all that I can not regard the matter as quite settled, because I feel constrained to raise the following objection: 'Your definition would certainly be right, if I only knew that the light by means of which the observer at *M* perceives the lightning flashes travels along the length *A—M* with the same velocity as along the length *B—M*. But an examination of this supposition would only be possible if we already had at our disposal the means of measuring time. It would thus appear as though we were moving here in a logical circle.'

"After further consideration you cast a somewhat disdainful glance at me—and rightly so—and you declare: 'I maintain my previous definition nevertheless, because in reality it assumes absolutely nothing about light. There is only *one* demand to be made of the definition of simultaneity, namely, that in every real case it must supply us with an empirical decision as to whether or not the conception which has to be defined is fulfilled. That light requires the same time to traverse the path *A—M* as for the path *B—M* is in reality *neither a supposition nor a hypothesis* about the physical nature of light, but a *stipulation* which I can make of my own free-will in order to arrive at a definition of simultaneity.' . . . We are thus led also to a definition of 'time' in physics."[1]

[1] Einstein, *Relativity*, pp. 26–28; italics are the author's.

As this example from the theory of relativity well illustrates, we can not even ask the questions which discovered law would answer until we have first by *a priori* stipulation formulated definitive criteria. Such concepts are not verbal definitions, nor classifications merely; they are themselves laws which prescribe a certain uniformity of behavior to whatever is thus named. Such definitive laws are *a priori;* only so can we enter upon the investigation by which further laws are sought. Yet it should also be pointed out that such *a priori* laws are subject to abandonment if the structure which is built upon them does not succeed in simplifying our interpretation of phenomena. If, in the illustration given, the relation "simultaneous with," as defined, should not prove transitive—if event *A* should prove simultaneous with *B*, and *B* with *C*, but not *A* with *C*—this definition would certainly be rejected.

And thirdly, there is that *a priori* element in science—as in other human affairs—which constitutes the criteria of the real as opposed to the unreal in experience. An object itself is a uniformity. Failure to behave in certain categorical ways marks it as unreal. Uniformities of the type called "natural law" are the clues to reality and unreality. A mouse which disappears where no hole is, is no real mouse; a landscape which recedes as we approach is but illusion. As the queen remarked in the episode of the wishing-carpet, "If this were real, then it would be a miracle. But miracles do not happen. Therefore I shall wake presently." That the uniformities of natural law are the only reliable criteria of the real, is inescapable. But such a criterion is *ipso facto a priori*. No conceivable experience could dictate the alteration of a law so long as failure to obey that law marked the content of experience as unreal.

This is one of the puzzles of empiricism. We deal with experience: what any reality may be which underlies experience, we have to learn. What we desire to discover is natural law, the formulation of those uniformities which obtain amongst the real. But experience as it comes to us contains not only the real but all the content of illusion, dream, hallucination, and mistake. The *given* contains both real and unreal, confusingly intermingled. If we ask for uniformities of this unsorted experience, we shall not find them. Laws which characterize all experience, of real and unreal both, are non-existent and would in any case be worthless. What we seek are the uniformities of the *real;* but *until we have such laws, we can not sift experience and segregate the real.*

The obvious solution is that the enrichment of experience, the separation of the real from the illusory or meaningless, and the formulation of natural law, all grow up together. If the criteria of the real are *a priori,* that is not to say that no conceivable character of experience would lead to alteration of them. For example, spirits can not be photographed. But if photographs of spiritistic phenomena, taken under properly guarded conditions, should become sufficiently frequent, this *a priori* dictum would be called in question. What we should do would be to redefine our terms. Whether "spook" was spirit or matter, whether the definition of "spirit" or of "matter" should be changed; all this would constitute one interrelated problem. We should reopen together the question of definition or classification, of criteria for this sort of real, and of natural law. And the solution of one of these would mean the solution of all. Nothing could *force* a redefinition of spirit or of matter. A sufficiently fundamental relation to human bent, to human interests, would guarantee continuance unaltered even in the face of unintelligible and baffling experiences. In such problems, the mind finds itself uncompelled save by its own purposes and needs. I *may* categorize experience as I will; but *what* categorical distinctions will best serve my interests and objectify my own intelligence? What the mixed and troubled experience shall be—that is beyond me. But what I shall do with it—that is my own question, when the character of experience is sufficiently before me. I am coerced only by my own need to understand.

It would indeed be inappropriate to characterize as *a priori* a law which we are wholly prepared to alter in the light of further experience, even though in an isolated case we should discard as illusory any experience which failed to conform. But the crux of the situation lies in this; beyond such principles as those of logic, which we seem fully prepared to maintain no matter what, there must be further and more particular criteria of the real prior to any investigation of nature whatever. We can not even interrogate experience without a network of categories and definitive concepts. And we must further be prepared to say what experimental findings will answer what questions, and how. Without tests which represent anterior principle, there is no question which experience could answer at all. Thus the most fundamental laws in any category—or those which we regard as most fundamental—are *a priori,* even though continued failure to render experience intelligible in such terms might result eventually in the abandonment of that category altogether. Matters so comparatively small as the behavior of Mercury and of starlight passing the sun's limb may, if there be persistent failure to bring them within the field of previously accepted modes of explanation, result in the abandonment of the independent categories of space and time. But without the definitions, fundamental principles, and tests, of the type which constitute such categories, no experience whatever could prove or disprove anything. And to that mind which should find independent space and time absolutely necessary conceptions, no possible experiment could prove the principles of relativity. "There must be some error in the experimental findings, or some law not yet discovered," represents an attitude which can never be rendered impossible. And the only sense in which it could be proved unreasonable would be the pragmatic one of comparison with another method of categorical analysis which more successfully reduced all such experience to order and law.

At the bottom of all science and all knowledge are categories and definitive concepts which represent fundamental habits of thought and deep-lying attitudes which the human mind has taken in the light of its total experience. But a new and wider experience may bring about some alteration of these attitudes, even though by themselves they dictate nothing as to the content of experience, and no experience can conceivably prove them invalid.

Perhaps some will object to this conception on the ground that only such principles should be designated *a priori* as the human mind *must* maintain, no matter what; that if, for example, it is shown possible to arrive at a consistent doctrine of physics in terms of relativity, even by the most arduous reconstruction of our fundamental notions, then the present conceptions are by that fact shown not to be *a priori*. Such objection is especially likely from those who would conceive the *a priori* in terms of an absolute mind or an absolutely universal human nature. We should readily agree that a decision by popular approval or a congress of scientists or anything short of such a test as would bring to bear the full weight of human capacity and interest, would be ill-considered as having to do with the *a priori.* But we wish to emphasize two facts: first, that in the field of those conceptions and principles which have altered in human history, there are those which could neither be proved nor disproved by any experience, but represent the uncompelled initiative of human thought—that without this uncompelled initiative no growth of science, nor any science at all, would be conceivable. And second, that the difference between such conceptions as are, for example, concerned in the decision of relativity versus absolute space and time, and those more permanent attitudes such as are vested in the laws of logic, there is only a difference of degree. The dividing line between the *a priori* and the *a posteriori* is that between principles and definitive concepts which *can* be maintained in the face of all experience and those genuinely empirical generalizations which *might* be proven flatly false. The thought which both rationalism and empiricism have missed is that there are principles, representing the initiative of mind, which impose upon experience no limitations whatever, but that such conceptions are still subject to alteration on pragmatic grounds when the expanding boundaries of experience reveal their infelicity as intellectual instruments.

Neither human experience nor the human mind has a character which is universal, fixed, and absolute. "The human mind" does not exist at all save in the sense that all humans are very much alike in fundamental respects, and that the language habit and the enormously important exchange of ideas has greatly increased our likeness in those respects which are here in question. Our categories and definitions are peculiarly social products, reached in the light of experiences which have much in common, and beaten out, like other pathways, by the coincidence of human purposes and the exigencies of human coöperation. Concerning the *a priori* there need be neither universal agreement nor complete historical continuity. Conceptions, such as those of logic, which are least likely to be affected by the opening of new ranges of experience, represent the most stable of our categories; but none of them is beyond the possibility of alteration.

Mind contributes to experience the element of order, of classification, categories, and definition. Without such, experience would be unintelligible. Our knowledge of the validity of these is simply consciousness of our own fundamental ways of acting and our own intellectual intent. Without this element, knowledge is impossible, and it is here that whatever truths are necessary and independent of experience must be found. But the commerce between our categorical ways of acting, our pragmatic interests, and the particular character of experience, is closer than we have realized. No explanation of any one of these can be complete without consideration of the other two.

Pragmatism has sometimes been charged with oscillating between two contrary notions; the one, that experience is "through and through malleable to our purpose," the other, that facts are "hard" and uncreated by the mind. We here offer a mediating conception: through all our knowledge runs the element of the *a priori,* which is indeed malleable to our purpose and responsive to our need. But throughout, there is also that other element of experience which is "hard," "independent," and unalterable to our will.

Willard Van Orman Quine

A Dogma of Empiricism

Modern empiricism has been conditioned in large part by two dogmas. One is a belief in some fundamental cleavage between truths which are *analytic,* or grounded in meanings independently of matters of fact, and truths which are *synthetic,* or grounded in fact. The other dogma is *reductionism*: the belief that each meaningful statement is equivalent to some logical construct upon terms which refer to immediate experience. Both dogmas, I shall argue, are ill-founded. One effect of abandoning them is, as we shall see, a blurring of the supposed boundary between speculative metaphysics and natural science. Another effect is a shift toward pragmatism.

1. BACKGROUND FOR ANALYTICITY

Kant's cleavage between analytic and synthetic truths was foreshadowed in Hume's distinction between relations of ideas and matters of fact, and in Leibniz's distinction between truths of reason and truths of fact. Leibniz spoke of the truths of reason as true in all possible worlds. Picturesqueness aside, this is to say that the truths of reason are those which could not possibly be false. In the same vein we hear analytic statements defined as statements whose denials are self-contradictory. But this definition has small explanatory value; for the notion of self-contradictoriness, in the quite broad sense needed for this definition of analyticity, stands in exactly the same need of clarification as does the notion of analyticity itself. The two notions are the two sides of a single dubious coin.

Kant conceived of an analytic statement as one that attributes to its subject no more than is already conceptually contained in the subject. This formulation has two shortcomings: it limits itself to statements of subject-predicate form, and it appeals to a notion of containment which is left at a metaphorical level. But Kant's intent, evident more from the use he makes of the notion of analyticity than from his definition of it, can be restated thus: a statement is analytic when it is true by virtue of meanings and independently of fact. Pursuing this line, let us examine the concept of *meaning* which is presupposed.

Meaning, let us remember, is not to be identified with naming. Frege's example of 'Evening Star' and 'Morning Star', and Russell's of 'Scott' and 'the author of *Waverley*', illustrate that terms can name the same thing but differ in meaning. The distinction between meaning and naming is no less important

---

From W. V. O. Quine, "Two Dogmas of Empiricism," *The Philosophical Review,* Vol. 60 (1951). Reprinted by permission of the author and of the editors of *The Philosophical Review.* The article can be found in Quine's *From a Logical Point of View,* 1953.

W. V. O. Quine (1908–) is Edgar Pierce Professor of Philosophy at Harvard University.

at the level of abstract terms. The terms '9' and 'the number of the planets' name one and the same abstract entity but presumably must be regarded as unlike in meaning; for astronomical observation was needed, and not mere reflection on meanings, to determine the sameness of the entity in question.

The above examples consist of singular terms, concrete and abstract. With general terms, or predicates, the situation is somewhat different but parallel. Whereas a singular term purports to name an entity, abstract or concrete, a general term does not; but a general term is *true of* an entity, or of each of many, or of none. The class of all entities of which a general term is true is called the *extension* of the term. Now paralleling the contrast between the meaning of a singular term and the entity named, we must distinguish equally between the meaning of a general term and its extension. The general terms 'creature with a heart' and 'creature with kidneys', for example, are perhaps alike in extension but unlike in meaning.

Confusion of meaning with extension, in the case of general terms, is less common than confusion of meaning with naming in the case of singular terms. It is indeed a commonplace in philosophy to oppose intension (or meaning) to extension, or, in a variant vocabulary, connotation to denotation.

The Aristotelian notion of essence was the forerunner, no doubt, of the modern notion of intension or meaning. For Aristotle it was essential in men to be rational, accidental to be two-legged. But there is an important difference between this attitude and the doctrine of meaning. From the latter point of view it may indeed be conceded (if only for the sake of argument) that rationality is involved in the meaning of the word 'man' while two-leggedness is not; but two-leggedness may at the same time be viewed as involved in the meaning of 'biped' while rationality is not. Thus from the point of view of the doctrine of meaning it makes no sense to say of the actual individual, who is at once a man and a biped, that his rationality is essential and his two-leggedness accidental or vice versa. Things had essences, for Aristotle, but only linguistic forms have meanings. Meaning is what essence becomes when it is divorced from the object of reference and wedded to the word.

For the theory of meaning a conspicuous question is the nature of its objects: what sort of things are meanings? A felt need for meant entities may derive from an earlier failure to appreciate that meaning and reference are distinct. Once the theory of meaning is sharply separated from the theory of reference, it is a short step to recognizing as the primary business of the theory of meaning simply the synonymy of linguistic forms and the analyticity of statements; meanings themselves, as obscure intermediary entities, may well be abandoned.

The problem of analyticity then confronts us anew. Statements which are analytic by general philosophical acclaim are not, indeed, far to seek. They fall into two classes. Those of the first class, which may be called *logically true,* are typified by:

(1) No unmarried man is married.

The relevant feature of this example is that it not merely is true as it stands, but remains true under any and all reinterpretations of 'man' and 'married'. If we suppose a prior inventory of *logical* particles, comprising 'no', 'un-', 'not', 'if', 'then', 'and', etc., then in general a logical truth is a statement which is true and remains true under all reinterpretations of its components other than the logical particles.

But there is also a second class of analytic statements, typified by:

(2) No bachelor is married.

The characteristic of such a statement is that it can be turned into a logical truth by putting synonyms for synonyms; thus (2) can be turned into (1) by putting 'unmarried man' for its synonym 'bachelor'. We still lack a proper characterization of this second class of analytic statements, and therewith of analyticity generally, inasmuch as we have had in the above description to lean on a notion of "synonymy" which is no less in need of clarification than analyticity itself.

. . .

2. DEFINITION

There are those who find it soothing to say that the analytic statements of the second class reduce to those of the first class, the logical truths, by *definition*; 'bachelor', for example, is *defined* as 'unmarried man'. But how do we find that 'bachelor' is defined as 'unmarried man'? Who defined it thus, and when? Are we to appeal to the nearest dictionary, and accept the lexicographer's formulation as law? Clearly this would be to put the cart before the horse. The lexicographer is an empirical scientist, whose business is the recording of antecedent facts; and if he glosses 'bachelor' as 'unmarried man' it is because of his belief that there is a relation of synonymy between those forms, implicit in general or preferred usage prior to his own work. The notion of synonymy presupposed here has still to be clarified, presumably in terms relating to linguistic behavior. Certainly the "definition" which is the lexicographer's report of an observed synonymy cannot be taken as the ground of the synonymy.

Definition is not, indeed, an activity exclusively of philologists. Philosophers and scientists frequently have occasion to "define" a recondite term by paraphrasing it into terms of a more familiar vocabulary. But ordinarily such a definition, like the philologist's, is pure lexicography, affirming a relation of synonymy antecedent to the exposition in hand.

Just what it means to affirm synonymy, just what the interconnections may be which are necessary and sufficient in order that two linguistic forms be properly describable as synonymous, is far from clear; but, whatever these interconnections may be, ordinarily they are grounded in usage. Definitions reporting selected instances of synonymy come then as reports upon usage.

There is also, however, a variant type of definitional activity which does not limit itself to the reporting of preëxisting synonymies. I have in mind what Carnap calls *explication*—an activity to which philosophers are given, and scientists also in their more philosophical moments. In explication the purpose is not merely to paraphrase the definiendum into an outright synonym, but actually to improve upon the definiendum by refining or supplementing its meaning. But even explication, though not merely reporting a preëxisting synonymy between definiendum and definiens, does rest nevertheless on *other* preëxisting synonymies. The matter may be viewed as follows. Any word worth explicating has some contexts which, as wholes, are clear and precise enough to be useful; and the purpose of explication is to preserve the usage of these favored contexts while sharpening the usage of other contexts. In order that a given definition be suitable for purposes of explication, therefore, what is required is not that the definiendum in its antecedent usage be synonymous with the definiens, but just that each of these favored contexts of the definiendum, taken as a whole in its antecedent usage, be synonymous with the corresponding context of the definiens.

Two alternative definientia may be equally appropriate for the purposes of a given task of explication and yet not be synonymous with each other; for they may serve interchangeably within the favored contexts but diverge elsewhere. By cleaving to one of these definientia rather than the other, a definition of explicative kind generates, by fiat, a relation of synonymy between definiendum and definiens which did not hold before. But such a definition still owes its explicative function, as seen, to preëxisting synonymies.

There does, however, remain still an extreme sort of definition which does not hark back to prior synonymies at all: namely, the explicitly conventional introduction of novel notations for purposes of sheer abbreviation. Here the definiendum becomes synonymous with the definiens simply because it has been created expressly for the purpose of being synonymous with the definiens. Here we have a really transparent case of synonymy created by definition; would that all species of synonymy were as intelligible. For the rest, definition rests on synonymy rather than explaining it.

. . .

3. INTERCHANGEABILITY

A natural suggestion, deserving close examination, is that the synonymy of two linguistic forms consists simply in their interchangeability in all contexts without change of truth value—interchangeability, in Leibniz's phrase, *salva veritate*. Note that synonyms so conceived need not even be free from vagueness, as long as the vaguenesses match.

But it is not quite true that the synonyms 'bachelor' and 'unmarried man' are everywhere interchangeable *salva veritate*. Truths which become false under substitution of 'unmarried man' for 'bachelor' are easily constructed with the help of 'bachelor of arts' or 'bachelor's buttons'; also with the help of quotation, thus:

'Bachelor' has less than ten letters.

Such counterinstances can, however, perhaps be set aside by treating the phrases 'bachelor of arts' and 'bachelor's buttons' and the quotation ' 'bachelor' ' each as a single indivisible word and then stipulating that the interchangeability *salva veritate* which is to be the touchstone of synonymy is not supposed to apply to fragmentary occurrences inside of a word. This account of synonymy, supposing it acceptable on other counts, has indeed the drawback of appealing to a prior conception of "word" which can be counted on to present difficulties of formulation in its turn. Nevertheless some progress might be claimed in having reduced the problem of synonymy to a problem of wordhood. Let us pursue this line a bit, taking "word" for granted.

The question remains whether interchangeability *salva veritate* (apart from occurrences within words) is a strong enough condition for synonymy, or whether, on the contrary, some heteronymous expressions might be thus interchangeable. Now let us be clear that we are not concerned here with synonymy in the sense of complete identity in psychological associations or poetic quality; indeed no two expressions are synonymous in such a sense. We are concerned only with what may be called *cognitive* synonymy. Just what this is cannot be said without successfully finishing the present study; but we know something about it from the need which arose for it in connection with analyticity in §1. The sort of synonymy needed there was merely such that any analytic statement could be turned into a logical truth by putting synonyms for synonyms. Turning the tables and assuming analyticity, indeed, we could explain cognitive synonymy of terms as follows (keeping to the familiar example): to say that 'bachelor' and 'unmarried man' are cognitively synonymous is to say no more nor less than that the statement:

(3) All and only bachelors are unmarried men

is analytic.

What we need is an account of cognitive synonymy not presupposing analyticity—if we are to explain analyticity conversely with help of cognitive synonymy as undertaken in §1. And indeed such an independent account of cognitive synonymy is at present up for consideration, namely, interchangeability *salva veritate* everywhere except within words. The question before us, to resume the thread at last, is whether such interchangeability is a sufficient condition for cognitive synonymy. We can quickly assure ourselves that it is, by examples of the following sort. The statement:

(4) Necessarily all and only bachelors are bachelors

is evidently true, even supposing 'necessarily' so narrowly construed as to be truly applicable only to analytic statements. Then, if 'bachelor' and 'unmarried man' are interchangeable *salva veritate*, the result:

(5) Necessarily all and only bachelors are unmarried men

of putting 'unmarried man' for an occurrence of 'bachelor' in (4) must, like (4), be true. But to say that (5) is true is to say that (3) is analytic, and hence that 'bachelor' and 'unmarried man' are cognitively synonymous.

Let us see what there is about the above argument that gives it its air of hocus-pocus. The condition of interchangeability *salva veritate* varies in its force with variations in the richness of the language at hand. The above argument supposes we are working with a language rich enough to contain the adverb 'necessarily', this adverb being so construed as to yield truth when and only when applied to an analytic statement. But can we condone a language which contains such an adverb? Does the adverb really make sense? To suppose that it does is to suppose that we have already made satisfactory sense of 'analytic'. Then what are we so hard at work on right now?

Our argument is not flatly circular, but something like it. It has the form, figuratively speaking, of a closed curve in space.

Interchangeability *salva veritate* is meaningless until relativized to a language whose extent is specified in relevant respects. Suppose now we consider a language containing just the following materials. There is an indefinitely large stock of one-place predicates (for example, '*F*' where '*Fx*' means that *x* is a man) and many-place predicates (for example, '*G*' where '*Gxy*' means that *x* loves *y*), mostly having to do with extralogical subject matter. The rest of the language is logical. The atomic sentences consist each of a predicate followed by one or more variables '*x*', '*y*', etc.; and the complex sentences are built up of the atomic ones by truth functions ('not', 'and', 'or', etc.) and quantification. In effect such a language enjoys the benefits also of descriptions and indeed singular terms generally, these being contextually definable in known ways. Even abstract singular terms naming classes, classes of classes, etc., are contextually definable in case the assumed stock of predicates includes the two-place predicate of class membership. Such a language can be adequate to classical mathematics and indeed to scientific discourse generally, except in so far as the latter involves debatable devices such as contrary-to-fact conditionals or modal adverbs like 'necessarily'. Now a language of this type is extensional, in this sense: any two predicates which agree extensionally (that is, are true of the same objects) are interchangeable *salva veritate*.

In an extensional language, therefore, interchangeability *salva veritate* is no assurance of cognitive synonymy of the desired type. That 'bachelor' and 'unmarried man' are interchangeable *salva veritate* in an extensional language assures us of no more than that (3) is true. There is no assurance here that the extensional agreement of 'bachelor' and 'unmarried man' rests on meaning rather than merely on accidental matters of fact, as does the extensional agreement of 'creature with a heart' and 'creature with kidneys'.

For most purposes extensional agreement is the nearest approximation to synonymy we need care about. But the fact remains that extensional agreement falls far short of cognitive synonymy of the type required for explaining analyticity in the manner of §1. The type of cognitive synonymy required there is such as to equate the synonymy of 'bachelor' and 'unmarried man' with the analyticity of (3), not merely with the truth of (3).

So we must recognize that interchangeability *salva veritate*, if construed in relation to an extensional language, is not a sufficient condition of cognitive synonymy in the sense needed for deriving analyticity in the manner of §1. If a language contains an intensional adverb 'necessarily' in the sense lately noted, or other particles to the same effect, then interchangeability *salva veritate* in such a language does afford a sufficient condition of cognitive synonymy; but such a language is intelligible only in so far as the notion of analyticity is already understood in advance.

. . .

4. SEMANTICAL RULES

Analyticity at first seemed most naturally definable by appeal to a realm of meanings. On refinement, the appeal to meanings gave way to an appeal to synonymy or definition. But definition turned out to be a will-o'-the-wisp, and synonymy turned out to be best understood only by dint of a prior appeal to analyticity itself. So we are back at the problem of analyticity.

I do not know whether the statement 'Everything green is extended' is analytic. Now does my indecision over this example really betray an incomplete understanding, an incomplete grasp of the "meanings", of 'green' and 'extended'? I think not. The trouble is not with 'green' or 'extended', but with 'analytic'.

It is often hinted that the difficulty in separating analytic statements from synthetic ones in ordinary language is due to the vagueness of ordinary language and that the distinction is clear when we have a precise artificial language with explicit "semantical rules." This, however, as I shall now attempt to show, is a confusion.

The notion of analyticity about which we are worrying is a purported relation between statements and languages: a statement *S* is said to be *analytic for* a language *L*, and the problem is to make sense of this relation generally, that is, for variable '*S*' and '*L*'. The gravity of this problem is not perceptibly less for artificial languages than for natural ones. The problem of making sense of the idiom '*S* is analytic for *L*', with variable '*S*' and '*L*,' retains its stubbornness even if we limit the range of the variable '*L*' to artificial languages. Let me now try to make this point evident.

For artificial languages and semantical rules we look naturally to the writings of Carnap. His semantical rules take various forms, and to make my point I shall have to distinguish certain of the forms. Let us suppose, to begin with, an artificial language L_0 whose semantical rules have the form explicitly of a specification, by recursion or otherwise, of all the analytic statements of L_0. The rules tell us that such and such statements, and only those, are the analytic statements of L_0. Now here the difficulty is simply that the rules contain the word 'analytic', which we do not understand! We understand what expressions the rules attribute analyticity to, but we do not understand what the rules attribute to those expressions. In short, before we can understand a rule which begins 'A statement *S* is analytic for language L_0 if and only if . . . ', we must understand the general relative term 'analytic for'; we must understand '*S* is analytic for *L*' where '*S*' and '*L*' are variables.

Alternatively we may, indeed, view the so-called rule as a conventional definition of a new simple symbol 'analytic-for-L_0', which might better be written untendentiously as '*K*' so as not to seem to throw light on the interesting word 'analytic'. Obviously any number of classes *K*, *M*, *N*, etc. of statements of L_0 can be specified for various purposes or for no purpose; what does it mean to say that *K*, as against *M*, *N*, etc., is the class of the "analytic" statements of L_0?

By saying what statements are analytic for L_0 we explain 'analytic-for-L_0' but not 'analytic', not 'analytic for'. We do not begin to explain the idiom '*S* is analytic for *L*' with variable '*S*' and '*L*', even if we are content to limit the range of '*L*' to the realm of artificial languages.

Actually we do know enough about the intended significance of 'analytic' to know that analytic statements are supposed to be true. Let us then turn to a second form of semantical rule, which says not that such and such statements are analytic but simply that such and such statements are included among the truths. Such a rule is not subject to the criticism of containing the un-understood word 'analytic'; and we may grant for the sake of argument that there is no difficulty over the broader term 'true'. A semantical rule of this second type, a rule of truth, is not supposed to specify all the truths of the language; it merely stipulates, recursively or otherwise, a certain multitude of statements which, along with others unspecified, are to count as true. Such a rule may be conceded to be quite clear. Derivatively, afterward, analyticity can be demarcated thus: a statement is analytic if it is (not merely true but) true according to the semantical rule.

Still there is really no progress. Instead of appealing to an unexplained word 'analytic', we are now appealing to an unexplained phrase 'semantical rule'. Not every true statement which says that the statements of some class are true can count as a semantical rule—otherwise *all* truths would be "analytic" in the sense of being true according to semantical rules. Semantical rules are distinguishable, apparently, only by the fact of appearing on a page under the heading 'Semantical Rules'; and this heading is itself then meaningless.

We can say indeed that a statement is *analytic-for-*L_0 if and only if it is true according to such and such specifically appended "semantical rules," but then we find ourselves back at essentially the same case which was originally discussed: 'S is analytic-for-L_0 if and only if. . . .' Once we seek to explain 'S is analytic for L' generally for variable 'L' (even allowing limitation of 'L' to artificial languages), the explanation 'true according to the semantical rules of L' is unavailing; for the relative term 'semantical rule of' is as much in need of clarification, at least, as 'analytic for'.

It may be instructive to compare the notion of semantical rule with that of postulate. Relative to a given set of postulates, it is easy to say what a postulate is: it is a member of the set. Relative to a given set of semantical rules, it is equally easy to say what a semantical rule is. But given simply a notation, mathematical or otherwise, and indeed as thoroughly understood a notation as you please in point of the translations or truth conditions of its statements, who can say which of its true statements rank as postulates? Obviously the question is meaningless—as meaningless as asking which points in Ohio are starting points. Any finite (or effectively specifiable infinite) selection of statements (preferably true ones, perhaps) is as much *a* set of postulates as any other. The word 'postulate' is significant only relative to an act of inquiry; we apply the word to a set of statements just in so far as we happen, for the year or the moment, to be thinking of those statements in relation to the statements which can be reached from them by some set of transformations to which we have seen fit to direct our attention. Now the notion of semantical rule is as sensible and meaningful as that of postulate, if conceived in a similarly relative spirit—relative, this time, to one or another particular enterprise of schooling unconversant persons in sufficient conditions for truth of statements of some natural or artificial language L. But from this point of view no one signalization of a subclass of the truths of L is intrinsically more a semantical rule than another; and, if 'analytic' means 'true by semantical rules', no one truth of L is analytic to the exclusion of another.

It might conceivably be protested that an artificial language L (unlike a natural one) is a language in the ordinary sense *plus* a set of explicit semantical rules—the whole constituting, let us say, an ordered pair; and that the semantical rules of L then are specifiable simply as the second component of the pair L. But, by the same token and more simply, we might construe an artificial language L outright as an ordered pair whose second component is the class of its analytic statements; and then the analytic statements of L become specifiable simply as the statements in the second component of L. Or better still, we might just stop tugging at our bootstraps altogether.

Not all the explanations of analyticity known to Carnap and his readers have been covered explicitly in the above considerations, but the extension to other forms is not hard to see. Just one additional factor should be mentioned which sometimes enters: sometimes the semantical rules are in effect rules of translation into ordinary language, in which case the analytic statements of the artificial language are in effect recognized as such from the analyticity of their specified translations in ordinary language. Here certainly there can be no thought of an illumination of the problem of analyticity from the side of the artificial language.

From the point of view of the problem of analyticity the notion of an artificial language with semantical rules is a *feu follet par excellence*. Semantical rules determining the analytic statements of an artificial language are of interest only in so far as we already understand the notion of analyticity; they are of no help in gaining this understanding.

Appeal to hypothetical languages of an artificially simple kind could conceivably be useful in clarifying analyticity, if the mental or behavioral or cultural factors relevant to analyticity—whatever they may be—were somehow sketched into the simplified model. But a model which takes analyticity merely as an irreducible character is unlikely to throw light on the problem of explicating analyticity.

It is obvious that truth in general depends on both language and extralinguistic fact. The statement 'Brutus killed Caesar' would be false if the world had been different in certain ways, but it would also be false if the word 'killed' happened rather to have the sense of 'begat'. Thus one is tempted to suppose in general that the truth of a statement is somehow analyzable into a linguistic component and a factual component. Given this supposition, it next seems reasonable that in some statements the factual component should be null; and these are the analytic statements. But, for all its a priori reasonableness, a boundary between analytic and synthetic statements simply has not been drawn. That there is such a distinction to be drawn at all is an unempirical dogma of empiricists, a metaphysical article of faith.

. . .

Rudolf Carnap

Meaning and Synonymy in Natural Languages

1. MEANING ANALYSIS IN PRAGMATICS AND SEMANTICS

The analysis of meanings of expressions occurs in two fundamentally different forms. The first belongs to *pragmatics*, that is, the empirical investigation of historically given *natural languages*. This kind of analysis has long been carried out by linguists and philosophers, especially analytic philosophers. The second form was developed only recently in the field of symbolic logic; this form belongs to *semantics* (here understood in the sense of pure semantics, while descriptive semantics may be regarded as part of pragmatics), that is, the study of constructed *language systems* given by their rules.

The theory of the relations between a language—either a natural language or a language system—and what language is about may be divided into two parts which I call the theory of extension and the theory of intension, respectively. The first deals with concepts like denoting, naming, extension, truth, and related ones. (For example, the word 'blau' in German, and likewise the predicate '*B*' in a symbolic language system if a rule assigns to it the same meaning, denote any object that is blue; its extension is the class of all blue objects; 'der Mond' is a name of the moon; the sentence 'der Mond ist blau' is true if and only if the moon is blue.) The theory of intension deals with concepts like intension, synonymy, analyticity, and related ones; for our present discussion let us call them "*intension concepts*". (I use 'intension' as a technical term for the meaning of an expression or, more specifically, for its designative meaning component; see below. For example, the intension of 'blau' in German is the property of being blue; two predicates are synonymous if and only if they have the same intension; a sentence is analytic if it is true by virtue of the intensions of the expressions occurring in it.)

From a systematic point of view, the description of a language may well begin with the theory of intension and then build the theory of extension on its basis. By learning the theory of intension of a language, say German, we learn the intensions of the words and phrases and finally of the sentences. Thus the theory of intension of a given language *L* enables us to *understand*

From Rudolf Carnap, "Meaning and Synonymy in Natural Languages," *Philosophical Studies,* Vol. 6 (1955). Reprinted by permission of the author, *Philosophical Studies,* and the University of Minnesota Press. The essay in its entirety can be found in Carnap's *Meaning and Necessity,* 2nd ed., 1956.

Rudolf Carnap (1891–) was born in Germany and came to the United States in 1936. He was Professor of Philosophy at the University of Chicago from 1936 to 1952 and at the University of California, Los Angeles, from 1954 until his retirement in 1961.

the sentences of *L*. On the other hand, we can apply the concepts of the theory of extension of *L* only if we have, in addition to the knowledge of the theory of intension of *L*, also sufficient empirical knowledge of the relevant facts. For example, in order to ascertain whether a German word denotes a given object, one must first understand the word, that is, know what is its intension, in other words, know the general condition which an object must fulfil in order to be denoted by this word; and secondly he must investigate the object in question in order to see whether it fulfils the condition or not. On the other hand, if a linguist makes an empirical investigation of a language not previously described, he finds out first that certain objects are denoted by a given word, and later he determines the intension of the word.

Nobody doubts that the pragmatical investigation of natural languages is of greatest importance for an understanding both of the behavior of individuals and of the character and development of whole cultures. On the other hand, I believe with the majority of logicians today that for the special purpose of the development of logic the construction and semantical investigation of language systems is more important. But also for the logician a study of pragmatics may be useful. If he wishes to find out an efficient form for a language system to be used, say, in a branch of empirical science, he might find fruitful suggestions by a study of the natural development of the language of scientists and even of the everyday language. Many of the concepts used today in pure semantics were indeed suggested by corresponding pragmatical concepts which had been used for natural languages by philosophers or linguists, though usually without exact definitions. Those semantical concepts were, in a sense, intended as explicata for the corresponding pragmatical concepts.

In the case of the semantical intension concepts there is an additional motivation for studying the corresponding pragmatical concepts. The reason is that some of the objections raised against these semantical concepts concern, not so much any particular proposed explication, but the question of the very existence of the alleged explicanda. Especially *Quine's* criticism does not concern the formal correctness of the definitions in pure semantics; rather, he doubts whether there are any clear and fruitful corresponding pragmatical concepts which could serve as explicanda. That is the reason why he demands that these pragmatical concepts be shown to be scientifically legitimate by stating empirical, behavioristic criteria for them. If I understand him correctly, he believes that, without this pragmatical substructure, the semantical intension concepts, even if formally correct, are arbitrary and without purpose. I do not think that a semantical concept, in order to be fruitful, must necessarily possess a prior pragmatical counterpart. It is theoretically possible to demonstrate its fruitfulness through its application in the further development of language systems. But this is a slow process. If for a given semantical concept there is already a familiar, though somewhat vague, corresponding pragmatical concept and if we are able to clarify the latter by describing an operational procedure for its application, then this may indeed be a simpler way for refuting the objections and furnish a practical justification at once for both concepts.

The purpose of this paper is to clarify the nature of the pragmatical concept of intension in natural languages and to outline a behavioristic, operational procedure for it. This will give a practical vindication for the semantical intension concepts; ways for defining them, especially analyticity, I have shown in a previous paper ["Meaning Postulates"]. By way of introduction I shall first (in § 2) discuss briefly the pragmatical concepts of denotation and extension; it seems to be generally agreed that they are scientifically legitimate.

2. THE DETERMINATION OF EXTENSIONS

We take as example the German language. We imagine that a linguist who does not know anything about this language sets out to study it by observing the linguistic behavior of German-speaking people. More specifically, he studies the German language as used by a given person Karl at a given time. For simplicity, we restrict the discussion in this paper mainly to predicates applicable to observable things, like 'blau' and 'Hund'. It is generally agreed that, on the basis of spontaneous or elicited utterances of a person, the linguist can ascertain whether or not the person is willing to apply a given predicate to a given thing, in other words, whether the predicate denotes the given thing for the person. By collecting results of this kind, the linguist can determine first, the extension of the predicate 'Hund' within a given region for Karl, that is, the class of the things to which Karl is willing to apply the predicate, second, the extension of the contradictory, that is, the class of those things for which Karl denies the application of 'Hund', and, third, the intermediate class of those things for which Karl is not willing either to affirm or to deny the predicate. The size of the third class indicates the degree of vagueness of the predicate 'Hund', if we disregard for simplicity the effect of Karl's ignorance about relevant facts. For certain predicates, e.g., 'Mensch', this third class is relatively very small; the degree of their extensional vagueness is low. On the basis of the determination of the three classes for the predicate 'Hund' within the investigated region, the linguist may make a hypothesis concerning the responses of Karl to things outside of that region, and maybe even a hypothesis concerning the total extension in the universe. The latter hypothesis cannot, of course, be completely verified, but every single instance of it can in principle be tested. On the other hand, it is also generally agreed that this determination of extension involves uncertainty and possible error. But since this holds for all concepts of empirical science, nobody regards this fact as a sufficient reason for rejecting the concepts of the theory of extension. The sources of uncertainty are chiefly the following: first, the linguist's acceptance of the result that a given thing is denoted by 'Hund' for Karl may be erroneous, e.g., due to a misunderstanding or a factual error of Karl's; and, second, the generalization to things which he has not tested suffers, of course, from the uncertainty of all inductive inference.

3. THE DETERMINATION OF INTENSIONS

The purpose of this paper is to defend the thesis that the analysis of intension for a natural language is a scientific procedure, methodologically just as sound as the analysis of extension. To many linguists and philosophers this thesis will appear as a truism. However, some contemporary philosophers, especially Quine and White believe that the pragmatical intension concepts are foggy, mysterious, and not really understandable, and that so far no explications for them have been given. They believe further that, if an explication for one of these concepts is found, it will at best be in the form of a concept of degree. They acknowledge the good scientific status of the pragmatical concepts of the theory of extension. They emphasize that their objection against the intension concepts is based on a point of principle and not on the generally recognized facts of the technical difficulty of linguistic investigations, the inductive uncertainty, and the vagueness of the words of ordinary language. I shall therefore leave aside in my discussion these difficulties, especially the two mentioned at the end of the last section. Thus the question is this: *granted that the linguist can determine the extension of a given predicate, how can he go beyond this and determine also its intension?*

The technical term 'intension', which I use here instead of the ambiguous word 'meaning', is meant to apply only to the cognitive or designative meaning component. I shall not try to define this component. It was mentioned earlier that determination of truth presupposes knowledge of meaning (in addition to knowledge of facts); now, cognitive meaning may be roughly characterized as that meaning component which is relevant for the determination of truth. The non-cognitive meaning components, although irrelevant for questions of truth and logic, may still be very important for the psychological effect of a sentence on a listener, e.g., by emphasis, emotional associations, motivational effects.

It must certainly be admitted that the pragmatical determination of intensions involves a new step and therefore a new methodological problem. Let us assume that two linguists, investigating the language of Karl, have reached complete agreement in the determination of the extension of a given predicate in a given region. This means that they agree for every thing in this region, whether or not the predicate in question denotes it for Karl. As long as only these results are given, no matter how large the region is—you may take it, fictitiously, as the whole world, if you like—it is still possible for the linguists to ascribe to the predicate different intensions. For there are more than one and possibly infinitely many properties whose extension within the given region is just the extension determined for the predicate.

Here we come to the core of the controversy. It concerns the nature of a linguist's assignment of one of these properties to the predicate as its intension. This assignment may be made explicit by an entry in the German-English dictionary, conjoining the German predicate with an English phrase. The linguist declares hereby the German predicate to be synonymous with the English phrase. *The intensionalist thesis* in pragmatics, which I am defending, says that the assignment of an intension is an empirical hypothesis which, like any other hypothesis in linguistics, can be tested by observations of language behavior. On the other hand, *the extensionalist thesis* asserts that the assignment of an intension, on the basis of the previously determined extension, is not a question of fact but merely a matter of choice. The thesis holds that the linguist is free to choose any of those properties which fit to the given extension; he may be guided in his choice by a consideration of simplicity, but there is no question of right or wrong. Quine seems to maintain this thesis; he says: "The finished lexicon is a case evidently of *ex pede Herculem*. But there is a difference. In projecting Hercules from the foot we risk error but we may derive comfort from the fact that there is something to be wrong about. In the case of the lexicon, pending some definition of synonymy, we have no stating of the problem; we have nothing for the lexicographer to be right or wrong about."

I shall now plead for the intensionalist thesis. Suppose, for example, that one linguist, after an investigation of Karl's speaking behavior, writes into his dictionary the following:

(1) *Pferd*, horse,

while another linguist writes:

(2) *Pferd*, horse or unicorn.

Since there are no unicorns, the two intensions ascribed to the word 'Pferd' by the two linguists, although different, have the same extension. If the extensionalist thesis were right, there would be no way for empirically deciding between (1) and (2). Since the extension is the same, no response by Karl, affirmative or negative, with respect to any actual thing can make a difference between (1) and (2). But what else is there to investigate for the linguist beyond Karl's responses concerning the application of the predicate to all the cases that can be found? The answer is, he must take into account not only the actual cases, but also possible cases.[1] The most direct way of doing this would be for the linguist to use, in the German questions directed to Karl, modal expressions corresponding to "possible case" or the like. To be sure, these expressions are usually rather ambiguous; but this difficulty can be overcome by giving suitable explanations and examples. I do not think that there is any objection of principle against the use of modal terms. On the other hand, I think that their use is not necessary. The linguist could simply describe for Karl cases, which he knows to be possible, and leave it open whether there is anything satisfying those descriptions or not. He may, for example, describe a unicorn (in German) by something corresponding to the English formulation: "a thing similar to a horse, but having only one horn in the middle of the forehead". Or he may point toward a thing and then describe the intended modification in words, e.g.: "a thing like this one but having one horn in the middle of the forehead". Or, finally, he might just point to a picture representing a unicorn. Then he asks Karl whether he is willing to apply the word 'Pferd' to a thing of this kind. An affirmative or a negative answer will constitute a confirming instance for (2) or (1) respectively. This shows that (1) and (2) are different empirical hypotheses.

All *logically possible* cases come into consideration for the determination of intensions. This includes also those cases that are causally impossible, i.e., excluded by the laws of nature holding in our universe, and certainly those that are excluded by laws which Karl believes to hold. Thus, if Karl believes that all *P* are *Q* by a law of nature, the linguist will still induce him to consider things that are *P* but not *Q*, and ask him whether or not he would apply to them the predicate under investigation (e.g., 'Pferd').

The inadequacy of the extensionalist thesis is also shown by the following

[1] Some philosophers have indeed defined the intension of a predicate (or a concept closely related to it) as the class of the possible objects falling under it. For example, C. I. Lewis defines: "The comprehension of a term is the classification of all consistently thinkable things to which the term would correctly apply." I prefer to apply modalities like possibility not to objects but only to intensions, especially to propositions or to properties (kinds). (Compare *Meaning and Necessity*, pp. 66 f.) To speak of a possible case means to speak of a kind of objects which is possibly non-empty.

example. Consider, on the one hand, these customary entries in German-English dictionaries:

(3) *Einhorn*, unicorn. *Kobold*, goblin,

and, on the other hand, the following unusual entries:

(4) *Einhorn*, goblin. *Kobold*, unicorn.

Now the two German words (and likewise the two English words) have the same extension, viz., the null class. Therefore, if the extensionalist thesis were correct, there would be no essential, empirically testable difference between (3) and (4). The extensionalist is compelled to say that the fact that (3) is generally accepted and (4) generally rejected is merely due to a tradition created by the lexicographers, and that there are no facts of German language behavior which could be regarded as evidence in favor of (3) as against (4). I wonder whether any linguist would be willing to accept (4). Or, to avoid the possibly misguiding influence of the lexicographers' tradition, let us put the question this way: would a man on the street, who has learned both languages by practical use without lessons or dictionaries, accept as correct a translation made according to (4)?

In general terms, the determination of the intension of a predicate may start from some instances denoted by the predicate. The essential task is then to find out what variations of a given specimen in various respects (e.g., size, shape, color) are admitted within the range of the predicate. The intension of a predicate may be defined as its range, which comprehends those possible kinds of objects for which the predicate holds. In this investigation of intension, the linguist finds a new kind of vagueness, which may be called *intensional vagueness*. As mentioned above, the extensional vagueness of the word 'Mensch' is very small, at least in the accessible region. First, the intermediate zone among animals now living on earth is practically empty. Second, if the ancestors of man are considered, it is probably found that Karl cannot easily draw a line; thus there is an intermediate zone, but it is relatively small. However, when the linguist proceeds to the determination of the *intension* of the word 'Mensch', the situation is quite different. He has to test Karl's responses to descriptions of strange kinds of animals, say intermediate between man and dog, man and lion, man and hawk, etc. It may be that the linguist and Karl know that these kinds of animals have never lived on earth; they do not know whether or not these kinds will ever occur on earth or on any other planet in any galaxy. At any rate, this knowledge or ignorance is irrelevant for the determination of intension. But Karl's ignorance has the psychological effect that he has seldom if ever thought of these kinds (unless he happens to be a student of mythology or a science-fiction fan; and therefore never felt an urge to make up his mind to which of them to apply the predicate 'Mensch'. Consequently, the linguist finds in Karl's responses a large intermediate zone for this predicate, in other words, a high intensional vagueness. The fact that Karl has not made such decisions means that the intension of the word 'Mensch' for him is not quite clear even to himself, that he does not completely understand his own word. This lack of clarity does not bother him much because it holds only for aspects which have very little practical importance for him.

The extensionalist will perhaps reject as impracticable the described procedure for determining intensions because, he might say, the man on the street is unwilling to say anything about nonexistent objects. If Karl happens to be over-realistic in this way, the linguist could still resort to a lie, reporting, say, his alleged observations of unicorns. But this is by no means necessary. The tests concerning intensions are independent of questions of existence. The man on the street is very well able to understand and to answer questions about assumed situations, where it is left open whether anything of the kind described will ever actually occur or not, and even about nonexisting situations. This is shown in ordinary conversations about alternative plans of action, about the truth of reports, about dreams, legends, and fairy tales.

Although I have given here only a rough indication of the empirical procedure for determining intensions, I believe that it is sufficient to make clear that it would be possible to write along the lines indicated a manual for determining intensions or, more exactly, for testing hypotheses concerning intensions. The kinds of rules in such a manual would not be essentially different from those customarily given for procedures in psychology, linguistics, and anthropology. Therefore the rules could be understood and carried out by any scientist (provided he is not infected by philosophical prejudices).

4. INTENSIONS IN THE LANGUAGE OF SCIENCE

The discussions in this paper concern in general a simple, pre-scientific language, and the predicates considered designate observable properties of material bodies. Let us now briefly take a look at the *language of science*. It is today still mainly a natural language (except for its mathematical part), with only a few explicitly made conventions for some special words or symbols. It is a variant of the pre-scientific language, caused by special professional needs. The degree of precision is here in general considerably higher (i.e., the degree of vagueness is lower) than in the everyday language, and this degree is continually increasing. It is important to note that this increase holds not only for extensional but also for intensional precision; that is to say that not only the extensional intermediate zones (i.e., those of actual occurrences) but also the intensional ones (i.e., those of possible occurrences) are shrinking. In consequence of this development, also the intension concepts become applicable with increasing clarity. In the oldest books on chemistry, for example, there were a great number of statements describing the properties of a given substance, say water or sulphuric acid, including its reactions with other substances. There was no clear indication as to which of these numerous properties were to be taken as essential or definitory for the substance. Therefore, at least on the basis of the book alone, we cannot determine which of the statements made in the book were analytic and which synthetic for its author. The situation was similar with books on zoology, even at a much later time; we find a lot of statements, e.g., on the lion, without a clear separation of the definitory properties. But in chemistry there was an early development from the state described to states of greater and greater intensional precision. On the basis of the theory of chemical elements, slowly with increasing explicitness certain properties were selected as essential. For a compound, the molecular formula (e.g., 'H_2O') was taken as definitory, and later the molecular structure diagram. For the elementary substances, first certain experimental properties were more and more clearly selected as definitory, for example the atomic weight, later the position in Mendeleev's system. Still later, with a differentiation of the various isotopes, the nuclear composition was regarded as definitory, say characterized by the number of protons (atomic number) and the number of neutrons.

We can at the present time observe the advantages already obtained by the explicit conventions which have been made, though only to a very limited extent, in the language of empirical science, and the very great advantages effected by the moderate measure of formalization in the language of mathematics. Let us suppose—as I indeed believe, but that is outside of our present discussion—that this trend toward explicit rules will continue. Then the practical question arises whether rules of extension are sufficient or whether it would be advisable to lay down also rules of intension. In my view, it follows from the previous discussion that rules of intension are required, because otherwise intensional vagueness would remain, and this would prevent clear mutual understanding and effective communication.

5. THE GENERAL CONCEPT OF THE INTENSION OF A PREDICATE

We have seen that there is an empirical procedure for testing, by observations of linguistic behavior, a hypothesis concerning the intension of a predicate, say 'Pferd', for a speaker, say Karl. Since a procedure of this kind is applicable to any hypothesis of intension, the general concept of the intension of any predicate in any language for any person at any time has a clear, empirically testable sense. This general concept of intension may be characterized roughly as follows, leaving subtleties aside: the intension of a predicate '*Q*' for a speaker *X* is the general condition which an object *y* must fulfil in order for *X* to be willing to ascribe the predicate '*Q*' to *y*. (We omit, for simplicity, the reference to a time *t*.) Let us try to make this general characterization more explicit. That *X* is able to use a language *L* means that *X* has a certain system of interconnected dispositions for certain linguistic responses. That a predicate '*Q*' in a language *L* has the property *F* as its intension for *X*, means that among the dispositions of *X* constituting the language *L* there is the disposition of ascribing the predicate '*Q*' to any object *y* if and only if *y* has the property *F*. (*F* is here always assumed to be an observable property, i.e., either directly observable or explicitly definable in terms of directly observable properties.) (The given formulation is oversimplified, neglecting vagueness. In order to take vagueness into account, a pair of intensions F_1, F_2 must be stated: *X* has the disposition of ascribing affirmatively the predicate '*Q*' to an object *y* if and only if *y* has F_1; and the disposition of denying '*Q*' for *y* if and only if *y* has F_2. Thus, if *y* has neither F_1 nor F_2, *X* will give neither an affirmative nor a negative response; the property of having neither F_1 nor F_2 constitutes the zone of vagueness, which may possibly be empty.)

The concept of intension has here been characterized only for thing-predicates. The characterization for expressions of other types, including sentences, can be given in an analogous way. The other concepts of the theory of intension can then be defined in the usual way; we shall state only those for 'synonymous' and 'analytic' in a simple form without claim to exactness.

Two expressions are *synonymous* in the language L for X at time t if they have the same intension in L for X at t.

A sentence is *analytic* in L for X at t if its intension (or range or truth-condition) in L for X at t comprehends all possible cases.

A language L was characterized above as a system of certain dispositions for the use of expressions. I shall now make some remarks on the *methodology of dispositional concepts.* This will help to a clearer understanding of the nature of linguistic concepts in general and of the concept of intension in particular. Let D be the disposition of X to react to a condition C by the characteristic response R. There are in principle, although not always in practice, two ways for ascertaining whether a given thing or person X has the disposition D (at a given time t). The first method may be called *behavioristic* (in a very wide sense); it consists in producing the condition C and then determining whether or not the response R occurs. The second way may be called the *method of structure analysis.* It consists in investigatig the state of X (at t) in sufficient detail such that it is possible to derive from the obtained description of the state with the help of relevant general laws (say of physics, physiology, etc.) the responses which X would make to any specified circumstances in the environment. Then it will be possible to predict, in particular, whether, under the condition C, X would make the response R or not; if so, X has the disposition D, otherwise not. For example, let X be an automobile and D be the ability for a specified acceleration on a horizontal road at a speed of 10 miles per hour. The hypothesis that the automobile has this ability D may be tested by either of the following two procedures. The behavioristic method consists in driving the car and observing its performance under the specified conditions. The second method consists in studying the internal structure of the car, especially the motor, and calculating with the help of physical laws the acceleration which would result under the specified conditions. With respect to a psychological disposition and, in particular, a linguistic disposition of a person X, there is first the familiar behavioristic method and second, at least theoretically, the method of a micro-physiological investigation of the body of X, especially the central nervous system. At the present state of physiological knowledge of the human organism and especially the central nervous system, the second method is, of course, not practicable.

. . .

I have tried to show in this paper that in a pragmatical investigation of a natural language there is not only, as generally agreed, an empirical method for ascertaining which objects are denoted by a given predicate and thus for determining the extension of the predicate, but also a method for testing a hypothesis concerning its intension (designative meaning). The intension of a predicate for a speaker X is, roughly speaking, the general condition which an object must fulfil for X to be willing to apply the predicate to it. For the determination of intension, not only actually given cases must be taken into consideration, but also possible cases, i.e., kinds of objects which can be described without self-contradiction, irrespective of the question whether there are any objects of the kinds described. The intension of a predicate can be determined for a robot just as well as for a human speaker, and even more completely if the internal structure of the robot is sufficiently known to predict how it will function under various conditions. On the basis of the concept of intension, other pragmatical concepts with respect to natural languages can be defined, synonymy, analyticity, and the like. The existence of scientifically sound pragmatical concepts of this kind provides a practical motivation and justification for the introduction of corresponding concepts in pure semantics with respect to constructed language systems.

H. P. Grice and P. F. Strawson

In Defense of a Dogma

In his article "Two Dogmas of Empiricism," Professor Quine advances a number of criticisms of the supposed distinction between analytic and synthetic statements, and of other associated notions. It is, he says, a distinction which he rejects. We wish to show that his criticisms of the distinction do not justify his rejection of it.

. . .

Is there . . . a presumption in favor of the distinction's existence? Prima facie, it must be admitted that there is. An appeal to philosophical tradition is perhaps unimpressive and is certainly unnecessary. But it is worth pointing out that Quine's objection is not simply to the words "analytic" and "synthetic," but to a distinction which they are supposed to express, and which at different times philosophers have supposed themselves to be expressing by means of such pairs of words or phrases as "necessary" and "contingent," "a priori" and "empirical," "truth of reason" and "truth of fact"; so Quine is certainly at odds with a philosophical tradition which is long and not wholly disreputable. But there is no need to appeal only to tradition; for there is also present practice. We can appeal, that is, to the fact that those who use the terms "analytic" and "synthetic" do to a very considerable extent agree in the applications they make of them. They apply the term "analytic" to more or less the same cases, withhold it from more or less the same cases, and hesitate over more or less the same cases. This agreement extends not only to cases which they have been *taught* so to characterize, but to new cases. In short, "analytic" and "synthetic" have a more or less established philosophical *use*; and this seems to suggest that it is absurd, even senseless, to say that there is no such

---

From H. P. Grice and P. F. Strawson, "In Defense of a Dogma," *The Philosophical Review,* Vol. 65 (1956). Reprinted by permission of the authors and of the editors of *The Philosophical Review.*

H. P. Grice (1913–) is Fellow of St. John's College, Oxford.

distinction. For, in general, if a pair of contrasting expressions are habitually and generally used in application to the same cases, *where these cases do not form a closed list,* this is a sufficient condition for saying that there are *kinds* of cases to which the expressions apply; and nothing more is needed for them to mark a distinction.

In view of the possibility of this kind of argument, one may begin to doubt whether Quine really holds the extreme thesis which his words encourage one to attribute to him. It is for this reason that we made the attribution tentative. For on at least one natural interpretation of this extreme thesis, when we say of something true that it is analytic and of another true thing that it is synthetic, it simply never is the case that we thereby mark a distinction between them. And this view seems terribly difficult to reconcile with the fact of an established philosophical usage (i.e., of general agreement in application in an open class). For this reason, Quine's thesis might be better represented not as the thesis that there is *no difference at all* marked by the use of these expressions, but as the thesis that the nature of, and reasons for, the difference or differences are totally misunderstood by those who use the expressions, that the stories they tell themselves *about* the difference are full of illusion.

We think Quine might be prepared to accept this amendment. If so, it could, in the following way, be made the basis of something like an answer to the argument which prompted it. Philosophers are notoriously subject to illusion, and to mistaken theories. Suppose there were a particular mistaken theory about language or knowledge, such that, seen in the light of this theory, some statements (or propositions or sentences) appeared to have a characteristic which no statements really have, or even, perhaps, which it does not make sense to suppose that any statement has, and which no one who was not consciously or subconsciously influenced by this theory would ascribe to any statement. And suppose that there were other statements which, seen in this light, did not appear to have this characteristic, and others again which presented an uncertain appearance. Then philosophers who were under the influence of this theory would tend to mark the supposed presence or absence of this characteristic by a pair of contrasting expressions, say "analytic" and "synthetic." Now in these circumstances it still could not be said that there was no distinction at all being marked by the use of these expressions, for there would be at least the distinction we have just described (the distinction, namely, between those statements which appeared to have and those which appeared to lack a certain characteristic), and there might well be other assignable differences too, which would account for the difference in appearance; but it certainly could be said that *the* difference these philosophers supposed themselves to be marking by the use of the expressions simply did not exist, and perhaps also (supposing the characteristic in question to be one which it was absurd to ascribe to any statement) that these expressions, as so used, were senseless or without meaning. We should only have to suppose that such a mistaken theory was very plausible and attractive, in order to reconcile the fact of an established philosophical usage for a pair of contrasting terms with the claim that *the* distinction which the terms purported to mark did not exist at all, though not with the claim that there simply did not exist a difference of any kind between the classes of statements so characterized. We think that the former claim would probably be sufficient for Quine's purposes.

But to establish such a claim on the sort of grounds we have indicated evidently requires a great deal more argument than is involved in showing that certain explanations of a term do not measure up to certain requirements of adequacy in philosophical clarification—and not only more argument, but argument of a very different kind. For it would surely be too harsh to maintain that the *general* presumption is that philosophical distinctions embody the kind of illusion we have described. On the whole, it seems that philosophers are prone to make too few distinctions rather than too many. It is their assimilations, rather than their distinctions, which tend to be spurious.

So far we have argued as if the prior presumption in favor of the existence of the distinction which Quine questions rested solely on the fact of an agreed *philosophical* usage for the terms "analytic" and "synthetic." A presumption with only this basis could no doubt be countered by a strategy such as we have just outlined. But, in fact, if we are to accept Quine's account of the matter, the presumption in question is not only so based. For among the notions which belong to the analyticity-group is one which Quine calls "cognitive synonymy," and in terms of which he allows that the notion of analyticity could at any rate be formally explained. Unfortunately, he adds, the notion of cognitive synonymy is just as unclarified as that of analyticity. To say that two expressions x and y are cognitively synonymous seems to correspond, at any rate roughly, to what we should ordinarily express by saying that x and y have the same meaning or that x means the same as y. If Quine is to be consistent in his adherence to the extreme thesis, then it appears that he must maintain not only that the distinction we suppose ourselves to be marking by the use of the terms "analytic" and "synthetic" does not exist, but also that the distinction we suppose ourselves to be marking by the use of the expressions "means the same as," "does not mean the same as" does not exist either. At least, he must maintain this insofar as the notion of *meaning the same as,* in its application to predicate-expressions, is supposed to differ from and go beyond the notion of *being true of just the same objects as.* (This latter notion—which we might call that of "coextensionality"—he is prepared to allow to be intelligible, though, as he rightly says, it is not sufficient for the explanation of analyticity.) Now since he cannot claim this time that the pair of expressions in question (viz., "means the same," "does not mean the same") is the special property of philosophers, the strategy outlined above of countering the presumption in favor of their marking a genuine distinction is not available here (or is at least enormously less plausible). Yet the denial that the distinction (taken as different from the distinction between the coextensional and the non-coextensional) really exists, is extremely paradoxical. It involves saying, for example, that anyone who seriously remarks that "bachelor" means the same as "unmarried man" but that "creature with kidneys" does not mean the same as "creature with a heart"—supposing the last two expressions to be coextensional—*either* is not in fact drawing attention to any distinction at all between the relations between the members of each pair of expressions *or* is making a philosophical mistake about the nature of the distinction between them. In either case, what he says, taken as he intends it to be taken, is senseless or absurd. More generally, it involves saying that it is always senseless or absurd to make a statement of the form "Predicates x and y in fact apply to the same objects, but do not have the same meaning." But the paradox is more violent than this. For we frequently talk of the presence or absence of relations of synonymy between kinds of expressions—e.g., conjunctions, particles of many kinds, whole sentences—where there does not appear to be any obvious substitute for the ordinary notion of synonymy, in the way in which coextensionality is said to be a substitute for synonymy of predicates. Is all such talk meaningless? Is all talk of correct or incorrect *translation* of sentences of one language into sentences of another meaningless? It is hard to believe that it is. But if we do successfully make the effort to believe it, we have still harder renunciations before us. If talk of sentence-synonymy is meaningless, then it seems that talk of sentences having a meaning at all must be meaningless too. For if it made sense to talk of a sentence having a meaning, or meaning something, then presumably it would make sense to ask "What does it mean?" And if it made sense to ask "What does it mean?" of a sentence, then sentence-synonymy could be roughly defined as follows: Two sentences are synonymous if and only if any true answer to the question "What does it mean?" asked of one of them, is a true answer to the same question, asked of the other. We do not, of course, claim any clarifying power for this definition. We want only to point out that if we are to give up the notion of sentence-synonymy as senseless, we must give up the notion of sentence-significance (of a sentence having meaning) as senseless too. But then perhaps we might as well give up the notion of sense. . . .

We have argued so far that there is a strong presumption in favor of the existence of the distinction, or distinctions, which Quine challenges—a presumption resting both on philosophical and on ordinary usage—and that this presumption is not in the least shaken by the fact, if it is a fact, that the distinctions in question have not been, in some sense, adequately clarified. It is perhaps time to look at what Quine's notion of adequate clarification is.

The main theme of his article can be roughly summarized as follows. There is a certain circle or family of expressions, of which "analytic" is one, such that if any one member of the circle could be taken to be satisfactorily understood or explained, then other members of the circle could be verbally, and hence satisfactorily, explained in terms of it. Other members of the family are: "self-contradictory" (in a broad sense), "necessary," "synonymous," "semantical rule," and perhaps (but again in a broad sense) "definition." The list could be added to. Unfortunately each member of the family is in as great need of explanation as any other. We give some sample quotations: "The notion of self-contradictoriness (in the required broad sense of inconsistency) stands in exactly the same need of clarification as does the notion of analyticity itself." Again, Quine speaks of "a notion of synonymy which is in no less need of clarification than analyticity itself." Again, of the adverb "necessarily," as a candidate for use in the explanation of synonymy, he says, "Does the adverb *really make sense?* To suppose that it does is to suppose that we have already *made satisfactory sense* of 'analytic.'" To make "satisfactory sense" of one of these expressions would seem to involve two things. (1) It would seem to involve providing an explanation which does not incorporate any expression belonging to the family-circle. (2) It would seem that the explanation provided must be of the same general character as those rejected explanations which do incorporate members of the family-circle (i.e., it must specify some feature common and peculiar to all cases to which, for example, the word "analytic" is to be applied; it must have the same general form as an explanation beginning, "a statement is analytic if and only if . . ."). It is true that Quine does not explicitly state the second requirement; but since he does not even consider the question whether any other kind of explanation would be relevant, it seems reasonable to attribute it to him. If we take these two conditions together, and generalize the result, it would seem that Quine requires of a satisfactory explanation of an expression that it should take the form of a pretty strict definition but should not make use of any member of a group of interdefinable terms to which the expression belongs. We may well begin to feel that a satisfactory explanation is hard to come by. The other element in Quine's position is one we have already commented on in general, before enquiring what (according to him) is to count as a satisfactory explanation. It is the step from "We have not made satisfactory sense (provided a satisfactory explanation) of *x*" to "*x* does not make sense."

It would seem fairly clearly unreasonable to insist *in general* that the availability of a satisfactory explanation in the sense sketched above is a necessary condition of an expression's making sense. It is perhaps dubious whether *any* such explanations can *ever* be given. (The hope that they can be is, or was, the hope of reductive analysis in general.) Even if such explanations can be given in some cases, it would be pretty generally agreed that there [are] other cases in which they cannot. One might think, for example, of the group of expressions which includes "morally wrong," "blameworthy," "breach of moral rules," etc.; or of the group which includes the propositional connectives and the words "true" and "false," "statement," "fact," "denial," "assertion." Few people would want to say that the expressions belonging to either of these groups were senseless on the ground that they have not been formally defined (or even on the ground that it was impossible formally to define them) except in terms of members of the same group. It might, however, be said that while the unavailability of a satisfactory explanation in the special sense described was not a *generally* sufficient reason for declaring that a given expression was senseless, it was a sufficient reason in the case of the expressions of the analyticity group. But anyone who said this would have to advance a reason for discriminating in this way against the expressions of this group. The only plausible reason for being harder on these expressions than on others is a refinement on a consideration which we have already had before us. It starts from the point that "analytic" and "synthetic" themselves are technical philosophical expressions. To the rejoinder that other expressions of the family concerned, such as "means the same as" or "is inconsistent with," or "self-contradictory," are not at all technical expressions, but are common property, the reply would doubtless be that, to qualify for inclusion in the family circle, these expressions have to be used in specially adjusted and precise senses (or pseudo-senses) which they do not ordinarily possess. It is the fact, then, that all the terms belonging to the circle are *either* technical terms *or* ordinary terms used in specially adjusted senses, that might be held to justify us in being particularly suspicious of the claims of members of the circle to have any sense at all, and hence to justify us in requiring them to pass a test for significance which would admittedly be too stringent if generally applied. This point has some force, though we doubt if the special adjustments spoken of are in every case as considerable as it suggests. (This seems particularly doubtful in the case of the word "inconsistent"—a perfectly good member of the non-technician's meta-logical vocabulary.) But though the point has some force, it does not have whatever force would be required to justify us in insisting that the expressions concerned should pass exactly that test for significance which is in question. The fact, if it is a fact, that the expressions cannot be explained in precisely the way which Quine seems to require, does not mean that they cannot be explained at all. There is no need to try to pass them off as expressing innate ideas. They can be and are explained, though in other and less formal ways than that which Quine considers. (And the fact that they are so explained fits with the facts, first, that there is a generally agreed philosophical use for them, and second, that this use is technical or specially adjusted.) To illustrate the point briefly for one member of the analyticity family. Let us suppose we are trying to explain to someone the notion of *logical impossibility* (a member of the family which Quine presumably regards as no clearer than any of the others) and we decide to do it by bringing out the contrast between logical and natural (or causal) impossibility. We might take as our examples the logical impossibility of a child of three's being an adult, and the natural impossibility of a child of three's understanding Russell's Theory of Types. We might instruct our pupil to imagine two conversations one of which begins by someone (X) making the claim:

(1) "My neighbor's three-year-old child understands Russell's Theory of Types,"

and the other of which begins by someone (Y) making the claim:

(1′) "My neighbor's three-year-old child is an adult."

It would not be inappropriate to reply to X, taking the remark as a hyperbole:

(2) "You mean the child is a particularly bright lad."

If X were to say:

(3) "No, I mean what I say—he really does understand it,"

one might be inclined to reply:

(4) "I don't believe you—the thing's impossible."

But if the child were then produced, and did (as one knows he would not) expound the theory correctly, answer questions on it, criticize it, and so on, one would in the end be forced to acknowledge that the claim was literally true and that the child was a prodigy. Now consider one's reaction to Y's claim. To begin with, it might be somewhat similar to the previous case. One might say:

(2′) "You mean he's uncommonly sensible or very advanced for his age."

If Y replies:

(3′) "No, I mean what I say,"

we might reply:

(4′) "Perhaps you mean that he won't grow any more, or that he's a sort of freak, that he's already fully developed."

Y replies:

(5′) "No, he's not a freak, he's just an adult."

At this stage—or possibly if we are patient, a little later—we shall be inclined to say that we just don't understand what Y is saying, and to suspect that he just does not know the meaning of some of the words he is using. For unless he is prepared to admit that he is using words in a figurative or unusual sense, we shall say, not that we don't believe him, but that his words have *no* sense. And whatever kind of creature is ultimately produced for our inspection, it will not lead us to say that what Y said was literally true, but at most to say that we now see what he meant. As a summary of the difference between the two imaginary conversations, we might say that in both cases we would tend to begin by supposing that the other speaker was using words in a figurative or unusual or restricted way; but in the face of his repeated claim to be speaking literally, it would be appropriate in the first case to say that we did not believe him and in the second case to say that we did not understand him. If, like Pascal, we thought it prudent to prepare against very long chances, we should in the first case know what to prepare for; in the second, we should have no idea.

We give this as an example of just one type of informal explanation which we might have recourse to in the case of one notion of the analyticity group. (We do not wish to suggest it is the only type.) Further examples, with different though connected types of treatment, might be necessary to teach our pupil the use of the notion of logical impossibility in its application to more complicated cases—if indeed he did not pick it up from the one case. Now of course this type of explanation does not yield a formal statement of necessary and sufficient conditions for the application of the notion concerned. So it does not fulfill one of the conditions which Quine seems to require of a satisfactory explanation. On the other hand, it does appear to fulfill the other. It breaks out of the family circle. The distinction in which we ultimately come to rest is that between not believing something and not understanding something; or between incredulity yielding to conviction, and incomprehension yielding to comprehension. It would be rash to maintain that *this* distinction does not need clarification; but it would be absurd to maintain that it does not exist. In the face of the availability of this informal type of explanation for the notions of the analyticity group, the fact that they have not received another type of explanation (which it is dubious whether *any* expressions *ever* receive) seems a wholly inadequate ground for the conclusion that the notions are pseudo-notions, that the expressions which purport to express them have no sense. To say this is not to deny that it would be philosophically desirable, and a proper object of philosophical endeavor, to find a more illuminating general characterization of the notions of this group than any that has been so far given. But the question of how, if at all, this can be done is quite irrelevant to the question of whether or not the expressions which belong to the circle have an intelligible use and mark genuine distinctions.

So far we have tried to show that sections 1 to 4 of Quine's article—the burden of which is that the notions of the analyticity group have not been satisfactorily explained—do not establish the extreme thesis for which he appears to be arguing.

. . .

There are two further points worth making which arise out of the first two sections.

(1) One concerns what Quine says about *definition* and *synonymy*. He remarks that definition does not, as some have supposed, "hold the key to synonymy and analyticity," since "definition—except in the extreme case of the explicitly conventional introduction of new notations—hinges on prior relations of synonymy." But now consider what he says of these extreme cases. He says: "Here the definiendum becomes synonymous with the definiens simply because it has been expressly created for the purpose of being synonymous with the definiens. Here we have a really transparent case of synonymy created by definition; would that all species of synonymy were as intelligible." Now if we are to take these words of Quine seriously, then his position *as a whole* is incoherent. It is like the position of a man to whom we are trying to explain, say, the idea of one thing fitting into another thing, or two things fitting together, and who says: "I can understand what it means to say that one thing fits into another, or that two things fit together, in the case where one was specially made to fit the other; but I cannot understand what it means to say this in any other case." Perhaps we should not take Quine's words here too seriously. But if not, then we have the right to ask him exactly what state of affairs he thinks *is* brought about by explicit definition, what relation between expressions *is* established by this procedure, and why he thinks it unintelligible to suggest that the same (or a closely analogous) state of affairs, or relation, should exist in the absence of this procedure. For our part, we should be inclined to take Quine's words (or some of them) seriously, and reverse his conclusions; and maintain that the notion of synonymy by explicit convention would be unintelligible if the notion of synonymy by usage were not presupposed. There cannot be law where there is no custom, or rules where there are not practices (though perhaps we can understand better what a practice is by looking at a rule).

(2) The second point arises out of a paragraph . . . of Quine's [article]. We quote:

> I do not know whether the statement "Everything green is extended" is analytic. Now does my indecision over this example really betray an incomplete understanding, an incomplete grasp, of the "meanings" of "green" and "extended"? I think not. The trouble is not with "green" or "extended," but with "analytic."

If, as Quine says, the trouble is with "analytic," then the trouble should doubtless disappear when "analytic" is removed. So let us remove it, and replace it with a word which Quine himself has contrasted favorably with "analytic" in respect of perspicuity—the word "true." Does the indecision at once disappear? We think not. The indecision over "analytic" (and equally, in this case, the indecision over "true") arises, of course, from a further indecision: viz., that which we feel when confronted with such questions as

"Should we count a *point* of green light as *extended* or not?" As is frequent enough in such cases, the hesitation arises from the fact that the boundaries of application of words are not determined by usage in all possible directions. But the example Quine has chosen is particularly unfortunate for his thesis, in that it is only too evident that our hesitations are not *here* attributable to obscurities in "analytic." It would be possible to choose other examples in which we should hesitate between "analytic" and "synthetic" and have few qualms about "true." But no more in these cases than in the sample case does the hesitation necessarily imply any obscurity in the notion of analyticity; since the hesitation would be sufficiently accounted for by the same or a similar kind of indeterminacy in the relations between the words occurring within the statement about which the question, whether it is analytic or synthetic, is raised.

. . .

For Further Reading

Aune, Bruce, "Is There an Analytic Apriori?," *Journal of Philosophy,* Vol. 60 (1963).
Austin, J. L., *Philosophical Papers,* 1961, Chap. 1.
Ayer, A. J., *Language, Truth and Logic,* 2nd ed., 1950, Chap. 4.
Bennett, Jonathan F., "Analytic-Synthetic," *Proceedings of the Aristotelian Society,* Vol. 59 (1958–59).
Black, Max, "Necessary Statements," *The Philosophical Review,* Vol. 67 (1958).
Broad, C. D., *Examination of McTaggart's Philosophy,* Vol. 1, 1933, pp. 38–53.
Coffey, Peter, *Epistemology,* 1917, Vol. 1, Chap. 8.
Cohen, L. Jonathan, *The Diversity of Meaning,* 1962, Chap. 6.
Cohen, Morris R., *Reason and Nature,* 1931, Chap. 3, Section V.
Dewey, John, *Logic,* 1938, Chaps. 1, 14, and 20.
Frege, Gottlob, *The Foundations of Arithmetic,* 1950, Chaps. 1 and 5.
James, William, *The Principles of Psychology,* 1890, Vol. 2, Chap. 28.
Kemeny, J. G., "Analyticity versus Fuzziness," in Gregg, J. R., and Harris, F. T. (eds.), *Form and Strategy in Science,* 1964.
Laird, John, *Knowledge, Belief, and Opinion,* 1930, Chaps. 8, 9, and 10.
Lewis, C. I., *Mind and the World Order,* 1929, Chaps. 7, 8, and 9.
Mates, Benson, "Synonymy," in Linsky, L. (ed.), *Semantics and the Philosophy of Language,* 1952, Chap. 7.
Pap, Arthur, *Semantics and Necessary Truth,* 1958, Chaps. 5 and 7.
Robinson, Richard, "Necessary Propositions," *Mind,* Vol. 67 (1958).
Sellars, Wilfrid, "Is There a Synthetic A Priori? " *Science, Perception, and Reality,* 1963, Chap. 10.
Waismann, Friedrich, "Analytic-Synthetic," *Analysis,* Vol. 11 (1951), pp. 53–61.
Walsh, W. H., "Analytic/Synthetic," *Proceedings of the Aristotelian Society,* Vol. 54 (1953–54).
White, Morton, "The Analytic and the Synthetic: An Untenable Dualism," in Hook, S. (ed.), *John Dewey: Philosopher of Science and Freedom,* 1950.
———, *Toward Reunion in Philosophy,* 1956, Chaps. 7, 8, and 9.

4
UNIVERSALS

It is a commonplace that most words we use are general (that is, unlike proper names, they can be predicated of an indefinite number of things or occurrences), and that the statements we make in communicating with family and friends as well as in the various branches of specialized inquiry all contain general terms. It is equally obvious that even statements about particular events contain such terms, because the traits or relational patterns attributed to the things under discussion are either known to be recurrent or are in principle repeatable. What is often called "the problem of universals" has emerged in the attempts that have been going on since Greek antiquity to understand and interpret these apparently unproblematic and generally uncontested commonplaces.

However, despite its suggestion that there is just one problem, the designation in fact covers a multitude of different ones—though it is by no means entirely clear what exactly is the point at issue in some of the problems, or where one problem ends and another begins. But at any rate, two groups of questions about universals are frequently distinguished, which for convenient reference we shall label as "ontological" and "epistemological," respectively.

The first group is closely related to the themes discussed in Chapter 1, Section B (Problems of Meaning: Meaning and Reference) and deals with the kind of "reality" or "ontological status" that is to be assigned to the connotations (or "meanings") of general terms. An example will serve to indicate how questions of this sort come to be asked. The early classifications of living organisms were based on the observation that some organisms strongly resemble each other in certain easily recognizable features, but differ markedly in those features from other organisms, and the assumption was eventually made that living things fall into distinct and fixed natural kinds or species. In consequence, although observation shows that no two individual organisms are absolutely alike, members of the same species were held to have something basic in common—indeed, according to a historically influential view, a common character that "explains" why the things possessing it exhibit certain distinctive and invariably conjoined traits. It has also been obvious to many thinkers that when some individual organism is said, for example, to be a man, the general term "man" stands for this common character. Moreover, since by hypothesis the stipulated character can be manifested in an indefinitely large number of individuals who may be widely separated in space and time, many philosophers have concluded that in thinking of the term's connotation the object of our thought cannot be anything occupying a place and occurring at a date, but must be a nonspatial and atemporal entity called a "universal." To this it should be added that the meanings of general terms may be interconnected, and that in mathematics as well as elsewhere the truth of statements about relations between meanings can be established as necessary and without recourse to observation. It has therefore been often claimed that the possibility of a priori knowledge in mathematics and other disciplines can be accounted for only on the assumption that the subject matter of these disciplines consists of universals and their relations.

The notion of universals thus has its genesis in attempts directed to different though connected objectives: to make intelligible the recurrent patterns found in experience and to clarify the use of general terms. However, the introduction of the notion leads directly to further questions about the sort of "existence" or "ontological status" that is to be attributed to universals, and it leads also to questions about how universals are related to particulars. The various positions that have been taken on these ontological issues are frequently divided into three main types. According to the so-called "realistic" view, universals are "objectively real," in the sense that their "existence" does not depend on the presence of human minds. But while the "extreme realism" advocated by Plato maintains that universals exist *ante rem* (independently of any spatiotemporal particulars that may embody them), the "moderate realism" of Aristotle holds that universals exist only *in re* (only as embodied in such particulars). One form of Platonic realism is defended in Russell's article in this chapter, and Plato's own views are described and criticized in the selection from Aristotle. Aristotelian realism, as interpreted by St. Thomas and formulated by a modern scholastic philosopher, is presented in the selection from Coffey.

The second type of view on the nature of universals is known as "conceptualism." According to it, universals are simply ways of thinking about particular things and do not exist independently of or external to human minds. Conceptualism has a number of variant forms, one of which is advocated in the selection from Locke in Chapter I, and another in the article by Hume in the present chapter.

Finally, the third type of doctrine about universals is called "nominalism." It is usually described as the view maintaining that words alone are universal, and that the only attribute common to the things designated by a general term is the common name given to them. However, it is doubtful whether anyone has consistently held such a thesis, and thinkers who are traditionally classified as nominalists (for example, Hobbes) do not deny that things receive a common name for reasons that are not wholly arbitrary—for the most part because there are certain resemblances between them. What they do deny is that the individual objects designated by a general term possess an attribute that is identical in all of them, and what they emphasize is the conventional character of classification, the indeterminate range of application of most words, and the role played by language in the intellectual organization of experience. Indeed, recent thinkers with nominalistic leanings deal with the ontological problem of universals almost exclusively from the perspective of logical grammar. Much of their effort is devoted to trying to show that the problem as traditionally pursued is the product of confused or inadequate conceptions about language; and some of them have reformulated the problem in order to make it unquestionably meaningful and entirely precise, so that it is transformed into a question about the grounds for choosing between linguistic frameworks that differ in the kinds of locution that can be constructed in them. The articles by Pears, Quine, Carnap, and Alston in the present chapter, as well as the selection from Waismann in Chapter 1, illustrate in one way or another current nominalistic tendencies. Pears argues that the notion of universals is largely the result of misconceived attempts to explain naming; Quine maintains that while the use of certain types of expressions implies a commitment to the "reality" of "abstract entities" such as universals, the fact that general terms occur in the statements we make does not by itself imply such a commitment; Carnap denies that any ontological commitments to universals are involved in the adoption of a linguistic framework, whatever its expressive means may be; and although Alston offers a critique of attempts to eliminate ontological commitments by the use of linguistic techniques, he stresses the importance of such techniques for avoiding the reification of universals and other confusions.

The second group of problems about universals—those problems we have called "epistemological"—is centered around the inclusive question of what the grounds are, if any, for maintaining that the use of general terms can be understood only on the assumption that at least some of them stand for universals. However, philosophers who deal with the question usually do so by discussing a congeries of more specific ones, including some that are partly if not entirely questions for experimental psychology. Even a bare catalogue of the various issues philosophers have raised in this connection would require many pages, but the following half dozen questions will indicate the sorts of problem that continue to receive attention. (1) What function (or functions) do general terms perform in the acquisition of knowledge and the communication of thought? (2) What are the prerequisites involving sensory or introspective experience, if any, for the ability to use general terms and understand their connotations? (3) What mental occurrences are associated with the use of general terms, and how do images, ideas, or other psychic events—which are all particular existents—achieve generality of reference? (4) Does the use of general terms presuppose that the things of which they are correctly predicated possess an identical common character, or is it possible to account for the use of general terms on the supposition that their predication involves only observations of resemblances between things and no commitment at any point to the existence of common characters? (5) Are there criteria for determining unambiguously whether or not a statement implies any assumption concerning the reality of universals? (6) Are assumptions about the existence of universals or other abstract entities comparable to scientific theories that postulate the existence of "unobservable" entities (such as electrons) and, in any case, on what grounds is the validity or acceptability of such assumptions to be assessed?

These questions are discussed in this chapter with unequal attention to details. The first is touched upon only briefly in Carnap's article; the second is examined from the perspective of scholastic philosophical psychology in the selection from Coffey; the third receives considerable notice in the selection from Hume, and some attention also from Coffey; the fourth is briefly discussed in the article by Russell; and the final two are the main concern of the essays by Quine and Carnap.

Bertrand Russell

The World of Universals

At the end of the preceding chapter we saw that such entities as relations appear to have a being which is in some way different from that of physical objects, and also different from that of minds and from that of sense-data. In the present chapter we have to consider what is the nature of this kind of being, and also what objects there are that have this kind of being. We will begin with the latter question.

The problem with which we are now concerned is a very old one, since it was brought into philosophy by Plato. Plato's "theory of ideas" is an attempt to solve this very problem, and in my opinion it is one of the most successful attempts hitherto made. The theory to be advocated in what follows is largely Plato's, with merely such modifications as time has shown to be necessary.

The way the problem arose for Plato was more or less as follows. Let us consider, say, such a notion as *justice*. If we ask ourselves what justice is, it is natural to proceed by considering this, that, and the other just act, with a view to discovering what they have in common. They must all, in some sense, partake of a common nature, which will be found in whatever is just and in nothing else. This common nature, in virtue of which they are all just, will be justice itself, the pure essence the admixture of which with facts of ordinary life produces the multiplicity of just acts. Similarly with any other word which may be applicable to common facts, such as "whiteness" for example. The word will be applicable to a number of particular things because they all participate in a common nature or essence. This pure essence is what Plato calls an "idea" or "form." (It must not be supposed that "ideas," in his sense, exist in minds, though they may be apprehended by minds.) The "idea" *justice* is not identical with anything that is just: it is something other than particular things, which particular things partake of. Not being particular, it cannot itself exist in the world of sense. Moreover it is not fleeting or changeable like the things of sense: it is eternally itself, immutable and indestructible.

Thus Plato is led to a supra-sensible world, more real than the common world of sense, the unchangeable world of ideas, which alone gives to the world of sense whatever pale reflection of reality may belong to it. The truly real world, for Plato, is the world of ideas; for whatever we may attempt to say about things in the world of sense, we can only succeed in saying that they participate in such and such ideas, which, therefore, constitute all their

---

From Bertrand Russell, *The Problems of Philosophy,* Chap. 9, published by Oxford University Press, London, and reprinted with their permission. This book first appeared in 1912.

character. Hence it is easy to pass on into a mysticism. We may hope, in a mystic illumination, to *see* the ideas as we see objects of sense; and we may imagine that the ideas exist in heaven. These mystical developments are very natural, but the basis of the theory is in logic; and it is as based in logic that we have to consider it.

The word "idea" has acquired, in the course of time, many associations which are quite misleading when applied to Plato's "ideas." We shall therefore use the word "universal" instead of the word "idea," to describe what Plato meant. The essence of the sort of entity that Plato meant is that it is opposed to the particular things that are given in sensation. We speak of whatever is given in sensation, or is of the same nature as things given in sensation, as a *particular*; by opposition to this, a *universal* will be anything which may be shared by many particulars, and has those characteristics which, as we saw, distinguish justice and whiteness from just acts and white things.

When we examine common words, we find that, broadly speaking, proper names stand for particulars, while other substantives, adjectives, prepositions, and verbs stand for universals. Pronouns stand for particulars, but are ambiguous: it is only by the context or the circumstances that we know what particulars they stand for. The word "now" stands for a particular, namely the present moment; but like pronouns, it stands for an ambiguous particular, because the present is always changing.

It will be seen that no sentence can be made up without at least one word which denotes a universal. The nearest approach would be some such statement as "I like this." But even here the word "like" denotes a universal, for I may like other things, and other people may like things. Thus all truths involve universals, and all knowledge of truths involves acquaintance with universals.

Seeing that nearly all the words to be found in the dictionary stand for universals, it is strange that hardly anybody except students of philosophy ever realises that there are such entities as universals. We do not naturally dwell upon those words in a sentence which do not stand for particulars; and if we are forced to dwell upon a word which stands for a universal, we naturally think of it as standing for some one of the particulars that come under the universal. When, for example, we hear the sentence, "Charles I's head was cut off," we may naturally enough think of Charles I, of Charles I's head, and of the operation of cutting off *his* head, which are all particulars; but we do not naturally dwell upon what is meant by the word "head" or the word "cut," which is a universal. We feel such words to be incomplete and insubstantial; they seem to demand a context before anything can be done with them. Hence we succeed in avoiding all notice of universals as such, until the study of philosophy forces them upon our attention.

Even among philosophers, we may say, broadly, that only those universals which are named by adjectives or substantives have been much or often recognised, while those named by verbs and prepositions have been usually overlooked. This omission has had a very great effect upon philosophy; it is hardly too much to say that most metaphysics, since Spinoza, has been largely determined by it. The way this has occurred is, in outline, as follows: Speaking generally, adjectives and common nouns express qualities or properties of single things, whereas prepositions and verbs tend to express relations between two or more things. Thus the neglect of prepositions and verbs led to the belief that every proposition can be regarded as attributing a property to a single thing, rather than as expressing a relation between two or more things. Hence it was supposed that, ultimately, there can be no such entities as relations between things. Hence either there can be only one thing in the universe, or, if there are many things, they cannot possibly interact in any way, since any interaction would be a relation, and relations are impossible.

The first of these views, which was advocated by Spinoza, and is held in our own day by Mr. Bradley and many other philosophers, is called *monism;* the second, which was advocated by Leibniz, but is not very common nowadays, is called *monadism,* because each of the isolated things is called a *monad.* Both these opposing philosophies, interesting as they are, result, in my opinion, from an undue attention to one sort of universals, namely the sort represented by adjectives and substantives rather than by verbs and prepositions.

As a matter of fact, if any one were anxious to deny altogether that there are such things as universals, we should find that we cannot strictly prove that there are such entities as *qualities, i.e.* the universals represented by adjectives and substantives, whereas we can prove that there must be *relations, i.e.* the sort of universals generally represented by verbs and prepositions. Let us take in illustration the universal *whiteness.* If we believe that there is such a universal, we shall say that things are white because they have the quality of whiteness. This view, however, was strenuously denied by Berkeley and Hume, who have been followed in this by later empiricists. The form which their denial took was to deny that there are such things as "abstract ideas." When we want to think of whiteness, they said, we form an image of some particular white thing, and reason concerning this particular, taking care not to deduce anything concerning it which we cannot see to be equally true of any other white thing. As an account of our actual mental processes, this is no doubt largely true. In geometry, for example, when we wish to prove something about all triangles, we draw a particular triangle and reason about it, taking care not to use any characteristic which it does not share with other triangles. The beginner, in order to avoid error, often finds it useful to draw several triangles, as unlike each other as possible, in order to make sure that his reasoning is equally applicable to all of them. But a difficulty emerges as soon as we ask ourselves how we know that a thing is white or a triangle. If we wish to avoid the universals *whiteness* and *triangularity,* we shall choose some particular patch of white or some particular triangle, and say that anything is white or a triangle if it has the right sort of resemblance to our chosen particular. But then the resemblance required will have to be a universal. Since there are many white things, the resemblance must hold between many pairs of particular white things; and this is the characteristic of a universal. It will be useless to say that there is a different resemblance for each pair, for then we shall have to say that these resemblances resemble each other, and thus at last we shall be forced to admit resemblance as a universal. The relation of resemblance, therefore, must be a true universal. And having been forced to admit this universal, we find that it is no longer worth while to invent difficult and unplausible theories to avoid the admission of such universals as whiteness and triangularity.

Berkeley and Hume failed to perceive this refutation of their rejection of "abstract ideas," because, like their adversaries, they only thought of *qualities*, and altogether ignored *relations* as universals. We have therefore here another respect in which the rationalists appear to have been in the right as against the empiricists, although, owing to the neglect or denial of relations, the deductions made by rationalists were, if anything, more apt to be mistaken than those made by empiricists.

Having now seen that there must be such entities as universals, the next point to be proved is that their being is not merely mental. By this is meant that whatever being belongs to them is independent of their being thought of or in any way apprehended by minds. We have already touched on this subject at the end of the preceding chapter, but we must now consider more fully what sort of being it is that belongs to universals.

Consider such a proposition as "Edinburgh is north of London." Here we have a relation between two places, and it seems plain that the relation subsists independently of our knowledge of it. When we come to know that Edinburgh is north of London, we come to know something which has to do only with Edinburgh and London: we do not cause the truth of the proposition by coming to know it, on the contrary we merely apprehend a fact which was there before we knew it. The part of the earth's surface where Edinburgh stands would be north of the part where London stands, even if there were no human being to know about north and south, and even if there were no minds at all in the universe. This is, of course, denied by many philosophers, either for Berkeley's reasons or for Kant's. But we have already considered these reasons, and decided that they are inadequate. We may therefore now assume it to be true that nothing mental is presupposed in the fact that Edinburgh is north of London. But this fact involves the relation "north of," which is a universal; and it would be impossible for the whole fact to involve nothing mental if the relation "north of," which is a constituent part of the fact, did involve anything mental. Hence we must admit that the relation, like the terms it relates, is not dependent upon thought, but belongs to the independent world which thought apprehends but does not create.

This conclusion, however, is met by the difficulty that the relation "north of" does not seem to *exist* in the same sense in which Edinburgh and London exist. If we ask "Where and when does this relation exist?" the answer must be "Nowhere and nowhen." There is no place or time where we can find the relation "north of." It does not exist in Edinburgh any more than in London, for it relates the two and is neutral as between them. Nor can we say that it exists at any particular time. Now everything that can be apprehended by the senses or by introspection exists at some particular time. Hence the relation "north of" is radically different from such things. It is neither in space nor in time, neither material nor mental; yet it is something.

It is largely the very peculiar kind of being that belongs to universals which has led many people to suppose that they are really mental. We can think *of* a universal, and our thinking then exists in a perfectly ordinary sense, like any other mental act. Suppose, for example, that we are thinking of whiteness. Then *in one sense* it may be said that whiteness is "in our mind." We have here the same ambiguity as we noted in discussing Berkeley. . . . In the strict sense, it is not whiteness that is in our mind, but the act of thinking of whiteness. The connected ambiguity in the word "idea," which we noted at the same time, also causes confusion here. In one sense of this word, namely the sense in which it denotes the *object* of an act of thought, whiteness is an "idea." Hence, if the ambiguity is not guarded against, we may come to think that whiteness is an "idea" in the other sense, *i.e.* an act of thought; and thus we come to think that whiteness is mental. But in so thinking, we rob it of its essential quality of universality. One man's act of thought is necessarily a different thing from another man's; one man's act of thought at one time is necessarily a different thing from the same man's act of thought at another time. Hence, if whiteness were the thought as opposed to its object, no two different men could think of it, and no one man could think of it twice. That which many different thoughts of whiteness have in common is their *object,* and this object is different from all of them. Thus universals are not thoughts, though when known they are the objects of thoughts.

We shall find it convenient only to speak of things *existing* when they are in time, that is to say, when we can point to some time *at* which they exist (not excluding the possibility of their existing at all times). Thus thoughts and feelings, minds and physical objects *exist.* But universals do not exist in this sense; we shall say that they *subsist* or *have being,* where "being" is opposed to "existence" as being timeless. The world of universals, therefore, may also be described as the world of being. The world of being is unchangeable, rigid, exact, delightful to the mathematician, the logician, the builder of metaphysical systems, and all who love perfection more than life. The world of existence is fleeting, vague, without sharp boundaries, without any clear plan or arrangement, but it contains all thoughts and feelings, all the data of sense, and all physical objects, everything that can do either good or harm, everything that makes any difference to the value of life and the world. According to our temperaments, we shall prefer the contemplation of the one or of the other. The one we do not prefer will probably seem to us a pale shadow of the one we prefer, and hardly worthy to be regarded as in any sense real. But the truth is that both have the same claim on our impartial attention, both are real, and both are important to the metaphysician. Indeed no sooner have we distinguished the two worlds than it becomes necessary to consider their relations.

Aristotle

The Platonic Theory of Forms

VI

When he was young, Plato spent much of his time with Cratylus, picking up from him Heraclitean ideas—for example, that all perceptible things are constantly changing state, and that it is therefore impossible to know anything about them with any precision; and Plato still believed all this when he was older. Socrates, on the other hand, did not attempt to deal with the behavior of all things, but only with the behavior of people; he tried to understand the general principles of human action, and he was the first to give serious attention to precise formulations in this field. Plato accepted Socrates' conclusions, but thought that general laws and precise statements could not be applied to the perceptible world, since it is impossible to formulate truly objective characterizations of the ever-changing objects we perceive. For this reason Plato concluded that precision can be attained only when dealing with other things, which he called "predicates that exist separate from physical reality." According to him, perceptible objects correspond to these pure predicates and are named after them; and he held that all the perceptible objects which are described by the same word are so described because they all share the features that some one of the pure predicates possesses. The only thing new here was the terminology: the Pythagoreans had said that real things are patterned after numbers, while Plato, changing the terminology, said that real things share the attributes of pure predicates. Neither of them undertook to specify just *how* things share the attributes of numbers or are patterned after pure predicates. Plato also held that the mathematical properties of real objects occupy an intermediate position between pure predicates and the real objects themselves. In his theory, mathematical properties are different from perceptible things because they do not change with time, and they are different from pure predicates because some of them are similar to others, while each pure predicate is unique.

Because Plato thought that pure predicates make things what they are, he believed that the basic features of pure predicates must at the same time be the basic features of an explanation of the real world. For this reason he held that the material composition of any actual object [1] is determined by a specified

[1] Which is one of the basic features of an explanation of the real world, given in Aristotle's list above.

range of magnitudes [2]; and that the essential defining characteristic of any actual object [3] is the characteristic which enables us to grasp the object as one thing.[4] For each pure predicate is basically determined by a specified range of magnitudes; and all predicates share one feature, that each is a unique entity which can be grasped as a single idea.

. . .

His is not however a reasonable explanation, since in fact the relationship between objects and predicates is quite different from that pictured by him. According to his school, matter serves many purposes in that many things are formed out of any given mass of matter, while each pure predicate serves only one purpose, to give its properties to matter once and for all.[5] What we observe, however, is that any one table, for example, is composed once and for all out of one specific piece of matter, while the carpenter who gave the mass of matter (which became a table) its property of being a table—though, to be sure, he is only one man—can impart the features of a table over and over again to matter, and so make many tables. In fact, the relationship between predicates and objects is analogous to the relationship between males and females: one act of copulation impregnates one female, but the male can inseminate more than one female. These, then, are the *correct* analogies to draw with the primary entities in Plato's theory: pure predicates and undefined matter.

We have now completed our review of Plato's way of looking at the subject we are studying. If we bear in mind our own classification of the various elements that can enter into satisfactory explanations, it is clear that Plato uses only two of these elements: the fundamental defining characteristics of a thing, which make it just what it is; and that to which these characteristics are applied. When he is talking about the real world, *the pure predicates* are the factors that determine that each thing be just what it is and nothing else; when he is talking about the realm of pure predicates, *the one feature all predicates share in common*—the property each has of being *one* thing—determines that each predicate be just what it is and nothing else.[6] When he is talking about perceptible objects (whose characteristics are defined by the pure predicates), then the thing to which the predicates apply—namely, matter—is *twofold* in nature, since it can vary in spatial extension between *large* and *small* extent; and when he is talking about the realm of pure predicates (whose characteristic property is the one feature all predicates share of being unique), then the things to which the feature of being unique applies (that is, the predicates) are also *twofold* in nature, since they vary in the extent of their

2 Which is one of the basic features of pure predicates (see the next sentence).

3 Another basic feature of an explanation of the real world.

4 Another basic feature of pure predicates (see the next sentence).

5 That is, one predicate applies once and for all to all bodies which it modifies. In other words, just one abstract predicate will do to represent the common property shared by all objects in the set of objects to which the predicate applies; while any one mass of matter can be in more than one such set.

6 Hence the property of being one thing has the same relation to pure predicates as pure predicates have to matter.

range of application from predicates having *large* ranges to predicates having *small* ranges (which are less inclusive).[7]

. . .

IX

In attempting to explain the world around us they [the school which talks about pure predicates] introduced a set of entities equal in number to perceptible objects but completely different from them—as if a person who wanted to count a certain number of objects thought that he could not count them as long as there are only a few, but that he could if he added some more! In any case, in their theory there are at least as many pure predicates (about the same number) as there are real objects, although the people who introduced them meant to explain *real* objects by transcending the perceptible world and having recourse to the realm of pure predicates. In this theory, to each object in the real world there corresponds something else described by the same word; and beyond these new entities, which describe the fundamental properties of the real objects whose name they bear, there lies the one feature common to all predicates, transcending the diversity of the predicates, and representing a third basic element in this theory in addition to perceptible objects and to the unchanging predicates.

Now the proofs that pure predicates exist are not real proofs. Some of them contain faulty reasoning, and others end up with kinds of pure predicates no one believes to exist. For example, the following arguments fall into the first category: (1) The argument which starts from the assumption that we have a clear picture of the various particular things that exist. According to this argument, there corresponds a pure predicate to each particular thing we have a clear picture of. (2) The argument that there are certain objects that have in common one particular feature. According to this argument, *everything* that can be asserted of an object is a pure predicate. (3) The argument that starts from the fact that we can somehow conceive of an object after it has disappeared. According to this argument, there are pure predicates corresponding to objects which are subject to change since a picture of their earlier state always remains after they have changed.

Examples of arguments whose reasoning is better, but which end up with kinds of pure predicates no one believes to exist, are: (1) Arguments from which it can be concluded that there are pure predicates of relation. (No one holds that objects which enter into a given relation form a single class to which a separate predicate corresponds.) (2) Arguments of the "third man" type.

In general, we find that all the arguments used to prove the existence of pure predicates overthrow beliefs which the proponents of the theory consider even more fundamental than the belief in the existence of pure predicates!

[7] Hence predicates (the objects to which uniqueness applies) have the same basic twofold nature, variation in extent between large and small extremes, as has matter (the stuff to which predicates apply). Aristotle's point in these two sentences is that Plato uses only *two* of Aristotle's four classes of factors that go into an explanation, and he uses the *same two* when he speaks of the real world and when he speaks of the realm of pure predicates (relative to which the property of *being one and the same for all time* is in turn a "higher" pure predicate).

Such arguments, for example, show that the concept of number is more fundamental than the concept "two," and that a relation into which a thing enters is more fundamental than the thing itself [8]; and they lead to all the other basic contradictions that follow from this theory when it is taken to its logical conclusion.

According to the arguments brought for the existence of predicates as separate entities, there will be pure predicates corresponding to a variety of things and not only to particular objects. This is because it is possible to form an integrated conception of many other things besides particular objects, since we can form a clear picture not only of a particular object but also of many other things. (Here I am bringing only one of a thousand possible arguments against the theory.) However, it follows logically from their theory that the only pure predicates that can exist are those corresponding to particular objects, since for every pure predicate there must be some other thing that possesses the attributes of the predicate.

Furthermore, when they talk about an object sharing the attributes of a pure predicate, they do not include among the attributes that that object possesses attributes which are secondary or derivative—that is, among the attributes the object possesses, they do not include attributes that the pure predicate of the object possesses. For example, an object that shares the attributes of the pure predicate "having two parts" shares only in a *secondary* sense the attribute "unchanging," in so far as "unchanging" happens to be a property of the pure predicate "having two parts." [9] This means, then, that an object can only share the attributes of a pure predicate which represents the essential primary characteristics of the object.[10]

Now, the features that mark the essential primary characteristics of an *object in the world around us* are the same features that mark these characteristics *in the realm of pure predicates*. This is just what these people mean by the statement that there is something else corresponding to objects in the real world—that there is one entity having the same features that a number of such objects has. One of two possibilities must hold: (1) The features of pure predicates may in fact be *the same* as those of the objects which share the attributes of the pure predicates. If this is so, the argument they use leads directly to the conclusion that there exists *something else* in which both the object and its corresponding predicate share. For example, suppose we had an object having two parts in the real world of physical change, and a predicate (possessing the same features) corresponding to this object in the realm of unchanging pure predicates. The "twoness" of these, which is exactly the same in both, and is a feature both share in common, is also a feature of the pure predicate which represents the cardinal number "two," as well as of anything at all that has two parts. (2) The features of pure predicates may *not* be the same as those of the objects that share the attributes of the pure predicates. If this is so, a pure predicate and the object that shares its attributes just *happen* to be referred to by the same word. It is as if someone decided to call

[8] This is so since the relation between an object and the pure predicate which corresponds to it is more fundamental than the object itself.

[9] Thus, as might be expected, an object having two parts is *not* said to *possess* the attributes of the pure predicate "unchanging."

[10] And hence, again, the result is that the only pure predicates that can exist are those corresponding to particular objects.

a block of wood and a person named Callias "a man," though the two had no observable features in common! [11]

The main problem in this theory is the way the pure predicates are related to the things we perceive—either to the unchanging bodies we observe in the skies, or to the ever-changing objects we observe around us. The pure predicates are not, for example, the factors responsible for motion and change in perceptible bodies. Nor are they in the least useful for extending our knowledge to anything else beyond themselves. For according to the theory they are not even the inherent primary characteristics of perceptible objects; if they were, they would be *in* the objects in the perceptible world. Nor do they contribute in any way towards making objects what they are, since they are in no way a part of the objects that share their attributes. If they *were* among the ingredient parts of the objects that share their attributes, a case *might* perhaps be made that they somehow explain something about these objects, just as it might seem that the reason a white object is white is that white particles are among its ingredients. This view, however, first proposed by Anaxagoras and later held by Eudoxus and others, is also easily overthrown. For it is easy to show that many absurdities follow from such an opinion.

Furthermore, things cannot in any way be said to arise from pure predicates. It is not enough merely to say that pure predicates are models whose features other things share—statements like this do not mean anything, and are little more than poetical metaphors. What does the job? What actually patterns real objects after these models?

Again, a given object can be just like something, or come to be just like something, without being actually copied from it as from a model. Whether or not there is another Socrates around, Socrates can become just as he is; similarly Socrates could become just as he is without any help from the outside, even if there happened to be an unchanging immortal Socrates off somewhere!

Yet again, a single object can have more than one archetype, and thus can share the features of more than one pure predicate. For example, the predicates "animal" and "biped" both apply to man, as well as the predicate "man." [12]

Furthermore, the pure predicates represent the attributes not only of perceptible objects, but of other pure predicates as well. For example, since there can be a class of predicates, there can be a predicate representing the common property shared by the predicates in this class. Thus the predicates in such a class will be both archetypes [13] and objects [14] at the same time.[15]

Again, it hardly seems possible that the essential characteristics of an object can exist separate from the object they characterize. How then can pure predicates, which represent the essential characteristics of objects, exist separately?

In the *Phaedo* it says that pure predicates cause things to be what they are, or to change into something else. Now on the one hand they cannot cause

11 This argument reduces the theory to a triviality. Aristotle's point is that, since either (1) or (2) must hold, the theory must be wrong.

12 This is another difficulty in talking of objects patterned after predicates. How do you decide after which predicate a given object is patterned? If it is patterned after a large number, by what mechanism is a single object patterned after more than one predicate?

13 They will be archetypes of the perceptible objects which share their properties.

14 These objects are those to which the predicate representing the common property of the class applies.

15 Thus the distinction between predicates and objects, which was the whole point of the theory, falls away.

things to be what they are, because the pure predicates are there all the time, while objects get to share their attributes only when something comes along and starts things going.[16] On the other hand, pure predicates cannot cause things to change into something else, because objects that have the properties of a given predicate (such as "house" or "ring") change into other things no longer having the properties of that predicate; and in such cases too it is patent that there must be some other factor[17] (like the one we just referred to above) to cause them to change the way they do.[18]

Peter Coffey

Moderate Realism

SCHOLASTIC THEORY OF ABSTRACTION

In tracing the transition from sense to intellect, and the relations between the respective objects of sense and intellect, it is well to distinguish between facts and theory. The facts are revealed by introspection, and the most important among them are the following. By the operation of the external and internal senses, and by our consciousness of these cognitive activities, we are made aware of concrete, individual data or objects or phenomena,—things, events, sense feelings, sensible qualities, etc.—a conscious stream or manifold of impressions. Each of these we apprehend intellectually as an abstract thought-object, as an isolated aspect of the sense-manifold, and thus we gradually come into possession of a stock of abstract and universal concepts or thought-objects whereby we *interpret* the individual data of sense and acquire *knowledge* of what we believe to be the real universe or totality of things.

So much for the facts. Now inasmuch as these thought-objects are not innate, inasmuch as we identify them in judgment with the individual data of sense, it follows that the intellect must somehow apprehend them to the data of sense and as constituting the intelligible natures or essences of these latter. When, therefore, sense perceives its data in the concrete, intellect must simultaneously exercise a power of apprehending them in the abstract. So much at

[16] Therefore pure predicates cannot cause things to become what they are, because whenever a cause is present its effect must be felt; the predicates are present always, but the objects which feel their effects are not.

[17] Other than the pure predicates.

[18] Either way, then, the pure predicates are not the factors which cause things to be or become what they are.

From Peter Coffey, *Epistemology,* Vol. 1, Chap. 9, published by Longmans, Green & Co. Limited, London, 1917, and reprinted with their permission.

Peter Coffey (1876–1943) was Professor of Logic and Metaphysics at Maynooth College, Ireland.

least is clear,—whatever account we may be able to give of the actual operation of this faculty of abstraction. . . .

The schoolmen called this *abstractive faculty* of intellect the *Intellectus Agens*,—the νοῦς ποιητικός,—after Aristotle,—and endeavoured by an introspective analysis of the whole process of conception to trace the transition to the latter from the concrete individual percepts or imagination images of sense consciousness. . . . The theory itself is purely psychological and keeps close to all the facts revealed by introspection. Its main points are as follows:—

Intellect, like sense, is a passive faculty inasmuch as it is not always in act, not always consciously operating. It has therefore to be reduced from potentiality to actual operation by some appropriate motive force or stimulus. This actualization takes place simultaneously with the exercise of sense cognition. This latter results in the sense apprehension or sense awareness of some concrete individual sense *datum*. This *datum*, present to sense consciousness through the percept or *phantasma*, is, however, sensible, organic, material. Of itself it is incapable of determining the intellect to *its* appropriate operation; for the intellect is a spiritual faculty, belonging to a higher domain than that of sense, and its operation is therefore an effect which transcends the causal influence of anything in the domain of sense. There must be, therefore, in the intellect itself a power of determining itself, on the occasion of actual sense cognition, to its own appropriate mode of cognition. By virtue of this abstractive faculty, or *intellectus agens*, there is produced in the understanding or *intellectus possibilis*,—*i.e.* in the intellect considered in its state of potentiality,—an appropriate *cognitional determinant*, a *species intelligibilis impressa*, an immaterial or spiritual modification whereby the understanding conceives or apprehends immaterially and in the abstract,—through an appropriate intellectual act or process and its product or term, the *species intelligibilis expressa*, or *verbum mentale*,—that which was given in sense consciousness in its concrete, numerical, space-and-time individuality.

. . .

Thus, then, for the conscious intellectual conception of any thought-object there is required the co-operation of a twofold cause or principle: on the one hand the presence in sense consciousness of an individual, concrete sense *datum* or *phantasma*, and on the other hand the abstractive power, on the part of the intellect, so to modify or determine itself by the *species intelligibilis impressa* that it apprehends in this individual *datum*, by means of the product or term of conception (the *verbum mentale*), the abstract thought-object which expresses more or less inadequately the essence or intelligible reality of the individual sense *datum*. We assume here that the sense *datum* makes us directly aware of *reality*. And the mental product of conception, the *species intelligibilis expressa* or *verbum mentale* is the *medium* or *means* whereby we are made *intellectually* aware of the *thought*-object which is potentially in the sense datum, constituting the *reality* revealed to sense consciousness in this latter.

Intellectual cognition is an interpretation of reality by means of abstract thought-objects used as predicates in judgment. Reality is given through sense-data, and in these the intellect apprehends its abstract thought-objects. This does not imply that all intellectually knowable reality is merely material or sensible; for, as we pointed out above, intellect apprehends, in the sense-data, modes of reality that transcend sense, and can infer from sense-data the actuality or actual existence of positively suprasensible or spiritual modes of reality. But it does imply that the concepts or thought-objects by which our intellect apprehends such suprasensible realities, being abstracted from sense-data and being primarily and properly representative of such data, do not represent suprasensible realities intuitively, adequately, and positively, but only analogically and inadequately.

Furthermore, the mental product of the conception process, the *verbum mentale*, the entire *intellectual* modification whereby the intellect is cognitively assimilated to the reality, *is not itself the object of which the intellect becomes aware*—just as we shall see later that the *species sensibilis expressa* is not the object of which sense becomes aware. It is that which gives the reality an *esse ideale*, which constitutes the reality present to intellect.

What the intellect consciously apprehends, in and through the *verbum mentale,* is the object of the concept, the thought-object. If this thought-object be itself called the *verbum mentale*, this latter term is being used in its objective sense, synonymously with the objective sense of the term *concept.*

. . .

If the thought-objects apprehended by the intellect in and through its concepts, turn out to be real, to be aspects of reality, it would appear at first sight that, according to the theory of conception just outlined, reality is so directly revealed to the intellect as to preclude the possibility of error. But the possibility of error is really quite consistent with the direct and immediate revelation of abstract aspects of reality to intellect in conception. For it is only in judgments that error can occur. Now all judgments are either judgments of existence or judgments of essence: they either affirm or deny the actual existence or happening of some thought-object, or else affirm or deny the real and intrinsic possibility of some thought-object. Judgments of the former class can clearly be erroneous even though the apprehended thought-object be real, for though real it need not be actually existent. It is by series of judgments of the latter class that we form complex concepts, and here too the judgment may be erroneous; for the synthesis or complex judged to be intrinsically possible need not be really so, even though each of the simpler conceptual factors or thought-objects composing it may be itself possible. Only in regard to the most elementary, axiomatic syntheses is the intellect infallible. But furthermore, and finally, our conception of the simplest, unanalysable thought-objects, even although it is invariably accompanied by the implicit judgment that these objects are real, cannot be said to be itself, and apart from this judgment, true or false. Conception and concepts may have *real objectivity*, inasmuch as the conceived object is—as we hope to show presently—real; but it is only the interpretation of these concepts that sets up between the mind and reality the relation we call truth or error.

REALITY OF OBJECTS OF CONCEPTION: MODERATE REALISM EXPLAINED

The thought-object is, as we have seen, abstract. That is to say, it is devoid of all the time-and-space conditions and limitations which individuate the sense-object and make the latter a numerically singular or individual, concrete and incommunicable, datum of experience. That which is apprehended by sense in the individualizing conditions which we describe as "material" or "sensible" is apprehended by intellect in abstraction from these conditions,—in a state which, therefore, characterizes the object as "immaterial" (negatively) or "intelligible".

The *reason* of this is that the material reality, given in sense consciousness, must, in order to be apprehended by the intellect, be made present to the intellect, and must, as thus present to the intellect, be conformed to the *immaterial* or *spiritual* mode of being of the intellect: according to the principle that whatever is thus in, or present to, a knowing subject must assume the mode of being of this latter, cognition being a sort of mental reproduction, in the knowing subject, of the known object.

The *consequences* of this abstract character of the thought-object are very important. The first of them is that, when it is regarded in itself and as to its positive content, it is *neither singular nor universal,* it is apprehended neither as *numerically one, individualized, incommunicable* (as it is grasped by sense), nor on the other hand as conceptually one but *common to many, predicable of many* (as it is grasped by a subsequent reflective act of the intellect formally universalizing it). A realization of this fact is of the first importance towards a right solution of the "Universals" problem.

. . .

No doubt, being a definite object of thought, and having a definite content or meaning whereby it can be consciously distinguished from other abstract thought-objects, it may be said to have a conceptual or formal unity; but in its abstract, absolute condition, and as yet not consciously related by the intellect to the individual object or objects of sense, from which it was abstracted, or made an object of reflex intellectual contemplation, it can be truly said to be neither singular nor universal.

Now the thought-object, considered in this abstract condition as object of direct intellectual conception, has been called by scholastics the *direct,* or *metaphysical,* or *fundamental,* or *potential* "universal". And when they say that "universals" are "fundamentally" in things or reality,—"*Universale est . . . fundamentaliter in re,*"—they mean that it is this abstract thought-object which, as to its content, is *real,* or *in things independently of our thought.*

The next important consequence of this abstract character of the object of conception is that, precisely because it is apprehended by intellect in the abstract, it is seen, by comparison with the corresponding individual sense-object (percept or imagination phantasm) which is simultaneously present in consciousness, to be not only in this latter object, and identical with it, and predicable of it, but *to be capable of indefinitely repeated realizations* in an indefinite multitude of other and similar sense-objects. By this act of intellectual reflection the object is apprehended to be potentially or actually "*common to many*," "predicable of many"; in other words it is *formally universalized*. When thus apprehended as susceptible of indefinite multiplication or realization in the domain of sense, the thought-object is called a *reflex*, or *logical*, or *formal* universal. And when scholastics say that "universals" are "formally" in the mind,—"*Universale est formaliter in mente*,"—they mean that the object of thought or conception considered *as a universal,—i.e.* as something common or communicable to, and realizable in, and predicable of, many things,—is only in the mind, and is, as such, not independent of thought. In other words, it is *because* the object is a *thought*-object, *or* in virtue of its being present to intellect, *or by reason of the esse ideale* or mode in which it is present to, and apprehended by intellect, *or* on account of the *immateriality* of the presence it has in the intellect, and not otherwise, *that it is a universal.* As it really exists in any individual *datum* of sense, as it is apprehended through the percept or phantasm, it is individualized, singular, incommunicable; only as it is apprehended in the abstract by the intellect, and in that "immaterial" or "intelligible" condition seen by a reflex act of thought to be susceptible of indefinitely manifold realizations, is it "common to many things," or "formally universal". . . .

What we may call the content or connotation of the concept is real, is in extramental reality; but it is not real in the manner in which it is conceived, *i.e.* as a universal; for as a universal it cannot be extramental, it can only be a *thought*-object. "Universals considered formally as universals are only in the mind. But the natures themselves, which are thus universalized by the thought process, are extramentally real." [St. Thomas]

The content or object of the concept is itself extramentally real—in the individual realities apprehended through sense. The universality which characterizes it as a thought-object is, however, no part or mode of its extramental reality, but is only a mode of its apprehension by intellect, a mental mode, a logical entity whose sole objectivity is that which it has for reflex thought. "The nature itself which is apprehended by intellect, which is abstracted and universalized, has its real being in the individual things [of sense]. But its actual presence to and apprehension by intellect, its abstractness and universality, are in the intellect. . . . The humanity which is apprehended as an object of thought by intellect is to be found really only in this or that individual man; but the apprehension of humanity without its individualizing conditions, its being subjected to abstraction and universalization,—all this belongs to humanity only inasmuch as it is perceived by intellect." [St. Thomas]

On the one hand, then, as against Conceptualism, we attain, through conception, to an object which is real; on the other hand, however, as against Extreme Realism, this object is not real *as a universal*, as something formally "common to many". "Humanity is something *in the real order*, but in the real order it is not *a universal*, inasmuch as outside the mind (or, in other words, independently of thought) there is no such thing as *a humanity* '*common to many*'; it is on becoming present to intellect, as a thought-object, that it receives, through the conception process, a mode or 'intention' whereby it is constituted a universal, or class-concept." [St. Thomas]

A clear apprehension of the fact that the abstract *thought-object* considered in the absolute, as a "fundamental" or "metaphysical" universal, is as such not yet judged to be "one-common-to-many" or "formally universal," or on the other hand to be "numerically manifold" in distinct individuals,—is absolutely essential to a right solution of the "universals" problem; for it is the universal considered thus in the absolute that forms the rational connecting link between the "formal universal" of intellect and the "individuals" of sense, and thus solves the apparent antinomy which emerges from a comparison of intellectual cognition with sense cognition.

. . .

Now when we predicate the universal of the singular, in judgment, it is the absolute content of the universal concept and not its universal mode, or, in other words, the metaphysical universal and not the formal universal, that we so predicate. And we are justified in doing so.

On the one hand, the content of the universal concept—*i.e.* the fundamental or metaphysical universal, the universale *in se*—is not *other* than its individual realizations in the manifold singular subjects of which it is predicated. The absolute nature or object signified by "man" is really in this, that, and the other individual man, in John and James and Thomas, etc. It is really in them, but, of course, with this difference in each, that it has in each *individualizing characteristics* which are not included in it as it is when considered *in itself*, in its abstract condition as an object of thought, apart from the singulars of which it is predicated. In any individual man there are individualizing notes that are not in the abstract thought-object "man"; but there is nothing in the latter that is not in the former. The content of the abstract concept gives, therefore, an insight into the individual, which is *inadequate*, no doubt, but *faithful* as far as it goes. If it be a transcendental or generic concept of the individual it gives a comparatively shallow and superficial insight into the reality of the latter; and even if it be a *specific* concept, a concept of the *species infirma* of the individual, it is still inadequate inasmuch as it abstracts from what makes up the individuality or *essentia atoma* of the individual. But, so far as it goes, the content of the abstract concept, the metaphysical universal, reveals *what is really in* the individuals of sense. But the formally universal concept has precisely the same content as the abstract concept, *viz.* the thought-object considered *quoad rem*, fundamentally, absolutely, or in itself. The universal concept is, therefore, *objectively real.*

On the other hand, the *formal universality* of this abstract thought-object adds *nothing real* to its content, but only a logical relation, an *intentio logica* or *ens rationis;* for what transforms the abstract thought-object or metaphysical universal into a formal universal is the relation of universality, or "communicability to many," or identity *quoad rem* with its manifold individual realizations,—a logical relation which the intellect superadds to it by a reflective act comparing it as it is in itself with its actual and possible concrete individual embodiments. Therefore this act of reflective comparison whereby the thought-object is made formally universal does not in any way transform or metamorphose or falsify its *objective reality*. And finally we do not, in judgment, predicate this *formal universality*, this *intentio universalitatis*, this mental or logical mode of the concept, of the individual, or attribute it to the individual; it is only the content of the formal universal, *i.e.* only the fundamental or metaphysical universal, that we identify with the individual in judgment: and thus we avoid the antinomy or contradiction of asserting the same thing to be both singular and universal.

. . .

There are therefore "universal" *thought*-objects, but there are no "universal" realities. Whatever is real, whatever actually exists or can exist is individual. When we think of "universality" we are thinking of an object which is an *ens rationis*, a purely logical relation, which has no objectivity other than what it has in and for thought: our concept of "universality" is a *secunda intentio mentis*, a reflex or logically universal concept. When, on the other hand, we think of "singularity," "individuality," "particularity," we are thinking of an object which is real: our concept is a *prima intentio mentis*, a direct universal concept,—like that of "whiteness," or "virtue," or "humanity," for instance,—because "particularity" is a real characteristic of real things: individuals are real. Take any class of the individuals revealed through sense perception,—men, for instance. The *human nature* of each individual is a distinct reality, really distinct and separate from the human nature of every other human individual. But these really and numerically distinct *human natures* are apprehended by intellect in the process of conception *without the features that differentiate them* in each; and therefore that which constitutes each of the individuated natures appears first to intellect *as to what it is essentially* (the fundamental or metaphysical universal), and in the abstract as a definite conceptual object, and then, by reflection on it in comparison with the individuals, as universal, or "one-common-to-all-of-them".

Why are manifold individuals classified under a common or universal concept? Because they are really identical, or constitute one reality? No; for they are not really one; but because they are *similar*. Why are they similar? What constitutes or makes them similar? What is "similarity"? Is similarity partial *real* identity? No; similarity is a partial *conceptual* or *logical* identity: each individual of the manifold is so constituted that some factor of each, isolated by the abstractive power of the intellect from the other factors, appears to intellect as one definite self-identical object, and is apprehended as universal or as "one-common-to-all". The concept of "similarity," like that of "particularity," is a concept of something real: it has for its object a *real* relation grounded on the real natures of the individual things.

David Hume

Of Abstract Ideas

OF ABSTRACT IDEAS

A very material question has been started concerning *abstract* or *general* ideas, *whether they be general or particular in the mind's conception of them.* A [1] great philosopher has disputed the receiv'd opinion in this particular, and has asserted, that all general ideas are nothing but particular ones, annexed to a certain term, which gives them a more extensive signification, and makes them recall upon occasion other individuals, which are similar to them. As I look upon this to be one of the greatest and most valuable discoveries that has been made of late years in the republic of letters, I shall here endeavour to confirm it by some arguments, which I hope will put it beyond all doubt and controversy.

'Tis evident, that in forming most of our general ideas, if not all of them, we abstract from every particular degree of quantity and quality, and that an object ceases not to be of any particular species on account of every small alteration in its extension, duration and other properties. It may therefore be thought, that here is a plain dilemma, that decides concerning the nature of those abstract ideas, which have afforded so much speculation to philosophers. The abstract idea of a man represents men of all sizes and all qualities; which 'tis concluded it cannot do, but either by representing at once all possible sizes and all possible qualities, or by representing no particular one at all. Now it having been esteemed absurd to defend the former proposition, as implying an infinite capacity in the mind, it has been commonly infer'd in favour of the latter; and our abstract ideas have been suppos'd to represent no particular degree either of quantity or quality. But that this inference is erroneous, I shall endeavour to make appear, *first*, by proving, that 'tis utterly impossible to conceive any quantity or quality, without forming a precise notion of its degrees: And *secondly* by showing, that tho' the capacity of the mind be not infinite, yet we can at once form a notion of all possible degrees of quantity and quality, in such a manner at least, as, however imperfect, may serve all the purposes of reflexion and conversation.

To begin with the first proposition, *that the mind cannot form any notion of quantity or quality without forming a precise notion of degrees of each*; we may prove this by the three following arguments. First, We have observ'd, that whatever objects are different are distinguishable, and that whatever objects

[1] Dr. *Berkeley.*

From David Hume, *A Treatise of Human Nature,* Book I, Part I, Section 7, first published in 1739.

are distinguishable are separable by the thought and imagination. And we may here add, that these propositions are equally true in the *inverse,* and that whatever objects are separable are also distinguishable, and that whatever objects are distinguishable are also different. For how is it possible we can separate what is not distinguishable, or distinguish what is not different? In order therefore to know, whether abstraction implies a separation, we need only consider it in this view, and examine, whether all the circumstances, which we abstract from in our general ideas, be such as are distinguishable and different from those, which we retain as essential parts of them. But 'tis evident at first sight, that the precise length of a line is not different nor distinguishable from the line itself; nor the precise degree of any quality from the quality. These ideas, therefore, admit no more of separation than they do of distinction and difference. They are consequently conjoined with each other in the conception; and the general idea of a line, notwithstanding all our abstractions and refinements, has in its appearance in the mind a precise degree of quantity and quality; however it may be made to represent others, which have different degrees of both.

Secondly, 'tis confest, that no object can appear to the senses; or in other words, that no impression can become present to the mind, without being determin'd in its degrees both of quantity and quality. The confusion, in which impressions are sometimes involv'd, proceeds only from their faintness and unsteadiness, not from any capacity in the mind to receive any impression, which in its real existence has no particular degree nor proportion. That is a contradiction in terms; and even implies the flattest of all contradictions, *viz.* that 'tis possible for the same thing both to be and not to be.

Now since all ideas are deriv'd from impressions, and are nothing but copies and representations of them, whatever is true of the one must be acknowledg'd concerning the other. Impressions and ideas differ only in their strength and vivacity. The foregoing conclusion is not founded on any particular degree of vivacity. It cannot therefore be affected by any variation in that particular. An idea is a weaker impression; and as a strong impression must necessarily have a determinate quantity and quality, the case must be the same with its copy or representative.

Thirdly, 'tis a principle generally receiv'd in philosophy, that every thing in nature is individual, and that 'tis utterly absurd to suppose a triangle really existent, which has no precise proportion of sides and angles. If this therefore be absurd in *fact and reality*, it must also be absurd *in idea*; since nothing of which we can form a clear and distinct idea is absurd and impossible. But to form the idea of an object, and to form an idea simply is the same thing; the reference of the idea to an object being an extraneous denomination, of which in itself it bears no mark or character. Now as 'tis impossible to form an idea of an object, that is possest of quantity and quality, and yet is possest of no precise degree of either; it follows, that there is an equal impossibility of forming an idea, that is not limited and confin'd in both these particulars. Abstract ideas are therefore in themselves individual, however they may become general in their representation. The image in the mind is only that of a particular object, tho' the application of it in our reasoning be the same, as if it were universal.

This application of ideas beyond their nature proceeds from our collecting all their possible degrees of quantity and quality in such an imperfect manner as may serve the purposes of life, which is the second proposition I propos'd to explain. When we have found a resemblance among several objects, that often occur to us, we apply the same name to all of them, whatever differences we may observe in the degrees of their quantity and quality, and whatever other differences may appear among them. After we have acquired a custom of this kind, the hearing of that name revives the idea of one of these objects, and makes the imagination conceive it with all its particular circumstances and proportions. But as the same word is suppos'd to have been frequently applied to other individuals, that are different in many respects from that idea, which is immediately present to the mind; the word not being able to revive the idea of all these individuals, only touches the soul, if I may be allow'd so to speak, and revives that custom, which we have acquir'd by surveying them. They are not really and in fact present to the mind, but only in power; nor do we draw them all out distinctly in the imagination, but keep ourselves in a readiness to survey any of them, as we may be prompted by a present design or necessity. The word raises up an individual idea, along with a certain custom; and that custom produces any other individual one, for which we may have occasion. But as the production of all the ideas, to which the name may be apply'd, is in most cases impossible, we abridge that work by a more partial consideration, and find but few inconveniences to arise in our reasoning from that abridgment.

For this is one of the most extraordinary circumstances in the present affair, that after the mind has produc'd an individual idea, upon which we reason, the attendant custom, reviv'd by the general or abstract term, readily suggests any other individual, if by chance we form any reasoning, that agrees not with it. Thus shou'd we mention the word, triangle, and form the idea of a particular equilateral one to correspond to it, and shou'd we afterwards assert, *that the three angles of a triangle are equal to each other*, the other individuals of a scalenum and isoceles, which we overlook'd at first, immediately crowd in upon us, and make us perceive the falshood of this proposition, tho' it be true with relation to that idea, which we had form'd. If the mind suggests not always these ideas upon occasion, it proceeds from some imperfection in its faculties; and such a one as is often the source of false reasoning and sophistry. But this is principally the case with those ideas which are abstruse and compounded. On other occasions the custom is more entire, and 'tis seldom we run into such errors.

Nay so entire is the custom, that the very same idea may be annext to several different words, and may be employ'd in different reasonings, without any danger of mistake. Thus the idea of an equilateral triangle of an inch perpendicular may serve us in talking of a figure, of a rectilineal figure, of a regular figure, of a triangle, and of an equilateral triangle. All these terms, therefore, are in this case attended with the same idea; but as they are wont to be apply'd in a greater or lesser compass, they excite their particular habits, and thereby keep the mind in a readiness to observe, that no conclusion be form'd contrary to any ideas, which are usually compriz'd under them.

Before those habits have become entirely perfect, perhaps the mind may not be content with forming the idea of only one individual, but may run over several, in order to make itself comprehend its own meaning, and the compass of that collection, which it intends to express by the general term. That we may fix the meaning of the word, figure, we may revolve in our mind the ideas of circles, squares, parallelograms, triangles of different sizes and proportions, and may not rest on one image or idea. However this may be, 'tis certain *that* we form the idea of individuals, whenever we use any general term; *that* we seldom or never can exhaust these individuals; and *that* those, which remain, are only represented by means of that habit, by which we recall them, whenever any present occasion requires it. This then is the nature of our abstract ideas and general terms; and 'tis after this manner we account for the foregoing paradox, *that some ideas are particular in their nature, but general in their representation.* A particular idea becomes general by being annex'd to a general term; that is, to a term, which from a customary conjunction has a relation to many other particular ideas, and readily recalls them in the imagination.

The only difficulty, that can remain on this subject, must be with regard to that custom, which so readily recalls every particular idea, for which we may have occasion, and is excited by any word or sound, to which we commonly annex it. The most proper method, in my opinion, of giving a satisfactory explication of this act of the mind, is by producing other instances, which are analogous to it, and other principles, which facilitate its operation. To explain the ultimate causes of our mental actions is impossible. 'Tis sufficient, if we can give any satisfactory account of them from experience and analogy.

First then I observe, that when we mention any great number, such as a thousand, the mind has generally no adequate idea of it, but only a power of producing such an idea, by its adequate idea of the decimals, under which the number is comprehended. This imperfection, however in our ideas, is never felt in our reasonings; which seems to be an instance parallel to the present one of universal ideas.

Secondly, we have several instances of habits, which may be reviv'd by one single word; as when a person, who has by rote any periods of a discourse, or any number of verses, will be put in remembrance of the whole, which he is at a loss to recollect, by that single word or expression, with which they begin.

Thirdly, I believe every one, who examines the situation of his mind in reasoning, will agree with me, that we do not annex distinct and compleat ideas to every term we make use of, and that in talking of *government*, *church*, *negotiation*, *conquest*, we seldom spread out in our minds all the simple ideas, of which these complex ones are compos'd. 'Tis however observable, that notwithstanding this imperfection we may avoid talking nonsense on these subjects, and may perceive any repugnance among the ideas, as well as if we had a full comprehension of them. Thus if instead of saying, *that in war the weaker have always recourse to negotiation*, we shou'd say, *that they have always recourse to conquest*, the custom, which we have acquir'd of attributing certain relations to ideas, still follows the words, and makes us immediately perceive the absurdity of that proposition; in the same manner as one particular idea may serve us in reasoning concerning other ideas, however different from it in several circumstances.

Fourthly, As the individuals are collected together, and plac'd under a general term with a view to that resemblance, which they bear to each other, this relation must facilitate their entrance in the imagination, and make them be suggested more readily upon occasion. And indeed if we consider the common progress of the thought, either in reflexion or conversation, we shall find great reason to be satisfy'd in this particular. Nothing is more admirable, than the readiness, with which the imagination suggests its ideas, and presents them at the very instant, in which they become necessary or useful. The fancy runs from one end of the universe to the other in collecting those ideas, which belong to any subject. One would think the whole intellectual world of ideas was at once subjected to our view, and that we did nothing but pick out such as were most proper for our purpose. There may not, however, be any present, beside those very ideas, that are thus collected by a kind of magical faculty in the soul, which, tho' it be always most perfect in the greatest geniuses, and is properly what we call a genius, is however inexplicable by the utmost efforts of human understanding.

Perhaps these four reflexions may help to remove all difficulties to the hypothesis I have propos'd concerning abstract ideas, so contrary to that, which has hitherto prevail'd in philosophy. But to tell the truth I place my chief confidence in what I have already prov'd concerning the impossibility of general ideas, according to the common method of explaining them. We must certainly seek some new system on this head, and there plainly is none beside what I have propos'd. If ideas be particular in their nature, and at the same time finite in their number, 'tis only by custom they can become general in their representation, and contain an infinite number of other ideas under them.

Before I leave this subject I shall employ the same principles to explain that *distinction of reason*, which is so much talk'd of, and is so little understood, in the schools. Of this kind is the distinction betwixt figure and the body figur'd; motion and the body mov'd. The difficulty of explaining this distinction arises from the principle above explain'd, *that all ideas, which are different, are separable.* For it follows from thence, that if the figure be different from the body, their ideas must be separable as well as distinguishable; if they be not different, their ideas can neither be separable nor distinguishable. What then is meant by a distinction of reason, since it implies neither a difference nor separation?

To remove this difficulty we must have recourse to the foregoing explication of abstract ideas. 'Tis certain that the mind wou'd never have dream'd of distinguishing a figure from the body figur'd, as being in reality neither distinguishable, nor different, nor separable; did it not observe, that even in this simplicity there might be contain'd many different resemblances and relations. Thus when a globe of white marble is presented, we receive only the impression of a white colour dispos'd in a certain form, nor are we able to separate and distinguish the colour from the form. But observing afterwards a globe of black marble and a cube of white, and comparing them with our former object, we find two separate resemblances, in what formerly seem'd, and really is, perfectly inseparable. After a little more practice of this kind, we begin to distinguish the figure from the colour by a *distinction of reason*; that is, we consider the figure and colour together, since they are in effect the same and undistinguishable; but still view them in different aspects, according to the resemblances, of which they are susceptible. When we wou'd consider only the figure of the globe of white marble, we form in reality an idea both of the figure and colour, but tacitly carry our eye to its resemblance with the globe of black marble: And in the same manner, when we wou'd consider its colour only, we turn our view to its resemblance with the cube of white marble. By this means we accompany our ideas with a kind of reflexion, of which custom renders us, in a great measure, insensible. A person, who desires us to consider the figure of a globe of white marble without thinking on its colour, desires an impossibility; but his meaning is, that we shou'd consider the colour and figure together, but still keep in our eye the resemblance to the globe of black marble, or that to any other globe of whatever colour or substance.

David F. Pears

Universals

'Do universals exist?' This question was debated so long and vehemently because it was mistaken for a factual question about some airy realm of being. But why was this mistake made? One diagnosis is that general words were tacitly assimilated to proper names,[1] and that, when this practice is exposed, it becomes harmless but pointless.[2] But this is a description of what happened rather than an explanation; it gives something more like a symptom than a cause. Could so many philosophers have been so silly in such a simple way? Even moderate scepticism on this point would lead to an attempt to supplement this suggestion. This article is such an attempt.

'Universals exist' has a deceptive logic. Realists offer it as the conclusion of many arguments: but unlike the premisses of these arguments, it cannot be understood as a verifiable statement of fact. On the other hand, if it is taken merely as an esoteric way of stating those premisses over again, the vehemence of the controversy becomes inexplicable. Faced with this difficulty of interpretation, some modern philosophers suggest that it is no good puzzling about its literal meaning, just as it is no good puzzling about the literal meaning of dreams. For traditional philosophy provided a small set of possible conclusions to arguments about the generality of thought and language, and tradition was strong. If a tribe educated its children to dream according to a tradition which restricted their manifest dream contents within narrow limits, it would be difficult to discover their much more varied latent dream contents.[3]

[1] Cf. J. S. Mill, *Examination of Sir William Hamilton's Philosophy* (5th edn., London, 1878) chap. xvii, p. 381, and Berkeley, *Principles of Human Knowledge,* Introduction § 18.
[2] Cf. M. Lazerowitz, 'The Existence of Universals' (*Mind,* 1946, pp. 1ff.).
[3] Cf. Freud, *The Interpretation of Dreams,* tr. A. A. Brill (London, 1913), p. 166.

From D. F. Pears, "Universals," in A. G. N. Flew (ed.), *Logic and Language,* second series, Blackwell, Oxford, 1953. Reprinted with permission.
D. F. Pears (1921–) is Fellow of Corpus Christi College, Oxford.

Similarly, although realists are argumentative, it is difficult to answer the question why they maintain that universals exist. Any answer must be based on a selection from among the many reasons which they themselves proffer: and a good selection will be diagnostic; it will successfully explain the doctrine. There is no sharp boundary here between descriptions of the premisses of philosophical arguments and diagnoses of their conclusions: because success in explaining, which is the criterion of a diagnosis, is a matter of degree, and because the reasons which philosophers themselves give for their doctrines sometimes completely explain why they held them. Quine's remark, that realists find a universal for every property which can be existentially generalized,[4] is an extremely brief description. The thesis of Berkeley and Mill was more than this: it was a diagnosis, but an inadequate one. I shall try to provide a less inadequate diagnosis.

'Because universals exist' is the answer to at least two general questions: 'Why are things what they are'? [5] and 'Why are we able to name things as we do'? Though Plato and Aristotle sometimes distinguished these two questions, it was characteristic of Greek thought to confuse them. Yet they can be clearly distinguished, the first requiring a dynamic answer from scientists, and the second a static answer from logicians. Now philosophy has often staked premature claims in the territory of science by giving quick comprehensive answers to questions which really required laborious detailed answers. And clearly this is what happened to the first of the two questions. When detailed causal answers were provided to it, the comprehensive answer 'Because universals exist' was no longer acceptable or necessary.[6] But what would detailed answers to the second question be like? Presumably they would be explanations of the meanings of words. But philosophers are easily led to neglect such detailed progressive answers to the second question, and to seek instead a comprehensive and ultimate explanation of naming. For, though comprehensive answers to the first question are clearly futile, there are no obvious penalties attached to answering the second question in a comprehensive way. Yet, I shall argue—and this will be my first thesis—that any comprehensive explanation of naming is necessarily circular: and that philosophers think that, in spite of this disadvantage, such explanations have some point largely because they wrongly assimilate naming to natural processes. Yet surely naming cannot be utterly artificial? My second thesis will be that the desire to understand naming leads to a hunt for a completely satisfactory analogy: but that all other processes either already contain the very feature of naming which was puzzling, or else are too natural or too artificial to be really analogous; and that it was the inevitable oscillation between these three points which prolonged the controversy about universals.

It is unnecessary to produce evidence that philosophers who proposed the existence of universals thought that they were explaining the unity of classes and hence the possibility of naming. What is debatable is whether this was an important motive, and this can be decided only in the sequel. My first thesis,

[4] Cf. 'Designation and Existence' in Feigl and Sellars, *Readings in Philosophical Analysis* (New York, 1949), p. 48.

[5] Aristotle criticized Plato's theory largely as an inadequate answer to this question.

[6] Socrates in the *Phaedo* (100d) says that it is the only acceptable answer to the first question. But the advance of science has undermined this thesis more thoroughly than the advance of logic has undermined the thesis that it is an acceptable answer to the second question.

which I must now try to establish, is that realism is necessarily a circular explanation of naming. Now the answer to the question 'Why are we able to name things as we do?' is 'The reason varies'. For it is always possible with more or less ingenuity, depending on the degree of atomicity of the name, to give a detailed informative reason; and this reason will vary with the name. But ultimately there must be some exit from the maze of words, and, wherever this exit is made, it will be impossible to give an informative reason except by pointing. For the only other way of giving an informative reason is to give a new word, and this would prevent the exit from the maze of words from being made at this place.[7] Still at the place where the exit is made it is always possible to give a detailed reason like 'We are able to call things red because they are red', which is too obviously circular even to look informative. Or alternatively it is possible to say 'We are able to call things φ because they are φ', and this is a general reason which is almost as obviously circular and uninformative. What philosophers who propose the existence of universals do is to propose a general reason which looks informative because it shifts to another level, but unfortunately is not. It merely marks time: but marking time can look very like marching if only the movements of the performers are watched, and not the ground which they profess to be covering. Yet this ground could not be covered. For the reason could not be informative even if it were detailed; since there could be a non-circular answer to the question 'What universal?' only if the exit from the maze of words were made at some different point, which would merely put off the moment of embarrassment from which in the end neither speech nor thought can be saved. Thus realism fails to escape the limitations of all explanations of naming; that they can be informative only if they are not general but detailed, and then only if they are not given at the point where an exit is made from the maze of words.

Uninformative answers have their point. They are silencing. What is wrong with realism is not this, but that it masquerades as an answer which advances knowledge one step further. The analytic machine acquires a momentum which carries it beyond the point where it ought to stop. And there is an inveterate philosophical habit which strengthens the tendency to go beyond this point, or rather to think that one has gone beyond it. 'A thing is called by a certain name because it instantiates a certain universal' is obviously circular when particularized, but it looks imposing when it is left in this general form. And it looks imposing in this general form largely because of the inveterate philosophical habit of treating the shadows cast by words and sentences as if they were separately identifiable. Universals, like facts and propositions, are such shadows; and too often philosophers by appealing to them in general terms have produced in their readers a feeling of satisfaction which ought to have been produced only by specifying them.[8] But universals are specifiable

[7] Cf. the view sketched by Socrates in the *Theaetetus* 201e–202c, and Antisthenes' view given by Aristotle in *Met.* H, 1043 b 23–32; also L. Wittgenstein, *Tractatus* 5; M. Schlick, *Grundzüge der Naturphilosophie* (Vienna, 1948), p. 21; and A. J. Ayer, *Thinking and Meaning* (London, 1947), p. 28.

[8] The same trick is played by those who say that laws of nature exhibit connections between universals. This gives the impression that we could independently know the eternal framework in which temporal things move and change, rather as we independently know how a piston must move by looking at a cylinder: cf. what Köhler says about Aristotle's astronomy and Descartes' neurology (*Gestalt Psychology*, London, 1930, pp. 82–6).

only by reference to words. Similarly facts may be brute and propositions may be definite, but what exactly it is about them which is brute or definite can be be specified only by reference to the sentences which were the unacknowledged starting-points. In all these cases it is tacit re-duplication which makes philosophers think that they can enjoy the benefits of specifying without actually specifying. Yet the explanation of naming is incomplete until a particular universal is specified, and, when it is specified, the explanation immediately fails through circularity. Naming is hazardous,[9] and any attempt to make it foolproof by basing it on an independent foundation must fail in this way. It is impossible to cross the gap between language and things without really crossing it.[10]

Since the failure of realism to perform this feat is inevitable, its rivals fail too. Nominalism, conceptualism and imagism,[11] in so far as they are rivals of realism, are attempts to provide a unity which will explain naming. Nominalism says that a name is merely connected with a multitude of things, sometimes adding that these things are similar. Conceptualism says that the name is not directly connected with the things but only via a concept, thus changing the nodal point. Imagism says that the nodal point is an image. And realism says that there is really no nodal point, since a name, though it appears to be connected with a multitude of things is all the time connected with only one thing, a universal. This is an over-simplification of what these theories say about the One and the Many; but it is enough for my next purpose, which is to show that these rivals of realism cannot produce a non-circular explanation of naming at those points where an exit is made from the maze of words.

The two psychological theories say that one word can apply to many things only because of the mediation of a concept or of an image. Locke's abstract general idea is 'the workmanship of the understanding, but has its foundation in the similitudes of things'.[12] And Berkeley replaces it by an idea which 'considered in itself is particular but becomes general by being made to represent or stand for all other particular ideas of the same sort'.[13] But what similitudes, and what representation? In the end both Locke's concept and Berkeley's image are completely identifiable only by their use.[14] Of course we can partly identify images by describing their features: and in this way we may even almost completely identify them, since certain images most naturally stand for certain things. And the same could be said of concepts, if they were not merely philosophers' reifications of mental processes. But this will not completely identify either of them, since thought may not follow the most natural course; nor is it always clear which is the most natural course. It is not so much that thinking is speaking as that thinking is like speaking in the only way that matters: it uses one thing as a symbol to stand for many things. And the only tool which could not be used differently is the use. Even

9 Cf. Bradley, *Appearance and Reality,* p. 22 and p. 533; and C. S. Peirce, *Collected Papers* (vol. I, para. 145): 'Direct experience is neither certain nor uncertain, because it affirms nothing—it just is.'

10 Cf. Stuart Hampshire, 'Scepticism and Meaning' (*Philosophy,* July 1950, p. 245).

11 Cf. H. H. Price, *Thinking and Representation* (British Academy Lecture, 1946).

12 Locke, *Essay concerning Human Understanding,* Bk. III, chap. III, § xiii.

13 Berkeley, *Principles of Human Knowledge,* Introduction, § 12.

14 This is due to Wittgenstein: cf. e.g. *Tractatus,* 3.326, 'In order to recognize the symbol in the sign we must consider the significant use'.

something which had its use written on it could be used differently.[15] And, if the psychological tool, whether concept or image, can be completely identified only by the things on which it is used, it cannot explain naming without circularity. For, unless we point, the use can be specified only by backward reference to the name. Nor is this circularity surprising. For psychological tools have no advantage over words: they are like them in being symbols, and unlike them only in being shadowy symbols.

The type of nominalism which says that a name is applied to a number of things which are similar immediately falls into the same circularity. For 'similar' is an incomplete predicate, anything being similar to anything in some way, perhaps a negative way.[16] And in the end the kind of similarity which is meant can be specified only by a backward reference to the name. Equally the type of nominalism which merely says that a name is applied to a class of things cannot say which class without a backward reference to the name. Here the circularity is so obvious and there is so little to cushion the shock of the realization that naming is naming that this type of nominalism seems hardly tenable. For, however strongly nominalists react against realism, they can never quite escape its influence: once somebody had said that universals exist it could never be quite the same again. Surely, one wants to protest, there must be some way of giving the class besides reference to the name? Well there is, of course, enumeration. But this answer seems to fail to allow for the possibility of ever using the name correctly in any synthetic sentence. For, if the class is given by enumeration, surely every use of the name must be either incorrect or analytic? Since, if to call a thing 'φ' is to include it in the class of things called 'φ', then surely either it is incorrect to call it 'φ' or else the class cannot be given without reference to it? It is the example of realism which encourages these protests. But it is a bad example. Such neatness is not to be had. For, first of all, these classes cannot be given by enumeration of all their members, since, except for words belonging to dead languages, they are never complete. Nor is it true even that each member must either contribute or not contribute towards giving a class; since a name may be applied to the same thing twice, once analytically and once synthetically, and even a single use of a name may be synthetic for the speaker and analytic

[15] W. T. Stace in 'Russell's Neutral Monism' in *The Philosophy of Bertrand Russell*, pp. 381–3, complains that neither Berkeley's precise image nor Russell's vague image (in *An Inquiry into Meaning and Truth*) succeeds in explaining the generality of thought. But no description of any item of mental furniture which included only its momentary properties and not its habitual use could possibly explain the generality of thought.

[16] Hence the point of many riddles. Cf. Stuart Hampshire, 'Scepticism and Meaning' (*Philosophy*, July 1950, p. 238). Also Plato, *Protagoras* 331 d. The Platonic theory avoids the 'similarity' difficulty, but not of course the general difficulty of which this is only one form. Speusippus, who abandoned the Platonic theory, seems to have held that, since every species is like every other species in some way, it is impossible to define one species without defining every other species. Cf. Aristotle, *Post. An.* 97 a 6–11. Cf. H. Cherniss, *Aristotle's criticism of Plato and the Academy* (I. 60), quoted by W. D. Ross in his note on this passage. J. Stenzel, in Pauly-Wissowa Real-Encyclopädie, *s.v.* Speusippus, pp. 1650 and 1655, brings out the affinity between Speusippus' view and Post-Kantian Idealism. Cf. Brand Blanshard on individuals (not species). 'One never gets what is fully particular until one has specified its relations of every kind with everything else in the universe', *The Nature of Thought* (London, 1939), vol. I, p. 639. Curiously enough N. R. Campbell arrives independently at a similar conclusion about species, when he is discussing the definition of such substances as silver, mercury or lead (*Physics. The Elements*, Cambridge, 1920, p. 50). All attempts to explain the unity of a species by similarity—whether by similarity of the individuals to one another, or by similarities and differences between the species and other species—suffer from the same incompleteness.

for the hearer. In fact the disjunction 'Analytic or Synthetic' cannot be applied simply to the addition of a member to a class without further caveats. But this in itself is not enough to remove the difficulty; it only makes it reappear in a new form. For if the addition of a member to a class can be synthetic for the speaker and analytic for a subsequent lexicographer, then to what class was the member added? Surely we now have two classes on our hands instead of one? An analogy will help us to deal with this new form of the difficulty. Naming is like electing the sort of member who makes a difference to a club. Strictly we cannot say without qualification to what club he was elected, since it was one club before he was elected and another club after he was elected. The club building might be pointed out, and of course there is no parallel move in the case of naming, although realism pretends that there is. But, even if there were no building or anything else of that kind, the puzzle about the two clubs would not be very perplexing. Similarly, when we reject the simple application of the dichotomy 'Analytic or Synthetic' the resulting puzzle about two classes is not very perplexing. All that is necessary is to point out that a class is incompletely given by a changing quorum. This may be untidy, but why not? There is something radically wrong with a request to be given a class which is not satisfied either with a reference to the name or with progressive enumeration. It is a request to be given something without being given it; as if somewhere, if only philosophers searched long enough, there could be found something which possessed all the advantages of a word and none of its disadvantages, an epistemological vehicle which carried all its destinations.

I now turn to my second thesis, that nothing is sufficiently like naming without being too like naming. Defenders of realism, like defenders of the other theories of naming, might object that the criticism contained in my first thesis is obvious, superficial and directed against a man of straw. For realism does not offer a non-circular detailed explanation of naming—how could it?—but simply gives a general characterization of the sort of unity which makes naming possible. But notice how very like a dream realism is. Taken literally it seems to be of little importance. But, if it is taken as the expression of a doctrine which, if *per impossibile* it were true, would give it great importance, the suggestion is immediately repudiated. Yet it does express such a doctrine, even if its exponents intermittently deny that it does; and it is to the devious expression of this doctrine that it owes most of its attractiveness. Its manifest content is little more than a harmless caprice, but its latent content is a serious error.

But has realism no point when it is taken simply as a general characterization of the sort of unity which makes naming impossible? One might answer that it has no point, and that it succeeds in appearing to have some point only by the device of inventing a new comprehensive term: and that this device is considered effective only in philosophy, since outside philosophy it is too obviously like making an impressive gesture in the direction of the interesting object, opening one's mouth and saying absolutely nothing. But such a denial would be tantamount to a denial that any general characterization of the sort of unity which makes naming possible could have a point. And surely such a denial would be wrong, since something can be done towards explaining the general possibility of naming by finding analogous processes? For instance, what makes naming possible is one thing which is in many things as an ingredient.[17] But does this analogy throw much light on naming? Any feature of logical mixing which is at all interesting seems to distinguish it from all other sorts of mixing. The values of an unrestricted variable are strange receptacles. What prevents contrary ingredients from being put in together, or an implicans from appearing without its implicate, is never the causal consequences. And anyway the whole notion of mixing ingredients which were not there before the mixing is peculiar. Could there be a logical conjuring trick?

Here defenders of realism might object that a new misunderstanding had replaced the old one. For, if realism is to be understood, not only must a general characterization of naming be allowed, but also the verification principle must not be applied too crudely. And anyway, if mixing is not a good analogy, this only means that some better analogy must be sought. This objection might lead to a tolerant examination of other analogies.[18] But fortunately it also opens up a short cut to the heart of the matter, which I shall soon take. Now it would be taking too short a cut to repeat the platitude that naming is *sui generis*. For it is natural to seek an analogy even if the search can never be completely successful. And anyway Butler's truism applies to everything. What is needed in order to explain the peculiar persistence of the debate about universals is something slightly longer, a demonstration that no analogy can be sufficiently close to satisfy philosophers without being too close.

It is most natural to seek a visible process as an analogy to naming, particularly for the Greeks who began this controversy.[19] Now previously I insisted that it is impossible in the end to give a detailed non-circular description of what makes it possible to name anything. Here, however, it would be unfair to object that, if naming in general is compared to a visible process, still that process itself must be named. For this sort of circularity is the inevitable result of the philosopher's predicament. However, it is dangerous to begin speaking at all where so little can be said. For it is fatally easy to think that one has separate access to what makes a name applicable just because one has separate access to whatever stands for this in the analogy. But, waiving this, let us now take the short cut and ask what sort of visible process could be analogous to naming. Let us try a rough analogy and say that one word is connected with many objects in the same way that the estuary of a river is connected with its many sources. But this analogy fails because this connection just happens naturally. We might then try to mend the analogy by saying that water follows the easiest course. But this could be called choice only anthropomorphically, in an extended and weak sense of 'choice'. In order to introduce choice in a restricted, strong sense, it is necessary to alter the analogy and say that people by directing the streams choose which sources shall feed the river. But, if the first process was too natural to be like naming, the second is too artificial, since, for the analogy to work, the sources ought to have something in common besides the fact that the river is fed from them. And it is difficult to find an analogy which is neither too natural nor too artificial. The

17 Cf. A. N. Whitehead, *Science and the Modern World* (Cambridge, 1928), pp. 197ff. For a criticism of this analogy, cf. Bentham, *Works,* vol. VIII, p. 335.

18 Metaphors must not be dismissed just because they are metaphors, as, e.g. 'copying' and 'participation' are by Aristotle, *Met.* 991 a 20.

19 Cf. J. Stenzel, *Plato's Method of Dialectic* (Oxford, 1940), p. 37.

characteristic of naming which is difficult to match is that the objects have something in common besides being called by one name, but nothing in common which counts except that in virtue of which they are called by one name. And this characteristic can be matched only by allowing that something makes it convenient but not absolutely necessary for people to canalize streams into the river in the way they do, and that whatever it is which makes this choice convenient is the only thing common to the sources which counts. But this compromise between the two extremes introduces into the analogy the very feature which it was intended to explain. For just how something works in influencing usage was what was to be explained. Nor is there a fourth alternative. So after all even general analogical characterizations of naming do fall into a circularity which is closely related to the type of circularity which my first thesis exposed. Neither in detail nor in general is it possible to step outside language.

This short way with analogies looks too superficial. For suppose that it is granted that one of the things that metaphysicians do is to seek the unattainable: that they hunt for definitions which would in no way involve their definienda,[20] and for analogies which would in no way involve what they were intended to explain. Yet even so metaphysics is a natural and inevitable pursuit, since the easiest way to discover how far one can go is to try to go one stage farther. And anyway there is a difference between complete failure and partial success; since, so long as analogies do not reach the point of self-frustration they get better and better as they approach it. These two qualifications are just but they only serve to strengthen my thesis that it was oscillation between the three points which prolonged the controversy about universals. For unless the possible analogies are mapped out in this simple way, it seems always conceivable that some altogether better analogy might lurk in an unexplored corner.

And what more are the rival theories of naming doing than seeking a completely satisfactory analogy? It is only jargon which makes them appear to be doing something more. The type of nominalism which suggests that things which are called by one name have only their name in common represents the extreme of artificiality.[21] It suggests that there are never any ways of telling even approximately whether a word is used in one sense or two senses. At the other extreme stands the type of realism which suggests that there is always one method of getting a precise answer to this question. In between are all the other theories of naming, which allow that it is neither impossible for the lexicographer to succeed in answering this question nor impossible for him to fail. None of these middle theories is really wrong, since of course we do bestow common names on certain chosen groups of things which exhibit certain similarities (else why should we do it?) or instantiate certain universals (why else were they invented?). But on the other hand none of them goes deep enough to satisfy the true metaphysician who is in all of us; since though they take us to the bottom of naming, we were in a simpler way already there, and they do not succeed in showing us how naming is founded on something else which lies even deeper. Hence each of these middle theories (except imagism, which says something empirical which seems to be false)

[20] Cf. J. Wisdom, 'Metaphysics and Verification' (*Mind*, 1938, pp. 465ff.).

[21] There are traces of such an extreme form of nominalism in Hobbes. Cf. *Leviathan*, Pt. I, chap. IV, p. 13 (Everyman edition).

develops its own thesis with embarrassing success up to a point, and can discredit its rivals only by accusing them of not going beyond that point. But, since naming cannot be explained by anything which really goes beyond a reasoned choice of usage, this is an unfair accusation. And its unfairness is concealed from those who make it only because each tacitly and wrongly assumes that his own theory alone does go beyond this point. Thus moderate nominalists maintain that similarity is a better explanation of the unity of a class than the presence of a universal. (But why should people not *just* recognize the presence of universals?) And moderate realists retort that this admits the existence of at least one universal, similarity. (But why should the presence of a universal explain the recognition of similarity if it cannot explain the recognition of anything else? Why should people not *just* recognize similarity?) Really these are not two arguments but two bare assertions of superiority. They are manoeuvres which are carried out in a way which suggests that they are difficult and that they must be advances: but both these suggestions are false. Yet these theories do seem to be striving towards something. And they are. Their goal is the unattainable completely satisfactory explanation of naming. And, as so often happens in metaphysics, progress is measured by distance from the starting-point and not by proximity to the goal whose unattainability each uses against its rivals without allowing it to deter itself.

Thus theories of naming, which seem to flout the verification principle without therefore saying nothing, can be interpreted as disguised analogies. And, though there is a common limit beyond which they cannot go, the success with which they stealthily approach this limit, camouflaged in the technical terms of epistemology, varies. But if this almost mechanical oscillation is avoided what else can be said about naming? Certainly as the first part of this article showed, detailed answers to the question why we name things as we do will in the end be circular. Only the trick of giving a general answer as if it were a detailed one cloaks their failure. If a word is explained ostensively, then however difficult this process may be it really is explained ostensively. It is no good trying to combine the concreteness of ostensive definition with the clarity of verbal definition. Verbal definitions have such an easy task just because ostensive definitions have such a difficult task. Surveyors find it easier to fix the positions of points which they can visit than to fix the positions of points which they cannot visit. Similarly it is easy to fix the relative positions of words: but the points in things to which words are related are in the end inaccessible to logicians.

Then what else can be said about naming? How *does* the lexicographer tell when a word is used in two senses rather than in one sense? Surely there must be something in common to all well constructed series of things? Yes, just that they *are* well constructed. For this question already contains the equivalent of any possible comprehensive answer which could be given to it. And, though in one way it is hard to see what detailed answers could be given to it, in another way it is only too easy to see. For we never reach a point where an exit *must* be made from the maze of words. Admittedly, if a verbal explanation is given at one point, it is only successful if at some other point a connection with things is already understood; and at some points it is more natural not to offer more words. But at no point is an exit obligatory. So, if detailed reasons why we call a thing what we do are required, it is easy to give them; but never ultimately or in the end, since here *ex vi termini* it is impossible to give them. But philosophers tend to ignore this kind of detailed answer and press on. But where to? Perhaps to experimental psychology, in order to discover how changes in the sense organs, in training and in interests alter the ways in which people group things. But this sort of investigation only gives the varying tests of the good construction of a series, and not its essence. But what could its essence be? When general analogical characterizations of naming have been mentioned, and detailed reasons why we call particular things by particular names, and the psychological background of all this, what is left? The desire to go on explaining naming is to some extent the result of the way these three fields have been confused, and to some extent the result of a natural feeling that in such a vast territory there might be something which lies outside these three fields. But above all it is the result of the Protean metaphysical urge to transcend language.

Willard Van Orman Quine

On What There Is

A curious thing about the ontological problem is its simplicity. It can be put in three Anglo-Saxon monosyllables: "What is there?" It can be answered, moreover, in a word—"Everything"—and everyone will accept this answer as true. However, this is merely to say that there is what there is. There remains room for disagreement over cases; and so the issue has stayed alive down the centuries.

Suppose now that two philosophers, McX and I, differ over ontology. Suppose McX maintains there is something which I maintain there is not. McX can, quite consistently with his own point of view, describe our difference of opinion by saying that I refuse to recognize certain entities. I should protest of course that he is wrong in his formulation of our disagreement, for I maintain that there are no entities, of the kind which he alleges, *for* me to recognize; but my finding him wrong in his formulation of our disagreement is unimportant, for I am committed to considering him wrong in his ontology anyway.

When *I* try to formulate our difference of opinion, on the other hand, I seem to be in a predicament. I cannot admit that there are some things which McX countenances and I do not, for in admitting that there are such things I should be contradicting my own rejection of them.

It would appear, if this reasoning were sound, that in any ontological dis-

From W. V. O. Quine, "On What There Is," *Review of Metaphysics*, Vol. 2 (1948). Reprinted by permission of the author and of *The Review of Metaphysics*. The article can also be found in his *From a Logical Point of View*, 1953.

pute the proponent of the negative side suffers the disadvantage of not being able to admit that his opponent disagrees with him.

This is the old Platonic riddle of non-being. Non-being must in some sense be, otherwise what is it that there is not? This tangled doctrine might be nicknamed *Plato's beard;* historically it has proved tough, frequently dulling the edge of Occam's razor.

It is some such line of thought that leads philosophers like McX to impute being where they might otherwise be quite content to recognize that there is nothing. Thus, take Pegasus. If Pegasus *were* not, McX argues, we should not be talking about anything when we use the word; therefore it would be nonsense to say even that Pegasus is not. Thinking to show thus that the denial of Pegasus cannot be coherently maintained, he concludes that Pegasus is.

McX cannot, indeed, quite persuade himself that any region of space-time, near or remote, contains a flying horse of flesh and blood. Pressed for further details on Pegasus, then, he says that Pegasus is an idea in men's minds. Here, however, a confusion begins to be apparent. We may for the sake of argument concede that there is an entity, and even a unique entity (though this is rather implausible), which is the mental Pegasus-idea; but this mental entity is not what people are talking about when they deny Pegasus.

. . .

The notion that Pegasus must be, because it would otherwise be nonsense to say even that Pegasus is not, has been seen to lead McX into an elementary confusion. Subtler minds, taking the same precept as their starting point, come out with theories of Pegasus which are less patently misguided than McX's, and correspondingly more difficult to eradicate. One of these subtler minds is named, let us say, Wyman. Pegasus, Wyman maintains, has his being as an unactualized possible. When we say of Pegasus that there is no such thing, we are saying, more precisely, that Pegasus does not have the special attribute of actuality. Saying that Pegasus is not actual is on a par, logically, with saying that the Parthenon is not red; in either case we are saying something about an entity whose being is unquestioned.

. . .

Wyman's overpopulated universe is in many ways unlovely. It offends the aesthetic sense of us who have a taste for desert landscapes, but this is not the worst of it. Wyman's slum of possibles is a breeding ground for disorderly elements. Take, for instance, the possible fat man in that doorway; and, again, the possible bald man in that doorway. Are they the same possible man, or two possible men? How do we decide? How many possible men are there in that doorway? Are there more possible thin ones than fat ones? How many of them are alike? Or would their being alike make them one? Are no *two* possible things alike? Is this the same as saying that it is impossible for two things to be alike? Or, finally, is the concept of identity simply inapplicable to unactualized possibles? But what sense can be found in talking of entities which cannot meaningfully be said to be identical with themselves and distinct from one another? These elements are well nigh incorrigible. By a Fregean therapy of individual concepts, some effort might be made at rehabilitation; but I feel we'd do better simply to clear Wyman's slum and be done with it.

Possibility, along with the other modalities of necessity and impossibility and contingency, raises problems upon which I do not mean to imply that we should turn our backs. But we can at least limit modalities to whole statements. We may impose the adverb 'possibly' upon a statement as a whole, and we may well worry about the semantical analysis of such usage; but little real advance in such analysis is to be hoped for in expanding our universe to include so-called *possible entities*. I suspect that the main motive for this expansion is simply the old notion that Pegasus, e.g., must be because it would otherwise be nonsense to say even that he is not.

. . .

I have spoken disparagingly of Plato's beard, and hinted that it is tangled. I have dwelt at length on the inconveniences of putting up with it. It is time to think about taking steps.

Russell, in his theory of so-called singular descriptions, showed clearly how we might meaningfully use seeming names without supposing that the entities allegedly named be. The names to which Russell's theory directly applies are complex descriptive names such as 'the author of *Waverly*', 'the present King of France', 'the round square cupola on Berkeley College'. Russell analyzes such phrases systematically as fragments of the whole sentences in which they occur. The sentence 'The author of *Waverly* was a poet', e.g., is explained as a whole as meaning 'Someone (better: something) wrote *Waverly* and was a poet, and nothing else wrote *Waverly*'. (The point of this added clause is to affirm the uniqueness which is implicit in the word 'the', in '*the* author of *Waverly*'.) The sentence 'The round square cupola on Berkeley College is pink' is explained as 'Something is round and square and is a cupola on Berkeley College and is pink, and nothing else is round and square and a cupola on Berkeley College'.

The virtue of this analysis is that the seeming name, a descriptive phrase, is paraphrased *in context* as a so-called incomplete symbol. No unified expression is offered as an analysis of the descriptive phrase, but the statement as a whole which was the context of that phrase still gets its full quota of meaning —whether true or false.

The unanalyzed statement 'The author of *Waverly* was a poet' contains a part, 'the author of *Waverly*', which is wrongly supposed by McX and Wyman to demand objective reference in order to be meaningful at all. But in Russell's translation, 'Something wrote *Waverly* and was a poet and nothing else wrote *Waverly*', the burden of objective reference which had been put upon the descriptive phrase is now taken over by words of the kind that logicians call bound variables, variables of quantification: namely, words like 'something', 'nothing', 'everything'. These words, far from purporting to be names specifically of the author of *Waverly,* do not purport to be names at all; they refer to entities generally, with a kind of studied ambiguity peculiar to themselves. These quantificational words or bound variables are of course a basic part of language, and their meaningfulness, at least in context, is not to be challenged. But their meaningfulness in no way presupposes there being either the author of *Waverly* or the round square cupola on Berkeley College or any other specifically preassigned objects.

Where descriptions are concerned, there is no longer any difficulty in affirming or denying being. 'There *is* the author of *Waverly*' is explained by Russell as meaning 'Someone (or, more strictly, something) wrote *Waverly* and nothing else wrote *Waverly*'. 'The author of *Waverly* is not' is explained, correspondingly, as the alternation 'Either each thing failed to write *Waverly* or two or more things wrote *Waverly*.' This alternation is false, but meaningful; and it contains no expression purporting to designate the author of *Waverly*. The statement 'The round square cupola on Berkeley College is not' is analyzed in similar fashion. So the old notion that statements of non-being defeat themselves goes by the board. When a statement of being or non-being is analyzed by Russell's theory of descriptions, it ceases to contain any expression which even purports to name the alleged entity whose being is in question, so that the meaningfulness of the statement no longer can be thought to presuppose that there be such an entity.

Now what of 'Pegasus'? This being a word rather than a descriptive phrase, Russell's argument does not immediately apply to it. However, it can easily be made to apply. We have only to rephrase 'Pegasus' as a description, in any way that seems adequately to single out our idea: say 'the winged horse that was captured by Bellerophon'. Substituting such a phrase for 'Pegasus', we can then proceed to analyze the statement 'Pegasus is', or 'Pegasus is not', precisely on the analogy of Russell's analysis of 'The author of *Waverly* is' and 'The author of *Waverly* is not'.

In order thus to subsume a one-word name or alleged name such as 'Pegasus' under Russell's theory of description, we must of course be able first to translate the word into a description. But this is no real restriction. If the notion of Pegasus had been so obscure or so basic a one that no pat translation into a descriptive phrase had offered itself along familiar lines, we could still have availed ourselves of the following artificial and trivial-seeming device: we could have appealed to the *ex hypothesi* unanalyzable, irreducible attribute of *being Pegasus,* adopting, for its expression, the verb 'is-Pegasus', or 'pegasizes'. The noun 'Pegasus' itself could then be treated as derivative, and identified after all with a description: 'the thing that is-Pegasus', 'the thing that pegasizes'.

If the importing of such a predicate as pegasizes seems to commit us to recognizing that there is a corresponding attribute, pegasizing, in Plato's heaven or in the mind of men, well and good. Neither we nor Wyman nor McX have been contending, thus far, about the being or non-being of universals, but rather about that of Pegasus. If in terms of pegasizing we can interpret the noun 'Pegasus' as a description subject to Russell's theory of descriptions, then we have disposed of the old notion that Pegasus cannot be said not to be without presupposing that in some sense Pegasus is.

Our argument is now quite general. McX and Wyman supposed that we could not meaningfully affirm a statement of the form 'So-and-so is not', with a simple or descriptive singular noun in place of 'so-and-so', unless so-and-so be. This supposition is now seen to be quite generally groundless, since the singular noun in question can always be expanded into a singular description, trivially or otherwise, and then analyzed out à la Russell.

We cannot conclude, however, that man is henceforth free of all ontological commitments. We commit ourselves outright to an ontology containing numbers when we say there are prime numbers between 1000 and 1010; we commit ourselves to an ontology containing centaurs when we say there are centaurs; and we commit ourselves to an ontology containing Pegasus when we say Pegasus is. But we do not commit ourselves to an ontology containing Pegasus or the author of *Waverly* or the round square cupola on Berkeley College when we say that Pegasus or the author of *Waverly* or the cupola in question is *not*. We need no longer labor under the delusion that the meaningfulness of a statement containing a singular term presupposes an entity named by the term. A singular term need not name to be significant.

. . .

Now let us turn to the ontological problem of universals: the question whether there are such entities as attributes, relations, classes, numbers, functions. McX, characteristically enough, thinks there are. Speaking of attributes, he says: "There are red houses, red roses, red sunsets; this much is prephilosophical common-sense in which we must all agree. These houses, roses, and sunsets, then, have something in common; and this which they have in common is all I mean by the attribute of redness." For McX, thus, there being attributes is even more obvious and trivial than the obvious and trivial fact of there being red houses, roses, and sunsets. This, I think, is characteristic of metaphysics, or at least of that part of metaphysics called ontology: one who regards a statement on this subject as true at all must regard it as trivially true. One's ontology is basic to the conceptual scheme by which he interprets all experiences, even the most commonplace ones. Judged within some particular conceptual scheme—and how else is judgment possible?—an ontological statement goes without saying, standing in need of no separate justification at all. Ontological statements follow immediately from all manner of casual statements of commonplace fact, just as—from the point of view, anyway, of McX's conceptual scheme—'There is an attribute' follows from 'There are red houses, red roses, red sunsets.'

Judged in another conceptual scheme, an ontological statement which is axiomatic to McX's mind may, with equal immediacy and triviality, be adjudged false. One may admit that there are red houses, roses, and sunsets, but deny, except as a popular and misleading manner of speaking, that they have anything in common. The words 'houses', 'roses', and 'sunsets' denote each of sundry individual entities which are houses and roses and sunsets, and the word 'red' or 'red object' denotes each of sundry individual entities which are red houses, red roses, red sunsets; but there is not, in addition, any entity whatever, individual or otherwise, which is named by the word 'redness', nor, for that matter, by the word 'househood', 'rosehood', 'sunsethood'. That the houses and roses and sunsets are all of them red may be taken as ultimate and irreducible, and it may be held that McX is no better off, in point of real explanatory power, for all the occult entities which he posits under such names as 'redness'.

One means by which McX might naturally have tried to impose his ontology of universals on us was already removed before we turned to the problem of universals. McX cannot argue that predicates such as 'red' or 'is-red', which we all concur in using, must be regarded as names each of a single universal entity in order that they be meaningful at all. For, we have seen that being a name of something is a much more special feature than being meaningful. He cannot even charge us—at least not by *that* argument—with having posited an attribute of pegasizing by our adoption of the predicate 'pegasizes'.

However, McX hits upon a different stratagem. "Let us grant," he says, "this distinction between meaning and naming of which you make so much. Let us even grant that 'is red', 'pegasizes', etc., are not names of attributes. Still, you admit they have meanings. But these *meanings,* whether they are *named* or not, are still universals, and I venture to say that some of them might even be the very things that I call attributes, or something to much the same purpose in the end."

For McX, this is an unusually penetrating speech; and the only way I know to counter it is by refusing to admit meanings. However, I feel no reluctance toward refusing to admit meanings, for I do not thereby deny that words and statements are meaningful. McX and I may agree to the letter in our classification of linguistic forms into the meaningful and the meaningless, even though McX construes meaningfulness as the *having* (in some sense of 'having') of some abstract entity which he calls a meaning, whereas I do not. I remain free to maintain that the fact that a given linguistic utterance is meaningful (or *significant,* as I prefer to say so as not to invite hypostasis of meanings as entities) is an ultimate and irreducible matter of fact; or, I may undertake to analyze it in terms directly of what people do in the presence of the linguistic utterance in question and other utterances similar to it.

The useful ways in which people ordinarily talk or seem to talk about meanings boil down to two: the *having* of meanings, which is significance, and *sameness* of meaning, or synonymy. What is called *giving* the meaning of an utterance is simply the uttering of a synonym, couched, ordinarily, in clearer language than the original. If we are allergic to meanings as such, we can speak directly of utterances as significant or insignificant, and as synonymous or heteronymous one with another. The problem of explaining these adjectives 'significant' and 'synonymous' with some degree of clarity and rigor—preferably, as I see it, in terms of behavior—is as difficult as it is important. But the explanatory value of special and irreducible intermediary entities called meanings is surely illusory.

Up to now I have argued that we can use singular terms significantly in sentences without presupposing that there be the entities which those terms purport to name. I have argued further that we can use general terms, e.g., predicates, without conceding them to be names of abstract entities. I have argued further that we can view utterances as significant, and as synonymous or heteronymous with one another, without countenancing a realm of entities called meanings. At this point McX begins to wonder whether there is any limit at all to our ontological immunity. Does *nothing* we may say commit us to the assumption of universals or other entities which we may find unwelcome?

I have already suggested a negative answer to this question, in speaking of bound variables, or variables of quantification, in connection with Russell's theory of descriptions. We can very easily involve ourselves in ontological commitments, by saying, e.g., that *there is something* (bound variable) which red houses and sunsets have in common; or that *there is something* which is a prime number between 1000 and 1010. But this is, essentially, the *only* way we can involve ourselves in ontological commitments: by our use of bound variables. The use of alleged names is no criterion, for we can repudiate their namehood at the drop of a hat unless the assumption of a corresponding entity can be spotted in the things we affirm in terms of bound variables. Names are in fact altogether immaterial to the ontological issue, for I have shown, in connection with 'Pegasus' and 'pegasize', that names can be converted to descriptions, and Russell has shown that descriptions can be eliminated. Whatever we say with help of names can be said in a language which shuns names altogether. To be is, purely and simply, to be the value of a variable. In terms of the categories of traditional grammar, this amounts roughly to saying that to be is to be in the range of reference of a pronoun. Pronouns are the basic media of reference; nouns might better have been named pro-pronouns. The variables of quantification, 'something', 'nothing', 'everything', range over our whole ontology, whatever it may be; and we are convicted of a particular ontological presupposition if, and only if, the alleged presuppositum has to be reckoned among the entities over which our variables range in order to render one of our affirmations true.

We may say, e.g., that some dogs are white, and not thereby commit ourselves to recognizing either doghood or whiteness as entities. 'Some dogs are white' says that some things that are dogs are white; and, in order that this statement be true, the things over which the bound variable 'something' ranges must include some white dogs, but need not include doghood or whiteness. On the other hand, when we say that some zoölogical species are cross-fertile, we are committing ourselves to recognizing as entities the several species themselves, abstract though they be. We remain so committed at least until we devise some way of so paraphrasing the statement as to show that the seeming reference to species on the part of our bound variable was an avoidable manner of speaking.

If I have been seeming to minimize the degree to which in our philosophical and unphilosophical discourse we involve ourselves in ontological commitments, let me then emphasize that classical mathematics, as the example of primes between 1000 and 1010 clearly illustrates, is up to its neck in commitments to an ontology of abstract entities. Thus it is that the great mediaeval controversy over universals has flared up anew in the modern philosophy of mathematics. The issue is clearer now than of old, because we now have a more explicit standard whereby to decide what ontology a given theory or form of discourse is committed to: a theory is committed to those and only those entities to which the bound variables of the theory must be capable of referring in order that the affirmations made in the theory be true.

. . .

I have argued that the sort of ontology we adopt can be consequential—notably in connection with mathematics, although this is only an example. Now how are we to adjudicate among rival ontologies? Certainly the answer is not provided by the semantical formula "To be is to be the value of a variable"; this formula serves rather, conversely, in testing the conformity of a given remark or doctrine to a prior ontological standard. We look to bound variables in connection with ontology not in order to know what there is, but in order to know what a given remark or doctrine, ours or someone else's, *says* there is; and this much is quite properly a problem involving language. But what there is is another question.

In debating over what there is, there are still reasons for operating on a semantical plane. One reason is to escape from the predicament noted at the beginning of the paper: the predicament of my not being able to admit that there are things which McX countenances and I do not. So long as I adhere to my ontology, as opposed to McX's, I cannot allow my bound variables to refer to entities which belong to McX's ontology and not to mine. I can, however, consistently describe our disagreement by characterizing the statements which McX affirms. Provided merely that my ontology countenances linguistic forms, or at least concrete inscriptions and utterances, I can talk about McX's sentences.

. . .

Our acceptance of an ontology is, I think, similar in principle to our acceptance of a scientific theory, say a system of physics: we adopt, at least insofar as we are reasonable, the simplest conceptual scheme into which the disordered fragments of raw experience can be fitted and arranged. Our ontology is determined once we have fixed upon the over-all conceptual scheme which is to accommodate science in the broadest sense; and the considerations which determine a reasonable construction of any part of that conceptual scheme, e.g. the biological or the physical part, are not different in kind from the considerations which determine a reasonable construction of the whole. To whatever extent the adoption of any system of scientific theory may be said to be a matter of language, the same—but no more—may be said of the adoption of an ontology.

But simplicity, as a guiding principle in constructing conceptual schemes, is not a clear and unambiguous idea; and it is quite capable of presenting a double or multiple standard. Imagine, e.g., that we have devised the most economical set of concepts adequate to the play-by-play reporting of immediate experience. The entities under this scheme—the values of bound variables—are, let us suppose, individual subjective events of sensation or reflection. We should still find, no doubt, that a physicalistic conceptual scheme, purporting to talk about external objects, offers great advantages in simplifying our over-all reports. By bringing together scattered sense events and treating them as perceptions of one object, we reduce the complexity of our stream of experience to a manageable conceptual simplicity. The rule of simplicity is indeed our guiding maxim in assigning sense data to objects: we associate an earlier and a later round sensum with the same so-called penny, or with two different so-called pennies, in obedience to the demands of maximum simplicity in our total world-picture.

Here we have two competing conceptual schemes, a phenomenalistic one and a physicalistic one. Which should prevail? Each has its advantages; each has its special simplicity in its own way. Each, I suggest, deserves to be developed. Each may be said, indeed, to be the more fundamental, though in different senses: the one is epistemologically, the other physically, fundamental.

The physical conceptual scheme simplifies our account of experience because of the way myriad scattered sense events come to be associated with single so-called objects; still there is no likelihood that each sentence about physical objects can actually be translated, however deviously and complexly, into the phenomenalistic language. Physical objects are postulated entities which round out and simplify our account of the flux of experience, just as the introduction of irrational numbers simplifies laws of arithmetic. From the point of view of the conceptual scheme of the elementary arithmetic of rational numbers alone, the broader arithmetic of rational and irrational numbers would have the status of a convenient myth, simpler than the literal truth (namely the arithmetic of rationals) and yet containing that literal truth as a scattered part. Similarly, from a phenomenalistic point of view, the conceptual scheme of physical objects is a convenient myth, simpler than the literal truth and yet containing that literal truth as a scattered part.

Now what of classes or attributes of physical objects, in turn? A platonistic ontology of this sort is, from the point of view of a strictly physicalistic conceptual scheme, as much of a myth as that physicalistic conceptual scheme itself was for phenomenalism. This higher myth is a good and useful one, in turn, in so far as it simplifies our account of physics. Since mathematics is an integral part of this higher myth, the utility of this myth for physical science is evident enough.

. . .

In earlier pages I undertook to show that some common arguments in favor of certain ontologies are fallacious. Further, I advanced an explicit standard whereby to decide what the ontological commitments of a theory are. But the question what ontology actually to adopt still stands open, and the obvious counsel is tolerance and an experimental spirit. Let us by all means see how much of the physicalistic conceptual scheme can be reduced to a phenomenalistic one; still physics also naturally demands pursuing, irreducible *in toto* though it be. Let us see how, or to what degree, natural science may be rendered independent of platonistic mathematics; but let us also pursue mathematics and delve into its platonistic foundations.

From among the various conceptual schemes best suited to these various pursuits, one—the phenomenalistic—claims epistemological priority. Viewed from within the phenomenalistic conceptual scheme, the ontologies of physical objects and mathematical objects are myths. The quality of myth, however, is relative; relative, in this case, to the epistemological point of view. This point of view is one among various, corresponding to one among our various interests and purposes.

Rudolf Carnap

Empiricism, Semantics, and Ontology

LINGUISTIC FRAMEWORKS

Are there properties, classes, numbers, propositions? In order to understand more clearly the nature of these and related problems, it is above all necessary to recognize a fundamental distinction between two kinds of questions concerning the existence or reality of entities. If someone wishes to speak in his language about a new kind of entities, he has to introduce a system of new ways of speaking, subject to new rules; we shall call this procedure the construction of a linguistic *framework* for the new entities in question. And now we must distinguish two kinds of questions of existence: first, questions of the existence of certain entities of the new kind *within the framework;* we call them *internal questions;* and second, questions concerning the existence or reality *of the system of entities as a whole,* called *external questions.* Internal questions and possible answers to them are formulated with the help of the new forms of expressions. The answers may be found either by purely logical methods or by empirical methods, depending upon whether the framework is a logical or a factual one. An external question is of a problematic character which is in need of closer examination.

THE WORLD OF THINGS

Let us consider as an example the simplest kind of entities dealt with in the everyday language: the spatio-temporally ordered system of observable things and events. Once we have accepted the thing language with its framework for things, we can raise and answer internal questions, e.g., "Is there a white piece of paper on my desk?", "Did King Arthur actually live?", "Are unicorns and centaurs real or merely imaginary?", and the like. These questions are to be answered by empirical investigations. Results of observations are evaluated according to certain rules as confirming or disconfirming evidence for possible answers. (This evaluation is usually carried out, of course, as a matter of habit rather than a deliberate, rational procedure. But it is possible, in a rational reconstruction, to lay down explicit rules for the evaluation. This is one of the main tasks of a pure, as distinguished from a psychological, epistemology.) The concept of reality occurring in these internal questions

---

Reprinted from *Meaning and Necessity,* 2nd ed., by Rudolf Carnap by permission of The University of Chicago Press. Copyright 1956 by The University of Chicago Press. The essay published in *Meaning and Necessity* is a slightly revised version of "Empiricism, Semantics, and Ontology," *Revue Internationale de Philosophie,* Vol. 4 (1950). The first section of that essay has been deleted here.

is an empirical, scientific, non-metaphysical concept. To recognize something as a real thing or event means to succeed in incorporating it into the system of things at a particular space-time position so that it fits together with the other things recognized as real, according to the rules of the framework.

From these questions we must distinguish the external question of the reality of the thing world itself. In contrast to the former questions, this question is raised neither by the man in the street nor by scientists, but only by philosophers. Realists give an affirmative answer, subjective idealists a negative one, and the controversy goes on for centuries without ever being solved. And it cannot be solved because it is framed in a wrong way. To be real in the scientific sense means to be an element of the system; hence this concept cannot be meaningfully applied to the system itself. Those who raise the question of the reality of the thing world itself have perhaps in mind not a theoretical question as their formulation seems to suggest, but rather a practical question, a matter of a practical decision concerning the structure of our language. We have to make the choice whether or not to accept and use the forms of expression in the framework in question.

In the case of this particular example, there is usually no deliberate choice because we all have accepted the thing language early in our lives as a matter of course. Nevertheless, we may regard it as a matter of decision in this sense: we are free to choose to continue using the thing language or not; in the latter case we could restrict ourselves to a language of sense-data and other "phenomenal" entities, or construct an alternative to the customary thing language with another structure, or, finally, we could refrain from speaking. If someone decides to accept the thing language, there is no objection against saying that he has accepted the world of things. But this must not be interpreted as if it meant his acceptance of a *belief* in the reality of the thing world; there is no such belief or assertion or assumption, because it is not a theoretical question. To accept the thing world means nothing more than to accept a certain form of language, in other words, to accept rules for forming statements and for testing, accepting, or rejecting them. The acceptance of the thing language leads, on the basis of observations made, also to the acceptance, belief, and assertion of certain statements. But the thesis of the reality of the thing world cannot be among these statements, because it cannot be formulated in the thing language or, it seems, in any other theoretical language.

The decision of accepting the thing language, although itself not of a cognitive nature, will nevertheless usually be influenced by theoretical knowledge, just like any other deliberate decision concerning the acceptance of linguistic or other rules. The purposes for which the language is intended to be used, for instance, the purpose of communicating factual knowledge, will determine which factors are relevant for the decision. The efficiency, fruitfulness, and simplicity of the use of the thing language may be among the decisive factors. And the questions concerning these qualities are indeed of a theoretical nature. But these questions cannot be identified with the question of realism. They are not yes-no questions but questions of degree. The thing language in the customary form works indeed with a high degree of efficiency for most purposes of everyday life. This is a matter of fact, based upon the content of our experiences. However, it would be wrong to describe this situation by saying: "The fact of the efficiency of the thing language is confirming evidence for the reality of the thing world"; we should rather say instead: "This fact makes it advisable to accept the thing language".

THE SYSTEM OF NUMBERS

As an example of a system which is of a logical rather than a factual nature let us take the system of natural numbers. The framework for this system is constructed by introducing into the language new expressions with suitable rules: (1) numerals like "five" and sentence forms like "there are five books on the table"; (2) the general term "number" for the new entities, and sentence forms like "five is a number"; (3) expressions for properties of numbers (e.g., "odd", "prime"), relations (e.g., "greater than"), and functions (e.g., "plus"), and sentence forms like "two plus three is five"; (4) numerical variables ("*m*", "*n*", etc.) and quantifiers for universal sentences ("for every *n*, . . .") and existential sentences ("there is an *n* such that . . .") with the customary deductive rules.

Here again there are internal questions, e.g., "Is there a prime number greater than a hundred?" Here, however, the answers are found, not by empirical investigation based on observations, but by logical analysis based on the rules for the new expressions. Therefore the answers are here analytic, i.e., logically true.

What is now the nature of the philosophical question concerning the existence or reality of numbers? To begin with, there is the internal question which, together with the affirmative answer, can be formulated in the new terms, say, by "There are numbers" or, more explicitly, "There is an *n* such that *n* is a number". This statement follows from the analytic statement "five is a number" and is therefore itself analytic. Moreover, it is rather trivial (in contradistinction to a statement like "There is a prime number greater than a million", which is likewise analytic but far from trivial), because it does not say more than that the new system is not empty; but this is immediately seen from the rule which states that words like "five" are substitutable for the new variables. Therefore nobody who meant the question "Are there numbers?" in the internal sense would either assert or even seriously consider a negative answer. This makes it plausible to assume that those philosophers who treat the question of the existence of numbers as a serious philosophical problem and offer lengthy arguments on either side, do not have in mind the internal question. And, indeed, if we were to ask them: "Do you mean the question as to whether the framework of numbers, *if* we were to accept it, would be found to be empty or not?", they would probably reply: "Not at all; we mean a question *prior* to the acceptance of the new framework". They might try to explain what they mean by saying that it is a question of the ontological status of numbers; the question whether or not numbers have a certain metaphysical characteristic called reality (but a kind of ideal reality, different from the material reality of the thing world) or subsistence or status of "independent entities". Unfortunately, these philosophers have so far not given a formulation of their question in terms of the common scientific language. Therefore our judgment must be that they have not succeeded in giving to the external question and to the possible answers any cognitive content. Unless and until they supply a clear cognitive interpretation, we are justified in our suspicion that their question is a pseudo-question, that is, one disguised in the form of a theoretical question while in fact it is non-theoretical; in the present case it is the practical problem whether or not to incorporate into the language the new linguistic forms which constitute the framework of numbers.

. . .

THE SYSTEM OF THING PROPERTIES

The thing language contains words like "red", "hard", "stone", "house", etc., which are used for describing what things are like. Now we may introduce new variables, say "*f*", "*g*", etc., for which those words are substitutable and furthermore the general term "property". New rules are laid down which admit sentences like "Red is a property", "Red is a color", "These two pieces of paper have at least one color in common" (i.e., "There is an *f* such that *f* is a color, and . . ."). The last sentence is an internal assertion. It is of an empirical, factual nature. However, the external statement, the philosophical statement of the reality of properties—a special case of the thesis of the reality of universals—is devoid of cognitive content.

. . .

WHAT DOES ACCEPTANCE OF A KIND OF ENTITIES MEAN?

Let us now summarize the essential characteristics of situations involving the introduction of a new kind of entities, characteristics which are common to the various examples outlined above.

The acceptance of a new kind of entities is represented in the language by the introduction of a framework of new forms of expressions to be used according to a new set of rules. There may be new names for particular entities of the kind in question; but some such names may already occur in the language before the introduction of the new framework. (Thus, for example, the thing language contains certainly words of the type of "blue" and "house" before the framework of properties is introduced; and it may contain words like "ten" in sentences of the form "I have ten fingers" before the framework of numbers is introduced.) The latter fact shows that the occurrence of constants of the type in question—regarded as names of entities of the new kind after the new framework is introduced—is not a sure sign of the acceptance of the new kind of entities. Therefore the introduction of such constants is not to be regarded as an essential step in the introduction of the framework. The two essential steps are rather the following. First, the introduction of a general term, a predicate of higher level, for the new kind of entities, permitting us to say of any particular entity that it belongs to this kind (e.g., "Red is a *property*", "*Five is a number*"). Second, the introduction of variables of the new type. The new entities are values of these variables; the constants (and the closed compound expressions, if any) are substitutable for the variables. With the help of the variables, general sentences concerning the new entities can be formulated.

After the new forms are introduced into the language, it is possible to formulate with their help internal questions and possible answers to them. A question of this kind may be either empirical or logical; accordingly a true answer is either factually true or analytic.

From the internal questions we must clearly distinguish external questions, i.e., philosophical questions concerning the existence or reality of the total system of the new entities. Many philosophers regard a question of this kind as an ontological question which must be raised and answered *before* the introduction of the new language forms. The latter introduction, they believe, is legitimate only if it can be justified by an ontological insight supplying an affirmative answer to the question of reality. In contrast to this view, we take the position that the introduction of the new ways of speaking does not need any theoretical justification because it does not imply any assertion of reality. We may still speak (and have done so) of "the acceptance of the new entities" since this form of speech is customary; but one must keep in mind that this phrase does not mean for us anything more than acceptance of the new framework, i.e., of the new linguistic forms. Above all, it must not be interpreted as referring to an assumption, belief, or assertion of "the reality of the entities". There is no such assertion. An alleged statement of the reality of the system of entities is a pseudo-statement without cognitive content. To be sure, we have to face at this point an important question; but it is a practical, not a theoretical question; it is the question of whether or not to accept the new linguistic forms. The acceptance cannot be judged as being either true or false because it is not an assertion. It can only be judged as being more or less expedient, fruitful, conducive to the aim for which the language is intended. Judgments of this kind supply the motivation for the decision of accepting or rejecting the kind of entities.

Thus it is clear that the acceptance of a linguistic framework must not be regarded as implying a metaphysical doctrine concerning the reality of the entities in question. It seems to me due to a neglect of this important distinction that some contemporary nominalists label the admission of variables of abstract types as "Platonism". This is, to say the least, an extremely misleading terminology. It leads to the absurd consequence, that the position of everybody who accepts the language of physics with its real number variables (as a language of communication, not merely as a calculus) would be called Platonistic, even if he is a strict empiricist who rejects Platonic metaphysics.

. . .

ABSTRACT ENTITIES IN SEMANTICS

The problem of the legitimacy and the status of abstract entities has recently again led to controversial discussions in connection with semantics. In a semantical meaning analysis certain expressions in a language are often said to designate (or name or denote or signify or refer to) certain extra-linguistic entities. As long as physical things or events (e.g., Chicago or Caesar's death) are taken as designata (entities designated), no serious doubts arise. But strong objections have been raised, especially by some empiricists, against abstract entities as designata, e.g., against semantical statements of the following kind:

(1) "The word 'red' designates a property of things";
(2) "The word 'color' designates a property of properties of things";
(3) "The word 'five' designates a number";
(4) "The word 'odd' designates a property of numbers";
(5) "The sentence 'Chicago is large' designates a proposition".

Those who criticize these statements do not, of course, reject the use of the expressions in question, like "red" or "five"; nor would they deny that these expressions are meaningful. But to be meaningful, they would say, is not the same as having a meaning in the sense of an entity designated. They reject the belief, which they regard as implicitly presupposed by those semantical statements, that to each expression of the types in question (adjectives like "red", numerals like "five", etc.) there is a particular real entity to which the expression stands in the relation of designation. This belief is rejected as incompatible with the basic principles of empiricism or of scientific thinking. Derogatory labels like "Platonic realism", "hypostatization", or " 'Fido'-Fido principle" are attached to it. The latter is the name given by Gilbert Ryle to the criticized belief, which, in his view, arises by a naïve inference of analogy: just as there is an entity well known to me, viz. my dog Fido, which is designated by the name "Fido", thus there must be for every meaningful expression a particular entity to which it stands in the relation of designation or naming, i.e., the relation exemplified by "Fido"-Fido. The belief criticized is thus a case of hypostatization, i.e., of treating as names expressions which are not names. While "Fido" is a name, expressions like "red", "five", etc., are said not to be names, not to designate anything.

Our previous discussion concerning the acceptance of frameworks enables us now to clarify the situation with respect to abstract entities as designata. Let us take as an example the statement:

(*a*) " 'Five' designates a number".

The formulation of this statement presupposes that our language L contains the forms of expressions which we have called the framework of numbers, in particular, numerical variables and the general term "number". If L contains these forms, the following is an analytic statement in L:

(*b*) "Five is a number".

Further, to make the statement (*a*) possible, L must contain an expression like "designates" or "is a name of" for the semantical relation of designation. If suitable rules for this term are laid down, the following is likewise analytic:

(*c*) " 'Five' designates five".

(Generally speaking, any expression of the form " '. . .' designates . . ." is an analytic statement provided the term ". . ." is a constant in an accepted framework. If the latter condition is not fulfilled, the expression is not a statement. Since (*a*) follows from (*c*) and (*b*), (*a*) is likewise analytic.

Thus it is clear that *if* someone accepts the framework of numbers, then he must acknowledge (*c*) and (*b*) and hence (*a*) as true statements. Generally speaking, if someone accepts a framework for a certain kind of entities, then he is bound to admit the entities as possible designata. Thus the question of the admissibility of entities of a certain type or of abstract entities in general as designata is reduced to the question of the acceptability of the linguistic framework for those entities. Both the nominalistic critics, who refuse the status of designators or names to expressions like "red", "five", etc., because they deny the existence of abstract entities, and the skeptics, who express doubts concerning the existence and demand evidence for it, treat the question of existence as a theoretical question. They do, of course, not mean the internal question; the affirmative answer to *this* question is analytic and trivial and too obvious for doubt or denial, as we have seen. Their doubts refer rather to the system of entities itself; hence they mean the external question. They believe that only after making sure that there really is a system of entities of the kind in question are we justified in accepting the framework by incorporating the linguistic forms into our language. However, we have seen that the external question is not a theoretical question but rather the practical question whether or not to accept those linguistic forms. This acceptance is not in need of a theoretical justification (except with respect to expediency and fruitfulness), because it does not imply a belief or assertion. Ryle says that the "Fido"-Fido principle is "a grotesque theory". Grotesque or not, Ryle is wrong in calling it a theory. It is rather the practical decision to accept certain frameworks. Maybe Ryle is historically right with respect to those whom he mentions as previous representatives of the principle, viz. John Stuart Mill, Frege, and Russell. If these philosophers regarded the acceptance of a system of entities as a theory, an assertion, they were victims of the same old, metaphysical confusion. But it is certainly wrong to regard *my* semantical method as involving a belief in the reality of abstract entities, since I reject a thesis of this kind as a metaphysical pseudo-statement.

. . .

Let us take as example the natural numbers as cardinal numbers, i.e., in contexts like "Here are three books". The linguistic forms of the framework of numbers, including variables and the general term "number", are generally used in our common language of communication; and it is easy to formulate explicit rules for their use. Thus the logical characteristics of this framework are sufficiently clear (while many internal questions, i.e., arithmetical questions, are, of course, still open). In spite of this, the controversy concerning the external question of the ontological reality of the system of numbers continues. Suppose that one philosopher says: "I believe that there are numbers as real entities. This gives me the right to use the linguistic forms of the numerical framework and to make semantical statements about numbers as designata of numerals". His nominalistic opponent replies: "You are wrong; there are no numbers. The numerals may still be used as meaningful expressions. But they are not names, there are no entities designated by them. Therefore the word "number" and numerical variables must not be used (unless a way were found to introduce them as merely abbreviating devices, a way of translating them into the nominalistic thing language)." I cannot think of any possible evidence that would be regarded as relevant by both philosophers, and therefore, if actually found, would decide the controversy or at least make one of the opposite theses more probable than the other. (To construe the numbers as classes or properties of the second level, according to the Frege-Russell method, does, of course, not solve the controversy, because the first philosopher would affirm and the second deny the existence of the system of classes or properties of the second level.) Therefore I feel compelled to regard the external question as a pseudo-question, until both parties to the controversy offer a common interpretation of the question as a cognitive question; this would involve an indication of possible evidence regarded as relevant by both sides.

. . .

CONCLUSION

For those who want to develop or use semantical methods, the decisive question is not the alleged ontological question of the existence of abstract entities but rather the question whether the use of abstract linguistic forms or, in technical terms, the use of variables beyond those for things (or phenomenal data), is expedient and fruitful for the purposes for which semantical analyses are made, viz. the analysis, interpretation, clarification, or construction of languages of communication, especially languages of science. This question is here neither decided nor even discussed. It is not a question simply of yes or no, but a matter of degree. . . .

The acceptance or rejection of abstract linguistic forms, just as the acceptance or rejection of any other linguistic forms in any branch of science, will finally be decided by their efficiency as instruments, the ratio of the results achieved to the amount and complexity of the efforts required. To decree dogmatic prohibitions of certain linguistic forms instead of testing them by their success or failure in practical use, is worse than futile; it is positively harmful because it may obstruct scientific progress. The history of science shows examples of such prohibitions based on prejudices deriving from religious, mythological, metaphysical, or other irrational sources, which slowed up the developments for shorter or longer periods of time. Let us learn from the lessons of history. Let us grant to those who work in any special field of investigation the freedom to use any form of expression which seems useful to them; the work in the field will sooner or later lead to the elimination of those forms which have no useful function. *Let us be cautious in making assertions and critical in examining them, but tolerant in permitting linguistic forms.*

William Payne Alston

Ontological Commitments

During the past half-century many philosophers have occupied themselves with translating one linguistic expression into another, or with providing general schema for such translations. And some of them, sensitive to charges of engaging in parlor games during working hours, have tried, in various ways, to exhibit the serious value of such activities. I want to consider one very popular sort of philosophic translation—the sort which goes from sentences of the form 'There are P's' (or from other sentences which obviously imply sentences of this form, such as 'The P is R') to sentences of some other form. And I want to consider one very common explanation of the point of such translations—viz., that they enable us to avoid "ontological commitments" to P's. It will be my contention that this explanation is basically confused, and that it only succeeds in raising a dust which obstructs our view of the real point of such translations.

Let's begin by considering an example from Morton White's recent book, *Toward Reunion in Philosophy*. He is speaking of the sentences 'There is a difference in age between John and Tom' and 'There is a possibility that James will come.'

"How, then, can we clarify these puzzling sentences and yet avoid the unwelcome conclusion that there are possibilities and age-differences in our universe . . .

"In the case of 'There is a difference in age between John and Tom,' we might begin by saying that we understand the relational predicate 'is as old as' and that we test statements of the form 'x is as old as y' without having to see that x has some queer thing called an age, that y has one, and that these ages are identical. In that event, the belief of the ordinary man that there is a difference in age between John and Tom would be rendered in language that is not misleading by saying instead, simply, 'It is not the case that John is as old as Tom.' We might offer an analogous translation of 'There is a possibility that James will come' in which we replace it by some statement about the statement 'James will come,' for example by the statement that this statement is not certainly false. . . . what we have done is to show that we *need not assert the existence* of age-differences or the existence of possibilities in communicating what we want to communicate." (Pp. 68–69.)

Here are several philosophically interesting translations of this sort (which I shall call 'existential reduction'):

From W. P. Alston, "Ontological Commitments" (with footnotes omitted), *Philosophical Studies,* Vol. 9 (1958). Reprinted by permission of the author, *Philosophical Studies,* and the University of Minnesota Press.

William P. Alston (1921–   ) is Professor of Philosophy at the University of Michigan.

1. There is a possibility that James will come.
2. The statement that James will come is not certainly false.

3. There is a meaning which can be given to his remarks.
4. His remarks can be understood in a certain way.

5. There are many virtues which he lacks.
6. He might conceivably be much more virtuous than he is.

7. There are facts which render your position untenable.
8. Your position is untenable in the light of the evidence.

Now it is puzzling to me that anyone should claim that these translations "show that we need not assert the existence of" possibilities, meanings, virtues, and facts "in communicating what we want to communicate." For if the translation of (1) into (2), for example, is adequate, then they are normally used to make the same assertion. In uttering (2) we would be making the same assertion as we would make if we uttered (1), i.e., the assertion that there is a possibility that James will come. And so we would be asserting that there is a possibility (committing ourselves to the existence of a possibility) just as much by using (2) as by using (1). If, on the other hand, the translation is not adequate, it has not been shown that we can, by uttering (2), communicate what we wanted to communicate when we uttered (1). Hence the point of the translation cannot be put in terms of some assertion or commitment from which it saves us.

This dilemma has more than a passing resemblance to the "paradox of analysis," which was extensively discussed a short while ago. (If x is adequately analyzable as y, then 'x' and 'y' must be synonymous. But if so, how can we convey any information by saying 'x is y.') Some philosophers attempted (unsuccessfully in my opinion) to resolve the paradox of analysis by pointing out differences between the meanings of 'x' and 'y' which were sufficient to make the analysis informative, but not so great so to render it invalid. Similar gambits might be tried here, although the omens are no more favorable than before.

A. It may be said that (1) differs from (2) only in carrying an imputation of 'ultimate reality' to possibilities, in implying that possibilities are among the 'ultimate furniture of the universe.' Thus in replacing (1) with (2) we continue to say everything we have any need or right to say, sloughing off only the groundless, and gratuitous, attribution of ultimate reality.

Before we can accept this account we must understand what is meant by 'ultimate reality' and this is not altogether easy. What can be meant by 'taking possibilities to be ultimately real,' other than simply asserting, seriously and with full awareness of what we are doing, that, for example, there is a possibility that James will come? And this can be done by the use of (2) as well as (1). But suppose that some meaning can be given to the phrase 'ultimate reality,' such that (2) does not carry with it an implication of the ultimate reality of possibilities. It is still worthy of note that no one has given adequate reason for the supposition that (1), as ordinarily used, carries any such implication either. What evidence is there that the ordinary man in uttering (1), or the scientist in uttering a sentence like 'There are fourteen electrons in this atom,' is asserting the ultimate reality of possibilities or electrons in any sense which goes beyond the serious and deliberate use of these sentences to make assertions? Of course a philosopher who utters such sentences as 'Possibilities are ultimately real,' 'Possibilities are objective entities,' etc., is asserting the *ultimate* reality of possibilities if anyone ever is. But does that justify us in saying that he is making the same assertion when he utters (1)? Well, perhaps the fact that he uses these queer sentences is an indication that his use of (1) carries a metaphysical implication. But if it does then precisely for that reason he will not admit that by using (2) he can just as well say what he wanted to say when he used (1). This is our problem all over again. Wherever (1), unlike (2), does carry a metaphysical force, the translation is not adequate. Thus the analysis would only have the virtue of showing us that we could say what we want to say without making an ontological commitment to possibilities, except where we want to make an ontological commitment to possibilities. In this case it would be less than a parlor game.

B. Alternatively, admitting that talk of 'ultimate reality' is unclear, or even unintelligible, one might locate the value of the analysis in the dissolution of this unclarity, i.e., in the fact that (2) says everything that is clearly said by (1) but without these confused suggestions of *ultimate* reality. But does (1) as ordinarily used carry such suggestions? Even if it does and even if this account is substantially correct, it offers no aid and comfort to the ontological interpretation. The ontological interpretation presupposes that there is an activity called 'admitting the (ultimate) existence of possibilities' which we might or might not perform, and the performance or nonperformance of which hinges on whether we employ (1) or (2) to say what we want to say (or on whether we use (1) with or without the realization that it can be translated by (2)). But to say that phrases like 'ultimate existence' are unintelligible is to say that we can't understand what such an activity would be, or what it would be like to perform it, and so are unable to specify what admission it is from which the translation saves us. In other words, on the present account, what the translation enables us to avoid is not certain commitments or assertions, but certain confusions. This clue will be taken up later. But first—back to the ontologist.

These moves have not proved fruitful. But there is indeed one thing, not yet explicitly mentioned, which the translation of (1) into (2) does enable us to avoid, and that is the *sentence,* (1). More generally the schema of which this translation is an instance enables us to say what we want to say without having to use any sentences of this form, i.e., any sentence beginning with 'There is (are),' followed by 'a possibility . . .' 'the possibility . . .' ('possibilities . . .' 'some possibilities . . . '), etc. And the hard-pressed ontologist may make a stand here by roundly declaring that the ability to avoid sentences of this form is what he *means* by avoiding an ontological commitment. That is, he will define 'ontological commitment to possibilities' as the inability to say what we want to say without using such sentences.

To be at all plausible this definition will have to be patched up. As it stands, we could avoid an ontological commitment to possibilities simply by introducing a new word as synonymous with 'there is,' or with 'possibility.' This makes the game too easy. The rules can be tightened by requiring that the restatement consist only of existing expressions with their established meanings. But that won't be enough. No one could consider the translation of (1) into 'The possibility exists that James will come' to constitute an evasion of an ontological commitment. The trouble is that there are a number of expressions in common use ('. . . exists,' 'some . . .') which do essentially the same job as 'there is'; let us speak of these expressions as having an explicitly existential force. The sort of translation we are trying to specify is a translation from a sentence which contains one of these expressions, along with the crucial predicate terms, into a sentence which does not. Taking account of this let us restate the definition of ontological commitment as follows:

I. One is ontologically committed to P's if and only if he is unable to say what he wants to say without using a sentence of the form 'There is (are) a P . . . (the P . . ., P's . . ., etc.)' or some other sentence which deviates from this form only by replacing 'there is' by some other expression with explicit existential force or by replacing 'P' by a synonym (together with such grammatical changes as are required by these replacements, as in the change from 'There are some lions in this country' to 'Lions exist in this country').

By a not so fortuitous circumstance this criterion is substantially equivalent to Quine's famous criterion for ontological commitment.

II. We are convicted of a particular ontological presupposition if, and only if, the alleged presuppositum has to be reckoned among the entities over which our variables range in order to render one of our affirmations true. (*From a Logical Point of View,* p. 13.)

An entity is assumed by a theory if and only if it must be counted among the values of the variables in order that the statements affirmed in the theory be true. (*Ibid.,* p. 103.)

The equivalence can be seen as follows. The variables of a theory must range over P's in order to make the affirmations of that theory true if and only if one of those affirmations is either 'There are P's' or some statement which implies 'There are P's,' such as 'There are R's and all R's are P's.' Of course Quine's criterion applies explicitly only to "theories" which are in quantificational form. But he himself points out that the criterion is applicable to theories otherwise expressed provided they can be translated into this form. And I see no reason why any English sentence beginning with 'there is' cannot be translated into one beginning '$\exists$x.' In fact II can be viewed as a narrower version of I, since '$\exists$x' is one of the expressions which does essentially the same job as 'there is.' Hence although the following remarks will be explicitly directed, for the most part, to I, they will, I believe, apply equally to II.

Do we, then, adequately bring out the merits of existential reduction by saying that it enables us to avoid "ontological commitments," in the sense specified by these criteria? These criteria do point up the way in which such translations enable us to cut down the number of sentences of an explicitly existential form which we use (or to reduce the range of our variables). And in certain contexts this may be a virtue. There may be desires, widespread among logicians, which are satisfied by such reductions. And for certain purposes of theory construction or formalization it might be desirable to have as narrow a range of variable substitutions as possible. But it is at best misleading, and at worst flatly incorrect, to record this achievement by saying that we have avoided making an ontological commitment to P's, or avoided asserting the existence of P's. For the achievement consists, to return to our chief example, in finding some other sentence which can be used to make the same statement which one had been making in uttering (1). And, in any ordinary sense of these terms, whether a man admits (asserts) the existence of possibilities depends on what statement he makes, not on what sentence he uses to make that statement. One admits that possibilities exist whenever he assertorially utters (1), *or any other sentence which means the same* (would ordinarily be used to make the same statement). It is a question of *what* he says, not of *how* he says it. Hence he cannot repudiate his admission by simply changing his words.

A man who was afraid of policemen would be reassured if he were convinced that there are no policemen. But he would not be reassured if he were convinced that one could express all one's beliefs in a language which took not policemen, but rather policemanship, as values of variables (that one could avoid locutions like 'There is a policeman around the corner' in favor of 'Policemanship is exemplified around the corner'). Nor could we convince a scientist that the assumption of the existence of electrons can be dispensed with, simply by providing a way of translating every sentence of the form '$(\exists x)$ (x is an electron . . .)' into another sentence which has the same meaning but which does not require variables to range over electrons, though he would be convinced if we could provide a theory which did the same jobs as his electronic theory but contained no individual sentences which were synonymous with his sentences asserting the existence of electrons. That is, in any context where questions of existence arise the problem is whether or not we shall assert *that* so-and-so exists, not whether we shall choose some particular way of making this assertion. This means that assertion of existence, commitment to existence, etc., does not consist in the inflexible preference for one verbal formulation over any other, however gratifying such preferences may be to logicians, and that the use of the phrase 'ontological commitment' here is unjustifiable and misleading.

Of course Quine could say that the notational question is what he is interested in and that, ordinary usage be damned, this is what he is using 'ontological commitment' to mean. But the whole point of his using 'ontological commitment' for this purpose rather than some other phrase (and the associated use of cognate expressions like 'believe in the existence of,' 'countenance abstract entities,' etc.) is to associate, or identify, the terminological problem with existential problems as they are ordinarily conceived, and so transfer to the former the interest and importance which attaches to the latter. Otherwise why present the values of variables formula as a criterion for 'ontological commitment' instead of just as something which is interesting in its own right? The fact that Quine intends his criterion to be more than just notational in import is further brought out by (1) his insistence that ontological questions (as he formulates them) are not different in kind from scientific questions; (2) his use of considerations other than notational convenience (queerness, unobservability) in deciding what values of variables it might be desirable to avoid.

Thus in the last analysis the ontological interpretation can offer no rationale of existential reduction other than the notational convenience attaching to the avoidance of certain verbal forms. But surely this sort of analysis has more significance than that. To get at its significance I shall relapse for a moment into ontological terminology and ask the hitherto neglected question 'Why should anyone wish to avoid an ontological commitment to, for example, possibilities?' More generally, why do the ontological analysts bend their efforts toward escaping from ontological commitments to "abstract entities" (attributes, classes, possibilities, meanings, facts, etc.) rather than to "concrete entities" (physical objects, events, persons, etc.). The reasons most commonly cited are these (Ockham's razor is not relevant here, since the question is not why we should ever try to avoid ontological commitments, but why we should aim at paring off abstract rather than concrete entities):

1. Possibilities, etc., are queer.
2. Possibilities, etc., are obscure in their nature.
3. Possibilities, etc., are unobservable (there is no empirical reason for supposing that there are any such things).

Obviously these reasons are not expressed very clearly. To say that a possibility is queer or obscure is no argument against its existence; on the contrary it is a conclusive argument for its existence. Possession of any characteristic entails, or presupposes, existence. And the unobservability of possibilities is not a matter of fact like the unobservability of mangoes on my desk or of unicorns. It is rather that we can't understand what it would be like to empirically observe a possibility.

These complaints are captious. But they do show that the objections to abstract entities would be more precisely expressed by talking not about possibilities, but about what people say about possibilities. It is because people sometimes say (and ask) such queer and obscure things about possibilities, and talk about them in empirically untestable ways, that our ontological analysts are so loath to "make an ontological commitment to possibilities," i.e., are so loath to use a sentence like (1). More specifically, the tendency to shy away from sentences like (1) is due to the fact that people who attach a great deal of importance to such sentences (and resist replacing them with sentences of other forms) are liable to:

1. Ask such puzzling questions as 'Are possibilities eternal?' 'Can a proposition be immediately intuited?' 'What are the parts of a fact?' 'Are there negative facts as well as positive ones?'
2. Propound 'theories' which are unintelligible, or at least such that we cannot find any relevant arguments for or against them. For example, "Possibilities contain in their essence a reference to actuality' 'Every true statement corresponds with a fact' 'Attributes have an existence independent of their exemplifications' 'Meanings are known by intuition.'
3. Take the existence (or *ultimate* existence) of such entities as problematic, subject to proof or disproof, even after ordinary sentences like (1) have been accepted, without giving an intelligible account of the difference between asserting ultimate existence in this problematic sense and simply assenting to the ordinary sentence.

But if (1) and (2) are synonymous, why should (1) and not (2) suffer this abuse, and how can the replacement of (1) with (2) alleviate the situation?

It is at this point that the real virtue of this sort of translation can be seen. Consider the following parallels:

There is a possibility that James will come
There is a fruit that James will eat

There is a meaning which can be given to his words
There is a chair which can be given to his aunt

There are many virtues which he lacks
There are many articles of clothing which he lacks

In each case the strong verbal similarity provides a temptation to assimilate the two sorts of existents, i.e., to suppose that we can talk of one in the same way as the other. Since chairs have spatial locations, we are apt to ask about the (ontological) locus of meanings. (See Whitehead on God as the locus of "eternal objects.") Physical objects like chairs and fruits consist of parts which can be specified, unless they are atomic; and so we are led into asking whether facts or propositions are atomic, and if not what their parts are like. Since this is a story which has been often, and ably, told in the recent literature, I shall not elaborate it further. The moral to be drawn here is that the only "ontological commitment" to possibilities which there is any reason to consider undesirable is the tendency to talk about possibilities in inappropriate ways ("category mistakes").

It is the seductive grammatical family likenesses of sentences like (1) which render them objectionable, not any assertion of the existence of possibilities they carry with them, in any intelligible sense of that term. And the point of translating (1) into (2) lies in the fact that once anyone sees that what he says when he uses (1) can be just as well said by using (2), the power of the grammatical lure will be broken. To see that one can say that there is a possibility that James will come, by using either of two sentences of quite different grammatical forms, is to see that possibilities do not *have* to be talked about in the way which would be suggested by either of these forms, and hence that one does not *have* to ask about possibilities the same sort of questions one asks about chairs. To put it in a rather dangerous way, he sees that possibilities do not exist in the same way as chairs. Of course the translation doesn't prove that the same questions cannot be asked about possibilities and about chairs. It is rather that the realization that the translation holds relieves us of the compulsion to ask these questions about possibilities in spite of the impossibility of really making sense of them.

Thus we can make explicit the virtues of existential reduction, taking account of the (unconfused) motives which have led people to perform it, without having to say what we have seen to be untenable—viz., that it enables us to avoid admitting the existence of something.

This way of looking at the matter should also free us from the supposition, which the ontological account might suggest, that when we utter (1) we are inevitably saying something false, at least if we haven't seen that it can be translated into (2), whereas we wouldn't be subject to any such danger in using (2), even if we didn't realize that it is translatable into (1). This gives rise to the idea that there is something inherently objectionable about (1), a sort of ontological taint. But when we see that the point of the translation is the neutralizing of tendencies to confusions, we see that the problem is essentially a strategic one. One is not necessarily misled by (1), with or without a translation, nor is one necessarily safe from confusion by using (2). The translation is a device for removing confusions wherever they arise. They usually arise in connection with (1), in which case we show that (2) can be used to say the same thing; but the reverse procedure might conceivably be useful. Just as no sentence is necessarily misleading, so none is guaranteed, by its form, to be used without confusion. The supposition to the contrary is one of the unfortunate effects of philosophic preoccupation with artificial languages.

For Further Reading

Aaron, R. I., *The Theory of Universals,* 1952, Part II.

Aquinas, St. Thomas, *Treatise on Man,* trans. by James F. Anderson, 1962, Questions 84 and 85.

Bambrough, Renford, "Universals and Family Resemblance," *Proceedings of the Aristotelian Society,* Vol. 61 (1960–61).

Berkeley, George, *Principles of Human Knowledge,* Parags. 6 through 20.

Bernays, Paul, "On Platonism in Mathematics," in Benacerraf, P., and Putnam, H. (eds.), *Philosophy of Mathematics,* 1964.

Bochenski, I. M., Church, Alonzo, and Goodman, Nelson, *The Problem of Universals,* 1956.

Brandt, Richard B., "Languages of Realism and Nominalism," *Philosophy and Phenomenological Research,* Vol. 17 (1957).

Cohen, L. Jonathan, *The Diversity of Meaning,* 1962, Chap. 4.

Cournot, Antoine A., *An Essay on the Foundations of Our Knowledge,* 1956, Chap. 11.

James, William, *The Principles of Psychology,* 1890, Vol. 1, Chap. 12.

Moore, G. E., *Some Main Problems of Philosophy,* 1953, Chaps. 17 and 18.

Pap, Arthur, "Nominalism, Empiricism, and Universals," *Philosophical Quarterly,* Vol. 9 (1959) and Vol. 10 (1960).

Plato, *Parmenides,* Part I; *Phaedo.*

Quine, W. V. O., *Word and Object,* 1960, Chap. 7.

Ramsey, Frank P., "Universals," *The Foundations of Mathematics,* 1931, Chap. 4.

Reid, Thomas, Essay V, Chap. 6, in Woozley, A. D. (ed.), *Essays on the Intellectual Powers of Man,* 1941.

Stout, A. K., "Nature of Universals and Propositions," *Studies in Philosophy and Psychology,* 1930, Chap. 17.

Thompson, Manley, "Abstract Entities," *Philosophical Review,* Vol. 69 (1960).

Further Reading

5

INDUCTION AND ITS JUSTIFICATION

A comparison of the arguments used in pure mathematics with those employed in, say, physics or courts of law reveals a fundamental logical difference between them. In mathematics, proof is exclusively deductive. It consists in showing that the statements asserted as theorems can be derived from given assumptions according to rules, which are known to transmit to the conclusion of an argument the truth of its conjoined premises. In consequence, if the premises of an argument are known to be true, there can be no doubt as to the truth of its conclusion. No area of inquiry, including physics and the law, can do without deductive reasoning. However, in the empirical sciences as well as in the management of human affairs, statements about matters of fact are not established by arguments that are purely deductive: such statements are accepted on evidence that does not have demonstrative force. In these domains, accordingly, even arguments that are universally regarded as unquestionably cogent may have true premises but their conclusions may nevertheless turn out to be false. Arguments of this sort, which are governed by rules that do not invariably transmit the truth of their premises to their conclusions and thus involve a transition to statements not necessitated by the premises, are generally called "nondemonstrative," "probabilistic," or "inductive." (It should be noted, however, that the word "inductive" is also used frequently in a more restricted sense for a particular type of nondemonstrative reasoning—namely, for arguments in which a conclusion about an entire class or population is based on observations concerning samples drawn from that class. But in this introduction we shall use the word in its inclusive sense.)

This basic difference between arguments was already recognized in Greek antiquity, and its study has been a major preoccupation of logicians since Aristotle. Such a study involves two distinct but closely related tasks: the formal one of codifying and developing systematically the various types of demonstrative and nondemonstrative inference; and the justificatory one of making clear the grounds, if any, for holding them to be "sound" or "valid." However, logicians have been far more successful in the execution of these tasks for deductive arguments than for inductive ones. Much was accomplished even in ancient times in analyzing and validating the more elementary forms of demonstrative reasoning (for example, the type of deduction called syllogistic), and during the past hundred years unprecedented advances have been made in constructing comprehensive systems of deductive logic, in which endless arrays of types of necessary inference are presented and shown to be valid. Moreover, though there has been and continues to be disagreement on questions concerning the foundations of deductive logic, the questions deal chiefly with matters irrelevant to the types of deductive proof most frequently used in empirical inquiry. The forms of deductive argument logicians have codified are in the main as noncontroversial as are most of the achievements of mathematics.

Nothing nearly like this can be said about the logic of nondemonstrative inference: its codification is at best much less complete than the standard formulations of deductive arguments; there is no generally accepted classification of its varieties; and competent students continue to disagree on the validity of many particular types of inductive reasoning, as well as on the justifications that have been proposed for those commonly held to be sound. It is also pertinent to note that while the explicit analysis of inductive arguments was initiated by Aristotle, the formal task of codifying them systematically did not properly begin until the nineteenth century, when the mathematical theory of probability reached a degree of development sufficient to permit its use as a comprehensive framework within which the articulation of their detailed structures could be attempted. Since Charles Peirce, at any rate, the study of nondemonstrative inference has usually been embedded in discussions of probability, with theorems in the calculus of probability (especially when supplemented by ideas taken from theoretical statistics) often construed as formulas of valid inductive reasoning.

As the selections from Peirce and Reichenbach in the present chapter indicate, the theory of probability has been of undoubted value in systematizing the logic of induction and in supplying suggestions for establishing its validity. Nevertheless, it is still a moot question whether the standard calculus of probability in any of its formulations is relevant to the analysis of nondemonstrative arguments and, even if assumed to be relevant, whether it provides a uniformly adequate codification of them. Moreover, the word "probability" is ambiguous. At least three distinct meanings of the word, which are currently under active discussion, can be specified: probability as a purely logical relation akin to the relation of entailment, as a measure of subjective credence, and as a relative frequency in the long run. Logicians differ over the sense in which the word is to be understood if the theorems of the probability calculus are to serve as rules for assessing the probative force of evidence in inductive reasoning. For example, according to the so-called "theorem of inverse probability," the probability of a hypothesis *h* (for example, Newton's law of gravitation) is increased by the addition of new evidence *e* (for example, the discovery in 1930 of the hitherto unknown planet Pluto at a certain location in the heavens) in proportion to the antecedent improbability of *e*. But this theorem is entirely otiose for evaluating the weight of evidence if the meaning of "probability" is indeterminate, or if the meaning assigned to the term is such that the "antecedent improbability" mentioned in the theorem cannot be ascertained.

However, with the exception of the selection from Peirce, which does include a simple classification of nondemonstrative arguments, the articles in this chapter—including Mill's account of reasoning by analogy—are concerned almost exclusively with the validation of such arguments rather than with the formal task of systematizing them. The problem of justifying claims to knowledge of universal truths does not arise in its modern form in Aristotle's discussion of induction, since he believed that by reflecting on sensory experience (or induction) the human mind can apprehend with certainty the truth of the universal and basic premises of every science. This historically influential view of the mind's alleged power to discover the indubitable nature of things was vigorously challenged by Hume. Attempts to answer his "skeptical doubts" about the "rational" character of inductive arguments are legion, but most of the proposed answers fall into a small number of distinctive groups, which we will briefly describe: (1) answers which in effect try to convert inductive arguments into deductive ones, by adding to the premises of the former some general assumption about the character of the universe (for example, the so-called "principle of the uniformity of nature"); (2) answers which maintain that the "rationality" of various rules of nondemonstrative inference is self-evident, or that the validity of those rules is "presupposed" by all significant discourse (for example, the rule that the conjunction of two logically independent hypotheses is supported by given evidence to a lesser degree than is the support supplied by that evidence to just one of the hypotheses); (3) answers which try to show that rules governing inductive arguments can be justified by arguments that are themselves inductive, but that nevertheless do not beg the question of the validity of induction; (4) answers which offer a "tautologous" justification of inductive rules, by arguing that since the aim of inquiry is allegedly to discover the limits of the relative frequencies with which events of various kinds occur, then the use of certain "self-corrective" rules for inferring the values of those limits is bound in the long run to achieve the goal of inquiry—provided that the relative frequencies do indeed have determinate limiting values, though no assurance can be given that the proviso is ever satisfied; and, finally, (5) answers which "resolve" the problem of justifying induction by attempting to show that the problem is in fact spurious and requires no answer.

Each type of answer continues to have proponents, although not all the types are represented in this chapter. Mill's justification of induction illustrates the first type, and some of the difficulties in his approach to the problem are discussed by Peirce. Unlike Mill, both Peirce and Reichenbach base their accounts of nondemonstrative reasoning on a frequency interpretation of probability. However, while Reichenbach's proposed justification of induction falls unambiguously into the fourth group, Peirce's views on this question are not so readily classified. Much that he says in this connection appears to make him a proponent of the fourth type of answer to the problem of justification; but his discussion of the problem also contains suggestions for solving it that places his answer into the third group as well. The fifth type of approach to the problem is illustrated in Strawson's article, and a critique of his argument is contained in the selection from Salmon.

Aristotle

How the Basic Truths of Science Come to Be Known

I

. . .

2. We suppose ourselves to possess unqualified scientific knowledge of a thing, as opposed to knowing it in the accidental way in which the sophist knows, when we think that we know the cause on which the fact depends, as the cause of that fact and of no other, and, further, that the fact could not be other than it is. Now that scientific knowing is something of this sort is evident—witness both those who falsely claim it and those who actually possess it, since the former merely imagine themselves to be, while the latter are also actually, in the condition described. Consequently the proper object of unqualified scientific knowledge is something which cannot be other than it is.

There may be another manner of knowing as well—that will be discussed later. What I now assert is that at all events we do know by demonstration. By demonstration I mean a syllogism productive of scientific knowledge, a syllogism, that is, the grasp of which is *eo ipso* such knowledge. Assuming then that my thesis as to the nature of scientific knowing is correct, the premisses of demonstrated knowledge must be true, primary, immediate, better known than and prior to the conclusion, which is further related to them as effect to cause. Unless these conditions are satisfied, the basic truths will not be 'appropriate' to the conclusion. Syllogism there may indeed be without these conditions, but such syllogism, not being productive of scientific knowledge, will not be demonstration. The premisses must be true: for that which is non-existent cannot be known—we cannot know, e.g., that the diagonal of a square is commensurate with its side. The premisses must be primary and indemonstrable; otherwise they will require demonstration in order to be known, since to have knowledge, if it be not accidental knowledge, of things which are demonstrable, means precisely to have a demonstration of them. The premisses must be the causes of the conclusion, better known than it, and prior to it; its causes, since we possess scientific knowledge of a thing only when we know its cause; prior, in order to be causes; antecedently known, this antecedent knowledge being not our mere understanding of the meaning, but knowledge of the fact as well. Now 'prior' and 'better known' are ambiguous terms, for

---

From Aristotle, *Analytica Posteriora,* Books I and II, trans. by G. R. G. Mure, published by The Clarendon Press, Oxford, 1928, and reprinted with their permission.

there is a difference between what is prior and better known in the order of being and what is prior and better known to man. I mean that objects nearer to sense are prior and better known to man; objects without qualification prior and better known are those further from sense. Now the most universal causes are furthest from sense and particular causes are nearest to sense, and they are thus exactly opposed to one another. In saying that the premisses of demonstrated knowledge must be primary, I mean that they must be the 'appropriate' basic truths, for I identify primary premiss and basic truth.

A 'basic truth' in a demonstration is an immediate proposition. An immediate proposition is one which has no other proposition prior to it. A proposition is either part of an enunciation, i.e. it predicates a single attribute of a single subject. If a proposition is dialectical, it assumes either part indifferently; if it is demonstrative, it lays down one part to the definite exclusion of the other because that part is true. The term 'enunciation' denotes either part of a contradiction indifferently. A contradiction is an opposition which of its own nature excludes a middle. The part of a contradiction which conjoins a predicate with a subject is an affirmation; the part disjoining them is a negation. I call an immediate basic truth of syllogism a 'thesis' when, though it is not susceptible of proof by the teacher, yet ignorance of it does not constitute a total bar to progress on the part of the pupil: one which the pupil must know if he is to learn anything whatever is an axiom. I call it an axiom because there are such truths and we give them the name of axioms *par excellence*. If a thesis assumes one part or the other of an enunciation, i.e. asserts either the existence or the non-existence of a subject, it is a hypothesis; if it does not so assert, it is a definition. Definition *is* a 'thesis' or a 'laying something down', since the arithmetician lays it down that to be a unit is to be quantitatively indivisible; but it is not a hypothesis, for to define what a unit is is not the same as to affirm its existence.

Now since the required ground of our knowledge—i.e. of our conviction—of a fact is the possession of such a syllogism as we call demonstration, and the ground of the syllogism is the facts constituting its premisses, we must not only know the primary premisses—some if not all of them—beforehand, but know them better than the conclusion: for the cause of an attribute's inherence in a subject always itself inheres in the subject more firmly than that attribute, e.g. the cause of our loving anything is dearer to us than the object of our love. So since the primary premisses are the cause of our knowledge—i.e. of our conviction—it follows that we know them better—that is, are more convinced of them—than their consequences, precisely because our knowledge of the latter is the effect of our knowledge of the premisses. Now a man cannot believe in anything more than in the things he knows, unless he has either actual knowledge of it or something better than actual knowledge. But we are faced with this paradox if a student whose belief rests on demonstration has not prior knowledge; a man must believe in some, if not in all, of the basic truths more than in the conclusion. Moreover, if a man sets out to acquire the scientific knowledge that comes through demonstration, he must not only have a better knowledge of the basic truths and a firmer conviction of them than of the connexion which is being demonstrated: more than this, nothing must be more certain or better known to him than these basic truths in their character as contradicting the fundamental premisses which lead to the opposed and erroneous conclusion. For indeed the conviction of pure science must be unshakable.

3. Some hold that, owing to the necessity of knowing the primary premisses, there is no scientific knowledge. Others think there is, but that all truths are demonstrable. Neither doctrine is either true or a necessary deduction from the premisses. The first school, assuming that there is no way of knowing other than by demonstration, maintain that an infinite regress is involved, on the ground that if behind the prior stands no primary, we could not know the posterior through the prior (wherein they are right, for one cannot traverse an infinite series): if on the other hand—they say—the series terminates and there are primary premisses, yet these are unknowable because incapable of demonstration, which according to them is the only form of knowledge. And since thus one cannot know the primary premisses, knowledge of the conclusions which follow from them is not pure scientific knowledge nor properly knowing at all, but rests on the mere supposition that the premisses are true. The other party agrees, with them as regards knowing, holding that it is only possible by demonstration, but they see no difficulty in holding that all truths are demonstrated, on the ground that demonstration may be circular and reciprocal.

Our own doctrine is that not all knowledge is demonstrative: on the contrary, knowledge of the immediate premisses is independent of demonstration. (The necessity of this is obvious; for since we must know the prior premisses from which the demonstration is drawn, and since the regress must end in immediate truths, those truths must be indemonstrable.) Such, then, is our doctrine, and in addition we maintain that besides scientific knowledge there is its originative source which enables us to recognize the definitions.

. . .

9. It is no less evident that the peculiar basic truths of each inhering attribute are indemonstrable; for basic truths from which they might be deduced would be basic truths of all that is, and the science to which they belonged would possess universal sovereignty. This is so because he knows better whose knowledge is deduced from higher causes, for his knowledge is from prior premisses when it derives from causes themselves uncaused: hence, if he knows better than others or best of all, his knowledge would be science in a higher or the highest degree. But, as things are, demonstration is not transferable to another genus, with such exceptions as we have mentioned of the application of geometrical demonstrations to theorems in mechanics or optics, or of arithmetical demonstrations to those of harmonics.

It is hard to be sure whether one knows or not; for it is hard to be sure whether one's knowledge is based on the basic truths appropriate to each attribute—the differentia of true knowledge. We think we have scientific knowledge if we have reasoned from true and primary premisses. But that is not so: the conclusion must be homogeneous with the basic facts of the science.

10. I call the basic truths of every genus those elements in it the existence of which cannot be proved. As regards both these primary truths and the attri-

butes dependent on them the meaning of the name is assumed. The fact of their existence as regards the primary truths must be assumed; but it has to be proved of the remainder, the attributes. Thus we assume the meaning alike of unity, straight, and triangular; but while as regards unity and magnitude we assume also the fact of their existence, in the case of the remainder proof is required.

. . .

31. Scientific knowledge is not possible through the act of perception. Even if perception as a faculty is of 'the such' and not merely of a 'this somewhat', yet one must at any rate actually perceive a 'this somewhat', and at a definite present place and time: but that which is commensurately universal and true in all cases one cannot perceive, since it is not 'this' and it is not 'now'; if it were, it would not be commensurately universal—the term we apply to what is always and everywhere. Seeing, therefore, that demonstrations are commensurately universal and universals imperceptible, we clearly cannot obtain scientific knowledge by the act of perception: nay, it is obvious that even if it were possible to perceive that a triangle has its angles equal to two right angles, we should still be looking for a demonstration—we should not (as some say) possess knowledge of it; for perception must be of a particular, whereas scientific knowledge involves the recognition of the commensurate universal. So if we were on the moon, and saw the earth shutting out the sun's light, we should not know the cause of the eclipse: we should perceive the present fact of the eclipse, but not the reasoned fact at all, since the act of perception is not of the commensurate universal.

. . .

II

19. As to the basic premisses, how they become known and what is the developed state of knowledge of them is made clear by raising some preliminary problems.

We have already said that scientific knowledge through demonstration is impossible unless a man knows the primary immediate premisses. But there are questions which might be raised in respect of the apprehension of these immediate premisses: one might not only ask whether it is of the same kind as the apprehension of the conclusions, but also whether there is or is not scientific knowledge of both; or scientific knowledge of the latter, and of the former a different kind of knowledge; and, further, whether the developed states of knowledge are not innate but come to be in us, or are innate but at first unnoticed. Now it is strange if we possess them from birth; for it means that we possess apprehensions more accurate than demonstration and fail to notice them. If on the other hand we acquire them and do not previously possess them, how could we apprehend and learn without a basis of preexistent knowledge? For that is impossible, as we used to find in the case of demonstration. So it emerges that neither can we possess them from birth, nor can they come to be in us if we are without knowledge of them to the extent of having no such developed state at all. Therefore we must possess a capacity of some sort, but not such as to rank higher in accuracy than these developed states. And this at least is an obvious characteristic of all animals, for they possess a congenital discriminative capacity which is called sense-perception. But though sense-perception is innate in all animals, in some the sense-impression comes to persist, in others it does not. So animals in which this persistence does not come to be have either no knowledge at all outside the act of perceiving, or no knowledge of objects of which no impression persists; animals in which it does come into being have perception and can continue to retain the sense-impression in the soul: and when such persistence is frequently repeated a further distinction at once arises between those which out of the persistence of such sense-impressions develop a power of systematizing them and those which do not. So out of sense-perception comes to be what we call memory, and out of frequently repeated memories of the same thing develops experience; for a number of memories constitute a single experience. From experience again—i.e. from the universal now stabilized in its entirety within the soul, the one beside the many which is a single identity within them all—originate the skill of the craftsman and the knowledge of the man of science, skill in the sphere of coming to be and science in the sphere of being.

We conclude that these states of knowledge are neither innate in a determinate form, nor developed from other higher states of knowledge, but from sense-perception. It is like a rout in battle stopped by first one man making a stand and then another, until the original formation has been restored. The soul is so constituted as to be capable of this process.

Let us now restate the account given already, though with insufficient clearness. When one of a number of logically indiscriminable particulars has made a stand, the earliest universal is present in the soul: for though the act of sense-perception is of the particular, its content is universal—is man, for example, not the man Callias. A fresh stand is made among these rudimentary universals, and the process does not cease until the indivisible concepts, the true universals, are established: e.g. such and such a species of animal is a step towards the genus animal, which by the same process is a step towards a further generalization.

Thus it is clear that we must get to know the primary premisses by induction; for the method by which even sense-perception implants the universal is inductive. Now of the thinking states by which we grasp truth, some are unfailingly true, others admit of error—opinion, for instance, and calculation, whereas scientific knowing and intuition are always true: further, no other kind of thought except intuition is more accurate than scientific knowledge, whereas primary premisses are more knowable than demonstrations, and all scientific knowledge is discursive. From these considerations it follows that there will be no scientific knowledge of the primary premisses, and since except intuition nothing can be truer than scientific knowledge, it will be intuition that apprehends the primary premisses—a result which also follows from the fact that demonstration cannot be the originative source of demonstration, nor, consequently, scientific knowledge of scientific knowledge. If, therefore, it is the only other kind of true thinking except scientific knowing, intuition will be the originative source of scientific knowledge. And the originative source of science grasps the original basic premiss, while science as a whole is similarly related as originative source to the whole body of fact.

David Hume

Skeptical Doubts Concerning the Operations of the Understanding

PART I

All the objects of human reason or inquiry may naturally be divided into two kinds, to wit, "Relations of Ideas," and "Matters of Fact." Of the first kind are the sciences of Geometry, Algebra, and Arithmetic, and, in short, every affirmation which is either intuitively or demonstratively certain. *That the square of the hypotenuse is equal to the square of the two sides* is a proposition which expresses a relation between these figures. *That three times five is equal to the half of thirty* expresses a relation between these numbers. Propositions of this kind are discoverable by the mere operation of thought, without dependence on what is anywhere existent in the universe. Though there never were a circle or triangle in nature, the truths demonstrated by Euclid would forever retain their certainty and evidence.

Matters of fact, which are the second objects of human reason, are not ascertained in the same manner, nor is our evidence of their truth, however great, of a like nature with the foregoing. The contrary of every matter of fact is still possible, because it can never imply a contradiction and is conceived by the mind with the same facility and distinctness as if ever so conformable to reality. *That the sun will not rise tomorrow* is no less intelligible a proposition and implies no more contradiction than the affirmation *that it will rise.* We should in vain, therefore, attempt to demonstrate its falsehood. Were it demonstratively false, it would imply a contradiction and could never be distinctly conceived by the mind.

It may, therefore, be a subject worthy of curiosity to inquire what is the nature of that evidence which assures us of any real existence and matter of fact beyond the present testimony of our senses or the records of our memory. This part of philosophy, it is observable, had been little cultivated either by the ancients or moderns; and, therefore, our doubts and errors in the prosecution of so important an inquiry may be the more excusable while we march through such difficult paths without any guide or direction. They may even prove useful by exciting curiosity and destroying that implicit faith and security which is the bane of all reasoning and free inquiry. The discovery of defects in the common philosophy, if any such there be, will not, I presume, be a discouragement, but rather an incitement, as is usual, to attempt something more full and satisfactory than has yet been proposed to the public.

From David Hume, *An Inquiry Concerning Human Understanding,* Section IV, first published in 1748.

All reasonings concerning matter of fact seem to be founded on the relation of *cause* and *effect*. By means of that relation alone we can go beyond the evidence of our memory and senses. If you were to ask a man why he believes any matter of fact which is absent, for instance, that his friend is in the country or in France, he would give you a reason, and this reason would be some other fact: as a letter received from him or the knowledge of his former resolutions and promises. A man finding a watch or any other machine in a desert island would conclude that there had once been men in that island. All our reasonings concerning fact are of the same nature. And here it is constantly supposed that there is a connection between the present fact and that which is inferred from it. Were there nothing to bind them together, the inference would be entirely precarious. The hearing of an articulate voice and rational discourse in the dark assures us of the presence of some person. Why? Because these are the effects of the human make and fabric, and closely connected with it. If we anatomize all the other reasonings of this nature, we shall find that they are founded on the relation of cause and effect, and that this relation is either near or remote, direct or collateral. Heat and light are collateral effects of fire, and the one effect may justly be inferred from the other.

If we would satisfy ourselves, therefore, concerning the nature of that evidence which assures us of matters of fact, we must inquire how we arrive at the knowledge of cause and effect.

I shall venture to affirm, as a general proposition which admits of no exception, that the knowledge of this relation is not, in any instance, attained by reasonings *a priori*, but arises entirely from experience, when we find that any particular objects are constantly conjoined with each other. Let an object be presented to a man of ever so strong natural reason and abilities—if that object be entirely new to him, he will not be able, by the most accurate examination of its sensible qualities, to discover any of its causes or effects. Adam, though his rational faculties be supposed, at the very first, entirely perfect, could not have inferred from the fluidity and transparency of water that it would suffocate him, or from the light and warmth of fire that it would consume him. No object ever discovers, by the qualities which appear to the senses, either the causes which produced it or the effects which will arise from it; nor can our reason, unassisted by experience, ever draw any inference concerning real existence and matter of fact.

This proposition, *that causes and effects are discoverable, not by reason, but by experience*, will readily be admitted with regard to such objects as we remember to have once been altogether unknown to us, since we must be conscious of the utter inability which we then lay under of foretelling what would arise from them. Present two smooth pieces of marble to a man who has no tincture of natural philosophy; he will never discover that they will adhere together in such a manner as to require great force to separate them in a direct line, while they make so small a resistance to a lateral pressure. Such events as bear little analogy to the common course of nature are also readily confessed to be known only by experience, nor does any man imagine that the explosion of gunpowder or the attraction of a loadstone could ever be discovered by arguments *a priori*. In like manner, when an effect is supposed to depend upon an intricate machinery or secret structure of parts, we make no difficulty in attributing all our knowledge of it to experience. Who will assert that he can give the ultimate reason why milk or bread is proper nourishment for a man, not for a lion or tiger?

But the same truth may not appear at first sight to have the same evidence with regard to events which have become familiar to us from our first appearance in the world, which bear a close analogy to the whole course of nature, and which are supposed to depend on the simple qualities of objects without any secret structure of parts. We are apt to imagine that we could discover these effects by the mere operation of our reason without experience. We fancy that, were we brought on a sudden into this world, we could at first have inferred that one billiard ball would communicate motion to another upon impulse, and that we needed not to have waited for the event in order to pronounce with certainty concerning it. Such is the influence of custom that where it is strongest it not only covers our natural ignorance but even conceals itself, and seems not to take place, merely because it is found in the highest degree.

But to convince us that all the laws of nature and all the operations of bodies without exception are known only by experience, the following reflections may perhaps suffice. Were any object presented to us, and were we required to pronounce concerning the effect which will result from it without consulting past observation, after what manner, I beseech you, must the mind proceed in this operation? It must invent or imagine some event which it ascribes to the object as its effect; and it is plain that this invention must be entirely arbitrary. The mind can never possibly find the effect in the supposed cause by the most accurate scrutiny and examination. For the effect is totally different from the cause, and consequently can never be discovered in it. Motion in the second billiard ball is a quite distinct event from motion in the first, nor is there anything in the one to suggest the smallest hint of the other. A stone or piece of metal raised into the air and left without any support immediately falls. But to consider the matter *a priori*, is there anything we discover in this situation which can beget the idea of a downward rather than an upward or any other motion in the stone or metal?

And as the first imagination or invention of a particular effect in all natural operations is arbitrary where we consult not experience, so must we also esteem the supposed tie or connection between the cause and effect which binds them together and renders it impossible that any other effect could result from the operation of that cause. When I see, for instance, a billiard ball moving in a straight line toward another, even suppose motion in the second ball should by accident be suggested to me as the result of their contact or impulse, may I not conceive that a hundred different events might as well follow from that cause? May not both these balls remain at absolute rest? May not the first ball return in a straight line or leap off from the second in any line or direction? All these suppositions are consistent and conceivable. Why, then, should we give the preference to one which is no more consistent or conceivable than the rest? All our reasonings *a priori* will never be able to show us any foundation for this preference.

In a word, then, every effect is a distinct event from its cause. It could not, therefore, be discovered in the cause, and the first invention or conception of it, *a priori*, must be entirely arbitrary. And even after it is suggested, the conjunction of it with the cause must appear equally arbitrary, since there are always many other effects which, to reason, must seem fully as consistent and natural. In vain, therefore, should we pretend to determine any single event or infer any cause or effect without the assistance of observation and experience.

. . .

PART II

But we have not yet attained any tolerable satisfaction with regard to the question first proposed. Each solution still gives rise to a new question as difficult as the foregoing and leads us on to further inquiries. When it is asked, *What is the nature of all our reasonings concerning matter of fact?* the proper answer seems to be, That they are founded on the relation of cause and effect. When again it is asked, *What is the foundation of all our reasonings and conclusions concerning that relation?* it may be replied in one word, *experience.* But if we still carry on our sifting humor and ask, *What is the foundation of all conclusions from experience?* this implies a new question which may be of more difficult solution and explication. Philosophers that give themselves airs of superior wisdom and sufficiency have a hard task when they encounter persons of inquisitive dispositions, who push them from every corner to which they retreat, and who are sure at last to bring them to some dangerous dilemma. The best expedient to prevent this confusion is to be modest in our pretensions and even to discover the difficulty ourselves before it is objected to us. By this means we may make a kind of merit of our very ignorance.

I shall content myself in this section with an easy task and shall pretend only to give a negative answer to the question here proposed. I say, then, that even after we have experience of the operations of cause and effect, our conclusions from that experience are *not* founded on reasoning or any process of the understanding. This answer we must endeavor both to explain and to defend.

It must certainly be allowed that nature has kept us at a great distance from all her secrets and has afforded us only the knowledge of a few superficial qualities of objects, while she conceals from us those powers and principles on which the influence of these objects entirely depends. Our senses inform us of the color, weight, and consistency of bread, but neither sense nor reason can ever inform us of those qualities which fit it for the nourishment and support of the human body. Sight or feeling conveys an idea of the actual motion of bodies, but as to that wonderful force or power which would carry on a moving body forever in a continued change of place, and which bodies never lose but by communicating it to others, of this we cannot form the most distant conception. But notwithstanding this ignorance of natural powers[1] and principles, we always presume when we see like sensible qualities that they have like secret powers, and expect that effects similar to those which we have experienced will follow from them. If a body of like color and consistency with that bread which we have formerly eaten be presented to us, we make no scruple of repeating the experiment and foresee with certainty like nourishment and support. Now this is a process of the mind or thought of which I would willingly know the foundation. It is allowed on all hands that

[1] The word "power" is here used in a loose and popular sense. The more accurate explication of it would give additional evidence to this argument.

there is no known connection between the sensible qualities and the secret powers, and, consequently, that the mind is not led to form such a conclusion concerning their constant and regular conjunction by anything which it knows of their nature. As to past *experience*, it can be allowed to give *direct* and *certain* information of those precise objects only, and that precise period of time which fell under its cognizance: But why this experience should be extended to future times and to other objects which, for aught we know, may be only in appearance similar, this is the main question on which I would insist. The bread which I formerly ate nourished me; that is, a body of such sensible qualities was, at that time, endued with such secret powers. But does it follow that other bread must also nourish me at another time, and that like sensible qualities must always be attended with like secret powers? The consequence seems nowise necessary. At least, it must be acknowledged that there is here a consequence drawn by the mind that there is a certain step taken, a process of thought, and an inference which wants to be explained. These two propositions are far from being the same: *I have found that such an object has always been attended with such an effect,* and *I foresee that other objects which are in appearance similar will be attended with similar effects.* I shall allow, if you please, that the one proposition may justly be inferred from the other: I know, in fact, that it always is inferred. But if you insist that the inference is made by a chain of reasoning, I desire you to produce that reasoning. The connection between these propositions is not intuitive. There is required a medium which may enable the mind to draw such an inference, if indeed it be drawn by reasoning and argument. What that medium is I must confess passes my comprehension; and it is incumbent on those to produce it who assert that it really exists and is the original of all our conclusions concerning matter of fact.

This negative argument must certainly, in process of time, become altogether convincing if many penetrating and able philosophers shall turn their inquiries this way, and no one be ever able to discover any connecting proposition or intermediate step which supports the understanding in this conclusion. But as the question is yet new, every reader may not trust so far to his own penetration as to conclude, because an argument escapes his inquiry, that therefore it does not really exist. For this reason it may be requisite to venture upon a more difficult task, and, enumerating all the branches of human knowledge, endeavor to show that none of them can afford such an argument.

All reasonings may be divided into two kinds, namely, demonstrative reasoning, or that concerning relations of ideas, and moral reasoning, or that concerning matter of fact and existence. That there are no demonstrative arguments in the case seems evident, since it implies no contradiction that the course of nature may change and that an object, seemingly like those which we have experienced, may be attended with different or contrary effects. May I not clearly and distinctly conceive that a body, falling from the clouds and which in all other respects resembles snow, has yet the taste of salt or feeling of fire? Is there any more intelligible proposition than to affirm that all the trees will flourish in December and January, and will decay in May and June? Now, whatever is intelligible and can be distinctly conceived implies no contradiction and can never be proved false by any demonstrative argument or abstract reasoning *a priori.*

If we be, therefore, engaged by arguments to put trust in past experience and make it the standard of our future judgment, these arguments must be probable only, or such as regard matter of fact and real existence, according to the division above mentioned. But that there is no argument of this kind must appear if our explication of that species of reasoning be admitted as solid and satisfactory. We have said that all arguments concerning existence are founded on the relation of cause and effect, that our knowledge of that relation is derived entirely from experience, and that all our experimental conclusions proceed upon the supposition that the future will be conformable to the past. To endeavor, therefore, the proof of this last supposition by probable arguments, or arguments regarding existence, must be evidently going in a circle and taking that for granted which is the very point in question.

In reality, all arguments from experience are founded on the similarity which we discover among natural objects, and by which we are induced to expect effects similar to those which we have found to follow from such objects. And though none but a fool or madman will ever pretend to dispute the authority of experience or to reject that great guide of human life, it may surely be allowed a philosopher to have so much curiosity at least as to examine the principle of human nature which gives this mighty authority to experience and makes us draw advantage from that similarity which nature has placed among different objects. From causes which appear similar, we expect similar effects. This is the sum of all our experimental conclusions. Now it seems evident that, if this conclusion were formed by reason, it would be as perfect at first, and upon one instance, as after ever so long a course of experience; but the case is far otherwise. Nothing so like as eggs, yet no one, on account of this appearing similarity, expects the same taste and relish in all of them. It is only after a long course of uniform experiments in any kind that we attain a firm reliance and security with regard to a particular event. Now, where is that process of reasoning which, from one instance, draws a conclusion so different from that which it infers from a hundred instances that are nowise different from that single one? This question I propose as much for the sake of information as with an intention of raising difficulties. I cannot find, I cannot imagine any such reasoning. But I keep my mind still open to instruction if anyone will vouchsafe to bestow it on me.

Should it be said that, from a number of uniform experiments, we *infer* a connection between the sensible qualities and the secret powers, this, I must confess, seems the same difficulty, couched in different terms. The question still occurs, On what process of argument is this *inference* founded? Where is the medium, the interposing ideas which join propositions so very wide of each other? It is confessed that the color, consistency, and other sensible qualities of bread appear not of themselves to have any connection with the secret powers of nourishment and support; for otherwise we could infer these secret powers from the first appearance of these sensible qualities without the aid of experience, contrary to the sentiment of all philosophers, and contrary to plain matter of fact. Here, then, is our natural state of ignorance with regard to the powers and influence of all objects. How is this remedied by experience? It only shows us a number of uniform effects resulting from certain objects, and teaches us that those particular objects, at that particular time, were endowed with such powers and forces. When a new object endowed with similar sensible qualities is produced, we expect similar powers and forces, and look for a like effect. From a body of like color and consistency with bread, we expect like nourishment and support. But this surely is a step or progress of the mind which wants to be explained. When a man says, *I have found, in all past instances, such sensible qualities, conjoined with such secret powers,* and when he says, *similar sensible qualities will always be conjoined with similar secret powers,* he is not guilty of a tautology, nor are these propositions in any respect the same. You say that the one proposition is an inference from the other; but you must confess that the inference is not intuitive, neither is it demonstrative. Of what nature is it then? To say it is experimental is begging the question. For all inferences from experience suppose, as their foundation, that the future will resemble the past and that similar powers will be conjoined with similar sensible qualities. If there be any suspicion that the course of nature may change, and that the past may be no rule for the future, all experience becomes useless and can give rise to no inference or conclusion. It is impossible, therefore, that any arguments from experience can prove this resemblance of the past to the future, since all these arguments are founded on the supposition of that resemblance. Let the course of things be allowed hitherto ever so regular, that alone, without some new argument or inference, proves not that for the future it will continue so. In vain do you pretend to have learned the nature of bodies from your past experience. Their secret nature, and consequently all their effects and influence, may change without any change in their sensible qualities. This happens sometimes, and with regard to some objects. Why may it not happen always, and with regard to all objects? What logic, what process of argument secures you against this supposition? My practice, you say, refutes my doubts. But you mistake the purport of my question. As an agent, I am quite satisfied in the point; but as a philosopher who has some share of curiosity, I will not say skepticism, I want to learn the foundation of this inference. No reading, no inquiry has yet been able to remove my difficulty or give me satisfaction in a matter of such importance. Can I do better than propose the difficulty to the public, even though, perhaps, I have small hopes of obtaining a solution? We shall at least, by this means, be sensible of our ignorance, if we do not augment our knowledge.

I must confess that a man is guilty of unpardonable arrogance who concludes, because an argument has escaped his own investigation, that therefore it does not really exist. I must also confess that, though all the learned, for several ages, should have employed themselves in fruitless search upon any subject, it may still, perhaps, be rash to conclude positively that the subject must therefore pass all human comprehension. Even though we examine all the sources of our knowledge and conclude them unfit for such a subject, there may still remain a suspicion that the enumeration is not complete or the examination not accurate. But with regard to the present subject, there are some considerations which seem to remove all this accusation of arrogance or suspicion of mistake.

It is certain that the most ignorant and stupid peasants, nay infants, nay even brute beasts, improve by experience and learn the qualities of natural objects by observing the effects which result from them. When a child has felt the sensation of pain from touching the flame of a candle, he will be careful not to put his hand near any candle, but will expect a similar effect from a cause which is similar in its sensible qualities and appearance. If you assert, therefore, that the understanding of the child is led into this conclusion by any process of argument or ratiocination, I may justly require you to produce that argument, nor have you any pretense to refuse so equitable a demand. You cannot say that the argument is abstruse and may possibly escape your inquiry, since you confess that it is obvious to the capacity of a mere infant. If you hesitate, therefore, a moment or if, after reflection, you produce an intricate or profound argument, you, in a manner, give up the question and confess that it is not reasoning which engages us to suppose the past resembling the future, and to expect similar effects from causes which are to appearance similar. This is the proposition which I intended to enforce in the present section. If I be right, I pretend not to have made any mighty discovery. And if I be wrong, I must acknowledge myself to be indeed a very backward scholar, since I cannot now discover an argument which, it seems, was perfectly familiar to me long before I was out of my cradle.

John Stuart Mill

Of the Ground of Induction and the Evidence for the Law of Universal Causation

OF THE GROUND OF INDUCTION

AXIOM OF THE UNIFORMITY OF THE COURSE OF NATURE

Induction properly so called, as distinguished from those mental operations, sometimes, though improperly, designated by the name, which I have attempted [earlier] to characterize, may, then, be summarily defined as generalization from experience. It consists in inferring from some individual instances in which a phenomenon is observed to occur that it occurs in all instances of a certain class, namely, in all which *resemble* the former in what are regarded as the material circumstances.

In what way the material circumstances are to be distinguished from those which are immaterial, or why some of the circumstances are material and others not so, we are not yet ready to point out. We must first observe that there is a principle implied in the very statement of what induction is; an assumption with regard to the course of nature and the order of the universe, namely, that there are such things in nature as parallel cases; that what happens once will, under a sufficient degree of similarity of circumstances, happen

From John Stuart Mill, *A System of Logic,* 10th ed., Book III, Chaps. 3 and 21, Longmans, Green & Co., London, 1879.

again, and not only again, but as often as the same circumstances recur. This, I say, is an assumption involved in every case of induction. And, if we consult the actual course of nature, we find that the assumption is warranted. The universe, so far as known to us, is so constituted that whatever is true in any one case is true in all cases of a certain description; the only difficulty is to find what description.

This universal fact, which is our warrant for all inferences from experience, has been described by different philosophers in different forms of language: that the course of nature is uniform; that the universe is governed by general laws; and the like. . . .

Whatever be the most proper mode of expressing it, the proposition that the course of nature is uniform is the fundamental principle or general axiom of induction. It would yet be a great error to offer this large generalization as any explanation of the inductive process. On the contrary, I hold it to be itself an instance of induction, and induction by no means of the most obvious kind. Far from being the first induction we make, it is one of the last or, at all events, one of those which are latest in attaining strict philosophical accuracy. As a general maxim, indeed, it has scarcely entered into the minds of any but philosophers; nor even by them, as we shall have many opportunities of remarking, have its extent and limits been always very justly conceived. The truth is that this great generalization is itself founded on prior generalizations. The obscurer laws of nature were discovered by means of it, but the more obvious ones must have been understood and assented to as general truths before it was ever heard of. We should never have thought of affirming that all phenomena take place according to general laws if we had not first arrived, in the case of a great multitude of phenomena, at some knowledge of the laws themselves, which could be done no otherwise than by induction. In what sense, then, can a principle which is so far from being our earliest induction be regarded as our warrant for all the others? In the only sense in which (as we have already seen) the general propositions which we place at the head of our reasonings when we throw them into syllogisms ever really contribute to their validity. As Archbishop Whately remarks, every induction is a syllogism with the major premise suppressed; or (as I prefer expressing it) every induction may be thrown into the form of a syllogism by supplying a major premise. If this be actually done, the principle which we are now considering, that of the uniformity of the course of nature, will appear as the ultimate major premise of all inductions and will, therefore, stand to all inductions in the relation in which, as has been shown at so much length, the major proposition of a syllogism always stands to the conclusion, not contributing at all to prove it, but being a necessary condition of its being proved; since no conclusion is proved for which there cannot be found a true major premise.

The statement that the uniformity of the course of nature is the ultimate major premise in all cases of induction may be thought to require some explanation. The immediate major premise in every inductive argument it certainly is not. Of that, Archbishop Whately's must be held to be the correct account. The induction, "John, Peter, etc., are mortal, therefore all mankind are mortal," may, as he justly says, be thrown into a syllogism by prefixing as a major premise (what is at any rate a necessary condition of the validity of the argument), namely, that what is true of John, Peter, etc., is true of all mankind. But how came we by this major premise? It is not self-evident; nay, in all cases of unwarranted generalization, it is not true. How, then, is it arrived at? Necessarily either by induction or ratiocination; and if by induction, the process, like all other inductive arguments, may be thrown into the form of a syllogism. This previous syllogism it is, therefore, necessary to construct. There is, in the long run, only one possible construction. The real proof that what is true of John, Peter, etc., is true of all mankind can only be that a different supposition would be inconsistent with the uniformity which we know to exist in the course of nature. Whether there would be this inconsistency or not may be a matter of long and delicate inquiry, but unless there would, we have no sufficient ground for the major of the inductive syllogism. It hence appears that, if we throw the whole course of any inductive argument into a series of syllogisms, we shall arrive by more or fewer steps at an ultimate syllogism which will have for its major premise the principle or axiom of the uniformity of the course of nature.[1]

. . .

THE QUESTION OF INDUCTIVE LOGIC STATED

In order to [reach] a better understanding of the problem which the logician must solve if he would establish a scientific theory of induction, let us compare a few cases of incorrect inductions with others which are acknowledged to be legitimate. Some, we know, which were believed for centuries to be correct were nevertheless incorrect. That all swans are white cannot have been a good induction, since the conclusion has turned out erroneous. The experience, however, on which the conclusion rested was genuine. From the earliest records, the testimony of the inhabitants of the known world was unanimous on the point. The uniform experience, therefore, of the inhabitants of the known world, agreeing in a common result, without one known instance of deviation from that result, is not always sufficient to establish a general conclusion.

But let us now turn to an instance apparently not very dissimilar to this. Mankind were wrong, it seems, in concluding that all swans were white; are we also wrong when we conclude that all men's heads grow above their shoulders and never below, in spite of the conflicting testimony of the naturalist Pliny? As there were black swans, though civilized people had existed for three thousand years on the earth without meeting with them, may there not

[1] But though it is a condition of the validity of every induction that there be uniformity in the course of nature, it is not a necessary condition that the uniformity should pervade all nature. It is enough that it pervades the particular class of phenomena to which the induction relates. An induction concerning the motions of the planets or the properties of the magnet would not be vitiated though we were to suppose that wind and weather are the sport of chance, provided it be assumed that astronomical and magnetic phenomena are under the dominion of general laws. Otherwise the early experience of mankind would have rested on a very weak foundation, for in the infancy of science it could not be known that *all* phenomena are regular in their course.

Neither would it be correct to say that every induction by which we infer any truth implies the general fact of uniformity *as foreknown*, even in reference to the kind of phenomena concerned. It implies *either* that this general fact is already known, *or* that we may now know it; as the conclusion, the Duke of Wellington is mortal, drawn from the instances A, B, and C, implies either that we have already concluded all men to be mortal, or that we are now entitled to do so from the same evidence. A vast amount of confusion and paralogism respecting the grounds of induction would be dispelled by keeping in view these simple considerations.

also be "men whose heads do grow beneath their shoulders," notwithstanding a rather less perfect unanimity of negative testimony from observers? Most persons would answer, No; it was more credible that a bird should vary in its color than that men should vary in the relative position of their principal organs. And there is no doubt that in so saying they would be right; but to say why they are right would be impossible without entering more deeply than is usually done into the true theory of induction.

Again, there are cases in which we reckon with the most unfailing confidence upon uniformity, and other cases in which we do not count upon it at all. In some we feel complete assurance that the future will resemble the past, the unknown be precisely similar to the known. In others, however invariable may be the result obtained from the instances which have been observed, we draw from them no more than a very feeble presumption that the like result will hold in all other cases. That a straight line is the shortest distance between two points we do not doubt to be true even in the region of the fixed stars.[2] When a chemist announces the existence and properties of a newly-discovered substance, if we confide in his accuracy, we feel assured that the conclusions he has arrived at will hold universally, though the induction be founded but on a single instance. We do not withhold our assent, waiting for a repetition of the experiment; or if we do, it is from a doubt whether the one experiment was properly made, not whether if properly made it would be conclusive. Here, then, is a general law of nature inferred without hesitation from a single instance, a universal proposition from a singular one. Now mark another case, and contrast it with this. Not all the instances which have been observed since the beginning of the world in support of the general proposition that all crows are black would be deemed a sufficient presumption of the truth of the proposition to outweigh the testimony of one unexceptionable witness who should affirm that, in some region of the earth not fully explored, he had caught and examined a crow and had found it to be gray.

Why is a single instance, in some cases, sufficient for a complete induction, while, in others, myriads of concurring instances, without a single exception known or presumed, go such a very little way toward establishing a universal proposition? Whoever can answer this question knows more of the philosophy of logic than the wisest of the ancients and has solved the problem of induction.

OF THE EVIDENCE OF THE LAW OF UNIVERSAL CAUSATION

THE LAW OF CAUSALITY DOES NOT REST ON AN INSTINCT

We have now completed our review of the logical processes by which the laws or uniformities of the sequence of phenomena and those uniformities in their co-existence which depend on the laws of their sequence are ascertained or tested. As we recognized in the commencement and have been enabled to see more clearly in the progress of the investigation, the basis of all these logical operations is the law of causation. The validity of all the inductive methods depends on the assumption that every event, or the beginning of every phenomenon, must have some cause, some antecedent, on the exist-

[2] In strictness, wherever the present constitution of space exists, which we have ample reason to believe that it does in the region of the fixed stars.

ence of which it is invariably and unconditionally consequent. In the method of agreement this is obvious, that method avowedly proceeding on the supposition that we have found the true cause as soon as we have negatived every other. The assertion is equally true of the method of difference. That method authorizes us to infer a general law from two instances: one, in which A exists together with a multitude of other circumstances, and B follows; another, in which, A being removed and all other circumstances remaining the same, B is prevented. What, however, does this prove? It proves that B, in the particular instance, cannot have had any other cause than A; but to conclude from this that A was the cause or that A will on other occasions be followed by B is only allowable on the assumption that B must have some cause, that among its antecedents in any single instance in which it occurs, there must be one which has the capacity of producing it at other times. This being admitted, it is seen that in the case in question that antecedent can be no other than A; but that, if it be no other than A, it must be A is not proved; by these instances at least, but taken for granted. There is no need to spend time in proving that the same thing is true of the other inductive methods. The universality of the law of causation is assumed in them all.

But is this assumption warranted? Doubtless (it may be said) *most* phenomena are connected as effects with some antecedent or cause, that is, are never produced unless some assignable fact has preceded them, but the very circumstance that complicated processes of induction are sometimes necessary shows that cases exist in which this regular order of succession is not apparent to our unaided apprehension. If, then, the processes which bring these cases within the same category with the rest require that we should assume the universality of the very law which they do not at first sight appear to exemplify, is not this a *petitio principii?* Can we prove a proposition by an argument which takes it for granted? And if not so proved, on what evidence does it rest?

For this difficulty, which I have purposely stated in the strongest terms it will admit of, the school of metaphysicians who have long predominated in this country find a ready salvo. They affirm that the universality of causation is a truth which we cannot help believing, that the belief in it is an instinct, one of the laws of our believing faculty. As the proof of this, they say, and they have nothing else to say, that everybody does believe it, and they number it among the propositions, rather numerous in their catalogue, which may be logically argued against and perhaps cannot be logically proved, but which are of higher authority than logic, and so essentially inherent in the human mind that even he who denies them in speculation shows by his habitual practice that his arguments make no impression upon himself.

Into the merits of this question, considered as one of psychology, it would be foreign to my purpose to enter here, but I must protest against adducing, as evidence of the truth of a fact in external nature, the disposition, however strong or however general, of the human mind to believe it. . . .

Were we to suppose (what it is perfectly possible to imagine) that the present order of the universe were brought to an end, and that a chaos succeeded in which there was no fixed succession of events, and the past gave no assurance of the future; if a human being were miraculously kept alive to witness this change, he surely would soon cease to believe in any uniformity, the uniformity itself no longer existing. If this be admitted, the belief in uniformity either is not an instinct, or it is an instinct conquerable, like all other instincts, by acquired knowledge.

. . .

—BUT ON AN INDUCTION BY SIMPLE ENUMERATION

As was observed in a former place, the belief we entertain in the universality, throughout nature, of the law of cause and effect is itself an instance of induction, and by no means one of the earliest which any of us, or which mankind in general, can have made. We arrive at this universal law by generalization from many laws of inferior generality. We should never have had the notion of causation (in the philosophical meaning of the term) as a condition of all phenomena unless many cases of causation, or, in other words, many partial uniformities of sequence, had previously become familiar. The more obvious of the particular uniformities suggest and give evidence of the general uniformity, and the general uniformity, once established, enables us to prove the remainder of the particular uniformities of which it is made up. As, however, all rigorous processes of induction presuppose the general uniformity, our knowledge of the particular uniformities from which it was first inferred was not, of course, derived from rigorous induction, but from the loose and uncertain mode of induction *per enumerationem simplicem*, and the law of universal causation, being collected from results so obtained, cannot itself rest on any better foundation.

It would seem, therefore, that induction *per enumerationem simplicem* not only is not necessarily an illicit logical process, but is in reality the only kind of induction possible, since the more elaborate process depends for its validity on a law itself obtained in that inartificial mode. Is there not, then, an inconsistency in contrasting the looseness of one method with the rigidity of another, when that other is indebted to the looser method for its own foundation?

The inconsistency, however, is only apparent. Assuredly, if induction by simple enumeration were an invalid process, no process grounded on it could be valid; just as no reliance could be placed on telescopes if we could not trust our eyes. But though a valid process, it is a fallible one, and fallible in very different degrees; if, therefore, we can substitute for the more fallible forms of the process an operation grounded on the same process in a less fallible form, we shall have effected a very material improvement. And this is what scientific induction does.

. . .

IN WHAT CASES SUCH INDUCTION IS ALLOWABLE

Now the precariousness of the method of simple enumeration is in an inverse ratio to the largeness of the generalization. The process is delusive and insufficient, exactly in proportion as the subject-matter of the observation is special and limited in extent. As the sphere widens, this unscientific method becomes less and less liable to mislead, and the most universal class of truths, the law of causation, for instance, and the principles of number and of geometry, are duly and satisfactorily proved by that method alone, nor are they susceptible of any other proof.

With respect to the whole class of generalizations of which we have recently treated, the uniformities which depend on causation, the truth of the remark just made follows by obvious inference from the principles laid down in the preceding chapters. When a fact has been observed a certain number of times to be true and is not in any instance known to be false, if we at once affirm that fact as a universal truth or law of nature without either testing it by any of the four methods of induction or deducing it from other known laws, we shall, in general, err grossly, but we are perfectly justified in affirming it as an empirical law, true within certain limits of time, place, and circumstance, provided the number of coincidences be greater than can with any probability be ascribed to chance. The reason for not extending it beyond those limits is that the fact of its holding true within them may be a consequence of collocations which cannot be concluded to exist in one place because they exist in another, or may be dependent on the accidental absence of counteracting agencies, which any variation of time or the smallest change of circumstances may possibly bring into play. If we suppose, then, the subject-matter of any generalization to be so widely diffused that there is no time, no place, and no combination of circumstances but must afford an example either of its truth or of its falsity, and if it be never found otherwise than true, its truth cannot be contingent on any collocations, unless such as exist at all times and places; nor can it be frustrated by any counteracting agencies, unless by such as never actually occur. It is, therefore, an empirical law co-extensive with all human experience; at which point the distinction between empirical laws and laws of nature vanishes, and the proposition takes its place among the most firmly established as well as largest truths accessible to science.

Charles Sanders Peirce

The Classification of Arguments, the Probability of Induction, and the Order of Nature

DEDUCTION, INDUCTION, AND HYPOTHESIS

The chief business of the logician is to classify arguments; for all testing clearly depends on classification. The classes of the logicians are defined by certain typical forms called syllogisms. For example, the syllogism called Barbara is as follows:

S is M, M is P;
Hence, S is P.

Or, to put words for letters—

Enoch and Elijah were men, all men die;
Hence, Enoch and Elijah must have died.

The "is P" of the logicians stands for any verb, active or neuter. It is capable of strict proof (with which, however, I will not trouble the reader) that all arguments whatever can be put into this form; but only under the condition that the *is* shall mean "*is* for the purposes of the argument" or "is represented by." Thus, an induction will appear in this form something like this:

These beans are two-thirds white,
But, the beans in this bag are (represented by) these beans;
∴ The beans in the bag are two-thirds white.

But, because all inference may be reduced in some way to *Barbara,* it does not follow that this is the most appropriate form in which to represent every kind of inference. On the contrary, to show the distinctive characters of different sorts of inference, they must clearly be exhibited in different forms peculiar to each. *Barbara* particularly typifies deductive reasoning; and so long as the *is* is taken literally, no inductive reasoning can be put into this form. *Barbara* is, in fact, nothing but the application of a rule. The so-called major premiss lays down this rule; as, for example, *All men are mortal.* The other or minor

From C. S. Peirce, "Deduction, Induction and Hypothesis," *Popular Science Monthly,* Vol. 13 (1878); "The Doctrine of Chances" and "The Probability of Induction," *Ibid.,* Vol. 12 (1878); and "The Order of Nature," *Ibid.,* Vol. 12. This selection is taken from four of the six articles Peirce published under the general title "Illustrations of the Logic of Science." The articles are reprinted in *Collected Papers of Charles Sanders Peirce,* Vol. 5, 1934, and Vol. 6, 1935.

premiss states a case under the rule; as, *Enoch was a man.* The conclusion applies the rule to the case and states the result: *Enoch is mortal.* All deduction is of this character; it is merely the application of general rules to particular cases. Sometimes this is not very evident, as in the following:

All quadrangles are figures,
But no triangle is a quadrangle;
Therefore, some figures are not triangles.

But here the reasoning is really this:

Rule. —Every quadrangle is other than a triangle.
Case. —Some figures are quadrangles.
Result. —Some figures are not triangles.

Inductive or synthetic reasoning, being something more than the mere application of a general rule to a particular case, can never be reduced to this form.

If, from a bag of beans of which we know that ⅔ are white, we take one at random, it is a deductive inference that this bean is probably white, the probability being ⅔. We have, in effect, the following syllogism:

Rule. —The beans in this bag are ⅔ white.
Case. —This bean has been drawn in such a way that in the long run the relative number of white beans so drawn would be equal to the relative number in the bag.
Result. —This bean has been drawn in such a way that in the long run it would turn out white ⅔ of the time.

If instead of drawing one bean we draw a handful at random and conclude that about ⅔ of the handful are probably white, the reasoning is of the same sort. If, however, not knowing what proportion of white beans there are in the bag, we draw a handful at random and, finding ⅔ of the beans in the handful white, conclude that about ⅔ of those in the bag are white, we are rowing up the current of deductive sequence, and are concluding a rule from the observation of a result in a certain case. This is particularly clear when all the handful turn out one color. The induction then is:

These beans were in this bag.
These beans are white.
∴All the beans in the bag were white.
Which is but an inversion of the deductive syllogism:
Rule.—All the beans in the bag were white.
Case.—These beans were in the bag.
Result.—These beans are white.

So that induction is the inference of the *rule* from the *case* and *result.*

But this is not the only way of inverting a deductive syllogism so as to produce a synthetic inference. Suppose I enter a room and there find a number of bags, containing different kinds of beans. On the table there is a handful of white beans; and, after some searching, I find one of the bags contains white beans only. I at once infer as a probability, or as a fair guess, that this handful was taken out of that bag. This sort of inference is called *making an hypothesis.* It is the inference of a *case* from a *rule* and a *result.* We have, then—

DEDUCTION

Rule.—All the beans from this bag are white.
Case.—These beans are from this bag.
∴*Result.*—These beans are white.

INDUCTION

Case.—These beans are from this bag.
Result.—These beans are white.
∴*Rule.*—All the beans from this bag are white.

HYPOTHESIS

Rule.—All the beans from this bag are white.
Result.—These beans are white.
∴*Case.*—These beans are from this bag.

We, accordingly, classify all inference as follows:

Inference

Deductive or Analytic   Synthetic

Induction   Hypothesis

Induction is where we generalize from a number of cases of which something is true, and infer that the same thing is true of a whole class. Or, where we find a certain thing to be true of a certain proportion of cases and infer that it is true of the same proportion of the whole class. Hypothesis is where we find some very curious circumstance, which would be explained by the supposition that it was a case of a certain general rule, and thereupon adopt that supposition. Or, where we find that in certain respects two objects have a strong resemblance, and infer that they resemble one another strongly in other respects.

I once landed at a seaport in a Turkish province; and, as I was walking up to the house which I was to visit, I met a man upon horseback, surrounded by four horsemen holding a canopy over his head. As the governor of the province was the only personage I could think of who would be so greatly honored, I inferred that this was he. This was an hypothesis.

Fossils are found; say, remains like those of fishes, but far in the interior of the country. To explain the phenomenon, we suppose the sea once washed over this land. This is another hypothesis.

Numberless documents and monuments refer to a conqueror called Napoleon Bonaparte. Though we have not seen the man, yet we cannot explain what we have seen, namely, all these documents and monuments, without supposing that he really existed. Hypothesis again.

As a general rule, hypothesis is a weak kind of argument. It often inclines our judgment so slightly toward its conclusion that we cannot say that we believe the latter to be true; we only surmise that it may be so. But there is no difference except one of degree between such an inference and that by which we are led to believe that we remember the occurrences of yesterday from our feeling as if we did so.

. . .

THE DOCTRINE OF CHANCES

. . .

III

To get a clear idea of what we mean by probability, we have to consider what real and sensible difference there is between one degree of probability and another.

The character of probability belongs primarily, without doubt, to certain inferences. Locke explains it as follows: After remarking that the mathematician positively knows that the sum of the three angles of a triangle is equal to two right angles because he apprehends the geometrical proof, he thus continues: "But another man who never took the pains to observe the demonstration, hearing a mathematician, a man of credit, affirm the three angles of a triangle to be equal to two right ones, *assents* to it; *i.e.,* receives it for true. In which case the foundation of his assent is the probability of the thing, the proof being such as, for the most part, carries truth with it; the man on whose testimony he receives it not being wont to affirm anything contrary to, or besides his knowledge, especially in matters of this kind." The celebrated *Essay Concerning Human Understanding* contains many passages which, like this one, make the first steps in profound analyses which are not further developed. It was shown in the first of these papers that the validity of an inference does not depend on any tendency of the mind to accept it, however strong such tendency may be; but consists in the real fact that, when premisses like those of the argument in question are true, conclusions related to them like that of this argument are also true. It was remarked that in a logical mind an argument is always conceived as a member of a *genus* of arguments all constructed in the same way, and such that, when their premisses are real facts, their conclusions are so also. If the argument is demonstrative, then this is always so; if it is only probable, then it is for the most part so. As Locke says, the probable argument is "*such as* for the most part carries truth with it."

According to this, that real and sensible difference between one degree of probability and another, in which the meaning of the distinction lies, is that in the frequent employment of two different modes of inference, one will carry truth with it oftener than the other. It is evident that this is the only difference there is in the existing fact. Having certain premisses, a man draws a certain conclusion, and as far as this inference alone is concerned the only possible practical question is whether that conclusion is true or not, and between existence and non-existence there is no middle term. "Being only is and nothing is altogether not," said Parmenides; and this is in strict accordance with the analysis of the conception of reality given in the last paper. For we found that the distinction of reality and fiction depends on the supposition that sufficient investigation would cause one opinion to be universally received and all others to be rejected. That presupposition, involved in the very conceptions of reality and figment, involves a complete sundering of the two. It is the heaven-and-hell idea in the domain of thought. But, in the long run, there is a real fact which corresponds to the idea of probability, and it is that a given mode of inference sometimes proves successful and sometimes not, and that in a ratio ultimately fixed. As we go on drawing inference after inference of the given kind, during the first ten or hundred cases the ratio of successes may be expected to show considerable fluctuations; but when we come into the thousands and millions, these fluctuations become less and less; and if we continue long enough, the ratio will approximate toward a fixed limit. We may, therefore, define the probability of a mode of argument as the proportion of cases in which it carries truth with it.

The inference from the premiss, A, to the conclusion, B, depends, as we have seen, on the guiding principle, that if a fact of the class A is true, a fact of the class B is true. The probability consists of the fraction whose numerator is the number of times in which both A and B are true, and whose denominator is the total number of times in which A is true, whether B is so or not. Instead of speaking of this as the probability of the inference, there is not the slightest objection to calling it the probability that, if A happens, B happens. But to speak of the probability of the event B, without naming the condition, really has no meaning at all. It is true that when it is perfectly obvious what condition is meant, the ellipsis may be permitted. But we should avoid contracting the habit of using language in this way (universal as the habit is), because it gives rise to a vague way of thinking, as if the action of causation might either determine an event to happen or determine it not to happen, or leave it more or less free to happen or not, so as to give rise to an *inherent* chance in regard to its occurrence. It is quite clear to me that some of the worst and most persistent errors in the use of the doctrine of chances have arisen from this vicious mode of expression.[1]

IV

But there remains an important point to be cleared up. According to what has been said, the idea of probability essentially belongs to a kind of inference which is repeated indefinitely. An individual inference must be either true or false, and can show no effect of probability; and, therefore, in reference to a single case considered in itself, probability can have no meaning. Yet if a man had to choose between drawing a card from a pack containing twenty-five red cards and a black one, or from a pack containing twenty-five black cards and a red one, and if the drawing of a red card were destined to transport him to eternal felicity, and that of a black one to consign him to everlasting woe, it would be folly to deny that he ought to prefer the pack containing the larger proportion of red cards, although, from the nature of the risk, it could not be repeated. It is not easy to reconcile this with our analysis of the conception of chance. But suppose he should choose the red pack, and should draw the wrong card, what consolation would he have? He might say that he had acted in accordance with reason, but that would only show that his reason was absolutely worthless. And if he should choose the right card, how could he regard it as anything but a happy accident? He could not say that if he had

[1] The conception of probability here set forth is substantially that first developed by Mr. Venn, in his *Logic of Chance*. Of course, a vague apprehension of the idea had always existed, but the problem was to make it perfectly clear, and to him belongs the credit of first doing this.

drawn from the other pack, he might have drawn the wrong one, because an hypothetical proposition such as, "if A, then B," means nothing with reference to a single case. Truth consists in the existence of a real fact corresponding to the true proposition. Corresponding to the proposition, "if A, then B," there may be the fact that *whenever* such an event as A happens such an event as B happens. But in the case supposed, which has no parallel as far as this man is concerned, there would be no real fact whose existence could give any truth to the statement that, if he had drawn from the other pack, he might have drawn a black card. Indeed, since the validity of an inference consists in the truth of the hypothetical proposition that *if* the premisses be true the conclusion will also be true, and since the only real fact which can correspond to such a proposition is that whenever the antecedent is true the consequent is so also, it follows that there can be no sense in reasoning in an isolated case, at all.

. . .

THE PROBABILITY OF INDUCTION

. . .

Late in the last century, Immanuel Kant asked the question, "How are synthetical judgments *a priori* possible?" By synthetical judgments he meant such as assert positive fact and are not mere affairs of arrangement; in short, judgments of the kind which synthetical reasoning produces, and which analytic reasoning cannot yield. By *a priori* judgments he meant such as that all outward objects are in space, every event has a cause, etc., propositions which according to him can never be inferred from experience. Not so much by his answer to this question as by the mere asking of it, the current philosophy of that time was shattered and destroyed, and a new epoch in its history was begun. But before asking *that* question he ought to have asked the more general one, "How are any synthetical judgments at all possible?" How is it that a man can observe one fact and straightway pronounce judgment concerning another different fact not involved in the first? Such reasoning, as we have seen, has, at least in the usual sense of the phrase, no definite probability; how, then, can it add to our knowledge? This is a strange paradox; the Abbé Gratry says it is a miracle, and that every true induction is an immediate inspiration from on high. I respect this explanation far more than many a pedantic attempt to solve the question by some juggle with probabilities, with the forms of syllogism, or what not. I respect it because it shows an appreciation of the depth of the problem, because it assigns an adequate cause, and because it is intimately connected—as the true account should be—with a general philosophy of the universe. At the same time, I do not accept this explanation, because an explanation should tell *how* a thing is done, and to assert a perpetual miracle seems to be an abandonment of all hope of doing that, without sufficient justification.

It will be interesting to see how the answer which Kant gave to his question about synthetical judgments *a priori* will appear if extended to the question of synthetical judgments in general. That answer is, that synthetical judgments *a priori* are possible because whatever is universally true is involved in the conditions of experience. Let us apply this to a general synthetical reasoning. I take from a bag a handful of beans; they are all purple, and I infer that all the beans in the bag are purple. How can I do that? Why, upon the principle that whatever is universally true of my experience (which is here the appearance of these different beans) is involved in the condition of experience. The condition of this special experience is that all these beans were taken from that bag. According to Kant's principle, then, whatever is found true of all the beans drawn from the bag must find its explanation in some peculiarity of the contents of the bag. This is a satisfactory statement of the principle of induction.

When we draw a deductive or analytic conclusion, our rule of inference is that facts of a certain general character are either invariably or in a certain proportion of cases accompanied by facts of another general character. Then our premiss being a fact of the former class, we infer with certainty or with the appropriate degree of probability the existence of a fact of the second class. But the rule for synthetic inference is of a different kind. When we sample a bag of beans we do not in the least assume that the fact of some beans being purple involves the necessity or even the probability of other beans being so. On the contrary, the conceptualistic method of treating probabilities, which really amounts simply to the deductive treatment of them, when rightly carried out leads to the result that a synthetic inference has just an even chance in its favour, or in other words is absolutely worthless. The colour of one bean is entirely independent of that of another. But synthetic inference is founded upon a classification of facts, not according to their characters, but according to the manner of obtaining them. Its rule is, that a number of facts obtained in a given way will in general more or less resemble other facts obtained in the same way; or, *experiences whose conditions are the same will have the same general characters.*

In the former case, we know that premisses precisely similar in form to those of the given ones will yield true conclusions, just once in a calculable number of times. In the latter case, we only know that premisses obtained under circumstances similar to the given ones (though perhaps themselves very different) will yield true conclusions, at least once in a calculable number of times. We may express this by saying that in the case of analytic inference we know the probability of our conclusion (if the premisses are true), but in the case of synthetic inferences we only know the degree of trustworthiness of our proceeding. As all knowledge comes from synthetic inference, we must equally infer that all human certainty consists merely in our knowing that the processes by which our knowledge has been derived are such as must generally have led to true conclusions.

Though a synthetic inference cannot by any means be reduced to deduction, yet that the rule of induction will hold good in the long run may be deduced from the principle that reality is only the object of the final opinion to which sufficient investigation would lead. That belief gradually tends to fix itself under the influence of inquiry is, indeed, one of the facts with which logic sets out.

THE ORDER OF NATURE

I

In the last [section] we examined the nature of inductive or synthetic reasoning. We found it to be a process of sampling. A number of specimens of a class are taken, not by selection within that class, but at random. These specimens will agree in a great number of respects. If, now, it were likely that a second lot would agree with the first in the majority of these respects, we might base on this consideration an inference in regard to any one of these characters. But such an inference would neither be of the nature of induction, nor would it (except in special cases) be valid, because the vast majority of points of agreement in the first sample drawn would generally be entirely accidental, as well as insignificant. To illustrate this, I take the ages at death of the first five poets given in Wheeler's *Biographical Dictionary*. They are:

Aagard, 48.
Abeille, 70.
Abulola, 84.
Abunowas, 48.
Accords, 45.

These five ages have the following characters in common:

1. The difference of the two digits composing the number, divided by three, leaves a remainder of *one*.
2. The first digit raised to the power indicated by the second, and divided by three, leaves a remainder of *one*.
3. The sum of the prime factors of each age, including one, is divisible by three.

It is easy to see that the number of accidental agreements of this sort would be quite endless. But suppose that, instead of considering a character because of its prevalence in the sample, we designate a character before taking the sample, selecting it for its importance, obviousness, or other point of interest. Then two considerable samples drawn at random are extremely likely to agree approximately in regard to the proportion of occurrences of a character so chosen. *The inference that a previously designated character has nearly the same frequency of occurrence in the whole of a class that it has in a sample drawn at random out of that class is induction.* If the character be not previously designated, then a sample in which it is found to be prevalent can only serve to suggest that it *may be* prevalent in the whole class. We may consider this surmise as an inference if we please—an inference of possibility; but a second sample must be drawn to test the question of whether the character actually is prevalent. Instead of designating beforehand a single character in reference to which we will examine a sample, we may designate two, and use the same sample to determine the relative frequencies of both. This will be making two inductive inferences at once; and, of course, we are less certain that both will yield correct conclusions than we should be that either separately would do so. What is true of two characters is true of any limited number. Now, the number of characters which have any considerable interest for us in reference to any class of objects is more moderate than might be supposed. As we shall be sure to examine any sample with reference to these characters, they may be regarded not exactly as predesignated, but as predetermined (which amounts to the same thing); and we may infer that the sample represents the class in all these respects if we please, remembering only that this is not so secure an inference as if the particular quality to be looked for had been fixed upon beforehand.

The demonstration of this theory of induction rests upon principles and follows methods which are accepted by all those who display in other matters the particular knowledge and force of mind which qualify them to judge of this. The theory itself, however, quite unaccountably seems never to have occurred to any of the writers who have undertaken to explain synthetic reasoning. The most widely-spread opinion in the matter is one which was much promoted by Mr. John Stuart Mill—namely, that induction depends for its validity upon the uniformity of Nature—that is, on the principle that what happens once will, under a sufficient degree of similarity of circumstances, happen again as often as the same circumstances recur. The application is this: The fact that different things belong to the same class constitutes the similarity of circumstances, and the induction is good, provided this similarity is "sufficient." What happens once is, that a number of these things are found to have a certain character; what may be expected, then, to happen again as often as the circumstances recur consists in this, that all things belonging to the same class should have the same character.

This analysis of induction has, I venture to think, various imperfections, to some of which it may be useful to call attention. In the first place, when I put my hand in a bag and draw out a handful of beans, and, finding three-quarters of them black, infer that about three-quarters of all in the bag are black, my inference is obviously of the same kind as if I had found any larger proportion, or the whole, of the sample black, and had assumed that it represented in that respect the rest of the contents of the bag. But the analysis in question hardly seems adapted to the explanation of this *proportionate* induction, where the conclusion, instead of being that a certain event uniformly happens under certain circumstances, is precisely that it does not uniformly occur, but only happens in a certain proportion of cases. It is true that the whole sample may be regarded as a single object, and the inference may be brought under the formula proposed by considering the conclusion to be that any similar sample will show a similar proportion among its constituents. But this is to treat the induction as if it rested on a single instance, which gives a very false idea of its probability.

In the second place, if the uniformity of Nature were the sole warrant of induction, we should have no right to draw one in regard to a character whose constancy we knew nothing about. Accordingly, Mr. Mill says that, though none but white swans were known to Europeans for thousands of years, yet the inference that all swans were white was "not a good induction," because it was not known that color was a usual generic character (it, in fact, not being so by any means). But it is mathematically demonstrable that an inductive inference may have as high a degree of probability as you please independent of any antecedent knowledge of the constancy of the character inferred. Before it was known that color is not usually a character of *genera*, there was certainly a considerable probability that all swans were white. But the further study of the *genera* of animals led to the induction of their non-uniformity in regard to color. A deductive application of this general proposition would have gone far to overcome the probability of the universal whiteness of swans before the black species was discovered. When we do know anything in regard to the general constancy or inconstancy of a character, the application of that general knowledge to the particular class to which any induction relates, though it serves to increase or diminish the force of the induction, is, like every application of general knowledge to particular cases, deductive in its nature and not inductive.

In the third place, to say that inductions are true because similar events happen in similar circumstances—or, what is the same thing, because objects similar in some respects are likely to be similar in others—is to overlook those conditions which really are essential to the validity of inductions. When we take all the characters into account, any pair of objects resemble one another in just as many particulars as any other pair. If we limit ourselves to such characters as have for us any importance, interest, or obviousness, then a synthetic conclusion may be drawn, but only on condition that the specimens by which we judge have been taken at random from the class in regard to which we are to form a judgment, and not selected as belonging to any sub-class. The induction only has its full force when the character concerned has been designated before examining the sample. These are the essentials of induction, and they are not recognized in attributing the validity of induction to the uniformity of Nature. The explanation of induction by the doctrine of probabilities, given in the last of these papers, is not a mere metaphysical formula, but is one from which all the rules of synthetic reasoning can be deduced systematically and with mathematical cogency. But the account of the matter by a principle of Nature, even if it were in other respects satisfactory, presents the fatal disadvantage of leaving us quite as much afloat as before in regard to the proper method of induction. It does not surprise me, therefore, that those who adopt this theory have given erroneous rules for the conduct of reasoning, nor that the greater number of examples put forward by Mr. Mill in his first edition, as models of what inductions should be, proved in the light of further scientific progress so particularly unfortunate that they had to be replaced by others in later editions. One would have supposed that Mr. Mill might have based an induction on *this* circumstance, especially as it is his avowed principle that, if the conclusion of an induction turns out false, it cannot have been a good induction. Nevertheless, neither he nor any of his scholars seem to have been led to suspect, in the least, the perfect solidity of the framework which he devised for securely supporting the mind in its passage from the known to the unknown, although at its first trial it did not answer quite so well as had been expected.

II

When we have drawn any statistical induction—such, for instance, as that one-half of all births are of male children—it is always possible to discover, by investigation sufficiently prolonged, a class of which the same predicate may be affirmed universally; to find out, for instance, *what sort of* births are of male children. The truth of this principle follows immediately from the theorem that there is a character peculiar to every possible group of objects. The form in which the principle is usually stated is, that *every event must have a cause.*

But, though there exists a cause for every event, and that of a kind which is capable of being discovered, yet if there be nothing to guide us to the discovery; if we have to hunt among all the events in the world without any scent; if, for instance, the sex of a child might equally be supposed to depend on the configuration of the planets, on what was going on at the antipodes, or on anything else—then the discovery would have no chance of ever getting made.

That we ever do discover the precise causes of things, that any induction whatever is absolutely without exception, is what we have no right to assume. On the contrary, it is an easy corollary, from the theorem just referred to, that every empirical rule has an exception. But there are certain of our inductions which present an approach to universality so extraordinary that, even if we are to suppose that they are not strictly universal truths, we cannot possibly think that they have been reached merely by accident. The most remarkable laws of this kind are those of *time* and *space.* With reference to space, Bishop Berkeley first showed, in a very conclusive manner, that it was not a thing *seen,* but a thing *inferred.* Berkeley chiefly insists on the impossibility of directly seeing the third dimension of space, since the retina of the eye is a surface. But, in point of fact, the retina is not even a surface; it is a conglomeration of nerve-needles directed toward the light and having only their extreme points sensitive, these points lying at considerable distances from one another compared with their areas. Now, of these points, certainly the excitation of no one singly can produce the perception of a surface, and consequently not the aggregate of all the sensations can amount to this. But certain relations subsist between the excitations of different nerve-points, and these constitute the premises upon which the hypothesis of space is founded, and from which it is inferred. That space is not immediately perceived is now universally admitted; and a mediate cognition is what is called an inference, and is subject to the criticism of logic. But what are we to say to the fact of every chicken as soon as it is hatched solving a problem whose data are of a complexity sufficient to try the greatest mathematical powers? It would be insane to deny that the tendency to light upon the conception of space is inborn in the mind of the chicken and of every animal. The same thing is equally true of time. That time is not directly perceived is evident, since no lapse of time is present, and we only perceive what is present. That, not having the idea of time, we should never be able to perceive the flow in our sensations without some particular aptitude for it, will probably also be admitted. The idea of force—at least, in its rudiments—is another conception so early arrived at, and found in animals so low in the scale of intelligence, that it must be supposed innate. But the innateness of an idea admits of degree, for it consists in the tendency of that idea to present itself to the mind. Some ideas, like that of space, do so present themselves irresistibly at the very dawn of intelligence, and take possession of the mind on small provocation, while of other conceptions we are prepossessed, indeed, but not so strongly, down a scale which is greatly extended. The tendency to personify every thing, and to attribute human characters to it, may be said to be innate; but it is a tendency which is very soon overcome by civilized man in regard to the greater part of the objects about him. Take such a conception as that of gravitation varying inversely as the square of the distance. It is a very simple law. But to say that it is simple is merely to say that it is one which the mind is particularly adapted to apprehend with facility. Suppose the idea of a quantity multiplied into another had been no more easy to the mind than that of a quantity raised to the power indicated by itself—should we ever have discovered the law of the solar system?

It seems incontestable, therefore, that the mind of man is strongly adapted to the comprehension of the world; at least, so far as this goes, that certain conceptions, highly important for such a comprehension, naturally arise in his mind; and, without such a tendency, the mind could never have had any development at all.

How are we to explain this adaptation? The great utility and indispensableness of the conceptions of time, space, and force, even to the lowest intelligence, are such as to suggest that they are the results of natural selection. Without something like geometrical, kinetical, and mechanical conceptions, no animal could seize his food or do anything which might be necessary for the preservation of the species. He might, it is true, be provided with an instinct which would generally have the same effect; that is to say, he might have conceptions different from those of time, space, and force, but which coincided with them in regard to the ordinary cases of the animal's experience. But, as that animal would have an immense advantage in the struggle for life whose mechanical conceptions did not break down in a novel situation (such as development must bring about), there would be a constant selection in favor of more and more correct ideas of these matters. Thus would be attained the knowledge of that fundamental law upon which all science rolls; namely, that forces depend upon relations of time, space, and mass. When this idea was once sufficiently clear, it would require no more than a comprehensible degree of genius to discover the exact nature of these relations. Such an hypothesis naturally suggests itself, but it must be admitted that it does not seem sufficient to account for the extraordinary accuracy with which these conceptions apply to the phenomena of Nature, and it is probable that there is some secret here which remains to be discovered.

John Stuart Mill

Of Analogy

VARIOUS SENSES OF THE WORD ANALOGY

The word Analogy, as the name of a mode of reasoning, is generally taken for some kind of argument supposed to be of an inductive nature, but not amounting to a complete induction. There is no word, however, which is used more loosely, or in a greater variety of senses, than Analogy. It sometimes stands for arguments which may be examples of the most rigorous Induction. Archbishop Whately, for instance, following Ferguson and other writers, defines Analogy conformably to its primitive acceptation, that which was given to it by mathematicians, Resemblance of Relations. In this sense, when a country which has sent out colonies is termed the mother country, the expression is analogical, signifying that the colonies of a country stand in the same *relation* to her in which children stand to their parents. And if any inference be drawn from this resemblance of relations, as, for instance, that obedience or affection is due from colonies to the mother country, this is called reasoning by analogy. Or if it be argued that a nation is most beneficially governed by an assembly elected by the people, from the admitted fact that other associations for a common purpose, such as joint-stock companies, are best managed by a Committee chosen by the parties interested; this, too, is an argument from analogy in the preceding sense, because its foundation is, not that a nation is like a joint-stock company, or Parliament like a board of directors, but that Parliament stands in the same *relation* to the nation in which a board of directors stands to a joint-stock company. Now, in an argument of this nature, there is no inherent inferiority of conclusiveness. Like other arguments from resemblance, it may amount to nothing, or it may be a perfect and conclusive induction. The circumstance in which the two cases resemble, may be capable of being shown to be the *material* circumstance; to be that on which all the consequences, necessary to be taken into account in the particular discussion, depend. In the example last given, the resemblance is one of relation; the *fundamentum relationis* being the management by a few persons, of affairs in which a much greater number are interested along with them. Now, some may contend that this circumstance which is common to the two cases, and the various consequences which follow from it, have the chief share in determining all the effects which make up what we term good or bad administration. If they can establish this, their argument has the force of a rigorous induction; if they cannot, they are said to have failed in proving the analogy

From John Stuart Mill, *A System of Logic,* 10th ed., Book III, Chap. 20, Longmans, Green & Co., London, 1879.

between the two cases; a mode of speech which implies that when the analogy can be proved, the argument founded on it cannot be resisted.

NATURE OF ANALOGICAL EVIDENCE

It is on the whole more usual, however, to extend the name of analogical evidence to arguments from any sort of resemblance, provided they do not amount to a complete induction: without peculiarly distinguishing resemblance of relations. Analogical reasoning, in this sense, may be reduced to the following formula:—Two things resemble each other in one or more respects; a certain proposition is true of the one; therefore it is true of the other. But we have nothing here by which to discriminate analogy from induction, since this type will serve for all reasoning from experience. In the strictest induction, equally with the faintest analogy, we conclude because A resembles B in one or more properties, that it does so in a certain other property. The difference is, that in the case of a complete induction it has been previously shown, by due comparison of instances, that there is an invariable conjunction between the former property or properties and the latter property; but in what is called analogical reasoning, no such conjunction has been made out. There have been no opportunities of putting in practice the Method of Difference, or even the Method of Agreement; but we conclude (and that is all which the argument of analogy amounts to) that a fact *m*, known to be true of A, is more likely to be true of B if B agrees with A in some of its properties (even though no connexion is known to exist between *m* and those properties), than if no resemblance at all could be traced between B and any other thing known to possess the attribute *m*.

To this argument it is of course requisite, that the properties common to A with B shall be merely not known to be connected with *m*; they must not be properties known to be unconnected with it. If, either by processes of elimination, or by deduction from previous knowledge of the laws of the properties in question, it can be concluded that they have nothing to do with *m*, the argument of analogy is put out of court. The supposition must be that *m* is an effect really dependent on some property of A, but we know not on which. We cannot point out any of the properties of A, which is the cause of *m*, or united with it by any law. After rejecting all which we know to have nothing to do with it, there remain several between which we are unable to decide: of which remaining properties, B possesses one or more. This accordingly, we consider as affording grounds, of more or less strength, for concluding by analogy that B possesses the attribute *m*.

There can be no doubt that every such resemblance which can be pointed out between B and A, affords some degree of probability, beyond what would otherwise exist, in favour of the conclusion drawn from it. If B resembled A in all its ultimate properties, its possessing the attribute *m* would be a certainty, not a probability: and every resemblance which can be shown to exist between them, places it by so much the nearer to that point. If the resemblance be in an ultimate property, there will be resemblance in all the derivative properties dependent on that ultimate property, and of these *m* may be one. If the resemblance be in a derivative property, there is reason to expect resemblance in the ultimate property on which it depends, and in the other derivative properties dependent on the same ultimate property. Every resemblance which can be shown to exist, affords ground for expecting an indefinite number of other resemblances: the particular resemblance sought will, therefore, be oftener found among things thus known to resemble, than among things between which we know of no resemblance.

For example, I might infer that there are probably inhabitants in the moon, because there are inhabitants on the earth, in the sea, and in the air: and this is the evidence of analogy. The circumstance of having inhabitants is here assumed not to be an ultimate property, but (as is reasonable to suppose) a consequence of other properties; and depending, therefore, in the case of the earth, on some of its properties as a portion of the universe, but on which of those properties we know not. Now the moon resembles the earth in being a solid, opaque, nearly spherical substance, appearing to contain, or to have contained, active volcanoes; receiving heat and light from the sun, in about the same quantity as our earth; revolving on its axis; composed of materials which gravitate, and obeying all the various laws resulting from that property. And I think no one will deny that if this were all that was known of the moon, the existence of inhabitants in that luminary would derive from these various resemblances to the earth, a greater degree of probability than it would otherwise have: though the amount of the augmentation it would be useless to attempt to estimate.

If, however, every resemblance proved between B and A, in any point not known to be immaterial with respect to *m*, forms some additional reason for presuming that B has the attribute *m*; it is clear, *è contra*, that every dissimilarity which can be proved between them, furnishes a counter-probability of the same nature on the other side. It is not indeed unusual that different ultimate properties should, in some particular instances produce the same derivative property; but on the whole it is certain that things which differ in their ultimate properties, will differ at least as much in the aggregate of their derivative properties, and that the differences which are unknown will on the average of cases bear some proportion to those which are known. There will, therefore, be a competition between the known points of agreement and the known points of difference in A and B; and according as the one or the other may be deemed to preponderate, the probability derived from analogy will be for or against B's having the property *m*. The moon, for instance, agrees with the earth in the circumstances already mentioned; but differs in being smaller, in having its surface more unequal, and apparently volcanic throughout, in having, at least on the side next the earth, no atmosphere sufficient to refract light, no clouds, and (it is therefore concluded) no water. These differences, considered merely as such, might perhaps balance the resemblances, so that analogy would afford no presumption either way. But considering that some of the circumstances which are wanting on the moon are among those which, on the earth, are found to be indispensable conditions of animal life, we may conclude that if that phenomenon does exist in the moon, (or at all events on the nearer side,) it must be as an effect of causes totally different from those on which it depends here; as a consequence, therefore, of the moon's differences from the earth, not of the points of agreement. Viewed in this light, all the resemblances which exist become presumptions against, not in favour of, the moon's being inhabited. Since life cannot exist there in the manner in which it exists here, the greater the resemblance of the lunar world to the terrestrial in other respects, the less reason we have to believe that it can contain life.

There are, however, other bodies in our system, between which and the earth there is a much closer resemblance; which possess an atmosphere, clouds, consequently water (or some fluid analogous to it), and even give strong indications of snow in their polar regions; while the cold, or heat, though differing greatly on the average from ours, is, in some parts at least of those planets, possibly not more extreme than in some regions of our own which are habitable. To balance these agreements, the ascertained differences are chiefly in the average light and heat, velocity of rotation, density of material, intensity of gravity, and similar circumstances of a secondary kind. With regard to these planets, therefore, the argument of analogy gives a decided preponderance in favour of their resembling the earth in any of its derivative properties, such as that of having inhabitants; though, when we consider how immeasurably multitudinous are those of their properties which we are entirely ignorant of, compared with the few which we know, we can attach but trifling weight to any considerations of resemblance in which the known elements bear so inconsiderable a proportion to the unknown.

Besides the competition between analogy and diversity, there may be a competition of conflicting analogies. The new case may be similar in some of its circumstances to cases in which the fact *m* exists, but in others to cases in which it is known not to exist. Amber has some properties in common with vegetable, others with mineral products. A painting of unknown origin, may resemble, in certain of its characters, known works of a particular master, but in others it may as strikingly resemble those of some other painter. A vase may bear some analogy to works of Grecian, and some to those of Etruscan, or Egyptian art. We are of course supposing that it does not possess any quality which has been ascertained, by a sufficient induction, to be a conclusive mark either of the one or of the other.

ON WHAT CIRCUMSTANCES ITS VALUE DEPENDS

Since the value of an analogical argument inferring one resemblance from other resemblances without any antecedent evidence of a connexion between them, depends on the extent of ascertained resemblance, compared first with the amount of ascertained difference, and next with the extent of the unexplored region of unascertained properties; it follows that where the resemblance is very great, the ascertained difference very small, and our knowledge of the subject-matter tolerably extensive, the argument from analogy may approach in strength very near to a valid induction. If, after much observation of B, we find that it agrees with A in nine out of ten of its known properties, we may conclude with a probability of nine to one, that it will possess any given derivative property of A. If we discover, for example, an unknown animal or plant, resembling closely some known one in the greater number of the properties may observe in it, but differing in some few, we may reasonably expect to find in the unobserved remainder of its properties, a general agreement with those of the former; but also a difference corresponding proportionately to the amount of observed diversity.

It thus appears that the conclusions derived from analogy are only of any considerable value, when the case to which we reason is an adjacent case; adjacent, not as before, in place or time, but in circumstances. In the case of effects of which the causes are imperfectly or not at all known, when consequently the observed order of their occurrence amounts only to an empirical law, it often happens that the conditions which have coexisted whenever the effect was observed, have been very numerous. Now if a new case presents itself, in which all these conditions do not exist, but the far greater part of them do, some one or a few only being wanting, the inference that the effect will occur, notwithstanding this deficiency of complete resemblance to the cases in which it has been observed, may, though of the nature of analogy, possess a high degree of probability. It is hardly necessary to add that, however considerable this probability may be, no competent inquirer into nature will rest satisfied with it when a complete induction is attainable; but will consider the analogy as a mere guide-post, pointing out the direction in which more rigorous investigations should be prosecuted.

It is in this last respect that considerations of analogy have the highest scientific value. The cases in which analogical evidence affords in itself any very high degree of probability, are, as we have observed, only those in which the resemblance is very close and extensive; but there is no analogy, however faint, which may not be of the utmost value in suggesting experiments or observations that may lead to more positive conclusions. When the agents and their effects are out of the reach of further observation and experiment, as in the speculations already alluded to respecting the moon and planets, such slight probabilities are no more than an interesting theme for the pleasant exercise of imagination; but any suspicion, however slight, that sets an ingenious person at work to contrive an experiment, or affords a reason for trying one experiment rather than another, may be of the greatest benefit to science.

On this ground, though I cannot accept as positive truths any of those scientific hypotheses which are unsusceptible of being ultimately brought to the test of actual induction, such, for instance, as the two theories of light, the emission theory of the last century, and the undulatory theory which predominates in the present, I am yet unable to agree with those who consider such hypotheses to be worthy of entire disregard. As is well said by Hartley (and concurred in by a thinker in general so diametrically opposed to Hartley's opinions as Dugald Stewart), "any hypothesis which has so much plausibility as to explain a considerable number of facts, helps us to digest these facts in proper order, to bring new ones to light, and make *experimenta crucis* for the sake of future inquirers."[1] If an hypothesis both explains known facts, and has led to the prediction of others previously unknown, and since verified by experience, the laws of the phenomenon which is the subject of inquiry must bear at least a great similarity to those of the class of phenomena to which the hypothesis assimilates it; and since the analogy which extends so far may probably extend farther, nothing is more likely to suggest experiments tending to throw light upon the real properties of the phenomenon, than the following out such an hypothesis. But to this end it is by no means necessary that the hypothesis be mistaken for a scientific truth. On the contrary, that illusion is in this respect, as in every other, an impediment to the progress of

[1] Hartley's *Observations on Man,* vol. i, p. 16. The passage is not in Priestley's curtailed edition.

real knowledge, by leading inquirers to restrict themselves arbitrarily to the particular hypothesis which is most accredited at the time, instead of looking out for every class of phenomena between the laws of which and those of the given phenomena any analogy exists, and trying all such experiments as may tend to the discovery of ulterior analogies pointing in the same direction.

Hans Reichenbach

The Problem of Induction, and the Justification of the Principle of Induction

THE PROBLEM OF INDUCTION

The frequency interpretation has two functions within the theory of probability. First, a frequency is used as a *substantiation* for the probability statement; it furnishes the reason why we believe in the statement. Second, a frequency is used for the *verification* of the probability statement; that is to say, it is to furnish the meaning of the statement. These two functions are not identical. The observed frequency from which we start is only the basis of the probability inference; we intend to state another frequency which concerns *future observations*. The probability inference proceeds from a known frequency to one unknown; it is from this function that its importance is derived. The probability statement sustains a prediction, and this is why we want it.

It is the problem of induction which appears with this formulation. The theory of probability involves the problem of induction, and a solution of the problem of probability cannot be given without an answer to the question of induction. The connection of both problems is well known; philosophers such as Peirce have expressed the idea that a solution of the problem of induction is to be found in the theory of probability. The inverse relation, however, holds as well. Let us say, cautiously, that the solution of both problems is to be given within the same theory.

In uniting the problem of probability with that of induction, we decide unequivocally in favor of that determination of the degree of probability which mathematicians call the *determination a posteriori*. . . .

By "determination a posteriori" we understand a procedure in which the relative frequency observed statistically is assumed to hold approximately for

---

Hans Reichenbach (1891–1953) was born in Germany, taught at the University of Berlin, and was Professor of Philosophy at the University of California, Los Angeles, from 1938 until his death.

any future prolongation of the series. Let us express this idea in an exact formulation. We assume a series of events A and $\bar{A}$ (non-A); let n be the number of events, m the number of events of the type A among them. We have then the relative frequency

$$h^n = \frac{m}{n}$$

The assumption of the determination a posteriori may now be expressed:

> For any further prolongation of the series as far as s events $(s > n)$, the relative frequency will remain within a small interval around h^n; i.e., we assume the relation
>
> $$h^n - \epsilon \leqq h^s \leqq h^n + \epsilon$$
>
> where ϵ is a small number.

This assumption formulates the *principle of induction.* We may add that our formulation states the principle in a form more general than that customary in traditional philosophy. The usual formulation is as follows: induction is the assumption that an event which occurred n times will occur at all following times. It is obvious that this formulation is a special case of our formulation, corresponding to the case $h^n = 1$. We cannot restrict our investigation to this special case because the general case occurs in a great many problems.

The reason for this is to be found in the fact that the theory of probability needs the definition of probability as the limit of the frequency. Our formulation is a necessary condition for the existence of a limit of the frequency near h^n; what is yet to be added is that there is an h^n of the kind postulated for every ϵ however small. If we include this idea in our assumption, our postulate of induction becomes the hypothesis that there is a limit to the relative frequency which does not differ greatly from the observed value.

If we enter now into a closer analysis of this assumption, one thing needs no further demonstration: the formula given is not a tautology. There is indeed no logical necessity that h^s remains within the interval $h^n \pm \epsilon$; we may easily imagine that this does not take place.

The nontautological character of induction has been known a long time; Bacon had already emphasized that it is just this character to which the importance of induction is due. If inductive inference can teach us something new, in opposition to deductive inference, this is because it is not a tautology. This useful quality has, however, become the center of the epistemological difficulties of induction. It was David Hume who first attacked the principle from this side; he pointed out that the apparent constraint of the inductive inference, although submitted to by everybody, could not be justified. We believe in induction; we even cannot get rid of the belief when we know the impossibility of a logical demonstration of the validity of inductive inference; but as logicians we must admit that this belief is a deception—such is the result of Hume's criticism. We may summarize his objections in two statements:

1. We have no logical demonstration for the validity of inductive inference.
2. There is no demonstration a posteriori for the inductive inference; any such demonstration would presuppose the very principle which it is to demonstrate.

These two pillars of Hume's criticism of the principle of induction have stood unshaken for two centuries, and I think they will stand as long as there is a scientific philosophy.

. . .

Inductive inference cannot be dispensed with because we need it for the purpose of action. To deem the inductive assumption unworthy of the assent of a philosopher, to keep a distinguished reserve, and to meet with a condescending smile the attempts of other people to bridge the gap between experience and prediction is cheap self-deceit; at the very moment when the apostles of such a higher philosophy leave the field of theoretical discussion and pass to the simplest actions of daily life, they follow the inductive principle as surely as does every earth-bound mind. In any action there are various means to the realization of our aim; we have to make a choice, and we decide in accordance with the inductive principle. Although there is no means which will produce with certainty the desired effect, we do not leave the choice to chance but prefer the means indicated by the principle of induction. If we sit at the wheel of a car and want to turn the car to the right, why do we turn the wheel to the right? There is no certainty that the car will follow the wheel; there are indeed cars which do not always so behave. Such cases are fortunately exceptions. But if we should not regard the inductive prescription and consider the effect of a turn of the wheel as entirely unknown to us, we might turn it to the left as well. I do not say this to suggest such an attempt; the effects of skeptical philosophy applied in motor traffic would be rather unpleasant. But I should say a philosopher who is to put aside his principles any time he steers a motorcar is a bad philosopher.

It is no justification of inductive belief to show that it is a habit. It *is* a habit; but the question is whether it is a good habit, where "good" is to mean "useful for the purpose of actions directed to future events." If a person tells me that Socrates is a man, and that all men are mortal, I have the habit of believing that Socrates is mortal. I know, however, that this is a good habit. If anyone had the habit of believing in such a case that Socrates is not mortal, we could demonstrate to him that this was a bad habit. The analogous question must be raised for inductive inference. If we should not be able to demonstrate that it is a good habit, we should either cease using it or admit frankly that our philosophy is a failure.

Science proceeds by induction and not by tautological transformations of reports. Bacon is right about Aristotle; but the *novum organon* needs a justification as good as that of the *organon*. Hume's criticism was the heaviest blow against empiricism; if we do not want to dupe our consciousness of this by means of the narcotic drug of aprioristic rationalism, or the soporific of skepticism, we must find a defense for the inductive inference which holds as well as does the formalistic justification of deductive logic.

THE JUSTIFICATION OF THE PRINCIPLE OF INDUCTION

We shall now begin to give the justification of induction which Hume thought impossible. In the pursuit of this inquiry, let us ask first what has been proved, strictly speaking, by Hume's objections.

Hume started with the assumption that a justification of inductive inference is only given if we can show that inductive inference must lead to success. In other words, Hume believed that any justified application of the inductive inference presupposes a demonstration that the conclusion is true. It is this assumption on which Hume's criticism is based. His two objections directly concern only the question of the truth of the conclusion; they prove that the truth of the conclusion cannot be demonstrated. The two objections, therefore, are valid only in so far as the Humean assumption is valid. It is this question to which we must turn: Is it necessary, for the justification of inductive inference, to show that its conclusion is true?

A rather simple analysis shows us that this assumption does not hold. Of course, if we were able to prove the truth of the conclusion, inductive inference would be justified; but the converse does not hold: a justification of the inductive inference does not imply a proof of the truth of the conclusion. The proof of the truth of the conclusion is only a sufficient condition for the justification of induction, not a necessary condition.

The inductive inference is a procedure which is to furnish us the best assumption concerning the future. If we do not know the truth about the future, there may be nonetheless a best assumption about it, i.e., a best assumption relative to what we know. We must ask whether such a characterization may be given for the principle of induction. If this turns out to be possible, the principle of induction will be justified.

An example will show the logical structure of our reasoning. A man may be suffering from a grave disease; the physician tells us: "I do not know whether an operation will save the man, but if there *is* any remedy, it is an operation." In such a case, the operation would be justified. Of course, it would be better to know that the operation will save the man; but, if we do not know this, the knowledge formulated in the statement of the physician is a sufficient justification. If we cannot realize the sufficient conditions of success, we shall at least realize the necessary conditions. If we were able to show that the inductive inference is a necessary condition of success, it would be justified; such a proof would satisfy any demands which may be raised about the justification of induction.

Now obviously there is a great difference between our example and induction. The reasoning of the physician presupposes inductions; his knowledge about an operation as the only possible means of saving a life is based on inductive generalizations, just as are all other statements of empirical character. But we wanted only to illustrate the logical structure of our reasoning. If we want to regard such a reasoning as a justification of the principle of induction, the character of induction as a necessary condition of success must be demonstrated in a way which does not presuppose induction. Such a proof, however, can be given.

If we want to construct this proof, we must begin with a determination of the aim of induction. It is usually said that we perform inductions with the aim of foreseeing the future. This determination is vague; let us replace it by a formulation more precise in character:

> The aim of induction is to find series of events whose frequency of occurrence converges toward a limit.

We choose this formulation because we found that we need probabilities and that a probability is to be defined as the limit of a frequency; thus our determination of the aim of induction is given in such a way that it enables us to apply probability methods. If we compare this determination of the aim of induction with determinations usually given, it turns out to be not a confinement to a narrower aim but an expansion. What we usually call "foreseeing the future" is included in our formulation as a special case; the case of knowing with certainty for every event A the event B following it would correspond in our formulation to a case where the limit of the frequency is of the numerical value 1. Hume thought of this case only. Thus our inquiry differs from that of Hume in so far as it conceives the aim of induction in a generalized form. But we do not omit any possible applications if we determine the principle of induction as the means of obtaining the limit of a frequency. If we have limits of frequency, we have all we want, including the case considered by Hume; we have then the laws of nature in their most general form, including both statistical and so-called causal laws—the latter being nothing but a special case of statistical laws, corresponding to the numerical value 1 of the limit of the frequency. We are entitled, therefore, to consider the determination of the limit of a frequency as the aim of the inductive inference.

Now it is obvious that we have no guaranty that this aim is at all attainable. The world may be so disorderly that it is impossible for us to construct series with a limit. Let us introduce the term "predictable" for a world which is sufficiently ordered to enable us to construct series with a limit. We must admit, then, that we do not know whether the world is predictable.

But, if the world is predictable, let us ask what the logical function of the principle of induction will be. For this purpose, we must consider the definition of limit. The frequency h^n has a limit at p, if for any given ϵ there is an n such that h^n is within $p \pm \epsilon$ and remains within this interval for all the rest of the series. Comparing our formulation of the principle of induction . . . with this, we may infer from the definition of the limit that, if there is a limit, there is an element of the series from which the principle of induction leads to the true value of the limit. In this sense the principle of induction is a necessary condition for the determination of a limit.

It is true that, if we are faced with the value h^n for the frequency furnished by our statistics, we do not know whether this n is sufficiently large to be identical with, or beyond, the n of the "place of convergence" for ϵ. It may be that our n is not yet large enough, that after n there will be a deviation greater than ϵ from p. To this we may answer: We are not bound to stay at h^n; we may continue our procedure and shall always consider the last h^n obtained as our best value. This procedure must at some time lead to the true value p, if there is a limit at all; the applicability of this procedure, as a whole, is a necessary condition of the existence of a limit at p.

To understand this, let us imagine a principle of a contrary sort. Imagine a man who, if h^n is reached, always makes the assumption that the limit of the frequency is at $h^n + a$, where a is a fixed constant. If this man continues his procedure for increasing n, he is sure to miss the limit; this procedure must at sometime become false, if there is a limit at all.

We have found now a better formulation of the necessary condition. We must not consider the individual assumption for an individual h^n; we must take account of the procedure of continued assumptions of the inductive type. The applicability of this procedure is the necessary condition sought.

If, however, it is only the whole procedure which constitutes the necessary condition, how may we apply this idea to the individual case which stands before us? We want to know whether the individual h^n observed by us differs less than ϵ from the limit of the convergence; this neither can be guaranteed nor can it be called a necessary condition of the existence of a limit. So what does our idea of the necessary condition imply for the individual case? It seems that for our individual case the idea turns out to be without any application.

This difficulty corresponds in a certain sense to the difficulty we found in the application of the frequency interpretation to the single case. It is to be eliminated by the introduction of a concept already used for the other problem: the concept of posit.

If we observe a frequency h^n and assume it to be the approximate value of the limit, this assumption is not maintained in the form of a true statement; it is a posit such as we perform in a wager. We posit h^n as the value of the limit, i.e., we wager on h^n, just as we wager on the side of a die. We know that h^n is our best wager, therefore we posit it. There is, however, a difference as to the type of posit occurring here and in the throw of the die.

In the case of the die, we know the weight belonging to the posit: it is given by the degree of probability. If we posit the case "side other than that numbered 1," the weight of this posit is 5/6. We speak in this case of a posit with appraised weight, or, in short, of an *appraised posit*.

In the case of our positing h^n, we do not know its weight. We call it, therefore, a *blind posit*. We know it is our best posit, but we do not know how good it is. Perhaps, although our best, it is a rather bad one.

The blind posit, however, may be corrected. By continuing our series, we obtain new values h^n; we always choose the last h^n. Thus the blind posit is of an approximative type; we know that the method of making and correcting such posits must in time lead to success, in case there is a limit of the frequency. It is this idea which furnishes the justification of the blind posit. The procedure described may be called the *method of anticipation;* in choosing h^n as our posit, we anticipate the case where n is the "place of convergence." It may be that by this anticipation we obtain a false value; we know, however, that a continued anticipation must lead to the true value, if there is a limit at all.

. . .

These considerations lead, however, to a more precise formulation of the logical structure of the inductive inference. We must say that, if there is any method which leads to the limit of the frequency, the inductive principle will do the same; if there is a limit of the frequency, the inductive principle is a sufficient condition to find it. If we omit now the premise that there is a limit of the frequency, we cannot say that the inductive principle is the necessary condition of finding it because there are other methods using a correction c_n. There is a set of equivalent conditions such that the choice of one of the members of the set is necessary if we want to find the limit; and, if there is a limit, each of the members of the set is an appropriate method for finding it.

We mav say, therefore, that the *applicability* of the inductive principle is a necessary condition of the existence of a limit of the frequency.

The decision in favor of the inductive principle among the members of the set of equivalent means may be substantiated by pointing out its quality of embodying the smallest risk; after all, this decision is not of a great relevance, as all these methods must lead to the same value of the limit if they are sufficiently continued. It must not be forgotten, however, that the method of clairvoyance is not, without further ado, a member of the set because we do not know whether the correction c_n occurring here is submitted to the condition of convergence to zero. This must be proved first, and it can only be proved by using the inductive principle, viz., a method known to be a member of the set: this is why clairvoyance, in spite of all occult pretensions, is to be submitted to the control of scientific methods, i.e., by the principle of induction.

It is in the analysis expounded that we see the solution of Hume's problem. Hume demanded too much when he wanted for a justification of the inductive inference a proof that its conclusion is true. What his objections demonstrate is only that such a proof cannot be given. We do not perform, however, an inductive inference with the pretension of obtaining a true statement. What we obtain is a wager; and it is the best wager we can lay because it corresponds to a procedure the applicability of which is the necessary condition of the possibility of predictions. To fulfil the conditions sufficient for the attainment of true predictions does not lie in our power; let us be glad that we are able to fulfil at least the conditions necessary for the realization of this intrinsic aim of science.

Peter Frederick Strawson

The "Justification" of Induction

If someone asked what grounds there were for supposing that deductive reasoning was valid, we might answer that there were in fact no grounds for supposing that deductive reasoning was always valid; sometimes people made valid inferences, and sometimes they were guilty of logical fallacies. If he said that we had misunderstood his question, and that what he wanted to know was what grounds there were for regarding deduction *in general* as a valid method of argument, we should have to answer that his question was without sense, for to say that an argument, or a form or method of argument, was valid or invalid would *imply* that it was deductive; the concepts of validity and invalidity had application only to individual deductive arguments or forms of deductive argument. Similarly, if a man asked what grounds there were for

---

From P. F. Strawson, *Introduction to Logical Theory,* Chap. 9, published by John Wiley & Sons, Inc., New York, 1952, and reprinted with their permission.

thinking it reasonable to hold beliefs arrived at inductively, one might at first answer that there were good and bad inductive arguments, that sometimes it was reasonable to hold a belief arrived at inductively and sometimes it was not. If he, too, said that his question had been misunderstood, that he wanted to know whether induction in general was a reasonable method of inference, then we might well think his question senseless in the same way as the question whether deduction is in general valid; for to call a particular belief reasonable or unreasonable is to apply inductive standards, just as to call a particular argument valid or invalid is to apply deductive standards. The parallel is not wholly convincing; for words like 'reasonable' and 'rational' have not so precise and technical a sense as the word 'valid'. Yet it is sufficiently powerful to make us wonder how the second question could be raised at all, to wonder why, in contrast with the corresponding question about deduction, it should have seemed to constitute a genuine problem.

Suppose that a man is brought up to regard formal logic as the study of the science and art of reasoning. He observes that all inductive processes are, by deductive standards, invalid; the premises never entail the conclusions. Now inductive processes are notoriously important in the formation of beliefs and expectations about everything which lies beyond the observation of available witnesses. But an *invalid* argument is an *unsound* argument; an *unsound* argument is one in which *no good reason* is produced for accepting the conclusion. So if inductive processes are invalid, if all the arguments we should produce, if challenged, in support of our beliefs about what lies beyond the observation of available witnesses are unsound, then we have no good reason for any of these beliefs. This conclusion is repugnant. So there arises the demand for a justification, not of this or that particular belief which goes beyond what is entailed by our evidence, but a justification of induction in general. And when the demand arises in this way it is, in effect, the demand that induction shall be shown to be really a kind of deduction; for nothing less will satisfy the doubter when this is the route to his doubts.

Tracing this, the most common route to the general doubt about the reasonableness of induction, shows how the doubt seems to escape the absurdity of a demand that induction in general shall be justified by inductive standards. The demand is that induction should be shown to be a rational process; and this turns out to be the demand that one kind of reasoning should be shown to be another and different kind. Put thus crudely, the demand seems to escape one absurdity only to fall into another. Of course, inductive arguments are not deductively valid; if they were, they would be deductive arguments. Inductive reasoning must be assessed, for soundness, by inductive standards. Nevertheless, fantastic as the wish for induction to be deduction may seem, it is only in terms of it that we can understand some of the attempts that have been made to justify induction.

VIII

The first kind of attempt I shall consider might be called the search for the supreme premise of inductions. In its primitive form it is quite a crude attempt; and I shall make it cruder by caricature. We have already seen that for a particular inductive step, such as 'The kettle has been on the fire for ten minutes, so it will be boiling by now', we can substitute a deductive argument by introducing a generalization (e.g., 'A kettle always boils within ten minutes of being put on the fire') as an additional premise. This manoeuvre shifted the emphasis of the problem of inductive support on to the question of how we established such generalizations as these, which rested on grounds by which they were not entailed. But suppose the manoeuvre could be repeated. Suppose we could find one supremely general proposition, which taken in conjunction with the evidence for any accepted generalization of science or daily life (or at least of science) would entail that generalization. Then, so long as the status of the supreme generalization could be satisfactorily explained, we could regard all sound inductions to unqualified general conclusions as, at bottom, valid deductions. The justification would be found, for at least these cases. The most obvious difficulty in this suggestion is that of formulating the supreme general proposition in such a way that it shall be precise enough to yield the desired entailments, and yet not obviously false or arbitrary. Consider, for example, the formula: 'For all f, g, wherever n cases of $f . g$, and no cases of $f . \sim g$, are observed, then all cases of f are cases of g.' To turn it into a sentence, we have only to replace 'n' by some number. But what number? If we take the value of 'n' to be 1 or 20 or 500, the resulting statement is obviously false. Moreover, the choice of any number would seem quite arbitrary; there is no privileged number of favourable instances which we take as decisive in establishing a generalization. If, on the other hand, we phrase the proposition vaguely enough to escape these objections—if, for example, we phrase it as 'Nature is uniform'—then it becomes too vague to provide the desired entailments. It should be noticed that the impossibility of framing a general proposition of the kind required is really a special case of the impossibility of framing precise rules for the assessment of evidence. If we could frame a rule which would tell us precisely when we had *conclusive* evidence for a generalization, then it would yield just the proposition required as the supreme premise.

Even if these difficulties could be met, the question of the status of the supreme premise would remain. How, if a non-necessary proposition, could it be established? The appeal to experience, to inductive support, is clearly barred on pain of circularity. If, on the other hand, it were a necessary truth and possessed, in conjunction with the evidence for a generalization, the required logical power to entail the generalization (e.g., if the latter were the conclusion of a hypothetical syllogism, of which the hypothetical premise was the necessary truth in question), then the evidence would entail the generalization independently, and the problem would not arise: a conclusion unbearably paradoxical. In practice, the extreme vagueness with which candidates for the role of supreme premise are expressed prevents their acquiring such logical power, and at the same time renders it very difficult to classify them as analytic or synthetic: under pressure they may tend to tautology; and, when the pressure is removed, assume an expansively synthetic air.

In theories of the kind which I have here caricatured the ideal of deduction is not usually so blatantly manifest as I have made it. One finds the 'Law of the Uniformity of Nature' presented less as the suppressed premise of crypto-deductive inferences than as, say, the 'presupposition of the validity of inductive reasoning'.

' ' '

X

Let us turn from attempts to justify induction to attempts to show that the demand for a justification is mistaken. We have seen already that what lies behind such a demand is often the absurd wish that induction should be shown to be some kind of deduction—and this wish is clearly traceable in the two attempts at justification which we have examined. What other sense could we give to the demand? Sometimes it is expressed in the form of a request for proof that induction is a *reasonable* or *rational* procedure, that we have *good grounds* for placing reliance upon it. Consider the uses of the phrases 'good grounds', 'justification', 'reasonable', &c. Often we say such things as 'He has *every justification* for believing that *p*'; 'I have *very good reasons* for believing it'; 'There are *good grounds* for the view that *q*'; 'There is *good evidence* that *r*'. We often talk, in such ways as these, of justification, good grounds or reasons or evidence for certain beliefs. Suppose such a belief were one expressible in the form 'Every case of *f* is a case of *g*'. And suppose someone were asked what he meant by saying that he had good grounds or reasons for holding it. I think it would be felt to be a satisfactory answer if he replied: 'Well, in all my wide and varied experience I've come across innumerable cases of *f* and never a case of *f* which wasn't a case of *g*.' In saying this, he is clearly claiming to have *inductive* support, *inductive* evidence, of a certain kind, for his belief; and he is also giving a perfectly proper answer to the question, what he meant by saying that he had ample justification, good grounds, good reasons for his belief. It is an analytic proposition that it is reasonable to have a degree of belief in a statement which is proportional to the strength of the evidence in its favour; and it is an analytic proposition, though not a proposition of mathematics, that, other things being equal, the evidence for a generalization is strong in proportion as the number of favourable instances, and the variety of circumstances in which they have been found, is great. So to ask whether it is reasonable to place reliance on inductive procedures is like asking whether it is reasonable to proportion the degree of one's convictions to the strength of the evidence. Doing this is what 'being reasonable' *means* in such a context.

As for the other form in which the doubt may be expressed, viz., 'Is induction a justified, or justifiable, procedure?', it emerges in a still less favourable light. No sense has been given to it, though it is easy to see why it seems to have a sense. For it is generally proper to inquire *of a particular belief*, whether its adoption is justified; and, in asking this, we are asking whether there is good, bad, or any, evidence for it. In applying or withholding the epithets 'justified', 'well founded', &c., in the case of specific beliefs, we are appealing to, and applying, inductive standards. But to what standards are we appealing when we ask whether the application of inductive standards is justified or well grounded? If we cannot answer, then no sense has been given to the question. Compare it with the question: Is the law legal? It makes perfectly good sense to inquire of a particular action, of an administrative regulation, or even, in the case of some states, of a particular enactment of the legislature, whether or not it is legal. The question is answered by an appeal to a legal system, by the application of a set of legal (or constitutional) rules or standards. But it makes no sense to inquire in general whether the law of the land, the legal system as a whole, is or is not legal. For to what legal standards are we appealing?

The only way in which a sense might be given to the question, whether induction is in general a justified or justifiable procedure, is a trivial one which we have already noticed. We might interpret it to mean 'Are all conclusions, arrived at inductively, justified?', i.e., 'Do people always have adequate evidence for the conclusions they draw?' The answer to this question is easy, but uninteresting: it is that sometimes people have adequate evidence, and sometimes they do not.

XI

It seems, however, that this way of showing the request for a general justification of induction to be absurd is sometimes insufficient to allay the worry that produces it. And to point out that 'forming rational opinions about the unobserved on the evidence available' and 'assessing the evidence by inductive standards' are phrases which describe the same thing, is more apt to produce irritation than relief. The point is felt to be 'merely a verbal' one; and though the point of this protest is itself hard to see, it is clear that something more is required. So the question must be pursued further. First, I want to point out that there is something a little odd about talking of 'the inductive method', or even 'the inductive policy', as if it were just one possible method among others of arguing from the observed to the unobserved, from the available evidence to the facts in question. If one asked a meteorologist what method or methods he used to forecast the weather, one would be surprised if he answered: 'Oh, just the inductive method.' If one asked a doctor by what means he diagnosed a certain disease, the answer 'By induction' would be felt as an impatient evasion, a joke, or a rebuke. The answer one hopes for is an account of the tests made, the signs taken account of, the rules and recipes and general laws applied. When such a specific method of prediction or diagnosis is in question, one can ask whether the method is justified in practice; and here again one is asking whether its employment is inductively justified, whether it commonly gives correct results. This question would normally seem an admissible one. One might be tempted to conclude that, while there are many different specific methods of prediction, diagnosis, &c., appropriate to different subjects of inquiry, all such methods could properly be called 'inductive' in the sense that their employment rested on inductive support; and that, hence, the phrase 'non-inductive method of finding out about what lies deductively beyond the evidence' was a description without meaning, a phrase to which no sense had been given; so that there could be no question of justifying our selection of one method, called 'the inductive', of doing this.

However, someone might object: 'Surely it is possible, though it might be foolish, to use methods utterly different from accredited scientific ones. Suppose a man, whenever he wanted to form an opinion about what lay beyond his observation or the observation of available witnesses, simply shut his eyes, asked himself the appropriate question, and accepted the first answer that came into his head. Wouldn't this be a non-inductive method?' Well, let us suppose this. The man is asked: 'Do you usually get the right answer by your method?' He might answer: 'You've mentioned one of its drawbacks; I never do get the right answer; but it's an extremely easy method.' One might then be inclined to think that it was not a method of finding things out at all. But suppose he answered: Yes, it's usually (always) the right answer. Then we might be willing to call it a method of finding out, though a strange one. But, then, by the very fact of its success, it would be an inductively supported method. For each application of the method would be an application of the general rule, 'The first answer that comes into my head is generally (always) the right one'; and for the truth of this generalization there would be the inductive evidence of a long run of favourable instances with no unfavourable ones (if it were 'always'), or of a sustained high proportion of successes to trials (if it were 'generally').

So every successful method or recipe for finding out about the unobserved must be one which has inductive support; for to say that a recipe is successful is to say that it has been repeatedly applied with success; and repeated successful application of a recipe constitutes just what we mean by inductive evidence in its favour. Pointing out this fact must not be confused with saying that 'the inductive method' is justified by its success, justified because it works. This is a mistake, and an important one. I am not seeking to 'justify the inductive method', for no meaning has been given to this phrase. *A fortiori,* I am not saying that induction is justified by its success in finding out about the unobserved. I am saying, rather, that any successful method of finding out about the unobserved is necessarily justified by induction. This is an analytic proposition. The phrase 'successful method of finding things out which has no inductive support' is self-contradictory. Having, or acquiring, inductive support is a necessary condition of the success of a method.

Why point this out at all? First, it may have a certain therapeutic force, a power to reassure. Second, it may counteract the tendency to think of 'the inductive method' as something on a par with specific methods of diagnosis or prediction and therefore, like them, standing in need of (inductive) justification.

Wesley Charles Salmon

Should We Attempt to Justify Induction?

In the broadest sense, an inductive inference is any non-demonstrative inference to a matter of fact. An inductive rule, then, would be any non-deductive rule of inference for drawing matter of fact conclusions, provided that such a rule does not sanction drawing self-contradictory conclusions from any con-

---

From W. C. Salmon, "Should We Attempt to Justify Induction?" *Philosophical Studies,* Vol. 8 (1957). Reprinted by permission of the author, *Philosophical Studies,* and the University of Minnesota Press.

W. C. Salmon (1925–) is Professor of Philosophy at Indiana University.

sistent set of premises (including the null set). I regard the problem of justifying induction as the problem of justifying a choice from among the wide variety of possible inductive rules. . . .

In recent years a rather large number of philosophers have argued that the attempt to justify induction ought to be abandoned. They have supported this claim by arguments designed to show that a justification of induction is either impossible or unnecessary or both. Within this paper I shall call such philosophers "anti-warrantists"; those who believe it worthwhile to persist in attempting to find a justification of induction will be called "warrantists." The anti-warrantists have frequently charged that there is no genuine problem of justifying induction—if there appears to be a problem it is because of a misconception of the nature of induction or justification, or because of a similar kind of confusion. . . .

Let us now examine [one] argument of the anti-warrantist for the impossibility of justifying induction. According to this argument, justification consists in showing that whatever is to be justified conforms to certain already accepted principles or rules. In particular, an inference is justified if it can be shown to conform to the relevant rules of inference. Sometimes these rules can, in turn, be justified by reference to other rules or principles. But to ask for a justification of *all* rules of inference is without sense, for no rules or principles are available in terms of which a justification could possibly be given. When we have called into question so much that there no longer remain any rules or principles to which a justification could be referred, then we have reached the limits of justifiability. Thus, to question any particular inductive inference is legitimate, for it can be justified or refuted in terms of the general canons of induction, whereas, to question induction in general leaves no canons in terms of which the justification can occur. This view is held by Strawson.

If the foregoing theory is correct, empirical knowledge is, at bottom, a matter of convention. We choose, quite arbitrarily it would seem, some basic canons of induction; there is no possibility of justifying the choice. They are arbitrary in the sense that cognitive considerations do not force their acceptance. It is perfectly conceivable that someone else might select a different set of inductive canons, and if so, there would be no way of showing that one set was better than another for purposes of gaining factual knowledge. Yet, such a person would regard certain inferences as justified which we would regard as unjustified. He would hold certain conclusions to be well established while we would hold the same conclusions to be disconfirmed. This is the sense in which conventionalism follows from the Strawson theory.

Herbert Feigl has given an answer to this contention of Strawson, and it consists in providing a clear sense for the question of the justification of induction in general. Feigl distinguishes two kinds of justification. He calls the first of these "validation"; it is the kind of justification Strawson describes. An inference is validated by showing that it is governed by an accepted rule. A rule of inference is validated by showing that it can be derived from other accepted rules or principles. There is, however, a second form of justification called "vindication." This kind of justification consists in showing that a given decision, policy, or act is well adapted to achieving a certain end. Translated into Feigl's terminology, Strawson's thesis becomes the innocuous claim that it is impossible to validate induction in general; only particular inductive rules and inferences can be validated. However, the warrantist is not attempting to validate the basic inductive canons; he seeks to vindicate them. The warrantist intentionally goes beyond the limits of validation, but he does not go beyond the limits of justification. To maintain that he transgresses the limits of justification would be tantamount to a denial that vindication is a kind of justification. It is difficult to imagine any argument that could possibly support such a denial.

The appeal to vindication requires, obviously, some aims or goals in terms of which a vindication can be given. It is at this point that one of the main controversies in the whole philosophy of induction occurs. The practicalist wants to vindicate induction by reference to the aim of attaining correct predictions and true conclusions. The critic will immediately point out that it is impossible to prove that induction will ever achieve this goal. It might therefore be concluded that there is no possibility of ever vindicating induction.

There are two major alternatives at this point. On the one hand, we may revise our conception of the aim of induction in an attempt to escape the necessity of proving that induction is well suited to the aforementioned purpose of arriving at true conclusions. On the other hand, we may hold, as the practicalist does, that it is possible to show that some inductive rules are better suited than others to the purpose of arriving at true results, even though it is impossible to prove that one will be successful while another will not. Let us consider the first of these alternatives. A large number of authors have suggested that we might justify induction as a tool for establishing *reasonable* beliefs, since it is impossible to show that induction will lead to *true* beliefs. According to this view, induction could be vindicated as leading, not necessarily to true conclusions, but rather to reasonable ones. Strawson, not really content with a view which implies sheer conventionalism, argues for this kind of justification when he is not busy arguing that no justification is needed. The argument is based chiefly upon an analysis of the meaning of "reasonable" which purports to establish that reasonable beliefs, by definition, are beliefs which have good inductive support. Strawson says, "to call a particular belief reasonable or unreasonable is to apply inductive standards . . ." A little later, he further comments: "to ask whether it is reasonable to place reliance on inductive procedures is like asking whether it is reasonable to proportion the degree of one's convictions to the strength of the evidence. Doing this is what 'being reasonable' *means* in such a context."

It seems to me that there are fatal objections to this approach. The term "reasonable" is, after all, virtually a synonym of "justifiable." To have reasonable beliefs is to have beliefs that are well grounded by justifiable methods. "Reasonable," then, partakes of the same ambiguity as "justifiable"—one sense referring to validation, the other to vindication. Thus, believing reasonably in one sense means holding beliefs which are sanctioned by inductive and deductive canons. In this sense, reasonable beliefs are beliefs which have been arrived at by methods which can be *validated* by reference to the accepted principles of inductive and deductive inference. In the second sense, "reasonable" means the adoption of methods and techniques which will most efficiently bring about one's ends and goals. This sense of "reasonable" corresponds to *vindication*. It is clear that using inductive methods is reasonable in the sense of "reasonable" which corresponds to *validation*. Now the problem of the justification of induction assumes the form "Is there any justification for being reasonable?" It will not do to reply that this question has the obvious tautological answer "It is reasonable to be reasonable." In view of the two distinct meanings of "reasonable" this answer may be no tautology at all, for it may contain an equivocation on the term "reasonable." Therefore, we must not lightly dismiss the question about a justification for being reasonable.

If we ask, "Why be reasonable?" construing "reasonable" in the sense related to vindication, the answer is easy to find. Being reasonable, in this sense, means adopting methods which are best suited to the attainment of our ends. Since we are motivated to achieve our ends, the realization that a method is reasonable constitutes a sufficient reason for adopting that method. To be unreasonable, in this sense, is to invite frustration. If, however, we shift to the sense of "reasonable" which is associated with validation, the answer to the question "Why be reasonable?" is much less clear. Presumably, the answer would be that to be reasonable is to be scientific and to use methods which have worked well for us. To be unreasonable would be to hold beliefs which are ill grounded and which run great danger of being false. But in so saying, have we not begged the very question which is at issue in the problem of induction? Surely there is no particular intrinsic value in being scientific or proceeding in accord with the standard inductive methods. We adopt these methods because we regard them as the best methods for establishing matter of fact conclusions. But when the problem of induction is raised, the question at issue is whether the standard inductive methods are, in fact, well suited to the purpose of establishing these factual conclusions.

It may be that the two senses of "reasonable" which we have distinguished are extensionally equivalent—that procedures are reasonable in the one sense if and only if they are reasonable in the other. But it would be a mistake merely to assume that this is the case. When a term has two distinct definitions it is not permissible to assume that the two definitions are equivalent; if there is such equivalence it must be shown. This is especially true when there are arguments which indicate that the supposed equivalence may not hold. Hume's arguments are just such arguments. If we try to show that such equivalence does hold—if we try to show that the standard inductive methods are those best suited to the purpose of arriving at correct beliefs—we are undertaking the task of the warrantist.

In accord with the philosophic fashion of the times one may be tempted to ask what is the ordinary meaning of "reasonable." Perhaps the ordinary sense of "reasonable" ensures that proceeding according to the standard inductive rules is reasonable. This is probably true of the ordinary sense. But this only shows that ordinary usage is established by people who are unaware of Hume's arguments. To say that ordinary people are untroubled by Humean doubts about induction may simply mean that ordinary people are philosophically ignorant. They assume that the two senses of reasonable distinguished above are equivalent partly because they have never thought of the distinction and partly because, had they thought of the distinction, they would have been unaware of any considerations which would lead to the conclusion that possibly the two senses are not equivalent. To cite ordinary use in this context, then, does not solve the philosophic question. It sanctions neglect of the philosophic question by virtue of an equivocation.

The attempt to vindicate inductive methods by showing that they lead to reasonable belief is a failure. If we assume that inductive beliefs are reasonable in the sense of being based on justifiable methods of inference, we are begging the question. If we regard beliefs as reasonable simply because they are arrived at inductively, we still have the problem of showing that reasonable beliefs are valuable. This is the problem of induction stated in new words. If we regard beliefs as reasonable simply because they are arrived at inductively and we hold that reasonable beliefs are valuable for their own sake, it appears that we have elevated inductive method to the place of an intrinsic good. On this latter alternative it would seem that we use inductive methods, not because they enable us to make correct predictions or arrive at true explanations, but simply because we like to use them. It sounds very much as if the whole argument (that reasonable beliefs are, by definition, beliefs which are inductively supported) has the function of transferring to the word "inductive" all of the honorific connotations of the word "reasonable," quite apart from whether induction is good for anything. The resulting justification of induction amounts to this: If you use inductive procedures you can call yourself "reasonable"—*and isn't that nice!*

For Further Reading

Ambrose, Alice, "Justifying Inductive Inference," *Journal of Philosophy,* Vol. 44 (1947).

Barker, S. F., *Induction and Hypothesis,* 1957, Chaps. 8 and 9.

Berlin, Isaiah, MacDonald, Margaret, and Ryle, Gilbert, "Induction and Hypothesis," *Proceedings of the Aristotelian Society,* Supplementary Vol. 16 (1937).

Black, Max, "The Justification of Induction," *Language and Philosophy,* 1949.

———, "Inductive Support of Inductive Rules," *Problems of Analysis,* 1954.

Braithwaite, R. B., *Scientific Explanation,* 1953, Chap. 8.

Burks, Arthur W., "On the Presuppositions of Induction," *Review of Metaphysics,* Vol. 8 (1955).

Carnap, Rudolf, "The Aim of Inductive Logic," in Nagel, E., Suppes, P., and Tarski, A. (eds.), *Logic, Methodology and Philosophy of Science,* 1962.

Cassirer, Ernst, *Determinism and Indeterminism in Modern Physics,* 1956, Chap. 8.

———, *Substance and Function,* 1923, Chap. 5.

Cohen, Morris R., *Reason and Nature,* 1931, Chap. 3, Sections III and IV.

Feigl, Herbert, "The Logical Character of the Principle of Induction," in Feigl, H., and Sellars, W. (eds.), *Readings in Philosophical Analysis,* 1949.

Hobhouse, L. T., *The Theory of Knowledge,* 3rd ed., 1921, Part II, Chaps. 10 and 17.

Keynes, J. M., *A Treatise on Probability,* 1921, Part III.

Kneale, William, *Probability and Induction,* 1949, Part IV.

Laird, John, *Knowledge, Belief and Opinion,* 1930, Chaps. 17, 18, and 19.

Pap, Arthur, *An Introduction to the Philosophy of Science,* 1962, Chap. 13.
Popper, Karl R., *The Logic of Scientific Discovery,* 1959, Chap. 10.
Ramsey, Frank P., *The Foundations of Mathematics,* 1931, Chaps. 7 and 8.
Russell, Bertrand, *Human Knowledge,* 1948, Part V.
Whitely, C. H., "On the Justification of Induction," *Analysis,* Vol. 7 (1940).
Williams, Donald, *The Ground of Induction,* 1947, Chaps. 4 and 6.
Wright, G. H. von, *The Logical Problem of Induction,* 2nd ed., 1957, Chaps. 5 and 7.

6

SCEPTICISM AND EPISTEMOLOGICAL ORDER

The remainder of this book concerns what can be known or believed with warrant, with the aid of observation. This new topic contrasts with the content of the earlier part of the book (especially Chapters 3 and 5) in two major respects. First, the earlier chapters concerned what can be known *without* the aid of observation, or at least without the aid of observation beyond that required for knowing what is *meant* by certain statements. (There may be one exception, however, since some philosophers think that the rules of inductive inference can be justified by the past success of predicting in accordance with them.) Second, the earlier chapters were concerned with *necessary* features of the world, with what can be known to be true for every possible world; whereas the chapters to come are concerned with what can be known about our actual world—contingent facts that could conceivably have been different. This second contrast is connected with the first, since it has usually been thought (and with good reason) that contingent facts can be known only by observation, directly or indirectly.

It is convenient to discuss our new topic in two stages. The first stage will concern some quite general problems and will occupy the present chapter. The second stage, occupying the remaining chapters, will concern what can be believed with warrant and for what reasons, first about the material world and human perception of it, and finally about the mental states of other persons.

What are the "general problems"? We shall consider three. The first is a question about the role of *first premises* in the empirical sciences and everyday thinking about the world: whether, if scepticism is to be avoided, there *must be* some synthetic propositions that it is warranted to believe with some confidence without the logical support of already known propositions, and whether we can seriously claim to be warranted in believing any such propositions. The second question, which assumes that the answer to the first one is affirmative, asks what kinds of proposition these first premises are and what their subject matter is. The third question, of less importance, asks whether these premises, and indeed any synthetic proposition about the world, can be known with certainty.

In answer to the first of these questions, some philosophers hold that the propositions that a person knows can be arranged in an *epistemological order,* that the justification of a belief is at least often (and to some extent necessarily) *vertical,* and that some propositions are *basic,* or *independently credible.* Philosophers who talk in this way suppose that there is a class of propositions in which some—perhaps the highest—degree of confidence may properly be placed solely because of something other than the support they enjoy from their logical relations to other propositions in which belief is warranted. These are the basic or independently credible propositions. For example, it is often supposed that a person's beliefs about an experience he is currently having enjoy a high degree of independent credibility. According to philosophers who suppose this, the general procedure for justifying belief in any synthetic proposition is roughly as follows. First we identify some propositions that can be accepted as relevant premises, propositions that are independently credible. We then draw inferences according to acceptable *rules of inference,* deductive or inductive—rules for whose use the justification has hopefully already been provided. This will lead to theorems whose acceptance is warranted—and, by repetition of the process, eventually to theorems identical with the propositions that we were interested in appraising. In this way a pyramidal set of beliefs, it is supposed, may be shown to be warranted, all resting ultimately on a floor of independently credible propositions and connected to it by justified rules of inference. Philosophers have often thought of this pyramid as consisting of several distinguishable layers, each resting on a definite lower layer. For instance, some have held that propositions about a person's own experience form the ground layer, propositions about the past the next layer, and (resting on both the preceding layers) particular propositions about material things the next. On a higher level, it has been thought, are beliefs about laws of behavior of material things, and on a still higher level, beliefs about theoretical entities such as electrons and about the experience of other people. And so on.

Most philosophers today, however, tend to be sceptical about the possibility of distinguishing neat layers in this way, each one clearly dependent on the layer next below it; it is thought that the relations are too complex for this. What is seriously contended by philosophers who espouse the concept of epistemological order is that there is and must be a ground-floor level. According to these philosophers, a complete theory of knowledge would comprise a detailed description of the types of propositions that are independently credible and a detailed account of how, with rules of inference already justified, the fact that these are credible can be used to justify various beliefs ever more remote from the basic evidence. Let us call philosophers who give this general answer to our first question "inductivists." We may call those who differ "contextualists."

What is asserted by the opposition to the inductivists? In general the critics oppose the view that some special set of beliefs forms the floor of a pyramid of knowledge; indeed they reject the metaphor of a pyramid of knowledge altogether. These philosophers do not, however, embrace scepticism; they hold that warrant for believing a proposition does not depend on a logical relation between the proposition and a ground-floor set of beliefs. When, then, may a belief be called reasonable? On the details of their answer to this question, these philosophers differ greatly. Some hold that a belief in a proposition P is reasonable, as contrasted with disbelief in the proposition, if and only if adding it to the total corpus of one's current beliefs would result in a *more coherent* system of beliefs. In other words, the belief is reasonable if it enjoys what can be called *horizontal* logical support from a person's other beliefs. This view, often called the "coherence theory of truth" (but better entitled the "coherence theory of warranted belief"), is represented by the Blanshard selection in Chapter 2. (An inductivist can come close to the coherence theory, but he will give a special status to ground-floor beliefs.)

But a contextualist need not adopt the coherence theory. He may say that if there is doubt about a certain proposition, support of it must come from its logical relations to other propositions that are at the time not doubtful, but that nothing so grand as relations to the total system of beliefs need be investigated. If the epistemological status of these other propositions not currently in doubt is queried, he will reply that there is no point in questioning a belief except for some specific reason, and that when a belief is questioned for some specific reason there will always be numerous other beliefs which are not in question and which can serve as bases for adjudication of the particular problem that has arisen. No belief, he says, is sacrosanct, but beliefs can be assessed only one at a time and with a background of beliefs not currently in dispute. Epistemology, he will maintain, need undertake no general reconstruction of the basis for all beliefs at once, since there is no serious question —indeed there *could* not be—about all beliefs at once. The contextualist is apt to deplore any such wholesale enterprise, to insist that doubts are particular and occur in a context, so that what we may reasonably do to meet them will depend on the special situation.

On this issue, among the selections below, Russell and Price are on the side of the inductivists, with Peirce and Austin (and, of course, Blanshard in Chapter 2) forming the opposition.

Let us turn now to the second of our two main questions: *Which* beliefs are ground-floor beliefs, the absolutely first premises, the independently credible synthetic propositions? Evidently this question is one that agitates only inductivists and not contextualists. The central issue here is whether or not only beliefs about *one's own experience* have independently credible status. Philosophers who hold that only beliefs about one's own experience are independently credible differ among themselves on a second point: Do only beliefs about one's own *present* experience have this status, or are memory-beliefs about one's own *past* experience also independently credible? The status of beliefs about one's own past experience will be left for later discussion, particularly in Chapter 7; the present chapter concentrates on controversy about whether only beliefs about a person's own experience, sometime or other, are initially warranted. We shall call a philosopher an "empiricist" if he thinks that only such propositions are initially warranted, among the synthetic particular propositions a person might accept. (This terminology is slightly awkward, since it leads us to classify some writers, such as Bertrand Russell, by an appellation they would reject because they use the term "empiricist" in a slightly different way; but for present purposes it is convenient.) Among the authors whose work appears below, then, Russell and Price may be considered outstanding examples of empiricism.

One important point of debate about empiricism concerns whether it is possible to state clearly what its thesis is. For what is "experience"? Evidently empiricist philosophers are using this term in a technical and unordinary way. It will probably seem reasonably clear to the reader, however, after examining the papers that follow, which propositions the empiricists would say concern a person's own "experience": those about his feelings, emotional states, thoughts, and most of all those about *how things look, sound, feel, or smell to him*.

Nevertheless the matter is controversial. Moreover, even when it is conceded that it is clear what the thesis means, critics of empiricism say that it inevitably leads to scepticism, or that the whole concept of propositions about one's own experience is contradictory. What is the positive thesis of inductivists who criticize empiricism? For one thing, they often hold that beliefs about material objects are independently credible—that in various circumstances we have good reason for believing them, but reason other than their logical relations to any kind of "evidence." Austin, Malcolm, and Quinton, in the readings that follow, support some of these points against empiricism.

The third main question is of somewhat less importance, although it has been widely debated. It asks whether synthetic propositions can, with the aid of observation, be known to be true for certain. More specifically, discussion has centered on two subquestions. The first is whether there can be certain knowledge at least about one's own experience at the time one is having it. The second is whether there can be certain knowledge of facts of any other kind, and, if so, which kinds? One widely represented view is that a belief about one's own current experience is a case of certain knowledge, but no other belief in a synthetic proposition is so. This view is defended in the paper by Henle in the present chapter. Other philosophers have thought that there is *no* certainty whatever, and still other philosophers have thought that a good many propositions of quite different types can be known to be true with certainty.

The philosophers who have debated the issues described above agree on one point: it is not reasonable to remain a sceptic. There have been, however, and still are sceptics. The initial reading below is by a Greek sceptic, Sextus Empiricus. The second reading, by Descartes, portrays a sceptical position of a more extreme sort, although Descartes went on, later in the same book, to combat that point of view. There are different degrees of scepticism. An extreme sceptic claims that there is no proposition in which any person can reasonably place more confidence than in its contradictory. (Some sceptics include the thesis of scepticism itself in this dictum.) A less extreme sceptic excepts some propositions of pure logic or mathematics. And a still more moderate sceptic excepts beliefs about a person's own experience when the experience is simultanous with the belief. Sextus Empiricus represents this last, rather mild, form of the position.

Sextus Empiricus

Scepticism

BOOK I, CHAPTER 4: WHAT SCEPTICISM IS

Scepticism is an ability, or mental attitude, which opposes appearances to judgements in any way whatsoever, with the result that, owing to the equipollence of the objects and reasons thus opposed, we are brought firstly to a state of mental suspense and next to a state of "unperturbedness" or quietude. Now we call it an "ability" not in any subtle sense, but simply in respect of its "being able." By "appearances" we now mean the objects of sense perception, whence we contrast them with the objects of thought or "judgements." The phrase "in any way whatsoever" can be connected either with the word "ability," to make us take the word "ability," as we said, in its simple sense, or with the phrase "opposing appearances to judgements"; for inasmuch as we oppose these in a variety of ways—appearances to appearances, or judgements to judgements, or *alternando* appearances to judgements,—in order to ensure the inclusion of all these antitheses we employ the phrase "in any way whatsoever." Or, again, we join "in any way whatsoever" to "appearances and judgements" in order that we may not have to inquire how the appearances appear or how the thought-objects are judged, but may take these terms in the simple sense. The phrase "opposed judgements" we do not employ in the sense of negations and affirmations only but simply as equivalent to "conflicting judgements." "Equipollence" we use of equality in respect to probability and improbability, to indicate that no one of the conflicting judgements takes precedence of any other as being more probable. "Suspense" is a state of mental rest owing to which we neither deny nor affirm anything. "Quietude" is an untroubled and tranquil condition of soul.

CHAPTER 6: OF THE PRINCIPLES OF SCEPTICISM

The originating cause of Scepticism is, we say, the hope of attaining quietude. Men of talent, who were perturbed by the contradictions in things and in doubt as to which of the alternatives they ought to accept, were led on to inquire what is true in things and what false, hoping by the settlement of this question to attain quietude. The main basic principle of the Sceptic system is that of

---

Reprinted by permission of the publishers from Sextus Empiricus, *Outlines of Pyrrhonism,* trans. by R. G. Bury, Loeb Classical Library, Cambridge, Mass.: Harvard University Press, 1933.

One of the early Greek sceptics, Sextus Empiricus (*ca.* 160–210 A.D.), primarily summarized reasoning proposed by earlier sceptics, particularly Aenesidemus (*ca.* 100–40 B.C.), who had offered "Ten Tropes" for the refutation of nonsceptics.

opposing to every proposition an equal proposition; for we believe that as a consequence of this we end by ceasing to dogmatize.

CHAPTER 7: DOES THE SCEPTIC DOGMATIZE?

When we say that the Sceptic refrains from dogmatizing we do not use the term "dogma," as some do, in the broader sense of "approval of a thing" (for the Sceptic gives assent to the feelings which are the necessary results of sense-impressions, and he would not, for example, say when feeling hot or cold "I believe that I am not hot or cold"); but we say that "he does not dogmatize" using "dogma" in the sense, which some give it, of "assent to one of the non-evident objects of scientific inquiry"; for the Pyrrhonean philosopher assents to nothing that is non-evident. Moreover, even in the act of enunciating the Sceptic formulae concerning things non-evident—such as the formula "No more (one thing than another)," or the formula "I determine nothing," or any of the others which we shall presently mention—he does not dogmatize. For whereas the dogmatizer posits the things about which he is said to be dogmatizing as really existent, the Sceptic does not posit these formulae in any absolute sense; for he conceives that, just as the formula "All things are false" asserts the falsity of itself as well as of everything else, as does the formula "Nothing is true," so also the formula "No more" asserts that itself, like all the rest, is "No more (this than that)," and thus cancels itself along with the rest. And of the other formulae we say the same. If, then, while the dogmatizer posits the matter of his dogma as substantial truth, the Sceptic enunciates his formulae so that they are virtually cancelled by themselves, he should not be said to dogmatize in his enunciation of them. And, most important of all, in his enunciation of these formulae he states what appears to himself and announces his own impression in an undogmatic way, without making any positive assertion regarding the external realities.

CHAPTER 10: DO THE SCEPTICS ABOLISH APPEARANCES?

Those who say that "the Sceptics abolish appearances," or phenomena, seem to me to be unacquainted with the statements of our School. For, as we said above, we do not overthrow the affective sense impressions which induce our assent involuntarily; and these impressions are "the appearances." And when we question whether the underlying object is such as it appears, we grant the fact that it appears, and our doubt does not concern the appearance itself but the account given of that appearance—and that is a different thing from questioning the appearance itself. For example, honey appears to us to be sweet (and this we grant, for we perceive sweetness through the senses), but whether it is also sweet in its essence is for us a matter of doubt, since this is not an appearance but a judgement regarding the appearance. And even if we do actually argue against the appearances, we do not propound such arguments with the intention of abolishing appearances, but by way of pointing out the rashness of the Dogmatists; for if reason is such a trickster as to all but snatch away the appearances from under our very eyes, surely we should view it with suspicion in the case of things non-evident so as not to display rashness by following it.

CHAPTER 11: OF THE CRITERION OF SCEPTICISM

. . . Adhering, then, to appearances we live in accordance with the normal rules of life, undogmatically, seeing that we cannot remain wholly inactive. And it would seem that this regulation of life is fourfold, and that one part of it lies in the guidance of Nature, another in the constraint of the passions, another in the tradition of laws and customs, another in the instruction of the arts. Nature's guidance is that by which we are naturally capable of sensation and thought; constraint of the passions is that whereby hunger drives us to food and thirst to drink; tradition of customs and laws, that whereby we regard piety in the conduct of life as good, but impiety as evil; instruction of the arts, that whereby we are not inactive in such arts as we adopt. But we make all these statements undogmatically.

CHAPTER 13: OF THE GENERAL MODES LEADING TO SUSPENSION OF JUDGEMENT

Now that we have been saying[1] that tranquillity follows on suspension of judgement, it will be our next task to explain how we arrive at this suspension. Speaking generally, one may say that it is the result of setting things in opposition. We oppose either appearances to appearances or objects of thought to objects of thought or *alternando.* For instance, we oppose appearances to appearances when we say "The same tower appears round from a distance, but square from close at hand"; and thoughts to thoughts, when in answer to him who argues the existence of Providence from the order of the heavenly bodies we oppose the fact that often the good are ill and the bad fare well, and draw from this the inference that Providence does not exist. And thoughts we oppose to appearances, as when Anaxagoras countered the notion that snow is white with the argument, "Snow is frozen water, and water is black; therefore snow also is black." With a different idea we oppose things present sometimes . . . to things past or future, as, for instance, when someone propounds to us a theory which we are unable to refute, we say to him in reply "Just as, before the birth of the founder of the School to which you belong, the theory it holds was not yet apparent as a sound theory, although it was really in existence, so likewise it is possible that the opposite theory to that which you now propound is already really existent, though not yet apparent to us, so that we ought not as yet to yield assent to this theory which at the moment seems to be valid." . . .

CHAPTER 14: CONCERNING THE TEN MODES

The usual tradition amongst the older Sceptics is that the "modes" by which "suspension" is supposed to be brought about are ten in number; and they also give them the synonymous names of "arguments" and "positions." . . .

The *First* argument (or *Trope*), as we said, is that which shows that the same impressions are not produced by the same objects owing to the differences in animals. . . . Moreover, the differences found in the most important parts of the body, and especially in those of which the natural function

[1] [In Chapter 12, omitted here.]

is judging and perceiving, are capable of producing a vast deal of divergence in the sense-impressions. . . . Thus, sufferers from jaundice declare that objects which seem to us white are yellow. . . . Since, then, some animals have eyes which are yellow, others bloodshot, others albino . . . they probably, I suppose, have different perceptions of colour. . . . Again, when we press the eyeball at one side the forms, figures and sizes of the objects appear oblong and narrow. So it is probable that all animals which have the pupil of the eye slanting and elongated—such as goats, cats, and similar animals—have impressions of the objects which are different and unlike the notions formed of them by the animals which have round pupils. . . . Of the other sense-organs also the same account holds good. . . .

But if the same things appear different owing to the variety of animals, we shall, indeed, be able to state our own impressions of the real object, but as to its essential nature we shall suspend judgement. For we cannot ourselves judge between our own impressions and those of the other animals, since we ourselves are involved in the dispute and are, therefore, rather in need of a judge than competent to pass judgement ourselves. . . .

The *Second Mode* is . . . based on the differences in men. . . . For man, you know, is said to be compounded of two things, soul and body, and in both these we differ one from another. . . . Tiberius Caesar could see in the dark; and Aristotle tells of a Thracian who fancied that the image of a man was continually going in front of him.

But the greatest proof of the vast and endless differences in men's intelligence is the discrepancy in the statements of the Dogmatists concerning the right objects of choice and avoidance, as well as other things. . . . And the poet says: "One thing is pleasing to one man, another thing to another." . . . Seeing, then, that choice and avoidance depend on pleasure and displeasure, while pleasure and displeasure depend on sensation and sense-impression, whenever some men choose the very things which are avoided by others, it is logical for us to conclude that they are also differently affected by the same things, since otherwise they would all alike have chosen or avoided the same things. But if the same objects affect men differently owing to the differences in the men, then, on this ground also, we shall reasonably be led to suspension of judgement. For while we are, no doubt, able to state what each of the underlying objects appears to be, relatively to each difference, we are incapable of explaining what it is in reality. For we shall have to believe either all men or some. But if we believe all, we shall be attempting the impossible and accepting contradictories; and if some, let us be told whose opinions we are to endorse. . . . Moreover, he who maintains that we ought to assent to the majority is making a childish proposal, since no one is able to visit the whole of mankind and determine what pleases the majority of them. . . .

[The] *Third Mode* is . . . based on differences in the senses. That the senses differ from one another is obvious. Thus, to the eye paintings seem to have recesses and projections, but not so to the touch. . . .

Each of the phenomena perceived by the senses seems to be a complex: the apple, for example, seems smooth, odorous, sweet and yellow. But it is non-evident whether it really possesses these qualities only; or whether it has but one quality but appears varied owing to the varying structure of the sense-organs; or whether, again, it has more qualities than are apparent, some of which elude our perception. . . . If, however, it is possible that only those qualities which we seem to perceive subsist in the apple, or that a greater number subsist, or, again, that not even the qualities which affect us subsist, then it will be non-evident to us what the nature of the apple really is. And the same argument applies to all the other objects of sense. But if the senses do not apprehend external objects, neither can the mind apprehend them; hence, because of this argument also, we shall be driven, it seems, to suspend judgement regarding the external underlying objects. . . .

The *Fourth Mode* . . . is the Mode based, as we say, on the "circumstances." . . . Thus, according as the mental state is natural or unnatural, objects produce dissimilar impressions, as when men in a frenzy or in a state of ecstasy believe they hear daemons' voices, while we do not. . . . Also, the same water which feels very hot when poured on inflamed spots seems lukewarm to us. . . . Now should anyone say that it is an intermixture of certain humours which produces in those who are in an unnatural state improper impressions from the underlying objects, we have to reply that, since healthy persons also have mixed humours, these humours too are capable of causing the external objects—which really are such as they appear to those who are said to be in an unnatural state—to appear other than they are to healthy persons. . . .

Sleeping and waking, too, give rise to different impressions, since we do not imagine when awake what we imagine in sleep, nor when asleep what we imagine when awake; so that the existence or nonexistence of our impressions is not absolute but relative, being in relation to our sleeping or waking condition. Probably, then, in dreams we see things which to our waking state are unreal, although not wholly unreal; for they exist in our dreams, just as waking realities exist although non-existent in dreams.

Age is another cause of difference. For the . . . same sound seems to the [older] faint, but to the [younger] clearly audible. . . . Predispositions are a cause; for the same wine which seems sour to those who have previously eaten dates or figs, seems sweet to those who have just consumed nuts or chick-peas. . . .

Seeing then that the dispositions also are the cause of so much disagreement, and that men are differently disposed at different times, although, no doubt, it is easy to say what nature each of the underlying objects appears to each man to possess, we cannot go on to say what its real nature is, since the disagreement admits in itself of no settlement. For the person who tries to settle it is either in one of the afore-mentioned dispositions or in no disposition whatsoever. But to declare that he is in no disposition at all . . . is the height of absurdity. And if he is to judge the sense-impressions while he is in some one disposition, he will be a party to the disagreement. . . .

The *Fifth Argument* (or *Trope*) is that based on positions, distances, and locations; for owing to each of these the same objects appear different; for example, the same porch when viewed from one of its corners appears curtailed, but viewed from the middle symmetrical on all sides; and the same ship seems at a distance to be small and stationary, but from close at hand large and in motion; and the same tower from a distance appears round but from a near point quadrangular.

These effects are due to distances; among effects due to locations are the following: the light of a lamp appears dim in the sun but bright in the dark; and the same oar bent when in the water but straight when out of the water. . . .

Effects due to positions are such as these: the same painting when laid flat appears smooth, but when inclined forward at a certain angle it seems to have recesses and prominences. . . .

Since, then, all apparent objects are viewed in a certain place, and from a certain distance, or in a certain position, and each of these conditions produces a great divergency in the sense-impressions, as we mentioned above, we shall be compelled by this Mode also to end up in suspension of judgement. For in fact anyone who purposes to give the preference to any of these impressions will be attempting the impossible. . . .

The *Sixth Mode* is that based on admixtures, by which we conclude that, because none of the real objects affects our senses by itself but always in conjunction with something else, though we may possibly be able to state the nature of the resultant mixture formed by the external object and that along with which it is perceived, we shall not be able to say what is the exact nature of the external reality in itself. That none of the external objects affects our senses by itself but always in conjunction with something else, and that, in consequence, it assumes a different appearance, is, I imagine, quite obvious. Thus, our own complexion is of one hue in warm air, of another in cold, and we should not be able to say what our complexion really is, but only what it looks like in conjunction with each of these conditions. And the same sound appears of one sort in conjunction with rare air and of another sort with dense air; and odours are more pungent in a hot bath-room or in the sun than in chilly air; and a body is light when immersed in water but heavy when surrounded by air. . . . Probably, too, the mind itself adds a certain admixture of its own to the messages conveyed by the senses. . . . Thus . . . we see that, owing to our inability to make any statement about the real nature of external objects, we are compelled to suspend judgment.

The *Seventh Mode* is that based . . . on the quantity and constitution of the underlying objects, meaning generally by "constitution" the manner of composition. And it is evident that by this Mode also we are compelled to suspend judgement concerning the real nature of the objects. Thus, for example, the filings of a goat's horn appear white when viewed simply by themselves and without combination, but when combined in the substance of the horn they look black. And silver filings appear black when they are by themselves, but when united to the whole mass they are sensed as white. . . . Therefore in these cases, too . . . when it comes to the independent and real nature of the objects, this we shall be unable to describe because of the divergency in the sense-impressions which is due to the combinations. . . .

CHAPTER 15: OF THE FIVE MODES

The later Sceptics hand down Five Modes leading to suspension, namely these: the first based on discrepancy, the second on regress *ad infinitum,* the third on relativity, the fourth on hypothesis, the fifth on circular reasoning. That based on discrepancy leads us to find that with regard to the object presented there has arisen both amongst ordinary people and amongst philosophers an interminable conflict because of which we are unable either to choose a thing or reject it, and so fall back on suspension. The Mode based upon regress *ad infinitum* is that whereby we assert that the thing adduced as a proof of the matter proposed needs a further proof, and this again another, and so on *ad infinitum,* so that the consequence is suspension, as we possess no starting-point for our argument. The Mode based upon relativity . . . is that whereby the object has such or such an appearance in relation to the subject judging and to the concomitant percepts, but as to its real nature we suspend judgement. We have the Mode based on hypothesis when the Dogmatists, being forced to recede *ad infinitum,* take as their starting-point something which they do not establish by argument but claim to assume as granted simply and without demonstration. The Mode of circular reasoning is the form used when the proof itself which ought to establish the matter of inquiry requires confirmation derived from that matter; in this case, being unable to assume either in order to establish the other, we suspend judgement about both. . . .

BOOK II, CHAPTER 4: DOES A CRITERION OF TRUTH REALLY EXIST?

. . . In order to decide the dispute which has arisen about the criterion [of truth], we must possess an accepted criterion by which we shall be able to judge the dispute; and in order to possess an accepted criterion, the dispute about the criterion must first be decided. And when the argument thus reduces itself to a form of circular reasoning the discovery of the criterion becomes impracticable, since we do not allow them to adopt a criterion by assumption, while if they offer to judge the criterion by a criterion we force them to a regress *ad infinitum.* And furthermore, since demonstration requires a demonstrated criterion, while the criterion requires an approved demonstration, they are forced into circular reasoning.

CHAPTER 14: CONCERNING SYLLOGISMS

So then it is also superfluous, perhaps, to discuss in detail the much vaunted "syllogisms." . . . Yet perhaps it will not be amiss to go further and deal with them separately, especially since these thinkers pride themselves upon them. Now there is much that one can say by way of suggesting their unreality, but in an outline sketch it is sufficient to treat of them by the method which follows. . . .

Well then, the premiss "Every man is an animal" is established by induction from the particular instances; for from the fact that Socrates, who is a man, is also an animal, and Plato likewise, and Dion and each one of the particular instances, they think it possible to assert that every man is an animal; so that if even a single one of the particulars should apparently conflict with the rest the universal premiss is not valid; thus, for example, when most animals move the lower jaw, and only the crocodile the upper, the premiss "Every animal moves the lower jaw" is not true. So whenever they argue "Every man is an animal, and Socrates is a man, therefore Socrates is an animal," proposing to deduce from the universal proposition "Every man is an animal" the particular proposition "Socrates therefore is an animal," which in fact goes . . . to establish by way of induction the universal proposition, they fall into the error of circular reasoning, since they are establishing the universal proposition inductively by means of each of the particulars and deducing the particular proposition from the universal syllogistically. . . .

CHAPTER 15: CONCERNING INDUCTION

It is also easy, I consider, to set aside the method of induction. For, when they propose to establish the universal from the particulars by means of induction, they will effect this by a review either of all or of some of the particular instances. But if they review some, the induction will be insecure, since some of the particulars omitted in the induction may contravene the universal; while if they are to review all, they will be toiling at the impossible, since the particulars are infinite and definite. Thus on both grounds, as I think, the consequence is that induction is invalidated.

René Descartes

Meditations on First Philosophy

MEDITATION I

OF THE THINGS WHICH MAY BE BROUGHT WITHIN THE SPHERE OF THE DOUBTFUL.

It is now some years since I detected how many were the false beliefs that I had from my earliest youth admitted as true, and how doubtful was everything I had since constructed on this basis; and from that time I was convinced that I must once for all seriously undertake to rid myself of all the opinions which I had formerly accepted, and commence to build anew from the foundation, if I wanted to establish any firm and permanent structure in the sciences. But as this enterprise appeared to be a very great one, I waited until I had attained an age so mature that I could not hope that at any later date I should be better fitted to execute my design. This reason caused me to delay so long that I should feel that I was doing wrong were I to occupy in deliberation the time that yet remains to me for action. To-day, then, since very opportunely for the plan I have in view I have delivered my mind from every care [and am happily agitated by no passions] and since I have procured for myself an assured leisure in a peaceable retirement, I shall at last

---

From René Descartes, *Meditations on First Philosophy,* 2nd ed., 1642 (first published in 1641), in *The Philosophical Works of Descartes,* trans. by E. S. Haldane and G. R. T. Ross, published by Cambridge University Press, Cambridge, 1931, and reprinted with their permission.

René Descartes (1596–1650) was born in France but spent most of his life in Holland. He was one of the founders of modern epistemology and a mathematician ("Cartesian coordinates") as well.

seriously and freely address myself to the general upheaval of all my former opinions.

Now for this object it is not necessary that I should show that all of these are false—I shall perhaps never arrive at this end. But inasmuch as reason already persuades me that I ought no less carefully to withhold my assent from matters which are not entirely certain and indubitable than from those which appear to me manifestly to be false, if I am able to find in each one some reason to doubt, this will suffice to justify my rejecting the whole. And for that end it will not be requisite that I should examine each in particular, which would be an endless undertaking; for owing to the fact that the destruction of the foundations of necessity brings with it the downfall of the rest of the edifice, I shall only in the first place attack those principles upon which all my former opinions rested.

All that up to the present time I have accepted as most true and certain I have learned either from the senses or through the senses; but it is sometimes proved to me that these senses are deceptive, and it is wiser not to trust entirely to any thing by which we have once been deceived.

But it may be that although the senses sometimes deceive us concerning things which are hardly perceptible, or very far away, there are yet many others to be met with as to which we cannot reasonably have any doubt, although we recognise them by their means. For example, there is the fact that I am here, seated by the fire, attired in a dressing gown, having this paper in my hands and other similar matters. And how could I deny that these hands and this body are mine, were it not perhaps that I compare myself to certain persons, devoid of sense, whose cerebella are so troubled and clouded by the violent vapours of black bile, that they constantly assure us that they think they are kings when they are really quite poor, or that they are clothed in purple when they are really without covering, or who imagine that they have an earthenware head or are nothing but pumpkins or are made of glass. But they are mad, and I should not be any the less insane were I to follow examples so extravagant.

At the same time I must remember that I am a man, and that consequently I am in the habit of sleeping, and in my dreams representing to myself the same things or sometimes even less probable things, than do those who are insane in their waking moments. How often has it happened to me that in the night I dreamt that I found myself in this particular place, that I was dressed and seated near the fire, whilst in reality I was lying undressed in bed! At this moment it does indeed seem to me that it is with eyes awake that I am looking at this paper; that this head which I move is not asleep, that it is deliberately and of set purpose that I extend my hand and perceive it; what happens in sleep does not appear so clear nor so distinct as does all this. But in thinking over this I remind myself that on many occasions I have in sleep been deceived by similar illusions, and in dwelling carefully on this reflection I see so manifestly that there are no certain indications by which we may clearly distinguish wakefulness from sleep that I am lost in astonishment. And my astonishment is such that it is almost capable of persuading me that I now dream.

Now let us assume that we are asleep and that all these particulars, e.g. that we open our eyes, shake our head, extend our hands, and so on, are but false delusions; and let us reflect that possibly neither our hands nor our whole body are such as they appear to us to be. At the same time we must at least confess that the things which are represented to us in sleep are like painted representations which can only have been formed as the counterparts of something real and true, and that in this way those general things at least, i.e. eyes, a head, hands, and a whole body, are not imaginary things, but things really existent. For, as a matter of fact, painters, even when they study with the greatest skill to represent sirens and satyrs by forms the most strange and extraordinary, cannot give them natures which are entirely new, but merely make a certain medley of the members of different animals; or if their imagination is extravagant enough to invent something so novel that nothing similar has ever before been seen, and that then their work represents a thing purely fictitious and absolutely false, it is certain all the same that the colours of which this is composed are necessarily real. And for the same reason, although these general things, to wit, [a body], eyes, a head, hands, and such like, may be imaginary, we are bound at the same time to confess that there are at least some other objects yet more simple and more universal, which are real and true; and of these just in the same way as with certain real colours, all these images of things which dwell in our thoughts, whether true and real or false and fantastic, are formed.

To such a class of things pertains corporeal nature in general, and its extension, the figure of extended things, their quantity or magnitude and number, as also the place in which they are, the time which measures their duration, and so on.

That is possibly why our reasoning is not unjust when we conclude from this that Physics, Astronomy, Medicine and all other sciences which have as their end the consideration of composite things, are very dubious and uncertain; but that Arithmetic, Geometry and other sciences of that kind which only treat of things that are very simple and very general, without taking great trouble to ascertain whether they are actually existent or not, contain some measure of certainty and an element of the indubitable. For whether I am awake or asleep, two and three together always form five, and the square can never have more than four sides, and it does not seem possible that truths so clear and apparent can be suspected of any falsity [or uncertainty].

Nevertheless I have long had fixed in my mind the belief that an all-powerful God existed by whom I have been created such as I am. But how do I know that He has not brought it to pass that there is no earth, no heaven, no extended body, no magnitude, no place, and that nevertheless [I possess the perceptions of all these things and that] they seem to me to exist just exactly as I now see them? And, besides, as I sometimes imagine that others deceive themselves in the things which they think they know best, how do I know that I am not deceived every time that I add two and three, or count the sides of a square, or judge of things yet simpler, if anything simpler can be imagined? But possibly God has not desired that I should be thus deceived, for He is said to be supremely good. If, however, it is contrary to His goodness to have made me such that I constantly deceive myself, it would also appear to be contrary to His goodness to permit me to be sometimes deceived, and nevertheless I cannot doubt that He does permit this.

There may indeed be those who would prefer to deny the existence of a God so powerful, rather than believe that all other things are uncertain. But let us not oppose them for the present, and grant that all that is here said of a God is a fable; nevertheless in whatever way they suppose that I have arrived at the state of being that I have reached—whether they attribute it to fate or to accident, or make out that it is by a continual succession of antecedents, or by some other method—since to err and deceive oneself is a defect, it is clear that the greater will be the probability of my being so imperfect as to deceive myself ever, as is the Author to whom they assign my origin the less powerful. To these reasons I have certainly nothing to reply, but at the end I feel constrained to confess that there is nothing in all that I formerly believed to be true, of which I cannot in some measure doubt, and that not merely through want of thought or through levity, but for reasons which are very powerful and maturely considered; so that henceforth I ought not the less carefully to refrain from giving credence to these opinions than to that which is manifestly false, if I desire to arrive at any certainty [in the sciences].

But it is not sufficient to have made these remarks, we must also be careful to keep them in mind. For these ancient and commonly held opinions still revert frequently to my mind, long and familiar custom having given them the right to occupy my mind against my inclination and rendered them almost masters of my belief; nor will I ever lose the habit of deferring to them or of placing my confidence in them, so long as I consider them as they really are, i.e. opinions in some measure doubtful, as I have just shown, and at the same time highly probable, so that there is much more reason to believe in than to deny them. That is why I consider that I shall not be acting amiss, if, taking of set purpose a contrary belief, I allow myself to be deceived, and for a certain time pretend that all these opinions are entirely false and imaginary, until at last, having thus balanced my former prejudices with my latter [so that they cannot divert my opinions more to one side than to the other], my judgment will no longer be dominated by bad usage or turned away from the right knowledge of the truth. For I am assured that there can be neither peril nor error in this course, and that I cannot at present yield too much to distrust, since I am not considering the question of action, but only of knowledge.

I shall then suppose, not that God who is supremely good and the fountain of truth, but some evil genius not less powerful than deceitful, has employed his whole energies in deceiving me; I shall consider that the heavens, the earth, colours, figures, sound, and all other external things are nought but the illusions and dreams of which this genius has availed himself in order to lay traps for my credulity; I shall consider myself as having no hands, no eyes, no flesh, no blood, nor any senses, yet falsely believing myself to possess all these things; I shall remain obstinately attached to this idea, and if by this means it is not in my power to arrive at the knowledge of any truth, I may at least do what is in my power [i.e. suspend my judgment], and with firm purpose avoid giving credence to any false thing, or being imposed upon by this arch deceiver, however powerful and deceptive he may be. But this task is a laborious one, and insensibly a certain lassitude leads me into the course of my ordinary life. And just as a captive who in sleep enjoys an imaginary liberty, when he begins to suspect that his liberty is but a dream, fears to awaken, and conspires with these agreeable illusions that the deception may be prolonged, so insensibly of my own accord I fall back into my former opinions, and I dread awakening from this slumber, lest the laborious wakefulness which would follow the tranquillity of this repose should have to be spent not in daylight, but in the excessive darkness of the difficulties which have just been discussed.

MEDITATION II

OF THE NATURE OF THE HUMAN MIND; AND THAT IT IS MORE EASILY KNOWN THAN THE BODY.

The Meditation of yesterday filled my mind with so many doubts that it is no longer in my power to forget them. And yet I do not see in what manner I can resolve them; and, just as if I had all of a sudden fallen into very deep water, I am so disconcerted that I can neither make certain of setting my feet on the bottom, nor can I swim and so support myself on the surface. I shall nevertheless make an effort and follow anew the same path as that on which I yesterday entered, i.e. I shall proceed by setting aside all that in which the least doubt could be supposed to exist, just as if I had discovered that it was absolutely false; and I shall ever follow in this road until I have met with something which is certain, or at least, if I can do nothing else, until I have learned for certain that there is nothing in the world that is certain. Archimedes, in order that he might draw the terrestrial globe out of its place, and transport it elsewhere, demanded only that one point should be fixed and immoveable; in the same way I shall have the right to conceive high hopes if I am happy enough to discover one thing only which is certain and indubitable.

I suppose, then, that all the things that I see are false, I persuade myself that nothing has ever existed of all that my fallacious memory represents to me. I consider that I possess no senses; I imagine that body, figure, extension, movement and place are but the fictions of my mind. What, then, can be esteemed as true? Perhaps nothing at all, unless that there is nothing in the world that is certain.

But how can I know there is not something different from those things that I have just considered, of which one cannot have the slightest doubt? Is there not some God, or some other being by whatever name we call it, who puts these reflections into my mind? That is not necessary, for is it not possible that I am capable of producing them myself? I myself, am I not at least something? But I have already denied that I had senses and body. Yet I hesitate, for what follows from that? Am I so dependent on body and senses that I cannot exist without these? But I was persuaded that there was nothing in all the world, that there was no heaven, no earth, that there were no minds, nor any bodies: was I not then likewise persuaded that I did not exist? Not at all; of a surety I myself did exist since I persuaded myself of something [or merely because I thought of something]. But there is some deceiver or other, very powerful and very cunning, who ever employs his ingenuity in deceiving me. Then without doubt I exist also if he deceives me, and let him deceive me as much as he will, he can never cause me to be nothing so long as I think that I am something. So that after having reflected well and carefully examined all things, we must come to the definite conclusion that this proposition: I am, I exist, is necessarily true each time that I pronounce it, or that I mentally conceive it.

Bertrand Russell

Epistemological Order and the Premises of Knowledge

KNOWLEDGE OF FACTS AND KNOWLEDGE OF LAWS

When we examine our beliefs as to matters of fact, we find that they are sometimes based directly on perception or memory, while in other cases they are inferred. To common sense this distinction presents little difficulty: the beliefs that arise immediately from perception appear to it indubitable, and the inferences, though they may sometimes be wrong, are thought, in such cases, to be fairly easily rectified except where peculiarly dubious matters are concerned. I know of the existence of my friend Mr. Jones because I see him frequently: in his presence I know him by perception, and in his absence by memory. I know of the existence of Napoleon because I have heard and read about him, and I have every reason to believe in the veracity of my teachers. I am somewhat less certain about Hengist and Horsa, and much less certain about Zoroaster, but these uncertainties are still on a common-sense level, and do not seem, at first sight, to raise any philosophical issue.

This primitive confidence, however, was lost at a very early stage in philosophical speculation, and was lost for sound reasons. It was found that what I know by perception is less than had been thought, and that the inferences by which I pass from perceived to unperceived facts are open to question. Both these sources of skepticism must be investigated.

There is, to begin with, a difficulty as to what is inferred and what is not. I spoke a moment ago of my belief in Napoleon as an inference from what I have heard and read, but there is an important sense in which this is not quite true. When a child is being taught history, he does not argue: "My teacher is a person of the highest moral character, paid to teach me facts; my teacher says there was such a person as Napoleon; therefore probably there was such a person." If he did, he would retain considerable doubt, since his evidence of the teacher's moral character is likely to be inadequate, and in many countries at many times teachers have been paid to teach the opposite

---

From Bertrand Russell, *Human Knowledge: Its Scope and Limits*.

of facts. The child in fact, unless he hates the teacher, spontaneously believes what he is told. When we are told anything emphatically or authoritatively, it is an effort not to believe it, as anyone can experience on April Fools' Day. Nevertheless there is still a distinction, even on a common-sense level, between what we are told and what we know for ourselves. If you say to the child, "How do you know about Napoleon?," the child may say, "Because my teacher told me." If you say, "How do you know your teacher told you?," the child may say, "Why, of course, because I heard her." If you say, "How do you know you heard her?," he may say, "Because I remember it distinctly." If you say, "How do you know you remember it?," he will either lose his temper or say, "Well, I do remember it." Until you reach this point, he will defend his belief as to a matter of fact by belief in another matter of fact, but in the end he reaches a belief for which he can give no further reason.

There is thus a distinction between beliefs that arise spontaneously and beliefs for which no further reason can be given. It is the latter class of beliefs that are of most importance for theory of knowledge, since they are the indispensable minimum of premises for our knowledge of matters of fact. Such beliefs I shall call "data." In ordinary thinking they are *causes* of other beliefs rather than *premises* from which other beliefs are inferred; but in a critical scrutiny of our beliefs as to matters of fact we must whenever possible translate the causal transitions of primitive thinking into logical transitions, and only accept the derived beliefs to the extent that the character of the transitions seems to justify. For this there is a common-sense reason, namely, that every such transition is found to involve some risk of error, and therefore data are more nearly certain than beliefs derived from them. I am not contending that data are ever completely certain, nor is this contention necessary for their importance in theory of knowledge.

There is a long history of discussions as to what was mistakenly called "skepticism of the senses." Many appearances are deceptive. Things seen in a mirror may be thought to be "real." In certain circumstances, people see double. The rainbow seems to touch the ground at some point, but if you go there you do not find it. Most noteworthy in this connection are dreams: however vivid they may have been, we believe, when we wake up, that the objects which we thought we saw were illusory. But in all these cases the core of data is not illusory, but only the derived beliefs. My visual sensations, when I look in a mirror or see double, are exactly what I think they are. Things at the foot of the rainbow do really look colored. In dreams I have all the experiences that I seem to have; it is only things outside my mind that are not as I believe them to be while I am dreaming. There are in fact no illusions of the senses, but only mistakes in interpreting sensational data as signs of things other than themselves. Or, to speak more exactly, there is no evidence that there are illusions of the senses.

Every sensation which is of a familiar kind brings with it various associated beliefs and expectations. When, say, we see and hear an airplane, we do not merely have the visual sensation and the auditory sensation of a whirring noise; spontaneously and without conscious thought we interpret what we see and hear and fill it out with customary adjuncts. To what an extent we do this becomes obvious when we make a mistake—for example, when what we thought was airplane turns out to be a bird. I knew a road, along which I used often to go in a car, which had a bend at a certain place, and a whitewashed wall straight ahead. At night it was very difficult not to see the wall as a road going straight on up a hill. The right interpretation as a house and the wrong interpretation as an uphill road were both, in a sense, inferences from the sensational datum, but they were not inferences in the logical sense, since they occurred without any conscious mental process.

I give the name "animal inference" to the process of spontaneous interpretation of sensations. When a dog hears himself called in tones to which he is accustomed, he looks round and runs in the direction of the sound. He may be deceived, like the dog looking into the gramophone in the advertisement of "His Master's Voice." But since inferences of this sort are generated by the repeated experiences that give rise to habit, his inference must be one which has usually been right in his past life, since otherwise the habit would not have been generated. We thus find ourselves, when we begin to reflect, expecting all sorts of things that in fact happen, although it would be logically possible for them not to happen in spite of the occurrence of the sensations which give rise to the expectations. Thus reflection upon animal inference gives us an initial store of scientific laws, such as "Dogs bark." These initial laws are usually somewhat unreliable, but they help us to take the first steps toward science.

Everyday generalizations, such as "Dogs bark," come to be explicitly believed after habits have been generated which might be described as a preverbal form of the same belief. What sort of habit is it that comes to be expressed in the words "Dogs bark"? We do not expect them to bark at all times, but we do expect that *if* they make a noise it will be a bark or a growl. Psychologically, induction does not proceed as it does in the textbooks, where we are supposed to have observed a number of occasions on which dogs barked, and then proceeded consciously to generalize. The fact is that the generalization, in the form of a habit of expectation, occurs at a lower level than that of conscious thought, so that, when we begin to think consciously, we find ourselves believing the generalization, not, explicitly, on the basis of the evidence, but as expressing what is implicit in our habit of expectation. This is a history of the belief, not a justification of it.

Let us make this state of affairs somewhat more explicit. First comes the repeated experience of dogs barking, then comes the habit of expecting a bark, then, by giving verbal expression to the habit, comes belief in the general proposition "Dogs bark." Last comes the logician, who asks not "Why do I believe this?" but "What reason is there for supposing this true?" Clearly the reason, if any, must consist of two parts: first, the facts of perception consisting of the various occasions on which we have heard dogs bark; second, some principle justifying generalization from observed instances to a law. But this logical process comes historically after, not before, our belief in a host of common-sense generalizations.

The translation of animal inferences into verbal generalizations is carried out very inadequately in ordinary thinking, and even in the thinking of many philosophers. In what counts as perception of external objects there is much that consists of habits generated by past experience. Take, for example, our belief in the permanence of objects. When we see a dog or a cat, a chair or a table, we do not suppose that we are seeing something which has a merely momentary existence; we are convinced that what we are seeing has a past and a future of considerable duration. We do not think this about everything that we see; a flash of lightning, a rocket, or a rainbow is expected to disappear quickly. But experience has generated in us the expectation that ordinary solid objects, which can be touched as well as seen, usually persist, and can be seen and touched again on suitable occasions. Science reinforces this belief by explaining away apparent disappearances as transformations into gaseous forms. But the belief in quasi-permanence, except in exceptional cases, antedates the scientific doctrine of the indestructibility of matter, and is itself antedated by the animal expectation that common objects can be seen again if we look in the right place.

The filling out of the sensational core by means of animal inferences, until it becomes what is called "perception," is analogous to the filling out of telegraphic press messages in newspaper offices. The reporter telegraphs the one word "King," and the newspaper prints "His Gracious Majesty King George VI." There is some risk of error in this proceeding, since the reporter may have been relating the doings of Mr. Mackenzie King. It is true that the context would usually reveal such an error, but one can imagine circumstances in which it would not. In dreams, we fill out the bare sensational message wrongly, and only the context of waking life shows us our mistake.

The analogy to abbreviated press telegrams is very close. Suppose, for instance, you see a friend at the window of an incoming train, and a little later you see him coming toward you on the platform. The physical causes of your perceptions (and of your interpretation of them) are certain light signals passing between him and your eyes. All that physics, by itself, entitles you to infer from the receipt of these signals is that, somewhere along the line of sight, light of the appropriate colors has been emitted or reflected or refracted or scattered. It is obvious that the kind of ingenuity which has produced the cinema could cause you to have just these sensations in the absence of your friend, and that in that case you would be deceived. But such sources of deception cannot be frequent, or at least cannot have been frequent hitherto, since, if they were, you would not have formed the habits of expectation and belief in context that you have in fact formed. In the case supposed, you are confident that it is your friend, that he has existed throughout the interval between seeing him at the window and seeing him on the platform, and that he has pursued a continuous path through space from the one to the other. You have no doubt that what you saw was something solid, not an intangible object like a rainbow or a cloud. And so, although the message received by the senses contains (so to speak) only a few key words, your mental and physical habits cause you, spontaneously and without thought, to expand it into a coherent and amply informative dispatch.

This expansion of the sensational core to produce what goes by the somewhat question-begging name of "perception" is obviously only trustworthy in so far as our habits of association run parallel to processes in the external world. Clouds looked down upon from a mountain may look so like the sea or a field of snow that only positive knowledge to the contrary prevents you from so interpreting your visual sensations. If you are not accustomed to the gramophone, you will confidently believe that the voice you hear on the other side of the door proceeds from a person in the room that you are about to enter. There is no obvious limit to the invention of ingenious apparatus capable of deceiving the unwary. We know that the people we see on the screen in the cinema are not really there, although they move and talk and behave in a manner having some resemblance to that of human beings; but if we did not know it, we might at first find it hard to believe. Thus what we seem to know through the senses may be deceptive whenever the environment is different from what our past experience has led us to expect.

From the above considerations it follows that we cannot admit as data all that an uncritical acceptance of common sense would take as given in perception. Only sensations and memories are truly data for our knowledge of the external world. We must exclude from our list of data not only the things that we consciously infer, but all that is obtained by animal inference, such as the imagined hardness of an object seen but not touched. It is true that our "perceptions," in all their fullness, are data for psychology: we do in fact have the experience of believing in such-and-such an object. It is only for knowledge of things outside our own minds that it is necessary to regard only sensations as data. This necessity is a consequence of what we know of physics and physiology. The same external stimulus, reaching the brains of two men with different experiences, will produce different results, and it is only what these different results have in common that can be used in inferring external causes. If it is objected that the truth of physics and physiology is doubtful, the situation is even worse; for if they are false, nothing whatever as to the outer world can be inferred from my experiences. I am, however, throughout this work, assuming that science is broadly speaking true.

If we define "data" as "those matters of fact of which, independently of inference, we have a right to feel most nearly certain," it follows from what has been said that all my data are events that happen to me, and are, in fact, what would commonly be called events in my mind. This is a view which has been characteristic of British empiricism, but has been rejected by most Continental philosophers, and is not now accepted by the followers of Dewey or by most of the logical positivists. As the issue is of considerable importance, I shall set forth the reasons which have convinced me, including a brief repetition of those that have already been given.

There are, first, arguments on the common-sense level, derived from illusions, squinting, reflection, refraction, etc., but above all from dreams. I dreamed last night that I was in Germany, in a house which looked out on a ruined church; in my dream I supposed at first that the church had been bombed during the recent war, but was subsequently informed that its destruction dated from the wars of religion in the sixteenth century. All this, so long as I remained asleep, had all the convincingness of waking life. I did really have the dream, and did really have an experience intrinsically indistinguishable from that of seeing a ruined church when awake. It follows that the experience which I call "seeing a church" is not conclusive evidence that there is a church, since it may occur when there is no such external object as I suppose in my dream. It may be said that, though when dreaming I may *think* that I am awake, when I wake up I *know* that I am awake. But I do not see how we are to have any such certainty, I have frequently dreamed that I woke up; in fact once, after ether, I dreamed it about a hundred times in the course of one dream. We condemn dreams, in fact, because they do not fit into a proper context, but this argument can be made inconclusive, as in Calderon's play *La Vida es Sueño*. I do not believe that I am now dreaming, but I cannot prove that I am not. I am, however, quite certain that I am having certain experiences, whether they be those of a dream or those of waking life.

We come now to another class of arguments, derived from physics and physiology. This class of arguments came into philosophy with Locke, who used it to show that secondary qualities are subjective. This class of arguments is capable of being used to throw doubt on the truth of physics and physiology, but I will first deal with them on the hypothesis that science, in the main, is true.

We experience a visual sensation when light waves reach the eye, and an auditory sensation when sound waves reach the ear. There is no reason to suppose that light waves are at all like the experience which we call seeing something, or sound waves at all like the experience which we call hearing a sound. There is no reason whatever to suppose that the physical sources of light and sound waves have any more resemblance to our experiences than the waves have. If the waves are produced in unusual ways, our experience may lead us to infer subsequent experiences which it turns out that we do not have; this shows that even in normal perception interpretation plays a larger part than common sense supposes, and that interpretation sometimes leads us to entertain false expectations.

Another difficulty is connected with time. We see and hear now, but what (according to common sense) we are seeing and hearing occurred some time ago. When we both see and hear an explosion, we see it first and hear it afterward. Even if we could suppose that the furniture of our room is exactly what it seems, we cannot suppose this of a nebula millions of light-years away, which looks like a speck but is not much smaller than the Milky Way, and of which the light that reaches us now started before human beings began to exist. And the difference between the nebula and the furniture is only one of degree.

Then there are physiological arguments. People who have lost a leg may continue to feel pain in it. Dr. Johnson, disproving Berkeley, thought the pain in his toe when he kicked a stone was evidence for the existence of the stone, but it appears that it was not even evidence for the existence of his toe, since he might have felt it even if his toe had been amputated. Speaking generally, if a nerve is stimulated in a given manner, a certain sensation results, whatever may be the source of the stimulation. Given sufficient skill, it ought to be possible to make a man see the starry heavens by tickling his optic nerve, but the instrument used would bear little resemblance to the august bodies studied by astronomers.

The above arguments, as I remarked before, may be interpreted skeptically, as showing that there is no reason to believe that our sensations have external causes. As this interpretation concedes what I am at present engaged in maintaining—namely, that sensations are the sole data for physics—I shall not, for the moment, consider whether it can be refuted, but shall pass on to a closely similar line of argument which is related to the method of Cartesian doubt. This method consists in searching for data by provisionally rejecting everything that it is found possible to call in question.

Descartes argues that the existence of sensible objects might be uncertain, because it would be possible for a deceitful demon to mislead us. *We* should substitute for a deceitful demon a cinema in technicolor. It is, of course, also possible that we may be dreaming. But he regards the existence of our thoughts as wholly unquestionable. When he says, "I think, therefore I am," the primitive certainties at which he may be supposed to have arrived are particular "thoughts," in the large sense in which he uses the term. His own existence is an inference from his thoughts, an inference whose validity does not at the moment concern us. In the context, what appears certain to him is that there is doubting, but the experience of doubting has no special prerogative over other experiences. When I see a flash of lightning I may, it is maintained, be uncertain as to the physical character of lightning and even as to whether anything external to myself has happened, but I cannot make myself doubt that there has been the occurrence which is called "seeing a flash of lightning," though there may have been no flash outside my seeing.

It is not suggested that I am certain about all my own experiences; this would certainly be false. Many memories are dubious, and so are many faint sensations. What I am saying—and in this I am expounding part of Descartes' argument—is that there are some occurrences that I cannot make myself doubt, and that these are all of the kind that, if we admit a not-self, are part of the life of myself. Not all of them are sensations; some are abstract thoughts, some are memories, some are wishes, some are pleasures or pains. But all are what we should commonly describe as mental events in me.

My own view is that this point of view is in the right in so far as it is concerned with data that are matters of fact. Matters of fact that lie outside my experience can be made to seem doubtful, unless there is an argument showing that their existence follows from matters of fact within my experience together with laws of whose certainty I feel reasonably convinced. But this is a long question, concerning which, at the moment, I wish to say only a few preliminary words.

Hume's skepticism with regard to the world of science resulted from (a) the doctrine that all my data are private to me, together with (b) the discovery that matters of fact, however numerous and well selected, never logically imply any other matter of fact. I do not see any way of escaping from either of these theses. The first I have been arguing; I may say that I attach especial weight in this respect to the argument from the physical causation of sensations. As to the second, it is obvious as a matter of syntax to anyone who has grasped the nature of deductive arguments. A matter of fact which is not contained in the premises must require for its assertion a proper name which does not occur in the premises. But there is only one way in which a new proper name can occur in a deductive argument, and that is when we proceed from the general to the particular, as in "All men are mortal, therefore Socrates is mortal." Now, no collection of assertions of matters of fact is logically equivalent to a general assertion, so that, if our premises concern only matters of fact, this way of introducing a new proper name is not open to us. Hence the thesis follows.

If we are not to deduce Hume's skepticism from the above two premises, there seems to be only one possible way of escape, and that is to maintain that among the premises of our knowledge, there are some general propositions, or there is at least one general proposition, which is not analytically necessary, i.e., the hypothesis of its falsehood is not self-contradictory. A principle justifying the scientific use of induction would have this character. What is needed is some way of giving probability (not certainty) to the inferences from known matters of fact to occurrences which have not yet been, and perhaps never will be, part of the experience of the person making the inference. If an individual is to know anything beyond his own experiences up to the present moment, his stock of uninferred knowledge must consist not only of matters of fact but also of general laws, or at least a law, allowing him to make inferences from matters of fact; and such law or laws must, unlike the principles of deductive logic, be synthetic, i.e., not proved true by their falsehood being self-contradictory. The only alternative to this hypothesis is complete skepticism as to all the inferences of science and common sense, including those which I have called animal inferences.

SOLIPSISM

The doctrine called "solipsism" is usually defined as the belief that I alone exist. It is not one doctrine unless it is true. If it is true, it is the assertion that I, Bertrand Russell, alone exist. But if it is false, and I have readers, then for you who are reading this chapter it is the assertion that you alone exist. This is a view suggested by the conclusions reached in the preceding chapter, to the effect that all my data, in so far as they are matters of fact, are private to me, and that inferences from one or more matters of fact to other matters of fact are never logically demonstrative. These conclusions suggest that it would be rational to doubt everything outside my own experience, such as the thoughts of other people and the existence of material objects when I am not seeing them. It is this view that we are now to examine.

We must begin by giving more precision to the doctrine, and by distinguishing various forms that it may take. We must not state it in the words "I alone exist," for these words have no clear meaning unless the doctrine is false. If the world is really the common-sense world of people and things, we can pick out one person and suppose him to think that he is the whole universe. This is analogous to the people before Columbus, who believed the Old World to be the total of land on this planet. But if other people and things do not exist, the word "myself" loses its meaning, for this is an exclusive and delimiting word. Instead of saying, "Myself is the whole universe," we must say, "Data are the whole universe." Here "data" may be defined by enumeration. We can then say, "This list is complete; there is nothing more." Or we can say, "There is not known to be anything more." In this form, the doctrine does not require a prior definition of the Self, and what it asserts is sufficiently definite to be discussed.

We may distinguish two kinds of solipsism, which I shall call "dogmatic" and "skeptical" respectively. The dogmatic kind, in the above statement, says "There is nothing beyond data," while the skeptical kind says "There is not known to be anything beyond data." No grounds exist in favor of the dogmatic form, since it is just as difficult to disprove existence as to prove it, when what is concerned is something which is not a datum. I shall therefore say no more about dogmatic solipsism, and shall concentrate on the skeptical form.

The skeptical form of the doctrine is difficult to state precisely. It is not right to say, as we did just now, "Nothing is known except data," since someone else might know more; there is the same objection as there is to dogmatic solipsism. If we emend our statement by saying "Nothing is known *to me* except the following (giving a list of data)," we have again introduced the Self, which, as we saw, we must not do in defining our doctrine. It is not altogether easy to evade this objection.

I think we can state the problem with which solipsism is concerned as follows: "The propositions p_1, p_2, . . . p_n are known otherwise than by inference. Can this list be made such that from it other propositions, asserting matters of fact, can be inferred?" In this form we do not have to state that our list is complete, or that it embraces all that some one person knows.

It is obvious that if our list consists entirely of propositions asserting matters of fact, then the answer to our question is in the negative and skeptical solipsism is true. But if our list contains anything in the nature of laws the answer may be different. These laws, however, will have to be synthetic. Any collection of matters of fact is logically capable of being the whole; in pure logic, any two events are compossible, and no collection of events implies the existence of other events.

But before pursuing this line of thought let us consider different forms of solipsism.

Solipsism may be more drastic or less drastic; as it becomes more drastic it becomes more logical and at the same time more unplausible. In its least drastic form, it accepts all my mental states that are accepted by common sense or by orthodox psychology; i.e., not only those of which I am directly aware, but also those that are inferred on purely psychological grounds. It is generally held that at all times I have many faint sensations that I do not notice. If there is a ticking clock in the room, I may notice it and be annoyed by it, but as a rule I am quite unaware of it, even if it [is] easily audible whenever I choose to listen to it. In such a case one would naturally say that I am having auditory sensations of which I am not conscious. The same may be said, at most times, of objects in the periphery of my field of vision. If they are important objects, such as an enemy with a loaded revolver, I shall quickly become aware of them and bring them into the center of my visual field; but if they are uninteresting and motionless I shall remain unaware of them. Nevertheless it seems natural to suppose that I am in some sense seeing them.

The same sort of considerations apply to lapses of memory. If I look at an old diary, I find dinner engagements noted that I have completely forgotten, but I find it hard to doubt that I had the experience which common sense would describe as going to a dinner party. I believe that I was once an infant, although no trace of that period survives in my explicit memory.

Such inferred mental states are allowed by the least drastic form of solipsism. It merely refuses to allow inferences to anything other than myself and my mental states.

This, however, is illogical. The principles required to justify inferences from mental states of which I am aware to others of which I am not aware are exactly the same as those required for inferences to physical objects and to other minds. If, therefore, we are to secure the logical safety of which solipsism is in search, we must confine ourselves to mental states of which we are now aware. Buddha was admired because he could meditate while tigers roared around him; but if he had been a consistent solipsist he would have held that the noise of roaring ceased as soon as he ceased to notice it.

We thus arrive at a second form of solipsism, which says that the universe consists, or perhaps consists, of only the following items; and then we enumerate whatever, at the moment of speaking, we perceive or remember. And this will have to be confined to what I actually notice, for what I *could* notice is inferred. At the moment, I notice my dog asleep, and as a plain man I am convinced that I could have noticed him any time this last hour, since he has been consistently (so I believe) in my field of vision, but I have in fact been quite unaware of him. The thoroughgoing solipsist will have to say that when, during the last hour, my eye absent-mindedly rested on the dog, nothing whatever occurred in me in consequence; for to argue that I had a sensation which I did not notice is to allow an inference of the forbidden kind.

In regard to memory, the results of this theory are extremely odd. The things that I am recollecting at one moment are quite different from those that I am recollecting at another, but the thoroughgoing solipsist should only admit what I am remembering now. Thus his world will be one of disjointed fragments which change completely from moment to moment—change, I mean, not as to what exists now, but as to what did exist in the past.

But we have not done with the sacrifices which the solipsist must make to logic if he is to feel safe. It is quite clear that I can have a recollection without the thing remembered having happened; as a matter of logical possibility, I might have begun to exist five minutes ago, complete with all the memories that I then had. We ought therefore to cut out events remembered and confine the solipsist's universe to present percepts, including percepts of present states of mind which purport to be recollections. With regard to present percepts, this most rigorous type of solipsist (if he exists) accepts the premise of Descartes's *cogito,* with some interpretation. What he admits can only be correctly stated in the form: "A, B, C, . . . occur." To call A, B, C, . . . "thoughts" adds nothing except for those who reject solipsism. What distinguishes the consistent solipsist is the fact that the proposition "A occurs," if it comes in his list, is never inferred. He rejects as invalid all inferences from one or more propositions of the form "A occurs" to other propositions asserting the occurrence of something, whether named or described. The conclusions of such inferences, he maintains, may or may not happen to be true, but can never be known to be true.

Having now stated the solipsist position, we must inquire what can be said for and against it.

The argument for skeptical solipsism is as follows: From a group of propositions of the form "A occurs," it is impossible to infer by deductive logic any other proposition asserting the occurrence of something. If any such inference is to be valid, it must depend upon some non-deductive principle such as causality or induction. No such principle can be shown to be even probable by means of deductive arguments from a group of propositions of the form "A occurs." (I shall be concerned in a later chapter with the proof of this assertion.) For example, the validity of induction cannot be inferred from the course of events except by assuming induction or some equally questionable postulate. Therefore if, as empiricists maintain, all our knowledge is based on experience, it must be not only based on experience but confined to experience; for it is only by assuming some principle or principles which experience cannot render even probable that anything whatever can be proved by experience except the experience itself.

I think this argument proves that we have to choose between two alternatives. Either we must accept skeptical solipsism in its most rigorous form, or we must admit that we know, independently of experience, some principle or principles by means of which it is possible to infer events from other events, at least with probability. If we adopt the first alternative, we must reject far more than solipsism is ordinarily thought to reject; we cannot know of the existence of our own past or future, or have any ground for expectations as to our own future, if it occurs. If we adopt the second alternative, we must partially reject empiricism; we must admit that we have knowledge as to certain general features of the course of nature, and that this knowledge, though it may be caused by experience, cannot be logically inferred from experience. We must admit also that, if we have such knowledge, it is not yet explicit; causality and induction, in their traditional forms, cannot be quite true, and it is by no means clear what should be substituted for them. It thus appears that there are great difficulties in the way of accepting either alternative.

For my part, I reject the solipsist alternative and adopt the other. I admit, what is of the essence of the matter, that the solipsist alternative cannot be disproved by means of deductive arguments, provided we grant what I shall call "the empiricist hypothesis," namely, that what we know without inference consists solely of what we have experienced (or, more strictly, what we are experiencing) together with the principles of deductive logic. But we cannot know the empiricist hypothesis to be true, since that would be knowledge of a sort that the hypothesis itself condemns. This does not prove the hypothesis to be false, but it does prove that we have no right to assert it. Empiricism may be a true philosophy, but if it is it cannot be known to be true; those who assert that they know it to be true contradict themselves. There is therefore no obstacle *ab initio* to our rejecting the empiricist hypothesis.

As against solipsism it is to be said, in the first place, that it is psychologically impossible to believe, and is rejected in fact even by those who mean to accept it. I once received a letter from an eminent logician, Mrs. Christine Ladd Franklin, saying that she was a solipsist, and was surprised that there were no others. Coming from a logician, this surprise surprised me. The fact that I cannot believe something does not prove that it is false, but it does prove that I am insincere and frivolous if I pretend to believe it. Cartesian doubt has value as a means of articulating our knowledge and showing what depends on what, but if carried too far it becomes a mere technical game in which philosophy loses seriousness. Whatever anybody, even I myself, may argue to the contrary, I shall continue to believe that I am not the whole universe, and in this everyone will in fact agree with me, if I am right in my conviction that other people exist.

The most important part of the argument as to solipsism is the proof that it is only tenable in its most drastic form. There are various halfway positions which are not altogether unplausible, and have in fact been accepted by many philosophers. Of these the least drastic is the view that there can never be good grounds for asserting the existence of something which no one experiences; from this we may, with Berkeley, infer the unreality of matter while retaining the reality of mind. But this view, since it admits the experiences of others than myself, and since these experiences are only known to me by inference, considers that it is possible to argue validly from the existence of certain occurrences to the existence of others; and if this is admitted, it will be found that there is no reason why the inferred events should be experienced. Exactly similar considerations apply to the form of solipsism which believes that oneself has a past and a probable future; this belief can only be justified by admitting principles of inference which lead to the rejection of every form of solipsism.

We are thus reduced to the two extreme hypotheses as alone logically defensible. Either, on the one hand, we know principles of nondeductive inference which justify our belief, not only in other people, but in the whole physical world, including the parts which are never perceived but only inferred from their effects; or, on the other hand, we are confined to what may be called "solipsism of the moment," in which the whole of my knowledge is limited to what I am now noticing, to the exclusion of my past and probable future, and also of all those sensations to which, at this instant, I am not paying attention. When this alternative is clearly realized, I do not think that anybody would honestly and sincerely choose the second hypothesis.

If solipsism of the moment is rejected, we must seek to discover what are the synthetic principles of inference by the knowledge of which our scientific and common-sense beliefs are to be justified in their broad outlines. To this task we shall [later] address ourselves. . . . But it will be well first to make a survey, on the one hand of data, and on the other hand of scientific beliefs interpreted in their least questionable form. By analyzing the results of this survey we may hope to discover the premises which, consciously or unconsciously, are assumed in the reasonings of science.

Henry Habberley Price

The Concept of Sense-Data

THE GIVEN

Every man entertains a great number of beliefs concerning material things, e.g. that there is a square-topped table in this room, that the earth is a spheroid, that water is composed of hydrogen and oxygen. It is plain that all these beliefs are based on sight and on touch (from which organic sensation cannot be separated): based upon them in the sense that if we had not had certain

---

From H. H. Price, *Perception,* Robert M. McBride & Company, New York, 1933. Reprinted by permission of the author.

H. H. Price (1899–), now retired, has most recently been Wykeham Professor of Logic at Oxford University. Before that he was Fellow of Magdalen College, Oxford; Lecturer at the University of Liverpool, and Fellow of Trinity College, Oxford.

particular experiences of seeing and touching, it would be neither *possible* nor *reasonable* to entertain these beliefs. Beliefs about imperceptibles such as molecules or electrons or X-rays are no exception to this. Only they are based not directly on sight and touch, but indirectly. Their direct basis consists of certain other beliefs concerning scientific instruments, photographic plates, and the like. Thus over and above any intrinsic uncertainty that they themselves may have, whatever uncertainty attaches to these more basic beliefs is communicated to them. It follows that in any attempt either to analyse or to justify our beliefs concerning material things, the primary task is to consider beliefs concerning perceptible or 'macroscopic' objects such as chairs and tables, cats and rocks. It follows, too, that no theory concerning 'microscopic' objects can possibly be used to throw doubt upon our beliefs concerning chairs or cats or rocks, so long as these are based directly on sight and touch. Empirical Science can never be more trustworthy than perception, upon which it is based; and it can hardly fail to be *less* so, since among its non-perceptual premises there can hardly fail to be some which are neither self-evident nor demonstrable. Thus the not uncommon view that the world which we perceive is an illusion and only the 'scientific' world of protons and electrons is real, is based upon a gross fallacy, and would destroy the very premises upon which Science itself depends.

My aim in this book is to examine those experiences in the way of seeing and touching upon which our beliefs concerning material things are based, and to inquire in what way and to what extent they justify these beliefs. Other modes of sense-experience, e.g. hearing and smelling, will be dealt with only incidentally. For it is plain that they are only auxiliary. If we possessed them, but did not possess either sight or touch, we should have no beliefs about the material world at all, and should lack even the very conception of it. Possessing sight or touch or both, we can use experiences of these other senses as signs of obtainable but not at the moment actual experiences of seeing or touching, and thereby gain indirectly information which these inferior senses in themselves provide no hint of.

It may appear to some people that Science, particularly Physiology, can answer these questions for us. But it should already be clear that this is a mistake. Thus if it be said that when a man sees something, e.g. a tomato, light rays emanating from the object impinge upon his retina and this stimulates the optic nerve, which in turn causes a change in the optic centres in his brain, which causes a change in his mind: there are two comments to be made. 1. No doubt this is in fact a perfectly true account, but what are our *grounds* for believing it? Obviously they are derived from observation, and mainly if not entirely from visual observation. Thus the Physiologist has not explained in the least how visual observation justifies a man in holding a certain belief about a tomato, e.g. that it is spherical. All he has done is to put forward certain *other* beliefs concerning a retina and a brain. Those other beliefs have themselves to be justified in exactly the same way as the first belief, and we are as far as ever from knowing what way that is. Instead of answering our question, we have found another instance of it. Nor is this result surprising. Since the premises of Physiology are among the propositions into whose validity we are inquiring, it is hardly likely that its conclusions will assist us. 2. In any case, Science only professes to tell us what are the *causes* of seeing and touching. But we want to know what seeing and touching themselves *are.* This question lies outside the sphere of Science altogether.

Thus there is no short cut to our goal. We must simply examine seeing and touching for ourselves and do the best we can. What, then, is it to see or to touch something? Let us confine ourselves to sight for the moment and return to the instance of the tomato.

When I see a tomato there is much that I can doubt. I can doubt whether it is a tomato that I am seeing, and not a cleverly painted piece of wax. I can doubt whether there is any material thing there at all. Perhaps what I took for a tomato was really a reflection; perhaps I am even the victim of some hallucination. One thing however I cannot doubt: that there exists a red patch of a round and somewhat bulgy shape, standing out from a background of other colour-patches, and having a certain visual depth, and that this whole field of colour is directly present to my consciousness. What the red patch is, whether a substance, or a state of a substance, or an event, whether it is physical or psychical or neither, are questions that we may doubt about. But that something is red and round then and there[1] I cannot doubt. Whether the something persists even for a moment before and after it is present to my consciousness, whether other minds can be conscious of it as well as I, may be doubted. But that it now *exists,* and that *I* am conscious of it—by me at least who am conscious of it this cannot possibly be doubted. And when I say that it is 'directly' present to my consciousness, I mean that my consciousness of it is not reached by inference, nor by any other intellectual process (such as abstraction or intuitive induction), nor by any passage from sign to significate. There obviously must be some sort or sorts of presence to consciousness which can be called 'direct' in this sense, else we should have an infinite regress. Analogously, when I am in the situations called 'touching something', 'hearing it', 'smelling it', etc., in each case there is something which at that moment indubitably exists—a pressure (or prement patch), a noise, a smell; and that something is directly present to my consciousness.

This peculiar and ultimate manner of being present to consciousness is called *being given,* and that which is thus present is called a *datum.* The corresponding mental attitude is called *acquaintance, intuitive apprehension,* or sometimes *having.* Data of this special sort are called *sense-data.* And the acquaintance with them is conveniently called *sensing;* though sometimes, I think, this word is used in another sense. It is supposed by some writers that sense-data are mental events, and these writers appear to think that the word 'sensing', if used at all, ought to mean the coming-into-being of sense-data, not the intuitive apprehension of them. (For their coming-into-being will then be a mental process.) This seems to be a very inconvenient usage. We need some word for the intuitive apprehension of sense-data. We cannot say 'perceiving' (for that, as we shall see, has at least two other meanings already). And 'sensing' is the obvious word to use. At any rate in this book we shall always use it in this sense. When we have occasion to speak of the process which is the coming-into-being of a sense-datum we shall call it *sense-datum-genesis.*

It is true that the term 'given' or 'datum' is sometimes used in a wider and looser sense to mean 'that, the inspection of which provides a premise for in-

[1] 'There' means 'In spatial relations to other colour-patches present to my consciousness at the same time'.

ference'. Thus the data of the historian are the statements which he finds in documents and inscriptions: the data of the general are the facts reported by his aircraft and his intelligence service: the data of the detective are the known circumstances and known results of the crime; and so on. But it is obvious that these are only data relatively and for the purpose of answering a certain question. They are really themselves the results of inference, often of a very complicated kind. We may call them data *secundum quid*. But eventually we must get back to something which is a datum *simpliciter,* which is not the result of any previous intellectual process. It is with data *simpliciter,* or rather with one species of them, that we are concerned.

How do sense-data differ from other data, e.g. from those of memory or introspection? We might be tempted to say, in the manner in which they come to be given, viz. as a result of the stimulation of a sense-organ. This will not do. For first, the sense-organs are themselves material things, and it seems quite likely that the term 'material thing' cannot be defined except by reference to sense-data; and if so we should have a vicious circle. And secondly, even though we doubted the existence of all material things, including our own body and its organs, it would still be perfectly obvious that sense-data differ from other sorts of data. The only describable differentia that they seem to have is this, that they lead us to conceive of and believe in the existence of certain material things, whether they are in fact any such things or not. (Visual and tactual sense-data do this directly, the others indirectly, as explained above.) But it seems plain that there is also another characteristic common and peculiar to them, which may be called 'sensuousness'. This is obvious on inspection, but it cannot be described.

Does sensing differ from other forms of intuitive apprehension? Or is there only one sort of intuitive apprehension, and does the difference between (say) sensing, remembering and the contemplation of mental images lie only in the nature of the apprehensa? The question is difficult, nor does it seem very important. Perhaps we may say that there are two sorts of intuitive apprehension, one directed upon *facts,* e.g. the fact that I am puzzled or was puzzled, or again the fact that $2 + 2 = 4$, or that courage is good: another directed upon *particular existents,* e.g. this colour patch or this noise or that visual image, or again upon this feeling of disgust and that act of wondering. The first is apprehension *that,* the second is apprehension *of*. The term *acquaintance* is properly reserved for the second, and we shall so use it in future.

Are there several different sorts of acquaintance, e.g. sensing, self-consciousness, and contemplation of mental images? I cannot see that there are. The difference seems to be wholly on the side of the data. If so, *a fortiori* there are not different kinds of sensing. Visual sensing will simply be the acquaintance with colour-patches, auditory sensing the acquaintance with sounds, and so on; the acquaintance being the same in each case. No doubt there will be different kinds of *sense-datum-genesis,* just as there are different kinds of sense-data. And if any one likes to use the term 'visual sensing',[2] to mean the genesis of colour-patches and 'auditory sensing' to mean the genesis of noises, he may;

[2] The substitution of 'seeing' for visual sensing, 'hearing' for auditory sensing, etc., would make confusion even worse confounded. For in the ordinary sense of the word *see,* what I see is not a colour-patch, but a material thing, e.g. a table or a tomato. Likewise *hear, smell,* etc., are in ordinary usage ambiguous. I hear the train, or I hear a noise. I smell the rose, or I smell a smell.

and of course he is then entitled to say that there *are* different kinds of sensing. But this has not the slightest tendency to show that there are different kinds of sensing in *our* sense of the word (which is also the usual one).

If the term sense-datum is taken in the strictly limited meaning that we have given it, I do not see how any one can doubt that there are sense-data. Yet it is certain that many philosophers do profess to doubt this and even to deny it. Indeed the sense-datum has come in for a good many hard words. It has been compared to the Wild Goose which we vainly chase: or again it is the Will o' the Wisp which lures the Realist further and further from Reality. According to an eminent Idealist philosopher,[3] our modern interest in the sense-datum is just one more manifestation (among so many others) of the degeneracy of an age which prefers the childish, the easy, and the barbarous to the laborious achievement of Intelligence and Civilization. Or again—a charge hardly compatible with this—it is derided as the invention of sophisticated philosophers, as no datum at all. Nor are our opponents content with brilliant metaphors. They have plausible arguments to put forward, and these we must try to answer. It is obvious that we cannot do more than this. It is impossible from the nature of the case to *prove* that there are sense-data or data of any other sort. The utmost we can do is to remove misunderstandings which prevent people from searching for them and from acknowledging them when found. After that, we can only appeal to every man's own consciousness.

The doctrine that there are no sense-data may take two forms, a wider and a narrower, which are not always clearly separated.

1. It is said that the very notion of givenness is an absurd and self-contradictory notion, that from the nature of the case nothing can ever be given at all. This is the most radical criticism that we have to meet. It may be called the *A priori* Thesis.

2. There is also what may be called the Empirical Thesis. This does not say that there is an absurdity in the very notion of givenness. It only says that we can never in fact find anything which is given. And it concludes that either there is no Given at all, or if there is any, it is found only in the experience of new-born children, idiots, and people falling into or just coming out of fainting fits: in which case (it is urged) the Given is clearly of no importance to the philosopher, for it is quite beyond the reach of investigation, and therefore cannot be appealed to as evidence for anything.

Either of these theses if established would be very damaging. The *A priori* Thesis is the most radical, but also the easier to answer. The Empirical Thesis is the really difficult one to meet, and we shall have to make some concessions to it. Nevertheless, the arguments by which it is ordinarily supported are open to very grave objections.

The 'A priori' Thesis. The main argument in favour of this may be summed up as follows:

It is impossible to apprehend something without apprehending some at least of its qualities and relations. In the language of Cambridge logicians, what we apprehend is always a *fact*—something of the form 'that A is B' or 'the B-ness of A'. You cannot apprehend just A. For instance, you cannot apprehend a

[3] Professor H. J. Paton, *The Idea of the Self*. University of California Publications in Philosophy, vol. 8, pp. 76–7.

round red patch without apprehending that it is red and round and has certain spatial relations. But if we apprehend that it has these qualities and relations, we are not passively 'receiving' or (as it were) swallowing; we are actively thinking—judging or classifying—and it is impossible to do less than this.

To this I answer, it is very likely true, but it is irrelevant. The argument only proves that nothing stands *merely* in the relation of givenness to the mind, without also standing in other relations: i.e. that what is given is always also 'thought about' in some sense or other of that ambiguous phrase. But this does not have the slightest tendency to prove that *nothing is given at all.* The fact that A and B are constantly conjoined, or even necessarily connected, does not have the slightest tendency to prove that A does not exist.[4] How could it, since it itself presupposes the existence of A? That arguments of this sort should be so frequently used, and should be thought so conclusive, is one of the curiosities of philosophical controversy.

Secondly, we may attack the enemy on his own ground and ask him how we can think without having something to think about. This *subject* or *subject-matter* about which we think must be somehow brought before the mind, if we are to think about it, and it cannot always be brought there by previous thinking, or we should have an infinite regress. This means that something must be *given.* And sensing is one of the ways (I do not say the only one) in which subject-matters for thought are given to us. No doubt it is important to insist that this intuitive 'receiving' of a datum is never more than an element in our total state of mind. But still it *is* an element, and an essential one.

The Empirical Thesis. This maintains that it is in fact impossible to discover any data. For if we try to point to an instance, it is said, we shall have to confess that the so-called datum is not really given at all, but is the product of interpretation.

This doctrine is put forward both in the interests of Subjective Idealism, which holds that each mind lives in a private world of its own, and in the interests of that Objective or Rationalistic Idealism which holds that the world is entirely constructed by 'Thought', or by 'Mind' with a capital M. But it may be suspected that sometimes the one party uses arguments which are only appropriate to the other.

We must begin by protesting with Professor G. E. Moore against the word 'interpretation', which is used to cover several quite different processes and is at best only a metaphor. For instance, it may mean either *association of ideas,* or some form of *thinking.* We shall begin with the first.

Effects of Association. We can easily find cases where the Given seems to have been contaminated, as it were, by the effects of association. Thus it would be said that Visual Depth beyond a pretty short range is plainly not given, but is due to the revival, by association, of the traces of past kinaesthetic and tactual experience. Or again a distant snowy peak looks cold, but is it not obvious that its coldness cannot be given? The sounds of a foreign language, say Italian, sound quite different when I have learned to speak the language myself. They then fall apart, as it were, into words and word-groups, which

[4] A stands here for 'Givenness' and B for 'thought-of-ness'. The argument is the one commonly used against what is called *vicious abstraction.* Sometimes the conclusion is not that A does not exist but that A is identical with B: but here again it is presupposed in the premises that they are different—else how could they be necessarily connected?

they never did before. (At first I heard just one continuous sound.) This is due to the traces of the kinaesthetic experiences experienced in speaking the language oneself, and further to one's newly-acquired knowledge of what the words mean—for this knowledge too has left its 'traces'. But neither the kinaestheta nor the meanings can be *heard*. Both are 'read into' what we hear. Proof-reading and Psychic Blindness also provide instances. But here the effect of the traces is negative instead of positive. Instead of seeing what is not there, we fail to see what is there.

Objections to the Argument. Let us first take the argument on its own ground, without criticizing its premises. We must then answer that no doubt the facts are as stated, but they do not prove what is wanted. Indeed, if anything, they prove the very opposite, viz. that there *are* data and that we know what they are.

1. If nothing whatever is given to me when I look at the mountain or hear the sounds, the phrase 'due to association' loses all sense. Association is a relation, and if we speak of it, we imply that there are at least two terms to be associated: what is associated must be associated *with something*. When the mountain looks cold to me, the presence of the coldness to my mind is due to association. But with what is the coldness associated? Obviously with the colour and shape. These then *are* given: *their* presence cannot be explained by association, for they are what the associated qualities join on to. And if, preferring another metaphor, you say that what I see is 'contaminated by' the traces of past experiences, or 'overlaid with' them: I answer, that where there is contamination there must be something which is contaminated, and where there is overlaying there must be something which is overlaid.

2. Is it not dangerous to specify *what* characteristics are due to association? We are told 'What you see looks cold, distant and solid; and obviously coldness, distance and solidity cannot be given to sight'. But how does the critic know that they are not given to sight? The only answer must be: 'Because colour and two-dimensional shape are the only qualities that *are* given to sight'. But in that case there is after all a datum of sight, and the critic knows what it is.

3. Is it not dangerous to give a name to the associations, to speak of them, for instance, as *tactual* associations, *kinaesthetic* associations and the like? For this presupposes that the associated characteristics, though not given now, have been given in the past. For instance, if you say that the apparent coldness and solidity of the seen mountain-peak are due to tactual associations, and therefore are not given to sight at this moment, you admit that they have been given to touch in the past. Otherwise what is the sense of using the word 'tactual'? And even if, more wary, you merely say that the presence of these qualities is due just to the traces of past experience, we must press you to specify what kind of past experience. And you will be obliged to say, past *sense*-experience, and so you will have admitted that these qualities have been given in the past. Thus in order to prove that A *is* not given, one has to assume that B *has been* given.

So far we have been attacking the critics of the Given upon their own ground. And that ground is this. They begin by assuming that there is a distinction between 'the real given' or the given-as-it-is-in-itself on the one hand, and 'what the given seems to be' on the other. And they then argue that we cannot know what this given-as-it-is-in-itself is. That the argument when we pursue it into detail is incoherent, and proves the very opposite of what it is supposed to prove, we have seen. We must now attack the initial assumption and point out:

4. That the distinction between the Given as it really is and what the Given seems to be [5] is altogether untenable. I scarcely know how to prove this. Is it not just obvious that if something seems to be given, it is given? For in the sphere of the given (as in that of pleasure and pain) what seems, is. Indeed we might go farther. We might say that the notion of seeming has no *application* to the given: and that, by the very definitions of 'seeming' and of 'given'. When A seems to be B, this really means that some mind unreflectively believes A to be B, or as we say 'takes' it to be B. Now if so, there must be some *evidence* upon which this taking is (however hastily and unreflectively) based. Thus if it seems to me to be raining, the evidence is that I hear a pitter-patter sound. This does not *seem* to be a pitter-patter sound; it *is* one. And only because there *is* this sound can it seem to have a certain cause, viz. rain falling on the roof. And though the rain which there seems to be may not after all exist (for it may have been a shower of gravel or peas) the sound none the less exists, and does have a pitter-patter character. In short, the Given is by definition that which by being itself actual and intuitively apprehended, makes it possible for something else to seem to exist or to have a certain quality. Of course certain characteristics may be given which some philosopher thinks *ought not* to be given, e.g. solidity. So much the worse for him, that is all. He must have held a false theory of what is 'giveable'. If something is given, it is given, and we must just make the best of it. In a matter of this kind we cannot and will not accept the dictation of theorists.

To clinch my point, I will try to show how these errors may have arisen. They arise, I think, from a confusion between two standpoints or modes of investigation, (*a*) the physiological and (*b*) the immanent or phenomenological. The physiologist finds that many of the characteristics of the visual field are not due to the electromagnetic stimulus which affects the retina; or even that none of its characteristics are entirely due to this. He therefore concludes that those characteristics are not given. But we must point out that he is using the term 'given' in an utterly different sense from ours, a *causal* sense: he is using it to mean 'due to a physical stimulus external to the organism'—or he may even be meaning that this stimulus *is* what is given.

But our standpoint is quite a different one. We are asking what is *given to consciousness,* or presented to the mind. We are not inquiring into the causes which may have led to its being given. Further (as has been shown already), our standpoint is the more fundamental one. For the physiologist's only evidence for believing that there is an organism, and physical stimuli affecting it, is derived from observation: that is, from the presentation to him—to him, not to his organism—of data in *our* sense of the word.

To sum up this rather intricate discussion:

1. It is true that what is given now to a certain mind depends to a surprisingly large extent upon what has been given to that mind in the past. But this, so far from disproving the existence either of present or of past data, asserts the existence of both, and enables us to describe their nature in a way we could not do before.

[5] In his *Philosophical Studies,* pp. 243–7, Professor G. E. Moore has suggested that sense-data may seem to be what they are not. But he admits that this suggestion may be 'sheer nonsense'.

2. It is true that the facts concerning association adduced by our critics do make the causal explanation of the datum more complicated than one might expect. But to say that they prove that there are no data is to deny the very fact of association itself, which presupposes the existence of past data. And to say that the causal explanation of something is complicated is to assert, not to deny, the existence of the something to be explained.

3. The facts adduced do not hinder but help the Realist, that is, the man who wishes to use his data to gain knowledge or true belief about a Real which exists whether known and believed about or not. For the datum, it turns out, gives information not only about the present or the immediate past, but also—*via* earlier data—about the remote past. And the past is as much a part of the real world as the present, and quite as interesting. Moreover, the datum, we have found, gives information not merely about the non-mental, but also about the mind to which it is presented (e.g. a psycho-analyst can argue from the peculiarities of a man's data, say the hallucinations from which he suffers, to the existence of such and such a suppressed complex in the man's mind). Why should it be supposed that this would upset the Realist? The mind is just as much a part of the Real, and just as fit an object for inquiry, as any mountain-top or teacup. And if we can collect information about it from the given, so much the better for us. We ought to be glad that the given is so full of a number of things, and accept the gift in the spirit in which it is offered.

So much for the first sense of the word 'interpretation'. There are however two others which we must consider. And first, interpretation may mean *thinking* of some kind or other. To interpret something may mean to apprehend (immediately or inferentially), or again to believe or opine or conjecture, that it has a certain characteristic. Thus if on hearing a certain noise we infer that it is the signal for dinner, we should be said to be interpreting what we hear. And even if one merely judges that it is a loud shrill sound, even this would be called interpretation by the philosophers with whom we are now concerned.

I do not wish to maintain that the line between this intellectual sense of the word 'interpretation', and the associative sense of it which we discussed first, is altogether easy to draw. For it seems likely that association is on the one side more intellectual, on the other more plastic, and so to say less 'wooden' and external, than the traditional account of it would suggest. But that is a matter which we are not obliged for our present purposes to discuss. It is sufficient to point out that by interpretation people sometimes mean an 'unconscious' process, whose existence and nature can only be inferred from its results, and this is what we have already discussed under the name of association; whereas sometimes they mean an actually experienced activity, whose existence does not need to be inferred, because we are immediately aware of it in self-consciousness. It is this latter process which I have called the intellectual or 'thinking' sort of interpretation; and this is what we must now discuss.

The argument which we have to meet is as follows: Even if there be something which is given it is quite impossible for us to know it.[6] For if we attempt to describe any so-called datum, e.g. this view which I now see, the very act of describing alters it. What we have at the end of the process is not the

[6] On this view the distinction between knowledge by acquaintance and knowledge about does not arise. Indeed the whole contention is that there *is* no acquaintance.

datum but a set of propositions, and the only relic of the datum is the term 'this' which stands as their subject. Thus every attempt to describe the given is bound to fail. But if we cannot describe it, i.e. say what characters it has, we obviously do not know it. It is just the hypothetical and inaccessible somewhat which was present before the process of describing began. And this applies even to the very simplest and naïvest act of describing e.g. this is red, this is hard.

This argument, especially when adorned with a multitude of learned illustrations and expounded at many pages' length, is apt to seem very formidable. But we must point out that it rests on the assumption that *if I know or believe that something has a certain nature, it follows that it cannot possibly have the nature that I know or believe it to have*: i.e. that from the fact that I know or believe that A is B, it follows that A cannot really be B. This assumption when openly and unmetaphorically stated is so extraordinary that it is difficult at first sight to understand how any one can accept it. But I think that on further reflection we can find certain facts, and certain confused conceptions of these facts, which do tend to make it plausible.

1. In the first place, the describing of something is an *active* process, something that we *do*. It is no wonder that Idealist philosophers speak in this connexion of 'the work' of thought, for in any cases but the simplest, the describing of what we see or hear is exceedingly difficult. An indefinitely large amount of extraneous knowledge may be involved in it. The greatest concentration of attention, the most happy and illuminating facility in recalling appropriate parallels, may well be necessary. Any one can, indeed, grasp that this is a black cross on a white ground; but it needs a Conrad to describe the data presented to the voyager in the China seas, and all the labours of all the great painters scarcely suffice to enable us to comprehend the pattern of the prospect which we can see from our own front doors.

In face of such efforts as these, it may be asked, what becomes of our Given? Can it really be the same at the end of this work as it was at the beginning? To say that it is completely unaffected is surely to say that the *work* has had no result. Nor can we draw a line anywhere between the simple statement 'This is a black cross on a white ground' and the elaborate, subtle, tortuous passage (perhaps pages long) of the novelist or the traveller. If the second transforms the datum into something which is not a datum at all, so must the first. The datum-as-it-is-in-itself will be the unknowable limit of the series, which we approach more closely as our description becomes simpler and simpler, but never actually reach. Or will it even be that? For at which end of the series do we come nearest to the datum as it really is? Does a bovine *naïveté* really bring us nearer to it than subtilty and sophistication?—especially when we remember that *naïveté* itself is often a most laborious achievement, which only the most sophisticated can attain to. It seems impossible to say. In short, the pursuit of the datum in itself seems to be a perfect wild-goose chase. We do not even know where we are to look for it, or when in our blundering attempts we are beginning (as children say) to get 'warm'.

To all this kind of argumentation we must firmly answer, that it rests upon too narrow a notion of activity. Describing is a form of thinking, and thinking is an activity, often a very difficult one indeed. But it does not follow that it *alters* the thing about which we think. Practical activity does alter the thing upon which we act. For instance, the activity of walking alters the position and state of the walker's body: and the activity of beating some one alters the man who is beaten. But intellectual activity does not alter that upon which it is directed. If it alters anything, it alters only one's own mind, causing it to pass (say) from a state of uncertainty to a state of certainty, or from confusion to clarity.[7] Indeed that is the obvious difference between intellectual and practical activity. But though obvious, it is concealed from people for the following reasons. First, intellectual activity, though it does not itself alter the object, may lead to practical activity which does. If I had not understood that this was a wasp, I should not have hit it. Again, intellectual activity is, as it were, included in practical activity as an essential element. We 'control' our action by recognition of the circumstances, by the thought of a plan or principle which we are seeking to realize in or by the action, and by the apprehension of certain alternative ways of realizing it. There is no such thing as unintelligent action. *Das Thun ist auch Denken*. Further, even in the most purely theoretical activity we must attend, and attending seems to be a kind of willing. But these facts, though important, do not have the faintest tendency to show that intellectual activity and practical activity are identical, or even alike. As we have seen before, from the fact that A and B are connected, however intimately, we cannot infer that A is identical with B, still less that A does not exist.

So much for the first confusion which leads philosophers to think that if I know or believe that A is B, it follows that A cannot really be B.

. . .

3. The third confusion in the minds of those who hold that thought destroys or transforms the given which is thought about has to do with *attention*. Mr. Bradley somewhere asks 'Does attention change its object?' Like another famous doubter, he does not stay for an answer. But I think he means to suggest that attention does alter its object. And I think that many of the critics of the Given have tacitly adopted the suggestion, though without putting the issue in this plain way. It is thought that as we attend to something, this something becomes more and more 'clear', and at the same time more and more complex. It starts by being a mere 'something or other' and it ends by being (say) a Gothic pinnacle, or a group of oak-trees arranged in a quincunx.

This, I suppose, is the doctrine. Yet when plainly stated it is so extraordinary that it is hard to see how any one can have the audacity to hold it. To alter something is to cause a change in it. But the kind of change which is supposed to occur in the object of attention is altogether fantastic. In a genuine change the object passes from the possession of one determinate character to the possession of another at the same level of determinateness. Thus if it changes shape it may pass from circular to elliptical: if colour, from peacock green to turquoise blue. But the change which attention is supposed to cause is not of this sort at all. It is a passage *from the possession of a generic character to the possession of a specific one,* and from that to the possession of one still more specific: or again it is a passage from possession of an indeterminate character to the possession of more and more determinate ones. Thus in regard to shape,

[7] I understand that some of the schoolmen said that in the activity of thinking the intellect *perfects itself.*

the thing (as I attend to it) will first have just shape in general, then rectilinear shape in general, then it will become triangular, and lastly perhaps it will be an equilateral triangle. In regard to colour, it will first have colouredness in general, then it will be green, then bluish green, and finally peacock green.

Now is it not plain as day that this is not change at all? Change is the passage from one characteristic to another characteristic of *equal determinateness*. But this so-called change is in another dimension altogether: it is from the less determinate to the more determinate. Is it not obvious that the change—the growing determinateness—is simply in our mode of apprehension and not in the thing apprehended? It is we who apprehend more and more determinately the always fully determinate character which the thing all along possessed.

Further, the doctrine involves another absurdity: that of supposing that an entity can exist with only generic or indeterminate qualities, e.g. that a colour-patch can exist which is just coloured and is neither red nor green, blue nor yellow. Such would be the fate of all those unfortunate entities which do not happen to get attended to.

So much for the confusions which lead philosophers to think that the attempt to know anything about the Given must alter it, and to conclude that if anything is given at all, it is unknowable. We have tried to show that the intellectual activities of describing, comparing, etc., do not alter that which is 'analysed' or described, but merely reveal its nature and its relation to other things in the world.

. . .

We may sum up this discussion as follows. When I am in the situation which is described as seeing something, touching something, hearing something, etc., it is certain in each case that a colour-patch, or a pressure, or a noise exists at that moment and that I am acquainted with this colour-patch, pressure or noise. Such entities are called sense-data, and the acquaintance with them is conveniently called sensing; but it differs from other instances of acquaintance only in its object, not in its nature, and it has no species. The usual arguments against the reality and against the knowability of sense-data break down on examination. They only prove at most that there is no sense-datum which is not the object of other sorts of consciousness besides sensing, and that the causes of most sense-data are more complicated than might have been expected: and in these conclusions there is nothing to disturb us.

In conclusion we may point out that the admission that there are sense-data is not a very large one; it commits us to very little. It may be worth while to mention explicitly a number of things which we are *not* committed to.

1. We are not committed to the view that sense-data *persist*[8] through the intervals when they are not being sensed. We have only to admit that they *exist* at the times when they are being sensed.

2. We are not committed to the view that several minds can be acquainted with the *same* sense-datum. We have only to admit that every mind is acquainted with *some* sense-data from time to time.

[8] Or more strictly, that there are persistent *sensibilia* which become sense-data temporarily when they are sensed. Cf. Mr. Bertrand Russell's *Mysticism and Logic*, p. 148.

3. We are not committed to any view about what is called 'the status' of sense-data in the Universe, either as regards the *category* they fall under, or as regards their relations with other types of existent entities. They may be events, or substances, or states of substances. They may be physical; i.e. they may be parts of or events in material objects such as chairs and tables or (in another theory) brains. They may be mental, as Berkeley and many others have held. They may be neither mental nor physical.

4. We are not committed to any view about their *origin*. They may originate as a result of processes in material objects, or of mental processes, or of both. Or again, it may be that the boot is on the other leg: it may be that they are the ultimate constituents of the Universe, and material things (perhaps minds as well) may be just collections of them; in which case they 'just are', and have no origin and no explanation, since everything else is explained by reference to them.

Thus the term sense-datum is meant to be a *neutral* term. The use of it does not imply the acceptance of any particular theory. The term is meant to stand for something whose existence is indubitable (however fleeting), something from which all theories of perception ought to start, however much they may diverge later.

And I think that all past theories have in fact started with sense-data. The Ancients and the Schoolmen called them *sensible species*. Locke and Berkeley called them *ideas of sensation,* Hume *impressions,* Kant *Vorstellungen*. In the nineteenth century they were usually known as *sensations,* and people spoke of visual and auditory sensations when they meant colour-patches and noises; while many contemporary writers, following Dr. C. D. Broad, have preferred to call them *sensa*.

All these terms have the defect of begging questions. If we speak of *sensible species* we assume that sense-data are physical, a sort of effluences flying off the external objects into our sense-organs. If we use terms like *idea, impression,* and *sensation* we commit ourselves to the view that sense-data are mental events. *Sensum* is very much the best. But it is generally used to mean a 'third kind' of entity, neither mental nor physical. And although we are not at present in a position to assert that sense-data are physical or that they are mental, neither are we in a position to deny either of these alternatives. (Thus 'sense-data are sensa' is not a tautology, but a synthetic proposition.)

An incidental virtue of the term *sense-datum* is that it enables us to give a brief and intelligible account of the traditional theories concerning perception and the external world, and so to make use of the work of our predecessors without wasting time in tedious historico-lexicographical investigations.

THE NATURE OF SENSE-DATA

. . .

We can now turn to our main problem. And first, it is fairly clear that sense-data are not *substances*. A colour-expanse, for instance, or a smell is created *ex nihilo* when suitable bodily and mental states are present; and when the bodily and mental state comes to an end, the sense-data vanish again *in nihilum*. In this respect, sense-data are unlike any substances known to us. It is not as if they were put together out of pre-existing particulars, and resolved again into these: they come into being at a stroke, and go out of being at a stroke.

Moreover, even creation is too mild a word. For according to our ordinary notion of creation (whether there are any instances of this notion or not), the thing created, once it has come into existence, goes on existing of itself, and has, so to speak, an intrinsic being of its own. But with sense-data this does not happen. It is not enough that there should be the appropriate cerebral and mental state at the beginning; it is not as if the body and mind of the percipient, having started the sense-datum off on its career could then (so to speak) leave it to itself, as the God of Deism was supposed to have left His creatures. On the contrary, they must *continue* in that state if the sense-datum is to continue in existence: if I shut my eyes, or change my mental 'attitude', the sense-datum ceases to be. When I open them again, or return to my previous 'attitude', a new one comes into being, exactly like the old perhaps, but still numerically different from it.

It is true that a brief interruption of the *physical stimulus* is not by itself sufficient to annihilate the sense-datum. A blink for instance, or the momentary obscuration of the object by some other object which passes in front of it, as when a cat walks in front of the coal-scuttle or a bough waving in the wind momentarily gets in the way of the view, would not necessarily annihilate the sense-datum of the coal-scuttle or of the distant mountain. Indeed, a gap is in some cases even necessary. When we hear a short spoken sentence, what we hear is one auditory sense-datum, with a certain form or pattern. And the nature of the pattern requires that there should be brief intervals of silence between the words: otherwise, what we sense is not one sense-datum, but a jumbled series. (The same will apply to a bar of music and to such sounds as the 'tick-tock' of the clock.) The rule seems to be, that so long as the same act of perceptual consciousness remains, the same sense-datum remains; this is in all cases consistent with a short break in the physical stimulus and in the consequent cerebral state (it is impossible to say in general how long the break can be), and sometimes even demands it.

This consideration does seem to refute the view that sense-data are *momentary* existents. It might be argued that since the sense-datum ceases to exist as soon as the mental and physical states upon which it depends come to an end, therefore even when these states continue throughout a period (as when we watch something intently throughout a certain half-minute) there is not really a single continuing sense-datum, but only an uninterrupted series of sense-data exactly resembling each other. For, it may be said, at any moment during the period we *might* have stopped watching, or the stimulus might have ceased, and if either of these things had happened, the sense-datum *would* have been annihilated: and does not this show that the sense-datum existing at any moment was wholly dependent for its existence upon the cerebral and mental state of that moment, so that there was not one sense-datum persisting throughout the period, but a continuous process of annihilation and re-creation?

The conclusion, however, does not follow. The argument ignores the fact that the unity of a sense-datum—that which makes it *a* sense-datum—depends in part upon what is called its form-quality, and that this in turn depends upon the 'meaning' which the sense-datum has for us: i.e. upon the perceptual (or otherwise 'meaningful'[9]) disposition which the physical stimulus evokes in us. Certainly if the act of perceptual consciousness[10] is momentary, then the sense-datum is momentary too: but it is very doubtful whether any mental act can be literally momentary, and certain that most are not. Thus it is highly probable that every sense-datum has a finite duration, and certain that most have.

On the other hand, it is also clear that the duration is at the best very small, probably never more than a few seconds (it will depend upon our 'span of attention' which is notoriously never great); so that although the annihilation and re-creation of sense-data is not continuous, it certainly does happen and is indeed extremely frequent. Thus these considerations about form-quality do not materially weaken our argument that sense-data, being subject to creation and annihilation, cannot be substances.

Moreover, even if there is not continuous creation of sense-data, there is a process very much like it which may be called their *conservation*. A sense-datum does indeed persist and retain its numerical identity through a certain period, but, so to speak, this persistence is not *its* fault, being entirely dependent upon the persistence of the originating conditions cerebral and mental, and ceasing when these cease. Now it is true that in the case of an ordinary substance, e.g. an organism, certain states of other things are necessary conditions of its persistence, e.g. a certain kind of atmosphere and a certain temperature in surrounding objects. But these conditions, though necessary, are not sufficient: certain internal states of the organism itself are also necessary. With the sense-datum, on the other hand, the external conditions are not only necessary but sufficient to its preservation. It does not contribute to its own preservation in any way whatever: its persistence, like its origination, is wholly 'parasitic'. And in this it is wholly unlike anything ordinarily called a substance.

Further, though sense-data persist through time, it is very doubtful whether they can be said to *change*. Consider, for instance, the sound 'tick-tock'. We cannot say that this changes from 'tick' into 'tock'. For until the 'tock' has arrived, the sense-datum is not there at all. The transition from tick to tock is not a change *in* the sense-datum; it is the becoming *of* the sense-datum. Indeed, if we may parody the remark of Solon,[11] we may say that the sense-datum does not exist until it is dead. But now if sense-data cannot change, they obviously cannot be substances, and though they persist through time, they do not persist in the way that substances do.

On these grounds it seems clear that sense-data are not substances, but *events* or *occurrences*.[12] (Perhaps it would be more accurate to speak of

[9] As when a spoken word brings to mind a certain concept. Here, too, the noise gets its form-quality from its 'meaningfulness' (if we had not understood the language, it would not have stood out as one individual auditory datum, but would have been lost in the general clatter). In this case, however, the meaning is non-perceptual.

[10] Perhaps it may be well to remind the reader that I am drawing a sharp distinction between the act of *sensing* and the *perceptual* act.

[11] Herodotus, Book I.

[12] In Mr. W. E. Johnson's language, they are *events*, not *occurrents* (*Logic*, vol. ii, p. xxi). For an occurrent is characterized by only one quality throughout its extent, and a sense-datum always has several qualities. Indeed, a single sense-datum may even display two contrasted determinates of the same determinable in different parts of itself: for instance, it may be black and white. Thus when we look at a black and white cat, we sense one single sense-datum which is black in one part and white in another.

'colorations' or 'colour-geneses' rather than colour-expanses, and of 'sonifications' and 'odorifications' instead of sounds and smells. But as this usage is very clumsy, we shall not adopt it.) We may still call them particular existents, for happening or occurring is one way of existing: but they do not exist in the way in which tables or trees do.[13]

Now if sense-data are not substances but events, it is natural to ask what substance they are phases of. For it is commonly held that every event is a phase of some substance or, as Mr. Johnson says, 'inheres in' it.[14] To this question three answers have been offered:

1. That they are phases of the objects that we perceive by means of them (are 'physical').
2. That they are phases of the percipient's mind (are 'mental').
3. That they are phases of the percipient's brain (are 'cerebral').

PERCEPTUAL ACCEPTANCE

. . . Suppose . . . that I see a tree, in that sense of the word in which 'to see' stands for a specific form of consciousness, distinct from but accompanying sensing, and does not merely convey that the tree is present to my senses, i.e. that I am sensing a sense-datum which does in fact belong to the tree.

Now in the first place it is clear that this perceptual consciousness is not a form of *knowing*. It is neither 'knowledge by acquaintance' (as sensing is) nor is it 'knowledge of facts about'. For it may be mistaken. It may be that the thing is not a tree but something else. It may be not over there but somewhere else (I may have been deceived by a mirror image); it may not have the size or the shape I take it to have. Or perhaps I am even having a complete hallucination and there is no material object present to my senses at all.

Accordingly certain philosophers, notably Reid, have described perceptual consciousness as *belief*; and this seems a plausible suggestion. But unfortunately we here encounter a difficulty of terminology, since the word is sometimes used in a very wide sense and sometimes in a narrow one. It seems best to follow Cook Wilson in restricting the expression 'to believe that S is P' to that state of mind in which, being aware of certain facts, (1) we know that they are evidence for S's being P, (2) we know that they do *not* make it certain that S is P, (3) we have towards the problematic conception S-P a feeling of confidence capable of varying in strength.[15] Now if this be so,

[13] Some readers may think that I have gone to excessive pains in disproving a view which is obviously false. Who ever thought that sense-data were substances? The reply is that some philosophers have not clearly enough distinguished between those particular existents which are substances and those which are not: accordingly it is supposed that when we say that sense-data are particulars, we mean that they are the same sort of beings as chairs or trees; and it is accordingly inferred that there are no such entities.

[14] Mr. Johnson distinguishes between *characterizing* which is a relation between 'substantives' and 'adjectives', and *inherence* which is a relation between events and continuants. Thus in the case of inherence, *both* the terms of the relation are 'substantives'. Since 'inhering' is not always distinguished from characterizing, it is necessary to warn the reader that we shall use it here in Mr. Johnson's sense.

[15] Cf. *Statement and Inference*, Part II, ch. 3. On 'problematic conceptions', cf. the same work, Part III, ch. 5.

belief includes or at any rate is conditioned by a form of *inference*; for the apprehension that a set of premises ABC are evidence for (or make probable) a particular conclusion is no less to be called inference than the apprehension that a certain other set, say ABCDE, necessitate that conclusion. But as we have seen, the Causal Theory was obliged to admit that in perceptual consciousness as we have it now (whatever it may have been in our infancy) there is no trace of inference, though according to that theory only inference could justify it.

Further, it follows from this account of belief, that we cannot strictly be said to believe without evidence[16]: what is so described is not belief but something else. Moreover, since *ex hypothesi* we know that the evidence does not amount to proof, we cannot believe that S is P, without knowing that, after all, S may not be P. Belief even at its firmest is never wholly undoubting; we are still aware that, after all, we may be wrong. Or, if we cease to be aware of that, we have slipped out of belief into another state of mind.

Now perceptual consciousness is not like this. Let us grant for argument's sake that the existence of a sense-datum of such and such a sort, taken along with some further facts already known, does in fact make it probable (if not on causal grounds, then on some others) that there now exists a tree having such and such characteristics. Nevertheless, in my act of perceptual consciousness I am not *apprehending* that this conclusion is made probable: the notion of probability does not enter my head at all. There may be facts about my sense-datum which could be used by an external philosopher as evidence for the existence of the tree if he knew them. But I, the subject of the perceptual act, do not use them so. I am in a state of mind which is, so to speak, below the level of evidence-using.

This state of mind much more resembles what Cook Wilson calls *being under an impression that* than what he calls belief. In 'being under an impression' we simply jump straight from the awareness of A to the thought of B, without any preliminary wondering or considering of evidence, indeed without any rational process whatever; for instance, we jump from hearing a knock on the door to the thought that our friend Jones has arrived.[17] And as there has been no consideration of evidence, so there is no consciousness that we may be wrong: one just has not raised the question whether one is liable to be wrong or not. We may also appeal once again to the time-honoured analogy of reading print. The reader does not say to himself 'These words here are evidence that Caesar crossed the Rubicon: so on the whole I believe that he actually did'. One simply passes straight from the written symbols to the propositions which they signify. Only in our case there is not even a passage. The two states of mind, the acquaintance with the sense-datum and the perceptual consciousness of the tree, just arise together. The sense-datum is presented to us, and the tree dawns on us, all in one moment.

[16] Still less can we believe contrary to the evidence. The schoolboy who defined faith as '*believing* what you know ain't true' was guilty of a contradiction; and would still have been so, even if he had said only 'believing what you know to be improbable'.

[17] This is vulgarly called 'jumping to conclusions': which of course may happen to be true ones, and indeed are likely to be true more often than not, since our associative dispositions (to which such jumps are due) have been acquired through experience of often-repeated and therefore probably regular conjunctions.

The two modes of 'presence to the mind', utterly different though they are, can only be distinguished by subsequent analysis.

Agreeably with this, there is in an act of perceptual consciousness no element of doubt, no awareness of insufficiency or inconclusiveness, as there is in belief proper; and in this again it resembles both reading and 'being under an impression that'. True, it may have to be revised later, as when we correct an illusion or hallucination. We may say that *in fact* it is always provisional and liable to correction. But this provisionality is not present to the mind of the conscious subject himself: not because he has asked himself 'Am I liable to be mistaken about this?' and decided that he is not, but because he simply has not raised the question at all. When he does raise the question and asks himself 'But is this really a tree?', at once he slips out of the perceptual consciousness of the tree, not indeed into mere sensing, but into a less determinate consciousness whose object is 'a material thing of some kind or other'. And so long as he retains this doubt, it is possible for him to believe that on the whole the thing is a tree after all, but it is not possible for him to *see* it as a tree; on the other hand, he cannot hold this belief unless he still sees it as some body or other.

Accordingly it would be nearer the mark to describe perceptual consciousness (in this its simplest and primary form) not as belief, but as *absence of disbelief* [18]: or again as 'the not doubting that'. Perhaps, however, the best term is *acceptance* or *taking for granted*. And we shall in future call this primary form of perceptual consciousness *perceptual acceptance*.

What then is it that is taken for granted? That there exists a material thing: and not merely that there exists some material thing or other somewhere or other, but a material thing such that this sense-datum which I now sense belongs to it.[19] Nor is this definite enough. The material thing, whose existence we take for granted, is still further specified as having a *front surface* of a certain sort, where 'front' means nearer than its other surfaces to the point of view at which the perceptually-conscious subject is. (What the thing's back surface or sides or insides may be is not as yet specified. In the primary perceptual act we only take for granted that it has some sort of back surface or other; what sort, we leave it to subsequent acts to determine.)

But in what way exactly is the front surface thus specified? What nature it is taken to have obviously depends partly upon the nature of the present sense-datum; but partly also on our acquired dispositions. Thus if the thing is very familiar to us, we still attribute to it a front surface of a highly determinate kind even when the sense-datum is excessively faint and undifferentiated: as when I recognize a familiar house at a good distance off, or in a mist. Here, however, we shall neglect this effect of acquired dispositions in order to study the perceptual consciousness as far as possible in its most elementary form. And it is in any case necessary to go back to this form of it, if we can. For everything was once unfamiliar to us, and the acquired dispositions which we have now were only built up by the repetition of acts of a more elementary type in which no acquired dispositions were present. Thus in any case we

[18] Cf. the description of the attitude of the reader of poetry or fiction as 'a willing suspension of disbelief'. Only in our case the suspension is neither willing nor unwilling; it is just automatic.

[19] Thus to perceive in Reid's sense is to take for granted that you are perceiving in Professor Moore's sense

come back in the end to the specification of the front surface by the sense-datum alone.

But in what manner the sense-datum specifies the front surface it is not easy to be sure. On the one hand we might be tempted to say that we take the sense-datum to *be* the front surface of the material thing,[20] or to be *coincident* therewith: (so that Naïve Realism would be perfectly right, provided we substituted 'taking for granted' for 'knowing'). This is plausible for touch and for vision at a fairly short range: thus it is plausible to say that I take the brown sense-datum which I sense at this moment to *be* the surface of the table at which I am writing. But when we turn to long-range vision we get into difficulty. Thus when two men are present to my senses, one five feet off and one a hundred yards off, I do not take for granted that the distant one is smaller than the other, or that he has a flat face; yet there can be no doubt that the sense-datum belonging to him is sensibly smaller than that belonging to the other man, and that it is flat.

Further, as Professor G. E. Moore has pointed out, the ordinary percipient when he sees something cannot be said to take for granted that his sense-datum is 'in Physical Space', as it would have to be if it were, or were *coincident* with, the surface of a material thing: nor yet that it is not in Physical Space. At the level of perceptual consciousness the question simply is not raised. The truth is, I think, that perceptual consciousness (in this respect as in others) is, so to speak, more negative than positive. It is rather that we do not assert a difference between the sense-datum and the surface, than that we do assert their identity.

Now of course we may ask, what is *in fact* the spatial relation between the sense-datum and the surface of the material thing? And it is a plausible answer that one single sense-datum taken alone cannot be said to stand in any spatial relation with any material thing, i.e. to be anywhere in 'Physical Space' at all: what has position in Physical Space being a certain sort of *group* of sense-data taken collectively. Now this might lead us into a second temptation. We might be tempted to say: what we take for granted in perceptual consciousness is that this present sense-datum is a member of a group which taken as a whole is, or is coincident with, the front surface of a material thing. But this, too, we must resist, for it is an 'over-rationalization' of the perceptual state of mind; we should be making the plain man, or indeed the plain animal, into a philosopher. If there really is the material thing, and if it really has the surface which the perceptual subject takes it to have (and of course the act of perceptual acceptance is always liable to be erroneous), then the sense-datum really was a member of such a group. But it does not follow that the conscious subject himself either takes it to be a member of such a group, or takes it not to be: the question whether it is or isn't simply has not occurred to him.

The most we can say is this: in perceptual consciousness, we do not regard the single sense-datum as *completely* specifying the shape, size and situation of the front surface of the material thing which we are taking to exist. We regard it as *restricting the possibilities* to a greater or less extent; we leave the complete specification of them to subsequent sense-data. Thus if the present

20 Or as Professor H. A. Prichard has expressed it, 'We straight off mistake a colour for a body' (where 'colour' means 'colour-expanse').

sense-datum is triangular I take it that the thing's front surface is not circular or square,[21] but I am by no means sure that it has not wavy edges, rounded corners, and a different relation of height to base. The degree in which the sense-datum is taken to restrict the possibilities depends mainly on two factors: its degree of differentiation, and in the case of sight its 'stereoscopic' character. When the sense-datum is flat, and uniform in colour and outline, we only make a 'rough shot' at the shape of the thing's front surface: we take it to be 'fairly large', 'more or less round' or 'broader than it is high'. When the sense-datum is full of detail and completely stereoscopic, we are very much more definite in our taking (though of course the resources of language may fail us if we attempt to state it in words), e.g. we take the front surface to be about seven feet by three, approximately rectangular in shape, and divided into panels. But the back and side surfaces, though we take for granted that there are some, still remain unspecified; we assume, too, that even the front surface could still be specified more, if we looked closer or used a magnifying glass, though only in relatively minor respects. Here we are less inclined to admit a non-identity of the sense-datum and the thing's surface, if we are asked. But still it would be false to say that we do positively take them to be identical.

To sum up this part of our discussion: What the perceptually conscious subject takes for granted when he senses a particular visual or tactual sense-datum is that there now exists a material thing to which this sense-datum belongs; and that this thing has a front surface of a certain general character, to be more exactly determined by subsequent perceptual acts. What general character the surface is taken to have, and how determinate that character is, does depend upon the nature of the present sense-datum. But it is not true that he takes the sense-datum to be identical with the surface, though (his state being an unreflective one) he does fail to distinguish them.

21 Of course I might be wrong even in this, owing to some complicated optical conditions. But we are here discussing what I *take* to be the case, not what *is* the case. Nor are we yet asking how we know whether it is the case or not.

Charles Sanders Peirce

A Critique of Cartesianism

SOME CONSEQUENCES OF FOUR INCAPACITIES

THE SPIRIT OF CARTESIANISM

Descartes is the father of modern philosophy, and the spirit of Cartesianism—that which principally distinguishes it from the scholasticism which it displaced—may be compendiously stated as follows:

1. It teaches that philosophy must begin with universal doubt; whereas scholasticism had never questioned fundamentals.

2. It teaches that the ultimate test of certainty is to be found in the individual consciousness; whereas scholasticism had rested on the testimony of sages and of the Catholic Church.

3. The multiform argumentation of the middle ages is replaced by a single thread of inference depending often upon inconspicuous premisses.

4. Scholasticism had its mysteries of faith, but undertook to explain all created things. But there are many facts which Cartesianism not only does not explain but renders absolutely inexplicable, unless to say that "God makes them so" is to be regarded as an explanation.

In some, or all of these respects, most modern philosophers have been, in effect, Cartesians. Now without wishing to return to scholasticism, it seems to me that modern science and modern logic require us to stand upon a very different platform from this.

1. We cannot begin with complete doubt. We must begin with all the prejudices which we actually have when we enter upon the study of philosophy. These prejudices are not to be dispelled by a maxim, for they are things which it does not occur to us *can* be questioned. Hence this initial skepticism will be a mere self-deception, and not real doubt; and no one who follows the Cartesian method will ever be satisfied until he has formally recovered all those beliefs which in form he has given up. It is, therefore, as useless a preliminary as going to the North Pole would be in order to get to Constantinople by coming down regularly upon a meridian. A person may, it is true, in the course of his studies, find reason to doubt what he began by believing; but in that case he doubts because he has a positive reason for it, and not on

---

Reprinted by permission of the publishers from *Collected Papers of Charles Sanders Peirce,* Volume V, edited by Charles Hartshorne and Paul Weiss, Cambridge, Mass.: The Belknap Press of Harvard University Press, Copyright, 1934, 1962, by the President and Fellows of Harvard College. This selection originally appeared in "Some Consequences of Four Incapacities," *Journal of Speculative Philosophy,* Vol. 2 (1868), and "The Fixation of Belief," *Popular Science Monthly,* Vol. 12 (1877).

account of the Cartesian maxim. Let us not pretend to doubt in philosophy what we do not doubt in our hearts.

2. The same formalism appears in the Cartesian criterion, which amounts to this: "Whatever I am clearly convinced of, is true." If I were really convinced, I should have done with reasoning and should require no test of certainty. But thus to make single individuals absolute judges of truth is most pernicious. The result is that metaphysicians will all agree that metaphysics has reached a pitch of certainty far beyond that of the physical sciences—only they can agree upon nothing else. In sciences in which men come to agreement, when a theory has been broached it is considered to be on probation until this agreement is reached. After it is reached, the question of certainty becomes an idle one, because there is no one left who doubts it. We individually cannot reasonably hope to attain the ultimate philosophy which we pursue; we can only seek it, therefore, for the *community* of philosophers. Hence, if disciplined and candid minds carefully examine a theory and refuse to accept it, this ought to create doubts in the mind of the author of the theory himself.

3. Philosophy ought to imitate the successful sciences in its methods, so far as to proceed only from tangible premisses which can be subjected to careful scrutiny, and to trust rather to the multitude and variety of its arguments than to the conclusiveness of any one. Its reasoning should not form a chain which is no stronger than its weakest link, but a cable whose fibers may be ever so slender, provided they are sufficiently numerous and intimately connected.

4. Every unidealistic philosophy supposes some absolutely inexplicable, unanalyzable ultimate; in short, something resulting from mediation itself not susceptible of mediation. Now that anything *is* thus inexplicable can only be known by reasoning from signs. But the only justification of an inference from signs is that the conclusion explains the fact. To suppose the fact absolutely inexplicable, is not to explain it, and hence this supposition is never allowable.

. . . A piece entitled "Questions concerning certain Faculties claimed for Man" . . . has been written in this spirit of opposition to Cartesianism. That criticism of certain faculties resulted in four denials, which for convenience may here be repeated:

1. We have no power of Introspection, but all knowledge of the internal world is derived by hypothetical reasoning from our knowledge of external facts.
2. We have no power of Intuition, but every cognition is determined logically by previous cognitions.
3. We have no power of thinking without signs.
4. We have no conception of the absolutely incognizable.

These propositions cannot be regarded as certain; and, in order to bring them to a further test, it is now proposed to trace them out to their consequences.

. . .

THE FIXATION OF BELIEF

. . .

DOUBT AND BELIEF

We generally know when we wish to ask a question and when we wish to pronounce a judgment, for there is a dissimilarity between the sensation of doubting and that of believing.

But this is not all which distinguishes doubt from belief. There is a practical difference. Our beliefs guide our desires and shape our actions. The Assassins, or followers of the Old Man of the Mountain, used to rush into death at his least command, because they believed that obedience to him would insure everlasting felicity. Had they doubted this, they would not have acted as they did. So it is with every belief, according to its degree. The feeling of believing is a more or less sure indication of there being established in our nature some habit which will determine our actions.[1] Doubt never has such an effect.

Nor must we overlook a third point of difference. Doubt is an uneasy and dissatisfied state from which we struggle to free ourselves and pass into the state of belief; [2] while the latter is a calm and satisfactory state which we do not wish to avoid, or to change to a belief in anything else.[3] On the contrary, we cling tenaciously, not merely to believing, but to believing just what we do believe.

Thus, both doubt and belief have positive effects upon us, though very different ones. Belief does not make us act at once, but puts us into such a condition that we shall behave in some certain way, when the occasion arises. Doubt has not the least such active effect, but stimulates us to inquiry until it is destroyed. This reminds us of the irritation of a nerve and the reflex action produced thereby; while for the analogue of belief, in the nervous system, we must look to what are called nervous associations—for example, to that habit of the nerves in consequence of which the smell of a peach will make the mouth water.[4]

[1] Let us recall the nature of a sign and ask ourselves how we can know that a feeling of any sort is a sign that we have a habit implanted within us.

We can understand one habit by likening it to another habit. But to understand what any habit is, there must be some habit of which we are directly conscious in its generality. That is to say, we must have a certain generality in our direct consciousness. Bishop Berkeley and a great many clear thinkers laugh at the idea of our being able to imagine a triangle that is neither equilateral, isosceles, nor scalene. They seem to think the object of imagination must be precisely determinate in every respect. But it seems certain that something general we must imagine. I do not intend [here] to go into questions of psychology. It is not necessary for us to know in detail how our thinking is done, but only how it can be done. Still, I may as well say, at once, that I think our direct consciousness covers a duration of time, although only an infinitely brief duration. At any rate, I can see no way of escaping the proposition that to attach any general significance to a sign and to know that we do attach a general significance to it, we must have a direct imagination of something not in all respects determinate.—1893.

[2] In this, it is like any other stimulus. It is true that just as men may, for the sake of the pleasures of the table, like to be hungry and take means to make themselves so, although hunger always involves a desire to fill the stomach, so for the sake of the pleasures of inquiry, men may like to seek out doubts. Yet, for all that, doubt essentially involves a struggle to escape it.—1893.

[3] I am not speaking of secondary effects occasionally produced by the interference of other impulses.

[4] Doubt, however, is not usually hesitancy about what is to be done then and there. It is anticipated hesitancy about what I shall do hereafter, or a feigned hesitancy about a fictitious state of things. It is the power of making believe we hesitate, together with the pregnant fact that the decision upon the merely make-believe dilemma goes toward forming a bona fide habit that

THE END OF INQUIRY

The irritation of doubt causes a struggle to attain a state of belief. I shall term this struggle *Inquiry,* though it must be admitted that this is sometimes not a very apt designation.

The irritation of doubt is the only immediate motive for the struggle to attain belief. It is certainly best for us that our beliefs should be such as may truly guide our actions so as to satisfy our desires; and this reflection will make us reject every belief which does not seem to have been so formed as to insure this result. But it will only do so by creating a doubt in the place of that belief.[5] With the doubt, therefore, the struggle begins, and with the cessation of doubt it ends. Hence, the sole object of inquiry is the settlement of opinion. We may fancy that this is not enough for us, and that we seek, not merely an opinion, but a true opinion. But put this fancy to the test, and it proves groundless; for as soon as a firm belief is reached we are entirely satisfied, whether the belief be true or false. And it is clear that nothing out of the sphere of our knowledge can be our object, for nothing which does not affect the mind can be the motive for mental effort. The most that can be maintained is, that we seek for a belief that we shall *think* to be true. But we think each one of our beliefs to be true, and, indeed, it is mere tautology to say so.[6]

That the settlement of opinion is the sole end of inquiry is a very important proposition. It sweeps away, at once, various vague and erroneous conceptions of proof. A few of these may be noticed here.

1. Some philosophers have imagined that to start an inquiry it was only necessary to utter a question whether orally or by setting it down upon paper, and have even recommended us to begin our studies with questioning everything! But the mere putting of a proposition into the interrogative form does not stimulate the mind to any struggle after belief. There must be a real and living doubt, and without this all discussion is idle.[7]

---

will be operative in a real emergency. It is these two things in conjunction that constitute us intellectual beings.

Every answer to a question that has any meaning is a decision as to how we would act under imagined circumstances, or how the world would be expected to react upon our senses. Thus, suppose I am told that if two straight lines in one plane are cut by a third making the sum of the internal angles on one side less than two right angles, then those lines if sufficiently produced will meet on the side on which the said sum is less than two right angles. This means to me that if I had two lines drawn on a plane and wished to find where they would meet, I could draw a third line cutting them and ascertaining on which side the sum of the two interval angles was less than two right angles, and should lengthen the lines on that side. In like manner, all doubt is a state of hesitancy about an imagined state of things.—1893.

[5] Unless, indeed, it leads us to modify our desires.—1903.

[6] For truth is neither more nor less than that character of a proposition which consists in this, that belief in the proposition would, with sufficient experience and reflection, lead us to such conduct as would tend to satisfy the desires we should then have. To say that truth means more than this is to say that it has no meaning at all.—1903.

[7] So long as we cannot put our fingers on our erroneous opinions, they remain our opinions, still. It will be wholesome enough for us to make a general review of the causes of our beliefs; and the result will be that most of them have been taken upon trust and have been held since we were too young to discriminate the credible from the incredible. Such reflections may awaken real doubts about some of our positions. But in cases where no real doubt exists in our minds inquiry will be an idle farce, a mere whitewashing commission which were better let alone. This fault in philosophy was very widespread in those ages in which Disputations were the principal exercises in the universities; that is, from their rise in the thirteenth century down to the middle of the eighteenth, and even to this day in some Catholic institutions. But since those disputations went out of vogue, this philosophic disease is less virulent.—1893.

2. It is a very common idea that a demonstration must rest on some ultimate and absolutely indubitable propositions. These, according to one school, are first principles of a general nature; according to another, are first sensations. But, in point of fact, an inquiry, to have that completely satisfactory result called demonstration, has only to start with propositions perfectly free from all actual doubt. If the premisses are not in fact doubted at all, they cannot be more satisfactory than they are.[8]

3. Some people seem to love to argue a point after all the world is fully convinced of it. But no further advance can be made. When doubt ceases, mental action on the subject comes to an end; and, if it did go on, it would be without a purpose.[9]

METHODS OF FIXING BELIEF

If the settlement of opinion is the sole object of inquiry, and if belief is of the nature of a habit, why should we not attain the desired end, by taking as answer to a question any we may fancy, and constantly reiterating it to ourselves, dwelling on all which may conduce to that belief, and learning to turn with contempt and hatred from anything that might disturb it? This simple and direct method is really pursued by many men. . . . A man may go through life, systematically keeping out of view all that might cause a change in his opinions, and if he only succeeds—basing his method, as he does, on two fundamental psychological laws—I do not see what can be said against his doing so. It would be an egotistical impertinence to object that his procedure is irrational, for that only amounts to saying that his method of settling belief is not ours. He does not propose to himself to be rational, and, indeed, will often talk with scorn of man's weak and illusive reason. So let him think as he pleases.

But this method of fixing belief, which may be called the method of tenacity, will be unable to hold its ground in practice. The social impulse is against it. The man who adopts it will find that other men think differently from him, and it will be apt to occur to him, in some saner moment, that their opinions are quite as good as his own, and this will shake his confidence in his belief. This conception, that another man's thought or sentiment may be equivalent to one's own, is a distinctly new step, and a highly important one. It arises from an impulse too strong in man to be suppressed, without danger of destroying the human species. Unless we make ourselves hermits, we shall necessarily influence each other's opinions; so that the problem becomes how to fix belief, not in the individual merely, but in the community.

Let the will of the state act, then, instead of that of the individual. Let an institution be created which shall have for its object to keep correct doctrines

[8] We have to acknowledge that doubts about them may spring up later; but we can find no propositions which are not subject to this contingency. We ought to construct our theories so as to provide for such discoveries; first, by making them rest on as great a variety of different considerations as possible, and second, by leaving room for the modifications which cannot be foreseen but which are pretty sure to prove needful. Some systems are much more open to this criticism than others. All those which repose heavily upon an "inconceivability of the opposite" have proved particularly fragile and short-lived. Those, however, which rest upon positive evidences and which avoid insisting upon the absolute precision of their dogmas are hard to destroy. —1893.

[9] Except that of self-criticism. Insert here a section upon self-control and the analogy between Moral and Rational self-control.—1903.

before the attention of the people, to reiterate them perpetually, and to teach them to the young; having at the same time power to prevent contrary doctrines from being taught, advocated, or expressed. Let all possible causes of a change of mind be removed from men's apprehensions. Let them be kept ignorant, lest they should learn of some reason to think otherwise than they do. . . .

This method has, from the earliest times, been one of the chief means of upholding correct theological and political doctrines, and of preserving their universal or catholic character.

In judging this method of fixing belief, which may be called the method of authority, we must, in the first place, allow its immeasurable mental and moral superiority to the method of tenacity. Its success is proportionately greater; and, in fact, it has over and over again worked the most majestic results. The mere structures of stone which it has caused to be put together —in Siam, for example, in Egypt, and in Europe—have many of them a sublimity hardly more than rivaled by the greatest works of Nature. And, except the geological epochs, there are no periods of time so vast as those which are measured by some of these organized faiths. If we scrutinize the matter closely, we shall find that there has not been one of their creeds which has remained always the same; yet the change is so slow as to be imperceptible during one person's life, so that individual belief remains sensibly fixed. For the mass of mankind, then, there is perhaps no better method than this. If it is their highest impulse to be intellectual slaves, then slaves they ought to remain.

But no institution can undertake to regulate opinions upon every subject. Only the most important ones can be attended to, and on the rest men's minds must be left to the action of natural causes. This imperfection will be no source of weakness so long as men are in such a state of culture that one opinion does not influence another—that is, so long as they cannot put two and two together. But in the most priest-ridden states some individuals will be found who are raised above that condition. These men possess a wider sort of social feeling; they see that men in other countries and in other ages have held to very different doctrines from those which they themselves have been brought up to believe; and they cannot help seeing that it is the mere accident of their having been taught as they have, and of their having been surrounded with the manners and associations they have, that has caused them to believe as they do and not far differently. Nor can their candour resist the reflection that there is no reason to rate their own views at a higher value than those of other nations and other centuries; thus giving rise to doubts in their minds.

They will further perceive that such doubts as these must exist in their minds with reference to every belief which seems to be determined by the caprice either of themselves or of those who originated the popular opinions. The willful adherence to a belief, and the arbitrary forcing of it upon others, must, therefore, both be given up. A different new method of settling opinions must be adopted, that shall not only produce an impulse to believe, but shall also decide what proposition it is which is to be believed. Let the action of natural preferences be unimpeded, then, and under their influence let men, conversing together and regarding matters in different lights, gradually develop beliefs in harmony with natural causes. This method resembles that by which conceptions of art have been brought to maturity. The most perfect example of it is to be found in the history of metaphysical philosophy. Systems of this sort have not usually rested upon any observed facts, at least not in any great degree. They have been chiefly adopted because their fundamental propositions seemed "agreeable to reason." This is an apt expression; it does not mean that which agrees with experience, but that which we find ourselves inclined to believe. Plato, for example, finds it agreeable to reason that the distances of the celestial spheres from one another should be proportional to the different lengths of strings which produce harmonious chords. Many philosophers have been led to their main conclusions by considerations like this; [10] but this is the lowest and least developed form which the method takes, for it is clear that another man might find Kepler's theory, that the celestial spheres are proportional to the inscribed and circumscribed spheres of the different regular solids, more agreeable to *his* reason. But the shock of opinions will soon lead men to rest on preferences of a far more universal nature. Take, for example, the doctrine that man only acts selfishly—that is, from the consid-

[10] Let us see in what manner a few of the greatest philosophers have undertaken to settle opinion, and what their success has been. Descartes, who would have a man begin by doubting everything, remarks that there is one thing he will find himself unable to doubt, and that is, that he does doubt; and when he reflects that he doubts, he can no longer doubt that he exists. Then, because he is all the while doubting whether there are any such things as shape and motion, Descartes thinks he must be persuaded that shape and motion do not belong to his nature, or anything else but consciousness. This is taking it for granted that nothing in his nature lies hidden beneath the surface. Next, Descartes asks the doubter to remark that he has the idea of a Being, in the highest degree intelligent, powerful, and perfect. Now a Being would not have these qualities unless he existed necessarily and eternally. By existing necessarily he means existing by virtue of the existence of the idea. Consequently, all doubt as to the existence of this Being must cease. This plainly supposes that belief is to be fixed by what men find in their minds. He is reasoning like this: I find it written in the volume of my mind that there is something X, which is such a sort of thing that the moment it is written down it exists. Plainly, he is aiming at a kind of truth which saying so can make to be so. He gives two further proofs of God's existence. Descartes makes God easier to know than anything else; for whatever we think He is, He is. He fails to remark that this is precisely the definition of a *figment.* In particular, God cannot be a deceiver; whence it follows, that whatever we quite clearly and distinctly think to be true about any subject, must *be* true. Accordingly, if people will thoroughly discuss a subject, and quite clearly and distinctly make up their minds what they think about it, the desired settlement of the question will be reached. I may remark that the world has pretty thoroughly deliberated upon that theory and has quite distinctly come to the conclusion that it is utter nonsense; whence that judgment is indisputably right. . . .

Many critics have told me that I misrepresent the *a priori* philosophers, when I represent them as adopting whatever opinion there seems to be a natural inclination to adopt. But nobody can say the above does not accurately define the position of Descartes, and upon what does he repose except natural ways of thinking? Perhaps I shall be told however, that since Kant, that vice has been cured. Kant's great boast is that he critically examines into our natural inclinations toward certain opinions. An opinion that something is *universally* true clearly goes further than experience can warrant. An opinion that something is *necessarily* true (that is, not merely is true in the existing state of things, but would be true in every state of things) equally goes further than experience will warrant. Those remarks had been made by Leibniz and admitted by Hume; and Kant reiterates them. Though they are propositions of a nominalistic cast, they can hardly be denied. I may add that whatever is held to be precisely true goes further than experience can possibly warrant. Accepting those criteria of the origin of ideas, Kant proceeds to reason as follows: Geometrical propositions are held to be universally true. Hence, they are not given by experience. Consequently, it must be owing to an inward necessity of man's nature that he sees everything in space. Ergo, the sum of the angles of a triangle will be equal to two right angles for all the objects of our vision. Just that, and nothing more, is Kant's line of thought. But the dry-rot of reason in the seminaries has gone to the point where such stuff is held to be admirable argumentation. I might go through the *Critic of the Pure Reason,* section by section, and show that the thought throughout is precisely of this character. He everywhere shows that ordinary objects, such as trees and gold-pieces, involve elements not contained in the first presentations of sense. But we cannot persuade

eration that acting in one way will afford him more pleasure than acting in another. This rests on no fact in the world, but it has had a wide acceptance as being the only reasonable theory.[11]

This method is far more intellectual and respectable from the point of view of reason than either of the others which we have noticed. Indeed, as long as no better method can be applied, it ought to be followed, since it is then the expression of instinct which must be the ultimate cause of belief in all cases. But its failure has been the most manifest. It makes of inquiry something similar to the development of taste; but taste, unfortunately, is always more or less a matter of fashion, and accordingly metaphysicians have never come to any fixed agreement, but the pendulum has swung backward and forward between a more material and a more spiritual philosophy, from the earliest times to the latest. And so from this, which has been called the *a priori* method, we are driven, in Lord Bacon's phrase, to a true induction. We have examined into this *a priori* method as something which promised to deliver our opinions from their accidental and capricious element. But development, while it is a process which eliminates the effect of some casual circumstances, only magnifies that of others. This method, therefore, does not differ in a very essential way from that of authority. The government may not have lifted its finger to influence my convictions; I may have been left outwardly quite free to choose, we will say, between monogamy and polygamy, and, appealing to my conscience only, I may have concluded that the latter practice is in itself licentious. But when I come to see that the chief obstacle to the spread of Christianity among a people of as high culture as the Hindoos has been a conviction of the immorality of our way of treating women, I cannot help seeing that, though governments do not interfere, sentiments in their development will be very greatly determined by accidental causes. Now, there are some people, among whom I must suppose that my reader is to be found, who, when they see that any belief of theirs is determined by any circumstance extraneous to the facts, will from that moment not merely admit in words that that belief is doubtful, but will experience a real doubt of it, so that it ceases in some degree at least to be a belief.

To satisfy our doubts, therefore, it is necessary that a method should be found by which our beliefs may be determined by nothing human, but by some external permanency—by something upon which our thinking has

ourselves to give up the reality of trees and gold-pieces. There is a general inward insistence upon them, and that is the warrant for swallowing the entire bolus of general belief about them. This is merely accepting without question a belief as soon as it is shown to please a great many people very much. When he comes to the ideas of God, Freedom, and Immortality, he hesitates; because people who think only of bread and butter, pleasure and power, are indifferent to those ideas. He subjects these ideas to a different kind of examination, and finally admits them upon grounds which appear to the seminarists more or less suspicious, but which in the eyes of laboratorists are infinitely stronger than the grounds upon which he has accepted space, time, and causality. Those last grounds amount to nothing but this, that what there is a very decided and general inclination to believe must be true. Had Kant merely said, I shall adopt for the present the belief that the three angles of a triangle are equal to two right angles because nobody but brother Lambert and some Italian has ever called it in question, his attitude would be well enough. But on the contrary, he and those who today represent his school distinctly maintain the proposition is *proved*, and the Lambertists *refuted*, by what comes merely to general disinclination to think with them. . . .

[11] An acceptance whose real support has been the opinion that pleasure is the only ultimate good. But this opinion, or even the opinion that pleasure *per se* is any good at all, is only tenable so long as he who holds it remains without any distinct idea of what he means by "good."—1903.

no effect.[12] Some mystics imagine that they have such a method in a private inspiration from on high. But that is only a form of the method of tenacity, in which the conception of truth as something public is not yet developed. Our external permanency would not be external, in our sense, if it was restricted in its influence to one individual. It must be something which affects, or might affect, every man. And, though these affections are necessarily as various as are individual conditions, yet the method must be such that the ultimate conclusion of every man shall be the same. Such is the method of science. Its fundamental hypothesis, restated in more familiar language, is this: There are Real things, whose characters are entirely independent of our opinions about them; those Reals affect our senses according to regular laws, and, though our sensations are as different as are our relations to the objects, yet, by taking advantage of the laws of perception, we can ascertain by reasoning how things really and truly are; and any man, if he have sufficient experience and he reason enough about it, will be led to the one True conclusion. The new conception here involved is that of Reality. It may be asked how I know that there are any Reals. If this hypothesis is the sole support of my method of inquiry, my method of inquiry must not be used to support my hypothesis. The reply is this: 1. If investigation cannot be regarded as proving that there are Real things, it at least does not lead to a contrary conclusion; but the method and the conception on which it is based remain ever in harmony. No doubts of the method, therefore, necessarily arise from its practice, as is the case with all the others. 2. The feeling which gives rise to any method of fixing belief is a dissatisfaction at two repugnant propositions. But here already is a vague concession that there is some *one* thing which a proposition should represent. Nobody, therefore, can really doubt that there are Reals, for, if he did, doubt would not be a source of dissatisfaction. The hypothesis, therefore, is one which every mind admits. So that the social impulse does not cause men to doubt it. 3. Everybody uses the scientific method about a great many things, and only ceases to use it when he does not know how to apply it. 4. Experience of the method has not led us to doubt it, but, on the contrary, scientific investigation has had the most wonderful triumphs in the way of settling opinion. These afford the explanation of my not doubting the method or the hypothesis which it supposes; and not having any doubt, nor believing that anybody else whom I could influence has, it would be the merest babble for me to say more about it. If there be anybody with a living doubt upon the subject, let him consider it.

12 But which, on the other hand, unceasingly tends to influence thought; or in other words, by something Real.—1903.

John Langshaw Austin

Some Objections to Empiricist Epistemology

The pursuit of the incorrigible is one of the most venerable bugbears in the history of philosophy. It is rampant all over ancient philosophy, most conspicuously in Plato, was powerfully re-animated by Descartes, and bequeathed by him to a long line of successors. No doubt it has many motives and takes many forms, and naturally we can't go into the whole story now. In some cases the motive seems to be a comparatively simple hankering for something to be *absolutely certain*—a hankering which can be difficult enough to satisfy if one rigs it so that certainty is absolutely unattainable; in other cases, such as Plato's perhaps, what is apparently sought for is something that will be *always true*. But in the case now before us, which descends directly from Descartes, there is an added complication in the form of a general doctrine about knowledge. And it is of course knowledge, not perception at all, in which these philosophers are really interested. In Ayer's case this shows itself in the title of his book, as well as, *passim,* in his text; Price is more seriously interested than is Ayer in the actual facts about perception, and pays more attention to them—but still, it is worth noticing that, after raising the initial question, 'What is it to *see* something?', his very next sentence runs, 'When I see a tomato there is much that I *can doubt.*'[1] This suggests that he too is really interested, not so much in what seeing is, as in what one *can't* doubt.

In a nutshell, the doctrine about knowledge, 'empirical' knowledge, is that it has *foundations*. It is a structure the upper tiers of which are reached by inferences, and the foundations are the *data* on which these inferences are based. (So of course—as it appears—there just have to be sense-data.) Now the trouble with inferences is that they may be mistaken; whenever we take a step, we may put a foot wrong. Thus—so the doctrine runs—the way to identify the upper tiers of the structure of knowledge is to ask whether one might be mistaken, whether there is something that one *can doubt*; if the answer is Yes, then one is not at the basement. And conversely, it will be characteristic of the *data* that in their case no doubt is possible, no mistake can be made. So to find the data, the foundations, look for *the incorrigible.*

Now of course Ayer's exposition of this very old story is (or at any rate was when it was written) very up-to-date, very linguistic. He constantly reproves Price and his other predecessors for treating as questions of fact what are really questions of language. However, as we have seen, this relative sophistication

[1] [A. J. Ayer, *The Foundations of Empirical Knowledge,* 1947; H. H. Price, *Perception,* 1933.]

From J. L. Austin, *Sense and Sensibilia* (reconstructed from manuscript notes by G. J. Warnock), Chap. 10, published by The Clarendon Press, Oxford, 1962, and reprinted with their permission. Also available in paperback.

does not prevent Ayer from swallowing whole almost all the old myths and mistakes incorporated in the traditional arguments. Also, as we have seen, it is not really true that he himself believes the questions raised to be questions about language, though this is his official doctrine. And finally, as we shall see in a moment, the doctrine that the questions *are* questions about language leads him, in the course of expounding it, to make about language a number of rather serious mistakes.

. . .

We must go a bit further into [the] doctrine about 'two languages'. On this topic Ayer becomes involved in a *fracas* with Carnap, and it will be instructive to see how the argument between them goes.[2]

Carnap's doctrine on this subject, with which Ayer finds himself in partial disagreement, is to the effect that the (legitimate) indicative sentences of a language, other than those which are analytic, can be divided into two groups, one group consisting of 'empirically testable' sentences, the other of 'observation-sentences', or 'protocols'. A sentence belongs to the first group, is empirically testable, if and only if, as Ayer puts it, some observation-sentence is 'derivable from it in accordance with the established rules of the language'. About these observation-sentences themselves Carnap has two things to say. He says (*a*) that it is fundamentally just a matter of convention which observation-sentences are taken to be *true*; all we need bother about is to fix it so that the total corpus of sentences we assert is internally consistent; and (*b*) that it doesn't much matter what sort of sentence we classify as an observation-sentence; for 'every concrete sentence belonging to the physicalistic system-language can in suitable circumstances serve as an observation-sentence'.

Now Ayer disagrees with Carnap on both of these points. On the first he argues, vehemently and perfectly correctly, that if anything we say is to have any serious claim to be in fact true (or even false) of the world we live in, then of course there have to be some things we say the truth (or falsehood) of which is determined by non-verbal reality; it can't be that everything we say has merely to be assessed for consistency with other things we say.

On the second point it is not *quite* so clear where Ayer stands. He holds—and this looks reasonable enough—that the only sentences which can properly be called 'observation-sentences' are those which record 'observable states of affairs'. But what kind of sentences do this? Or, as Ayer puts it, is it possible 'to delimit the class of propositions that are capable of being directly verified'? The trouble is that it is not quite clear how he answers this question. He begins by saying that 'it depends upon the language in which the proposition is expressed'. There is evidently no serious doubt that propositions about sense-data can be directly verified. 'On the other hand, when we are teaching English to a child, we imply that propositions about material things can be directly verified.' Well, perhaps we do; but are we right in implying this? Ayer sometimes seems to say that we can at any rate get away with it: but it is difficult to see how he could really think so. For (apart from his tendency, already noted, to express the conviction that the only real facts are facts about sense-data) there is the point that observation-sentences are regarded by him, as by Carnap, as the *termini* of processes of verification; and Ayer repeatedly ex-

[2] Ayer, op. cit., pp. 84–92, 113–14 [Rudolf Carnap, *The Logical Syntax of Language,* 1937].

presses the view that propositions about 'material things' not only stand in need of verification themselves, but are actually incapable of being 'conclusively' verified. Thus, unless Ayer were prepared to say that propositions which *can't* be 'conclusively' verified *can* be 'directly' verified, and furthermore that they can figure as *termini* in processes of verification, he must surely deny that propositions about material things can be 'observation-sentences'. And in fact it is fairly clear, from the general trend of his argument as well as from its internal structure, that he does deny this. In the terms used by Carnap, his real view seems to be that propositions about 'material things' are 'empirically testable', propositions about sense-data are 'observation-sentences'; and whereas members of the first group are not conclusively verifiable, members of the second group are actually *incorrigible.*

We must now consider the rights and wrongs of all this. Ayer is right, we have said already, and Carnap wrong, on the question of connexion with non-verbal reality; the idea that nothing at all comes in but the consistency of sentences with each other is, indeed, perfectly wild. On the second question, however, Carnap is at least more nearly right than Ayer; there is indeed no special subclass of sentences whose business it is to count as evidence for, or to be taken as verifying, other sentences, still less whose special feature it is to be incorrigible. But Carnap is not *quite* right even about this; for if we consider just why he is nearly right, we shall see that the most important point of all here is one on which he and Ayer are both equally mistaken.

Briefly, the point is this. It seems to be fairly generally realized nowadays that, if you just take a bunch of sentences (or propositions,[3] to use the term Ayer prefers) impeccably formulated in some language or other, there can be no question of sorting them out into those that are true and those that are false; for (leaving out of account so-called 'analytic' sentences) the question of truth and falsehood does not turn only on what a sentence *is*, nor yet on what it *means*, but on, speaking very broadly, the circumstances in which it is uttered. Sentences are not *as such* either true or false. But it is really equally clear, when one comes to think of it, that for much the same reasons there could be no question of picking out from one's bunch of sentences those that are evidence for others, those that are 'testable', or those that are 'incorrigible'. What kind of sentence is uttered as providing evidence for what depends, again, on the circumstances of particular cases; there is no kind of sentence which *as such* is evidence-providing, just as there is no kind of sentence which *as such* is surprising, or doubtful, or certain, or incorrigible, or true. Thus, while Carnap is quite right in saying that there is no special kind of sentence which *has* to be picked out as supplying the evidence for the rest, he is quite wrong in supposing that *any* kind of sentence *could* be picked out in this way. It is not that it doesn't much matter how we do it; there is really no question of doing such a thing at all. And thus Ayer is also wrong in holding, as he evidently does hold, that the evidence-providing kind of sentences are always sense-datum sentences, so that *these* are the ones that ought to be picked out.

[3] The passage in which Ayer explains his use of this term (p. 102) obscures *exactly* the essential point. For Ayer says (*a*) that in his use 'proposition' designates a class of sentences that all have *the same meaning,* and (*b*) that 'consequently' he speaks of propositions, not sentences, as being true or false. But of course to know what a sentence *means* does *not* enable us to say that *it* is true or false; and that of which we can say that it is true or false is *not* a 'proposition', in Ayer's sense.

This idea that there is a certain kind, or form, of sentence which as such is incorrigible and evidence-providing seems to be prevalent enough to deserve more detailed refutation. Let's consider incorrigibility first of all. The argument begins, it appears, from the observation that there are sentences which can be identified as intrinsically more adventurous than others, in uttering which we stick our necks out further. If for instance I say 'That's Sirius', I am wrong if, though it is a star, that star is not Sirius; whereas, if I had said only 'That's a star', its not being Sirius would leave me unshaken. Again, if I had said only, 'That looks like a star', I could have faced with comparative equanimity the revelation that it isn't a star. And so on. Reflections of this kind apparently give rise to the idea that there is or could be a kind of sentence in the utterance of which I take no chances *at all*, my commitment is absolutely minimal; so that in principle *nothing* could show that I had made a mistake, and my remark would be 'incorrigible'.

But in fact this ideal goal is completely unattainable. There isn't, there couldn't be, any kind of sentence which as such is incapable, once uttered, of being subsequently amended or retracted. Ayer himself, though he is prepared to say that sense-datum sentences are incorrigible, takes notice of one way in which they couldn't be; it is, as he admits, always possible in principle that, however non-committal a speaker intends to be, he may produce the *wrong word,* and subsequently be brought to admit this. But Ayer tries, as it were, to laugh this off as a quite trivial qualification; he evidently thinks that he is conceding here only the possibility of slips of the tongue, purely 'verbal' slips (or of course of lying). But this is not so. There are more ways than these of bringing out the wrong word. I may say 'Magenta' wrongly either by a mere slip, having meant to say 'Vermilion'; or because I don't know quite what 'magenta' means, what shade of colour is called *magenta*; or again, because I was unable to, or perhaps just didn't, really notice or attend to or properly size up the colour before me. Thus, there is always the possibility, not only that I may be brought to admit that 'magenta' wasn't the right word to pick on for the colour before me, but *also* that I may be brought to see, or perhaps remember, that the colour before me just wasn't *magenta.* And this holds for the case in which I say, 'It seems, to me personally, here and now, as if I were seeing something magenta', just as much as for the case in which I say, 'That is magenta.' The first formula may be more cautious, but it isn't *incorrigible.*[4]

Yes, but, it may be said, even if such cautious formulae are not *intrinsically* incorrigible, surely there will be plenty of cases in which what we say by their utterance will *in fact* be incorrigible—cases in which, that is to say, nothing whatever could actually be produced as a cogent ground for retracting them. Well, yes, no doubt this is true. But then exactly the same thing is true of

[4] Ayer doesn't exactly *overlook* the possibility of misdescribing through inattention, failure to notice or to discriminate; in the case of sense-data he tries to *rule it out.* But this attempt is partly a failure, and partly unintelligible. To stipulate that a sense-datum has whatever qualities it appears to have is insufficient for the purpose, since it is *not* impossible to err even in saying only what qualities something appears to have—one may, for instance, not attend to its appearance carefully enough. But to stipulate that a sense-datum just is whatever the speaker takes it to be—so that if he *says* something different it must be a different sense-datum—amounts to making non-mendacious sense-datum statements true by *fiat*; and if so, how could sense-data be, as they are also meant to be, non-linguistic entities *of* which we are aware, *to* which we refer, that against which the factual truth of all empirical statements is ultimately to be tested?

utterances in which quite different forms of words are employed. For if, when I make some statement, it is true that nothing whatever could in fact be produced as a cogent ground for retracting it, this can only be because I am in, have got myself into, the very best possible position for making that statement —I have, and am entitled to have, *complete* confidence in it when I make it. But whether this is so or not is not a matter of what *kind of sentence* I use in making my statement, but of what *the circumstances are* in which I make it. If I carefully scrutinize some patch of colour in my visual field, take careful note of it, know English well, and pay scrupulous attention to just what I'm saying, I may say, 'It seems to me now as if I were seeing something pink'; and nothing whatever could be produced as showing that I had made a mistake. But equally, if I watch for some time an animal a few feet in front of me, in a good light, if I prod it perhaps, sniff, and take note of the noises it makes, I may say, 'That's a pig'; and this too will be 'incorrigible', nothing could be produced that would show that I had made a mistake. Once one drops the idea that there is a special *kind of sentence* which is *as such* incorrigible, one might as well admit (what is plainly true anyway) that *many* kinds of sentences may be uttered in making statements which are *in fact* incorrigible—in the sense that, when they are made, the circumstances are such that they are quite certainly, definitely, and un-retractably *true*.

Consider next the point about evidence—the idea that there is, again, some special kind of sentences whose function it is to formulate the evidence on which other kinds are based. There are at least two things wrong with this.

First, it is not the case, as this doctrine implies, that whenever a 'material-object' statement is made, the speaker must have or could produce evidence for it. This may sound plausible enough; but it involves a gross misuse of the notion of 'evidence'. The situation in which I would properly be said to have *evidence* for the statement that some animal is a pig is that, for example, in which the beast itself is not actually on view, but I can see plenty of pig-like marks on the ground outside its retreat. If I find a few buckets of pig-food, that's a bit more evidence, and the noises and the smell may provide better evidence still. But if the animal then emerges and stands there plainly in view, there is no longer any question of collecting evidence; its coming into view doesn't provide me with more *evidence* that it's a pig, I can now just *see* that it is, the question is settled. And of course I might, in different circumstances, have just seen this in the first place, and not had to bother with collecting evidence at all.[5] Again, if I actually see one man shoot another, I may *give* evidence, as an eye-witness, to those less favourably placed; but I don't *have* evidence for my own statement that the shooting took place, I actually *saw* it. Once again, then, we find that you have to take into account, not just the words used, but the situation in which they are used; one who says 'It's a pig' will sometimes have evidence for saying so, sometimes not; one can't say that the *sentence* 'It's a pig', as such, is of a kind for which evidence is essentially required.

But secondly, as the case we've considered has already shown, it is not the

[5] I have, it will be said, the 'evidence of my own eyes'. But the point of this trope is exactly that it does *not* illustrate the ordinary use of 'evidence'—that I *don't* have evidence in the ordinary sense.

case that the formulation of evidence is the function of any special sort of sentence. The evidence, if there is any, for a 'material-object' statement will usually be formulated in statements of just the same kind; but in general, *any* kind of statement could state evidence for *any* other kind, if the circumstances were appropriate. It is not true in general, for instance, that general statements are 'based on' singular statements and not vice versa; my belief that *this* animal will eat turnips may be based on the belief that most pigs eat turnips; though certainly, in different circumstances, I might have supported the claim that most pigs eat turnips by saying that this pig eats them at any rate. Similarly, and more relevantly perhaps to the topic of perception, it is not true in general that statements of how things are are 'based on' statements of how things appear, look, or seem and not vice versa. I may say, for instance, 'That pillar is bulgy' on the ground that it looks bulgy; but equally I might say, in different circumstances, 'That pillar looks bulgy'—on the ground that I've just built it, and I *built* it bulgy.

We are now in a position to deal quite briefly with the idea that 'material-object' statements are *as such* not conclusively verifiable. This is just as wrong as the idea that sense-datum statements are as such incorrigible (it is not just 'misleading', as Ayer is prepared to allow that it might be). Ayer's doctrine is that 'the notion of certainty does not apply to propositions *of this kind*'.[6] And his ground for saying this is that, in order to verify a proposition of this kind conclusively, we should have to perform the self-contradictory feat of completing 'an infinite series of verifications'; however many tests we may carry out with favourable results, we can never complete all the possible tests, for these are infinite in number; but nothing *less* than all the possible tests would be *enough*.

Now why does Ayer (and not he alone) put forward this very extraordinary doctrine? It is, of course, not true in general that statements about 'material things', as such, *need* to be 'verified'. If, for instance, someone remarks in casual conversation, 'As a matter of fact I live in Oxford', the other party to the conversation may, if he finds it worth doing, verify this assertion; but the *speaker*, of course, has no need to do this—he knows it to be true (or, if he is lying, false). Strictly speaking, indeed, it is not just that he has no *need* to verify his statement; the case is rather that, since he already knows it to be true, nothing whatever that he might do could *count* as his 'verifying' it. Nor need it be true that he is in this position by virtue of having verified his assertion at some previous stage; for of how many people really, who know quite well where they live, could it be said that they have at any time *verified* that they live there? When could they be supposed to have done this? In what way? And why? What we have here, in fact, is an erroneous doctrine which is a kind of mirror-image of the erroneous doctrine about evidence we discussed just now; the idea that statements about 'material things' *as such* need to be verified is just as wrong as, and wrong in just the same way as, the idea that statements about 'material things' *as such* must be based on evidence. And both ideas go astray, at bottom, through the pervasive error of neglecting *the*

[6] He is, incidentally, also wrong, as many others have been, in holding that the 'notion of certainty' *does* apply to 'the *a priori* propositions of logic and mathematics' as such. Many propositions in logic and mathematics are not certain at all; and if many are, that is not just because they *are* propositions in logic and mathematics, but because, say, they have been particularly firmly established.

circumstances in which things are said—of supposing that *the words alone* can be discussed, in a quite general way.

But even if we agree to confine ourselves to situations in which statements can be, and do need to be, verified, the case still looks desperate. Why on earth should one think that such verification can't ever be conclusive? If, for instance, you tell me there's a telephone in the next room, and (feeling mistrustful) I decide to verify this, how could it be thought *impossible* for me to do this conclusively? I go into the next room, and certainly there's something there that looks exactly like a telephone. But is it a case perhaps of *trompe l'oeil* painting? I can soon settle that. Is it just a dummy perhaps, not really connected up and with no proper works? Well, I can take it to pieces a bit and find out, or actually use it for ringing somebody up—and perhaps get them to ring me up too, just to make sure. And of course, if I do all these things, I *do* make sure; what more could possibly be required? This object has already stood up to amply enough tests to establish that it really is a telephone; and it isn't just that, for everyday or practical or ordinary purposes, enough is *as good as* a telephone; what meets all these tests just *is* a telephone, no doubt about it.

However, as is only to be expected, Ayer has a reason for taking this extraordinary view. He holds, as a point of general doctrine, that, though in his view statements about 'material things' are never strictly equivalent to statements about sense-data, yet 'to say anything about a material thing is to say something, but not the same thing about classes of sense-data'; or, as he sometimes puts it, a statement about a 'material thing' *entails* 'some set of statements or other about sense-data'. But—and this is his difficulty—there is no *definite* and *finite* set of statements about sense-data entailed by any statement about a 'material thing'. Thus, however assiduously I check up on the sense-datum statements entailed by a statement about a 'material thing', I can never exclude the possibility that there are *other* sense-datum statements, which it also entails, but which, if checked, would turn out to be untrue. But of course, if a statement may be found to entail a false statement, then it itself may thereby be found to be false; and this is a possibility which, according to the doctrine, cannot in principle be finally eliminated. And since, again according to the doctrine, verification just consists in thus checking sense-datum statements, it follows that verification can *never* be conclusive.[7]

Of the many objectionable elements in this doctrine, in some ways the strangest is the use made of the notion of entailment. What does the sentence, 'That is a pig', *entail*? Well, perhaps there is somewhere, recorded by some zoological authority, a statement of the necessary and sufficient conditions for belonging to the species *pig*. And so perhaps, if we use the word 'pig' strictly in that sense, to say of an animal that it's a pig will entail that it satisfies those conditions, whatever they may be. But clearly it isn't this sort of entailment that Ayer has in mind; nor, for that matter, is it particularly relevant to the use that non-experts make of the word 'pig'.[8] But what other kind of entailment is there?

[7] Material things are put together like jig-saw puzzles; but since the number of pieces in a puzzle is not finite, we can never know that any puzzle is perfect, there may be pieces missing or pieces that won't fit.

[8] Anyway, the official definition won't cover *everything*—freaks, for instance. If I'm shown a five-legged pig at a fair, I can't get my money back on the plea that being a pig entails having only four legs.

We have a pretty rough idea what pigs look like, what they smell and sound like, and how they normally behave; and no doubt, if something didn't look at all right for a pig, behave as pigs do, or make pig-like noises and smells, we'd say that it wasn't a pig. But are there—do there *have* to be—*statements* of the form, 'It looks . . .', 'It sounds . . .', 'It smells . . .', of which we could say straight off that 'That is a pig' entails them? Plainly not. We learn the word 'pig', as we learn the vast majority of words for ordinary things, ostensively—by being told, in the presence of the animal, '*That* is a pig'; and thus, though certainly we learn what sort of thing it is to which the word 'pig' can and can't be properly applied, we don't go through any kind of intermediate stage of relating the word 'pig' to a lot of *statements* about the way things look, or sound, or smell. The word is just not introduced into our vocabulary in this way. Thus, though of course we come to have certain expectations as to what will and won't be the case when a pig is in the offing, it is wholly artificial to represent these expectations in the guise of *statements entailed by* 'That is a pig.' And for just this reason it is, at best, wholly artificial to speak as if *verifying* that some animal is a pig consists in checking up on the statements entailed by 'That is a pig.' If we do think of verification in this way, certainly difficulties abound; we don't know quite where to begin, how to go on, or where to stop. But what this shows is, not that 'That is a pig' is very difficult to verify or incapable of being conclusively verified, but that this is an impossible travesty of verification. If the procedure of verification were rightly described in this way, then indeed we couldn't say just what would constitute conclusive verification that some animal was a pig. But this doesn't show that there is actually any difficulty at all, usually, in verifying that an animal is a pig, if we have occasion to do so; it shows only that what verification *is* has been completely misrepresented.[9]

We may add to this the rather different but related point that, though certainly we have more or less definite views as to what objects of particular kinds will and won't do, and of how they will and won't re-act in one situation or another, it would again be grossly artificial to represent these in the guise of definite entailments. There are vast numbers of things which I take it for granted that a telephone won't do, and doubtless an infinite number of things which it never enters my head to consider the possibility that it might do; but surely it would be perfectly absurd to say that 'This is a telephone' *entails* the whole galaxy of statements to the effect that it doesn't and won't do these things, and to conclude that I haven't *really* established that anything is a telephone until, *per impossibile,* I have confirmed the whole infinite class of these supposed entailments. Does 'This is a telephone' *entail* 'You couldn't eat it'? Must I try to eat it, and fail, in the course of making sure that it's a telephone?[10]

[9] Another way of showing that 'entailment' is out of place in such contexts: Suppose that tits, all the tits we've ever come across, are bearded, so that we are happy to say 'Tits are bearded.' Does this *entail* that what isn't bearded isn't a tit? Not really. For if beardless specimens are discovered in some newly explored territory, well, of course we weren't talking about *them* when we said that tits were bearded; we now have to think again, and recognize perhaps this new species of glabrous tits. Similarly, what we say nowadays about tits just doesn't refer *at all* to the prehistoric co-tit, or to remote future tits, defeathered perhaps through some change of atmosphere.

[10] Philosophers, I think, have taken too little notice of the fact that most words in ordinary use are defined ostensively. For example, it has often been thought to be a puzzle why A *can't*

The conclusions we have reached so far, then, can be summed up as follows:

1. There is no *kind* or *class* of sentences ('propositions') of which it can be said that *as such*

(*a*) they are incorrigible;
(*b*) they provide the evidence for other sentences; and
(*c*) they must be checked in order that other sentences may be verified.

2. It is not true of sentences about 'material things' that *as such*

(*a*) they must be supported by or based on evidence;
(*b*) they stand in need of verification; and
(*c*) they cannot be conclusively verified.

Sentences in fact—as distinct from *statements made in particular circumstances*—cannot be divided up *at all* on these principles, into two groups or any other number of groups. And this means that the general doctrine about knowledge which I sketched at the beginning of this section, which is the real bugbear underlying doctrines of the kind we have been discussing, is *radically* and *in principle* misconceived. For even if we were to make the very risky and gratuitous assumption that what some particular person knows at some particular place and time could systematically be sorted out into an arrangement of foundations and super-structure, it would be a mistake in principle to suppose that the same thing could be done for knowledge *in general*. And this is because there *could* be no *general* answer to the questions what is evidence for what, what is certain, what is doubtful, what needs or does not need evidence, can or can't be verified. If the Theory of Knowledge consists in finding grounds for such an answer, there is no such thing.

---

be B, if being A doesn't *entail* being not-B. But it is often just that 'A' and 'B' are brought in as, ostensively defined as, words for *different things*. Why can't a Jack of Hearts be a Queen of Spades? Perhaps we need a new term, 'ostensively analytic'.

Norman Malcolm

Wittgenstein's Philosophical Investigations

Ein Buch ist ein Spiegel; wenn ein Affe hineinguckt, so kann freilich kein Apostel heraussehen.
LICHTENBERG

An attempt to summarize the *Investigations*[1] would be neither successful nor useful. Wittgenstein compressed his thoughts to the point where further compression is impossible. What is needed is that they should be unfolded and the connections between them traced out. A likely first reaction to the book will be to regard it as a puzzling collection of reflections that are sometimes individually brilliant, but possess no unity, present no system of ideas. In truth the unity is there, but it cannot be perceived without strenuous exertion. Within the scope of a review the connectedness can best be brought out, I think, by concentrating on some single topic—in spite of the fact that there are no separate topics, for each of the investigations in the book crisscrosses again and again with every other one. In the following I center my attention on Wittgenstein's treatment of the problem of how language is related to inner experiences—to sensations, feelings, and moods. This is one of the main inquiries of the book and perhaps the most difficult to understand. I am sufficiently aware of the fact that my presentation of this subject will certainly fail to portray the subtlety, elegance, and force of Wittgenstein's thinking and will probably, in addition, contain positive mistakes.

References to Part I will be by paragraph numbers, e.g., (207), and to Part II by page numbers, e.g., (p. 207). Quotations will be placed within double quotation marks.

PRIVATE LANGUAGE

Let us see something of how Wittgenstein attacks what he calls "the idea of a private language." By a "private" language is meant one that not merely is not but *cannot* be understood by anyone other than the speaker. The reason

[1] Ludwig Wittgenstein, *Philosophical Investigations;* German and English in facing pages. Tr. by G. E. M. Anscombe (New York: The Macmillan Company, 1953).

From Norman Malcolm, *Knowledge and Certainty*. © 1963, by permission of Prentice-Hall, Inc., Englewood Cliffs, N. J. This selection originally appeared in "Wittgenstein's *Philosophical Investigations*," *Philosophical Review*, Vol. 63 (1954).

Norman Malcolm (1911–) has for many years been Professor of Philosophy at the Sage School of Philosophy, Cornell University. While a student at Cambridge University, he worked with and was a close friend of Ludwig Wittgenstein; among his many publications is *Ludwig Wittgenstein: A Memoir* (1958).

for this is that the words of this language are supposed to "refer to what can only be known to the person speaking; to his immediate private sensations" (243). What is supposed is that I "*associate* words with sensations and use these names in description" (256). I fix my attention on a sensation and establish a connection between a word and the sensation (258).

It is worth mentioning that the conception that it is possible and even necessary for one to have a private language is not eccentric. Rather it is the view that comes most naturally to anyone who philosophizes on the subject of the relation of words to experiences. The idea of a private language is presupposed by every program of inferring or constructing the 'external world' and 'other minds.' It is contained in the philosophy of Descartes and in the theory of ideas of classical British empiricism, as well as in recent and contemporary phenomenalism and sense-datum theory. At bottom it is the idea that there is only a contingent and not an *essential* connection between a sensation and its outward expression—an idea that appeals to us all. Such thoughts as these are typical expressions of the idea of a private language: that I know only from my *own* case what the word 'pain' means (293, 295); that I can only *believe* that someone else is in pain, but I *know* it if I am (303); that another person cannot have *my* pains (253); that I can undertake to call *this* (pointing inward) 'pain' in the future (263); that when I say 'I am in pain' I am at any rate justified *before myself* (289).

In order to appreciate the depth and power of Wittgenstein's assault upon it you must partly be its captive. You must feel the strong grip of it. The passionate intensity of Wittgenstein's writing is due to the fact that he lets this idea take possession of him, drawing out of himself the thoughts and imagery by which it is expressed and defended—and then subjecting those thoughts and pictures to fiercest scrutiny. What is written down represents both a logical investigation and a great philosopher's struggle with his own thoughts. The logical investigation will be understood only by those who duplicate the struggle in themselves.

One consequence to be drawn from the view that I know only from my *own* case what, say, 'tickling' means is that "I know only what *I* call that, not what anyone else does" (347). I have not *learned* what 'tickling' means, I have only called something by that name. Perhaps others use the name differently. This is a regrettable difficulty; but, one may think, the word will still work for me as a name, provided that I apply it consistently to a certain sensation. But how about 'sensation'? Don't I know only from my *own* case what *that* word means? Perhaps what I call a 'sensation' others call by another name? It will not help, says Wittgenstein, to say that although it may be that what I have is not what others call a 'sensation,' at least I have *something*. For don't I know only from my own case what 'having something' is? Perhaps my use of *those* words is contrary to common use. In trying to explain how I gave 'tickling' its meaning, I discover that I do not have the right to use any of the relevant words of our common language. "So in the end when one is doing philosophy one gets to the point where one would like just to emit an inarticulate sound" (261).

Let us suppose that I did fix my attention on a pain as I pronounced the word 'pain' to myself. I think that thereby I established a connection between the word and the sensation. But I did not establish a connection if subsequently

I applied that word to sensations other than pain or to things other than sensations, e.g., emotions. My private definition was a success only if it led me to use the word correctly in the future. In the present case, 'correctly' would mean '*consistently* with my own definition'; for the question of whether my use agrees with that of others has been given up as a bad job. Now how is it to be decided whether I have used the word consistently? What will be the difference between my having used it consistently and its *seeming* to me that I have? Or has this distinction vanished? "Whatever is going to seem right to me is right. And that only means that here we can't talk about 'right' " (258). If the distinction between 'correct' and 'seems correct' has disappeared, then so has the concept *correct*. It follows that the 'rules' of my private language are only *impressions* of rules (259). My impression that I follow a rule does not confirm that I follow the rule, unless there can be something that will prove my impression correct. And the something cannot be another impression —for this would be "as if someone were to buy several copies of the morning paper to assure himself that what it said was true" (265). The proof that I am following a rule must appeal to something *independent* of my impression that I am. If in the nature of the case there cannot be such an appeal, then my private language does not have *rules,* for the concept of a rule requires that there be a difference between 'He is following a rule' and 'He is under the impression that he is following a rule'—just as the concept of understanding a word requires that there be a difference between 'He understands this word' and 'He thinks that he understands this word' (cf. 269).

'Even if I cannot prove and cannot know that I am correctly following the rules of my private language,' it might be said, 'still it *may* be that I am. It has *meaning* to say that I am. The supposition makes sense: you and I *understand* it.' Wittgenstein has a reply to this (348–353). We are inclined to think that we know what it means to say 'It is five o'clock on the sun' or 'This congenital deaf-mute talks to himself inwardly in a vocal language' or 'The stove is in pain.' These sentences produce pictures in our minds, and it *seems* to us that the pictures tell us how to *apply* them—that is, tell us what we have to look for, what we have to do, in order to determine whether what is pictured is the case. But we make a mistake in thinking that the picture contains in itself the instructions as to how we are to apply it. Think of the picture of blindness as a darkness in the soul or in the head of the blind man (424). There is nothing wrong with it *as a picture*. "But *what* is its application?" What shall count for or against its being said that this or that man is blind, that the picture applies to him? The *picture* doesn't say. If you think that you understand the sentence 'I follow the rule that *this* is to be called "pain" ' (a rule of your private language), what you have perhaps is a picture of yourself checking off various feelings of yours as either being *this* or not. The picture appears to solve the problem of how you determine whether you have done the 'checking' right. Actually it doesn't give you even a hint in that direction; no more than the picture of blindness provides so much as a hint of *how* it is to be determined that this or that man is blind (348–353, 422–426, p. 184).

One will be inclined to say here that one can simply *remember* this sensation and by remembering it will know that one is making a consistent application of its name. But will it also be possible to have a *false* memory impression? On the private-language hypothesis, what would *show* that your memory impression is false—or true? Another memory impression? Would this imply that memory is a court from which there is no appeal? But, as a matter of fact, that is *not* our concept of memory.

> Imagine that you were supposed to paint a particular color "C," which was the color that appeared when the chemical substances X and Y combined.—Suppose that the color struck you as brighter on one day than on another; would you not sometimes say: "I must be wrong, the color is certainly the same as yesterday"? This shows that we do not always resort to what memory tells us as the verdict of the highest court of appeal [56].

There is, indeed, such a thing as checking one memory against another, e.g., I check my recollection of the time of departure of a train by calling up a memory image of how a page of the time-table looked—but "this process has got to produce a memory which is actually *correct*. If the mental image of the time-table could not itself be *tested* for correctness, how could it confirm the correctness of the first memory?" (265)

If I have a language that is really private (i.e., it is a logical impossibility that anyone else should understand it or should have any basis for knowing whether I am using a particular name consistently), my assertion that my memory tells me so and so will be utterly empty. 'My memory' will not even mean—my memory *impression*. For by a memory impression we understand something that is either accurate or inaccurate; whereas there would not be, in the private language, any *conception* of what would establish a memory impression as correct, any conception of what 'correct' would mean here.

THE SAME

One wants to say, 'Surely there can't be a difficulty in knowing whether a feeling of mine is or isn't the *same* as the feeling I now have. I will call this feeling "pain" and will thereafter call the *same* thing "pain" whenever it occurs. What could be easier than to follow that rule?' To understand Wittgenstein's reply to this attractive proposal we must come closer to this treatment of rules and of what it is to follow a rule. (Here he forges a remarkably illuminating connection between the philosophy of psychology and the philosophy of mathematics.) Consider his example of the pupil who has been taught to write down a cardinal number series of the form '0, n, 2n, 3n . . .' at an order of the form '+n,' so that at the order '+1' he writes down the series of natural numbers (185). He has successfully done exercises and tests up to the number 1,000. We then ask him to continue the series '+2' beyond 1,000; and he writes 1,000, 1,004, 1,008, 1,012. We tell him that this is wrong. His instructive reply is, "But I went on in the same way" (185). There was nothing in the previous explanations, examples, and exercises that made it *impossible* for him to regard that as the continuation of the series. Repeating *those* examples and explanations won't help him. One must say to him, in effect, 'That isn't what we *call* going on in the *same* way.' It is a fact, and a fact of the kind whose importance Wittgenstein constantly stresses, that it is *natural* for human beings to continue the series in the manner 1,002, 1,004, 1,006, given the previous training. But that is merely what it is—a fact of human nature.

One is inclined to retort, 'Of course he can misunderstand the instruction and misunderstand the order "+2"; but if he *understands* it he must go on in the right way.' And here one has the idea that "The understanding itself is a state which is the *source* of the correct use" (146)—that the correct continuation of the series, the right application of the rule or formula, springs from one's understanding of the rule. But the question of whether one understands the rule cannot be divorced from the question of whether one will go on in that one particular way that we call 'right.' The correct use is a criterion of understanding. If you say that knowing the formula is a state of the mind and that making this and that application of the formula is merely a *manifestation* of the knowledge, then you are in a difficulty: for you are postulating a mental apparatus that explains the manifestations, and so you ought to have (but do not have) a knowledge of the construction of the apparatus, quite apart from what it does (149). You would like to think that your understanding of the formula determines in advance the steps to be taken, that when you understood or meant the formula in a certain way "your mind as it were flew ahead and took all the steps before you physically arrived at this or that one" (188). But how you meant it is not independent of how in fact you use it. "We say, for instance, to someone who uses a sign unknown to us: 'If by "$x!2$" you mean x^2, then you get *this* value for y, if you mean $2x$, *that* one.'—Now ask yourself: how does one *mean* the one thing or the other by '$x!2$'?" (190). The answer is that his putting down *this* value for y shows whether he meant the one thing and not the other: "*That* will be how meaning it can determine the steps in advance" (190). How he meant the formula determines his subsequent use of it, only in the sense that the latter is a criterion of how he meant it.

It is easy to suppose that when you have given a person the order 'Now do the *same* thing,' you have pointed out to him the way to go on. But consider the example of the man who obtains the series 1, 3, 5, 7 . . . by working out the formula $2x + 1$ and then asks himself, "Am I always doing the same thing, or something different every time?" (226). One answer is as good as the other; it doesn't matter which he says, so long as he continues in the right way. If we could not observe his work, his mere remark 'I am going on in the same way' would not tell us what he was doing. If a child writing down a row of 2's obtained '2, 2, 2' from the segment '2, 2' by adding '2' once, he might deny that he had gone on in the *same* way. He might declare that it would be doing the same thing only if he went from '2, 2' to '2, 2, 2, 2' in *one* jump, i.e., only if he *doubled* the original segment (just as it doubled the original single '2'). That could strike one as a *reasonable* use of 'same.' This connects up with Wittgenstein's remark: "If you have to have an intuition in order to develop the series 1 2 3 4 . . . you must also have one in order to develop the series 2 2 2 2 . . ." (214). One is inclined to say of the latter series, 'Why, all that is necessary is that you keep on doing the *same* thing.' But isn't this just as true of the other series? In both cases one has already *decided* what the correct continuation is, and one calls that continuation, and no other, 'doing the same thing.' As Wittgenstein says: "One might say to the person one was training: 'Look, I always do the same thing. I . . .'" (223). And then one proceeds to show him what 'the same' *is*. If the pupil does not acknowledge that what you have shown him is the *same*, and if he is not persuaded by your examples and explanations to carry on as you wish him to—then you have reached bedrock and will be inclined to say "This is simply what I do" (217). You cannot give him more reasons than you yourself have for proceeding in that way. Your reasons will soon give out. And then you will proceed, without reasons (211).

PRIVATE RULES

All of this argument strikes at the idea that there can be such a thing as my following a rule in my private language—such a thing as naming something of which only I can be aware, 'pain,' and then going on to call the same thing, 'pain,' whenever it occurs. There is a charm about the expression 'same' which makes one think that there cannot be any difficulty or any chance of going wrong in deciding whether *A* is the *same* as *B*—as if one did not have to be *shown* what the 'same' is. This may be, as Wittgenstein suggests, because we are inclined to suppose that we can take the identity of a thing *with itself* as "an infallible paradigm" of the *same* (215). But he destroys this notion with one blow: "Then are two things the same when they are what *one* thing is? And how am I to apply what the *one* thing shows me to the case of two things?" (215).

The point to be made here is that when one has given oneself the private rule 'I will call this same thing "pain" whenever it occurs,' one is then free to do anything or nothing. That 'rule' does not point in any direction. On the private-language hypothesis, no one can teach me what the correct use of 'same' is. I shall be the sole arbiter of whether this is the *same* as that. What I choose to call the 'same' will *be* the same. No restriction whatever will be imposed upon my application of the word. But a sound that I can use *as I please* is not a *word*.

How would you teach someone the meaning of 'same'? By example and practice: you might show him, for instance, collections of the same colors and same shapes and make him find and produce them and perhaps get him to carry on a certain ornamental pattern uniformly (208). Training him to form collections and produce patterns is teaching him what Wittgenstein calls "techniques." Whether he has mastered various techniques determines whether he understands 'same.' The exercise of a technique is what Wittgenstein calls a "practice." Whether your pupil has understood any of the rules that you taught him (e.g., the rule: this is the 'same' color as that) will be shown in his practice. But now there cannot be a 'private' practice, i.e., a practice that cannot be exhibited. For there would then be no distinction between believing that you have that practice and having it. 'Obeying a rule' is itself a practice. "And to *think* one is obeying a rule is not to obey a rule. Hence it is not possible to obey a rule 'privately'; otherwise thinking one was obeying a rule would be the same thing as obeying it" (202, cf. 380).

If I recognize that my mental image is the 'same' as one that I had previously, how am I to know that this public word 'same' describes what I recognize? "Only if I can express my recognition in some other way, and if it is possible for someone else to teach me that 'same' is the correct word here" (378). The notion of the private language doesn't admit of there being 'some other way.' It doesn't allow that my behavior and circumstances can be so related to my utterance of the word that another person, by noting my behavior and circumstances, can discover that my use of the word is correct or incorrect. Can I discover this for myself, and how do I do it? That discovery would presuppose that I have a conception of correct use which comes from outside my private language and against which I measure the latter. If this were admitted, the private language would lose its privacy and its point. So it isn't admitted. But now the notion of 'correct' use that will exist within the private language will be such that if I *believe* that my use is correct then it is correct; the rules will be only impressions of rules; my 'language' will not be a language, but merely the impression of a language. The most that can be said for it is that I *think* I understand it (cf. 269).

SENSATIONS OF OTHERS

The argument that I have been outlining has the form of *reductio ad absurdum:* postulate a 'private' language; then deduce that it is not *language.* Wittgenstein employs another argument that is an external, not an internal, attack upon private language. What is attacked is the assumption that once I know from my *own* case what pain, tickling, or consciousness is, then I can transfer the ideas of these things to objects outside myself (283). Wittgenstein says:

> If one has to imagine someone else's pain on the model of one's own, this is none too easy a thing to do: for I have to imagine pain which I *do not feel* on the model of the pain which I *do feel.* That is, what I have to do is not simply to make a transition in imagination from one place of pain to another. As, from pain in the hand to pain in the arm. For I am not to imagine that I feel pain in some region of his body. (Which would also be possible.) [302]

The argument that is here adumbrated is, I think, the following: If I were to learn what pain is from perceiving my own pain then I should, necessarily, have learned that pain is something that exists only when *I* feel pain. For the pain that serves as my paradigm of pain (i.e., my own) has the property of existing only when *I* feel it.[2] That property is essential, not accidental; it is nonsense to suppose that the pain I feel could exist when I did not feel it. So if I obtain my *conception* of pain from pain that I experience, then it will be part of my conception of pain that *I* am the only being that can experience

[2] [This is an error. Apparently I fell into the trap of assuming that if two people, A and B, are in pain, the pain that A feels must be *numerically* different from the pain that B feels. Far from making this assumption, Wittgenstein attacks it when he says: "In so far as it makes *sense* to say that my pain is the same as his, it is also possible for us both to have the same pain" (*op. cit.,* 253). There is not some sense of "same pain" (*numerically* the same) in which A and B *cannot* have the same pain. "Today I have that same backache that you had last week" is something we say. "Same" means here, answering the same description. We attach no meaning to the "question" of whether the backache you had and the one I have are or are not "numerically" the same.

A more correct account of Wittgenstein's point in sec. 302 is the following: A proponent of the privacy of sensations rejects circumstances and behavior as a criterion of the sensations of others, this being essential to his viewpoint. He does not need (and could not have) a criterion for the existence of pain that he feels. But surely he will need a criterion for the existence of pain that *he* does *not* feel. Yet he cannot have one and still hold to the privacy of sensation. If he sticks to the latter, he ought to admit that he has not the faintest idea of what would count for or against the occurrence of sensations that he does not feel. His conclusion should be, not that it is a contradiction, but that it is unintelligible to speak of the sensations of others. (There is a short exposition of Wittgenstein's attack on the idea that we learn what sensation is *from our own case,* in "Knowledge of Other Minds," reprinted below, pp. 637–44.)]

it. For me it will be a *contradiction* to speak of *another's* pain. This strict solipsism is the necessary outcome of the notion of private language. I take the phrase "this is none too easy" to be a sarcasm.

One is tempted at this point to appeal to the 'same' again: "But if I suppose that someone has a pain, then I am simply supposing that he has just the same as I have so often had" (350). I will quote Wittgenstein's brilliant counterstroke in full:

> That gets us no further. It is as if I were to say: "You surely know what 'It is 5 o'clock here' means; so you also know what 'It's 5 o'clock on the sun' means. It means simply that it is just the same time there as it is here when it is 5 o'clock."—The explanation by means of *identity* does not work here. For I know well enough that one can call 5 o'clock here and 5 o'clock there "the same time," but what I do not know is in what cases one is to speak of its being the same time here and there.
>
> In exactly the same way it is no explanation to say: the supposition that he has a pain is simply the supposition that he has the same as I. For *that* part of the grammar is quite clear to me: that is, that one will say that the stove has the same experience as I, *if* one says: it is in pain and I am in pain [350].

EXPRESSIONS OF SENSATION

Wittgenstein says that he destroys "houses of cards" ("Luftgebäude": 118) and that his aim is to show one how to pass from disguised to obvious nonsense (464). But this is not all he does or thinks he does. For he says that he changes one's *way of looking at things* (144). What is it that he wishes to substitute for that way of looking at things that is represented by the idea of private language? One would *like* to find a continuous exposition of his own thesis, instead of mere hints here and there. But this desire reflects a misunderstanding of Wittgenstein's philosophy. He rejects the assumption that he should put forward a *thesis* (128). "We may not advance any kind of theory" (109). A philosophical problem is a certain sort of confusion. It is like being lost; one can't see one's way (123). Familiar surroundings suddenly seem strange. We need to command a view of the country, to get our bearings. The country is well known to us, so we need only to be *reminded* of our whereabouts. "The work of the philosopher consists in assembling reminders for a particular purpose" (127). "The problems are solved, not by giving new information, but by arranging what we have always known" (109). When we describe (remind ourselves of) certain functionings of our language, what we do must have a definite bearing on some particular confusion, some "deep disquietude" (111), that ensnares us. Otherwise our work is irrelevant—to *philosophy*. It is philosophically pointless to formulate a general theory of language or to pile up descriptions for their own sake. "This description gets its light, that is to say its purpose—from the philosophical problems" (109). Thus we may not complain at the absence from the *Investigations* of elaborate theories and classifications.

Wittgenstein asks the question "How do words *refer* to sensations?" transforms it into the question "How does a human being learn the meaning of the names of sensations?" and gives this answer: "Words are connected with the primitive, the natural expressions of the sensation and used in their place.

A child has hurt himself and he cries; and then the adults talk to him and teach him exclamations and, later, sentences. They teach the child new pain-behavior" (244). Wittgenstein must be talking about how it is that a human being learns to refer with words to his *own* sensations—about how he learns to use 'I am in pain'; not about how he learns to use 'He is in pain.' What Wittgenstein is saying is indeed radically different from the notion that I learn what 'I am in pain' means by fixing my attention on a 'certain' sensation and calling it 'pain.' But is he saying that what I do instead is to fix my attention on my *expressions* of pain and call them 'pain'? Is he saying that the word 'pain' means crying? "On the contrary: the verbal expression of pain replaces crying and does not describe it" (244). My words for sensations are used *in place of* the behavior that is the natural expression of the sensations; they do not *refer* to it.

Wittgenstein does not expand this terse reminder. He repeats at least once that my words for sensations are "tied up with my natural expressions of sensation" (256) and frequently alludes to the importance of the connection between the language for sensations and the behavior which is the expression of sensation (e.g., 288, 271). The following questions and objections will arise:

(1) What shows that a child has made this 'tie up'? I take Wittgenstein to mean that the child's utterances of the word for a sensation must, in the beginning, be frequently concurrent with some nonverbal, natural expression of that sensation. This concomitance serves as the criterion of his understanding the word. Later on, the word can be uttered in the absence of primitive expressions. ('It hurts' can be said without cries or winces.)

(2) In what sense does the verbal expression 'replace' the nonverbal expression? In the sense, I think, that other persons will react to the child's mere words in the same way that they previously reacted to his nonverbal sensation-behavior; they will let the mere words serve as a *new* criterion of his feelings.

(3) I feel inclined to object: 'But has the child *learned* what the words *mean?* Hasn't he merely picked up the *use* of the word from his parents?' My objection probably arises from assimilating the learning of the meaning of words to the labeling of bottles—a tendency that is easily decried but not easily resisted: 'Learning *ought* to consist in attaching the right name to the right object,' I should like to say (cf. 26). The example of 'the beetle in the box' is pertinent here (see 293). The aim of this fantasy is to prove that attending to a private object can have nothing to do with learning words for sensations. Suppose you wanted to teach a child what a tickling feeling is. You tickle him in the ribs, and he laughs and jerks away. You say to him, 'That's what the feeling of tickling is.' Now imagine that he felt something that you can't know anything about. Will this be of any interest to you when you decide from his subsequent use of the word 'tickling' whether he understands it? Others understand the word too. If each one has something that only he can know about, then all the somethings may be different. The something could even be nothing! Whatever it is, it can have no part in determining whether the person who has it understands the word. "If we construe the grammar of the expression of sensation on the model of 'object and name' the object drops out of consideration as irrelevant" (293, cf. 304).

My previous objection could be put like this: the teaching and learning of names of sensations cannot stop at the mere expressions of sensation; the names must be brought *right up* to the sensations themselves, must be applied *directly* to the sensations! Here we can imagine Wittgenstein replying, "Like *what,* e.g.?" as he replies to an analogous objection in a different problem (191). In *what* sense is Wittgenstein denying that names are applied directly to sensations? Do I have a model of what it would be to apply the name 'directly'? No. I have this picture—that learning the meaning of 'pain' is applying the sign 'pain' to pain itself. I have that picture, to be sure, but what does it teach me, what is its "application"? When shall I say that what it pictures has taken place, i.e., that someone has learned the meaning of 'pain'? It doesn't tell me; it is *only* a picture. It cannot conflict with, cannot refute, Wittgenstein's reminder of what it is that determines whether a child has learned the word for a sensation.

(4) Wittgenstein says that the verbal expressions of sensation can take the place of the nonverbal expressions and that in learning the former one learns "new pain-behavior." This seems to mean that the words (and sentences) for sensations are related to sensations in the same way as are the primitive expressions of sensations. I am inclined to object again. I want to say that the words are used to *report* the occurrence of a sensation and to inform others of it. The natural expressions, on the contrary, are not used to inform others; they are not 'used' at all; they have no purpose, no function; they *escape* from one. But I have oversimplified the difference, because (a) a sentence can be forced from one, can escape one's lips ('My God, it hurts!'), and (b) a natural expression of sensation can be used to inform another, e.g., you moan to let the nurse know that your pain is increasing (you would have suppressed the moan if she hadn't entered the room), yet the moan is genuine. Perhaps my objection comes to this: I don't *learn* to moan; I do learn the words. But this is the very distinction that is made by saying that moaning is a "natural," a "primitive," expression of sensation.

It is a mistake to suppose that Wittgenstein is saying that the utterance 'My leg hurts' is *normally called* an 'expression of sensation.' (Of course it isn't. For that matter, only a facial expression, not a groan, is called an '*expression* of pain.' But this is of no importance.) He is not reporting ordinary usage, but drawing our attention to an *analogy* between the groan of pain and the utterance of those words. The important similarity that he is trying to bring to light (here I may misinterpret him) is that the verbal utterance and the natural pain-behavior are each (as I shall express it) 'incorrigible.' A man cannot be in *error* as to whether he is in pain; he cannot say, 'My leg hurts,' by mistake, any more than he can groan by mistake. It is senseless to suppose that he has wrongly identified a tickle as pain or that he falsely believes that it is in his leg when in fact it is in his shoulder. True, he may be undecided as to whether it is best described as an 'ache' or a 'pain' (one is often hard put to give satisfactory descriptions of one's feelings); but his very indecision *shows* us what his sensation is, i.e., something between an ache and a pain. His hesitant observation, 'I'm not sure whether it is a pain or an ache,' is itself an *expression* of sensation. What it expresses is an indefinite, an ambiguous sensation. The point about the incorrigibility of the utterance 'I'm in pain' lies behind Wittgenstein's reiterated remark that 'I *know* I'm in pain' and 'I don't know whether I'm in pain' are both senseless (e.g., 246, 408).[3] Wherever it is *meaningless* to speak of 'false belief,' it is also meaningless to speak of 'knowledge'; and wherever you cannot say 'I don't know . . .' you also cannot say 'I know. . . .' Of course, a philosopher can say of me that I *know* I am in pain. But 'What is it supposed to mean—except perhaps that I *am* in pain?" (246).

There are many 'psychological' sentences, other than sentences about sensations, that are incorrigible, e.g., the *truthful* report of a dream is a criterion for the occurrence of the dream and, unless some other criterion is introduced, "the question cannot arise" as to whether the dreamer's memory deceives him (pp. 222–223). If one who has a mental image were asked whom the image is of, "his answer would be decisive," just as it would be if he were asked whom the drawing represents that he has just made (p. 177). When you say, 'It will stop soon,' and are asked whether you *meant* your pain or the sound of the piano-tuning, your truthful answer is the answer (666–684).

When Wittgenstein says that learning the words for sensations is learning "new pain-behavior" and that the words "replace" the natural expressions, he is bringing to light the arresting fact that my sentences about my present sensations have the same logical status as my outcries and facial expressions. And thus we are helped to "make a radical break with the idea that language always functions in one way, always serves the same purpose: to convey thoughts—which may be about houses, pains, good and evil, or anything else you please" (304).

This is not to deny that first-person sentences about sensations may, in other respects, be more or less like natural expressions of sensation. Wittgenstein's examples of the use of 'I am afraid' (pp. 187–188) show how the utterance of that sentence can be a cry of fear, a comparison, an attempt to tell someone how I feel, a confession, a reflection on my state of mind, or something in between. "A cry is not a description. But there are transitions. And the words 'I am afraid' may approximate more, or less, to being a cry. They may come quite close to this and also be *far* removed from it" (p. 189). The words 'I am in pain' "may be a cry of complaint, and may be something else" (p. 189); and 'it makes me shiver' may be a "shuddering reaction" or may be said "as a piece of information" (p. 174). If we pursue these hints, it is not hard to construct a list of examples of the use of the words 'My head hurts,' in which the variety is as great as in Wittgenstein's list for 'I am afraid.' E.g., compare 'Oh hell, how my head hurts!' with 'If you want to know whether to accept the invitation for tonight then I must tell you that my head hurts again.' In one case the sentence 'My head hurts' belongs to an exclamation of pain, not in the other. In saying that in *both* cases it is an 'expression' of pain, Wittgenstein stretches ordinary language and in so doing illuminates the hidden continuity between the utterance of that sentence and—expressions of pain.

CRITERION

That the natural pain-behavior and the utterance 'It hurts' are each incorrigible is what makes it possible for each of them to be a criterion of pain.

[3] It is interesting to note that as long ago as 1930 Wittgenstein had remarked that it has no sense to speak of *verifying* 'I have a toothache.' (See G. E. Moore, "Wittgenstein's Lectures in 1930-33," *Mind,* LXIII [1954], 14.)

With some reluctance I will undertake to say a little bit about this notion of 'criterion,' a most difficult region in Wittgenstein's philosophy. Perhaps the best way to elucidate it is to bring out its connection with *teaching* and *learning* the use of words. "When I say the ABC to myself, what is the criterion of my doing the same as someone else who silently repeats it to himself? It might be found that the same thing took place in my larynx and in his. (And similarly when we both think of the same thing, wish the same, and so on.) But then did we learn the use of the words, 'to say such-and-such to oneself,' by someone's pointing to a process in the larynx or the brain?" (376). Of course we did not, and this means that a physiological process is not our 'criterion' that *A* said such-and-such to himself. Try to imagine, realistically and in detail, how you would teach someone the meaning of 'saying the ABC silently to oneself.' This, you may think, is merely psychology. But if you have succeeded in bringing to mind what it is that would show that he *grasped* your teaching, that he *understood* the use of the words, then you have elicited the 'criterion' for their use—and that is not psychology. Wittgenstein exhorts us, over and over, to bethink ourselves of how we learned to use this or that form of words or of how we should teach it to a child. The purpose of this is not to bring philosophy down to earth (which it does), but to bring into view those features of someone's circumstances and behavior that *settle* the question of whether the words (e.g., 'He is calculating in his head') rightly apply to him. Those features constitute the 'criterion' of calculating in one's head. It is logically possible that someone should have been born with a knowledge of the use of an expression or that it should have been produced in him by a drug; that his knowledge came about by way of the normal process of teaching is not necessary. What is necessary is that there should be something on the basis of which we *judge* whether he *has* that knowledge. To undertake to describe this may be called a 'logical' investigation, even though one should arrive at the description by reflecting on that logically inessential process of teaching and learning.

If someone says, e.g., 'I feel confident . . . ,' a question can arise as to whether he understands those words. Once you admit the untenability of 'private ostensive definition' you will see that there must be a *behavioral* manifestation of the feeling of confidence (579). There must be behavior against which his words, 'I feel confident . . . ,' can be checked, if it is to be possible to judge that he does or does not understand them. Even if you picture a feeling of confidence as an "inner process," still it requires "outward criteria" (580).

Wittgenstein contrasts 'criterion' with 'symptom,' employing both words technically. The falling barometer is a 'symptom' that it is raining; its looking like *that* outdoors (think how you would teach the word 'rain' to a child) is the 'criterion' of rain (354). A process in a man's brain or larynx might be a symptom that he has an image of red; the criterion is "what he says and does" (377, 376). What makes something into a symptom of *y* is that experience teaches that it is always or usually associated with *y*; that so-and-so is the criterion of *y* is a matter, not of experience, but of "definition" (354). The satisfaction of the criterion of *y* establishes the existence of *y* beyond question; it repeats the kind of case in which we were taught to say '*y*.' The occurrence of a symptom of *y* may also establish the existence of *y* 'beyond question'—but in a different sense. The observation of a brain process may make it certain that a man is in pain—but not in the same way that his pain behavior makes it certain. Even if physiology has established that a specific event in the brain accompanies bodily pain, still it *could* happen (it makes sense to suppose) that a man might be in pain without that brain event occurring. But if the criterion of being in pain is satisfied then he *must* be in pain. Sometimes, and especially in science, we *change* our criteria: "what today counts as an observed concomitant of a phenomenon will tomorrow be used to define it" (79).

The preceding remarks point up the following question: Do the propositions that describe the criterion of his being in pain *logically imply* the proposition 'He is in pain'? Wittgenstein's answer is clearly in the negative. Pain-behavior is a criterion of pain only in *certain circumstances*. If we come upon a man exhibiting violent pain-behavior, couldn't something show that he is not in pain? Of course. For example, he is rehearsing for a play; or he has been hypnotized and told, 'You will act as if you are in pain, although you won't be in pain,' and when he is released from the hypnotic state he has no recollection of having been in pain; or his pain-behavior suddenly ceases and he reports in apparent bewilderment that it was as if his body had been possessed—for his movements had been entirely involuntary, and during the 'seizure' he had felt no pain; or he has been narrowly missed by a car and as soon as a sum for damages has been pressed into his hand, his pain-behavior ceases and he laughs at the hoax; or . . . , etc. The expressions of pain are a criterion of pain in *certain* "surroundings," not in others (cf. 584).

Now one would like to think one can still formulate a logical implication by taking a description of his pain-behavior and conjoining it with the negation of every proposition describing one of those circumstances that would count against saying he is in pain. Surely, the conjunction will logically imply 'He is in pain'! But this assumes there is a *totality* of those circumstances such that if none of them were fulfilled, and he was also pain-behaving, then he *could not but* be in pain (cf. 183). There is no totality that can be exhaustively enumerated, as can the letters of the alphabet. It is quite impossible to list six or nine such circumstances and then to say 'That is all of them; no other circumstances can be imagined that would count against his being in pain.' The list of circumstances has no 'all,' in that sense; the list is, not infinite, but *indefinite*. Therefore, entailment-conditions cannot be formulated; there are none.

The above thought is hard to accept. It is not in line with our *ideal* of what language should be. It makes the 'rules' for the use of 'He is in pain,' too vague, too loose, not really *rules*. Wittgenstein has deep and difficult things to say about the nature of this 'ideal': "We want to say that there can't be any vagueness in logic. The idea now absorbs us, that the ideal *'must'* be found in reality. Meanwhile we do not as yet see *how* it occurs there, nor do we understand the nature of this 'must.' We think it must be in reality; for we think we already see it there" (101). "The strict and clear rules of the logical structure of propositions appear to us as something in the background—hidden in the medium of the understanding" (102). "The more narrowly we examine actual language, the sharper becomes the conflict between it and our requirement. (For the crystalline purity of logic was, of course, not a *result of investigation:* it was a requirement.)" (107) What we need to do is to remove from our noses the logical glasses through which we look at reality (103). We must study the phenomenon of language, as it is, without preconceived ideas. One thing this study will teach us is that the criteria for the use of third-person psychological statements are not related to the latter by an entailment-relation.

Wittgenstein suggests that propositions describing the fulfillment of behavioral criteria are related to third-person psychological statements in the way that propositions describing sense-impressions are related to physical-object statements (compare 486 and p. 180). It does not *follow* from the propositions describing my sense-impressions that there is a chair over there (486). The relation cannot be reduced to a *simple* formula (p. 180). *Why* doesn't it follow? Wittgenstein does not say, but the reason would appear to be of the same sort as in the example of 'He is in pain.' The propositions describing my sense-impressions would have to be conjoined with the proposition that I am not looking in a mirror, or at a painted scenery, or at a movie film, or . . . , etc. Here too there cannot be an exhaustive enumeration of the negative conditions that would have to be added to the description of sense-impressions *if* 'There's a chair over there' *were* to be logically implied.

The puzzling problem now presents itself: if it does not *follow* from his behavior and circumstances that he is in pain, then how can it ever be *certain* that he is in pain? "I can be as *certain* of someone else's sensations as of any fact," says Wittgenstein (p. 224). How can this be so, since there is not a definite set of six or eight conditions (each of which would nullify his pain-behavior) to be checked off as not fulfilled? It *looks* as if the conclusion ought to be that we cannot 'completely verify' that he is in pain. This conclusion is wrong, but it is not easy to see why. I comprehend Wittgenstein's thought here only dimly. He says:

> A doctor asks: "How is he feeling?" The nurse says: "He is groaning." A report on his behavior. But need there be any question for them whether the groaning is really genuine, is really the expression of anything? Might they not, for example, draw the conclusion "If he groans, we must give him more analgesic"—without suppressing a middle term? Isn't the point the service to which they put the description of behavior [p. 179]?

One hint that I take from this is that there can be situations of real life in which a question as to whether someone who groans is pretending, or rehearsing, or hypnotized, or . . . , simply does not exist. "Just try—in a real case—to doubt someone else's fear or pain" (303). A doubt, a question, would be rejected as absurd by anyone who knew the actual surroundings. 'But might there not be still further surroundings, unknown to you, that would change the whole aspect of the matter?' Well, we go only *so* far—and then we are certain. "Doubting has an end" (p. 180). Perhaps we can *imagine* a doubt; but we do not take it seriously (cf. 84). Just as it becomes certain to us that there is a chair over there, although we can imagine a *possible* ground of doubt. There is a concept of certainty in these language-games only because we stop short of what is conceivable.

"'But, if you are *certain,* isn't it that you are shutting your eyes in face of doubt?'—They are shut" (p. 224). This striking remark suggests that what we sometimes do is draw a boundary around *this* behavior in *these* circumstances and say, 'Any additional circumstances that might come to light will be irrelevant to whether this man is in pain.' Just as we draw a line and say, 'No further information will have any bearing on whether there is a chair in the corner—that is settled.' If your friend is struck down by a car and writhes with a broken leg, you do not think: Perhaps it was prearranged in order to alarm me; possibly his leg was anaesthetized just before the 'accident' and he isn't suffering at all. Someone *could* have such doubts whenever another person was ostensibly in pain. Similarly: "I can easily imagine someone always doubting before he opened his front door whether an abyss did not yawn behind it; and making sure about it before he went through the door (and he might on some occasion prove to be right)—but that does not make me doubt in the same case" (84).

The man who doubts the other's pain may be neurotic, may 'lack a sense of reality,' but his reasoning is perfectly sound. *If* his doubts are true then the injured man is *not* in pain. His reaction is abnormal but not illogical. The certainty that the injured man is in pain (the normal reaction) ignores the endless doubts that *could* be proposed and investigated.

And it is important to see that the abnormal reaction *must* be the exception and not the rule. For if someone *always* had endless doubts about the genuineness of expressions of pain, it would mean that he was not using *any criterion* of another's being in pain. It would mean that he did not accept anything as an *expression* of pain. So what could it mean to say that he even had the *concept* of another's being in pain? It is senseless to suppose that he has this concept and yet always doubts.

THIRD-PERSON SENSATION-SENTENCES

Wittgenstein assimilates first-person, not third-person, sensation-sentences to *expressions* of sensation. I will say one or two things more about his conception of the use of third-person sensation-sentences.

(1) "Only of a living human being and what resembles (behaves like) a living human being can one say: it has sensations; it sees; is blind; hears; is deaf; is conscious or unconscious" (281). The *human* body and *human* behavior are the *paradigm* to which third-person attributions of consciousness, sensations, feelings, are related. (The use of first-person sensation-sentences is governed by *no* paradigm.) Thus there cannot occur in ordinary life a question as to whether other human beings ever possess consciousness, and I can have this question when I philosophize only if I forget that I use that paradigm in ordinary life. It is by analogy with the human form and behavior that I attribute consciousness (or unconsciousness) to animals and fish, the more remote the analogy the less sense in the attribution. (Just as it is by analogy with our ordinary language that anything is called 'language') (494). In order to imagine that a pot or a chair has thoughts or sensations one must give it, in imagination, something like a human body, face, and speech (282, 361). A child says that its doll has stomach-ache, but this is a "secondary" use of the concept of pain. "Imagine a case in which people ascribed pain *only* to inanimate things; pitied *only* dolls" (282, cf. 385, p. 216)! Wittgenstein means,

I think, that this is an impossible supposition because we should not want to say that those people *understood* ascriptions of pain. If they did not ever show pity for human beings or animals or expect it for themselves, then their treatment of dolls would not be *pity*.

(2) My criterion of another's being in pain is, first, his behavior and circumstances and, second, his words (after they have been found to be connected in the right way with his behavior and circumstances). Does it follow that my interest is in his behavior and words, not in his pain? Does 'He is in pain' *mean* behavior? In lectures Wittgenstein imagined a tribe of people who had the idea that their slaves had no feelings, no souls—that they were automatons—despite the fact that the slaves had human bodies, behaved like their masters, and even spoke the same language. Wittgenstein undertook to try to give sense to that idea. When a slave injured himself or fell ill or complained of pains, his master would try to heal him. The master would let him rest when he was fatigued, feed him when he was hungry and thirsty, and so on. Furthermore, the masters would apply to the slaves our usual distinctions between genuine complaints and malingering. So what could it mean to say that they had the idea that the slaves were automatons? Well, they would *look* at the slaves in a peculiar way. They would observe and comment on their movements *as if* they were machines. ('Notice how smoothly his limbs move.') They would discard them when they were worn and useless, like machines. If a slave received a mortal injury and twisted and screamed in agony, no master would avert his gaze in horror or prevent his children from observing the scene, any more than he would if the ceiling fell on a printing press. Here is a difference in 'attitude' that is not a matter of believing or expecting different facts.

So in the *Investigations,* Wittgenstein says, "My attitude towards him is an attitude towards a soul. I am not of the *opinion* that he has a soul" (p. 178). I do not *believe* that the man is suffering who writhes before me—for to what facts would a 'belief' be related, such that a change in the facts would lead me to alter it? I *react* to his suffering. I look at him with compassion and try to comfort him. If I complain of headache to someone and he says 'It's not so bad,' does this prove that he believes in something *behind* my outward expression of pain? "His attitude is a proof of his attitude. Imagine not merely the words 'I am in pain' but also the answer 'It's not so bad' replaced by instinctive noises and gestures" (310). The thought that behind someone's pain-behavior is the pain itself does not enter into our use of 'He's in pain,' but what does enter into it is our sympathetic, or unsympathetic, reaction to him. The fact that the latter does enter into our use of that sentence (but might not have) gives sense to saying that the sentence 'He is in pain' does not just *mean* that his behavior, words, and circumstances are such and such—although these are the criterion for its use.

When he groans we do not *assume,* even tacitly, that the groaning expresses pain. We fetch a sedative and try to put him at ease. A totally different way of reacting to his groans would be to make exact records of their volume and frequency—and do nothing to relieve the sufferer! But our reaction of seeking to comfort him does not involve a presupposition, for, "Doesn't a presupposition imply a doubt? And doubt may be entirely lacking" (p. 180).

FORM OF LIFE

The gestures, facial expressions, words, and activities that constitute pitying and comforting a person or a dog are, I think, a good example of what Wittgenstein means by a "form of life." One could hardly place too much stress on the importance of this latter notion in Wittgenstein's thought. It is intimately related to the notion "language-game." His choice of the latter term is meant to "bring into prominence the fact that the *speaking* of language is part of an activity, or of a form of life" (23; cf. 19). If we want to understand any concept we must obtain a view of the human behavior, the activities, the natural expressions, that surround the words for that concept. What, for example, is the concept of *certainty* as applied to *predictions?* The nature of my certainty that fire will burn me comes out in the fact that "Nothing could induce me to put my hand into a flame" (472). That reaction of mine to fire shows the *meaning* of certainty in this language-game (474). (Of course, it is *different* from the concept of certainty in, e.g., mathematics. "The kind of certainty is the kind of language-game" [p. 124].) But is my certainty justified? Don't I need reasons? Well, I don't normally think of reasons, I can't produce much in the way of reasons, and I don't feel a need of reasons (cf. 477). Whatever was offered in the way of reasons would not strengthen my fear of fire, and if the reasons turned out to be weak I still wouldn't be induced to put my hand on the hot stove.

As far as 'justification' is concerned, "What people accept as a justification—is shown by how they think and live" (325). If we want to elucidate the concept of justification we must take note of what people *accept* as justified; and it is clearly shown in our lives that we accept as justified both the certainty that fire will burn and the certainty that this man is in pain—even without reasons. Forms of life, embodied in language-games, teach us what justification is. As philosophers we must not attempt to justify the forms of life, to give reasons for *them*—to argue, for example, that we pity the injured man because we believe, assume, presuppose, or know that in addition to the groans and writhing, there is pain. The fact is, we pity him! "What has to be accepted, the given, is—so one could say—*forms of life*" (p. 226). What we should say is: *"This language-game is played"* (654).

From this major theme of Wittgenstein's thought one passes easily to another major theme—that "Philosophy simply puts everything before us, and neither explains nor deduces anything" (126). "It leaves everything as it is" (124).

Anthony M. Quinton

The Problem of Perception

The problem of perception is to give an account of the relationship of sense-experience to material objects. This relationship has traditionally been seen as logical, a matter of showing how beliefs about objects can be established or supported by what we know in immediate experience. For, it is held, only our knowledge of experience is direct, immediate, by acquaintance; what we know or claim to know about objects is indirect, derivative, by inference from what we know directly. Consequently if our beliefs about objects are to have any secure foundation, it must consist in what we know directly, by acquaintance, about sense-data. From this starting-point philosophers have gone on to present varying accounts of the type of inference involved. An extreme view is Hume's, that the passage from experiences to objects rests on 'a kind of fallacy or illusion'. Lockean causal theories assert that the connexion between experiences and objects is contingent and that knowledge of experience is good inductive evidence for beliefs, logically distinct from it about objects. The species of inference involved is transcendental hypothesis of the type to be found in scientific arguments for the existence of such unobservables as electrons or chromosomes. For phenomenalism the connexion between experiences and objects is necessary, to speak of objects is to speak in an abbreviated way about certain pervasive kinds of regularity in experience. The species of inference involved is simple inductive extrapolation. There are not two worlds, an inner and an outer, but two terminologies. The terminology of objects is used to refer to what is invariant as between the private worlds of experience.

Each view derives strength from the weaknesses of its opponent. The most emphasised weakness of phenomenalism is that, if it were true, unobserved objects would be mere possibilities and actual effects would have to arise from merely potential causes. Mill's view that objects are permanent possibilities of sensation is confronted by a fundamental and unargued incredulity. A more serious difficulty arises about the antecedents of the hypothetical statements which describe the permanent possibilities in question. For these antecedents mention objects. To assume, as phenomenalists often cheerfully do, that these references can be replaced by references to 'orienting experiences' is to beg the very question at issue. One cannot *assume* that statements about experiences are equivalent in meaning to statements about objects in order to *show* that they are. Against the causal theory it is argued that, given the sense-datum theory, it would be impossible ever to know that the

---

From A. M. Quinton, "The Problem of Perception," *Mind,* Vol. 44 (1955). Reprinted by permission of the author and of the editor of *Mind.*

For many years, A. M. Quinton (1926–) has been Fellow of New College, Oxford, and Lecturer in Philosophy at Oxford University.

logically distinct, unobservable, transcendental causes existed. For a causal inference is only legitimate if it is at least possible to obtain evidence for the existence of the cause which is independent of the events it is held to explain.

In the face of this impasse sense-datum theorists have tended to adopt a middle position of compromise. Causal theorists liken their procedure to the 'model-building' of natural scientists. The external world is a theoretical construction, fruitful and various in its predictive and explanatory consequences. Phenomenalists modify their thesis of the strict logical equivalence of statements about experiences and about objects, in view of the difficulties, in principle and practice, of translating one into the other. Both extremes are abandoned in favour of the view that it is a simple, convenient and fruitful theoretical construction. But this is rather a method of refusing to face the difficulties than of overcoming them. For what sort of theoretical construction is involved, a substantial model of the not-yet-observed like a theory of atomic structure or a mere *façon de parler* like theories of magnetic and gravitational fields?

My purpose in this paper is to overcome these difficulties by a more radical procedure, that of refuting the premise from which both problematic doctrines derive, that we are never directly aware of or acquainted with objects.

My principal target will be the conception of direct awareness or acquaintance itself. The sense-datum theory holds that corresponding to the two kinds of objects of knowledge are two kinds of knowledge—direct and indirect. Thus while no knowledge of material objects is direct, all or only knowledge of experience is direct. In more linguistic terms, while no statements about objects are basic, all or only statements about experience are basic. A piece of knowledge, then, is direct if, and only if, it can be expressed by a basic statement. But this translation is of little help since neither of the crucial terms, 'direct' and 'basic', is clearly intelligible, let alone more intelligible than the other.

Two main kinds of definition are commonly offered of these expressions, one in terms of certainty, the other in terms of inference. By the former I directly know that *p* (or '*p*' is a basic statement) if I know for certain that *p*. It is held that beliefs about objects are never certain, beliefs about experience are always certain and that for any uncertain belief to be even probable something else must be certain. Consequently all beliefs about objects that are to any extent probable must be logically derived from beliefs about experience. I shall hold that all three of the premises for this conclusion are false. The incorrigibility of statements about experience has been defended, notably by Ayer, on the ground that the only mistakes to which we are liable in making such statements are 'verbal'. I shall attempt to show that this too is false. Sometimes a definition in terms of inference is preferred. I directly know that *p* (or '*p*' is a basic statement) if I know that *p* without inference. It is not, of course, maintained that in coming to form a belief about an object I undertake any conscious process of reasoning. What is involved is 'implicit' inference. Nevertheless, it is held, reasons exist for beliefs about objects which it is the philosopher's business to render explicit and without reference to which no justification of these beliefs can be provided. I shall argue that there is no relevant sense of 'reason' in which a reason for them always exists.

Why should this have been thought to be so? The sense-datum theory, seemingly a variant of the empiricist principle that all our knowledge of matters of fact is based on sense-experience, tends to assume that principle's authority. But this, like other oracles, owes much of its reputation to ambiguity. It can be taken to assert three different things, two of which are uncontentious while the third deserves close inspection. First, it is an unexciting truth of physiology that sensations, physical stimulations of the sense-organs, are causally necessary conditions of our knowledge of matters of fact. Second, the establishment of any truth about objects logically requires that someone shall have seen, touched or otherwise perceived something. The chains of inference and testimony cannot hang unsupported but must terminate in observation. In this use 'sense-experience' does not mean anything so definite as 'sense-datum', it has no phenomenological flavour. Seeing a tomato is just as much an observation as seeing a round, red, shiny patch. Finally, 'based on sense-experience' can be taken to mean 'logically derived from sense-experience'. The logical derivation in question here is of statements about objects from statements about experiences. It is this third interpretation of the principle that constitutes the sense-datum theory and which I shall attempt to refute.

These definitions of 'direct' and 'basic' in terms of certainty and inference are not, however, the starting-points of sense-datum theories of perception. They are rather conclusions to the argument from illusion in terms of which the expressions 'direct' and 'basic' are normally introduced. This argument holds that objects are not always what they appear to be and that there need be no discoverable difference between two situations in one of which an object is and in the other is not what it appears to be. In consequence, all that we really know is what appears to be the case, since, even when what appears to be the case *is* the case, we cannot there and then tell whether it is or not. Since we know only what appears to be the case, the only things we really perceive are appearances. Some philosophers have protested weakly against the later stages of this argument. I hope to substantiate and fortify their protest.

The mistake lies in the identification of what appears to be the case with our sense-experience. We always know what appears to be the case. So it is appearances, not objects, that we really perceive. But what else are these appearances but our current sense-fields, our sense-experience? The three forms of words: 'this appears to be ϕ', 'there is a ϕ appearance', 'there is a ϕ sense-datum', are held to be equivalent in meaning. I shall argue that a statement of what appears to be the case is rarely a description of our sense-experience and is normally a modified, guarded claim about what *is* the case, expressing an inclination to believe something about objects. The ostensible firmness and incorrigibility of these assertions is a consequence, not of their referring to a class of private, given entities, but rather of the modesty of the claim they make. So what the argument from illusion establishes is not that we always infallibly know what our sense-experience is like, but only that, whether or not we *know* what is the case, we can always say, without much fear of contradiction, what we are inclined to *believe* is the case. These statements do not, then, express a special kind of direct knowledge by acquaintance nor are they premises from which statements about objects could be inferred. For they are not claims to knowledge at all, but more or less tentative expressions of belief, and what is tentatively affirmed is precisely the same as, and thus cannot be a premise for, what, in the conclusion of the supposed inference, we claim to know without hesitation. I shall argue, however, that we can, and rather infrequently do, describe our experience and that we can do this in statements containing such expressions as 'look', 'appear' and 'seem'.

The consequences of this distinction of 'appearances' from sense-data are that knowledge about experience is much less common than is widely supposed and that the greater part of our 'knowledge of appearances' is not capable of figuring as premises in inferences to beliefs about objects.

Before embarking on this another familiar argument for the sense-datum theory must be considered: what may be called the argument from scientific knowledge. There is conclusive evidence for the fact that many of our sense-experiences occur appreciably later than the events of which they give us knowledge, in particular the experiences caused by what is astronomically visible or less remotely audible. More generally, every sense-experience is at the end of a temporally extended causal chain whose first member is the supposedly perceived occurrence. Consequently, what we directly perceive, the object of acquaintance, cannot be the same as that about which we claim knowledge. But this involves no new issue of principle. It shows objects and experiences to be temporally distinct where the argument from illusion shows them to be much more generally different in character. It only shows that we do not directly perceive objects if the supposed consequence of the argument from illusion—that we perceive only our sense-experience directly—is already accepted.

The view common to all versions of the sense-datum theory that the perception of objects is really a kind of inference seems to arise from a belief that, while perception proper must be infallible, inference need not be, and thus that all mistakes are fallacies. But both perception and inference are learnt, intelligent activities which we can presumably perform with varying degrees of efficiency and success. That perception is an acquired skill has perhaps been an inducement to regard it as inference to those who suppose all intelligent activities to be species of reasoning.

Ultimately the problem of perception is that of the relation of thought or language to the world. There is a distressing correspondence with primitive cosmology. Some statements are supported by others, but what supports these others, what is tortoise to their elephant? For the whole system of knowledge cannot support itself in mid-air; it is not self-contained. There is a dilemma here. Either the ultimate support is logically related to the body of knowledge and is thus automatically brought inside the body of knowledge, since only statements can stand in logical relations, and, if so, the question of dependence on the extralinguistic world breaks out again. Or it is not and there is no answer in terms of correct inference to the request for a justification of reliance on this ultimate support.

Philosophers have sought to evade this dilemma by recourse to the Janus-faced notion of experience. The fact that we cannot, it seems, have an experience without somehow being conscious or aware of it has seemed to provide foundation-stones for the edifice of knowledge which are at once statements, capable of standing in logical relations to the rest of the structure, and parts, perhaps the sole constituents, of the extralinguistic world, self-describing entities. I shall contend that there are no such things and opt for the second horn of the dilemma which, as I hope to show, is a less painful resting-place than it might seem.

II

Our first problem is to evaluate the argument from illusion. From the unexceptionable premises that things are not always what they appear to be and that we cannot always tell, there and then, whether they are or not, it is concluded that we have direct knowledge only of appearances, never of objects. For there need be no immediately discoverable difference between two appearances of which one is in fact 'veridical' and the other 'delusive'. So what we really perceive are appearances, whether they are veridical or not depends on something that lies outside the perceptual situation. But what are these appearances that we perceive? They are, it is said, sense-data, the given, immediate experience, they are the current states of our sense-fields.

Of some uses of 'appear', 'seem', etc. it is clearly untrue to say that they figure in descriptions of experience. 'They appear to be away', said when the twice-rung doorbell of a house with drawn curtains remains unanswered, means much the same as 'they must be away' or 'they are probably away'. We are not here describing, but drawing conclusions from, what we observe. The word 'appear' serves to indicate that these conclusions are drawn with less than full confidence. There is nothing 'basic' about them.

But there is another use of 'appear' in which no reason can be given for statements containing it and which do report observations. 'It appears to be green' we might say of a distant house. If challenged we can only repeat, or perhaps correct, ourselves or protest, 'well, that is how it appears to me'. But such a statement would normally be made in answer to such questions as 'what colour is that house' and could be replaced by 'it's green, I think' or 'it's green, isn't it?' They report observations in a tentative way where we know, believe or suspect that the circumstances are unfavourable to an accurate report, that there is something wrong with or abnormal about the conditions of observation. They resemble ordinary categorical descriptions, 'that house is green', in subject-matter, but differ from them in expressing inclinations to believe rather than full beliefs.

There is a third use of 'appear', which resembles the one last mentioned, in that no reasons or evidence can be given for statements containing it, but differs from it in that certain conventional conditions of observation are supposed to obtain, whether they do or not. 'It looks to me (here, now) elliptical' we say of a plate we know to be tilted and round, supposing it to be at right angles to our line of vision. This statement answers the question 'how does it strike you, look to you, what exactly do you see?' It is replaceable by 'there is an elliptical patch in the centre of my visual field'. It is in this type of case only that the description of appearances and experience coincide.

Consider that old friend the stick half in, half out, of water. One might say of it (*a*) 'it is straight', (*b*) 'it looks bent but is really straight', (*c*) 'it looks bent', (*d*) 'it is bent'. Statement (*a*) is true, (*b*) describes the stick correctly and points out how one might be led to make a mistake about it if unaware of an abnormality (a refracting medium) in the conditions of observation, (*c*) gives tentative expression to the inclination mistakenly to believe (*d*) which is straightforwardly false. 'It looks bent' is the puzzling case. For it may be a guarded way of saying 'it is bent' (denied by 'it isn't bent') or a way of saying 'most people would be inclined to say it was bent' (denied by 'it doesn't') or a way of saying 'it looks bent to me, here, now' (which can only be denied by 'oh surely not').

So, even when not used to give tentative conclusions from evidence, the verb 'appear' and its cognates are seldom used to describe experience, but primarily to give tentative descriptions of objects. In other words, the 'appearances' that survive the argument from illusion as the proper objects of acquaintance are not ordinarily sense-experiences. These seemingly rock-bottom matters of fact are, in a way, incorrigible and, *ex hypothesi,* uninferred. But their incorrigibility is imperfect and spurious. Imperfect because both 'this is ϕ, I think' and 'this is ϕ, most people would say' can be contradicted (by 'it isn't' and 'they wouldn't') and revised accordingly. Spurious because it arises, not from their making a definite claim about something private, but from their making a weak, indefinite claim about something public. And, though uninferred, they cannot play the part of premises in inferences to categorical descriptions of objects. 'This appears to be ϕ' is no more evidence or a reason for 'this is ϕ' than are 'this may be ϕ' or 'this is probably ϕ'. All three are simply modified ways of saying 'this is ϕ', appropriate for one who is inclined, but not inclined quite confidently enough, to make the categorical statement itself.

This is not to deny that we can and do describe our experience. All I have tried to show is that we describe it very much less often than is usually supposed. Being unsure about the circumstances is a common enough occurrence. But the description of experience proper is a sophisticated procedure and one seldom called for. It is an essential accomplishment for painters, broadcasting engineers, doctors of the eye and ear, cooks and experimental psychologists. But unless we fall into their hands there is little need for us to become proficient in it. The sophistication arises with the deliberate supposition that conditions obtain which we have no reason to suppose do so in fact and perhaps every reason to suppose do not. The fact that we have laboriously to learn perspective drawing is an indication of this, as is the notorious unreliability of eye-witnesses.

That we seldom do describe our experience and then usually with difficulty does not entail that we could not set up and become proficient in the use of a private language. But it would involve a remarkable change in our attitude to the world. Normally we observe in a context of beliefs about where we are and what we are doing that the sophisticated naiveté of phenomenology would exclude. To attend to one's experience involves a radical shift in attitude, a determined effort to resist the solicitations of that submerged constellation of beliefs within which our perceptual discoveries are made.

To this extent, then, I am in sympathy with those who have argued that if the stick half in water looks bent then something really *is* bent. When I say the stick looks bent, I should discover, if I were to direct my attention to it, that my visual field contained a bent brown line. Whether it follows from this that I am in some way aware of this feature of my visual field is a question that will be answered later. But there is something to be said against this line of argument which is commonly ignored. No doubt when the stick looks bent, something else is bent. But consider these cases. I see a small glassy object in a radio shop and say 'that looks like a [tube]'. But in fact it is a wineglass. For this error there is no sensory cue; it is the outcome of my general beliefs about the contents of radio shops. Again, I see what is in fact half a pair of spectacles beside a box which I mistakenly suppose to be obscuring the rest. Even when I know better, it still looks just like a pair to me but it is unlikely that my visual field contains anything corresponding to the second lens.

I have been at pains to emphasise the uncommon and sophisticated nature of the description of experience because of the supposed consequence of the argument from illusion, that in every perceptual situation, even if no object is in fact perceived or if objects are misperceived, still something is perceived, our sense-experience. It would seem *prima facie* that one cannot be said to perceive something unless one is in a position to describe it. But I am not in a position to describe my experience unless I am in the appropriate, sophisticated, phenomenological frame of mind.

Normally if someone says mistakenly that he sees something we are not inclined to say that he really saw something else. We should say of Macbeth that he thought he saw the dagger, imagined he could see it, was under the impression he could see it, but that he did not actually see it at all. In cases of illusion, as against hallucination, there will be something that really is perceived, but it will be a perfectly ordinary public object, not a private experience. If I take a piece of mud on the doormat to be a letter, it will be said that what I actually saw was a piece of mud.

In general, it is not the case, when I am mistaken about what I claim to perceive, either that I am in a position to describe my experience or that I would be said really to have perceived my experience. There are reasons, nevertheless, which have led philosophers to believe that I am aware of my experience, acquainted with it, in such circumstances.

It is not only when in the hands of those professionally concerned with it that we attend to and describe our experience. We are sometimes forced to do so by total ignorance of the conditions of observation. Waking up in unfamiliar circumstances we may, if no other assumption seems inviting, suppose that the conventional phenomenological conditions obtain. In exceptional circumstances of this kind, as we come round from an anaesthetic for example, a description of our visual experience is a possible answer to the question 'can you see anything?' But it is worth noticing that in such cases we can also say, with even better warrant perhaps, 'no, just a lot of yellow streaks' instead of 'yes, a lot of yellow streaks'. Only in a very marginal sense is a description of one's visual experience to be called 'seeing' at all.

In a way, then, we can be said sometimes to 'see' our visual experience: when we are trying to describe it or when we are not in a position to describe anything else. But what of the case of a man lying in the sun on his back with his eyes open and his mind far away? Does he see the blue expanse with shifting white patches on it that he could describe if he were to turn his attention to his visual field? And what of the man who is carefully watching a hen to discover where the gap in the hen-run is? Does he see the green expanse of the downs beyond, that he would in fact find occupying the greater part of his visual field if he were to attend to it? Compare these cases with a less problematic kind of seeing. Suppose you show me round your garden and afterwards ask me 'did you see the tulip tree?' If I say 'no', you may say 'you must have done, it's right beside the summer-house I showed you'. If I still deny seeing it, even after another look to refresh my memory, then I cannot have seen it. Yet one might be inclined here to think that I must have seen it all the same. There it was, ten yards away, in broad daylight, right in the middle of my field of vision. But perhaps I was concentrating on the summer-house or thinking of something else altogether. One's visual field is in much the same case as the tulip tree in this example. However far one's attention may have strayed, it seems, nevertheless, that one is inescapably *confronted* by it. So philosophers have said that whenever we think we see anything we really do see the contents of our visual fields. But this is an extremely hypothetical kind of seeing. All we can say is that if I had been in a different frame of mind I should have noticed the tree; I should have been able to describe the contents of my visual field.

In every perceptual situation, then, we know what appears to be the case, but this is not usually to be in a position to describe our experience. It may be true that we can be said to have sense-experiences in every perceptual situation (they are, no doubt, the *causes* of our inclinations to believe) but this is quite another matter from being aware of them, noticing them, being in a position to describe them, and nothing less than this can be involved in the claim of the sense-datum theory that it is our experience which we really perceive.

But can having experiences and being aware of them be clearly distinguished in this way? For having an experience is a mental event of the kind, it would be argued, the only direct evidence for whose existence is its presence in consciousness. One might distinguish two senses of 'awareness'. In the wider sense I am aware of any mental event that I am in any way conscious of. In the narrower sense I am only aware of what I notice or attend to, of what I am in a position to describe, of what, in fact, I have some statable knowledge of. Now it might be argued that one was aware of all experience in the wider sense and that this was sufficient reason for saying that all experience was really perceived. I do not think that this distinction can be maintained. It is not that we are really aware of a great many things which we do not notice or attend to but rather that we suppose ourselves to have a great deal of experience for whose existence we have little or no direct evidence. For ordinarily 'be aware of' and 'notice' are largely interchangeable. Both imply claims to knowledge. There are differences of nuance: to become aware of a smell of decay is to have it borne in upon one, to notice a smell of decay is to have discovered it. In implying claims to knowledge both words resemble the perceptual verbs 'see', 'hear', etc. One cannot be aware *of* something without knowing something about it, being aware *that* something is the case.

Now we are, perhaps, usually vaguely aware of the character of our experience, but far too indefinitely for the knowledge involved to support the complicated structure of beliefs that the sense-datum theory would erect on it. The faint and undetailed nature of this underlying awareness of experience is attested to by the fact that when asked to recall our experience we have more or less to reconstruct it from the objects perceived. We attend to experience often enough to know the sort of experiences normally associated with various kinds of object in various conditions. When we transfer our attention from objects to experience an enormously richer awareness of the latter is obtained. We then suppose that we were in fact having experiences of as complex and detailed a kind while attending to the objects, although we were unaware of the complexity and detail. This move is not inference supported by recollection, but a convention. It is assumed that, given unchanged objects, medium, and sense-organs, a change of attention brings about no change in the associated experiences. The idealist's problem 'does attention alter its object'? is thus a matter of convention not of fact. The convention described here lays down that it does not. By this a distinction is introduced between experiences which we have and which we are aware of. It gives a sense to the expression 'unnoticed experience'. One could equally well, if not better, opt for the other alternative and speak, not of 'unnoticed', but of 'possible' experiences, that is the experiences one would be aware of were one to adopt the phenomenological frame of mind. There is a close analogy with the problem of unsensed sense-data. Should we speak with Russell of 'sensibilia' or with Ayer of 'possible sense-data'? In each case considerations of continuity urge one convention, conceptual economy and epistemological rigour the other. In our problem continuity makes a stronger claim. For while there is a clear distinction between sensed and unsensed sense-data, there would seem to be an unbroken continuum of grades of awareness. At any rate to have an experience of which one is not aware is not so much an event as the possibility of an event, it is to be able, by appropriately directing one's attention, to become aware of an experience. The nature of these possibilities is discovered inductively. I conclude that, whether we decide to say we have experiences of which we are not aware or merely that we could have them, anything we can say about them or their possibility depends on the limited number we are aware of. It is only these, meagre or absent in most perceptual situations, which we can be said to perceive.

III

I have argued that experience cannot be the sole object of acquaintance since it is not the case that in every perceptual situation we are aware of it. If this argument is accepted it can be reinforced—if not replaced—by considering what is *meant* by saying that experience alone is the object of acquaintance. I shall first consider the view that this is so because only of experience can we have certain knowledge.

That statements about objects can never be certain (an elliptical way of saying that we can never know for certain that they are true) is sometimes affirmed on the ground that they are empirical. For it is an essential feature of empirical statements that they can be shown to be false and, it is argued, if a statement can be false there can be reasonable doubt of its truth. But if there can be reasonable doubt of its truth it cannot be certain. This argument has the notorious consequence that only necessary truths can be certain. This is not, as some have argued, merely inconvenient in assimilating one useful distinction to another, it is the outcome of a definite mistake. For it is not correct to say that a statement is certain only if there *can* be no reasonable doubt of its truth; a statement is certain, rather, if there *is* no reasonable doubt of its truth.

This familiar argument, in trying to prove that no empirical statement is certain, tries to prove too much. For, if it were correct, the supposed difference in epistemological status between objects and experiences could not consist in a difference in respect of certainty between the statements describing them. I shall consider two arguments designed to show that, in fact, there is always reasonable doubt about descriptions of objects. Both assert that descriptions of objects have implications which inevitably 'go beyond' or 'lie outside' the current observation.

The first holds that there is no limit to the set of other statements which follow from a given statement about objects. For at any time, however remote from the time to which the original statement refers, evidence will exist and could be obtained for or against it. If at any time there is no evidence, however tenuous, for or against it, it is then untestable and, therefore, without meaning. At any rate the possibility of evidence arising for any statement, however remote its reference, cannot be ruled out. So, it is argued, however much favourable evidence for the truth of a statement may have accumulated, it is always possible that all the evidence to come may point to and, in the end, enforce the opposite conclusion.

If, as I shall argue later, it is also the case that descriptions of experience can be revised, that there can be evidence for and against them distinct from the occurrence of the experience itself, then precisely the same argument can be applied to them and so no difference in epistemological status is established. In effect this argument comes to the same as the previous one; revision in the face of unfavourable evidence is as much a universal feature of empirical statements as falsifiability.

But, waiving this point for the moment, the argument is fallacious in concluding that statements with 'open consequences' are never certain. For if the statement of unfavourable evidence q is remote, in the way described, from the original statement p, then q alone will not entail the falsity of p but only in conjunction with some generalization or law of nature r. So q will only falsify or disconfirm p to the extent that r is accepted as true and applicable. It is not p and q simply that are incompatible but *p, q and r*. If q turns out to be true we are not therefore compelled to abandon p. The more remote q is from p, the more tenuous the connexion, the more we shall be inclined to abandon r. This critical point between abandoning p and abandoning r in face of q may be hard to locate, but for every statement it will exist and for every statement circumstances can be indicated in which its 'logical neighbourhood' is so densely populated with favourable evidence that no remote unfavourable evidence whatever would be taken as refuting it. So it does not follow from the fact that the set of a statement's consequences is open that there is always reasonable doubt of its truth.

The second argument about implications asserts that statements about objects are always and necessarily predictive, that they always logically imply something which the current observation is not sufficient to establish. A statement about objects always forms part of a system of beliefs of varying size, at least including assumptions about the normality—or controllable abnormality—of the conditions of observation. But this has no disastrous consequences. In the first place, no infinite regress is generated. The entailed consequences (or assumptions about the conditions of observation) are themselves statements about objects, but *their* entailed consequences (or conditions) will not all be distinct from the original statement. The implications do not fray off endlessly into the unknown, they are, rather, elements in finite, and indeed decently small, systems of mutual support. And in the second place, arising out of this, it is wrong to regard statements about objects as necessarily predictive under all circumstances. For it is perfectly possible to establish all the members of such a set of mutually supporting statements. Knowledge of the conditions of observation constitutes just such a framework which a statement about objects completes, supports and is supported by. I am not here going back on my earlier criticism of the coherence theory. These coherent sets of statements are not self-sufficient. For their members are conventionally correlated with observed situations. Loose talk about semantic or ostensive rules has ignored the indeterminacy of this correlation, the existence of slack in the application of statements about objects which the systems in which they figure take up.

In the normal course of events it is not that the entailed consequences or conditions are yet to be discovered but that they are known already. This 'systematic' character of our knowledge of objects does indeed distinguish it from our knowledge of experience, consistently with what has gone before since it is the logical correlate of the perceptual as against the phenomenological frame of mind. In the extreme, limiting case (waking up, etc.), where we have no knowledge of the conditions, all descriptions of objects are likely to be less than certain. But we are not usually in this unfortunate position and single observations can give us certain knowledge about objects.

Even if statements about objects were never certain this would not prove them to be derived from statements about experience, if being less than certain were not identified with being probable and if it were not held that nothing can be probable unless something else is certain.

The crucial error in these interconnected doctrines is the supposition that certainty and probability are exhaustive as well as mutually exclusive. Any assertion made with full confidence may be called certain but only one kind of assertion made with less than full confidence is called probable. 'It appears to be cloudy over there' is perfectly good, if weak, evidence for 'it will probably rain'. Yet the whole point of saying that it appears to be, rather than that it is, cloudy over there is to indicate lack of confidence, uncertainty. That is, a less than certain conclusion can be based on less than certain premises which are not themselves the result of inference. The word 'probably' qualifies assertions which are both tentatively advanced, held to be less than certain, and are the conclusions of inferences. This latter characteristic allows us always to challenge, to ask for the reasons for, a statement that something is probably the case and warrants the view that probability is always relative to evidence. But this evidence may itself be tentative and less than certain. To express just this 'uninferred' hesitancy is, as was shown earlier, the principal office of the words 'look', 'appear' and 'seem'. But can we describe experience in this way? The sole use we have for forms of words where these verbs are reiterated (it seems to look ϕ) is where neither verb is used to describe experience (I am inclined to think that most people would say it was ϕ). But this does not entail that phenomenological uses of these verbs cannot be tentative, that 'this looks to me, here, now, ϕ' must be certain. To modify these we use adverbial devices like 'roughly', 'more or less', 'sort of' or add the rider 'I think'. We avoid 'appear' and its kin because they suggest assignable reservations, that we realise or suspect something to be amiss with the conditions of observation or, in non-perceptual uses ('he appears to have died about 300 B.C.'), that we realise that better evidence could, in principle, be obtained. But there are no better conditions in which to describe our experiences than those in which they occur, no better evidence than that they occur. The corrigibility of a statement, in other words, does not entail that 'appear' and the rest apply to it; they apply only where assignable reservations are indicated.

Less than certain statements are not all probable; they are so only if they are the conclusions of inferences, and the premises of these inferences may be less than certain without themselves being inferred. They will be what appears to be the case if I can assign the reservations from which my tentativeness arises or what is, I think, roughly the case, if I cannot.

Finally we must consider a familiar argument against the view that all descriptions of experience are certain. A statement of fact must be expressed by a sentence containing a predicate, a general or descriptive word, and must, therefore, involve the classification of what it refers to, the discrimination of this from other things to which the predicate does not apply. Things, including experiences, do not confront us already sorted out, classified, discriminated. And like any other learnt, regular procedure classification can be carried out wrongly. The use of predicates in classifying and discriminating is essentially a matter of relating what we are describing to the things which are the standard for the application of the predicate, with which it is conventionally correlated, by which it is 'ostensively defined'.

For we can and do revise our descriptions of experience, however convinced we were of their correctness at the time we made them. Such revision could only be excluded by the presumption that recollected experiences, formerly described as ϕ, and now recalled as noticeably different from something else we want to call ϕ, must always be misrecollected. But our recollections have a credibility of their own which does not depend on what is recollected matching something which we now describe with the same predicate we applied to it. Not only can we revise past descriptions of experience, we can also be hesitant about present descriptions. Sometimes we can find no precedent for a perfectly distinct and definite but unique impression; sometimes, while inclined to give a certain description, there is some peculiarity in the situation which we cannot precisely identify and which makes us hesitate. There is a range of cases between these extremes of inadequate vocabulary and indistinct experience.

Against this view it is argued that the errors corrected by such a revision are merely *verbal*. 'All that one can properly mean . . . by saying that one doubts whether this (sense-datum) is green is that one is doubting whether "green" is the correct word to use.' (Ayer). But what else is one doubting when one doubts whether this *object* is green? There is a difference, of course, in that one can have another, better, look at the object but not at the sense-datum. But it does not follow from this that all mistakes that do not depend on unfavourable conditions of observation are not really mistakes at all. What, after all, is a 'merely verbal' error? Properly speaking, only mistaken expressions of belief due to slips of the tongue or pen or laziness and inattention. Linguistic incapacity, the source of mistaken descriptions of experience, is quite another matter. Professor Ayer has recently argued that experience is described 'not by relating it to anything else but by indicating that a certain word applies to it in virtue of a meaning-rule of the language'. The suggestion is that the application of meaning-rules is such a simple matter that it is impossible to perform it wrongly except by a slip. But meaning-rules do not have the bemusing simplicity of their 'semantic' formulation (the word 'red' applies to red things). The class of things to which a predicate applies is indeterminately bounded. Some blue things are more obviously blue than others. Again we are not equally and perfectly accomplished in the application of all predicates. We can manage 'red' and 'round' fairly well, but are less efficient with 'mauve' and 'rhomboidal'. Even if we were trained up to the highest pitch of descriptive efficiency with the predicates we do understand, it is wrong to imagine that that notoriously blunt instrument, our descriptive vocabulary, would provide a precisely appropriate caption for every situation, that it could deal exhaustively with the fecundity of experience. Behind this theory of semantic rules lurks a pair of metaphysical assumptions: that universals, in one-one correlation with predicates, are wide open to some kind of direct apprehension and that there is a decent limit to their variety. The implied analogy with the rules by means of which the truths of mathematics and logic are established is misleading. These rules are precise, definite and can be clearly stated and communicated; careful tests can be made of whether they have been employed correctly. No such laborious check of the correct employment of 'meaning-rules' is possible with the private, fluid and unstable constituents of our sense-experience.

Lack of clarity about the relation between the mere occurrence of an experience and its description has contributed to the view that we cannot, without lying or slips, misdescribe experience. Experience just happens. But being what it is we cannot help being aware of it. Yet it occurs in every perceptual situation. This confusion of the phenomenologically scrutinised with the more or less hypothetical unnoticed experience is responsible for the view that simply to have an experience is to know it for what it is. Those who have, consistently enough, denied that experience as such is properly speaking either a kind of knowledge or true or false at all, have avoided the confusion at the cost of abolishing their problem. For from mere events nothing can be logically derived; only from statements, from what can be known to be true, can other statements be inferred.

I conclude that statements about objects and about experience are sometimes certain, sometimes not. In this respect there is no sharp distinction between the two. Whether a description of objects is certain will depend largely on the circumstances in which it is given and what is known about them. Its familiarity and stability will no doubt determine whether a description of experience is certain. We can err about both from linguistic incapacity and the loose correlation of language and the world, about objects on account of unfavourable conditions of observation and about experiences (and occasionally objects) on account of their evanescence. Such difference as there is between the respective sources of error is not sufficient to substantiate a theory of acquaintance or to show one category to be logically prior to the other.

IV

Some philosophers, realising that certainty as a criterion of acquaintance or basic statements is not sufficient to distinguish objects and experience in the way the sense-datum theory requires, have proposed a different definition in terms of inference. On this view we know directly, by acquaintance, what we know without inference; basic statements are primitive, uninferred; and, while no descriptions of experience are inferred, all descriptions of objects are. The task of theory of knowledge, it is held, is to make a rational reconstruction of our knowledge of matters of fact in which the uninferred premises from which alone this knowledge can be validly derived are explicitly set out. It is agreed that we are rarely, if ever, conscious of carrying out these inferences. It is thought, nevertheless, that experiential premises must somehow 'underlie' what we believe about objects.

If this account is correct two conditions must be satisfied. Statements about experience must count as reasons or evidence for statements about objects and they must in some, no doubt rather obscure, sense be accepted by those who make statements about objects. This second, seemingly platitudinous, requirement deserves emphasis. A fact cannot be a man's reason or evidence for an assertion unless, however implicitly, he is aware of it. Someone's implicit or unconscious awareness of facts about objects can be established by observation of his behaviour. But there is no such criterion available for detecting his awareness of his experience. The view, mistaken as I have argued, that we cannot help being aware of our experience no doubt explains why it has not been thought necessary to provide any criterion for the occurrence of this supposed awareness. If my argument against the view that in every perceptual situation we are aware of our own experience is accepted, it follows that the second condition of the inference theory is unsatisfied and that the theory is mistaken. For our experiences could only be our reasons or evidence for our beliefs about objects if we were to become aware of them through adopting a completely different, phenomenological, frame of mind in our traffic with the external world. Like any other facts, facts about experience must be discovered before they can be appealed to. But even if my argument on this is not accepted, the inference theory is mistaken since the first condition mentioned is not satisfied either.

The best proof that statements about experience were reasons or evidence for statements about objects would be that we did in fact commonly infer from the one to the other. This, however, is admittedly not the case. But, as it stands, this is of little importance. In the first place, the psychological criterion involved is exceedingly vague, seeming to do no more than mark off as cases of inference those in which a thoughtful pause supervenes between observation and announcement. Furthermore, there are many cases, unquestionably of knowledge by inference, where it is not in the least likely that any conscious process of reasoning has taken place. A girl, sitting in the drawing-room, hears the front door slam and says 'Father's home'. I hear a pattering on the roof and say 'it's raining'. I see a small pool on the kitchen floor and say 'the dog has misbehaved'. We only infer consciously in situations that are unfamiliar or complex, in the predicament of the weekend guest or the new boy on the first day of term. The detective, the busybody, the scientist are more or less professionally concerned to make the most of a small stock of data. Conscious, deliberate thinking is both exhausting and infrequent, a last resort to be appealed to only when all habitual capacities have failed. But most of our perceptual knowledge is of familiar states of affairs and acquired in familiar conditions.

That a statement is employed as a premise in a conscious process of reasoning is not the only feature of our use of that statement which shows it to count as a reason or evidence for the conclusion. More fundamental surely, is that we *give* it as our reason when challenged on the other.

Consider these five cases. I can at once reproduce the course of reasoning that led me to say that it is Mother's hat on top of the garage. This is conscious inference, where the reason given is a premise already consciously affirmed. Secondly, I can, without hesitation, answer 'by the way he sways about' when asked how I can tell someone is drunk, although I recollect no process of inferring. Thirdly, I may take some time over or require assistance in accounting for my claim that Towzer is ill by the glazed look in his eye. Fourthly, I may be unable to give any reason of my own and unwilling to accept any reason offered by another for my assertion that X dislikes Y. Yet commonly in this type of case I may be sure a reason does exist for my belief, may be extremely confident of the truth of my belief and turn out, in the end, to be quite right. Finally, consider standing in broad daylight three feet away from a large and perfectly normal chestnut cart-horse and saying 'that is a horse' or, more adventurously, 'that horse is brown'. This resembles the previous case in that one would be quite unable to give or accept any reason whatever for one's assertion. It differs from it in that one would not be in the very least abashed or apologetic about this. For, in these conditions, the challenge 'how can you tell?' is simply devoid of sense.

Still, if it were made, one might perhaps answer 'well, because it looks like a horse'. If this were intended as a description of one's experience, as interchangeable with 'there is now a shiny brown patch of a characteristic shape in the centre of my visual field', it would not be to answer the question but rather to change the subject, perhaps to offer a causal explanation of one's belief. But this interpretation proposed by the sense-datum theory, a wildly unnatural interpretation of what is, in the circumstances, a wildly unnatural remark, is surely mistaken. The statement would more naturally be intended and understood as a modification of, an infusion of tentativeness into, the original claim, expressing a lack of confidence inspired by the nagging question. As such it is not a reason. To repeat oneself in a more cautious way is not to substantiate but merely to attenuate one's original assertion. 'It looks like a horse' resembles 'it is probably a horse' or 'I think it's a horse' and not 'it has thick legs and no horns' which might be advanced to support the claim that some comparatively distant animal was a horse. For there are, of course, plenty of situations in which reasons do exist for statements about objects.

A statement cannot be inferred, then, if no reason or evidence for it exists, or, more exactly, if it does not make sense to ask for or give a reason for it. Whether or not it does make sense to ask for a reason depends on the circumstances in which the statement is made. The sentence, the form of words, 'that is a horse', may be used in an enormous variety of circumstances. In some of these it will make sense to ask 'how can you tell', in others not. The latter may be called the standard conditions of its use. It will be in such circumstances that the use of the sentence will normally be learnt. This accomplished, it will be possible to use it in an increasingly adventurous way in increasingly non-standard conditions. Connexions are established between assertions and their reasons through the discovery of a vast array of factual concomitances. That standard conditions are those in which we learn how to use a sentence helps to explain why the statements they are used to make are basic and uninferred. For in these conditions, they are directly correlated with an observable situation, they are not introduced by means of other statements. (This explains 'implicit inference'. I implicitly infer, acknowledge a reason for, a statement if I was introduced to it by means of other statements but can now make it without conscious consideration of them.) For some sentences there are no standard conditions (generalizations or such implicitly general sentences as 'she is naturally shy'). With others the nature of their standard conditions may vary from person to person. A wife will be able to tell at once that her husband is depressed where others have no inkling of the fact. (A difference in capacity that leads us to speak of intuition.) Again prolonged success in a certain nonstandard use of a sentence may lead us to incorporate the conditions of this use into the standard. I say 'it is raining' when I cannot actually see the rain falling but only drops of water bouncing off the wet street. The addition of unwillingness to inability to answer the question 'how can you tell?' shows that these conditions have become standard. Standard conditions are those in which we have a right to feel certain of the truth of an assertion. The suggestion of uncertainty conveyed by the protest 'that's only an inference' would be made more obviously by the equivalent protest 'you are in no position to be sure' (*i.e.* 'these are not standard conditions'.) The lawyer, who asks for a description of what one *actually* saw, devoid of inference and conjecture, is asking for a standard description, that is, a description for which the conditions one was then in were standard.

The notions of acquaintance and of the basic statements which it warrants have, therefore, a foundation in our ordinary way of thinking and speaking. The failure to locate them in their right place is due in part to the failure to distinguish between sentences and statements. For because of multiplicity of uses there are no 'basic sentences'. What we know for certain and without inference in any situation is what the circumstances we are in are the standard conditions for. This will normally be a statement about objects. But there are circumstances in which, knowing nothing about the conditions or that they are highly abnormal, we can take no description of objects as standard. In such a situation we can do no more than tentatively say what appears to be the case. If we are not prepared to do this we can, by an appropriate shift of attention, describe our experience. This last-ditch feature of statements about experience is another encouragement to the sense-datum theorist.

More important is the fact that standard conditions are not a perfect guarantee of the truth of a statement made in them. For standard conditions do not involve that all of a statement's entailed consequences have been established. The horse in the example may just possibly be a brilliantly contrived deception, a flat painted board. We could make our standard stringent enough to cater for this, by insisting on the establishment of entailed consequences, without abandoning statements about objects as basic. But it would be laborious and inconvenient to do so. The programme of convenience embodied in our actual standards is abetted by the order of nature which is uniform enough to make the risks of standard description negligible. Our standards depend on contingencies but some contingencies are highly reliable and regular. Error, as Descartes pointed out, is a product of the will rather than the understanding and arises almost entirely with nonstandard descriptions.

This minute residual imperfection is the ultimate source of the sense-datum theory. The metaphysical demand behind the theory is for an infallible basis for knowledge. So a new standard is proposed which is thought to be perfect. The justification of the new standard is that the knowledge of conditions required is always available, conditions are always standard for the description of experience. I have argued that we are not, in fact, always in standard conditions for the description of experience but rather that it is always in our power, by an appropriate shift of attention, to produce such conditions. If this is so, the sense-datum theory can be no more than the proposal of a new and exceedingly cumbrous way of thinking and speaking to be adopted from fear of a very minor risk. But whether it is true or not, whether the sense-datum theory is a proposal or, what it claims to be, an account of what actually occurs, the supposed improvement is illusory. For, in taking steps to set one exaggerated doubt at rest, it provides the opportunity for another to arise. Admittedly descriptions of experience, for which conditions are always standard, do not depend on a knowledge of conditions which may not be forthcoming. But they have weaknesses of their own. The objects we describe are largely stable and persistent; if we are unsure about them we can always look again. But experience is fleeting and momentary; to attend to it again is to make the insecure hypothesis that it has not changed. The systematic, mutually corroborative character of our beliefs about objects is not a weakness but a strength. Similarly the atomic, disconnected character of experiences, which has encouraged the view that they are self-describing entities, is a weakness. I conclude, then, that experiences are not only not in fact the basis of our empirical knowledge but that they would be inferior to the basis we have, since we are just as much open to error about them, though not entirely the same way; and we should have to revise our way of thinking and speaking completely to use them as a basis.

The relation between experiences and objects, then, neither is nor should be logical. On the contrary it is causal, a matter of psychological fact. Our beliefs about objects are based on experience in a way that requires not justification but explanation. Experiences are not *my* reasons for my beliefs about objects—to have an experience is not to know or believe anything which could be a reason in this sense—though they may be *the* reasons for my believing what I do from the point of view of the psychologist. They may, that is, be the causes of my beliefs and explain them. But they could only be my reasons for my beliefs about objects if I already knew something independently about the relations between experiences and objects.

We learn, it is said, to interpret our experiences, to give rein to Hume's principle of the imagination, to apply Kant's schematized category of substance. These forms of words at least point out that perception is an intelligent activity (not an infallible reflex), but they point it out so uncompromisingly that it is over-intellectualised. Interpreting experiences suggests literary scholarship or detective work. But not all intellectual processes are types of reasoning. These phrases refer to the psychological preconditions of recognizing objects for what they are. They point out that we must learn to use the language we do use, that this is an exercise of skill not an automatism and, further, that the situations in which any one sentence may be correctly uttered are extremely various. But they do not demand and could not evoke any logical justification of our practice of thinking and speaking of a common world of objects. We cannot set out the logical relation of an assertion about objects with the experiences that occasion it, because there is no such relation. This is not to sever language from the world altogether, the sin of the coherence theory. It is simply to say that the relations that obtain within the body of our knowledge do not also connect it with what is outside.

I have considered the three principal methods of establishing the sense-datum theory: the arguments from illusion, certainty and inference. Those who hold statements about experience to be basic have misconstrued all three. Statements about experience are not known in every perceptual situation, for we cannot know what we are not aware of, they are no more certain than statements about objects and they do not differ from all statements about objects in being uninferred. Doctrines about acquaintance and basic statements are the outcome of a search for perfect standard conditions. But no standard conditions are perfect and there is no reason to say that descriptions of experience are or ought to be our standard. Our empirical knowledge already has a basis and as good a one as we can obtain. It is to be found, as we should expect, in those situations in which the use of our language is taught and learnt.

Paul Henle

On the Certainty of Empirical Statements

In a recent issue of [*The Journal of Philosophy*], Professor W. T. Stace has argued that empirical statements are theoretically capable of the same sort of certainty as *a priori*.[1] There is much in his discussion which strikes me as wholly admirable—he holds that doubts about the principle of induction are not a proper basis for holding that empirical statements are merely probable; he shows that there is a sense in which both *a priori* and empirical statements are doubtful. So far, I believe, no sensible critic would disagree with him. His final conclusion, however, I can not accept, and for reasons which I believe Professor Stace himself would find congenial. Since the whole problem of

[1] "Are All Empirical Statements Merely Hypotheses?" [*The Journal of Philosophy*], Vol. XLIV (1947), pp. 29–39.

From Paul Henle, "On the Certainty of Empirical Statements," *The Journal of Philosophy,* Vol. 44 (1947). Reprinted by permission of Mrs. Paul Henle and of the editors of *The Journal of Philosophy.*

For most of his life, Paul Henle (1908–62) was Professor of Philosophy at the University of Michigan, although he was for a brief time at Northwestern University.

the certainty of empirical propositions is basic in contemporary theory of knowledge, it seems worth while to go into enough detail at least to sketch a theory of the matter.

It may be helpful in the first place to distinguish two grounds or sources of uncertainty. The first may be illustrated in the case of adding a column of figures. Granted the rules of addition and the usual conventions of symbolism, it is an *a priori* statement that the sum of 962, 435, and 851 is 2248; yet, having performed the addition, I may be uncertain of the result. The ground of this uncertainty may lie in the possibility of misapplying familiar rules, of treating, for example, a "5" as if it were a "6." Or, again, the mistake may be an error of memory, of forgetting what figure was being "carried" from one column to the next. Mistakes of this sort are not, of course, confined to arithmetic. In the heat of discussion I may mis-speak myself, choosing the wrong word to convey the sense I intend and may, in fact, say just the opposite of what I wish to.

A similar phenomenon, though it involves other factors as well, is found in the claim of many philosophers that their critics misunderstand them. Such misunderstanding is sometimes willful, and at other times is due to obscurity, but there seem to be some cases, at least, in which the philosopher, intent on making certain points, has magnified their place in his system, thereby giving a warped account of his position as a whole. Such a philosopher, re-reading his work in a perspective of years, might, if he were candid, admit that he had not said what he had intended. Warned by such examples, and assuming a standard sense of language, anyone might have doubts as to the correctness of his conclusions.

Here, then, we have a ground for uncertainty which, in the broadest sense of the term, might be called *linguistic*. It is characteristic of linguistic uncertainties that they are removed by performing over again the operations in which they are suspected. If I have doubts as to the correctness of an addition, I add again and repeat the addition until I get consistent results. If I doubt that I have said what I mean, I express my thought again and continue until I come to consistently equivalent statements. It is of course true that this procedure is not infallible. I may add a column half a dozen times and reach the same wrong result each time. Also, I fear, some of my ideas will never be expressed as they should be. This is a ground for claiming that all statements are infected with linguistic uncertainty, a sort of uncertainty no more characteristic of empirical judgments than of *a priori*. This point is made by Professor Stace and I concur wholeheartedly. If there is any basis for claiming that empirical judgments are merely probable in a sense that *a priori* judgments are certain, it must be that they involve a different ground of uncertainty. We turn to this.

Perhaps the commonest ground for uncertainty is insufficiency of evidence. It is for this reason that I am uncertain of the order in which the Platonic dialogues were written, or whether the Russians know how to make an atomic bomb, or countless other matters. Uncertainties of this sort are too well known to call for discussion, and may be referred to as *evidential* uncertainties. If evidential uncertainties are to be eliminated in any field, two conditions must be fulfilled: (1) there must be a maximum, or limit of evidence, beyond which added evidence can contribute nothing; and (2) that limit must be attained. If evidence can go on piling up without limit, always contributing something more towards certainty, it is clear that complete certainty can never be attained. Or, again, if such a limit exists, but has not been attained, certainty will be lacking. Our question then becomes, how do empirical and *a priori* statements compare with respect to the character of their evidence.

In general, when a proposition is asserted in mathematics, it is asserted as holding in some system. The evidence for it is its proof and, assuming the proof to be correct and the logic of the system fixed (i.e., neglecting linguistic uncertainties), no further evidence can be given or demanded. A second proof might, to be sure, add to one's feeling of security in the result, but only because of possible obscurities or lacunae in the first proof, that is to say, only because of linguistic uncertainties. Added proofs might possess an elegance or economy of assumption that the original lacked, but the fact remains that the original was a proof and that there is no accretion of further evidence. Thus both the limit of evidence and its attainment seem possible in mathematics and deductive reasoning generally.

Exactly the same considerations apply to statements made on the basis of definitions. If the definition and the syntax of the language are given, then, neglecting linguistic uncertainties, no further evidence is possible. Even in the case of synthetic *a priori* statements, if such exist, conclusive and complete evidence is claimed, either in the form of an immediate intuition or of a compelling deduction. Thus in *a priori* knowledge generally, the conditions of complete evidential certainty are met. It remains to consider empirical statements.

Professor Stace considers two types of empirical judgments, generalizations and attributions of a predicate to an individual. I shall argue that, in neither case, can complete certainty be obtained, even neglecting linguistic uncertainties. It will be convenient to begin with generalizations.

We may take as a specimen generalization a statement of Aristotle's: "No insect with only two wings has a sting in the rear" (*History of Animals* 532a 22). What is being asserted here is that three complex characteristics, (1) of being an insect, (2) of having two wings, (3) of *lacking* a sting in the rear, are conjoined in such manner that whenever the first two are present, the third is present also. Since there is nothing in the definition of a dipterous insect which prevents its having a sting in the rear, the assertion must be founded on observation. What is observed is the compresence of the characteristics. In any group of qualities observed to accompany each other on any given occasion, the compresence may be due to chance—they may just happen to appear together—or the connection may be universal, may be such that they always appear together. It is the latter that the generalization maintains. The evidence, however, is compatible with either alternative. The function of added evidence, i.e., more instances of the conjunction of the characteristics, is to decrease the probability that the joint appearance is due to chance and to increase the probability that the connection is universal. Thus the more diptera found which lack stings in the rear, the less likely that the examined specimens just happened to lack them and the more likely that Aristotle is correct.

It is clear, however, that any finite number of coincidences, however unlikely, is possible, so that the chance conjunction can never be completely ruled out. Thus any proof of a generalization must fall short of complete certainty. A judicious choice of instances on which to base the generalization may go far toward reducing the possibility of the effect being due to coincidence, but it can never obviate it.

The above discussion has proceeded on the assumption that certainty might be attained in a consideration of the individual instances from which the generalization was made. It assumed that, for example, in examining two-winged insects we did not include a mutilated bee or grasshopper by mistake. If certainty can not be attained in the instances, *a fortiori* it is unattainable in the generalization. It is to such particular situations, the second type discussed by Professor Stace, that we turn now.

Professor Stace takes as an example the statement "This key is made of iron." We may facilitate discussion by considering the simpler statement "This is made of iron." Professor Stace argues that, since iron is defined by a finite number of characteristics, a finite number of experiments, one decisive for each characteristic, should establish the truth of the statement. One such characteristic is being attracted by a magnet; thus, a magnet is brought near the object, and the test is completed.

Unfortunately, the matter is not so simple. In order for the test to be conclusive, it must be certain that it is really a magnet with which we have brought our object in contact. If there is no attraction, it may be because the object is not iron or because what I took to be a magnet actually is not one. To establish that the object is not iron, it is necessary first to establish that the putative magnet actually is one. One would be tempted in this case to conclude that since the presumed magnet is horse-shoe shaped, is of appropriate size, and is painted red everywhere except at its polished ends, it is of course a magnet. But this could be done only on the assumption of the generalization that all such objects are magnets. Since, as we have seen, no generalizations can be certain, the certainty that I have a magnet can not be established in this way. Indeed, if I have friends who are both machinists and practical jokers, and if the date is near April 1, I can not even have practical certainty. Instead of relying on such generalizations, I may decide to test whether or not I have a magnet; I may, for example, bring it near a compass needle, to see if one pole of the magnet repels one end of the needle. But this in turn, if the test is to be conclusive, requires that I know that I have a genuine compass, and the same problem with which we were faced before recurs.

All this has been on the assumption that the test of attraction has been negative. If it is positive, the question is the same. If there is attraction, it may be because the original object is iron and is being attracted by a magnet, or it may be because the object is of magnetized steel or nickel alloy and is attracting an unmagnetized iron horse-shoe. Once again it is necessary first to determine that I have a magnet to make the test conclusive.

This account of the way in which one verifies that a thing has a characteristic leads to an infinite regress. In showing that the statement "This is iron" involves for its verification the statement "This is a magnet" and that in turn the statement "That is a compass" and so on, one might be led to expect that not merely certainty, but also any degree of confirmation would be lost in the un-ending process. What is required is to show that not merely, negatively, there is no certainty attained in the process, but also, positively, that there is a gain in probability. The key to such an explanation lies in what might be called statements of appearance. These constitute the one class of empirical statements which may be evidentially certain.

Examples of statements of appearance are found in statements like the following "This looks red," "This tastes sweet," "That sounds like a Beethoven sonata," and the like. In each case an impression is being reported and nothing more. The statement "This looks red" is not disproved or contradicted if the object subsequently turns out to be orange and it may still be true that something sounded like a Beethoven sonata (to me and at the time) even though its author turns out to be Mozart or Haydn. Thus such statements can be certain just because they make no prediction and are not liable to refutation by the course of subsequent experience. Since they make claims only about an immediate appearance, their evidence may be given completely and all at once, with resulting evidential certainty.

Such statements, of course, are not statements about objects and events, but merely about appearances; none the less, they have evidential value for statements about objects and events. Thus the first judgment [2] one might make concerning the statement to be confirmed in our previous example, "This is made of iron," is that "This looks like iron" or "This feels like iron." Such reports of appearances need not of course be conclusive evidence for the statement about the object, but it is hard to see how they can avoid giving some confirmation. Unless there were some acquaintance with iron, it would be impossible to make the judgment. There is of course the possibility of faulty recollection, misinterpretation of data and the like, but granted all these, the mere fact that an object looks like something to some one is some evidence that it is that thing.

This last statement calls for some explanation. Suppose I judge "This looks like a parrot." The judgment, we have seen, is a mere report of appearances, making no claims beyond itself. But it is also a datum for explanation, giving rise to the question: how does it happen that there is such an appearance? *Prima facie* the simplest answer is that I am confronted with a parrot, that "This is a parrot." As the simplest explanation this answer is to be preferred and the judgment of appearance constitutes evidence for it. This is not to claim that the evidence is overwhelming or that there may not be stronger evidence leading to a contrary conclusion, but merely that there is some evidence. If I am on an Arctic exploratory expedition, I shall very likely conclude that it was not a parrot I saw. That is, there may be other factors ruling out the *prima facie* simplest explanation.

I do not claim that whenever one is confronted with an appearance, one can make a judgment of appearance. In many cases the appearance is confused or one does not know how to classify it. Thus in attempting to adjust a radio amplifier, a person with only an ordinarily sensitive ear may be in doubt as to whether or not it sounds "true." He may be totally unable to make up his mind. In such cases one attempts to find another set of appearances which he can judge. Thus a more accurate method of tuning the amplifier is to feed impulses of a given form into it and connect the output to an

[2] I speak of "judgments of experience" rather than "statements of experience" to avoid the question of veracity. "Judgment" is used as a synonym for "statement believed to be true by the person making it."

oscilloscope. It is both easier and more reliable to see if the form on the screen of the oscilloscope looks the right shape than to judge if something sounds true. Similarly, one reason for reducing scientific measurements to pointer readings is that judgments of appearance are thereby made easy. Again, a good deal of the art of a craftsman or a connoisseur lies in the ability to make judgments of appearance more reliable and more refined than those of the average person. So, there is no claim that judgments of appearance are always possible, or equally possible for all people; merely that, when they can be made, they are evidence.

To come back to our original statement, "This is made of iron": the verification may go indefinitely into the future, involving "This is a magnet," "That is a compass," and so on; but there will be increments of probability through judgments, "This looks like iron," "This looks like a magnet," "What looks like a magnet appears to be attracting this," and the like throughout the entire procedure. If the theory sketched here is correct, the process of verification yields some increase in probability but never complete certainty. And if this is the case, there is difference in evidential certainty between *a priori* statements and those empirical statements which represent generalizations or ascribe a characteristic to an object.

One final objection remains to be considered: I have defined evidential certainty in terms of the limit of evidence. It may well be objected that this amount of evidence is not necessary and that one may have certainty with something less than this ideal maximum. Along such lines, one would probably define certainty psychologically, either in terms of a willingness to act or in terms of a feeling of certainty. It is beside the point for this discussion to enquire whether or not the two definitions are equivalent, or even to formulate them carefully. What is important is to notice that these represent perfectly correct and usual senses of the term and in either of them certainty of empirical statements is possible. In some such sense, I may be certain that Jones was down-town this afternoon when the only evidence is that I saw some one who, I thought, looked like Jones. In such a sense also I can fairly readily become certain that "This is made of iron."

Certainties of this sort might aptly be called *practical* certainties. Practical certainty has a down-to-earth, hard-headed character and a freedom from merely chimerical doubts which would *prima facie* recommend it as a working concept more highly than the sort of certainty which I have outlined above. In order to defend the earlier concept, I should like to show that it is definable in terms of practical certainty.

We may begin by noticing that practical certainty depends not merely on evidence but also on the use to which a statement is to be put. I may be genuinely and completely certain that Jones was down-town this afternoon and may be ready to bet you five dollars on it. If, however, you wish me to bet five hundred dollars against your five, I may refuse. My willingness to act may not go that far, if certainty is being defined in those terms. Or, if certainty is being defined in terms of a feeling, the feeling may have changed under the stress of the proposal. Again, even if I were willing to take this bet, I might balk at giving odds of a thousand to one. These situations, varying in the strain they place on a certainty, are merely evidence that willingness to act is always willingness to act in some context, and that willingness to act in one situation does not necessarily imply willingness to act similarly in any situation. In short, willingness to act is relative, and relative not merely to the evidence, but to the consequences of the action as well. The same considerations apply to certainties defined in terms of feeling.

It is worth noticing that if, in the situation we have been considering, the evidence is not strong enough to induce me to make a hundred-to-one bet, additional evidence would lead me to. If, for example, I had stopped Jones on the street and spent a few minutes talking to him, I might be ready to give the odds. Similarly, in the case of the bit of iron, procedures of confirmation which would ordinarily appear silly, might become perfectly reasonable if enough depended on the identification. There is no difference in kind, moreover, between an extension of the investigation which seems far-fetched and that part which seems a natural precaution. It is merely an amassing of more evidence of the same sort, with the amount of evidence required increasing with the stake. This would naturally suggest a definition of the sort of certainty discussed previously as the limit of practical certainties as the stake increases without limit.

Thus, whether completeness of evidence be admitted in its own right or defined in terms of practical certainties, it must be considered. Once admitted, it serves as a means of distinguishing empirical from *a priori* statements with regard to evidential certainty, even though there is no difference with respect to linguistic uncertainties. I should add that the division of grounds of uncertainty into linguistic and evidential is not meant to be exhaustive. Undoubtedly, there are others and one's total uncertainty is a compound of all these factors. Still, [in] one dimension at least, none but empirical statements are uncertain.

For Further Reading

Armstrong, D. M., "Is Introspective Knowledge Incorrigible?" *Philosophical Review,* Vol. 72 (1963).
Ayer, A. J., *The Concept of a Person,* 1963, Chap. 3.
———, *The Foundations of Empirical Knowledge,* 1947, pp. 84–92.
———, "Philosophical Scepticism," in Lewis, H. D. (ed.), *Contemporary British Philosophy,* 1956.
———, *The Problem of Knowledge,* 1956, passim.
Blanshard, Brand, *The Nature of Thought,* 1939, Chaps. 25 and 26.
Bradley, F. H., *Essays in Truth and Reality,* 1914, pp. 107–10, 113–18, and Chap. 7.
Campbell, C. A., "Sense Data and Judgment in Sensory Cognition," *Mind,* Vol. 56 (1947).
"Can There Be a Private Language?" (Symposium), *Proceedings of the Aristotelian Society,* Supplementary Vol. 28 (1954).
Chisholm, R. M., "Foundations of Empirical Knowledge," in Schilpp, P. A. (ed.), *Philosophy of Bertrand Russell,* 1946.
———, *Perceiving: A Philosophical Study,* 1957, Chaps. 3–6.

Chisholm, R. M., "Theory of Knowledge," in Chisholm, R. M., *et al., Philosophy,* 1964, especially pp. 244–86.
Dewey, John, *Essays in Experimental Logic,* 1916, Chap. 11.
Ewing, A. C., *Idealism,* 1934, pp. 228–50.
Goodman, Nelson, Lewis, C. I., and Reichenbach, Hans, "The Experiential Element in Knowledge" (Symposium), *Philosophical Review,* Vol. 61 (1952).
Malcolm, Norman, "Certainty and Empirical Statements," *Mind,* Vol. 51 (1942).
———, "The Verification Argument," *Knowledge and Certainty,* 1964, pp. 1–56.
Moore, G. E., "Certainty," *Philosophical Papers,* 1959.
———, "A Defense of Common-Sense," in Muirhead, J. H. (ed.), *Contemporary British Philosophy,* 1925.
Nagel, Ernest, in Schilpp, P. A. (ed.), *Philosophy of Bertrand Russell,* 1946, pp. 329–38.
Perkins, Moreland, "Intersubjectivity and Gestalt Psychology," *Philosophy and Phenomenological Research,* Vol. 13 (1953).
Popper, K. R., *The Logic of Scientific Discovery,* 1959, pp. 98–111.
Price, H. H., *Truth and Corrigibility,* 1936.
———, "Appearing and Appearances," *American Philosophical Quarterly,* Vol. 1 (1964).
Russell, Bertrand, *An Inquiry into Meaning and Truth,* 1948, pp. 131–9, 150–65.
Ryle, Gilbert, "Sensation," in Lewis, H. D. (ed.), *Contemporary British Philosophy,* 1956.
Schlick, Moritz, "The Foundations of Knowledge," in Ayer, A. J. (ed), *Logical Positivism,* 1963.
Thomson, J. Jarvis, "Private Language," *American Philosophical Quarterly,* Vol. 1 (1964).
Wellman, Carl, "Wittgenstein and the Egocentric Predicament," *Mind,* Vol. 68 (1959).

7

TYPES OF EMPIRICAL KNOWLEDGE: PAST EVENTS

It will have been clear from the preceding chapter that some propositions about present occurrences have been relatively exempt from philosophical doubt; in particular, most philosophers have not doubted that a person can have knowledge, even certain and incorrigible knowledge, of what he is experiencing at any given moment. The ancient sceptics, for example, did not question the reliability of a person's beliefs about his experience at a time contemporaneous with that experience. It is a different story, however, with propositions about past events. The Greek sceptics questioned whether there is any reason for accepting any proposition about the past in preference to its contradictory—even propositions about a person's own experience in the immediate past. They affirmed that there is a logical gap between what statements about the past claim is the case and the evidence (if any) available for them at the time the statement is made; they questioned the rationality of moving from an affirmation of the evidence to an affirmation of propositions about the past.

Philosophers have quite properly thought that warrant for believing statements about past events is of crucial importance. Obviously, the status of any volume of history depends on the possibility of such warrant. But more important still, it is agreed that acceptance of any law of the nonformal sciences is justified only if one is warranted in believing the evidence of observation or experiment; for observation and experiment are the *only* reason for believing any structure of scientific theory. To believe, however, that there is observational or experimental evidence for a certain theory is to believe that certain events took place in the past—that certain experiments were performed with certain outcomes. If there is no warrant for belief that certain events occurred, there is no warrant for accepting any law or theory of the sciences.

But how may we justify such beliefs? A partial answer to this question is obvious and accepted by all: *If* we can justifiably believe the laws and theories of science, then to some extent we are justified in believing some propositions about the past. For just as these laws and theories, when taken with descriptions of a present state of affairs, enable us to *predict* events to come, so they enable us to *retrodict* events in the past. The laws of motion justify us in predicting an eclipse tomorrow; equally they enable us to retrodict an eclipse three thousand years ago. Or on a humbler level, just as what we know of human nature enables us to predict that the President of the United States will not declare for atheism tomorrow, so it enables us to retrodict that Queen Elizabeth was jealous of Mary Queen of Scots. Laws, taken with present evidence, then, have implications for the past as well as for the future.

This answer to our question, however, is only partial. For it tells us only that *if* we are justified in believing the laws and theories of science, *then* we are justified in accepting certain propositions about the past. But, as we observed above, we need to be justified in believing statements about particular events in the past in order to believe these laws and theories with warrant. And we hardly cite the laws and theories as observational grounds for the very statements needed to believe the laws and theories; we cannot pull ourselves up by our own bootstraps. So, most philosophers have thought, if science is to have a sound evidential foundation, there must be some warrant other than appeal to the laws and theories of science for believing some propositions about past events.

Only *most* philosophers have come to this conclusion, however. The contextualist (p. 372) need not agree. Here there is a major strategic issue for epistemology. If we were to follow the contextualist in his proposal that we worry only about one problem at a time, then, when we were inquiring about our warrant for believing any particular proposition about the past with which we happened to be concerned, we could reasonably take the whole corpus of scientific laws and theories as available premises for a solution. And similarly, if our doubt were about one general "law" of a science, we could properly use as premises propositions about past events that we do not seriously doubt. It is only if we undertook a *general reconstruction* of the total corpus of knowledge, all at once, that we would be faced with a serious problem about knowledge of past events.

We need not judge here which party is right in the controversy about what the epistemologist must do. Let us rather examine what the problem is, and whether and how it may be solved, *if* one decides that a general reconstruction of the corpus of knowledge is called for. We must consider, then, whether and how belief in propositions about past events is warranted, assuming that we cannot use as an evidential base any proposition we would not be warranted in believing unless we were already warranted in believing some propositions about the past.

Which kinds of propositions may, then, be accepted as premises for a solution of our present problem? (1) As has already been observed, most philosophers would accept propositions about one's own present experience. (2) Some philosophers would hold that some propositions about material objects, for example, that I am now sitting before a typewriter, can also be affirmed with warrant independently of any warrant to believe propositions about the past. This stand, however, is controversial. Perhaps most philosophers would deny the claim, saying, for example, that I am justified in believing there is a typewriter in front of me now only because I know that when I have been presented with an appearance like the present one on past occasions, there was usually or always a typewriter in front of me. (3) Most philosophers would agree that we can use as premises propositions to the effect that we at least *seem to remember* that we had certain experiences, or witnessed certain events, in the past. Most philosophers who reject the contextualist stand without embracing scepticism believe that such facts of ostensible recall are the key to warrant for believing propositions about the past. But how can we identify which propositions have the support of memory? If we are in no position to identify those propositions we seem to *remember* to be true, as distinct from those we merely fancy to be true, appeal to the support of memory cannot reasonably be made. Philosophers who doubt the wisdom of the whole reconstructive enterprise (those with contextualist learnings) are apt to doubt the very possibility of distinguishing propositions about fact that we *seem to remember* from other propositions we tend to accept. And on their behalf it must be said that the descriptions philosophers have offered (see the selection from Hume in this chapter) of what is specific to remembered facts (for example, that there are vivid images, or that the images have an aura of familiarity) have not been very convincing.

Suppose, however, that a philosopher assumes that premises of these various types can be used. How might he, without circularity, use them to show that we are warranted in believing propositions about the past? It is not obvious that even all these premises together will do the job. Bertrand Russell has often argued that there is no inconsistency in accepting all the particular propositions we can observe to be true about the world as it is at present, even including as a fact that people have the memorial beliefs we think they have, and at the same time asserting that no material or mental being existed five minutes ago. What lines of reasoning have been offered in justification of belief in propositions about the past?

1. Some philosophers have tried to argue inductively to the *reliability of memory as a faculty*. This path can easily become circular, however, since the occasions of past reliability of memory seem to be knowable only by the use of memory.

2. Other philosophers claim that unless at least some—or perhaps all—sets of one's memory judgments are accepted as initially warranted, we are condemned to scepticism. (By "initially warranted" is meant judgments that are more believable than their contradictories, at least until some are eliminated on the basis of their logical incoherence with other memory judgments or other premises.) One might say that this is a very pragmatic reason for accepting memory judgments, but if the function of epistemology is to separate the better from the worse beliefs, ultimately for the sake of action, a sceptical conclusion can well lead to a reconsideration of basic assumptions.

If this line of reasoning is adopted, however, it must still be decided exactly which propositions supported by memory are to be assigned such initial warrant.

2a. One class of propositions must certainly be assigned a high degree of warrant: those about one's own line of reasoning (including ostensible recall of various past experiences) when engaged in epistemological reflection. If it is not conceded that we are justified in thinking that we just now went through a certain line of reasoning or decided that we seemed to remember certain things, we shall not succeed in giving warrant to any beliefs by any line of reasoning. In other words we must, as C. I. Lewis says, trust propositions about the "epistemological present." Descartes tried to avoid the necessity of making this assumption by saying that with practice we might see all the steps in an argument intuitively, but this proposal seems unrealistic.

2b. Some philosophers claim that *any* proposition one seems to remember about one's *own past experience* is initially better warranted than the contradictory of it.

2c. Still other philosophers would extend this class of propositions somewhat, to include a carefully defined class of perceptual statements about material things, for example, "I remember that I just saw a brown square object."

3. Philosophers who accept (2) may then go on to use premises (a), (b), or (c) to show that the logical relations of the premises to one another will in the end warrant acceptance of some propositions as nearly certain, rejections of others as almost certainly false, and acceptance of some entirely different ones as at least highly probable. Examining these relations requires the use of probability logic and especially Bayes' theorem, but the details have not been fully worked out, so that the proposal remains, at present, rather programmatic.

4. Still other philosophers claim that, if we allow ourselves [following (2a)] the assumption that a certain large set of propositions about our own past experiences at least seems to be or to have been remembered, we can explain *this* fact in all its detail only by supposing that our own memory is a usually reliable instrument and that it has been interacting with events of a specific kind—roughly the events that we seem to remember having occurred. This kind of reasoning has to meet the sceptical objection of Descartes, the objection that our memories might have been created by a malicious demon who enjoys watching us believe false propositions about the past.

So much for the important lines of reasoning that have been used to justify belief in propositions about past events by argument from premises which can be known to be true even if knowledge of past events is not assumed.

It might be supposed, from the foregoing, that one *really* remembers a past event only (a) if one *seems* to remember that an event of a certain description occurred and (b) if such an event really did occur. This conclusion is mistaken, however, for it is possible for a person to have a seeming recollection of a past event and for the event really to have occurred as remembered, although no one would say that the person really remembered it if, for example, he was not even there. (It is said that George IV acquired such recollections of the Battle of Waterloo, at which he was not present.) Perhaps a better analysis of "*S* really remembers *E*" would expand the above suggestion into (a) *S* seems to remember that an event of description *E* occurred; (b) an event of description *E* really did occur; and (c) *S*'s seeming to remember such an event is a causal consequent of the occurrence of *E*, and it is a direct consequent in that it is independent of teaching or prompting by other persons. This topic of the nature of genuine recall is explored in some of the articles listed below for further reading.

The passages from Hume reprinted below have shaped the form taken by the problem of memory in the empiricist tradition. Ayer's discussion surveys the whole spectrum of problems about memory and the past. His defense of accepting propositions about the past appears to rely on the reasoning described under (2a), (2b), and perhaps (4) above. Lewis' very systematic examination of the problem seems to utilize, at one point or another, all but (1) and (2c). Malcolm attempts to use, in part, "ordinary language" methods to discredit some proposals about past events and our knowledge of them; most of his reasoning thus falls outside the possible arguments we have sketched, although his final pages perhaps approach (4).

David Hume

A Phenomenology of Recollection

OF THE IDEAS OF THE MEMORY AND IMAGINATION

We find, by experience, that when any impression has been present with the mind, it again makes its appearance there as an idea; and this it may do after two different ways: either when, in its new appearance, it retains a considerable degree of its first vivacity, and is somewhat intermediate betwixt an impression and an idea; or when it entirely loses that vivacity, and is a perfect idea. The faculty by which we repeat our impressions in the first manner, is called the *memory,* and the other the *imagination.* It is evident, at first sight, that the ideas of the memory are much more lively and strong than those of the imagination, and that the former faculty paints its objects in more distinct colors than any which are employed by the latter. When we remember any past event, the idea of it flows in upon the mind in a forcible manner; whereas, in the imagination, the perception is faint and languid, and cannot, without difficulty, be preserved by the mind steady and uniform for any considerable time. Here, then, is a sensible difference betwixt one species of ideas and another. But of this more fully hereafter.

There is another difference betwixt these two kinds of ideas, which is no less evident, namely, that though neither the ideas of the memory nor imagination, neither the lively nor faint ideas, can make their appearance in the mind, unless their correspondent impressions have gone before to prepare the way for them, yet the imagination is not restrained to the same order and form with the original impressions; while the memory is in a manner tied down in that respect, without any power of variation.

It is evident, that the memory preserves the original form, in which its objects were presented, and that wherever we depart from it in recollecting any thing, it proceeds from some defect or imperfection in that faculty. An historian may, perhaps, for the more convenient carrying on of his narration, relate an event before another to which it was in fact posterior; but then, he takes notice of this disorder, if he be exact; and, by that means, replaces the idea in its due position. It is the same case in our recollection of those places and persons, with which we were formerly acquainted. The chief exercise of the memory is not to preserve the simple ideas, but their order

From David Hume, *A Treatise of Human Nature,* Book I, Part I, Section 3, and Book I, Part III, Sections 4 and 5, first published from 1739 to 1740.

and position. In short, this principle is supported by such a number of common and vulgar phenomena, that we may spare ourselves the trouble of insisting on it any further.

. . .

OF THE COMPONENT PARTS OF OUR REASONINGS CONCERNING CAUSE AND EFFECT

Though the mind in its reasonings from causes or effects, carries its view beyond those objects which it sees or remembers, it must never lose sight of them entirely, nor reason merely upon its own ideas, without some mixture of impressions, or at least of ideas of the memory, which are equivalent to impressions. When we infer effects from causes, we must establish the existence of these causes; which we have only two ways of doing, either by an immediate perception of our memory or senses, or by an inference from other causes; which causes again we must ascertain in the same manner, either by a present impression or by an inference from *their* causes, and so on, till we arrive at some object, which we see or remember. It is impossible for us to carry on our inferences *in infinitum;* and the only thing that can stop them, is an impression of the memory or senses, beyond which there is no room for doubt or inquiry.

. . .

OF THE IMPRESSIONS OF THE SENSES AND MEMORY

In this kind of reasoning, then, from causation, we employ materials, which are of a mixed and heterogeneous nature, and which, however connected, are yet essentially different from each other. All our arguments concerning causes and effects consist both of an impression of the memory or senses, and of the idea of that existence, which produces the object of the impression, or is produced by it. Here, therefore, we have three things to explain, viz. *first,* the original impression. *Secondly,* the transition to the idea of the connected cause or effect. *Thirdly,* the nature and qualities of that idea.

As to those *impressions,* which arise from the *senses,* their ultimate cause is, in my opinion, perfectly inexplicable by human reason, and it will always be impossible to decide with certainty, whether they arise immediately from the object, or are produced by the creative power of the mind, or are derived from the Author of our being. Nor is such a question any way material to our present purpose. We may draw inferences from the coherence of our perceptions, whether they be true or false; whether they represent nature justly, or be mere illusions of the senses.

When we search for the characteristic, which distinguishes the *memory* from the imagination, we must immediately perceive, that it cannot lie in the simple ideas it presents to us; since both these faculties borrow their simple ideas from the impressions, and can never go beyond these original perceptions. These faculties are as little distinguished from each other by the arrangement of their complex ideas. For, though it be a peculiar property of the memory to preserve the original order and position of its ideas, while the imagination transposes and changes them as it pleases; yet this difference is not sufficient to distinguish them in their operation, or make us know the one from the other; it being impossible to recall the past impressions, in order to compare them with our present ideas, and see whether their arrangement be exactly similar. Since therefore the memory is known, neither by the order of its *complex* ideas, nor the nature of its *simple* ones; it follows, that the difference betwixt it and the imagination lies in its superior force and vivacity. A man may indulge his fancy in feigning any past scene of adventures; nor would there be any possibility of distinguishing this from a remembrance of a like kind, were not the ideas of the imagination fainter and more obscure.

It frequently happens, that when two men have been engaged in any scene of action, the one shall remember it much better than the other, and shall have all the difficulty in the world to make his companion recollect it. He runs over several circumstances in vain; mentions the time, the place, the company, what was said, what was done on all sides; till at last he hits on some lucky circumstance, that revives the whole, and gives his friend a perfect memory of everything. Here the person that forgets, receives at first all the ideas from the discourse of the other, with the same circumstances of time and place; though he considers them as mere fictions of the imagination. But as soon as the circumstance is mentioned that touches the memory, the very same ideas now appear in a new light, and have, in a manner, a different feeling from what they had before. Without any other alteration, beside that of the feeling, they become immediately ideas of the memory, and are assented to.

Since therefore the imagination can represent all the same objects that the memory can offer to us, and since those faculties are only distinguished by the different *feeling* of the ideas they present, it may be proper to consider what is the nature of that feeling. And here I believe every one will readily agree with me, that the ideas of the memory are more *strong* and *lively* than those of the fancy.

A painter, who intended to represent a passion or emotion of any kind, would endeavor to get a sight of a person actuated by a like emotion, in order to enliven his ideas, and give them a force and vivacity superior to what is found in those, which are mere fictions of the imagination. The more recent this memory is, the clearer is the idea; and when, after a long interval, he would return to the contemplation of his object, he always finds its idea to be much decayed, if not wholly obliterated. We are frequently in doubt concerning the ideas of the memory, as they become very weak and feeble; and are at a loss to determine whether any image proceeds from the fancy or the memory, when it is not drawn in such lively colors as distinguish that latter faculty. I think I remember such an event, says one; but am not sure. A long tract of time has almost worn it out of my memory, and leaves me uncertain whether or not it be the pure offspring of my fancy.

And as an idea of the memory, by losing its force and vivacity, may degenerate to such a degree, as to be taken for an idea of the imagination; so, on the other hand, an idea of the imagination may acquire such a force and vivacity, as to pass for an idea of the memory, and counterfeit its effects on the belief and judgment. This is noted in the case of liars; who by the frequent repetition of their lies, come at last to believe and remember them, as realities; custom and habit having, in this case, as in many others, the same influence on the mind as nature, and infixing the idea with equal force and vigor.

Thus it appears, that the *belief* or *assent,* which always attends the memory and senses, is nothing but the vivacity of those perceptions they present; and that this alone distinguishes them from the imagination. To believe is in this case to feel an immediate impression of the senses, or a repetition of that impression in the memory. It is merely the force and liveliness of the perception, which constitutes the first act of the judgment, and lays the foundation of that reasoning, which we build upon it, when we trace the relation of cause and effect.

Alfred Jules Ayer

Memory

HABIT MEMORY AND THE MEMORY OF EVENTS

Philosophers who write about memory are generally inclined to treat it as though it were analogous to perception. Though what is remembered is past, the remembering takes place in the present. It is therefore assumed that there must be some present content which gives, as it were, its flavour to a memory-experience. This present content, which is commonly thought of as a memory image, is treated as a private object, very much like a sense-datum. And just as sense-data appear to cut us off from physical objects, so these present contents of our memory-experiences appear to cut us off from the past. At this point, as we have remarked, the sceptic finds his opportunity. He argues, on grounds which we have already indicated, that since it is logically impossible that one should ever observe a past event, one can have no valid reason for believing that it occurred. Again, this argument may be met by denying the sceptic's premise. The analogy to holding that physical objects are directly perceived is to hold that we have the power of being directly acquainted with past events. But many philosophers find this answer unsatisfactory, or even unintelligible. They therefore seek other solutions. The analogy to the phenomenalist theory of perception is, as we have noted, the implausible view that statements about the past are reducible to statements about the present or future evidence that we have, or could obtain, in favour of them; evidence in which the occurrence of memory-experiences would play a part. There is no very strict analogy to the causal theory; but it is sometimes maintained that our trust in our memories can be justified by an induc-

---

From A. J. Ayer, *The Problem of Knowledge,* Chap. 4, published by Macmillan & Co. Ltd., London, St. Martin's Press, Inc., New York, and The Macmillan Company of Canada, Limited, 1956. Reprinted by permission of the publishers. This book is also available in paperback.

tive argument. The objection that this is no ordinary inductive argument may then lead to the conclusion that the deliverances of memory are justified in their own way. And here a parallel may be drawn with the general problem of induction. It may be argued that while the truth of any one belief which is supposed to be based on memory may be tested by reference to another, there can be no question of justifying memory as a whole: the demand for such a justification would be illegitimate.

Let us begin, as before, with the sceptic's original premise. The first point to notice is that, at best, it applies only to what may be called the memory of events. In a great many cases where one is said to remember something there is no question of one's even seeming to recall any past occurrence. The remembering consists simply in one's having the power to reproduce a certain performance. Thus, remembering how to swim, or how to write, remembering how to set a compass, or add up a column of figures is in every case a matter of being able to do these things, more or less efficiently, when the need arises. It can indeed happen, in cases of this sort, that people are assisted by actually recalling some previous occasion on which they did the thing in question, or saw it done, but it is by no means necessary that they should be. On the contrary, the better they remember, the less likely it is that they will have any such events in mind: it is only when one is in difficulties that one tries as it were to use one's recollections as a manual. To have learnt a thing properly is to be able to dispense with them.

But still, it may be argued, even if one remembers how to do things without having any conscious recollection of having done them before, or of having learned to do them, there must be at least an unconscious recollection. Otherwise how would one know what to do? But what does this 'unconscious recollection' amount to? Simply to the fact that one succeeds in doing whatever it may be, with the implication that this is the result of learning and practice. Certainly the causes of one's proficiency include one's past experiences. The reason why we speak of remembering in these contexts is just that we suppose ourselves to be dealing with things that have been learned. And it may be that these past experiences have left physical traces which are discernible, for instance, in our brains; the physical mechanism of this type of memory is not here in question. What we are concerned with is simply the description of these processes of remembering; and in this the hypothesis regarding physical traces plays no part, though it may in their explanation; it is not suggested that remembering how to do things actually involves inspecting one's own brain. But neither need it involve inspecting the past events, or any mental representatives of the past events, which are causally responsible for the present performance. One may say that they are recollected unconsciously, if one means no more by this than that one's present ability to remember is causally dependent upon them, and so in its way a sign of their having taken place. But it would be much less misleading to say that they are not recollected at all.

Philosophers have recognized the existence of this class of cases, and they have grouped them under the heading of 'habit-memory', in contrast to 'factual-memory', or the memory of events. What they have not always realized is how far the class extends. It covers not only the instances of knowing how to do things, in which, as we have seen, it is not necessary that one should also know that anything is the case, but also a great many instances in which the knowledge displayed is classified as knowledge of fact. Suppose that I am set to answer a literary *questionnaire,* and that I have to rely upon my memory. I shall, perhaps, succeed in remembering that such and such a poem continues in such and such a way, that So-and-so was the author of such and such a book, that a given incident appears in this novel rather than in that. But none of this need involve my having any recollection of a past event. I may recall some of the occasions on which I read, or was told about, the books in question, but equally I may not. Here again, the more readily my memory functions, the less likely it is that I shall engage in any reflections of this sort. Neither is it necessary that I should entertain any images. Some people may, indeed, assist their memories by visualizing the printed page; others, perhaps, by recalling the sound of a recitation; but these are personal peculiarities. Others, again, just write the answers down. The image, if it occurs, is simply an *aide-mémoire*; it does not go to constitute the memory. The proof that it is dispensable in these cases is that many people habitually dispense with it.

In the same way, a historian who remembers, for example, what the state of parties was throughout the reign of Queen Victoria, a biologist who remembers Lamarck's version of the theory of evolution, a mathematician who remembers Pythagoras's proof of the existence of irrational numbers, a jurist who remembers a point of corporation law, need none of them be recollecting any past event; nor need they be having any images. Their remembering just consists in their getting the answer right. Whether they are helped to do so by conjuring up images, or consciously delving into their past experience, is irrelevant. Once more, the more easily they remember, the less likely it is that they will need any assistance of this sort. And here the point is not that the word 'remember' is used dispositionally, so that one can properly be said to remember things that one is not actually thinking of. It is that when such dispositions are actualized, their actualization consists in nothing more than giving a successful performance. In this sense, to remember a fact is simply to be able to state it. The power is displayed in its exercise; and such exercises need not be accompanied by anything that one would be even tempted to call a memory-experience.

DISPENSABILITY OF MEMORY IMAGES

It is characteristic of this type of memory that it does not, except incidentally, yield knowledge of the past. Certainly, in the case of the historian, the facts which are remembered are facts about the past; but, so far as his exercise of memory goes, they might just as well not have been. His remembering them consists in his stating them correctly; it would therefore be just as much a display of memory, in this sense, if the facts that he remembered were like some scientific facts in having no specific reference to time, or if they referred to the present or even to the future; an astronomer may remember that an eclipse of the sun will take place at some future date. And not only is this type of memory not essentially linked with knowledge of the past. There are good reasons for saying that it is not a source of knowledge at all. The exercise of it is a manifestation of knowledge. But it is not by itself a ground for the acceptance of what is known. My readiness to say, for example, that

Peacock was the author of *Crotchet Castle* provides no evidence that he was the author, without some further assumption such as that I have made a special study of Peacock's work, or that I do not usually make statements of this sort unless I have checked my references. Unless there were independent reasons for believing that Peacock did write *Crotchet Castle,* my 'remembering' that he did would count for nothing. I may not myself know what these reasons are; I may well have forgotten how I ever came to have this information. But it is only these things, which I may not remember, that give any warrant for regarding what I do remember as a piece of knowledge. In short, if remembering consists, in these instances, in giving a successful performance, what makes the performance successful must be something other than the mere fact that it is given. It is not because one remembers them that one has reason to believe that the facts are so: it is because there is reason to believe that they are so that one is entitled to say that one remembers them.

But still, it may be argued, this is not the whole story. Suppose that my reason for being sure that Peacock wrote *Crotchet Castle* is that I was reading it only yesterday. How do I know that I was reading it only yesterday? Because I remember doing so. Or possibly because I find it noted in my diary. But how do I know that words which are written down in diaries do not spontaneously change their shape, so that what to-day appears as 'Peacock' might yesterday have appeared as 'Thackeray'? For all sorts of reasons. But when they are examined it will be found that at some point or other they all involve the fact that someone remembers that something was so. The observations which we use to check our memories are interpreted in the light of hypotheses which are themselves accepted on the basis of past experience. Which brings us back again to memory; but to memory in a different sense from that which we have so far been considering, the sense in which to remember something consists in recollecting a past event. And surely in this sense memory is a source of knowledge. The evidence that the past event occurred is to be found in the character of one's present memory-experience.

But what exactly is this experience? The usual assumption is that it consists primarily in the presence of a distinctive sort of image. Thus, Hume's analysis of memory is that it is simply a matter of having an idea, by which he means an image, which is a copy of some previous sense-impression. These ideas of memory are distinguished from impressions by the fact that they are fainter, and from ideas of imagination by the fact that they are livelier.[1] Russell, who in this as in other cases is inclined to follow Hume, sees, however, that this talk of faintness and liveliness is inadequate. According to him what makes the image a *memory* image is its being accompanied by a feeling of familiarity.[2] Assuming, as they both do, that the past event, or experience, which is remembered, cannot itself be present to the mind, they infer that something else must be; and an image then seems to be the only candidate.

Let us, however, look more closely at the facts. It is plausible to make the presence of an image a necessary feature of this type of memory, so long as one considers only visual examples, that is, so long as one confines one's analysis to the recollection of things seen. But what of the other senses? I

[1] *A Treatise of Human Nature,* Book I, Part I, section iii.
[2] *The Analysis of Mind,* Lecture IX.

remember speaking to a friend this morning on the telephone but I do not have an auditory image either of his voice or of my own. If I have any image at all in such a case, it is likely to be visual; a picture of my friend seated by his telephone, and possibly also of myself; in short, a picture of something that I did not actually see. But it very often happens that one remembers such conversations without having images of any kind whatever. In the same way, I remember that a moment ago I ran my hand over the surface of my writing-table: I remember how it felt in the sense that I can give a description of the feeling, but I do not have any tactual image of it. And even in the case where one remembers something that one has seen, there need not always be a present image. If I am asked whom I met at the party to which I went last night, I may answer without hesitation that So-and-so and So-and-so were there, without having any accompanying images of their faces. I may be able to obtain such images, if I make the effort, but I can very well remember what went on, I can give an account of the party, without having any images at all. Here once again, the better one's memory functions, the more readily one replies to the question as to what took place, the greater is the likelihood that no images intervene.

Moreover, even when there is an image, it appears to play only an auxiliary rôle. To begin with, it does not greatly matter what qualities it has. Though taken by some to be a copy of the scene which it helps one to remember, it may in fact bear very little resemblance to it. Not everybody is a very good visualizer: and even the images obtained by those who are will tend to be schematic; they will rarely, if ever, reproduce in every detail the forms and colours of the remembered scene. But so far as one's ability to remember goes, a 'bad' image may be just as serviceable as a good one. It is not as if one carefully inspected the image, as an intelligence officer inspects an aerial photograph, in the hope of finding in it a faithful reproduction of the past. It is rather as if the image were transparent: one has the impression of looking at the original picture *through* it, in much the same way as one grasps the sense of words through handwriting or print. There is this difference, however, that whereas, if the handwriting is very bad, it becomes difficult, if not impossible, to understand what it is meant to express, the image can be as fuzzy as you please without any detriment to the memory which it assists.

Neither is this simply a question of psychology. As a matter of logic, however faithful the image, it cannot be merely because of its fidelity that it signifies a past event. Considered simply as an object, it has the properties that it has: such and such an outline, such and such details, such and such a degree of vividness. Now it may be that this collection of properties bears a close resemblance to the collection of properties which characterized some previous occurrence, but this is not something that is detectable in the image taken by itself. Even if the image had, as it were, written on it its claim to be a copy of something else, this would, apart from the interpretation that we give it, be only one further feature of its appearance, an extra piece of decoration. And the same applies if one tricks the image out with feelings of familiarity. Unless these so-called feelings of familiarity are taken as comprising a judgement to the effect that something like this occurred before, they merely put an aura round the image, an aura which is no more capable than its other features of signifying anything else. In sum, a present image can refer to a past occurrence only in so far as it is so *interpreted*. But if a faithful image can be interpreted in this way, so can an unfaithful one. As in the case of any other symbol, it is the use that we make of its qualities that matters, the construction that we put upon them, not these qualities themselves. The memory image serves its purpose just in so far as it prompts one to form an accurate belief about one's past experience. But then we can form such beliefs without the assistance of an image. The proof that we can is, as I have argued, that we quite often do.

There would seem, then, to be no very sharp distinction between what is called habit-memory and what we have called the memory of events. In a case of habit-memory there may be an accompanying image, as when one is assisted to remember a quotation by visualizing it in print; and conversely, one can dispense with images in remembering an event. What is decisive in both cases is one's ability to give the appropriate performance, whether it be a matter of displaying some skill, stating a fact which may or may not have reference to the past, or describing, or, as it were, reliving a past experience. These performances may be stimulated by various means, including the presence of an image; but even in the case of the recollection of a past experience, these stimuli do not constitute the memory. The only thing that we have so far discovered to be essential is the true belief that the experience occurred; a belief which may consist in nothing more than a disposition to give a correct answer to any question as to what took place.

IN WHAT DOES REMEMBERING CONSIST?

All the same, it cannot be entirely correct to equate remembering an event with having a true belief about the past. I remember that the Battle of Waterloo was fought in 1815, but I certainly do not remember the Battle of Waterloo. One very good reason why I do not remember it is that I was not alive at the time. There is a sense, on the other hand, in which I do remember the Battle of Arnhem, even though I was not present at it. I remember hearing and reading about it. But then I also remember hearing and reading about the Battle of Waterloo. What is the difference which makes it correct to say that I remember the one but not the other? Only, it seems, that in the case of the Battle of Arnhem, the experiences which I remember having were roughly contemporaneous with the event. One speaks of remembering an event primarily in the case where one actually witnessed it; but in a derivative sense one can also be said to remember it if one witnessed some of its immediate effects.

Accordingly, it may be suggested that remembering an event is just a special instance of the sort of habit-memory which consists in remembering a fact. To remember an event is to be disposed to state a fact about the past, but not just any fact about the past: it must be a fact which one has oneself observed, either straightforwardly or, as it were, at second hand. What differentiates the memory of events from other memories of fact is that it ranges only over one's own previous experience. This does not mean that one remembers only one's past experiences, in the sense that one always puts oneself into the picture which one's recollection forms. One may do so, or one may not. The emphasis in memory may fall either on the situation of which one was in fact a witness, or on one's own feelings and attitude as a spectator. Very often the memory covers both. But even if one does not come into the picture, one must at least have provided the frame. In a looser sense we may be said to remember events which we have not personally witnessed, as in the example given above. But this is only an extension of the primary usage, according to which our recollection of events is limited to what we have experienced. This restriction provides a necessary condition for an event to be remembered: apart from it, the sufficient conditions are to be found in the analysis of habit-memory which we have already given.

This is an attractive suggestion, but it is open to two fatal objections. In the first place, it may be argued that the limitation to one's past experience is not necessary, on the ground that it is at least conceivable that one should recollect an event which one has not in fact experienced. And, secondly, it may be argued that even if this is a necessary factor, its combination with the others is not sufficient, on the ground that it is possible to believe truly that one has had a certain experience, without remembering it; from which it follows that remembering it cannot simply consist in holding the true belief.

In envisaging the possibility of recollecting an event which one has not in fact experienced, I am not now thinking of the cases where one's recollection is delusive. This raises a quite different problem, into which we shall enter later on. I am thinking rather of the abnormal cases in which people claim to remember the experiences of others; cases of alleged co-consciousness, or cases in which people profess to have 'recaptured' the experiences of the dead. It may be that the evidence for such phenomena is very dubious, but for the purpose of the present argument it does not matter whether we accept these claims or not. The mere fact that we can consider whether to accept them shows, it may be argued, that the power of remembering experiences which were not one's own, in exactly the same way as one remembers one's own experiences, is at least to be admitted as a logical possibility.

So strong, however, is our tendency to make the restriction to one's own experience a necessary condition for the recollection of events, that we may be reluctant to allow even these abnormal cases to constitute a possible exception to the rule. Thus, admitting it to be a fact that people do sometimes seem to have an accurate recollection of the experiences of others, that they seem to remember them as if they were their own, the inference which is sometimes drawn is that they really were their own. Their possession of this unusual power is appealed to as a proof of reincarnation. But even if we admit the facts, this method of describing them is not forced upon us. Rather than accept the hypothesis of a single person's inhabiting a series of bodies, which many would regard as preposterous, if not wholly unintelligible, we may maintain that these so-called memories are not memories at all, just on the ground that one cannot remember experiences that one has never had. Or, finally, it may be allowed that they are indeed memories, but memories of experiences which were not one's own. I am not now interested in deciding which of these three courses would be the best to take. My point is only that if it be admitted, as I think it must be, that the third course would be open to us, it follows that the restriction of the memory of events to the field of one's past experience is not logically necessary.

The same point may be illustrated by a less far-fetched example. It sometimes happens that people under hypnosis are able to remember things which they were not consciously aware of at the relevant time. Owing to some psychological impediment, a person may fail to see something that is staring him in the face. Subsequently, however, when he is hypnotized, he is able to describe it. This is generally taken as a proof that he really did see it in the first place. It is assumed that one can have experiences of which one is not conscious at the time that they occur. But if we do not like to make this assumption, it is open to us to take a different course. We can admit that the presence of the object left some physical trace upon the man, but still deny that he ever underwent the experience of seeing it; and from this it will follow that what he displays under hypnosis is the memory of an experience which he never actually had. Again, I do not wish to argue that this is the best way of accounting for the facts: all that is here required is the admission of its possibility.

Such an admission may come more easily once it is recognized that to hold a true belief about an event in one's past experience is not sufficient for remembering it. There is still a distinctive factor lacking. If someone whose word I trust describes an incident in my past of which he was a witness, I may be fully persuaded that the incident occurred; if I am an inveterate visualizer, I may even form a mental picture of it, and this mental picture may in fact be accurate: but still I do not remember it. For instance, I myself remember very little about my early childhood, but I have acquired beliefs about it which, judging by the evidence available, may very well be true. Now it sometimes happens that a belief of this sort transforms itself into a memory. The transformation may be uncertain. One says 'I do dimly recollect it', being still not quite sure whether one does or not, whether one has not been talked into 'remembering' something that one does not really remember at all. But it may also be that all of a sudden the event comes back to one quite clearly. One has no doubt that one remembers it. But what is it exactly that has happened? Not the acquisition of an image; for that may have existed already, as an accompaniment to the belief. Not even that the image becomes more vivid: this may indeed happen in some cases, but it is not essential; the process may take place without any alteration to the image, or in the absence of any image at all. The presence, then, of a peculiar feeling? Such feelings do indeed occur: no doubt they are what Russell had in mind when he spoke of the feeling of familiarity, but again they do not seem to be essential. At least I do not myself detect their presence on every occasion on which I exercise my recollection of a past event.

Perhaps the correct answer is that there is no one thing that is universally present in every such instance of remembering. Sometimes it is a matter of one's having an especially vivid image; sometimes, with or without an image, there is a feeling of familiarity; sometimes there is no specific mental occurrence: it is simply then a matter of one's seriously saying 'Yes, I do remember'. There can, indeed, be said to be distinctive memory-experiences, in the sense that remembering an event, whatever form it takes, 'feels different' from merely imagining it, or believing that it occurred. But these experiences do not essentially consist in the presence of a special sort of object. There is nothing in this field that corresponds to the sense-datum, even allowing sense-data to be admissible.

Neither is it the primary function of the verb 'to remember', or its equivalents, to describe any such experiences. It would, indeed, be incorrect to say that one remembered something, unless one were in the appropriate mental attitude, however little this may in fact amount to. But in claiming to remember one is not so much describing one's present state of mind as giving an assurance that the event occurred, at the same time implying that one is in a position to know that it occurred. If we wish to rebut such a claim, we do not set out to enquire into the person's state of mind. We try to show that he is mistaken in his account of the event in question; or else we may argue that he is not qualified to offer us a guarantee, or at least not the sort of guarantee that he professes to give us in saying 'I remember'. The event, we may say, took place a very long time ago; he has a strong unconscious motive for distorting the facts; he seems only to be repeating what he has heard from someone else; he was drunk at the time; he was not even there. Such arguments are not decisive. We have seen that in very exceptional cases one might even be driven to admit that someone remembered an experience which he himself had never had. But what might cause us to make this admission would not be an investigation into the person's mental state. It would be rather that we were impressed by the facts which his 'recollection' brought to light. The accuracy of his reports, assuming that we had some independent means of checking them, would outweigh the insufficiency of his credentials. We might in the end be willing to say that he remembered the events in question because we could not see how else he could know them. But commonly we are not so liberal. The usage of the verb 'to remember' is partly governed by our conception of what is memorable. People are not supposed to offer guarantees unless they are qualified to make them good. They may be lucky, but that does not absolve them. In the case of memory, as in that of knowledge in general, it is not always sufficient just to get the answer right.

MEMORY AND THE CONCEPT OF THE PAST

But how, it may be asked, can one ever be in a position to offer such a guarantee? Why should it ever be accepted? To say 'I remember' is supposed, in certain circumstances at least, to be a good answer to the question 'How do you know?' But, if our analysis is correct, it comes down to little more than a mere repetition of the claim to knowledge. Merely to say that one has had a certain experience is not to give any reason why one's statement should be believed; and the fact that it may in certain cases be accompanied by images or feelings of a special kind does not, on the face of it, make such a statement any the more credible. Admittedly, there is the further implication that one is in a position to know. If one's recollection is challenged in a given instance, to point out that it is the sort of experience that one would, in these conditions, be expected to remember, is, it would normally be thought, to give a good answer. But how is this view to be supported? If we had found by experience that events of the kind in question usually had happened when people subsequently said they had, we might be justified in applying the general rule to this particular case. But what experiences can we have had to justify the general rule? Only experiences of remembering, for which the same difficulty arises. It would appear that the most that we are entitled to say is that statements which are expressed by the use of the past tense are found in a very large measure to cohere with one another. But this is formally consistent with there never having been a past at all. So far as our analysis has taken us, it may even be wondered how anyone ever came to attach a meaning to talking of the past.

It is such difficulties as these that philosophers try to sweep away by arguing that memory makes us directly acquainted with the past. 'The pastness of [a remembered] object', says Samuel Alexander, 'is a datum of experience, directly apprehended.' 'The object', he goes on to explain, 'is compresent with me as *past*.'[3] And Professor Broad, who takes this theory seriously though he does not himself agree with it, argues that the fact that an event is past is not a reason why it should not still present itself to us.[4] To say that an event is past is not, in his view, to say that it does not now exist. On the contrary, he thinks that once an event has occurred, there is a sense in which it goes on existing for all time. It is, as it were, put in storage; and there is no *a priori* reason why we should not subsequently take it out and look at it.

This view of the past is fairly common, but what does it amount to? What proof could there possibly be that a past event either did or did not continue to exist? It is to be hoped that a great many statements about the past are true, and also that, somehow or other, we have good reason to believe that they are true. And if one likes to take this as a proof of the 'reality' of the past, well and good. But then in saying that the past is real, one will be saying nothing more than that these statements are true; one will not, in any sense, be giving an explanation of their truth. Neither does this make it clear what can be meant by saying that past events *continue* to exist. Perhaps just that they are preserved in memory. But in that case to say that they continue to exist is not to account for the possibility of their being remembered. It is just another, and misleading, way of saying that the possibility obtains.

Much the same objection applies to the view that memory makes us directly acquainted with the past. The claim that 'the pastness of a remembered object is a datum of experience' may be allowed to stand if it is intended merely as a psychological comment on the way in which our memory seems to function. It brings out the point, which we have already noted, that even when a memory-experience has a present content, in the form, say, of an image, the image does not seem to stand between us and the past; we say to ourselves, apparently of the image, 'this happened' rather than 'something like this happened'; treating the image as diaphanous, we tend psychologically to identify it with the past event. On the other hand, if this is meant to be an explanation of our ability to remember, it is completely worthless. For what conceivable proof could there be that an object which I am now recollecting is 'compresent with me as past' except just that I am now recollecting it? Here, as elsewhere, the naïve realist offers us, in the guise of an explanation, what is nothing more than a re-statement of the claim to knowledge.

But perhaps the naïve realist wishes not so much to give an explanation of our ability to remember as to make the point that there need be no question in this case of our having to justify an inference. His contention may be that some memories at least are self-guaranteeing. This position gains an unmerited

[3] *Space, Time and Deity*, vol. i, p. 113.
[4] *The Mind and its Place in Nature*, pp. 249 ff.

plausibility from the fact that the verb 'to remember', like the verb 'to know', is used in such a way that if something is remembered it follows that it was so. To speak of remembering what never happened would be self-contradictory. This does not mean, however, that one cannot think that one remembers something which in fact never happened, that memory-experiences cannot be delusive. On the contrary, it is certain that they sometimes are. For not only are there cases in which one person's memories, or alleged memories, contradict another's, but even a single person's 'memories' may be contradictory. He may 'remember' that a given event occurred, while also 'remembering' that at an earlier time he 'remembered' that it did not. Since the event either did or did not occur, the fact that both alternatives may be remembered is also a proof that some memory-experiences are veridical,[5] though it does not enable us to decide which they are. The point which is important here is that, whichever they are, they will not differ qualitatively from those that are delusive. And even if they did so differ, the support which this might be thought to give to the naïve realist's position would not be effective. He wishes to represent the act of remembering as being, in some instances at least, a cognitive performance which bears on itself the stamp of infallibility. But we have already demonstrated that there cannot be any such performances. It may be argued that, in favourable circumstances, the fact that someone is confident that he remembers puts it beyond doubt that the relevant statement about the past is true. But whatever the character of his experience, it must always be logically consistent with it that the statement in question should be false.

The remaining argument in favour of saying that we are directly acquainted with past events is that this alone explains how we come to have a conception of the past. But once more the explanation is spurious. As we have already remarked, the fact that an object was presented to us, with the words 'I am past' stamped, as it were, upon it, could not in itself give rise to any conception of the past at all. Unless the device, whatever it may be, is interpreted as referring to the past, it is nothing more than a decorative addition to the object. But if we are to interpret it as referring to the past, our conception of the past must be independent of it. Moreover, this conception cannot in any case have arisen *from* the exercise of memory. For we have seen that whatever the content of a memory-experience, it acquires its reference to the past only through being so interpreted. But from this it follows that the identification of anything as a memory presupposes an understanding of what is meant by being past. And if this understanding is presupposed by memory, it cannot be founded on it. Psychologically it may arise *with* the exercise of memory, but that is another question.

In any case, if we insist on looking for a 'simple idea', in Locke's sense, from which to derive the complex idea of memory, it is not difficult to find one. It can, I think, plausibly be maintained that the relation of temporal precedence is 'given' to us in experience. As a matter of empirical fact, one can see or hear A-following-B, in the same immediate fashion as one can see A-to the left of-B. And this relation of temporal precedence, coupled with the notion of the present, which may be defined ostensively, is all that is required to yield the concepts both of the past and of the future. Defining the present as the class of events which are contemporaneous with *this*, where

[5] Assuming, of course, that there has been a past.

this is any event that one chooses to indicate at the given moment, one can define the past as the class of events which are earlier than the present, and the future as the class of events which are later than the present. This brings out also the important point that events are not in themselves either past, present, or future. In themselves they stand in relations of temporal precedence which do not vary with time; if one event is ever earlier than another, it is always so. Or rather, since the position of events in time is fixed by their temporal relations, it makes no sense to apply temporal predicates to their possession of these relations themselves. What varies is only the point of reference which is taken to constitute the present. Every past event has been at different times both present and future; every future event will be present and then past; and every present event has been future and will be past. But these facts are not a source of contradiction, as some philosophers have supposed: nor are they an excuse for nonsensical talk about a multiplicity of temporal dimensions. The explanation of them is just that the point of present reference, by which we orient ourselves in time, the point of reference which is implied by our use of tenses, is continuously shifted. It is this shift of the point of reference in the direction of earlier to later, not any change in the temporal relationship of events, that constitutes the passage of time. 'Le temps ne s'en va pas, mais nous nous en allons' is not only a good epigram; it is a piece of accurate analysis.

This logical subordination of the idea of the passage of time to that of temporal succession should be enough to make the notion of the past, and so of memory, respectable to those who like to see their empirical concepts straightforwardly grounded in experience. I do not suggest, however, that this is how the concept of the past is actually acquired. Genetically, it may very well be that one does not first form a concept of the relation of temporal precedence, and then extrapolate it to events which are beyond the range of one's immediate experience. It seems to me more likely that the understanding of what it is for an event to be past develops *pari passu* with the understanding of the use of the past tense. It may be objected that in order to understand the use of the past tense one must already have a conception of the past; else how would one know to what the past tense applied? But this is to ignore the extent to which the formation of concepts is itself a function of the use of words. Logically it is because there can be events which are earlier than this that we have a use for saying 'it was so'. But psychologically it may be that we first acquire the habit of saying 'it was so' in a certain class of present situations, and only later identify the reference of such phrases with events which are earlier than this.

CONCERNING THE ANALYSIS OF STATEMENTS ABOUT THE PAST

However these psychological questions are to be settled, the logical difficulty remains. Assuming that we somehow become capable of understanding statements which are intended to refer to the past, what possible means have we of verifying them? We can note that they corroborate one another, but can we go any further than this? Is it not logically impossible that we should discover, by direct inspection of the past, whether any one of them is true? Memory would seem to be our only resource, and it has been shown that memory does not furnish us with any such power. But then what reason can we have for believing in the occurrence of any past events? We may have reason for believing in the occurrence of events which some practical difficulty prevents us from observing; but it is requisite that they should at least be theoretically observable.

It is their acceptance of this argument that has led some philosophers to identify statements which are ostensibly about the past with statements which are ordinarily taken as referring to the actual or possible evidence on which our beliefs about the past are, or might be, founded; that is, to statements which, on the face of it, are not about the past at all, but about the present and future. Rather than conclude that the statements by means of which we try to refer to the past are all of them unwarranted or, worse still, nonsensical, these philosophers prefer to hold that they do not mean what they seem to mean. By construing them as referring to the present or future evidence that is, or might be made, available, they think that they at least make sure that they are capable of being verified.

Apart from this one advantage this view would seem, however, to have nothing to commend it. To begin with, it makes the meaning of statements which are expressed in the past tense remarkably unstable. For with the passage of time the range of the evidence which is supposed to be within our reach will be continually changing. The events which it was within my power to observe when I began to write this paragraph have already disappeared into the past. So the interpretation of all the statements in the analysis of which a description of these events figured will have to be revised; the description of these events will have to be replaced by a description of whatever present or future events are regarded as evidence for *them*; and, as they too fall into the past, the revised version will constantly have to be revised again. It will follow also, what we have already found to be objectionable, that sentences in the past and present tenses cannot express the same statement. I describe to-day's weather by saying that the sun is shining; but if to-morrow I say 'the sun shone yesterday' I am taken to be referring not to what I now express by saying 'the sun is shining', for that will be inexpressible, but to what one will find if one looks up the records in a meteorological office, or reads the newspaper, or consults one's own or other people's recollections. The possibility that these records are deceitful does not arise, except in so far as they may contradict each other, or may be contradicted by further evidence. At any given moment, the truth or falsehood of a statement about an earlier event depends entirely on the evidence that may thenceforward be discoverable. If from a certain time onward all the available evidence will go to show that such and such an event has occurred, then, on this view, it will follow that it really has occurred. To deny that it had occurred would simply be to predict that there would be a breakdown in the run of the favourable evidence; that it was at some later moment going to point the other way. We are thus brought to an entirely pragmatic conception of the use of language. Except in so far as they describe what one is actually observing—a fleeting performance, since the facts do not stay on record—the indicative use of sentences is to announce our expectations of the future. The truth or falsehood of what they express is merely a matter of the extent to which these expectations are capable of being fulfilled.

Now it is certainly true that if, from a given moment onwards, all the available evidence goes to show that a certain event has occurred, no one who lives at any subsequent time will have any reason to suppose that it did not. But to allow this is surely not to allow that the statement that the event occurred is formally entailed by the evidence. The possibility that the evidence is deceptive must remain open; and this not only in the sense that further evidence may fail to corroborate it. It must be at least conceivable that the event did not in fact occur, even though from the time at which the question is raised all the evidence that will ever be forthcoming goes to show that it did. Not only for emotional, but also for logical reasons, we wish to deny that it is possible, by a suitable adjustment of the evidence, literally to manufacture the past. The fact that the argument leads to this result should make us suspect that its premises are faulty. Is this really the only interpretation of statements about the past that allows them to be verifiable?

If it is thought to be so, it is because of the assumption that once an event is past it is inaccessible: what is past is past and there can be no returning to it. But is it so certain that one can have no access to the past? We have already remarked that, in view of the fact that light and sound take time to reach us, there is a ground for saying that a great many, perhaps the majority, of our perceptions are perceptions of past events. But this, it will be argued, is beside the point. If our acceptance of certain physical theories, combined with a predilection for the language of naïve realism, induces us to say that we perceive the past, this will just be the way that we have chosen to describe, or to account for, a certain set of observations. By adopting such hypotheses as that light and sound waves have a finite velocity, we come to interpret our experiences in such a way that a difference is established between their time order and the time order of the physical events with which they are supposed to bring us into contact. In a rather simpler fashion, we might decide to say that to watch a news-reel in the cinema was an instance of observing the past. But the only way in which we can come to attach a meaning to any such locutions is through the application of some scientific theory, which one accepts on the basis of one's past experiences. And whatever tricks we may be able to play with the dating of physical events, our past experiences are not recapturable. Once they are gone, they are gone for ever.

But what is it that prevents one from recapturing a past experience? With the progress of science, why should not a time machine be constructible which would enable us to travel in time, as we already succeed in travelling in space? Why should one not literally relive the scenes of one's childhood, or, for that matter, enjoy in advance the experiences of one's old age? It may not be technically feasible, but surely the possibility can at least be envisaged. Has it not, indeed, already been envisaged by writers of science fiction? The answer to this is that there is no difficulty at all in supposing that one can have experiences which are exactly like the experiences of one's childhood: one can conceive of their being obtained through hypnotism, or the use of drugs; there is no need to have recourse to anything so dubious as a time machine. But they still would not be the same experiences; and the reason why they would not be the same is just that they would occur at a different date. Even if it were possible to have one's life over and over again, in the sense that whenever one reached a certain age one would proceed to undergo a series of experiences which were qualitatively the same in every detail as those that one had undergone since birth, this still would not constitute a literal recapture of the past. One term of the cycle would be necessarily different from another. There is, therefore, no possibility of travelling in time. To travel in space is to be at different places at different times; but the idea of being at different times at different times is simply nonsensical. One can imagine being projected back into the eighteenth century, in the sense that from a given moment onwards one would have only such experiences as would be appropriate to that period of history; but still they could not be identical with the experiences that anyone, oneself or another, had actually had before. For inasmuch as they would succeed one's present experiences, they could not also precede them. To assign to one and the same event two different places in the same time order is self-contradictory.

Thus the reason why the past cannot be recaptured is just that nothing is allowed to count as our recapturing it. It is a necessary fact that if one occupies the position in time that one does at any given moment, one does not at that moment also occupy a different position. If one event temporally precedes another, an experience which is strictly simultaneous with the second of these events cannot also be strictly simultaneous with the first. So, if observing a past event is taken as requiring one to have an experience which is earlier than any experience that one is actually having, it is a necessary fact that one cannot observe a past event.

But from the fact that one cannot now observe an event which took place at an earlier date, it does not follow that the event itself is to be characterized as unobservable.[6] We must distinguish here between things which are unobservable in themselves, in the sense that to talk of anyone's observing them is contradictory or nonsensical, and things which are unobservable by a given person, because of the situation in which he happens to be placed. We are not accustomed to regard events which are occurring at a different place from that in which we happen to be as being for that reason unobservable. Yet it is necessarily true that, being now where I am, I cannot make any of the observations which would require me to be somewhere else. It is true that I can change my position in space, whereas I cannot change my position in time: but to travel in space takes time, so that I cannot observe what is now going on elsewhere; the best that I can do is put myself into a position to observe what will be going on there at some future date. It is indeed conceivable that I should now be somewhere else; it is not a necessary fact that I am where I am. But then is it not conceivable that I should have lived at a different time? When people say, for example, that they would like to have lived in Ancient Greece, it is certainly not obvious that the wish that they express is self-contradictory. The question is difficult because it is not at all clear what is required for the preservation of one's personal identity. Our imagination, which allows us to roam freely about space, is also equal to the idea of a certain amount of transposition in time, but when the period in which it seeks to place us is extremely remote, there is an inclination to say that one would not in that case be the same person. But even if it were self-contradictory, as I do not think it is, to say of any event, which is in fact past though

[6] I have already developed this argument in a paper called 'Statements about the Past', published in the *Proceedings of the Aristotelian Society*, 1950–51, and reprinted in *Philosophical Essays*.

not described as being so, that I, being the person that I am, am now observing it, it still would not follow that the event itself was unobservable. The position is different if the event is described as being past, but then this is not a description of the event itself but only an indication of the speaker's temporal relation to it.

This is, indeed, the important point. The mistake which is made by those who think themselves obliged to turn statements about the past into statements about the present and future is that of supposing that a difference in the tense of an indicative sentence invariably makes a difference to the factual content of the statement which it expresses. It does make a difference in the cases where the tense is the only means employed for dating the event referred to. Clearly, if I now say that the sun is shining, I am making a different statement from that which I should be making if I were to say that the sun shone yesterday, or that it will shine to-morrow. But in all such cases one could convey the same information by making the dates explicit in a way that did not essentially involve the use of tenses, or of other temporal demonstratives such as the words 'yesterday' or 'to-morrow'. Instead of using the present tense and leaving it to be understood from the context what date I am referring to, I could record the occurrence of sunshine at a certain place on August 20th, A.D. 1955. And then it makes no difference to the content of the record whether it is the expression of a prediction, a contemporary observation, or an act of memory. If I am speaking before the event I shall make use of the future tense, and if I am speaking after the event I shall make use of the past tense, but the fact which I describe will be in either case the same. In such an instance, the substitution of one tense for another serves to give a different indication of the temporal position of the speaker with respect to the occurrence to which he is referring, but the meaning of the sentence is not otherwise affected. The truth or falsehood of a statement which purports to describe the condition of the weather at a given date is quite independent of the time at which it is expressed. By combining a description of the event in question with a reference to the temporal position of the speaker, the use of tenses brings together two pieces of information which are logically distinct. It does this in an economical fashion, but it is not indispensable. Either piece of information could perfectly well be given in a language that contained no tenses at all. The temporal position of the speaker, relatively to the event described, which is shown by this use of the present, past, or future tense, could itself be characterized by being explicitly assigned a date.

We come then to a conclusion which we have already anticipated in remarking that events, considered in themselves, are neither present, past, or future. For it follows from this that considering only the factual content of a statement, irrespective of the time at which it is expressed, no statement is as such about the past. It may describe an event which is earlier than the occasion of its being expressed, and it may itself refer to this temporal relationship. But both the characterization of the event and the account of its temporal relationship to a particular occasion of its being described are pieces of information that could be given at any time. The fact that they are given at one time rather than another may bear upon the strength of the reasons that we at present have for accepting them, but it has no bearing on their content. Thus, the analysis of a given statement is not affected by the question whether the statement is delivered before, or after, or simultaneously with the event to which it refers. From which it follows that inasmuch as the verifiability of a statement depends only on its meaning, a statement which is verifiable when the event to which it refers is present is equally verifiable when the event is future or past.

The importance of this argument is that it preserves us from having to accept an implausible analysis of statements about the past; it shows that there is no need for us to try to convert them into statements about the present or future. Even so, it may be objected, it does not take us very far. Let it be granted that statements about the past are verifiable in themselves. The fact remains that we, who happen to be living at a later time, are not, and could not be, in a position to verify them. It may, or may not, be conceivable that we should have occupied a different position in time. We have to accept the fact that we occupy the position that we do: and, this being so, there is no means now available to us of observing an event which would be accessible to us only if we occupied an earlier position. As has already been shown, there is nothing even that would count as our returning to the past. But this means that we are still confronted with the problem of showing how we can ever be justified in accepting statements which purport to describe these past events.

It might seem that if we are to be justified at all it must be by an inductive argument. We have, indeed, already established that one of the conditions which is ordinarily required for an inductive argument to be valid can be met; the conclusion is not as such unverifiable. But what is the evidence on which the argument would be based? There is not even a single instance in which anyone has actually observed the conjunction of a present and a past event; or rather, if there are said to be such instances, as in the cases where an event like a solar eclipse is calculated to be past at the time when it is observed, it is only in virtue of some scientific hypothesis which, as we have noted, would not itself be justifiable unless we had independent reasons for believing in the existence of certain past events. One may argue that if it is reasonable to expect a given process to continue into the future it must also be reasonable to infer that it grew out of the past. If 'change and decay in all around I see', there must be something that things have changed out of, as well as something that they are changing into. Not every process can start in mid-career, like Minerva springing fully armed from the head of Jove. But to speak of a process starting in mid-career is to imply that processes of its kind normally have antecedent phases. The change that I am said to see is mostly change that I remember. Our right to conceive of current processes as extending in both temporal directions is itself based upon our knowledge of the past. There would appear then to be no escaping from this circle. Any attempt to justify a statement about the past by an inductive argument is found at some point to involve the assumption that some statement about the past is true.

Indeed, it is obvious that this must be so. Since no event intrinsically points beyond itself, our reason for linking a later with an earlier event, for assuming that the one would not in the given circumstances have occurred unless the other had preceded it, must lie in our acceptance of some general hypothesis;

that is to say, we account for the later event by correlating it with the earlier. The hypothesis which gives us our warrant for doing this will itself be supported by evidence for which other hypotheses will provide a backing in its turn. There may thus be no statement about the past that one is not, if one accepts it, prepared to justify; even if the justification sometimes consists in nothing more than an appeal to memory, an appeal the force of which lies in the assumption that people are commonly in a position to know about the events which they claim to remember, that their reports of these events are to be trusted; and this is again a general assumption for which evidence can be adduced. So one statement about the past is used to justify another; but still there is no independent means of justifying them all. There is not, because there could not be. To obtain this justification one would have to be able to recapture the past in a way that has been shown to be logically impossible.

It does not follow, however, that we must renounce any claim to knowledge of the past. Historians cannot perform impossible feats of temporal projection; they cannot make a later event coincide with, or precede, an earlier event in the same time-series; but still there are canons of historical evidence. One authority is checked against another; psychological and economic laws are brought into play: in a considerable number of cases the evidence attains a strength which makes it proper to say that some statement about an earlier event is known to be true. Not that any such statement will be logically entailed by the evidence, except in such cases as the evidence is taken as including general propositions which themselves will draw their support from statements about the past. For instance, the statement that the earth is millions of years old is supported by a wealth of geological evidence; it would not be incorrect to say that we know it to be true. There are, however, people who for religious reasons prefer to believe that the earth came into existence only a few thousand years ago but already bearing perceptible signs of age. We may say that this is a silly view: if we know the other to be true, we know it to be false, but it is formally compatible with the evidence. Even the view that the earth and all its inhabitants had come into existence just at this moment would not be formally inconsistent with anything that one could now observe. What it would contradict would be the accepted interpretations and explanations of the phenomena; it would be an arbitrary denial of them, and all the more irresponsible in that it would furnish us with no other means of accounting for subsequent events. The case for the scientifically orthodox explanations is that they do explain.

Still it is logically conceivable that they are false. And if anyone chooses to make this a reason for withholding even a provisional judgement on them, if anyone chooses, in particular, to maintain that our being unable to recapture any past experience leaves it an entirely open question whether any statement about the past is true, I do not know what more there is left to say to him: any more than I know what there is to say to someone who maintains that the fact that scientific hypotheses go beyond their evidence deprives us of any right to form expectations of the future. We can say that he is irrational; but this will not worry him; our standard of rationality is just what he objects to. Our only resource is to point out, as we have done, that the proof that he requires of us is one that he makes it logically impossible for us to give. It is, therefore, not surprising that we cannot furnish it: it is no discredit to the proofs which we do rely on that they do not imply that we can achieve the impossible; it would be a discredit to them, rather, if they did.

Clarence Irving Lewis

Probable Knowledge and the Validity of Memory

. . . The assumption of certainty for memory in general would be contradicted by the fact that we remember remembering things and later finding them to be false. And memory in general being thus fallible, the claim of certainty for any particular memory, or class of them, becomes dubious. Such credence of any particular thing remembered, asks for some other and supporting ground beyond the immediate item which presents itself with the quality of recollection. And here we might well fall into despair; because we see in advance that in any attempt to provide for a memory such supporting grounds of its credibility, we are bound to encounter the same difficulty all over again, and in a more complex and aggravated form. Because we shall have to rest upon facts about like memories in the past and their subsequent confirmation —facts which can only be themselves disclosed by remembering.

The answer which, as we conceive, can be returned to the problem thus posed, has two parts. First; whatever is remembered, whether as explicit recollection or merely in the form of our sense of the past, is *prima facie* credible because so remembered. And second; when the whole range of empirical beliefs is taken into account, all of them more or less dependent upon memorial knowledge, we find that those which are most credible can be assured by their mutual support, or as we shall put it, by their *congruence.* Neither of these two theses is put forward as being self-evident, or even as having initial plausibility. Nor are we minded to put them forward as *ad hoc* postulates, which should be accepted on the ground that, granted these premises, the 'facts of knowledge' can be explained. Both of them should be submitted to an examination which is as careful as possible, and accepted only if they then appear compelling.

First, however, let us be quite clear why the usual conception of empirical knowledge as a vast and complex body of information, built up historically out of the experience of men, each advance supported by previous cognitive achievements, and the whole structure founded originally upon our data of

From C. I. Lewis, *An Analysis of Knowledge and Valuation* (incorporating the Paul Carus Lectures of 1945), Chap. 11, published by The Open Court Publishing Co., LaSalle, Ill., 1946, and reprinted with their permission.

sense—why this easily suggested picture, whatever its historical justification may be, affords no solution for the problem of the *validity* of empirical knowledge. All of one's empirical knowledge rests, ultimately, for its credibility, upon one's *own* experience. (And there is no empirical knowledge which belongs to men in general but to nobody in particular.) Reports by other persons, and other such indirect evidence, play an enormously large part, in the justification, as well as in the corroboration of it; but before such indirect evidence can play this supporting role, it is essential that there be some ground on which, for example, the credibility of another's report can be assessed. That ground will involve a reference to past experience of receiving such reports and finding them reliable, in measure, by reference to later confirmations of what was reported. It requires the report plus some such generalization from our own experience to give credibility. And since the report itself is, when received, a certain kind of experience of our own, the whole basis of belief must finally lie within the knower's own experience.

Similarly for our own experience. What we empirically know in the first person all goes back eventually to those critical items which may be labelled 'direct perception', like my present observation of the paper now before me. But for the objective empirical fact of this paper—or even for credibility of it —the presently given and indubitable data of sense are not sufficient. For credibility of the statement "White paper is now before me," I must have, in addition to the sense presentation, those generalizations which would not be available in the early experience of an infant, and which will enable prediction, with a degree of assurance, of the corroboration in further experience of what the reality of white paper before me would imply. Such generalizations are available to me by virtue of my past experience of comparable occasions. But they are available only as remembered. That is; what is available directly, to my present reflective examination of my present belief, is only given presentations having the qualitative character of memory, and not the facts of past experience which are requisite. Before I can accredit the present belief, on the basis of given sense data and a generalization about past like occasions, I must first accredit the presently given recollections or sense of past fact, which are the only available witnesses to actual past experience. I must find at least a degree of credibility attaching to the empirical judgment, "On past like occasions I had such and such experience"; and the present fact of memory, which suggests this judgment to me, is still not sufficient to assure the truth of it. In addition to the present data of recollection, a generalization is required to the effect that when such data of memory are given, the seemingly remembered experience may, with some degree of credibility, be accepted as actual. And that requisite generalization concerns the trustworthiness of memory in general, or of memories of a certain class which includes the present one. To establish that generalization, I must summon the evidence that I have, on past occasions, had experiences like this present one of remembering explicitly past facts, or of sensing them as belonging to my past, and that these past experiences of remembering later turned out to be genuinely indicative of past facts, in a sufficiently large proportion of cases to justify my accepting the present recollection as probably valid.

I could, doubtless, summon such evidence: I do on occasion, reflect upon the reliability of certain classes of my memories; for example, of my recollections of colors, or of names, or of the places where I put my things; and I do arrive at generalizations about the credibility of this or that kind of memorial presentation. But it is more in point to observe the general predicament of empirical knowledge which now becomes sufficiently evident. I set out to assess the credibility of an empirical fact believed, on the evidence of present data of sense. For this, a generalization concerning past like occasions of experience proved requisite. That had to be based on memory. But the mere fact of present memory was insufficient; both because memorial presentations, like sense presentations, are not equivalent to the empirical fact they suggest to us, and because, in particular, merely remembering—as certain of my memories themselves suggest—is not a completely trustworthy index of the facts remembered. Before I can assess my present belief, then, I am sent back to past experience, and must assess the credibility of particular items of memorial knowledge. These can only be assessed by reference to past experiences of remembering—which, in turn, are not presently given, but only evidenced in memory. There is no circularity here—as the merely verbal formulation might suggest: I could make the assessment of this particular memory in the general manner which is obvious. But what I observe is that I am certainly not going to be able in this process to come to the end of my problem of assessing the credibility of my present empirical belief; because at each step I shall be sent back to past experience; hence to the evidence of memory; and shall always find that the available evidence of memory is insufficient and requires itself a ground of credence, which, in turn, can only be found in past experience—as remembered—and so on. The general nature of memorial knowledge constitutes a Gordian knot. And no ultimate solution of the validity of probable knowledge is possible unless this can be untied.

As has been pointed out, this predicament is theoretical, not practical. Because memories, as well as beliefs suggested by sense perception, are confirmable as well as justifiable. And the practical resolution of any doubt as to the correctness of a memory, is to make some further test of it, by looking to some present or future consequence of its truth. If, for example, I wonder whether I am correct in remembering that I put my glasses on the mantel, I shall not pause overlong in reflecting on the grounds I have for trusting this particular recollection, but shall look and see. If my memory is corroborated in this way, that is much better evidence of its credibility (if I still have an interest in that) than any which I might get by summoning up anterior grounds for crediting it. But for the theoretical problem of the validity of my memorial belief as genuinely cognitive, this appeal to confirmation would be pointless. Because this theoretical problem concerns credibility *per se,* not the truth of what is credited; which last is the practical concern.

For the requisite analysis of knowledge, we are brought no nearer by observing that memories can be confirmed by sense experience, instead of regressively justified on antecedent grounds. Because our problem concerns the validity of belief as probable knowledge anterior to and independently of any corroboration by sense which is subsequent to the cognition under examination. And what we find with respect to that problem is that any solution involving the supposition that a belief is justified as probable on antecedent grounds which are either certain or, if only probable, then are such as have in turn their temporally prior grounds, and so on, until we come to final and sufficient grounds contained exclusively in direct empirical evidence—that this solution by way of a finite linear regress ending in given data which are wholly certain, is quite impossible.

What, in particular, makes it impossible, is the fact that the 'experience' looked to as the eventual foundation of our whole pyramidal structure of empirical beliefs, is mainly not given sense experience, at the time when we appeal to it, but past experience, available to us only as remembered. But no memory is epistemologically equivalent to the certainty of what is remembered: it is only evidence to be weighed in validating the empirical judgment that what is remembered actually took place. And the attempt to validate this judgment sends us in search of other requisite grounds, which in turn will involve other appeals to memory. Hence no regressus of this sort can be brought to termination in empirical certainties.

VII

The nature of this predicament almost inevitably suggests a coherence theory of truth as the solution of it. Specifically it suggests, as a possibility to be examined, that a body of empirical beliefs, each of which is less than certain and no one of which can be substantiated on empirically certain grounds, may nevertheless be justified as credible by their relation to one another. That possibility is indeed borne out by certain facts about conjoint probabilities which are simple and fairly obvious. But these pertinent facts are fundamentally different, in the logical significance of them, from those theses, put forward by British post-Kantian idealism, which have the best right, historically, to the label 'coherence theory of truth'. In order to mark our departure from that historical conception, we shall speak of the *congruence* of statements, instead of coherence; and shall assign to this term 'congruence' a definite and limited meaning. *A set of statements, or a set of supposed facts asserted, will be said to be congruent if and only if they are so related that the antecedent probability of any one of them will be increased if the remainder of the set can be assumed as given premises.*

This relation of congruence requires something more than merely the mutual consistency of a set of statements, but something less than that relation of a set or system such that each statement in it is logically deducible from the others, taken together as premises. If, however, we are not to repeat some of the fallacies of the historical coherence theory, it becomes vitally important to observe that neither mutual consistency throughout, nor what we call congruence of a set of statements, nor even that relation of a system in which every included statement is deducible from others which are included, can by itself assure even the lowest degree of probability for a body of empirical beliefs or suppositions in question. For that, it is absolutely requisite that some at least of the set of statements possess a degree of credibility antecedent to and independently of the remainder of those in question, and derivable from the relation of them to direct experience. It is on this point particularly that the historical coherence theory appears to be ambiguous: it seems never possible to be sure, in presentations of that conception, whether 'coherence' implies some essential relation to *experience,* or whether it requires only some purely logical relationship of the statements in question. Indeed, the so-called 'modern logic', associated with this theory, is such as totally to obscure the essential distinction between analytic truths of logic and those empirical truths which can only be assured by some reference beyond logic to given data of sense.

The mere relationship of consistency amongst statements believed—the fact that, together, they constitute a completely self-consistent system—provides by itself no ground whatever for rational credence of any one of them. This would be sufficiently evident if the body of statements in question should be small. No one would be so silly as to believe four statements, *'P'*, *'Q'*, *'R'*, *'S'*, because they were consistent, if there were no *other* reason to believe any one of them. Possibly, however, it will be replied that it is the size of the aggregate of statements believed which makes the difference here: that the 'whole of the truth' is consistent, and no non-fact is consistent with this whole of the truth; and hence that as the body of included beliefs approaches to such a comprehensive whole, complete consistency is increasingly good evidence of truth and therefore an increasingly good ground of rational credence.

Such reasoning, however, is a mere paralogism. The premises—that the whole of the truth is a completely consistent system, and that no non-fact is consistent with this whole—are obviously true, supposing that the phrase 'whole of the truth' means anything. But the conclusions drawn do not follow, and in fact find no basis whatever in any logic which is not itself born of confusion. If there is any consistent body of truth, then also there is a corresponding and equally self-consistent system of statements incorporating some which are false; or many such systems. That in the end only one sufficiently comprehensive system of statements would be found consistent, is a suggestion which runs counter to obvious facts about the nature of consistency and of systems: probably it strikes us as plausible because we are such poor liars, and are fairly certain to become entangled in inconsistencies sooner or later, once we depart from the truth. A sufficiently magnificent liar, however, or one who was given time and patiently followed a few simple rules of logic, could eventually present us with any number of systems, as comprehensive as you please, and all of them including falsehoods. Insofar as it is possible to deal with any such notion as 'the whole of the truth', it is the Leibnitzian conception of an infinite plurality of possible worlds which is justified, and not the conception of the historical coherence theory that there is just one all-comprehensive system, uniquely determined to be true by its complete consistency.

This point can be brought out without reference to those difficulties which must eventually defeat the human attempt to envisage any system of statements adequate to describe a possible world. First, let us remark a fact which is simple and commonplace. Empirical statements universally have the character of logical contingency: they cannot be certified as true by any logical character of them, nor can they be so certified as false. If we should have collated, up to a certain point, some body of such empirical statements believed, then for any empirical truth not already implied by or incompatible with what we thus believe, both that truth and the contradictory of it are entirely consistent with this body of antecedent beliefs. Let us suppose this set of statements believed to be self-consistent throughout; and let us label the conjoint statement of all these beliefs *'P'*. And let *'Q'* be any further contingent statement, whose truth is not yet determined. That '*Q*' is contingent means that '*Q*' and its contradictory, 'not-*Q*', are both of them self-consistent statements. That '*Q*' is not deducible from '*P*'—and hence is not already contained in the system '*P*'—means that everything contained in '*P*' is consistent with the falsity of '*Q*'. And that 'not-*Q*' is not deducible from '*P*'—and hence '*Q*' is not already determined to be false or disbelievable—means that everything in '*P*' is consistent with '*Q*'. To say that a body of antecedent beliefs '*P*' does not imply already the truth or the falsity of '*Q*', and to say that '*Q*' and its contradictory 'not-*Q*' are both of them completely consistent with everything in '*P*', are merely two ways of saying the same thing.

Second—and now we come nearer to the point in question—if we start with some set of contingent statements, '*P, Q, R,* . . .', and the problem be to determine the truth or falsity of one of them—say '*P*'—by reference to its consistency or inconsistency with comprehensive systems of possible empirical fact, then that problem has no solution. It is insoluble for the following reasons. For any pair of such propositions, '*P*' and '*Q*', if the conjoint statement '*P* and *Q*' is not consistent (i.e., if '*P*' is not consistent with '*Q*'), then '*P* and not-*Q*' will be consistent; and if 'not-*P* and *Q*' is not consistent, then 'not-*P* and not-*Q*' will be consistent. And for '*P*' and '*Q*' and any third contingent statement '*R*', the facts are similar. If '*P* and *Q*' is consistent, then either '*P* and *Q* and *R*' is consistent or '*P* and *Q* and not-*R*' is consistent; and if 'not-*P* and *Q*' is consistent, then either 'not-*P* and *Q* and *R*' is consistent or 'not-*P* and *Q* and not-*R*' will be consistent. Likewise for any compound statement '*M*', representing any already constructed system of possible empirical fact, and any remaining empirical alternative, '*N*' or 'not-*N*': if '*M* and *N*' is not consistent, then '*M* and not-*N*' must be consistent.

Thus if we start with any empirical belief or statement '*P*', we shall find that one or other of every pair of further empirical statements, '*Q*' and 'not-*Q*', '*R*' and 'not-*R*', etc., can be conjoined with '*P*' to form a self-consistent set. And exactly the same will likewise be true of its contradictory 'not-*P*'. *Every empirical supposition, being a contingent statement, is contained in some self-consistent system which is as comprehensive as you please.* And as between the truth of any empirical belief or statement '*P*' and the falsity of it (the truth of 'not-*P*') consistency with other possible beliefs or statements, or inclusion in comprehensive and self-consistent systems, provides no clue or basis of decision.

Unless there are *some* empirical truths known otherwise than by their relations of consistency or inconsistency with others, no empirical truth can ever be determined by the criterion of consistency. And when some empirical truths *are* antecedently known, no *further* empirical truth is in any wise determinable by appeal to considerations of consistency or inconsistency, except such as are determinable from what we already know or can determine by the familiar methods of ordinary logic. The attempt to determine any empirical truth not simply deducible from antecedently determined facts, by an appeal to consistency, is completely defeated by the elementary facts of logic.

. . .

VIII

What might with better reason suggest 'coherence' as justifying empirical belief, is consideration of certain facts about probability and about conjoint probabilities. It is relationships of the kind in question for which we have suggested the label 'congruence' instead of 'coherence'; and the main considerations which are in point have already been referred to in Chapter VIII [not reprinted here]. For example, one main method of inductive substantiation of empirical beliefs is that called 'hypothesis and verification'; and it can be claimed with some plausibility that the major part, or even the whole, of the business of inductive inference could be brought under the general principles of this method. By this procedure the probability of a hypothesis is weighed by looking to the truth or falsity of consequences of it, and by looking to the probability which such consequences have independently of the hypothesis. What are rated as consequences of a hypothesis are not—it should be observed —deductions from it. Deductive consequences may be included as a special case; but when a hypothesis *'H'* is said to have the consequence *'C'*, what typically is meant is that *'H'*, together with other statements which may reasonably be assumed, gives a high probability of *'C'*.[1] For instance, if the hypothesis that there are termites infesting a certain building is said to have the consequence that the walls of the building will sag, what is meant is that, given the premise of termites in the building, together with known facts about termites and about buildings, and the laws of physics, there arises a high probability of sagging walls. One would have to be a bit ingenious to supplement the stated hypothesis *'H'* with some set of other reasonable presumptions *'K'* in such wise that *'C'* would follow by the laws of deductive logic from *'HK'*. And even where this should be possible, it still goes beyond what would commonly be intended by calling *'C'* a consequence of *'H'*. For this usual meaning, it will be sufficient if there is a fairly high probability of *'C'* on the premises *'HK'*. Also, what figure as the pertinent facts *'K'* which are presumed, may, some of them, be premises which are not themselves so certain that failure of the consequences of *'HK'* could not lead to the repudiation of *'K'* instead of the repudiation of *'H'*. The whole set of statements in question, *'H'* and *'K'* and the various consequences, C_1, C_2, and so on, may be such that, antecedently to tests which are not yet made, each of them has some higher or lower degree of probability but none of them is certain—even when 'certain' means only 'practically' or 'scientifically' certain. A complete and careful logical analysis of this fairly frequent type of situation represents a kind of study which has never yet been carried out; and we shall not attempt it here. The most important considerations may be elicited without that, relying on facts which are obvious.

A point which particularly should draw our attention, is what can happen when various consequences of a single hypothesis are found to be true. If different consequences be verified, or independently confirmed, the conjoint fact of these separate confirmations may increase the probability of the hypothesis in a degree notably greater than that which any one of them alone would give, and greater than the sum of the increases which these confirmations would give separately. Specifically, if 'C_1' and 'C_2' be independent conse-

[1] It is not even essential that such a probability be high: in general, the same principle will apply wherever *'C'* is more probable than not.

quences of *'H'* (so related that supposing *'H'* false, the finding of one of them true would not increase the probability of the other), then the finding of *both* of them true will increase the probability of *'H'* in measure as this conjunction of circumstances (C_1 and C_2 both true), is improbable if *'H'* be false.

. . .

[The possible] example of relatively unreliable witnesses who independently tell the same circumstantial story, is another illustration of the logic of congruence; and one which is more closely typical of the importance of relations of congruence for determination of empirical truth in general. For any one of these reports, taken singly, the extent to which it confirms what is reported may be slight. And antecedently, the probability of what is reported may also be small. But congruence of the reports establishes a high probability of what they agree upon, by principles of probability determination which are familiar: on any other hypothesis than that of truth-telling, this agreement is highly unlikely; the story any one false witness might tell being one out of so very large a number of equally possible choices. (It is comparable to the improbability that successive drawings of one marble out of a very large number will each result in choice of the one white marble in the lot.) And the one hypothesis which itself is congruent with this agreement becomes thereby commensurately well established. It is the possible role of congruence in the determination of empirical truth which is dramatized in detective stories and mystery tales. Here various items of evidence are given initially, or introduced as the story unfolds; some as authenticated fact, and some having greater or smaller initial credibility. Taken separately, these afford small confirmation of the hypothesis which eventually gives the solution, and may not even serve to suggest it. Also, any single one of them is congruent with various alternative hypotheses. But the picture-puzzle relation of these items, at one stroke raises what was merely conjecturable before to the status of the highly probable, when the last piece of evidence fits into place. And if such light fiction typically exaggerates the part which congruence alone may play, still science has its detective stories in goodly number, and the logic of them is rather better than that of the thrillers.

It may also serve to emphasize the importance of congruence in the confirmation of empirical beliefs if we observe in how large a measure the final bases of credibility must be found in evidence having the character of 'reports' of one kind or another—reports of the senses, reports of memory, reports of other persons—and this label 'report' is appropriate just because such items do not fully authenticate what is 'reported'. 'Reports' also exemplify another feature which, more often than not, characterizes the confirmation of our beliefs through their congruent relations: namely, that where independent 'reports' mainly 'agree' what they agree upon may still become highly credible, in spite of some single report, or a few, which disagree. . . . If all the witnesses but one independently tell the same story, that story is still highly credible, and the disagreeing witness is probably to be discredited.

. . .

Yet we must not, without further ado, suppose it universally the case that no single item of evidence can outweigh congruence of other items or of our antecedent beliefs. If an unexamined coin should have fallen heads ten times in succession, there would be a considerable probability of its being a false coin; but a tail on the eleventh throw would discredit that presumption at once. 'Congruence' is a rather broad or weak relationship—though not quite so weak as consistency—and where it obtains, a variety of stronger relationships may also hold, or may fail to hold. It will be sufficiently evident that the logic of congruent sets would be a complex matter. We have spoken of it mainly in terms of 'hypothesis and verification'; partly because the logic of that method will be familiar. But plainly there is hardly a feature of the logic of induction which would not be involved. Indeed, it may well be said that 'congruence' is merely a suggestive name for a relation universally discoverable in those situations where inductive inference is possible. And if it should be added that real usefulness of it would depend upon that developed logic of induction which is here omitted, we should have no quarrel with that comment. However, it is likewise true that 'hypothesis and verification' is only a name for one mode of formulation which universally can be given to problems of inductive inference.[2]

Speaking in terms of this familiar method, the considerations needing to be weighed in determining any particular relationship of congruence, would include the following: (1) the other hypotheses, alternative to the one under consideration, which also might 'explain' (give a high probability of) those

[2] The distinction between 'the hypothesis' and its 'consequences' is often arbitrary to a degree, and made on grounds which are only in part logical. A good deal of logic was formerly written on the assumption—usually vague and unexpressed—that the consequences by which a hypothesis is confirmed are *deducible* from it. As has been noted this would be the case only exceptionally; very exceptionally in fact. Typically what is labelled 'hypothesis' is a member of a congruent set, selected by reference to one or more of the following considerations: (*a*) it is more general than its consequences, (*b*) it is relatively difficult to test directly, and is mainly to be confirmed by reference to its consequences, (*c*) it is that member of the set in whose confirmation we are particularly interested, (*d*) it is a statement whose addition to the set emphasizes the congruent relationship of the members.

There is one fallacy which, while seldom explicit, seems to color a good deal of discussion of the inductive procedure of hypothesis and verification: it seems to be assumed that an ideal case for exhibiting the logic of this method would be an instance in which the hypothesis, 'H', cannot be tested directly, but evidenced only by some set of consequences, '$C_1, C_2, \ldots C_n$'; and that if ideally chosen, these consequences would all be mutually independent. It should be noted that this ideal case is wholly impossible. In the nature of this case, either the remainder of the set of consequences, without reference to 'H', must afford some probability of a given consequence, 'C_m'—in which case this consequence is not independent of the others—or 'C_m' is not a consequence of 'H', or the other consequences, without 'C_m', afford no probability of the hypothesis. For example, suppose that zero comes up 'too often' on a roulette wheel, but that under the conditions no direct test of possible interference can be made. Then either this too frequent occurrence of zero must eventually establish a probability of its continuance for the future, or no smallest probability of interference could arise, no matter how often the zero comes up. And the difficulty of setting any criterion for determining how often, here, is 'too often', and how long continuation of this aberration is required for a probability as to the future, should warn us of dubiety in the presumption that two occurrences of zero are, logically considered, completely independent.

In general, the consequences of a hypothesis are independent only in the sense that the establishment of one does not increase the probability of another on the assumption that the hypothesis is *false*. And the whole set of consequences will be congruent *without the assumption* of the hypothesis. One manner in which this fact may be emphasized, is by the statement often made that inductive inference is, in reality, inference from particulars to particulars; the 'generalization' having no content save the included particulars. A not directly testable hypothesis likewise has no content beyond the testable consequences of it. And if these consequences be not of themselves a congruent set, then the hypothesis must be either empty or false.

items which are found true or for which a high degree of probability is independently established; (2) the antecedent credibility attaching to this hypothesis in comparison with alternatives; (3) the independence which the consequences have of one another (that is; whether, supposing 'H_1' *false*, the probability of a consequence, 'C_1', depends on that of another, 'C_2'); (4) the probability of each consequence on the supposition that the hypothesis in question holds.

. . .

Take the case of the unreliable observers who agree in what they report. In spite of the antecedent improbability of any item of such report, when taken separately, it may become practically certain, in a favorable case, merely through congruent relation to other such items, which would be similarly improbable when separately considered. On the general principle that, out of all the possible ways in which unreliable reporters can go wrong, their happening to tell independently just these stories which agree point for point, would be so thoroughly incredible on any other hypothesis than that of accurate telling of the truth. And similarly for memory: something I seem to remember as happening to me at the age of five may be of small credibility; but if a sufficient number of such seeming recollections hang together sufficiently well and are not incongruent with any other evidence, then it may become highly probable that what I recollect is fact. It becomes thus probable just in measure as this congruence would be unlikely on any other supposition which is plausible.

But still it is no logical relationship of statements believed which contributes the critical ground of their believability. Such logical relationship—at least the relation of complete consistency—is requisite as a *sine qua non* of probability. But if this congruent set of statements should be fabricated out of whole cloth, the way a novelist writes a novel, or if it should be set up as an elaborate hypothesis *ad hoc* by some theorist whose enthusiasm runs away with his judgment, such congruence would be no evidence of fact. If such merely logical relationship of statements were good reason for belief, then unreliable reporters would be working in the interest of truth if they got together and fudged their stories into agreement. And the hard-pressed undergraduate who works his 'experiment' backwards and gets his 'data' from the answer in the book, would be following a highly meritorious procedure which should be recommended to all scientists. The feature of such corroboration through congruence which should impress us, is the requirement that the items exhibiting these congruent relationships must—some of them at least—be *independently given facts* or have a probability which is antecedent. There must be *direct* evidence of something which would be improbable coincidence on any other hypothesis than that which is corroborated. The root of the matter is that the unreliable reporters do make such congruent reports without collusion; that we do find ourselves presented with recollections which hang together too well to be dismissed as illusions of memory. The indispensable item is some direct empirical datum; the actually given reports, the facts of our seeming to remember; and without that touchstone of presentation, relations of congruence would not advance us a step toward determination of the empirically actual or the validly credible. However important this relation of congruence in the building up of our structure of empirical beliefs, the foundation stones which must support the whole edifice are still those items of truth which are disclosed in given experience. All the facts of reality undoubtedly form a congruent set, and one comprising an untold number of subsets, each congruent within itself and congruently related with all the others. But that character of reality will not tell us which one, out of innumerably many such possible worlds, each of them overlapping logically with others, this world we live in is; any more than the completely congruent character and systematic unity of each of the various geometries, will determine for us which one of them applies to our space. To discover that kind of fact, we shall have to rely upon experience.

. . .

The application of our conclusions to the validation of memory is one which would, in all probability, have been obvious without this extended examination. Our only evidence of past experience, essential to the validity of any inductive establishment of empirical fact as probable, must be finally in the form of present 'reports' of past fact; particularly the reports of memory and of our present sense of past experience as having been thus and so. But the past is irrecoverable: we cannot go behind the epistemological present in any attempted justification of belief: and the presently given memorial items are not epistemically equivalent to the past experience which they represent, but are only surrogates of such past fact. They are, moreover, beset by the paradox that if memory in general is to be trusted, then *not all* memories are trustworthy; which estops us from any blanket assumption that what is remembered is true.

In this situation, the consideration of congruence supplies the missing link. It is not necessary to make this unwarranted assumption: it is only essential that the fact of present memory afford *some presumption* of the fact which is memorially presented. All that is needed is initial assumption that the mere fact of present rememberings renders what is thus memorially present in some degree credible. For the rest, the congruence of such items with one another and with present sense experience will be capable of establishing an eventual high credibility, often approximating to certainty, for those items which stand together in extensive relations of such congruence. Such establishment of high credibilities concerning what is past, by reference to congruence, will, moreover, be in full accord with our common-sense practices in the corroboration of past fact, and with our common understanding of the basis of our actual beliefs about the past. Furthermore, this logic of congruence is compatible with the fact that even though what is remembered or presents itself with the sense of pastness is *prima facie* credible for that reason, this initial credibility may be dispelled and give way to improbability in cases where the seemingly remembered item is incongruent with others which are congruent amongst themselves.

. . .

XI

There is, however, one further step which calls for examination, if this kind of final validation of empirical knowledge by reference to ultimate data in some sense presently given, and to the congruence of such data, is to be acceptable. It is essential to the argument that any item of our sense of past fact be *prima facie* credible; that such mnemic presentation itself should, before any further examination as to congruence, afford some probability of past fact. Just what degree of credibility thus attaches initially to the remembered, merely because remembered, we do not need to ask. It does not appear that we could, candidly, assign any particular degree to it. We seldom take cognizance of this initial presumption, because generalizations as to particular *classes* of our memories intervene between it and any matter to be attested by memory. That recollections of the recent past are comparatively reliable; of the remote past, unreliable; that our memory for faces and for what we have said is trustworthy, but our remembering of names and dates is not: such generalizations will be the proximate grounds on which the credibility of particular memories is assessed. But these are, of course, generalizations from past experience (of remembering, and of later confirming or disconfirming) and as such are presently available only in the form of remembered experience, and require for their own authentication the presumption of initial credibility of the merely remembered as such. And the degree of this initial credibility, we have said, is hardly assignable. But it does not need to be assigned. A larger or a smaller such initial probability would have no appreciable effect upon the eventually determinable probabilities in question beyond that of a difference in the *extent* of congruity with other mnemic items and with sense presentation which would be required for building up eventual probabilities sufficient for rational and practical reliance. If, however, there were *no* initial presumption attaching to the mnemically presented; no valid supposition of a real connection with past experience; then no extent of congruity with other such items would give rise to any eventual credibility. The coherence of a novel, or of the daydreams we are aware of fabricating as we go along, can never have the slightest weight toward crediting the content of them as fact, no matter how detailed and mutually congruent such items may be.

This assumption of initial credibility of mnemic presentation might be made without further ado: everyone in fact takes it for granted, in effect if not explicitly. But it seems undesirable thus to rest the final validity of empirical knowledge upon an *ad hoc* postulate, however agreeable to common sense. The analysis of knowledge, even though in some sense or some part a logical reconstruction rather than a psychological depiction, should be no mere attempt to find a set of postulates sufficient for what we already believe, but should be governed throughout by our final and best sense of fact. Furthermore, this assumption in question has a certain kind of justification, in the fact that mnemic perseveration of past experience; its present-as-pastness; is constitutive of the world we live in. It represents that continuing sense of a reality beyond the narrow confines of the merely sensibly presented; the only reality which as humans we can envisage; the only reality which could come before us to be recognized as such. If we adopt the Cartesian method of doubting everything which admits of doubt, we must stop short of doubting this. Because to doubt our sense of past experience as founded in actuality, would be to lose any criterion by which either the doubt itself or what is doubted could be corroborated; and to erase altogether the distinction between empirical fact and fantasy. In that sense, we have no rational alternative but to presume that anything sensed as past is just a little more probable than that which is incompatible with what is remembered and that with respect to which memory is blank. It would seem regrettable to have come so far in the attempt at complete validation of empirical knowledge and to stop short with no examination of this final point. Let us make trial of a Cartesian doubt that our sense of the past has any reliable connection with past actuality; even though this must be, in the nature of the case, an essay in the fantastic.

As a first step in such doubt, let us not deny that inductive generalization from the mnemically presented may be trusted, but let us suppose that a particular knower is subject to a systematic delusion of memory, which he has no reason to suspect, concerning—let us say—his experience of music. As he remembers it, whenever he has heard music in the past, it has been accompanied by kaleidoscopic patterns of imaged color. Now music is promised, and he predicts the like accompaniment on this occasion. This prediction is, for him, validly credible if the general principle of induction is valid: it is made in the light of the best and most pertinent evidence open to him, and that evidence justifies it.

Will such a knower later discover the delusive character of this class of his memories, through the test of experience? The supposition that he will, is supposition that the delusion will not persist. If it should persist, but should not extend to his sense experience when given, then he will find each further verifying experience a puzzling exception to all past experience as he will remember it, which he will take note of and resolve to bear in mind next time, as diminishing the credibility of similar predictions for the future. But on each occasion when this later becomes pertinent, he will again remember his past experience erroneously, and again credit prediction on the basis of his delusive recollections. And his judgment will again be completely valid, if judgments based on past experience as remembered are valid.

And now let us attempt to generalize this fantastic supposition. Let us suppose that everyone at every moment is subject to such systematic delusions in all sorts of ways. If that should be the case but these delusions should not extend to sense perception, then our sense experience is going to be highly surprising to us. And if we remain reasonable and minded to check generalizations made by their further confirmations and disconfirmations in experience, then we shall continually be noting the necessity of revising downward the credibility of recollections of one kind or another, because of our present disappointments in prediction. But also, we shall always be forgetting our disappointments, on each later occasion to which they would be pertinent, and remembering the general character of past experience in ways determined by our delusions instead of the ways in which it actually occurred. And our credible beliefs, formulated each time on the basis of past experience as remembered, will have the same logical validity that credible beliefs do in actual and normal experience. And in a community of persons subject to such tragic affliction, if some should busy themselves with the analysis of experience as cognitive, and raise the question of the validity of memory, they would be in exactly the same case as ourselves, and find the same reason for crediting memory in general that we do.

Suppose, then, the terrible thought occurs to us that our memories are in fact like that; and we tremble with fright about ourselves and our future. On calm reflection, however—in this exceptional moment of sane suspicion—we ought to observe that we are not going to suffer from this affliction so much as we might suppose. Because we are never going to be in position to substantiate this suspicion we now entertain. Our lives, as some outside omniscient observer would view them, are going to be a continual succession of disappointments of our cognitive expectations by our presented sense experience, but we are never going to know that general fact. Each disappointment is going to be strictly temporary, like the suffering some people suspect that they have endured under an anaesthetic, though the memory of it—they suppose—is later blocked. Also, what is a *cognitive* disappointment, may be in other respects a pleasant surprise. And on any grounds, *occasional* cognitive disappointments must be expected by anyone who commits himself to predictions which are less than certain. In short, we are going to lead quite normal lives.

Let it be admitted that this attempt of ours at a Cartesian doubt of the validity of memory has not been well carried out. It would in fact be impossible to carry it out consistently. If we have induced the reader to suppose momentarily that we have been logically cogent, however fantastic, that will be because we have unjustifiably capitalized on the suggestion of *systematic* delusion: a general *unreliability* of memory would be something quite different and must reveal itself, if we preserved our rationality, by its falling into incongruities. The attempt to carry through a circumstantial supposition that would actually conform to what we have attempted to suggest, must inevitably end in nonsense.

Still the point which we have so poorly illustrated should be obvious. The world as revealed to us by our sense of past experience must be the world we live in. Any suspicion we could entertain, and any generalization we could have reason to credit—including any about the nature of reality, or of life and experience, or about the relation between experience and reality, or about anything else—must be attested by its conformity with what the congruities of given experience and recollection will substantiate. That world our sense of which is a memorial precipitate of past experience, may be phenomenal, in whatever good or bad sense one may find to give to 'phenomenal' as compared with 'real'; but it is the only world with which we can be acquainted or in which we can raise any question admitting of possible answer. Our fantastic supposition above, if it should succeed in anything, would succeed only in conjuring up some unknowable *an sich* world, and would be merely an essay in bad metaphysics. We might as well have gone the whole length in one sweep and supposed that there is no such thing as past or future, but that humans, bounded in the nutshell of the here and now, count themselves kings of infinite time and space by a systematic delusion. But as the time-worn theme of Berkeley's idealism should have taught us, the distinction between an objectively real world and a sufficiently systematic delusion of one—congruent throughout—is a distinction which makes no discoverable difference, and is not the subject of any reasonable discussion. One can put it forward only by supposing himself both in and out of his 'merely phenomenal' world at one and the same time.

Our sense of a cumulative temporal experience, mnemically presented within the epistemological present, or in Kant's phrase, in the transcendental unity of apperception, not only is something of which we cannot divest ourselves; it is constitutive of our sense of the only reality by reference to which empirical judgments could have either truth or falsity or any meaning at all. Without it, there could be no answer to any question, nor any question to be answered, because there could be no such thing as fact and no intelligible discourse.

Norman Malcolm

Memory and the Past

I

I begin by quoting some well-known remarks by Russell in *The Analysis of Mind:*

> In investigating memory-beliefs, there are certain points which must be borne in mind. In the first place, everything constituting a memory-belief is happening now, not in that past time to which the belief is said to refer. It is not logically necessary to the existence of a memory-belief that the event remembered should have occurred, or even that the past should have existed at all. There is no logical impossibility in the hypothesis that the world sprang into being five minutes ago, exactly as it then was, with a population that "remembered" a wholly unreal past. There is no logically necessary connection between events at different times; therefore nothing that is happening now or will happen in the future can disprove the hypothesis that the world began five minutes ago. Hence the occurrences which are *called* knowledge of the past are logically independent of the past; they are wholly analyzable into present contents, which might, theoretically, be just what they are even if no past had existed.
>
> I am not suggesting that the non-existence of the past should be entertained as a serious hypothesis. Like all sceptical hypotheses, it is logically tenable, but uninteresting. All that I am doing is to use its logical tenability as a help in the analysis of what occurs when we remember.[1]

We must not be misled by Russell's remark that his "hypothesis" is not to be taken seriously. He was perfectly serious when he said that there is no logical impossibility in it, that it is "logically tenable." In later books he expresses the same thought. In *An Outline of Philosophy* he says that "there is no logical impossibility in the view that the world was created five minutes ago, complete with memories and records."[2] In *Human Knowledge* he says: "I might have

[1] Bertrand Russell, *The Analysis of Mind* (New York: The Macmillan Company, 1921), pp. 159–60.
[2] *An Outline of Philosophy* (New York: W. W. Norton & Company, Inc., 1927), p. 7.

come into existence a few moments ago, complete with just those recollections which I then had." [3]

Russell's belief in the logical tenability of his "hypothesis" greatly influenced his treatment of the topic of memory. A good part of the chapter on memory in *The Analysis of Mind* is presumably devoted to finding out "what occurs when we remember." If his "sceptical hypothesis" were tenable it would follow that remembering is logically independent of the past; and it would be a further consequence that there is little left for the philosophy of memory to do except to investigate what goes on in our minds when we remember. If the hypothesis were to appear untenable it would no longer seem obvious, as it did to Russell, that philosophy should be concerned with this. One would be free to think that what happens in our minds when we remember something has little if any philosophical interest.

The idea that it is logically possible that the world began five minutes ago, "complete with memories and records," is an astonishing thought partly because, as we first mull the idea over, we cannot get hold of anything which would prove that it is *not* a logical possibility. It is worth inquiring whether this can be done. What I wish to examine at first is not the question of whether it is logically possible that the world began five minutes ago, but the question of whether it is logically possible that the world began five minutes ago "complete with memories of an unreal past."

To begin with one might think it is self-contradictory to speak of *remembering incorrectly,* and if this were so the hypothesis would be self-contradictory. A. J. Ayer says that "the verb 'to remember,' like the verb 'to know,' is used in such a way that if something is remembered it follows that it was so. To speak of remembering what never happened would be self-contradictory." [4] Is this so? Let us look into the matter of usage.

The verb "remember" occurs in various locutions. One of these is the phrase "to remember that so-and-so." This is normally so used that it is improper to say such a thing as, "He remembers that so-and-so happened although it didn't happen." We have the authority of G. E. Moore for this.[5] But I want to prove the point by means of an example for which I am indebted to Professor Jaakko Hintikka. Suppose someone was taught that Columbus discovered America in 1392. Later he is asked, "When did Columbus discover America?", and he answers, "1392." Can we say he *remembers* that America was discovered in 1392? Of course not: anymore than we can say that he *knows* it was. If he had been taught that the date was 1492, and if when asked for the date he had answered "1492," it would have been right to say, "He remembers that 1492 is the date Columbus discovered America." In both cases he was taught something and in both cases he remembers what he was taught. The sole difference between the two cases is that the date is wrong in one and right in the other. The example provides a proof that one cannot remember that p when p is false. Sometimes we do say such a thing as "He *remembers* that there were four men in the room but actually there were only three." But this is carelessness or possibly sarcasm. It is exactly as wrong to speak this way as to say, "He *knows* that there were four men but actually there were only three."

[3] *Human Knowledge* (New York: Simon and Schuster, Inc., 1948), p. 228.
[4] *The Problem of Knowledge* (London: MacMillan & Co., Inc., 1956), p. 168.
[5] See his *Philosophical Papers* (New York: The Macmillan Company, 1959), p. 217.

The verb "remember" is used in other locutions. We say "As he remembers the dinner there was a lady seated on his left," or "That is how he remembers it," or "the way he remembers it is so-and-so." These locutions make it possible to speak of incorrect memory. Even if I know that at the dinner there was a gentleman, not a lady, on his left, I can still say, "That is how he remembers it—that there was a lady on his left." If someone claims to remember that *p,* and I wish to refer to his claim without committing myself to accepting *p* as true, I can say, "As he remembers it, *p,*" "According to his memory of the occasion, *p,*" and so on. But if I say "He remembers that *p,*" then I have committed myself: I have myself implied that I believe it is true that *p,* just as I have when I say "He knows that *p.*"

Thus it is not true without qualification, that "If something is remembered it follows that it was so." This holds for remembering *that* so-and-so, but not for those other locutions. If as Jones remembers it, *p,* and *p* is false, then Jones' memory is incorrect.

Let us look more closely at this notion of incorrect memory. If a man told us that once he lunched with Winston Churchill, and then it turned out that it was breakfast, not lunch, his memory was incorrect. He remembered the meal as lunch: here his memory was wrong. If the occasion had been a cocktail party then his memory of it as a meal was wrong. If he had never met Churchill at all, and had indeed never encountered any of the great ones of this world, and always took meals with his wife only, then there seems to be *no respect* in which his alleged memory of having lunched with the Prime Minister is *incorrect.* And also there is no respect in which it is correct.

One is reluctant to speak in this case of his "memory" of having lunched with the Prime Minister, and would prefer to speak of his "alleged" or "so-called" memory, or of his "claim" to remember so-and-so. Why is this? I believe it is because incorrect or erroneous memory is possible only in a context of correct memory. If I remember a dinner party which occurred in such and such a place, at such and such a time, attended by these persons and those persons, then there is room for some of my recollections of the occasion to be incorrect—for example, that there was a lady seated on my left. But if my belief about the supposed past incident was completely false—no social occasion of even approximately that description had occurred—one could not say that my memory was incorrect or erroneous. Or rather: you could say it, but you would not mean that I remembered the occasion, although incorrectly. You would mean that it was not memory at all. One could call it a "delusion of memory" or, a "delusive memory." But a memory which is totally delusive, as in the example, is not a memory. It stands to an erroneous memory as a counterfeit diamond stands to an imperfect diamond. The latter is a diamond, the other not. A totally delusive memory is no more a memory than a fictitious occurrence is something that happened, or no more than a painted fire is a fire. This is not quibbling. A painted fire does not have the important properties of fire and a totally delusive memory does not have the important properties of memory. Nothing could be more unsound, therefore, than to base one's philosophical treatment of memory on the notion of a total delusion of memory, as Russell does.

Two of the chief properties of memory are *present knowledge* and *previous knowledge* of what is remembered. My limits do not permit me to give these points the discussion they need, but I will offer the following brief considerations. Memory can be divided into correct and incorrect memory. It is pretty evident that correct memory of something involves both present and previous knowledge of it. It would be self-contradictory to say of someone that he *correctly remembers* the date of the battle of Austerlitz, but to add either that he *does not know* its date, or that he *did not know its date at any time prior* to his remembering it.

I think that incorrect memory of something involves correct memory of something and, therefore, both present and previous knowledge of the latter. Let us suppose that a man remembers the date of the battle of Austerlitz incorrectly. This can be so only if, in giving some date, he is referring to that battle. He must provide some correct information about the latter in order for it to be identified as the event whose date he purports to be giving. He must have some knowledge of it in order to be talking about *it*. And at least some part of his present knowledge of the battle of Austerlitz must be knowledge that he *previously* possessed. Otherwise it would not be a case of *remembering* its date even incorrectly.

Thus incorrect memory of an occurrence presupposes some correct memory of it. But one may also have incorrect memory relating to an event which did not occur and which, therefore, one does not refer to by means of some correct memory of *it*. How is this to be dealt with? Different kinds of cases are possible here. Someone could point at a man in plain sight and say "I met him last week." The event he refers to is meeting-*that*-man-last-week. His memory is wrong, let us suppose, because he and the man pointed at were in different parts of the world last week. His erroneous memory does not presuppose some correct memory of the event referred to, for it did not take place. Still, his memory might be partly correct, for it might be that he remembered meeting this man but is wrong about when it happened. Or it could be that he had never met this particular man, but had met one who could easily be mistaken for him. Correct memory would here be mixed in with incorrect memory. Another possibility would be that previously he had dreamt of meeting this man, or had hallucinated it, or had formed in some other way an erroneous impression of having met him. But if his present belief was based on a previous false impression, then the present belief would not involve an error of *memory*: the error would be in the original impression. Finally, if he had never met this man nor anyone who could be mistaken for him, and had not been under any previous erroneous impression of having met him, then if it seems to him that he remembers having met him, this would be a *delusion* of memory and not memory, not even incorrect or erroneous memory. What keeps it from being memory is that there is no element of knowledge in it.

It is interesting to observe a curious vacillation in *The Analysis of Mind* on the question of whether memory is knowledge. There is, on one hand, the thesis that memory is logically independent of the past, which entails that memory is not knowledge, since knowledge is certainly not logically independent of what is known, it being plainly self-contradictory to say, for example, "He knows that Napoleon won the Battle of Austerlitz although Napoleon actually lost it." When Russell says that occurrences of memory are "*called* knowledge of the past" he is insinuating that this is a common *error*.

But elsewhere in his discussion he assumes that memory *is* knowledge, as when he says that "there can be no doubt that memory forms an indispensable part of our knowledge of the past." [6]

Let us return now to Russell's hypothesis in which the people are supposed to remember, at the first moment of their creation, "a wholly unreal past." Since what is supposed to be remembered is *wholly* unreal, the so-called memories of the past involve no knowledge of the past, which implies that they are not memories. The hypothesis, as formulated by Russell, is self-contradictory. Can we turn it into a description of what is logically possible by formulating it in another way?

II

It may be thought that it is easy to achieve a revision of the hypothesis that avoids self-contradiction. Instead of saying that the newly created people remember things that did not happen, let us say that they *think* they remember those things, or that it *seems* to them that they remember them, or that they have *delusions* of memory. Is this a logical possibility?

I believe it is not. It involves a kind of logical incoherence different from the self-contradiction previously noted, and one that goes deeper. It may help to bring this to light to consider the example of a child who is learning to speak. Let us suppose he has begun to master the use of a few verbs in the present tense indicative. By saying that he has begun to master their use, I imply that when he uses them in sentences what he says is *true,* for the most part. He says "Mama is there" when it is true, mostly, that his mother is where he points. If he is asked whether she is there when she isn't, he will usually say she isn't. If what he says is not true, it will generally be evident that he is pretending, or perhaps that he is deceived by appearances.

Let us suppose that he has not yet used the past tense forms of any verbs. But now they begin to crop up in his speech. Let us imagine that when he speaks in the past tense what he says is always or nearly always false. He says his dog "was" barking when this was not so. If he says it only when the dog is just beginning to bark, it would be plausible to think that he has not yet differentiated past and present tense: there would be some justification for thinking he *means* that the dog *is* barking. If there was not that particular regularity one could not suppose he means *that.* If there was no other regularity it would be wrong to suppose he means anything. Certainly we should have no right to say, "As he remembers it the dog was barking."

Why would it be wrong to say this? I think the answer is that although a person can say what he remembers and what he thinks he remembers, this presupposes that he has some understanding of past tense speech. This in turn presupposes that the statements he makes with past tense sentences are mainly true. If this were not so then his sentences, even though they had past tense grammatical form, would not express statements *about the past.* It would not be *that* "language-game," but some other one, or none at all. Here we can make a comparison with chess, Wittgenstein's favorite analogy. It cannot be right to say that the members of a club who have the pastime of moving chess pieces on chess boards, are playing chess unless the moves they make are mostly legal chess moves. If in their play illegal moves were the

[6] *The Analysis of Mind,* p. 165.

rule and not the exception, then they would not be playing chess, but some other game, or none at all. In this analogy, legal moves correspond to true statements and illegal moves to false statements, about the past.

I am holding that Russell's "population" could not make false statements about past happenings unless their statements about the past were largely true. I rely, first of all, on Wittgenstein's familiar thesis that our concepts, our language-games, presuppose *agreement in judgments.* Wittgenstein asks: "Does it make sense to say that people generally agree in their judgment of colour? What would it be like for them not to? One man would say a flower was red which another called blue, and so on. But what right should we have to call these people's words 'red' and 'blue' *our* 'colour-words'?" [7] We can see that unless those people agreed almost completely with us in applying those words to things—agreed in saying that *this* is red and *that* is blue—their words would *not* be *our* color words. They would not be making color judgments.

This notion of agreement in judgments is of central importance in Wittgenstein's thought. As he says, "This consideration must . . . apply to mathematics too. If there were not complete agreement, then neither would human beings be learning the technique which we learn. It would be more or less different from ours up to the point of unrecognizability." [8] Here we are made to take note of the striking fact that there is a *normal* reaction to the explanations and examples that make up the instruction in elementary mathematics. Given a certain teaching everyone goes on in the same way. We agree that in taking such and such further steps we are doing the *same* as we were taught to do. We agree that doing *this* (not *that*) is what the rule, which we were taught, requires.

It is conceivable that someone should not have this normal reaction; conceivable that he should, as a matter of course, go on in a different way. It is even conceivable that he should be able to give a plausible explanation for saying that his way of going on is the *same* as the way he was taught, and that *our* way is *not* the same.

This is conceivable: but it does not happen, or only rarely. If this were not so, mathematics would not be possible; and the same holds for other areas of language. Agreement in judgments is "part of the framework on which the working of our language is based." [9]

The second point in support of my contention about Russell's "population" is that the concept of *truth* is bound up with the agreement in judgments that underlies our language-games. Wittgenstein puts to himself the question: "So you are saying that human agreement decides what is true and what is false?" He answers: "It is what human beings *say* that is true and false: and they agree in language." [10] In a sense, the question is answered in the affirmative. The existence of color judgments requires that there be a great many cases in which people agree that this is red and that is blue. The disagreement that there is in color judgments presupposes a background of overwhelming agreement. Furthermore, this agreement in language makes it *true* that this is red and that is blue.

[7] Ludwig Wittgenstein, *Philosophical Investigations,* tr. G. E. M. Anscombe (New York: The Macmillan Company, 1953), p. 226.
[8] *Ibid.*
[9] *Ibid.,* sec. 240.
[10] *Ibid.,* sec. 241.

The same holds for judgments about the past. People must agree, overwhelmingly, about what they have just noticed or observed, e.g., that the telephone *rang* or the lights *went out.* Otherwise they do not speak the same language. The agreement in language, which is necessary for agreement in judgments, is an agreement about *what to say.* And this brings in *truth.*[11] In order for there to be a past tense in our language there must be a multitude of cases in which we agree that so-and-so happened; and in which it is true that so-and-so happened, because that is how we speak. We "agree in language."

We have an inclination to imagine the past as *behind* us, *out of sight,* and to think that every proposition we make about it might be false. But in imagining this we assume all along that our propositions do *refer* to the past, are genuinely propositions *about* the past. When we think out what is involved in that *reference to the past,* which we took for granted, we see that it requires that many of those propositions about the past should be true.

In opposition to this, Russell's "hypothesis" requires that the newly created people should make judgments about the past, all of which are false. What criterion would there be, then, for saying that they have a past tense in their language? An omniscient observer ought to conclude that they do not have one. The case would be similar to that of a people who apparently speak English but whose "color judgments" are always or usually false. An observer ought to conclude that, contrary to what had first been supposed, they are not making color judgments. What originally looked like that has to be interpreted in some other way. The same holds for those sentences that at first appeared to express statements about the past.

Knowing how to use the past tense cannot be completely separated from actually using it correctly, and using it correctly cannot be completely separated from making many true statements with it. From Russell's hypothesis it really follows that the people do not make statements about the past. If one of them uttered the sentence "I did so-and-so" an observer would not be entitled to attribute to him the thought or seeming memory of having done so-and-so. If he said "*I seem to remember* doing so-and-so," that would not change matters. He cannot be saying what we should be saying if we uttered the same words. We cannot use their remarks as our criterion of their having thoughts about past events. They cannot give expression in language to seeming memories.

Nor can they express them in behavior. There is, of course, nonlinguistic behavior that expresses memory, e.g., a child buries a toy in the sand and then a little later digs it out again. Indeed, nonlinguistic memory behavior is, in a sense, more fundamental than memory language. In the beginning the latter can be taught and the understanding of it can be verified only by connecting it with the behavior of taking interest in objects, of being surprised by their disappearance, of pursuing them, searching for them, and so on. Against

[11] Notice the following remark by D. M. Armstrong: "We may concede Wittgenstein the point that: 'If language is to be a means of communication there must be agreement not only in definitions but also . . . in judgments' (*Investigations,* sec. 242). But notice that Wittgenstein only speaks of *agreements* in judgments, and not that the judgments that are agreed upon must be true" (*Perception and the Physical World* [New York: Humanities Press and London: Routledge & Kegan Paul, Ltd., 1961], p. 168, footnote). But what would be the standard of comparison in relation to which it would have *meaning* to say that those judgments were false?

a background of behavior that exhibited correct memory, there could be some behavior that expressed mere seeming memory, as when the child digs in the wrong place. But as in the case of language, the exception cannot be the rule. Russell's hypothesis requires that *all* the memory behavior of the newly created people should be erroneous, as well as all of their memory statements. In that case there would be nothing in their behavior that *looked* like memory—not even like delusive memory.

Russell's people could not give expression to seeming memories either in behavior or in language. But could they not *have* seeming memories? This question may feel as if it were significant. But how could it seem to someone that he remembers something, if there was no *expression* of memory? What would be supposed to happen? Saying the words "I remember so-and-so" would be irrelevant, since Russell's hypothesis, we have argued, is incompatible with there being any language of memory. What about imagery? But imagery may also figure in daydreams and expectations. Memory-images are images that go with remembering and seeming to remember. These latter concepts require something more than imagery; and what could this "more" be, if there was neither the behavior nor the language of memory? One is tempted to supplement the imagery with feelings of "familiarity," "pastness," or "fittingness," as philosophers have done. But these inventions could not turn images into memories or make them refer to the past.

Russell's people may be compared to the dog, in Wittgenstein's example, who can believe that his master is at the door but cannot be said to believe that his master will come the day after tomorrow.[12] He can express the first belief in behavior but not the second one. The dog's inability to have beliefs about the day after tomorrow is matched by the inability of Russell's people to have beliefs about the past. They will not have the necessary language or behavior.

I conclude that it is not intelligible that they should have *thoughts* about past happenings, or the *experience* of *seeming to remember* something. They cannot, therefore, have delusive memories.

III

I wish to consider one more possible revision of the hypothesis. Instead of trying to suppose that in the first moments after their creation the people seem to remember an unreal past, let us suppose that over a considerable period of time they exhibit normal memory-reactions in daily behavior and also gradually demonstrate a mastery of language, including the past tense. In all respects they appear like ourselves. But then they begin to express, in the language which they understand, apparent memories of "a wholly unreal past." The objections I previously made will not apply here, since these people have normal memories and a language they understand. Is this new supposition "logically tenable"?

We are entitled to suppose that their apparent memories are in *agreement:* for this is what Russell envisaged when he spoke of "a population that 'remembered' a wholly unreal past." Their apparent memories will largely agree with each other and *also* with the "records." For this is how things actually are with us, and it was Russell's intention to urge that it is logically possible

[12] *Philosophical Investigations,* p. 174.

that *this* world, *our* world, sprang into existence five minutes ago, "complete with memories and records."

But if there was this kind of agreement then the apparent memories would be verified as true. This is what the *verification* of apparent memories *means.* There is nothing else for it to mean since, as Russell remarks, "we cannot evoke the past bodily."[13] This comment about verification does not deny that "memory is true (or false) in virtue of a past event."[14] It merely says how it is determined what the past event was. And if the apparent memories were verified it would not be intelligible to hold that, nevertheless, the past they describe may not have existed.

Thus the twice revised hypothesis destroys itself again. The supposed unreal past has turned out to be real. Russell said that his sceptical hypothesis was logically tenable but uninteresting. I believe the exact opposite has proved to be the case.

IV

I have completed what I wish to say directly about memory in relation to Russell's hypothesis. The question inevitably arises whether or not it is a logical possibility that the world sprang into being five minutes ago; so I will make a few remarks about this. I am reluctant, however, to discuss exactly this question. If the world came into existence five minutes ago then the world came into existence. But the sentence "The *world* came into existence" is one that is notoriously difficult to understand. If the world came into existence, it would seem to follow that at one time there was no world. But what could this mean? If, like Wittgenstein in the *Tractatus,* we define "the world" as "everything that is the case," then if at one time there was no world would this mean that at one time there was *nothing* that was the case? One may reasonably doubt that this makes any sense. Yet we have difficulty in giving a meaning, other than the *Tractatus* does, to the phrase "the world." So I would rather not talk about the world.

I prefer to consider a sentence that is, in a sense, easier to understand: namely, the sentence "The *earth* sprang into being five minutes ago." There seems to be no conceptual difficulty in supposing that *the earth* came into existence and that, therefore, there was a time at which it did not exist. It is obvious, I think, that Russell would have held that it is logically possible that the earth came into existence five minutes ago. This would even seem to be a less radical assertion than the one about the world and one that is easier to defend.

To me it seems surprising that there is a strong tendency to assume that *of course* it is a *logical* possibility that the earth came into existence five minutes ago. Once we ask ourselves what conceivable fact could *support* the hypothesis about the earth, it will not appear obvious that it is a logical possibility. Russell remarked about his hypothesis that "nothing that is happening now or will happen in the future can disprove" it, and probably he would have agreed that nothing can *prove* it. It is worth dwelling on this. If the hypothesis were that the earth came into existence one million years ago, this could be a subject of inquiry, and it is conceivable there should be evidence, for or against

[13] *The Analysis of Mind,* p. 161.
[14] *Ibid.,* p. 165.

it, from geology, chemistry or radar astronomy. But nothing would count as evidence that the earth came into existence five minutes ago. Could a *document* (as Wittgenstein once asked ironically) be evidence for it; or a carbon-14 test, or someone's testimony? No one could seriously think so. The five-minute hypothesis is incompatible with the very concept of *evidence.* If a geologist thought it was a conceivable hypothesis that the earth came into existence one million years ago, he would surely imply that some discovery could be evidence for that hypothesis. A philosopher who puts forward the five-minute hypothesis does not imply this. There is "merely a difference in the quantity of time"; yet this has the consequence that one hypothesis is an empirical proposition, the other not.

Let us dwell on the point that the five-minute hypothesis is incompatible with our concept of evidence. Consider what would be implied by our "believing" that the earth and mankind have just come into existence. If one of us were to "believe" this he would have to renounce, not only his previous conception of his own identity, but his entire store of common knowledge—his knowledge of natural processes; his knowledge of the normal properties of anything, so that he would no longer know what wood, water, and fire are; his knowledge of how the words of his language are used or even that he has a language; of how people live, act, and react; of what interests them and what kinds of inquiries they make; of how measurements, experiments, and arguments are conducted, and when something is held to be proved. If he thought out the consequences of this hypothesis he would realize that it is not anything he could rationally believe, because "believing" it would mean that he no longer understood anything at all. If a man were to refuse to pay his income tax on the "ground" that the earth had come into existence only five minutes before, this would literally be (and not just be called) *madness.*

To accept this "hypothesis" as true would mean the destruction of *all* our thinking. This is why we could not rationally regard *any* future disclosure as evidence for it.

Perhaps we can conceive that Martian scientists (whose technology is wonderfully advanced in the imagination of philosophers) should demonstrate their ability to produce, instantaneously, planets with complete populations. But if those scientists were to maintain that they had done this very thing with the earth five minutes ago, the least we could think would be that it was a case of mistaken identity. England is part of the earth, and by "England" we *mean* a geographical and national entity with a long history. By "Bertrand Russell" I mean a man who has written many books, lived many years, and greatly contributed to the development of logic and philosophy. No one could understand what England is and who Bertrand Russell is and also believe that they are only five minutes old. The Martians must have got their planets mixed up.

If someone admitted that nothing could serve as evidence for the five-minute hypothesis but still maintained that it is a "logical possibility," what would he mean? He might be influenced by the consideration that the sentence "The earth came into existence five minutes ago" is not self-contradictory. It is true that one cannot deduce a contradiction by means of definitions and formal manipulations. But one cannot do this either with the sentence "All of our color judgments have been wrong," which nevertheless does not express a logical possibility. Nor can one do it with the sentence "I am unconscious." There is not just *one* brand of logical impossibility.

It may be that more influential than anything else is the thought that some being could have *observed* the earth's coming into existence five minutes ago "exactly as it then was," and now *knows* this to be a fact, whereas we earth-dwellers do not know it. This thought might be accompanied by quite definite imagery. The difficulty, however, has merely been transferred to another place. What could count as evidence that some being made that observation five minutes ago? If a voice were to announce this from the heavens, in impressive circumstances, the best we could do would be to treat it as a dark saying.

Russell, following Hume, claims that "There is no logically necessary connection between events at different times." This is obviously false: keeping a promise logically implies a prior event, and so does changing one's mind or winning a bet. From this doctrine Russell draws the conclusion that nothing can disprove the five-minute hypothesis, and he may think that this proves it to be a logical possibility. It is true that no one would think that something had *disproved* it. But this is for the same reason that no one would take anything as evidence for it, namely, that we cannot rationally think of it as "possibly true."

There is a temptation to think that *for human understanding* it is inconceivable that the earth and mankind came into existence five minutes ago, but that *in itself* it is a logical possibility. If it is admitted that the truth of this proposition would be incompatible with our concepts of evidence, of proof, and of possibility, then the notion must be that there is a framework of logical possibilities which is independent of our concepts and our application of language. I believe that this attractive notion is a mere piece of imagery.

For Further Reading

Alexander, Samuel, *Space, Time, and Deity,* 1920, Vol. 1, pp. 113–29.

Benjamin, B. S., "Remembering," *Mind,* Vol. 65 (1956).

Bradley, F. H., *Essays on Truth and Reality,* 1914, Chaps. 12 and 13.

Brandt, R. B., "The Epistemological Status of Memory Beliefs," *Philosophical Review,* Vol. 64 (1955).

——, "A Puzzle in Lewis' Theory of Memory," *Philosophical Studies,* Vol. 5 (1954).

Broad, C. D., *The Mind and its Place in Nature,* 1929, Chap. 5.

Frankfurt, Harry, "Memory and the Cartesian Circle," *Philosophical Review,* Vol. 71 (1962).

Furlong, E. J., "Memory," *Mind,* Vol. 57 (1948).

——, "Memory and the Argument from Illusion," *Proceedings of the Aristotelian Society,* 1954–55.

——, *A Study in Memory,* 1951.

Harrod, R. F., "Memory," *Mind,* Vol. 51 (1942).

——, *Foundations of Inductive Logic,* 1956, Chap. 8.

Holland, R. F., "The Empiricist Theory of Memory," *Mind,* Vol. 63 (1954).
Laird, John, *Knowledge, Belief, and Opinion,* 1930, pp. 292–307.
———, *A Study in Realism,* 1920, Chap. 3.
Malcolm, Norman, *Knowledge and Certainty,* 1963, pp. 203–40.
Price, H. H., "Memory Knowledge," *Proceedings of the Aristotelian Society,* Supplementary Vol. 15 (1936).
Reid, Thomas, *Essays on the Powers of the Human Mind,* 1808, Vol. 3, Chaps. 1 and 2.
Russell, Bertrand, *Analysis of Mind,* 1922, Chap. 9.
———, *Human Knowledge,* 1948, pp. 189–90.
———, *Inquiry into Meaning and Truth,* 1948, pp. 154–61.
Saunders, J. T., "Scepticism and Memory," *Philosophical Review,* Vol. 72 (1963).
Shoemaker, Sydney, *Self-Knowledge and Self-Identity,* 1963, Chap. 4.
Singer, Marcus, "Memory, Meaning, and the Moment of Creation," *Proceedings of the Aristotelian Society,* Vol. 63 (1962–63).
Stout, G. F., *Studies in Philosophy and Psychology,* 1930, Chap. 8.
Woozley, A. D., *Theory of Knowledge,* 1949, Chaps. 2 and 3.

8

TYPES OF EMPIRICAL KNOWLEDGE: THE MATERIAL WORLD

At present, with controversy in the physical sciences focused on atomic or subatomic structures, no one really doubts the warrant of such propositions as "There is an ink bottle in front of me." Humble propositions like this, however, are of supreme importance for science: it is only because we can know them to be true that we can test the more interesting and speculative propositions of, say, physics. It is perhaps even more important for understanding the logical basis of the physical sciences, however (since the physical sciences depend on *observation* for their evidence), that such propositions as "I *see* an ink bottle in front of me" are warranted. Observation statements like this, we should note, include a verb of perception followed by a reference to some physical thing. Such *perceptual statements* or *perceptual claims* are the primary concern of the present chapter.

Perceptual claims have puzzled philosophers since the earliest times, primarily because things are often different from the way they appear to be. The early Greeks noticed this disparity between appearance and reality: that straight sticks look bent when partially immersed in water, and that warm objects feel hot to a cold hand but cool to a fevered hand. One kind of problem raised by this disparity (although it would arise eventually even without the disparity) is the scientific one of understanding the mechanics of the perception process, the roles played by an organism and its environment (for example, the atmosphere) in the total event of perception. Although this problem is not philosophical, well-confirmed scientific theories of perception are of course something philosophers must bear in mind.

The disparity between appearance and reality also raises a three-part epistemological problem (although, again, it would arise even without the disparity) parallel to those discussed in the two previous chapters. (a) Exactly what do perceptual statements mean? (b) Exactly what kind of evidence is available to support them? (c) How may one justify passing from this evidence to the perceptual statement? The first of these questions is more complex than it might at first appear. Knowing what a perceptual statement (for example, "I see an ink bottle") means requires not only knowing what it is to *see* something, but knowing what the phrase referring to the material thing ("an ink bottle") means; hence it requires knowing what it is for there to *be* a material thing like an ink bottle. Theories of perception are ordinarily theories about all these problems at once: they take into account what it is for there to be a material thing, what it is for someone to see a material thing, what kind of evidence a person might have for saying that a material thing exists or that he sees it, and why or how this evidence is satisfactory (or unsatisfactory).

The foregoing statement of the problem is, however, somewhat deficient. It identifies a perceptual statement rather too narrowly as a reference to some physical *thing*. For when we say we hear sounds, have a sour taste in our mouths, see a rainbow or a shadow or a flash, it is possible at least in some cases that we are not referring to any physical *thing*. In order to broaden the definition of "perceptual statement" to include such statements, we can say that a perceptual statement is one which refers to some physical thing *or occurrence*. Some philosophers, however, would be unhappy even with this amendment, on the grounds that any talk of a "physical thing" or "physical occurrence" needs explanation. It is true that these phrases are philosophers' phrases more than scientists' or laymen's. The point, however, does not create serious difficulties, since all the important issues of principle can be raised even if we discuss only simple examples such as "I see an ink bottle."

Let us now turn to the types of answers that have been offered to the several epistemological questions about the perception of things and consider, first, theories about what it is for there to be a material object. What it is for there to be a material object sounds like a rather general scientific question to be answered by observation and hence unlike philosophy's usual conceptual questions that are answered by analyzing the meanings of terms or statements. But in this case the contrast is only apparent; the issue can be considered a question about the meanings of terms or statements if we draw a certain distinction. (a) Thus we might ask about a perception statement what in fact it *actually means* to the person who utters it; or, in other words, we might seek another statement synonymous with the perception statement but more analytic. (b) Or we might ask what a person *would presumably mean* by a perceptual statement if he were making the philosophical distinctions he ought to make, if he were not exceeding the evidence, and so on. This question is somewhat vague, but it is a fact that philosophical reflection often induces people to sharpen or alter their meanings; thus it is worth considering what thought a person *would* be expressing by his perceptual statement if he had reflected adequately on the process of perception. For instance, a phenomenalist might represent his theory as an account of what perceptual statements would mean if people were rational, precise, aware of the available evidence, and so on. The distinction here is between the *actual* meaning and the *ideal* meaning of perceptual statements. Now how does this distinction relate to the question of what it *is* for there to be a material object? What a person actually means by his talk of material things corresponds to what he *thinks* material objects are. In contrast, what he ideally would mean by his talk of material things might be said to correspond with what things *really* are. At any rate, whether or not this correspondence is exactly as suggested, it seems that there is no further problem about what a material thing really is once we have examined what our concepts are and what they would be if all the necessary distinctions and available evidence were taken into account. We must concede that philosophers have not all been perfectly clear on these matters: for instance, Berkeley sometimes advertises his view as the common-sense view, although at other times he seems to say that his view would be adopted only if some very sophisticated points were recognized.

Remembering that different accounts can concern either actual concepts or ideal concepts of material thinghood, then, what answers have been given to our first question? Some of the more important kinds of answer may be summarized as follows.

I. The first theory holds that material things are just as they look to be: their shape, size, color, and so forth is just as it appears. Furthermore, it supposes that physical things continue to exist when they are not being observed, and that they are, when unobserved, exactly as they are when observed. This "naive realist" view of objects is one that everyone has some inclination to hold, at least for the properties of objects disclosed by vision, although we all think too that things do not always look just as they are and hence recognize that some modifications are called for.

II. A very similar theory, associated with John Locke, is that whereas things are as they sometimes appear to be in some respects (shape, size, solidity, number), in some other respects they are quite unlike what they ever look to be. Thus, although many objects look colored and carry an odor, they are not really colored or odoriferous at all. All that we can say about these objects is that they have the capacity of *causing* in human beings the look of being colored and the experience of smelling a certain odor. Thus the theory is that although it is perfectly proper to say that an object is red, what this means is that the object has a certain causal property—the property of causing a human observer in normal circumstances to see a red appearance. (It is not contended that red objects necessarily cause birds or angels to see a red appearance.) In Locke's terminology, the properties things look to have and do have—properties, incidentally, that contemporary physics ascribes to things—are called primary; and the other properties, which things look to have but do not have (instead they possess corresponding causal powers), are called secondary.

III. A third theory moves still further from the first view, but in the same direction as the second. Whereas the second view affirms that what is true when a thing has a certain secondary quality (for example, is red) is that the object has a certain causal property, the third view holds that a primary quality too, at least in most cases, is some relational (possibly causal) property. Relativity theory has familiarized us with the idea that the size, shape, and velocity of objects are relational properties.

IV. The foregoing theories all assert that there are some facts about the material world entirely independent of how things *look* and in particular of how they look *to* anyone. The fourth view, however, denies this. In order to state this fourth view, it is convenient to use a technical term, "sense datum." When it looks to someone as if he were, for example, seeing a certain kind of thing, something is the case which is different from what would have been the case if it looked as if he were seeing a different sort of thing. Let us call this "something which is the case" a "sense datum." Thus we will use "sense datum of a certain sort" to describe the look or appearance of a thing to someone, whether veridical or illusory—and equally to describe the kind of hallucination a person might be having. To say that a person has a sense datum of a certain kind is not yet to say anything about the further status of the look or appearance: whether it is a physical thing or a part of a physical thing, or a state of a person's mind (or even of his brain), or a special kind of entity neither physical or mental. The careful reader of Price's selection in Chapter

6 will already be familiar with this terminology. Using the concept of a sense datum, we can say theories of the fourth kind hold that for a material object to have a physical property means certain sense data are occurring, or would occur under some conditions, or that certain events (sometimes called "sensibilia") are occurring which would be sense data of the requisite sort if only a mind were aware of them. Such views might be called "reductionist" in that the concept of a physical object with its properties is unnecessary as long as we have the concept of a sense datum with its qualities, and the concept of sense data occurring at the same time, actually or possibly, as other sense data with certain characters. Phenomenalism often provides a good example of this view (although the name is sometimes applied to a theory of the third type); for instance, some phenomenalists think that for there to be an ink bottle means that, were there a normal observer looking in a certain direction (the phenomenalist would phrase this in terms of sense data), he would have characteristic ink-bottle-like sense data. "Selective realism" is very similar: it holds that for there to be an ink bottle means that there actually are occurrences like those the phenomenalist describes, except that they may or may not have an observer. This view sometimes asserts that material things are groups of "sensibilia" (which need not be sensed in order to be real occurrences).

Before turning from these views about the nature of material thinghood to important proposals about what it is to perceive (see, hear, and so forth) a material thing, we must distinguish among several meanings of perception verbs (see, hear, and so forth). We sometimes say that an hallucinated person "sees bats" during his hallucination, although of course there are no bats around him. We might analyze this by saying that he "was being 'appeared to' in a bat-like way" and that he "took this experience to be the seeing [in another sense] of bats." This sense of "see" is not important for our purposes, however, and we shall ignore it. Using "see" in a second—and more important—way, we might say, "He was really seeing a large bird, but he thought he was seeing a jet plane." "See" in this sense might be said to mean "is visibly presented with." There are other meanings. An important one combines the first two, so that in that sense we "see" something only if we are visually presented with it and also take it that we are seeing a thing of the kind it really is.

Some important theories about what it is to "perceive" (see, hear, and so forth) a material object in the second meaning are as follows. (We should remember that these theories, like the ones about what it is for there to be a thing, can be construed either as theories about the *concepts* of perceiving, seeing, etc., or as theories about what perceiving, seeing, etc., really are.)

A. The first theory asserts that for a person to see a certain thing is for a *part of the surface* of that thing to be part of his visual field or identical with one of his visual sense data. (We should recall that "sense datum" has been so defined that the question of whether a sense datum is mental, physical, or something else is left open.) Combining this first theory about seeing with the first theory of what it is to be a material thing results in what is often called "the naive realist theory of perception." This theory is usually regarded as very difficult to defend: the occurrence of illusions, of distortions resulting from intervening media (air, lenses), and even from perspective, makes it difficult to identify a person's sense data with the surface of the object seen, except in very special cases.

B. A second theory is that perceiving is an unanalyzable relation, although we can distinguish seeing and hearing from each other as special modes of this relation much as we can distinguish red and green as different modes of color. It is a fundamental and also unanalyzable fact that persons are "appeared to" in a certain way by things, or that things appear in a certain way to persons, and we must let it go at that. Advocates of this view generally assert that there is no reason why, for instance, a red thing must *appear red* to a person—in appropriate circumstances it may appear black.

C. A very influential theory, espoused by John Locke and many others, holds that when a person sees an object *O* there is a sense datum in his visual field for which the object *O* is causally responsible, responsible in such a way that the sense datum can not be causally explained in full without reference to the object *O*. This theory is sometimes called "dualistic" because the sense datum is not identical with, or even any part of, the material thing. It is also sometimes called a "representative" theory because sense experience does not literally contain part of the object itself, but only some thing which stands in a certain relation to the object and which because of certain similarities to the object may be deemed its representative. This point of view is also called "the causal theory" of perception, for obvious reasons. The theory is most usually combined with the second (Lockian) theory about material thinghood, but with certain qualifications it can also be combined with some of the others, and in particular with phenomenalism.

D. Finally, it is sometimes said—in conjunction with some form of the fourth theory of material thinghood—that when a person sees an object there is a sense datum in his visual field that is a normal member of the "family" of sense data constituting the thing. Suppose, for instance, that one is looking at a penny. There will be a characteristic kind of sense datum in one's visual field and, if one shifts his point of view or makes other changes in his perceptual "stance," other sense data of a characteristic kind will occur. The initial (and the later) sense datum is said to belong to a family of sense data—the "penny" family. When any member of the family occurs in one's experience, one sees the penny. It should be noticed that there may be no inconsistency in defending the present and preceding views together: both may be true when one is seeing something.

So much for theories about what thinghood is and about what it is to perceive something. Let us turn now to the kinds of theory that answer the last two questions: what kind of evidence may be adduced to support perceptual statements ("I see an ink bottle"), and what kind of justification may be given for passing from the evidence to the perceptual claim?

1. The most familiar theory concerning evidence has, over the past three centuries, maintained that the evidence consists of present sense experiences and seeming recollections of past sense experiences. Given this basic evidence, it is then assumed that by some kind of reasoning (the kinds were examined in the preceding chapter) it can be shown to be reasonable to believe that past sense experiences did occur approximately as remembered. Accordingly a rather large reservoir of theorems—premises for further inferences—is available about past sense experience.

1a. One justification for belief in perceptual claims is, then, that given these premises about past sense experiences, we may pass, by induction, to some generalizations about what sense data may be experienced under various circumstances (for example, about what sense data I might experience, given that I am now seeing a penny-like sense datum, if I moved my position in various ways but kept the penny-like datum in the middle of my visual field). But according to some theories (for example, phenomenalism), there is a certain physical object if and only if certain statements about the sense data a person would experience under various possible circumstances are true. So the inference, by induction, of these general statements about sense data has already carried us to statements about material things. Moreover, at least according to the last theory of what it is to "see" a thing, the same inference will have led to the conclusion that one is *seeing* a thing of a certain kind. Given the premises about sense data, then, it is supposed that the principle of induction will justify at least certain perceptual claims.

1b. A second justification for perceptual claims, starting from the same type of premises about sense experience, uses a noninductive mode of inference. It may employ a causal axiom stating that every event is an instance of a causal law, and it may then propose possible causal antecedents for individual sense experiences, or for the sequences or patterns of sense data that may be discovered in the premises. According to this theory, the only plausible causal explanations of known sense data are physical objects of a certain sort. Further, it may be argued that a complete explanation of a particular sense datum requires—given other past experiences as collateral information—the assumption of a particular physical thing outside the nervous system of the perceiver. In this case the person may be said to be perceiving this object, at least if the causal theory (C, above) is accepted as expressing the nature of the perceptual relation. Incidentally, it need not be presupposed by this argument that it is self-evident that every event has a cause; it may simply be said that it is useful to assume that every event has a cause or that the assumption must be made for purposes of prediction. It may also be an oversimplification to say that every occurrence has a cause; it is perhaps more accurate to say that every event has a causal explanation and that some proposition about a physical object must play a role in causal explanations of sense experiences. H. H. Price and A. J. Ayer have criticized this type of reasoning; so has Berkeley, who claimed that physical objects cannot be causes of anything at all.

2. Some philosophers think we may start from a set of premises rather different from descriptions of the sense data present in perceiving and that we can reach propositions about material things by a much shorter route. For instance, A. M. Quinton (see Chapter 6) has held that in certain circumstances we may regard statements about things as ultimate premises, for which there is neither the need nor the possibility of further evidential support. With similar effect, R. M. Chisholm has included among premises the fact that a perceiver may *take* his sense experience to be the appearance to him of an object of a certain sort. Chisholm then affirms that we may adopt a new rule of inference: when a person takes an experience to be an experience of an object of a certain kind, he is warranted, at least until definite unfavorable evidence is found in his other experiences and takings, in believing that there *is* an object of that kind and that he is perceiving it.

3. Some other philosophers, for example, Peirce (see Chapter 6) and Grice, appear to think that we are often justified in using as premises, at any particular time, a quite large set of propositions about physical things and other persons, and even general laws about these. If this is true, the epistemologist does not have any general task of answering sceptical doubts about the existence, or perception, of material things in general. Might a philosopher who holds this view still be a phenomenalist? He might, for to say that we may claim to know certain things from the outset is not to say how the propositions known are to be analyzed. This philosopher would have a wide choice among theories both about what it is for there to be a material object of a certain kind and about what it is to perceive a physical object.

It may be helpful to classify the selections that follow according to the theories described above, and to comment briefly on the position of their authors in the stream of epistemological thought about perception. John Locke holds II.C.1b; his view is a classical (but in some ways rather primitive) formulation of this position. Berkeley represents IV.D.1a, as do John Stuart Mill and A. J. Ayer—a fact showing that the foregoing classifications require further refinement, since Berkeley is usually called a "subjective idealist" and Mill and Ayer "phenomenalists." R. M. Chisholm's paper is a criticism of the phenomenalist theory, by use of an argument that many philosophers today regard as sound. Barnes appears to represent III.B.3, or perhaps III.B.2. Most of his paper, however, is taken up with an attack on sense data, along lines that have appealed to many recent philosophers. Grice and Whiteley, like Locke, seem to hold II.C.1b. Grice's view is, of course, immensely more sophisticated than Locke's, and develops the causal analysis of perception in careful detail. Whiteley's paper concerns the type of argument by which the belief in physical things may be justified; it contains an interesting supplement to Chisholm's criticism of phenomenalism.

John Locke

A Causal Theory of Perception

SOME FURTHER CONSIDERATIONS CONCERNING OUR SIMPLE IDEAS

1. *Positive Ideas from privative Causes.* Concerning the simple ideas of sensation, it is to be considered, that whatsoever is so constituted in nature as to be able, by affecting our senses, to cause any perception in the mind, doth thereby produce in the understanding a simple idea, which, whatever be the external cause of it, when it comes to be taken notice of by our discerning

---

From John Locke, *An Essay Concerning Human Understanding,* Book II, Chaps. 8 and 9, and Book IV, Chap. 11, first published in 1690.

faculty, it is by the mind looked on and considered there to be a real positive idea in the understanding as much as any other whatsoever, though, perhaps, the cause of it be but a privation of the subject.

2. Thus the ideas of heat and cold, light and darkness, white and black, motion and rest, are equally clear and positive ideas in the mind; though, perhaps, some of the causes which produce them are barely privations in subjects from whence our senses derive those ideas. These the understanding, in its view of them, considers all as distinct positive ideas, without taking notice of the causes that produce them, which is an inquiry not belonging to the idea, as it is in the understanding, but to the nature of the things existing without us. These are two very different things, and carefully to be distinguished, it being one thing to perceive and know the idea of white or black, and quite another to examine what kind of particles they must be, and how ranged in the superficies, to make any object appear white or black.

. . .

7. *Ideas in the Mind, Qualities in Bodies.* To discover the nature of our ideas the better, and to discourse of them intelligibly, it will be convenient to distinguish them as they are ideas or perceptions in our minds, and as they are modifications of matter in the bodies that cause such perceptions in us, that so we may not think (as perhaps usually is done) that they are exactly the images and resemblances of something inherent in the subject; most of those of sensation being in the mind no more the likeness of something existing without us, than the names that stand for them are the likeness of our ideas, which yet upon hearing they are apt to excite in us.

8. Whatsoever the mind perceives in itself, or is the immediate object of perception, thought, or understanding, that I call idea; and the power to produce any idea in our mind, I call quality of the subject wherein that power is. Thus a snowball having the power to produce in us the ideas of white, cold, and round, the power to produce those ideas in us, as they are in the snowball, I call qualities; and as they are sensations or perceptions in our understandings, I call them ideas; which ideas, if I speak of sometimes as in the things themselves, I would be understood to mean those qualities in the objects which produce them in us.

9. *Primary Qualities.* Qualities thus considered in bodies are, first, such as are utterly inseparable from the body, in what state soever it be; such as in all the alterations and changes it suffers, all the force can be used upon it, it constantly keeps; and such as sense constantly finds in every particle of matter which has bulk enough to be perceived and the mind finds inseparable from every particle of matter, though less than to make itself singly be perceived by our senses, v. g., take a grain of wheat, divide it into two parts, each part has still solidity, extension, figure, and mobility; divide it again, and it retains still the same qualities; and so divide it on till the parts become insensible, they must retain still each of them all those qualities. For division (which is all that a mill, or pestle, or any other body, does upon another, in reducing it to insensible parts) can never take away either solidity, extension, figure, or mobility from any body, but only makes two or more distinct separate masses of matter, of that which was but one before; all which distinct masses, reckoned as so many distinct

bodies, after division, make a certain number. These I call original or primary qualities of body, which I think we may observe to produce simple ideas in us, viz., solidity, extension, figure, motion or rest, and number.

10. *Secondary Qualities.* Secondly, such qualities which in truth are nothing in the objects themselves, but powers to produce various sensations in us by their primary qualities, i.e., by the bulk, figure, texture, and motion of their insensible parts, as colours, sounds, tastes, &c., these I call secondary qualities. To these might be added a third sort, which are allowed to be barely powers, though they are as much real qualities in the subject, as those which I, to comply with the common way of speaking, call qualities, but for distinction, secondary qualities. For the power in fire to produce a new colour or consistency in wax or clay, by its primary qualities, is as much a quality in fire as the power it has to produce in me a new idea or sensation of warmth or burning, which I felt not before, by the same primary qualities, viz., the bulk, texture, and motion of its insensible parts.

11. *How primary Qualities produce their Ideas.* The next thing to be considered is, how bodies produce ideas in us; and that is manifestly by impulse, the only way which we can conceive bodies to operate in.

12. If then external objects be not united to our minds when they produce ideas therein, and yet we perceive these original qualities in such of them as singly fall under our senses, it is evident that some motion must be thence continued by our nerves or animal spirits, by some parts of our bodies, to the brain, or the seat of sensation, there to produce in our minds the particular ideas we have of them. And since the extension, figure, number, and motion of bodies of an observable bigness, may be perceived at a distance by the sight, it is evident some singly imperceptible bodies must come from them to the eyes, and thereby convey to the brain some motion, which produces these ideas which we have of them in us.

13. *How secondary.* After the same manner that the ideas of these original qualities are produced in us, we may conceive that the ideas of secondary qualities are also produced, viz., by the operations of insensible particles on our senses. For it being manifest that there are bodies and good store of bodies, each whereof are so small, that we cannot by any of our senses discover either their bulk, figure, or motion, as is evident in the particles of the air and water, and others extremely smaller than those, perhaps as much smaller than the particles of air and water, as the particles of air and water are smaller than peas or hail-stones; let us suppose at present, that the different motions and figures, bulk and number, of such particles, affecting the several organs of our senses, produce in us those different sensations which we have from the colours and smells of bodies; v. g., that a violet, by the impulse of such insensible particles of matter of peculiar figures and bulks, and in different degrees and modifications of their motions, causes the ideas of the blue colour and sweet scent of that flower to be produced in our minds; it being no more impossible to conceive that God should annex such ideas to such motions, with which they have no similitude, than that he should annex the idea of pain to the motion of a piece of steel dividing our flesh, with which that idea hath no resemblance.

14. What I have said concerning colours and smells may be understood also of tastes and sounds, and other the like sensible qualities; which, whatever reality

we by mistake attribute to them, are in truth nothing in the objects themselves, but powers to produce various sensations in us, and depend on those primary qualities, viz., bulk, figure, texture, and motion of parts, as I have said.

15. *Ideas of primary Qualities are Resemblances; of secondary, not.* From whence I think it easy to draw this observation, that the ideas of primary qualities of bodies are resemblances of them, and their patterns do really exist in the bodies themselves; but the ideas produced in us by these secondary qualities have no resemblance of them at all. There is nothing like our ideas existing in the bodies themselves. They are in the bodies we denominate from them, only a power to produce those sensations in us; and what is sweet, blue, or warm in idea, is but the certain bulk, figure, and motion of the insensible parts in the bodies themselves, which we call so.

16. Flame is denominated hot and light; snow, white and cold; and manna, white and sweet, from the ideas they produce in us; which qualities are commonly thought to be the same in those bodies that those ideas are in us, the one the perfect resemblance of the other, as they are in a mirror; and it would by most men be judged very extravagant if one should say otherwise. And yet he that will consider that the same fire that at one distance produces in us the sensation of warmth, does at a nearer approach produce in us the far different sensation of pain, ought to bethink himself what reason he has to say that this idea of warmth, which was produced in him by the fire, is actually in the fire; and his idea of pain, which the same fire produced in him the same way, is not in the fire. Why are whiteness and coldness in snow, and pain not, when it produces the one and the other idea in us; and can do neither, but by the bulk, figure, number, and motion of its solid parts?

17. The particular bulk, number, figure, and motion of the parts of fire or snow are really in them, whether any one's senses perceive them or not, and therefore they may be called real qualities, because they really exist in those bodies; but light, heat, whiteness, or coldness, are no more really in them than sickness or pain is in manna. Take away the sensation of them; let not the eyes see light or colours, nor the ears hear sounds; let the palate not taste, nor the nose smell; and all colours, tastes, odours, and sounds, as they are such particular ideas, vanish and cease, and are reduced to their causes, i.e., bulk, figure, and motion of parts.

18. A piece of manna of a sensible bulk is able to produce in us the idea of a round or square figure; and by being removed from one place to another, the idea of motion. This idea of motion represents it as it really is in the manna moving: a circle or square are the same, whether in idea or existence, in the mind or in the manna; and this both motion and figure are really in the manna, whether we take notice of them or no: this everybody is ready to agree to. Besides, manna, by the bulk, figure, texture, and motion of its parts, has a power to produce the sensations of sickness, and sometimes of acute pains or gripings in us. That these ideas of sickness and pain are not in the manna, but effects of its operations on us, and are nowhere when we feel them not, this also every one readily agrees to. And yet men are hardly to be brought to think that sweetness and whiteness are not really in manna, which are but the effects of the operations of manna, by the motion, size, and figure of its particles on the eyes and palate; as the pain and sickness caused by manna are confessedly nothing but the effects of its operations on the stomach and guts, by the size,

motion, and figure of its insensible parts, (for by nothing else can a body operate, as has been proved); as if it could not operate on the eyes and palate, and thereby produce in the mind particular distinct ideas, which in itself it has not, as well as we allow it can operate on the guts and stomach, and thereby produce distinct ideas, which in itself it has not. These ideas being all effects of the operations of manna on several parts of our bodies, by the size, figure, number, and motion of its parts; why those produced by the eyes and palate should rather be thought to be really in the manna, than those produced by the stomach and guts; or why the pain and sickness, ideas that are the effect of manna, should be thought to be nowhere when they are not felt; and yet the sweetness and whiteness, effects of the same manna on other parts of the body, by ways equally as unknown, should be thought to exist in the manna, when they are not seen or tasted, would need some reason to explain.

19. *Ideas of primary Qualities are Resemblances; of secondary, not.* Let us consider the red and white colours in porphyry: hinder light from striking on it, and its colours vanish, it no longer produces any such ideas in us; upon the return of light it produces these appearances on us again. Can any one think any real alterations are made in the porphyry by the presence or absence of light, and that those ideas of whiteness and redness are really in porphyry in the light, when it is plain it has no colour in the dark? It has, indeed, such a configuration of particles, both night and day, as are apt, by the rays of light rebounding from some parts of that hard stone, to produce in us the idea of redness, and from others the idea of whiteness; but whiteness or redness are not in it at any time, but such a texture that hath the power to produce such a sensation in us.

20. Pound an almond, and the clear white colour will be altered into a dirty one, and the sweet taste into an oily one. What real alteration can the beating of the pestle make in any body, but an alteration of the texture of it?

21. Ideas being thus distinguished and understood, we may be able to give an account how the same water, at the same time, may produce the idea of cold by one hand and of heat by the other; whereas it is impossible that the same water, if those ideas were really in it, should at the same time be both hot and cold; for if we imagine warmth, as it is in our hands, to be nothing but a certain sort and degree of motion in the minute particles of our nerves or animal spirits, we may understand how it is possible that the same water may, at the same time, produce the sensations of heat in one hand and cold in the other; which yet figure never does, that never producing the idea of a square by one hand which has produced the idea of a globe by another. But if the sensation of heat and cold be nothing but the increase or diminution of the motion of the minute parts of our bodies, caused by the corpuscles of any other body, it is easy to be understood, that if that motion be greater in one hand than in the other, if a body be applied to the two hands, which has in its minute particles a greater motion than in those of one of the hands, and a less than in those of the other, it will increase the motion of the one hand and lessen it in the other, and so cause the different sensations of heat and cold that depend thereon.

22. I have in what just goes before been engaged in physical inquiries a little further than perhaps I intended; but it being necessary to make the nature of sensation a little understood, and to make the difference between the qualities

in bodies, and the ideas produced by them in the mind, to be distinctly conceived, without which it were impossible to discourse intelligibly of them, I hope I shall be pardoned this little excursion into natural philosophy, it being necessary in our present inquiry to distinguish the primary and real qualities of bodies which are always in them, (viz., solidity, extension, figure, number, and motion, or rest, and are sometimes perceived by us, viz., when the bodies they are in are big enough singly to be discerned,) from those secondary and imputed qualities which are but the powers of several combinations of those primary ones, when they operate without being distinctly discerned; whereby we may also come to know what ideas are, and what are not, resemblances of something really existing in the bodies we denominate from them.

23. *Three Sorts of Qualities in Bodies.* The qualities, then, that are in bodies, rightly considered, are of three sorts.

First, the bulk, figure, number, situation, and motion or rest of their solid parts; those are in them, whether we perceive them or not; and when they are of that size that we can discover them, we have by these an idea of the thing as it is in itself, as is plain in artificial things. These I call primary qualities.

Secondly, the power that is in any body, by reason of its insensible primary qualities, to operate after a peculiar manner on any of our senses, and thereby produce in us the different ideas of several colours, sounds, smells, tastes, &c. These are usually called sensible qualities.

Thirdly, the power that is in any body, by reason of the particular constitution of its primary qualities, to make such a change in the bulk, figure, texture, and motion of another body, as to make it operate on our senses differently from what it did before. Thus the sun has a power to make wax white, and fire to make lead fluid. These are usually called powers.

The first of these, as has been said, I think may be properly called real, original, or primary qualities, because they are in the things themselves, whether they are perceived or not; and upon their different modifications it is that the secondary qualities depend.

The other two are only powers to act differently upon other things, which powers result from the different modifications of those primary qualities.

24. *The first are Resemblances; the second thought Resemblances, but are not; the third neither are, nor are thought so.* But though the two latter sorts of qualities are powers barely, and nothing but powers, relating to several other bodies, and resulting from the different modifications of the original qualities, yet they are generally otherwise thought of; for the second sort, viz., the powers to produce several ideas in us by our senses, are looked upon as real qualities in the things thus affecting us; but the third sort are called and esteemed barely powers; v. g., the idea of heat or light, which we receive by our eyes or touch from the sun, are commonly thought real qualities existing in the sun, and something more than mere powers in it. But when we consider the sun in reference to wax, which it melts or blanches, we look on the whiteness and softness produced in the wax, not as qualities in the sun, but effects produced by powers in it; whereas, if rightly considered, these qualities of light and warmth, which are perceptions in me when I am warmed or enlightened by the sun, are no otherwise in the sun, than the changes made in

the wax, when it is blanched or melted, are in the sun. They are all of them equally powers in the sun, depending on its primary qualities, whereby it is able, in the one case, so to alter the bulk, figure, texture, or motion of some of the insensible parts of my eyes or hands, as thereby to produce in me the idea of light or heat; and in the other, it is able so to alter the bulk, figure, texture, or motion of the insensible parts of the wax, as to make them fit to produce in me the distinct ideas of white and fluid.

25. The reason why the one are ordinarily taken for real qualities, and the other only for bare powers, seems to be, because the ideas we have of distinct colours, sounds, &c., containing nothing at all in them of bulk, figure, or motion, we are not apt to think them the effects of these primary qualities, which appear not, to our senses, to operate in their production, and with which they have not any apparent congruity or conceivable connexion. Hence it is that we are so forward to imagine that those ideas are the resemblances of something really existing in the objects themselves; since sensation discovers nothing of bulk, figure, or motion of parts in their production; nor can reason show how bodies, by their bulk, figure, and motion, should produce in the mind the ideas of blue or yellow, &c. But in the other case, in the operations of bodies, changing the qualities one of another, we plainly discover that the quality produced hath commonly no resemblance with anything in the thing producing it; wherefore we look on it as a bare effect of power. For though receiving the idea of heat or light from the sun, we are apt to think it is a perception and resemblance of such a quality in the sun; yet when we see wax, or a fair face, receive change of colour from the sun, we cannot imagine that to be the reception or resemblance of anything in the sun, because we find not those different colours in the sun itself. For our senses being able to observe a likeness or unlikeness of sensible qualities in two different external objects, we forwardly enough conclude the production of any sensible quality in any subject to be an effect of bare power, and not the communication of any quality, which was really in the efficient, when we find no such sensible quality in the thing that produced it; but our senses not being able to discover any unlikeness between the idea produced in us, and the quality of the object producing it, we are apt to imagine that our ideas are resemblances of something in the objects, and not the effects of certain powers placed in the modification of their primary qualities, with which primary qualities the ideas produced in us have no resemblance.

26. *Secondary Qualities twofold; first, immediately perceivable; secondly, mediately perceivable.* To conclude, beside those before-mentioned primary qualities in bodies, viz., bulk, figure, extension, number, and motion of their solid parts, all the rest whereby we take notice of bodies, and distinguish them one from another, are nothing else but several powers in them depending on those primary qualities, whereby they are fitted, either by immediately operating on our bodies, to produce several different ideas in us, or else, by operating on other bodies, so to change their primary qualities as to render them capable of producing ideas in us different from what before they did. The former of these, I think, may be called secondary qualities, immediately perceivable; the latter, secondary qualities, mediately perceivable.

OF PERCEPTION

1. *Perception the first simple Idea of Reflection.* Perception, as it is the first faculty of the mind exercised about her ideas, so it is the first and simplest idea we have from reflection, and is by some called thinking in general: though thinking, in the propriety of the English tongue, signifies that sort of operation in the mind about its ideas, wherein the mind is active; where it, with some degree of voluntary attention, considers anything. For in bare naked perception, the mind is, for the most part, only passive; and what it perceives, it cannot avoid perceiving.

2. *Is only when the Mind receives the Impression.* What perception is, every one will know better by reflecting on what he does himself, what he sees, hears, feels, &c., or thinks, than by any discourse of mine. Whoever reflects on what passes in his own mind cannot miss it; and if he does not reflect, all the words in the world cannot make him have any notion of it.

3. This is certain, that whatever alterations are made in the body, if they reach not the mind, whatever impressions are made on the outward parts, if they are not taken notice of within, there is no perception. Fire may burn our bodies with no other effect than it does a billet, unless the motion be continued to the brain, and there the sense of heat, or idea of pain, be produced in the mind, wherein consists actual perception.

4. How often may a man observe in himself, that whilst his mind is intently employed in the contemplation of some objects, and curiously surveying some ideas that are there, it takes no notice of impressions of sounding bodies made upon the organ of hearing, with the same alteration that uses to be for the producing the idea of sound! A sufficient impulse there may be on the organ; but if not reaching the observation of the mind, there follows no perception: and though the motion that uses to produce the idea of sound be made in the ear, yet no sound is heard. Want of sensation, in this case, is not through any defect in the organ, or that the man's ears are less affected than at other times when he does hear: but that which uses to produce the idea, though conveyed in by the usual organ, not being taken notice of in the understanding, and so imprinting no idea in the mind, there follows no sensation. So that wherever there is sense or perception, there some idea is actually produced, and present, in the understanding.

. . .

8. *Ideas of Sensation often changed by the Judgment.* We are further to consider concerning perception, that the ideas we receive by sensation are often in grown people altered by the judgment, without our taking notice of it. When we set before our eyes a round globe of any uniform colour, v. g., gold, alabaster, or jet, it is certain that the idea thereby imprinted on our mind is of a flat circle variously shadowed, with several degrees of light and brightness coming to our eyes. But we have by use been accustomed to perceive what kind of appearance convex bodies are wont to make in us, what alterations are made in the reflections of light by the difference of the sensible figures of bodies, the judgment presently, by an habitual custom, alters the appearances into their causes, so that from that which is truly variety of shadow or colour,

collecting the figure, it makes it pass for a mark of figure, and frames to itself the perception of a convex figure and an uniform colour, when the idea we receive from thence is only a plane variously coloured, as is evident in painting. To which purpose I shall here insert a problem of that very ingenious and studious promoter of real knowledge, the learned and worthy Mr. Molineux, which he was pleased to send me in a letter some months since; and it is this: "Suppose a man born blind, and now adult, and taught by his touch to distinguish between a cube and a sphere of the same metal, and nighly of the same bigness, so as to tell, when he felt one and the other, which is the cube, which the sphere. Suppose, then, the cube and sphere placed on a table, and the blind man be made to see: quaere, whether by his sight, before he touched them, he could now distinguish and tell which is the globe, which the cube?" To which the acute and judicious proposer answers, "Not. For though he has obtained the experience of how a globe, how a cube affects his touch, yet he has not yet obtained the experience, that what affects his touch so or so, must affect his sight so or so; or that a protuberant angle in the cube, that pressed his hand unequally, shall appear to his eye as it does in the cube." I agree with this thinking gentleman, whom I am proud to call my friend, in his answer to this problem; and am of opinion that the blind man, at first sight, would not be able with certainty to say which was the globe, which the cube, whilst he only saw them; though he could unerringly name them by his touch, and certainly distinguish them by the difference of their figures felt. This I have set down, and leave with my reader, as an occasion for him to consider how much he may be beholden to experience, improvement, and acquired notions, where he thinks he had not the least use of, or help from them; and the rather, because this observing gentleman further adds, that having, upon the occasion of my book, proposed this to divers very ingenious men, he hardly ever met with one that at first gave the answer to it which he thinks true, till by hearing his reasons they were convinced.

9. But this is not, I think, usual in any of our ideas, but those received by sight; because sight, the most comprehensive of all our senses, conveying to our minds the ideas of light and colours, which are peculiar only to that sense; and also the far different ideas of space, figure, and motion, the several varieties whereof change the appearances of its proper object, viz., light and colours; we bring ourselves by use to judge of the one by the other. This, in many cases, by a settled habit, in things whereof we have frequent experience, is performed so constantly and so quick, that we take that for the perception of our sensation, which is an idea formed by our judgment; so that one, viz., that of sensation, serves only to excite the other, and is scarce taken notice of itself; as a man who reads or hears with attention and understanding, takes little notice of the characters or sounds, but of the ideas that are excited in him by them.

10. Nor need we wonder that this is done with so little notice, if we consider how very quick the actions of the mind are performed; for as itself is thought to take up no space, to have no extension, so its actions seem to require no time, but many of them seem to be crowded into an instant. I speak this in comparison to the actions of the body. Any one may easily observe this in his own thoughts, who will take the pains to reflect on them. How, as it were in an instant do our minds with one glance see all the parts of a demonstration,

which may very well be called a long one, if we consider the time it will require to put it into words, and step by step show it another? Secondly, we shall not be so much surprised that this is done in us with so little notice, if we consider how the facility which we get of doing things by a custom of doing, makes them often pass in us without our notice. Habits, especially such as are begun very early, come at last to produce actions in us, which often escape our observation. How frequently do we, in a day, cover our eyes with our eyelids, without perceiving that we are at all in the dark! Men that by custom have got the use of a by-word, do almost in every sentence pronounce sounds which, though taken notice of by others, they themselves neither hear nor observe. And therefore it is not so strange that our mind should often change the idea of its sensation into that of its judgment, and make one serve only to excite the other, without our taking notice of it.

. . .

OF OUR KNOWLEDGE OF THE EXISTENCE OF OTHER THINGS

1. *It is to be had only by sensation.* The knowledge of our own being we have by intuition. The existence of a God reason clearly makes known to us, as has been shown.

The knowledge of the existence of any other thing we can have only by sensation: for there being no necessary connexion of real existence with any idea a man hath in his memory; nor of any other existence but that of God with the existence of any particular man: no particular man can know the existence of any other being, but only when, by actual operating upon him, it makes itself perceived by him. For the having the idea of anything in our mind no more proves the existence of that thing than the picture of a man evidences his being in the world, or the visions of a dream make thereby a true history.

2. It is therefore the actual receiving of ideas from without that gives us notice of the existence of other things, and makes us know that something doth exist at that time without us which causes that idea in us, though perhaps we neither know nor consider how it does it. For it takes not from the certainty of our senses, and the ideas we receive by them, that we know not the manner wherein they are produced: v. g., whilst I write this, I have, by the paper affecting my eyes, that idea produced in my mind, which whatever object causes, I call white; by which I know that that quality or accident (i. e., whose appearance before my eyes always causes that idea) doth really exist, and hath a being without me. And of this, the greatest assurance I can possibly have, and to which my faculties can attain, is the testimony of my eyes, which are the proper and sole judges of this thing; whose testimony I have reason to rely on as so certain, that I can no more doubt, whilst I write this, that I see white and black, and that something really exists that causes that sensation in me, than that I write or move my hand; which is a certainty as great as human nature is capable of, concerning the existence of anything but a man's self alone, and of God.

3. *This, though not so certain as demonstration, yet may be called knowledge, and proves the existence of things without us.* The notice we have by our

senses of the existing of things without us, though it be not altogether so certain as our intuitive knowledge, or the deductions of our reason employed about the clear abstract ideas of our own minds; yet it is an assurance that deserves the name of *knowledge*. If we persuade ourselves that our faculties act and inform us right concerning the existence of those objects that affect them, it cannot pass for an ill-grounded confidence: for I think nobody can, in earnest, be so sceptical as to be uncertain of the existence of those things which he sees and feels. At least, he that can doubt so far (whatever he may have with his own thoughts) will never have any controversy with me; since he can never be sure I say anything contrary to his opinion. As to myself, I think God has given me assurance enough of the existence of things without me; since by their different application I can produce in myself both pleasure and pain, which is one great concernment of my present state. This is certain, the confidence that our faculties do not herein deceive us is the greatest assurance we are capable of concerning the existence of material beings. For we cannot act anything but by our faculties, nor talk of knowledge itself, but by the help of those faculties which are fitted to apprehend even what knowledge is. But besides the assurance we have from our senses themselves, that they do not err in the information they give us of the existence of things without us, when they are affected by them, we are farther confirmed in this assurance by other concurrent reasons.

4. *Because we cannot have them but by the inlet of the senses.* First, It is plain those perceptions are produced in us by exterior causes affecting our senses, because those that want the organs of any sense never can have the ideas belonging to that sense produced in their minds. The organs themselves, it is plain, do not produce them; for then the eyes of a man in the dark would produce colours, and his nose smell roses in the winter: but we see nobody gets the relish of a pine-apple till he goes to the Indies where it is, and tastes it.

5. *Because an idea from actual sensation and another from memory are very distinct perceptions.* Secondly, Because sometimes I find that I cannot avoid the having those ideas produced in my mind. For though when my eyes are shut, or windows fast, I can at pleasure recall to my mind the ideas of light or the sun, which former sensations had lodged in my memory; so I can at pleasure lay by that idea, and take into my view that of the smell of a rose, or taste of sugar. But if I turn my eyes at noon towards the sun, I cannot avoid the ideas which the light or sun then produces in me. So that there is a manifest difference between the ideas laid up in my memory, and those which force themselves upon me, and I cannot avoid having. And therefore it must needs be some exterior cause, and the brisk acting of some objects without me, whose efficacy I cannot resist, that produces those ideas in my mind, whether I will or no. Besides, there is nobody who doth not perceive the difference in himself between contemplating the sun as he hath the idea of it in his memory, and actually looking upon it: of which two, his perception is so distinct, that few of his ideas are more distinguishable one from another. And therefore he hath certain knowledge that they are not both memory, or the actions of his mind, and fancies only within him; but that actual seeing hath a cause without.

6. *Pleasure or pain, which accompanies actual sensation, accompanies not the returning of those ideas without the external objects.* Thirdly, Add to this, that many of those ideas are produced in us with pain, which afterwards we

remember without the least offence. Thus the pain of heat or cold, when the idea of it is revived in our minds, gives us no disturbance; which, when felt, was very troublesome, and is again, when actually repeated: which is occasioned by the disorder the external object causes in our bodies when applied to it. And we remember the pain of hunger, thirst, or the headache, without any pain at all; which would either never disturb us, or else constantly do it as often as we thought of it, were there nothing more but ideas floating in our minds, and appearances entertaining our fancies, without the real existence of things affecting us from abroad. The same may be said of pleasure accompanying several actual sensations; and though mathematical demonstration depends not upon sense, yet the examining them by diagrams gives great credit to the evidence of our sight, and seems to give it a certainty approaching to that of the demonstration itself. For it would be very strange that a man should allow it for an undeniable truth, that two angles of a figure which he measures by lines and angles of a diagram, should be bigger one than the other, and yet doubt of the existence of those lines and angles which, by looking on, he makes use of to measure that by.

7. *Our senses assist one another's testimony of the existence of outward things.* Fourthly, Our senses, in many cases, bear witness to the truth of each other's report concerning the existence of sensible things without us. He that sees a fire may, if he doubt whether it be anything more than a bare fancy, feel it too, and be convinced by putting his hand in it; which certainly could never be put into such exquisite pain by a bare idea or phantom, unless that the pain be a fancy too; which yet he cannot, when the burn is well, by raising the idea of it, bring upon himself again.

Thus I see, whilst I write this, I can change the appearance of the paper; and by designing the letters, tell beforehand what new idea it shall exhibit the very next moment, barely by drawing my pen over it: which will neither appear (let me fancy as much as I will) if my hand stand still, or though I move my pen, if my eyes be shut; nor, when those characters are once made on the paper, can I choose afterwards but see them as they are; that is, have the ideas of such letters as I have made. Whence it is manifest that they are not barely the sport and play of my own imagination, when I find that the characters that were made at the pleasure of my own thoughts do not obey them; nor yet cease to be, whenever I shall fancy it, but continue to affect my senses constantly and regularly, according to the figures I made them. To which if we will add, that the sight of those shall, from another man, draw such sounds as I beforehand design they shall stand for, there will be little reason left to doubt that those words I write do really exist without me, when they cause a long series of regular sounds to affect my ears, which could not be the effect of my imagination, nor could my memory retain them in that order.

8. *This certainty is as great as our condition needs.* But yet, if after all this any one will be so sceptical as to distrust his senses, and to affirm that all we see and hear, feel and taste, think and do, during our whole being, is but the series and deluding appearances of a long dream whereof there is no reality; and therefore will question the existence of all things or our knowledge of anything: I must desire him to consider, that if all be a dream, then he doth but dream that he makes the question; and so it is not much matter that a

waking man should answer him. But yet, if he pleases, he may dream that I make him this answer, that the certainty of things existing *in rerum natura,* when we have the testimony of our senses for it, is not only as great as our frame can attain to, but as our condition needs. For our faculties being suited not to the full extent of being, nor to a perfect, clear, comprehensive knowledge of things free from all doubt and scruple; but to the preservation of us, in whom they are; and accommodated to the use of life: they serve to our purpose well enough, if they will but give us certain notice of those things which are convenient or inconvenient to us. For he that sees a candle burning, and hath experimented the force of its flame by putting his finger in it, will little doubt that this is something existing without him, which does him harm and puts him to great pain. And if our dreamer pleases to try whether the glowing heat of a glass furnace be barely a wandering imagination in a drowsy man's fancy, by putting his hand into it, he may perhaps be awakened into a certainty, greater than he could wish, that it is something more than bare imagination. So that this evidence is as great as we can desire, being as certain to us as our pleasure or pain, i. e., happiness or misery; beyond which we have no concernment, either of knowing or being. Such an assurance of the existence of things without us is sufficient to direct us in the attaining the good and avoiding the evil which is caused by them, which is the important concernment we have of being made acquainted with them.

9. *But reaches no farther than actual sensation.* In fine, then, when our senses do actually convey into our understandings any idea, we cannot but be satisfied that there doth something at that time really exist without us, which doth affect our senses, and by them give notice of itself to our apprehensive faculties, and actually produce that idea which we then perceive: and we cannot so far distrust their testimony as to doubt that such collections of simple ideas as we have observed by our senses to be united together, do really exist together. But this knowledge extends as far as the present testimony of our senses, employed about particular objects that do then affect them, and no farther. For if I saw such a collection of simple ideas as is wont to be called man, existing together one minute since, and am now alone, I cannot be certain that the same man exists now, since there is no necessary connexion of his existence a minute since with his existence now: by a thousand ways he may cease to be, since I had the testimony of my senses for his existence. And if I cannot be certain that the man I saw last to-day is now in being, I can less be certain that he is so who hath been longer removed from my senses, and I have not seen since yesterday, or since the last year; and much less can I be certain of the existence of men that I never saw. And therefore, though it be highly probable that millions of men do now exist, yet whilst I am alone writing this, I have not that certainty of it which we strictly call knowledge; though the great likelihood of it puts me past doubt, and it be reasonable for me to do several things upon the confidence that there are men (and men also of my acquaintance, with whom I have to do) now in the world: but this is but probability, not knowledge.

10. *Folly to expect demonstration in everything.* Whereby yet we may observe how vain it is to expect demonstration and certainty in things not capable of it, and refuse assent to very rational propositions, and act contrary to very plain and clear truths, because they cannot be made out so evident as to

surmount every the least (I will not say reason, but) pretence of doubting. He, that, in the ordinary affairs of life, would admit of nothing but direct plain demonstration, would be sure of nothing in this world but of perishing quickly.

George Berkeley

The Reduction of Objects to Experiences of a Mind

OF THE PRINCIPLES OF HUMAN KNOWLEDGE

PART FIRST

1. It is evident to any one who takes a survey of the *objects of human knowledge,* that they are either *ideas* actually imprinted on the senses; or else such as are perceived by attending to the passions and operations of the mind; or lastly, *ideas* formed by help of memory and imagination—either compounding, dividing, or barely representing those originally perceived in the aforesaid ways. By sight I have the ideas of light and colours, with their several degrees and variations. By touch I perceive hard and soft, heat and cold, motion and resistance; and of all these more and less either as to quantity or degree. Smelling furnishes me with odours; the palate with tastes; and hearing conveys sounds to the mind in all their variety of tone and composition.

And as several of these are observed to accompany each other, they come to be marked by one name, and so to be reputed as one *thing.* Thus, for example, a certain colour, taste, smell, figure and consistence having been observed to go together, are accounted one distinct thing, signified by the name apple; other collections of ideas constitute a stone, a tree, a book, and the like sensible things; which as they are pleasing or disagreeable excite the passions of love, hatred, joy, grief, and so forth.

2. But, besides all that endless variety of ideas or objects of knowledge, there is likewise Something which knows or perceives them; and exercises divers operations, as willing, imagining, remembering, about them. This perceiving, active being is what I call *mind, spirit, soul,* or *myself.* By which words I do not denote any one of my ideas, but a thing entirely distinct from them, wherein they exist, or, which is the same thing, whereby they are perceived; for the existence of an idea consists in being perceived.

From George Berkeley, *A Treatise Concerning the Principles of Human Knowledge,* first published in 1710, and *The Third Dialogue Between Hylas and Philonous,* first published in 1713.

George Berkeley (1685–1753), made Bishop of Cloyne in 1734, wrote several important philosophical works, especially in his early years. He lived for three years in Rhode Island during an attempt to found a university in the Bermudas that would extend its benefits to the Americans.

3. That neither our thoughts, nor passions, nor ideas formed by the imagination, exist without the mind is what everybody will allow. And to me it seems no less evident that the various sensations or ideas imprinted on the Sense, however blended or combined together (that is, whatever objects they compose), cannot exist otherwise than in a mind perceiving them. I think an intuitive knowledge may be obtained of this, by any one that shall attend to what is meant by the term *exist* when applied to sensible things. The table I write on I say exists; that is, I see and feel it: and if I were out of my study I should say it existed; meaning thereby that if I was in my study I might perceive it, or that some other spirit actually does perceive it. There was an odour, that is, it was smelt; there was a sound, that is, it was heard; a colour or figure, and it was perceived by sight or touch. This is all that I can understand by these and the like expressions. For as to what is said of the *absolute* existence of unthinking things, without any relation to their being perceived, that is to me perfectly unintelligible. Their *esse* is *percipi*; nor is it possible they should have any existence out of the minds or thinking things which perceive them.

4. It is indeed an opinion strangely prevailing amongst men, that houses, mountains, rivers, and in a word all sensible objects, have an existence, natural or real, distinct from their being perceived by the understanding. But, with how great an assurance and acquiescence soever this Principle may be entertained in the world, yet whoever shall find in his heart to call it in question may, if I mistake not, perceive it to involve a manifest contradiction. For, what are the forementioned objects but the things we perceive by sense? and what do we perceive besides our own ideas or sensations? and is it not plainly repugnant that any one of these, or any combination of them, should exist unperceived?

5. If we thoroughly examine this tenet it will, perhaps, be found at bottom to depend on the doctrine of *abstract ideas*. For can there be a nicer strain of abstraction than to distinguish the existence of sensible objects from their being perceived, so as to conceive them existing unperceived? Light and colours, heat and cold, extension and figures—in a word the things we see and feel—what are they but so many sensations, notions, ideas, or impressions on the sense? and is it possible to separate, even in thought, any of these from perception? For my part, I might as easily divide a thing from itself. I may, indeed, divide in my thoughts, or conceive apart from each other, those things which perhaps I never perceived by sense so divided. Thus, I imagine the trunk of a human body without the limbs, or conceive the smell of a rose without thinking on the rose itself. So far, I will not deny, I can abstract; if that may properly be called *abstraction* which extends only to the conceiving separately such objects as it is possible may really exist or be actually perceived asunder. But my conceiving or imagining power does not extend beyond the possibility of real existence or perception. Hence, as it is impossible for me to see or feel anything without an actual sensation of that thing, so is it impossible for me to conceive in my thoughts any sensible thing or object distinct from the sensation or perception of it. [In truth, the object and the sensation are the same thing, and cannot therefore be abstracted from each other.]

6. Some truths there are so near and obvious to the mind that a man need only open his eyes to see them. Such I take this important one to be, viz. that all the choir of heaven and furniture of the earth, in a word all those bodies which compose the mighty frame of the world, have not any subsistence with-

out a mind; that their *being* is to be perceived or known; that consequently so long as they are not actually perceived by me, or do not exist in my mind, or that of any other created spirit, they must either have no existence at all, or else subsist in the mind of some Eternal Spirit: it being perfectly unintelligible, and involving all the absurdity of abstraction, to attribute to any single part of them an existence independent of a spirit. [To be convinced of which, the reader need only reflect, and try to separate in his own thoughts the *being* of a sensible thing from its *being perceived.*]

7. From what has been said it is evident there is not any other Substance than *Spirit,* or that which perceives. But, for the fuller proof of this point, let it be considered the sensible qualities are colour, figure, motion, smell, taste, and such like, that is, the ideas perceived by sense. Now, for an idea to exist in an unperceiving thing is a manifest contradiction; for to have an idea is all one as to perceive: that therefore wherein colour, figure, and the like qualities exist must perceive them. Hence it is clear there can be no unthinking substance or *substratum* of those ideas.

8. But, say you, though the ideas themselves do not exist without the mind, yet there may be things like them, whereof they are copies or resemblances; which things exist without the mind, in an unthinking substance. I answer, an idea can be like nothing but an idea; a colour or figure can be like nothing but another colour or figure. If we look but never so little into our thoughts, we shall find it impossible for us to conceive a likeness except only between our ideas. Again, I ask whether those supposed *originals,* or external things, of which our ideas are the pictures or representations, be themselves perceivable or no? If they are, then *they* are ideas, and we have gained our point: but if you say they are not, I appeal to any one whether it be sense to assert a colour is like something which is invisible; hard or soft, like something which is intangible; and so of the rest.

9. Some there are who make a distinction betwixt *primary* and *secondary* qualities. By the former they mean extension, figure, motion, rest, solidity or impenetrability, and number; by the latter they denote all other sensible qualities, as colours, sounds, tastes, and so forth. The ideas we have of these last they acknowledge not to be the resemblances of anything existing without the mind, or unperceived; but they will have our ideas of the *primary qualities* to be patterns or images of things which exist without the mind, in an unthinking substance which they call Matter. By Matter, therefore, we are to understand an inert, senseless substance, in which extension, figure, and motion do actually subsist. But it is evident, from what we have already shewn, that extension, figure, and motion are only ideas existing in the mind, and that an idea can be like nothing but another idea; and that consequently neither they nor their archetypes can exist in an unperceiving substance. Hence, it is plain that the very notion of what is called *Matter* or *corporeal substance,* involves a contradiction in it. [Insomuch that I should not think it necessary to spend more time in exposing its absurdity. But, because the tenet of the existence of Matter seems to have taken so deep a root in the minds of philosophers, and draws after it so many ill consequences, I choose rather to be thought prolix and tedious than omit anything that might conduce to the full discovery and extirpation of that prejudice.]

10. They who assert that figure, motion, and the rest of the primary or orig-

inal qualities do exist without the mind, in unthinking substances, do at the same time acknowledge that colours, sounds, heat, cold, and suchlike secondary qualities, do not; which they tell us are sensations, existing in the mind alone, that depend on and are occasioned by the different size, texture, and motion of the minute particles of matter. This they take for an undoubted truth, which they can demonstrate beyond all exception. Now, if it be certain that those *original* qualities are inseparably united with the other sensible qualities, and not, even in thought, capable of being abstracted from them, it plainly follows that *they* exist only in the mind. But I desire any one to reflect, and try whether he can, by any abstraction of thought, conceive the extension and motion of a body without all other sensible qualities. For my own part, I see evidently that it is not in my power to frame an idea of a body extended and moving, but I must withal give it some colour or other sensible quality, which is acknowledged to exist only in the mind. In short, extension, figure, and motion, abstracted from all other qualities, are inconceivable. Where therefore the other sensible qualities are, there must these be also, to wit, in the mind and nowhere else.

. . .

14. I shall farther add, that, after the same manner as modern philosophers prove certain sensible qualities to have no existence in Matter, or without the mind, the same thing may be likewise proved of all other sensible qualities whatsoever. Thus, for instance, it is said that heat and cold are affections only of the mind, and not at all patterns of real beings, existing in the corporeal substances which excite them; for that the same body which appears cold to one hand seems warm to another. Now, why may we not as well argue that figure and extension are not patterns or resemblances of qualities existing in Matter; because to the same eye at different stations, or eyes of a different texture at the same station, they appear various, and cannot therefore be the images of anything settled and determinate without the mind? Again, it is proved that sweetness is not really in the sapid thing; because the thing remaining unaltered the sweetness is changed into bitter, as in case of a fever or otherwise vitiated palate. Is it not as reasonable to say that motion is not without the mind; since if the succession of ideas in the mind become swifter, the motion, it is acknowledged, shall appear slower, without any alteration in any external object?

15. In short, let any one consider those arguments which are thought manifestly to prove that colours and tastes exist only in the mind, and he shall find they may with equal force be brought to prove the same thing of extension, figure, and motion. Though it must be confessed this method of arguing does not so much prove that there is no extension or colour in an outward object, as that we do not know by sense which is the true extension or colour of the object. But the arguments foregoing plainly shew it to be impossible that any colour or extension at all, or other sensible quality whatsoever, should exist in an unthinking subject without the mind, or in truth that there should be any such thing as an outward object.

16. But let us examine a little the received opinion. It is said extension is a *mode* or *accident* of Matter, and that Matter is the *substratum* that supports it. Now I desire that you would explain to me what is meant by Matter's *support-*

ing extension. Say you, I have no idea of Matter; and therefore cannot explain it. I answer, though you have no positive, yet, if you have any meaning at all, you must at least have a relative idea of Matter; though you know not what it is, yet you must be supposed to know what relation it bears to accidents, and what is meant by its supporting them. It is evident *support* cannot here be taken in its usual or literal sense, as when we say that pillars support a building. In what sense therefore must it be taken? [For my part, I am not able to discover any sense at all that can be applicable to it.]

17. If we inquire into what the most accurate philosophers declare themselves to mean by *material substance,* we shall find them acknowledge they have no other meaning annexed to those sounds but the idea of Being in general, together with the relative notion of its supporting accidents. The general idea of Being appeareth to me the most abstract and incomprehensible of all other; and as for its supporting accidents, this, as we have just now observed, cannot be understood in the common sense of those words: it must therefore be taken in some other sense, but what that is they do not explain. So that when I consider the two parts or branches which make the signification of the words *material substance,* I am convinced there is no distinct meaning annexed to them. But why should we trouble ourselves any farther, in discussing this material *substratum* or support of figure and motion and other sensible qualities? Does it not suppose they have an existence without the mind? And is not this a direct repugnancy, and altogether inconceivable?

18. But, though it were possible that solid, figured, moveable substances may exist without the mind, corresponding to the ideas we have of bodies, yet how is it possible for us to know this? Either we must know it by Sense or by Reason. As for our senses, by them we have the knowledge only of our sensations, ideas, or those things that are immediately perceived by sense, call them what you will: but they do not inform us that things exist without the mind, or unperceived, like to those which are perceived. This the materialists themselves acknowledge.—It remains therefore that if we have any knowledge at all of external things, it must be by reason inferring their existence from what is immediately perceived by sense. But (I do not see) what reason can induce us to believe the existence of bodies without the mind, from what we perceive, since the very patrons of Matter themselves do not pretend there is any necessary connexion betwixt them and our ideas? I say it is granted on all hands (and what happens in dreams, frensies, and the like, puts it beyond dispute) that it is possible we might be affected with all the ideas we have now, though no bodies existed without resembling them. Hence it is evident the supposition of external bodies is not necessary for the producing our ideas; since it is granted they are produced sometimes, and might possibly be produced always, in the same order we see them in at present, without their concurrence.

19. But, though we might possibly have all our sensations without them, yet perhaps it may be thought easier to conceive and explain the manner of their production, by supposing external bodies in their likeness rather than otherwise; and so it might be at least probable there are such things as bodies that excite their ideas in our minds. But neither can this be said. For, though we give the materialists their external bodies, they by their own confession are

never the nearer knowing how our ideas are produced; since they own themselves unable to comprehend in what manner body can act upon spirit, or how it is possible it should imprint any idea in the mind. Hence it is evident the production of ideas or sensations in our minds, can be no reason why we should suppose Matter or corporeal substances; since that is acknowledged to remain equally inexplicable with or without this supposition. If therefore it were possible for bodies to exist without the mind, yet to hold they do so must needs be a very precarious opinion; since it is to suppose, without any reason at all, that God has created innumerable beings that are entirely useless, and serve to no manner of purpose.

. . .

22. I am afraid I have given cause to think I am needlessly prolix in handling this subject. For, to what purpose is it to dilate on that which may be demonstrated with the utmost evidence in a line or two, to any one that is capable of the least reflexion? It is but looking into your own thoughts, and so trying whether you can conceive it possible for a sound, or figure, or motion, or colour to exist without the mind or unperceived. This easy trial may perhaps make you see that what you contend for is a downright contradiction. Insomuch that I am content to put the whole upon this issue:—If you can but conceive it possible for one extended moveable substance, or in general for any one idea, or anything like an idea, to exist otherwise than in a mind perceiving it, I shall readily give up the cause. And, as for all that compages of external bodies you contend for, I shall grant you its existence, though you cannot either give me any reason why you believe it exists, or assign any use to it when it is supposed to exist. I say, the bare possibility of your opinions being true shall pass for an argument that it is so.

23. But, say you, surely there is nothing easier than for me to imagine trees, for instance, in a park, or books existing in a closet, and nobody by to perceive them. I answer, you may so, there is no difficulty in it. But what is all this, I beseech you, more than framing in your mind certain ideas which you call *books* and *trees,* and at the same time omitting to frame the idea of any one that may perceive them? But do not you yourself perceive or think of them all the while? This therefore is nothing to the purpose: it only shews you have the power of imagining, or forming ideas in your mind; but it does not shew that you can conceive it possible the objects of your thought may exist without the mind. To make out this, it is necessary that you conceive them existing unconceived or unthought of; which is a manifest repugnancy. When we do our utmost to conceive the existence of external bodies, we are all the while only contemplating our own ideas. But the mind, taking no notice of itself, is deluded to think it can and does conceive bodies existing unthought of, or without the mind, though at the same time they are apprehended by, or exist in, itself. A little attention will discover to any one the truth and evidence of what is here said, and make it unnecessary to insist on any other proofs against the existence of *material substance.*

. . .

25. All our ideas, sensations, notions, or the things which we perceive, by whatsoever names they may be distinguished, are visibly inactive: there is nothing of power or agency included in them. So that one idea or object of thought cannot produce or make any alteration in another. To be satisfied of the truth of this, there is nothing else requisite but a bare observation of our ideas. For, since they and every part of them exist only in the mind, it follows that there is nothing in them but what is perceived: but whoever shall attend to his ideas, whether of sense or reflexion, will not perceive in them any power or activity; there is, therefore, no such thing contained in them. A little attention will discover to us that the very being of an idea implies passiveness and inertness in it; insomuch that it is impossible for an idea to do anything, or, strictly speaking, to be the cause of anything: neither can it be the resemblance or pattern of any active being, as is evident from sect. 8. Whence it plainly follows that extension, figure, and motion cannot be the cause of our sensations. To say, therefore, that these are the effects of powers resulting from the configuration, number, motion, and size of corpuscles, must certainly be false.

26. We perceive a continual succession of ideas; some are anew excited, others are changed or totally disappear. There is therefore *some* cause of these ideas, whereon they depend, and which produces and changes them. That this cause cannot be any quality or idea or combination of *ideas,* is clear from the preceding section. It must therefore be a *substance*; but it has been shewn that there is no corporeal or material substance: it remains therefore that the cause of ideas is an incorporeal active substance or Spirit.

27. A Spirit is one simple, undivided, active being—as it perceives ideas it is called the *understanding,* and as it produces or otherwise operates about them it is called the *will.* Hence there can be no *idea* formed of a soul or spirit; for all ideas whatever, being passive and inert (vid. sect. 25), they cannot represent unto us, by way of image or likeness, that which acts. A little attention will make it plain to any one, that to have an idea which shall be *like* that active Principle of motion and change of ideas is absolutely impossible. Such is the nature of Spirit, or that which acts, that it cannot be of itself perceived, but only by the effects which it produceth. If any man shall doubt of the truth of what is here delivered, let him but reflect and try if he can frame the idea of any power or active being; and whether he has ideas of two principal powers, marked by the names *will* and *understanding,* distinct from each other, as well as from a third idea of Substance or Being in general, with a relative notion of its supporting or being the subject of the aforesaid powers—which is signified by the name *soul* or *spirit.* This is what some hold; but, so far as I can see, the words *will,* [*understanding, mind,*] *soul, spirit,* do not stand for different ideas, or, in truth, for any idea at all, but for something which is very different from ideas, and which, being an agent, cannot be like unto, or represented by, any idea whatsoever. [Though it must be owned at the same time that we have some *notion* of soul, spirit, and the operations of the mind, such as willing, loving, hating—inasmuch as we know or understand the meaning of these words.]

28. I find I can excite ideas in my mind at pleasure, and vary and shift the scene as oft as I think fit. It is no more than *willing,* and straightway this or that idea arises in my fancy; and by the same power it is obliterated and

makes way for another. This making and unmaking of ideas doth very properly denominate the mind active. Thus much is certain and grounded on experience: but when we talk of unthinking agents, or of exciting ideas exclusive of volition, we only amuse ourselves with words.

29. But, whatever power I may have over my own thoughts, I find the ideas actually perceived by Sense have not a like dependence on *my* will. When in broad daylight I open my eyes, it is not in my power to choose whether I shall see or no, or to determine what particular objects shall present themselves to my view: and so likewise as to the hearing and other senses; the ideas imprinted on them are not creatures of *my* will. There is therefore some other Will or Spirit that produces them.

30. The ideas of Sense are more strong, lively, and distinct than those of the Imagination; they have likewise a steadiness, order, and coherence, and are not excited at random, as those which are the effects of human wills often are, but in a regular train or series—the admirable connexion whereof sufficiently testifes the wisdom and benevolence of its Author. Now the set rules, or established methods, wherein the Mind we depend on excites in us the ideas of Sense, are called *the laws of nature*; and these we learn by experience, which teaches us that such and such ideas are attended with such and such other ideas, in the ordinary course of things.

31. This gives us a sort of foresight, which enables us to regulate our actions for the benefit of life. And without this we should be eternally at a loss: we could not know how to act anything that might procure us the least pleasure, or remove the least pain of sense. That food nourishes, sleep refreshes, and fire warms us; that to sow in the seedtime is the way to reap in the harvest; and in general that to obtain such or such ends, such or such means are conducive—all this we know, not by discovering any *necessary connexion* between our ideas, but only by the observation of the *settled laws* of nature; without which we should be all in uncertainty and confusion, and a grown man no more know how to manage himself in the affairs of life than an infant just born.

32. And yet this consistent uniform working, which so evidently displays the Goodness and Wisdom of that Governing Spirit whose Will constitutes the laws of nature, is so far from leading our thoughts to Him, that it rather sends them wandering after second causes. For, when we perceive certain ideas of Sense constantly followed by other ideas, and we know this is not of our own doing, we forthwith attribute power and agency to the ideas themselves, and make one the cause of another, than which nothing can be more absurd and unintelligible. Thus, for example, having observed that when we perceive by sight a certain round luminous figure, we at the same time perceive by touch the idea or sensation called heat, we do from thence conclude the sun to be the *cause* of heat. And in like manner perceiving the motion and collision of bodies to be attended with sound, we are inclined to think the latter the *effect* of the former.

33. The ideas imprinted on the Senses by the Author of nature are called *real things*: and those excited in the imagination, being less regular, vivid, and constant, are more properly termed *ideas* or *images of* things, which they copy and represent. But then our *sensations,* be they never so vivid and distinct, are nevertheless ideas: that is, they exist in the mind, or are perceived by it, as truly as the ideas of its own framing. The ideas of Sense are allowed to have

more reality in them, that is, to be more strong, orderly, and coherent than the creatures of the mind; but this is no argument that they exist without the mind. They are also less dependent on the spirit or thinking substance which perceives them, in that they are excited by the will of another and more powerful Spirit: yet still they are *ideas*: and certainly no idea, whether faint or strong, can exist otherwise than in a mind perceiving it.

. . .

57. But why they should suppose the ideas of sense to be excited in us by things in their likeness, and not rather have recourse to *Spirit,* which alone can act, may be accounted for. First, because they were not aware of the repugnancy there is, as well in supposing things like unto our ideas existing without, as in attributing to them power or activity. Secondly, because the Supreme Spirit which excites those ideas in our minds, is not marked out and limited to our view by any particular finite collection of sensible ideas, as human agents are by their size, complexion, limbs, and motions. And thirdly, because His operations are regular and uniform. Whenever the course of nature is interrupted by a miracle, men are ready to own the presence of a Superior Agent. But, when we see things go on in the ordinary course, they do not excite in us any reflexion; their order and concatenation, though it be an argument of the greatest wisdom, power, and goodness in their Creator, is yet so constant and familiar to us, that we do not think them the immediate effects of a *Free Spirit*; especially since inconsistency and mutability in acting, though it be an imperfection, is looked on as a mark of *freedom.*

. . .

139. But it will be objected that, if there is no *idea* signified by the terms *soul, spirit,* and *substance,* they are wholly insignificant, or have no meaning in them. I answer, those words do mean or signify a real thing; which is neither an idea nor like an idea, but that which perceives ideas, and wills, and reasons about them. What I am *myself*, that which I denote by the term *I*, is the same with what is meant by *soul,* or *spiritual substance.* [But if I should say that *I* was nothing, or that *I* was an *idea* or *notion,* nothing could be more evidently absurd than either of these propositions.] If it be said that this is only quarrelling at a word, and that, since the immediate significations of other names are by common consent called *ideas,* no reason can be assigned why that which is signified by the name *spirit* or *soul* may not partake in the same appellation. I answer, all the unthinking objects of the mind agree in that they are entirely passive, and their existence consists only in being perceived: whereas a *soul* or *spirit* is an active being, whose existence consists, not in being perceived, but in perceiving ideas and thinking. It is therefore necessary, in order to prevent equivocation and confounding natures perfectly disagreeing and unlike, that we distinguish between *spirit* and *idea.*

. . .

145. From what hath been said, it is plain that we cannot know the existence of *other spirits* otherwise than by their operations, or the ideas by them, excited in us. I perceive several motions, changes, and combinations of ideas, that inform me there are certain particular agents, like myself, which accompany them, and concur in their production. Hence, the knowledge I have of other spirits is not immediate, as is the knowledge of my ideas; but depending on the intervention of ideas, by me referred to agents or spirits distinct from myself, as effects or concomitant signs.

146. But, though there be some things which convince us human agents are concerned in producing them, yet it is evident to everyone that those things which are called the Works of Nature, that is, the far greater part of the ideas or sensations perceived by us, are *not* produced by, or dependent on, the wills of *men*. There is therefore some other Spirit that causes them; since it is repugnant that they should subsist by themselves. . . . But, if we attentively consider the constant regularity, order, and concatenation of natural things, the surprising magnificence, beauty and perfection of the larger, and the exquisite contrivance of the smaller parts of the creation, together with the exact harmony and correspondence of the whole, but above all the never-enough-admired laws of pain and pleasure, and the instincts or natural inclinations, appetites, and passions of animals;—I say if we consider all these things, and at the same time attend to the meaning and import of the attributes One, Eternal, Infinitely Wise, Good, and Perfect, we shall clearly perceive that they belong to the aforesaid Spirit, 'who works all in all' and 'by whom all things consist.'

147. Hence, it is evident that God is known as certainly and immediately as any other mind or spirit whatsoever, distinct from ourselves. We may even assert that the existence of God is far more evidently perceived than the existence of men; because the effects of Nature are infinitely more numerous and considerable than those ascribed to human agents. There is not any one mark that denotes a man, or effect produced by him, which does not more strongly evince the being of that Spirit who is the Author of Nature. For it is evident that, in affecting other persons, the will of man hath no other object than barely the motion of the limbs of his body; but that such a motion should be attended by, or excite any idea in the mind of another, depends wholly on the will of the Creator. He alone it is who, 'upholding all things by the word of His power,' maintains that intercourse between spirits whereby they are able to perceive the existence of each other. And yet this pure and clear Light which enlightens every one is itself invisible [to the greatest part of mankind].

. . .

THE THIRD DIALOGUE BETWEEN HYLAS AND PHILONOUS

. . .

Hyl. Since therefore you have no *idea* of the mind of God, how can you conceive it possible that things should exist in *His* mind? Or, if you can conceive the mind of God, without having an idea of it, why may not I be allowed to conceive the existence of Matter, notwithstanding I have no idea of it?

Phil. As to your first question: I own I have properly no *idea,* either of God or any other spirit; for these being active, cannot be represented by things perfectly inert, as our ideas are. I do nevertheless know that I, who am a spirit or thinking substance, exist as certainly as I know my ideas exist. Farther, I know what I mean by the terms *I* and *myself*; and I know this immediately or intuitively, though I do not perceive it as I perceive a triangle, a colour, or a sound. The Mind, Spirit, or Soul is that indivisible unextended thing which thinks, acts, and perceives. I say *indivisible,* because unextended; and *unextended,* because extended, figured, moveable things are ideas; and that which perceives ideas, which thinks and wills, is plainly itself no idea, nor like an idea. Ideas are things inactive, and perceived. And Spirits a sort of beings altogether different from them. I do not therefore say my soul is an idea, or like an idea. However, taking the word *idea* in a large sense, my soul may be said to furnish me with an idea, that is, an image or likeness of God—though indeed extremely inadequate. For, all the notion I have of God is obtained by reflecting on my own soul, heightening its powers, and removing its imperfections. I have, therefore, though not an inactive idea, yet in *myself* some sort of an active thinking image of the Deity. And, though I perceive Him not by sense, yet I have a notion of Him, or know Him by reflexion and reasoning. My own mind and my own ideas I have an immediate knowledge of; and, by the help of these, do mediately apprehend the possibility of the existence of other spirits and ideas. Farther, from my own being, and from the dependency I find in myself and my ideas, I do, by an act of reason, necessarily infer the existence of a God, and of all created things in the mind of God. So much for your first question. For the second: I suppose by this time you can answer it yourself. For you neither perceive Matter objectively, as you do an inactive being or idea; nor know it, as you do yourself, by a reflex act; neither do you mediately apprehend it by similitude of the one or the other; nor yet collect it by reasoning from that which you know immediately. All which makes the case of *Matter* widely different from that of the *Deity.*

[*Hyl.* You say your own soul supplies you with some sort of an idea or image of God. But, at the same time, you acknowledge you have, properly speaking, no *idea* of your own soul. You even affirm that spirits are a sort of beings altogether different from ideas. Consequently that no idea can be like a spirit. We have therefore no idea of any spirit. You admit nevertheless that there is spiritual Substance, although you have no idea of it; while you deny there can be such a thing as material Substance, because you have no notion or idea of it. Is this fair dealing? To act consistently, you must either admit Matter or reject Spirit. What say you to this?

Phil. I say, in the first place, that I do not deny the existence of material substance, merely because I have no notion of it, but because the notion of it is inconsistent; or, in other words, because it is repugnant that there should be a notion of it. Many things, for aught I know, may exist, whereof neither I nor any other man hath or can have any idea or notion whatsoever. But then those things must be possible, that is, nothing inconsistent must be included in their definition. I say, secondly, that, although we believe things to exist which we do not perceive, yet we may not believe that any particular thing exists, without some reason for such belief: but I have no reason for believing the existence of Matter. I have no immediate intuition thereof: neither can I immediately from my sensations, ideas, notions, actions, or passions, infer an unthinking, unperceiving, inactive Substance—either by probable deduction, or necessary consequence. Whereas the being of my Self, that is, my own soul, mind, or thinking principle, I evidently know by reflexion. You will forgive me if I repeat the same things in answer to the same objections. In the very notion or definition of *material Substance,* there is included a manifest repugnance and inconsistency. But this cannot be said of the notion of Spirit. That ideas should exist in what doth not perceive, or be produced by what doth not act, is repugnant. But, it is no repugnancy to say that a perceiving thing should be the subject of ideas, or an active thing the cause of them. It is granted we have neither an immediate evidence nor a demonstrative knowledge of the existence of other finite spirits; but it will not thence follow that such spirits are on a foot with material substances: if to suppose the one be inconsistent, and it be not inconsistent to suppose the other; if the one can be inferred by no argument, and there is a probability for the other; if we see signs and effects indicating distinct finite agents like ourselves, and see no sign or symptom whatever that leads to a rational belief of Matter. I say, lastly, that I have a notion of Spirit, though I have not, strictly speaking, an idea of it. I do not perceive it as an idea, or by means of an idea, but know it by reflexion.

Hyl. Notwithstanding all you have said, to me it seems that, according to your own way of thinking, and in consequence of your own principles, it should follow that *you* are only a system of floating ideas, without any substance to support them. Words are not to be used without a meaning. And, as there is no more meaning in *spiritual Substance* than in *material Substance,* the one is to be exploded as well as the other.

Phil. How often must I repeat, that I know or am conscious of my own being; and that *I myself* am not my ideas, but somewhat else, a thinking, active principle that perceives, knows, wills, and operates about ideas. I know that I, one and the same self, perceive both colours and sounds: that a colour cannot perceive a sound, nor a sound a colour: that I am therefore one individual principle, distinct from colour and sound; and, for the same reason, from all other sensible things and inert ideas. But, I am not in like manner conscious either of the existence or essence of Matter. On the contrary, I know that nothing inconsistent can exist, and that the existence of Matter implies an inconsistency. Farther, I know what I mean when I affirm that there is a spiritual substance or support of ideas, that is, that a spirit knows and perceives ideas. But, I do not know what is meant when it is said that an unperceiving substance hath inherent in it and supports either ideas or the archetypes of ideas. There is therefore upon the whole no parity of case between Spirit and Matter.]

John Stuart Mill

The Psychological Theory of the Belief in an External World

We have seen Sir W. Hamilton at work on the question of the reality of Matter, by the introspective method, and, as it seems, with little result. Let us now approach the same subject by the psychological. I proceed, therefore, to state the case of those who hold that the belief in an external world is not intuitive, but an acquired product.

This theory postulates the following psychological truths, all of which are proved by experience, and are not contested, though their force is seldom adequately felt, by Sir W. Hamilton and the other thinkers of the introspective school.

It postulates, first, that the human mind is capable of Expectation. In other words, that after having had actual sensations, we are capable of forming the conception of Possible sensations; sensations which we are not feeling at the present moment, but which we might feel, and should feel if certain conditions were present, the nature of which conditions we have, in many cases, learned by experience.

It postulates, secondly, the laws of the Association of Ideas. So far as we are here concerned, these laws are the following: 1st. Similar phaenomena tend to be thought of together. 2d. Phaenomena which have either been experienced or conceived in close contiguity to one another, tend to be thought of together. The contiguity is of two kinds; simultaneity, and immediate succession. Facts which have been experienced or thought of simultaneously, recall the thought of one another. Of facts which have been experienced or thought of in immediate succession, the antecedent, or the thought of it, recalls the thought of the consequent, but not conversely. 3d. Associations produced by contiguity become more certain and rapid by repetition. When two phaenomena have been very often experienced in conjunction, and have not, in any single instance, occurred separately either in experience or in thought, there is produced between them what has been called Inseparable, or less correctly, Indissoluble Association: by which is not meant that the association must inevitably last to the end of life—that no subsequent experience or process of thought can possibly avail to dissolve it; but only that as long as no such experience or process of thought has taken place, the association is irresistible; it is impossible for us to think the one thing disjoined from the other. 4th. When an

---

From John Stuart Mill, *An Examination of Sir William Hamilton's Philosophy,* Chap. 11, 1865.

association has acquired this character of inseparability—when the bond between the two ideas has been thus firmly riveted, not only does the idea called up by association become, in our consciousness, inseparable from the idea which suggested it, but the facts or phaenomena answering to those ideas, come at last to seem inseparable in existence: things which we are unable to conceive apart, appear incapable of existing apart; and the belief we have in their co-existence, though really a product of experience, seems intuitive. Innumerable examples might be given of this law. One of the most familiar, as well as the most striking, is that of our acquired perceptions of sight. Even those who, with Mr. Bailey, consider the perception of distance by the eye as not acquired, but intuitive, admit that there are many perceptions of sight which, though instantaneous and unhesitating, are not intuitive. What we see is a very minute fragment of what we think we see. We see artificially that one thing is hard, another soft. We see artificially that one thing is hot, another cold. We see artificially that what we see is a book, or a stone, each of these being not merely an inference, but a heap of inferences, from the signs which we see, to things not visible.

Setting out from these premises, the Psychological Theory maintains, that there are associations naturally and even necessarily generated by the order of our sensations and of our reminiscences of sensation, which, supposing no intuition of an external world to have existed in consciousness, would inevitably generate the belief, and would cause it to be regarded as an intuition.

What is it we mean when we say that the object we perceive is external to us, and not a part of our own thoughts? We mean, that there is in our perceptions something which exists when we are not thinking of it; which existed before we had ever thought of it, and would exist if we were annihilated; and further, that there exist things which we never saw, touched, or otherwise perceived, and things which never have been perceived by man. This idea of something which is distinguished from our fleeting impressions by what, in Kantian language, is called Perdurability; something which is fixed and the same, while our impressions vary; something which exists whether we are aware of it or not, and which is always square (or of some other given figure) whether it appears to us square or round, constitutes altogether our idea of external substance. Whoever can assign an origin to this complex conception, has accounted for what we mean by the belief in matter. Now, all this, according to the Psychological Theory, is but the form impressed by the known laws of association, upon the conception or notion, obtained by experience, of Contingent Sensations; by which are meant, sensations that are not in our present consciousness, and perhaps never were in our consciousness at all, but which, in virtue of the laws to which we have learned by experience that our sensations are subject, we know that we should have felt under given supposable circumstances, and under these same circumstances, might still feel.

I see a piece of white paper on a table. I go into another room, and though I have ceased to see it, I am persuaded that the paper is still there. I no longer have the sensations which it gave me; but I believe that when I again place myself in the circumstances in which I had those sensations, that is, when I go again into the room, I shall again have them; and further, that there has been no intervening moment at which this would not have been the case. Owing to this law of my mind, my conception of the world at any given instant consists, in only a small proportion, of present sensations. Of these I may at the time have none at all, and they are in any case a most insignificant portion of the whole which I apprehend. The conception I form of the world existing at any moment, comprises, along with the sensations I am feeling, a countless variety of possibilities of sensation; namely, the whole of those which past observation tells me that I could, under any supposable circumstances, experience at this moment, together with an indefinite and illimitable multitude of others which though I do not know that I could, yet it is possible that I might, experience in circumstances not known to me. These various possibilities are the important thing to me in the world. My present sensations are generally of little importance, and are moreover fugitive: the possibilities, on the contrary, are permanent, which is the character that mainly distinguishes our idea of Substance or Matter from our notion of sensation. These possibilities, which are conditional certainties, need a special name to distinguish them from mere vague possibilities, which experience gives no warrant for reckoning upon. Now, as soon as a distinguishing name is given, though it be only to the same thing regarded in a different aspect, one of the most familiar experiences of our mental nature teaches us, that the different name comes to be considered as the name of a different thing.

There is another important peculiarity of these certified or guaranteed possibilities of sensation; namely, that they have reference, not to single sensations, but to sensations joined together in groups. When we think of anything as a material substance, or body, we either have had, or we think that on some given supposition we should have, not some *one* sensation, but a great and even an indefinite number and variety of sensations, generally belonging to different senses, but so linked together, that the presence of one announces the possible presence at the very same instant of any or all of the rest. In our mind, therefore, not only is this particular Possibility of sensation invested with the quality of permanence when we are not actually feeling any of the sensations at all; but when we are feeling some of them, the remaining sensations of the group are conceived by us in the form of Present Possibilities, which might be realized at the very moment. And as this happens in turn to all of them, the group as a whole presents itself to the mind as permanent, in contrast not solely with the temporariness of my bodily presence, but also with the temporary character of each of the sensations composing the group; in other words, as a kind of permanent substratum, under a set of passing experiences or manifestations: which is another leading character of our idea of substance or matter, as distinguished from sensation.

Let us now take into consideration another of the general characters of our experience, namely, that in addition to fixed groups, we also recognize a fixed Order in our sensations; an Order of succession, which, when ascertained by observation, gives rise to the ideas of Cause and Effect, according to what I hold to be the true theory of that relation, and is in any case the source of all our knowledge *what* causes produce what effects. Now, of what nature is this fixed order among our sensations? It is a constancy of antecedence and sequence. But the constant antecedence and sequence do not generally exist between one actual sensation and another. Very few such sequences are presented to us by experience. In almost all the constant sequences which occur in Nature, the antecedence and consequence do not obtain between sensations, but between the groups we have been speaking about, of which a very small portion is actual sensation, the greater part being permanent possibilities of sensation, evidenced to us by a small and variable number of sensations actually present. Hence, our ideas of causation, power, activity, do not become connected in thought with our sensations as *actual* at all, save in the few physiological cases where these figure by themselves as the antecedents in some uniform sequence. Those ideas become connected, not with sensations, but with groups of possibilities of sensation. The sensations conceived do not, to our habitual thoughts, present themselves as sensations actually experienced, inasmuch as not only any one or any number of them may be supposed absent, but none of them need be present. We find that the modifications which are taking place more or less regularly in our possibilities of sensation, are mostly quite independent of our consciousness, and of our presence or absence. Whether we are asleep or awake, the fire goes out, and puts an end to one particular possibility of warmth and light. Whether we are present or absent, the corn ripens, and brings a new possibility of food. Hence we speedily think to learn of Nature as made up solely of these groups of possibilities, and the active force in Nature as manifested in the modification of some of these by others. The sensations, though the original foundation of the whole, come to be looked upon as a sort of accident, depending on us, and the possibilities as much more real than the actual sensations, nay, as the very realities of which these are only the representations, appearances, or effects. When this state of mind has been arrived at, then, and from that time forward, we are never conscious of a present sensation without instantaneously referring it to some one of the groups of possibilities into which a sensation of that particular description enters; and if we do not yet know to what group to refer it, we at least feel an irresistible conviction that it must belong to some group or other; *i. e.*, that its presence proves the existence, here and now, of a great number and variety of possibilities of sensation, without which it would not have been. The whole set of sensations as possible, form a permanent background to any one or more of them that are, at a given moment, actual; and the possibilities are conceived as standing to the actual sensations in the relation of a cause to its effects, or of canvas to the figures painted on it, or of a root to the trunk, leaves, and flowers, or of a substratum to that which is spread over it, or, in transcendental language, of Matter to Form.

When this point has been reached, the permanent Possibilities in question have assumed such unlikeness of aspect, and such difference of position relatively to us, from any sensations, that it would be contrary to all we know of the constitution of human nature that they should not be conceived as, and believed to be, at least as different from sensations as sensations are from one another. Their groundwork in sensation is forgotten, and they are supposed to be something intrinsically distinct from it. We can withdraw ourselves from any of our (external) sensations, or we can be withdrawn from them by some other agency. But though the sensations cease, the possibilities remain in existence; they are independent of our will, our presence, and everything which belongs to us. We find, too, that they belong as much to other human or sentient beings as to ourselves. We find other people grounding their expectations and conduct upon the same permanent possibilities on which we ground ours. But we do not find them experiencing the same actual sensa-

tions. Other people do not have our sensations exactly when and as we have them: but they have our possibilities of sensation; whatever indicates a present possibility of sensations to ourselves, indicates a present possibility of similar sensations to them, except so far as their organs of sensation may vary from the type of ours. This puts the final seal to our conception of the groups of possibilities as the fundamental reality in Nature. The permanent possibilities are common to us and to our fellow-creatures; the actual sensations are not. That which other people become aware of when, and on the same grounds as I do, seems more real to me than that which they do not know of unless I tell them. The world of Possible Sensations succeeding one another according to laws, is as much in other beings as it is in me; it has therefore an existence outside me; it is an External World.

. . .

Matter, then, may be defined, a Permanent Possibility of Sensation. If I am asked whether I believe in matter, I ask whether the questioner accepts this definition of it. If he does, I believe in matter: and so do all Berkeleians. In any other sense than this, I do not. But I affirm with confidence, that this conception of Matter includes the whole meaning attached to it by the common world, apart from philosophical, and sometimes from theological, theories. The reliance of mankind on the real existence of visible and tangible objects, means reliance on the reality and permanence of Possibilities of visual and tactual sensations, when no such sensations are actually experienced. We are warranted in believing that this is the meaning of Matter in the minds of many of its most esteemed metaphysical champions, though they themselves would not admit as much: for example, of Reid, Stewart, and Brown. For these three philosophers alleged that all mankind, including Berkeley and Hume, really believed in Matter, inasmuch as unless they did, they would not have turned aside to save themselves from running against a post. Now, all which this manoeuvre really proved is, that they believed in Permanent Possibilities of Sensation. We have therefore the sanction of these three eminent defenders of the existence of matter, for affirming, that to believe in Permanent Possibilities of Sensation *is* believing in Matter. It is hardly necessary, after such authorities, to mention Dr. Johnson, or any one else who resorts to the *argumentum baculinum* of knocking a stick against the ground. Sir W. Hamilton, a far subtler thinker than any of these, never reasons in this manner. He never supposes that a disbeliever in what he means by Matter, ought in consistency to act in any different mode from those who believe in it. He knew that the belief on which all the practical consequences depend, is the belief in Permanent Possibilities of Sensation, and that if nobody believed in a material universe in any other sense, life would go on exactly as it now does. He, however, did believe in more than this, but, I think, only because it had never occurred to him that mere Possibilities of Sensation could, to our artificialized consciousness, present the character of objectivity which, as we have now shown, they not only can, but unless the known laws of the human mind were suspended, must necessarily, present.

Perhaps it may be objected, that the very possibility of framing such a notion of Matter as Sir W. Hamilton's—the capacity in the human mind of imagining an external world which is anything more than what the Psychological Theory makes it—amounts to a disproof of the theory. If (it may be said) we had no revelation in consciousness, of a world which is not in some way or other identified with sensation, we should be unable to have the notion of such a world. If the only ideas we had of external objects were ideas of our sensations, supplemented by an acquired notion of permanent possibilities of sensation, we must (it is thought) be incapable of conceiving, and therefore still more incapable of fancying that we perceive, things which are not sensations at all. It being evident, however, that some philosophers believe this, and it being maintainable that the mass of mankind do so, the existence of a perdurable basis of sensations, distinct from sensations themselves, is proved, it might be said, by the possibility of believing it.

Let me first restate what I apprehend the belief to be. We believe that we perceive a something closely related to all our sensations, but different from those which we are feeling at any particular minute; and distinguished from sensations altogether, by being permanent and always the same, while these are fugitive, variable, and alternately displace one another. But these attributes of the object of perception are properties belonging to all the possibilities of sensation which experience guarantees. The belief in such permanent possibilities seems to me to include all that is essential or characteristic in the belief in substance. I believe that Calcutta exists, though I do not perceive it, and that it would still exist if every percipient inhabitant were suddenly to leave the place, or be struck dead. But when I analyze the belief, all I find in it is, that were these events to take place, the Permanent Possibility of Sensation which I call Calcutta would still remain; that if I were suddenly transported to the banks of the Hoogly, I should still have the sensations which, if now present, would lead me to affirm that Calcutta exists here and now. We may infer, therefore, that both philosophers and the world at large, when they think of matter, conceive it really as a Permanent Possibility of Sensation. But the majority of philosophers fancy that it is something more; and the world at large, though they have really, as I conceive, nothing in their minds but a Permanent Possibility of Sensation, would, if asked the question, undoubtedly agree with the philosophers: and though this is sufficiently explained by the tendency of the human mind to infer difference of things from difference of names, I acknowledge the obligation of showing how it can be possible to believe in an existence transcending all possibilities of sensation, unless on the hypothesis that such an existence actually is, and that we actually perceive it.

The explanation, however, is not difficult. It is an admitted fact, that we are capable of all conceptions which can be formed by generalizing from the observed laws of our sensations. Whatever relation we find to exist between any one of our sensations and something different from *it*, that same relation we have no difficulty in conceiving to exist between the sum of all our sensations and something different from *them*. The differences which our consciousness recognizes between one sensation and another, give us the general notion of difference, and inseparably associate with every sensation we have, the feeling of its being different from other things; and when once this association has been formed, we can no longer conceive anything, without being able, and even being compelled, to form also the conception of something different from it. This familiarity with the idea of something different from *each* thing we know, makes it natural and easy to form the notion of something different from *all* things that we know, collectively as well as individually. It is true we can form no conception of what such a thing can be; our notion of it is merely negative; but the idea of substance, apart from the impressions it makes on our senses, *is* a merely negative one. There is thus no psychological obstacle to our forming the notion of a something which is neither a sensation nor a possibility of sensation, even if our consciousness does not testify to it; and nothing is more likely than that the Permanent Possibilities of sensation, to which our consciousness does testify, should be confounded in our minds with this imaginary conception. All experience attests the strength of the tendency to mistake mental abstractions, even negative ones, for substantive realities; and the Permanent Possibilities of sensation which experience guarantees, are so extremely unlike in many of their properties to actual sensations, that since we are capable of imagining something which transcends sensation, there is a great natural probability that we should suppose these to be it.

But this natural probability is converted into certainty, when we take into consideration that universal law of our experience which is termed the law of Causation, and which makes us unable to conceive the beginning of anything without an antecedent condition, or Cause. The case of Causation is one of the most marked of all the cases in which we extend to the sum total of our consciousness, a notion derived from its parts. It is a striking example of our power to conceive, and our tendency to believe, that a relation which subsists between every individual item of our experience and some other item, subsists also between our experience as a whole, and something not within the sphere of experience. By this extension to the sum of all our experiences, of the internal relations obtaining between its several parts, we are led to consider sensation itself—the aggregate whole of our sensations—as deriving its origin from antecedent existences transcending sensation. That we should do this, is a consequence of the particular character of the uniform sequences, which experience discloses to us among our sensations. As already remarked, the constant antecedent of a sensation is seldom another sensation, or set of sensations, actually felt. It is much oftener the existence of a group of possibilities, not necessarily including any actual sensations, except such as are required to show that the possibilities are really present. Nor are actual sensations indispensable even for this purpose; for the presence of the object (which is nothing more than the immediate presence of the possibilities) may be made known to us by the very sensation which we refer to it as its effect. Thus, the real antecedent of an effect—the only antecedent which, being invariable and unconditional, we consider to be the cause—may be, not any sensation really felt, but solely the presence, at that or the immediately preceding moment, of a group of possibilities of sensation. Hence it is not with sensations as actually experienced, but with their Permanent Possibilities, that the idea of Cause comes to be identified: and we, by one and the same process, acquire the habit of regarding Sensation in general, like all our individual sensations, as an Effect, and also that of conceiving as the causes of most of our individual sensations, not other sensations, but general possibilities of sensation. If all these considerations put together do not completely explain and account for our conceiving these Possibilities as a class of independent and substantive entities, I know not what psychological analysis can be conclusive.

It may perhaps be said, that the preceding theory gives, indeed, some account of the idea of Permanent Existence which forms part of our conception of matter, but gives no explanation of our believing these permanent objects to be external, or out of ourselves. I apprehend, on the contrary, that the very idea of anything out of ourselves is derived solely from the knowledge experience gives us of the Permanent Possibilities. Our sensations we carry with us wherever we go, and they never exist where we are not; but when we change our place we do not carry away with us the Permanent Possibilities of Sensation: they remain until we return, or arise and cease under conditions with which our presence has in general nothing to do. And more than all—they are, and will be after we have ceased to feel, Permanent Possibilities of sensation to other beings than ourselves. Thus our actual sensations and the permanent possibilities of sensation, stand out in obtrusive contrast to one another: and when the idea of Cause has been acquired, and extended by generalization from the parts of our experience to its aggregate whole, nothing can be more natural than that the Permanent Possibilities should be classed by us as existences generically distinct from our sensations, but of which our sensations are the effect.

The same theory which accounts for our ascribing to an aggregate of possibilities of sensation, a permanent existence which our sensations themselves do not possess, and consequently a greater reality than belongs to our sensations, also explains our attributing greater objectivity to the Primary Qualities of bodies than to the Secondary. For the sensations which correspond to what are called the Primary Qualities (as soon at least as we come to apprehend them by two senses, the eye as well as the touch) are always present when any part of the group is so. But colors, tastes, smells, and the like, being, in comparison, fugacious, are not, in the same degree, conceived as being always there, even when nobody is present to perceive them. The sensations answering to the Secondary Qualities are only occasional, those to the Primary, constant. The Secondary, moreover, vary with different persons, and with the temporary sensibility of our organs: the Primary, when perceived at all, are, as far as we know, the same to all persons and at all times.

Alfred Jules Ayer

The Constitution of Material Things

CONCERNING PHENOMENALISM

The problem of specifying the relationship of material things to sense-data, to which the causal theory of perception has been shown to provide so unsatisfactory an answer, is apt to be obscured by being represented as a problem about the inter-relationship of two different classes of objects. There is, indeed, a sense in which it is correct to say that both sense-data and material things exist, inasmuch as sentences that are used to describe sense-data and sentences that are used to describe material things both very frequently express true propositions. But it would not be correct to infer from this that there really were both material things and sense-data, in the sense in which it can truly be said that there really are chairs as well as tables, or that there are tastes as well as sounds. For whereas, in these cases, the existential propositions refer to different empirical "facts", this does not hold good in the case of sense-data and material things. All the same, the term "material thing" is not synonymous with any term or set of terms that stand for species of sense-data. It is indeed logically necessary that any situation that in any degree establishes the existence of a material thing should also establish the existence of a sense-datum; for we have constructed the sense-datum language in such a way that whenever it is true that a material thing is perceived, it must also be true that a sense-datum is sensed; and this applies also to the cases where the existence of the material thing is inferred from observations of its "physical effects". But it is not wholly a matter of convention that a situation which establishes the existence of a sense-datum should also be evidence in some degree for the existence of a material thing. For this depends, as I shall show, upon certain special features of our sensory experience, which it might conceivably not have possessed. Moreover, while a situation which directly establishes the existence of a sense-datum does so conclusively, no such situations can conclusively establish the existence of a material thing. The degree to which the existence of the material thing is established will depend upon the character of the sense-data in question, and especially upon the nature of the contexts in which they occur; but whatever the strength of this evidence may be, it will always be logically compatible with the hypothesis that this material thing is not in all respects what it appears to be, or even that it does not exist at all. Additional evidence may weaken this hypothesis to an extent that makes it very foolish still to entertain it; but it may also substantiate it, as the fact that there

From A. J. Ayer, *The Foundations of Empirical Knowledge,* Chap. 5, published by Macmillan & Co. Ltd., London, St. Martins Press, Inc., New York, and The Macmillan Company of Canada, Limited, 1947. Reprinted by permission of the publishers.

are illusions shows. At the same time, it is to be remarked that this additional evidence, whether favourable or not, will always consist in the occurrence of further sense-data. Indeed there is nothing else in which one can legitimately suppose it to consist, once one has accepted the rule that the word "sense-datum" is to be used to stand for whatever is, in fact, observed. And since it is impossible, by any valid process of inference, to make a transition from what is observed to anything that is conceived as being, in principle, unobservable, all that the evidence in question will be evidence for or against is the possible occurrence of further sense-data still. And from this it seems to follow that, even though the term "material thing" is not synonymous with any set of terms that stand for species of sense-data, any proposition that refers to a material thing must somehow be expressible in terms of sense-data, if it is to be empirically significant.

A common way of expressing this conclusion is to say that material things are nothing but collections of actual and possible sense-data. But this is a misleading formula and one that provokes objections which a more accurate way of speaking might avoid. Thus, it is sometimes argued, by those who reject this "phenomenalistic" analysis of the nature of material things, that to conceive of such things as houses or trees or stones as mere collections of actual and possible sense-data is to ignore their "unity" and "substantiality", and that, in any case, it is hard to see how anything can be composed of so shadowy a being as a possible sense-datum. But these objections are founded upon the mistaken assumption that a material thing is supposed to consist of sense-data, as a patchwork quilt consists of different coloured pieces of silk. To remove this misconception, it must be made clear that what the statement that material things consist of sense-data must be understood to designate is not a factual but a linguistic relationship. What is being claimed is simply that the propositions which are ordinarily expressed by sentences which refer to material things could also be expressed by sentences which referred exclusively to sense-data; and the inclusion of possible as well as actual sense-data among the elements of the material things must be taken only to imply a recognition that some of these statements about sense-data will have to be hypothetical. As for the belief in the "unity" and "substantiality" of material things, I shall show that it may be correctly represented as involving no more than the attribution to visual and tactual sense-data of certain relations which do, in fact, obtain in our experience. And I shall show that it is only the contingent fact that there are these relations between sense-data that makes it profitable to describe the course of our experience in terms of the existence and behaviour of material things.

It may seem that an attempt to carry out this plan of "reducing" material things to sense-data would be at variance with my previous attempt to draw a sharp distinction between them. But the purpose of making this distinction was simply to increase the utility and clarity of the sense-datum language by ensuring that its sentences should not be of the same logical form as those that refer to material things. And here it may be explained that two sentences may be said to have the same logical form if they can be correlated in such a way that to each expression that occurs in either one of them there corresponds in the other an expression of the same logical type; and that two expressions may be said to be of the same logical type if any sentence that significantly contains either one of them remains significant when the other is put in its place. It follows that if sentences referring to sense-data are of a different logical form from sentences referring to material things, it must not be assumed that precisely the same things can be said about them. To say, for example, that this was being written with a "pennish" group of sense-data, instead of saying that it was being written with a pen, would be neither true nor false but nonsensical. But this does not rule out the possibility that a proposition which is expressed by a sentence referring to a material thing can equally well be expressed by an entirely different set of sentences, which refer to sense-data; and this is what those who assert that material things are "logical constructions" out of sense-data must be understood to claim. Their view is sometimes put in the form of an assertion that "to say anything about a material thing is to say something, but not the same thing about classes of sense-data"; [1] but if this is taken to imply that any significant statement about a material thing can actually be translated, without alteration of meaning, into a definite set of statements about sense-data, it is not strictly accurate, for a reason I shall presently give.

An objection which is often brought against phenomenalists is that they begin with a false conception of the nature of "perceptual situations". Thus, it is held by some philosophers that what is directly observed is usually not a sense-datum at all, but a material thing; so that the view that material things must be reducible to sense-data, on the ground that these alone are observable, is fundamentally erroneous. But this . . . is not the expression of a disagreement about any matter of fact, but only of a preference for a different form of language. It is indeed legitimate to use the phrase "direct observation" in such a way that things like houses and trees and stones can properly be said to be directly observable; and this usage can perfectly well be made to cover the case of delusive as well as veridical perceptions, provided that it is allowed that what is "directly observed" may not in fact exist, and that it may not really have the properties that it appears to have. But I have shown that it is also legitimate to use the phrase "direct observation" in such a way that it is only what is designated by the term "sense-datum", or some equivalent term, that can be said to be directly observable; and that it is this usage that, for my present purpose, is to be preferred. And one reason why it is to be preferred is to be found in the fact, which I have already mentioned, that whereas the proposition that a sense-datum is veridically sensed does not entail that any material thing is veridically perceived, the proposition that a material thing is veridically perceived can always be represented as entailing that some sense-datum or other is veridically sensed. Indeed, it is inconceivable that any sense-datum should not be sensed veridically, since it has been made self-contradictory to say of an experienced sense-datum that it does not exist or that it does not really have the properties that it appears to have. And because there is this logical relationship between "perceiving a material thing" and "sensing a sense-datum", it follows that, while a reference to a material thing will not elucidate the meaning of a sentence which is used to describe a sense-datum, except in so far as the poverty of our language may make it convenient to identify this sense-datum as one of a type that is ordinarily asso-

[1] *Vide* A. E. Duncan-Jones, "Does Philosophy Analyse Common Sense?" *Aristotelian Society Supplementary Proceedings,* 1937, pp. 140–41.

ciated with a special sort of material thing, a reference to sense-data will provide a general elucidation of the meaning of statements about material things by showing what is the kind of evidence by which they may be verified. And this may be regarded as the purpose of the phenomenalist analysis.

Besides the philosophers who maintain that material things are themselves "directly observed", there are others who object to phenomenalism on the ground that even if the occurrence of illusions shows that what is directly observed is not a material thing, it is still not just a sense-datum. Thus Professor Stout, for one, has argued that "the evidence of sense-perception flatly contradicts phenomenalism", on the ground that to regard what is immediately experienced as being just a sensible appearance is to ignore an essential factor which he calls "perceptual seeming".[2] According to him, it is because of "perceptual seeming" that one is able to "perceive one thing as behind another, although it is so hidden that there is no sensible appearance of it", or that one can "perceive things as having insides, when they are not transparent".[3] But while this line of argument may have some force against those who employ a physiological criterion for determining the character of sense-data, it does not affect us at all, inasmuch as our use of the word sense-datum is not bound up with any special empirical theory about the nature of what is given. If one accepts the view of certain psychologists that there are experiences that may properly be described as experiences of "seeing the inside of a solid object" or "seeing an object when it is screened by another", then the inference one must draw is not that what is observed on such occasions is "more than a mere sense-datum", but that the character of people's visual sense-fields is empirically different from what a misplaced attention to the laws of physiology might lead one to suppose. It is true that the terms in which the psychologists describe such experiences are not purely sensory; but the reason for this is that it is only by referring to material things that they can actually expect to make their meaning understood. We must not, therefore, be misled into supposing that what they are intending to describe is anything more than a sensory phenomenon. The statement that someone is having the experience of "seeing the inside of a solid object" must not, in this context, be taken to exclude the possibility that no such physical object is actually there.

It may, however, be admitted that not only in cases of this sort, but in the vast majority of cases in which one senses a visual or tactual sense-datum, one tends to take it for granted that there is a physical object "there"; and it may be that this is what Professor Stout is referring to when he talks of "perceptual seeming". But this is a fact that I do not think any phenomenalist would wish to deny. The view that material things are, in the sense I have just explained, logical constructions out of sense-data does not imply that "perceiving a material thing" need involve any conscious process of inference from the occurrence of one sense-datum to the possible occurrence of another. The phenomenalist is perfectly free to admit that the sensing of a visual or tactual sense-datum is, in most cases, accompanied by an unreflecting assumption of the existence of some material thing. But the question in which he is interested is, What exactly is it that is here unreflectingly assumed? And

[2] "Phenomenalism", *Proceedings of the Aristotelian Society*, 1938–9, pp. 1–18.
[3] *Loc. cit.* pp. 10–11.

his answer, which certainly cannot be refuted by any such appeal to psychology as Professor Stout relies on, is that it is the possibility of obtaining further sense-data.

It would seem that the best way to justify the claim that "to say anything about a material thing is always to say something, though not the same thing, about certain sense-data", would be to provide a number of specimen translations. But this is what no one has ever yet been able to do. It may be suggested that the reason why it has never been done is that no one has yet devised a sufficiently elaborate vocabulary. With our current resources of language we are able to classify visual sense-data only in a very general way, tactual data even less specifically, and kinaesthetic data hardly at all: and the result is that when we wish to distinguish the sense-data that belong to one sort of material thing from those that belong to another we are unable to achieve it except by referring to the material things in question. But suppose that someone took the trouble to name all the different varieties of sensible characteristics with which he was acquainted. Even so, he would still not be able to translate any statement about a material thing into a finite set of statements about sense-data. It is not inconceivable that someone should construct and make use of such a sensory language, though in practice he would find it very difficult to make himself understood; but what he succeeded in expressing by these means would never be precisely equivalent even to the singular statements that we make about material things. For when statements are equivalent to one another, they can always be represented as standing in a relationship of mutual entailment. And, in the case I am now considering, this condition cannot be fulfilled.

I have indeed already admitted that no finite set of singular statements about sense-data can ever formally entail a statement about a material thing, inasmuch as I have recognized that statements about material things are not conclusively verifiable. For when we try to reproduce the content of a statement about a material thing by specifying the empirical situations that would furnish us with direct tests of its validity, we find that the number of these possible tests is infinite. Admittedly, when someone makes a statement of this kind he does not actually envisage an infinite series of possible verifications. He may very well be satisfied, in familiar circumstances, with the single sense-experience on which his statement is based; and if he does think it necessary to test it further, the subsequent occurrence, in the appropriate conditions, of only a limited number of "favourable" sense-data will be sufficient, in the absence of contrary evidence, to convince him that it is true. And this is an entirely reasonable procedure, as I have shown. But the fact remains that however many favourable tests he may make he can never reach a stage at which it ceases to be conceivable that further sense-experience will reverse the verdict of the previous evidence. He will never be in a position to demonstrate that he will not subsequently have experiences that will entitle him to conclude that his original statement was false after all. And this implies that the content of a statement about a material thing cannot be exhaustively specified by any finite number of references to sense-data. This difficulty could indeed be met by introducing into the sense-datum language a suitable set of expressions which would be understood to refer to infinite series of sense-data. But I am afraid that most philosophers would not admit that this gave them the sort of translation that they wanted. For all that would seem to be achieved by the introduction of these new expressions would be a mere renaming of material things.

But not only is the occurrence of any one particular, finite series of sense-data never formally sufficient to establish the truth of a statement about a material thing; it is never even necessary. There is, indeed, a sense in which it can be said that every statement about a material thing entails some set of statements or other about sense-data, inasmuch as it is only by the occurrence of some sense-datum that any statement about a material thing is ever in any degree verified. But there is no set of statements about the occurrence of particular sense-data of which it can truly be said that precisely this is entailed by a given statement about a material thing. And the reason for this is that what is required to verify a statement about a material thing is never just the occurrence of a sense-datum of an absolutely specific kind, but only the occurrence of one or other of the sense-data that fall within a fairly indefinite range. In other words, not only can we go on testing a statement about a material thing as long as we like without being able to arrive at a formal demonstration of its truth; but for any test that we actually do carry out there are always an indefinite number of other tests, differing to some extent either in respect of their conditions or their results, which would have done just as well. And this means that if we try to describe what at any given moment would afford us direct evidence for the truth of a statement about a material thing by putting forward a disjunction of statements about sense-data, we shall find once again that this disjunction will have to be infinite.[4]

But if one infers from this that sentences referring to material things cannot be translated, without alteration of meaning, into sentences referring to sense-data, one must not then conclude that to speak about a material thing is to speak about something altogether different from sense-data, or that it is to speak about sense-data but about something else besides. For that would be a mistake analogous to that of supposing that because sentences referring indefinitely to what is red cannot be translated into [a] finite number of sentences referring to particular red things, therefore "redness" is the name of an object with a distinct existence of its own, or that because sentences referring to "someone" cannot be translated into a finite disjunction of sentences referring to particular persons, therefore "someone" is the name of a peculiar being, a "subsistent entity" perhaps, who is distinct from any person that one can actually meet. If we cannot produce the required translations of sentences referring to material things into sentences referring to sense-data, the reason is not that it is untrue that "to say anything about a material thing is always to say something about sense-data", but only that one's references to material things are vague in their application to phenomena and that the series of sense-data that they may be understood to specify are composed of infinite sets of terms.

This does not mean, however, that nothing can be done in the way of "analysing material things in terms of sense-data". It would not, indeed, be profitable to seek in any such analysis a means of distinguishing one material thing from another. It is not by a verbal analysis in terms of sense-data that one can hope to make clear what is meant, for example, by "a pen" as

[4] Cf. John Wisdom, "Metaphysics and Verification", *Mind,* October 1938, pp. 478–81.

opposed to "a pencil", or by "a steamship" as opposed to "a canoe". One can give a verbal, as well as an ostensive, indication of the meaning of such words; but it will not exclude the use of other expressions that belong to a physical rather than to a purely sensory terminology. At the same time, there are certain general features about the way in which any expression referring to a material thing applies to phenomena that one can profitably undertake to analyse. That is to say, one may be able to explain what are the relations between sense-data that make it possible for us successfully to employ the physical terminology that we do. If I may now use the metaphor of construction without being misunderstood, I can describe the task I am about to undertake as that of showing what are the general principles on which, from our resources of sense-data, we "construct" the world of material things.

Roderick Milton Chisholm

The Problem of Empiricism

Professor C. I. Lewis, in Book II of his Carus Lectures, *An Analysis of Knowledge and Valuation,* defends the thesis that the meaning of any statement which refers to a material thing may be fully conveyed in statements which refer solely to sense-data or the sensible appearances of things. His account is perhaps the clearest and most careful defence of this empirical thesis which has yet appeared and, in consequence, it enables us to state, more clearly than has been possible before, the characteristic difficulties of empiricism.

According to Professor Lewis, an analysis of the meaning of any ordinary thing statement, such as "This thing is red" or "That is a doorknob," will show that the statement entails an unlimited number of statements referring solely to sense-data. The sense-datum statements are "analytic consequences" of the thing statement; that this is so in any particular case "is certifiable *a priori,* either by reference to logical rules or by reference to meanings involved or by both together" (p. 249). The relation which thing statement bears to sense-datum statement is similar to that which "*T* is red" bears to "*T* is colored" (*ibid.*). Since the full meaning of any thing statement may be conveyed in the sense-datum statements which it entails, thing statements may be said to be "translatable" into sense-datum statements (p. 181).[1] The prin-

[1] Seldom, of course, does anyone ever *formulate* any sense-datum statements and, as Professor Lewis admits (p. 173), it may be questioned whether the terms of ordinary language are adequate to convey judgments about sense-data. Although he finds it convenient to present his conclusions by reference to relations between *statements,* his theory does not purport to be a linguistic analysis. The problem is an epistemological one, concerning our beliefs or judgments about material things, and could be discussed without reference to statements at all. The pres-

From R. M. Chisholm, "The Problem of Empiricism," *The Journal of Philosophy,* Vol. 45 (1948). Reprinted by permission of the author and of the editors of *The Journal of Philosophy.*

cipal difficulty with this view concerns the first step: the problem of showing that any ordinary thing statement has, as analytic consequences, statements which refer solely to sense-data.

The roots of the difficulty are the familiar facts sometimes referred to as "the relativity of sense perception." Whether a material thing will ever present, say, a red appearance or sense-datum depends partly upon the thing and partly upon the conditions under which it is observed. If one knew that the thing were red and that the lighting conditions were normal, one could predict that, to a normal observer, the thing would present a red appearance. If one knew that the lights were out, or that the observer had a certain type of color blindness, one could predict that the thing would present some other appearance. And so on, for any other thing and its possible appearances. To calculate the appearances with complete success, it is necessary to know both the thing-perceived and the (subjective and objective) observation-conditions, for it is the thing-perceived and the observation-conditions working jointly which determine what is to appear. Professor Lewis believes that "This thing is red" entails as analytic consequences an unlimited number of statements referring solely to what might appear. But the facts of "perceptual relativity" suggest that it doesn't entail *any* statement about sense-data; they suggest that a sense-datum statement is entailed only when "This thing is red" is taken in conjunction with *another* thing statement referring to observation-conditions. The translatability thesis requires that *both* observation-conditions and things-perceived be definable in terms of what might appear. But the facts of perceptual relativity indicate that it is the joint operation of things-perceived and observation-conditions which determines what is to appear; hence the task of the empiricist would seem to be similar to that of an economist who hoped to define *both* supply and demand in terms of possible prices.

The complexity of the problem will become evident if, before turning to the details of Professor Lewis's view, we consider a simple example. Consider the thing statement

(*P*) This is red.

and the sense-datum statement

(*R*) Redness will appear.

May we say that *P* entails *R?* Possibly it will be immediately evident that no contradiction is involved in affirming *P* and denying *R*. The following considerations, however, may make the matter clearer.

Taken in conjunction with some *other* thing statement, referring to observation-conditions, *P* does entail *R*. The other statement could be

(*Q*) This is observed under normal conditions; and if this is red and is observed under normal conditions, redness will appear.

But taken in conjunction, not with *Q,* but with still *another* thing statement, also referring to observation-conditions, *P* entails not-*R*. This other thing statement could be

---

ent issues, however, may be brought into clearer focus if we follow Professor Lewis and discuss the relations between statements. It should be noted that Professor Lewis does not use the brief terms "thing statement" and "sense-datum statement."

(*S*) This is observed under conditions which are normal except for the presence of blue lights; and if this is red and is observed under conditions which are normal except for the presence of blue lights, redness will not appear.

So far as ordinary usage is concerned, it is quite evident that the statement *S* is logically consistent with *P*; there is no contradiction involved in affirming one and denying the other. But the conjunction of *P* and *S*, if they are logically consistent, must entail everything that *P* entails and cannot entail anything logically inconsistent with what *P* entails. If *P* and *S* entail not-*R*, it is impossible that *P* entail *R*. Hence "This is red" (*P*) does not entail "Redness will appear" (*R*).

We may draw a similar conclusion with respect to any other categorical sense-datum statement *R′*. Although there may be a statement about observation-conditions, *Q′*, such that "This is red" (*P*) and *Q′* entail *R′*, there is also a statement about observation-conditions, *S′*, such that *P* and *S′* entail not-*R′*. Hence *P* does not entail *R′*.

Professor Lewis admits that no thing statement, such as "This is red," entails any categorical sense-datum statement, such as "Redness will appear"; he admits further that "This is red" does not entail any sense-datum conditional, such as "If such-and-such should appear, then such-and-such would appear" (p. 237). The sort of sense-datum statement which is entailed is considerably more complicated. It is a conditional of the form: "If such-and-such a presentation (or sense-datum) should appear and such-and-such feelings of action (also sense-data) should appear, then in all probability such-and-such another sense-datum would appear" (cf. pp. 248 ff). For reasons essential to his account of knowledge and action, the antecedent of the sense-datum statement must refer both to some "sensory clue" and to a feeling of activity, and the consequent must be prefaced by some such phrase as "in all probability." These complications, however, do not affect the principle now under discussion.

We may utilize the above letters again in discussing Professor Lewis's view. One of his examples is the thing statement

(*P*) There really is a doorknob in front of me and to the left.

One of the complicated sense-datum statements which are analytic consequences of this might be

(*R*) If I should seem to see such a doorknob and if I should seem to myself to be initiating a certain grasping motion, then in all probability the feeling of contacting a doorknob would follow.[2]

According to Professor Lewis, *R* is an analytic consequence of *P*; or, in other words, *P* entails *R*. But, again, if *P* entails *R*, then it is logically impossible that there be a statement *S*, consistent with *P* and such that *P* and *S* entail not-*R*. Hence, if there is such a statement *S*, *P* does not entail *R*. Is there, then, such a statement *S*?

It should be remarked that we are not asking whether there is such a statement *S* which is *true*. For Professor Lewis's theory concerns the *meaning*

[2] Cf. *op. cit.*, pp. 240, 248–249. We are to suppose, of course, that the words which appear in this statement are in what Professor Lewis calls the "expressive language," referring solely to sense-data.

of thing statements, what is certifiable *a priori* by reference to logic and the meanings of terms. If there is a statement S, which in conjunction with P entails not-R, then, whether or not S is true, the theory—at least in application to this case—is mistaken.

Clearly there are many such statements S. One might be

(S) I am unable to move my limbs and my hands but am subject to delusions such that I think I'm moving them; I often seem to myself to be initiating a certain grasping motion, but, when I do, I never have the feeling of contacting anything.

This statement in conjunction with P entails not-R. There is no reason to suppose that S is inconsistent with P. Hence it is false that P entails R. Similarly, for any other complex sense-datum statement R' which might be thought to be an analytic consequence of P, it would seem to be possible to formulate a statement S', consistent with P, and such that P and S' entail not-R'.

Thus it remains to be seen in what sense *any* sense-datum statement can be regarded as an analytic consequence of "This thing is red" or "That is a doorknob." [3]

It was suggested above that statements such as "This thing is red" entail sense-datum statements only when taken in conjunction with some *other* thing statement pertaining to observation-conditions. Thus, in our earlier example, "This is red" (P) does entail a sense-datum statement when it is conjoined with our statement Q: "This is observed under normal conditions; and if this is red and is observed under normal conditions, redness will appear." Without seeking to beg any questions, we might call the latter part of Q a *psychophysical* statement, for it refers to sense-data which will appear under certain physical conditions. The sense-datum statement ("Redness will appear") is entailed, not by the thing statement ("This is red") but by the conjunction of: (i) the thing statement; (ii) the statement about observation-conditions ("This is observed under normal conditions"); and (iii) the psychophysical statement ("If this is red and is observed under normal conditions, redness will appear"). As we have seen, the thing statement, "This is red," if conjoined with a different statement about observation-conditions and with a different psychophysical statement, may entail a different sense-datum statement.

It could be contended that the psychophysical statement (iii) is analytic, that "If this is observed under normal conditions, redness will appear" is an analytic consequence of "This is red." This fact would be of little use to the translatability program, however. For this method of deriving sense-datum statements from "This is red" proceeds by utilizing additional thing state-

[3] A. J. Ayer, who also defends the translatability thesis, admits that no thing statement, such as "This thing is red," entails any particular sense-datum statement. But, he holds, the thing statement does entail numerous disjunctive "sets" of sense-data statements, "where the defining characteristic of the set is that all its members refer to sense-contents that fall within a certain specifiable range" (*Language, Truth and Logic,* 2nd edition, p. 13; cf. *Foundations of Empirical Knowledge,* pp. 240–241). E.g., each member of a set might refer to some specific shade of red, not referred to by the other members, but all of the sense-data referred to would fall within the "fairly indefinite range" of redness. The view that the thing statement entails such a set, however, is subject to the difficulties noted above in the case of single statements; for, again, it would seem to be possible to find another thing statement which, taken in conjunction with "This thing is red," entails the contradictory of any set which Mr. Ayer might mention.

ments ("This is observed under normal conditions," referring presumably to lighting arrangements, ocular conditions, and so on). Instead of eliminating thing statements in this manner, therefore, we would be multiplying them. And the new thing statements would present our old difficulties again.[4]

The translatability thesis, however, does claim to provide an account of the respect in which our knowledge of things is founded in, and is verifiable and falsifiable in, sense experience. If we deny this thesis we must provide an alternative account of the manner in which such experience may be said to justify our knowledge of things.[5] This is not the place to pursue this further question in detail; but it is relevant to note that, in principle, the problem becomes similar to that of the validity of memory and that Professor Lewis's own method of treating the latter problem may in fact be applicable to both problems. The possibility of our having any knowledge at all, he believes, requires that we make two assumptions about memory: "First; whatever is remembered, whether as explicit recollection or merely in the form of our sense of the past, is *prima facie* credible because so remembered. And second; when the whole range of empirical beliefs is taken into account, all of them more or less dependent upon memorial knowledge, we find that those which are most credible can be assured by their mutual support, or . . . *congruence*" (p. 334). If thing statements are not translatable into sense-datum statements, it may be that the validity of our perceptual knowledge of things requires similar assumptions. It may be that whenever the presence of a sense-datum leads one to accept a belief about a material thing (e.g., whenever, as a matter of fact, the presence of a red sense-datum leads one to accept the belief that one is observing a red thing) the belief which is thus "perceptually accepted" is *prima facie* credible because it is so accepted. Indeed Mr. Price has said as much. And it may be that when the whole range of our perceptual beliefs are taken into account, all of them more or less dependent upon our perceptual acceptances, we find that those which are most credible can be assured by their mutual support. These assumptions do not claim any faculties for man which are not involved in Professor Lewis's defence of memory. Whether they will suffice for justifying perceptual knowledge, however, is a question which can be answered only on the basis of a discussion as thorough as the one which Professor Lewis devotes to memory.

[4] Cf. H. H. Price, *Hume's Theory of the External World*, pp. 183–188.

[5] Similarly, we should have to reconsider the thesis, fundamental to Professor Lewis's views (as well as to Mr. Ayer's), that a synthetic statement is meaningful only to the extent to which it refers to possible experience. But it is reasonable to suppose that the acceptability of such a criterion of meaning should be secondary to considerations such as those discussed above.

Winston H. F. Barnes

The Myth of Sense-Data

I

Our knowledge of the physical world is subject to many doubts and uncertainties but we commonly see no reason to doubt certain facts. We all agree, when we are out of the study, that we sometimes see tables and chairs, hear bells and clocks, taste liquids, smell cheeses, and feel the woollen vests that we wear next to our skin in winter. To put the matter generally, we agree that we perceive physical objects, physical objects being such things as tables, chairs and cheeses, and perceiving being a generic word which comprehends the specific activities of seeing, hearing, tasting, smelling, and feeling. These activities are invariably directed upon an object or objects; and this fact distinguishes them from other activities of ours—if that be the right word—such as feeling pained or feeling tired, which go on entirely within ourselves. We take it for granted that by means of the former activities we become aware of the existence, and acquainted with the qualities, of physical objects, and we further regard the kind of acquaintance which we acquire in this way as a basis for the far reaching and systematic knowledge of the physical world as a whole, which is embodied in the natural sciences.

Let us call experiences such as seeing a table, hearing a bell, etc., perceptual experiences; and the statements which assert the existence of such experiences perceptual statements. Many philosophers have cast doubt upon the claims made by such perceptual statements. They have produced arguments to show that we never perceive physical objects, and that we are in fact subject to a constant delusion on this score. As these arguments are by no means easily refuted and are such as any intelligent person interested in the matter will sooner or later come to think of, they are well worth considering. Moreover, certain modern philosophers claim to show by these arguments not only that we do not perceive physical objects but that what we do perceive is a different sort of thing altogether, which they call a sense-datum. They are obliged to invent a new term for it because no one had previously noticed that there were such things. This theory is obviously important because it not only claims to settle the doubts which we cannot help feeling when we reflect on our perceptual experience, but it makes the astonishing claim that we have all failed to notice a quite peculiar kind of entity, or at least have constantly made mistakes

---

From W. H. F. Barnes, "The Myth of Sense-Data," *Proceedings of the Aristotelian Society,* Vol. 45 (1944–45). Reprinted by permission of the author and of the secretary and editor of the Aristotelian Society.

Winston H. F. Barnes (1909–) is Vice-Chancellor of the University of Liverpool. He has been Professor of Philosophy at the University of Edinburgh.

about its nature. I hope to show that the sense-datum theory is beset by internal difficulties; that it is not necessitated by the doubts we have about our perceptual experience; and finally that the doubts which are caused in us by a little reflection are allayed by further reflection.

The arguments which philosophers such as Professors Russell, Broad and Price use to demonstrate that we perceive not physical objects but sense-data, are many and various, and no good purpose would be served by stating them all, even if that were possible. Undoubtedly, however, these arguments do cause us to doubt whether we are acquainted with physical objects when we think we are; and, these doubts demand to be resolved in one way or another. If there is such a thing as a problem of perception, it must consist in reviewing the doubts which arise in our minds in this way. I shall select for brief statement three typical arguments so as to make clear the difficulties which are thought to justify the negative conclusion that we do not perceive physical objects and the positive conclusion that we perceive sense-data. There are two *caveats* to be registered. First, in compressing the arguments into a small compass I cannot hope to do full justice to the arguments, many and various, used by the sense-datum philosophers. I must leave it to the reader to decide whether I represent their general line of argument correctly or not. More than this I cannot hope to do; nor do I think more is necessary. Secondly, I should not be in the least surprised to be told that I already have misrepresented some of these philosophers by stating as one of their contentions that we do not perceive physical objects. Some of them would maintain that in some peculiar, or Pickwickian sense, to use Professor Moore's term, we do perceive physical objects. However, as, on their view, we do not perceive physical objects in the sense in which we think we perceive them, and we do perceive sense-data in precisely this sense, the misrepresentation is purely verbal and should mislead no one.[1]

I now proceed to state the three arguments. They are all taken from visual experience, and they all pose in one way or another what we may call the "appearance-reality" problem of perception.

(1) A penny appears circular to an observer directly above it, but elliptical to an observer a few paces away. It cannot *be* both elliptical and circular at one and the same time. There is no good reason for supposing that the penny reveals its real shape to an observer in one position rather than to an observer in any other position. The elliptical appearance and the circular appearance cannot be identified with the penny or any parts of it, but they are entities of some kind. It is things of this sort which are called sense-data.

(2) The stick which looks straight in the air looks angularly bent when

[1] The sense in which, on the sensum theory, we perceive [sense data], is described as *direct perception* or *direct apprehension* by the exponents of the theory to distinguish it from the perception or apprehension of physical objects which the theory as sometimes expounded allows to be possible. (*The Philosophy of G. E. Moore,* pp. 629, 640–643.) This distinction is usually drawn by those philosophers who accept the position taken up by the philosophy of analysis that there are many statements such as 'I see the table,' 'I hear the bell,' which are certainly true, although the analysis of them requires careful thought; and at the same time are convinced by arguments which claim to show that we cannot in fact see the table in the ordinary sense of the word see. I can see no really important difference, however, between the two statements: (1) I see only sense-data in the sense in which I have been accustomed to think I see physical objects, and my relation to the physical object is not that of seeing but that of R. (2) I see only sense-data in the sense in which I have been accustomed to think I see physical objects, but I do see physical objects in the sense that I have a relation R to them.

in water. There are good reasons for thinking that no such change of shape takes place in the stick. Yet there *is* something straight in the one case and something bent in the other, and there is no good reason for supposing either is less or more of an existent than the other. The straight-stick appearance and the bent-stick appearance are sense-data.

(3) There may seem to be things in a place when in fact there are no such things there, as illustrated by the mirages which appear in the desert and the highly coloured rodents which appear to habitual drunkards. Not unrelated to this type of experience is the one in which we see double. If an eyeball is pressed by the forefinger while one is looking at a candle flame, two flames are seen. Although it would be possible to say that one of the flames is the actual object and the other is something else, to be called a sense-datum, it seems even more evident here than in the previous instances that there is no good reason for distinguishing between the two in this way.

In all these cases there is a suggestion that what we see in certain cases cannot be a physical object or the surface of a physical object, but is some kind of non-physical entity. It is non-physical entities of this kind which are called sense-data. The argument goes even further by urging that, if in some cases we see non-material things, it is possible and indeed likely, that we do so in all cases. This plausible suggestion is accepted by certain sense-datum theorists such as Professor Broad and is extended to cover all forms of perceiving. With the acceptance of this suggestion we reach the basic position taken by one form of the sense-datum theory, viz., we perceive only sense-data, and consequently have no direct acquaintance through our senses with physical objects.

It is clear that, on this view, the term sense-datum has as part of its connotation, the not being a physical body.[2] As everything I experience is a sense-datum, the sense-experience of a table, for example, differs not at all, in itself, from an hallucination or an illusion. These latter again seem to differ only in degree from the images we have while we are day dreaming, or those we have while dreaming in the proper sense, or again from the after-images, or as they are more properly called, the after-sensations which sometimes follow our visual sensations. All these appearances would be regarded by certain philosophers as in principle of the same kind. This position is paradoxical to common-sense which regards perceptual experience as giving first-hand acquaintance with physical objects, and hallucinations and illusions as failing precisely in this respect. The common-sense ground for the distinction however is removed by the sense-datum theorist, and if in fact he does believe in physical objects, he has to substitute a new ground of a far more subtle and elaborate nature. In some cases he may prefer to get along altogether without physical objects, and may even urge that if we once give up the common-sense ground of distinction as untenable there is no other ground for believing in them.[3] Such questions as these, however, are domestic problems of sense-datum theorists and need not detain us, as we are intent on coming to grips with

[2] "In the common usage, some characteristic which entailed 'not a physical reality' was put into the connotation of 'sense-datum'; 'sense-datum' was so used that it would be a contradiction to say of any object that it was *both a physical reality and also* a 'sense-datum'." (*The Philosophy of G. E. Moore,* p. 634.)

[3] As Dr. Luce does, in his "Immaterialism." (Annual Philosophical Lecture, British Academy, 1944.)

the basis of the theory itself. It is important to note, however, that once the sense-datum theory is developed in the form stated above, it follows that, even if physical objects exist, they are never present in perceptual experience; and it becomes an open question whether they have any existence at all.

II

I shall consider later whether the arguments for the existence of sense-data in the sense indicated are valid. First, however, I want to state three considerations regarding the sense-datum itself. The first is of a very general nature and calculated to make us wonder whether a theory which departs so radically from common sense can be true; the second points out what extraordinary existents sense-data would be if there were such things; the third is directed to show that the kind of difficulty the theory was carefully framed to meet tends to break out anew within the theory.[4]

(1) The general consideration concerning the sensum theory is as follows: If the theory is true, then in all our perceptual experience sensa are interposed between us and the physical world, whereas it is one of our most strongly held beliefs that in perception we are face to face with the physical world. I do not wish to suggest that no attempt can be made to answer this obvious objection. The sensum theory can and does urge that in a Pickwickian sense of the term *perceive* we do perceive physical objects, i.e., we perceive sensa which are related in certain ways to physical objects. Nevertheless there is no doubt that, when presented with this type of explanation, we are apt to feel that we have been given a very inferior substitute in exchange for the direct acquaintance with physical objects which we have been called upon to surrender. . . .

Not only do we feel that sensa are an inadequate substitute for the physical objects which we claim to be confronted with in perception, but they seem to be embarrassingly numerous. Every appearance, however evanescent and fleeting, can claim to be an existent. As ordinary men, we contrast the intermittent character of our perceptual experience, broken as it is by sleep, lack of attention and change of place, with the permanent or relatively permanent and continuing status of physical objects. The changing facets of our perceptual experience we distribute carefully, crediting some to the physical world and disowning others as apparent only. The sensum theory credits all alike to reality, since it considers each and every one to be an individual entity. It is from this beginning that the wilder excesses of realism took their origin, in which not only reality but mind-independence was credited lavishly to almost anything that could be named, until the world began to take on the appearance of a great museum in which a few of the contents were real operative beings but the vast majority were exhibits only, ready to be produced on the appropriate occasion, but possessed of no other ground of existence.

[4] As the form of sense-datum theory now to be considered is that which has been most clearly worked out by Prof. Broad, I propose to substitute for the word *sense-datum* in this section the word *sensum* which Prof. Broad himself uses in its place. We shall see later that what Prof. Moore and others have to say about sense-data makes it advisable to have different words for the two theories, distinguished as follows: *sense-datum,* the immediate object in perception which may or may not be identical with a part of a physical object; *sensum,* the immediate object in perception, taken to be non-physical. Prof. Price, whose views are very like those of Prof. Broad, speaks of sense-data, but would, if he had accepted this rule for the use of the two words, have spoken of sensa.

I am not inclined to over-estimate the effect that a general consideration of this kind can be expected to have, but it is not lightly to be dismissed. There are philosophers to whom a single departure from the norms of common sense acts only as a stimulus to further more exciting philosophical adventures in the realms of speculation, but I confess that, for my part, I regard such a departure rather as a danger signal, warning that it would be wise to consider whether the steps which have led to this departure are as secure as they appear to be.

It is one thing to assert of a theory, however, that it presents us with a large number of existents which seem unnecessary and which, if they existed, would make it difficult to justify our acquaintance with physical objects; it is quite another to show that the existents are not merely unnecessary but are open to grave objections. This is the second point to which we must now turn.

(2) There are two reasons for considering sensa to be very objectionable existents.

(i) In the first place, unlike physical objects they do not always obey the Law of Excluded Middle. If I contemplate an object at some distance, it often happens that I am uncertain whether it is circular or polygonal. It is necessary for me to approach closer before I can determine the matter with certainty. On the sensum theory, the mode in which the object appeared to me at first is a sensum, and every sensum *is* what it appears to be. Now this sensum appears neither circular nor non-circular. Therefore it is neither circular nor non-circular. Let us be quite clear on this point. It is not that I do not know whether it is circular or non-circular, though in fact it must be one or the other. It really is neither one nor the other. This kind of experience is more common than one is perhaps inclined to believe at first. When an optician asks you to read those minute letters inscribed at the bottom of his chart, there comes a time when you are compelled to say "I am not sure whether it is an M or an N," because the shape you see is sufficiently indeterminate for you to think it may be either. Of course, some eminent philosophers have thought that reality did not obey the Law of Excluded Middle, but it would be surprising to find Professor Broad in their company.

It is tempting to urge that we *must* know the shape of the sensum because an artist can sit down and draw something which reproduces the shape. A little reflection, however, will show that what the artist does is to draw something which, having a certain definite shape, will appear at a certain distance to be as indeterminate in shape as the object itself appeared. In other words, what the artist does is the same in principle as what a joiner might do by building another object like the first one which would give rise to the same sort of appearance as the first one. So far as I can see, all so-called sensa, i.e., colours, sounds, smells, etc., are indeterminate in this way, though under favourable conditions the range of indeterminacy is so limited that it is, for practical purposes, not of any importance.

(ii) The second reason for considering sense-data to be objectionable existents, though closely connected with the former is less formidable; but is worth mentioning because it leads up to a number of very interesting considerations. It is a necessary consequence of the fact that a sense-datum *is* what it appears to be that there is no possibility of making further discoveries about its nature. It is always possible to get to know more and more about a particular existent, such as an apple or a squirrel, and, so far as we can tell, this process need never come to an end. There is no progress to be made in our knowledge of any particular sensum. This contention may seem to go too far in view of the revelations which philosophers claim to have about sensa. It can, however, be justified. Our knowledge of things is increased either by observation or by experiment. Experiment, as a means of gaining knowledge of sensa, is clearly ruled out, since it is obvious that any movement on my part or interference with the conditions will only cause one sensum to be replaced by another. It does, however, seem as though I might increase my knowledge of a particular sensum by observing it more closely than I had done. Rather, we must say, "by observing it more closely than I am doing," for clearly, my closer observation can only yield me more knowledge if it follows uninterruptedly upon my first. It will not do for me to come back at 5 p.m. to a closer study of the sensum which my table presented at 3 p.m. Can I gain more knowledge by continuing to observe it at 3 p.m.? I think we must say that I cannot. If we were to maintain that this was possible, and that something in the sensum previously unobserved might by observation be brought to light, we should need some criterion for making certain that it was the same sensum which we were observing at a later date as at an earlier date. *But no observation or experiment can yield a criterion.* The sensum theorists offer us little help on this point. The only thing is to fall back on the principle that a sensum is what it appears to be. If we interpret this as meaning it is all that it appears to be *and nothing more,*[5] then the possibility of learning anything about a sensum is cut away at once, for the very good reason that we know all there is to know about it by simply having it. It is, I think, a very odd fact, if true, that there are existents such that their being known at all entails their being completely known.

. . .

The moral of this is that those who believe in sensa tell us so little about the laws of their existence that we are at liberty to make a variety of assumptions on quite fundamental points. For example, how do we determine the duration of a sensum? If I blink my eyes while looking at a red patch are there two sensa separated in time, or is there only one interrupted in its career? If a change occurs in my visual field has the sensum changed or been replaced by another? If the latter, is there any reason why, when no change is observed, a sensum should not be replaced by another exactly like it? It may be said that to answer these questions is not important. I am inclined to agree that it is not; but the only reason I can see for this is that, sensa being wholly fictitious entities, we can attribute to them what qualities we please.[6]

Let us consider in a more particular way the arbitrary character of the sensum theory. Prof. Broad allows that a sensum may move across one's visual field; but he would not I think, allow that it can change in size or qualities. Take the simple case where I am watching a cinema screen on which is de-

[5] We shall see later that there are difficulties about other interpretations.

[6] This fact is at the bottom of Mr. Ayer's contention that the sensum theory is really only an alternative language, but we shall see later that there is more to it than this.

picted a round red patch moving across a background of different colour. Here, according to Prof. Broad, is a single sensum moving across my visual field. Supposing the round red patch remains stationary but slowly contracts in size before finally disappearing. Here, presumably, is a succession of sensa. Supposing, now, the red patch moves across the screen and as it does so it diminishes in size, have we one or a succession of sensa? The answer would have to be, I think: "A succession." There would seem, then, no reason for supposing that where the size of the moving patch is constant, there should not also be a succession of sensa. If this is so, sensa do not move, they merely rise up one after another in a certain spatial order. We could equally well allow, on the other hand, that sensa not only move but change in shape, size, colour, etc. In fact, if the essential characteristic of a sensum is that it is what it appears to be, then there is a very good case for taking this view, since there certainly *appear* to be changes in the colour and shape as well as the position of what we experience through our senses. What is worth remarking is that there is nothing which enables us to consider one alternative nearer the truth than the other. As long as this kind of question can be decided only arbitrarily, it is clear that there is no way of determining the number of sensa. So we find them to have another peculiar property for existents; they are not numerable.

. . .

Before turning to consider the validity of the reasoning which is used to prove the existence of sensa, there is one other point which merits attention. One of the most serious arguments against the sensum theory is that, if it is true, it is extremely difficult to explain how from knowledge of our sensa we could come to knowledge of material things; and yet, according to Prof. Broad, "all that I ever come to know about physical objects and their qualities seems to be based upon the qualities of the sensa that I become aware of in sense-perception." [7] But an even greater difficulty faces us, viz., that of being assured that material things exist at all, i.e., relatively permanent things with certain qualities and interacting with one another. Prof. Broad says: ". . . there is nothing in my sensa to force me logically to the conclusion that there must be something beyond them, having the constitutive properties of physical objects. The belief that our sensa are appearances of something more permanent and complex than themselves seems to be primitive, and to arise inevitably in us with the sensing of the sensa. It is not reached by inference, and could not logically be justified by inference. On the other hand, there is no possibility of either refuting it logically, or of getting rid of it, or—so far as I can see—of co-ordinating the facts without it." [8] Prof. Luce thinks otherwise. In rejecting the existence of physical objects over and above sensa he says: "To accept both the sense-datum *and* matter is to turn the one world into two." [9]

If I believed in sensa I should be found on the side of Dr. Luce, for the difficulties of distinguishing between a primitive belief and a primitive delusion seem to me insuperable.

[7] *Scientific Thought*, p. 241.
[8] *Scientific Thought*, p. 268.
[9] "Immaterialism" (Annual Philosophical Lecture, British Academy, 1944), p. 6.

III

So far we have been considering the difficulties that arise from holding that sensa form a class of existents totally different from physical objects. Though the difficulties are perhaps not sufficiently serious to destroy the theory, they seem to me quite serious enough to make it desirable to look carefully into the considerations put forward for inducing belief in such entities.

These considerations seem to me to reduce to one fundamental argument, and this argument seems to me to be false, though plausible. If I am right, then the reason for believing in sensa goes.

I quoted earlier three typical arguments for the existence of sensa. I now wish to examine carefully a single argument which embodies the principle of these and other similar arguments. No one will deny, I think, that a situation may exist in which the following three propositions are true:

(i) I see the rose.
(ii) The rose appears pink to me.
(iii) The rose is red.

The belief in sensa is reached by arguing, not unplausibly, that since what I am seeing appears pink, there exists something which *is* pink; and since the rose is red, not pink, it cannot be the rose which is pink; therefore what I am seeing is something other than the rose. Whereupon the term sensum is invented and given as a name to this existent and others like it. And so we reach the conclusion:

(iv) I see a pink sensum.

The argument is fallacious. *That something appears pink to me is not a valid reason for concluding either that that thing is pink or that there is some other thing which is pink.* From the fact that a thing *looks* pink I can sometimes with the help of certain other propositions infer that it *is* pink or that it *is* red; I may also, with the help of certain other propositions, be able to infer that something in some other place is pink, e.g., the electric light bulb which is illuminating the rose. But I cannot infer, as is proposed, *merely from the three facts that I am seeing something, that it looks pink and that it is red, that there is a pink something where the thing appears pink to me.*

This, when we examine it, is the foundation stone on which the great edifice of the sensum theory has been raised. Is it surprising that the upper storeys present doubts and perplexities? But there is worse to come. Not only is the argument fallacious but the conclusion contradicts one of the premises, viz., (i) I see a rose. It does so because, in order that the conclusion should seem at all plausible, it has been assumed that, if I were to see a rose which actually possessed a red colour, I should see it as red, i.e., it would necessarily appear red to me. This again is an assumption in contradiction with propositions (ii) and (iii) taken together. As soon as this self-induced contradiction is discovered by the sensum theorists, repair work is put in hand on one or other of alternative lines: (*a*) It is accepted that I do not see the rose, and an account is given of the relation in which I *do* stand to the rose and which has been mistaken for seeing. A little reflection, of course, soon convinces those who go this way that, if this is true, it is not only roses that are born to blush unseen, but the whole world of material things. In this way sensa become an impenetrable barrier barring for ever our acquaintance through the senses with the world of material things. This is strong meat for any but really metaphysical natures, and fortunately for the sensum theory there is another way of making the necessary repairs. (*b*) The alternative procedure is something like this: It is certain that I do see the rose. I have convinced myself, however, by argument that one thing I undoubtedly see, in a plain unvarnished use of the word *see*, is a pink rose-figured sensum. Hence the sense in which I see the rose must be different, i.e., "seeing" is systematically ambiguous and what exactly is meant by seeing the rose needs to be elucidated. Seeing a rose and seeing a pink rose-figured sensum are then distinguished as quite different ways of seeing and it is convenient to refer to seeing a sensum as "directly seeing," and seeing a rose as "seeing."[10] The analysis of seeing the rose can then be made in terms of directly seeing a certain sort of sensum and at the same time having perceptual assurance that . . . etc., the complete analysis varying from one philosopher to another.[11]

There is another way in which an attempt may be made to justify the conclusion of the argument we have condemned as fallacious. I have argued that from the fact that something which is red appears pink, it does not follow that a pink sensum exists. It may be said that the existence of a pink sensum, while not following from the premises, is justified by a direct appeal to our sense experience. "I see it, therefore it is." The argument can be stated as follows: "I certainly see a pink something and to say that there is nothing pink is to say that I have no reason for believing in what I see now; and if I cannot believe in what I see now, how can I believe in what I see on any occasion, or any one else in what he sees on any occasion? If you deny the existence of this pink patch, you deny the existence altogether of the world revealed by the senses." The answer to this objection is simple, if we reflect, viz., "You never can believe in what you see on any occasion, it always may mislead you as to what the thing is. If you wish to state only that something appears to be so and so, this can safely be done. But this is not a statement about something made on the basis of a piece of evidence, it is a statement of the piece of evidence itself, which you already have before you without clothing it in words." Modes of appearance are clues to the nature of what exists, not existents. I submit that it is improper to ask whether the pink mode of appearing, which is how the rose appears to me, exists. You may ask whether the rose exists and whether it is red or pink; and in answering this question account must be taken of how it appears under different conditions and to different people. Although modes of appearance are not existents, they are the material and the only material on which thinking can operate to discover the nature of existing things; and it is an epistemological ideal that if we were to discover

[10] Prof. Moore makes this use of the two terms. It is worth pointing out that in ordinary language we should be ready to say that we were directly seeing the rose; in contrast, for example to seeing it as reflected in a mirror or seeing it through a microscope, where the indirectness would consist, no doubt, to our minds, in the interposition of a further medium between our eyes and the object in addition to the usual light and air. There is still an air of paradox, consequently, about the way in which the words seeing and directly seeing are used by sensum theorists.

[11] Philosophers tend to adopt the second alternative because it enables them to eat their cake and have it. They continue on this matter to speak with the vulgar and think with the learned, following in this respect the good Bishop of Cloyne, the inventor of philosophical analysis.

completely the nature of existing things, there would be nothing left in the modes of appearance which would not entirely harmonise with our system of knowledge and find its explanation there.

. . .

VI

I now propose to state briefly the lines of an alternative account to the sensum theory. The account is quite simple and is implicit in the foregoing discussion. I can claim no great originality for it as it is substantially the theory put forward by Prof. Dawes Hicks[12] and called by Prof. Broad the Multiple Relation Theory of Appearance. I can claim only that I arrived at it by a somewhat different line of thought and for that reason my statement of it may have some interest. I propose to call it simply the theory of appearing. I hope to show that it is the theory implicit in common sense and that it can be defended against the more obvious objections.

We saw that the sensum theory was led into difficulties by concluding from the propositions (i) I see the rose, (ii) The rose appears pink to me, and (iii) The rose is red, to a proposition (iv) I see a pink sensum. To attain consistency it was necessary to distinguish between the meaning which the word *see* has in proposition (i) and that which it has in proposition (iv). It is obvious, however, when we reflect, that propositions such as (i) must be incomplete versions of propositions such as (ii), e.g., "I see the rose as pink" is the expanded form of the proposition (i), which says the same thing as proposition (ii), but begins with me and proceeds to the rose, instead of beginning with the rose and proceeding to me. It is evident, further, if this is so, that *see* must have the same sense but in the reverse direction, as *appears*.

The account I put forward, then, is that objects themselves appear to us in sense-perception; that they in general appear in sense-perception to have those qualities which they in fact have; that where they appear to have qualities which they do not in fact have, these instances are more properly regarded as their failing in differing degrees to appear to have the properties they do have, such failure being accounted for by the conditions under which they are perceived. We must be quite bold at this point and admit at once that on this account of the matter a thing can possess a certain quality and at the same time appear to some one to possess another quality, which it could not actually possess in conjunction with the former quality. Let us be quite clear about what we are saying. When I see a circular penny as elliptical I am seeing the circular surface of the penny, not some elliptical substitute. This circular surface, it is true, appears elliptical to me, but that fact has no tendency to show that I am not directly aware of the circular surface. Aeneas was none the less in the presence of his mother Venus though she concealed from him the full glory of her godhead.

It is clear that, on this theory, perception has a much closer resemblance to thinking than would be allowed by the sensum theorists. For (i) it may have a content more or less false to the real, as thought may; and (ii) this content does not exist independent of the act of perceiving any more than the content

[12] In his *Critical Realism*.

of a false proposition.[13] The chief objection to this contention is stated by Prof. Broad as follows: "It is very hard to understand how we could seem to ourselves to *see* the property of bentness exhibited in a concrete instance, if in fact *nothing* was present to our minds that possessed that property." [14] I can see no great difficulty in this, and we have seen how the attempt to escape from the imagined difficulty leads to difficulties. Fourteen years later Prof. Broad himself was not so sure for he says: "Now one may admit that a certain particular might seem to have a characteristic which differs from and is incompatible with the characteristic which it does have. But I find it almost incredible that one particular extended patch should seem to be two particular extended patches at a distance apart from each other." [15] Prof. Price finds the same difficulty, for he says: "It is not really sense to say 'To me the candle appears double. . . 'doubled' is not really a predicate at all." [16]

Seven years have passed since Prof. Broad wrote the latter of his two quoted statements so it may be that he now finds the assertion more credible. I certainly find nothing incredible in it. No doubt it is impossible for one candle to *be* two candles but there seems no reason why it should not appear to be any number of things. Finally, hallucinations and delusions need present no insuperable difficulties. There appeared to Lady Macbeth to be a dagger but there was no dagger in fact. Something appeared to be a dagger, and there are certainly problems concerning exactly what it is in such circumstances appears to be possessed of qualities which it does not possess. It is easy of course to object that an illusory dagger is not just nothing. The answer is neither "Yes, it is" nor "No, it isn't," but "An illusory dagger is a misleading expression if used to describe an element in the situation." It is misleading also in some degree to say that there exists "a dagger-like appearance," though we need not be misled by such a use of the word *appearance* if we are careful. Strictly speaking, however, there are no such things as appearances. To suppose that there are would be like supposing that because Mr. X put in an appearance, there must have been something over and above Mr. X which he was kind enough to put in. "Mr. X appeared": that is the proper mode of expression if we are to avoid difficulties.[17]

An existent must be determinate and we saw that what are alleged to be existents and called sense-data could not meet this demand. To give rise to similar difficulties by speaking of appearances, thereby seeming to condone treating the modes in which things appear as existents, would be most inappropriate. That a thing, though wholly determinate, should fail to reveal its full determinate character to a single *coup d'oeil* is surely to be expected and our theory derives support from the fact that objects do not always appear in their fully determinate nature.

There is another point about our account of the matter. It allows that it

[13] It is a salutary reflection in this connection that the spiritual home of the sensum at one time opened its gates wide to an even more peculiar entity, the proposition.

[14] *Scientific Thought,* p. 241.

[15] *Mind and Its Place in Nature,* p. 188.

[16] *Perception,* pp. 62–3.

[17] Cf. the judicious remark of Prof. Dawes Hicks: "When, in ordinary language, we speak of the objective constituent of a perceptual situation as being the 'appearance of' a physical object we mean not that it is the appearance which appears but that it is the physical object which appears" (*Critical Realism,* p. 55). Even so, it is better to avoid the noun altogether, or at least always to test out the validity of its use by mentally translating into the verb.

is *possible* for certain people at certain times to become acquainted through perception with things as they are, not merely as they appear to be. This can be seen best as follows. The word *sense-datum* was substituted for the word *appearance* to emphasise that there is an indubitable element in sense experience, in contrast with the use of the term *appearance* by philosophers who denied the existence of any such given, and who used the contrast between appearance and reality to grind a metaphysical axe of their own. But, as was pointed out by Prof. Moore, the term was often used with the connotation "not a physical reality." If this connotation is accepted, it follows that, however extensive our acquaintance with sense-data, we are no whit nearer to becoming acquainted with physical objects, and it is even difficult to see how we can know *about* these latter. This is the "great barrier" objection to the theory as held by Prof. Broad and his followers. Even for those who avoid putting into the term sense-datum this unwarrantable connotation the term is apt to give rise to unnecessary difficulties. For example, Mr. Wisdom, more careful than most philosophers not to be misled by the term, writes: "I should agree that it is unplausible to say that, although when I see a thing in bad light my corresponding sense-datum is not identical with the observed surface of the thing, nevertheless, when the light changes, the corresponding sense-datum which I then obtain is identical with the observed surface, I cannot say why I find this unplausible, but I do. I find such a discontinuity, such a popping in and out of the material world on so slight a provocation, most objectionable."[18] If we are content to talk in terms of appearance or, better still, of things appearing, we shall not have pseudo-problems of this kind. We need have no heart-burning about the following statement: "Although when I see a thing in bad light the surface does not appear to me in every respect as it really is, nevertheless, when the light is adequate, it does." The reason we are now talking better sense is that the language of appearance permits us to maintain (*a*) that a thing can not only appear what it is not, but what it is: (*b*) that a thing's appearing what it is not is best understood as a deviation from its appearing what it is. A terminology which purports to be neutral and yet makes these propositions sound absurd has prejudged the issue in a most unfortunate manner.[19]

On the theory outlined it is easy to explain how we can come to know about material objects for in all our perception we are perceiving material objects even though we are not always completely successful in perceiving them exactly as they are. On the sensum theory, as we have seen, it is difficult to explain why knowledge of sensa should contribute towards knowledge of material things; how we could ever have been led to the belief in material things; and, still less, how we could justify the belief.

Finally, the account of the matter I have given is, I think, remarkably close to common sense. As Prof. Broad claims that this type of theory departs as widely from common sense as the sensum theory this claim needs to be defended. He argues that, as commonly used, a statement such as "I see a table"

[18] *Problems of Mind and Matter*, p. 156.

[19] In fairness to Mr. Wisdom it must be pointed out that immediately after making the statement quoted, he goes on to say something which, if I understand it rightly, is very like what I have said except that (*a*) he calls that which appears a sense-datum and (*b*) identifies it with an object's surface.

involves the unexpressed theory that there is a situation involving two constituents, myself and the table, related by a relation of seeing, a relation which proceeds from me to the table. This theory, ascribed to common sense, Prof. Broad calls naïve realism.[20] Now it is only plausible to maintain that this theory is held by the ordinary man if carefully selected perceptual statements concerning objects at close range are considered. If we regard the whole range of perceptual situations the common sense belief is quite different. This belief involves that in perceptual situations objects reveal more or less of their nature to us; and common sense would find no difficulty in admitting that there are cases where very little of the nature of the object of perception is revealed. For example, statements of the following type are a commonplace: "I can just see something, but I cannot make out what it is," "I think I can see something there but I cannot be sure," "It looks like a house, but it may be just an outcrop of rock." Instances could be multiplied indefinitely. Common sense would not scruple to admit that objects do not always have the qualities which they seem to have when seen, heard, tasted, touched or smelt. It accepts without flinching that the hills which look purple in the distance are really green. It is indeed a platitude enshrined in proverbial literature that "things are seldom what they seem."

I draw attention to these elementary facts, in the first place, to point out that the only naïveté about naïve realism is that philosophers should have thought the ordinary man believed it. More important, however, is that these facts show the common sense view not to involve belief in a simple two-termed relation between me and the things I perceive, in which no possibility of illusion can arise, but a relation in which there is the possibility of the object's nature being revealed to a greater or less degree. It is true, of course, that the plain man no less than the philosopher sometimes puts as the object of *see* not the material thing but the *how it appears* as when, looking into the distance, one says "I can see a purple haze; it may be mountains or cloud." No violence is done to his language if it is rewritten "I see something as purple and hazy" or "There is something which appears purple and hazy." It is the lack of sufficient information to establish the nature of the object appearing which leads to the varying form of statement.

In concluding, I do not wish to suggest that no problems beset the theory of appearing. For example the two cases of a thing's appearing double and of something appearing to be where there is no such thing, present the problem: Is the apparent expanse in these cases the actual surface of any object? If so, of what object? I must, however, defer the inquiry into this and other problems to a future occasion, when I can consider the affinities of this theory with the different but closely related theory of multiple inherence and at the same time discuss some of the points in Prof. Dawes Hicks' exposition with which I am not perfectly satisfied. Here I have only been able to indicate the possibility of such an account as an appendix to my main task which has been to criticise those theories which make the notion of sense-datum fundamental in their explanations of perception.

[20] "Naïve Realism . . . is the explicit formulation of the belief which forms *an essential part* of the perceptual situation as such." *The Mind and Its Place in Nature,* p. 243.

H. P. Grice

The Causal Theory of Perception

I

The Causal Theory of Perception (CTP) has for some time received comparatively little attention, mainly, I suspect, because it has been generally assumed that the theory either asserts or involves as a consequence the proposition that material objects are unobservable, and that the unacceptability of this proposition is sufficient to dispose of the theory. I am inclined to regard this attitude to the CTP as unfair or at least unduly unsympathetic and I shall attempt to outline a thesis which might not improperly be considered to be a version of the CTP, and which is, if not true, at least not too obviously false.

What is to count as holding a causal theory of perception? (1) I shall take it as being insufficient merely to believe that the perception of a material object is always to be causally explained by reference to conditions the specification of at least one of which involves a mention of the object perceived; that, for example, the perception is the terminus of a causal sequence involving at an earlier stage some event or process in the history of the perceived object. Such a belief does not seem to be philosophical in character; its object has the appearance of being a very general contingent proposition; though it is worth remarking that if the version of the CTP with which I shall be primarily concerned is correct, it (or something like it) will turn out to be a necessary rather than a contingent truth. (2) It may be held that the elucidation of the notion of perceiving a material object will include some reference to the rôle of the material object perceived in the causal ancestry of the perception or of the sense-impression or sense-datum involved in the perception. This contention is central to what I regard as a standard version of the CTP. (3) It might be held that it is the task of the philosopher of perception not to elucidate or characterize the ordinary notion of perceiving a material object, but to provide a rational reconstruction of it, to replace it by some concept more appropriate to an ideal or scientific language: it might further be suggested that such a redefinition might be formulated in terms of the effect of the presence of an object upon the observer's sense-organ and nervous system or upon his behaviour or "behaviour-tendencies" or in terms of both of these effects. A view of this kind may perhaps deserve to be called a causal theory of perception; but I shall not be concerned with theories on these lines. (4) I shall distinguish from the adoption of a CTP the attempt to provide for a wider or narrower range of propositions ascribing properties to material objects a certain

---

From H. P. Grice, "The Causal Theory of Perception," *Proceedings of the Aristotelian Society,* Supplementary Vol. 35 (1961). Reprinted by permission of the author and of the secretary and editor of the Aristotelian Society.

sort of causal analysis: the kind of analysis which I have in mind is that which, on *one* possible interpretation, Locke could be taken as suggesting for ascriptions of, for example, colour and temperature; he might be understood to be holding that such propositions assert that an object would, in certain standard conditions, cause an observer to have certain sorts of ideas or sense-impressions.

In Professor Price's *Perception,*[1] there appears a preliminary formulation of the CTP which would bring it under the second of the headings distinguished in the previous paragraph. The CTP is specified as maintaining (1) that in the case of all sense-data (not merely visual and tactual) "belonging to" simply means *being caused by,* so that '*M* is present to my senses' will be equivalent to '*M* causes a sense-datum with which I am acquainted'; (2) that perceptual consciousness is fundamentally an inference from effect to cause. Since it is, I think, fair to say [2] that the expression "present to my senses" was introduced by Price as a special term to distinguish one of the possible senses of the verb "perceive", the first clause of the quotation above may be taken as propounding the thesis that "I am perceiving *M*" (in one sense of that expression) is to be regarded as equivalent to "I am having (or sensing) a sense-datum which is caused by *M*." (The second clause I shall for the time being ignore.) I shall proceed to consider at some length the feature which this version of the CTP shares with other non-causal theories of perception, namely, the claim that perceiving a material object involves having or sensing a sense-datum; for unless this claim can be made out the special features of the CTP become otiose.

II

The primary difficulty facing the contention that perceiving involves having or sensing a sense-datum is that of giving a satisfactory explanation of the meaning of the technical term 'sense-datum'. One familiar method of attempting this task is that of trying to prove, by means of some form of the Argument from Illusion, the existence of objects of a special sort for which the term 'sense-datum' is offered as a class-name. Another method (that adapted in a famous passage by Moore) is that of giving directions which are designed to enable one to pick out items of the kind to which the term 'sense-datum' is to be applied. The general character of the objections to each of these procedures is also familiar, and I shall, for present purposes, assume that neither procedure is satisfactory.

Various philosophers have suggested that though attempts to indicate, or demonstrate the existence of, special objects to be called sense-data have all failed, nevertheless the expression 'sense-datum' can (and should) be introduced as a technical term; its use would be explicitly defined by reference to such supposedly standard locutions as "So-and-so looks Φ (*e.g.,* blue) to me", "It looks (feels) to me as if there were a Φ so-and-so", "I seem to see something Φ" and so on. Now as the objection to such proposals which I have in mind is one which might be described as an objection in principle, it is not to my present purpose to consider how in detail such an explicit definition of the notion of a sense-datum might be formulated. I should, however, remark that this programme may be by no means so easy to carry through as the

[1] P. 66.
[2] *Cf. ibid.,* pp. 21–25.

casual way in which it is sometimes proposed might suggest; various expressions are candidates for the key rôle in this enterprise *e.g.*, "looks ("feels" etc.), "seems", "appears" and the more or less subtle differences between them would have to be investigated; and furthermore even if one has decided on a preferred candidate, not all of its uses would be suitable; if for example we decide to employ the expressions "looks" etc., are we to accept the legitimacy of the sentence "It looks indigestible to me" as providing us with a sense-datum sentence "I am having an indigestible visual sense-datum"?

. . .

V

I hope that I may have succeeded in disposing of what I have found to be a frequently propounded objection to the idea of explaining the notion of a sense-datum in terms of some member or members of the suggested family of locutions. Further detailed work would be needed to find the most suitable member of the family, and to select the appropriate range of uses of the favoured member when it is found; and, as I have indicated, neither of these tasks may be easy. I shall, for present purposes, assume that some range of uses of locutions of the form "It looks (feels, etc.) to *X* as if" has the best chance of being found suitable. I shall furthermore assume that the safest procedure for the Causal Theorist will be to restrict the actual occurrences of the term "sense-datum" to such classificatory labels as "sense-datum statement" or "sense-datum sentence"; to license the introduction of a "sense-datum terminology" to be used for the re-expression of sentences incorporating the preferred locutions seems to me both unnecessary and dangerous. I shall myself, on behalf of the CTP, often for brevity's sake talk of sense-data or sense-impressions; but I shall hope that a more rigorous, if more cumbrous, mode of expression will always be readily available. I hope that it will now be allowed that, interpreted on the lines which I have suggested, the thesis that perceiving involves having a sense-datum (involves its being the case that some sense-datum statement or other about the percipient is true) has at least a fair chance of proving acceptable.

I turn now to the special features of the CTP. The first clause of the formulation quoted above[3] from Price's *Perception* may be interpreted as representing it to be a necessary and sufficient condition of its being the case that *X* perceives *M* that *X*'s sense-impression should be causally dependent on some state of affairs involving *M*. Let us first enquire whether the suggested condition is necessary. Suppose that it looks to *X* as if there is a clock on the shelf; what more is required for it to be true to say that *X* sees a clock on the shelf? There must, one might say, actually be a clock on the shelf which is in *X*'s field of view, before *X*'s eyes. But this does not seem to be enough. For it is logically conceivable that there should be some method by which an expert could make it look to *X* as if there were a clock on the shelf on occasions when the shelf was empty: there might be some apparatus by which *X*'s cortex could be suitably stimulated, or some technique analogous to post-hypnotic suggestion. If such treatment were applied to *X* on an occasion when there actually

[3] P. 595 *supra*.

was a clock on the shelf, and if *X*'s impressions were found to continue unchanged when the clock was removed or its position altered, then I think we should be inclined to say that *X* did not see the clock which was before his eyes, just because we should regard the clock as playing no part in the origination of his impression. Or, to leave the realm of fantasy, it might be that it looked to me as if there were a certain sort of pillar in a certain direction at a certain distance, and there might actually be such a pillar in that place; but if, unknown to me, there were a mirror interposed between myself and the pillar, which reflected a numerically different though similar pillar, it would certainly be incorrect to say that I saw the first pillar, and correct to say that I saw the second; and it is extremely tempting to explain this linguistic fact by saying that the first pillar was, and the second was not, causally irrelevant to the way things looked to me.

There seems then a good case for allowing that the suggested condition is necessary; but as it stands it can hardly be sufficient. For in any particular perceptual situation there will be objects other than that which would ordinarily be regarded as being perceived, of which some state or mode of functioning is causally relevant to the occurrence of a particular sense-impression: this might be true of such objects as the percipient's eyes or the sun. So some restriction will have to be added to the analysis of perceiving which is under consideration. Price[4] suggested that use should be made of a distinction between "standing" and "differential" conditions: as the state of the sun and of the percipient's eyes, for example, are standing conditions in that (roughly speaking) if they were suitably altered, all the visual impressions of the percipient would be in some respect different from what they would otherwise have been; whereas the state of the perceived object is a differential condition in that a change in it would affect only some of the percipient's visual impressions, perhaps only the particular impression the causal origin of which is in question. The suggestion then is that the CTP should hold that an object is perceived if and only if some condition involving it is a differential condition of some sense-impression of the percipient. I doubt, however, whether the imposition of this restriction is adequate. Suppose that on a dark night I see, at one and the same time, a number of objects each of which is illuminated by a different torch; if one torch is tampered with, the effect on my visual impressions will be restricted, not general; the objects illuminated by the other torches will continue to look the same to me. Yet we do not want to be compelled to say that each torch is perceived in such a situation; concealed torches may illuminate. But this is the position into which the proposed revision of the CTP would force us.

I am inclined to think that a more promising direction for the CTP to take is to formulate the required restriction in terms of the way in which a perceived object contributes towards the occurrence of the sense-impression. A conceivable course would be to introduce into the specification of the restriction some part of the specialist's account, for example to make a reference to the transmission of light-waves to the retina; but the objection to this procedure is obvious; if we are attempting to characterize the ordinary notion of perceiving, we should not explicitly introduce material of which someone who is perfectly capable of employing the ordinary notion might be ignorant.

[4] *Op. cit.*, p. 70.

I suggest that the best procedure for the Causal Theorist is to indicate the mode of causal connexion by examples; to say that, for an object to be perceived by *X*, it is sufficient that it should be causally involved in the generation of some sense-impression by *X* in the kind of way in which, for example, when I look at my hand in a good light, my hand is causally responsible for its looking to me as if there were a hand before me, or in which . . . (and so on), *whatever that kind of way may be;* and to be enlightened on that question one must have recourse to the specialist. I see nothing absurd in the idea that a non-specialist concept should contain, so to speak, a blank space to be filled in by the specialist; that this is so, for example, in the case of the concept of seeing is perhaps indicated by the consideration that if we were in doubt about the correctness of speaking of a certain creature with peculiar sense-organs as *seeing* objects, we might well wish to hear from a specialist a comparative account of the human eye and the relevant sense-organs of the creature in question. We do not, of course, ordinarily need the specialist's contribution; for we may be in a position to say that the same kind of mechanism is involved in a plurality of cases without being in a position to say what that mechanism is.[5]

At this point an objection must be mentioned with which I shall deal only briefly, since it involves a manoeuvre of the same general kind as that which I discussed at length earlier in this paper. The CTP as I have so expounded it, it may be said, requires that it should be linguistically correct to speak of the causes of sense-impressions which are involved in perfectly normal perceptual situations. But this is a mistake; it is quite unnatural to talk about the cause, say, of its looking to *X* as if there were a cat before him unless the situation is or is thought to be in some way abnormal or delusive; this being so, when a cause can, without speaking unnaturally, be assigned to an impression, it will always be something other than the presence of the perceived object. There is no natural use for such a sentence as "The presence of a cat caused it to look to *X* as if there were a cat before him"; yet it is absolutely essential to the CTP that there should be.

In reply to this objection I will make three points. (1) If we are to deal sympathetically with the CTP we must not restrict the Causal Theorist to the verb 'cause'; we must allow him to make use of other members of the family of causal verbs or verb-phrases if he wishes. This family includes such expressions as "accounts for", "explains", "is part of the explanation of", "is partly responsible for", and it seems quite possible that some alternative formulation of the theory would escape this objection. (2) If I regard myself as being in a position to say "There is a cat", or "I see a cat", I naturally refrain from making the weaker statement "It looks to me as if there were a cat before me", and so, *a fortiori,* I refrain from talking about the cause of its looking to me thus. But, if I was right earlier in this paper, to have made the weaker statement would have been to have said something linguistically correct and true, even if misleading; is there then any reason against supposing that it could have been linguistically correct and true, even if pointless or misleading,

[5] It might be thought that we need a further restriction, limiting the permissible degree of divergence between the way things appear to *X* and the way they actually are. But objects can be said to be seen even when they are looked at through rough thick glass or distorting spectacles, in spite of the fact that they may then be unrecognizable.

to have ascribed to a particular cause the state of affairs reported in the weaker statement? (3) *X* is standing in a street up which an elephant is approaching; he thinks his eyes must be deceiving him. Knowing this, I could quite naturally say to *X*, "The fact that it looks to you as if there is an elephant approaching is accounted for by the fact that an elephant is approaching, not by your having become deranged." To say the same thing to one's neighbour at the circus would surely be to say something which is true, though it might be regarded as provocative.

I have extracted from the first clause of the initial formulation of the CTP an outline of a causal analysis of perceiving which is, I hope, at least not obviously unacceptable. I have of course considered the suggested analysis only in relation to seeing; a more careful discussion would have to pay attention to nonvisual perception; and even within the field of visual perception the suggested analysis might well be unsuitable for some uses of the word 'see', which would require a stronger condition than that proposed by the theory.

VI

Is the CTP, as so far expounded, open to the charge that it represents material objects as being in principle unobservable, and in consequence leads to scepticism about the material world? I have some difficulty in understanding the precise nature of the accusation, in that it is by no means obvious what, in this context, is meant by "unobservable".

(1) It would be not unnatural to take "unobservable" to mean "incapable of being perceived". Now it may be the case that one could, without being guilty of inconsistency, combine the acceptance of the causal analysis of perceiving with the view that material objects cannot in principle be perceived, if one were prepared to maintain that it is in principle impossible for material objects to cause sense-impressions but that this impossibility has escaped the notice of common sense. This position, even if internally consistent, would seem to be open to grave objection. But even if the proposition that material objects cannot be perceived is consistent with the causal analysis of perceiving, it certainly does not appear to be a consequence of the latter; and the exposition of the CTP has so far been confined to the propounding of a causal analysis of perceiving.

(2) The critic might be equating "unobservable" with "not directly observable"; and to say that material objects are not directly observable might in turn be interpreted as saying that statements about material objects lack that immunity from factual mistake which is (or is supposed to be) possessed by at least some sense-datum statements. But if "unobservable" is thus interpreted, it seems to be *true* that material objects are unobservable, and the recognition of this truth could hardly be regarded as a matter for reproach.

(3) "Observation" may be contrasted with "inference" as a source of knowledge and so the critic's claim may be that the CTP asserts or implies that the existence of particular material objects can only be a matter of inference. But in the first place, it is not established that the acceptance of the causal analysis of perceiving commits one to the view that the existence of particular material objects is necessarily a matter of inference (though this view is explicitly asserted by the second clause of Price's initial formulation of the CTP); and secondly, many of the critics have been phenomenalists,

who would themselves be prepared to allow that the existence of particular material objects is, in some sense, a matter of inference. And if the complaint is that the CTP does not represent the inference as being of the right kind, then it looks as if the critic might in effect be complaining that the Causal Theorist is not a Phenomenalist. Apart from the fact that the criticism under discussion could now be made only by someone who not only accepted Phenomenalism but also regarded it as the only means of deliverance from scepticism, it is by no means clear that to accept a causal analysis of perceiving is to debar oneself from accepting Phenomenalism; there seems to be no patent absurdity in the idea that one could, as a first stage, offer a causal analysis of '*X* perceives *M*', and then re-express the result in phenomenalist terms. If the CTP is to be (as it is often regarded as being) a rival to Phenomenalism, the opposition may well have to spring from the second clause of the initial formulation of the theory.

There is a further possibility of interpretation, related to the previous one. If someone has seen a speck on the horizon which is in fact a battleship, we should in some contexts be willing to say that he has seen a battleship; but we should not, I think, be willing to say that he has observed a battleship unless he has recognized what he has seen as a battleship. The criticism levelled at the CTP may then be that it asserts or entails the impossibility in principle of *knowing*, or even of being reasonably assured, that one is perceiving a particular material object, even if one is in fact perceiving it. At this point we must direct our attention to the second clause of the initial formulation of the CTP, which asserted that "perceptual consciousness is fundamentally an inference from effect to cause". I shall assume (I hope not unreasonably) that the essence of the view here being advanced is that anyone who claims to perceive a particular material object *M* may legitimately be asked to justify his claim; and that the only way to meet this demand, in the most fundamental type of case, is to produce an acceptable argument to the effect that the existence of *M* is required, or is probably required, in order that the claimant's current sense-impressions should be adequately accounted for. A detailed exposition of the CTP may supplement this clause by supplying general principles which, by assuring us of correspondences between causes and effects, are supposed to make possible the production of satisfactory arguments of the required kind.

It is clear that, if the Causal Theorist proceeds on the lines which I have just indicated, he cannot possibly be accused of having *asserted* that material objects are unobservable in the sense under consideration; for he has gone to some trouble in an attempt to show how we may be reasonably assured of the existence of particular material objects. But it may be argued that (in which is perhaps a somewhat special sense of "consequence") it is an unwanted consequence of the CTP that material objects are unobservable: for if we accept the contentions of the CTP (1) that perceiving is to be analysed in causal terms, (2) that knowledge about perceived objects depends on causal inference, and (3) that the required causal inferences will be unsound unless suitable general principles of correspondence can be provided, then we shall have to admit that knowledge about perceived objects is unobtainable: for the general principles offered, apart from being dubious both in respect of truth and in respect of status, fail to yield the conclusions for which they are designed; and more successful substitutes are not available. If this is how the criticism of the CTP is to be understood, then I shall not challenge it, though I must confess to being in some doubt whether this is what actual critics have really meant. My comment on the criticism is now that it is unsympathetic in a way that is philosophically important.

There seem to me to be two possible ways of looking at the CTP. One is to suppose an initial situation in which it is recognized that, while appearance is ultimately the only guide to reality, what appears to be the case cannot be assumed to correspond with what is the case. The problem is conceived to be that of exhibiting a legitimate method of arguing from appearance to reality. The CTP is then regarded as a complex construction designed to solve this problem; and if one part of the structure collapses, the remainder ceases to be of much interest. The second way of looking at the CTP is to think of the causal analysis of perceiving as something to be judged primarily on its intrinsic merits and not merely as a part of a solution to a prior epistemological problem, and to recognize that some version of it is quite likely to be correct; the remainder of the CTP is then regarded as consisting (1) of steps which appear to be forced upon one if one accepts the causal analysis of perceiving, and which lead to a sceptical difficulty, and (2) a not very successful attempt to meet this difficulty. This way of looking at the CTP recognizes the possibility that we are confronted with a case in which the natural dialectic elicits distressing consequences (or rather apparent consequences) from true propositions. To adopt the first attitude to the exclusion of the second is both to put on one side what may well be an acceptable bit of philosophical analysis and to neglect what might be an opportunity for deriving philosophical profit from the exposure of operations of the natural dialectic. This, I suggest, is what the critics have tended to do; though, no doubt, they might plead historical justification, in that the first way of looking at the CTP may have been that of actual Causal Theorists.

It remains for me to show that the CTP can be looked upon in the second way by exhibiting a line of argument, sceptical in character, which incorporates appropriately the elements of the CTP. I offer the following example. In the fundamental type of case, a *bona fide* claim to perceive a particular material object *M* is based on sense-datum statements; it is only in virtue of the occurrence of certain sense-impressions that the claimant would regard himself as entitled to assert the existence of *M*. Since the causal analysis of perceiving is to be accepted, the claim to perceive *M* involves the claim that the presence of *M* causally explains the occurrence of the appropriate sense-impressions. The combination of these considerations yields the conclusion that the claimant accepts the existence of *M on the grounds that* it is required for the causal explanation of certain sense-impressions; that is, the existence of *M* is a matter of causal inference from the occurrence of the sense-impressions. Now a model case of causal inference would be an inference from smoke to fire; the acceptability of such an inference involves the possibility of establishing a correlation between occurrences of smoke and occurrences of fire, and this is only possible because there is a way of establishing the occurrence of a fire otherwise than by a causal inference. But there is supposed to be no way of establishing the existence of particular material objects except by a causal inference from sense-impressions; so such inferences cannot be rationally justified. The specification of principles of correspondence is of course an attempt to avert this consequence by rejecting the smoke-fire model. [If this model is rejected recourse may be had to an assimilation of material objects to such entities as electrons, the acceptability of which is regarded as being (roughly) a matter of their utility for the purposes of explanation and prediction; but this assimilation is repugnant for the reason that material objects, after having been first contrasted, as a paradigm case of uninvented entities, with the theoretical constructs or *entia rationis* of the scientist, are then treated as being themselves *entia rationis*.]

One possible reaction to this argument is, of course, "So much the worse for the causal analysis of perceiving"; but, as an alternative, the argument itself may be challenged, and I shall conclude by mentioning, without attempting to evaluate, some ways in which this might be done. (1) It may be argued that it is quite incorrect to describe many of my perceptual beliefs (*e.g.*, that there is now a table in front of me) as "inferences" of any kind, if this is to be taken to imply that it would be incumbent upon me, on demand, to justify by an argument (perhaps after acquiring further data) the contention that what appears to me to be the case actually is the case. When, in normal circumstances, it looks to me as if there were a table before me, I am entitled to say flatly that there is a table before me, and to reject any demand that I should justify my claim until specific grounds for doubting it have been indicated. It is essential to the sceptic to assume that any perceptual claim may, without preliminaries, be put on trial and that innocence, not guilt, has to be proved; but this assumption is mistaken. (2) The allegedly 'fundamental' case (which is supposed to underlie other kinds of case), in which a perceptual claim is to be establishable purely on the basis of some set of sense-datum statements, is a myth; any justification of a particular perceptual claim will rely on the truth of one or more further propositions about the material world (for example, about the percipient's body). To insist that the 'fundamental' case be selected for consideration is, in effect, to assume at the start that it is conceptually legitimate for me to treat as open to question all my beliefs about the material world at once; and the sceptic is not entitled to start with this assumption. (3) It might be questioned whether, given that I accept the existence of *M* on the evidence of certain sense-impressions, and given also that I think that *M* is causally responsible for those sense-impressions it follows that I accept the existence of *M on the grounds that* its existence is required in order to account for the sense-impressions. (4) The use made of the smoke-fire model in the sceptical argument might be criticized on two different grounds. *First,* if the first point in this paragraph is well made, there are cases in which the existence of a perceived object is not the conclusion of a causal inference, namely those in which it cannot correctly be described as a matter of inference at all. *Secondly,* the model should never have been introduced; for whereas the proposition that fires tend to cause smoke is supposedly purely contingent, this is not in general true of propositions to the effect that the presence of a material object possessing property *P* tends to (or will in standard circumstances) make it look to particular persons as if there were an object possessing *P*. It is then an objectionable feature of the sceptical argument that it first treats non-contingent connexions as if they were contingent, and then complains that such connexions cannot be established in the manner appropriate to contingent connexions. The non-contingent character of the proposition that the presence of a red (or round) object tends to make it look to particular people as if there were something red (or round) before them does not, of course, in itself preclude the particular fact that it looks to me as if there were something red before me from being explained by the presence of a particular red object; it is a non-contingent matter that corrosive substances tend to destroy surfaces to which they are applied; but it is quite legitimate to account for a particular case of surface-damage by saying that it was caused by some corrosive substance. In each case the effect might have come about in some other way.

VII

I conclude that it is not out of the question that the following version of the CTP should be acceptable: (1) It is true that *X* perceives *M* if, and only if, some present-tense sense-datum statement is true of *X* which reports a state of affairs for which *M*, in a way to be indicated by example, is causally responsible, and (2) a claim on the part of *X* to perceive *M*, if it needs to be justified at all, is justified by showing that the existence of *M* is required if the circumstances reported by certain true sense-datum statements, some of which may be about persons other than *X*, are to be causally accounted for. Whether this twofold thesis deserves to be called a Theory of Perception I shall not presume to judge; I have already suggested that the first clause neither obviously entails nor obviously conflicts with Phenomenalism; I suspect that the same may be true of the second clause. I am conscious that my version, however close to the letter, is very far from the spirit of the original theory; but to defend the spirit as well as the letter would be beyond my powers.

C. H. Whiteley

Physical Objects

The problem I shall discuss is What reason have we for believing that there are physical objects? My purpose is not either to raise or to dispel doubts as to the existence of physical objects; this doubt constitutes a medical rather than a philosophical problem. The point of asking the question is that, while there can be no reasonable difference of opinion as to whether there are physical objects, there can be and is reasonable difference of opinion as to how the notion of a physical object is to be analysed; and if we are clear as to what

From C. H. Whiteley, "Physical Objects," *Philosophy*, Vol. 34 (1959). Reprinted by permission of the author and of the editor of *Philosophy*.

C. H. Whiteley (1911–) is Professor of Philosophy at the University of Birmingham. He has been a Visiting Professor at Brown University.

grounds there are for believing in physical objects, we shall also be clearer as to what sort of physical objects we have grounds for believing in. Also, it is worth while to inquire which other beliefs are logically connected with, and which are logically independent of, the belief in physical objects.

I make one important assumption at the outset: namely, that by a physical object or process we mean something that exists or occurs apart from and independently of our perceptions, and of our experiences of other kinds. The distinction between the physical or "real" world and the "subjective" or "imaginary"—illusions, hallucinations, after-images, shadows, rainbows, mental pictures, what we merely suppose, imagine or expect—is a distinction between things and events which exist or occur whether anybody is aware of them or not, and things and events which have their being only as and when somebody is aware of them. A belief in physical objects is a belief in things which are sometimes at least unobserved by the believer.

It is obvious that the existence of such things is not a question to be settled by sense-perception alone. That there is a material world cannot be established or even made plausible merely by looking, listening, touching; it is not *given* in the way in which the existence of something red and something round, of sounds, smells, aches, feelings of sadness, can be given. I do not mean that the something red or round cannot be a physical object; I mean that it cannot be known to be a physical object just by looking at it or otherwise perceiving it. For I cannot, simply by perceiving something, tell whether that something continues to exist when I cease to perceive it. This logical necessity is not evaded by naïve realism, which holds that the something red or round which appears to sight is (usually at least) identical with a physical object; for though this may be so, we cannot know it just by looking. Nor is it evaded by phenomenalism; for no phenomenalist does or plausibly could analyse statements about physical objects into statements asserting the *actual* occurrence of sense-data; he must add statements about what sense-data *would* be sensed if certain conditions were fulfilled; and this fact is not given by sense-perception, but reasons for it are required. That there are physical objects is not something we observe or perceive, but something we suppose or assume (to call it a "hypothesis" or "postulate" is to suggest something rather too deliberate and self-conscious). In old-fashioned language, it is a transcendent belief; it goes beyond the evidence.

Thus there is no logical absurdity in denying or refusing to admit the existence of a material world. To say that there are no physical objects, while doubtless very foolish, does not involve a man in any logical contradiction, nor does it force him to shut his eyes to any patent and indisputable facts. An intellectually indolent percipient, whose few wants were supplied independently of his own efforts, might well abstain from supposing that there was a physical world. There is some evidence that young babies, who are more or less in this situation, do not believe that there are any material things—do not believe, for instance, that the rattle just dropped from the hand and the visitor just departed from the room are now anywhere at all.

If somebody did behave like this, in what way would he be worse off, and what other beliefs would he be debarred from entertaining? I answer—and this is my principal point—that he would be unable to make valid generalizations, or reliable forecasts of his future experience. He would have to do without the belief in an order in nature, in regular sequences of events, in causal laws. For if I confine myself to what I myself observe or am aware of, I can make no valid generalizations concerning the concomitance or sequence of types of phenomena. I find only that phenomena of one type are quite often accompanied or followed by phenomena of another type, but sometimes not. There is no type of sense-datum A of which it is true that whenever it occurs another type of sense-datum B accompanies or follows or precedes it. And this is the case however complex you make your . . . A and your B. This point has often been overlooked. People know quite well that lightning is always accompanied by thunder, barking by the presence of dogs, that green apples are always sour, and the ground always gets dark and sticky after a heavy fall of rain; and they talk about these as though they were *phenomenal* regularities—as though the seeing of lightning always went along with the hearing of thunder, and so forth. But this is of course not the case. If, as some people have said, it was the business of science to disclose the order or regularity in phenomena, meaning by phenomena what we see and hear and feel, science would be a very unrewarding pursuit. For phenomena are disorderly and irregular, and scientists cannot make them out any different.

Many philosophers have indeed thought that natural regularities could be conceived without the postulation of actual unobserved things and events, if instead we postulate that certain phenomena would occur or would have occurred, given certain unfulfilled conditions. Instead of saying that whenever I hear barking there exists an actual dog, perceived or unperceived, I am to say that whenever I hear barking, I should perceive a dog if certain conditions were fulfilled—if my eyes were open and my sight normal, if there was an adequate amount of light, if I looked in the right direction and there was no opaque obstacle in my line of vision, etc. Such an interpretation in terms of possible phenomena would relieve us of any need to postulate another order of physical events over and above perceptual events, and would in this way be more economical. There are, however, three ways in which phenomenal generalizations of this kind cannot take the place of physical generalizations.

(1) A physical generalization associates one uniform property with another uniform property: I mean that when something is asserted to be universally true of dogs, or pieces of iron, or cases of pneumonia, or falling bodies of a weight of ten pounds, it is assumed that there is some physical property or group of properties which is common to all dogs, pieces of iron, etc. Phenomenal generalizations, however, concern associations between sets of diverse phenomena. If we wish to correlate the auditory phenomenon of barking with visual phenomena we must specify a set of canine sense-data, or views of dogs, which are not all alike in any sensory property, but form one class only in virtue of a very complex set of relations.

(2) A physical generalization applies to *all* cases of a given type, and the study of nature aims at reducing to laws all events and all features of events. But phenomenal generalizations can never apply to all cases of a given type, but only to some of them, namely to those cases in which the supplementary conditions for observation are fulfilled. The physical generalization "There's no smoke without fire" applies to all instances of smoke, whether or not either the smoke or the fire is observed. But the corresponding phenomenal generalization brings under a uniformity-rule only those cases in which both the

smoke and the fire are observed. Observed smoke can be correlated with observed fire; but when I observe the smoke but not the fire, the observed smoke is correlated with nothing, and is an instance of no natural law (except in the forced and trivial sense in which a white cat with brown eyes and quick hearing is an instance of the law that all white cats with blue eyes are deaf); it forms no part of the order of nature.

(3) A phenomenal generalization must always include a reference to conditions of observation, whereas physical generalizations are independent of these. We can say without qualification "Whenever it thunders, it lightens". But we can say "Whenever thunder is heard, lightning is seen" only if we add "provided that there is an observer with adequate eyesight, facing in the appropriate direction, having his eyes open and his view not obscured by any opaque object, etc." This difference does not merely prevent the phenomenal generalization from adequately replacing the physical one. It also means that there can be no generalizations on the phenomenal level which are universally valid. For it is impossible to give in purely phenomenal terms an adequate statement of all the conditions required for perceiving lightning besides the occurrence of lightning. It is curious that the analysis of physical-object statements in terms of sense-data and the analysis of causation in terms of regular sequence should have been so often advocated by the same philosophers. For if we restrict our attention to phenomena, we can find no instances for the regular-sequence concept of cause to apply to.

If, therefore, I am to make reliable generalizations about the course of events, and reliable forecasts about my future experiences, I must suppose that there are unperceived as well as perceived events. Thus the connection between the category of substance and that of cause is, as Kant suggested, not fortuitous but necessary. We do not discover that there are (perfect) regularities in nature, that is, in the physical world, as we discover that there are (imperfect) regularities amongst phenomena. On the contrary, the regularity is essential to the concept of nature; the assumption that the physical world is orderly is inseparable from the assumption that the physical world exists. It is only to the extent that I assume it to be orderly that I have any grounds for believing that there is a physical world at all. This may help to account for our strong inclination to regard physical determinism as a necessary *a priori* truth.

What, then, is the sort of supposition which will make it possible to believe in regular sequences and concomitances in the world, and to regulate our expectations accordingly? A simple and comprehensive answer cannot be given to this question. The precise character of the suppositions we make about physical objects and processes is subject to variation for different kinds of case, and to modification with the improvement of our knowledge. One can, however, indicate the general line which must be followed.

There are, amongst the events which we are aware of, certain associations of characteristics which, while not invariable, are very common: for example, the association between the sound of barking and the sight of dogs, between the visual appearance of oranges and their characteristic flavour, between the brightness of sunshine and felt warmth, between the kinaesthetic sensations of speech and the sound of my own voice, between the visible immersion of a lump of sugar in a cup of tea and its gradual disappearance, between the various members of the visible sequence black-coal . . . flame . . . red-coal . . . ashes, between the patter of raindrops, the sight of rain falling, the feeling of dampness on exposed parts of the body, and the darkening of the soil or pavement. (These are, of course, examples of several different kinds of association.)

The supposition required has two parts: (1) That to these imperfect phenomenal regularities there corresponds in each case a perfect physical regularity, that is, in each case in which there is a frequent association between phenomenal characteristics there are some corresponding physical characteristics which are invariably associated. Whereas the sound of barking is often but not always accompanied by the sight of a dog, there is some type of event, physical barking, which is always accompanied by the presence of some one type of physical object, a dog. Whereas the visual brightness of sunshine is only sometimes accompanied by a feeling of warmth, there is a physical entity, sunlight, and a physical entity, heat, which always goes with it. Whereas a person may be seen setting off from A and arriving at B without being seen at intermediate places at intermediate times, physical passage from A to B involves the temporally continuous traversing of a spatially continuous path. In general, whenever there is an imperfect but frequent association between a phenomenal characteristic A and a phenomenal characteristic B, there is a thing or process having a characteristic corresponding to A which is invariably associated with a thing or process having a characteristic corresponding to B. Thus whenever I hear barking, there exists a physical dog, whether or not there also occurs the experience of my seeing him.

(2) The existence of the corresponding physical thing, or the occurrence of the corresponding physical process, is a necessary but not a sufficient condition for the awareness of the phenomenal characteristic. There can be no hearing of barks without there being (physical) barks; but there can be barks without the hearing of barks. The further conditions, other than the existence of the dog or the occurrence of the bark, which are required if I am to have the corresponding perception of the dog or the bark, may be called the observation-conditions. Some of these conditions are pretty easy to discover. For instance, if I am to see anything at all, there must be a certain amount of light (but not enough to dazzle), and my vision must not be blocked by any obstacle. Other observation-conditions can only be discovered by much experimental research: for instance, the need for air or some other transmitting medium in the case of hearing, the need for integrity of the optic nerves in the case of sight. The occurrence of the appropriate sense experience is determined jointly by the corresponding physical process and the relevant observation-conditions. (These conditions, of course, concern the properties of other physical things and processes, so that we cannot say just what they are without knowing something about physical things other than the one to be perceived. Learning about the properties of dogs, and learning about the properties of light and the human sense-organs, go hand in hand.) Thus the assumption of a physical world involves two supposed sets of regularities: an association between one physical characteristic and another, and an association between physical processes together with observation-conditions on the one hand and sense-experiences on the other.

So far, the physical world has been presented as a set of processes which occur independently of perceptions, which are related by laws of sequence and concomitance to other processes, and which together with the relevant observation-conditions determine specific sense-experiences of ours. These are purely relational properties; and nothing has been said so far about any other properties that physical objects may possess. On the view here advocated, namely that the justification of a belief in a physical world is that it makes possible the formulation of laws of nature, the only positive reason for attributing a property to physical objects would be that by assuming physical objects to possess this property we can account for the character of our perceptions, and explain how we come to perceive this rather than that, now rather than then. One way of accounting for the character of our perceptions would be to suppose that the sensory qualities which are present in them (the particular colours, sounds, tastes, etc.) are properties of physical objects, and persist unperceived just as they appear when perceived. This is naïve realism. A completely naïve-realist theory would hold that all sensory qualities are properties of physical objects, and exist independently of perception; other theories are naïvely realistic to the extent that they identify the properties of physical things with those properties which are present in sense-experience.

Now the investigation of the properties of physical things is the business of the science of physics. And contemporary physics is not naïvely realistic in any degree. The properties which it attributes to physical objects are not sensory properties, but hypothetical properties defined by their relations to one another and to certain kinds of perceptions. The reason for this is often misunderstood. Philosophical criticism of naïve realism is apt to concentrate on the "argument from illusion", that is, on the *deceptiveness* of sense-perception. This is the wrong sort of criticism. Our perceptions can sometimes mislead us (that is, lead us to form false expectations about other perceptions to come) only because they also, and more often, lead us to form true expectations; perception could not be systematically misleading. But the question whether our perceptions induce in us true or false expectations is quite independent of the question whether they show us the permanent characteristics of material things. The damaging criticisms of naïve realism rest on this principle: given that the physical object corresponding to a given sense-datum is something which, in conjunction with the relevant observation-conditions, determines the characteristics of that sense-datum, then if a given characteristic can be shown to be determined by the observation-conditions, there can be no reason for attributing it to the corresponding physical object. The successive modifications in our concept of the physical world arise from our increasing knowledge of the dependence of sensory properties upon observation-conditions. The challenge to naïve realism with respect to colours comes from optics. The challenge to naïve realism with respect to space and time comes from relativity-theory. The challenge to naïve realism with respect to beauty and ugliness comes from our understanding of the dependence of aesthetic delight and disgust upon the dispositions and past experiences of the subject.

In abandoning naïve realism, scientific theory only carries further a process which pre-scientific common sense has already begun. The common-sense view of the physical world is by no means a purely naïve-realist view. When I look at an object from different angles and in different lights successively, the sensory properties which appear to me are many and various. Common sense does not hold that all these various sensory properties belong to the physical object and exist apart from my perception. Were that so, there would have to be either a multitude of physical objects or a constantly changing object to possess all these different properties. Common sense holds, on the contrary, that there is but one object with one shape, size, colour etc., which are unchanging throughout my changing perceptions. This postulation of a single set of physical properties corresponding to a multiplicity of sensory properties is the first and fundamental step away from naïve realism. A Berkeleian analysis, which reverses this step, is a greater affront to common sense and provokes more resistance from it than a Lockean analysis which takes a step or two further in the same direction.

It is a belief of common sense that at least some sensory properties are not properties of physical objects, but are due to conditions of observation (quantity and quality of light, distance, defects of vision, etc.). As to whether *any* sensory properties are also physical properties, I am not convinced that common sense has any clear and consistent view. Of course we say that grass is green and roses are red. But does this mean more than that if we look at them under suitable conditions green and red are the colours we shall see? It is not clear to me that common sense is committed to the belief that objects have any colours when unperceived. (Examining the way we talk about the matter is of no help. Given that a certain piece of cloth looks bluish in artificial light and greyish in daylight, are we to presume that its colour changes with changes in the light, and say "It *is* blue in artificial light and grey in daylight", or are we to presume that it has a colour independently of the light, and say "It is really grey, but it looks blue in artificial light"? Ordinary idiom allows us to say either of these things indifferently.) By contrast, there are some properties which common sense does attribute to physical objects apart from perception—size and weight, for instance. When I conclude that this brick must have made that hole in the window, though nobody saw it do so, I credit the brick with having a size and weight at a time when it was not being perceived. But size and weight are not sensory properties. Blueness is a way things look; but heaviness is not a way things look or feel. A thing can, of course, look or feel heavy; but its *being* heavy is something different—it is heavy if it will hold down or make dents in other objects, if you can't lift it with one hand, and so on; and these causal characteristics are not ways of looking or feeling. Properties like size and weight, which common sense does attribute to unperceived objects, bear the same sort of relation to sense-experience as the concepts of modern physics. Thus it seems to me that one can abandon naïve realism in all its forms without abandoning any belief to which common sense is committed.

To sum up. That there are physical objects is a supposition, not a datum. The use of the supposition is to account for the regularities in sensory phenomena, to enable the course of events to be set in a framework of regular sequences and concomitances. It is confirmed by the success we achieve in ordering our experiences by its aid, in making our generalizations continually more extensive and more exact. Being a supposition, and not an inevitable and invariable category of thought, it is subject to modification as we learn more about the conditions under which perception takes place. Scientific concepts are related to sense-experience in a remoter and more complex fashion than common-sense concepts of physical objects. But they are not of an entirely different order. The common-sense concept of "table" is not, like "blue" or "bang" or "stench", a merely phenomenal concept; it is explanatory and theoretical.

For Further Reading

Armstrong, D. M., *Perception and the Physical World,* 1961.
Austin, J. L., *Sense and Sensibilia,* 1962.
Ayer, A. J., *Foundations of Empirical Knowledge,* 1947.
———, *Language, Truth, and Logic,* 1948, Chap. 7.
———, *Philosophical Essays,* 1954, Chaps. 4–6.
———, *The Problem of Knowledge,* 1956, Chap. 3.
Berlin, Isaiah, "Empirical Propositions and Hypothetical Statements," *Mind,* Vol. 59 (1950).
Broad, C. D., "Berkeley's Denial of Immaterial Substance," *Philosophical Review,* Vol. 63 (1954).
———, *The Mind and Its Place in Nature,* 1929, Chap. 4.
———, "Phenomenalism," *Proceedings of the Aristotelian Society,* Vol. 15 (1914–15).
———, *Scientific Thought,* 1927, Part II.
Chisholm, R. M., *Perceiving: A Philosophical Study,* 1957.
———, "The Theory of Appearing," in Black, M. (ed.), *Philosophical Analysis,* 1950.
———, "Theory of Knowledge," in R. M. Chisholm, *et al., Philosophy,* pp. 312–24.
Feigl, Herbert, "Existential Hypotheses," *Philosophy of Science,* Vol. 17 (1950).
Firth, Roderick, "Phenomenalism," in *American Philosophical Assn., Eastern Division,* Vol. 1 (1952).
———, "Radical Empiricism and Perceptual Relativity," *Philosophical Review,* Vol. 59 (1950).
———, "Sense Data and the Percept Theory," *Mind,* Vols. 58 and 59 (1949 and 1950).
Grice, H. P., "The Causal Theory of Perception," *Proceedings of the Aristotelian Society,* Supplementary Vol. 35 (1961).
Hardie, W. F. R., "Ordinary Language and Perception," *Philosophical Quarterly,* Vol. 5 (1955).
———, "Paradox of Phenomenalism," *Proceedings of the Aristotelian Society,* Vol. 46 (1945–46).
Hirst, R. J., *The Problems of Perception,* 1959.
———, Wyburn, G. M., and Pickford, R. W., *Human Senses and Perception,* 1964, Part III.
Lean, Martin, *Sense Perception and Matter,* 1953.
Lewis, C. I., *An Analysis of Knowledge and Valuation,* 1946, Chaps. 7–9.
———, *Mind and the World Order,* 1929.
———, "Reply to Chisholm," *Journal of Philosophy,* Vol. 45 (1948).

Lovejoy, A. O., *The Revolt Against Dualism,* 1930.
Marhenke, P., "Phenomenalism," in Black, M. (ed.), *Philosophical Analysis,* 1950.
Moore, G. E., *Philosophical Papers,* 1959, Chap. 7.
———, *Philosophical Studies,* 1922.
———, *Some Main Problems of Philosophy,* 1953, Chaps. 2 and 5–7.
———, "Visual Sense Data," in Mace, C. A. (ed.), *British Philosophy at Mid-Century,* 1957, pp. 205–11.
Mundle, C. W. K., "Common Sense *vs.* Hirst's Theory of Perception," *Proceedings of the Aristotelian Society,* Vol. 60 (1959–60).
Price, H. H., "The Argument from Illusion," in Lewis, H. D. (ed.), *Contemporary British Philosophy,* 1956.
———, *Hume's Theory of the External World,* 1940.
———, "Mill's View of the External World," *Proceedings of the Aristotelian Society,* Vol. 27 (1926–27).
———, *Perception,* 1933, *passim.*
Russell, Bertrand, *The Analysis of Matter,* 1927.
———, *Mysticism and Logic,* 1932.
———, *Our Knowledge of the External World,* 1928.
———, *The Problems of Philosophy,* Chaps. 1–3.
Ryle, Gilbert, *Concept of Mind,* 1949, Chap. 7.
———, *Dilemmas,* 1954, Chap. 7.
"Seeming" (Symposium), *Proceedings of the Aristotelian Society,* Supplementary Vol. 26 (1952).
Sellars, Wilfrid, *Science, Perception, and Reality,* 1963, Chap. 3.
Stace, W. T., "The Refutation of Realism," *Mind,* Vol. 43 (1934).
———, *Theory of Knowledge and Existence,* 1932, Chap. 6.

9

TYPES OF EMPIRICAL KNOWLEDGE: THE CONSCIOUS STATES OF OTHER PERSONS

It is often clear to us that a person is in a particular perceptual state: that Mr. X sees Mr. Y, that Mr. X does not hear what is being said, or that Mr. X smells smoke. A great deal about the opinions of other persons sometimes seems clear as well: we think we know their views on politics, theology, history, and the qualities of themselves and other persons. Again, we assume we have considerable knowledge of the moods and affective states of other persons: they are angry, happy, sad, remorseful, fearful, or in pain.

The traditional sceptic finds a familiar problem in these beliefs: a gap between the evidence and our supposed knowledge. This gap may lead him to adopt a sceptical form of solipsism (see the Russell selection in Chapter 6). But, since the charges of the sceptic concerning beliefs about the past and about physical things may have been met by various kinds of reasoning in the preceding two chapters, the question now is whether knowledge of the conscious states of other persons involves a *special type* of problem—one that cannot be solved by the forms of reasoning used earlier. Many contemporary philosophers think it does.

Whether a special problem exists depends on what it is for a person to perceive, for something to look red to him, for him to have an opinion, to be in pain, and so on. In other words, it depends on an analysis of perceiving, looking red, having an opinion, being in pain, and so on. There is one way of construing these things so that there is no special problem, and persons who do so are often called "logical behaviorists." According to their view all of these things share, at least roughly, the logical structure of the property "water solubility"; they are construed as *behavioral dispositions of the body* of the person to whom the property is ascribed. And, of course, the belief that a body has a certain behavioral disposition can be justified, given appropriate observations of its past behavior, by forms of inference we have already discussed—indeed by a rather simple form of inductive generalization based on how the body behaved earlier under certain circumstances.

Few, if any, current philosophers espouse logical behaviorism; thus no example of the view appears below. Some psychologists, however, do accept it at least for certain predicates. For instance, they suggest that what it is for a rat to *think* there is water at the end of a certain runway is for it to be the case that, after being deprived of water for three hours, he will if placed at a choice-point very probably go down the runway and have a drink. The reasons contemporary philosophers are dubious about the validity of logical behaviorism, at least for human beings, are, first, that whatever behavioral definition may be offered for "X believes Y," "X wants Y," it is easy to specify conditions in which the defining phrase might apply to an individual but not the definiendum, and conversely. Perhaps we should say it is *relatively* easy, for the issue is controversial: some would say that when the definition has become suitably complex such conditions cannot be specified. Second, philosophers point out that it is possible, when analyzing one's own conscious states, to *distinguish* belief or desire, say, from the actions referred to in a behavioristic definition of those states; for instance, they hold that it is one thing to want a drink and another to express this want in behavior in any way, that it is not *contradictory* to assert that either the want or the behavior occurred without the other.

But if predicates like wanting, thinking, and feeling cannot be defined as dispositions to behave in certain ways, is there anything general that can be said about what they mean? Many philosophers—this is the standard or traditional view—would say that what these predicates have in common is that part of their meaning is to designate some quality or relation which, for the person who has it and no one else, is open to direct inspection. For instance, part of what it is to be anxious, these philosophers would say, is for a person to have a feeling which he himself can be aware of by introspection, but which no one else can discern except by inference. It may even be said that since a person can inspect his own conscious states directly he can have *certain* knowledge of them. He is at least in a privileged position: he has direct access to his conscious states whereas other people can only reflect and guess. Philosophers agree, however, that not all properties of a mind can be analyzed simply in this way. For instance, to love someone is not just for an inspectable feeling to occur: it is rather, at least in part, for it to be the case that in certain complex circumstances, certain feelings *would* occur. Nevertheless, it is characteristic of the predicates in question that an analysis of them includes reference to directly inspectable events.

When a person says one of these states exists in *another* person, he is not in a position himself to observe the state that he asserts is present—only the other person can do that. It is generally thought, however, that the property he ascribes to the other person by using a phrase like "X is angry about Y" is exactly the same as the one he would ascribe to himself by using the same phrase. Not that every philosopher has agreed with this: some have thought that when one applies a word like "angry" to one's self, its meaning cannot be analyzed by reference to dispositions to behave in certain ways; whereas when one applies such a word to another, its meaning is different and can be accounted for satisfactorily through logical behaviorism. This proposal, however, seems far-fetched, and it is doubtful that many still defend it.

Philosophers have seen a special epistemological problem in justifying the ascription of mental states to other persons, then, because the property one wants to ascribe to someone else is in principle observable only by that someone else. Similarly, one's own observation of such properties will be limited to one's own case. Thus it seems that the ascription of such a property to another person must be based on *observation* of the property only in *one's own case*. This seems very different from ordinary inductive generalization, which moves from the observation of several cases (preferably under varying conditions) to the ascription of a property to an unobserved case. How then can an inferred conclusion about the state of another's mind be justified?

The sceptic, of course, will say that it cannot be. Other philosophers who are not sceptics (for example, Wittgenstein and Malcolm) have also thought that if the above statement of the problem were correct, no justification of our beliefs about other minds would be possible. Indeed, they would go further and say that if one holds that there is only private access to mental states, then not only can we not make judgments with warrant about the mental states of others; we cannot even have justified opinions about our own. There can not, it is said, be talk or thought in symbols about any essentially private facts (see the paper by Malcolm in this chapter). It is for this reason that Wittgenstein and Malcolm have sought a theory of mental properties midway between the above traditional view and that of logical behaviorism.

Rightly or wrongly, however, most philosophers have thought that the ascription of mental properties to others is warranted even if the traditional concept of mental states is preserved. Some, in fact, have thought that no inference is needed, for they have supposed that there is direct intuitive awareness of others' minds—a supposition which, of course, precludes the "private access" view of mental states. Price adverts to such a theory in his article in this chapter, although it has few if any defenders among philosophers today. Other philosophers have thought that the inference can after all be viewed as a straightforward inductive generalization on the grounds that while it is true that inductive generalization requires several instances, the many observations one can make of one's self on different occasions are sufficient to meet this requirement. Others say we can properly generalize from the reliability of a person's testimony on publicly observable facts to his general veracity and reliability—and hence to the propriety of accepting his testimony on matters (such as his having a headache) that only he can observe.

Still other philosophers, however, think that conclusions about the mental states of other persons require a mode of reasoning different from those that can be used to reach the other kinds of warranted belief we have considered. If they are right in this, the "problem" of other minds is indeed a *special* problem. They suggest that "analogical reasoning" must be used. For instance, Bertrand Russell affirms in the selection in this chapter the widely held view that a principle of analogy must be permitted if we are to infer from our data the conclusions we all share about the minds of others.

What, however, is the principle of analogy? This term is applied to various closely related forms of inference. One of these forms can be explained as follows (although Russell and some other philosophers have a somewhat different form of inference in mind). Consider two objects, A and B. Then consider the abstract properties they are known to have in common and call these the "known positive analogy." Consider further the properties in which they are known to differ and call these the "known negative analogy." Take the *number* of properties in the known positive analogy to form the numerator of a fraction whose denominator is the *sum* of this number and the number of the properties in the known negative analogy. This fraction will be $P/P + N$. We may then say that one uses an "argument by analogy" if one infers when A is known to have some property I but it is impossible to determine by observation whether or not B has it, that the *probability* that B also has I is $P/P + N$. The principle of analogy is used to support the inference to conscious states of others in what is perhaps an obvious way. Suppose I dislocate my knee, grasp it and stifle groans after I have done so, and at the same time experience severe pain. When I subsequently observe another person—who has a body very similar to mine—dislocate his knee and mumble what appear to be stifled groans, I may properly infer that he probably is feeling pain very similar to what I felt. And the same for other states of mind. The question of why we should accept arguments by analogy of course remains.

There are additional questions about analogical reasoning beyond the acceptance of the general principle. How do we decide how may properties two things have in common? Could we not, with some ingenuity, always find an indefinitely large number? (For example, should disjunctive properties be included?) What becomes of our fraction if it depends so much on ingenuity? Should we not differentiate between important and unimportant properties? However, it must be noted that some writers (for example, J. M. Keynes) find analogy not a dubious principle greatly inferior to induction but a principle central to inductive inference.

For philosophers who accept neither analogical reasoning nor inductive generalization as justifications for the inference of the conscious states of others, there is another possibility. They might claim that our beliefs about the conscious states of others are *hypotheses* which function in our explanation of observable events roughly as the theory of electrons functions in physics. The hypothesis, for instance, that a person has just received bad news may be used to explain why he is not making any witty sallies and why he looks so tense or faraway. No other known type of hypothesis—certainly not a physiological one—will do as well. There is of course one difference between such hypotheses and theories in physics: no one ever observes electrons (for instance) directly, but everyone does observe some mental states (his own) directly; this is a good reason for refusing to view the concept of mental states merely as a useful fiction. Reasoning to hypothetical beliefs about the minds of other persons in order to explain what we observe is discussed in H. H. Price's selection in this chapter.

If this theory is accepted, then the kind of inference necessary to justify beliefs that others are in a certain state of mind is not special. What is special is the problem of describing in detail what kinds of observed behavior the hypothesis of mental events explains, and just exactly how the explanation is accomplished.

Henry Habberley Price

Our Evidence for the Existence of Other Minds

I

In ordinary life everyone assumes that he has a great deal of knowledge about other minds or persons. This assumption has naturally aroused the curiosity of philosophers; though perhaps they have not been as curious about it as they ought to have been, for they have devoted many volumes to our consciousness of the material world, but very few to our consciousness of one another. It was thought at one time that each of us derives his knowledge of other minds from the observation of other human organisms. I observe (it was said) that there are a number of bodies which resemble my own fairly closely in their shape, size, and manner of movement; I conclude by analogy that each of these bodies is animated by a mind more or less like myself. It was admitted that this argument was not demonstrative. At the best it would only provide evidence for the existence of other minds, not proof; and one's alleged knowledge of other minds would only be, at the most, well-grounded opinion. It was further admitted, by some philosophers, that our belief in the existence of other minds was probably not *reached* by an argument of this sort, indeed was not reached by an argument at all, but was an uncritical and unquestioning taking-for-granted, a mere piece of primitive credulity; but, it was claimed, the belief can only be justified by an argument of this sort.

This theory, which may be called the Analogical Theory, has come in for a good deal of criticism, and has now been generally abandoned. Perhaps it has sometimes been abandoned for the wrong reasons; for some of its critics (not all) seem to have overlooked the distinction between the genesis of a belief and its justification. However this may be, I shall not discuss the theory any further at present. My aim in this paper is to consider certain other theories which have been or might be suggested in its place, and to develop one of them at some length.

With the abandonment of the Analogical Theory a very different view, which I shall call the Intuitive Theory, came into favour. It was maintained that each of us has a direct and intuitive apprehension of other minds, just as he has of his own, or at least that he intuitively apprehends some other minds on some occasions, for instance in a conversation or a quarrel. It was said that there is social consciousness as well as self-consciousness, a direct awareness of the "thou" as well as a direct awareness of the "me." I wish

From H. H. Price, "Our Evidence for the Existence of Other Minds," *Philosophy,* Vol. 13 (1938). Reprinted by permission of the author and of the editor of *Philosophy.*

to emphasize that this consciousness was held to be a form of knowing, not merely belief (however well-grounded), still less taking for granted. And I think it would have been said to be knowing by acquaintance—extrospective acquaintance as we might call it—though doubtless this acquaintance would make possible a certain amount of "knowledge about," just as when I am acquainted with a noise I may know about the noise that it is shrill or louder than some previous noise.

This view might be worked out in several different ways. Do I have extrospective acquaintance with foreign selves, or only with foreign psychical events, from which foreign selves can somehow be inferred? Or would it be said that foreign selves, and my own self too, are only logical constructions out of extrospectible or introspectible data? Again, is my extrospective acquaintance confined to human minds, or does it extend to sub-human and super-human ones, if such there be? It is certain that some who held this kind of theory thought that it did extend to super-human minds at any rate; for they thought that religious experience, or at any rate one of the types of experience covered by that label, was an extrospective acquaintance with the Divine Mind. And I suppose that some might claim an extrospective acquaintance with what we may call ex-human minds, minds which once animated human bodies, but now animate them no longer (and perhaps with ex-animal minds, if there are any?).

We should also have to ask just what the special circumstances are which make this extrospective acquaintance possible. For clearly it does not occur in all circumstances. Otherwise we should never be deceived by waxworks; we could tell at a glance whether the man we see lying by the roadside is unconscious, or dead, or only shamming; and we should know at once whether the words we hear are uttered by a gramophone or by an animate and conscious human organism.

I do not propose to pursue these questions any further. I only mention them to suggest that the theory requires a more detailed and thorough working out than it has yet received. But perhaps it is well to add that it derives no support whatever from the phenomena of telepathy. No doubt there is strong empirical evidence for the occurrence of telepathy. But the telepathic relation appears to be causal, not cognitive; it is more like infection than like knowledge. An event E_1 in mind No. 1 causes an event E_2 in mind No. 2, without any discoverable physical intermediary. It may be that E_2 resembles E_1 fairly closely. For instance, E_1 might be the seeing of a certain scene accompanied by a feeling of horror, and E_2 might be the imaging of a visual image closely resembling that scene, accompanied by a similar feeling of horror. But E_2 is not a *knowing* of E_1; just as, when you have scarlet fever and I catch it from you, my fever is not a knowing of yours.

. . .

II

The suggestion I wish to examine is that one's evidence for the existence of other minds is derived primarily from the understanding of language. I shall use the word "language" in a wide sense, to include not only speech and writing, but also signals such as waving a red flag, and gestures such as beckoning and pointing. One might say, the suggestion is that one's evidence for the existence of other minds comes from *communication*-situations. But this would be question-begging. For communication is by definition a relation between two or more minds. Thus if I have reason to believe that a communication is occurring, I must already have reason to believe that a mind other than my own exists. However, it would be true, according to the theory which I am about to consider, that the study of communication is of fundamental importance. For according to it one's most important evidence for the existence of another mind is always also evidence for the occurrence of communication between that mind and oneself. Even so, the word "communication" has to be taken in a wide sense, as the word "language" has to be. Utterances which I am not intended to hear, and writings or signals which I am not intended to see, will have to be counted as communications, provided I do in fact observe and understand them. In other words, we shall have to allow that there is such a thing as involuntary communication.

Let us consider some instances. Suppose I hear a foreign body[1] utter the noises "Look! there is the bus." I understand these noises. That is to say, they have for me a *symbolic* character, and on hearing them I find myself entertaining a certain proposition, or if you like entertaining a certain thought. (It does not matter how they came to have this symbolic character for me. The point is that they do have it now, however they got it.) As yet I only *entertain* what they symbolize, with perhaps some slight inclination towards belief; for as yet I have no decisive ground for either belief or disbelief. However, I now proceed to look round; and sure enough there is the bus, which I had not seen before, and perhaps was not expecting yet. This simple occurrence, of hearing an utterance, understanding it and then verifying it for oneself, provides some evidence that the foreign body which uttered the noises is animated by a mind like one's own. And at the same time it provides evidence that the mind in question is or recently has been in a determinate state. Either it has been itself observing the bus, or it has been observing some other physical object or event from which the advent of the bus could be inferred.

Now suppose that I frequently have experiences of this sort in connection with this particular foreign body. Suppose I am often in its neighbourhood, and it repeatedly produces utterances which I can understand, and which I then proceed to verify for myself. And suppose that this happens in many different kinds of situations. I think that my evidence for believing that this body is animated by a mind like my own would then become very strong. It is true that it will never amount to demonstration. But in the sphere of matters of fact it is a mistake to expect demonstration. We may expect it in the spheres of Pure Mathematics and Formal Logic, but not elsewhere. So much at least we may learn from Hume. If I have no direct extrospective acquaintance with other minds, the most that can be demanded is adequate *evidence* for their existence. If anyone demands *proof* of it his demand is nonsensical, at least if the word "proof" is used in the strict sense which it bears in Pure Mathematics. It is not that the demand unfortunately cannot

[1] I use a phrase "a foreign body" to mean "a body other than my own." As we shall see, it need not be a *human* body.

be fulfilled, owing to the limitations of human knowledge. It is that it cannot really be made at all. The words which purport to formulate it do not really formulate anything.

To return to our argument: the evidence will be strongest where the utterance I hear gives me new information; that is to say, where it symbolizes something which I do *not* already believe, but which I subsequently manage to verify for myself. For if I did already believe it at the time of hearing, I cannot exclude the possibility that it was my own believing which caused the foreign body to utter it. And this might happen even if my own believing were, as we say, "unconscious"; as when I have been believing for many hours that to-day is Saturday, though until this moment I have not thought about the matter. I know by experience that my believings can cause my own body to utter symbolic noises; and for all I can tell they may sometimes cause a foreign body to do the same. Indeed, there is some empirical evidence in favour of this suggestion. The utterances of an entranced medium at a spiritualistic séance do sometimes seem to be caused by the unspoken beliefs of the sitters. That one mind—my own—can animate two or more bodies at the same time is therefore not an absurd hypothesis, but only a queer one. It cannot be ruled out of court *a priori,* but must be refuted by specific empirical evidence.

It might, however, be suggested that we are demanding too much when we require that the foreign utterance should convey new information. Would it not be sufficient if the information, though not new, was, so to speak, *intrusive*—if it broke in upon my train of thought, and had no link, either logical or associative, with what I was thinking a moment before? Thus, suppose that while I am engaged in a mathematical calculation I suddenly hear a foreign body say "to-day is Saturday." I did in a sense believe this already. I have received no new information. Still, the utterance has no logical relevance to the propositions which were occupying my mind, and there was nothing in them to suggest it by association. Would not the hearing of this utterance provide me with evidence for the existence of another mind? I admit that it would, but I think the evidence would be weak. For I know by experience that my powers of concentration are exceedingly limited. Sentences proceeding from my own unconscious sometimes break in upon my train of thought in just this intrusive way. It is true that they usually present themselves to my mind in the form of verbal images. But occasionally they are actually uttered in audible whispers, and sometimes they are uttered aloud. How can I tell that these same unconscious processes in myself may not sometimes cause a foreign body to utter such intrusive noises? Their intrusive character is no bar to their unconscious origin. What we require is that they should symbolize something which I did not believe beforehand at all, even unconsciously. It is still better if they symbolize something which I *could* not have believed beforehand because I was not in a position to make the relevant perceptual observations. For instance, I hear a foreign body say "there is a black cloud on the horizon" at a time when my back is turned to the window, and then I turn round and see the cloud for myself. Or I am walking in pitch darkness in a strange house, and hear someone say "there are three steps in front of you," which I had no means of guessing beforehand; and I then verify the proposition for myself by falling down the steps.

III

It follows from what has been said that if there were a foreign body which never uttered anything but platitudes, I should be very doubtful whether it was independently animated, no matter how closely it resembled my own. In the instance given ("to-day is Saturday," when I already believe that to-day *is* Saturday) the platitude was a *singular* platitude, stating a particular matter of fact. But there are also *general* platitudes. Among these some are empirical, such as "there is always a sky above us," "all cats have whiskers"; while others are *a priori,* such as "2 + 2 = 4," or "it is either raining or not raining," and are true at all times and in all possible worlds. If there was a body which uttered only singular platitudes, I should be inclined to conclude (as we have said) that it was not independently animated; I should suspect that its noises were caused by my own believings, conscious and unconscious. If it uttered nothing but general platitudes, I might doubt whether it was animated at all. I should be inclined to think that it was a mere mechanism, a sort of talking penny-in-the-slot machine, especially if its repertoire of platitudes was limited; though it might occur to me to wonder whether any intelligent being had constructed it.

So far, then, it appears that if the noises uttered by a foreign body (or its visible gesticulations) are to provide adequately strong evidence for the existence of another mind, they must give me information. They must symbolize something which I did not know or believe beforehand, and which I then proceed to verify for myself. If these conditions are fulfilled, I have evidence of the occurrence of a foreign act of perceiving—an act of perceiving which did not form part of my own mental history. But it is not really necessary that the information conveyed should be a singular proposition, restricted to one single perceptible situation. It might be general, as if I hear a foreign body say "some cats have no tails," or "all gold dissolves in *aqua regia.*" Neither of these is restricted to one single perceptible object or situation. Still, they are both empirical, and there is a sense in which even the second can be empirically verified, or at any rate confirmed, by suitable observations and experiments. Clearly such utterances as these do give me evidence for the existence of another mind; but not in the way that the previous utterances did, such as "there is the bus," or "there is a black cloud on the horizon now." They do not show that a specific perceptual act falling outside my own mental history is now occurring, or has just occurred. In one way they show something less—merely that some perceivings of cats or of gold have occurred at some time or other. But in another way they show something more: namely, that a foreign act of *thinking* is occurring or has recently occurred, directed upon the *universals* "cat," "tail," "gold," and "aqua regia." (Or if it be objected that even perceiving involves some thinking, directed upon universals in abstraction from their instances.)

. . .

IV

In the situations hitherto mentioned the noises which I hear and understand are uttered by a foreign organism which I observe. And the foreign organism is more or less similar to my own. But of course I need not actually observe it. It suffices if I hear an intelligible and informative utterance proceeding from a megaphone or a telephone, from the next room or from behind my back. It may, however, be thought that such a foreign organism must be in principle observable if I am to have evidence of the existence of another mind, and further that it must be more or less similar to my own organism. But I believe that both of these opinions are mistaken, as I shall now try to show by examples.

There is a passage in the Old Testament which reads, "Thou shalt hear a voice behind thee saying, 'This is the way, walk ye in it.'" Now suppose that something like this did actually occur. For instance, I am lost on a mountain-top, and I hear a voice saying that on the other side of such-and-such a rock there is a sheep-track which leads down the mountain. After the best search that I can make, I can find no organism from which the voice could have proceeded. However, I go to the rock in question, and I do find a sheep-track which leads me down safely into the valley. Is it not clear that I should then have good evidence of the existence of another mind? The fact that so far as I can discover there was no organism, human or other, from which the voice proceeded makes no difference, provided I hear the noises, understand them, and verify the information which they convey. Now suppose I go up the mountain many times, and each time I hear an intelligible set of noises, conveying information which is new to me and subsequently verified; but I never find an organism from which they could have proceeded, search as I may. I should then have reason for concluding that the place was "haunted" by an unembodied mind. Such things do not happen, no doubt. But still there is no contradiction whatever in supposing them. The point is that if they did happen they would provide perfectly good evidence for the existence of another mind. And this is sufficient to show that the presence of an observable organism is not essential; *a fortiori,* the presence of an observable organism more or less resembling my own is not essential.

. . .

It appears then that I could conceivably get strong evidence of the existence of another mind even if there was no observable organism with which such a mind could be connected. This incidentally is a new and fatal argument against the old Analogical Theory which was referred to at the beginning of this paper. For that theory maintained that one's evidence of the existence of other minds could *only* come from observing foreign bodies which resemble one's own. It is also clear that even when I do observe a foreign body producing the relevant utterances, that body need not be in the least like my own. There is no logical absurdity in the hypothesis of a rational parrot or a rational caterpillar. And if there was such a creature, I could have as good evidence of its rationality as I have in the case of my human neighbours; better evidence indeed than I can have in the case of a human idiot. There is no *a priori* reason why even vegetable organisms should not give evidence of being animated by rational minds, though as it happens they never do. If the rustlings of the leaves of an oak formed intelligible words conveying new information to me, and if gorse-bushes made intelligible gestures, I should have evidence that the oak or the gorse-bush was animated by an intelligence like my own.

. . .

V

I have now tried to show by a number of examples that it is the perceiving and understanding of noises and other symbols which gives one evidence for the existence of other minds. I think it is clear that the situations I have described do provide evidence for this conclusion. But exactly *how* they do so is not yet clear. Before we discuss this question, however, there are three preliminary points to be made.

First, it is necessary to insist that there is nothing recondite about this evidence for the existence of other minds. It is not the sort of evidence which only philosophers or scientists or other experts can discover. Perhaps I have spoken as if it were suddenly presented to the notice of an intelligent and reflective adult, who has reached years of discretion without ever finding any good reasons for believing in the existence of another mind, and now finds some for the first time. But of course this is not really the position. The evidence I have spoken of is available to anyone, however youthful and inexperienced, as soon as he has learned the use of language. All that is required is that he should be able to receive information by means of words or other symbols, and that he should be able to distinguish between observing something and being told about it. (Perhaps he is not *self*-conscious until he is able to draw this distinction. If so, we may agree with those who say that consciousness of self and consciousness of others come into being simultaneously, though not with their further contention that consciousness of others is a form of acquaintance or intuitive knowledge.) Thus by the time that he has reached years of discretion evidence of the sort described is exceedingly familiar to him, little though he may have reflected upon it.

The second point is more serious. It may be objected that one cannot learn to understand language unless one *already* believes (or knows?) that the noises one hears are produced by a mind other than oneself. For if not, how would it ever occur to one that those queer noises which one hears are symbols at all? Must one not assume from the start that these noises are *intended* to stand for something? Then, but not otherwise, one can proceed to discover what in particular they stand for.

To this I reply, at first it does not occur to one that the noises *are* symbols. One has to discover this for oneself. And one discovers it by learning to *use* them as symbols in one's own thinking. One begins by merely noticing a correlation between a certain type of object and a certain type of noise, as one might notice a correlation between any other two types of entities which are frequently combined, say, thunder and lightning. The correlation is at first far from complete, for one sometimes observes the object without hearing the noise. But gradually one comes to imitate the noise for oneself. And thus the correlation becomes more nearly complete; if no foreign body says "cat" when I see a cat, I shall say "cat" myself. Thus a strong association is set up in my mind between that type of noise and that type of object. The next step after this is certainly a mysterious one, the more so as it is perhaps not literally a "next" step, but merely the continuation and completion of something which has been going on from the start. But the mystery has nothing to do with awareness of other people's intentions. It has to do with what used to be called the abstraction of universals from particulars. We must suppose that all conscious beings have the power of recognizing that two or more particulars are similar to each other. No consciousness devoid of this power would be of the faintest use to its possessor; so it must be assumed that the lower animals, if they are conscious at all, can recognize at least some similarities, namely, those which are important for their biological welfare. But only some conscious beings can single out within the similar particulars that common factor in respect of which they are similar, and can conceive of it in abstraction; that is, at times when they are not actually perceiving or remembering any particular of the sort in question. This conceiving of universals in the absence of their instances is what we commonly call thinking. And it is for this that symbols are required; conversely, noises and the like only become symbols in so far as they are used as means to such conceiving. For example, I have seen many cats, and for some time I have found that the noise "cat" occurs when I see one (whether it is uttered by a foreign body or by myself, or by both). I must now attend to the common feature of all these objects, and learn to associate the noise with that. Then, when I hear the noise in future, whether uttered by myself or not, it will bring that common feature—that universal—before my mind, even if no cat is actually being perceived by me. When this happens, and not till then, the noise "cat" has become a symbol for me. The process is very puzzling, and I do not profess to have given anything like an adequate account of it. But whatever difficulties there may be about it, it does not seem to presuppose at any stage that one has a prior knowledge of other minds, or even a prior belief in their existence.

. . .

VI

We may now return to the main argument. We have described a number of situations in which the perceiving and understanding of symbols gives one evidence of the existence of another mind. But how exactly do they provide evidence for this conclusion? Let us confine ourselves for simplicity to the cases in which the evidence comes from the hearing of sounds. Two conditions, we have seen, must be fulfilled. The first, and most important, is that they must have a symbolic character. And they must be symbolic *for me.* It is obvious that the characteristic of being symbolic is a relational character. An entity S is only a symbol in so far as it stands for some object—whatever the right analysis of "standing for" may be. It is no less obvious, though sometimes forgotten, that the relation is not a simple two-term relation. It involves at least three terms: the entity S, the object O, and in addition a mind or minds. S symbolizes O *to someone.* The relation is more like "to the right of" than it is like "larger than." A is to the right of B from somewhere, from a certain limited set of places. From other places it is not to the right of B, but to the left of it, or in front of it or behind it.

But if the hearing or seeing of S, or its presentation to me in the form of an image, is to provide me with evidence of the existence of another mind, it is not sufficient that S should symbolize some object to someone. It must symbolize some object *to me*. I myself must understand it. Otherwise all I know about it is that it is a noise or black mark having such-and-such sensible qualities. It is true that if I heard sounds uttered in the Arabic language, which I do not understand, I could reasonably conclude to the existence of another mind. But only by analogy. The sounds have some similarity to others which *are* symbolic to me; I therefore assume that they, too, might come to be symbolic to me if I took the trouble.

Secondly, it is essential, I think, that the sounds should symbolize to me something *true or false*. They must propound *propositions* to me. It is not, however, necessary that they should have the grammatical form of a statement. A single word may propound a proposition. Thus the word "snake" may be equivalent to "there is a snake in the immediate neighbourhood." Again, the phrase "the bus" may be equivalent to "the bus is now approaching." Must the proposition propounded be such that I can *test* it, whether in fact I do test it or not? It must certainly be such that I know what the world would be like if it were true. Otherwise I have not understood the symbols: for me they are not symbols at all. But it is not necessary that I should be able to discover by direct observation that the world is in fact like that, or is not. Otherwise I could not understand statements about the remote past, whereas actually I can understand them perfectly well.

The third condition is the one which we have already emphasized. The noises must not only be symbolic to me; they must give me information. The proposition which they propound must be new to me. That is, it must be new to me as a whole, though of course its constituents and their mode of combination must be familiar to me; otherwise I do not understand the utterance. If it is not new (i.e. new as a whole) the noises do still give evidence of the occurrence of a mental act other than the present act which understands them, and even of a mental act which is in a sense "foreign." But as we have seen, it might conceivably be an unconscious mental act of my own. And this greatly diminishes the evidential value of the utterance.

Now suppose these conditions are fulfilled. I hear noises which are symbolic to me; they propound to me something true or false; and what they propound is new to me. For instance, I hear the noises "here is a black cat" at a time when I do not myself see the cat and was not expecting it to appear. How exactly does this situation provide me with evidence of the existence of another mind? (It is well to insist once again that evidence, not proof, is all that can be demanded.)

It might be said: I have direct access to a number of cognitive acts by my own introspection. I find that these acts are usually accompanied by noises, audible or imaged. Moreover, I find by introspection that an act directed upon one sort of object, e.g. a cat, is usually accompanied by one sort of noise; and that an act directed upon another sort of object, e.g. blackness, is usually accompanied by another sort of noise. Thus there is a correspondence between the noises and the acts. Differences in the noises are accompanied by differences in the "direction" of the acts. When the object of the act is complex, I usually find a corresponding complexity in the noise. If n_1 usually accompanies an act directed upon O_1 and n_2 usually accompanies an act directed upon O_2, then I find that the complex noise n_1n_2 is usually accompanied by an act directed upon the complex object O_1O_2. And the structure of the complex noise (the way the constituent noises are arranged) varies with the structure of the object-complex upon which the accompanying act is directed. In this way, it may be said, I know from introspection that, when the noise-complex "here is a black cat" occurs, it is usually accompanied by a specific sort of cognitive act, namely, by the seeing and recognizing of a black cat. But this time it cannot have been a cognitive act of my own, for *I* was not seeing any black cat at the time when the noise-complex occurred. It must therefore have been a foreign cognitive act, an act extraneous to myself, and therefore presumably forming part of the history of some *other* mind.

However, such an account of the matter is not altogether satisfactory. The relation between the noises and the mental acts is really much more intimate than this. It is not a mere accompanying. If it were, the noises would not be functioning as *symbols*. When I am thinking I am always aware of symbols of some sort or another. But they do not just occur along with the thinking. The occurrence of them, whether in a sensible or an imaged form, is an integral part of the thinking itself. One might even define thinking as awareness by means of symbols. Perhaps, indeed, I can *perceive* without symbols. But in fact symbols usually are present to my mind in perceiving as well. And if they are present, again they do not merely accompany the perceiving. They enable me to analyse what I perceive, to recognize and classify the various factors in it, so that the perceiving turns into what philosophers call perceptual judgment, a piece of intelligent or thoughtful perceiving.

Thus the argument should be restated as follows: I know from introspection that noises of this sort frequently function as *instruments to* a certain sort of mental act (not merely accompany it). Therefore they are probably functioning as instruments to an act of that sort in the present case. But in the present case the act is not mine.

But there is still a further amendment to be made. There is a sense in which the noises *are* functioning as symbolic instruments to a mental act of my own. For after all, I do understand them. It is true that I am not seeing the black cat. But I do entertain the thought that a black cat is in the neighbourhood. And I think this *by means of* the noises that I hear. But if the noises are in any case functioning as instruments to a mental act of my own, what need have I to suppose that there is also some other mental act—some foreign one—to which they are instrumental?

To clear up this point, we must distinguish two different ways in which symbols can be instrumental to cognitive acts. We must distinguish *spontaneous* thinking from *imposed* thinking. In the present case, my entertaining of the thought that there is a black cat in the room is *imposed* by the noises which I hear. What causes me to use these noises as symbols is the noises themselves, or rather my hearing of them. When I hear them, they arouse certain cognitive dispositions in me (dispositions arising from my learning of English, which are there whether I like it or not); and the result is that I am forced to use them for the entertaining of a certain determinate thought, one which but for them I should not on this occasion have entertained.

But how did these noises happen to present themselves to me? I did not originate them, either consciously, or—so far as I can discover—unconsciously either. And how did they happen to be arranged in just that way? They are so arranged that they make up a whole which is for me a single complex symbol, symbolizing something true or false about the world. That is how they manage to impose an act of thought upon me, which many of the noises I hear do not, striking and complicated though they be. How did this remarkable combination of events come about? How is it that each of the noises was for me a symbol, and how is it, moreover, that they were so combined as to make a single complex symbol, symbolizing something true or false? Well, I know from my own experience how it might have happened, because I know what happens in *spontaneous* thinking. In the spontaneous acts of thinking which introspection reveals to me, noises often function as symbolic instruments. And when they do, they are not usually found in isolation. They are ordered into complexes, each of which is symbolic as a whole and signifies something true or false. It would not be correct to say that I find two acts occurring at once: on the one hand, an act of spontaneous thinking, on the other an act of spontaneously producing symbols and ordering them into a symbol-complex which is true or false as a whole. What happens is that the producing of the significant symbol-complex occurs *in the process of performing* the spontaneous act of thinking. Sometimes this spontaneous act of thinking is concerned with something which I am perceiving. It is then a so-called perceptual judgment.

Thus I can now guess how the noises which I hear have come about, and how they have come to be such and so arranged that I am made to use them as instruments for an act of imposed thinking. For I know by introspection that just such noises, and just such an arrangement of them, are often produced in the course of acts of spontaneous thinking. This makes it likely that here, too, they were produced in the course of an act of spontaneous thinking. But in this case no spontaneous thinking of that particular sort was occurring in myself. Therefore in this case the spontaneous act of thinking must have been a *foreign* act, occurring in some other mind. If the noises are "here is a black cat," the act was probably a perceptual judgment, occasioned by the perceiving of a black cat. But if on investigating the matter for myself I find no black cat, the evidence for a foreign act of thinking still stands. (As we pointed out earlier, false information is just as evidential as true.) Only I shall then have to conclude that this act of thinking was not a perceptual judgment after all, but a piece of fiction-making or story-telling.

In this instance the noise-complex was already familiar to me as a whole. I have often seen black cats and said to myself "here is a black cat." But this is not always so. When I hear a complex noise and find myself using it as an instrument for an act of imposed thinking, it frequently happens that the complex as a whole is one which I am not familiar with. Thus the noise-complex, "the steward of Common-Room keeps a tame mongoose," may be one which I have never myself made use of in an act of spontaneous thinking.

Still, if I hear it, it will impose an act of thinking on me; not less so if I am sure that what I am being made to think of is false. And it will accordingly provide me with evidence of a foreign act of spontaneous thinking. This is because I often have used the *constituents* of the noise-complex in the course of my own spontaneous thinkings, for instance the noises "mongoose" and "steward" and "Common-Room." Moreover, although this actual combination of noises is new to me, the *manner* of combination, the structure which the noise-complex has, is perfectly familiar. I have often used it myself in the course of my spontaneous thinkings. Thus the noise-complex as a whole functions as a symbol for me, and imposes an act of thinking on me, even though I have never made use of it in any of my own spontaneous thinkings.

VII

We must now raise certain general questions about this argument for the existence of other minds. Though very different in detail from the one used by the old Analogical Theory, it is clearly an argument from analogy. The form of the argument is: situations *a* and *b* resemble each other in respect of a characteristic C_1; situation *a* also has the characteristic C_2; therefore situation *b* probably has the characteristic C_2 likewise. The noises I am now aware of closely resemble certain ones which I have been aware of before (in technical phraseology, they are *tokens* of the same *type*), and the resemblance covers both their qualities and their manner of combination. Those which I was aware of before functioned as symbols in acts of spontaneous thinking. Therefore these present ones probably resemble them in that respect too; they too probably function as instruments to an act of spontaneous thinking, which in this case is not my own.

But the argument is not only analogical. The hypothesis which it seeks to establish may also be considered in another way. It provides a simple *explanation* of an otherwise mysterious set of occurrences. It explains the curious fact that certain noises not originated by me nevertheless have for me a symbolic character, and moreover are combined in complexes which are symbolic for me as wholes (i.e. propound propositions). Many varieties of sounds occur in the world, and of these only a relatively small proportion are symbolic for me. Those which are symbolic for me can occur in a variety of combinations, and the number of mathematically possible combinations of them is very large; of these combinations only a small proportion "make sense," that is, result in noise-complexes which are symbolic for me *as wholes*. But if there is another mind which uses the same symbols as I do and combines them according to the same principles, and if this mind has produced these noises in the course of an act of spontaneous thinking: then I can account for the occurrence of these noises, and for the fact that they are combined in one of these mathematically-improbable combinations. When I say that these facts are "explained" or "accounted for" by our hypothesis, I mean that if the hypothesis is true these facts are instances of a rule which is already known to hold good in a large number of instances. The rule is, that symbolically-functioning noises combined in symbolically-functioning combinations are produced in the course of acts of spontaneous thinking; and the instances in which it is already known to hold good have been presented to me by introspection.

It may be objected by some that the hypothesis is worthless because it is *unverifiable*. Accordingly it may be said that it has no explanatory power at all, nor can any argument (analogical or other) do anything to increase its probability. For being unverifiable, it is nonsensical; that is, the words which purport to formulate it do not really formulate anything which could conceivably be true or even false.

Now it is true that the hypothesis of the existence of other minds is "unverifiable" in a very narrow sense of that word, namely, if verifying a proposition entails observing some event or situation which makes it true. I cannot *observe* another mind or its acts—unless extrospective acquaintance is possible, which there is no reason to believe it is. But the hypothesis is a perfectly conceivable one, in the sense that I know very well what the world would have to be like if the hypothesis were true—what sorts of entities there must be in it, and what sort of events must occur in them. I know from introspection what acts of thinking and perceiving are, and I know what it is for such acts to be combined into the unity of a single mind (however difficult it may be to give a satisfactory philosophical *theory* of such unity). Moreover, the hypothesis *is* verifiable in what is called the "weak" sense. I know what it would be like to find evidence to support it, because I have in fact found a great deal of evidence which does support it; and this evidence can be increased without assignable limit. It seems to me to be a mistake to demand that all the different types of hypothesis should be verifiable in the same manner. What is to be demanded is, first, that the hypothesis should be conceivable (otherwise certainly it is nonsense); and secondly that it should be verifiable or refutable in its own appropriate manner, in accordance with the methods suitable to that particular sort of subject-matter.

However, it is instructive to ask what one would be left with if one refused to entertain the hypothesis of the existence of other minds on the ground of its unverifiability. It would still remain the case that one thinks by means of symbols. Further, the distinction between spontaneous and imposed thinking would still hold good. Nor could one possibly deny that in imposed thinking one acquires information which one did not possess before. It is a rock-bottom fact, and one must accept it whatever philosophy one holds, that the thinking imposed by heard or seen symbols enlarges one's consciousness of the world far beyond the narrow limits to which one's own perception and one's own spontaneous thinking would confine it.[2] An extreme empiricist must accept this fact like anyone else. But the purity of his principles prevents him from attempting any explanation of it, since they force him to conclude that the hypothesis of other minds is nonsensical. So he must just be content to accept the fact itself. Or perhaps he may say: what I *mean* by asserting that there are other minds is simply this fact, that my own consciousness of the world is constantly being enlarged by the hearing of noises and the seeing of marks which are symbolic to me, and by the consequent acts of imposed thinking which go on in me; so that "you" is just a label for certain pieces of information which I get in this fashion, and "Jones" is a label for certain other pieces of information, and so on. In that case he, too, can admit that there are other minds. Indeed, he can say it is a certainty that there are, and not merely (as we have suggested) a hypothesis for which there is strong evidence. But obviously he is giving a very strange sense to the phrase "other minds," a sense utterly different from the one which he gives to the phrase "my own mind."

If I am right, there is no need to go to such lengths. One has evidence of

[2] Here we may note that even the most rigorous course of Cartesian doubt requires the use of symbols. One cannot doubt without symbols to bring before one's mind the proposition which is to be doubted. And philosophical doubt, which is concerned with complicated and highly abstract matters, is scarcely conceivable without the use of *verbal* symbols. We may conjecture that Descartes himself conducted his doubt in French, with some admixture of Latin.

the existence of other minds in the ordinary literal sense of the word "mind," the sense in which one applies the word to oneself. Nevertheless, the argument I have offered does have its sceptical side. Any mind whose existence is to be established by it must be subject to certain restrictive conditions, which follow from the nature of the argument itself. In the first place, it must use symbols which I can understand; and I shall only be able to do this if I am able to use them myself. It is true that I may be able to guess that certain noises or marks are symbolic even if I cannot myself understand them. But this, as we have seen, is because they have a fairly close resemblance to other noises or marks which I do understand. If I never understood *any* of the noises or marks which I hear or see, I should have no evidence for the existence of other minds. (Strictly speaking we ought to add "tactual data" as well. They, too, may be symbols for the person who feels them, as the case of Helen Keller shows.)

There is a second restriction of great importance: any mind whose existence is to be established by such an argument must be aware of the same world as I am aware of. It must be such that the world which I am aware of is *public* to me and to it, *common* to both of us. This restriction really follows from the first. Unless the foreign symbols refer to objects which I too am aware of they will not be for me symbols at all. These public entities need not be sense-data. Sense-data might still be private, as many philosophers hold. It might even be, as some hold, that the sense-datum analysis of perception is mistaken from beginning to end, and that sensing is not a cognitive process at all, but is merely the being in a certain state ("seeing bluely," or the like). But still, if I am to have evidence of your existence, there must be publicity *somewhere*. Somehow or other we must both have access to one and the same world; if not by sensing, then by some other form of consciousness which sensing makes possible. Suppose this was not so. Suppose that there is another mind which is not aware of the same world which I am aware of, and suppose that it somehow produces noises which I hear or marks which I see. When it makes these noises, obviously I shall not have the faintest idea what it is talking about. How can I, since *ex hypothesi* the noises do not refer to any objects which I am aware of? But this is equivalent to saying that I have no reason whatever for thinking that it is *talking* at all. And so I shall have no reason whatever for believing that it exists, or even for suspecting that it does. The noises which I hear, even though in fact they state the profoundest truths, will be for me mere noises, like the soughing of the wind or the roaring of waves.

It appears, then, that any evidence which I can have of the existence of another mind must also be evidence that the other mind is aware of the same world as I am aware of myself. Philosophers have sometimes suggested that each mind perhaps lives in a private world of its own. Probably no one believes this. But some people have been worried by the suggestion. They have suspected that though incredible it could not be rationally refuted, and have had recourse to mysterious acts of faith to get them out of their difficulty. But the difficulty does not exist, for this speculation of philosophers is nothing but a baseless fancy. The theory is such that there could not conceivably be any evidence in favour of it. Any relevant evidence one can get is bound from the nature of the case to tell against it. Any evidence that I can get of your existence is bound also to be evidence that you do not *live* in a private world, but in the public world which is common to all intelligences, or at least to all those which can have any good reason to believe in one another's existence.

. . .

VIII

. . . [It] remains to ask how one [learns] that other minds experience emotions and volitions. The evidence so far considered, derived from the informative side of language, shows only that they are percipients and thinkers. In other words, how does one learn that there *is* an emotive element in most or all of the utterances which one hears and understands, and likewise in writing and gesture?

Let us first consider utterances expressive of volitions. How do I get my evidence that other minds experience volitions? It is because I first get evidence that they are entertaining certain thoughts, and then find that the objective world is being altered in such a way as to conform to those thoughts. For instance, I am seeing a door and I notice that it is open. I then hear the words "that the door has got to be shut." At present, we are assuming, the expressive element in language conveys nothing to me (we are trying to explain by what process it comes to do so). So at present I can make nothing of the words "has got to," nor yet of the determined tone in which they are said. It is just a curious auditory quality which the noises have. But I *can* understand the words "that door" and "be shut," both of which refer to certain objective entities which I am aware of: the one to a certain material thing which I observe, the other to an objective universal which I am familiar with. Thus they bring before my mind *a proposition,* the proposition "the door is shut." Now this is a piece of information. It tells me something new which I did not believe before; I did not believe it before, because I believed the contrary, and indeed I still do. So far, then, I have merely received a piece of false information; still it *is* information, and therefore gives me evidence of the existence of a foreign mind which is holding a false belief, or at least entertaining a false proposition. But now a curious thing happens. The organism from which the utterance emanated proceeds to move in such a way that the door *is* shut. The situation is so altered that the information which was false before is now made true. Here, then, I have got evidence of the occurrence of a foreign thought which *affects the objective world.* There was a thought with which the objective state of affairs did not correspond; and immediately afterwards the objective state of affairs is altered so that it does correspond with this thought. Apparently this thought has somehow brought about its own verification. It was false when first uttered, but it has altered the situation in such a way as to make itself true.

Normally this alteration comes about by the intermediation of certain movements in the organism from which the utterances proceeded; it gets up and shuts the door. But even if I observed no organism, I could still get evidence of the existence of a foreign volition. Let us reconsider our previous instance of a disembodied voice. Suppose I heard such voice saying, "Let there be a thunderstorm"; and suppose there promptly was a thunderstorm, although hitherto there had been no sign that any such event was likely to happen (the sky, we will assume, was perfectly clear at the moment when the utterance occurred). And suppose that there were many instances of this sort of thing; many occasions when this voice made an utterance conveying a proposition which was false at the time, but was followed by an objective change which verified it—a surprising change, which no previously observable feature in the situation made probable. I should then have good evidence for thinking that the voice proceeded from a foreign thinker whose thoughts could directly alter the objective world. Such "telekinetic" action of unembodied minds does not in fact happen. But there is no logical absurdity in it. And it is no more difficult to understand how a mind can directly cause changes in the atmosphere than to understand how it can directly cause changes in an organism, which after all is only a complex material object.

We now see how one discovers that certain utterances are expressive of volitions. If one is to discover this, the utterance which expresses the volition must also have an *informative* side. It must among other things propound a proposition, one which is at the moment false. I learn that it is expressive of a volition because of the effects by which it is followed. And when I recognize that a sentence is expressive of a volition without actually observing the physical change which fulfils it, I do so by noticing that it resembles other utterances which *have* been observed to have such effects. It resembles them in respect of tone of voice, or in grammatical structure (by containing verbs in the imperative mood), or in respect of the gestures which accompany it. So I conclude that it, like them, is probably followed by an objective change which verifies it.

Thus it is quite wrong to suppose that the utterance "directly conveys" a foreign volition. There is no question of an immediate and infallible revelation, giving me direct insight into the volition of another person. The "conveying" is a misleading name for an induction which I have to do for myself, by observing that noises uttered in a certain tone of voice are frequently followed by objective changes which verify the propositions they propound.

Let us now turn to utterances expressive of emotion. Emotions are intimately related to thinking on the one hand, to action on the other; and in virtue of these two relations, they are also intimately related to the objective world. Every emotion includes some thinking, and this thinking is not a mere accompaniment, but is an integral part of the emotion itself. The thinking may consist in holding a false belief, as when one is afraid of a purely imaginary danger. But even so, certain objective universals must be present to the mind; else there could be no belief, not even a false one. I may be afraid of a lion outside a door, when in fact there is no lion within miles. But in order to have this "groundless" fear, I must conceive of *lionhood* and *outsideness.* It follows that any utterance which completely expresses an emotion must also propound a proposition, true or false. If someone says in a horror-struck voice, "Oh! a snake!" he is incidentally making a statement which gives me information; the information is, that there is a snake in the immediate neighbourhood. But how do I learn that the tone in which he speaks *is* a tone of horror? I answer, I learn it inductively. I discover by repeated observation that when an object is spoken of in that tone of voice, certain consequences are liable to follow. The objective situation is liable to change in a remarkable manner.

The relation between the snake and the organism from which the noise proceeded does not usually remain what it was. The noise-making organism runs away, or strikes the snake with a stick. So when I hear that tone of voice again I conclude that such objective consequences are again likely to occur. We have seen that such utterances do propound propositions, and so give evidence of the occurrence of a foreign thought. But I have now found that when the utterance is in that tone of voice the foreign thought in question is a *tendencious* thought, one which tends to change the objective world in certain ways. And I can correlate differences in tone of voice (and in gesture or facial configuration) with different sorts of objective changes which are liable to follow. Thus I distinguish different sorts of tendencious thoughts, one tending to the avoidance of the object which the thought refers to, another tending to the pursuit of it, another to the destruction of it, and so on. And these are the different emotional attitudes.

It follows, and indeed is obvious in any case, that emotional attitudes and volitions are closely connected. Nevertheless, they are not expressed by the same sort of utterance. I discover that an utterance expresses a volition when I find that though false at the moment of its occurrence it results in an objective change which brings the facts into conformity with it. But utterances expressing emotions are related to subsequent objective changes in a more complex way than this. The objective change which follows varies with the specific quality of the utterance. This is not surprising. There is only one way of willing—setting yourself to bring into being the objective situation which you have thought of. But there are many different kinds of emotional attitude; one leads you to alter the objective world in one way, another in another way.

There are, however, certain emotional attitudes which appear not to influence conduct at all, and so do not affect the objective world; for instance, emotions about the past. How am I to discover that an emotion of this sterile kind is occurring in a foreign mind? The utterance which expresses it will indeed propound a proposition to me, and so give me evidence of the occurrence of a foreign thought. But it may seem that in this case the thought has no tendenciousness about it. To this I reply that if the foreign utterance really does express an emotion (and of course hypocrisy is always possible), then the thought of which it gives evidence *is* tendencious, though in rather a different way. Let us consider an emotion directed upon a historical character. Suppose that a man admires the Emperor Valentinian I. If he does, his thinking about that emperor does have effects, effects which it would not have if instead of admiring he disapproved of him. It does not affect the thinker's actions, but it does affect the course of his subsequent thoughts, and this will be revealed by subsequent utterances. We shall find, for instance, that he tends to talk about the good qualities of his hero rather than the bad ones: say, about his military efficiency rather than his atrocious bad temper. If we do not find this, we shall suspect that his utterance did not express emotion at all, but was merely a piece of hypocrisy. Thus in these cases the tendencious character of the thinking lies in the selective control which it exercises upon later thinkings, in directing the thinker's attention upon one set of facts rather than another, and even causing him to ignore certain facts altogether. Thus we may say that in these cases, as in the others, the emotion reveals itself by its tendency to affect one's subsequent relations with objects: only "objects" must be understood to include thinkable objects as well as perceived ones, and "relations" must cover cognitive relations as well as practical ones.

Bertrand Russell

Analogy

The postulates hitherto considered have been such as are required for knowledge of the physical world. Broadly speaking, they have led us to admit a certain degree of knowledge as to the space-time structure of the physical world, while leaving us completely agnostic as regards its qualitative character. But where other human beings are concerned, we feel that we know more than this; we are convinced that other people have thoughts and feelings that are qualitatively fairly similar to our own. We are not content to think that we know only the space-time structure of our friends' minds, or their capacity for initiating causal chains that end in sensations of our own. A philosopher might pretend to think that he knew only this, but let him get cross with his wife and you will see that he does not regard her as a mere spatio-temporal edifice of which he knows the logical properties but not a glimmer of the intrinsic character. We are therefore justified in inferring that his skepticism is professional rather than sincere.

The problem with which we are concerned is the following. We observe in ourselves such occurrences as remembering, reasoning, feeling pleasure, and feeling pain. We think that sticks and stones do not have these experiences, but that other people do. Most of us have no doubt that the higher animals feel pleasure and pain, though I was once assured by a fisherman that "Fish have no sense nor feeling." I failed to find out how he had acquired this knowledge. Most people would disagree with him, but would be doubtful about oysters and starfish. However this may be, common sense admits an increasing doubtfulness as we descend in the animal kingdom, but as regards human beings it admits no doubt.

It is clear that belief in the minds of others requires some postulate that is not required in physics, since physics can be content with a knowledge of structure. My present purpose is to suggest what this further postulate may be.

It is clear that we must appeal to something that may be vaguely called "analogy." The behavior of other people is in many ways analogous to our own, and we suppose that it must have analogous causes. What people say is what we should say if we had certain thoughts, and so we infer that they probably

---

From Bertrand Russell, *Human Knowledge: Its Scope and Limits,* Part VI, Chap. 8.

have these thoughts. They give us information which we can sometimes subsequently verify. They behave in ways in which we behave when we are pleased (or displeased) in circumstances in which we should be pleased (or displeased). We may talk over with a friend some incident which we have both experienced, and find that his reminiscences dovetail with our own; this is particularly convincing when he remembers something that we have forgotten but that he recalls to our thoughts. Or again: you set your boy a problem in arithmetic, and with luck he gets the right answer; this persuades you that he is capable of arithmetical reasoning. There are, in short, very many ways in which my responses to stimuli differ from those of "dead" matter, and in all these ways other people resemble me. As it is clear to me that the causal laws governing my behavior have to do with "thoughts," it is natural to infer that the same is true of the analogous behavior of my friends.

The inference with which we are at present concerned is not merely that which takes us beyond solipsism, by maintaining that sensations have causes about which *something* can be known. This kind of inference, which suffices for physics, has already been considered. We are concerned now with a much more specific kind of inference, the kind that is involved in our knowledge of the thoughts and feelings of others—assuming that we have such knowledge. It is of course obvious that such knowledge is more or less doubtful. There is not only the general argument that we may be dreaming; there is also the possibility of ingenious automata. There are calculating machines that do sums much better than our schoolboy sons; there are gramophone records that remember impeccably what So-and-so said on such-and-such an occasion; there are people in the cinema who, though copies of real people, are not themselves alive. There is no theoretical limit to what ingenuity could achieve in the way of producing the illusion of life where in fact life is absent.

But, you will say, in all such cases it was the thoughts of human beings that produced the ingenious mechanism. Yes, but how do you know this? And how do you know that the gramophone does *not* "think"?

There is, in the first place, a difference in the causal laws of observable behavior. If I say to a student, "Write me a paper on Descartes' reasons for believing in the existence of matter," I shall, if he is industrious, cause a certain response. A gramophone record might be so constructed as to respond to this stimulus, perhaps better than the student, but if so it would be incapable of telling me anything about any other philosopher, even if I threatened to refuse to give it a degree. One of the most notable peculiarities of human behavior is change of response to a given stimulus. An ingenious person could construct an automaton which would always laugh at his jokes, however often it heard them; but a human being, after laughing a few times, will yawn, and end by saying, "How I laughed the first time I heard that joke."

But the differences in observable behavior between living and dead matter do not suffice to prove that there are "thoughts" connected with living bodies other than my own. It is probably possible theoretically to account for the behavior of living bodies by purely physical causal laws, and it is probably impossible to refute materialism by external observation alone. If we are to believe that there are thoughts and feelings other than our own, that must be in virtue of some inference in which our own thoughts and feelings are relevant, and such an inference must go beyond what is needed in physics.

I am, of course, not discussing the history of how we come to believe in other minds. We find ourselves believing in them when we first begin to reflect; the thought that Mother may be angry or pleased is one which arises in early infancy. What I am discussing is the possibility of a postulate which shall establish a rational connection between this belief and data, e.g., between the belief "Mother is angry" and the hearing of a loud voice.

The abstract schema seems to be as follows. We know, from observation of ourselves, a causal law of the form "A causes B," where A is a "thought" and B a physical occurrence. We sometimes observe a B when we cannot observe any A; we then infer an unobserved A. For example: I know that when I say, "I'm thirsty," I say so, usually, because I am thirsty, and therefore, when I hear the sentence "I'm thirsty" at a time when I am not thirsty, I assume that someone else is thirsty. I assume this the more readily if I see before me a hot, drooping body which goes on to say, "I have walked twenty desert miles in this heat with never a drop to drink." It is evident that my confidence in the "inference" is increased by increased complexity in the datum and also by increased certainty of the causal law derived from subjective observation, provided the causal law is such as to account for the complexities of the datum.

It is clear that in so far as plurality of causes is to be suspected, the kind of inference we have been considering is not valid. We are supposed to know "A causes B," and also to know that B has occurred; if this is to justify us in inferring A, we must know that *only* A causes B. Or, if we are content to infer that A is probable, it will suffice if we can know that in most cases it is A that causes B. If you hear thunder without having seen lightning, you confidently infer that there was lightning, because you are convinced that the sort of noise you heard is seldom caused by anything except lightning. As this example shows, our principle is not only employed to establish the existence of other minds but is habitually assumed, though in a less concrete form, in physics. I say "a less concrete form" because unseen lightning is only abstractly similar to seen lightning, whereas we suppose the similarity of other minds to our own to be by no means purely abstract.

Complexity in the observed behavior of another person, when this can all be accounted for by a simple cause such as thirst, increases the probability of the inference by diminishing the probability of some other cause. I think that in ideally favorable circumstances the argument would be formally as follows:

From subjective observation I know that A, which is a thought or feeling, causes B, which is a bodily act, e.g., a statement. I know also that, whenever B is an act of my own body, A is its cause. I now observe an act of the kind B in a body not my own, and I am having no thought or feeling of the kind A. But I still believe, on the basis of self-observation, that only A can cause B; I therefore infer that there was an A which caused B, though it was not an A that I could observe. On this ground I infer that other people's bodies are associated with minds, which resemble mine in proportion as their bodily behavior resembles my own.

In practice, the exactness and certainty of the above statement must be softened. We cannot be sure that, in our subjective experience, A is the only cause of B. And even if A is the only cause of B in our experience, how can we know that this holds outside our experience? It is not necessary that we should know this with any certainty; it is enough if it is highly probable. It is the assumption of probability in such cases that is our postulate. The postulate may therefore be stated as follows:

If, whenever we can observe whether A and B are present or absent, we find that every case of B has an A as a causal antecedent, then it is probable that most B's have A's as causal antecedents, even in cases where observation does not enable us to know whether A is present or not.

This postulate, if accepted, justifies the inference to other minds, as well as many other inferences that are made unreflectingly by common sense.

Norman Malcolm

Knowledge of Other Minds

I

I believe that the argument from analogy for the existence of other minds still enjoys more credit than it deserves, and my first aim will be to show that it leads nowhere. J. S. Mill is one of many who have accepted the argument and I take his statement of it as representative. He puts to himself the question, "By what evidence do I know, or by what considerations am I led to believe, that there exist other sentient creatures; that the walking and speaking figures which I see and hear, have sensations and thoughts, or in other words, possess Minds?" His answer is the following:

> I conclude that other human beings have feelings like me, because, first, they have bodies like me, which I know, in my own case, to be the antecedent condition of feelings; and because, secondly, they exhibit the acts, and other outward signs, which in my own case I know by experience to be caused by feelings. I am conscious in myself of a series of facts connected by an uniform sequence, of which the beginning is modifications of my body, the middle is feelings, the end is outward demeanor. In the case of other human beings I have the evidence of my senses for the first and last links of the series, but not for the intermediate link. I find, however, that the sequence between the first and last is as regular and constant in those other cases as it is in mine. In my own case I know that the first link produces the last through the intermediate link, and could not produce it without. Experience, therefore, obliges me to conclude that there must be an intermediate link; which must either be the same in others as in myself, or a different one: I must either believe them to be alive, or to be automatons: and by believing them to be alive, that is, by supposing the link to be of the same nature

From Norman Malcolm, *Knowledge and Certainty*. © 1963, by permission of Prentice-Hall, Inc., Englewood Cliffs, N. J. This selection was first published as "Knowledge of Other Minds," *The Journal of Philosophy*, Vol. 56 (1959).

as in the case of which I have experience, and which is in all other respects similar, I bring other human beings, as phenomena, under the same generalizations which I know by experience to be the true theory of my own existence.[1]

I shall pass by the possible objection that this would be very *weak* inductive reasoning, based as it is on the observation of a single instance. More interesting is the following point: suppose this reasoning could yield a conclusion of the sort "It is probable that that human figure (pointing at some person other than oneself) has thoughts and feelings." Then there is a question as to whether this conclusion can *mean* anything to the philosopher who draws it, because there is a question as to whether the sentence "That human figure has thoughts and feelings" can mean anything to him. Why should this be a question? Because the assumption from which Mill starts is that he has *no criterion* for determining whether another "walking and speaking figure" does or does not have thoughts and feelings. If he had a criterion he could apply it, establishing with certainty that this or that human figure does or does not have feelings (for the only plausible criterion would lie in behavior and circumstances that are open to view), and there would be no call to resort to tenuous analogical reasoning that yields at best a probability. If Mill has no criterion for the existence of feelings other than his own then in that sense he does not understand the sentence "That human figure has feelings" and therefore does not understand the sentence "It is *probable* that that human figure has feelings."

There is a familiar inclination to make the following reply: "Although I have no criterion of verification still I *understand,* for example, the sentence 'He has a pain.' For I understand the meaning of 'I have a pain,' and 'He has a pain' means that he has the *same* thing I have when I have a pain." But this is a fruitless maneuver. If I do not know how to establish that someone has a pain then I do not know how to establish that he has the *same* as I have when I have a pain.[2] You cannot improve my understanding of "He has a pain" by this recourse to the notion of "the same," unless you give me a criterion for saying that someone *has* the same as I have. If you can do this you will have no use for the argument from analogy: and if you cannot then you do not understand the supposed conclusion of that argument. A philosopher who purports to rely on the analogical argument cannot, I think, escape this dilemma.

There have been various attempts to repair the argument from analogy. Mr. Stuart Hampshire has argued[3] that its validity as a method of inference can be established in the following way: others sometimes infer that I am feeling giddy from my behavior. Now I have direct, noninferential knowledge, says Hampshire, of my own feelings. So I can check inferences made about me against the facts, checking thereby the accuracy of the "methods" of inference.

All that is required for testing the validity of any method of factual inference is that each one of us should sometimes be in a position to confront the conclusions

[1] J. S. Mill, *An Examination of Sir William Hamilton's Philosophy,* 6th ed. (London: Longmans, 1889), pp. 243–44.

[2] "It is no explanation to say: the supposition that he has a pain is simply the supposition that he has the same as I. For *that* part of the grammar is quite clear to me: that is, that one will say that the stove has the same experience as I, *if* one says: it is in pain and I am in pain" (Ludwig Wittgenstein, *Philosophical Investigations* [New York: Macmillan Company, 1953], §350).

[3] "The Analogy of Feeling," *Mind,* LXI (1952), 1–12.

of the doubtful method of inference with what is known by him to be true independently of the method of inference in question. Each one of us is certainly in this position in respect of our common methods of inference about the feelings of persons other than ourselves, in virtue of the fact that each one of us is constantly able to compare the results of this type of inference with what he knows to be true directly and non-inferentially; each one of us is in the position to make this testing comparison, whenever he is the designated subject of a statement about feelings and sensations. I, Hampshire, know by what sort of signs I may be misled in inferring Jones' and Smith's feelings, because I have implicitly noticed (though probably not formulated) where Jones, Smith and others generally go wrong in inferring my feelings [pp. 4–5].

Presumably I can also note when the inferences of others about my feelings do not go wrong. Having ascertained the reliability of some inference-procedures I can use them myself, in a guarded way, to draw conclusions about the feelings of others, with a modest but justified confidence in the truth of those conclusions.

My first comment is that Hampshire has apparently forgotten the purpose of the argument from analogy, which is to provide some probability that "the walking and speaking figures which I see and hear, have sensations and thoughts" (Mill). For the reasoning that he describes involves the assumption that other human figures *do* have thoughts and sensations: for they are assumed to *make inferences* about me from *observations* of my behavior. But the philosophical problem of the existence of other minds *is* the problem of whether human figures other than oneself do, among other things, make observations, inferences, and assertions. Hampshire's supposed defense of the argument from analogy is an *ignoratio elenchi.*

If we struck from the reasoning described by Hampshire all assumption of thoughts and sensations in others we should be left with something roughly like this: "When my behavior is such-and-such there come from nearby human figures the sounds 'He feels giddy.' And generally I do feel giddy at the time. Therefore when another human figure exhibits the same behavior and I say 'He feels giddy,' it is probable that he does feel giddy." But the reference here to the sentence-like sounds coming from other human bodies is irrelevant, since I must not assume that those sounds express inferences. Thus the reasoning becomes simply the classical argument from analogy: "When my behavior is such-and-such I feel giddy; so probably when another human figure behaves the same way he feels the same way." This argument, again, is caught in the dilemma about the criterion of the *same.*

The version of analogical reasoning offered by Professor H. H. Price[4] is more interesting. He suggests that "one's evidence for the existence of other minds is derived primarily from the understanding of language" (p. 429). His idea is that if another body gives forth noises one understands, like "There's the bus," and if these noises give one new information, this "provides some evidence that the foreign body which uttered the noises is animated by a mind like one's own. . . . Suppose I am often in its neighborhood, and it repeatedly produces utterances which I can understand, and which I then proceed to verify for myself. And suppose that this happens in many different kinds of situation. I think that my evidence for believing that this body is animated by a

[4] "Our Evidence for the Existence of Other Minds," *Philosophy,* XIII (1938), 425–56.

mind like my own would then become very strong" (p. 430). The body from which these informative sounds proceed need not be a human body. "If the rustling of the leaves of an oak formed intelligible words conveying new information to me, and if gorse bushes made intelligible gestures, I should have evidence that the oak or the gorse bush was animated by an intelligence like my own" (p. 436). Even if the intelligible and informative sounds did not proceed from a body they would provide evidence for the existence of a (disembodied) mind (p. 435).

Although differing sharply from the classical analogical argument, the reasoning presented by Price is still analogical in form: I know by introspection that when certain combinations of sounds come from me they are "symbols in acts of spontaneous thinking"; therefore similar combinations of sounds, not produced by me, "probably function as instruments to an act of spontaneous thinking, which in this case is not my own" (p. 446). Price says that the reasoning also provides an *explanation* of the otherwise mysterious occurrence of sounds which I understand but did not produce. He anticipates the objection that the hypothesis is nonsensical because unverifiable. "The hypothesis is a perfectly conceivable one," he says, "in the sense that I know very well what the world would have to be like if the hypothesis were true—what sorts of entities there must be in it, and what sorts of events must occur in them. I know from introspection what acts of thinking and perceiving are, and I know what it is for such acts to be combined into the unity of a single mind . . ." (pp. 446–47).

I wish to argue against Price that no amount of intelligible sounds coming from an oak tree or a kitchen table could create any probability that it has sensations and thoughts. The question to be asked is: What would show that a tree or table *understands* the sounds that come from it? We can imagine that useful warnings, true descriptions and predictions, even "replies" to questions, should emanate from a tree, so that it came to be of enormous value to its owner. How should we establish that it understood those sentences? Should we "question" it? Suppose that the tree "said" that there was a vixen in the neighborhood, and we "asked" it "What is a vixen?" and it "replied," "A vixen is a female fox." It might go on to do as well for "female" and "fox." This performance might incline us to say that the tree understood the words, in contrast to the possible case in which it answered "I don't know" or did not answer at all. But would it show that the tree understood the words in the same sense that a person could understand them? With a person such a performance would create a presumption that he could make correct *applications* of the word in question: but not so with a tree. To see this point think of the normal teaching of words (e.g., "spoon," "dog," "red") to a child and how one decides whether he understands them. At a primitive stage of teaching one does not require or expect definitions, but rather that the child should *pick out* reds from blues, dogs from cats, spoons from forks. This involves his looking, pointing, reaching for and going to the right things and not the wrong ones. That a child says "red" when a red thing and "blue" when a blue thing is put before him, is indicative of a mastery of those words *only* in conjunction with the other activities of looking, pointing, trying to get, fetching and carrying. Try to suppose that he says the right words but looks at and reaches for the wrong things. Should we be tempted to say that he has mastered the use of those words? No, indeed. The disparity between words and behavior would make us say that he does not understand the words. In the case of a tree there could be no disparity between its words and its "behavior" because it is logically incapable of behavior of the relevant kind.

Since it has nothing like the human face and body it makes no sense to say of a tree, or an electronic computer, that it is looking or pointing at or fetching something. (Of course one can always *invent* a sense for these expressions.) Therefore it would make no sense to say that it did or did not understand the above words. Trees and computers cannot either pass or fail the tests that a child is put through. They cannot even take them. That an object was a source of intelligible sounds or other signs (no matter how sequential) would not be enough by itself to establish that it had thoughts or sensations. How informative sentences and valuable predictions could emanate from a gorse bush might be a grave scientific problem, but the explanation could never be that the gorse bush has a mind. Better no explanation than nonsense!

It might be thought that the above difficulty holds only for words whose meaning has a "perceptual content" and that if we imagined, for example, that our gorse bush produced nothing but pure mathematical propositions we should be justified in attributing thought to it, although not sensation. But suppose there was a remarkable "calculating boy" who could give right answers to arithmetical problems but could not apply numerals to reality in empirical propositions, i.e., he could not *count* any objects. I believe that everyone would be reluctant to say that he *understood* the mathematical signs and truths that he produced. If he could count in the normal way there would not be this reluctance. And "counting in the normal way" involves looking, pointing, reaching, fetching, and so on. That is, it requires the human face and body, and human behavior—or something similar. Things which do not have the human form, or anything like it, not merely do not but *cannot* satisfy the criteria for thinking. I am trying to bring out part of what Wittgenstein meant when he said, "We only say of a human being and what is like one that it thinks" (*Investigations,* §360), and "The human body is the best picture of the human soul" (*ibid.,* p. 178).

I have not yet gone into the most fundamental error of the argument from analogy. It is present whether the argument is the classical one (the analogy between my body and other bodies) or Price's version (the analogy between my language and the noises and signs produced by other things). It is the mistaken assumption that *one learns from one's own case* what thinking, feeling, sensation are. Price gives expression to this assumption when he says: "I know from introspection what acts of thinking and perceiving are . . ." (*op. cit.,* p. 447). It is the most natural assumption for a philosopher to make and indeed seems at first to be the only possibility. Yet Wittgenstein has made us see that it leads first to solipsism and then to nonsense. I shall try to state as briefly as possible how it produces those results.

A philosopher who believes that one must learn what thinking, fear, or pain is "from one's own case," does not believe that the thing to be observed is one's behavior, but rather something "inward." He considers behavior to be related to the inward states and occurrences merely as an accompaniment or possibly an effect. He cannot regard behavior as a *criterion* of psychological phenomena: for if he did he would have no use for the analogical argument (as was said before) and also the priority given to "one's own case" would be pointless. He believes that he notes something in himself that he calls "thinking" or "fear" or "pain," and then he tries to infer the presence of the *same* in others. He should then deal with the question of what his criterion of the *same* in others is. This he cannot do because it is of the essence of his viewpoint to reject circumstances and behavior as a criterion of mental phenomena in others. And what else could serve as a criterion? He ought, therefore, to draw the conclusion that the notion of thinking, fear, or pain in others is in an important sense meaningless. He has no idea of what would count for or against it.[5] "That there should be thinking or pain other than my own is unintelligible," he ought to hold. This would be a rigorous solipsism, and a correct outcome of the assumption that one can know only from one's own case what the mental phenomena are. An equivalent way of putting it would be: "When I say 'I am in pain,' by 'pain' I mean a certain inward state. When I say '*He* is in pain,' by 'pain' I mean *behavior*. I cannot attribute pain to others *in the same sense* that I attribute it to myself."

Some philosophers before Wittgenstein may have seen the solipsistic result of starting from "one's own case." But I believe he is the first to have shown how that starting point destroys itself. This may be presented as follows: one supposes that one inwardly picks out something as thinking or pain and thereafter identifies it whenever it presents itself in the soul. But the question to be pressed is, Does one make *correct* identifications? The proponent of these "private" identifications has nothing to say here. He feels sure that he identifies correctly the occurrences in his soul; but feeling sure is no guarantee of being right. Indeed he has no idea of what being *right* could mean. He does not know how to distinguish between actually making correct identifications and being under the impression that he does. (See *Investigations,* §§258–59.) Suppose that he identified the emotion of anxiety as the sensation of pain? Neither he nor anyone else could know about this "mistake." Perhaps he makes a mistake *every* time! Perhaps all of us do! We ought to see now that we are talking nonsense. We do not know what a *mistake* would be. We have no standard, no examples, no customary practice, with which to compare our inner recognitions. The inward identification cannot hit the bull's-eye, or miss it either, because there is no bull's-eye. When we see that the ideas of correct and incorrect have no application to the supposed inner identification, the latter notion loses its appearance of sense. Its collapse brings down both solipsism and the argument from analogy.

II

This destruction of the argument from analogy also destroys the *problem* for which it was supposed to provide a solution. A philosopher feels himself in a difficulty about other minds because he assumes that first of all he is acquainted with mental phenomena "from his own case." What troubles him is how to make the transition from his own case to the case of others. When his thinking is freed of the illusion of the priority of his own case, then he is able to look at the familiar facts and to acknowledge that the circumstances,

[5] One reason why philosophers have not commonly drawn this conclusion may be, as Wittgenstein acutely suggests, that they assume that they have "an infallible paradigm of identity in the identity of a thing with itself" (*Investigations,* §215).

behavior, and utterances of others actually are his *criteria* (not merely his evidence) for the existence of their mental states. Previously this had seemed impossible.

But now he is in danger of flying to the opposite extreme of behaviorism, which errs by believing that through observation of one's own circumstances, behavior, and utterances one can find out that one is thinking or angry. The philosophy of "from one's own case" and behaviorism, though in a sense opposites, make the common assumption that the first-person, present-tense psychological statements are verified by self-observation. According to the "one's own case" philosophy the self-observation cannot be checked by others; according to behaviorism the self-observation would be by means of outward criteria that are available to all. The first position becomes unintelligible; the second is false for at least many kinds of psychological statements. We are forced to conclude that the first-person psychological statements are not (or hardly ever) verified by self-observation. It follows that they have no verification at all; for if they had a verification it would have to be by self-observation.

But if sentences like "My head aches" or "I wonder where she is" do not express observations then what do they do? What is the relation between my declaration that my head aches and the fact that my head aches, if the former is not the report of an observation? The perplexity about the existence of *other* minds has, as the result of criticism, turned into a perplexity about the meaning of one's own psychological sentences about oneself. At our starting point it was the sentence "*His* head aches" that posed a problem; but now it is the sentence "*My* head aches" that puzzles us.

One way in which this problem can be put is by the question, "How does *one know when to say* the words 'My head aches'?" The inclination to ask this question can be made acute by imagining a fantastic but not impossible case of a person who has survived to adult years without ever experiencing pain. He is given various sorts of injections to correct this condition, and on receiving one of these one day, he jumps and exclaims, "Now I feel pain!" One wants to ask, "How did he *recognize* the new sensation as a pain?"

Let us note that if the man gives an answer (*e.g.,* "I knew it must be pain because of the way I jumped") then he proves by that very fact that he has not mastered the correct use of the words "I feel pain." They cannot be used to state a *conclusion.* In telling us *how* he did it he will convict himself of a misuse. Therefore the question "How did he recognize his sensation?" requests the impossible. The inclination to ask it is evidence of our inability to grasp the fact that the use of this psychological sentence has nothing to do with recognizing or identifying or observing a state of oneself.

The fact that this imagined case produces an especially strong temptation to ask the "How?" question shows that we have the idea that it must be more difficult to give the right name of one's sensation *the first time.* The implication would be that it is not so difficult *after* the first time. Why should this be? Are we thinking that then the man would have a paradigm of pain with which he could compare his sensations and so be in a position to know right off whether a certain sensation was or was not a pain? But the paradigm would be either something "outer" (behavior) or something "inner" (perhaps a memory impression of the sensation). If the former then he is misusing the first-person sentence. If the latter then the question of whether he compared *cor-*

rectly the present sensation with the inner paradigm of pain would be without sense. Thus the idea that the use of the first-person sentences can be governed by paradigms must be abandoned. It is another form of our insistent misconception of the first-person sentence as resting somehow on the identification of a psychological state.

These absurdities prove that we must conceive of the first-person psychological sentences in some entirely different light. Wittgenstein presents us with the suggestion that the first-person sentences are to be thought of as similar to the natural nonverbal, behavioral expressions of psychological states. "My leg hurts," for example, is to be assimilated to crying, limping, holding one's leg. This is a bewildering comparison and one's first thought is that two sorts of things could not be more unlike. By saying the sentence one can make a *statement;* it has a *contradictory;* it is *true* or *false;* in saying it one *lies* or *tells the truth;* and so on. None of these things, exactly, can be said of crying, limping, holding one's leg. So how can there be any resemblance? But Wittgenstein knew this when he deliberately likened such a sentence to "the primitive, the natural, expressions" of pain, and said that it is "new pain-behavior" (*ibid.,* §244). This analogy has at least two important merits: first, it breaks the hold on us of the question "How does one *know when to say* 'My leg hurts'?" for in the light of the analogy this will be as nonsensical as the question "How does one know when to cry, limp, or hold one's leg?"; second, it explains how the utterance of a first-person psychological sentence by another person can have *importance* for us, although not as an identification—for in the light of the analogy it will have the same importance as the natural behavior which serves as our preverbal criterion of the psychological states of others.

Alfred Jules Ayer

The Meaning of Statements About the Mental States of Others

WHAT CAN WE COMMUNICATE?

Now the obvious answer to the question how we know about the experiences of others is that they are communicated to us, either through their natural manifestations in the form of gestures, tears, laughter, play of feature and so forth, or by the use of language. A very good way to find out what another person is thinking or feeling is to ask him. He may not answer, or if he does answer he may not answer truly, but very often he will. The fact

From A. J. Ayer, *The Problem of Knowledge,* published by Macmillan & Co. Ltd., London, St. Martin's Press, Inc., New York, and The Macmillan Company of Canada, Limited, 1956. Reprinted by permission of the publishers.

that the information which people give about themselves can be deceptive does not entail that it is never to be trusted. We do not depend on it alone: it may be, indeed, that the inferences which we draw from people's non-verbal behaviour are more secure than those that we base upon what they say about themselves, that actions speak more honestly than words. But were it not that we can rely a great deal upon words, we should know very much less about each other than we do.

At this point, however, a difficulty arises. If I am to acquire information in this way about another person's experiences, I must understand what he says about them. And this would seem to imply that I attach the same meaning to his words as he does. But how, it may be asked, can I ever be sure that this is so? He tells me that he is in pain, but may it not be that what he understands by pain is something quite different from anything that I should call by that name? He tells me that something looks red to him, but how do I know that what he calls 'red' is not what I should call 'blue', or that it is not a colour unlike any that I have ever seen, or that it does not differ from anything that I should even take to be a colour? All these things would seem to be possible. Yet how are such questions ever to be decided?

In face of this difficulty, some philosophers have maintained that experiences as such are incommunicable.[1] They have held that in so far as one uses words to refer to the content of one's experiences, they can be intelligible only to oneself. No one else can understand them, because no one else can get into one's mind to verify the statements which they express. What can be communicated, on this view, is structure. I have no means of knowing that other people have sensations or feelings which are in any way like my own. I cannot tell even that they mean the same by the words which they use to refer to physical objects, since the perceptions which they take as establishing the existence of these objects may be utterly different from any that I have ever had myself. If I could get into my neighbour's head to see what it is that he refers to as a table, I might fail to recognize it altogether, just as I might fail to recognize anything that he is disposed to call a colour or a pain. On the other hand, however different the content of his experience may be from mine, I do know that its structure is the same. The proof that it is the same is that his use of words agrees with mine, in so far as he applies them in a corresponding way. However different the table that he perceives may be from the table that I perceive, he agrees with me in saying of certain things that they are tables and of others that they are not. No matter what he actually sees when he refers to colour, his classification of things according to their colour is the same as mine. Even if his conception of pain is quite different from my own, his behaviour when he says that he is in pain is such as I consider to be appropriate. Thus the possible differences of content can, and indeed must be disregarded. What we can establish is that our experiences are similarly ordered. It is this similarity of structure that provides us with our common world: and it is only descriptions of this common world, that is, descriptions of structure, that we are able to communicate.

On this view, the language which different people seem to share consists, as it were, of flesh and bones. The bones represent its public aspect; they serve

[1] This view was current, at one time, in the Vienna Circle. Cf. M. Schlick, *Allgemeine Erkenntnislehre,* and R. Carnap, *Der logische Aufbau der Welt.*

alike for all. But each of us puts flesh upon them in accordance with the character of his experiences. Whether one person's way of clothing the skeleton is or is not the same as another's is an unanswerable question. The only thing that we can be satisfied about is the identity of the bones.

This theory has, I think, a certain plausibility. Its weakness appears when one tries to make it more precise. For what exactly is this distinction between structure and content supposed to be? Can one find any examples of a statement which is purely about structure, a statement which belongs entirely to the public part of language? Descriptions of spatial relationships, perhaps, where the terms between which the relations hold are left qualitatively unidentified? But what anyone understands by such words as 'above' or 'beyond' or 'to the left of' depends no less upon the character of his experience than what he understands by 'sweet' or 'blue'. Even the understanding of so bare a statement as that two things are similar in some respect requires that similarity be identifiable in one's experience. If I cannot know that another person means the same as I do by 'table' I cannot know that he means the same by 'similarity'. Even the use of numerals, in the expression of statements which are not wholly formal, cannot be understood unless one can interpret the results of counting or measuring operations. And how can I be sure that my neighbour's interpretation is the same as mine? How can I be sure that if I were to perceive what he counts as a group of four things I should not reckon them to be four hundred? I am not saying, indeed, that I have any serious reason for entertaining doubts on such a point; but only that if there are reasons for doubt they apply to any descriptive use of language, to the attribution of relations as much as to the attribution of qualities, to statements about structure no less than to statements about content.

But what of the argument that other people's behaviour, while revealing nothing of the content of their experience, does at least show me that its structure is the same as that of mine? It is suggested that even if I cannot know that someone else means the same as I do by the words he uses, I do know that he applies them to the same things. But if I can know nothing whatsoever about the content of his experience, then I cannot know even that he does apply his words in a way that is formally consistent with my own. For all that I can tell, what sounds to me like a repetition of the same word does not sound so to him, what looks to me like an object of the same type as those to which the word was previously applied does not look so to him. The fact that he behaves as if we understood each other, that he responds in the appropriate way to my statements or requests, may prove that our respective worlds are somehow geared together, but it does not prove that their structure is the same. Once more, I am not maintaining that different people do not understand each other, or that this is not proved by their behaviour. I am maintaining only that there is no warrant here for separating structure and content, for arguing that structure can be communicated whereas content cannot. Indeed, this whole attempt to draw a distinction within descriptive language between what can and cannot be communicated appears to me misguided. If there were something that my neighbour could not communicate to me, I should be left in ignorance of his meaning: I should not know what he was talking about. But if I am in a position to say what it is that he has failed to communicate to me, he has in fact succeeded. To say, for example, that he cannot tell me that he is in pain implies that I understand what is meant by his being in pain: for otherwise I should attach no meaning to saying that *this* was what he could not tell me. But if I understand what is meant by his being in pain, there is no reason in logic why he should not be able to tell me that he is in pain. And the same applies to any other statement that he may choose to make about the content of his experience. What the analysis of these statements is, whether, for example, they have a different meaning for him from the meaning that they have for me, is another question. We shall return to it later on.

THE THESIS OF PHYSICALISM

This mistake of supposing that only structure is communicable arises from a combination of errors. The philosophers who made it assumed that for a language to be public it must be used to refer to public objects. But they also believed that to make an empirical statement was ultimately to refer to one's own experiences. And since they held that all one's experiences were private to oneself, they seemed bound to conclude that an empirical statement could never be public; that it could be intelligible only to the person who made it. But finding this result too paradoxical, they sought to mitigate the privacy of experiences by assigning them a common structure. And so they came to hold that structure, being the only common object, was the only thing communicable. But in the first place it is false that for a language to be public it must refer to public objects. What makes a language public is that one person's use of it is intelligible to another: and, as I hope to show presently, from the fact that one cannot literally share the experiences of another person it does not follow that one cannot understand what he says about them. And, secondly, it is also false that in making an empirical statement one is always referring to one's own experiences. Empirical statements may be said to refer to experiences, in the sense that it is only through the occurrence of some experience that they can be shown to be true or false, but it need not be one's own experience; it need not be the experience of any given person. To put it another way, in the case where an empirical statement does not itself record an actual or possible experience, it may be required that some such 'experiential' statement be derivable from it: but this experiential statement may be impersonal. If it is true, it will in fact be because someone has the experience in question. But its truth need not depend upon the identity of the person who has the experience. Some other person might have done as well.

The same errors have been responsible for what is known as the thesis of physicalism; the thesis that when one appears to be speaking about minds one is really always speaking about bodies; or, to put it more precisely, that to say anything about a person's thoughts or feelings, or sensations, or private experiences of any kind, is always equivalent to saying something about his physical condition, or behaviour, where this applies to the statements that one makes about oneself as well as to those that one makes about other people. For the ground on which this thesis is maintained is that it is only if such statements are interpreted 'physicalistically' that they can convey any information from one person to another. Otherwise, not only should we not be able to communicate our experiences; we should not, so it is argued, even be able to exchange any information about physical objects. Thus Carnap, who uses the expression 'physical language' to designate the class of statements which ostensibly refer to physical objects or occurrences, and the expression 'protocol language' to designate the class of statements which ostensibly refer to a person's private experiences, maintains that our understanding of the physical language requires that the protocol language be included in it. He holds that 'physical statements' must entail 'protocol statements' in order to be verifiable. Were this not so, 'physical statements would float in a void disconnected, in principle, from all experience'. But if protocol statements are deducible from physical statements they must, he thinks, themselves refer to physical facts. For the only alternative is that physical statements refer to the contents of experience; and Carnap argues that this is excluded by the fact that experiences are private. If S_1 and S_2 are different people, 'S_1's protocol language refers to the content of S_1's experience, S_2's protocol language to the content of S_2's experience. What can the intersubjective physical language refer to? It must refer to the content of the experiences of both S_1 and S_2. This is however impossible for the realms of experience of two persons do not overlap.' He therefore concludes that 'there is no solution free from contradictions in this direction'.[2]

Once more it is assumed that if experiences are private they are describable only in a private language; and from this it is inferred that if protocol statements were interpreted purely as records of experience, the fact that they were entailed by physical statements would mean that the public language, which we use to refer to physical objects, would dissolve into a set of private languages, having nothing in common with each other. But this conclusion does not hold. The statements of what Carnap calls the physical language may be said to refer to experiences, in the sense that they are verified by them. But in that case, as we have already remarked, they refer to them neutrally. Let us suppose, for example, that S_1 verifies a physical statement p by having an experience e_1 and that S_2 verifies p by having an experience e_2. So long as e_1 and e_2 are both of the appropriate type, they respectively justify S_1 and S_2 in accepting p; and the fact that they are not identical with one another does not lead to any contradiction at all. Thus, the answer to Carnap's question 'What can the intersubjective physical language refer to?' is that it refers, in this sense, neither to the 'private world' of S_1 nor to that of S_2, but to the experiences of anyone you please.

It does not follow from this that the thesis of physicalism is false. Independently of this fallacious argument, it might still be the case that every assertion of what would appear to be a mental fact is logically equivalent to the assertion of some physical fact. But when it is considered on its own merits, this thesis does not appear at all convincing. Certainly, in one's own case, it seems necessary to distinguish the sensations, or images, or feelings that one has from the physical states or actions by which they are manifested. However intimate the relation may be between an 'inner' experience and its 'outward' expression, it is not necessary that the one should accompany the other.

[2] R. Carnap, *The Unity of Science*, p. 82.

I can behave as if I had thoughts, or sensations, or feelings that I in fact do not have; and I can have thoughts or feelings that I keep entirely to myself. No doubt I could always express them if I chose; perhaps I am always disposed to express them; but this is not to say that my having them consists in nothing more than my being disposed to perform certain actions, or utter certain words. Again, it may be argued that every so-called mental event has its physiological counterpart, that each of one's experiences is, as it were, recorded on one's brain. This is a physiological hypothesis which has yet to be adequately verified, but it may very well be true. Even so, it would not follow that the experience was identical with its physical correlate, that to describe one's sensations or feelings was logically equivalent to describing the condition of one's brain. For the existence of this psycho-physical parallelism, if it does exist, is a scientific *discovery*. The connection between the mental and the physical events has to be established by experiment. But this implies that they are not identical. For if they were identical, experiments would not be needed. The connection could be established by logic alone.

The question whether one can have experiences which find no 'external' expression is complicated by the fact that a number of the words which seem to stand for mental events or processes are actually used in such a way that they include a reference to physical behaviour. Thus to be angry, or jealous, or bored, or gay, or happy is not merely, or even primarily, to have a special feeling; it is also to display certain physical signs, to behave, or be disposed to behave, in the appropriate fashion. If I go only by introspection I may mistake my mood; other people who note only my demeanour may judge the state of my feelings better than I do myself. But from the fact that we speak of feelings in a wider as well as in a narrower sense, the fact that what might pass for a description of one's feeling is commonly taken to imply rather more than the existence of the feeling as something privately and immediately felt, it does not follow that these feelings, in the narrow 'mental' sense, do not exist at all: nor does it follow that they cannot be described. And when it comes to other mental phenomena, such as sensations or images, the connection with physical events seems wholly synthetic; the descriptions which we give of them would not ordinarily be construed as entailing any reference to what is publicly observable.

Finally, the argument which Carnap brings in favour of physicalism, that otherwise 'physical statements would float in a void disconnected, in principle, from all experience', actually works the other way. For the whole point of 'protocol statements' was that they characterized experiences. It was this that gave them their privileged position. But if they themselves are to be construed as statements about the condition of one's body, they will no longer play this special rôle. Like other physical statements, they will have to be empirically verifiable: but their translation into the class of physical statements will leave us without any means of describing the experiences by which they or their fellows are to be verified. The place that they were designed to occupy in language could indeed be left vacant; one may know what experiences are required to verify a given physical statement, without in fact having the resources for describing them: but it must be possible that such descriptions should be found.

For Further Reading

Alexander, Peter, "Other People's Experience," *Proceedings of the Aristotelian Society,* Vol. 51 (1950–51).
Aune, Bruce, "On Thought and Feeling," *Philosophical Quarterly,* Vol. 13 (1963).
Baier, Kurt, "Pains," *Australasian Journal of Philosophy,* Vol. 40 (1962).
Eaton, R. M., *General Logic,* 1931, pp. 550–66.
Hampshire, Stuart, "The Analogy of Feeling," *Mind,* Vol. 61 (1952).
Hempel, C. G., "The Logical Analysis of Psychology," in Feigl, H., and Sellars, W. (eds.), *Readings in Philosophical Analysis,* 1949.
Jones, J. R., "Our Knowledge of Other Persons," *Philosophy,* Vol. 25 (1950).
Keynes, J. M., *A Treatise on Probability,* pp. 257–78.
Köhler, Wolfgang, *Gestalt Psychology,* 1947, Chap. 7.
Shearn, M., "Other People's Sense Data," *Proceedings of the Aristotelian Society,* Vol. 50 (1949–50).
Strawson, P. F., *Individuals,* 1959, Chap. 3.
Thomson, James, "The Argument from Analogy and Our Knowledge of Other Minds," *Mind,* Vol. 60 (1951).
Whiteley, C. A., "Behaviorism," *Mind,* Vol. 70 (1961).
Wisdom, John, Austin, J. L., and Ayer, A. J., "Other Minds" (Symposium), *Proceedings of the Aristotelian Society,* Supplementary Vol. 20 (1946).

10

THE MEANING AND JUSTIFICATION OF EPISTEMIC STATEMENTS

In the General Introduction we pointed out that it is convenient to divide the theory of knowledge into two parts, "theory of knowledge proper" and "meta-epistemology." The former consists in a systematic formulation and reasoned defense of general epistemological principles; the latter consists in an explanation of the meaning of epistemological terms (such as "know" and "probable") and of auxiliary terms essential to that meaning, and in a general theory of how epistemological principles can be validated. Earlier selections have been devoted to explanations of these auxiliary terms ("meaning," "reference," "truth") and to the theory of knowledge proper. They have not, however, given concentrated attention to the meaning of epistemological terms themselves or to the question of how, in general, epistemological principles may be supported.

These topics have been touched on in many selections—those on the coherence and instrumentalist theories of truth; those on the analytic-synthetic distinction and the possibility of a priori knowledge; some of those on the problem of induction and on epistemological order and scepticism; and so on. Nevertheless, they have not been discussed systematically, nor has any reading been directed to them. The present chapter, Roderick M. Chisholm's "The Nature and Justification of Epistemic Statements," fills this gap.

It might seem more logical to have placed this selection first than last. For how can we discuss epistemological questions in an intelligent and orderly way unless we have already determined what epistemological statements mean and how they may be supported? The topic, however, is very abstract—so abstract that most people find it more illuminating to begin their epistemological studies with a relatively simple intuitive understanding of relatively concrete statements, and to come to theories about the meaning and justification of epistemological statements only after they have the kind of background provided by the earlier selections in this book.

The extract that follows comprises two sections from Chisholm's *Perceiving: A Philosophical Study*. The first puts forward proposals about the logical relation of various epistemological concepts (such as "certain" and "evidence") to one another. The second discusses various types of theory about the meaning of the epistemological terms mentioned in the General Introduction: nonnaturalism, naturalism, and noncognitivism in epistemology. Chisholm finds noncognitivism the most acceptable of these, and he develops its implications for the study of epistemology.

Roderick Milton Chisholm

The Nature and Justification of Epistemic Statements

EPISTEMIC TERMS

II

"Adequate evidence"—like "acceptable," "unreasonable," "indifferent," "certain," "probable," and "improbable"—is a term we use in appraising the epistemic, or cognitive, worth of propositions, hypotheses, and beliefs. The statements in which we express such appraisal—for example, "'We do not have adequate evidence for believing that acquired characteristics are inherited," "The astronomy of Ptolemy is unreasonable," and "In all probability, the accused is innocent"—are similar in significant respects to "Stealing is wicked," "We ought to forgive our enemies," and other statements expressing our ethical or moral appraisals. Many of the characteristics which philosophers and others have thought peculiar to ethical statements also hold of epistemic statements. And when we consider the application of "evident" and our other epistemic terms, we meet with problems very much like those traditionally associated with "right," "good," and "duty."

I shall propose definitions of several important epistemic terms. The definitions are intended to be adequate only to some of the epistemic uses of the terms defined. Many of the terms I shall define have other, nonepistemic uses I shall not mention. And there are many terms having important epistemic uses which I shall not attempt to define; the epistemic uses of such terms, I believe, can be defined by means of the epistemic vocabulary presented here. The definitions make use of one undefined epistemic locution. This is the locution: *"h* is more worthy of S's belief than *i,"* where "S" may be replaced by the name of a person and *"h"* and *"i"* by names of propositions, statements, or hypotheses. An alternative reading is *"h* is more acceptable than *i* for S." [Later] I shall discuss the application of our epistemic vocabulary and . . . the meaning of our undefined locution.

III

A proposition, statement, or hypothesis is *unreasonable* if it is less worthy of belief than is its denial or contradictory. Let us say, then:

(2) "It would be *unreasonable* for S to accept *h*" means that non-*h* is more worthy of S's belief than *h*.

If S *does* accept *h,* we may say, of course, that it *is* unreasonable of him to do so. When it is clear from the general context what subject S is intended, we may say, elliptically, that a proposition, statement, or hypothesis is unreasonable.

"Absurd" and "preposterous" are sometimes synonyms of "unreasonable" in its present sense. And the belief—or feeling—that a proposition is unreasonable may also be expressed by means of imperatives. If I say to you, "Don't count on seeing me before Thursday," I may mean that it would be unreasonable of you to believe that you will see me before Thursday.

Whenever it would be unreasonable for a man to accept a certain proposition, then he may be said to have *adequate evidence* for its contradictory. Our next definition is:

(3) "S has *adequate evidence* for *h*" means that it would be unreasonable for S to accept non-*h*.

When it is clear what subject S is intended, then we may speak elliptically, once again, and say that a proposition, statement, or hypothesis is *evident.* The expression "adequate evidence" as it is used in this definition should be thought of as a single term; I use it because it seems to be ordinarily used in such contexts. An alternative locution which I shall also use is "*h* is evident for S."

As examples of propositions which are evident, we could cite what a man knows or perceives to be true. But we are not defining "adequate evidence" in terms [of] "know" or "perceive." In definition . . . (6) we shall define "know" in terms of "adequate evidence." There are, moveover, propositions for which a man may have adequate evidence without knowing or perceiving them to be true. For there are times when, as we would ordinarily say, the available evidence may favor some proposition which is false; at such times, a false proposition is more worthy of one's belief than is a true proposition. Thus it may be true that a man is going to win a lottery and yet unreasonable for him to believe that he is. But once the drawings are announced, the belief may no longer be unreasonable.

The example indicates that our definitions should contain temporal references. For a proposition may be evident at one date and unreasonable at another. The phrase "at *t*" could be inserted in our definitions: a proposition would then be said to be evident *at a time t* provided only that its contradictory is unreasonable at *t;* and so on. But, for simplicity, I shall not make these temporal references explicit.

The *evident,* according to our definition, is more worthy of belief than is the unreasonable. But there is another sense of the phrase "worthy of belief" in which we can say, more simply, that the *true* is more worthy of belief than the false. If the evident, as I have suggested, is sometimes false, then there are hypotheses which, in the one sense, are more worthy of belief than are their contradictories but which, in the other, are less. This twofold sense of "worthy" is not peculiar to our epistemic terms, but holds of ethical terms generally. Following Richard Price, let us distinguish between the *absolute* and the *practical* senses of these terms.[1]

[1] See Richard Price, *Review of the Principal Questions of Morals* (Oxford, 1948; first published in 1787), ch. viii. Compare H. A. Prichard's "Duty and Ignorance of Fact," reprinted in his *Moral Obligation* (Oxford, 1950), and W. D. Ross, *Foundations of Ethics* (London, 1939), ch. vii.

Using the ethical term "right" in its *absolute* sense, we may say that no one can ever know what actions are right; for no one can ever know what *all* of the consequences of any action will be. In this absolute sense of "right," perhaps it would have been right for someone to have killed Hitler and Stalin when they were infants; perhaps their parents acted (absolutely) wrongly in allowing them to live.[2] But in the *practical* sense of "right" such killings would *not* have been right. It was not possible, when Hitler and Stalin were infants, for anyone to foresee the harm they would do and, I think we may assume, there is no motive which would have justified putting them to death. If we try, as some philosophers do, to restrict "right" and "wrong" and other ethical terms to their absolute use, then other terms must take over their practical use. We might then say of the killings we have been discussing that, although they might have been right, they would hardly have been *praiseworthy*—or that, although they would not have been wrong, they would certainly have been *blameworthy*.

We cannot know, of any action, whether it is right or wrong in the absolute senses of these terms unless we know what all of its consequences are going to be. But, I believe, we can know, of any contemplated act of our own, whether it is right or wrong in the practical senses of these terms; we can know of any act we contemplate whether that act would be praiseworthy or blameworthy.

When it is said, then, that people ought to believe what is evident and that they ought not to believe what is unreasonable, "ought" has its practical use. But when it is said that they ought to believe what is true and that they ought not to believe what is false, "ought" has its absolute use.[3] Our locution "*h* is more worthy of belief than *i*" is to be taken in its practical sense. And all of the other epistemic terms to be used here are, similarly, to be taken in a practical and not in an absolute sense.

IV

Let us say that a proposition, statement, or hypothesis is acceptable provided only that it is not unreasonable.

(4) "*h* is *acceptable* for S" means: it is false that it would be unreasonable for S to accept *h*.

In other words, if the contradictory of a proposition is not evident, then the proposition is acceptable. "Justifiable," "reasonable," or "credible" might be used in place of "acceptable" here; I have avoided them, however, because in their ordinary use in such contexts they are often taken as synonymous with "evident." The modal term "*possible*" is sometimes used as a synonym of "acceptable"; when a man says, "It is possible that we will have good news tomorrow," he may mean it is not unreasonable of us to believe that we will have good news tomorrow.

[2] Compare Bertrand Russell, *Human Knowledge* (New York, 1948), pt. v, ch. vi.

[3] There is a useful discussion of this distinction in R. B. Braithwaite, *Scientific Explanation* (Cambridge, 1953), pp. 279 ff. In *The Origin of the Knowledge of Right and Wrong* (London, 1902), sec. 23, Franz Brentano says in effect that we ought to believe only what is true. In a colloquium entitled "The Normative in the Descriptive," Konstantin Kolenda and Abraham Edel say we ought to believe only what is true, while Alan Ross Anderson, Max Black, and Irving Copi say there are times when we need not believe what is true (*Review of Metaphysics,* X [1956], 106–121).

In his lecture "The Ethics of Belief," W. K. Clifford said, "It is wrong to believe upon insufficient evidence."[4] His ethics was somewhat more rigid than that suggested here, for he held that, for each of us, there is a large class of propositions concerning which we ought to withhold both assent and denial. But I have suggested, in effect, that a proposition should be treated as innocent until proven guilty. It is only when we have adequate evidence for the contradictory of a proposition that it is unreasonable for us to accept the proposition. We have adequate evidence for the proposition that Eisenhower was President in 1956; hence it is unreasonable for us to accept the proposition that he was *not* President in 1956. We do not now have adequate evidence for the proposition that a Republican will be President in 1975; Clifford would say, therefore, that we ought not to believe that a Republican will be President in 1975. I suggest that we *may* believe this, that the proposition is "acceptable" in the sense defined above.[5] But to say that we have a right to believe it is not to say that we have a right to bet our savings on it.

We may say that a hypothesis is acceptable for someone without implying that it is always reasonable for him to *act upon* it; indeed, we may say that he has *adequate evidence* for a hypothesis without implying that it is always reasonable for him to act upon it. And in saying that in a certain instance it may be reasonable for a man to act upon a hypothesis, we do not imply that the hypothesis is one for which he has adequate evidence. A man may have adequate evidence for believing he will win if he plays Russian roulette; he may also have adequate evidence for believing he will be paid $10 if he does win. But it would be foolish of him to play, despite the fact that, in so doing, he would be acting upon hypotheses for which he has adequate evidence. On the other hand, a swimmer may have adequate evidence for the hypothesis that he cannot swim ashore and yet be in a position wherein it would be unreasonable of him *not* to act upon it. And often, when we take precautionary measures—when we buy insurance, for example—we are justified in acting on hypotheses which are unreasonable and which we believe to be false. In deciding whether to act upon a hypothesis we must consider, not only the evidence that bears upon the hypothesis itself, but also the evidence that bears upon the "utility" or "moral gain" of acting upon it. We should try to decide, for example, what the value of acting upon the hypothesis would be if the hypothesis were true, what the "disvalue" of acting upon the hypothesis would be if the hypothesis were false, and we must try to compare these values and disvalues.[6] And we should also consider whether we ought to inquire further—whether we ought to seek out *additional* evidence. I have adequate evidence for the hypothesis that this is a piece of paper and in setting out to write I may be satisfied with the evidence at hand; but before betting my savings on the hypothesis I should make a more thorough investigation.

[4] W. K. Clifford, *Lectures and Essays,* vol. II (London, 1879). It should be noted that our definitions, as they now stand, have this limitation: they do not enable us to formulate Clifford's position, for we cannot consistently say that a hypothesis and its contradictory are *both* unreasonable.

[5] Compare this dialogue from Sheridan's *The Rivals:* "Absolute: 'Sure, Sir, this is not very reasonable, to summon my affection for a lady I know nothing of.' Sir Anthony: 'I am sure, Sir, 'tis more unreasonable in you to object to a lady you know nothing of' " (quoted by J. M. Keynes in *A Treatise on Probability* [London, 1921], p. 41).

[6] These concepts are discussed with more exactness in writings on probability. See, for example, Rudolf Carnap, *Logical Foundations of Probability* (Chicago, 1950), pp. 226–279.

The question whether to *accept* a certain hypothesis—whether to *believe* it—is thus easier to answer than the question of whether to *act upon* it.[7] In deciding whether to accept it, we need not consider the "utility" or "moral gain" that would result from acting upon it. And we need not consider whether we ought to make further inquiry and investigation.

If a proposition, statement, or hypothesis is acceptable but not evident, then its contradictory is also acceptable but not evident. Such a proposition might be called epistemically indifferent. We may add, then, the following definition:

(5) "*h* is *indifferent* for S" means: (i) it is false that S has adequate evidence for *h* and (ii) it is also false that S has adequate evidence for non-*h*.

The hypothesis that it will rain in London a year from today is, for most of us, epistemically indifferent; we do not have adequate evidence either for it or for its contradictory. If a proposition or hypothesis is indifferent, its contradictory is also indifferent. An indifferent proposition is thus one which is neither evident nor unreasonable. According to Clifford, no proposition is epistemically indifferent. According to the "absolute skeptic," all propositions are epistemically indifferent.[8]

. . .

VI

Let us now consider the epistemic uses of "know"—its uses in such statements as "He knows the earth to be round" and "The speaker knows that the hall is filled."

A number of authors have tried to reduce this epistemic sense of know—*knowing that*—to a kind of verbal *knowing how*. "Knowing that some fact is the case is to know how to tell the truth about matters of a certain kind."[9] Knowing that the earth is round, according to this conception, differs from knowing how to swim only in that a different kind of skill or aptness is involved, namely, "the capacity to state correctly what is the case."[10] If, by "the capacity to state correctly what is the case," we were to mean merely "the capacity to utter words truly describing what is the case," then this capacity, like the ability to swim, *would* be a kind of aptness of the body. But if we define "knowing that the earth is round" in terms of *this* capacity—the capacity to utter the sentence "The earth is round" (or some other sentence having the same meaning)—then we must say, of most of those people who believe that the earth is *flat*, that they *know* that it is round. For most of those people are capable of uttering the sentence "The earth is round." Hence a qualification must be introduced in the phrase "the capacity of uttering words truly describ-

[7] I suggest that the concept of *acting upon* a hypothesis must be defined by reference to *action*, *purpose*, and *belief* in some such way as this. "In acting A, S is *acting upon h*" means: in acting A, S is trying to produce E; and he is acting as we would act if, further, (i) he believed *h* and (ii) he believed that A will result in E if and only if *h* is true. I shall not discuss the concepts of *purpose* and *action* [here].

[8] See Sextus Empiricus, *Outlines of Pyrrhonism*, bk. I, especially pp. 9, 112, and 123 of vol. I of *Sextus Empiricus* (Loeb Classical Library, London, 1933).

[9] John Watling, "Inferences from the Known to the Unknown," *Proceedings of the Aristotelian Society*, LV (1954–1955), 58.

[10] John Hartland-Swann, "The Logical Status of 'Knowing That,'" *Analysis*, XVI (1956), 114.

ing what is the case" if this phrase is to provide us with an adequate definition of *knowing that.*

A definition of *knowing that* should be adequate, moreover, to the distinction between *knowing* and *believing truly.* If I now predict the winner on the basis of what the tea leaves say, then, even though my prediction may be true, I cannot now be said to *know* that it is true.

"Knowing that," I suggest, has at least two epistemic senses. In what follows, I shall confine "know" to the broader of these senses and use "certain" for the narrower sense. The following, then, will be our definition of "know":

(6) "S *knows* that *h* is true" means: (i) S accepts *h;* (ii) S has adequate evidence for *h;* and (iii) *h* is true.

If we wish to avoid the term "true," we may substitute this formulation:

> "S knows that . . ." means: (i) S accepts the hypothesis (or proposition) that . . . ; (ii) S has adequate evidence for the hypothesis (or proposition) that . . . ; and (iii). . . .

The term "accepts" which appears in (6) has not been previously defined; I shall discuss it in detail [later]. "Assumes" is an alternative: for "S accepts *h*" is replaceable by "S assumes that *h* is true"; and "S accepts the proposition or hypothesis that *x* is *f*" is replaceable by "S assumes that *x* is *f*."

If a man knows, say, that the hall has been painted, then, according to our definition, he accepts the hypothesis that it has been painted, he has adequate evidence for this hypothesis, and, finally, the hall *has* been painted. On the other hand, if he accepts the hypothesis, has adequate evidence for it, but does not *know* that it is true, then the hall has not been painted.

Should we say that, if S knows *h* to be true, then S *believes* that *h* is true? (It should be noted that *believing* a proposition is not the same as asserting, proclaiming, or announcing that one believes it. When we *assert* a proposition and when we *say* that we believe it, then, unless we are lying, we are *acting upon* the proposition. . . . There is a sense of "believe," in its ordinary use, which is such that "S believes that *h* is true" entails "S does *not* know that *h* is true." If I *know* that La Paz is in Bolivia, I'm not likely to say, "I believe that La Paz is in Bolivia," for "I *believe* that La Paz is in Bolivia" suggests I don't know that it is. In this use, "S believes that *h* is true" means that S accepts *h* but does not know that *h* is true. Hence, if we interpret "believe" in this way, we cannot say that *knowing* entails *believing.* There is still another use of "believe" which is such that the expression *"I* believe"—an expression in the first person—entails "I know," or at least entails "I have adequate evidence." If a man says, "His policy, I believe, will not succeed," the parenthetical expression may be intended to express the claim to know or the claim to have adequate evidence that the policy will not succeed.[11]

But "believe" is also used to mean the same as "accept," in the sense in which "accept" is meant above, and in this use *knowing* does entail *believing.* I may believe that *x* is *f,* in this third sense of "believe," and yet not *say,* "I

[11] Compare J. O. Urmson, "Parenthetical Verbs," *Mind,* vol. LXI (1952), reprinted in Antony Flew, ed., *Essays in Conceptual Analysis* (London, 1956).

believe that *x* is *f*"; for, as we have noted, when "I believe" is used in this construction (in contrast with its parenthetical use) it is ordinarily intended to express doubt or hesitation. *You* may say of me, however, "He believes that *x* is *f* and, for all I know, he *knows* that *x* is *f*."

But even if there is a sense of "believe," or "accept," in which *knowing* entails *believing,* or *accepting,* we must not think of knowing as being, in any sense, a "species of" believing, or accepting. A man can be said to believe firmly, or reluctantly, or hesitatingly, but no one can be said to *know* firmly, or reluctantly, or hesitatingly. Professor Austin has noted that, although we may ask, "*How* do you know?" and "*Why* do you believe?" we may not ask, "*Why* do you know?" or "*How* do you believe?" The relation of knowing to believing, in the present sense of "believe," is not that of falcon to bird or of airedale to dog; it is more like that of arriving to traveling. *Arriving* entails *traveling*—a man cannot arrive unless he has traveled—but arriving is not a species of traveling.

When we exhort people epistemically, we say, not "You ought to *believe h,*" but "You ought to *know h.*" If I say to my friend, "you ought to know *h*," it is likely that I accept *h* and believe that he has adequate evidence for *h;* hence the only additional condition I'm exhorting him to meet is that of believing *h.* Or it may be that I claim to know *h* myself and am suggesting that he ought to make further inquiry or investigation (see Section IV, p. 654) and that when he does he will then have adequate evidence for *h.* Similar remarks hold of such statements as "You ought to have *known h.*"

. . .

VII

The term "certain," like "know," is used in many ways. Sometimes it is a synonym for the modal term "necessary"; sometimes one is said to be certain of a proposition only if one is unable to doubt it or if one accepts it with a "maximum degree of confidence"; and sometimes one is said to be certain only if one *knows* that one knows. But the sense of "certain" which is of most importance epistemically, I think, is this:

(7) "S is *certain* that *h* is true" means: (i) S knows that *h* is true and (ii) there is no hypothesis *i* such that *i* is more worthy of S's belief than *h.*

We could avoid "true," if we chose, in the manner suggested in connection with the definition of "know" above.

Sometimes the locution "S is certain" is used to mean merely that S *feels sure.* And in this use, of course, "S is certain" does not imply that S knows. I felt sure that my candidate would win the election, but since he did not, I could not have known that he would.

The present epistemic concept of *certainty* may be illustrated by a quotation from Moritz Schlick. He does not use our epistemic terms, but he is telling us, in effect, that, although statements made by scientists may be evident, they are not certain and that there are other statements which, in contrast with those of the scientists are certain.

> I do have trust in those good fellows, but that is only because I have always found them to be trustworthy whenever I was able to test their enunciations. I assure you most emphatically that I should *not* call the system of science true if I found its consequences incompatible with my own observations of nature, and the fact that it is adopted by the whole of mankind and taught in all the universities would make no impression on me. If all the scientists in the world told me that under certain experimental conditions I must see three black spots, and if under those conditions I saw only one spot, no power in the universe could induce me to think that the statement "there is now only one black spot in the field of vision" is false.[12]

This passage might be interpreted as saying that, at the present moment, there is no hypothesis, not even the best-confirmed hypotheses of science, which is more acceptable than the hypothesis that there is now only one black spot in the field of vision.

But we need not say, as Cardinal Newman did, that certitude is "indefectible" and permanent—that "whover loses his conviction on a given point is thereby proved not to have been certain of it."[13] For definition (7), like our other definitions, should be thought of as containing a temporal reference. Even if a man in the position Schlick describes above is *now* certain of the proposition expressed by "There is only one black spot in the field of vision," a proposition about what is to be seen today, he will not be certain about today's black spots tomorrow. And it may well be that at some later date this true proposition about today will become unreasonable.

We need not say that people are certain of all those propositions which they know to be true or which they perceive to be true. A man may know or perceive that there is smoke along the harbor without being certain—for there may be other propositions which, for him, are even more worthy of belief. In one of its many senses, "There *appears* to me to be smoke along the harbor," if it is true, expresses a proposition which, for any subject, no matter what he may be perceiving, is more acceptable than the proposition that there *is* smoke there. This point . . . is sometimes obscured by the other uses which "certain," "know," and "appear" happen to have in ordinary discourse.

It would be strange to say, "Not only do I *know* that that is true—I am *certain* of it." For one way of saying, "I am certain," in the present sense of the word, is to say, "I know," with emphasis.[14] Moreover, the negative expression "I am *not* certain that . . ." is often used to mean, not simply "It is false that I am certain that . . . ," but, more strongly, "I do not believe, and am indeed inclined to doubt, that. . . ." I may say, "I'm not certain I can attend the meeting," in order to convey my belief that I probably won't attend the meeting. But in saying above that *knowing* and *perceiving* do not imply *being*

[12] Moritz Schlick, "Facts and Propositions," *Analysis*, II (1935), 70. Compare Norman Malcolm on "the strong sense of 'know,' " in "Knowledge and Belief," *Mind*, LXI (1952), 178–189.

[13] *The Grammar of Assent*, ch. vii.

[14] A. D. Woozley contrasts this "certifying" or "guaranteeing" character of "I know that" with the tentativeness expressed by "I am certain," when "I am certain" means merely that I feel sure; see his *Theory of Knowledge* (London, 1949), pp. 187–189. Compare J. L. Austin, "Other Minds," *Proceedings of the Aristotelian Society*, suppl. vol. XX (1946), especially pp. 170–174, reprinted in Antony Flew, ed., *Logic and Language*, 2d ser. In "Ordinary Language and Absolute Certainty," Paul Edwards points out ambiguities in uses of "certain" (*Philosophical Studies*, I [1950]).

certain, I mean merely that there are some propositions which are even more worthy of our belief than many of those which we know or perceive to be true.

KNOWING ABOUT EVIDENCE

I

If we know that charity is a mark of what is right, then any test enabling us to decide that a certain act is an instance of charity would also enable us to decide that the act is right. If we *know* that the act is a charitable one, we also know that it is right. Hence, to the general question "How do you tell whether or not a given act is right?" we may be tempted to reply: "By finding out whether or not it has a 'right-making' characteristic." But to the question "How do you tell whether or not a given characteristic is a 'right-making' characteristic?" we must reply, . . . "By finding out whether or not it applies to actions which are right."

How, then, did we come to decide that acts of charity are right? More generally, how do we learn *which* characteristics are the ones that are "right-making"?

The relation of *evidence* to what I have called the "marks of evidence" is like that of *right* to what philosophers have called the "right-making" characteristics. Concerning both relations, we may ask the same sort of puzzling—and difficult—questions.

II

Should we say that ostensible ethical generalizations, such as "Every act of charity is right," are *analytic* statements and thus, in one important sense, not really generalizations at all? If "Every act of charity is right" is analytic, then it is like "Every square is rectangular" and "Every quadruped has feet" in that its denial is contradictory and in that the meaning of the predicate term may be said to be included in that of the subject. But we have said that a "right-making" characteristic, such as we are supposing charity to be, is one we can describe in language which is "ethically neutral." *Being charitable* can be described without using "right" or any term synonymous with "right." And, more generally, it is one thing to say, of some "right-making" characteristic, that it applies to a certain action and it is quite another thing to say that that action is *right.* A man who is morally perverse may affirm that a certain act is an act of charity and yet deny that it is right. We may condemn his moral judgment; but we would not condemn his *logic,* as we would if he were to deny that some squares are rectangles. It would seem to be a mistake, then, to identify the characteristic of *being right* with any of those characteristics which go to make up being charitable.[15] And therefore it would also seem to be a mistake to say, of the statement "Every act of charity is right," that it is an analytic statement.

[15] Bentham, according to Sidgwick, having seen that "being conducive to the general happiness" is a sign or mark of rightness, made the mistake of supposing that rightness is the *same* as being conducive to the general happiness (Henry Sidgwick, *Methods of Ethics* [London, 1893], p. 26). Bentham's mistake, if Sidgwick's charge is justified, was that of supposing that being "right-making" is the same as being right. This mistake is one form of what G. E. Moore has called the "naturalistic fallacy."

But if "Every act of charity is right" is a *synthetic* statement, it is quite unlike the ordinary generalizations of science. Although we have spoken of "marks of rightness," the relation of *being a "right-making" characteristic*—in our example, *being an act of charity*—to *being right* is not like that of symptom to disorder. If doctors know that there is some symptom—say, a certain marking on the skin—which is invariably accompanied by neuritis, their information was acquired, presumably, as a result of someone's inductions. People who display the symptoms were examined, people who display neuritis were examined, and it was noticed that all of the people in the first class were also members of the second. But it would not be accurate to say that "Every act of charity is right" was ever established or confirmed in the same sort of way. It would not be accurate to say that someone examined certain people who were found to be acting charitably, then examined certain people who were found to be acting rightly, and then noticed that all of the people in the first group were also in the second. Professor Ayer has put this point by saying that ethical generalizations, about the goodness or badness of certain types of situation, or the rightness or wrongness of certain types of action, are not "scientific" generalizations. For if they *were* scientific generalizations, he writes,

> then the goodness or badness of the situation, the rightness or wrongness of the action, would have to be something apart from the situation, something independently verifiable, for which the facts adduced as reasons for the moral judgment were evidence. But in these moral cases the two coincide. There is no procedure of examining the value of the facts, as distinct from examining the facts themselves. We may say that we have evidence for our moral judgments, but we cannot distinguish between pointing to the evidence itself and pointing to that for which it is supposed to be evidence. Which means that in the scientific sense it is not evidence at all.[16]

If we believe that charity is an invariable mark of rightness, we do not even feel the need to justify our belief by means of an inductive generalization; we do not feel the need to take samples or perform experiments. Why take the trouble to examine acts of charity to *find out* whether they are right? An "experiment in the imagination" will do. We need only *think about* various types of charitable action and if we consider all the relevant possibilities we will then be in a position to decide whether or not every act of charity is right.

But if someone were to *disagree* with us, holding that charity is *not* a "right-making" characteristic, or even holding that charity is "wrong-making," that every act of charity would be *wrong*, what kind of argument or evidence could we use to show him that he was mistaken? We cannot establish our own moral principle—that every act of charity would be *right*—by the usual

[16] A. J. Ayer, *Philosophical Essays* (London, 1954), p. 237. Compare the following quotation from *Butler's Moral Philosophy*, by Austin Duncan-Jones: "If there are categorical obligations, and if no statement that a categorical obligation exists can be resolved into statements about obligation-bearing qualities; and if, further, no amount of knowledge about obligation-bearing qualities would, by itself, tell us what our obligations were, it follows that knowledge of obligation—supposing that we can know them—must be obtained by some quite distinct process, different from any process by which we get to know the facts of the physical world, or human history, or human psychology" (p. 162).

inductive procedure of science, nor can we establish it by showing it to be a consequence of the principles of logic or mathematics.[17]

III

All of the foregoing applies, *mutatis mutandis,* to the relation between *evidence* and *marks of evidence,* to the relation between evidence and "evidence-bearing" characteristics. The statement that being appeared to, or that taking, is a mark of evidence is not an analytic statement; it is not like "All squares are rectangles." Nor is it a statement which seems to require—or which could have—any inductive evidence. If we are able to make a decision about such a statement, if we can decide whether or not to accept it, then we can do so merely by thinking of the various possibilities and without "examining" particular cases. For epistemic reasoning and discourse are very much like ethical reasoning and discourse.

In opposing Clifford's ethics of belief, I suggested [earlier] that a proposition should be regarded as innocent until proven guilty, that we may accept any proposition we would like to accept provided only that we do not have adequate evidence for its contradictory. In saying this, I was guided, in part, by what I believed to be the skeptical consequences of accepting Clifford's ethics. If Clifford were to reject my reasoning, if he were to say that no demonstration of skeptical consequences would invalidate his principle, our dispute would be like an ethical one and we would have difficulty in settling upon any method of resolving it.

Presenting "the problem of the criterion," . . . I suggested that we cannot decide what any of the marks of evidence are—we cannot decide what characteristics or events are "evidence-making"—until we are able to say which of our beliefs are evident. If we are able to show that we have a rule, enabling us to distinguish good apples from bad apples, then we know which apples are bad and which apples are good. And if we are to choose among a number of such rules, our decision will depend, in part, upon what we know about the goodness and badness of the apples.

[Earlier] we chose among a number of possible marks of evidence and we made our decision, apparently, by reference to what we knew about the kind of evidence that is available to us. We rejected "empiricism" because of what we judged to be its defects: for empiricism seems to imply, as Hume had seen, that it is in vain for us to ask whether there be body. We rejected the unqualified "taking" criterion because of what we judged to be its excesses: for, if we accept the "taking" criterion, then we must say, of what seem to be the most unacceptable of prejudices, that they are constantly made evident in the experience of those who have them. And we said, of the "sensibly-taking" criterion, that it seemed to be acceptable: for if we accept the "sensibly-taking" criterion, then, apparently, we can describe as evident just those propositions which we *want* to describe as evident. And therefore we may say, . . . "If, according to the 'sensibly-taking' criterion, no one has adequate evidence for the propositions of electronics and quantum physics, and if we *want* to be

17 See Bertrand Russell's account of a debate between Buddha and Nietzsche, in his *A History of Western Philosophy* (New York, 1945), pp. 270 ff. Compare C. L. Stevenson, "The Nature of Ethical Disagreement," in H. Feigl and W. S. Sellars, eds., *Readings in Philosophical Analysis* (New York, 1949).

able to say that these propositions are evident to someone, then we may reject the 'sensibly-taking' criterion."

In his *History of Western Philosophy,* Bertrand Russell said that St. Thomas has "little of the true philosophic spirit." For St. Thomas, according to Russell, "is not engaged in an inquiry, the result of which it is impossible to know in advance. Before he begins to philosophize, he already knows the truth; it is declared in the Catholic Faith."[18] But similarly, when we set out to solve the problem of the criterion, we already knew which propositions are the ones that are evident; we knew in advance that skepticism with regard to the senses is mistaken. Hence one might say that, if St. Thomas' philosophy constitutes "special pleading" for certain propositions of theology, our philosophy constitutes "special pleading" for certain propositions of science and common sense.[19]

What if a theologian or a mystic were to tell us that no criterion of evidence is adequate unless it describes marks of evidence enabling us to say that there are people who have evidence for certain propositions about God and his attributes?

Leon Chwistek, describing the epistemic principles, which most of us profess, as the "criteria of sound reason," considers a bookkeeper who, in a moment of fatigue, loses his faith in these criteria. If the bookkeeper's friends cannot lead him out of this situation, they will

> regard him as insane and put him in a sanitarium. In such an event he obviously will not believe that he has been justly treated. On the contrary, he will be convinced that the concept of reality [evidence] they employ in putting him out of the way is not worthy of serious consideration. To the argument that it is not possible to remain alive for long if daily life is disregarded, he could simply retort: Why should one remain alive? It is far better really to have enjoyed one brief glimpse of true reality than to have lived in unenlightened error for a long time.[20]

Can we say, to the skeptic, the mystic, and the bookkeeper, that the procedure we have followed is not itself an instance of "special pleading"? Can we say, concerning the propositions *we* want to count as evident, that they are propositions which, prior to our philosophical inquiry, we *knew* to be evident? Can we say, more generally, that *epistemic* statements express propositions for which we can have evidence, or which we can know to be true? [21]

[18] Russell, *A History of Western Philosophy,* p. 463.

[19] Compare Russell's own description of the inquiry he was later to undertake in his *Human Knowledge:* "If I ever have the leisure to undertake another serious investigation of a philosophical problem, I shall attempt to analyse the inferences from experience to the world of physics, assuming them capable of validity, and seeking to discover what principles of inference, if true, would make them valid. Whether these principles, when discovered, are accepted as true, is a matter of temperament; what should not be a matter of temperament should be the proof that acceptance of them is necessary if solipsism is to be rejected" (quoted from "My Mental Development," in P. A. Schilpp, ed., *The Philosophy of Bertrand Russell* [The Library of Living Philosophers, vol. V, Evanston, Ill., 1944], p. 16).

[20] Leon Chwistek, *The Limits of Science* (New York, 1948), pp. 288–289. Chwistek adds that "although there is no way of convincing the over-tired bookkeeper that the multiplication table is correct, there are no good reasons to question it."

[21] This "objective" conception has been clearly and explicitly defended in scholastic writings on epistemology; among the best of these, I think, are Cardinal Mercier's *Critériologie générale* and P. Coffey's *Epistemology* (London, 1917). In *Human Knowledge,* Russell makes use of the undefined term "degree of credibility" and says this about our knowledge of credibility: "We

Much of what may be said of our knowledge of *ethics,* or right and wrong, may also be said about our knowledge of *evidence*. In what follows, let us consider our ethical and epistemic convictions together. I use the word "conviction" instead of "belief," and instead of "approval" and "disapproval," in order not to prejudge the issues that will be raised.

IV

It is illuminating to compare our ethical and epistemic convictions with our *feelings* or *emotions*. For many of the statements in which we express our feelings and emotions resemble the ethical and epistemic statements we have been discussing.

If we were to approach "the theory of humor" in the way we have approached the theories of ethics and evidence, we would try to formulate general propositions relating the ostensible characteristic of *being amusing* to the *marks* of being amusing—to "amusement-bearing" qualities. Combining various suggestions which have been made about humor, a philosopher might say: "Whenever a pretentious person is exhibited as functioning like a machine, then, provided the exhibition is surprising but not completely implausible, it is amusing." The philosopher's statement could be construed in the way we have construed the ethical and epistemic statements of our examples. We could show that his statement is not analytic; a man could deny the statement without contradicting himself. And we could show that his statement is not a synthetic statement arrived at by inductive procedures. It is not a statement which can be falsified by showing, say, that, Navahos are *not* amused in the situations described. For (our philosopher could say) if Navahos do not laugh under the condition he has described, then either their sense of humor is perverted or it is not yet developed. To decide whether or not to accept the general statement about *being amusing,* we do not need to examine actual cases. It is enough to "examine possible cases"—to think about various possible situations and then to decide, with respect to each, whether or not it *would* be amusing. And therefore, our philosopher might conclude, his generalization is a *synthetic* statement we can know *a priori* to be true.

But it is simpler to say that *being amused* is not a state which is either true or false. Being amused at the comedian's dance is *not* like expecting the post office soon to be painted. If I expect the post office to be painted, then I am in a state which is true if and only if the post office *is* about to be painted. And the words in which I express this state—"The post office is soon to be painted"—are, similarly, true if and only if the post office *is* soon to be painted. But if I am amused at the comedian's dance, my amusement is not thereby true or false. I may express my amusement in the indicative sentence "The comedian's

---

must hold that the degree of credibility attached to a proposition is itself sometimes a datum. I think we should also hold that the degree of credibility to be attached to a *datum* is sometimes a datum, and sometimes (perhaps always) falls short of certainty. We may hold, in such a case, that there is only one datum, namely a proposition with a degree of credibility attached to it, or we may hold that the datum and its degree of credibility are two separate data. I shall not consider which of these two views should be adopted" (pp. 381–382). Compare G. E. Moore, *Some Problems of Philosophy* (London, 1953), chs. vi and vii; H. A. Prichard, "Does Moral Philosophy Rest upon a Mistake?" *Mind,* vol. XXI (1912), reprinted in Prichard's *Moral Obligation* and in W. S. Sellars and John Hospers, eds., *Readings in Ethical Theory* (New York, 1952); and C. I. Lewis, *An Analysis of Knowledge and Valuation,* ch. xi.

dance is funny." But we need not say, of my state and of the words which express it, that "they are true if and only if the comedian's dance *is* funny."

To say that the dance is funny is to report or express the fact that one is amused; it is *not* to say that the dance has a certain characteristic in virtue of which one's laughter or amusement is *correct* or *true*. But to say that the post office will soon be painted is to say more than that one believes or expects that the post office will soon be painted; it is to say, rather, that the post office has a certain characteristic—or is going to have a certain characteristic—in virtue of which one's belief, or expectation, is true. I think that most people would say, more generally, with respect to our feelings or emotions, that even though these feelings or emotions may frequently be said to have objects—one may be pleased, or disturbed, or unconcerned, about some *x* being *f*—these feelings are neither true nor false, neither correct nor mistaken.

Since the statements expressing what I have called our ethical and epistemic convictions resemble some of those expressing our emotions or feelings, and since the respect in which they resemble the statements expressing our emotions or feelings is one in which they differ from the generalizations of science and mathematics, we may be tempted to say that our ethical and epistemic convictions *also* resemble our emotions or feelings in being neither true nor false, in being neither correct nor mistaken. If we decide to say this, then the terms "approval" and "disapproval" may be more accurate in the present context than the word "conviction." The statement "He morally approved of the official's refusal to testify" would be like "He was amused by the comedian's dance," and unlike "He expected the post office soon to be painted," in that the verb is *not* replaceable by "believe" and an adjective designating some characteristic. "He morally approved of the official's refusal to testify" would *not* mean that the official's refusal to testify had a certain characteristic—that of *being right*—in virtue of which the moral approval was either true or false.

Some of the philosophers who have taken this view of our ethical or epistemic convictions—or, rather, of our ethical or epistemic *approvals* and *disapprovals*—have said that the statements in which we ostensibly express these approvals and disapprovals have the same meaning as do the statements in which we might *report* these approvals and disapprovals. If a man says, "The official acted rightly in refusing to betray his friends," then, according to this "psychologistic" conception, he is saying merely, "I approve of the official's refusal to betray his friends." And if a man says, "It would be unreasonable to suppose that the crisis will soon be over," then, according to this conception, he is saying merely, "I disapprove of accepting the hypothesis that the crisis will soon be over." Hence, if we accept this conception, we could say that, even if our approvals and disapprovals are neither true nor false, neither correct nor mistaken, our ethical and epistemic *statements* are statements which are either true or false. Similarly, even though the state of being amused is neither true nor false, neither correct nor mistaken, such statements as "That dance was very funny" are either true or false. For "That dance was very funny" is a *report* of someone's amusement: "I was very amused by that dance."

This "psychologistic" interpretation of our ethical and epistemic convictions has at least one implausible consequence. If "psychologism" were true, then, in order to show that a particular moral or epistemic statement is true, it would be sufficient to show that the person who made the statement did in fact make the appraisal which such a statement would normally express. And in order to show that such a statement is false, it would be sufficient to show that the person did *not* make the appraisal which the statement would normally express. For example, in order to show that "The official's act was right" is true, it would be sufficient to show that the person who made the statement approved of the official's act; and in order to show that it is false, it would be sufficient to show that the person did not approve of the official's act.[22]

If we are to say that our moral and epistemic convictions—our approvals and disapprovals—are *neither* true nor false, it would seem reasonable also to say that the statements in which these approvals and disapprovals are normally expressed are, similarly, neither true nor false. Instead of interpreting these statements "psychologistically," we might interpret them "emotively," or "performatively." We could say that such statements as "He acted rightly" and "That hypothesis is unreasonable" are like "Would that he were to return," "The Lord be praised," and "Do not cross the street," which are *not* used to say what could be true or false. These statements perform a variety of linguistic functions; they express or give vent to one's feelings; they influence the behavior and feelings of other people; and they are used to make ceremony. But according to this "emotive" conception, they are not used to say what is true or false. And the approvals and disapprovals which they express are not states which are true or false.[23]

We could accept an "emotive," or "performative," interpretation of *epistemic* statements and yet retain an "objective" interpretation of *probability* statements. For it is convenient to restrict "probability" to those statements which describe relative frequencies or which state the degree of confirmation that one hypothesis may have in relation to another. . . . However, such probability statements will not tell us anything of epistemic significance—will not tell us what is evident or what we have a right to believe—unless we apply the principles of probability to statements for which we have adequate evidence.[24]

The "emotive," or "performative," conception of ethical and epistemic statements shares the economy and simplicity of "psychologism" without having its implausible consequences. We need no longer say that, in order to show that "The official acted rightly" is true, it is sufficient to show that the person who said it did in fact approve of the official's action. For we can no longer say that "The official acted rightly" is true.

But what reason do we have for saying that our ethical and epistemic

[22] Compare the criticism of "psychologism" in Gottlob Frege, *Die Grundlagen der Arithmetic* (Breslau, 1884), pp. 36–38; Edmund Husserl, *Logische Untersuchungen* (Halle, 1929), I, 50–191; Desiré Mercier, *Critériologie générale*, pp. 172–217; A. Meinong, "Für die Psychologie und gegen den Psychologismus in der allgemeinen Werttheorie," *Logos*, III (1912), 1–14; and Rudolf Carnap, *Logical Foundations of Probability*, pp. 37–42.

[23] Anders Wedberg, in "Bertrand Russell's Empiricism," has suggested that our inability to use the terms "knowledge" and "true belief" interchangeably "is explained by the fact that 'knowledge' expresses something which the phrase 'true belief' does not express, namely an actual belief feeling of a special kind" (*Adolf Phalén in Memoriam* [Uppsala, 1937], p. 351). See also C. H. Whiteley, "More about Probability," *Analysis*, vol. VIII (1948); R. F. Atkinson, " 'Good,' 'Right,' and 'Probable,' in *Language, Truth, and Logic*," *Mind*, vol. LXIV; and Stephen Toulmin, "Probability," *Proceedings of the Aristotelian Society*, Suppl. vol. XXIV (1950).

[24] J. N. Findlay suggests an "emotive" interpretation of probability statements in "Probability without Nonsense," *Philosophical Quarterly*, II (1952), 218–219. But he does not restrict "probability" in the way I have proposed. . . .

convictions—our approvals and disapprovals—are neither true nor false? If we can find a good reason for accepting such a view of ethical statements and convictions, we can also find a good reason for accepting such a view of epistemic statements and convictions.

V

Those who say that our ethical convictions are neither true nor false often appeal to arguments which are inconclusive. They may point out (i) that no statement is true or false unless it is a "factual" or "descriptive" statement and (ii) that the statements which express our moral convictions are not "factual" or "descriptive." (The technical terms I have put in quotation marks may, of course, be replaced by others—for instance, by "scientific," "verifiable," or "cognitive.") But we find, on analyzing such arguments, that one of the two premises (it may be either) is taken to be analytic—as derivable from statements explicating the terms in quotation marks—and that the other premise is not defended at all.

The best reason for saying that our moral and epistemic convictions are neither true nor false seems to me to be this: If we say, of these convictions and of the statements in which they are expressed, that they *are* either true or false, and if we say, further, that some of them can be *known* to be true or to be false, then, as I have noted, we seem committed to saying that there are synthetic statements, about ethics and about evidence, which we know *a priori* to be true or to be false. Hence, to avoid the doctrine of the synthetic *a priori,* we may classify moral and epistemic convictions with such states as that of *being amused* and say that they are *neither* true nor false. The view that such convictions and the statements expressing them are neither true nor false is simpler and more economical than its contradictory and leads to fewer puzzling questions.

We should remind ourselves, however, that "simplicity" and "economy" alone do *not* constitute sufficient reason for accepting any view, philosophical or otherwise. One might argue that our ostensible beliefs about the past are really not beliefs—that they are attitudes which are neither true nor false—and that the statements in which they are expressed ("I saw him at the meeting yesterday"), although capable of performing many linguistic functions, are neither true nor false. Such a conception would have the advantage of economy and simplicity, for it would dispense with the notion of the past and thus enable us to avoid a number of puzzling questions about our memory. A similar conception might be applied to the notion of *future,* or to that of *time* generally. In these instances, however, the economy and simplicity of the view in question do not constitute a sufficient reason for accepting it.

Yet there is one significant difference between our beliefs about the past and our moral and epistemic convictions. In discussing the concept of *sensibly taking, . . .* we described a source of evidence—other than seeming-to-remember—for statements about the past. We said that if, with respect to two events, a man *takes* one of them to occur before the other, he thereby has adequate evidence for believing that the one occurred before the other. We said the words "before" and "after" describe certain sensible relations. There is a respect, therefore, in which the concept of something being *past* can be said to be exemplified in our experience. But there is no similar respect in which the concepts of *rightness* or of *evidence* can be said to be exemplified in our experience. For we did not say that the word "evidence" —or "good" or "right"—describes any sensible characteristic. Our theory of evidence, it could be said, does not allow anyone to have evidence for statements about evidence; it doesn't tell us that there is anything which is a *mark of evidence* for statements about evidence.

In formulating our theory of evidence, we seem to have been guided by what, in advance, we wished to regard as evident. The good apples had already been separated from the bad ones. What, then, if the mystic or the bookkeeper had expressed a different conception? Suppose the mystic or the bookkeeper had classified the apples differently—and, in consequence, had described some other experiences as marks of evidence?

I do not feel that we can reply to the mystic and the bookkeeper unless we are prepared to accept the doctrine of the synthetic *a priori.*

For Further Reading

Austin, J. L., *Philosophical Papers,* 1961, pp. 67–71.
Ayer, A. J., *The Problem of Knowledge,* 1956, Chap. 1.
Barnes, W. H. F., "Knowing," *Philosophical Review,* Vol. 72 (1963).
Chisholm, R. M., "Evidence as Justification," *Journal of Philosophy,* Vol. 68 (1961).
———, and Firth, Roderick, "Ultimate Evidence" (Symposium), *Journal of Philosophy,* Vol. 53 (1956).
Harrison, Jonathan, "Knowing and Promising," *Mind,* Vol. 71 (1962).
Malcolm, Norman, *Knowledge and Certainty,* 1963, Chap. 2.
Moore, G. E., "Certainty" and "A Defense of Common Sense," *Philosophical Papers,* 1959.
Prichard, H. A., *Knowledge and Perception,* 1950, pp. 71–103.
Russell, Bertrand, *The Problems of Philosophy,* Chap. 13.
Toulmin, S. E., "Probability," in Flew, A. G. N. (ed.), *Essays in Conceptual Analysis,* 1956.
Urmson, J. O., "Some Questions Concerning Validity," in Flew, *Essays in Conceptual Analysis,* 1956.
Woozley, A. D., "Knowing and Not Knowing," *Proceedings of the Aristotelian Society,* Vol. 52 (1951–52).